JIM MURRAY'S
WHISKEY
BIBLE
2021

This edition first published 2020 by Dram Good Books Ltd

10 9 8 7 6 5 4 3 2 1

The "Jim Murray's" logo and the "Whiskey Bible" logo are trade marks of Jim Murray.

Text, tasting notes & rankings, artwork, Jim Murray's logo and the Whiskey Bible logo copyright © Jim Murray 2020

Design copyright © Dram Good Books Ltd 2020

For information regarding using tasting notes from Jim Murray's Whiskey Bible contact: Dram Good Books Ltd, Unit 2, Barnstones Business Park, Litchborough, U.K., NN12 8JJ Tel: 44 (0)117 317 9777. Or contact us via www.whiskybible.com

A CIP catalogue record for this book is available from the British Library

ISBN: 978-0-9932986-7-7

Printed in Belgium by Graphius Group.

Written by: Jim Murray
Edited by: Peter Mayne and David Rankin
Design: Jim Murray, Vincent Flint-Hill and James Murray
Maps: James Murray, Rob-indesign and Vincent Flint-Hill
Production: Vincent Flint-Hill
Chief Researcher: Vincent Flint-Hill
Crunchy, shell-rich Eggs on Incinerated Toast: Jane Garnett
Sample Research: Vincent Flint-Hill, Ally Telfer, Julia Nourney, Kelly May
Sales: info@whiskybible.com
PA to Jim Murray: Jane Garnett
European Dictionary: Julie Nourney, Tom Wyss, Mariette Duhr-Merges, Stefan Baumgart, Erik Molenaar, Jürgen Vromans, Henric Molin and Kalle Valkonen.

Author's Note
I have used the spelling "whiskey" or "whisky" depending on how the individual distillers prefer. All Scotch is "whisky". So is Canadian. All Irish, these days, is "whiskey", though that was not always the case. In Kentucky, bourbon and rye are spelt "whiskey", with the exception of the produce of the early Times/Old Forester Distillery and Maker's Mark which they bottle as "whisky". In Tennessee, it is a 50-50 split: Dickel is "whisky", while Daniel's is "whiskey".

Introduction

When I write the introduction to the Whisky Bible – always the very last task I perform for each year's edition – I usually find it one of the easier parts of putting this annual publication together.

But this year: just where do I start....?

After a day's tasting, I would normally read a book, listen to some classical music, spend an hour of getting whisky out of my head and then go to bed to be up bright and early for another full day's tasting. Or maybe nip over to my local pub for a quiet half pint with my dearest friends and catch up on the world and lives of others.

That was the past. Normality. This has been 2020 and nothing is normal. So this year I have been tasting and sometimes, instead of reading, going on to Youtube and watching the cult 1967 British TV series, The Prisoner. I hadn't ever seen it before but for some reason I was determined to watch it now. And then, halfway through the series, I realised the choice had probably been a subliminal one.

Because I was informed very early on by a doctor friend of mine, and some time before it became public knowledge, that there appeared to be yet unproven link between Covid-19 and the loss of taste and smell. It was, I was told, an early sign of having caught the virus, and the length of this loss of sensation was still unknown: it might be temporary, it might be permanent. Like so much with this invisible invader, very little was known.

And so I had to tell my staff that my isolation had to continue. I had been tasting the North American whiskies at my base in Kentucky when Donald Trump announced flights from Britain were going to be suspended. I had a choice: stay in Frankfort and write the entirety of the Bible from there, or go back to the UK and be by my production facilities. The realisation that I had only two more months of travel insurance made the decision for me. So back I flew from, driving down to Nashville to catch the flight to London – and having been through two international airports, straight into self-imposed quarantine.

Since that date in March I have left my village only three times...and it is now August. Aware that should I catch the virus, there was the real possibility of no Jim Murray's Whisky Bible 2021.

No wonder I became so wrapped up with Patrick McGoohan and The Prisoner...

My brilliant team carried on working, too. At first from home and then, when it was considered safe enough, back in the office. And they were allowed into my house, attired in masks and gloves. As I write this, that is still the situation.

And so I have tasted another 1,252 whiskies for the Whisky Bible. Which unplanned and by freak chance was the exact same number of whiskies as last year – except it has been completed a month and three days earlier. It would have been finished even earlier still had it not been for a surfeit of sulphur-treated sherry butts which slowed my daily output of tasting notes from about 15 a day to less than 10. It also resulted in the putting on of weight as I tried to rescue my taste buds with cheese and other agents which have some success of neutralising the offending off-notes.

Ironically, I had been speaking on the phone to a number of blenders and one commented about how sulphur was no longer a problem in the whisky industry. Contrary to his assertion I can vouch that the problem hasn't gone away and appears in no great hurry to.

Indeed, this year can be marked by the polarisation in the standard of whiskies that I came across. Yes, there were far too many poor ones for my liking. And, for some reason, way too many brands have become sherry dependent in character, either becoming dull or wrecked by a poor nose and/or finish. I had also noticed that caramel was creeping back into the blending lab. I suspect a lot of this is to do with chasing the Asian market. Being holed up, a prisoner in my own lab and faced with an increase in very bland or sub-standard whiskies, and exsiting on a diet of tasteless food to preserve my taste buds, my mood at times was not the greatest.

But, equally, I found myself blown away with truly magnificent whiskies from every corner of the globe. The vast majorities of the bourbons were an absolute treat and the malts out of England and Wales also warmed the heart, as well as Scandinavia and Belgium in particular.

And, of course Scotland, where whiskies from a distillery built in 2014 delighted with the beauty of its youth while Gordon and MacPhail supplied a 1956 bottling that took literally hours to unravel.

Even better, the three whiskies to be named the Whisky Bible's World Whisky of the Year, runner-and third-placed had never been in the top three before...

So, a year to remember for so many reasons. I just hope that I will soon be able to find a way to travel the world and discuss these whiskies with you personally...

Stay safe.

Jim Murray
Willow Cottage
Somewhere in rural Northamptonshire
August 2020

Contents

JIM MURRAY'S
WHISKEY
BIBLE
2021

DRAM GOOD BOOKS

How to Read The Bible

The whole point of this book is for the whiskey lover – be he or she an experienced connoisseur or, better fun still, simply starting out on the long and joyous path of discovery – to have ready access to easy-to-understand information about as many whiskies as possible. And I mean a lot. Thousands.

This book does not quite include every whiskey on the market... just by far and away the vast majority. And those that have been missed this time round – either through accident, logistics or design – will appear in later editions once we can source a sample.

WHISKEY SCORING

The marking for this book is tailored to the consumer and scores run out just a little higher than I use for my own personal references. But such is the way it has been devised that it has not affected my order of preference.

Each whiskey is given a rating out of 100. Twenty-five marks are given to each of four factors: nose (n), taste (t), finish (f), balance and overall complexity (b). That means that 50% of the marks are given for flavour alone and 25% for the nose, often an overlooked part of the whiskey equation. The area of balance and complexity covers all three previous factors and a usually hidden one besides:

Nose: this is simply the aroma. Often requires more than one inspection as hidden aromas can sometimes reveal themselves after time in the glass, increased contact with air and changes in temperature. The nose very often tells much about a whisky, but – as we shall see – equally can be quite misleading.

Taste: this is the immediate arrival on the palate and involves the flavour profile up to, and including, the time it reaches maximum intensity and complexity.

Finish: often the least understood part of a tasting. This is the tail and flourish of the whiskey's signature, often revealing the effects of ageing. The better whiskies tend to finish well and linger without too much oak excess. It is on the finish, also, that certain notes which are detrimental to the whiskey may be observed. For instance, a sulphur-tarnished cask may be fully revealed for what it is by a dry, bitter residue on the palate which is hard to shake off. It is often worth waiting a few minutes to get the full picture of the finish before having a second taste of a whiskey.

Balance: This is the part it takes a little experience to appreciate but it can be mastered by anyone. For a whiskey to work well on the nose and palate, it should not be too one-sided in its character. If you are looking for an older whiskey, it should have evidence of oak, but not so much that all other flavours and aromas are drowned out. Likewise, a whisky matured or finished in a sherry butt must offer a lot more than just wine alone and the greatest Islay malts, for instance, revel in depth and complexity beyond the smoky effects of peat.

Each whisky has been analysed by me without adding water or ice. I have taken each whiskey as it was poured from the bottle and used no more than warming in an identical glass to extract and discover the character of the whisky. To have added water would have been pointless: it would have been an inconsistent factor as people, when pouring water, add different amounts at varying temperatures. The only constant with the whiskey you and I taste will be when it has been poured directly from the bottle.

Even if you and I taste the same whiskies at the same temperature and from identical glasses – and even share the same values in whiskey – our scores may still be different. Because a factor that is built into my evaluation is drawn from expectation and experience. When I sample a whisky from a certain distillery at such-and-such an age or from this type of barrel or that, I would expect it to offer me certain qualities. It has taken me 30 years to acquire this knowledge (which I try to add to day by day!) and an enthusiast cannot be expected to learn it overnight. But, hopefully, Jim Murray's Whiskey Bible will help...!

SCORE CHART

Within the parentheses **()** is the overall score out of 100.

0–50.5 Nothing short of absolutely diabolical.
51–64.5 Nasty and well worth avoiding.
65–69.5 Very unimpressive indeed.
70–74.5 Usually drinkable but don't expect the earth to move.
75–79.5 Average and usually pleasant though sometimes flawed.
80–84.5 Good whisky worth trying.
85–89.5 Very good to excellent whiskies definitely worth buying.
90–93.5 Brilliant.
94–97.5 Superstar whiskies that give us all a reason to live.
98–100 Better than anything I've ever tasted!

KEY TO ABBREVIATIONS & SYMBOLS

% Percentage strength of whiskey measured as alcohol by volume. **b** Overall balance and complexity. **bott** Date of bottling. **nbc** No bottling code. **db** Distillery bottling. In other words, an expression brought out by the owners of the distillery. **dist** Date of distillation or spirit first put into cask. **f** Finish. **n** Nose. **nc** Non-coloured. **ncf** Non-chill-filtered. **sc** Single cask. **t** Taste. ◇ New entry for 2021. ⊙ Retasted – no change. ⊙⊙ Retasted and re-evaluated. **v** Variant
🏆 2021 Category Winner. 🏆 2021 Category Runner-up.

Finding Your Whiskey

Worldwide Malts: Whiskies are listed alphabetically throughout the book. In the case of single malts, the distilleries run A–Z style with distillery bottlings appearing at the top of the list in order of age, starting with youngest first. After age comes vintage. After all the "official" distillery bottlings are listed, next come other bottlings, again in alphabetical order. Single malts without a distillery named (or perhaps named after a dead one) are given their own section, as are vatted malts.

Worldwide Blends: These are simply listed alphabetically, irrespective of which company produces them. So "Black Bottle" appears ahead of "White Horse" and Japanese blends begin with "Ajiwai Kakubin" and end with "Za". In the case of brands being named after companies or individuals the first letter of the brand will dictate where it is listed. So William Grant, for instance, will be found under "W" for William rather "G" for Grant.

Bourbon/Rye: One of the most confusing types of whiskey to list because often the name of the brand bears no relation to the name of the distillery that made it. Also, brands may be sold from one company to another, or shortfalls in stock may see companies buying bourbons from another. For that reason all the brands have been listed alphabetically with the name of the bottling distiller being added at the end.

Irish Whiskey: There are four types of Irish whiskey: (i) pure pot still; (ii) single malt, (iii) single grain and (iv) blended. Some whiskies may have "pure pot still" on the label, but are actually single malts. So check both sections.

Bottle Information

As no labels are included in this book I have tried to include all the relevant information you will find on the label to make identification of the brand straightforward. Where known I have included date of distillation and bottling. Also the cask number for further recognition. At the end of the tasting notes I have included the strength and, if known, number of bottles (sometimes abbreviated to btls) released and in which markets.

PRICE OF WHISKEY

You will notice that Jim Murray's Whiskey Bible very rarely refers to the cost of a whiskey. This is because the book is a guide to quality and character rather than the price tag attached. Also, the same whiskies are sold in different countries at varying prices due to market forces and variations of tax, so there is a relevance factor to be considered. Equally, much depends on the size of an individual's pocket. What may appear a cheap whiskey to one could be an expensive outlay to another. With this in mind prices are rarely given in the Whiskey Bible.

How to Taste Whiskey

It is of little use buying a great whisky, spending a comparative fortune in doing so, if you don't get the most out of it.

So when giving whisky tastings, no matter how knowledgeable the audience may be I take them through a brief training schedule in how to nose and taste as I do for each sample included in the Whisky Bible.

I am aware that many aspects are contrary to what is being taught by distilleries' whisky ambassadors. And for that we should be truly thankful. However, at the end of the day we all find our own way of doing things. If your old tried and trusted technique suits you best, that's fine by me. But I do ask you try out the instructions below at least once to see if you find your whisky is talking to you with a far broader vocabulary and clearer voice than it once did. I strongly suspect you will be pleasantly surprised – amazed, even - by the results.

Amusingly, someone tried to teach me my own tasting technique some years back in an hotel bar. He was not aware who I was and I didn't let on. It transpired that a friend of his had been to one of my tastings a few years earlier and had passed on my words of "wisdom". I'd be lying if I said I didn't smile when he informed me it was called "The Murray Method." It was the first time I had heard the phrase... though certainly not the last!

"THE MURRAY METHOD"

1. Drink a black, unsweetened, coffee or chew on 90% minimum cocoa chocolate to cleanse the palate, especially of sugars.

2. Find a room free from distracting noises as well as the aromas of cooking, polish, flowers and other things which will affect your understanding and appreciation of the whisky.

3. Make sure you have not recently washed your hands using heavily scented soap or are wearing a strong aftershave or perfume.

4. Use a tulip shaped glass with a stem. This helps contain the alcohols at the bottom yet allows the more delicate whisky aromas you are searching for to escape.

5. Never add ice. This tightens the molecules and prevents flavours and aromas from being released. It also makes your whisky taste bitter. There is no better way to get the least from your whisky than by freezing it.

6. Likewise, ignore any advice given to put the bottle in the fridge before drinking.

7. Don't add water! Whatever anyone tells you. It releases aromas but can mean the whisky falls below 40%... so it is no longer whisky. Also, its ability to release flavours and aromas diminishes quite quickly. Never add ridiculous "whisky rocks" or other supposed tasting aids.

8. Warm the undiluted whisky in the glass to body temperature before nosing or tasting. Hence the stem, so you can cradle in your hand the curve of the thin base. This excites the molecules and unravels the whisky in your glass, maximising its sweetness and complexity.

9. Keep an un-perfumed hand over the glass to keep the aromas in while you warm. Only a minute or two after condensation appears at the top of your glass should you extend your arms, lift your covering hand and slowly bring the glass to your nose, so the alcoholic vapours have been released before the glass reaches your face.

10. Never stick your nose in the glass. Or breathe in deeply. Allow glass to gently touch your top lip, leaving a small space below the nose. Move from nostril to nostril, breathing normally. This allows the aromas to break up in the air, helping you find the more complex notes.

11. Take no notice of your first mouthful. This is a marker for your palate.

12. On second, bigger mouthful, close your eyes to concentrate on the flavour and chew the whisky - moving it continuously around the palate. Keep your mouth slightly open to let air in and alcohol out. It helps if your head is tilted back very slightly.

13. Occasionally spit – if you have the willpower! This helps your senses to remain sharp for the longest period of time.

14. Look for the balance of the whisky. That is, which flavours counter others so none is too dominant. Also, watch carefully how the flavours and aromas change in the glass over time.

15. Assess the "shape" and mouthfeel of the whisky, its weight and how long its finish. And don't forget to concentrate on the first flavours as intensely as you do the last. Look out for the way the sugars, spices and other characteristics form.

16. Never make your final assessment until you have tasted it a third or fourth time.

17. Be honest with your assessment: don't like a whisky because someone (yes, even me!), or the label, has tried to convince you how good it is.

18. When you cannot discriminate between one whisky and another, stop immediately.

Bible Thumping
Old Malt of Dreams
Young Dram of Vision

Living, as I do, part of the year on the edge of the beautiful Cotswolds in England and in the historic centre of an old Kentucky town for the remainder, I get the chance to observe people closely.

And what folk crave, I have noted, is the past.

In England they come in their hundreds and they come in their thousands. By car, by coach, by train they pile into quaint Oxfordshire and Gloucestershire towns and villages to feast their eyes on architecture that had gone out of fashion when Queen Victoria still sat upon the throne; and built from stone now far too expensive to be used by builders of today and to designs that would never get past today's health and safety maniacs at the local town hall. They will find rail lines along which steam trains, themselves puffing, hissing and creaking dinosaurs of a bygone age restored to life, billowing smuts into their delighted passengers' eyes; sedate churches dating from just after the Normans put an arrow into the less than delighted King Harold's eye nearly a millennia before; marvel at the straightness of the Roman roads from almost a thousand years before Harold, and linger over the fine artwork of mosaics of a long lost Roman villa unearthed close by one of those ancient trackways.

Then, that night, they will stay at a hotel that was once a coaching inn, the arched entry into the courtyard a giveaway; or they will escape from other tourists and find an ancient pub sitting by the sleepy, ambling River Windrush and drink beer made at the nearby Donnington Brewery where time, like its brewing methods, have stood still and you can sit there devouring your lip-smacking pint of nostalgia, of 'Ye Olde England'.

This is what people come in their droves to find. The remaining vestiges of an authentic, somehow gentler world. Just as in Frankfort tourists wander among the noble houses of a once frontier town; each proud home a bold and elegant statement to claim from the untamed forests and rivers civilization and order.

I watch people deeply breathe in the past, filling their lungs and souls with yesteryear and sometimes share discussions with them about the importance of these treasures in reminding us of context; as these structures, these smoke belching machines, either side of the pond, were the result of men with big ideas and a vision that sculpted the society in which they lived, usually for the better. Progress.

Yet despite progress, it is hard to find anyone who would not wish to travel back in time to when those towns and villages did not attract tourists, but just bustled along with the ordinary business of the day. Even with its attendant hardships and daily discomforts.

With the imprisoning advent of Covid-19, with the continued pressure of now being in an increasingly humourless society hell-bent on apportioning blame and embracing a new form of puritanism, the average, normal, sensible, decent human being, with normal, sensible, decent values and with not the slightest need for safe spaces or recourse to pressure groups is bewildered by how quickly society has changed (very much for the worse) and seeks solace in the past. Where, if the remaining architecture is to go by, common sense, good taste and pride abounded.

And so I chat to them in pubs in the Cotswolds, or bars and diners in Kentucky. Lovely people feasting on the receding remnants of a lost world.

What I have noticed over the years are that these people share a common ground with a large portion of whisky drinkers I have met. So many, from the UK to Kentucky, through to China, Japan, back round to India and through Europe and back to the UK again, simply gorge on nostalgia.

They love to know how long a distillery has been functioning. That the whisky is made today just as it was when the owner wore a top hat and the workers would smoke from a clay pipe. The number of times I have spoken to people at shows, or just privately in conversation, who have told me that they chose one bottle to buy over another because of the antiquity and history of the distillery. And in the case of people new to whisky, it was obvious that this provenance gave it an upper hand on another whisky they had considered buying. Their reasonable logic: if a distillery has lasted this long, then it must be good.

There is a certain truth to that. When United Distillers and others made a ruthless cull of their distilleries during the great Whisky Loch of the 1980s - when overproduction and a declining demand put huge strains on the industry as the value of maturing stock plummeted – two types of distilleries were found in the cross hairs of the accountants and production executives: small, two-still distilleries which were labour-intensive and produced a litre of alcohol at a relatively uneconomic rate, and distilleries that blenders believed made sub-standard spirit. I'll let you guess which one of these two Port Ellen fell under.

Then, history did not matter. Because what counted was quality and economics. And if their own blenders could do without the new make and blenders from other companies had no call for it within a reciprocal agreement, then that distillery's days were numbered. Whenever it was built.

Of course, today marketing types would never admit that. They will use the age of the distillery not only as a selling product but a form of guarantee that the whisky must be good because there is 150 years, or whatever, of distilling skill behind every bottle produced.

Those of us in the industry know that is complete stuff and nonsense. But for people new to whisky and, perhaps from a holiday that involved a distillery tour or two, it is quite easy to go along with that thinking.

Because, as we see with people thronging to the Cotswolds, or wandering the elegant, ageless streets of downtown Frankfort, or clambering around Stonehenge, the Pyramids of Egypt, the remains of Pompei, there is a natural desire to flock to the past and embrace it. To drink it in and be sated.

It is this natural desire for the past that falsely makes us automatically believe that anything which comes from it cannot be other than authentic and built upon generations of craft and knowledge. It cannot, therefore, be bad.

But here's the rub, as tourists to Shakespeare's Stratford-on-Avon might say. Think of a once great, all-conquering football team that first lost its trophy-winning manager, then its star centre-back and, finally, fatally, its record goalscorer. The board of directors decided not to spend as before. So they now invest moderately instead of once buying only best, recruiting only the most talented as they long did. The new manager deploys tactics that are negative and eschews entertainment for safety. And from once lording it among the élite, providing the finest football you had ever seen, it was now down among the also rans.

You turn up to the wonderful stadium, historic and proud and full of so many great memories. You enter full to the brim with expectation, but where once you watched poetry you now witness the prosaic.

And so it might be with a whisky. The bottle looks exactly the same, the label invites you in – but what is in the glass has little to do with the distillery at its zenith.

It might be a change of staff, a change of barrel type, a change to the distillation process, a change of blender. It might be one of those things, a combination of some – or the whole shooting match.

For a distillery's past does not guarantee its present or future. The performance and fate of a distillery is seldom linear.

Yet, very often, new distilleries, or even new distilling nations, are given very little chance. Perception has defeated them in the eyes of the public. How can they be compared to a distillery dating back to the 1830s or, lord forgive us, 1608 (a word to the wise: no distillery on the planet goes back to 1608, no matter what anyone claims).

Of course there are whisky lovers out there with open minds and willing to take on any whisky at face value. But, sadly, the majority don't. This year, as last year, the Annandale distillery in the Lowlands of Scotland has picked up an Award in the Whisky Bible for its single malt. This is remarkable, since the distillery has been going since only 2014.

When touring China last year I was asked about this on several occasions, usually along the lines of "what were you thinking of giving high awards to such a young and virtually unknown distillery?"

Again, the question was asked on the premise that it has to be older, centuries-established distilleries which produce the best whisky. They simply could not compute that a distillery that had been around only five years or so was not only able to make truly brilliant whisky, but something that could stand shoulder-to-shoulder – and even slightly above the rest.

Likewise, English, Welsh and Indian whiskies. Their presence on the international stage is, in whisky terms, recent. So to the perception of many – and here I include to a degree buyers and importers I have met – they cannot be taken as seriously as even the most mundane, sloppily distilled, appallingly matured Scotch single malt. The fact the distillery is firstly, located in Scotland and, secondly, as old as the hills means to these people that the whisky must be good. I can understand that perception with people in their first five or ten years of learning about whisky. But I find that thinking a little harder to forgive with people I meet in the trade itself.

Bible Thumping

It is understandable that in the sea of whisky that these days engulfs us in liquor stores and supermarkets, the natural instinct is to cling to the lifebuoy of age, tradition and history.

But the one thing that tasting 1,250 whiskies a year for this book has reinforced in my mind, is that for people to really enjoy whisky of whatever type, then they have to let go of the past and learn to swim. Some ancient distilleries, like Buffalo Trace and Glen Grant, have stayed true to their greatness. Others, alas, haven't. While some new distilleries, like Paul John in India, St George's in England and Annandale in Scotland have filled the void by concentrating on excellence. Of course, some of the newbies have not been quite as successful.

The secret, though, is having that open mind, free from marketing hype, and the bravery to go out and discover which whiskies remain as beautiful landmarks of the past. And which new whiskies represent the present at its best and perhaps the near future, too...

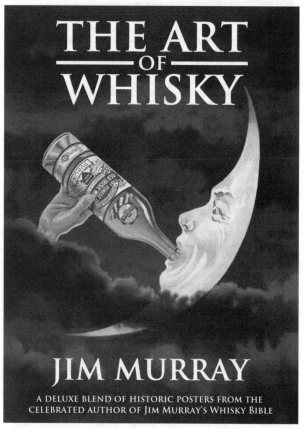

Immortal Drams:
The Whiskey Bible
Winners 2004-2020

	World Whisky of the Year	Second Finest Whisky of the Year	Third Finest Whisky of the Year
2004	George T Stagg	N/A	N/A
2005	George T Stagg	N/A	N/A
2006	George T Stagg	Glen Moray 1986	N/A
2007	Old Parr Superior 18 Years Old	Buffalo Trace Twice Barreled	N/A
2008	Ardbeg 10 Years Old	The Ileach Single Islay Malt Cask Strength	N/A
2009	Ardbeg Uigedail	Nikka Whisky Single Coffey Malt 12 Years	N/A
2010	Sazerac Rye 18 Years Old (bottled Fall 2008)	Ardbeg Supernova	Amrut Fusion
2011	Ballantine's 17 Years Old	Thomas H Handy Sazerac Rye (129 proof)	Wiliam Larue Weller (134.8 proof)
2012	Old Pulteney Aged 21 Years	George T Stagg	Parker's Heritage Collection Aged 10 Years
2013	Thomas H Handy Sazerac Rye (128.6 proof)	William Larue Weller (133.5 proof)	Ballantine's 17 Years Old
2014	Glenmorangie Ealanta 1993	William Larue Weller (123.4 proof)	Thomas Handy Sazerac Rye (132.4 proof)
2015	Yamazaki Single Malt Sherry 2013	William Larue Weller (68.1 abv)	Sazerac Rye 18 Years Old (bottled Fall 2013)
2016	Crown Royal Northern Harvest Rye	Pikesville 110 Proof Straight Rye	Midleton Dair Ghaelach
2017	Booker's Rye 13 Years, 1 Month, 12 Days	Glen Grant 18 Year Old	William Larue Weller (134.6 proof)
2018	Colonel E.H. Taylor 4 Grain Aged 10 Years	Redbreast Aged 21 Years	Glen Grant 18 Year Old
2019	William Larue Weller (128.2 proof)	Glen Grant Aged 18 Years	Thomas Handy Sazerac Rye (127.2 proof)
2020	1792 Full Proof Kentucky Bourbon	William Larue Weller (125.7 proof)	Thomas Handy Sazerac Rye (128.8 proof)

Who has won this year? You are one page away...

Jim Murray's Whiskey Bible Awards 2021

Fifteen years ago The Whisky Bible shook the Canadian whisky world by naming Alberta Premium the country's finest native spirit.

What bemused millions of Canadian whisky lovers (as opposed to lovers of Canadian whisky) was that it was the brand - often sold in plastic bottles – they walked past without even a second glance on the way to the more exclusive and higher-priced whiskies in their search for excellence. And the most common comment when I spoke to Canadians after giving this award and they had had a chance to grab a bottle: "I had no idea it was this good". Not least because I'm pretty sure I had never met a single person who had ever drank it neat.

Indeed, around the globe, people rarely considered Canada a country from which truly world-class whisky could be found.

But now, for the second time in five years, Canada find themselves top of the tree once more: Alberta Premium has cracked it big time. Not that this is standard AP. Or their 25-year-old which some years back also deserved the widest audience. This is unfettered Alberta Premium at full cask strength and tasting just as I has tasted in their warehouses direct from the barrel when I first explored their contents over 25 years ago.

With this most true of Canadian ryes, boasting the most startling lucidity on the palate imaginable, seemingly each grain of rye coerced into giving its naked all, Canadians – and the world – are now spoiled for choice. Five years ago it was Crown Royal Northern Harvest Rye which strode the world; now it is this. Both 97.5 pointers. And one costing just $32 Canadian, the other double that – but both just tiny sums for such quality.

If that proves a surprise, then what about Mithuna from the Paul John Distillery from India coming in as the world's third best whisky? Of all the 1,252 whiskies I tasted this year, this had the most complete, longest and most spectacular finish of them all – kind of out Larue Wellering this year's William Larue Weller: a startling claim in itself.

Sandwiched between these two surprise outsiders and coming home second was, inevitably, a bourbon from the Buffalo Trace distillery. But, again, it was a newbie to the Whisky Bible podium. The stunning Stagg Junior seems to have taken the place in quality long held by George T Stagg, the first-ever World Whisky of the Year for the Whisky Bible, awarded for the 2004 edition.

The World Single Cask of the Year was a straight battle between a breath-taking bourbon and Scotch. Curiously, both whiskies were brought out to mark the centenary of the birth of two legends within the industry and with whom I'd had the honour of working in my whisky career: George Urquhart of Gordon and MacPhail and Elmer T Lee of Buffalo Trace, the latter becoming a mentor and close friend. It was, however, the extraordinary 1956 Glen Grant from Gordon and MacPhail that emerged as victor. Just.

2021 World Whiskey of the Year
Alberta Premium Cask Strength Rye

Second Finest Whiskey in the World
Stagg Jr Barrel Proof

Third Finest Whiskey in the World
Paul John Mithuna

Single Cask of the Year
Gordon & MacPhail Mr George
Centenary Edition Glen Grant 1956

SCOTCH

Scotch Whisky of the Year
Glen Grant Aged 15 Years Batch Strength
Single Malt of the Year (Multiple Casks)
Glen Grant Aged 15 Years Batch Strength
Single Malt of the Year (Single Cask)
Gordon & MacPhail Mr George Centenary Edition Glen Grant 1956
Scotch Blend of the Year
Ballantine's 30 Years Old
Scotch Grain of the Year
The Perfect Fifth Cambus 1979
Scotch Vatted Malt of the Year
Compass Box The Spice Tree

Single Malt Scotch

No Age Statement
Glen Grant Rothes Chronicles Cask Haven
10 Years & Under (Multiple Casks)
Octomore Edition 10.3 Aged 6 Years
10 Years & Under (Single Cask)
Annandale Vintage Man O'Words 2015
11-15 Years (Multiple Casks)
Glen Grant Aged 15 Years Batch Strength
11-15 Years (Single Cask)
Gordon & MacPhail Connoisseurs Choice Caol Ila Aged 15 Years
16-21 Years (Multiple Casks)
Knockando Aged 21 Years Master Reserve
16-21 Years (Single Cask)
The First Editions Longmorn Aged 21 Years
22-27 Years (Multiple Casks)
Old Pulteney 25 Year Old
22-27 Years (Single Cask)
Golden Glen Glenlossie Aged 22 Years
28-34 Years (Multiple Casks)
Glenfiddich 30 Years Old
28-34 Years (Single Cask)
The Perfect Fifth Aberlour 1989
35-40 Years (Multiple Casks)
Port Ellen 9 Rogue Casks 40 Year Old
35-40 Years (Single Cask)
The Whisky Agency Lochside 1981
41 Years & Over (Multiple Casks)
Tomatin Warehouse 6 Collection 1977
41 Years & Over (Single Cask)
Gordon & MacPhail Mr George Centenary Edition Glen Grant 1956

BLENDED SCOTCH

No Age Statement (Standard)
White Horse
No Age Statement (Premium)
Johnnie Walker Blue Label Ghost & Rare
5-12 Years
Johnnie Walker Black Label Aged 12 Years
13-18 Years
Ballantine's Aged 17 Years
19 - 25 Years
Dewar's Aged 25 Years The Signature
26 - 39 Years
Ballantine's 30 Year Old
40 Years & Over
Whyte & Mackay Aged 50 Years

IRISH WHISKEY

Irish Whiskey of the Year
Midleton Barry Crockett Legacy
Irish Pot Still Whiskey of the Year
Midleton Barry Crockett Legacy
Irish Single Malt of the Year
Bushmills Port Cask Reserve

Irish Blend of the Year
Bushmills Black Bush
Irish Single Cask of the Year
Redbreast Dream Cask Aged 28 Years

AMERICAN WHISKEY

Bourbon of the Year
Stagg Jr Barrel Proof
Rye of the Year
Thomas H. Handy Sazerac
US Micro Whisky of the Year Multiple Cask
Garrison Brothers Balmorhea 2020 Release
US Micro Whisky of the Year Single Cask
Woodinville Straight Bourbon Private Select
American Blended Whiskey of the Year
Michter's Celebration Sour Mash Whiskey

BOURBON

No Age Statement (Multiple Barrels)
Stagg Jr Barrel Proof
No Age Statement (Single Barrel)
Elmer T. Lee 100 Year Tribute Kentucky Bourbon
9 Years & Under
Bib & Tucker Bourbon Aged 6 Years
10 - 12 Years
Michter's Single Barrel 10 Year Old Bourbon
11 - 15 Years
Knob Creek Aged 15 Years
16 Years & Over
Michter's 20 Year Old Kentucky Straight Bourbon

RYE

No Age Statement
Thomas H. Handy Sazerac
Up to 10 Years
Wild Turkey Cornerstone
11-15 Years
Van Winkle Family Reserve 13 Years Old
Over 15 Years
Sazerac 18 Years Old
Single Cask
Michter's 10 Years Old Single Barrel Straight Rye

CANADIAN WHISKY

Canadian Whisky of the Year
Alberta Premium Cask Strength Rye

JAPANESE WHISKY

Japanese Whisky of the Year
Nikka Whisky Single Malt Yoichi Apple Brandy Wood Finish
Japanese Single Grain of the Year
Makoto Single Grain Whisky Aged 23 Years
Japanese Single Malt of the Year
Nikka Whisky Single Malt Yoichi Apple Brandy Wood Finish
Japanese Single Cask of the Year
The Matsui Single Cask Mizunara Cask

EUROPEAN WHISKY

European Whisky of the Year Multiple Cask
PUNI Aura Italian Single Malt
European Whisky of the Year Single Cask
Braeckman Belgian Single Grain Whiskey Single Barrel Aged 12 Years

WORLD WHISKIES

Asian Whisky of the Year
Paul John Mithuna
Southern Hemisphere Whisky of the Year
Adams Distillery Tasmanian Cask Strength

*Overall age category and/or section winners are presented in **bold**.*

The Whiskey Bible Liquid Gold Awards (97.5-94)

Jim Murray's Whiskey Bible is delighted to again make a point of celebrating the very finest whiskies you can find in the world. So we salute the distillers who have maintained or even furthered the finest traditions of whisky making and taken their craft to the very highest levels. And the bottlers who have brought some of them to us.

After all, there are over 4,500 different brands and expressions listed in this guide and from every corner of the planet. Those which score 94 and upwards represents only a very small fraction of them. These whiskies are, in my view, the élite: the finest you can currently find on the whiskey shelves of the world. Rare and precious, they are Liquid Gold.

So it is our pleasure to announce that all those scoring 94 and upwards automatically qualify for the Jim Murray's Whiskey Bible Liquid Gold Award. Congratulations!

97.5
Scottish Single Malt
Glenmorangie Ealanta 1993 Vintage
Old Pulteney Aged 21 Years
Scottish Blends
Ballantine's 17 Years Old
Irish Pure Pot Still
Midleton Dair Ghaelach Grinsell's Wood Ballaghtobin Estate
Bourbon
1792 Full Proof Kentucky Straight Bourbon
Colonel E.H. Taylor Four Grain Bottled in Bond Aged 12 Years
Stagg Jr Barrel Proof
William Larue Weller 125.7 proof
William Larue Weller 128.2 proof
William Larue Weller 135.4 proof
American Straight Rye
Booker's Rye 13 Years, 1 Month, 12 Days
Pikesville Straight Rye Aged at Least 6 Years
Thomas H. Handy Sazerac Straight Rye
Canadian Blended
Alberta Premium Cask Strength Rye
Crown Royal Northern Harvest Rye

97
Scottish Single Malt
Ardbeg 10 Years Old
Bowmore Aged 19 Years The Feis Ile Collection
Glenfiddich 50 Years Old
Glen Grant Aged 15 Years Batch Strength 1st Edition bott code: LRO/HI16
Glen Grant Aged 18 Years Rare Edition
Glen Grant Aged 18 Years Rare Edition bott code: LRO/EE04
Glen Grant Aged 18 Years Rare Edition bott code: LRO/EE03
Gordon & MacPhail Mr George Centenary Edition Glen Grant 1956
The Macphail 1949 China 70th Anniversary Glen Grant Special Edition 1
The Last Drop Glenrothes 1970
Scottish Grain
The Last Drop Dumbarton 1977
Scottish Blends
Compass Box The Double Single
The Last Drop 1971 Blended Scotch Whisky
Irish Pure Pot Still
Redbreast Aged 21 Years
Bourbon
Elmer T. Lee 100 Year Tribute Kentucky Straight Bourbon Whiskey
Old Forester
William Larue Weller 128 proof
American Straight Rye
Thomas H. Handy Sazerac 125.7 proof
Thomas H. Handy Sazerac 127.2 proof
Thomas H. Handy Sazerac 128.8 proof

Canadian Blended
Canadian Club Chronicles: Issue No. 1 Water of Windsor Aged 41 Years
Crown Royal Northern Harvest Rye
Indian Single Malt
Paul John Mithuna

96.5
Scottish Single Malt
The Perfect Fifth Aberlour 1989
Annandale Man O' Sword Smoulderingly Smoky
Ardbeg 20 Something
Ardbeg 21 Years Old
Berry Bros & Rudd Ardmore 9 Years Old
Bowmore Black 50 Year Old
Octomore Edition 10.3 Aged 6 Years
Dramfool Port Charlotte 2002 16 Years Old
Old Malt Cask Bunnahabhain Aged 27 Years
Caol Ila 30 Year Old
Convalmore 32 Year Old
Glencadam Aged 18 Years
Glenfiddich 30 Years Old
Glen Grant Aged 15 Years Batch Strength 1st Edition bott code: LRO/FG 19
The Glenlivet Cipher
Golden Glen Glenlossie Aged 22 Years
Highland Park 50 Years Old
The Perfect Fifth Highland Park 1987
Gordon & MacPhail Private Collection Inverleven 1985
Berry Bros & Rudd Arran 21 Years Old
Kilchoman Private Cask Release
Knockando Aged 21 Years Master Reserve
AnCnoc Cutter
AnCnoc Rutter
Laphroaig Aged 27 Years
Loch Lomond Organic Aged 17 Years
The Whisky Agency Lochside 1981
The First Editions Longmorn Aged 21 Years
Port Ellen 39 Years Old
Gleann Mór Port Ellen Aged Over 33 Years
Talisker Aged 25 Years
Tomatin 36 Year Old American & European Oak
Tullibardine 1970
Port Askaig 100 Proof
Arcanum Spirits TR21INITY Aged Over 21 Years
Glen Castle Aged 28 Years
Whisky Works 20 Year Old Speyside 2019/WV02./CW
Scottish Grain
Berry Bros & Rudd Cambus 26 Years Old
The Perfect Fifth Cambus 1979
The Whisky Barrel Dumbarton 30 Year Old
Scottish Blends
The Antiquary Aged 35 Years
Dewar's Aged 18 Years The Vintage
Dewar's Double Double Aged 27 Years Blended Scotch Whisky

Johnnie Walker Blue Label The Casks Edition
The Last Drop 1965
The Last Drop 56 Year Old Blend
Royal Salute 32 Years Old
Teacher's Aged 25 Years

Irish Pure Pot Still
Midleton Barry Crockett Legacy
Redbreast Aged 32 Years Dream Cask

Bourbon
1792 Bottled In Bond Kentucky Straight Bourbon
Blanton's Uncut/Unfiltered
Bulleit Bourbon Blender's Select No. 001
Colonel E.H. Taylor 18 Year Marriage BiB
Colonel E H Taylor Single Barrel BiB
George T. Stagg 116.9 proof
George T. Stagg 129.2 proof
George T. Stagg 144.1 proof
Michter's 20 Year Old Kentucky Straight Bourbon batch no. 18I1370
Michter's 20 Year Old Kentucky Straight Bourbon batch no. 19H1439, bott code: A192421439

American Straight Rye
Knob Creek Cask Strength

American Microdistilleries
Garrison Brothers Balmorhea Texas Straight Bourbon Whiskey
Garrison Brothers Balmorhea Texas Straight Bourbon Whiskey dist 2014
Garrison Brothers Balmorhea Texas Straight Bourbon Whiskey dist 2015
Woodinville Straight Bourbon Whiskey Private Select

American/Kentucky Whiskey Blends
Michter's Celebration Sour Mash Whiskey Release No. 3

Whiskey Distilled From Bourbon Mash
Knaplund Straight Bourbon Whiskey Atlantic Aged

Canadian Blended
Canadian Club Chronicles Aged 42 Years

Japanese Single Malt
Nikka Whisky Single Malt Yoichi Apple Brandy Wood Finish

English Single Malt
The English Single Malt Aged 11 Years
The Norfolk Farmers Single Grain Whisky
The Norfolk Single Grain Parched

Welsh Single Malt
Penderyn Icons of Wales No 5 Bryn Terfel
Penderyn Rhiannon
Penderyn Single Cask no. 182/2006

Belgian Single Malt
Belgian Owl 12 Years Vintage No. 07 First Fill Bourbon Single Cask No 4275925
Belgian Owl Single Malt The Private Angels 60 Months
Braeckman Belgian Single Grain Whiskey Single Barrel Aged 10 Years

Danish Single Malt
Thy Whisky No. 9 Bøg Single Malt

Italian Single Malt
PUNI Aura Italian Single Malt

Indian Single Malt
Paul John Single Cask Non Peated #4127

Taiwanese Single Malt
Kavalan 40th Anniversary Single Malt Selected Wine Cask Matured Single Cask
Nantou Distillery Omar Cask Strength

96

Scottish Single Malt
Annandale Vintage Man O'Words 2015
Ardbeg 1977

Ardbeg Provenance 1974
The Balvenie The Week of Peat Aged 14 Years
Octomore 7.1 5 Years Old
Glenwill Caol Ila 1990
Gordon & MacPhail Connoisseurs Choice Caol Ila Aged 15 Years
Gordon & MacPhail Private Collection Dallas Dhu 1969
The Dalmore Candela Aged 50 Years
Gordon & MacPhail Glen Albyn 1976
The Whisky Shop Glendronach Aged 26 Years
Glenfarclas The Family Casks 1978 W18
Glenfarclas The Family Casks 1988 W18
Glenfarclas The Family Casks 1995 W18
Glenfiddich Fire & Cane
Glen Grant Aged 10 Years
Glen Grant Rothes Chronicles Cask Haven First Fill Casks bott code: LRO/FG 26
Glen Grant Rothes Chronicles Cask Haven The Macphail 1949 China 70th Anniversary
Glen Grant Special Edition 2
Glen Scotia 45 Year Old
Cadenhead's Cask Strength Glentauchers Aged 41 Years
The Glenturret Fly's 16 Masters Edition
Highland Park Loki Aged 15 Years
Highland Park Aged 25 Years
Highland Park 2002
Highland Park Sigurd
Kilchoman 10 Years Old
Lagavulin Aged 12 Years
Lagavulin 12 Year Old
Cadenhead's Lagavulin 11 Year Old
Laphroaig Lore
Laphroaig PX Cask
Laphroaig Quarter Cask
Loch Lomond 10 Year Old 2009 Alvi's Drift Muscat de Frontignan Finish
G&M Private Collection Longmorn 1966
Port Ellen 9 Rogue Casks 40 Year Old
Old Pulteney Aged 25 Years
Artful Dodger Springbank 18 Year Old 2000
The Perfect Fifth Springbank 1993
Gordon & MacPhail Private Collection St. Magdalene 1982
Ledaig Dùsgadh 42 Aged 42 Years
Tomatin Warehouse 6 Collection 1977
Compass Box Myths & Legends I
Glen Castle Islay Single Malt 1989 Vintage Cask 29 Years Old
Abbey Whisky Anon. Batch 3 Aged 30 Years
Whiskey Bottle Company Cigar Malt Lover Aged 21 Years

Scottish Vatted Malt
Compass Box The Spice Tree
Glen Castle Blended Malt 1992 Sherry Cask
Glen Castle Blended Malt 1990 Sherry Cask Matured 28 Years Old

Scottish Grain
SMWS Cask G14.5 31 Year Old
Single Cask Collection Dumbarton 30 Years Old
The Cooper's Choice Garnheath 48 Year Old
Port Dundas 52 Year Old
The Sovereign Blended Grain 28 Years Old

Scottish Blends
Ballantine's Aged 30 Years
Ballantine's Finest
Ballantine's Limited release no. A27380
Dewar's Aged 25 Years The Signature
Grant's Aged 12 Years
Islay Mist Aged 17 Years
Johnnie Walker Blue Label Ghost & Rare
Oishii Wisukii Aged 36 Years
Royal Salute 21 Years Old
Whyte & Mackay Aged 50 Years

Irish Pure Pot Still
Method and Madness Single Pot Still
Powers Aged 12 Years John's Lane Release
Redbreast Aged 12 Years Cask Strength batch no. B1/18
Redbreast Dream Cask Aged 28 Years

Bourbon
Ancient Ancient Age 10 Years Old
Bib & Tucker Small Batch Aged 6 Years
Colonel E.H. Taylor Barrel Proof
Elijah Craig Barrel Proof Kentucky Straight Bourbon Aged 12 Years
Michter's Single Barrel 10 Year Old Kentucky Straight Bourbon barrel no. 19D662
Old Grand-Dad Bonded 100 Proof
Pappy Van Winkle 15 Years Old
Pappy Van Winkle Family Reserve Kentucky Straight Bourbon Whiskey 15 Years Old
Stagg Jr
Very Old Barton 100 Proof

American Straight Rye
Colonel E.H. Taylor Straight Rye BiB
J Mattingly House Money Small Batch Rye Whiskey Aged 4 Years
Michter's 10 Years Old Single Barrel Kentucky Straight Rye barrel no. 19F965
Sazerac Rye
Sazerac 18 Years Old bott Summer 2018
Sazerac 18 Years Old bott Summer 2019
Van Winkle Family Reserve Kentucky Straight Rye Whiskey 13 Years Old No. 99A
Wild Turkey Master's Keep Cornerstone Aged a Minimum of 9 Years

American Microdistilleries
Balcones Peated Texas Single Malt Aged 26 Months in American Oak
291 Barrel Proof Aged 2 Years
Garrison Brothers Cowboy Bourbon Barrel Proof Aged Four Years
Grand Traverse Michigan Wheat 100% Straight Rye Wheat Whiskey Bottled in Bond
Rock Town Single Barrel Rye Whiskey Aged 32 Months
The Notch Single Malt Whisky Aged 15 Years
Woodinville Bottled-in-Bond Straight Bourbon Whiskey Pot Distilled

Canadian Blended
Crown Royal Noble Collection 13 Year Old Bourbon Mash
Crown Royal Special Reserve
Heavens Door The Bootleg Series Canadian Whisky 26 Years Old 2019
J. P. Wiser's 35 Year Old
Lot No. 40 Rye Whisky

Japanese Single Malt
Chichibu 2012 Vintage
The Hakushu Paul Rusch 120th Anniversary
Nikka Coffey Malt Whisky
ePower Komagatake
The Matsui Single Cask Mizunara Cask
The Yamazaki Single Malt Aged 18 Years

English Single Malt
Cotswolds Single Malt Whisky Peated Cask Batch No. 01/2019
The English Single Malt Triple Distilled

Welsh Single Malt
Penderyn Portwood Single Cask 12 Year Old

Australian Single Malt
Adams Distillery Tasmanian Single Malt Whisky Cask Strength

Belgian Single Malt
Belgian Owl Single Malt 12 Years Vintage No 6 Single First Fill Bourbon Cask No 4018737
Belgian Owl Single Malt 12 Years Single Cask No 14018725

Czech Republic Single Malt
Gold Cock Single Malt 2008 Virgin Oak

Danish Single Malt
Copenhagen Single Malt First Edition
Stauning Kaos

German Single Malt
Hercynian Willowburn Exceptional Collection Aged 5 Years Single Malt

Swedish Single Malt
Mackmyra Svensk Single Cask Whisky Reserve The Dude of Fucking Everything

Swiss Single Malt
Langatun Old Woodpecker Organic

Indian Single Malts
Paul John Kanya
Paul John Single Cask Non Peated #6758
Paul John Single Cask Peated #6355
Paul John Select Cask Peated
Paul John Tula

95.5

Scottish Single Malt
Ardbeg An Oa
Ardbeg Grooves Committee Release
Balblair 2000 2nd Release
Ben Nevis 32 Years Old 1966
The BenRiach Aged 12 Years Matured In Sherry Wood
Benromach 30 Years Old
Benromach Organic 2010
Bowmore 20 Years Old 1997
Octomore Edition 10.4 Aged 3 Years
The First Editions Bruichladdich Aged 28 Years 1991
Caol Ila Aged 25 Years
Fadandel.dk Caol Ila Aged 10 Years
The Dalmore Visitor Centre Exclusive Abbey Whisky Glendronach 1993
Glenfarclas 105
Glenfarclas The Family Casks 1979 W18
Glenfarclas The Family Casks 1989 W18
Glenfiddich Aged 15 Years Distillery Edition
Glenfiddich Project XX
Glengoyne 25 Year Old
Glen Grant Aged 10 Years bott code: LRO/GE01
Gordon & MacPhail Private Collection Glen Grant 1948
The Glenlivet Archive 21 Years of Age
The Whisk(e)y Company The Spirit of Glenlossie Aged 22 Years
Glenmorangie 25 Years Old
Glenmorangie Private Edition 9 Spios
Glen Moray Chardonnay Cask 2003
The Singleton of Glen Ord 14 Year Old
The Singleton Glen Ord Distillery Exclusive
The Last Drop Glenrothes 1970
Whisky Illuminati Glentauchers 2011
G&M Rare Old Glenury Royal 1984
Highland Park Aged 18 Years
Fadandel.dk Orkney Aged 14 Years
AnCnoc 1999
Lagavulin Aged 8 Years
Loch Lomond The Open Special Edition Distiller's Cut
The Macallan Fine Oak 12 Years Old
Cadenhead's Whisky & More Baden Miltonduff 10 Year Old
Old Pulteney Aged 15 Years
Gordon & MacPhail Connoisseurs Choice Pulteney Aged 19 Years
Rosebank 21 Years Old
Springbank 22 Year Old Single Cask
Tomatin Warehouse 6 Collection 1975
Port Askaig Islay Aged 12 Years Spring Edition
Arcanum Spirits Arcanum One 18 Years Old

Compass Box Myths & Legends III
Whisky Illuminati Artis Secretum 2011

Scottish Vatted Malt
Compass Box The Lost Blend
Wemyss Malts Spice King Batch Strength

Scottish Blends
Artful Dodger Blended Scotch 41 Year Old
Ballantine's Aged 30 Years
The Chivas 18 Ultimate Cask Collection
First Fill American Oak
Chivas Regal Aged 25 Years
James Buchanan's Aged 18 Years
Johnnie Walker Black Label 12 Years Old
Royal Salute 21 Year Old The Lost Blend
Royal Salute 62 Gun Salute

Irish Pure Pot Still
Redbreast Aged 12 Years Cask Strength
batch no. B2/19

Irish Single Malt
Bushmills Aged 21 Years
Bushmills Port Cask Reserve
The Irishman Aged 17 Years
J. J. Corry The Flintlock No. 1 16 Year Old
Kinahan's Special Release Project 11 Year Old

Bourbon
Blade and Bow 22 Year Old
Buffalo Trace Single Oak Project Barrel #27
Buffalo Trace Single Oak Project Barrel #30
Eagle Rare Aged 10 Years
Elmer T Lee Single Barrel Kentucky
Straight Bourbon Whiskey
Frankfort Bourbon Society Elijah Craig
Small Batch Serial No 4718833
Knob Creek Aged 9 Years
Michter's Single Barrel 10 Year Old Kentucky
Straight Bourbon barrel no. 19D625
Old Forester 1920 Prohibition Style
Pappy Van Winkle Family Reserve Kentucky
Straight Bourbon Whiskey 23 Years Old
Parker's Heritage Collection 24 Year Old
Bottled in Bond Bourbon
Rock Hill Farms Single Barrel Bourbon
Weller Antique 107
Weller C.Y.P.B Wheated Straight Bourbon
Wild Turkey Rare Breed Barrel Proof
William Larue Weller 135.4 proof

Tennessee Whiskey
Uncle Nearest 1820 Aged 11 Years

American Straight Rye
Knob Creek Rye Single Barrel Select
Wild Turkey 101 Kentucky Straight Rye

American Microdistilleries
Horse Soldier Reserve Barrel Strength
Bourbon Whiskey
Burns Night Single Malt
Balcones FR.OAK Texas Single Malt Whisky
Aged at least 36 Months in Oak
Corsair Dark Rye American Rye Malt
Whiskey Aged 8 Months
Garrison Brothers Cowboy Bourbon Barrel
Proof Aged Five Years
Cadenhead's Garrison Brothers 2014
Laws Whiskey House Four Grain Straight
Bourbon Whiskey Barrel Select Aged 8 Years
Woodinville Cask Strength Straight Bourbon

Canadian Single Malt
Lohin McKinnon Peated Single Malt Whisky
Forty Creek Copper Pot Reserve
Shelter Point Single Cask Virgin Oak Finish

Canadian Blended
Crown Royal Northern Harvest Rye
Gibson's Finest Rare Aged 18 Years

Japanese Vatted Malt
Nikka Taketsuru Pure Malt

Japanese Single Grain
Makoto Single Grain Whisky Aged 23 Years

English Single Malt
Bimber Distillery Single Malt London
Cotswolds Single Malt Whisky Founder's
Choice STR
The English Single Malt Whisky 'Lest We
Forget' 1914 - 1918

Welsh Single Malt
Penderyn Celt
Penderyn Legend
Penderyn Madeira Finish
Penderyn Rich Oak
Penderyn Single Cask no. 2/2006
Penderyn Ex-Madeira Single Cask no. M524

Australian Single Malt
Bakery Hill Peated Malt Cask Strength
Single Malt Whisky
Heartwood Night Thief
Limeburners Western Australia Single Malt
Whisky Port Cask Cask Strength

Austrian Single Malt
J.H. Original Rye Whisky 6 Jahre Gelagert

Corsican Single Malt
P & M Aged 13 Years Corsican Single Malt

Danish Single Malt
Stauning Peat
Stauning Rye The Master Distiller

French Single Malt
Kornog En E Bezh 10 Year Old
Kornog Saint Erwan 2018

German Single Malt
Feller New Make Barley Malt Peated

Swedish Single Malt
High Coast Distillery Visitor Center Cask
Mackmyra Brukswhisky art nr. MB-003
Mackmyra Brukswhisky art nr. MB-004
Mackmyra Single Cask 2nd Fill ex-Bourbon
Cask Fat Nr 11638
Mackmyra Svensk Rök
Mackmyra Svensk Moment 22
Smögen Primör Revisited Single Malt 2019

Swiss Single Malt
Langatun 10 Year Old Chardonnay
Langatun Cardeira Cask Finish Single Malt

Indian Single Malt
Amrut Greedy Angels Peated Rum Finish
Chairman's Reserve 10 Years Old
Amrut Peated Port Pipe Single Cask
Paul John Christmas Edition

95 (New Entries Only)

Scottish Single Malt
Berry Bros & Rudd Allt-á-Bhainne 23 Year Old
The Whisky Chamber Annandale 4 Jahre
The Balvenie Double Wood Aged 17 Years
Woolf/Sung The Lowest Tide Bowmore 26
Year Old 1991
Bruichladdich Black Art 7 Aged 25 Years
Octomore Edition 10.1 Aged 5 Years
Port Charlotte Aged 10 Years
Port Charlotte Islay Barley 2011 Aged 6 Years
Glenfiddich Winter Storm Aged 21 Years
Icewine Cask Finish Experiment
Glenmorangie Grand Vintage 1997
Glen Moray Aged 21 Years Portwood Finish
Laphroaig 10 Year Old
Loch Lomond Aged 18 Years
Loch Lomond Aged 18 Years Inchmurrin
Wilson & Morgan Barrel Selection Macduff
Old Malt Cask Miltonduff Aged 25 Years
The Whisky Agency Springbank 1991
Compass Box Myths & Legends II
Wemyss Malts Nectar Grove Blended Malt

Scottish Vatted Malt
Compass Box The Peat Monster
Wemyss Malts Peat Chimney Blended Malt

Scottish Blends
Johnnie Walker Black Label Aged 12 Years
Irish Pure Pot Still
Method and Madness Single Pot Still
Redbreast Lustau Edition Sherry Finish
Irish Single Malt
Bushmills Distillery Reserve Single Malt Aged 12 Years
Artful Dodger Irish Single Malt 15 Year Old
Irish Blends
Bushmills Black Bush
Bourbon
Booker's Kentucky Straight Bourbon Aged 6 Years, 6 Months, 19 Days
Eagle Rare 17 Years Old
J Mattingly Bobo's Bourbon Larceny Barrel Proof batch no. B520
Larceny Barrel Proof batch no. A1200
American Straight Rye
Sagamore Spirit Straight Rye Double Oak
American Microdistilleries
Balcones Peated Texas Single Malt Whisky Aged at least 36 Months in Oak
Balcones True Blue Cask Strength Straight Corn Whiskey Aged at least 31 Months in Oak
Dry Fly Straight Wheat Whiskey Cask Strength Aged 3 Years
Lone Elm Single Barrel Texas Straight Wheat
Garrison Brothers Texas Straight Bourbon Whiskey 2020 Release
Kings County Distillery Empire Rye Aged 2 Years or More
Rock Town Arkansas Straight Rye Whiskey Aged 2.5 Years
Blackback Straight Rye Whiskey Alpha Series Aged 4 Years
Other American Whiskey
Sagamore Spirit Calvados Finish
Japanese Single Malt
Meiyo Pure Malt Aged 15 Years Edition 2020
Nikka Taketsuru Pure Malt Whisky
The Essence of Suntory Whisky Yamazaki
English Single Malt
Filey Bay Yorkshire Whisky First Release
Welsh Single Malt
Penderyn Legend
Penderyn Sherrywood
Penderyn Single no. 71/2007
Australian Single Malt
Chief's Son Single Malt 900 Standard
Cradle Mountain The Long Trek
Lark Distillery Sherry Matured & Finished
Sullivans Cove French Oak
Sullivans Cove Old & Rare American Oak
Iniquity Gold Label Single Malt Batch 005
Danish Single Malt
Stauning Port Smoke Cask Strength
Finnish Single Malt
Teerenpeli Kaski Single Malt Whisky
Norwegian Single Malt
Myken Artic Single Malt Whisky Octave Symphony 2020 4 Year Old
Swiss Single Malt
Langatun 10 Year Second Edition Single Malt
Indian Single Malt
Paul John Single Cask Peated #6086

94.5 (New Entries Only)
Scottish Single Malt
eSpirits Shop Selection Aberlour 24 Year Old
Old Malt Cask Balmenach Aged 14 Years
Glen Grant Aged 12 Years bott code: LRO/HI18
Gordon & MacPhail Connoisseurs Choice Glenlivet Aged 14 Years
Glen Moray Rhum Agricole Cask Finish Project
Glen Scotia Victoriana Cask Strength

Signatory Vintage Glentauchers 22 Year Old
Deer, Bear & Moose Inchgower Aged 22 Years
Liquid Treasures Inchfad 14 Year Old
Tomatin 21 Year Old
Fadandel.dk Tomatin 10 Year Old
Tullibardine The Murray Cask Strength
Scottish Vatted Malt
Compass Box The Circle
Scyfion Choice Westport 1996
Scottish Grain
Artful Dodger Cameronbridge 35 Year Old
Liquid Treasures From Miles Away Cameronbridge 38 Year Old
Single & Single Invergordon 5 Years Old
Scottish Blends
Compass Box Rogue's Banquet
Islay Mist Aged 21 Years
The Sovereign 45 Years Old Blended Scotch White Horse
Irish Pure Pot Still
Hinch Single Pot Still
Irish Blends
Jameson The Cooper's Croze
Bourbon
1792 Aged 12 Years Straight Bourbon
Elijah Craig Barrel Proof Kentucky Straight
Mayor Pingree Aged 7 Years Straight Bourbon Whiskey
Wild Turkey Rare Breed Barrel Proof
American Straight Rye
Elijah Craig Kentucky Straight Rye Whiskey
Sagamore Spirit Straight Rye Whiskey Barrel Select Aged 6 Years
American Microdistilleries
Balcones Texas Blue Corn Bourbon Aged at least 34 Months in Oak
Copperworks American Single Malt Whiskey Release No. 027 Aged 31 Months
Copperworks American Single Malt Whiskey Cask No. 187 Aged 29 Months
Ironroot Ichor Straight Bourbon Whiskey Aged 48 Months
Kings County Distillery Straight Bourbon Blender's Reserve Aged 5 Years
Koval Single Barrel Bourbon Whiskey
Reservoir Distillery Bourbon 100% Corn Aged a Minimum of 2 Years
Rock Town Single Barrel Rye Aged 30 Months
The Notch Single Malt Aged 12 Years
Woodinville Cask Strength Straight 100% Rye Whiskey
Canadian Single Malt
Forty Creek Confederation Oak Reserve
Canadian Blended
Crown Royal Northern Harvest Rye
English Single Malt
Cotswolds Single Malt Whisky Blenheim Palace Single Cask
Filey Bay Yorkshire Single Malt Whisky Moscatel Finish
Welsh Single Malt
Penderyn Single Cask no. PT267
Penderyn Single Cask no. 078-2
Belgian Single Malt
Belgian Owl Single Malt 40 Months First Fill Bourbon Single Cask No 6631688
Belgian Owl Single Malt 12 Years Vintage No 5 Single First Fill Bourbon Cask No 4279860
Braeckman Belgian Single Grain Whiskey Single Barrel Aged 12 Years
Danish Single Malt
Stauning Rye
Stauning Rye Rum Cask Finish
German Single Malt
Salamansar Single Cask Whisky Batch no. 1

Derrina Hafermalz Schwarzwälder Single Malt
Rye Schwäbischer Roggenmalz-Whisky
St. Kilian Signature Edition Three

Israeli Single Malt
The Milk & Honey Distillery Single Cask La Maison Du Whisky 2019

Norwegian Single Malt
Myken Artic Single Malt Whisky Peated Sherry 2019 3 Year Old

Swedish Single Malt
Mackmyra Moment Lava
Mackmyra Single Cask 2nd Fill ex-Bourbon Cask Fat Nr 11641

Swiss Single Malt
Langatun Founder's Reserve 10 Year Old

Indian Single Malt
Paul John Distillery Edition

94 (New Entries Only)

Scottish Single Malt
Old Malt Cask Allt A'Bhainne Aged 27 Years
The Whisky Chamber Ardmore 10 Jahre
Cask & Thistle Ben Nevis Aged 22 Years
Blair Athol Distillery Exclusive Bottling Bowmore Aged 15 Years
Wemyss Malts Kilning The Malt Bowmore 1996 23 Years Old
Octomore Edition 10.2 Aged 8 Years
Fadandel.dk Bruichladdich 15 Year Old
Liquid Treasures Bunnahabhain 11 Year Old
Artful Dodger Caol Ila 9 Year Old 2008
The Single Cask Caol Ila 2007
G&M Private Collection Coleburn 1981
Cragganmore 15 Years Old 150th Anniversary
Fadandel.dk Dalmore 11 Year Old
Glen Grant Aged 10 Years code: LRO/GD26
Glenmorangie Signet
The First Editions Glen Moray Aged 25 Years
Glen Scotia Vintage 1991
The Great Drams Glentauchers 10 Years Old
Jura Aged 21 Years Tide
Kingsbarns Dream to Dram
Knockando Aged 18 Years
anCnoc 12 Years Old
Chapter 7 Miltonduff 21 Year Old 1998
The First Editions Miltonduff Aged 29 Years
Tamnavulin Red Wine Cask Edition No. 01
Acla Selection Tobermory 23 Year Old
Liquid Treasures Ledaig 13 Year Old
Single & Single Ledaig 2005 13 Years Old
Elements of Islay CL13
Kingsbury Gold Kilbride 13 Year Old

Scottish Vatted Malt
Black Tartan 88 31 Year Old

Scottish Grain
The Whisky Gallery The Magician North British Aged 5 Years

Scottish Blends
Grand Macnish Double Matured Aged 15 Years Sherry Cask Edition
Islay Mist Aged 10 Years
Johnnie Walker Double Black

Irish Pure Pot Still
Green Spot
Redbreast Aged 21 Years

Irish Single Malt
The Tyrconnell Single Malt Irish Whiskey Aged 16 Years
Bushmills Rum Cask Reserve

Irish Blends
Egan's Centenary

Bourbon
Baker's Kentucky Straight Bourbon Single Barrel Aged 8 Years, 6 Months
Bomberger's Declaration 2019 Release Bourbon 30

Bulleit Bourbon Frontier Whiskey
Michter's Single Barrel 10 Year Old Kentucky Straight Bourbon barrel no. 20C363
Old Forester 1870 Original Batch
The Single Cask Heaven Hill 2009
Smooth Ambler Contradiction Bourbon
Weller Full Proof Kentucky Straight Bourbon

Tennessee Whiskey
Joe Got a Gun Single Barrel #1

American Straight Rye
New Riff Balboa Rye Whiskey Bottled in Bond

American Straight Wheat
Bernheim Original 7 Year Aged Kentucky Straight Wheat Whiskey

American Microdistilleries
Tire Fire Single Malt
Copperworks American Single Malt Whiskey Release No. 020 Aged 34 Months
Copperworks American Single Malt Whiskey Release No. 025 Aged 43 Months
291 Bad Guy Colorado Bourbon Whiskey Aged 324 Days Aspen Stave Finished
Iron Smoke Casket Strength Straight Bourbon Whiskey Aged a Minimum of 2 Years
Kings County Distillery Peated Rye Aged 2 Years or More
Christine Single Barrel Virginia Bourbon Whiskey Riggleman Reserve
Westland Single Cask Aged 46 Months

Other American Whiskey
Taconic Distillery Mizunara Cask

Canadian Single Malt
Two Brewers Yukon Single Malt Release 16

Japanese Single Malt
Chichibu On The Way 2019

Japanese Vatted Malt
Kamiki Blended Malt Whisky Sakura Wood

English Single Malt
The English Single Malt Whisky Small Batch Release Rum Cask Matured

Welsh Single Malt
Penderyn Legend
Penderyn Myth
Penderyn Peated

Australian
Bakery Hill Death or Glory
Launceston Distillery Cask Strength Tawny Cask Matured Tasmanian Single Malt Whisky
Limeburners Western Australia Single Malt Whisky Darkest Winter Cask Strength
Heartwood Market Correction Tasmanian Single Malt Whisky

Danish Single Malt
Lindorm Danish Single Malt 2nd Edition
Mosgaard Organic Single Malt Whisky

Finnish Single Malt
Teerenpeli Savu Single Malt Whisky

French Single Malt
ER 2015 Single Malt Whisky Tourbé No. 001

German Single Malt
Aureum Single Malt Whisky 10 Year Old Cask Strength
Feller Torf Single Malt
Derrina Müsli Schwarzwälder Single Grain
Palatinatus Single Malt Whisky Single Cask German Oak 2014
Sild Crannog Single Malt Whisky 2019

Portuguese Single Malt
Woodwork Madeira Cask Strength Single Malt

New Zealand Single Malt
The New Zealand Whisky Collection The Oamaruvian 18 Year Old

Taiwanese Single Malt
Golden Gate Sunset Kavalan Single Malt Whisky Sherry Cask

American Whiskey

During the early Spring of last year I took a very long drive. It was from Texas to Kentucky, taking me on a route which cut through the Ozark Mountains in both Arkansas and Missouri, where I dropped in on a forest in which oaks had been felled for the making of bourbon barrels. And then stood beside the stumps of departed trees holding in my hands the last acorns they had ever deposited.

I stopped at quite a few liquor stores en-route, also. And found something possibly even more astonishing. Where, once, the whisk(e)y shelves had contained an ever-increasing number of single malt Scotch whiskies, now they contained bourbon and rye.

Kentucky bourbon, Colorado bourbon, Texas bourbon. They were all there. Alongside ryes and Tennessee and various types of whiskeys from the smaller concerns that had mushroomed up around the country since the turn of the century. It seemed that in mid-America at least bourbon and rye had Scotch whisky on the run: a nation had fallen back in love with its national whiskey.

And that can hardly be surprising when the consistency of Kentucky bourbon and rye in particular has been unrelentingly good. Indeed, for the last three years running, it was a bourbon whiskey which scooped the Jim Murray Whisky Bible World Whisky of the Year with three different brands: E H Taylor, William Larue Weller and the 1792 Barton. And with Booker's Rye winning in 2017, that means Kentucky whiskey had scooped the top award for four years running.

This year, the astonishing cask strength Alberta Premium Rye had ended Kentucky's domination, taking the Whisky Bible World Whisky of the Year crown back to Canada. Even so, it was Stagg Junior from Buffalo Trace which came in a very close second – both winner and second place on 97.5 points. This bourbon is really a chip off the old block: George T Stagg was the Bible's first-ever World Whisky of the Year.

In Texas, so high is the standard of the whiskeys there, I was recently able to travel to the State to carry out a whiskey shootout between 11 of their distilleries there to see which, through blind tasting, the assembled crowd appreciated most. It was Garrison Brothers' Balmorhea. This enormous bourbon this year completed the hat-trick of picking up Microdistillery Whisky of the Year with another stupendous bottling.

A quarter of a century ago the liquor store owners from New York to San Francisco were telling me that bourbon and rye would soon be a thing of the past as single malts moved in. Bourbon is well and truly back. And, as the top awards of Jim Murray's Whisky Bible underlines, with very good reason.

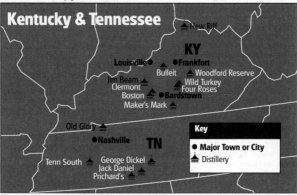

Bourbon Distilleries

Bourbon confuses people. Often they don't even realise it is a whiskey, a situation not helped by leading British pub chains, such as Wetherspoon, whose bar menus list "whiskey" and "bourbon" in separate sections. And if I see the liqueur Southern Comfort listed as a bourbon one more time I may not be responsible for my actions.

Bourbon is a whiskey. It is made from grain and matured in oak, so really it can't be much else. To be legally called bourbon it must have been made with a minimum of 51% corn and matured in virgin oak casks for at least two years. Oh, and no colouring can be added other than that which comes naturally from the barrel.

Where it does differ, from, say Scotch, is that the straight whiskey from the distillery may be called by something other than that distillery name. Indeed, the distillery may change its name which has happened to two this year already and two others in the last three or four. So, to make things easy and reference as quick as possible, I shall list the Kentucky-based distilleries first and then their products in alphabetical order along with their owners and operational status.

Bourbon Distillery List

Bardstown	**Lexington**	Jim Beam Urban Stillhouse
Barton 1792	Barrel House	Kentucky Peerless
Rebell Yell	Bluegrass	Michter's Fort Nelson
Willett Distillery	James E. Pepper	Michter's Shively
	Town Branch	Old Forester
		Rabbit Hole
		Stitzel Weller
	Louisville	
	Angel's Envy	
Frankfort	Bernheim.	**Shelbyville**
Buffalo Trace	Evan Williams	Bulleit Distilling Co.
Castle & Key	Heaven Hill Bernheim	Jeptha Creed
Glenns Creek		

Jim Murray's Whisky Bible 2021 American Whiskies of the Year

Bourbon of the Year	Stagg Jr Barrel Proof
Second Finest Bourbon of the Year	William Larue Weller
Rye of the Year	Thomas H. Handy Sazerac
Second Finest Rye of the Year	Wild Turkey Cornerstone
US Micro Whisky of the Year Multiple Barrels	Garrison Brothers Balmorhea Texas Straight Bourbon Whiskey 2020 Release
US Micro Whisky of the Year Single Barrel	Woodinville Straight Bourbon Whiskey Private Select cask no. 1953

Jim Murray's Whisky Bible American Whiskey Award Winners

	Overall Winner	Bourbon	Rye	Microdistilleries
2004-2006	George T. Stagg	George T. Stagg	Sazerac Rye 18 Years Old	McCarthy's Oregan Single Malt
2007	Buffalo Trace Experimental	Buffalo Trace Experimental	Rittenhouse Rye 21 Barrel No.28	McCarthy's Oregan Single Malt
2008	George T. Stagg 70.3%	George T. Stagg 70.3%	Old Potrero Hotaling's 11 Essay	Old Potrero Hotaling's 11 Essay
2009	George T. Stagg (144.8 Proof)	George T. Stagg (144.8 Proof)	Rittenhouse Rye 23 Barrel No.8	Stranahan's Colorado 5 Batch 11
2010	Sazerac Rye 18 (Fall 2008)	George T. Stagg (144.8 Proof)	Sazerac Rye 18 (Fall 2008)	N/A
2011	Thomas H. Handy Rye (129 Proof)	William Larue Weller (134.8 Proof)	Thomas H. Handy Rye (129 Proof)	N/A
2012	George T. Stagg (143 Proof)	George T. Stagg (143 Proof)	Thomas H. Handy Rye (126.9 Proof)	N/A
2013	Thomas H. Handy Rye (128.6 Proof)	William Larue Weller (133.5 Proof)	Thomas H. Handy Rye (128.6 Proof)	Balcones Brimstone
2014	William Larue Weller (123.4 Proof)	William Larue Weller (123.4 Proof)	Thomas H. Handy Rye (132.4 Proof)	Cowboy Bourbon Whiskey
2015	William Larue Weller	William Larue Weller	Sazerac Rye 18 (Fall 2013)	Arkansas Single Barrel Reserve #190
2016	Pikesville Straight Rye (110 Proof)	William Larue Weller	Pikesville Straight Rye (110 Proof)	Notch 12 Year Old
2017	Booker's Rye 13 Years 1 Mo 12 Days	William Larue Weller (134.6 Proof)	Booker's Rye 13 Years 1 Mo 12 Days	Garrison Brothers Cowboy 2009
2018	Colonel E.H. Taylor Four Grain	Colonel E.H. Taylor Four Grain	Thomas H. Handy Rye (126.2 Proof)	Balcones Texas Blue Corn
2019	William Larue Weller (128.2 Proof)	William Larue Weller (128.2 Proof)	Thomas H. Handy Rye (127.2 Proof)	Garrison Brothers Balmorhea
2020	1792 Full Proof Bourbon	1792 Full Proof Bourbon	Thomas H. Handy Rye (128.8 Proof)	Garrison Brothers Balmorhea

Bourbon

⟡ **1792 Aged 12 Years Kentucky Straight Bourbon Whiskey** nbc db **(94.5) n24** those busy small grains – a kind of 1792 Distillery trademark– are burbling and bubbling away under the red liquorice, the rye in particular surfacing for a quick stab before vanishing again. Despite the good age, the tannins remain restrained and delicately in keeping with the grains. The softer corn gently offers an enticing bready sweetness; **t24** the delivery is all about the corn oil. So sensual, every nuance just melts into the next. Light acacia and ulmo honey mix for a controlled sweetness; the red liquorice is a meagre nod towards the big age. But, as usual, the star turn is the bubbling grains busily frothing away; **f23** surprisingly quiet. But, as usual below the surface, so much is happening...; **b23.5** the usual 1792 complexity mixed with sleek curves. Nowhere near in the same league as last year's world conquering Full Proof version. But for a gentle perambulation among the unsung small grains, this is as good a route as you can take... *48.3% (96.6 proof).*

1792 Bottled In Bond bott code: L172731504:465 db **(93) n23 t23.5 f23 b23.5** An unusually salty resonance to this which travels from the nose to the very last moments of the finish. Certainly does a job in sharpening up the flavour profile! *50% (100 proof).*

1792 Bottled In Bond Kentucky Straight Bourbon bott code: L183471505565 **(96.5) n24 t24 f24 ...b24.5** Well, it's only gone and improved, hasn't it..!!! I just wish this distillery would give a whiskey I could seriously pan..! Just so damn, indecently beautiful...! *50% (100 proof).*

1792 Full Proof Kentucky Straight Bourbon bott code: L18135513:425 **(97.5) n24 t24.5 f24 b25** Sings on the nose and palate like a wood thrush in a Kentucky forest: melodious, mysterious and slightly exotic. On this evidence Buffalo Trace has a threat to its world supremacy – from a rival distillery...they own! This is a whiskey of stand out, almost stand-alone beauty. Finding fault is not easy with something this intense and magnificently rich. If this is not World Whisky of the Year for 2020, then its master will be something to marvel at. *62.5% (125 proof).*

1792 Single Barrel Kentucky Straight Bourbon nbc **(90.5) n22.5** a lovely hickory-liquorice mix with spices in healthy mode; **t22** a creamy and peppery start, the corn oils high on the early flavour profile. The toffees and vanillas take their time to make a mark but get there at their own pace; **f23** more complex now as the tannins and vanillas appear more harmonised and the sugars now deliciously integrated; **b23** typical of a single cask, offering some of what you expect from a distillery though not necessarily all. Delicious and more mouth-filling as it progresses. *44% (88 proof). sc.*

1792 Small Batch bott code: L173111514:395 **(94) n23 t24 f23.5 b23.5** Yet again a 1792 expression pulls off Whisky Bible Liquid Gold status. Astonishing. *46.85% (93.7 proof).*

1792 Small Batch Kentucky Straight Bourbon bott code: L190461512595 **(94) n23.5 t24 f23 b23.5** On the lighter side of the 1782 spectrum, though definitely within the distillery's new orbit. Where there is often a rich wave of soft tannins, here it concentrates on the defter vanillas, at times delicate to the point of fragility, though the trademark weight and gravitas is not far behind... *46.85% (93.7 proof).*

Abraham Bowman Limited Edition Viriginia Sweet XVI Bourbon dist 4-26-02, bott 4-26-18 **(95.5) n23.5 t24.5 f23.5 b24** Probably the most outrageously complex and full-flavoured Virginia whiskey I have ever encountered in bottled form...Just amazin'! *58% (116 proof).*

⟡ **American Eagle Tennessee Bourbon Aged 4 Years** bott code: L927704 db **(91) n22.5** such an attractive mix between mildly damp muscovado sugar and drier, powdery hickory; **t23** any specialist in Bowmore will immediately recognise an earthy Victory V cough sweet assembly which apes that distillery remarkably from how it was 15 years ago. The hickory really does do a star turn...; **f22.5** a light oiling of corn heralds the arrival of the delicate spices; **b23** an attractive bourbon very much of the hickory persuasion. Enticing, soft, good corn involvement and well distributed spice. A very sound whiskey. *40%.*

⟡ **American Eagle Tennessee Bourbon Aged 12 Years** bott code: L9053HA12 db **(84.5) n21 t22 f20 b21.5** When I tasted this earlier in the year, I was quite impressed. This bottling seems to have dropped a notch. The nose warns of an unhappy alliance between the spirit and oak. The unhappy finish confirms it dramatically. *43%.*

American Rockies Small Batch Bourbon Whiskey (76) n19 t22 f17 b18 Sweet, soft, fruity and rounded. But very dull. With an unattractive furry finish to boot. Just not sure what all these fruit notes are doing in a bourbon. *44% (88 proof).*

Ancient Age bott code: 03072163212:09F **(94) n24 t23.5 f22.5 b24** Though at times a little youthful and proudly possessing a little nip to the delivery, this still exudes Buffalo Trace character and class and a lot more inner oomph than when I first encountered this brand decades ago – indeed, when the distillery was still called Ancient Age. Enough oak to make a comfortable foil for the busy small grain. Salivating, complex and deeply satisfying, especially when the burnt honey begins to make itself heard. A classic name and my word, this bottling shows it in a classic light. *40% (80 proof)*

Ancient Age Kentucky Straight Bourbon bott code: L190240120:254 **(93)** n23 t23 f23.5 **b23.5** Very similar to the bottling code above One very slight difference here is just a slight downturn in the intensity of the honey while the spices, perhaps with a fraction less to counter it, have a marginally louder voice. Perhaps not quite the same balance, but the finish goes on so much longer. *40% (80 proof).*

Ancient Age Bonded (92) n23 t24 f23 b23. Unmistakably Buffalo Trace... with balls. *50%*

Ancient Ancient Age 10 Years Old (96) n23.5 t24 f24 b24.5. This whiskey is like shifting sands: same score as last time out, but the shape is quite different again. Somehow underlines the genius of the distillery that a world class whiskey can reach the same point of greatness, but by taking two different routes...However, in this case the bourbon actually finds something a little extra to move it on to a point very few whiskeys very rarely reach... *43%*

Ancient Ancient Age 10 Star (94.5) n23 t24 f23.5 b24. A bourbon which has slipped effortlessly through the gears over the last decade. It is now cruising and offers so many nuggets of pure joy this is now a must have for the serious bourbon devotee. Now a truly great bourbon which positively revels in its newfound complexity: a new 10 Star is born... *45%*

Ancient Age 10 Star Kentucky Straight Bourbon bott code: L182010116 **(94)** n22.5 t23.5 f24 b24 A bourbon which had lost its way slightly in recent years. And though it still splutters about a bit for identity and rhythm on the nose, there is no doubting it is right back on track with some taste-bud catching moments. It is at times, monumental. *45% (90 proof).*

Ancient Age 90 bott code: 03072173209:38W **(88.5)** n22 t22 f22.5 b22 An emboldened bourbon showing little of genteel complexity of the standard Ancient Age. Delicious, though! *45% (90 proof)*

Ancient Age 90 Kentucky Straight Bourbon Whiskey bott code: B1310606 **(93.5)** n23 t23 f23.5 b24 More of the same as above, though now is a lot more vibrant. A little more stark tannin on the nose to this one and an infinitely more lush and bold delivery. If the layering was good before, then now it is excellent with not just an extra layer or two of strata to negotiate but much more Manuka honey coming through at the death. How can two whiskeys be outwardly so similar, yet so different? A bit like having a polished Jaguar XK against a slightly dusty one. *45% (90 proof).*

◈ **Baker's Kentucky Straight Bourbon Single Barrel Aged 8 Years, 3 Months** dist 10-2011, warehouse CL-Z, serial no. 000289669 db **(93)** n23.5 the gentlest phenol note clings to the dull tannin and spice. Very genteel and delicate; t23.5 light hickory had brushed the nose, so gently, you may not have noticed. But it certainly on display here, unambiguous and in full bloom. Despite the softly, softly tactics, there is a still some profound bourbon at work, the Demerara sugars intensifying things further; f22.5 a discreet nod towards the custard-rich tannin; b23.5 just amazing that the distillery that brings you the occasionally pulverising Knob Creek can also caress you so tenderly with a Baker's like this... *53.5% (107 proof). sc.*

◈ **Baker's Kentucky Straight Bourbon Single Barrel Aged 8 Years, 6 Months** dist 01-2011, warehouse CL-D db **(94)** n23.5 almost a light smokiness to soften the impact of the prevailing tannins. A dusting of hickory and a small pinch of spice compliments the light maple syrup and molasses mix; t24 silky corn oils abound and ensures a sublime counter for the most prickly of spices that try to puncture the sugary frame. So chewy and elegant; f23 just a trace of bitterness follows the hefty liquorice; b23.5 surely Jim Beam's Clermont Distillery has to be the most under-rated in the world: familiarity breeding contempt, I suppose. But this single barrel shows you in no uncertain terms just how high grade and beautifully complex their output can be. *53.5% (107 proof). sc.*

Barrel Bourbon Cask Strength Aged 9.5 Years batch 015 **(88)** n22 t23 f21 b22 An interesting bottling which fits cosily together in places and falls apart slightly in others. Overall, though, enjoyable. *53.8% (107.6 proof). Distilled in Tennessee and Kentucky.*

Barrel Whiskey Infinite Barrel Project Cask Strength bott June 1 2018 **(85.5)** n21 t22.5 f20.5 b21.5 A strange, thin Tennessee whiskey with a mysterious sub-plot of gin-like botanicals. Which will doubtless appeal to some. *59.3% (118.6 proof). Distilled in Tennessee.*

Basil Hayden's Kentucky Straight Bourbon Whiskey bott code L5222 **(87)** n22.5 t22 f21 b21.5. Bigs up the bitter marmalade but a relatively thin bourbon with not enough depth to entirely manage the flattening and slightly unflattering vanilla. The usual rye-based backbone has gone missing. *40% (80 proof)*

Bib and Tucker Small Batch Bourbon Aged 6 Years batch no 018 **(88.5)** n22 t22 f22.5 b22 Bit of a straight up and downer, with the complexity at last formulating towards the finale. About as easy-going and even as it gets. *46% (92 proof).*

◈ **Bib & Tucker Small Batch Bourbon Aged 6 Years** batch no. 21 **(96)** n24 if you find any whiskey on the planet shewing more hickory on the nose than this, please let me know; t24.5 this is thick corn-oil rammed bourbon sporting the most pleasing and untamed chicory coffee and liquorice spine The spices are gentle by comparison; f23.5 lots of vanilla, dried molasses and still that chicory...; **b24** a far more intense and captivating bourbon than the last bottling I sampled. This is Tennessee bourbon to put hairs on your chest. I'd love to see this at full strength, I can tell you! A whiskey demanding to be served in a dirty glass. I absolutely love this! *46% (92 proof).* 🍷

Blade & Bow batch SW-B1 **(84) n21.5 t21.5 f20 b21.** A simple, if at times massively sweet, offering which minimises on complexity. *45.5%*

Blade and Bow 22 Year Old (95.5) n24 t24 f23.5 b24 This may not be the oldest bourbon brand on the market, but it creaks along as though it is. Every aspect says "Old Timer". But like many an old 'un, has a good story to tell... in this case, exceptional. *46% (92 proof)*

Blade & Bow DeLuxe batch WLCFSS-2 **(88.5) n22.5 t22.5 f21 b22.5** A steady ship which, initially, is heavy on the honey. *46%*

Blanton's (92) n21.5 t24 f23 b23.5. If it were not for the sluggish nose this would be a Whisky Bible Liquid Gold award winner for sure. On the palate it shows just why little can touch Buffalo Trace for quality at the moment... *40%*

◈ **Blanton's** dumped 10-10-19 Warehouse H Rick 1 db **(84.5) n21 t22 f20 b21.5** Well, what do you know? A Blanton's firing off only half its cylinders at most. Both the nose and finish are strangely muffled and muted. And despite a brief moment of juicy brilliance on delivery, the musty, bitter finale confirms all is not well. My God! This bourbon is made by humans after all... *46.5% (93 proof).*

Blanton's Gold Edition Bourbon Whiskey dumped 15 Jan 19, barrel no 131, Warehouse H, Rick 15 **(90) n22 t23 f22 b23** The last time I tasted a Blanton's Gold, I was stopped in my tracks and knew I had, in my glass, some kind of major Whisky Bible award winner. And so it proved. This time the key honey notes crucial to greatness are thin on the ground. And, lovely whiskey though it may be, this one is no award winner..! *51.5% (103 proof). sc.*

Blanton's The Original Single Barrel Bourbon Whiskey dumped 7 March 19, barrel no 199, Warehouse H Rick 11 **(94) n24 t23.5 f23 b23.5** Not sure bourbon gets any friendlier and sweeter than this without losing shape. Superb! *46.5% (93 proof). sc.*

Blanton's Single Barrel Kentucky Straight Bourbon dumped 30th April 18, barrel no 126, Warehouse H Rick 52 **(94.5) n23.5 t24 f23 b24** A very long journey from beginning to end: intriguing as you are never sure what will be happening next. *46.5% (93 proof). sc.*

Blanton's Uncut/Unfiltered (96.5) n25 t24 f23.5 b24. Uncut. Unfiltered. Unbelievable. *65.9%*

Bomberger's Declaration Kentucky Straight Bourbon 2018 Release batch no. 18C317, bott code: A18096317 **(95) n23.5 t24 f23.5 b24** A breath-taking whiskey which, despite its seemingly soft and inclusive nature, is huge in personality. *54% (108 proof). 1,658 bottles. Bottled by Michter's Distillery.*

◈ **Bomberger's Declaration Kentucky Straight Bourbon 2019 Release** batch no. 19G1234, bott code: A192071234 **(94) n23.5** I'm almost drooling at the interplay between red and black liquorice. Top grade marzipan cementing it all together; **t24** the criss-crossing of caramels, milky marzipan, praline and corn oils is sublime. There is even a lime-blossom honey note to give a delicate fruity gloss to the sweetness; **f23** still those corn oils ooze, though the spices arrive to give them a bit of a late jolt; **b23.5** proper bourbon, this. Ticks every box. And there is nothing more dangerous than a Bomberger that ticks... *54% (108 proof). 2,577 bottles. Bottled by Michter's Distillery.*

Bondi Bourbon Whiskey Aged 4 Years (85) n20.5 t21.5 f21.5 b21.5 Rammed full of varied honey notes, the feintiness on both the nose and delivery can't be entirely ignored. Still. Chewy and attractive late on. *40% (80 proof).*

◈ **Booker's Kentucky Straight Bourbon Aged 6 Years, 6 Months, 19 Days** batch no. 2019-04 db **(95) n23.5** the small grains are punchy and confident; the backdrop is almost like a stick of candy (presumably with "Booker's" written right through it); a lovely eucalyptus and liquorice lilt, to...; **t24** the crispness hinted at on the nose is apparent here from the very first moment of delivery. The liquorice almost has a cough sweet quality....accompanied by a cube of Demerara sugar; **f23.5** dries with the hefty liquorice and light molasses; **b24** huge! Not a bourbon to be trifled with. And you will note that despite its enormity there is not a single off-key moment, not a single false step. *63.5% (126.1 proof).*

Boone County Eighteen 33 Straight Bourbon Aged 12 Years nbc **(94.5) n23.5 t24 f23 b24** Sits as beautifully on the plate as it does in the glass. Gorgeous! *45.4% (90.8 proof). Distilled at DSP-IN-1 (MGP, Indiana, presumably.).*

◈ **Bourbon 30 (91) n22 t23.5 f22.5 b23** A sturdy, highly attractive bourbon making maximum use of the small grains to really ramp up the complexity. Beautifully deft sugars give an extra crispness...while the small grains fizz and nip. Vanilla everywhere! Love the late spice, too. Great stuff...!! *45% (90 proof).*

◈ **Bourbon 30 (94) n23.5 t23.5 f23 b24** A little more oily than their 45% bottling with far more corn visible on the nose and, especially, the delivery. Much more roasty, headstrong liquorice forming the meat of the body. In fact, just a little more everything compared to the

45%, chest-beating liquorice especially. The late spices here aren't afraid to pack a punch, either... Truly classic high class bourbon. Delicious. *50% (100 proof).*

Bowman Brothers Small Batch Virginia Straight Bourbon bott code: L183540513 **(93)** n23.5 t23 f23 b23.5 A significant improvement on the last Small Batch I encountered with much more confidence and depth on the finish. The coffee note hangs wonderfully... *45% (90 proof).*

Bowman Brothers Virginia Small Batch bott code: 71600080ASB08:22 **(88.5)** n22 t23 f21.5 b22 A lovely bourbon, though the sugars are thinly spread. *45% (90 proof)*

Buffalo Trace (92.5) n23 t23 f23.5 b23. Easily one of the lightest BTs I have tasted in a very long while. The rye has not just taken a back seat, but has fallen off the bus. *46%*

Buffalo Trace Kentucky Straight Bourbon bott code: L190400220 **(94)** n23.5 t23.5 f23 b24 A huge whiskey dressed up as something altogether more modest. But get the temperature right on this and watch it open up like a petal in sunlight. A true anywhere, anytime bourbon with hidden sophistication. *45% (90 proof).*

Buffalo Trace Single Oak Project Barrel #132 (r1yKA1 *see key below*) db **(95)** n24 t23.5 f23.5 b24. This sample struck me for possessing, among the first batch of bottlings, the classic Buffalo Trace personality. Afterwards they revealed that it was of a profile which perhaps most closely matches their standard 8-year-old BT. Therefore it is this one I shall use as the tasting template. *45% (90 Proof)*

Key to Buffalo Trace Single Oak Project Codes

Mash bill type: r = rye; w = wheat
Entry strength: A = 125; B = 105
Tree grain: 1 = course; 2 = average; 3 = tight
Seasoning: 1 = 6 Months; 2 = 12 Months
Tree cut: x = top half; y = bottom half
Char: All #4 except * = #3
Warehouse type: K = rick; L = concrete

Buffalo Trace Single Oak Project Barrel #1 (r3xKA1*) db **(90.5)** n22 t23 f23 b22.5. *45%*
Buffalo Trace Single Oak Project Barrel #2 (r3yKA1*) db **(91.5)** n23 t23 f22.5 b23. *45%*
Buffalo Trace Single Oak Project Barrel #3 (r2xKA1) db **(90.5)** n22.5 t23 f22.5 b22.5. *45%*
Buffalo Trace Single Oak Project Barrel #4 (r2yKA1) db **(92)** n23 t23 f23 b23. *45%*
Buffalo Trace Single Oak Project Barrel #5 (r2xLA1*) db **(89)** n23 t22.5 f21.5 b22. *45%*
Buffalo Trace Single Oak Project Barrel #6 (r3yLA1*) db **(90)** n23 t22 f23 b22.5. *45%*
Buffalo Trace Single Oak Project Barrel #7 (r3xLA1) db **(90.5)** n23 t22.5 f22.5 b22.5. *45%*
Buffalo Trace Single Oak Project Barrel #8 (r3yLA1) db **(92.5)** n23 t23 f23.5 b23. *45%*
Buffalo Trace Single Oak Project Barrel #9 (r3xKA2*) db **(90)** n22 t22.5 f23 b22.5. *45%*
Buffalo Trace Single Oak Project Barrel #10 (r3yKA2*) db **(93)** n23.5 t23.5 f22.5 b23.5. *45%*
Buffalo Trace Single Oak Project Barrel #11 (r3xKA2) db **(94.5)** n23 t24 f23.5 b24. *45%.*
Buffalo Trace Single Oak Project Barrel #12 (r3yKA2) db **(92)** n24 t23 f22.5 b22.5. *45%.*
Buffalo Trace Single Oak Project Barrel #13 (r3xLA2*) db **(89.5)** n22 t23 f22 b22.5. *45%*
Buffalo Trace Single Oak Project Barrel #14 (r3yLA2*) db **(95)** n24 t24 f23 b24. *45%*
Buffalo Trace Single Oak Project Barrel #15 (r3xLA2) db **(90.5)** n22.5 t23 f22 b23. *45%.*
Buffalo Trace Single Oak Project Barrel #16 (r3yLA2) db **(91.5)** n22.5 t23.5 f22.5 b23. *45%*
Buffalo Trace Single Oak Project Barrel #17 (r3xKB1*) db **(88.5)** n21.5 t22.5 f22.5 b22. *45%*
Buffalo Trace Single Oak Project Barrel #18 (r3yKB1*) db **(92.5)** n23 t23 f23.5 b23. *45%*
Buffalo Trace Single Oak Project Barrel #19 (r3xKB1) db **(93)** n23.5 f23 b23.5. *45%.*
Buffalo Trace Single Oak Project Barrel #20 (r3yKB1) db **(95)** n23.5 t24 f23 b23.5. *45%.*
Buffalo Trace Single Oak Project Barrel #21 (r3xLB1*) db **(92)** n23 t23 f23 b23. *45%*
Buffalo Trace Single Oak Project Barrel #22 (r3yLB1*) db **(91)** n22 t23.5 f22.5 b23. *45%*
Buffalo Trace Single Oak Project Barrel #23 (r3xLB1) db **(89)** n21 t22.5 f22.5 b23. *45%.*
Buffalo Trace Single Oak Project Barrel #24 (r3yLB1) db **(90)** n22 t23 f22.5 b22.5. *45%.*
Buffalo Trace Single Oak Project Barrel #25 (r3xKB2*) db **(90.5)** n22.5 t23 f22.5 b22.5. *45%*
Buffalo Trace Single Oak Project Barrel #26 (r3yKB2*) db **(89.5)** n22 t23.5 f22 b22. *45%*
Buffalo Trace Single Oak Project Barrel #27 (r3xKB2) db **(95.5)** n23 t24 f24.5 b24. *45%.*
Buffalo Trace Single Oak Project Barrel #28 (r3yKB2) db **(94.5)** n23 t24 f23.5 b24. *45%*
Buffalo Trace Single Oak Project Barrel #29 (r3xLB2*) db **(91)** n23 t22.5 f23 b22.5. *45%*
Buffalo Trace Single Oak Project Barrel #30 (r3yLB2*) db **(95.5)** n23.5 t24 f24 b24. *45%*
Buffalo Trace Single Oak Project Barrel #31 (r3xLB2) db **(87.5)** n22 t22 f21.5 b22. *45%.*
Buffalo Trace Single Oak Project Barrel #32 (r3yLB2) db **(90.5)** n23.5 t23 f21.5 b22.5. *45%.*
Buffalo Trace Single Oak Project Barrel #33 (w3xKA1*) db **(94.5)** n24 t23.5 f23 b24. *45%.*
Buffalo Trace Single Oak Project Barrel #34 (w3yKA1*) db **(90)** n21.5 t23.5 f22.5 b22.5. *45%*
Buffalo Trace Single Oak Project Barrel #35 (w3xKA1) db **(89.5)** n22 t22 f23 b22.5. *45%.*
Buffalo Trace Single Oak Project Barrel #36 (w3yKA1) db **(91.5)** n23 t23 f22.5 b23. *45%*
Buffalo Trace Single Oak Project Barrel #37 (w3xLA1*) db **(90)** n21 t23 f22 b22. *45%*
Buffalo Trace Single Oak Project Barrel #38 (w3yLA1*) db **(87.5)** n22 t23.5 f20.5 b21.5. *45%*

Buffalo Trace Single Oak Project Barrel #39 (w3xLA1) db (87) n21.5 t22 f21.5 b22. 45%
Buffalo Trace Single Oak Project Barrel #40 (w3xLA1) db (93) n23 t23 f23.5 b23.5. 45%
Buffalo Trace Single Oak Project Barrel #41 (w3xKA2*) db (92.5) n22 t23 f23.5 b24. 45%
Buffalo Trace Single Oak Project Barrel #42 (w3yKA2*) db (85.5) n22 t21.5 f21 b21. 45%
Buffalo Trace Single Oak Project Barrel #43 (w3xKA2) db (89) n22 t23 f22 b22. 45%
Buffalo Trace Single Oak Project Barrel #44 (w3yKA2) db (89) n23 t23 f21 b22. 45%
Buffalo Trace Single Oak Project Barrel #45 (w3xLA2*) db (87) n23 t22 f21 b21. 45%.
Buffalo Trace Single Oak Project Barrel #46 (w3yLA2*) db (88) n21.5 t22 f22.5 b22. 45%
Buffalo Trace Single Oak Project Barrel #47 (w3xLA2) db (88.5) n22.5 t22 f22 b22. 45%.
Buffalo Trace Single Oak Project Barrel #48 (w3yLA2) db (90.5) n22 t23 f22.5 b23. 45%.
Buffalo Trace Single Oak Project Barrel #49 (w3xKB1) db (93) n24 t23 f23 b23. 45%
Buffalo Trace Single Oak Project Barrel #50 (w3yKB1*) db (88) n21.5 t23 f21.5 b22. 45%
Buffalo Trace Single Oak Project Barrel #51 (w3xKB1) db (89.5) n23 t23 f21.5 b22. 45%
Buffalo Trace Single Oak Project Barrel #52 (w3yKB1) db (87.5) n21.5 t22 f22 b22. 45%
Buffalo Trace Single Oak Project Barrel #53 (w3xLB1*) db (91) n22 t23 f23 b23. 45%
Buffalo Trace Single Oak Project Barrel #54 (w3yLB1*) db (89) n22 t23 f22.5 b22.5. 45%
Buffalo Trace Single Oak Project Barrel #55 (w3xLB1) db (89) n22 t22 f23 b22. 45%.
Buffalo Trace Single Oak Project Barrel #56 (w3yLB1) db (91) n24 t22.5 f22 b22.5. 45%
Buffalo Trace Single Oak Project Barrel #57 (w3xKB2*) db (94) n23 t23.5 f23.5 b24. 45%
Buffalo Trace Single Oak Project Barrel #58 (w3yKB2*) db (90.5) n22.5 t23 f22.5 b22.5. 45%
Buffalo Trace Single Oak Project Barrel #59 (w3xKB2) db (92) n22 t23.5 f23 b23.5. 45%
Buffalo Trace Single Oak Project Barrel #60 (w3yKB2) db (87.5) n22.5 t22.5 f21 b21.5. 45%
Buffalo Trace Single Oak Project Barrel #61 (w3xLB2*) db (94.5) n24 t23 f23.5 b24. 45%
Buffalo Trace Single Oak Project Barrel #62 (w3yLB2*) db (88) n22 t22.5 f21.5 b22. 45%
Buffalo Trace Single Oak Project Barrel #63 (w3xLB2) db (95.5) n24 t23 f24 b24.5. 45%
Buffalo Trace Single Oak Project Barrel #64 (w3yLB2) db (91) n22.5 t23.5 f22.5 b23. 45%
Buffalo Trace Single Oak Project Barrel #65 (r2yKA1) db (91) n23.5 t22 f23 b22.5. 45%
Buffalo Trace Single Oak Project Barrel #66 (r2xKA1*) db (88.5) n22.5 t22.5 f21.5 b22. 45%
Buffalo Trace Single Oak Project Barrel #67 (r2xKA1) db (89.5) n22 t23 f22.5 b22. 45%
Buffalo Trace Single Oak Project Barrel #68 (r2yKA1) db (92) n22.5 t23 f23.5 b23. 45%
Buffalo Trace Single Oak Project Barrel #69 (r2xLA1*) db (94.5) n23 t24 f23.5 b24. 45%
Buffalo Trace Single Oak Project Barrel #70 (r2yLA1*) db (91.5) n22.5 t23 f23 b23. 45%
Buffalo Trace Single Oak Project Barrel #71 (r2xLA1) db (92) n22.5 t23 f23.5 b23. 45%
Buffalo Trace Single Oak Project Barrel #72 (r2yLA1) db (89) n22.5 t23 f21.5 b22. 45%
Buffalo Trace Single Oak Project Barrel #73 (r2xKA2*) db (87.5) n21.5 t22 f22 b22. 45%
Buffalo Trace Single Oak Project Barrel #74 (r2yKA2*) db (88) n22 t22 f22 b22. 45%
Buffalo Trace Single Oak Project Barrel #75 (r2xKA2) db (91.5) n23 t22.5 f23 b23. 45%
Buffalo Trace Single Oak Project Barrel #76 (r2yKA2) db (89) n22.5 t22.5 f22 b22. 45%
Buffalo Trace Single Oak Project Barrel #77 (r2xLA2*) db (88) n22 t23 f21 b22. 45%.
Buffalo Trace Single Oak Project Barrel #78 (r2yLA2*) db (89) n22.5 t22 f22.5 b22. 45%
Buffalo Trace Single Oak Project Barrel #79 (r2xLA2) db (93) n23 t23.5 f23 b23.5. 45%.
Buffalo Trace Single Oak Project Barrel #80 (r2yLA2) db (91.5) n22.5 t23 f23 b23. 45%.
Buffalo Trace Single Oak Project Barrel #81 (r2yKB1*) db (94) n23 t23 f24 b24. 45%.
Buffalo Trace Single Oak Project Barrel #82 (r2yKB1*) db (91.5) n22.5 t23.5 f22.5 b23. 45%
Buffalo Trace Single Oak Project Barrel #83 (r2xKB1) db (92) n22.5 t23 f23.5 b23. 45%.
Buffalo Trace Single Oak Project Barrel #84 (r2yKB1) db (94) n23.5 t24 f23 b23.5. 45%.
Buffalo Trace Single Oak Project Barrel #85 (r2xLB1*) db (88.5) n21.5 t22.5 f22 b22.5. 45%
Buffalo Trace Single Oak Project Barrel #86 (r2yLB1*) db (90) n22.5 t22 f23 b22.5. 45%
Buffalo Trace Single Oak Project Barrel #87 (r2xLB1) db (93.5) n22.5 t23.5 f23.5 b24. 45%.
Buffalo Trace Single Oak Project Barrel #88 (r2yLB1) db (89) n23.5 t22 f21.5 b22. 45%
Buffalo Trace Single Oak Project Barrel #89 (r2xKB2*) db (89.5) n22 t22.5 f22 b22.5. 45%
Buffalo Trace Single Oak Project Barrel #90 (r2yKB2*) db (94) n23.5 t24 f23 b23.5. 45%
Buffalo Trace Single Oak Project Barrel #91 (r2xKB2) db (86.5) n21.5 t22 f21.5 b21.5. 45%
Buffalo Trace Single Oak Project Barrel #92 (r2yKB2) db (91) n22 t23 f23 b23. 45%
Buffalo Trace Single Oak Project Barrel #93 (r2xLB2*) db (89) n22.5 t22 f22 b22.5. 45%
Buffalo Trace Single Oak Project Barrel #94 (r2yLB2*) db (92.5) n22.5 t24 f23 b23. 45%
Buffalo Trace Single Oak Project Barrel #95 (r2xLB2) db (94) n23 t23.5 f23.5 b24. 45%
Buffalo Trace Single Oak Project Barrel #96 (r2yLB2) db (89) n22 t23.5 f21.5 b22. 45%
Buffalo Trace Single Oak Project Barrel #97 (w2xKA1*) db (87) n22.5 t22 f21.5 b21.5. 45%
Buffalo Trace Single Oak Project Barrel #98 (w2yKA1*) db (93) n23 t23.5 f23 b23.5. 45%
Buffalo Trace Single Oak Project Barrel #99 (w2xKA1) db (86.5) n22 t22 f21 b21.5. 45%
Buffalo Trace Single Oak Project Barrel #100 (w2yKA1) db (94) n23 t23.5 f23.5 b24. 45%
Buffalo Trace Single Oak Project Barrel #101 (w2xLA1) db (96) n23.5 t24 f23.5 b25. 45%
Buffalo Trace Single Oak Project Barrel #102 (w2yLA1*) db (88.5) n22 t22 f22.5 b22. 45%

Buffalo Trace Single Oak Project Barrel #103 (w2xLA1) db (89) n22.5 t22 f22 b22.5. 45%
Buffalo Trace Single Oak Project Barrel #104 (w2xLA1) db (91) n23 t23 f22.5 b22.5. 45%
Buffalo Trace Single Oak Project Barrel #105 (w2xKA2*) db (89) n22.5 t22 f22.5 b22. 45%
Buffalo Trace Single Oak Project Barrel #106 (w2yKA2*) db (92.5) n24 t23 f23 b23.5. 45%
Buffalo Trace Single Oak Project Barrel #107 (w2xKA2) db (93.5) n23.5 t23 f23 b24. 45%
Buffalo Trace Single Oak Project Barrel #108 (w2yKA2) db (94) n22.5 t24 f23.5 b24. 45%
Buffalo Trace Single Oak Project Barrel #109 (w2xLA2*) db (87.5) n21.5 t23.5 f21 b21.5. 45%
Buffalo Trace Single Oak Project Barrel #110 (w2yLA2*) db (90) n22 t22.5 f22.5 b23. 45%
Buffalo Trace Single Oak Project Barrel #111 (w2xLA2) db (89) n22.5 t22.5 f22 b22. 45%
Buffalo Trace Single Oak Project Barrel #112 (w2yLA2) db (90) n21.5 t23 f22.5 b23. 45%
Buffalo Trace Single Oak Project Barrel #113 (w2xKB1*) db (88) n22.5 t22 f22 b21.5. 45%
Buffalo Trace Single Oak Project Barrel #114 (w2yKB1*) db (90) n22 t23 f22 b23. 45%
Buffalo Trace Single Oak Project Barrel #115 (w2xKB1) db (88.5) n22 t22.5 f22 b22. 45%
Buffalo Trace Single Oak Project Barrel #116 (w2yKB1) db (90.5) n22 t22 f23.5 b23. 45%
Buffalo Trace Single Oak Project Barrel #117 (w2xLB1*) db (82.5) n20 t20.5 f22 b20. 45%
Buffalo Trace Single Oak Project Barrel #118 (w2yLB1*) db (86) n20.5 t21.5 f22 b22. 45%
Buffalo Trace Single Oak Project Barrel #119 (w2xLB1) db (93.5) n22.5 t24 f23.5 b23.5. 45%
Buffalo Trace Single Oak Project Barrel #120 (w2xLB1) db (89.5) n23 t22 f22.5 b22. 45%
Buffalo Trace Single Oak Project Barrel #121 (w2xKB2*) db (89) n22.5 t23 f21.5 b22. 45%
Buffalo Trace Single Oak Project Barrel #122 (w2yKB2*) db (93) n22 t23.5 f23.5 b24. 45%
Buffalo Trace Single Oak Project Barrel #123 (w2xKB2) db (85.5) n21 t22 f21 b21.5. 45%
Buffalo Trace Single Oak Project Barrel #124 (w2yKB2) db (90.5) n22.5 t23 f22.5 b22.5. 45%
Buffalo Trace Single Oak Project Barrel #125 (w2xLB2*) db (93) n24 t22 f22.5 b22.5. 45%
Buffalo Trace Single Oak Project Barrel #126 (w2yLB2*) db (90) n22 t23 f22.5 b22.5. 45%
Buffalo Trace Single Oak Project Barrel #127 (w2xLB2) db (85.5) n21.5 t22 f21 b21. 45%.
Buffalo Trace Single Oak Project Barrel #128 (w2yLB2) db (89) n21.5 t22 f22.5 b22.5. 45%
Buffalo Trace Single Oak Project Barrel #129 (r1xKA1*) db (88) n22.5 t22 f22 b22. 45%
Buffalo Trace Single Oak Project Barrel #130 (r1yKA1*) db (92.5) n22 t23.5 f23 b24. 45%
Buffalo Trace Single Oak Project Barrel #131 (r1xKA1) db (92.5) n23 t23 f23.5 b23. 45%
Buffalo Trace Single Oak Project Barrel #132 See above.
Buffalo Trace Single Oak Project Barrel #133 (r1xLA1*) db (89) n22.5 t23 f21 b22.5. 45%
Buffalo Trace Single Oak Project barrel #134 (r1yLA1*) db (91.5) n22 t23.5 f23 b23. 45%
Buffalo Trace Single Oak Project Barrel #135 (r1xLA1) db (92.5) n23 t23 f23.5 b23. 45%
Buffalo Trace Single Oak Project Barrel #136 (r1yLA1) db (92) n23.5 t22.5 f23 b23. 45%
Buffalo Trace Single Oak Project Barrel #137 (r1xKA2*) db (90.5) n22 t23.5 f22 b23. 45%
Buffalo Trace Single Oak Project Barrel #138 (r1yKA2*) db (87) n22.5 t21.5 f21.5 b21.5. 45%
Buffalo Trace Single Oak Project Barrel #139 (r1xKA2) db (88) n22.5 t22 f21.5 b22. 45%.
Buffalo Trace Single Oak Project Barrel #140 (r1yKA2) db (93) n23 t24 f23 b23. 45%
Buffalo Trace Single Oak Project Barrel #141 (r1xLA2) db (90) n23.5 t22 f22.5 b22. 45%.
Buffalo Trace Single Oak Project Barrel #142 (r1yLA2*) db (89.5) n22.5 t22.5 f22 b22.5. 45%
Buffalo Trace Single Oak Project Barrel #143 (r1xLA2) db (88.5) n22.5 t22.5 f21.5 b22. 45%
Buffalo Trace Single Oak Project Barrel #144 (r1yLA2) db (91) n23 t22.5 f22.5 b22.5. 45%.
Buffalo Trace Single Oak Project Barrel #145 (r1xKB1*) db (91) n22.5 t22 f23.5 b23. 45%
Buffalo Trace Single Oak Project Barrel #146 (r1yKB1*) db (93) n23 t24 f22 b24. 45%
Buffalo Trace Single Oak Project Barrel #147 (r1xKB1) db (93) n23.5 t23 f23.5 b23. 45%.
Buffalo Trace Single Oak Project Barrel #148 (r1yKB1) db (94) n22.5 t24 f23.5 b24. 45%
Buffalo Trace Single Oak Project Barrel #149 (r1xLB1*) db (92) n22.5 t23.5 f23 b23. 45%
Buffalo Trace Single Oak Project Barrel #150 (r1yLB1*) db (93) n23 t23.5 f23 b23.5. 45%
Buffalo Trace Single Oak Project Barrel #151 (r1xLB1) db (91.5) n22 t23 f23.5 b23. 45%.
Buffalo Trace Single Oak Project Barrel #152 (r1yLB1) db (81.5) n21 t20.5 f20 b20.5. 45%
Buffalo Trace Single Oak Project Barrel #153 (r1xKB2*) db (94) n23.5 t23.5 f23 b24. 45%
Buffalo Trace Single Oak Project Barrel #154 (r1yKB2*) db (92) n22.5 t23 f23 b23.5. 45%
Buffalo Trace Single Oak Project Barrel #155 (r1xKB2) db (93) n23 t24 f22.5 b23.5. 45%.
Buffalo Trace Single Oak Project Barrel #156 (r1yKB2) db (85.5) n22 t21 f21.5 b21. 45%
Buffalo Trace Single Oak Project Barrel #157 (r1xLB2*) db (84.5) n21 t21.5 f20.5 b21. 45%
Buffalo Trace Single Oak Project Barrel #158 (r1yLB2*) db (88) n22 t22 f22 b22. 45%
Buffalo Trace Single Oak Project Barrel #159 (r1xLB2) db (88) n20.5 t22.5 f22 b22.5. 45%
Buffalo Trace Single Oak Project Barrel #160 (r1yLB2) db (92.5) n23.5 t23 f22 b23. 45%
Buffalo Trace Single Oak Project Barrel #161 (w1xKA1*)db (87) n21 t22 f22 b22. 45%
Buffalo Trace Single Oak Project Barrel #162 (w1yKA1*) db (88.5) n22 t22 f22.5 b22. 45%
Buffalo Trace Single Oak Project Barrel #163 (w1xKA1) db (90) n23 t22.5 f22 b22.5. 45%
Buffalo Trace Single Oak Project Barrel #164 (w1yKA1) db (94.5) n23.5 t23 f24 b24. 45%
Buffalo Trace Single oak Project Barrel #165 (w1xLA1*) db (91.5) n22.5 t23 f23 b23. 45%
Buffalo Trace Single Oak Project Barrel #166 (w1yLA1*) db (91) n22 t23 f23 b23. 45%

Buffalo Trace Single Oak Project Barrel #167 (w1yLB1) db (94) n23.5 t23.5 f23 b24. 45%

Buffalo Trace Single Oak Project Barrel #168 (w1xLA1) db (89.5) n22 t23 f22 b22.5. 45%

Buffalo Trace Single Oak Project Barrel #169 (w1xKA2*) db (94) n23.5 t23.5 f23 b24. 45%

Buffalo Trace Single Oak Project Barrel #170 (w1yKA2*) db (92.5) n22.5 t23 f23.5 b23.5. 45%

Buffalo Trace Single Oak Project Barrel #171 (w1xKA2) db (88.5) n22 t23 f21.5 b22. 45%.

Buffalo Trace Single Oak Project Barrel #172 (w1yKA2) db (90.5) n22.5 t23 f22.5 b22.5. 45%

Buffalo Trace Single Oak Project Barrel #173 (w1yLA2*) db (91) n23.5 t23 f22 b22.5. 45%.

Buffalo Trace Single Oak Project Barrel #174 (w1yLA2*) db (89) n22 t22.5 f22.5 b22. 45%

Buffalo Trace Single Oak Project Barrel #175 (w1xLA2) db (91.5) n21.5 t23 f24 b23. 45%.

Buffalo Trace Single Oak Project Barrel #176 (w1yLA2) db (89) n21.5 t22.5 f22.5 b22.5. 45%.

Buffalo Trace Single Oak Project Barrel #177 (w1xKB1*) db (87) n21.5 t22 f22 b21.5. 45%

Buffalo Trace Single Oak Project Barrel #178 (w1yKB1*) db (88.5) n22.5 t23 f21.5 b21.5. 45%

Buffalo Trace Single Oak Project Barrel #179 (w1xKB1) db (88) n21 t22 f22.5 b22.5. 45%

Buffalo Trace Single Oak Project Barrel #180 (w1yKB1) db (92) n22 t23.5 f23 b23.5. 45%

Buffalo Trace Single Oak Project Barrel #181 (w1xKB1*) db (94.5) n22.5 t24.5 f23 b23.5. 45%

Buffalo Trace Single Oak Project Barrel #182 (w1yLB1*) db (86) n21.5 t21.5 f22 b21. 45%

Buffalo Trace Single Oak Project Barrel #183 (w1xLB1) db (95.5) n24 t24 f23.5 b24. 45%.

Buffalo Trace Single Oak Project Barrel #184 (w1yLA1) db (93) n23.5 t23 f23.5 b23.5. 45%

Buffalo Trace Single Oak Project Barrel #185 (w1xKB2*) db (92.5) n23 t23.5 f23 b23. 45%

Buffalo Trace Single Oak Project Barrel #186 (w1yKB2*) db (90) n23 t22.5 f22 b22.5. 45%

Buffalo Trace Single Oak Project Barrel #187 (w1xKB2) db (88) n22 t22 f22 b22. 45%

Buffalo Trace Single Oak Project Barrel #188 (w1yKB2) db (90) n21.5 t23.5 f22.5 b22.5. 45%

Buffalo Trace Single Oak Project Barrel #189 (w1xLB2*) db (88.5) n24 t22 f21 b21.5. 45%

Buffalo Trace Single Oak Project Barrel #190 (w1yLB2*) db (94) n23.5 t24 f23 b23.5. 45%

Buffalo Trace Single Oak Project Barrel #191 (w1xLB2) db (94.5) n23 t23.5 f24 b24. 45%

Buffalo Trace Single Oak Project Barrel #192 (w1yLB2) db (94.5) n23 t24 f23.5 b24. 45%

Buffalo Trace Experimental Collection Seasoned Staves - 36 Months dist 10-26-09, barrelled 10-27-09, bott 11/26/2018, still proof: 130, entry proof: 125, warehouse/ floor: K/7, rick/row/slot: 7/1/1-4, charred white oak, age at bottling: 9 years, evaporation: 28.1% db **(92.5) n23 t23.5 f23 b23** A really fascinating experiment, comparing this with the 48 month seasoned staves. Here the whisky is burnished gold; the 48 month is deep amber. From tip to toe this is all about subtlety with all the leading notes, from the red liquorice and corn oils in pastel shades and no particularly firm form. Only the delivery offers something firm and crystalline as the Demerara sugars make a crisp entry. The remainder is all super-soft and vanilla rich. 45% (90 proof).

Buffalo Trace Experimental Collection Seasoned Staves - 48 Months dist 10-26-09, barrelled 10-27-09, bott 11/26/2018, still proof: 130, entry proof: 125, warehouse/ floor: K/7, rick/row/slot: 7/1/1-4, charred white oak, age at bottling: 9 years, evaporation: 29.7% db **(95) n23.5 t24 f23.5 b24** As the richer colour suggests, there is more going on here and the extra intervention of the oak brings about a sturdier bourbon. There is still the meaningful Demerara, but now it is backed by liquorice-edged tannin both on nose and delivery and greater weight all round. It is even juicier and more salivating! The spices have certainly upped their game and have make their mark two thirds the way in. This is a better-balanced and more confident bourbon shewing a lot more of everything...and in perfect balance and equal measures, too... Fascinating! 45% (90 proof).

Bulleit Bourbon (87) n21.5 t22 f21.5 b22. Vanilla-fashioned on both nose and flavour development. If it was looking to be big and brash, it's missed the target. If it wanted to be genteel and understated with a slightly undercooked feel yet always friendly, then bullseye... 45% (90 proof)

◈ **Bulleit Bourbon Frontier Whiskey** bott code: L9197ZB001 **(94)** n23.5 an unusually crisp bourbon: Demerara sugars vie with corn, a brisk spiciness and even a little salt for top billing. Mint and green apple also makes their mark. Imagine a view for miles around from a hill on a chilled Fall morning, the air crystal clear and still, the shapes and colours ahead of you vivid and undistorted...that is this nose to a tee...; **t23.5** from such a nose you expect the flavours to be no less precise and sharp. And you are not let down, though a little corn oil does now start to have a gentle impact on proceedings. But still it is about those sugars, as well as vanillas which slowly inveigle their way into a position of strength. The whole is a brilliantly salivating pastiche, because if you are not concentrating, you might just for a moment mistake this for a rye; **f23** despite the oils and growing oaks, this still retains its brown sugar clarity and its small grain complexity rightly to the very end; **b24** in style this has just about become a stand-alone bourbon, with a crisp character all its own: like a rye, but chiselled from corn. It has been fascinating watching the quality of this brand rise quite dramatically in recent years and now enjoys a consistency and dependability which makes it an easy 'go to' bourbon. As for that unique clarity of flavour, have to say I now regularly use this brand to help re-set my taste buds after they have been clattered into submission and disabled by some sulphur-ruined Scotch or Irish. A magnificent every day non-age statement bourbon but boasting a cut-glass rye edge. *45% (90 proof).*

Bulleit Bourbon 10 Year Old (90) n23 t22.5 f22 b22.5 Not remotely spectacular. But does the simple things deliciously. *45.6% (91.2 proof)*

⬦ **Bulleit Bourbon Frontier Whiskey Aged 10 Years** bott code: L9229R60010249 **(92.5)** n24 the spices are more brazen and serious here, the tannins thicker set and borderline chocolatey. A little hickory with the dried date. Dense, meaningful and means business...; t23.5 sumptuous oils link arms with the liquorice, hickory and molasses for a classic well-aged bourbon lift off. A moment or two of black cherry, too...; f22 just tires very slightly as it loses the sugars. Chalky oak remains...; b23 "but how can a 10-year-old bourbon be not as good as a younger one with no age statement?" I hear you ask. Well, there is nothing wrong with this. It is just less brilliant! Definitely upped in whiskey values since I last encountered it. But that extra tannin, which giving extra intensity depth, does slightly lose the complexity and harmony of the standard Bulleit as the spaces in which the younger bourbon could perform have now been filled in. That said, there are a few moments of whiskey heaven just after delivery as that classic hickory note kicks in with the dark sugars. *45.6% (91.2 proof).*

Bulleit Bourbon Barrel Strength (91.5) n22.5 t22.5 f23.5 b23 The extra oils at full strength make such a huge difference in seeing the fuller picture. *59.6% (119.2 proof)*

⬦ **Bulleit Bourbon Frontier Whiskey Blender's Select No. 001** bott code: L0023ZB001 **(96.5)** n23.5 so fascinating how the corns oils merge with a serious oak input. And yet rye notes still abound to give it that crisp outline so easily distinguishable in the standard bottling...; t24.5 one of the deliveries of the year. Rye hits every taste bud on your palate with a laser-precision sharpness, almost setting your mouth on edge with its incredibly full-flavoured vigour. Once past the rye, the older elements kick in with a dark chocolate intensity, matching cherries and hickory and thick molasses; f24 long...could it be anything else? Still the corn oils hold their ground, but the spices are more keen now. The small grain still pulse to their rye-rich beat while the cocoa mingles with the oils...; b24.5 an extraordinary halfway house between the standard Bulleit and their 10-year-old, with the all the richness and gravitas of the older whiskey married with the vivaciousness of the younger bottling. So much rye to be found...yet never quite has the chance to dominate, such is the labyrinthine complexity of this stunning whiskey. One of the bourbons of 2021, to be sure...and truly world class. *50% (100 proof).*

Clarke's Old Kentucky Straight Sour Mash Whisky Bourbon (88.5) n22.5 t22 f22 b22. Honest and hugely impressive bourbon. The rich colour – and remember straight bourbon cannot be falsely coloured – tells its own tale. *40%. Aldi.*

Clyde May's Straight Bourbon batch CR 079 recipe no 2. **(95)** n23.5 t24 f23.5 b24 Though from a Florida company, this busy Kentucky bourbon sings pure Bluegrass. Love it! *46% (92 proof). ncf. Distilled in Kentucky*

⬦ **Colonel E.H. Taylor 18 Year Marriage Bottled in Bond** bott code: L201270114:141 db **(96.5)** n24 here we go: a 20 minute nose. Just one of those indecipherable bourbons where the citrus tones are so deeply intertwangled with the red liquorice, hickory and earthier tannins that is almost impossible to pick them apart. Almost... Though what is very noticeable here is the lack of spice: an oaky nip apart, there is none...; t24 think of a dark, cold Sunday afternoon after an exhausting week and you are tangled up in bed all day with the one you deeply love, never leaving the warmth of the arms, legs and blankets that envelope you: an experience beyond bliss. And here we have it in liquid form, the corn oils the comforting blanket, the small grains and oak providing the electric touches and profound warmth, that erotic bitter-sweet touch that send tingles through your body; f24 so long. So relaxed. So complex. There is that toastiness of old age you know is coming. But so beautifully aligned are the dark sugars, there is not a jot of bitterness...nor excessive sweetness, either. At last, though, come the spices...a warming buzz as gentle and in keeping with the rest of this love story...; b24.5 well this marriage lasted twice as long as mine and was a least twice as good... *50% (100 proof).*

⬦ **Colonel E.H. Taylor Amaranth Grain of the Gods Bottled in Bond** bott code: L191800112:17K db **(91.5)** n23 unlike any other Buffalo Trace whiskey I have ever nosed. There is an aching dullness to this; a gap where so much else should be. But there is also a true uniqueness to the spices which buzz seemingly at first without a sting, but over time build up and then attack without mercy...; t23 soft and enveloping. Like the nose, there is a certain character to this unlike anything I have yet encountered in a bourbon. First the corn oils hug you tight and kiss, but slowly a dull and half-heartedly bitter dryness begins to fashion its personality; f22.5 light heather honey on the delicately bitter fade; b23 not sure amaranth grain is a true cereal, but if it is good enough for BT, then it is good enough for me. I'm presuming that the amaranth has usurped the rye for this bottling as I can't locate any of the sharp sugary tones normally associated with that grain and the bitterness towards the end is most un Colonel Taylor-ish. Different and thoroughly enjoyable stand-alone bottling, with moments of brilliance, but not a patch of the distillery's usual genius. *50% (100 proof).*

Colonel E.H. Taylor Barrel Proof bott code: B1319909:44M **(93) n23 t23.5 f23 b23.5** It is as though every last trace of natural caramel has been sucked from the barrel... *67.7% (135.4 proof).*

Colonel E.H. Taylor Barrel Proof bott code: L81313910:20M db **(96) n24.5 t24 f23.5 b24** This, amazingly, is the 19,999th whiskey I have tasted for the Jim Murray's Whisky Bible since it first began in 2003. I chose E H Taylor as I have had (very happy) memories going back over 25 years of trying to piece together and discover where his distillery was. And really, if you are going to taste a special bourbon, then it really should be at a strength nature intended. And as for the whiskey itself...? Just another exhibition from this distillery of truly astonishing bourbon making. *67.7% (135.4 proof).*

Colonel E.H. Taylor Four Grain Bottled in Bond Aged 12 Years db **(97.5) n24.5 t24.5 f24 b24.5** Unquestionably one of the greatest whiskeys bottled worldwide in the last 12 months, simply because of the unfathomable depths of its complexity. Every aspect of great whiskey making clears its respective hurdle with yards to spare: brewing, distilling, maturation...the nose and taste confirms that a team of people knew exactly what they were doing...and achieved with rare distinction what they set out to do. Forget about the sheer, undiluted beauty of this bourbon: for me, it is simply a true honour – and thrill - to taste. *50% (100 proof).*

Colonel E.H. Taylor Seasoned Wood db **(93.5) n25 t24 f21.5 b23** I am sitting in my garden in near darkness tasting and writing this, the near-thousand-year-old church just 75 yards or so behind me clanging out that it is ten of the clock. Although mid-July, it is the first day warm enough in this apology of a British summer where I have been able to work outside. Oddly, it reminded me when I used to write my books and chapters on bourbon in the grounds of Buffalo Trace in the 1990s, the sun also set and a warm breeze kissing my face. No possums here for company, although the bats are already circling me, kindly protecting me from midges. And as I can't read the label of the whiskey, it makes my senses all the more alive. A whiskey, though not perfect, for when the sun sets but your day is really about to begin... *50% (100 proof)*

Colonel E H Taylor Single Barrel Bottled in Bond bott code: L190740114 **(96.5) n24 t24 f24 b24.5** Absolutely no single cask whiskey, of any type, has the right to be this good. How on earth does it achieve this balance? So many nuances, yet each in league or sympathetic to another? A world single cask of the year contender for certain. Breathtaking. *50% (100 proof). sc.*

Colonel E.H. Taylor Small Batch Bottled in Bond nbc **(94.5) n23.5 t23.5 f23.5 b24** Just balances out so beautifully. *50% (100 proof).*

Colonel E.H. Taylor Small Batch Bottled in Bond bott code: L190980115:45D **(90) n23 t23 f22 b22** Well, I'd not have recognised this as a Colonel Taylor offering unless I had opened the bottle and poured it myself. Not a patch on the exquisite single barrel and, for all its caramel softness and other riches, still one for a dirty glass... *50% (100 proof).*

◇ **Coopers' Craft Barrel Reserve** bott code: SS3501815 db **(92) n22.5** can you get a tang to the nose...? Well, you do here: the tannins have a distinct sharpness to them, almost a degree of phenol. Curious, and intriguing, especially when the rye grains get into their stride; **t23.5** what a wonderful delivery. There is a moulded crispness to this, again the ryes seeming to be at the vanguard. But soon a wonderful oaky resonance kicks in, full of chocolate and liquorice; **f23** layered molasses, spices and vanilla...; **b23** a distinctly different slant to a bourbon with the emphasis placed where it usually isn't, the pace of development slightly skewed. Fascinating. *50% (100 proof). Chiseled & Charred Collection.*

◇ **David Nicholson 1843 Kentucky Straight Bourbon Whiskey** bott code: LF3936 **(91.5) n22.5** not so much a nose as a whisper, or a hint. Deft hickory strolls across a light corn-oiled backdrop; **t23** again, the corn leads the way. But at relaxed intervals degrees of peppered muscovado sugars and red liquorice add extra depth...though with no great conviction; **f23** decidedly spicy now, with a little heather honey sweetening the liquorice and vanilla fade; **b23** an engagingly timid bourbon which wins your heart with its polite and well-mannered ways. *50% (100 proof).*

◇ **David Nicholson Reserve Kentucky Straight Bourbon Whiskey** bott code: LF4223 **(90.5) n22.5** remarkably similar to the 1843! **t23** ah! A much more robust delivery with those pepper spices released on kick-off and soon joining a leathery-liquorice attack. Early heather-honey, too...; the corn oils gang up massively; **f22.5** a lot of spicy corn; **b22.5** an example of a little more meaning a little less. Delicious bourbon, for sure, but not quite so well-balanced or teasing as the 1843. *50% (100 proof).*

Eagle Rare Aged 10 Years bott code: L172800119:194 **(95.5) n23.5 t24 f24 b24** To the British and Europeans Eagle Rare means Crystal Palace not losing a game...very rare indeed. In the US it will probably mean a lot more to those who once hankered after Ancient Age 10, as this is not the Single Barrel incarnation. And while Crystal Palace may be pointless, literally, this striking whiskey most certainly isn't... That's one soaring, beautiful eagle... *45% (90 proof)*

Eagle Rare Aged 10 Years Single Barrel (89) n21.5 t23 f22 b22.5. A surprising trip, this, with some dramatic changes en route. *45%*

Eagle Rare 17 Years Old bott Summer 2017 db **(94.5) n24 t23.5 f23 b24** Just goes a fraction easier on both the sugars and cocoa here. But the toastiness always remains in control and impressively underscores the big age. *45% (90 proof).*

Eagle Rare 17 Years Old bott Summer 2018 db **(95) n24 t24 f23 b24** This version goes into cream toffee overload. But, it does it so well... *50.5% (101 proof).*

⬧ **Eagle Rare 17 Years Old** bott Summer 2019 db **(95) n24** a punchy, sporty and spicy mix of toffee and impressive hickory. A real livewire for its years; **t23.5** the age is apparent from first sip with the tannins on the attack and deep hickory tones taking huge strides around the palate. The sugars are muted by toffee and tannin but some well spiced molasses do help soften the mid-ground; **f23.5** a much greater accent here on the caramels leached from the oak; **b24** the rich caramel thread found in this whiskey could so easily become its tomb, as with many bourbons that toffee note strangles the life out of all development. Not here: the hickory and spice in tandem produce some truly wonderful moments. *50.5% (101 proof).*

Early Times Bottled-in-Bond Straight Bourbon bott code: A146171040 3131550 **(94) n23 t23.5 f23.5 b24** They call this "Old Style", and it really is. A blast from the past bourbon, oozing personality. A bit of a stunner. *50% (100 proof).*

Elijah Craig Barrel Proof Kentucky Straight Bourbon batch no. C917 db **(95) n23.5 t24 f23.5 b24** A bourbon which is winner just for much for its rich texture as it is the subtle complexities of its nose and delivery. A real honey – in every sense! *65.5% (131 proof).*

⬧ **Elijah Craig Barrel Proof Kentucky Straight Bourbon** batch no. B520 db **(94.5) n23.5** the sweeter, lighter notes are pure toffee-apple. The duskier, more moody moments are dried dates and walnut. With the odd red liquorice note piping in for good measure...; **t24** there are controlled explosions. And there are controlled explosions. And this is a very controlled explosion! The spices and maple syrup arrive hand-in-hand, while the liquorice ticks along effortlessly – the whole being wonderfully salivating. Together, and backed up by the alcohol...boom..! **f23.5** a mild fade, really. The sugars stand their ground, inviting the gentle waves of tannin onto them; **b23.5** unambiguous quality! *63.6% (127.2 proof).*

Elijah Craig Barrel Proof Kentucky Straight Bourbon batch no. C918 db **(94.5) n23.5 t24 f23 b24** Just classic stuff! All the usual cast members of red liquorice and Manuka honey are trotted out to make their bow, but there is a slight saltiness to this bottling also...something that isn't usually in the script. Intense, yet at the same time restrained; the burnt toast and marmalade towards the finish works rather well and fits the narrative. *65.7% (131.4 proof).*

Elijah Craig Barrel Proof Kentucky Straight Bourbon Aged 12 Years batch no. A119 db **(96) n24 t24.5 f23.5 b24** When you get this degree of toastiness from a bourbon, either there has been one hell of an average temperature rise over the last dozen years in Kentucky. Or this has been plucked from near the top of a warehouse, where it has been cooking happily for over a decade. The result is bourbon that takes no prisoners. It is also a fascinating bourbon, not just because of the intensity of the blood oranges on the nose or the prickle of the splinters on the palate. But it is because it shews an inordinate degree of copper in the flavour profile, the mid-point to the finish in particular. It is as though something was just done to the still, maybe some repair work, just prior to this being distilled. And that to the blindingly busy small grain input and the result is a bourbon of cor blimey richness! *67.6% (135.2 proof).*

Elijah Craig Barrel Proof Kentucky Straight Bourbon Aged 12 Years batch no. B519 db **(90.5) n22.5 t23 f22 b23** One of those quietly delicious bourbons which is saturated in caramel and goes for mouthfeel effect over complexity. Mouth-puckering on delivery, this is sticky whiskey on the palate so thick is that corn oil. But the growth of cocoa and spice is nothing to quibble about. *61.1% (122.2 proof).*

⬧ **Elijah Craig Barrel Proof Kentucky Straight Bourbon Aged 12 Years** batch no. C919 db **(90.5) n23** rock hard and brittle, the rye pings around the nose like a pinball machine; **t23** this is eye-watering fare! The lack of metal within the framework of this bourbon leaves the grains to go gung-ho at the taste buds, almost with a salty relish. Salivating almost to a painful doubt, the liquorice appears to be dosed up with more steroids than a Russian shot-putter...holy crap....!!! **f22** having pulled myself off the floor, dusted myself down and re-found my seat, I settle down to find a rather bitter and toasty finale; **b22.5** good grief!!! The original Heaven Hill distillery could never have made a bourbon this uncompromising, this harrowing... The old stills always would have injected extra copper to soften even their most unforgiving grain-led creations. This is as memorable as it is different...and scary! *68.4% (136.8 proof).*

Elijah Craig Small Batch Kentucky Straight Bourbon db **(89.5) n22.5 t22.5 f22 b22.5** About as quiet and understated as Elijah Craig ever gets. *47% (94 proof).*

⬧ **Elmer T. Lee 100 Year Tribute Kentucky Straight Bourbon Whiskey** bott code: L192240121:22K db **(97) n24.5** if anyone asks: "please show me the perfect bourbon aroma"...open a bottle of this, pour, and give them 20 minutes with this work of art. Don't let them drink. Just allow them to be absorbed by the ultimate rye recipe aroma with its sexy hints of mint and eucalyptus, suggesting very good age. This is a single barrel, so can't assure them they'll get exactly this, but if this is a random example, they will be on their knees in worshipful prayer...as I am...; **t24** I actually laughed when I tasted this: the nose is all about subtlety yet crisp and precise notes...and that's exactly what turns up in the first ten seconds on the palate. No bourbon I have tasted this year, be it single barrel or not, has managed to get the softness of the corn and the salivating jaggedness of the grain so brilliantly matched. The sugars are as brittle as the grains, the tannins as earthy as the corn is flighty. In the meantime, spices rumble pitch perfect...; **f24** just more of the same for a ridiculously long finale. The only thing that doesn't seem to fade is the spice. Oh, and Elmer's legacy...; **b24.5** I had the great fortune not only to know Elmer but have him as my mentor as I got to grips with the complex world of bourbon whiskey. I know that this particular barrel would have blown him away as it is choc-a-bloc with all the features and devices he thought sacred within a bourbon. Knowing him so intimately, before tasting I had feared that this tribute would be a bit of a let-down. I really should have known better. As a mark of respect to Elmer, I left this to be the final whiskey tasted for the Jim Murray Whisky Bible 2021, the 1,252nd whisky in all. It is just as well. Because, just like Elmer T Lee, this would have been a very hard, if not impossible, act to follow... *50% (100 proof).* 🏆

Elmer T Lee Single Barrel Kentucky Straight Bourbon Whiskey bott code: L18199011025K **(95.5) n24 t24 f23.5 b24** A peach of a single cask. The great man would have celebrated this one... *45% (90 proof). sc.*

Evan Williams 23 Years Old (94) n22 t23.5 f24.5 b24. Struts his stuff, refusing to allow age to slow him or dim the shine from his glowing grains. Now oak has taken its toll. This seems older than its 23 years... Or so I first thought. Then a light shone in my soul and it occurred to me: hang on...I have wines going back to the last century. For the older ones, do I not allow them to breathe? So I let the whiskey breathe. And, behold, it rose from the dead. This Methuselah of a whiskey had come alive once more...and how!! *53.5%*

Ezra Brooks Bourbon Whiskey bott code: A193180914 **(90) n22.5 t22.5 f22 b23** A truly classic young to medium bourbon which celebrates the beautiful arrangement come to between the corn and tannin. An absolutely classic old style of bourbon that the grandfather of whoever distilled this would instantly recognise. *40% (80 proof).*

◈ **Falls Church Distillers Church Bourbon Whiskey** batch no. 19, American oak barrels **(87.5) n21.5 t22.5 f21.5 b22** Certainly likes to go worship at the Hickory Church of Latter Day Bourbon, boasting all kinds of cough sweet richness, and softer liquorice and vanillas, too. If they could just cut down on some of the superficial oils this really would be very impressive. *40% (80 proof).*

Four Roses Bourbon bott code: 2018/11/20 db **(88) n24 t22.5 f20 b21.5** After a few years with a little extra weight behind it, the standard Four Roses has reverted back to a light and flimsy style recognisable to those of us who encountered it between the 1970s and late 1990s. One of the most fragile Kentucky bourbons in the market place, but profiting from a sublime nose. *40%.*

Four Roses Single Barrel warehouse No. LE, barrel no. 4-25, bott code: 1400 05218 0655 db **(91) n23 t23 f22 b23** A very distinctive style of bourbon: crisp caramelised shell around the house light corn and vanilla. *50%.*

Four Roses Small Batch bott code: 1316 14318 1363 db **(95) n23.5** a halfway house between an assertive confidence on the nose and its trademark appealing, understated fruitiness. All spruced up with a little salt and pepper...and pine; **t24** a beautiful delivery with some real age shewing from the very first moment. The oils are, as near as damn it, perfect, adding just the right weight to further enrich the crackling, spiced-up caramelized sugars and add lustre to the hugely intense, almost concentrated corn sub-stratum; **f23.5** long and luxurious. The spices are like a dog with a bone, refusing to let go. But the vanilla is of epic proportions and rich enough to easily contain the light liquorice notes which flicker late on; **b24** a hugely satisfying, high quality bourbon. Undisputed class. *45%.*

Frankfort Bourbon Society Buffalo Trace Single Barrel Select (86) n21.5 t22 f21. b21.5 A spluttering bourbon in part, haunted by a lactic note visible on both the nose and finish. At least the denser, sugar-spiced high points are truly majestic. *45% (90 proof).*

Frankfort Bourbon Society Elijah Craig Small Batch Serial No 4718833 bott Fall 2018 **(95.5) n24 t24 f23.5 b24.** This gem of a barrel was hand-picked by members of the Frankfort Bourbon Society and I suspect that had they had a hundred stabs at the stocks, they would not have come away with something more alluring and complex than this. *47% (94 proof).*

Frankfort Bourbon Society Knob Creek Single Barrel Reserve Aged 9 Years Barrel No 6225 bott Spring 2018 **(95) n23.5 t24 f23.5 b24** Unusual for a single barrel to so comprehensively typify an entire brand. Bold, bracing and brilliant! *60% (120 proof).*

Frankfort Bourbon Society Weller Antique 107 Single Barrel Select Serial (94) n23 t23.5 f23.5 b24 Despite the relative youth of this bourbon, the effect of the wheat is astonishing, radiating its spicy intent from the very first moment. But only when the honey catches up and mingles with an exquisite feel for balance do things become truly special. Tasting this on a day when Frankfort, Ky, dropped to around minus 15 degrees – one of the coldest days here in many a year – those warming spices came in most welcome...even though the bourbon was not swallowed! *53.5% (107 proof).*

George T. Stagg db **(97)** n24 t24.5 f24 b24.5 Amazing consistency: this is the fourth year running it has been given a score of 96.5 or above - a Stagg-ering achievement. *72.05% (144.1 proof).*

George T. Stagg db **(97)** n24 t24.5 f24 b24.5 Funny: I nosed this and I thought: "T-bone steak."Huge whiskey deserving to be the warm-up act for a meal at either RingSide Steakhouse, Portland or Barberian's Steak House in Toronto or even some outdoor parrilla in Uruguay. It is the kind of whiskey that demands something very special: it just refuses, point-blanc, to do ordinary... *64.6% (129.2 proof).*

George T. Stagg db **(96)** n24 t24.5 f23.5 b24.5 As a George T Stagg goes, this is a bit of a wimp: some 20 proof weaker than some of its incarnations. So for those of you of a delicate disposition, you might be able to tackle this tamed monster for once. *62.45% (124.9 proof).*

⬙ **George T. Stagg** db **(96.5)** n24 soft, genteel, quietly spoken caramels....hang on a minute: what am I saying...? This is George T Stagg, isn't it? Just checked the sample...yep, it certainly is. And in a yielding pose I have never quite seen before. Light kumquat and thin liquorice help jazz up the complexity; t24 much more gripping on the palate than nose, again with a thick blend of toffee and liquorice. Superb spices on delivery and a clever sprinkling of dark sugars all over the piece; f24.5 as is so often the case, the heftier, drier notes gang up on the finish. This time they work quite beautifully in conjunction with the dried dates and molasses. Meanwhile, the toasty corn oil lingers...; b24 on nosing this I did the kind of double take James Finlayson would have been proud of in a Laurel and Hardy film. Stagg...at this strength? I was expecting the usual low 70% abv or high 60s, perhaps. But less than 60%....? A very different George T Stagg to what we have seen over the years. But the pedigree remains... *58.45% (116.9 proof).*

H. Deringer Bourbon Whiskey (88) n21.5 t22 f22 b22.5 Despite the huge, weighty bottle, this is the lighter side of bourbon whiskey with vanilla and sugars in quiet agreement. *40%. Aiko Importers, Inc.*

Hancock's President's Reserve Single Barrel bott code: B1710117:26K **(90.5)** n22.5 t23 f22.5 b22.5 A joyous Bourbon that gives the impression that it is performing well within itself. *44.45% (88.9 proof)*

Hartfield & Co Whisky batch 2.5 month **(81.5)** n20 t21 f20 b20.5 So here it is: the first whiskey legally produced from Bourbon County, Kentucky (which gave the unique whiskey its name) since before prohibition arrived in Kentucky in 1919. A nutty, sweet, largely off-key whiskey, this probably isn't the best made you can find in the State, and hopefully future bottlings will have a cleaner cut and far more copper interaction. But it is enjoyable for what it is, a nutty chewy whisky full of caramel and thinned honey which some of the 26 distillers closed down in Bourbon County exactly a century ago might have looked upon with a degree of awe... And certainly the bottle will be a collectors' item... *50% (100 proof). Distilled from Corn, rye and barley.*

⬙ **Heaven Hill Bottled in Bond 7 Years Old Kentucky Straight Bourbon Whiskey** nbc db **(90)** n22.5 toasted mallows amid lightweight red liquorice and rich corn oil: soft for a BIB would be an understatement...; t23 luxurious: a massaging of the taste buds with vanilla kneaded in to every available nerve ending. Above average oils, as well as heather-honey and marzipan; f22 drier, broader and starker, with a more vigorous spice buzz now; b22.5 a satisfying, if at times docile, BIB. *50% (100 proof).*

Hogs 3 Bourbon Aged Over 3 Years (86.5) n22.5 t21.5 f21 b21.5 A bang on standard mid-towards upper warehouse Kentucky 3-year-old with plenty of juicy but ungainly vanilla, Demerara sugar and citrus.... and absolutely no frills. *40% (80 proof). Quality Spirits International.*

I.W. Harper Kentucky Straight Bourbon 15 Year Old (94.5) n23.5 t23.5 f24 b23.5 Class in a glass. *43% (86 Proof)*

⬙ **J Mattingly Bobo's Bourbon Small Batch Bourbon Whiskey (95)** n23 t24 f24 b24 A brilliant sharpness to the small grains underlines the excellence of both the distillate the high-grade casks. Presumably a rye mashbill, for no other reason than the extraordinary crispness and salivating qualities of the treacle and vanilla mix. That said, some fair spices abound (well within the scope of a wheated mashbill) always balanced within limits...and then the amazing dark chocolate fade...complete with bewildering spice and thick molasses. What amazing balance and complexity...just...wow! If anyone doesn't appreciate this for what it is, they wouldn't know a truly great bourbon if it hit them around the head with a with a 32oz bone-in ribeye steak. (CV) *61.5% (123 proof). Distilled in Kentucky and Indiana*

◌ **J Mattingly Ripcord Single Barrel Straight Whiskey** (83.5) n21 t22 f20 b20.5 You know how amazingly good Bobos Bourbon (above) is. Well, this just isn't...Just way too liquorice dominated, bitter and tart. If this was a real ripcord, you'd end up crashing to the ground... *55% (110 proof).Distilled in Indiana sc.*

James E. Pepper 1776 Straight Bourbon Whiskey Aged Over 3 Years (91.5) n23 t23 f22.5 b23 Beautiful old school bourbon. *50% (100 proof). ncf.*

Jim Beam Black Double Age Aged 8 Years (93) n23 t24 f22.5 b23.5. Rather than the big, noisy, thrill-seeking JB Black, here it is in quiet, reflective, sophisticated mode. Quite a shift. But no less enjoyable. *43% (86 proof)*

◌ **Jim Beam Bonded 100 Proof** bott code: L8 305 (90) n22.5 pretty much classic with some major crunchy Demerara sugars at play as well as the light spices which are a bit more active than of old; t23 those spices fizz on impact and though the tannins weigh in delightfully, feels a little bit younger than some other bottlings; f22 an interesting mix of aged toastiness and younger corn-rich bourbon; b22.5 satisfyingly salivating with lots to chew on here and offers some truly classical moments. That said, thins out late on as a younger style takes control... *50% (100 proof).*

Jim Beam Signature Craft Aged 12 Years db (92.5) n23 t23.5 f23 b23 Classic Beam: big rye and massive fruit. Quite lovely. 43%.

Jim Beam Repeal Batch Bourbon bott code: L8226FFE222730700 db (89) n22 t22.5 f22 b22.5 Good, honest, unspectacular, understated but unerringly delicious and charming bourbon bottled to celebrate the 85th Anniversary of the repeal of Prohibition. On this evidence, I think they should equally celebrate the 86th anniversary... *43% (86 proof). ncf*

John E. Fitzgerald Very Special Reserve Aged 20 Years (93) n22.5 t24 f23 b23.5 A bourbon lover's bourbon! *45% (90 proof)*

John J Bowman Single Barrel Virginia Straight Bourbon bott code: L172010507:28B (93) n23 t23.5 f23 b23.5 This is very high quality bourbon making the most of both its big toastiness and its more intrinsic honey tones. Simple...yet devastatingly complex... *50%*

John J Bowman Single Barrel Virginia Straight Bourbon bott code: L190070510 (94.5) n23 t24 f23.5 b24 A very different animal to the Small Batch with a greater emphasis on the sugars and just more all round drama and muscularity. Stunning. *50% (100 proof). sc.*

◌ **Kentucky Owl Bourbon Whiskey** batch no. 9 (90.5) n23 goes for the bourbon jugular from the very first sniff: abounding with toasty tannins and crisp dark sugars from the very start, the intensity shows no sign of abating. A few spices are on the prowl, too, as the hefty liquorice tones make their stunning statement; t23 a touch oiler than the nose lets on. This thickens the sticky heather honey further and by the time the big liquorice appears we are in the midst of a pretty spicy soup; f22 just bitters out a tad a those oils extra are played out; b22.5 if, like me, you are a pretty serious birdwatcher then you know just how captivating the sight of an owl in full swoop can be. Trust me: despite those extra oils, this will captivate you... *63.8% (1276 proof). 11,595 bottles.*

Kentucky Owl Confiscated bott code: 3158860834 (80) n19 t22 f19 b20 From the moment the boiled cabbage nose hits you, this is one very disappointing whiskey. Stands up to scrutiny on delivery, where the intense caramels and vanillas combine rather well. But the dirty, buzzy finale is also a let down. Not a bourbon, in this form, I could give two hoots about, to be honest. *48.2% (96.4 proof).*

Kentucky Tavern Straight Kentucky Bourbon bott code: L190081510 (92) n22.5 t23 f23 b23.5 What a great improvement on when I last tasted this several years back. Much more depth, balance and chewability. One of the biggest – and most pleasant - surprises of my tasting day. Delicious! *40% (80 proof).*

◌ **Knob Creek 100 Proof Small Batch** bott code:: L9/55 CLH290 (89) n22.5 light with a walnut and vanilla lead; a gentle marmalade edge, too...; t22.5 takes a while for the oils to build and find their direction. In the mean-time delicate vanilla and spices help get the juices flowing, with light molten Demerara sugars at play; f21.5 thin, with a vague toastiness; b22.5 "Since 1992" chirps the label. But if you tasted that original Knob Creek against this, you might have a few problems spotting the relationship. This is the lightest of the Knob Creeks I have ever encountered, with a youthful zestiness to where you would normally find heady, rumbling dark sugars and tannin. Enjoyable, drinkable bourbon? Of course. But a chest-hair curling Knob Creek to chew on until your jaw drops, as of old? Nope. *50%.*

Knob Creek 25th Anniversary Single Barrel barrelled 2/25/2004 db (93) n23 t24 f23 b23 A caramel-rich critter, yes-siree! But let it hang around the glass a bit and a rich liquorice edginess will develop... *62% (124 proof). sc.*

Knob Creek Aged 9 Years bott code L6154 (95.5) n23.5 t24 f23.5 b24.5 Seems like more barrels have been included from the lower echelons of the warehouse. Lighter, sweeter and more feminine. One of the most complex Knob Creeks I have ever encountered: a true Kentucky belle! *50% (100 proof)*

⟪⟫ **Knob Creek Aged 12 Years** bott code: L9252CLA db **(93.5) n23.5** lurking caramels have to make way for the kumquats, In turn they cede to the growing rye influence within the mashbill. Spices abound no matter in this complex aroma; **t23.5** surprisingly juicy and refreshing for its age. The sugars have solidified with the small grains to salivating effect. Juicy dates merge with the molasses at the midpoint to terrific effect; **f23** remains toasty and dries as a mark of respect to its good age; **b23.5** needs the full Murray Method of tasting to really get this engine to fire up. Too cool and the caramels swamp everything. When warmed slightly, the small grains go into complexity overdrive. 50% (100 proof).

⟪⟫ **Knob Creek Aged 15 Years** release no. KC001, bott code: L0139CLJ db **(92.5) n23** distinctly nutty, with fluting hickory and surprisingly delicate sugars. Even the spices have a relaxed and light touch; **t23** none of the normal butch liquorice on delivery you'd expect from Knob Creek. Instead, the brown sugars are of the same delicate nature revealed on the nose, man-marking the tannins and ensuring the age has a bigger mark on the label than it does in the glass. A very soft liquorice tone mingles well with the semi-fizzing spice; **f23** light butterscotch and vanilla points towards the extra caramels from the oak working in tandem with the corn oils. Incredibly soft...; **b23.5** it is a curious thing that when Knob Creek first came into the market, the style chosen – and from much younger barrels than used here – was intensity married with complexity: Knob Creek was a huge, uncompromising bourbon; but one always celebrating its role as the gentle giant. Here the bourbon is markedly older. But it appears the blender has decided to pick a slightly different type of barrel, those it appears that were lodged in the lower rungs of the warehouse rather than somewhere much higher up, as had previously been the case. So this is a surprise bourbon, not at all expected. Muscle makes way for elegance, baritone for tenor. 50% (100 proof). ⚘

⟪⟫ **Larceny Barrel Proof** batch no. A1200, bott code: A32291246 db **(95) n23.5** the liquorice comes at you as though in three dimensions. Pleasingly salty, too, which appears to up both the sharpness and complexity level up a notch; **t24** my god...!! That is bourbon...!!! The delivery just doesn't bite, but it nibbles, kisses and caresses. As on the nose, the liquorice is of nearly unbelievable intensity, rounded by the corn oils but polished by the Demerara sugars; as for the spices....hang on to your John Fitzgerald Treasury Agent hat....as I'm doing right now, as I happen to be wearing one...; **f23.5** long, thanks to those solid corn oils and slow melting of the dark sugars. Much more chocolatey tones towards the death; **b24** if you don't track down a bottle of this stunning batch, then you have just committed one hell of a crime...!!! 61.6% (123.2 proof).

⟪⟫ **Larceny Barrel Proof** batch no. B520 db **(95) n23.5** a remarkable re-run of batch A1200, though with a tad more caramel; **t24** very much on the same course as A1200, though slightly saltier here giving the loftier tannins a keener feel. There is a salivating sharpness to this, though the liquorice is slightly subdued by the corn oils. A light heather honey gloss here, too...; **f23.5** much spicier and aloof. The cocoa enters late into the game. But so delicious...; **b24** a glorious variation on a theme from batch A1200 but fractionally less complex. But it is like choosing between one Dashiell Hammett novel and another... 60.6% (122.2 proof).

⟪⟫ **Liquid Treasures 10th Anniversary Heaven Hill 10 Year Old** bourbon barrel, dist 2009, bott 2019 **(88.5) n22 t22 f22.5 b22** Heaven Hickory: the most one-dimensional bourbon I have tasted this year. But is it thoroughly enjoyable? Yep! 50.2%. sc. 161 bottles.

Maker's 46 (95) n23.5 t24.5 f23 b24 Some people have a problem with oak staves. I don't: whisky, after all, is about the interaction of a grain spirit and oak. This guy is all about the nose and, especially, the delivery. With so much controlled honey on show, it cannot be anything other than a show-stopper. Frankly, magnificent. I think I've met my Maker's... 47% (94 proof)

Maker's 46 barrel finished with oak staves, bott code: L6155MMB 00651 1233 **(89) n22.5 t22.5 f22 b22** Maker's at its most surprisingly genteel. 47% (94 proof).

⟪⟫ **Mayor Pingree Aged 7 Years Straight Bourbon Whiskey** batch no. 4 db **(94.5) n24** super high-class. The lavender, mint and light eucalyptus mingles sublimely with the molasses to present a chest-beating aroma. A little French mustard offers extra prickle; **t23.5** the subtlety of the sugars is in keeping with the nose. The drier tannins and spices have the upper hand but the liquorice has an almost puckering quality; **f23.5** brilliant layers of dry cocoa powder; **b23.5** distilled in Lawrenceburg, Indiana, the label confirms. The announcement had already been made on the nose... Casks almost certainly picked from the higher points of the warehouse. 59% (118 proof). ncf sc.

McAffee's Benchmark Old No 8 Brand Kentucky Straight Bourbon bott code: L190260113 **(87.5) n22 t22 f21.5 b22** A good, honest, unspectacular bourbon which ticks all the boxes without for a moment trying to go into superdrive. Lays on the natural caramels thickly, then some low voltage spice to stir things up. The sugars are on a slow build, but get there. 40% (80 proof).

Michter's 20 Year Old Kentucky Straight Bourbon batch no. 18I1370, bott code: A182681370 **(96.5) n24 t24 f24 b24.5** When people ask me why I think that bourbon has the edge over Scotch at the moment, perhaps I should point them in the direction of a bottling like this to give them some understanding as to why... One of the best 20+ year-old bourbons I have ever encountered. *57.1% (114.2 proof). 463 bottles.*

❖ **Michter's 20 Year Old Kentucky Straight Bourbon** batch no. 19H1439, bott code: A192421439 **(96.5) n24.5** you know when the toastiness is this deep, yet so magnificently well balanced that a treat awaits. There is a slightly acrid bite to the tannins, but the interwoven liquorice and molasses keeps everything where it should be. Helped along massively by an orange blossom honey and maple syrup backdrop. A Murray-Method 15-minute nose, please...; **t24** the heart-winning array of sugars on the nose seem to join forces and harden slightly to form the main thrust of the early part of the delivery. Quickly, though, a massive liquorice and hickory surge take over, everything lubricated by the still game corn oils; the spices threaten but stay busy but relatively delicate; **f23.5** much quieter with spices still wittering away among the lush hickory and mocha, **b24.5**. When this bourbon was distilled, it was unlikely a barrel could reach this degree of antiquity and still taste as wonderfully complete as this. Then, if a bourbon reached its second decade, it was one that had slipped through the net and had not been especially cared for. Meaning, nearly always, they were too old and clogged with oak. Not this fellow. This is an old timer all right. But beautifully manicured and more beautiful now than at any previous time in its life. A privilege to taste. *57.1% (114.2 proof). 440 bottles.* 🍷

Michter's Single Barrel 10 Year Old Kentucky Straight Bourbon barrel no. 19D625, bott code: A19095625 **(95.5) n24.5 t23.5 f23.5 b24** An incredibly beautiful whiskey. A contender for the single barrel of the year, for sure... *47.2% (94.4 proof). sc.*

Michter's Single Barrel 10 Year Old Kentucky Straight Bourbon barrel no. 19D662, bott code: A19099662 **(96) n24 t24 f23.5 b24.5** A classic top quarter of warehouse 10-year-old (barrel 625, above, was much nearer midpoint) which has seen some heat action and ensures maximum depth and entertainment for its age. Beautifully made, too...! *47.2% (94.4 proof). sc.*

❖ **Michter's Single Barrel 10 Year Old Kentucky Straight Bourbon** barrel no. 20C363, bott code: A200700363 **(94) n23.5** an adorable shimmering sweetness to the high-flying liquorice: this is a top dollar aroma typical of the house style understatement; **t23.5** the most curious delivery: for the first flavour wave or two...nothing seems to be there. But this is the lull before the storm, because we are then met by a minty-liquorice arrival that, via the corn oil, moves into full-blown chocolate milkshake. Then, by the midpoint, stunning liquorice. But there is also a strangeness - a unique numbing note, too, that you can sometimes find when first chewing a walnut; **f23** almost a slight phenolic smokiness to the fading vanilla and liquorice; **b24** a truly unique bourbon profile that certainly knows how to surprise and entertain! *47.2% (94.4 proof). sc.* 🍷

Michter's Small Batch Kentucky Straight Bourbon batch no. L18F873, bott code: A8172873 **(87.5) n22 t22.5 f21 b22** An attractive, slightly minty and ungainly offering with extra bitterness to the toastiness, especially at the death. Some subtle orange blossom honey aids the sweetness. *45.7% (91.4 proof).*

❖ **Michter's Small Batch Kentucky Straight Bourbon** batch no. 20C430, bott code: A200830430 **(92) n23** exceptionally nutty and deft. Strives towards power but settles on an understated richness, with a flickering of mocha and citrus imposing itself gently on the nuttiness; **t23.5** the lightest corn oils wash over the taste buds and leave drier toastier tannins as beached driftwood; the midpoint seems to gather up all the stray nuttiness; **f22.5** bitters slightly, but cocoa to the rescue..; the oils hang around longer than first expected; **b23** a deceptively weighty bourbon which is an essay in genteel understatement. Complex and fascinating, especially in the many guises the cocoa creates. *45.7% (91.4 proof).*

Michter's Small Batch Original Sour Mash batch no. L18V1608, bott code: A183041608 **(92) n23.5 t23 f22.5 b23** One of the weaker Michter's by strength, but lacks nothing in subtlety. *43% (86 proof).*

❖ **New Riff Backsetter Bourbon Bottled in Bond** db **(87) n22.5 t22 f21 b21.5** One of the sweetest bourbons I've encountered for a little while: the expected liquorice and toasty molasses making way for an infinitely more honeyed style with a heather honey forging ahead of the later maple syrup. Strangely tangy, though: a bit like particularly virile marmalade. *50% (100 proof). ncf.*

New Riff Kentucky Straight Bourbon Aged At Least 4 Years dist Fall 2014, bott Fall 2018 nbc **(91.5) n22 t23.5 f22.5 b23.5** I will have to get to Newport, on the opposite banks of the Ohio to Cincinnati, to see this excellent new Kentucky distillery in action. This is as big and impressive as the river that flows astride the two towns. *50% (100 proof). 65% corn, 30% rye 5% malted barley.*

❖ **New Riff Kentucky Straight Bourbon Whiskey Bottled in Bond** dist Fall 2015, bott Spring 2020 db **(87) n22 t22.5 f21 b21.5** An oily cove with the odd tell-tale sign of wider cut. The massive natural caramels do al they can to hush it up. *50% (100 proof). ncf.*

❖ **New Riff Single Barrel Kentucky Straight Bourbon Whiskey** barrel no. 15-6995, dist Fall 2015, bott Fall 2019 db **(89) n22.5** tantalisingly light with a lot of warming tannin nibble; the toffee slowly gathers forces; **t22.5** fat and explosive. Massive amounts if caramels take up the mid-ground; **f21.5** bitters slightly; **b22.5** maybe a little too much extracted from the still by this distillery's usually high standards. *56.75% (113.5 proof). ncf sc.*

⬦ **New Riff Single Barrel Kentucky Straight Bourbon Whiskey** barrel no. 16-7128, dist Spring 2016, bott Spring 2020 db (**92**) **n22.5** gorgeous oaky toffee layering, offset by a subtle rye nip: the small grains are working busily here; **t23.5** magnificently two toned: the corn oils and tannins engage as one to create a toffee-laden, delightfully sweet massage while simultaneously the spices are pinching and punching, refusing to allow the softer tones to either settle or dominate; **f22.5** beautifully layered vanilla, the spices still flickering; **b23.5** a rich, sweet and satisfying bourbon. *56.6% (113.2 proof). ncf sc.*

Old Charter 8 bott code: B170871 10:094 (**91**) **n22.5 t23 f22.5 b23** A wonderfully oily affair which sticks to the palate like a limpet. From taste alone, appears no longer to be an 8-year-old but has retained the number 8. Probably a mix of years as the layering and complexity is significant. *40% (80 proof)*

Old Charter 8 Kentucky Straight Bourbon bott code: L183420122 (**92**) **n22.5 t23.5 f22.5 b23.5** Very similar to the bottling above, except here the sugars, up in attack earlier, gleam and sparkle while the later spices bristle a little more aggressively: slightly more polarisation, but more polish, too. Such great stuff! *44% (88 proof).*

Old Charter Oak Mongolian Oak Kentucky Straight Bourbon (**92**) **n22 t23.5 f23 b23.5** How strange that just two or three weeks ago I was in London, being booked up for a whisky tasting next year in Mongolia. And now here I am in Kentucky tasting a bourbon matured in Mongolian oak, the first such whiskey I have ever heard of. Talk about whisky being an international spirit these days... This is very different to any bourbon I have tasted before: positively schizoid. Starts off, unmistakably, as a bourbon, though offering a unique profile, and finishes something much closer in style to Speyside single malt but taking a previously uncharted route between the two empires: less Murray Method than Marco Polo. Not exactly a silk road of a bourbon but as intriguing as it is delicious. *45% (90 proof).*

Old Carter Straight Bourbon Barrel Strength Batch 1 (**91.5**) **n22 t23.5 f23 b23** The nose may be slightly cumbersome and plodding, like the horse on the label, but as soon as it hits the palate you know you are backing a winner. *54.45% (108.8 proof). 1567 bottles.*

⬦ **Old Ezra Aged 7 Years Kentucky Straight Bourbon** bott code: LF4227 (**92**) **n22.5** light and citrussy, with more than a degree of freshly cut kumquat; **t23.5** the tannins aren't exactly thin on the ground, but they are a little stand-offish. This makes for a small grain bonanza: intricate and busy with the liquorice on a slow build; the clever weighting (and waiting!) of the molasses is understated but essential; **f23** heftier now with the desired liquorice-hickory combination; **b23** essentially, a light and complex bourbon with, presumably, the majority of barrels gleaned from the lower floors. *50.5% (101 proof).*

Old Fitzgerald Bottled-in-Bond Aged 9 Years Fall 2018 Edition made: Fall 2008, bott 05/23/2018 db (**93.5**) **n23.5 t23.5 f23 b24** Middle aged wheated bourbon at its deliciously complex best. *50% (100 proof).*

Old Fitzgerald Bottled-in-Bond Aged 13 Years Spring 2019 Edition made: Fall 2005, bott 01/30/2019 db (**95**) **n23.5 t24 f23.5 b24** A very different animal to their 9-year-old offering, which is tighter and with a more precise game plan. By contrast, this drifts and is less attentive to the wheat...though you never lose sight of it. *50% (100 proof).*

⬦ **Old Fitzgerald Bottled-in-Bond Aged 15 Years Fall 2019 Edition** made: Fall 2004, bott Fall 2019 db (**89**) **n23** though the tannins have a much chunkier feel to previous Old Fitzes I have tasted in recent years, and the marmalade far thicker cut, there is still an enigmatic weight to this which charms rather than bludgeons...; **t22** the corn oil has thickened to chewable proportions; the molasses oozes rather than runs, making it slightly over-sweet...; **f22** hefty spice among the planks of oak; **b22** Old Fitz is feeling his years in this one... *50% (100 proof).*

Old Forester bott code: A083151035 db (**94.5**) **n23.5 t23.5 f23.5 b24** Solid as a rock: a classic and criminally under-rated bourbon which is wonderfully true to the distillery. *43%.*

⬦ **Old Forester** bott code: A115192109 db (**96.5**) **n24** hang on....wait... This one has so much more than might first be spotted. So rare to find liquorice on a layered footing, almost alternating between red and black; the sugars and honeys are also mottled and streaked, no dominating factor, but a mix between crisper Demerara and more embracing acacia honey. Meanwhile the tannins cajole and tease, one moment shewing the vital part they play, then equally aloof and distant... This is such a classic, old-style type of bourbon...; **t24.5** what a delivery!! I mean...just brain-pummellingly stunning. You think, OK: here comes the liquorice...but instead the small grains turn up in force and momentarily dominate, the tannins having suddenly vanished to the back benches. Again the sugars are crisp and play into the hands of the more salivating part of the story. And only then do those liquorice notes start edging their way back into the game, growing in depth, but never over-stepping the mark...; **f23.5** long, elegant and still improbably salivating and complex. Much more emphasis on the red liquorice now, and the sugars which seem to bring the spices into play (far more than when slightly warmed)... The layering of the vanillas alongside the dovetailing of the small grains deserve a standing ovation...; **b24.5** having taken it right through the Murray Method, this is one of those very rare whiskies – maybe one in between 300 and 400 - which can be found at its absolute best at ordinary room temperature. Then the influence of the oils is arrested and the grains become the dominating force. And the degree of layering takes a good half hour to fathom. So far this whiskey has taken me around two hours to tame. It is, unquestionably the best whiskey I have tasted so far this year, either for the Bible, or in general whisky work. And, do you know what else I love. No corks. No wax. You are just a bottle top click away from true bourbon genius... *43% (86 proof).*

◇ **Old Forester** bott code: A115191606 db **(91)** **n22.5** the mild vanilla and hickory make for the most gentle of aromas; **t22.5** a corn-ucopia of oils – then the hickory sets in...; **f23** back to the vanilla...and, of course, hickory; **b23** simplistic – and really goes to town on the hickory! *50% (100 proof).*

◇ **Old Forester 1870 Original Batch** bott code: F050191128702394 db **(94)** **n23.5** unmistakable Old Forester crispness and rigidity to the rye and tannin mix: the molasses could almost crumble...; **t23.5** salivating – and a complete transfer off the nose to the palate...; **f24** seems to up the stakes slightly by piling in with extra hickory and now ulmo honey, too... **b24** simply glorious bourbon! *45% (90 proof).*

Old Forester 1897 Bottled in Bond bott code: L297811823 **(92.5)** **n22.5** takes time for the layering to harmonise, but given patience and warmth it gets there. Ultimately weighty with toasted yams and walnuts; **t23.5** sonorously rich on delivery, the corn oils really making a full impact from the first. Burnt fudge and toasty tannin sticks like a limpet to the roof of the mouth; **f23** so chewy and deep, hefty molasses clinging to the overdone toast as perfected by my wonderful PA, Jane; **b23.5** the toast starts to slowly smoulder in a gorgeous bourbon that creeps up and mugs you. Surprisingly rich and just so lush. *50% (100 proof).*

Old Forester 1910 Old Fine Whisky nbc **(92)** **n23 t23.5 f22.5 b23** The kind of dark, hefty bourbon this distillery has long championed. Substantial and satisfying. *46.5% (93 proof).*

Old Forester 1920 Prohibition Style nbc **(95.5)** **n23.5** deep rumbling like a barely audible cello, a salty edge gives extra life to the seemingly moribund tannin and slowly, the complexity levels rise as floral and treacle notes rise and then merge; **t24** exemplary mouthfeel: silky soft but daggers of spice pierce the cosiness. The sugars are profound yet controlled, all of the darker style, especially molasses; **f24** still spicy and busy with a mix of Manuka and heather honeys dovetailing and mingling sublimely with the varied toasty oaks; **b24** just oozes with classic Old Forester depth and oomph! A classic of its style. *57.5% (115 proof).*

Old Forester Statesman bott code: L2337123:49 db **(92.5)** **n23 t23.5 f23 b23.5** A very laid back and relaxed Forester. *47.5% (95 proof).*

Old Grand-Dad **(90.5)** **n22 t23 f23 b23.5.** This one's all about the small grains. A busy, lively bourbon, this offers little to remind me of the original Old Grand-Dad whiskey made out at Frankfort. That said, this is a whisk(e)y-lover's whiskey: in other words the excellence of the structure and complexity outweighs any historical misgivings. Enormously improved and now very much at home with its own busy style. *43%*

Old Grand-Dad 80 Proof bott code: L7119FFB140640030 **(87)** **n21.5 t22.5 f21 b22** Steady and pretty light weight. Doesn't have quite the same backbone as the 43%. But who cannot fall for the charm of delicate citrus and chalky vanillas? Just enough liquorice and rye juiciness to lift it into the easy drinking category. *40% (80 proof).*

Old Grand-Dad Bonded 100 Proof **(95)** **n23 t24.5 f23.5 b24** A brilliant bourbon built for the Bottled in Bond category, the extra oils ramping up the rye to significant and disarming effect. Classically beautiful, a bourbon that appears to be just getting better and better. *50% (100 proof).*

Old Grand-Dad Bonded 100 Proof bott code 258/17 **(96)** **n23 t24.5 f24 b24.5** For a bourbon, I have tasted rye less rye-like than this. A bourbon standing erect, proud pretty much top of its game wallowing in its faultless distillation and maturation; indeed, probably the best Grand-Dad Bonded I have yet encountered, which really is saying something over so many years! Glorious. *50% (100 proof).*

Old Pepper Straight Bourbon Whiskey Aged 10 Years new white oak barrel, barrel no. L18U **(90.5)** **n23 t23.5 f21.5 b22.5** Pepper by name, pepper by nature...! *56.9% (113.8 proof). sc.*

Old Rip Van Winkle Aged 10 Years bott code: B17053113:497 **(91.5)** **n23 t23.5 f22 b23** Those who know the Weller Antique 107 will find this enjoyable, but just a little lacking in body by comparison. *53.5% (107 proof).*

Old Rip Van Winkle Aged 10 Years bott code: B1705307:267 db **(93.5)** **n24 t23 f23 b23.5** There is something of the old Ancient Age 10 in this, you know... *53.5% (107 proof).*

Old Taylor 6 Kentucky Straight Bourbon bott code: B1631608446 **(90)** **n22.5 t23 f22 b22.5** Exactly as above. Except we now see a little more corn oil and rye glisten on the finish. What a lovely old-fashioned kind of bourbon this is, especially for Old Timers like me...! *40% (80 proof).*

Old Virginia Kentucky Straight Bourbon Aged 6 Years bott code: L833901B **(91.5)** n23 t22.5 f23 b23 The kind of old-fashioned style bourbon I fell in love with over 40 years ago... *40%.*

Orphan Barrel Rhetoric Aged 24 Years bott code: L8059K1002 **(95)** n24 t24 f23.5 b23.5 An unusual bourbon for this kind of great age. Usually they head down a heavy duty tannin route. Instead this one almost drowns in natural creamy caramels. Almost as meek as Theresa May when facing the EU bully boys though, of course, nothing on the planet is that pathetic. *45.4%*

Pappy Van Winkle Family Reserve 15 Years Old bott code: L172520110:237 **(96)** n24 t23.5 f24 b24.5 Weller Antique fans will possibly find a closer match here structure-wise than the 10-year-old. While those in pursuit of excellent bourbon should just linger here awhile. Anyone other than true bourbon lovers need not sample. But there again... *53.5%*

Pappy Van Winkle Family Reserve Kentucky Straight Bourbon Whiskey 15 Years Old bott code: L181340105:017 db **(96)** n24 t24.5 f23.5 b24 Usually I spit everything I taste. I accidentally found myself swallowing a drop of this without thinking. A bourbon-lover's bourbon... *53.5% (107 proof).*

Pappy Van Winkle's Family Reserve 20 Years Old bott code: L172640108:18N **(95)** n24 t22.5 f24.5 b24 An ancient bourbon, so should be a flavour powerhouse. But this is all about understatement and complexity. *45.2% (90.4 proof).*

Pappy Van Winkle Family Reserve Kentucky Straight Bourbon Whiskey 20 Years Old bott code: L18233C10723N db **(85.5)** n21 t22.5 f21 b21 Some profound vanilla and citrus moments on delivery. But the nose tells you things aren't as they should be and the finale confirms it. One or two casks used here that have gone through the top, bringing out some pretty tired notes from the oak. Just never comfortable in its own skin. *45.2% (90.4 proof).*

Pappy Van Winkle's Family Reserve 23 Years Old bott code: L1707013:20N **(94.5)** n24.5 t23 f23.5 b23.5 I well remember the first Pappy boasting this kind of age: it was horrifically over-oaked and lacked any form of meaningful structure. Well, this also has the odd moment where the tannins are slightly out of control, especially just after delivery. But the structure to this is sound, the complexity a joy. And as for the nose....wow! *47.8% (95.6 proof).*

Pappy Van Winkle Family Reserve Kentucky Straight Bourbon Whiskey 23 Years Old bott code: L180590111:08N db **(95.5)** n24 t24 f23.5 b24 One of the holy grails of bourbon is to produce consistently a 23- to 25-year-old which is still sweet and not tannin dominated: no easy ask. This has certainly moved a little way towards that, shewing some of the character of the last bottling I tasted, although this is unquestionably drier. At least on the nose a decisive sweetness I detected and there are still sugars enough to give some fabulous moments on the palate. The tannins do, though, still have the biggest say. But remember: this whiskey has matured for a very long time. In the glass it takes well over an hour to get the best out of it: the secrets of such an ancient bourbon are always revealed tantalisingly slowly... *47.8% (95.6 proof).*

Parker's Heritage Collection 24 Year Old Bottled in Bond Bourbon dist Fall 90 **(95.5)** n24 t24 f23.5 b24 For my 999th whisky for the 2018 Bible, thought I'd take on the oldest commercially bottled Kentucky bourbon I can ever remember seeing. Had no idea how this one would go, as the heat of the Midwest means there is little room for the whiskey to manoeuvre. What we actually have is a bourbon in previously unchartered territory and clearly experiencing new, sometimes mildly bewildering, sensations, having proudly gone where no bourbon has gone before... *50%.*

Quarter Horse Kentucky Bourbon Whiskey Aged a Minimum of 1 Year in New Oak (87) n21.5 t23 f21.5 b21.5 An intriguing whiskey which simultaneously shews its youth and the spirit and maturity from the cask. The creamy toffee notes on delivery and follow through are superb. For a Quarter Horse it's not half bad... *46% (92.*

Rebel Yell Kentucky Straight Bourbon Whiskey bott code: A305181406 **(88)** n22.5 t22 f21 b22 When, back in 1992 I had set off on my uncertain future as the world's first full time whisky writer, the London underground was festooned with adverts for Rebel Yell, complete with Confederate flag, if memory serves over the passing quarter of a century. It was United Distillers' (now Diageo) great hope of conquering the world with bourbon. They didn't and the company, with their fingers scorched, turned their backs on not only what was actually a very good bourbon, but the entire genre. They had gone in all guns blazing, when in fact what bourbon needed – after so many decades of decline - was a softly softly approach. This doesn't have quite the richness of that defeated Rebel Yell from a previous era, but the delicate nature of the sweetness is very attractive. *40% (80 proof).*

◇◇ **Rebel Yell Single Barrel Aged 10 Years Kentucky Straight Bourbon Whiskey** barrel no: 5083248, dist 09/06 **(93)** n23 beautifully scented: lavender weaves in and out of the soft and sweetened liquorice: as tender and gentle as it gets...; t23.5 intricate and spicy from the moment it touches the taste buds, there is a light viscosity to the corn oils which helps to accentuate the light lemon-zesty quality of the sugars; f23 a marked chalkiness is attached to the drier elements here. The spices rumble mildly, the sugars pulse with a friendly beat while the tannins build but with a light coffee roastiness; **b23.5** a subtle and satisfying wheated bourbon. *50% (100 proof). sc.*

Rebel Yell Small Batch Reserve Kentucky Straight Bourbon Whiskey (94.5) n23.5 t24 f23 **b23.5** A full on, toasty bourbon making the most of the ample spices on hand. *45.3% (90.6 proof).*

◆ **Redemption Bourbon Aged No Less Than 2 Years** batch no. 029, bott code: L9269607:16 **(83.5)** n22 t22.5 f19 b20 Certainly kicks off well enough both on nose and delivery with an attractive mix of vanilla and liquorice. But the finish is curiously bitter: not a trait one normally associates with bourbon. Some decent redeeming muscovado sugars at play. *42% (84 proof).*

◆ **Redemption High Rye Bourbon Aged No Less Than 2 Years** batch no. 122, bott code: L9262600:23 **(91)** n22.5 a bright interplay of rye and black liquorice; big toasty molasses, too; **t23** though the corn is reduced here, its oil makes the first move before the toastier tannins dig in. Well spiced with an understated rye-fruit back kick; **f22.5** it's all about the spice; **b23** so much better than the last Redemption High Rye I encountered. Surprisingly well spiced for a bourbon sporting a rye content weighing at a hefty 38% of the mash bill. *46% (92 proof).*

◆ **Redwood Empire Pipe Dream Bourbon Whiskey Aged at least 4 Years** bott code: L19 1760 **(91.5)** n23 Victory V cough candy ground down and mixed in with Demerara sugar. Like....wow!! **t23** like nose, like delivery...hickory runs amok and not even a dose of molasses can lasso it in. Takes quite a creamy turn once the corn oils kick into action; **f22.5** takes on a toasty hue and burnt liquorice; **b23** for a whiskey of this age, the hickory content is high. And a very sweet hickory at that. Very distinctive bourbon. *45%.*

Rock Hill Farms Single Barrel Bourbon bott code: B1717118:40K **(95)** n24 t24 f23.5 b24 Almost impossible to find fault with this. Anyone who loves whisky, bourbon in particular, will simply groan in pleasure in the same way your leg might jolt out when the knee is tapped. The only fly in the ointment is that I cannot tell you the barrel or bottling, because it isn't marked on the bottle. This really is bourbon at it sexiest. *50% (100 proof)*

Rock Hill Farms Single Barrel Bourbon bott code: L18102010829K **(95.5)** n24 t24 f23.5 b24 Take a bet on this and you are likely to be a winner. A true bourbon connoisseur's favourite.... *50%*

Russell's Reserve Kentucky Straight Bourbon 10 Years Old bott code: LL/GI210755 db **(92.5)** n23 t23 f23 b23.5 One of the softest decade-old bourbons I have tasted in a very, very long time. *45% (90 proof).*

Russell's Reserve Single Barrel no 17-0208 Rickhouse B Floor 6 17 2 **(95.5)** n23.5 t24 f23.5 **b24.5** So understated, this bourbon communicates in gentle whispers. Comes across sweet as honey but thickens into a gentle giant - yet all the time the balance is never threatened, only continually enhanced. Sublime. *55% (110 proof). Selected by the Frankfort Bourbon Society*

Seven Devils Straight Bourbon Whiskey (82.5) n20 t21.5 f20.5 b20.5 Nutty, caramel-laden and sweet, there is a buzz on the palate to this which suggests the distillate has not been quite as well made as it could be. Doesn't sit right, despite (or maybe because of) the praline. *45% (90 proof). Bottled by Koenig Distillery*

Shenk's Homestead Kentucky Sour Mash 2018 Release batch no. 18C322, bott code: A18094322 **(89)** n22.5 t22.5 f22 b22 A pleasant, non-taxing, small grain dominated bourbon, but with a curious lack of body. *45.6% (91.2 proof). 2,691 bottles. Bottled by Michter's Distillery.*

◆ **Shenk's Homestead Kentucky Sour Mash 2019 Release** batch no. 19G1139, bott code: A191861139 **(88)** n22.5 t22.5 t22 f21.5 b22 Exceptionally gentle whiskey boasting modest but important kumquat note on both nose and body and a shimmering, slightly metallic heather honey sweetness. A tad bitter late on. *45.6% (91.2 proof). 2,882 bottles. Bottled by Michter's Distillery.*

◆ **The Single Cask Heaven Hill 2009** barrel, cask no. 152724 **(94)** n23.5 t24 f23 b23.5 HH at is busiest, though not quite brightest. The liquorice and brief maple syrup mix are the highlight, just after delivery. But the toastiness is a little aggressive and, ultimately, on the bitter side. Even so, there is much to enjoy elsewhere, especially with the corn oils, spices and, above all, the controlled depth of the Victory V cough sweet-style hickory. Lovely stuff! *62.5%. nc ncf sc.*

◆ **Smooth Ambler Contradiction Bourbon** a blend of straight bourbons blended in West Virginia, Tennessee and Indiana, batch 273 **(94)** n23.5 ah...such layering!! The vanillas, sugars and lightest of spices each appear to have about the same degree of intensity, with none wanting to outdo the other. This, really, is how it should be...; again, hickory appears on the menu...; **t24** when cold, this can be a little tight and heady. Opened using the Murray Method, the sugars spring to life and kick-start that hickory note to brilliant effect. Real Fisherman's Friends cough sweets at work here; **f23** dry and toasty with the molasses seemingly having an element of charcoal...; **b23.5** if this whiskey had a middle name, it would be Complexity... and you would hear no contradictions from me...! *46% (92 proof).*

◆ **Smooth Ambler Old Scout Straight Bourbon** batch No 55 distilled in Indiana **(92)** n23 sharp and yeasty, there is almost a staccato trill to the sugars; there is a hickory fingerprint everywhere; **t23** a hickory lead on delivery refuses to back down even when the molasses and tannins begin to gang together. The spices appear initially on the warpath, but soon back down; **f22.5** the corn oils bring matters to a soothing conclusion; **b23.5** non-spectacular but thoroughly enjoyable bourbon that wears its excellence well. *49.5% (99 proof).*

◇ **Spirits of French Lick The Wheater Straight Bourbon Whiskey** batch no. 4 **(92) n23 t23 f22.5 b23.5** This mixing of two-year-old French Lick and 7-year-old Wyoming Wheated bourbons has to be one of the creamiest of this style I have ever encountered. The nose is fat and friendly with a light brushing of cinnamon on the ginger and over cooked toast. However, the sugars are first on parade on the palate, most of the presenting a toasty Demerara style. However, those corn oils insist on being counted to ensure a lush and lingering mouthfeel. The toastiness increases as the spices mount but red liquorice balances things neatly. Wonderfully flavoursome! (CV) *51% (102 proof).*

Stagg Jr bott code: B1707310457 **(96) n24 t24.5 f23.5 b24** I well remember the first Stagg Junior I encountered. Which though truly excellent, skimped a little too much on the sugars and struggled to find its balance and, thus, full potential. Certainly no such worries with this bottling: indeed, the honey is remarkable for its abundance. Staggering... *64.75% (129.5 proof)*

◇ **Stagg Jr Barrel Proof** bott code: L192940114.09D db **(97.5) n24** the dense nose is crammed with toasty sugar and tub-thumping tannins. Only the light maple syrup softness of the corn oils prevents a full-on assault of all the darker, weightier aspects...; **t25** oh...those corns oils again! This time fully coats the palate and acts as the adhesive on which the concentrated toasty-molasses stick. The small grains ping and pound around lustily and in full salivation mode. Meanwhile, the battle between sweeter molasses and torched tannins is a bitter one... literally...; **f24** cocoa, dark liquorice and so much toastiness...; **b24.5** it may be called Junior. But it is towering over Daddy these days.... Spectacularly mind-blowing! *64.2% (128.4 proof).* 🏆

Ten High Kentucky Bourbon bott code: L172211518053 **(72) n19 t19 f16 b18** Docile, unusually sweet early on but the finish never quite feels right, the flavours jarring badly. Bitter at the death. This is a bourbon...? *40% (80 proof).*

Treaty Oak Distilling Red Handed Bourbon Whiskey db **(90) n22 t23 f22.5 b22.5** As thick cut as a Texas steak....and no less juicy! *47.5% (95 proof).*

Van Winkle Special Reserve 12 Years Old Lot "B" bott code: L172550110:147 **(93.5) n23 t23 f24 b23.5** Those looking for comparisons between certain Weller products and Van Winkle's might find this particular bottling a little better weighted, less forthright and more complex. *45% (90 proof)*

Van Winkle Special Reserve 12 Years Old Lot "B" Batch Bourbon Whiskey bott code: L181300112 **(94.5) n23.5 t23.5 f23 b23.5** Roughly consistent in quality to the bottling above, but better here and takes a slightly different route - by putting its foot on the toastiness and steering by some very impressive waxy Manuka honey. For those who like their bourbon hairy, bristling with spice, honey and big oak interaction. *45.2% (90.4 proof).*

Very Old Barton bott code: L17/60111:104 **(87.5) n22 t22 f21.5 b22** Attractive, brittle and with a delicious slow burn of first delicate, then broader hickory tones. The small grains fizz and dazzle in typical VOB style. If anything, slightly undercooked at this strength, and missing the extra oils, too. *40% (80 proof)*

Very Old Barton 6 bott code: 907:104 **(93) n22 t24 f23.5 b23.5** The VOB 6, when the number stood for the years, has for the last quarter of a century been one of my bourbons of choice: an understated classic. This version has toned down on the nose very slightly and the palate underlines a far less definite oak-to-grain parry and counter-thrust. That said, still a bourbon which mesmerises you with its innate complexity and almost perfect weight and pace on the palate. One that has you instinctively pouring a second glass. *45% (90 proof)*

Very Old Barton 86 Proof bott code: B1635619:024 **(89) n21.5 t22.5 f22.5 b22.5** It is not the three percent extra alcohol which makes the difference here: simply the marriage of barrels. These ones have allowed the rye tones within the small grain to positively shine...; *43% (86 proof)*

Very Old Barton 90 Proof Kentucky Straight Bourbon bott code: L181370113 **(92) n22.5 t23.5 f23 b23** Gorgeous whiskey, though not perhaps the tour de force of previous bottlings. *45% (90 proof).*

Very Old Barton 100 Proof bott code: L17/640102:074 **(96) n23.5 t24.5 f23.5 b24.5** Here's a challenge for you: find fault with this whiskey... Brilliant bourbon of the intense yet sophisticated variety. *50% (100 proof)*

Very Old Barton Kentucky Straight Bourbon bott code: 3820123 **(87.5) n22 t22 f21.5 b22** A consistent bourbon (just noticed I have marked it identically to the last bottling!) giving a limited but delightful account of the VIB brand, ensuring the busy small grains keeps on scrambling around the palate and just enough liquorice and hickory meets the onrushing caramel and praline. Deceptively delicious. *40% (80 proof).*

Virginia Gentleman (90.5) n22 t23 f23 b23.5. A Gentleman in every sense: and a pretty sophisticated one at that. *40% (80 Proof)*

Weller Aged 12 Years bott code: B17081 20:56 **(91)** n22.5 t23 f22.5 b23 Firm, crunchy, sweet bourbon and very warming... 45% (90 proof)

Weller Aged 12 Years Kentucky Straight Bourbon Whiskey bott code: L190790117 **(91.5)** n22.5 t23.5 f22.5 b23 Spookily similar to the bottling above, the only noticeable difference being the degree of waxy honey on delivery. 45% (90 proof).

Weller Antique 107 bott code: B17044 17:374 **(95.5)** n23.5 t24.5 f23.5 b24 The higher strength has helped bring the best from the great whiskey as the oils are left unchecked and allowed to help the other elements cast their magic spells. To add water to this, especially, would be sacrilege. 53.5% (107 proof)

Weller Antique 107 Kentucky Straight Bourbon bott code: L190170117 **(88)** n22 t23 f21 b22 Enjoyable, but nothing like the Antique 107 I have become used to swooning over. Attractive, but some antiques are more desired than others. 53.5% (107 proof).

Weller C.Y.PB Wheated Kentucky Straight Bourbon bott code: L18163011042N **(95.5)** n24 t24 f23.5 b24 Has all the chutzpah of a wheated bourbon that knows it's damn good and goes out to shock. Enjoy the myriad little favour and spice explosions. And the deceptive depth.... 47.5% (95 proof).

⟡ **Weller Full Proof Kentucky Straight Bourbon** bott code: L192200103:21B db **(94)** n23 dense, toasty yet never dry or aggressive. The corn oils play a vital role in keeping things level with the wheat ensuring the aroma is constantly on the move with a controlled spiciness; t23.5 mouth-filling, again with the oils taking an early lead. But soon those spices bulldoze their way in and this time shew limited restraint. Salivating and eye-watering as the small grains batter the taste buds while a gorgeous mocha note forms at the midpoint as the tannins reveal they mean business...; f23.5 more mocha with a hickory side-dish; b24 a thick knife, fork and spoon bourbon that you can make a right meal from. Fabulous balance to the intensity here. And who doesn't love bourbon in their dark chocolate mousse... 57% (114 proof).

⟡ **Weller Single Barrel Kentucky Straight Bourbon** bott code: 30022133321 db **(91.5)** n23.5 the wheat isn't shy here and literally peppers you from the first warming sniff. Light hickory and molasses shew superb oak integration and complexity; t23 momentarily a sweet delivery – sweeter than most Wellers. But that shock of sugar soon passes and those tannins which set about the nose are soon playing a part here, as are the light corn oils which have a delightful softening effect; f22 spicy, dry and possessing some very late molasses; b23 a beautifully competent, undemonstrative wheated bourbon which never puts a foot out of place and enjoys a quiet complexity. 48.5% (97 proof). sc.

Weller Special Reserve bott code: L172080115:014 **(93)** n23 t23.5 f23 b23.5 Imperiously excellent, yet somehow given to understatement. 45% (90 proof)

Weller Special Reserve Kentucky Straight Bourbon bott code: L19018 0118 **(94)** n23 t23.5 f24 b24 Almost too soft and easy to drink. A thousand kisses in a glass.. 45% (90 proof).

Western Gold 6 Year Old Bourbon Whiskey (91.5) n22 t23 f22.5 b23 Taken from barrels sitting high in the warehouse, that's for sure. You get a lot for your six years... 40%.

The Whisky Shop Maker's Mark batch no. 002, oak staves with barrel finish **(94.5)** n23.5 t24 f23 b24 So rare to find Maker's Mark at this strength. The kind of whisky that give wheated bourbon lovers a little stiffy... 54.95%.

Widow Jane Straight Bourbon Whiskey Aged 10 Years barrel no. 1785, bott 2018 **(95)** n23.5 t23.5 f24 b24 This is one very passionate Widow... 45.5% (91 proof). sc.

Wilcox Bourbon Whiskey (73.5) n19 t19 f17.5 b18 When you buy a bourbon whiskey, you have in your mind a clean, complex Kentuckian. Not sure who made this, but far too feinty for its own good with none of the liquorice and honey notes you should rightfully expect. A very poor representation of bourbon, and not remotely in the true Kentucky style. 40% (80 proof). BBC Spirits.

Wild Turkey 81 Proof bott code: LL/DF291109 db **(91.5)** n23 t23 f22.5 b23 A much sweeter, more relaxed bottling than the old 40% version, gathering up honey notes like a wild turkey hoovering up summer berries. 40.5% (81 proof).

⟡ **Wild Turkey 81 Proof** bott code: LL/HA040353 db **(92)** n22.5 much more emphasis on the hickory here than any 81 proof Turkey I've before encountered. An old-fashioned suet pudding depth, perhaps with a slab of butter; t23.5 oh, wow...! That is huge hickory now, just as the nose promises, a little heather-honey ensuring the sugars are well represented; f22.5 long with a broad brush of corn oil. Spices infiltrate late and with limitation; b23 more oak interaction with this feller than any other 81 proof I've encountered. Lays on the hickory with a trowel: delicious! 40.5% (81 proof).

Wild Turkey 101 Proof bott code: LL/GE170523 db **(93)** n23 t23.5 f23 b23.5 Perhaps now the most corn-rich of all the major Kentucky bourbons. 50.5% (101 proof).

⟡ **Wild Turkey 101 Proof** bott code: LL/HH300747 db **(93)** n23.5 there's a real nip to this these days: a squadron of spices are scrambled from the first moment, red liquorice required to restore calm; **t23.5** it is the mouthfeel as much as the flavour which blows you away here: the corn oils are set on "extra lush" mode while gentle maple syrup mixes in with the hickory to form a beautifully salivating experience; **f23** now the spices tingle teasingly, a light liquorice note emphasising the oaky depth; **b23** the astonishing overall softness on the palate is counterintuitive to the slight aggression on the nose. I've been savouring this whisky for over 30 years. And still it has the ability to surprise. *50.5% (101 proof).*

Wild Turkey Kentucky Spirit Single Barrel barrel no. 0401, warehouse A, rick no. 6, bott 01/14/19, bott code: LL/HA152135 db **(89) n22.5 t23 f21.5 b22** A real enjoyable softie if, perhaps, a tad one dimensional. *50.5% (101 proof). sc.*

Wild Turkey Longbranch oak and Texas mesquite charcoal refined bott code: LL/GI180207 db **(91.5) n23 t23 f22.5 b23** Mesquite must be America's answer to peat: here there is a just a light touch, barely noticeable until the finish, and emphasised by the very late warmness to the finale itself. *43% (86 proof).*

⬧ **Wild Turkey Longbranch** bott code: LL/HD261325 db **(92.5) n23** slightly spiced chocolate cookie, which is how I think I remember the last bottling of this: consistent...; **t23** gorgeous Demerara sugars waft over the pillow of soft corn oils. Caramels and delicate spices entwine; **f23** this whiskey has been filtered over mesquite charcoal. Last time I tasted it, the unique influence was little more than a caress or a soft dab. Here, unlike last time and for the better, those spices grow and congregate....with a little maple syrup for company; **b23.5** "Mesquite must be America's answer to peat" I thought as I nosed and tasted this. "Have I written that before about this?" I mused. I had. And it is... *43% (86 proof).*

Wild Turkey Rare Breed Barrel Proof bott code: LL/GD020831 db **(95.5) n23.5 t24 f24 b24** A clever glass bottle, its roundness reinforcing the mouthfeel and character of the bourbon itself: one of the most rounded in all Kentucky. In some ways this whiskey is the blueprint for bourbon: its characteristics embrace what we mentally define as bourbon. *58.4% (116.8 proof).*

⬧ **Wild Turkey Rare Breed Barrel Proof** bott code: LL/HA140731 db **(94.5) n23.5** despite the strength, no bullying on the nose here: a little orange blossom honey and hickory intertwangle with no little panache; **t24** blood orange and hickory merge on impact, then a joyful exhibition of crème brulé and molasses; **f23** dryer than usual, a more powdery feel to the vanilla. The gentle spices and toasted sugars ensure the balance; **b24** hickory is all the rage with Wild Turkey this year: another bottling that is leading with that delightful trait. However, have noticed the honey level has receded slightly. *58.4% (116.8 proof).*

Wilderness Trail Single Barrel Kentucky Straight Bourbon BIB Sweet Mash barrel no 14E23 **(83.5) n20.5 t21.5 f21 b20.5** A hot, aggressive bourbon with more bite than spice. The corn element ticks the right boxes and does a great job, but this bourbon struggles to find its rhythm despite an attractive mocha finale. *50% (100 proof). ncf. 245 bottles. 64% corn, 24% wheat 12% malted barley. sc.*

William Larue Weller db **(96) n24 t24.5 f23.5 b24** the most relaxed and lightly spiced Weller since its first launch. May lack its inherent oomph, but the deft, complex notes are still one of life's great pleasures... *67.7% (135.4 proof).*

William Larue Weller db **(97.5) n24 t25 f24 b24** ...The most delicious lesson in whiskey structure imaginable. This was my 1,263rd and final new whiskey for the Jim Murray Whisky Bible 2019. Did I leave the very best until last....? *64.1% (128.2 proof).*

William Larue Weller db **(97.5) n25 t24.5 f23.5 b24.5** I have before me a glass of whiskey. It is pure amber in colour and has won more top honours, including World Whisky of the Year, in Jim Murray's Whisky Bible than any other brand. For that reason the sample before me is, as I nose and taste it on the evening of 26th August 2019, the 20,000th whisky I have specifically tasted for this book since it was first published in 2003. There really could be no other I could possibly bestow this personal honour upon. It is a landmark whiskey in every sense... Oh, once again, I have not been let down. I will have to wait to see if this is World Whisky of the Year once more: on the evidence before me it will be close. But I do know no whiskey will better its truly perfect nose... *62.85% (125.7 proof).*

⬧ **William Larue Weller** db **(97) n24.5** the spices meander their way through the moderately sweetened corn oils to glorious effect. Anyone who has walked bluebell woods in early spring and breathed in that earthy freshness will recognise the properties at work, the natural order of things: that impossible balance between sweet and dusky which seems beyond the creation of man; **t24** a delicate mintiness on the nose is partially matched on delivery, which is cool and sharp. The peppers are abroad early and salivating; the tannins are a pace behind and gathering weight; **f24** oh...just one of the finishes of the year. High class artisanal brown bread, husks 'n' all, beautifully damp and intense as the wheat thickens. The sugars grow more toasty by the minute, starting as Demerara but finishing as molasses with a light touch of Manuka honey, too. But the coup-de-gras is a late tannin and spice mix which elevates the sugars while the dense wheat is allowed to form the deeper base notes; **b24.5** has a subtly different approach to last year's William Larue Weller, which was enormous with all its knees and elbows protruding among the massive favour values. This is more reserved, yet no less powerful or complex. Tells a similar story, but in a much quieter voice, seemingly understated. Unless you pay attention... 64% (128 proof). 🍷

Winchester Bourbon Whiskey Aged a Minimum of 6 Months in New Oak bott code: L219A090024564 **(85.5) n21.5 t22 f21 b21** That is one very curious bourbon with an arrangement of tobacco and leather on the nose and thick corn oil and orange blossom honey on delivery. A little chunky and feinty towards the close, but the spices do a good job. Complex and decidedly idiosyncratic. 45% (90 proof

⬦ **Woodford Reserve Distiller's Select Batch 500 (87.5) n21.5 t22 f22 b22** A steady, laid-back bourbon, happy to wallow in its own understatement. The nose is light with a gentle sweet, hickory theme; the taste is no more taxing and relying on a thin-ish spicy sweetness amid the gentle tannins. Attractive and undemanding. 43.2%. (86.4 proof).

⬦ **Yellowstone Aged 9 Years Kentucky Straight Bourbon Whiskey 2019 Edition** bott code: 211 19 **(93.5) n23.5** the dry black peppers almost set you a-sneezin'...!!! There's some serious tannins abroad...; **t23.5** so the instant low voltage hit of molasses comes as a bit of a surprise. But soon the drier tones are catching up, the rich corn oils softening the blow and giving the midground more to chew on; **f23** the almost crunchy tannins more to a more burnt toast dryness; **b23.5** remarkable for its almost unremitting dryness. The delicate sweetness does just the job required. 50.5% (101 proof). Limestone Branch Distillery Co.

Yellowstone Select Kentucky Straight Bourbon Whiskey (90.5) n22.5 t22.5 f22.5 b23 A good, solid Kentucky bourbon, shewing more body and balance than the Yellowstone of yesteryear. 46.5% (93 proof).

⬦ **Yellowstone Select Kentucky Straight Bourbon Whiskey** bott code: 311 19 **(92.5) n23** classically bright and teaming with Demerara but balanced superbly by a sharper kumquat tannin note; **t23** stays on the house classic theme of liquorice and thin manuka honey, dried with dovetailing hickory; **f23** leaves a trail of tannins and light spices in its wake. Brilliant corn oils keeps the sugars lingering; **b23.5** a good, honest Kentucky bourbon which pulls no punches. Just a little more confident and assertive than the last bottling I found. 46.5% (93 proof). Bottled by Limestone Branch Distillery Co.

Tennessee Whiskey

Heaven's Door Tennessee Bourbon Whiskey 10 Year Old bott code: 10/25/18 **(85) n21.5 t22.5 f20 b21** I'm knock-knock-knocking this Heaven's Door: far too heavy, I'm afraid. But, wow! What a delivery...!!! 50% (100 proof).

Heaven's Door Tennessee Bourbon Whiskey Aged for a Minimum of 7 Years bott code: 2019/04/120555 **(94) n23 t24 f23.5 b23.5** Another bewildering whiskey type to contend with in the USA. Now it is Tennessee Bourbon. I presume that is a bourbon whiskey made in Tennessee but without deploying the charcoal mellowing process. Whatever, it is quite Heavenly.... 45% (90 proof).

⬦ **Joe Got a Gun** batch no. 1, bott code: 10/07/19 **(88.5) n23 t22 f21.5 b22** The nose has star billing here. Such a charming marriage between hickory and citrus. On the palate it proves a little more workaday, but still shewing much to enjoy. The sugars, though toasty are elegantly done. Perhaps a shade too much chalkiness on the finale, though. 40%. BBC Spirits.

⬦ **Joe Got a Gun Single Barrel #1** bott code: 10/07/19 **(94) n23.5** the hickory here has dropped the citrus evident on their other bottling and instead has lassoed chunkier, toastier sugars to take its place. Look out, also, for the sublime chocolate fudge candy; **t23.5** those sugars are on instant full blast: toasty, sharp with the hickory arriving as back-up rather than leading the way. As the tannins arrive, so does a countering light lime blossom honey sweetness; **f23** the slight extra strength helps allow extra oils carry the sugars the distance – a minor failing of the batch No 1, which is a little too underpowered. This retains excellent chewability; **b24** a far more masculine bottling than their batch no 1. The tannins are not shy and give a delicious account of themselves. A quite superb Tennessee. Joe's gun has hit the bullseye with this one... 45%. sc. 300 bottles. BBC Spirits.

⬦ **Obtainium Tennessee Rye Whiskey** db **(83) n21 t21.5 f20 b20.5** Far too dependent on the blood orange core. Sharp, fruity, ultimately bitter and, overall, just awry with the rye... 57.8% (115.6 proof).

⬦ **Uncle Nearest 1820 Premium Whiskey Aged 11 Years** barrel no. US.21, bott 11/5/19 **(95.5) n24** sticks immaculately to the hickory script. Allows itself to ab lib with some lighter red liquorice notes and even the odd eucalyptus quote. But this is wonderfully delivered – and almost hard to move on to the tasting bit, so hard is it to prize the proboscis from the glass...; **t24** you know when you have a massage and the oils applied are just the right stickiness and temperature spot on...? Well so this feels on delivery. Which is a great start when those corn oils serve up a nutty sweetness which melts into the hickory and mocha; ulmo honey provides the even and laid-back sweetness; **f23.5** and with oils come length of finish....and this is long! A little salty praline drifts into view and lingers...; **b24** I have waited all day to get through the previously scheduled whiskeys to taste this I was so looking forward to it! It was worth the wait as this has not just stayed true to form but improved magnificently on the last excellent bottle of this I encountered. Real, rich chewing whiskey! What a treat! *58.6% (1171 proof). sc. 126 bottles.*

Uncle Nearest 1820 Premium Whiskey Aged 11 Years Nearest Green Single Barrel barrel no. US-1 **(94.5) n23 t24 f23.5 b24** A real roller coaster of a ride. Let's get back on again... *576%*

Uncle Nearest 1820 Premium Whiskey Aged 11 Years Nearest Green Single Barrel barrel no. US-2 **(92.5) n23 t23 f23 b23.5** Have to applaud the delicate nature of this whiskey and its superior layering. Just too easy to enjoy. *55.1% (110.2 proof). 146 bottles.*

Uncle Nearest 1856 Premium Whiskey (89.5) n22 t22.5 f22.5 b22.5 No bells and whistles. Just a slow radiating of gentle sugar and tannin tones. Easy sipping. *50% (100 proof).*

◇ **Uncle Nearest 1856 Premium Whiskey** bott code: 192451651 **(91.5) n23** cheerful spices infiltrate the liquorice lead; **t23** beautifully mouth-filling and rounded from the get-go with immediate corn oil and molasses impact. Excellent, lip-smacking vanilla layering ensures considerably complexity; **f22.5** the spices continue their excellent work, now teaming up with a far chunkier degree of hickory; **b23** a lustier, busier incarnation than the last bottling of 1856 I encountered. Thoroughly enjoyable. *50% (100 proof).*

◇ **Uncle Nearest 1884 Small Batch Whiskey** bott code: 10/29/20191007 **(90.5) n22.5** pleasing, multi-layered and always light. The hickory and vanilla undulations boast a light orange blossom honey thread; **t22** the delivery is very light in body and immediately moves into spiced hickory mode. Again, excellent layering; **f23** now really hits the high points. The previous delicate nature of the whiskey now moves into a phase of intensity, the vanilla and hickory holding equal shares; **b23** perhaps noticeable for its significant lack of corn oils. Delicate and leans towards a hickory persona. A covertly complex and delightful Tennessee. *46.5% (93 proof).*

GEORGE DICKEL

George Dickel Aged 17 Years bott code: L6154K1001 db **(94) n24 t24 22.5 b23.5** The oldest George Dickel I have ever encountered has held its own well over the years. A defiant crispness to the piece makes for memorable drinking, though it is the accommodating and comfortable nose which wins the greatest plaudits... *43.5% (87 proof).*

George Dickel Barrel Select (90.5) n21 t23 f23.5 b23 The limited nose makes the heart sink. What happens once it hits the palate is another story entirely. Wonderful! *43%*

George Dickel Distillery Reserve Collection 17 Year Old (91.5) n23.5 t23.5 f21.5 b23 Outside of a warehouse, I'm not sure I've encountered a Tennessee whiskey of this antiquity before. I remember one I tasted some while back, possibly about a year older or two older than this, was black and like tasting eucalyptus concentrate. This is the opposite, showing extraordinary restraint for its age, an almost feminine charm. *43.5%*

George Dickel No. 12 bott code: L7034R60011402 db **(89) n21.5 t23.5 f22 b22** In a way, a classic GD where you feel there is much more still in the tank... *45% (90 proof).*

JACK DANIEL

Jack Daniel's 120th Anniversary of the White Rabbit Saloon (91) n22.5 t23.5 f22 b23 On its best-behaved form. After the delivery, the oils are down a little, so not the usual bombastic offering from JD. Nonetheless, this is pure class and the clever use of sugars simply make you drool... *43%. Brown-Forman.*

Jack Daniel's Gentleman Jack bott code: 141734518B db **(90.5) n22.5 t22.5 f22.5 b23** A Jack that can vary slightly in style. A couple of months back I included one in a tasting which was much fuller bodied and dripping in maple syrup. This one is infinitely more laid back. *40% (80 proof).*

Jack Daniel's Old No.7 Brand (Black Label) (92) n23 t23 f22.5 b23.5. Actually taken aback by this guy. The heavier oils have been stripped and the points here are for complexity...that should shock a few old Hell's Angels I know. *40%*

Jack Daniel's No. 27 Gold Double Barrelled extra matured in maple barrels **(82) n21 t21.5 f19 b20.5.** Pleasant enough. But it appears the peculiar tannins from the maple barrels have just done slightly too good a job of flattening out the higher, more complex notes from the grains themselves. Slightly bitters towards the finish also. Tennessee Gold with precious little sparkle at all... *40%*

Jack Daniel's Master Distiller Series No 1 db **(90.5) n24 t22 f22 b22.5** no mistaking the JD pedigree. Just a few telling extra degrees of fruit. *40%*

Jack Daniel's Single Barrel Select barrel no. 18-7604, rick no. R-18, bott 10 18 18 db **(94) n23 t23.5 f23.5 b24** Outwardly very similar to a standard Jack, only with a few extra waves of honey and a little less fat around the edges. More subtle but incontrovertible evidence that JD is a far better distillery than most connoisseurs give it credit for. *45% (90 proof). sc.*

Jack Daniel's Straight Rye Whiskey bott code: L184601033 db **(87.5) n**21.5 **t**23 **f**21.5 **b**21.5 For some reason the rye refuses to take pole position and is lost behind a series of pretty ordinary corn and oak-vanilla notes, though the cool mintiness is a classy touch. Pleasant and plodding without being in any way - well, except minty moments - exciting or stimulating...as a good rye should always be! *45% (90 proof).*

Corn Whiskey

◇◇◇ **Obtainium Kentucky Corn Whiskey** db **(92.5) n**23 very confident nose: presses the gentle heather honey into immediate action while spices purr away...; **t**23.5 what a stunning mix of corn oil and ulmo honey. Salivating, chewy but with enough about it to really gear up on the far weightier oak tones; **f**23 that corn oil just refuses to go away, staying intact for the duration. Lots of vanilla and butterscotch to keep the sweetness level. And still those spices pound...; **b**23 now that's pretty good corn whiskey! Beautifully made and matured. *63.1% (126.2 proof).*

Straight Rye

Basil Hayden's Rye Whiskey 2017 Release re-barreled in charred oak quarter casks, bott code: L7129CLA 153330822 **(88.5) n**23 **t**22 **f**21.5 **b**22 You can have too much of a good thing and it appears here the quarter casks have managed to overdose this rye with a surfeit of caramel. *40% (80 proof).*

Booker's Rye 13 Years, 1 Month, 12 Days batch no. 2016-LE db **(97.5) n**25 **t**24 **f**24 **b**24.5 This was a rye made in the last days of when Jim Beam's Yellow Label was at its very peak. Then, it was the best rye commercially available. Today, it is simply a staggering example of a magnificent rye showing exactly what genius in terms of whiskey actually means. If this is not World Whisky of the Year for 2017, it will be only fragments of molecules away... *68.1% (136.2 proof)*

Bulleit 95 Rye bott code: L6344R60010848 **(83) n**20.5 **t**22 **f**20 **b**20.5 In some 30 years of tasting rye from the great Lawrenceburg, Indiana, distillery, this has to be the weirdest batch I have yet encountered. The highly unusual and mildly disturbing tobacco note on the nose appears to be a theme throughout the tasting experience. A rye which rallies briefly on delivery but ultimately falls flat on its face. *45% (90 proof).*

◇◇◇ **Bulleit 95 Rye Frontier Whiskey** bott ode: L9145R60011708 **(86.5) n**21.5 **t**23 **f**20.5 **b**21.5 An upgrade on the last bottling, but still that mysterious tobacco note issuing from an Indiana distillery which was once the byword for pristine, super-pure nosing and tasting rye. When the grain does burst through it is sharp, salivating and full of its old Demerara sugar crispness. Lots of chocolate to be had, too, even if there is a strange buzz to the finish. And if you are into tobacco, this Bulleit's got your name on it. *45% (90 proof).*

Colonel E.H. Taylor Straight Rye Bottled in Bond bott code: L1728501 **(94.5) n**23.5 **t**24 **f**23.5 **b**23.5 Nothing like the big rye lift I found on the previous E. H. Taylor rye: this is happier to play the subtle game with a slow build rather than a naked graininess. A genuine surprise package. *50% (100 proof).*

Colonel E.H. Taylor Straight Rye Bottled in Bond bott code: L182130113:007 **(96) n**24 **t**24 **f**24 **b**24 hose were the very simplified notes of a long and beautiful story... *50% (100 proof).*

◇◇◇ **Elijah Craig Kentucky Straight Rye Whiskey** first to char oak barrels, bott code: A35292135 db **(94.5) n**23 a thickset aroma: the tannins have sprawled themselves all over the nose. But kumquat, crisp rye and a squadron of spices do manage to puncture through the oaky wall... with a bit of effort; **t**24 just one of those whiskeys where I quietly sighed to myself in delight as the richness of the delivery caught me slightly off guard. Sweet chestnut mixes with dates and ever-increasing degrees of rye. A light golden syrup thins the Manuka honey; **f**23.5 gentle, toasty spices and red liquorice. Some natural caramels from the oak spills over...; **b**24 superbly made. And as relaxed yet beautifully busy as ol' Earl Scruggs on his banjo. And just as note perfect... *47% (94 proof).*

◇◇◇ **Ezra Brooks Kentucky Straight Rye Whiskey** bott code: A129171852 **(91.5) n**23 lovely mix of mint and sherbet, with a vanilla-rye backdrop; **t**23.5 such a lush mouthfeel... and just hark at those spices digging in early and with a purpose. The sugars are decidedly of icing sugar, melt-in-the-mouth variety; **f**22 just a little bitterness (as you always get after that kind of sugar attack) despite the rye and oak buzz; **b**23 pretty classic rye of the old school. Go back 25 years, pick a rye up off the shelf...and here you go! *45% (90 proof).*

Frankfort Bourbon Society Knob Creek Single Barrel Select Rye Barrel No 7540 bott Fall 2018 **(88.5) n**22 **t**23 **f**21.5 **b**22 One of the spicier rye whiskeys you are likely to encounter. Pleasant, but the inert nature of the vanilla and the rapid loss of sugars make this a bit of an also ran in Knob Creek terms. *57.5% (115 proof).*

Highspire Whiskey 100% Rye Grain Aged 4 Months oak, finished with oak staves, batch no 3 **(73.5) n**18.5 **t**19 **f**18 **b**18 Youthful and a rather feinty. Both the rye and tannin are there in spades, but with little integration; some hefty flavours, especially on the oak side which somehow over-dominates the grain. An interesting young whiskey, but the oak seems forced and at no times forms an attractive allegiance with the rye. I think they need to go a little gentler on this one. 40% (80 proof). Distilled by Kindred Distilled Spirits Crestwood, Ky.

⬧ **High West Whiskey Rendezvous Rye** batch no. 19K12 **(93.5) n23.5** puckering grain nibbles on the nose; Demerara sugars slowly melting with the spices. The rye is wonderfully bold; **t23.5** initially a soft delivery with chewy oils. But hardens as the grains make their stand. Increasingly sharp and salivating as the sugars leave it to the rye to ensure the entertainment; **f23** light minty chocolate. And rye...! **b23.5** one of those ryes where you find yourself slapping the back of your head to overcome the eye-watering sharpness of the grain. 46% (92 proof). nc ncf. A blend of straight rye whiskies.

⬧ **J Mattingly House Money Small Batch Rye Whiskey Aged 4 Years (96)** n23.5 t24 f24.5 **b24** If you see the magic words "Distilled in Indiana" attached to any rye whiskey, then you know there is a high possibility that you are in for something world class. Only Lawrenceburg Indiana produces a rye that can give Buffalo Trace a run for its money...and here you can see exactly why. The grain itself takes first, second and third position on both nose and delivery before the softer and beautifully balancing chocolate mousse accepts a humble but vital position of second in command. The spices are far more restrained than most ryes, but still make a telling contribution as they represent their tannins in their splendidly refined and elegant pose. Added to this, there is a concentrated rye Demerara sugar crispness to the very end which melds with unbelievable finesse with the mocha. Fantastic rye of the very highest calibre: unquestionably the finest made anywhere in the world outside Kentucky. 57% (114 proof) distilled in Indiana.

James E. Pepper 1776 Straight Rye Whiskey (88.5) n22 t22.5 f21.5 b22.5 Not technically quite on the ball, but the intensity of the rye deserves a standing ovation. 50% (100 proof). ncf.

James E. Pepper 1776 Straight Rye Whiskey Barrel Proof (87.5) n22 t22 f21.5 b22 On the nose, delivery and finish there is evidence of a wider than normal cut here, giving the whisky a slightly murky feel. Great rye contribution and spices. But the oils are a bit OTT. 57.8% (115.6 proof). ncf.

Jim Beam Pre-Prohibition Style Rye db **(95) n23 t24.5 f23.5 b24** Very similar to how Jim Bean Yellow Label was over 20 years ago. In other words: simply superb! 45% (90 Proof)

Kentucky Owl Aged 10 Years Kentucky Straight Rye Whiskey bott Nov 18 **(90.5) n22.5 t23.5 f21.5 b23** Unlike their pretty poor bourbon offering, this rye is more Owl than Ow! 57% (114 proof).

Knob Creek Cask Strength warehouse A, barreled 2009, 2018 release, bott code: L8106CLA **(96.5) n24 t24 f24 b24.5** Knob Creek rye has always been excellent, but having tasted Jim Beam's rye output for some 40 years I always thought it delivered within itself. Now this one is much closer to what I had been expecting. Brilliant! And the first rye to give the great rye of Buffalo Trace a serious run for their money. Indeed; this is going for a head to head... 59.8% (119.6 proof).

Knob Creek Cask Strength Rye db **(95) n24 t24 f3.5 b23.5** Another unforgettable rye from Knob Creek, not least for the amount of hairs you'll find on your chest the next day. This is uncompromising in every sense of the word, but scores a little lower than last year's award winner as the tannin just seems a little tighter and less willing to give the grain full scope. The delivery, though...just type-it on...!!! 63.1% (126.2 proof).

Knob Creek Rye Single Barrel Select barrel no. 7809 **(95.5) n23.5 t24 f23.5 b24.5** A cleverly selected bottle by Kelly May, who appears to have eschewed the usual pile-driver Knob Creek style for a nuanced and satisfying rye where both the barrel and grain appear to have an equal say. Stunning stuff! Just hope you can get to their bar before this little classic runs out! Certainly one of my favourite ryes for 2019 and unquestionably one of the most enigmatic... 57.5% (115 proof). Selected by Kelly May of Bourbon on Main, Frankfort, Ky. sc.

Knob Creek Straight Rye Whiskey (92.5) n23.5 t23.5 f22.5 b23 a slightly more genteel rye than I expected, if you compare standard Knob Creek to their usual bourbon. 50% (100 proof).

Knob Creek Straight Rye Whiskey batch L5349CLA **(92.5) n23.5 t23.5 f22.5 b23** Curious: just checked: I scored a batch from last year at 92.5 also. Can't say this isn't consistent quality...! 50%

Michter's 10 Years Old Single Barrel Straight Rye barrel no. 16A113 **(88) n22.5 t23 f20.5 b22** Michter's and rye go together like all the great names of America and success: like David Beckham and football, Christopher Nolan and Hollywood directing, Hugh Laurie and Hollywood acting, my old Fleet Street colleague Piers Morgan and chat shows, my girlfriend's old chum Simon Cowell and talent shows. This, though, isn't quite in the same league as the bottle I tasted from them last year, which was in a Saville Row suit compared to the dowdy hand-me-down here. Enjoyable, but by Michter's high standards... 46.4% (92.8 proof).

⬧ **Michter's 10 Years Old Single Barrel Kentucky Straight Rye** barrel no. 19F965, bott code: A19156965 **(96) n24.5** soft, chocolate mint with well ripened banana and fig. The spices, light liquorice and molasses underline an aged feel to this. The rye is enigmatic, but there is a vaguely crisp form should you remember to look for it; **t24** the gentleness of the nose is transferred to the palate along with the chocolate mint. The tannins kick in with some rousing spices while vanilla begins to really make its mark at the midpoint. When you spot those crunchier, more salivating notes...well, then rye ahoy! **f23.5** mildly drier as the tannin embraces the liquorice note at the expense of the cocoa; **b24** interesting how the rye itself takes a back seat and intervenes only when the chocolate richness of the oak becomes slightly too dominant. Doesn't possess the obvious rye-rich traits of their barrel 19H1321, but the whole works far, far better. 46.4% (92.8 proof). sc. 🍷

❖ **Michter's 10 Years Old Single Barrel Kentucky Straight Rye** barrel no. 19H1321, bott code: A192341321 **(93.5) n24** when you get a layer of eucalyptus quite this well entrenched on the nose you know that the barrel has spent a fair bit of time giving its best to maturing whiskey. And when, despite all those obvious signs of age, the grain still has a vitality and firmness, then you know this has been very well distilled, too...; **t23.5** salivating and lightly spiced on impact, the oils are equally vital in the shape and feel of this rye. The toastier tones of the tannin work stunningly well with the more bullish aspects of the crisp grain; **f22.5** takes a relaxed, easy route thanks to the drier, lightly liquorice-coated tannins. Some good molasses and spice on the curiously tangy fade...; **b23.5** radiates great age. Wears its vintage well and with great pride. 46.4% (92.8 proof). sc.

Michter's Barrel Strength Kentucky Straight Rye barrel no. 19C467, bott code: A19071467 **(94.5) n23.5 t24 f23 b24** One or two moments here are pure textbook rye. Just savour that amazing sharpness and clarity on delivery! 56% (112 proof). sc.

Michter's Barrel Strength Kentucky Straight Rye barrel no. 19C386, bott code: A19066388 **(94) n24 t23.5 f23 b23.5** A full-bloodied rye that isn't for the squeamish. 55% (110 proof). sc.

Michter's Single Barrel Kentucky Straight Rye barrel no. L18F881, bott code: 8173881 **(88.5) n22 t22 f22 b22.5** A pretty low voltage rye. 42.4% (84.8 proof). sc.

❖ **Michter's Single Barrel Kentucky Straight Rye** barrel no. 20C549, bott code: A200950549 **(89.5) n22.5** quite a vanilla-rich flourish to this. The grain keeps itself surprisingly low key; **t22.5** sharp – almost eye-wateringly so. As on the nose, the rye doesn't come at you directly, but hides behind the skirts of the vanillin. The sugars expected are replaced by an almost puckering fruitiness to the rye – very unusual...indeed, intriguing. A little cocoa by the midpoint; **f22** dry and spicy, the rye has now almost vanished altogether; **b22.5** a highly distinctive rye that refuses to keep to the script. Follows no usual set pattern and insists on following its own singular route. 42.4% (84.8 proof). sc.

❖ **New Riff Backsetter Rye Bottled in Bond** db **(86) n21 t22.5 f21 b21.5** Well, that was an experience! The nose works you hard to find the rye. The flavours are flowing and full on. But, again, in a very idiosyncratic style. Pleasant enough, but not exactly what I look for in a classic rye style. Still, the acacia honey middle works well with the oaky vanillas. But not a patch on New Riff's straight rye. 50% (100 proof). ncf

❖ **New Riff Balboa Rye Whiskey Bottled in Bond** dist Jun 14, bott Nov 19 db **(94) n24 t23.5 f23 b23.5** A good old-fashioned 4-year-old rye very much in the Kentucky tradition. Quite beautifully distilled – as clean and technically excellent as any outside the Kentucky and Indiana big boys. One of those stunners that is all about crisp grain and molten Demerara. Lip-smacking and enough sweetness and chocolate to make up for the late oils on the finale. 50% (100 proof). ncf.

❖ **New Riff Kentucky Straight Rye Whiskey Bottled in Bond** dist Fall 2015, bott Fall 2019 db **(92.5) n22.5** a little oilier and enclosed than the Balboa, not this time shewing the crisper elements but far earthier ones; **t23.5** rye on steroids. The intensity of the salivating grain is there from the very first moment of the very first mouthful. Only a cluster of tannin notes make any kind of impact around it...well apart from the concentrated Demerara sugar, of course...; **f23** the rye still radiates, but is more subdued now. Far more toffee and chocolate to be getting on with; **b23.5** at times this seems a bit of a bruiser. But for all its chunky oils, the rye itself come through unmolested and clear. 50% (100 proof). ncf.

❖ **New Riff Single Barrel Kentucky Straight Rye Whiskey** barrel no. 15-6614, dist Fall 2015, bott Fall 2019 db **(91) n22** a little sluggish with the odd little chirrup from the grain; **t23.5** far more on the ball delivery than the lay nose might have you believing. As is the house style, the rye is sharp and unambiguous, the dark sugars dovetailing. Tannins take on a light hickory hue; **f22.5** dulls down as the spices and oils arrive; **b23** though the flavour profile keeps you entertained with its big rye presence, it never quite hits a rhythm. 56.15% (112.3 proof). ncf sc.

❖ **New Riff Single Barrel Kentucky Straight Rye Whiskey** barrel no. 16-7625, dist Spring 2016, bott Spring 2020 db **(93) n23** really well made rye, this. Love the touch of lavender decorating the grain; **t23.5** mouth-filling with molasses and heather honey prepping the way for the sharper rye personality. Soft and oily rather than crisp and fruity; **f23** such a great finish with the praline working so well with the grain; **b23.5** that's much more like it. Better made and better balanced. 55.9% (111.8 proof). ncf sc.

Old Forester Straight Rye 100 proof bott code A016 191607 **(93)** n23 t23.5 f23 b23.5 Beautifully made, beautifully devised...and a beautiful, slightly rugged, experience. *50% (100 proof). 65% rye, 20% malted barley 15% corn*

Old Pepper Straight Rye Whiskey Aged Over 2 Years barrel no. G18Q **(88.5)** n21.5 t23.5 f21 b22.5 Perhaps technically not quite perfect, but the flavour profile on delivery warrants a standing ovation. *55.35% (110.7 proof). sc.*

Peerless Straight Rye Aged 3 Years batch 150812105 **(84.5)** n22 t21 f20.5 b21 A new whiskey distilled in Louisville. Peerless might not be quite the way to describe it. A tad feinty, alas, *54.55% (109.1 proof).*

Pikesville Straight Rye Whiskey Aged at Least 6 Years (97.5) n24.5 t24.5 f24 b24.5 The most stunning of ryes and the best from Heaven Hill for some time. *55% (110 Proof)*

Rebel Yell Small Batch Rye Aged 24 Months bott code: A075181421 **(83.5)** n21.5 t21.5 f21.5 b19 Normally ryes coming out of Indiana score highly, as they should because with Buffalo Trace the output from there represents, on their day, the best rye in the world. However, this is a classic example of when a whiskey is undercooked; it is way too young in that the grain and tannin are barely on speaking terms. Negligible balance, though the light liquorice note early on in delivery and late spices do salvage something. *45% (90 proof).*

Redemption Riverboat Rye (78) n19 t21 f19 b19. Dry, weirdly off key and oily – and holed below the water line. *40%*

Redemption Rye (85.5) n22 t22.5 f20 b21. The tobacco nose is a bit of a poser: how did that get there? Or the spearmint, which helps as you try to chew things over in your mind. The big rye wave on delivery is supported by mixed dark sugars yet something ashy about the finish. *46%*

◇ **Redemption Rye Aged No Less Than 2 Years** batch no. 259, bott code: L9169607:27 **(86.5)** n22 t23 f20 b21.5 Bright, brittle rye but always with a feintiness lurking in the wings. The delivery, though, is rye at its most beautifully intense and pure. *46% (92 proof).*

◇ **Redwood Empire Emerald Giant Rye Whiskey Aged at least 3 Years** bott code: L19 1490 **(86)** n22 t21.5 f21 b21.5 While the grain may be stark, the tobacco note tends to knock this whiskey sygogglin, as the moonshiners of the south Appalachians might say. Never seems to be on an even keel, thought the odd sharp note is more than attractive. *45%.*

Russell's Reserve Kentucky Straight Rye 6 Years Old bott code: LL/GD240744 db **(94)** n23.5 t23.5 f23 b24 All incredibly charming and understated – a bit like Jimmy Russell himself... *45% (90 proof).*

Sagamore Spirit Straight Rye Whiskey batch no. 7C **(90.5)** n23.5 t23 f21.5 b22.5 Very attractive rye, but seems underpowered and slightly lacking in the oils required for the expected rich finish. *41.5% (83 proof).*

◇ **Sagamore Spirit Straight Rye Whiskey Barrel Select Aged 6 Years** barrel no. 2, floor 3, rack 2, new charred oak barrels **(94.5)** n23.5 the nose screams "Indiana" even before you check the label. A unique cut-grass crispness to the grain, Demerara sugars flickering around; a little orange-blossom honey leavens the intensity; t24 an eye-rolling eruption of sharp rye, as promised on the nose. Continuously salivating, this soon evolved into a thicker beast with superb mocha notes mingling with the sticky butterscotch tart; f23 the rye-flavoured Demerara sugars just keep on crunching on; b23 when top form Indiana rye is at work, what's not to like...? Oh, and one of those rare whiskies at its best when at ambient room temperature than slightly warmed. *55% (110 proof). sc. Bottled for Ryeday 13.*

Sagamore Spirit Straight Rye Whiskey Cask Strength batch no. 4A **(95)** n24 t24 f23.5 b23.5 Wow! What a way to start another Whisky Bible tasting day...!!! *56.1% (112.2 proof).*

Sagamore Spirit Straight Rye Whiskey Double Oak batch no. 2C **(91)** n24 t23 f21.5 b22.5 Beautiful in part but a little too intense with the oak late on. *48.3% (96.6 proof).*

◇ **Sagamore Spirit Straight Rye Whiskey Double Oak** batch no. 4A, new charred oak barrels **(95)** n23 the rye takes a more subdued stance. But the thicker tannins have rye leaking from every pore; t24 now, that is one very complex whisky. Not your Indiana CrunchFest. This is like rye wrapped in a blanket of tannin and soothed and massaged with chocolate and hickory; f24 the rye gets a clearer pathway towards the finale when the Demerara sugars come back out to play. Excellent spice, too...; b24 it may sound strange but there is a distinctive bourbon type feel to the rye, perhaps from the ratio of tannin to grain. A serious mouthful just laden with flavours. Superb. *48.3% (96.6 proof).*

Sazerac Rye bott code: L172540108: 414 ref 1A 5C VT 15C **(96)** n24 t24.5 f23.5 b24 The nose and delivery are just about as good as it gets. Anyone thinking of making a clean and succulent rye whiskey should plant this on a dais and bow to it every morning before heading into the stillroom... *45% (90 proof).*

Sazerac 18 Years Old bott Summer 2018 db **(96)** n24.5 t24.5 f23 b24 I have chosen this as my 1,250th whisky for the Whisky Bible 2020 (and 20,026th whiskey sample tasted for the book) because, many years ago, I (with my blending hat on) played a part in the development of this whisky – for which I was given the priceless very first bottle off the production line as a token of thanks. Sadly, it was stolen just a few days later in New York at a Whiskey Festival there. But I can still remember vividly as Elmer T Lee and I pieced this whiskey together how it might taste and feel in the mouth. And, you know, some 15 years or so on it really hasn't altered that much, other than in this case finish perhaps... But someone, somewhere - hopefully with a guilty conscience - might be able to be able to tell me differently... 45% (90 proof).

 Sazerac 18 Years Old bott Summer 2019 db (**96**) **n24.5** the sensuality of the age on this rye is akin to having a lover who has enjoyed many summers and knows exactly how to please. Just effortlessly finding those g spots on your nose and teasing you with a balmy mintiness, then caressing and kissing you with rye-stained sugars that are dark, slightly salty like sweat but, oh, so ridiculously sweet and tender...; **t24** possibly the softest delivery of any of the near 1,250 whiskeys I have tasted so far this year. Lands like a butterfly on the palate and immediately opens up to reveal a slight eucalyptus earthiness to counter the sharper, sweeter grains which abounds with a mix of Demerara sugars, molasses and red liquorice; **f23** not quite as long as some previous Sazerac 18s, but determined to extract every last delicate nuance from the grain to complement the gathering butterscotch; **b24.5** this is simply a whiskey with a greatness all its own. What can you say...? *45% (90 proof).*

 Thomas H. Handy Sazerac db (**97**) **n24.5** the spices nibble, bite, nip and comes close to drawing blood. The grains are jagged and crisp...shards of rye that cut deep. A light floral edge accompanies the vivid fruit. This is sharp and delectable. Rye with a three dimensional firmness; **t24.5** one of the deliveries of the year. As near as damn it getting a 25 for its intensity and elan. There's a real brazen bite to this: you feel you are both being attacked by the grain, the clothing to your taste buds being ripped aside, while simultaneously being kissed better by the oils... incredible...; **f24** rich chocolate, black cherry... and yet more and more insistent, relentless, rye...; **b24** I am often asked by those unable to track down either Sazerac, or, at best, just one: "what is the difference between these two whiskeys?" The answer, as demonstrated for the Whisky Bible 2021, is that one is an old hand that's been about a bit that effortlessly displays every trick in the book how to seduce you; the other comes at you like a vixen and has you groaning with pleasure before you know where you are. Do you want your love making gentle... or a little bit rough? This is the little bit rough...but there is no less pleasure... *62.85% (125.7 proof).*

Thomas H. Handy Sazerac Straight Rye (**97.5**) **n24 t24.5 f24.5 b24.5** This was World Whisky of the Year last year and anyone buying this on the strength of that will not be disappointed. Huge whiskey with not even the glimmer of a hint of an off note. Magnificent: an honour to taste and rye smiles all round... *66.2%. ncf.*

Thomas H. Handy Sazerac Straight Rye (**95.5**) **n24 t24 f23.5 b24** Perhaps because this has become something of a softie, without all those usual jagged and crisp rye notes, it doesn't quite hit the spot with quite the same delicious drama. Still a beauty, though. *64.6%*

Thomas H. Handy Sazerac db (**97**) **n24 t24.5 f24 b24.5** Just one of those must have whiskeys. Dramatic. And dreamy. All in one. *63.6% (127.2 proof).*

Thomas H. Handy Sazerac db (**97**) **n24 t24.5 f24 b24.5** Rye whiskey par excellence. How can one grain do so much to the taste buds? As bewildering as it is beautiful. *64.4% (128.8 proof).*

Treaty Oak Distilling Red Handed Rye Whiskey Aged 10 Years db (**91**) **n22 t23 f22.5 b23.5** A very odd rye, where the tannins appear half-hearted and happy to allow the grain a bigger say than normal. Different, but delicious. *50% (100 proof).*

Van Winkle Family Reserve Rye 13 Years Old batch Z2221 (**90**) **n22.5 t23.5 f22 b22** A hard-as-nails, uncompromising rye with a slightly tangy finish. A whiskey to break your teeth on... *47.8% (95.6 proof)*

Van Winkle Family Reserve Kentucky Straight Rye 13 Years Old No. 99A bott code: L180400107:23N db (**96**) **n24.5 t24 f23.5 b24** Quite simply, textbook rye whiskey... *47.8%*

 Wild Turkey Master's Keep Cornerstone Aged a Minimum of 9 Years batch no. 21587, bott code: LLJHE301949 db (**96**) **n23.5** some serious age present here: this looks like mid- to top-warehousing for the tannins to make this kind of impact. The spice prickle appears to confirm this, also. A much more classic crisp rye note than often found with WT, which with the spice makes for a firm and bristling nose...; **t24** just huge with the sugars coming from too distinct directions, but merging sublimely. One is from the tannins, offering a classic light liquorice, molassed sweetness; the other stems directly from the leading grain. The oils offer just the right degree of give to ensure good length and a cushion for when these two worlds collide...; **f24** stunning chocolate mousse. The rye appears to provide the brittle Demerara sugars designed to balance the rich cocoa to near perfection; **b24.5** easily the most profound rye whiskey I have ever seen carrying the Wild Turkey name. Easy for the chocolate off the oak to overwhelm the rye and the rye to also for an imbalance with the chocolate. Instead, they support each other magnificently. *54.5% (109 proof).*

Wild Turkey Rye bott code: 194712P22:59 db **(91.5)** n23 t23 f22.5 b23 A perfectly graceful, well-made rye. But at this strength a bit like Rolls Royce powered by a lawnmower engine. *40.5% (81 proof).*

◇ **Wild Turkey Rye 81 Proof** bott code: LL/GE250429:59 db **(92.5)** n23.5 probably the most minty WT rye I've encountered for a good while, a slight spearmint touch to this on top of the brisk, fruitier rye. Not unattractive at all...; **t23** salivating, even slightly sharp in its proferring of the essential rye tones which gives this bottling a decided grainy fizz. Still minty, though the classic crisp dark sugars associated with rye are there in force; **f22.5** the tannins have the best of it, drying to the point of losing the rye altogether. Busily spiced. **b23.5** a greatly improved rye than in recent years, here really displaying the grain to excellent effect. The finish has a slight tang, but, that apart, spends its tine moulding the mint to the sugars. One characterful whiskey... *40.5% (81 proof).*

Wild Turkey 101 Kentucky Straight Rye bott code: LL/GH130429 db **(95.5)** n23.5 full, rich and with the rye shewing sharp enough to cut the glass in two...; **t24** stunning delivery. This is a mouth-filler, at first you think lots of natural caramel and vanilla. But as the dust settles you realise the rye is at the very heart of the mêlée, ram-rod hard, mouth-puckeringly sharp and radiating a sumptuous fruitiness. Elsewhere the spices dazzle and the tannins rumble; **f23.5** long, thanks to the fabulous oils that keep both the spices and the grain on song; **b24.5** simply magnificent. The kind of whiskey, when you spot in the bar, it is almost impossible not to order. *50.5% (101 proof).*

Straight Wheat Whiskey

◇ **Bernheim Original 7 Years Aged Kentucky Straight Wheat Whiskey** bott code: A33582052 db **(94)** n23.5 the nutty spiciness sits comfortably with the gentle tannins and growing chicory. Slightly minty for good measure; **t23.5** the softness yields to slightly firmer Demerara note which kick up the salivation levels. Almost immediately spices move in to keep the juices flowing. A lovely mocha background makes for an even softer midpoint; **f23** fabulously earthy now and showing magnificent depth, despite the muscovado sugars trying to keep it afloat; **b24** a step up from the last Bernheim I tasted, the spices and sugars this time working in breathtaking tandem. The bass notes even deeper than the lower recesses of Larry Kass's voice, though that seems hardly possible...(hope you are enjoying your retirement, Larry!) What a treat this whiskey is! *45% (90 proof).*

American Microdistilleries
Alabama
JOHN EMERALD DISTILLING COMPANY Opelika, Alabama.

John's Alabama Single Malt Whiskey Aged Less Than 4 Years batch no. 102 db **(86)** n21.5 t22 f21 b21.5 This distillery has the propensity towards going for a wider cut during distillation, ramping up the oils and spices in the process. Makes for an uneven affair, though very much to type the caramels are lush and chewy. *43% (86 proof).*

John's Alabama Single Malt Aged Less Than 4 Years batch no. 103 db **(89)** n22.5 t22.5 f22 b22 A little extra thrust from the delicate smoke makes a huge difference. *43%.*

John's Alabama Single Malt Whiskey Aged Less Than 4 Years batch no. 104 db **(88)** n22 t23 f21 b22 Presumably the horse on the label of this whisky was presented to Troy... *43%*

Alaska
ALASKA DISTILLERY Wasilla, Alaska.

Alaska Proof Bourbon db **(86)** n22 t22.5 f20 b21.5. It must be Alaska and the lack of pollution or something. But how do these guys make their whiskey quite so clean....? For a rugged, wild land, it appears to concentrate on producing a bourbon which is borderline ethereal and all about sugary subtlety. The downside is that such lightness allows any weakness in the wood or distillation to be flagged up, though with nobody saluting. *40% (80 proof)*

Arizona
HAMILTON DISTILLERS Tuscon, Arizona.

Whiskey Del Bac Dorado Mesquite Smoked Single Malt batch MC16-1, bott 29 Feb 16 db **(94)** n23 t23.5 f24b23.5 Dang! I'd sure like to see a bottle of this come sliding up to me next time I'm-a-drinkin' in the Crystal Palace Saloon Bar in Tombstone, yesiree! And I'd take my own dirty glass – one smoked with mesquite!! *45% (90 proof). ncf.*

SANTAN SPIRITS Chandler, Arizona.

◇ **Sacred Stave American Single Malt Whiskey** finished in American red wine barrels db **(85.5)** n20.5 t22.5 f21 b21.5 A bit of a wide cut here which has a few problems gelling with a fruit influence so far as harmony is concerned. But plenty to enjoy of the creamy crescendo just after delivery when the malt's sharper, more vivid qualities take on a purer form. *45% (90 proof).*

⬦ **Sacred Stave American Single Malt Whiskey Cask Strength** F.O. Moorvedre barrels, finished in American red wine barrels db **(88) n22 t23 f21 b22** Impressed that even through the slapped on fruit the malt has its moments to intensify and shine: unusual, that. The house feinty style does ensure a degree of murkiness. But there is also a pleasing toffee-raisin mixing with the malt and spices for the attractive, mildly charismatic middle. 63.9% (127.8 proof).

⬦ **Butcher Jones American Straight Rye Whiskey Cask Strength** char #3 barrels db **(90.5) n22.5** one of the most intense, unyielding and truly unambiguous rye noses of the year. A little bit of feint is mixed in, but the sharpness of the grain is superb; **t23.5** hold on tight! The combination of the high strength and the concentrated intensity of the grain appears to drill holes into your taste buds. Again, as on the nose, there is the murky evidence of a wide cut. But it is like making love in the middle of a thunderstorm: forget the off-putting noise around you and concentrate on the highly pleasurable bits; **f22** more off-putting noise...; **b22.5** for those who like rye whiskey with hairs on... *64.7% (129.7 proof).*

Arkansas
ROCK TOWN DISTILLERY Little Rock, Arkansas.

Rock Town 8th Anniversary Arkansas Rye Whiskey 4 Years Old Bottled in Bond db **(92) n23.5 t23 f22.5 b23** A very pure rye for the rye purists... *50%. ncf. 475 bottles.*

⬦ **Rock Town Arkansas Barley Straight Bourbon Whiskey Aged 2.8 Years** batch no. 3 db **(93) n23** light liquorice amid the chocolate orange; **t23.5** eye-watering juiciness to the grains which are young and vibrant. As in the nose, the liquorice plays a major role adding both a flighty sweetness and depth; **f23** always a great sign when molasses leave it late to emerge; **b23.5** high grade, complex and deeply satisfying bourbon 46% *(92 proof).*

Rock Town Arkansas Bourbon Whiskey Aged 19 Months batch no. 62 db **(91.5) n23 t23 f22.5 b23** An undemonstrative exhibition of quality. *46%.*

Rock Town Arkansas Rye Whiskey Aged 23 Months batch no. 23 db **(94.5) n24 t23.5 f23 b24** Sharper than a Harvard graduate. And worth a whole lot more... *46%.*

Rock Town Arkansas Single Malt Aged 3 Years finished in Cognac casks db **(90) n22.5 t23 f22 b22.5** A pathetic 90 for their Single malt. What are you thinking of? I thought you had turned your back on excellent and gone for a grade or two higher. *46%.*

⬦ **Rock Town Arkansas Straight Golden Promise Bourbon Whiskey Aged 2.4 Years** batch no. 2 db **(92) n22.5** gentle strains of heather honey; **t23.5** that is huge jump for nose to delivery: on the nose, the honey almost apologetic. Here it intensifies, fortifies itself with rabid spices...and goes for the jugular; **f23** gloriously toasty. Honey has made way for very dry molasses and liquorice; **b23** having previous tasted this at half this age, I can confirm it has moved on very positively in the passing year... *46% (92 proof).*

⬦ **Rock Town Arkansas Straight Rye Whiskey Aged 2.5 Years** batch no. 26 db **(95) n24** classic! Clean, crisp, chiselling. The fruitiness here is set in stone. So intense...! **t23.5** the rye runs amok. Pulsating grain with light tannins and a spicy back up; **f23.5** sensuous brown sugars, a lick of red liquorice...and then still that concentrated rye....; **b24** for unerring consistency, this has to be the brightest star in the Rock Town firmament. Just as beautifully distilled and matured, seemingly extracting every last atom of beauty from each grain. *46% (92 proof).*

⬦ **Rock Town Bottled-in-Bond Arkansas Straight Bourbon Whiskey Aged 4 Years** batch no. 1 db **(91.5) n22.5** clean and softly honeyed enough to be distilled American breakfast cereal...; **t23.5** brilliant display of mixed brown sugars – embedded in heather honey, of course...; **f22.5** bitters out slightly as the oily residue wells up. But now it is the turn of the liquorice and cough sweet hickory to have a big say; **b23** after a run of three RT whiskeys with big feints – something I have never encountered before – it is great to be back tasting a bourbon from them of the type of quality I usually associate with them 50% *(100 proof).*

⬦ **Rock Town Chocolate Malt Straight Bourbon Whiskey Aged 2.4 Years** batch no. 2 db **(93) n23.5** some green corn oils work closely with the weightier and noticeable malt; **t23** silky soft oils, again the corn coming up fast, strong, sweet and in very juicy fashion. Then towards the midpoint the chocolate malt hits overdrive; **f23** chocolate lime; **b23.5** a typically big-favour Rock Town. *46% (92 proof).*

Rock Town Four Grain Sour Mash Bourbon Whiskey Aged 20 Months batch no. 7 db **(86.5) n22 t22 f21 b21.5** A much drier, slightly bitter version with as much oil from the distillation as the corn. *46%.*

⬦ **Rock Town Four Grain Sour Mash Straight Bourbon Whiskey Aged 2.5 Years** batch no. 14 db **(86.5) n21.5 t22.5 f20.5 b22** Another big, oily offering from their Four Grain stable. Lots of maple syrup and liquorice work hard to keep the bourbon on course, but the finale is on the bitter as well as oily side. *46% (92 proof).*

Rock Town Single Barrel Barley Bourbon Whiskey Aged 26 Months cask no. 7 db **(95.5)** n23.5 t24.5 f23.5 b24 They should call themselves Choc Town after this stunner...One of the non-Kentucky bourbons of the year. And the best thing I have yet encountered from this outstanding distillery...*56%. sc.*

Rock Town Single Barrel Bourbon Whiskey Aged 20 Months cask no. 661 db **(95.5)** n24 t23.5 f24 b24 Rock Town have upped their game a few notches, and in so doing have taken the micros into a whole new ball park... *59.39%. sc.*

Rock Town Single Barrel Bourbon Whiskey Aged 22 Months cask no. 494 db **(90)** n22.5 t23 f22 b22.5 An oily but entirely delicious bourbon. *578%. sc.*

Rock Town Single Barrel Bourbon Whiskey Aged 24 Months cask no. 614 db **(91.5)** n23 t23.5 f22 b23 Thank God! Just an ordinary excellent whiskey from Rock Town instead of outrageously brilliant! I was getting worn out... *56.83%. sc.*

◈ **Rock Town Single Barrel Bourbon Whiskey Aged 48 Months** 53 gallon cask, cask no. 434 db **(95)** n23.5 a little saltiness to the tannins. Dried orange peel, too; t24 one of the most complex deliveries from Rock Town this year: puckering tannins – and there's that salty disposition, too, seemingly lifting all the vanillas and sugars to far more lurid heights. The liquorice gives the follow through the full bourbon works...wow! Superb molasses at the midpoint; f23.5 settles for a dry-ish, sophisticated mocha and toast fade; b24 brilliant. *58.6% (1172 proof). sc.*

Rock Town Single Barrel Four Grain Sour Mash Bourbon Whiskey Aged 26 Months cask no. 41 db **(95.5)** n24 t24 f23.5 b24 A few months ago I was in Little Rock, but my insane schedule – plus some ill luck with the car I had hired – meant I had no time to visit the distillery. Next time I shall somehow engineer a day or two. Because what they are achieving at this distillery deserves all the publicity it can get. This is another classic and actually eclipses the brilliant Cask No 7.... *58.8%. sc.*

◈ **Rock Town Single Barrel Four Grain Sour Mash Bourbon Whiskey Aged 27 Months** 25 gallon cask, cask no. 66 db **(87.5)** n22 t22.5 f21 b22 Rock Town is one of the few distilleries that could come up with this kind of careless cut and still come away smelling of bourbon... just love the liquorice, slightly overdone toast and then a big dose of manuka honey. *56.7% (113.4 proof). sc.*

◈ **Rock Town Single Barrel French Oak Single Malt Whiskey Aged 39 Months** 250L cask, cask no. 65 db **(91)** n22.5 rolls its sleeves up and means business: oily, but without the feinty threat. Bread pudding and molten Demerara; t23 boldly gets into its stride. Harnesses the oils thicken up the spiced manuka honey even further; f22.5 drier, toasty and sensibly spiced; b23 c'est magnifique! *55.6% (111.2 proof). sc.*

Rock Town Single Barrel Peach Wood Smoked Bourbon Whiskey Aged 23 Months cask no. 2 db **(88)** n22.5 t22.5 f21 b22 Anyone who has driven the back roads from Rock Town to the Ozark mountains will have experienced the extraordinary undulating character of the highway, with one blind peak following another. Up, down, up, down...for miles. And so it is with this bourbon, the smokiness playing hide and seek with the sweeter elements. *56%. sc.*

◈ **Rock Town Single Barrel Rye Whiskey Aged 30 Months** 15 gallon cask, cask no. 160 db **(94.5)** n23.5 just fabulous: the grain is dual toned: hard on the outside with a soft rye middle... or is it the other way round? Certainly, a little mocha is in on the act; t23.5 toasted honeycomb coats the rock-hard shell of the fruity rye. Luxurious and juicy all at once; f23.5 long, with the oils gathering in typical RT style. Chocolate transforms to mocha; b24 if anyone goes into the business of making chocolate rye candy, they'll be on a winner... *61% (122 proof). sc.*

Rock Town Single Barrel Rye Whiskey Aged 32 Months cask no. 109 db **(96)** n23.5 t24 f24.5 b24 I'm not sure any micro distillery makes their cuts any cleaner than these guys. Just put them into the Premier class... *59.88%. sc.*

California
ALCHEMY DISTILLERY Arcata, California.

Boldt Cereal Killer Straight Rye Whiskey Aged 2 Years batch no. 8 **(94.5)** n23.5 t24 f23 b24 Don't know about cereal killer: more the Rye Ripper! *62% (124 proof). nc sc.*

Boldt Cereal Killer Straight Triticale Whiskey Aged 2 Years batch no. 10 **(94)** n23.5 t24 f23 b23.5 In the 20,000 whiskies I have tasted for the Whisky Bible since 2003 this may be the first time I have tasted mash made from Triticale. This is one big-arsed killer and I can see this being a massive whiskey favourite among Star Trek fans...and Tribbles. *62.5% (125 proof). nc sc.*

Boldt Cereal Killer Straight Wheat Whiskey Aged 2 Years batch no. 4 **(92)** n22.5 t23.5 f23 b23 Sticking very much to the wheat whiskey style, this is some spicy cuss.. *61.5% sc.*

CHARBAY DISTILLERY Napa Valley, California.

Charbay 1999 Pilsner Whiskey Release III Double Alambic Charentais Pot Distilled Whiskey aged 6 years in new American white oak barrels and 8 additional years in stainless steel tanks db **(84.5) n21 t22 f21.5 b20** Just a point: you can't age for 8 years in stainless steel tanks. The moment it leaves the barrel the aging process stops: the term makes no sense. Lots of sugars at play and a distinctive fruity and spicy edge, though harmonisation is at a premium. *66.2%.*

GRIFFO DISTILLERY Petaluma, California.

Belgian Hen Single Malt Whiskey db **(83.5) n21 t21.5 f20 b21** Well, that was different. Less single malt. More lightly spiced soft centred orange liqueur chocolate. *46% (92 proof).*

Stony Point Whiskey db **(85) n20 t22 f21.5 b21.5** Makes up for the tobacco feinty tones with a rush of muscovado sugars. Good texture and chewability and spice. *47% (94 proof).*

Stout Barreled Whiskey db **(84.5) n21 t22 f20 b21.5** Robust, sweet and full bodied. But I must say I have a problem with hops in whisky. Sorry. *45% (90 proof).*

LOST SPIRITS DISTILLERY Monterey County, California.

Abomination The Crying of the Puma Heavily Peated Malt (93) n23.5 t24 f22.5 b23 An utterly baffling experience. This is, for all intents and purposes a Scotch whisky: at least in personality. If this was distilled in the US, then they have cracked it. The thing I particularly couldn't work out was an unrecognisable fruit edge. And after tasting I dug out the bottle and read the small print (so small, the detail was left off the heading by my researchers) that Riesling seasoned oak staves had been used. From the bizarre label and even brand name to the battle on your palate this is a bewildering and nonsensical whisky – if it is whisky at all, as the term is never used. But wholly delicious if raw...and boasting an impact that blows the taste buds' doors down... *54%. nc ncf.*

SONOMA DISTILLING COMPANY Rohnert Park, California.

Sonoma Bourbon Whiskey nbc, db **(87.5) n21.5 t23 f21 b22** Big and flavoursome, they just need to get that cut reduced slightly so all the oils belong to the corn and are not from elsewhere. The small grains pulse out a lot of coffee-rich vitality and there are fabulous molasses in midstream. But the finish is slightly undone by the feints. *46% (92 proof). 70% corn (CA & Midwest), 25% wheat (CA & Canada) & 5% Malted Barley (Wyoming).*

Sonoma Cherrywood Rye Whiskey lot: CR01AC db **(91) n22.5 t23.5 f22 b23** When the rye pops through, it rips... *47.8% (95.6 proof). 80% rye (California & Canada), 10% wheat (California) & 10% cherrywood smoked malted barley.*

Sonoma Rye Whiskey nbc, db **(89.5) n22.5 t23 f21.5 b22.5** A rye that could do with a polish when distilling, but the sheer enormity of the rye wins through in the glass...and your heart. *46.5% (93 proof). 80% rye (California & Canada) & 20% malted rye (United Kingdom).*

ST GEORGE SPIRITS Alameda, California.

Baller Single Malt Whiskey Aged 3 Years batch no. BW-5 db **(87) n22.5 t22 f21 b21.5** The nose made me laugh out loud: only one distillery on the planet can produce something that outrageously apple strewn...Elsewhere, though, I'm not so sure. After the initial big malt delivery, it then zips of into European style malt, the type where hops are at play. Certainly there is an imbalance to the marauding light bitterness which undermines what should be, one feels, a fragile and juicy malt. *47% (94 proof).*

Breaking & Entering American Whiskey Aged no less than 2.5 Years batch no. 06302018 **(92) n23 t24 f22 b23** The crisp apple aroma wafted through long before I realised this was from St George. Not only breaking and entering, but St George has left his fingerprints everywhere... *47% (94 proof).*

St. George Single Malt Whiskey batch no. SM018 db **(88) n22.5 t22 f21.5 b22** Definitely shewing signs of a wider cut these days. Gets away with it, but a return to a cleaner style might be the way forward. Characterful, nonetheless. *43% (86 proof).*

STARK SPIRITS Pasadena, California.

◇ **Stark Spirits California Single Malt Whiskey** American oak barrels, batch no. 52-13, bott 10-1-19 db **(88) n21.5 t22 f22.5 b22** Well, certainly no shortage of character on this chap! Takes a little time to settle down, and the slight feinty nose explains exactly why. But the barley hits its straps about a third of the way in and the oils from the generous cut helps elongate the growing gristy sugars. The finish has a satisfying degree of banana and custard as well as malt. Certainly grows on you! *46% (92 proof).*

◇ **Stark Spirits Peated Single Malt Whiskey** American oak barrels, batch no. 4, bott 8-2-19 db **(92) n23.5** a technically sound aroma, seemingly clean off the still with only the beautifully sweet phenols offering their gentle depth. A true delight...; **t23** again the peat is to the fore, but it is as much noticeable for its sleight of hand as it is its smoky quality. Everything understated with toasted mallows sweetening further the smoky grist; the underlying sugars of a crystalised molassed style; **f22** there must have been a wide-ish cut after all, as the hefty oils gang up in force; **b23.5** well, they may have got the nose all wrong for batch 52-13. But here are no complaints here. A far better distillation, helped along further by some pretty decent peat. *46% (92 proof).*

Colorado
10TH MOUNTAIN WHISKEY & SPIRIT COMPANY Vail, Colorado.
10th Mountain Rocky Mountain Bourbon Whiskey Aged 6 Months db **(92)** n22 t23 f23.5 b23.5 The youth of the spirit is apparent on the nose where slightly more hostile tannins have not yet had a chance to say howdy to the corn. But once on the palate the entire story changes as the maple syrup and molasses – and, amazingly, even liquorice already – makes a far better attempt to find a happy medium with the grain. Beautifully made and a really sumptuous and spice-ridden offering. *46% (92 proof).*

AXE AND THE OAK Colorado Springs, Colorado.
Axe and the Oak Bourbon Whiskey batch no. 20 db **(86.5)** n20.5 t22.5 f21.5 b22 Although this is batch number 20, you still get the feeling this is a work in progress. The nose at times displays some most unbourbon-like traits with far more of the still and/or fermentation room than opened cask. But the whiskey recovers with admirable calm: on the palate the corn oils establish themselves and the rye present kicks in with a firm sweetness while the tannins crank up the light liquorice and spice. The soft chocolate mousse on the finish works well with the molasses. Promising. 46% (92 proof).

Axe and the Oak Cask Strength Bourbon Whiskey batch no. 1 db **(87.5)** n21 t23 f21.5 b22 Big, bustling, no-prisoners whiskey which reveals quite a wide cut. That adds extra weight for sure, but a tanginess interrupts the flow of the excellent liquorice and molasses tones which had made the delivery and immediate aftermath something genuinely to savour. Get the cut right on the run and this will be one hell of a bourbon. *64.4% (128.8 proof).*

BLACK BEAR DISTILLERY Green Mountain Falls, Colorado.
◈ **Black Bear Bourbon Irish Style Colorado Whiskey** finished in sherry casks db **(88)** n21.5 t22.5 f22 b22 Quite a bulky whiskey, with the additional fatness of the grape adding to the oils from the generous cut. Technically, doesn't pull up any trees. But it is impossible not to be drawn towards the delicious mix of blackcurrant pastel candy and mocha. Genuinely tasty whiskey and great fun. Oh, and lip-smackingly salivating to boot. *45% (90 proof).*

BRECKENRIDGE DISTILLERY Breckenridge, Colorado.
Breckenridge Bourbon Whiskey db **(84.5)** n21 t21.5 f21 b21 Definitely on the flat side, with a dusty, dry character. *43% (86 proof).*

Breckenridge Colorado Bourbon Whiskey Single Barrel barrel no. 12H 31-1db **(88.5)** n22 t22.5 f22 b22 This distillery has certainly created a style all its own. *46% (92 proof). sc.*

Breckenridge Colorado Whiskey Powder Hound batch no. 1 db **(91)** n22 t23.5 f22 b23.5 Despite a slight blemish at the death, this is probably the most complex and well balanced whiskey I have yet seen from this distillery. *45% (90 proof).*

Breckenridge Dark Arts batch no. 5 db **(87.5)** n20 t24 f21 b22.5 I appear to have missed out on batch 4 (apologies) but this appears to have started when batch 3 ended. Some of the sensations on delivery are borderline orgasmic, the golden syrup, praline and barley melding together with the spices with uncanny intuition and balance. But, once more, the very wide cut has a negative effect on both nose and finish. As for the delivery and aftershocks, though: world class! *46% (92 proof). Whiskey distilled from malt mash.*

Breckenridge High Proof Blend Aged a Minimum of at least Two Years db **(90)** n22.5 oily and happy to take the liquorice route; t23.5 powering flavours for the first moment. The explosion of heather honey and molasses on delivery is exceptionally beautiful. Goes through the hickory, spice and caramel gears with ease; f21.5 just a little on the bitter and oily side; b22.5 maybe not technically perfect, but some of those honey tones are pure 24 carat... *52.5% (105 proof). A blend of straight bourbon whiskeys.*

DEERHAMMER DISTILLING COMPANY Buena Vista, Colorado.
Deerhammer American Single Malt Whiskey virgin oak barrel #2 char, batch no. 32 db **(87.5)** n21.5 t23.5 f20.5 b22 This, like most Colorado whiskeys, is huge. Had the cut been a little less generous, the oils a little less gripping and tangy, this would have scored exceptionally highly. For there is no doubting the deliciousness of the big toasted malt, the kumquat citrus element, the moreishness of the heavyweight dark fudge and the magnificent Java coffee. All these make a delivery and follow through to remember. I look forward to the

next bottling where hopefully the cut is a little more careful: a very significant score awaits as this is borderline brilliant... 46% (92 proof). 870 bottles.

DISTILLERY 291 Colorado Springs, Colorado.

291 Bad Guy Colorado Bourbon Whiskey Aged 291 Days distilled from a bourbon mash, American oak barrel, aspen stave finished, batch no. 4 db (95) n24.5 t24 f23 b23.5 This distillery was always very good. Now it is hitting genius status on a regular basis. 60.6% (121.1 proof).

⬥ **291 Bad Guy Colorado Bourbon Whiskey Aged 324 Days Aspen Stave Finished** American oak barrel, batch no. 5 db (94) n23.5 deeply pleasing signature here, with a jaunty peppery note attached to the salty toasted honeycomb; t23.5 a gripping blend of molasses and heather honey coats the palate as deeper, more black liquorice and spice form the tongue-lashing backbone; f23 oilier than usual, but those deeply toasted dark sugars do an impressive job of hanging on in there; b24 less fruity on character than some previous bottlings, tasting this after their 50%abv Small Batch, below, this Bad Guy is the very much the good guy. And at 123.4 proof, they can still show that making good bourbon is as easy as ABC... 61.6% (123.4 proof). 1,257 bottles.

291 Barrel Proof Colorado Whiskey Aged Less Than 2 Years distilled from a rye malt mash, American oak barrel, aspen stave finished, batch no. 378 db (87.5) n21.5 t23.5 f21 b21.5 Never quite the star turn of the Distillery 291 range, though I feel it should be. Always big on the rye but intensity is never matched with clarity with the finish offering touch a bit too much oil. But that delivery...? Wow! 64.6% (129.3 proof). sc. 47 bottles.

291 Barrel Proof Colorado Whiskey Aged 2 Years distilled from a bourbon mash, American oak barrel, aspen stave finished, barrel no. 398 db (96) n24 t24.5 f23.5 b24 I have just had to abandon tasting a batch of Scotch single malts for the Bible as 40% of them had been sulphur tarnished and my tortured taste buds were on the point of catastrophic failure. So I found this cask specially to bring back some life into my palate - as well as a will to live - where before there had been nearly none. And if you want to add restorative to the adjectives for this whiskey, go right ahead. You wouldn't be wrong! 65.3% (130.6 proof). sc. 57 bottles.

291 Barrel Proof Colorado Whiskey Aged 2 Years distilled from a bourbon mash, American oak barrel, aspen stave finished, barrel no. 383 db (93.5) n23 t23.5 f23.5 b23.5 No doubt in my mind that Distillery 291 are getting their bourbons pretty much on the money and they are consistently better than both their malt and rye. Surely this will be their main thrust forward... 64.8% (129.6 proof). sc. 42 bottles.

291 E Colorado Whiskey Single Malt Whiskey Aged 479 Days American oak barrel, aspen stave finished, batch no. 4 db (88.5) n22 t23 f21.5 b22 Well, it may have been matured in an American oak barrel but this is dripping with fruit... 61.1% (122.2 proof). 281 bottles.

291 E Colorado Whiskey Single Malt Whiskey Aged 479 Days American oak barrel, aspen stave finished, batch no. 5 db (92) n23 t23.5 f22.5 b23 How it all began, with their single malt. This is much cleaner distilled than in those early day and less oak in play. What a beauty! 62% (124.1 proof). 362 bottles.

⬥ **291 E Colorado Whiskey Aged 578 Days Aspen Stave Finished** American oak barrel, finished in cherry and Peach Nine barrels, batch no. 6 db (93) n23 t23.5 f23 b23.5 A rampant, super-complex whiskey which started life as a bourbon before it lost that status among foreign timbers. The nose is as parched, peppery and prickly as you are likely to find while the delivery compensates with an avalanche of Demerara sugars and heather honey. But it is those spices which take star billing. Though there is nothing wrong with the chocolate toffee finish, either. The finale, however, is as dry as it gets.... 61.3% (122.6 proof). 303 bottles.

⬥ **291 HR Colorado Bourbon Whiskey Aged at Least 1 Year** American oak barrel, batch no. 23 db (92.5) n23 seemingly soft, with all its fancy intertwangling honey and vanilla tones. But those of us who have been around bourbon a long, long time know when to beware...and there is something of the devil lurking here... t23 the first moments make you doubt yourself as the sugars are natural though refined - if you know what I mean? – while the rye detaches itself from the corn oil. Then whooomph! Up it goes, a powering beast of a spice kick that sears your tonsils...; f23.5 one of those rare whiskeys that leaves the best to last. Goes into overdrive with a massive Sumatra coffee presence, though this is almost more Kama Sutra. So much tannic liquorice burning off, too...; b23 for a bourbon, the rye has a lot to say for itself. A muscular, no-prisoners taken whiskey that is not for the squeamish.... 60.9% (121.9 proof). 458 bottles.

⬥ **291 Small Batch Colorado Bourbon Whiskey Aspen Stave Finished** batch no. 1 db (83.5) n21.5 t21 f20.5 b20.5 Heavy handed and feinty, this is not a patch on their normal high-quality whiskey. There is a brief flirtation with honey early on, but nothing to (bees) wax lyrical about. 50% (100 proof). 1,226 bottles.

⬥ **291 Small Batch Colorado Rye Whiskey Aspen Stave Finished** batch no. 1 db (86) n21 t23 f20.5 b21.5 Astonishingly sweet rye that celebrates concentrated molasses as much as it does the grain. A slightly over-generous cut robs this rye of any chance of greatness, and makes for some hard work on both the nose and finish. But as for that salivating delivery: no complaints there. *50.8% (101.7 proof). 1,185 bottles.*

DOWNSLOPE DISTILLING Centennial, Colorado.

◇ **Downslope Double Diamond Rye/Malt Whiskey Aged 3 Years** bourbon cask finish, cask no. 326 db **(89)** n22 t22.5 f22 b22.5 A blend of 60% rye and 40% malted barley certainly shows the rye, which is tight and fruity. Don't know if it is the word association with Double Diamond, an old British bottled beer of my youth, but I also pick up a vaguely hop-type note to this, too. But it's the rye which runs the show here big time. *45% (90 proof). sc.*

◇ **Downslope Double Diamond Straight Rye Whiskey Aged 3 Years** cask no. WR-235 db **(87.5)** n22 t23 f20.5 b22 Downslope certainly know how to make their rye talk. This is at its fruitiest and most eye-watering. A light vanilla sub-plot is hard to engage with when the grain is being so attention seeking and bolshy. There is still that mysterious house bitterness that is vaguely hoppy in style and slightly unravels some of the earlier good. If they could dispense with that, they would be operating at a different level. *45% (90 proof). sc.*

LAWS WHISKEY HOUSE Denver, Colorado.

◇ **Laws Whiskey House Centennial Straight Wheat Whiskey Bonded** batch no. 1 db **(87.5)** n21.5 t22.5 f21.5 b22 A charming grain that strives for finesse over power. And achieves in it in the most part as the playful sugars join the usual wheat-induced spice to tease and tingle. The trouble with finesse is that any cracks show in double measure, and here cloying oiliness of the feints can be seen clearly. But there is no faulting the delivery where the grain is seen at its very brightest. *50% (100 proof).*

A.D. Law Four Grain Straight Bourbon Whiskey Aged Over 3 Years batch no. 18 db **(82)** n21 t21 f20 b20 The cuts are all wrong here leaving the feints far too much say. *47.5% (90 proof).*

◇ **Laws Whiskey House Four Grain Straight Bourbon Whiskey Aged 3 Years** batch no. 20 db **(88.5)** n22 t23 f21.5 b22 Plucked from the warehouse at not quite the time when it wanted to be. From the nose through to the finale, you get the feel of a bourbon only half cooked. That said, still makes for a very tasty meal with more natural caramel than your average toffee factory. This ensures, along with the sterling corn oil, a soft countenance; the spices and busy grains guarantee a warming one, too... No feints, beautifully made, excellent oak involvement...just needed a bit of extra time... *47.5% (95 proof).*

A.D. Law Four Grain Straight Bourbon Whiskey Aged 6 Years Bottled in Bond batch no. A-19 db **(93.5)** n23.5 t23.5 f23 b23.5 High class bourbon. Love it! *50% (100 proof).*

A.D. Law Four Grain Straight Bourbon Whiskey Aged 6 Years 1 Month Cask Strength barrel no. 342 db **(94.5)** n23.5 t24 f23.5 b23.5 This is one of those brands where you are never quite sure what you are going to get from the bottle quality-wise. Well, three cherries on this one... b23.5 *56.4% (112.8 proof). sc.*

◇ **Laws Whiskey House Four Grain Straight Bourbon Whiskey Barrel Select Aged 8 Years** barrel no. 66 db **(95.5)** n24 talk about busy....the grains are chattering away crisply and sharply. Theirs is a hubbub of complexity; t24.5 what a delivery...just what a delivery! One of the best of the year for certain, not least because of the charm of the early mix of ulmo and heather honeys. This lays the friendliest of platforms on which those ridiculously complex grains can perform. Tart grain notes dart around the palate, hitting random targets at will. Light caramels drift into a heftier molasses and liquorice mix. The mouthfeel is one of light oils and drier oaks...and always lip-smacking and chewy; f23 long with an unusual praline on slightly burnt toast; b24 this distillery's four grain bourbon is a Laws unto itself...especially when it reaches 8 years, as I believe this has. Monumentally magnificent. *55% (110 proof). sc.* 🍷

◇ **Laws Whiskey House Four Grain Straight Bourbon Whiskey Bonded Aged 6 Years** batch no. 2 db **(87)** n21.5 t23 f21 b21.5 The feints may be a little top heavy on both the nose and finish. But the delivery is outrageously boisterous cramming almost indecent amounts of molasses into the few spaces left by the thick liquorice. Deliciously flawed. *50% (100 proof).*

◇ **Laws Whiskey House Henry Road Straight Malt Whiskey Bonded 4 Years Old** batch no. 1 db **(93)** n23 on a warm Spring day, the cherry blossom trees in my English garden offer a sweet aroma not unlike this. A little diced apple, too, mingles with the warmer, earthier tannins; t23.5 poundingly rich and spicy from the get go, the molasses on the nose spread themselves around the palate like you might lounge about your sofa; f23 huge waves of caramels leeched from the oak thicken as the malt begins to concentrate; b23.5 if this is Batch One, I can't wait for the next ones. Congratulations to all at Laws for producing such an outstanding malt whiskey first time out. *50% (100 proof).*

◇ **Laws Whiskey House San Luis Valley Straight Rye Whiskey Cask Aged 3 Years** barrel no. 152 db **(81.5)** n20 t22.5 f19 b20 For a while this recovers impressively from an indifferent nose that is technically way off beam. Rye often yields a fruity persona and here we have, quite uniquely, blood orange and kumquat in equal measure. Sadly the finale apes the nose's ungainly feints. *56.8% (113.6 proof). sc.*

⟫ **Laws Whiskey House San Luis Valley Straight Rye Aged 6 Years Bonded** batch 1 db **(86) n21 t23 f20 b22** An historic whiskey by all accounts: the first-ever to be Bottled in Bond in Colorado's rich history. Sadly, the back label also mentions tobacco notes, and that usually spells a problem. Not because I don't smoke – and never have - but a tobacco aroma and taste is, 99 times out of 100, associated with feints. And there is no escaping that the cut on this was as wide as the Colorado River. But, that said, it also relishes its kumquat and ginger main show and simply revels in the massive molasses they melt into. And despite the obvious weakness on nose and finish, there is also no getting away from the mind-boggling intensity of the grain itself. *50% (100 proof).*

A.D. Law Straight Rye Whiskey Aged Over 3 Years batch no. 1 db **(77.5) n18.5 t21 f19 b19** I think the distillery went through a little period when they really weren't getting all their feints out of their middle cut. A shame. *50% (100 proof).*

A.D. Law Straight Rye Whiskey Aged 6 Years Bottled in Bond batch no. A-19 db **(87) n22 t22.5 f21 b21.5** There are times you can tell from the sheer élan of the early Demerara reminds you that this distillery is capable of making stupendous rye. But there is a slight dulling buzz note to this especially towards the finish that shews that the cut was just a shade too generous for greatness. Much to enjoy, though. *50% (100 proof).*

A.D. Law Straight Rye Whiskey Aged 6 Years 5 Months Cask Strength barrel no. 46 db **(92.5) n23 t23.5 f22.5 b23.5** When this distillery get their cuts right, they make a formidable rye whiskey. *58.4% (116.8 proof).*

LEOPOLD BROS Denver, Colorado.

Leopold Bros Maryland-Style Rye Whiskey barrel no. 174 db **(77.5) n20.5 t19 f19 b19** Because of the vast over generosity of the cut, their bourbon shows more rye character than this actual rye does. Very much in the German mould of whisky making with those feints offering a distinct nougat style. Badly needs a far more disciplined approach to their cut points. Their bourbon shews they have much more to offer than this. *43%. sc. American Small Batch Whiskey Series.*

Leopold Bros Straight Bourbon Cask Select barrel no. 135, bott 11 Mar 19 db **(87.5) n22 t22.5 f21 b22** Really interesting here how the rye plays such a significant role in the flavour personality of this bourbon. The given mash bill reveals 17% malted barley to 15% rye, yet it is that latter grain that can be found in all the highlights. Especially on the nose and eye-watering delivery. Good spice, but just need to get the feints down a little to make the most of the growing honey tones. Seriously promising. *50%. sc.*

SPIRIT HOUND DISTILLERS Lyons, Colorado.

Spirit Hound Distillers Bottled in Bond Straight Malt Whiskey 4 Years Old barrel no. 13 db **(85.5) n21 t22 f21 b21.5** The chocolatey nutty nougat reveals that this is an early example of the distillery's work, before the distiller had worked out the better cut points (as exhibited in the later barrel 93 below). Despite some faults, including perhaps not quite enough copper at play, there are enough ulmo honey spots to make for some attractive moments. *50%. sc.*

Spirit Hound Distillers Cask Strength Straight Malt Whiskey 2 Years Old barrel no. 93 db **(93) n23 t23.5 f23 b23.5** The balance on the delivery is pretty close to perfect. A fantastic exhibition of controlled sugars. A three course meal of a malt. *63% (126 proof). sc. 72 bottles.*

Spirit Hound Distillers Straight Malt Whiskey 2 Years Old barrel no. 66 db **(88.5) n21.5 t22.5 f22 b22.5** Not sure this distillery benefits from lower strengths, which allows the drier notes to dominate. But there is a big malt theme if you can tune into it. *45% (90 proof). sc.*

VAPOR DISTILLERY Boulder, Colorado.

Boulder Spirits American Single Malt Whiskey Peated Aged for 2 Years 53 gallon white oak barrels db **(91.5) n23 t23 f22.5 b23** An impressive malt which eschews the chance to go OTT with the peat. Good call, as the subtlety of this malt is its making...that and the very high quality distillate. *46% (92 proof).*

Boulder Spirits Straight Bourbon Whiskey Aged for 2 Years 53 gallon white oak barrels db **(88.5) n22 t23 f21.5 b22** Pretty well made and matured. Doubtless the perfect whiskey to get stoned on. *42% (84 proof).*

WOOD'S HIGH MOUNTAIN DISTILLERY Salida, Colorado.

⟫ **Wood's Alpine Rye Whiskey Aged 2 Years** batch no. 16 db **(87) n21 t22 f22 b22** These guys really go for their rye full throttle. The grains thump into the taste buds with purpose and vigour – and make a point of hanging around on the chewy oils. But the nose is a little murkier than the last bottling I sampled, the wider cut making its mark. *49% (98 proof).*

◇◇ **Wood's Sawatch American Malt Whiskey Aged 4 Years** batch no. 2 db **(87)** n22 t22 f21 b22 Just as you get the rye in their rye, so the barley (well, they say "Malt" but it has a barley-esque quality) leaves nothing to the imagination here, a juicy grassiness dominating. Again, a wide cut makes for a hefty experience, some mocha arriving late on. *49% (98 proof).*

◇◇ **Wood's Tenderfoot American Malt Whiskey Aged 18 Months** batch no. 66 db **(88)** n21.5 t22 f22.5 b22 A cleaner distillate than the 4-year-old means the grain here piles in at its most juicy and grassy. More melt-in-the mouth sugars, too, and though the house cocoa turns up towards the end as expected, there is far more layering from the grain now. *45% (90 proof).*

Florida
FISH HAWK SPIRITS Gainesville, Florida.

Sui Generis Conquistador 1513 batch no. 6 db **(68)** n21 t20 f12 b15 I had learned the hard way, from tasting their other two whiskies first, to wait until the finish kicked in before even beginning to form a view. And, again, the awful finish makes what goes on before almost irrelevant. *40% (80 proof).*

Sui Generis Silver Queen batch no. 2 db **(70)** n17 t18 f17 b18 There are no words. Perhaps other than "fish".... *40% (80 proof).*

Sui Generis Siren Song batch no. 6 db **(78)** n21 t22 f17 b18 Where the Silver Queen was dethroned (and hopefully guillotined), at least this Siren Song has some allure. The big salty nose and big sweet delivery make some kind of sense. But this song goes horribly out of tune as the fade beckons. *40% (80 proof).*

FLORIDA FARM DISTILLERS Umatilla, Florida.

◇◇ **Palm Ridge Golden Handmade Micro Batch Wheated Florida Whiskey** nbc db **(92)** n22.5 full of the vitality of Florida youth, the grain has a jauntiness to its step while the sugars err on the side of golden syrup; t23..... on the subject of golden syrup, that is a close proximity to the mouthfeel of this little beauty. A slightly wide cut is detected, but the marriage of intense wheat and layered muscovado sugars make for an impressive match; f23.5 just love the patient finish, the continuous waves of vanilla of varying hue, the spice-pricked chalkier tannins and, for the most part, those deft balancing sugars; b23 a massive personality and an exhibition of controlled sugars. *45% (90 proof). ncf.*

◇◇ **Palm Ridge Rye Handmade Micro Batch Florida Rye Whiskey** nbc db **(88)** n21 t23.5 f21.5 b22 A bit of a heavy-handed, clumsy fumble of a rye. Where they got away with a slightly wide cut on their wheat, they were unable to pull off the trick quite so well here with this unforgiving grain. Certainly a delivery to remember with the rye in almost insanely intense form, and is worth finding a bottle of this to experience rye on steroids. However, the finish drops away alarmingly as the over-egged cut moves in with its heavier oils. A genuine Jekyll and Hyde rye. *50% (100 proof). ncf.*

MANIFEST DISTILLING Jacksonville, Florida.

◇◇ **Manifest 100% Rye** Batch 1 db **(86.5)** n20.5 t21.5 f23 b21.5 A very untidy rye, not least with a bitter-ish tobacco note on the nose and very little structure to the delivery. However, at around the midpoint it throws off its shackles and displays both the grain and a gorgeous chocolate milkshake note off to superb effect, the sparkling Demerara on the finale rounding things off superbly. Worth investigating just for that dreamy finish. *50% (100 proof).*

◇◇ **Manifest Straight Rye** Batch 12 db **(83)** n20 t20 f22 b21 Similar style to their 100% Rye Batch 1 (above) except the tobacco note might appeal more to a heavy smoker. *50% (100 proof).*

Georgia
ASW DISTILLERY Atlanta, Georgia.

◇◇ **Burns Night Single Malt** db **(95.5)** n24 what a clever nose! The barley has a gristy quality, fresh and sweet. But it is never allowed to get too flighty as the most delicate of smoky tones acts as ballast; t24 a stunning delivery, not least because the heather honey has almost an arrogant sneer, so beautiful does it know it is... Wonderfully waxy, and still with that modest but perfect smokiness to add exactly the right amount of weight; f23.5 long, again with those smoky notes intertwining with a surprising degree of residual honey. A lovely butterscotch fade is as soft as a silk and eiderdown pillow, though still those most gentle of phenols ensures there is substance, too....; b24 I tasted this after their Tire Fire, as this contained the feints from that distillate...so one must assume there was a lot, as Tire Fire is so clean. I suspect this is better quality whiskey than Rabbie Burns ever got his lips around... This will be in the running for micro-distillery whiskey of the year for certain... Magnificent: such a classy, classy act... *46% (92 proof).*

⬦ **Fiddler Unison Bourbon (91.5)** n23 goes big on the liquorice style; some excellent countering manuka honey; t23.5 big and chewy, this one is all about boldness. As on the nose, the liquorice is the lead player, at first coming in thick and fast, but then deciding to play a more layered game. This allows the most delicate of spices to balance out the thick manuka honey and molasses countering sweetness. The result is a pulsating pleasure; f22 now the corn has its say...; b23 a thoughtful blend of bourbons which suggests boldness, but always with a touch of elegance not far away... 45% (90 proof).

⬦ **Maris Otter Single Varietal Single Malt** db **(88.5)** n21.5 t23.5 f21.5 b22 A malt that a tasting glass does well to hold, for this is bursting with the most intense barley flavours imaginable. The slightly wide-ish cut means a few oils get in on the act, too, making thing a much heavier whiskey than is best for this grain. That said, the blend of ulmo and heather honeys on delivery really are a joy, as is the waxiness they form. A unique single malt style and, with a tighter cut, one to be seriously reckoned with further down the line. 46% (92 proof).

⬦ **Resurgent Rye** db **(87)** n20.5 t22.5 f22 b22 Thunders out the grain on delivery, both in juicier crisp and drier, oilier, rounded form. A chewing rye, not least because the cut here has been a little on the generous side. But if nothing else that means the spices on the finish are really something to behold. A rye that lets you know it....!! 67.2% (134.4 proof).

⬦ **Tire Fire Single Malt** db **(94)** n23.5 yes, there is a little of the blazing tire to this. But if that was all, the score would be low. The phenols are much more ambiguous than that, and there is also something of a crofter's peat fire, as well...after he's thrown a few pencils and erasers on, too...; t23.5 forget the smoke. For a moment just concentrate on the improbable softness of that delivery: the lightest of friendly oils offering a touch of manuka honey to ensure balance; f23 those embers take on a slight butterscotch note. Spices arrive, small and prickly. Then some moist ginger cake to absorb the remaining smoke; b24 amazing what can be achieved when you get those cuts right! Beautifully made and smoky malt with finesse. The best peated from America I have tasted this year. Superb! 45.5% (91 proof).

SWAMP FOX DISTILLING CO. Buena Vista, Georgia.

⬦ **Swamp Fox Distilling Co. F. Marion Single Barrel Continental Whiskey Aged 3 Months Minimum** nbc db **(62)** n15 t17.5 f14 b15.5 Words fail me. I have no idea what this whiskey is trying to achieve. Or even why it is in a bottle. 41% (82 proof). sc.

⬦ **Swamp Fox Distilling Co. Kettle Creek Malt Whiskey Aged 3 Months Minimum** nbc db **(80.5)** n19 t21 f20 b20.5 There is a house pattern here of off-key nose and finish and huge, mind-stunning delivery. But, again, those tobacco notes tend to point towards a distillation where the heart is over enlarged. 50% (100 proof).

⬦ **Swamp Fox Distilling Co. King's Town Rye Whiskey Aged 3 Months Minimum** nbc db **(76.5)** n19.5 t20 f18 b19 When a new distillery breezes into town, there is nothing more I like than to taste their whiskey, put my arms around their shoulders and say: "well done, lads". Sadly, I'm not getting much of a chance here. The mixture of mouldy, dank straw and tobacco points towards a number of failures which even a few rounds of sharp rye notes can't repair. 50% (100 proof).

⬦ **Swamp Fox Distilling Co. Will O' The Wisp White Whiskey Aged 3 Months Minimum** nbc db **(84)** n20.5 t21.5 f21 b21 This young whiskey is vibrant and bursting at the seams with busy sugars and complex compound grains. It is undone, though, by the tobacco notes from the distillation which undermines both the nose and finish in particular. 50% (100 proof).

Illinois
BLAUM BROS Galena, Illinois.

Blaum Bros Bourbon Aged 3 Years db **(81)** n19.5 t22 f19 b20.5 A curious bourbon, this. Has the complex spice make up of a cake mix. Exceptionally sweet and leaves the tongue buzzing... 50% (100 proof).

Blaum Bros Fever River Rye Aged 2 Years new American oak, finished in Port and Madeira barrels db **(86.5)** n21.5 t21.5 f22 b21.5 Less bizarre spices at play here, the wine casks making for a friendlier, after experience with an attractive complexity that now makes sense. 40% (80 proof).

Blaum Bros Straight Bourbon Whiskey 4 Years Old db **(86)** n21 t22 f21.5 b21.5 Lots of Victory V/Fisherman's Friend cough sweet hickory to this. A touch of the Bowmores... 50%

Blaum Bros Straight Rye Whiskey 4 Years Old db **(90.5)** n23 t23 f22 b22.5 A sturdy and steady rye with just the right degree of brittleness. 50% (100 proof).

FEW SPIRITS DISTILLERY Evanston, Illinois.

FEW American Whiskey Aged at Least 1 Year batch no. 18H30, bott code: FS 18297 333 db **(90)** n22 t23 f22.5 b22.5 They've cracked it...! 46.5% (93 proof).

FEW Bourbon Whiskey batch no. 18K14, bott code: 318 347 1555 db (**95**) **n**23.5 **t**24 **f**23.5 **b**24 This distillery has moved a long way in a relatively short space of time. A real force for quality now on the US whiskey scene. 46.5% (93 proof).

FEW Rye Whiskey batch no. 18E30 db (**94**) **n**23.5 **t**24 **f**23 **b**23.5 The cleanest FEW whisky I have tasted to date, the grain positively sparkles. And the way this whiskey has panned out... regrets? Too FEW to mention...... 46.5% (93 proof).

KOVAL DISTILLERY Chicago, Illinois.

Koval Bourbon Single Barrel Whiskey barrel no. 3060 db (**93**) **n**23.5 **t**23.5 **f**22 **b**23 Although small batch bourbon makers, these guys really are the real deal. Not entirely technically flawless, but enough beauty and brilliance in the glass to forgive easily. 47%. Sc.

◈ **Koval Single Barrel Bourbon Whiskey** cask no. 4Q3P7W db (**94.5**) **n**23.5 I could stick my snout in this glass all day long! Oozing liquorice, but seemingly dipped in thick heather honey; **t**24 the corn oils do a blinding job of holding together the sweeter, honeyed elements and the toastier tannins. Big under blustering or bullying; the slow spice build is masterful; **f**23 warmly spiced ulmo honey and vanilla. Long and luxuriant; **b**24 technically on the money and ticks all the bourbon boxes. Big and rich in honey. 47%. sc.

Koval Four Grain Single Barrel Whiskey barrel no. WB5K42 db (**87.5**) **n**21 **t**23 **f**21.5 **b**22 A busy, bitty and entertaining whiskey with one of the most intrinsic and captivating deliveries of the year. Fabulous layering with the busy-ness of those grains working to startling effect, especially when the soft bruyere honey kicks in. But just a little too wide a cut for true greatness, though the late spiced chocolate notes do make some amends. 55%. sc.

◈ **Koval Single Barrel Four Grain Whiskey** cask no. NB6M34 db (**84.5**) **n**19 **t**23.5 **f**21 **b**21 After finding their Four Grain sporting a wide cut last year, I was expecting service to return to normal this. Sadly not. The feints are even more exaggerated this time out making the nose challenging and the dying embers very untidy. However, the delivery is a different matter, and you feel like forgiving the whiskey's sins simply for the sheer joy of the heather honey and ginger delivery and follow through. That may well be short, but it really is perfectly formed. 47%. sc.

Koval Wheat Single Barrel Whiskey charred barrel, barrel no. FE8X10 db (**93.5**) **n**23.5 **t**23.5 **f**23 **b**23.5 Wheat whiskey can be a little spicy....and this is very spicy. You don't need to check the label to confirm the grain. 55%. sc.

WHISKEY ACRES DISTILLING CO. DeKalb, Illinois.

◈ **Whiskey Acres Distilling Co. Straight Bourbon Whiskey Aged at Least 2 Years** db (**91.5**) **n**23.5 chocolate sauce on vanilla ice cream: and I mean thick chocolate...the liquorice and molasses give this a real old-fashioned bourbon feel...; **t**22.5 still on the heavy side, the corn oils respond to sweeten while the liquorice delves deep; **f**22.5 a little manuka honey battling it out with the various oils; **b**22.5 you can see what a difference two extra years of working those stills has made. A much more sympathetic cut. Still plenty of oils to make for a chewathon, but now the tannins really come out to play. 43.5% (87 proof). ncf.

◈ **Whiskey Acres Distilling Co. Straight Bourbon Whiskey Bottled-in-Bond Aged at Least 4 Years** db (**87**) **n**22.5 **t**22 **f**21 **b**21.5 Bottled-in-Bond...and Big! The wide cut has meant little too much feint has entered the system here. The nose has a magnificent heather- and manuka honey mix to compensate and enough salivating corn oil on delivery melds with the maple syrup to make for and enjoyable delivery. The finish, though, is not quite so forgiving. 50% (100 proof). ncf.

◈ **Whiskey Acres Distilling Co. Straight Rye Whiskey Aged at Least 2 Years** db (**92**) **n**23.5 I just love it when the rye comes at you from the glass like a laser. The cleanest cut of all their whiskeys and it pays dividends on the nose at least: beautiful! **t**23 the grain enjoys a lustre which allows the rye to sparkle in its sharpness. A very light feint note mixes with the tannins to form a light toffee note that transforms into mocha; **f**22.5 spices warm matters considerably; **b**23 an incredibly tasty rye where the flavours are impossible to tame. Rich and vibrating with rye intensity. Again, a slightly cleaner cut and we'd be talking top drawer whiskey. 43.5% (87 proof). ncf.

Indiana
SPIRITS OF FRENCH LICK West Baden Springs, Indiana.

◈ **Spirits of French Lick Lee W. Sinclair 4 Grain Indiana Straight Bourbon Whiskey** db (**89**) **n**22.5 the four grains combine to offer attractive complexity. The oats – as oats often do – have a slightly louder voice than most; **t**23 a sweet caress on entry followed by a decent dollop of ulmo honey, spices and polite tannin; **f**21.5 the spices keep nagging; there is a late metallic tartness; **b**22 silky and soft thanks probably to the oat contingent, the aroma of which is definitely easy to spot. 45% (90 proof).

Iowa
CAT'S EYE DISTILLERY Bettendorf, Iowa.

◈ **Cat's Eye Distillery Essence of Iowa** db **(87)** n21.5 t22 f21.5 b22 Ah! So this is what Iowa smells like, is it? Well, for those who have never been there, let me tell you it has a distinctive citrus lightness to the aroma, though at times it can come through quite sharply. Strange, as I always though Iowa smelt like cheese. To taste, there is a very sweet vanilla lead, the corn oils filling the palate to generate a lush and friendly mouthfeel. Perhaps a little tangy at the death. But, in essence, Iowa is a very friendly place, indeed. 40% (80 proof).

Kentucky
GLENNS CREEK DISTILLERY Frankfort, Kentucky.

Glenns Creek Café Olé Kentucky Bourbon Barrel No 1 Aged At Least 1 Year (94) n23 t23.5 f23.5 b24 The thing about big David Meier the distiller is that he like to make whiskies more enormous than himself. And, my word...has he succeeded here! Stupendous whisky! 57% sc.

Millville Malt barrel 1 db **(91.5)** n23 t23.5 f21.5 b23.5 A distillery located just a mile or two from my house on Glenn's Creek has come up with a malt that defies belief. Massive attention to detail on the cuts has paid dividends and has ensured a clean yet majestically rich addition to the malt whisky lexicon. 57.1% (114.2 proof)

Glenns Creek OCD#5 (94.5) n23 t24 f23.5 b24 This is one quirky distillery. But, by thunder, it knows how to make truly great bourbon. 57.8 % (115.6 proof).

Ryskey barrel 4 single barrel double oaked db **(92.5)** n23.5 t23.5 f22 b23 The usual excellence from the Lawrenceburg, Indiana, distillery but given a curious twist but the stirring in of some muscular tannin. Attractive and intriguing. 59.3% (118.6 proof) distilled Indiana – oak staves added at Glenns Creek.

Stave + Barrel Bourbon single barrel, double aged db **(88.5)** n22 t23 f21.5 b22 Full flavoured and salivating, but as well balanced as their Ryskey. 57.9% (115.8 proof) distilled Indiana. Toasted staves added at Glenns Creek.

O. Z. TYLER Owensboro, Kentucky.

O.Z. Tyler Kentucky Bourbon Aged a Year and a Day Minimum (83) n20 t21 f21 b21 A tight, nutty bourbon shewing good late chocolate and molasses. But the youth of the whiskey means it has little ability to relax, although decent oils allow the sugars to distribute evenly. No off notes: just green and undercooked. Would love to see this at four or five times this age... 45%

Maryland
MISCELLANEOUS DISTILLERY Mt Airy, Maryland.

◈ **Brill's Batch Bourbon Whiskey Aged 420 Days** batch no. 8 db **(88.5)** n22 t22.5 f22 b22 Pretty well distilled bourbon with specific emphasis on a maple syrup sweetness allowed to drier tannins. A salivating sharpness works particularly well just after the delivery. A light liquorice fade. 44% (88 proof).

◈ **Gertrude's 100% Rye Whiskey Aged 7 Months** batch no. 9 db **(87)** n20.5 t23 f21.5 b22 Maryland is one of the original homes of rye whiskey, so it is always engaging to taste the spirit from there. The only fault here is the wide cut which allows more feint in than the grain can handle. But, that said, the type of grain is never in question because the rye announces itself in deliciously muscular fashion, both the fruitiness and crisp sugar quality is very much in evidence and certainly knows how to create a crescendo. One compensation of the extra cut is the richness of the chocolate on the finish. If this could be a bit cleaner this really has potential for excellence. 50% (100 proof).

OLD LINE SPIRITS Baltimore, Maryland.

Old Line Single Malt American Whiskey Aged at Least One Year (87.5) n22 t22 f21.5 b22 A beautifully calm and majestic malt whisky which suffers a little from being a touch too round and elegant. Beautifully distilled, the thinned Manuka honey and natural caramels appear to fill every gap, other than a slight bitterness at the death. At times, though, spends a little too much time in the doldrums. 43% (86 proof). Distilled at Middle West Spirits.

Old Line Single Malt American Whiskey Cask Strength Aged at Least One Year batch no. 1M **(92)** n22.5 t23.5 f23 b23 An altogether more impressive sailing than their 43% version. Not least because the oils, destroyed at the weaker strength, are able to encourage the richer segments of the malt to work full speed ahead. Excellent. 60% (120 proof). Distilled at MWS.

TOBACCO BARN DISTILLERY Hollywood, Maryland.

◈ **Tobacco Barn Distillery Small Batch Straight Bourbon Whiskey Aged More Than 3 Years** batch no. 17 A-8 db **(82)** n20 t21 f20.5 b20.5 Some of the first American whiskey

I ever tasted – way back in 1974 - was made in Maryland, where I was staying at the time. That came from a Seagrams plant, long since closed. It was very different to this, I remember, as this flags up its small distillery credentials with its very wide cut. Ironically, those feints wrap tobacco feel around the whiskey. Whether that was on purpose or not I can't say. But I hope future bottlings will show greater restraint in the still house. *45% (90 proof). 402 bottles.*

Massachusetts
TRIPLE EIGHT DISTILLERY Nantucket, Massachusetts.

◇ **Nor' Easter Bourbon Whiskey A Blend** nbc db **(73.5) n19 t19.5 f17 b18** Not sure how much of this was distilled in Nantucket: very little or none, I suspect. Doesn't contain their usual classy touch and instead relies on a minty, milky nose and flavour profile which is hardly up to the great name of this distillery. This Nor' easter has sunk this whiskey with all hands lost... *44.4% (88.8 proof).*

◇ **The Notch Single Malt Whisky Aged 12 Years** batch no. 003, dist 2005, bott 2018 db **(94.5) n23.5** a teasing combination of dried citrus peel – lime mostly – pistachio nuttiness and thick vanilla layers of tannin. For its time in an American warehouse, very understated and delicately nuanced; **t24** the sugars may have been muzzled on the nose, but they break free here with relish. Mostly gristy, castor sugar early on, it solidifies as the delicate honey tones begin to gather in force. The intense butterscotch and vanilla grows and captivates; **f23** a slight bitterness as the oak grumbles slightly, but the roasty element to the oak compensates with an elegantly dry finale; **b24** there is a reason why America's good and great gravitate to Nantucket. For the whiskey, of course... *48% (96 proof).*

◇ **The Notch Single Malt Whisky Aged 15 Years** batch no. 001, dist 2002, bott 2018 db **(96) n24** a faint bourbon touch to this malt as a light liquorice note jousts with the salty heather honey. Shards of marmalade and marzipan also to be found is sexy quantities. A distinctly islandy feel to this malt...which after spending 15 years on an island is perhaps not surprising...; **t23.5** again an early saline announcement underlines the island credentials, and equally adds sharpness to the citrus tones that fly the flag from lime to thin kumquat in equal measure. The spices put a warming spotlight on the tannins yet, against the odds, the barley is still juicy and active; **f24** long and fabulously weighted. The sugars and spices are in a constant battle for supremacy but neither wins while a salty mocha note and a light buttery oiliness gives the finish a real panache; **b24.5** unquestionably one of the great island malt whiskies outside Scotland. Exudes class from first sniff to last, fading salty signal. Truly brilliant. *48% (96 proof).* ☕

◇ **The Notch Single Malt Whisky Peated** nbc db **(92.5) n23 t23 f23 b23.5** Triple Eight's trademark super-clean malt allows the light smoke far greater licence than a more clumsily distilled malt would allow. The result is an essay of charm and subtlety. Indeed, the peat has the lightest of footprints, but is confident enough to ensure weight is added to the juicy cream toffee malt. Spices give the gentle marmalade notes a little extra zip. *52% (104 proof).*

Michigan
GRAND TRAVERSE DISTILLERY Traverse City, Michigan.

◇ **Grand Traverse Distillery Bourbon Aged at Least 4 Years** bott code: 192090524 db **(84.5) n21 t21.5 f21 b21** Huge toffee from start to finish. And no shortage of Demerara sugars, too. But there is no escaping the feints from the overly generous cut. *46% (92 proof).*

◇ **Grand Traverse Distillery Michigan Wheat 100% Straight Rye Wheat Whiskey Bottled in Bond** bott code: 192090514 db **(96) n23.5** elegant and complex, this is a far too rare example of where the style's usual peppery nose harmonises to a fault with the layered vanillas and touch-tight brown sugars; **t24** must have been distilled from silk worms that lived on a diet of wheat. Has an oatmeal stout softness to the piece that is shaken out of its sleepy state by the most preposterous degree of controlled spice. The kind of whiskey makes you laugh, as you can hardly believe its dash and depth. The midground is a blend of outrageously spiced manuka honey and pure toffee; **f24** long with lingering coffee and toffee....and buzzing spice, of course...; **b24.5** it is hard to imagine a modestly-sized distillery making a wheat whiskey any better than this. On this evidence, the usage of wheat for bread should be banned and it should all be sent to Grand Traverse... *50% (100 proof).*

◇ **Grand Traverse Distillery Ole George 100% Straight Rye Whiskey** bott code: 192090320 db **(90.5) n23** quite an unusual mix of paprika, cloves and juniper nuzzle into the vaguely oily rye; **t23** a generous cut really puts the cat amongst the pigeons. The caramel is already at its toffee-creamiest and the additional oils make this one of the silkiest and most chewy ryes of the year. Technically not 100% at the races, but the complexity levels leap off the graph; **f22** bitters out a tad too enthusiastically. Some grains stand their ground, though; **b22.5** the sheer force of personality means it escapes censure for any lapse. *46.5% (93 proof).*

⟐ **Grand Traverse Distillery Ole George Double Barrel 100% Straight Rye Whiskey** French white oak finish db **(89.5) n21.5** quite a tart nose where the tannins have a sweet, spicy gruffness, the grain itself not finding its usual crystal clear voice; **t23** the oils confirm a slightly wide cut. But it is the layering of the oaky sugars that really captures the attention. This is by no means usual in a rye, though the grains have recovered now to resume their usual crisp stance; **f22** slightly bitter, but that is caused by the vivid starkness of the deeper toasty oak notes again the prevailing sugars; **b23** a very different fingerprint to any rye I have tasted before: the sugar seems natural enough and just keeps on coming – and it transpired that toasted French white oak was used in a finishing process. Which would, indeed, ramp up the natural sugar content... Clever whiskey. *46.5% (93 proof).*

JOURNEYMAN DISTILLERY Three Oaks, Michigan.

Journeyman Buggy Whip Wheat Whiskey batch 38 db **(94.5) n24 t23.5 f23 b24** I'll climb aboard this buggy any day. What a beautiful wheat whiskey this is...cracking, in fact...! *45% (90 proof).*

Journeyman Corsets, Whips and Whiskey 100% Wheat Whiskey batch no. 7 db **(89.5) n22 t23 f22 b22.5** One mouthful of this and I thought: "Oh, yes! The cough syrup distillery!" And sure enough this was one the one whose whiskey, a year or two back, reminded me of pleasant medication I had taken as a child. *64.5% (129 proof).*

Journeyman Featherbone Bourbon Whiskey batch 72 db **(84) n21 t21.5 f20 b21.5** The first mouthful of this flung me back 50 years to when I was a kid tucked up in bed and having to swallow a couple of spoons-worth of cherry-flavoured cough syrup. I can picture their salesmen getting people to gather round and peddling this as Dr Journeyman's Elixir for Coughs and Colds. In truth, though, a forceful corn-rich, oily, muscovado-sugared bag of tricks. *45% (90 proof).*

Journeyman Silver Cross Whiskey batch 61 db **(86) n22 t22 f20.5 b21.5** I am a fan of this fascinating distillery, that's for sure, and wondering what they are up to next. Not sure if this was designed to ward off vampires, but to be on the safe side I tasted this long after the sun set. A serious mish-mash of a whiskey which celebrated a rich ulmo-honey sweetness, but is ultimately undone by a bitterness which, sadly, no amount of sugar can keep fully under control and gets you in the neck in the end... *45% (90 proof).*

NEW HOLLAND BREWING COMPANY Holland, Michigan.

New Holland Beer Barrel Bourbon bott code: 192201 db **(80.5) n22 t21.5 f18 b19** It was doing so well until that heavy hop kicked in on the finish: the bourbon notes on this are as good as anything I've encountered from this distillery. I want my hops with my beer, not whisky. I just don't even begin to understand the concept of this style of whisk(e)y. Sorry. *40% (80 proof).*

New Holland Beer Barrel Rye American white oak db **(80) n21 t21 f19 b19** Were this from Speyside, I dare-say it would be called hopscotch... The hoppiest whisk(e)y I have tasted anywhere in the world. Apart from a brief chocolate intervention, this is seriously not my kind of thing. I mean: I love whisky and I love beer. But just not together. Less befuddled by it than befuggled... *40% (80 proof).*

Pitchfork Wheat Michigan-Grown Wheat Whiskey aged 14 months, American oak barrels db **(93) n22.5 t23.5 f23.5 b23.5** So love it! Like a digestive biscuit you want to dunk in your coffee...By far and away the best thing I have ever seen from this distillery: this really is top drawer microdistillery whiskey just brimming with flavours and personality. Genuinely impressed. *45% (90 proof).*

Zeppelin Bend Straight Malt Whiskey American oak barrels db **(84.5) n21 t21.5 f21 b21** The Zep is back!! Not seen it for a while and this is a new model. Actually, in some ways barely recognise it from the last one I saw about five years ago. Much more effervescent than before, though that curious hop note I remember not only persists but appears to have been upped slightly. *45% (90 proof).*

VALENTINE DISTILLING CO. Ferndale, Michigan.

Mayor Pingree Small Batch Bourbon Whiskey batch no. 39 db **(89.5) n23.5 t22.5 f21.5 b22** A very different animal, or mayor, and obviously distilled in different stills from their 9- and 10-year-old Mayor Pingree brands. A little confusing for the punter but a very attractive if under-stated micro-bourbon without doubt. *45% (90 proof).*

Montana
MONTGOMERY DISTILLERY Missoula, Montana.

Montgomery American Single Malt Whiskey Aged 5 Years American white oak barrels, dist 2013 db **(84) n20.5 t22.5 f20.5 b20.5** That's a pretty hefty middle cut there and the resulting oils make for a lot of chewing. A toffee-nougat nose sets the scene but the delivery of intense bruyere honey is exceptionally beautiful. Sadly, those feints kick in with a vengeance further down the line. *45% (90 proof). 1,750 bottles. Third Release.*

⬦ **Sudden Wisdom Straight Rye Whiskey Aged 3 Years** new American white oak barrels, bott code: 19258 0856 db **(85) n21.5 t21.5 f21 b21** I tasted this unaware of this distillery's dallying with hoppy whiskey, as there is nothing on the label to suggest traditional beer is in any way involved. Yet the first thing I spotted on the nose and on the delivery was a distinct hoppiness which out-punched the rye. A shame, as this is well distilled and if the grain had been allowed to shine to its fullest extent, this could have been a cracker. *45% (90 proof).*

New England
SONS OF LIBERTY Rhode Island, New England.
Battle Cry American Single Malt Whiskey db **(77.5) n19 t21 f18 b19.5** A sweet, nutty whisky weakened by the butyric-like off notes. *46% (92 proof).*

New York
BLACK BUTTON DISTILLING Rochester, New York.
⬦ **Empire Rye Whiskey Aged at least 2 Years** distilled from New York State rye & malted barley, batch no. 3 db **(85) n20 t23.5 f20.5 b21** The tobacco smoke underlines the wide cut on this. Technically imperfect it may be, but the delivery and immediate follow-through is gripping - and delicious! For a moment it is like distilled mead as the honey takes on a concentrated form you so very rarely see. The tannins are multi-layered and the chocolate tones have a touch of intense Lubek marzipan at work. The finish, as one might suspect, leaves a little to be desired. But this is all about a follow-through that transfixes and, frankly, blows you away! *42% (84 proof). ncf.*

BREUCKELEN DISTILLING Brooklyn, New York.
77 Whiskey Bonded Rye Aged 4 Years American oak barrels db **(86.5) n21.5 t22 f21.5 b21.5** Big flavoured and butch, but a few too many nougat and tobacco notes point an accusing finger towards the cut. Plenty to enjoy, but perhaps not up to Breuckelen's usual very high standards. *50% (100 proof).*

⬦ **77 Whiskey Bonded Rye Distilled From 100% Rye Aged 6 Years** db **(91) n22.5** the expected rye freshness has been quietened by a massive toffee statement; **t23.5** the house lushness on delivery coats the palate with an attractive combination of creamy caramels and toasty molasses. As on the nose, the rye character is struggling to make its mark overtly though there is no doubting the delicious properties to be chewed on here, especially when the spices turn up. Look closely, though and you can find the brittle grains under the caramels. And once you spot them, the more revealing they become; **f22** chocolate eclairs...with spice; **b23** a beautifully understated rye whiskey. 50% (100 proof).

77 Whiskey Bonded Rye & Corn Aged 4 Years American oak barrels db **(95) n23.5 t24 f23.5 b24** There you go: Breuckleyn back on track with a spot edition of their signature brand. Sings from the glass like a barber-shop quartet. *50% (100 proof).*

77 Whiskey Local Corn 700 Days Old db **(92) n23 t23.5 f22.5 b23** It is as if very single atom of sugar has been sucked out of the oak though, thankfully, baser tannins give balance. Remarkable and delicious! *45% (90 proof).*

⬦ **77 Whiskey Distilled From 100% Corn 1377 Days Old** American oak barrels db **(92) n23** gorgeous corn oil fattened further by light ulmo honey and punctuated with spice; **t23.5** that is one delightful delivery: just as on the nose the corn is in full swing and creates a mouthfeel to die for. Warmed acacia honey or molten sugars on porridge springs to mind; **f22.5** just bitters slightly though the tannins are well layered; **b23** the mark of a good corn whiskey is the honey hanging off the clean oils. And this has it by the bushel: a corn-ucopia, you might say... *45% (90 proof).*

77 Whiskey Local Rye & Corn 538 Days Old American oak barrels db **(92.5) n22.5 t23.5 f23 b23.5** The 377th whisky tasted for my Bible 2018 just had to be this. I remember last year tasting a younger version of this which was quite astonishing. Here the rye, which was so prominent last time, has been overtaken by the corn which has clipped its brittle wings. Still an astounding experience, nonetheless... *45% (90 proof).*

⬦ **77 Whiskey Distilled From Local Rye & Corn 655 Days Old** American oak barrels db **(87) n22 t22.5 f21 b21.5** An extraordinary degree of citrus on the nose – it is almost like opening up a pack of fruit pastel candy – sends this whiskey into unusual territory and it doesn't end there! The palate is awash with all kinds of dark sugars with an under note of fruit and spice. A little thin. Which doesn't help the finish ward off a slight bitterness. A distinctly idiosyncratic style. *45% (90 proof).*

◈ **77 Whiskey Distilled From New York Wheat 624 Days Old** American oak barrels db **(89.5)** n22 a little nip, but nothing like you might expect from this grain. In its place is friendly and not unattractive toffee and nut combination; t23 those caramels really go to town from the first moment. A little mocha and maple syrup continue the sweet and super-soft theme; f22 at least some spices arrive, but in muted fashion; b22.5 wheat whiskeys tend to be ablaze with spices. This, however, follows the distillery style of succulent sweetness. *45% (90 proof).*

◈ **Brownstone Malt Whiskey 6 Years Old** batch no. 1 db **(87.5)** n21.5 t21 f23 b22 OK. So we accept that the nutty-nougat element on both nose and delivery yells of over-egged feints. But once you get past that...just...wow! As thick, rich and chocolatey as any malt you could hope for, with a superb spiced Jaffa Cake. A finish to be savoured... *50% (100 proof).*

Project No 1: Wheated Straight Bourbon Bottled in Bond Aged 4 Years dist 2013 db **(88)** n22 t22.5 f21.5 b22 A bit heavy on the oils, but the wheat and associated spices make their mark. *50% (100 proof).*

Project No 2: Single Malt Whiskey Bottled in Bond Aged 4 Years dist 23 Mar 13, bott 26 Feb 18 db **(84.5)** n21 t21 f21.5 b21 Sweet and widely cut. A project still in development, I suspect... *50% (100 proof).*

COOPERSTOWN DISTILLERY Cooperstown, New York.

Cooper's Classic American Whiskey bourbon mash finished in French oak barrels, bott code. 148 10 db **(90.5)** n22.5 t22.5 f23 b22.5 Plugs into the sugars and takes full voltage. *45%.*

Cooper's Legacy Bourbon Whiskey Grant's Recipe bott code. 147 02 db **(95)** n23.5 t24 f23.5 b24 I'd like, with this exceptional bourbon, to raise a toast to my son, James', new (indeed, first) dog: Cooper. Named, naturally, after Dale Cooper of Twin Peaks fame. Dale whippet. Dale bourbon. *50% (100 proof).*

Cooper's Ransom Rye Whiskey db **(86.5)** n21 t22 f21.5 b22 If they could just keep the cut points a little more tight, they'd really have some rye here. Despite the light feints the rye does at times sparkle with commendable crispness. *51% (102 proof).*

FINGER LAKES DISTILLING Burdett, New York.

McKenzie Wheated Bourbon Whiskey Bottled in Bond Aged a Minimum of 4 Years American oak db **(93)** n23 t23.5 f23 b23.5 Rich, full flavoured and well powered. Not a bourbon for the faint of heart. Beautifully constructed and structured. *50% (100 proof). ncf.*

McKenzie Straight Rye Whiskey Aged a Minimum of 3 Years American oak db **(90)** n23 t23.5 f21 b22.5 Just adore the intermittent crispness of the grain. Great stuff. *45.5% (91 proof). ncf.*

HIGH PEAKS DISTILLING LLC Lake George, New York.

◈ **High Peaks Cloudsplitter Aged 2 Years** db **(91)** n23 the lightness of the smoke is beguiling. They call it wispy, and that is exactly right. Never forms into a solid, instead attaches gently to the sweet barley to offer a shadow of depth; t23 playful smoke and spice dovetail with the gentle mix of sweet barley and dry, toasty raisin; the mouthfeel is always soft, mildly oiled and favours the vague ulmo honey tones; f22 dries quite quickly as those raisins hit home. A little tangy and untidy at the very death, but forgivable; b23 their label is interesting. They are one of the few distilleries that boast of refined cuts...and that is what they had, because the distillate is feint free. But they fall into the trap of saying that sherry sweetens: most actually impart a dryness, which I feel has happened here. No complaints from me, as that has certainly upped the sophistication of this hugely attractive malt. *46%.*

HILLROCK ESTATE DISTILLERY Hudson Valley, New York.

◈ **Hillrock Double Cask Rye Whiskey** barrel no. OSR DC Rye 1 db **(77)** n20 t20.5 f17.5 b19 Tomorrow I have to drastically cut short my time at my home and tasting room on the banks of the Kentucky River to return to England. The President has decreed that no more incoming craft will be allowed to travel from the UK because of the C-19 crisis. I could have stayed here and worked on, but there was a chance my health insurance would have run out before the travel ban was lifted...so I have booked a flight home later today. I have worked all day and into the early hours of the morning, trying to keep away from the wine finishes and hop-fermented whiskeys which would have so drastically slowed down my palate and ability to work. My last whiskey before I leave is this one, simply because I wanted to taste one of the great Dave Pickerell's creations, from a distiller I have known and admired now for a quarter of a century, before heading back. That said, this distillery's track record with finishing leaves a little to be desired, not seeming to understand the damage that sulphur can cause to a whiskey. I picked this one because it said it was double matured in American wood. Even so, the grim finish is one that would have seen me off for the night anyway, as it is unforgiving in its bitterness and furriness. As long as I live, I will never understand why any American distilling company would like to ape the very worst of Scotch whisky, repeating the mistakes that has allowed true bourbon and rye whiskey to sail above most Scotch single malts in quality. *53.6% (107.2 proof). sc.*

IRON SMOKE WHISKEY Fairport, New York.

Iron Smoke Casket Strength Straight Bourbon Whiskey Aged A Minimum of Two Years batch no. 1, bott 12/27/18 db **(94.5)** n23.5 t23.5 f23.5 b24 After having tasted the latest Apple Wood version, normal service is resumed with this superbly distilled and beautifully functioning bourbon. *60% (120 proof).*

⬙ **Iron Smoke Casket Strength Straight Bourbon Whiskey Aged a Minimum of 2 Years** batch no. 2, bott 7-11-19 db **(94)** n23.5 their signature smokiness has slightly run out of ink. Youthful, greenish and angular; t24 wow..!! That youthfulness is confirmed on impact: the juiciness is rumbustious and salivating in the extreme. The sugars are borderline crunchy, the grains are almost pre-pubescent. But together the palate is left rocking by the end product of this improbable combination; f23 bitters slightly as the tannins at last get a foothold...; b23.5 might be a little less wheat in the mash bill here as the usual smokiness (carried on that one particular grain) is much less evident than usual. It doesn't appear to suffer from that fact, either... *60% (120 proof).*

Iron Smoke Four Grain Bourbon With Apple Wood Smoked Wheat Aged A Minimum of Two Years batch no. 24, bott 5/7/19 db **(91.5)** n22.5 t23 f22.5 b23.5 Considering it was only the wheat that was smoked, this is one big ass Kentuckian. And they have pulled it off beautifully by, somehow, getting the balance near enough spot on, despite the cut being wider than usual. Superb. *40% (80 proof).*

⬙ **Iron Smoke Special Reserve Single Barrel Straight Bourbon Whiskey Aged a Minimum of 2 Years** barrel no. 246, dist 8/19/15 db **(92)** n22 the smoked apple wood holds the upper hand; t23.5 serenely soft and sweet, garrulous Demerara notes chattering away two to the dozen, some light timber ensuring a backbone; f23 just love the red and black liquorice interplay with the spiced smokiness forming the backdrop; b23.5 a unique Iron Smoke style here beautifully played out. *45% (90 proof). sc. MAHAN Liquor.*

Iron Smoke Special Reserve Single Barrel Straight Bourbon Whiskey Aged A Minimum of Two Years batch no. 380, bott 12/18/18 db **(93)** n22.5 t23.5 f23 b23.5 A thoroughly lip-smacking, though ultimately dry version. *45% (90 proof). Bottled exclusively for Whole Foods.*

⬙ **Iron Smoke Special Reserve Single Barrel Straight Bourbon Whiskey Aged a Minimum of 2 Years** barrel no. 515, dist 9/28/16, bott 12-6-19 db **(92)** n22.5 slightly extra pungency on the smoke itself gives this an uncommon weightiness for an American whiskey; t23 much spicier than earlier bottlings of their Special Reserve, though the sugars are still in full teeth-attacking mode...; f23 earthier finish as the smoke reconnects, the spices quieten and the tannins oscillate; b23.5 Iron Smoke in its typically full on demeanour. *45% (90 proof). sc. DW Select Batch no. 2.*

⬙ **Iron Smoke Straight Four Grain Bourbon Whiskey Aged a Minimum of 2 Years** batch no. 29, bott 11-22-19 db **(87.5)** n22 t22.5 f21 b22 I was really looking forward to this bottling as in the past their Four Grain has been a source of delight. And while this isn't bad, it doesn't hit the heights expected due to a slightly over-enthusiastic oiliness. What we used to call "dirty" in the old days isn't exactly that here, but the hefty cut combined with the smoke makes for a complex but testing bourbon. *40% (80 proof).*

KINGS COUNTY DISTILLERY Brooklyn, New York.

⬙ **Kings County Distillery Bottled-in-Bond Empire Rye Four Years Old** dist Spring 2015, bott Fall 2019 db **(90.5)** n22 slightly extra on the cut leaves louder oils to drown out some of the rye intensity; t23.5 sweet, oily and juicy, the spices take no time in running the show. Brilliant mocha, liquorice and molasses at the midpoint, but it is fleeting; f22 dry and oily. The vanilla has a dusty quality; b23 very oily and, spices apart, moderately subdued by comparison to their sublime 51% version. *50% (100 proof).*

⬙ **Kings County Distillery Empire Rye Aged 2 Years or More** batch no. 4 db **(95)** n23.5 lavender and spice add even further complexity to an already intense and noisy toasted rye; t24 as deliveries go, this falls into the bloody brilliant category. Salivating on impact, the grain, at its most toasty and brittle, immediately slugs it out with a thick wave of molasses. It takes some time for the tannins to make themselves heard...which they certainly do; f23.5 there is a dropped intro' on spices, but though arriving late, they make their mark and bond cheerfully with the lingering molasses; b24 easily among the best ryes made outside Kentucky. As huge and complex as it is superb.... *51% (102 proof).*

⬙ **Kings County Distillery Peated Rye Aged 2 Years or More** batch no. 2 db **(94)** n23 anyone who has lived around farm stock will soon recognise this earthy aroma...; t24 it is the mouthfeel itself that first grabs the headlines. Then the subtlety and superb weight to the flavours that begin to draw your attention. Silky and inviting, it at first appears to be in neutral. Slowly, thanks to one gently lapping wave after another the tide of rye is soon caressing your taste buds, a well-behaved spice ensuring a muted liveliness; **f23** the peat returns to gently take control. A light toasted molasses note keeps it good and perfectly balanced company; **b24** from those who brought you Peated Bourbon, Kings Country now offer their Peated Rye version. It takes a while or the palate to adjust to these unusual signals, but once it does it is a joy all the way... Brilliant! *45% (90 proof).*

⟳ **Kings County Distillery Straight Bourbon Blender's Reserve Aged 5 Years** batch no. 1 db **(94.5) n23** acacia honey and nuts in tandem. Red liquorice makes a case for the tannin..; **t23.5** a juicy, sugary and always gripping delivery. The toastier tones crash through with minimum subtlety. Liquorice and hickory abound...; **f24** more of the same, with some superb small grain complexity dancing around the palate until very late on; how the molasses and maple syrup mix lasts quite this long and to such spellbinding effect, is anyone's guess. Breathtaking! What a magnificent finale...; **b24** this distillery is seriously impressing me... Another big experience... *52.5% (105 proof).*

TACONIC DISTILLERY Stanfordville, New York.

Taconic Dutchess Private Reserve Straight Bourbon Whiskey db **(86) n21.5 t22 f21 b21.5.** A pretty bourbon, with the sugars sitting in the right place, if sometimes over enthusiastically. Good spice balance, roastiness and generous oils. Also, some decent rye in that mash bill it seems. *45%*

Taconic Straight Bourbon Whiskey db **(92.5) n23 t23.5 f23 b23** I well remember their bourbon from last year: this appears to have upped a gear...not only in strength but in far better usage of the sugars. *57.5% (115 proof).*

Taconic Straight Rye Whiskey db **(91.5) n22.5 t23.5 f22.5 b23** If memory serves, this is the same distillery which came up with a resounding rye last year. This, though, has a different feel with the oak enclosing in on the grain like a python gets all up close and personal to a lamb. *57.5% (115 proof).*

TOMMYROTTER DISTILLERY Buffalo, New York.

Tommyrotter Triple Barrel American Whiskey batch no. 3 French oak Finish **(88.5) n22 t22.5 f22 b22** Despite using three barrels, it as though the caramel has merged many of the facets to create a continuous flavour stream. Not as a complex as I hoped for, but not a whiskey to turn down a second glass of. *46% (92 proof). nc ncf.*

WIDOW JANE DISTILLERY Brooklyn, New York.

Baby Jane Bourbon Whiskey batch no.1 db **(85.5) n21 t22 f21 b21.5** Jane is a chubby little thing, displaying plenty of baby fat. Sweet, though, with an enjoyable molasses and nougat theme. *45.5% (91 proof).*

North Carolina
BLUE RIDGE DISTILLING CO. Golden Valley, North Carolina.

Defiant American Single Malt 100% malted barley, bott code: 307/18 04:43 L32 db **(81.5) n18 t22.5 f20.5 b20.5** Wow! I see they have done nothing to reduce the cut since I last tasted this, resulting in a challengingly feinty nose. Must say, though, that the malty, ulmo honey on delivery is a delicious surprise! *41% (81 proof).*

Defiant Rye Whisky bott code: 066/18 05:26 L32 db **(86.5) n21.5 t22 f21.5 b21.5** With the exception of slightly more honey on delivery, the tasting notes (and quality of rye) remains absolutely identical to the last time I tasted this! *46% (92 proof).*

⟳ **Defiant Rye Whisky** bott code: 082/19 db **(84.5) n20.5 t21 f22 b21** A nougat-laden rye which tends to suggest, correctly, that the cut is a lot less disciplined than it should be. The grain appears to manifest itself with an attractive honeyed swirl towards the midpoint. *46% (92 proof).*

BROAD BRANCH DISTILLERY Winston-Salem, North Carolina.

⟳ **Broad Branch Rye Fidelity Aged 6 Years** charred new oak barrels, barrel no. 37 db **(85) n21 t22 f20.5 b21.5** There is no doubting the intensity of the rye itself which blends in with the vanillas and butterscotch from the oak to good effect. And the heather honey at the midpoint is truly superb. The spices are also in fine fettle. However, the smokiness claimed on the back label comes from the cut being a little too generous for its own good. Indeed, those minor feints have enough influence to slightly lessen the complexity on the finish and leave an oily residue. It will be interesting to see if future bottlings reflect a correction of this. What we are looking for is High Fidelity... *45% (90 proof). ncf sc.*

Ohio
AMERICAN FREEDOM DISTILLERY Columbus, Ohio

◇◇◇ **Soldier Commanders Select Bourbon Whiskey Aged 12 Years** db (82.5) n20 t21.5 f21 b20 One of the most yeasty whiskeys I have tasted in many a year. A defiant steak of hickory and liquorice gives it its bourbon stripes. 48.5% (97 proof).

◇◇◇ **Horse Soldier Premium Straight Bourbon Whiskey Aged a Minimum of 2 Years** db (89.5) n22 light but very true: no off notes and clean. A little black cherry on the red liquorice; t22.5 pretty young, but proud with it, too. Old enough for the tannins to make their mark, the delicate hickory tones melding with the thin molasses; f22.5 dries, but elegantly so, upping the vanilla and oak presence; b22.5 unerringly pleasant and polite. 43.5% (87 proof). ncf.

◇◇◇ **Horse Soldier Reserve Barrel Strength Bourbon Whiskey** db (95.5) n23.5 salty – not sure if these are horse soldiers or marines: there is something of the coast about this one; t24.5 stunning! The delivery I have been waiting for all day and after 12 hours of tasting it has finally arrived. Liquorice, muscovado sugars, toasty tannins, burnt caramel...they all gang up, not in a polite line, but explode together on entry. The palate is like some kind of spectrometer as it picks off and identifies the constituent parts...; f23.5 long, with the dark sugars lingering with intent; b24 uncannily beautiful. 58.45% (116.9 proof).

◇◇◇ **Horse Soldier Signature Small Batch Bourbon Whiskey** db (91) n22 a little small grain storm here; t23.5 you expect a minor explosion on delivery and those small grains duly oblige. So much honey yet still it is puckeringly tart and lively, you get the distinct feeling that a spicy onslaught isn't far away....and that arrives on cue, too...! f22.5 ulmo honey, vanilla and outlandish spice; b23 this isn't a small batch whiskey: it's a very naughty boy. A bourbon that refuses to behave... 47.5% (95 proof).

MIDDLE WEST SPIRITS Columbus, Ohio

OYO Michelone Reserve Bourbon Whiskey db (86) n22.5 t22 f20 b21.5 A mainly attractive, restrained bourbon showing limited age and therefore depth. Lovely small grains to the busy nose and the sugars rise early before the buttery spices begin, but runs out of steam quite soon after. Not too happy with the tangy finish. 45% (90 proof).

OYO Oloroso Wheat Whiskey db (88) n23.5 t22.5 f20 22 As any good wheat whiskey should, this radiates spices with abandon. The fruit helps paper over some cracks in the distillate, especially towards the weak finish. 51% (102 proof).

Oregon
CLEAR CREEK DISTILLERY Portland, Oregon.

McCarthy's Oregon Single Malt Aged 3 Years batch W16-01, bott 6 May 16 db (88.5) n22 t23 f21.5 b22 For the first time since I tasted their first bottlings – in the days when my beard was still black – this whiskey has changed. Appears to have far less copper in the system to give the normal all-round richness; this is quite apparent on the nose and finish in particular. But they appear to have upped the peat ratio to good effect. 42.5% (85 proof)

HOUSE SPIRITS DISTILLERY Portland, Oregon.

◇◇◇ **Westward American Single Malt Whiskey** new American oak barrels, bott code: L9 067 0010 db (84) n21.5 t22 f20.5 b20 Well, it is certainly different. Not sure the last time I tasted such a dramatic variance between the sweetness and bitterness. Or such huge but random flavours. The problem is that it never quite resolves itself. Or finds something close to balance. Love the delivery, when the gristy barley sweetness is just budding. But from then after, it is every man for himself: American Pioneer spirit, indeed! 45% (90 proof). ncf.

OREGON SPIRIT DISTILLERS Bend, Oregon.

◇◇◇ **Oregon Spirit Distillers Straight American Bourbon Aged 4 Years** charred new American oak barrels, barrel series no. 150704 db (88.5) n22 t23 f21 b22.5 A truly lovely bourbon of the nutty and enigmatically sweet style basting a deeply enjoyable mouthfeel. The finish is perhaps its Achilles heel with a little too much dryness present and even a degree of bitterness. But until then both the nose and delivery rejoice in its hazelnut praline persona and its softness of touch. The strands of Lubeck marzipan are also to be celebrated and admired. (CV) 47% (94 proof).

RANSOM SPIRITS Sheridan, Oregon.

Ransom The Emerald 1865 batch no. 005 db (86.5) n21 t23 f21 b21.5 "This whiskey rings a bell", thought I. Brilliant delivery, magnificently complex grains at play, but OTT feints. I've tasted this one before, I concluded. And, on checking in a previous Bible, I see I had a couple of years back, though an earlier bottling and then not called The Emerald. Brilliant Irish style mix of malted and unmalted barley. But just need to sort that cut out. 43.8%.

Ransom Rye, Barley, Wheat Whiskey Aged a Minimum of 2 Years batch no. 003 db **(85.5)** n21 t22 f21 b21.5 A little too much earthiness to this for its own good, meaning the wheat has to fight hard to get its sweet and spicy message out there. Needs a tad more copper in the system to get the most out of this whiskey, as a metallic spark appears missing. Just love this distillery's labels, by the way: real class. *63.4%.*

ROGUE SPIRITS Newport, Oregon.

Rogue Dead Guy Whiskey ocean aged in oak barrels at least 1 year db **(86)** n22.5 t22 f20.5 b21. Ah, I remember this guy from a year or two back: I had a bone to pick with him about his finish. Well, not the preferred drink of the Grim Reaper now, and makes good use of its malty, peppery structure. The finish is still a bit tangy and salty. But a big improvement.*40% (80 proof).*

Pennsylvania
DAD'S HAT RYE DISTILLERY Bristol, Pennsylvania.

Dad's Hat Pennsylvania Straight Rye Whiskey Aged Minimum 3 Years db **(91.5)** n23 t23.5 f22 That persistent vague bitterness does gather momentum towards the end; b23 the truest rye I have seen from you yet: I take my hat off to you guys...quite literally...! *47.5% (95 proof).*

South Carolina
PALMETTO DISTILLERY Anderson, South Carolina.

◈ **Palmetto SC Whiskey** bott code: 325 04 db **(85)** n21.5 t23 f19.5 b21 Prefer this to the last bottling I sampled. Here the emphasis is on chocolate-caramel with a delicious spiced ulmo honey back up. But the cut here is a little tardy, which damages both the nose and, especially, the finish. But I'm clinging on to the memories of the rousing delivery – and so are my taste buds.... *44.65% (89.3 proof).*

Tennessee
CORSAIR ARTISAN DISTILLERY Nashville, Tennessee.

◈ **Corsair Dark Rye American Rye Malt Whiskey Aged 8 Months** batch no. 3 db **(95.5)** n23.5 a lovely double header: at once a real hardness to the rye, revealing a brittleness that you feel can crack at any moment, and at the same time a deft, teasing, caressing counternote with a mild acidic pungency to the vaguely smoky toastiness; **t24.5** there is probably no grain on the planet so full-flavoured as malted rye. And I include peated malt amongst that. Here, you feel it has been taken about as far as it can go – and in so doing all those amazing juicy, salivating vaguely fruity rye tones are wrung out onto a grateful palate like moisture is expelled by a mangle. At all times there's little escape from the gentle allure of delicate heather-honey, too...; **f23.5** light, playful spice and then a slow build-up of subtle cocoa tones; **b24** I am assuming that the rye has been roasted into chocolate form in the same way chocolate malt is made from barley (and first used in a whisky by Glenmorangie a good decade or so ago). With rye having a far starker flavour profile than barley, the chocolate effect has to work harder to make an impact. But it certainly does as those sweet cocoa notes filter through at the finale. A whiskey-lover's whisky. *42.5% (85 proof). 385 bottles.*

◈ **Corsair Triple Smoke American Single Malt Whiskey Aged 8 Months** batch no. 319 db **(92.5)** n24 there may be cherry and beechwood smoke involved here, but it is the peat reek which holds the upper hand, the finer phenols ensuring a sweeter edge. Fruity, phenolic and fun...; **t22.5** a bit of a ham-fisted entry onto the palate, with too much happening here. This is young spirit at play and the tannins haven't had time to tame the wilder elements. Can't say it isn't juicy, though or that the journey doesn't offer some wild scenes; the consistent softness to the mouthfeel is a bonus; **f23** the finish has fun untangling itself and allowing more delicate pastel shades to breeze around. Outstanding bitter-sweet balance **b23** bottled a tad too young, despite the high pleasure value. Even so, a very complex offering. *40% (80 proof). 252 bottles.*

Texas
BALCONES DISTILLERY Waco, Texas.

Balcones 1 Texas Single Malt Aged at Least 26 Months in Oak batch no. SM19-1, bott 3.12.19 db **(84.5)** n22 t21.5 f20 b21 Nowhere near Balcones's normal high standard with the cut as wide as a Texas rib eye, even more fatty and thick but with nothing like the taste. Some big natural caramel and lighter molasses...but it isn't enough. This weekend of 20-21 July 2019 I am tasting all my remaining Texas whiskeys for this forthcoming Bible. Because it was 50 years ago this weekend that man first walked on the Moon, an event I remember vividly as a child watching in thrilled awe on our black and white television with my now departed parents. And Texas played a key part in that amazing event, something that will never be forgotten by those who witnessed it. Houston: this whiskey has a slight problem... *53%. nc ncf.*

Balcones Brimstone Texas Scrub Oak Smoked Whisky Aged At Least 1 Day In Oak batch no. BRM18-1, bott 1-23-18 db (**93**) n23.5 t23.5 f22.5 b23.5 I can neither add nor subtract from my tasting notes to the previous bottling. Actually, upon refection, I can. An extra half point for some clever extra spices on delivery... 53% (106 proof). nc ncf.

Balcones Brimstone Redux Aged 33 Months in American Oak barrel no. 4880 db (**94**) n23.5 t24 f22.5 b24 Welcome to Texas's very own Tannin Fest...in a bottle... Phew...! One of a kind, for sure. 64.9% (129.8 proof). sc.

Balcones FR.OAK Texas Single Malt Whisky Pot Distilled Aged At Least 35 Months In Oak batch no. FROAK18-1, bott 4-27-18 db (**92.5**) n21.5 t24 f23.5 b23.5 Discernible barley gets lost in a forest of sweet tannin. 59.9% (119.8 proof). nc ncf. Tenth Anniversary.

◇ **Balcones FR.OAK Texas Single Malt Whisky Aged at least 36 Months in Oak** batch no. FROAK19-1, bott 5/30/19 db (**95.5**) n24 t24 f23.5 b24 While I was mightily impressed with their previous French Oak matured malt, this one has really knocked me back in my chair with delight. You get the feeling that they have quickly learned how to better control the more masculine chars of the French tannin and nowhere better does this shew but on the rich but magnificently complex nose. The sugars are pristine and sharp, the liquorice tones mingling and with and controlling the spices. You expect this to fall apart slightly on delivery, but it doesn't. Indeed the early Demerara sugars mutate into molasses while, against the odds, the barley itself can be detected alive and well clinging to the roof the mouth, with a burnt raisin, fruity muscovado sugar accompaniment. Perhaps only Texas can provide us with a malt this mind-bogglingly big....(CV) 61.9% (123.8 proof). nc ncf.

Balcones Peated Texas Single Malt Aged 26 Months in American Oak barrel no. 10472 db (**96**) n24 t24 f24 b24 There's no smoke without fire...and this has both. Enormous and really cleanly and beautifully made. Rarely has peated malt and new oak been so happily married. One of the greatest malt whiskeys ever produced in the USA. 63% (126 proof). sc.

◇ **Balcones Peated Texas Single Malt Whisky Aged at least 36 Months in Oak** batch no. PEAT19-1, bott 10.26.19 db (**95**) n24 t24.5 f23 b23.5 It is interesting how extra time in cask can subtract as well as add. That last peated malt was about year younger if I remember correctly. The smoke and tannin fitted like a hand in glove. This is still a significantly stunning malt, on the nose especially, where the peat forms pretty patterns as it dovetails with the tannin. But the extra oak here has slightly nudged the balance – so this is now drier overall and the bigger flavours seemingly weighted towards the overture on the palate. Having said that, the mix of heather and ulmo honeys and the upping of the spice means you are still in for a spectacular treat and, make no mistake, this is one of the great malt whiskeys produced anywhere in the USA during the last year. 65.2% (130.4 proof). nc ncf.

◇ **Balcones Texas Blue Corn Bourbon Aged at least 34 Months in Oak** batch no. BCB19-1, bott 6.25.19 db (**94.5**) n23 t24 f23.5 b24 After the disappointment of the wheated bourbon, normal service has been resumed....and with interest! All kinds of dark sugars vie for pole position on both nose and delivery. But the hickory and cream toffee mix meet with bold spices so both nose and delivery are treated to a scintillating experience. Wonderful finish, also, with that creaminess increasing as the corn is gather and the ulmo honey adding just the right touch of elegant sweetness to a bourbon so big. (CV) 65% (130 proof). nc ncf.

Balcones Texas Rye 100 Proof Aged at Least 15 Months in Oak batch no. RYE0019-1 db (**85.5**) n20 t22.5 f21.5 b21.5 Another strange rye offering from Balcones who definitely have some room for improvement with consistency with this style of whiskey. The nose is definitely broken, but once passed the oils on delivery, the grain really zeros into the taste buds and hits its target unerringly. Too short lived though as the fade shews a little attractive rye sweetness. 50%. nc ncf.

Balcones Texas Rye Cask Strength Aged at Least 27 Months in Oak batch no. RCS19-1 db (**95**) n23 t24 f23.5 b24.5 Every bit as beautiful and on the money as their 15-month old rye was lacklustre. It is this type of excellence I normally associate with this distillery. 63.3%. nc ncf.

Balcones Texas Single Malt Rum Cask Finished Aged at Least 27 Months in Oak batch no. SMR19-1, bott 1.15.19 db (**91.5**) n22.5 t23.5 f22.5 b23 Rum cask whiskeys have a tendency to be hard as nails. This is one very big nail... 63.5%. nc ncf.

Balcones Texas Single Malt Single Barrel Aged at Least 24 Months in Oak cask no. 17222, American oak cask, dist 5.3.17, bott 6.13.19 db (**88**) n22.5 t22 f21.5 b22 Enjoyable and another that is not quite up the distillery's usual brilliant standard. 64%. nc ncf sc.

Balcones Texas Single Malt Single Barrel Aged at Least 65 Months in Oak cask no. 2642, American oak cask, dist 1.8.14, bott 6.11.19 db (**95**) n23.5 t24 f23.5 b24 So thick and dense, probably has more gravitational pull than that Moon these Texans went out and lassoed 50 years ago... 66.4%. nc ncf sc.

Balcones Texas Single Malt Single Barrel Aged at Least 60 Months in Oak cask no. 2504, American oak cask, dist 2.17.14, bott 2.20.19 db (**94.5**) n23.5 t24 f23 b24 A wonderfully honeyed and metallic malt from when the stills were younger and at times upping the richness dramatically. A five-year-old with an attractive aloofness. *64.8%. nc ncf sc.*

◈ **Balcones Texas Wheated Bourbon Aged at least 34 Months in Oak** batch no. WHB19-1, bott 9.2.19 db **(83.5) n21 t21.5 f20 b21** Unusually feinty for a Balcones. This is a distillery that has rightly earned its high reputation of getting its cuts right, so when even a relatively marginal off-cut can be noticed, then it sends shock waves. Of the favour profile, after the big vanilla and caramel statement the extra spices certainly point towards the wheat but, overall, this is a pretty coarse experience for a Balcones. (CV) *61.3% (122.6 proof). nc ncf.*

◈ **Balcones True Blue Cask Strength Straight Corn Whiskey Aged at least 31 Months in Oak** batch no. TCB19-1, bott 6.27.19 db **(95) n23.5 t24 f23.5 b24** Ye Gods...!!! This is so good. Pretty estery on the nose and with mocha on both the aroma and finish there is something of old, high grade Demerara Pot Still rum about this: that is a hell of a compliment, believe me. This is a chewing whiskey of the highest order. Sweet chestnuts are noticeable at almost every point, as is the high quality of the distillate – the cut is clean but has enough corn oils to make the enjoyment last for a very impressive amount of time. Love the controlled spice, too, so as not to distract from the complex whole. Brilliant! (CV) *63.1% (126.2 proof). nc ncf.*

DALLAS DISTILLERIES Garland, Texas.
Herman Marshall Texas Bourbon batch 18/12 **(90.5) n22.5 t23 f22.5 b22.5** A very confident and beautifully-made Texan which never sits shy. *46% (92 proof).*

DEVILS RIVER WHISKEY San Antonio, Texas.
Devils River Barrel Strength Texas Bourbon batch SW8325 **(87.5) n22 t21.5 f22 b22** A light, delicate Texan with the emphasis on a vanilla and almost cream soda theme. Busy spices up the salivation levels to a considerable degree, while the light oils from the uncut spirit stretch the icing sugar almost to breaking point. Nothing like so hefty as your average Texas bourbon despite the strength. And as the bottle suggests: "sin responsibly". *48.5% (117 proof).*

FIRESTONE AND ROBERTSON DISTILLING CO LTD Fort Worth, Texas.
TX Texas Straight Bourbon bott code: 20181214B **(91) n22.5 t23 f22.5 b23** A well-made, satisfying whiskey. Once you get past its unusual firmness on both nose and palate, it becomes pretty easy to start picking out the impressive layering and balance. Another quality bourbon from Texas. *45% (90 proof). Firestone and Robertson Distilling Co Ltd.*

FIVE POINTS DISTILLING Forney, Texas.
◈ **Lone Elm Single Barrel Texas Straight Wheat Whiskey** barrel no. 100 barreled 9/13 db **(95) n23.5 t24 f23.5 b24** You could stand a spoon up in a glass of this monster whiskey. This is as thick on the palate as whiskey gets and the world's oak tannins appear to be having their annual congress there. Heavily represented is the maple syrup branch of oaky sugars which dominate both the nose and early delivery. And they need to be there, or this would be a puckering-fest, as the tannins are relentless; this is a whiskey to appeal to the Pappy Van Winkle devotees....and those with a good half hour to spare just to understand what kind of mighty straight wheat they are dealing with here. Plenty of mocha and liquorice concentrate, too, which arrive and disappear in the myriad layers. With this much outrageous oak on show, mind the splinters... (CV) *53.8% (1076proof).*

◈ **Lone Elm Texas Straight Wheat Whiskey** db **(87) n21 t22.5 f21.5 b22** Texas doesn't really do subtle. And there is no evidence of it here, either. The cut is a wide one, without any major problem from feints. This means the extra oils plus the oils off the grain make for a spirit very high in viscosity: this is a chewing, not a sippin' whiskey. Superb initial delivery, with liquorice levels high. The sugars are as thick as the oils, but wilt slightly as the tannins bite and the oils thicken at the death. Not technically perfect for sure, but the sweet-dry ratio makes for a fascinating experience. (CV) *45% (90 proof).*

GARRISON BROTHERS Hye, Texas.
Garrison Brothers Balmorhea Texas Straight Bourbon Whiskey db **(96.5) n24 t24.5 f24; b24** The quality of their whiskey is simply ridiculous. The smaller independent distilleries from outside Kentucky are just not supposed to be this good.... If it doesn't win some kind of Whisky Bible gong, then the standard this year must be extraordinary... *57.5% (115 proof).*

Garrison Brothers Balmorhea Texas Straight Bourbon Whiskey #1 panhandle white corn, corn harvest 2013, dist 2014, bott 2019 db **(96.5) n24** a Sea of Tranquillity as a small step of crisp grain becomes a giant step for Texas bourbon kind...; **t24** with raging spices, corn and ultra-toasty tannins, delivered at an uncompromising 115 proof, the arrival is an Ocean of Storms. Oaky liquorice and thick natural caramel. Soon a Sea of Nectar swells as the astonishing blend of corn oils, heather honey and Manuka honeys converge and intertwangle; **f24** at last settles into a Sea of Serenity as the tannins calm to the honey's soothing tune...; **b24.5** tasting this just about 50 years ago to the very minute of the first man setting foot on the Moon. He had started his journey in Texas...of course... And the whiskey? Out of this world class... *57.5% (115 proof).*

◇ **Garrison Brothers Balmorhea Texas Straight Bourbon Whiskey 2020 Release** food grade #1 white corn, dist 2015 db **(96.5) n24** such a quiet, confident intensity: like a sportsman about to do battle, in the zone and certain in his own mind he will win. Crisp fruity grain, red liquorice and a sprinkling of spice. But that intensity....wow! **t24.5** corn oils and concentrated Demerara sugars make for a simultaneously fat, weighty, yet mouth-watering delivery before the more eye-watering grains get going. For all the trademark intensity (and, my word, this is really intense) a much more even ride through the gears than some previous years...; **f23.5** a slightly toastier finale than usual – maybe from a deeper char or older bourbon than usual. But here the slightly burnt and bitter aspect works beautifully with the molasses; **b24.5** almost exactly a year ago today (20th July 2019, today is 19th July 2020) I tasted last year's bottling the exact moment 50 years to the second man first walked on the moon – the crew having been supported by their team in Houston, Texas. Today, I taste this on the final day of tasting for the Jim Murray Whiskey Bible 2021: this is number 1,244 with just eight more to do. So I am ending my own epic journey through a Covid-19 ridden world, by far the hardest assignment of my long whiskey life. But when you encounter a whiskey like this and can help the world to share such beauty, you know that four months of near total isolation was in fact worth it... *57.5% (115 proof).* 🦃

Garrison Brothers Cowboy Bourbon Barrel Proof Aged Four Years #1 panhandle white corn, corn harvest 2011, dist 2012, bott 2017 db **(96) n24 t24 f24 b24** These guys have proved once again that they do a mighty mean four-year-old... another improbably spectacular bourbon from Garrison Brothers. *68.5% (137 proof).*

Garrison Brothers Cowboy Bourbon Barrel Proof Aged Five Years #1 panhandle white corn, corn harvest 2011, dist 2012 db **(95.5) n24** this liquorice and honey festooned nose has been branded with the Garrison Bothers mark...; **t24** as huge as it may be, this is so stunningly controlled. The liquorice looks as though it about to stampede when the rich caramels lasso it back under control. The heather honey and tannin mix really is something...; **f23.5** after the bucking bronco of a delivery, this settles for a quiet finale to die for caramel and vanillas...just so well weighted...; **b24** a macho bourbon at first but shows a far softer side when needed. The epitome of a balanced whiskey. *66.95% (133.9 proof).*

Garrison Brothers Texas Straight Bourbon Whiskey Single Barrel Aged Three Years #1 panhandle white corn, corn harvest 2011, cask no. 3433, dist 2012 db **(93.5) n23 t23.5 f23.5 b23.5** Delicious, but Garrison's whiskey at this strength always seems a fraction under par. *47% (94 proof). sc.*

Garrison Brothers Texas Straight Bourbon Whiskey Single Barrel #1 panhandle white corn, corn harvest 2013, dist 2014, barrel no. 6103 db **(93.5) n23.5 t24 f22.5 b23.5** Delicious, yet a surprisingly muted Garrison Brothers bourbon. *47% (94 proof). sc. 63 bottles.*

Garrison Brothers Texas Straight Bourbon Whiskey 2019 #1 panhandle white corn, corn harvest 2013, dist 2014 db **(95) n23.5 t24 f23.5 b24** Garrison Bros going all soft and touchy-feely. A rare example of their bourbon offering nothing other than subtlety. *47% (94 proof).*

◇ **Garrison Brothers Texas Straight Bourbon Whiskey 2020 Release** #1 panhandle white corn db **(94.5) n24** any more layers to this and I might need to drill a core sample for a closer look, something they are quite good at in Texas. A fascinating honey-themed mini-giant: it sets off as though it means business with an oily kick of liquorice but settles on a charming variation of heather and ulmo honey themed notes; **t23** a little more feint than usual and this stokes up the toastier liquorice and eucalyptus notes. The honey hums quietly; **f23.5** I expected molasses... and get molasses. A rich vanilla and corn oil which seems to hold those honey variants as on the nose...; **b24** wanted to finish the day's tasting on a high – and even better still, a Hye!! You see I've just tasted a succession of pretty average American whiskies, and needed my confidence restored. This was earmarked for tomorrow... but great whiskey has long been regarded as an excellent restorative. And, trust me, on the evidence of this it certainly is... One of those big whiskies with a gentle but charismatic character that needs you to taste as many times as you need to listen to a Handel cantata before you fully appreciate the intricate accord. *47% (94 proof).*

◇ **Cadenhead's Garrison Brothers 2014** cask no. 7117, bott 2020 db **(95.5) n24 t24 f23.5 b24** What a sensational representation of this great distillery. The nose with a purity and surety of intent and intensity is unique to this Texas whiskey landmark: the blend of molasses and Manuka honey, an unerring, linear broadcast of muzzled sweetness...the liquorice and vanillas calm those sugars. The spices, also, ensure balance is honoured. And that's just on the nose. On the palate it is less a whiskey and more a rambling story to be told over a campfire. The liquorice doesn't tighten and cramp as it sometimes can, not least because of the lashings of ulmo and heather honey that pitches in to offer both a balancing sweetness but the softest, most yielding mouthfeel. Coffee and hickory abounds, too, drying and softening further. As they say in them thar parts....Yep! 60.1% (120.2 proof). 81 bottles. Selected by Peter Siegenthaler.

⌘ **Cadenhead's Garrison Brothers 2015** cask no. 9057, bott 2019 db **(93) n23.5 t23.5 f23 b23** An unusually mild Garrison Brothers bourbon which reaches for the toffee within itself rather than the liquorice. And finds it! As soft and even as Garrison gets – almost to the point of docility. But if you love concentrated cream toffee, all polished off with a delightful coating of hickory, then you won't be disappointed. Have to admit I was a little surprised by this. But certainly not disappointed... 47% (92 proof). 63 bottles. Selected by Peter Siegenthaler.

IRONROOT REPUBLIC DISTILLING Denison, Texas.

Ironroot Harbinger Bourbon 199 Edition Aged 30 Months db **(91) n23 t23.5 f21.5 b23** More like Iron Boot, such is the kick to this one...absolutely delicious Texas bourbon. 60.1%

⌘ **Ironroot Harbinger Straight Bourbon Whiskey 32 Months Aged H20A Edition** db **(91.5) n23.5** not too much to quibble about here. Thumpingly crisp on the honeyed tannins, the liquorice and hickory keeps the peppery spices good company. Exceptionally well balanced; **t23** shifts through the bourbon gears effortlessly. The corn oils always keep things in check, even when the spices and Demerara sugars begin bullying the toasty tannins; **f22** dries and oils up as a little feint seepage comes through at the end; **b23** one of the rising stars of Texas whiskey is shining brightly here. Lovely stuff! 57.5% (115 proof). ncf.

⌘ **Ironroot Hubris Straight Corn Whiskey 31 Months Aged 2020 Edition** db **(87.5) n22 t22.5 f21 b22** Yay!! How I love to see straight corn whiskey – nowhere near enough of it made. This one displays above average spice – especially on the husky delivery - but there is a muffled bitterness on both the nose the palate. The sugars are relaxed but of a light mollassed variety. Decent and doesn't stint on entertainment value. But you get the feeling that better will be coming down the line. 58.90% (117.8 proof). ncf.

⌘ **Ironroot Ichor Straight Bourbon Whiskey 46 Months Aged** db **(93) n23.5** hang on tight, ladies and gentlemen. The first message from this aroma is that we're about to be taken on a foot to the floor ride. This is heavy duty bourbon: the aromas are thick and weighty. So hefty that the spices seem crushed just by the intent of the tannin alone...; **t24** just wow....!! A good three minutes of chewing required for this one. The corn oil is in concentrated form, thick and sticky with it. But the burnt toffee works so well with the molasses and peppers. Maybe, though, it is that giant wave of eucalyptus that pounds the taste buds early on that sets the scene and takes the breath away most. Had to say...this layered giant offers a quite incredible delivery and midpoint, which is deliciously cocoa-rich by the way...; **f22** the finish is usually the weak spot of Ironroot and, comparatively, it is here also with a little bitterness digging in; **b23.5** 61.5% (123 proof). ncf. 5th Anniversary.

Ironroot Harbinger XC Straight Bourbon 2018 Edition Aged 24 Months db **(88) n21.5 t22.5 f21.5 b22.5** Though the nose gets this one off to a wobbly start, its improvement is immediate and impressive. 45% (90 proof).

⌘ **Ironroot Ichor Straight Bourbon Whiskey Aged 48 Months** db **(94.5) n23.5** ribbons of rich liquorice are slowly consumed by clouds of hickory; **t24** a big nose has suddenly got bigger on delivery. This is no sipping whiskey: this is one to masticate until every last atom of sweetness has been drawn from the molasses in order to take on the fabulous, though dry hickory; **f23** teaming with toasty tannins to the very last; **b24** a bourbon behemoth very much of the hickory kind. Beautiful! 61.5% (123 proof). ncf. 5th Anniversary bottling.

KIEPERSOL DISTILLERY Tyler, Texas.

Jimmy's 100 Texas Straight Bourbon db **(86) n21.5 t22 f22 b20.5** It is not the extra strength of alcohol that is the problem here, but the unforgiving nature of the oak. To carry this amount of tannin in a bourbon there must be balancing sugars, and most have been spent here. That said, for those looking at pure oomph and eye-watering wood, you may have found your perfect mate. 50% (100 proof).

Jimmy's Through Heroes Eyes Texas Straight Bourbon db **(91) n22 t23 f22.5 b22.5** A clean, well-made bourbon with a big spicy depth. From a distance, Jimmy's Second World War goggles look like a pair of peaches on the label...and ironically there is a delicate hint of peach in the whiskey. 45% (90 proof).

RANGER CREEK DISTILLING, San Antonio, Texas.

Ranger Creek .36 Straight Texas Bourbon Aged For a Minimum of 2 Years db **(91) n23 t23 f22 b22.5** Not technically perfect, but the nose and taste profile cannot be faulted, nor the subtle range of honeys at play. 48% (96 proof).

Ranger Creek Rimfire Mesquite Smoked Texas Single Malt batch 1 **(85)** n21.5 t22 f20.5 **b21.** As I have never tasted anything smoked with mesquite before – especially whiskey – I will have to guess that it is the tree of the semi-desert which is imparting a strange, mildly bitter tang on the finish. Whether it is also responsible for the enormous degree of creamed toffee, I am also not sure. Enjoyable, fascinating even...but something the ol' taste buds need a bit of acclimatising to. *43% (86 proof)*

TAHWAHKARO DISTILLERY Grapevine, Texas.

Tahwahkaro TAH Four Grain Bourbon Whiskey Aged Not Less Than 1 Year batch 1 **(79)** n19 t21 f19 b20 A very first effort from a new Texas distillery. Shows some lovely toffee apple touches and certainly not short on sugars and character. But appears to need a little extra copper contact to clean up the nose and finish as well as a slightly more precise cut off the stills. *48% (96 proof).*

TREATY OAK DISTILLING Ranch Drippings Springs, Texas.

Treaty Oak Distilling Ghost Hill Texas Bourbon Whiskey db **(87)** n22 t21 f22 b22 The good folk of Treaty Oak actually let us into the make-up of their mash bill: 57% Texas corn, 32% Texas wheat, 11% American barley (are we to infer that Texas is a separate country from America..?) No doubt some Texans will raise a glass of this to toast that notion...They will enjoy this whiskey, but that is providing they forgive the very slight indiscretions in the distilling itself which results in a sometimes sharp, often jarring but always full-favoured bourbon. Some real cough sweet hickory depth to this, too. *47.5% (95 proof).*

YELLOW ROSE DISTILLING Houston, Texas.

Yellow Rose Outlaw Batch Bourbon batch 16-33, made from 100% corn db **(94)** n24 t23.5 f23 b23.5 Outlaw? This should be made both legal and compulsory. Really high grade corn whiskey, even if they do call it, outlawishly, bourbon. *46% (92 proof).*

Virginia
CATOCTIN CREEK DISTILLERY Loudoun County, Virginia.

Braddock Oak Single Barrel Rye Whisky batch B17K1 db **(90)** n22.5 t23 f22 b22.5 It is heart-warming to see a distillery dedicated to making rye. Still the odd technical off-note but I am sure this will be corrected with time and experience. Plenty here to savour. *46% sc.*

Catoctin Creek Cask Proof Roundstone Rye Whisky batch B17A2, charred new oak barrels db **(85)** n21.5 t22.5 f22 b22 So much flavour. But needs to get those cuts cleaner to maximise the rye profile. *57.8% (115.6 proof). ncf.*

Catoctin Creek Roundstone Cask Proof Edition Rye Whiskey batch no. 18919 db **(87)** n20.5 t23.5 f21 b22 Presumably German stills at work here as that unmistakable light feint note just chips the top off the peak of the higher rye notes. Masses of charm and flavour on delivery, and buckets of spice, too. With a little cleaning up, this could be such a substantial and classy whiskey. *58% (116 proof). ncf sc. 125 bottles.*

Catoctin Creek Roundstone Distillers Edition Rye Whiskey batch no. 18621 db **(87.5)** n21 t22.5 f22 b22 This is cleaner than Cask Proof above. But it just its lacks muscular rye complexity and is much more happy for a dithering grain note to merge with the tannins and lingering oils to form a slightly nutty chocolate theme. *46% (92 proof). ncf sc.*

Catoctin Creek Roundstone Rye Whisky batch B17G1, charred new oak barrels db **(88)** n21.5 t23.5 f21 b22 The brighter end of the distillery's narrow spectrum: the rye here really is deliciously on song! *46% (92 proof). ncf.*

Catoctin Creek Roundstone Single Barrel Virginia Rye Whiskey batch no. 19A01 db **(88)** n19.5 t23 f22.5 b23 Again, the wide cut acts as a bit of a ball and chain around this whiskey. But when it gets rolling, the salivating qualities of the crisp rye and then chocolate and honey notes are really impressive. Most enjoyable. *40% (80 proof). ncf sc.*

COPPER FOX DISTILLERY Sperryville, Virginia.

⬦ **Copper Fox Original American Single Malt** batch no. 159, finished in a second used bourbon barrel db **(93.5)** n22.5 as always, it is the phenols you spot first, but here it appears to have been refined slightly so the applewood dominates no more than the peat might on a Caol Ila; **t24** gorgeous oils make the most of the maple syrup and spice delivery: stunning! The mid-ground is malt, alternating with the spice; **f23** though warm, the vanillas from the tannins cut an elegant dash; **b24** technically, as good as anything I have seen from this distillery. Superbly distilled and very cleverly engineered in the cask to really pump out the personality. Big stuff! *48% (96 proof). ncf.*

⬦ **Copper Fox Original Rye** batch no. 136, finished in a second used bourbon barrel db **(92)** n22 just a slight stain of tobacco smoke on the otherwise crisp and fruity rye; **t24** while the first wave of the delivery is untidy, the second and the next dozen or so after are pure gold...or do I mean copper? The grain revels in its intensity and the rye, momentarily exploding out into toasted honeycomb candy, flexes its considerable muscle; **f22.5** a little drier and just a slight remnant of a generous cut; **b23.5** a couple of days ago I was out walking in the glorious, lonely countryside around my UK home and, once more, I came face to face with a fox - just how I had done on the day I last tasted this whiskey. Once more we stood eye to eye regarding the other...until finally off he trotted in his own time. On the way back home I pondered this incident and I hoped my research team had come up with Rick Wasmund's latest rye. And what do you know... *45% (90 proof). ncf.*

RESERVOIR DISTILLERY Richmond, Virginia.

Reservoir Distillery Bourbon Whiskey year 18, batch no. 1 db **(94.5) n23.5 t23.5 f23.5 b24** They have excelled: a Reservoir that is so damned good... *50% (100 proof).*

⬧ **Reservoir Distillery Bourbon 100% Corn Aged a Minimum of 2 Years** 5 gallon barrels db **(94.5) n23 t24 f23.5 b24** A very well made Corn Whiskey (hang on: they are mysteriously still calling this a bourbon..) which successfully extracts the full oily value from the grain and sets about using its considerable charm to further the cause of the ulmo honey and butterscotch...not to mention the profound spice. It is all rather beautiful...and technically of a very high standard. *50% (100 proof).*

⬧ **Reservoir Distillery Grey Ghost Bourbon 2019 100% Corn Aged 4.5 Years** 5 gallon barrels db **(83.5) n21 t20 f21.5 b21.5** Nowhere near as well made as the 2-year-old corn, above, and abounds in one too many slightly off-key notes. All rather green, too, despite its age. *50% (100 proof).*

⬧ **Reservoir Distillery Holland's Milkman Aged a Minimum of 2 Years** 5 gallon barrels, aged milk stout beer barrel finish db **(87) n21.5 t23 f22 b20.5** Can't say I'm much a fan of the prevailing hop note, as modest as it is. But there is just enough in there to upset the balance what had previously been an excellent joust between the sharp tannins and the milk chocolate. *53.5% (107 proof).*

⬧ **Reservoir Distillery Hunter & Scott Bourbon Aged 1.5 Years** 5 and 10 gallon barrels db **(91.5) n22 t23.5 f23 b23** Be thankful that the tannins have thrown in some genuinely toasty, almost earthy, elements here. Otherwise those sugars would spin out of control. Rarely have I seen such concentrated forms of Demerara let loose in a whiskey, linking up with the corn oil to not just hit but remain at every taste bud it can find. Those with a sweet tooth will merrily kill for this. Those of us with more moderate tastes will also find themselves seduced. One way or another, you stand no chance: just enjoy... *45% (90 proof).*

⬧ **Reservoir Distillery Hunter & Scott Rye Aged 1.5 Years** 5 and 10 gallon barrels db **(93.5) n23.5 t23.5 f23 b23.5** Although matured in very small barrels, it is still the grain that has star billing on both nose and delivery. Everything about this whiskey is intense and urgent: the rye is piercing, almost shrill, on the nose, the sturdy oak no more than a dais; and so it is on delivery – exactly. There is something of the chocolate liqueur on the finale. One hell of a rye! *45% (90 proof).*

⬧ **Reservoir Distillery Maison de Cuivre Aged a Minimum of 2 Years** 5 gallon barrels, Merlot barrel finish db **(92.5) n23.5 t23 f22.5 b23.5** First thing to report is that the Merlot barrel is free of sulphur. And those of you who have found whisky matured in Merlot elsewhere around the world will know, that has not always been the case....with dire consequences. Some lovely dry pepper notes ingratiate both on nose and delivery into a more robust liquorice note. If there is a fruitiness to be found, it seems more like small grains going about their work rather than any grape. Just-so amounts of maple syrup enter the fray from just before the midpoint and hang around, even blending into a little cocoa late on. An elegant, often brisk but never brusque whisky *50% (100 proof).*

Reservoir Distillery Rye Whiskey year 18, batch no. 1 db **(89) n22.5 t23 f21 b22** An annoying bitter note just takes the edge off what would have been a superb rye. Grrrr! *50% (100 proof).*

⬧ **Reservoir Distillery Rye Whiskey 100% Rye Aged a Minimum of 2 Years** 5 gallon barrels db **(81) n21 t21.5 f19 b19.5** A strange one, this. The nose gives mixed messages, both of lively rye and something very amiss. The delivery initially follows the route of the sharp heart-warming grain. But even as the ulmo honey begins to appear, so do the myriad puckering, tangy faults. A whiskey probably lost somewhere in the fermentation, I suspect. *50% (100 proof).*

Reservoir Distillery Wheat Whiskey year 18, batch no. 1 db **(93) n24 t24 f22 b23** A top (reservoir) dog wheat whiskey. A *50% (100 proof).*

⬧ **Reservoir Distillery Wheat Whiskey 100% Wheat Aged a Minimum of 2 Years** 5 gallon barrels db **(89) n21.5 t23 f22 b22.5** All kinds of crispy Demerara sugar on display here and makes for some duet when the spices are unleashed by the wheat. A curious bitter thread runs throughout this. Big stuff, all the same. *50% (100 proof).*

SILVERBACK DISTILLERY Afton, Virginia.

◆ **Blackback Straight Bourbon Whiskey Aged 3 Years** batch no. 18 db **(89) n22.5** soft and eschews a roasty style for a more relaxed caramel and cod liver oil one...; **t22.5** the house style of molten sugar has its fingerprints all over this from the start. Does finally tart and toast up a little, but then a lovely hazelnut praline depths develops; **f22** lots of nutty vanilla, though thins out quickly; **b22** for those who prefer their bourbons a little nutty... *43% (86 proof). sc.*

◆ **Blackback Straight Rye Whiskey Alpha Series Aged 4 Years** barrel no. 51 db **(95) n23.5** fruity and crisp as every self-respecting rye whiskey should be. Impressively intense, too. So much so, the nose has the spicy quality of a Grand-cru wine...but without the grape...; **t24.5** I am astounded. This is absolutely sublime rye that gives a master class in how to be both bold and assertive yet yielding enough to allow the tannins to make an impassioned contribution. Like on the nose, one is reminded of a Chateau Lafite, or Margeaux...but without the grape. How it pulls off this amazing trick, I really don't know.... As for the grain input...just bloody wow!!! **f23** OK, just a little too oily at the very death – so this was made by humans after all. But before we get to that point there is a wonderfully glazed molasses moment or three, where the rye appears to be captured in the molten sugars but able to radiate its crisp, slightly chocolatey message...; **b24** not sure if this is a Virginian rye or from Pennsylvania. Surely the latter: after all, it was there that rye whiskey was perfected. And while this may not be perfect, they have had a damn good try in making it so. The impact of the rye is truly thrilling. Make no mistake: this is a stunning rye whiskey. *55% (110 proof). sc.*

◆ **Blackback Straight Rye Whiskey Lucky 13 Aged 3 Years** batch no. 25 db **(87) n22 t23 f20.5 b21.5** A liquorice-laden rye thumping its chest with personality. But not distilled to the same degree of excellence as their Alpha Series Rye (above), resulting in a tangy finish. Can't fault the second and third flavour-waves after delivery, though – a gorgeous molasses and mocha concoction that is immensely pleasing. *43% (86 proof).*

◆ **Christine Single Barrel Virginia Bourbon Whiskey Riggleman Reserve** batch no. 1 db **(94) n23.5** both curvaceous and with a playful spicy nip at the same time...intriguing... and classically bourbony; **t23.5** full-bodied and rounded from the off: kind of like the nose, but now with much more flesh on the bone. The spices are launched from every angle and in increasing intensity. Natural caramels. Form a chewy bridge on which the manuka honey and liquorice crosses. This is very serious, beautifully structured bourbon...; **f23** drying, toasty tannins begin to bite deep. A shell of molasses ensures the balance is never breeched; **b24** I have never met Christine Riggleman. But if she is anything like this whiskey, then I'd sure like to. Distinguished and a little classy. *56% (112 proof). sc. 179 bottles.*

VIRGINIA DISTILLERY CO. Lovinston, Virginia.

Virginia Distillery Co. Courage & Conviction Prelude American Single Malt Whisky db **(88) n22 t22.5 f21.5 b22** Everything about this youthful single malt screams "new distillery!". And what a gorgeous distillery this is, located in the stunning highlands of Virginia, close to the Blue Ridge Mountains. Even if the Scotch Whisky Association arrogantly believe that only Scotland possesses such things as highlands and litigiously and ridiculously claim otherwise should any distillery in the world dare mention the fact. Virginia has them also. There's a little feint on the early nose, but this soon burns off with a little Murray Method handling, then an overriding degree of copper and light vanilla. But the nose is ostensibly buttered up new make – and from new stills. The flavour profile is rich from the wide cut but then increasingly, and deliciously, malty. Fascinating! I have seen some of what is coming further down the line. It is ,technically better than this, as you would expect from a fledgling copper pot still distillery, And promising some glorious days ahead. *46% (92 proof).*

Washington
BAINBRIDGE ORGANIC DISTILLERS Bainbridge Island, Washington.

Bainbridge Battle Point Organic Wheat Whiskey db **(87.5) n21.5 t23 f21 b22** A charming if single-paced wheat whiskey with only a modest degree of the usual spice one associates with this grain type. The delivery, with its mix of silky tannins, lightened molasses and caramel is its high point by a distance; the finish has a slightly bitter edge at the death. Very well distilled without doubt. *43% (86 proof).*

Bainbridge Battle Point Two Islands Organic Wheat Whiskey Islay cask db **(95) n23.5 t24 f23.5 b24** Now the Japanese cask (below) may not work quite as had been hoped, but this certainly does! Has to be one of the surprise packages of the year. An exercise in poise and balance: just so effortlessly and gracefully beautiful. *43% (86 proof).*

CHAMBERS BAY DISTILLERY University Place, Washington.

◆ **Chambers Bay Captain's Reserve Bottled-in-Bond Bourbon Boathouse-Aged a minimum of Five Years** barrel no. 45 db **(87) n22 t22.5 f20.5 b22** Tasting the five- against the three-year-old suggests that in those intervening two years the distillery's fermentation and distilling abilities rose significantly. This has swarths of vanilla, salt and toffee. But underneath all that is a rather heavyweight and clumsy spirit whose weaknesses are evident at the death: there are no similar faults with the three year-old. 50% (100 proof). sc.

◈ **Chambers Bay Greenhorn Bourbon Micro-barrel Aged a minimum of One Year** batch no. 15 db **(86) n21.5 t21.5 f21.5 b21.5** Well it certainly is green, the youth apparent with every atom of aroma and flavour. On the subject of the nose, how about that vanilla coffee...? It is like going into a west coast coffee house for the 30-somethings... On the palate juicy and tart but, overall, a significant step up from previous bottlings. 44% (88 proof).

◈ **Chambers Bay Straight Bourbon Whiskey Bourbon Boathouse-Aged a minimum of Three Years** batch no. 07 db **(91.5) n22.5** the oak offers a pleasing drying effect; a little salty, too...; **t23** explosive sugars on delivery. A little light hickory gets lost under the growing spice; **f23** decent oils ensure length and chewability. The spices provide late bite while the dried maple syrup also lasts the course; **b23** anchors away for a full-bodied bourbon that gets the liquorice and spice mix pretty ship shape. 47.5% (95 proof).

COPPERWORKS Seattle, Washington.

Copperworks American Single Malt Whiskey Release No. 013 Aged 30 Months new American oak, five malt & pale malt recipe db **(87.5) n22 t22 f21.5 b22** Soft and sensual from nose to tail, again the accent is on toffee. Still that mystery bitterness creeps around. But this is a very relaxed malt. 51% (102 proof). 1,740 bottles.

Copperworks American Single Malt Whiskey Release No. 014 Aged 38 Months Wine Barrel Select new American oak, cask no. 102, five malt recipe db **(91.5) n22.5 t23.5 f22.5 b23** What a treat that was! The mystery house bitterness is all but eradicated; while there a fruit pastille quality to the sweetness. 57.1% (114.2 proof). sc. 224 bottles.

Copperworks American Single Malt Whiskey Release No. 015 Aged 36 Months new American oak, cask no. 115, five malt recipe db **(86.5) n22 t21.5 f21.5 b21.5** Far less fruit influence than Release 14, so the toffee and house bitterness make a much bigger stand. Chewy and well-weighted. 57.7% (115.4 proof). sc. 222 bottles.

Copperworks American Single Malt Whiskey Release No. 016 Aged 38 Months new French oak, cask no. 97, five malt recipe db **(92) n23 t23.5 f22.5 b23** They have now added a chocolate note to their repertoire, and it suits them well. Love whiskey. 58.9% (117.8 proof). sc.

◈ **Copperworks American Single Malt Whiskey Release No. 017 Aged 25 Months Collaboration Cask** new American oak, finished for 6 months in Amaro Amorino, pale malt recipe db **(82.5) n20 t22 f20 b20.5** Well, I didn't expect that! Yes, I was prepared for a subtle orange infusion. But the effects of the liqueur hits you right between the eyes – and on the nose in particular. You look for an aroma, but find a perfume... A malt that will thrill liqueur lovers, but has left a maligne effect on old traditionalists like me. That said, there are a few passing moments when the malt does get a word in edgeways. The bitter finale, after so much early sweetness, was a foregone certainty. 50% (100 proof). 290 bottles.

◈ **Copperworks American Single Malt Whiskey Release No. 019 Aged 34 Months** new American oak, cask no. 138, Knutzen Farms Alba Skagit Valley Malting db **(91.5) n23** booming tannins serve up nuts and spices in almost equal measure; slightly buttery, too. The sugars are as dark and toasty as they come...; **t23** salivating on delivery despite the muscular oak presence. The gristy sugars and liquorice-led oils ensures the balance lasts; **f22.5** long, still toasty and a light fade of manuka honey; **b23** extracts every last flavour profile from the virgin oak, but still allows the lightening barley to have its say. Impressive. 50% (100 proof). sc. 264 bottles.

◈ **Copperworks American Single Malt Whiskey Release No. 020 Aged 34 Months** new American oak, cask no. 142, Knutzen Farms Alba Skagit Valley Malting db **(94) n23** backs off from the full-frontal tannins displayed in Release 19 and opts for a more subtle, honeyed approach – though the oak is never far away; the sweetened stewed gooseberries is both a surprise and a delight...; **t23.5** sugary oils arrive in double quick time...and soon it becomes apparent that the sweetness is malt-led; varying layers of vanilla move into butterscotch. The oak infusion is chalky and deft. The spices grow almost without notice until they are well upon you...; **f23.5** sharp and the barley continues its juicy parade with subtle strata of ulmo honey and over-ripe greengage; still those spices pulse...; **b24** such an understated malt, its shyness almost hiding the enormity of the whiskey. Almost... 50% (100 proof). sc. 262 bottles.

◈ **Copperworks American Single Malt Whiskey Release No. 021 Aged 38 Months** new American oak, alba, five malt & pale malt recipe db **(89) n22** there's that mystery minor hop note again! Though this is all about cream toffee; **t22.5** one of those sensuous deliveries which starts soft and innocently – and very much staying on the cream toffee threat – then suddenly takes off with a malty-tannin kick...; **f22** ....then quietens for the slightly bitter, vaguely hoppy finish; **b22.5** pretty docile by Copperworks' standards. Wish I knew why the odd bottle of theirs sports a distinct hoppy note. *50% (100 proof). 1,760 bottles.*

⬥ **Copperworks American Single Malt Whiskey Release No. 022 Aged 29 Months** new American oak, pale malt recipe db (**86.5**) **n21 t22 f21.5 b22** Enjoyable, but pretty one-dimensional by their standards (and overly bitter, too), the caramel always in the ascendancy. If this malt were a colour, it'd be beige.... *51% (102 proof). 1,707 bottles.*

⬥ **Copperworks American Single Malt Whiskey Release No. 023 Aged 29 Months** new American oak, pale malt & five malt recipe db (**86.5**) **n21.5 t22.5 f21 b21.5** The sharp and awkward nose is countered by super-soft delivery. Creamy textured with thick vanilla and light molasses interference from the tannins. Finally, spicy yet bitter-sweet, then emphasis on the bitter. So, in all, about as well disciplined as a bunch of kids after eating highly coloured candy. *50% (100 proof). 1,329 bottles.*

⬥ **Copperworks American Single Malt Whiskey Brewery Casks Release No. 024 Aged 29 Months** new American oak, finished for 2 months in a Three Magnets Copperworks Tompkins Imperial Stout cask, five malt recipe db (**93**) **n22.5** one of the most tame noses they have ever produced, yet there is an enticing quality to its creamy maltiness; **t23** the malt announces itself in juicy fashion before that creamy character takes charge once more. There is a playful pepperiness playing little power games; **f23.5** a truly delicious confection of milky chocolate; **b24** creamy-textured and initially well spiced, it at first appears rather monotoned by this distillery's high standards. But a serious dose of the Murray Method soon changes the perspective of things – quite dramatically in the end - and slowly you are able to tease out its extraordinary charm and complexity. Truly a one-off in style and mood for the 2021 Whisky Bible, and not a bad choice for its 900th whisky... *50% (100 proof). 500 bottles.*

⬥ **Copperworks American Single Malt Whiskey Release No. 025 Aged 43 Months** new American oak, cask no. 148, queen's pale & alba recipe db (**94**) **n23.5** so sensual and attractive with the heather-honey notes purring from the glass, some keen barley notes not that far behind. For a moment or two a vague bourbon-style liquorice is to be had; **t23.5** a spectacular entry followed by a gorgeous mouthfeel: shimmering and salivating first with malt, then that heather honey as on the aroma...and finally a little salty kick; **f23** plenty of bitter chocolate. Still salty too; **b24** the extra months appear to make a telling difference with the honey far more relaxed and settled. Settled in Seattle. Beautifully. *56.1% (112.2 proof). sc. 167 bottles.*

⬥ **Copperworks American Single Malt Whiskey Release No. 026 Aged 31 Months** new American oak, cask no. 200, five malt recipe db (**92**) **n22** creamy and full of caramels; **t23.5** whoomph! Goes up like a national forest during an illegal barbecue: the spices seer into the taste buds as light maple syrup and liquorice try to douse the flames. Slowly a crescendo of spiced chocolate forms...; at times the oils are something to be believed; **f23** despite a nagging low key bitterness, the mix of chocolate-flavoured molasses and spices continue to melt the heart...; **b23.5** one of the spiciest Copperworks I've ever encountered. But the balancing sugars border on magical. *57.4% (114.8 proof). sc. 232 bottles.*

⬥ **Copperworks American Single Malt Whiskey Release No. 027 Aged 31 Months** new American oak, cask no. 205, five malt recipe db (**94.5**) **n23** one of the fattest noses on the malt scene: muscovado sugar, ulmo honey and lashings of vanilla to the fore...; **t23.5** ever licked the remains of a pot of ulmo honey...No? You have now...; **f24** the creamy butterscotch-vanilla blend and ulmo honey embrace the drier, spicier tannins and are easily their match; **b24** malt that is both lush and luscious.... *57.6% (115.2 proof). sc. 230 bottles.*

⬥ **Copperworks American Single Malt Whiskey Release No. 028 Aged 30 Months** new American oak, cask no. 207, five malt recipe db (**93**) **n23** a flicker of liquorice here, hickory there...and malt everywhere...; **t23.5** fabulously estery, the malt goes into mouth-watering ecstasy. The barley is rich and topped with no shortage of marzipan; **f23** bitters slightly in the house style, but the spices and hang-on sugars do a superb countering job; **b23.5** another example of the big jump in quality in the mid to late 20s bottling, to the earlier American cask ones. *58.8% (117.6 proof). sc. 230 bottles.*

⬥ **Copperworks American Single Malt Whiskey Aged 33 Months** new American oak, cask no. 108, five malt recipe db (**84**) **n20 t22.5 f20.5 b21** One very strange beast. A great distance away from Releases 19 and 20, this has some technical, feinty flaws on both the nose and finish that cannot easily be overlooked. However, those extra oils certainly boost up both the intensity and sweetness of the huge malt on delivery. *57% (114 proof). sc. 100 bottles. Proof Washington Distillers Festival release.*

⬥ **Copperworks American Single Malt Whiskey Cask No. 187 Aged 29 Months** new American oak, pale malt recipe db (**94.5**) **n23.5** maybe this is why it;s called Copperworks: there is copper all over this like mint sauce all over a shoulder of lamb. And, my word...it works...! **t24** that slightly metallic sharpness does a great job of offering a spice to the heather-honey that dominates. The barley is profound and juicy; **f23.5** still attractively coppery with a plethora of dark sugars and chocolate...then a nagging bitter note...hmmm; **b23.5** just that little bit of mysterious inherent hop-like bitterness prevents this from going onto a greater score still. But just be thankful for the fabulous. *64% (128 proof). sc. 100 bottles. Proof of Washington Distillers Festival 2019.*

DRY FLY DISTILLING Spokane, Washington.

◈◈ **Dry Fly Straight Bourbon 101 Whiskey Aged 4 Years** bott 12/30/19 db **(88.5) n21.5 t23.5 f21.5 b22** A decent bourbon that pitches on the toffee-mocha side of the wicket with the emphasis on subtlety rather than power. Let down slightly by just a fraction too wide of a cut which undermines the finish. Frustrating, as this is on the cusp of excellence. *50.5% (101 proof).*

◈◈ **Dry Fly Straight Triticale Whiskey Aged 4 Years** bott 11/15/19 db **(89.5) n23.5** make no mistake: this is a great nose. If it has set out to be delicate and complex, then it has succeeded. Anyone who can remember biting into a toffee apple, to be left with that clean, enticing green apple and caramel aroma will appreciate this. There is also a peppery element, but it is every bit as subtle as the fruit and toffee...; **t23** I can count three different layers of sweetness here, each with varying intensity. The delivery is salivating, the grains offering a degree of sweet gristiness before the thin ulmo honey moves in; **f21** there had been signs of bitterness forming from about a third the way in and on the finish, just as the spices try to take hold, they become a little nagging; **b22** one of those frustrating whiskeys where the nose cannot be matched by what follows after, though that would have been a tall order. Please give this one at least ten minutes nosing before tasting.. *45% (90 proof).*

◈◈ **Dry Fly Straight Wheat Whiskey Aged 3 Years** bott 01/20/20 db **(90) n22.5 t23 f22 b22.5** The one thing you must say about this distillery's whiskey is its remarkable consistency of quality. Here again, we have a well-made whiskey with no pretensions of breath-taking greatness, but does what you'd like it to do well. In this case it displays the wheat to good effect, maximising the spices to counter the bready sugars. This one peaks on delivery and displays a languid chewiness to the lightly molassed cream toffee. Impressive. (CV) *45% (90 proof).*

◈◈ **Dry Fly Straight Wheat Whiskey Cask Strength Aged 3 Years** bott 12/09/19 db **(95) n23.5 t24 f23.5 b24** No doubt about it: Dry Fly are making a massive statement with this one! Beautifully distilled and very sympathetically matured, they have hit the big time thanks to the understated complexity and even more quietly spoken enormity. Like their 45% version, there is a bread-like quality to this - on the palate especially. But the charm is all in the molten Demerara sugars mixing it with the kind of fiery spices only wheat whiskey can produce, with all this to the backdrop of as clean and intense wheat as you likely to find this year. A deft oiliness makes for a sensual mouthfeel, the grains are still young enough to induce some major salivation. A whiskey which takes this distillery up another notch and one I hope they use as their benchmark for greater things. Not just superb; this is a true classic (CV) *60% (120 proof).*

◈◈ **O'Danaghers Whiskey American Caledonian Single Potstill Aged 5 Years Single Barrel** db **(88.5) n22 t22.5 f21.5 b22.5** This offers an interesting variation to their Hibernian version (below). By comparison to this plodder, the Hibs bottling is flighty and lively. This appears to rejoice in its lumbering style though, paradoxically, it shews more fruitiness than its lighter, sweeter twin. The oak is offering a tad more tannin and the spices can do battle with a more molassed sweetness. Yet, for all this, the Pot Still style is less pronounced, even cryptic. A big, dense whiskey that needs chewing - and then chewing some more.... *45% (90 proof). sc.*

◈◈ **O'Danaghers Whiskey American Hibernian Triple Distilled Potstill Aged 5 Years Single Barrel** bott 11/23/19 db **(89.5) n22 t23 f22 b22.5** Over a quarter of a century ago, I took on the old guard at Irish Distillers to ensure that the production of Irish Pot Still would not be phased out, or even reduced. It was certainly on their minds. So, it is heart-warming to see, so many years on, a distillery from the Washington State part of Ireland adding to the growing number of pure Pot Still brands. In all honesty, I can't say the not unattractive nose much reminds me of the original stuff. And must also say that the cut has been quite clever here to allow the subtleties of the unmalted grains to shew. The sweet lightly honeyed juiciness on the palate is sheer Dry Fly in style – and for an extended moment or two there is a glimpse of the true Pot Still style, especially when the acacia honey kicks in against a semi-murky, more bitter back drop: a hard trick to pull off. I really hope they keep working at perfecting this. For this is a cracking effort worthy of investigation. "...whiskey in the Celtic tradition from the auld sod" says the label. To be sure. And reviewed by one, an' all... *45% (90 proof). sc.*

WESTLAND DISTILLERY Seattle, Washington.

Westland Distillery cask no. 922 db **(93) n22.5 t24 f23 b23.5** A must grape style sharpness to this on the nose and a much sweeter grist and muscovado sugar on delivery, with everything delivered in stark and concentrated form. Balances out beautifully and helped, like most Westland whiskys, with a rich textured mouthfeel to die for. *61.2% (122.4 proof). sc*

Westland Distillery cask no. 4274 db **(94) n23 t24 f23 b24** Breathtaking use of tannin here. The oak has been pulled and stretched into different shapes, weights and flavours. But it is the praline depth which wins your heart, accompanied by lychee. The last of the four Westlands I tasted for the 2020 Bible and if an American micro has sent me four better and more varied whiskeys on average, then they have escaped my mind. *49.5% (99 proof). sc*

⬧ **Westland Distillery Colere Edition Aged 4 Years** db **(90) n23 t23 f22 b22** A highly perfumed cedary whisky which is never less than full-flavoured. If you are not into big tannins, you might have problems here as you'll find them smeared in abundance all over the nose and very dry finish. The light acacia honey on delivery is probably the one and only concession to softness. *50% (100 proof).*

⬧ **Westland Distillery Garryana 3|1** bott 2018 db **(92.5) n23 t23 f23.5 b23** From the rich, honeyed and oily school of malt. The mouthfeel has a gloss which perfectly reflects the dark sugars to be found on the spicy nose. But the spice, though present, is far more restrained on the palate until it accumulates at the strangely sweet and dry finale. Certainly complex. *56% (112 proof).*

⬧ **Westland Distillery Garryana 4|1** bott 2019 db **(90.5) n22 t22.5 f23 b23** A much slimmer version where, compared to 3/1, they have eschewed the honey and oils for a more dusty, drier tannin and spice take on things. A little molasses thickens the sweetness very late on and helps bring on the even later chocolate. A very subtle whisky. *50% (100 proof).*

Westland Distillery Peat Week Fifth Annual Edition db **(95) n23.5 t24 f23.5 b24** My tasting notes are just about identical to their Fourth Annual Edition. Except this has just a little more stand-alone phenol; and some extra citrus and even raspberry jam has got into the mix. Bravo! *50% (100 proof). nc ncf.*

⬧ **Westland Distillery Peat Week 6th Annual Edition** db **(93) n23.5 t23 f23 .b23.5** A far more youthful nature on both nose and delivery than previous bottlings. And that youth means the peat has a far more solid, chunky persona than before. No stinting on the smoke whatsoever, nor the gristy sugars. Raw and rewarding. *60.4% (120.8 proof).*

Westland Distillery Reverie fig. 1 db **(91) n22.5 t23.5 f22 b23** A beautifully made malt that has no second thoughts about fully embracing the fruitier side of life. Some lovely maple syrup and spice fills the gaps. Salivating and with a top-notch mouthfeel throughout. *50% (100 proof). nc ncf. Distillery Exclusive.*

⬧ **Westland Distillery Single Cask Aged 46 Months** cask no. 3204 db **(94) n23.5 t23.5 f23 b24** A luxurious whisky which makes no attempt to compromise on its depth and richness. A mix of maple syrup and Demerara sugar helps illuminate a fruity character to the sweetness while the tannins are both huge but always kept under control and in overall context. The fact there is no massive age is always evident. But it doesn't really matter. When all the pieces of the jigsaw fit this comfortably together, age is immaterial... *60% (120 proof). sc*

WOODINVILLE WHISKEY CO. Woodinville, Washington.

⬧ **Woodinville Bottled-in-Bond Straight Bourbon Whiskey Pot Distilled** db **(96) n24** the liquorice is borderline punchy, the molasses astride sweet and toasty stools, the small grains busy and buzzy, the honey veering towards orange blossom. And the softness and balance heading towards perfection...; **t24.5** I have just exhaled with a groan of pleasure of spitting the first mouthfull, so immediately complete is this bourbon I could also have groaned from the sheer injustice to having to spit: what a waste! The delivery is equal to almost anything found ten years or younger in Kentucky. The corn oils and ulmo honey have formed an unholy partnership, surely. How else can this be explained? When you finally descend from your fluffy little bourbon cloud to concentrate on what is happening next, you'll find a slow advance of toastiness, more a heather-honey and light molasses mix now with a spring of spices forming into playful creeks around the palate; **f23.5** only on the finish does the very slightest of feint notes become apparent. But this is forgiven, as the extra oils have contributed to overall richness. Now, though, it is time to enjoy the tannin-fed vanillas...; **b24** happy anniversary to unquestionably one of the greatest bourbon distilleries outside Kentucky. The whiskey used here has a maximum 10-year-old age statement. But it isn't so much the age as the stunning layering of this classic bourbon. As always, a joy to taste. *50% (100 proof). 10 Years Anniversary Edition.*

⬧ **Woodinville Cask Strength Straight 100% Rye Whiskey** db **(94.5) n23.5** cleanly distilled so the rye, unmolested, offers its sharp, mildly fruity, Demerara sugar-sweet, firm signature; **t23.5** as it should be: immediately salivating, crisp and firm, there is a genuine crunchiness to the grain: you half expect your teeth to shatter as you chew it; Light liquorice tones reminds you that the tannins are around; **f23.5** the rye seems to echo around the palate while the chocolate moves in for dessert; **b24** when a rye is crisp, salivatingly fruity and offers an enigmatic sweetness, then you know it has done its job. *59.24% (118.48 proof).*

◈ **Woodinville Cask Strength Straight Bourbon Whiskey** cask no. 1528, bott 4/22/20 db **(95.5)** n23.5 wave upon wave of caramel laps gently at the nose. The corn oils are outstanding. A little golden syrup and molasses give a toasted, glossy sweetness. Technically excellent bourbon; t24 what a beautiful delivery, making a nonsense of the 62% abv. This is super-soft, the corn oil acting like shock absorbers and allowing the custard and hickory duet to thrive. Even so, like every great bourbon there is a threat or the actuality of serious toastiness, and it isn't lacking here...; f24 even at the death you are salivating! The small grains have awoken and join the spices to tease; b24 just so staggeringly well made. 61.91% (123.82 proof). sc.

◈ **Woodinville Straight 100% Rye Whiskey Pot Distilled** db **(88)** n22.5 t22 f21.5 b22 An attractive rye, though the grain plays second fiddle to a chalky vanilla lead. Very dry despite the odd heather honey cameo appearance. Do really like the rich copper which infiltrates this, though the distillate isn't up to the usual sky-high standard.. 45% (90 proof).

◈ **Woodinville Straight Bourbon Whiskey Pot Distilled** db **(92.5)** n23.5 such satisfying caramel. A little ulmo honey and hickory adds shape..; t23.5 the house style volley of muted sugars makes for the most pleasant of deliveries. Slowly the hickory and molasses unfurl to take hold; f22 a little dry and bitter as the oils gather. The spices now become quite loud...; b23.5 a charming bourbon that appears to be operating well within its range. I think this is the definition of easy drinking... 45% (90 proof).

◈ **Woodinville Straight Bourbon Whiskey Private Select** cask no. 1953 db **(96.5)** n24.5 oh, just get a load of that kumquat peel and liquorice. One of the most Kentuckian noses outside Kentucky. Though the theme is soft and inviting, there is a fabulous steeliness to the crisp Demerara sugars and intent on the spices; t24 salivating yet toasty on impact, the sugars and toastier tannins go head to head with gusto. The citrus on the nose acts like a bucking bronco between the delivery and midpoint while the house style enveloping corn oils as usual team up with light ulmo honey to form the most soothing balm; f24 vanilla, butterscotch and light molasses create an exit of refined elegance. And it's in no hurry to go...; b24 to put it simply: this is fantastic, flawless bourbon. And, I'd so love to see this follow hard on the heels of a 12 ounce ribeye! Probably because it has taken me longer to analyse this bourbon than it would to fight my way through the steak. It is to my great shame that I have been neither to the Woodinville distillery near Seattle (I was going to visit once, unannounced, but after the dreadful experience of driving through the Canadian border - on the Canadian side, as usual - from Vancouver I hadn't quite lost the will to live, but I certainly wasn't in the right frame of mind for congenial discourse) nor Bern's Steak House in Tampa, a restaurant that has been on my must experience list for 30 years but still eluding a tick. There's only the little matter of a 3,000 mile drive between these two establishments. But once it becomes safe to travel again, after being cooped up in the same place for two months on Covid Lockdown.... just give me a map! 61.6% (123.20 proof). sc. Bottled for Bern's Steak House 2020. ☙

◈ **Woodinville Triple Barrel Blended Whiskey Pot Distilled** bott 9 Feb 20 db **(88.5)** n22 t23 f21 b22.5 Sweet and lush, there is almost a maltiness to this whiskey. As much butterscotch as you can imagine and no shortage of dark sugars, too. Spices are in no hurry to arrive but boost the dry finish when they do. Very pleasant, indeed. 45.5% (91 proof).

West Virginia
SMOOTH AMBLER Greenbrier County, West Virginia.
◈ **Smooth Ambler Big Level Wheated Bourbon** batch 49 db **(91)** n23 have to say that that is one quite brilliant nose: the wheat kicks up a storm of minor spices while the hickory-liquorice spice has a fair bit of muscle attached; t22 a slightly weaker delivery than nose as there are quite a few oils vying to be top dog here, leaving dusky sugars to carry the load; by the midpoint things are starting to make sense; f23.5 so it all about the finish, then. For that is where the grains, corn oils and busy tannin hit maximum harmony. Light spice and hickory on the heather honey afterglow....; b22.5 a really impressive bourbon bursting with depth and personality. 50% (100 proof).

American/Kentucky Whiskey Blends
Ancient Age Preferred Blended Whiskey bott code: L181271517082 **(70)** n18 t19 f16 b17 Remains thin gruel for those looking for the richness of an Ancient Age bourbon. But this is a blend, and a very ordinary one at that. The nose has improved a tad, but the finish falls apart more than it once did. 40% (80 proof).

◈ **Falls Church Distillers Church Whiskey** batch no. 3, used American oak bourbon barrels **(86.5)** n21 t22 f21.5 b22 Pretty attractive, as American blends go. Thin in part, but no stinting on the fuller-bodied liquorice. 40% (80 proof).

Lewis & Clark American Whiskey bott 30 Aug 18, bott code: L1656 003075 **(85.5)** n21 t21 f22 b21.5 A silky Toffee Fest. Thoroughly attractive and enjoyable in its own way, but don't expect any great complexity. 40% (80 proof). BBC Spirits.

Little Book Chapter 02: Noe Simple Task Blended Straight Whiskey (91) n22.5 t23 f22.5 **b23** Very distinctive Beam-like elements which is taking blended American whiskey into higher, more rarified atmosphere. *60.55% (121.1 proof).*

⬦ **Michter's Celebration Sour Mash Whiskey Release No. 3 (96.5)** n24 a nose to make you swoon. This radiates old age like a perfectly cut diamond radiates money. This has been withdrawn from the warehouse at optimum time: there is an equilibrium to the dried kumquat peel the ulmo and manuka honey blend, the high grade – almost pure – vanilla, the lightest of spice prickle attached to the relaxed tannin. Wow...! **t24.5** just about the best delivery of all the whiskies so far this year – and this is number 605. From the very first corn oil-cushioned landing, the flavours explode and then explode again – a series of eruptions that leave you salivating. Following on the nose, that ulmo-manuka mix forms an impressive stage, but now the tannins are far more to be reckoned with than on the nose, the spices noisier but never rowdy, the liquorice deeper, but never without a sugary chaperone. Simply beautiful...; **f23.5** it is here you know that the barrel has been plucked from the warehouse at just the right time. For there is never a trace of bitterness...just a continuing procession of controlled toasty notes. The honey does that rarest of things: it actually carries its bat, making it from the first moment on delivery, to the final drying toasty sunset; **b24.5** I have tasted some pretty average whisky for the last three or four days, my taste buds being assaulted by one sulphur-ruined sherry butt after another. Then, as you begin to wilt and wonder "what is the point?", you come across a whiskey like this. And then you remember. No wonder American whiskey keeps on winning so many awards when they can come up with releases like this. *57.8% (115.6 proof). 277 bottles.* 🏆

Mulholland Distilling American Whiskey (87.5) n21.5 t22.5 f21.5 **b22** Fat, exceptionally sweet and a little monotone. That said, has a kick in the right place and a lovely chewing whiskey. Just needs a tidy up at the finish, a change in flavour stance, a bit of complexity... And, dare I say it? A little drive... *50% (100 proof).*

⬦ **Redwood Empire Lost Monarch A Blend of Straight Whiskies Aged at least 3 Years** bott code: L19 1506 **(92.5)** n24 riddled with rye, this is crisp and sexy in the extreme. Fresh cut apple, a sprinkle of ginger and a ring of tannin begin to emerge; **t23** a slightly confused fusion at first, perhaps because of the early arrival of the oak. But the rye soon puffs out its chest to make its presence felt, though the crispness evident on the nose has been softened by the tannin; oily and toasty, a mix of orange blossom and manuka honeys gives a degree of choreographed restraint; **f22.5** buzzes with restrained spice; **b23** a style of nose I had previously only ever experienced in my own blending lab...for the last 30 years! With the emphasis, inevitably, on the rye, they have done an excellent job of marrying rye and bourbon together to produce a wonderfully emphatic and rich whiskey with no quarter asked or given. Seeing as this whiskey is in honour of the most colossal of the giant redwoods, the hugeness of the whiskey is in perfect keeping, though perhaps a 101 strength might also have added to the controlled enormity. *45%.*

Whisky Jewbilee Straight Rye 5 Years and Straight Bourbon 12 Years (94.5) n23.5 t23.5 f23.5 **b24** Both whiskies comes from the Midwest Grain's fabled Lawrenceburg Indiana distillery which makes the only rye in the US able to stand proud against Buffalo Trace. A rye intense but very unusual whisky which cannot be faulted in any way...well, so few bottles being available apart...; *53% (106 proof). Jewish Whisky Company. 280 Bottles*

Widow Jane Aged 10 Years batch no. 60, bott 2018 db **(94)** n23 t24 f23.5 b23.5 This is one widow that has been married beautifully..... *45.5% (91 proof). ncf.*

Whiskey Distilled From Bourbon Mash

⬦ **Angel's Envy Cask Strength Kentucky Straight Bourbon Whiskey Finished in Port Wine Barrels** bott 2019 db **(87)** n22.5 t22 f21 b21.5 At this strength a grain and grape should be singing from the same hymn sheets, Here they are at war though. I admit I do love the hickory foreground desperately trying to act as peacemaker. An aggressive piece of work, saved by the odd charming moment or two. *61.2% (122.4 proof).*

⬦ **Angel's Envy Kentucky Straight Bourbon Whiskey Finished in Port Wine Barrels** db **(86.5)** n22 t22 f21 b21.5 A curious whiskey, though not with serious presence. There are some standard bourbon markers of note, the liquorice in particular. But the whole deal is eclipsed by a strange sultana stranglehold. Not unattractive. But infuriatingly frustrating as a whiskey as it falls between two stools with minimal harmony. *43.3% (86.6 proof).*

⬦ **Artful Dodger Heaven Hill Bourbon 10 Year Old** port pipe **(81.5)** n20 t21.5 f21 b19 Hard to know how to describe this. The fruit is all over the corn oil, while the tannins, the hickory in particular look ether isolated or lost. Lacks cohesion and balance: a real mess. *59.3%.*

⬦ **Blood Oath Pact No.5 2019 Release** bott 1/17/2019 **(87.5)** n22 t23.5 f20.5 b21.5 The usual glassy feel to the palate, by no means unusual with rum cask finishes with any spirit, dampens the fun on this whiskey that had been distilled from bourbon mash. So it is principally all about the strikingly wonderful delivery, at once sweet and peppery, then broadened in character with lovely chocolate lime candy, all mixed in with powering liquorice. The thin finish is a disappointment by comparison. 49.3% (98.6 proof). *Kentucky straight bourbon whiskey finished in Caribbean rum casks. Lux Row Distillers.*

◈ **Cadée Distillery Deceptivus Bourbon Whiskey** finished in Portuguese Port barrels **(86.5) n21.5 t22 f21 b22** What was once bourbon has been lost in a sea of Demerara sugars and grape. Soft and sweet, it benefits from the volley of spices unleashed at the midway point. *42.5% (85 proof).*

Isaac Bowman Straight Bourbon Finished in Port Barrels bott code: L190390513 db **(90) n22.5 t23 f22 b22.5** Interesting that when Scotch, for instance, is finished in Port, there is a definite pinkish tinge to the final whisky. Not here, though: just an extra degree of richness to the gold. An attractive whisky, amazingly sensual and soft throughout, which loses its bourbon character from the very first sniff. The fact that the wine cask is clean as a nut helps enormously. *46% (92 proof).*

Jim Beam Bourbon Finished in PX Sherry Casks Distiller's Masterpiece db **(66.5) n21.5 t19 f12 b14** An uncompromising dullard of a whiskey with virtually no personality once we get past the one third mark: I'm not sure this even makes it as far as half way. A serious waste of good bourbon, as Jim Beam makes some of the finest in the world without question. But why they should ruin it by putting it in a PX cask is entirely beyond me. Do they not understand that the quality of Scotch whisky has often been compromised by the use of an intensely sweet sherry barrel which allows the OTT sugars to neutralise the complexity of a spirit by gaudily filling in the gaps? It does the same nullifying job here, alas. Certainly it gives it a fruity, plummy, spicy lift on the nose that is limited but not at all unpleasant. And the initial arrival mirrors this big spice and fruit thrust, and even maybe a little rye may come into play. Then after that...tumbleweed. Just a flat line of a whiskey: it is dead. Bereft of life. It is an ex-bourbon. The Scots have been shooting themselves in the foot using these casks for a while, giving bourbon a significant advantage over them. Why Kentuckians would want to emulate their failures defeats me, especially when they have their rivals on the back foot. And, to cap it all...there is a distinct, uncomfortable, frankly unpleasant, dirty buzz of sulphur on the finish...another often fatal weakness of sherry-matured Scotch. A dreadful, flawed finish that haunts you for a long time afterwards, A special award for the most self-defeating nonsensical Kentucky whiskey of the year, surely. And please, may this be an end of this sherry finish nonsense, the glutinous, whiskey-killing PX in particular. NB: Over an hour after having tasted this my taste buds have still not sufficiently recovered to carry on working, so my day's tasting has come to an end. If only the industry could pull itself away from the worthless, navel-gazing hype. And think, instead, what past generations of lifetime bourbon distillers would have done: the Beams, the Lees, the Blantons, the Taylors: they saw greatness in American whiskey with virgin oak. Suddenly, the transitory marketing people in their world of hype and instant experts know better. Yeah. Right... *50% (100 proof).*

◈ **Knaplund Straight Bourbon Whiskey Atlantic Aged** batch no. B201 **(96.5) n24** a curiously salty edge to his rumbustious bourbon. This is rich, full-frontal stuff shewing the standard hickory and honey requirement of a very good bourbon, but sharpened in its presentation. Allow to dry in the glass and you are treated to a spectacular display of heather and ulmo honey; **t24** good grief! This is profound and, again there is a saline drift to this, tough the sugars seems a little more advanced and intense, taking a more cloying maple syrup route; **f24** although it dries, and even gets thicker in body, this succeeds so beautifully because everything is either counter-weighted or staggered. It is an orderly retreat with what seems almost a maltiness at the death. Sublime...; **b24.5** no, it's not your imagination. This really is a salty bourbon! What started life as a pretty decent bourbon, has become more interesting still. Uniquely so! As an experiment, you could say that this was one hell of a success as this is one of the most complex whiskies of 2021... *50% (100 proof). Distilled in the US, aged at the Atlantic sea and bottled in Denmark by Knaplund Distillery.*

Legent Kentucky Straight Bourbon Partially Finished in Wine and Sherry Casks (88.5) n23 t23.5 f20 b22 "East is east and west is west and never the twain shall meet"...well, so wrote my former fellow Savilian, Rudyard Kipling. And I think in the same poem he gave us "a gift for a gift". Well here there has been a gift for a gift and the twain have met, for this is a joint creation by Fred Noe of Jim Beam and Shinji Fukuyo, chief blender at Suntory, Japan. A highly attractive piece, let down very slightly by a finishing note you will never find at Suntory, but no stranger to sherry or wine casks. It certainly ain't bourbon, but who cares? There are some moments even Kipling might have struggled to find the words for... *47% (94 proof).*

Michter's Toasted Barrel Finish Kentucky Straight Bourbon batch no. 18H1191 **(89) n22 t22.5 f22 b22.5** As is so often the case, the extra toasting has resulted in a massive dollop of natural caramels which levels slightly the peaks and troughs. Attractive, but quite restrained. *45.7% (91.4 proof).*

Micther's Toasted Barrel Finish Kentucky Straight Bourbon batch no. 18H1193, bott code: A182751193 **(92.5)** n23 t23.5 f23 b23 A much perkier and altogether more entertaining bottling than 1191, making far better use of both corn and sugars. *45.7% (91.4 proof).*

◇◇◇ **Old Charter Oak French Oak Barrel Aged** bott code: L191610118:38M db **(88)** n23.5 t22 f20.5 b22 I was wondering how they were going to square virgin French oak and the Kentucky climate. And the answer is: with difficulty. Few quercus are quite so quirky as France's: it is like handling TNT on roller skates. As expected, the nose is an enjoyable ejaculation of varied sugary tones, and from that standpoint truly beautiful, if on the sweet side. Less traditional bourbon liquorice, more boiled sugar candy on a warm day. The delivery runs truer to normal bourbon lines, though perhaps here the corn oils and flavours are more elevated than normal. It was the finish I feared for – and not without reason as the bitterness was to be expected and arrived on cue. Still, not often you find blood orange in a bourbon...but there it is! Butch stuff. *46% (92 proof).*

Parker's Heritage Collection 12th Edition Aged 7 Years bourbon finished in orange Curacao barrels db **(87)** n17 t17 f17 b18 Oh, dear. It's whisky, Jim; but not as we know it... *55% (110 proof).*

◇◇◇ **Rebel Yell Kentucky Straight Bourbon** finished in French oak barrels, bott code: A207192107 **(82.5)** n21 t22 f20.5 b19 A dull, unbalanced whiskey (not straight bourbon), where the French oak does what French oak does best: dominate. The entirely avoidable result was something that was probably once very good, now becoming weighed down and lop-sided as the tannins first wipe out the charm of the grains and then any hope of subtle oaky layering. Instead we get a straight race between corn oils, molasses, liquorice and tannin. But never, sadly, shall they mix. *45% (90 proof). Lux Row Distillers.*

◇◇◇ **Rock Town Single Barrel Cognac Cask Bourbon Whiskey Aged 21 Months** 450L cask, cask no. 759 db **(86.5)** n21.5 t22.5 f21.5 b21 Thin and bottled at a time when cask and grain were still struggling to find common ground. At least the delivery has an entertaining tannin surge, accompanied by light cocoa. *578% (115.6 proof). sc.*

◇◇◇ **Woodinville Straight Bourbon Whiskey Finished in Port Casks Pot Distilled** db **(80.5)** n21.5 t21 f19.5 b18.5 Nothing technically wrong with this whiskey, except maybe for a niggardly finish. However, I don't actually understand it. There you have one of the finest bourbon whiskeys made anywhere in the world, and you throw a lush port cover over it. It is like a Klingon Cloaking Device: the whiskey itself has vanished, and now there is fruit from the port and little else besides. I know they say the market demands this. Fine. But all I can see is a total waste of great whiskey. *45% (90 proof).*

Whiskey Distilled From Malt Mash

Battle Cry American Single Malt Whiskey finished in Sauternes wine barrels db **(71)** n18 t19 f16 b18 When even something as magical as a Sauternes cask fails to deal with the fire on the throat and the persistent weaknesses of the spirit, you know it's back to the drawing board. Less Battle Cry: more hara kiri... *46% (92 proof).*

Battle Cry American Single Malt Whiskey finished in oloroso sherry barrels, batch no. 2 db **(80)** n20 t21 f19 b20 An acceptable malt which does little to entertain other than allow the richer notes of the oloroso to show a sweet, fruit cake intensity. Still a bit of flame-thrower late on, though. *46% (92 proof). 625 bottles.*

◇◇◇ **Copperworks American Single Malt Whiskey Release No. 018 Aged 32 Months** new American oak (90%) and Oloroso sherry (10%), five malt & pale malt recipe db **(89)** n22.5 firm spices ricochet around the Demerara sugars; the lightest trace of toasted raisin; t23 big chewy delivery with a mouth-watering kumquat and barley depth; f21.5 just a faint hint of something a little bitter and furry; b22 an attractive malt where the flavours arrive in solid, rather than pastel, shades. *48.5% (97 proof). 1,220 bottles.*

◇◇◇ **Copperworks American Single Malt Whiskey Release No. 029 Aged 31 Months** new American oak, cognac & oloroso casks, full pint, five malt & pale malt recipe db **(83)** n21 t21.5 f20 b20.5 A real mess. Drier than the Gobi desert. Just doesn't work. *50% (100 proof).*

◇◇◇ **Downslope Double Diamond Malt Whiskey Aged 4 Years** Cognac cask finish, cask no. WR-260 db **(87)** n21.5 t22.5 f21 b22 Rather lacks the finesse that their previous Cognac Cask Finish displayed. But at least the juicy barley on delivery has not been taken out of its stride. The odd bit of chocolate lurks, too. *40% (80 proof). sc.*

New Holland Zeppelin Bend Reserve American Single Malt sherry cask finish db **(87)** n22 t21.5 f22 b21.5 My Panama off to the chaps at Zep Bend for finding some outstanding sherry casks to help infuse the most wonderful, succulent grape note to this mouth-filling malt and slow-burning cocoa. Rich fruit cake at its most moist and spicy, though a slight, off-key hop note somewhat paddles against the style and grain. Otherwise, close to being a stunner. *45% (90 proof).*

Uprising American Single Malt Whiskey finished in Pedro Ximenez sherry barrels, batch no. 4 db **(83.5)** n21.5 t21 f20 b21 A hot, mildly aggressive whisky where for once the PX is a force for good by sculpting an intensely rich, sugary grapeyness to fill in the plot holes of the malt itself. *46% (92 proof). 900 bottles.*

◈ **Westward American Single Malt Oregon Stout Cask** new American oak barrels, bott code: L9 067 0015 db (**86**) **n21.5 t22.5 f21 b21** There is a fragmentary moment, just after delivery, when all is right in the world: the malt has blossomed like a rhododendron on steroids, the palate is thick with delightful gristy sugars and light maple syrup....then the darker clouds return. Again, it is in the form of bitterness from the distillate. Technically flawed, but those malty moments, plus some late dark chocolate, which ensures some delicious moments. *45% (90 proof). ncf.*

◈ **Westward American Single Malt Whiskey Single Barrel Selection** Pinot finish Suzor Wines, barrel no. 1+3, bott code: L9 067 0013 db (**83.5**) **n21 t22.5 f19.5 b20.5** If you can't get decent Pinot Noir barrels when based in Oregon, you might as well call it a day. For my money, some of the finest Pinots I've ever encountered came from that State and there is a golden moment on delivery when a charmingly understated fruity richness fills the mouth and thrills the taste buds. However, the Pinot has a bit of a fight on its hands as the base malt stills bears many scars in its distillation, the feints not conceding ground without a fight. *45% (90 proof). ncf.*

Whiskey Distilled From Rye Mash

◈ **Angel's Envy Rye Whiskey Finished in Caribbean Rum Casks** bott 2019 db (**91.5**) **n23.5 t22.5 f22.5 b23** The spiciest and most beautifully balanced of all this style of whisky on the planet, It is like tasting distilled Christmas cake. Indeed, a seasonal whiskey seasoned almost to perfection. Don't see this lasting more than a day on the shelves in Germany...! *50% (100 proof).*

James E. Pepper 1776 Straight Rye Whiskey PX Sherry Finish batch no. PX3 (**72.5**) **n18.5 t19 f17 b18** Fails on so many levels, hard to know where to begin. Flat and overly sweet in part, overly bitter in others. When will this PX finish insanity end? At least it was sulphur free.... *50% (100 proof). ncf.*

◈ **Cadée Distillery Cascadia Rye Whiskey** finished in Portuguese Port barrels (**75**) **n19 t23 f13 b18** While the nose doesn't work – the rye and fruit are never on the same wavelength – the same can't be said for the delivery, which strikes like an iron hand in a velvet glove. Sublime bitter-sweet tones soon moves towards full-blown spices. Loses its way again on the finish, which is a little harsh, bitter and furry. But that's what happens when you deploy sulphur-treated European casks *43.5% (87 proof).*

Cadée Distillery Rye Whiskey (**93**) **n23.5 t23 f23.5 b23** Have to admit, when I tasted this a rye type crossed my mind: then I looked at the label and spotted where it was actually made.... *42% (84 proof). Distilled in Indiana.*

◈ **Grand Traverse Distillery Ole George Rye Whiskey Finished in Maple Syrup Barrels** bott code: 9259 1 438 db (**87**) **n22 t22.5 f21 b21.5** The maple has far less effect than might be envisaged. Certainly no complaints about the delivery and follow-through profile which abounds in both juicy rye notes and enthusiastic spices. The balance elsewhere, though, doesn't hit quite the same high water mark. *50% (100 proof).*

◈ **Grand Traverse Distillery Ole George Rye Whiskey Finished in Sherry Casks** db (**77**) **n20.5 t22.5 f16 b18** Just a word about putting excellent rye into sherry butts. Don't. *50% (100 proof).*

Heaven's Door Straight Rye Whiskey finished in Vosges oak barrels, bott code: 2019/19/11172 (**87.5**) **n22 t23 f21 b21.5** Not entirely sure what the point was of using these secondary barrels for maturation. The visible rye seems very high class. But there is dumbing down on both nose and palate with more seemingly taken away than added late on. Even so, some attractive moments, especially when the rye goes into super-fruity mode. *46% (92 proof).*

◈ **Knaplund Rye Whiskey Atlantic Aged** batch no. 02 (**92**) **n22.5** nothing like the same start lavishness of the bourbon nose. This is more conservative and oak inclined. Indeed, the rye has taken a back seat here; **t22.5** soft and lethargic, this is a smorgasbord of vanilla and ulmo honey notes with more variations than you can wave a pork chop at. Only towards the midpoint do we really get the rye itself making a stand, doused though it is in vanilla; **f23.5** ridiculously gentle and wonderful interplay between rye, the most delicate of spices and that ultra complex vanilla; **b23.5** a whiskey where the whole is bigger than the sum of its parts. Shyly beautiful. *50% (100 proof). Distilled in the US, aged at the Atlantic sea and bottled in Denmark by Knaplund Distillery.*

◈ **Laws Whiskey House Experimental Barrel Rye Whiskey Finished in Sauternes Casks** dist 16 Jan 16, bott 25 Feb 19 db (**68**) **n16 t22 f14 b16** Ignore the nose, which is a chaotic mish-mash of aggressive tones hardly on speaking terms. And the finish, which reveals sulphur in its naggingly unattractive and furry form. But if you must taste this, then concentrate on the delivery alone. For you are given ten seconds of brilliance as the sharp rye grain hits like a laser beam into the sweet fruit. But it is all far too brief. If you play with the type of barrels which have done so much to damage Scotch, then expect to be damaged yourself. *50% (100 proof). ncf. 1,450 bottles*

Micther's Toasted Barrel Finish Kentucky Straight Rye batch no. 18H1329, bott code: A182471329 **(89.5) n22 t23 f22 b22.5** Toasted barrel often equates to greater sugar. And that's what we have here – seemingly to the detriment of the rye. Pleasant but, for rye, a little on the dull side. *54.7% (109.4 proof).*

◈ **Minor Case Straight Rye Whiskey Sherry Cask Finished Aged 24 Months** bott code: 178 19 **(78) n21 t22 f17 b18** Though sherry cask finished, this is dominated on both nose and delivery by all kinds of citrus. Sadly, a bitter and off-key finish (tragically typical of the finishing cask type) undermines the whiskey altogether. *45% (90 proof). Bottled by Limestone Branch Distillery.*

◈ **Obtainium Polish Rye Whiskey** port barrel finish db **(84.5) n22 t21.5 f21 b20** As far as I can see, this is a well-made whiskey. But why Port has been involved I have no idea as the fruit makes a complete mess of the grain. The balance has been severely compromised. *57.45%*

WhistlePig Old World Cask Finish Rye Whiskey Aged 12 Years 100% Oloroso sherry cask finish, bott code: 20190214ADLWT38 **(77.5) n23.5 t22 f15 b17** The back label claims this to be a straight rye whiskey. How can it be if it has spent time in a non-virgin oak cask, ie. Sherry...? This is beginning to grate on me seriously now. And to make matters worse, we have a spoiled whiskey. Initially, the nose is stunning, just twitching with cut glass rye. The delivery is a natural follow on of delicious crisp juiciness and then about halfway in it all starts crumbling. The fabulous rye begins to get lost behind a non-specific cloud, then a tingling bitterness creeps in, the tongue going numb. A problem more associated with Scotch or Irish. Not rye. So you have top class rye, probably the best whiskey style in the world...and you then put this liquid gold into the very worst, most ruinous casks on the planet. I really don't understand what is going on. *43% (86 proof). Bottled for Master of Malt.*

Widow Jane Whiskey Distilled From A Rye Mash Oak & Apple Wood Aged batch no. 13 db **(86) n22 t21.5 f21 b21.5** Sweet, firm, has a few teeth that aren't afraid to nip – and a slight tobacco note on the nose. Plenty to chew on, for sure. *45.5% (91 proof).*

Whiskey Distilled From Wheat Mash

◈ **Laws Whiskey House Experimental Barrel Straight Wheat Whiskey Finished in Curaçao Casks** dist 22 Apr 15, bott 22 Mar 19 db **(84.5) n22 t22.5 f21 b21** So overwhelming is the orange influence, this is not a nose any whiskey lover can take too seriously. That said, the delivery is another matter entirely with a sublime chocolate orange explosion with a fascinating spice sub-plot. The finish bitters out and wanders hopelessly off course. *47.5% (95 proof). ncf. 390 bottles.*

White Dog

Buffalo Trace White Dog Mash #1 bott code: L181550112 **(94) n23 t24 f23 b24** Almost exactly as above: no change, other than being slightly more salivating. But talk about consistent...! *57% (114 proof).*

Buffalo Trace White Dog Rye Mash bott code: L180080113 **(95.5) n23 t24.5 f24 b24** Just so consistent by comparison to the last bottling, though half a mark off for a slight drop in copper contact. If I was ever to be converted to regularly imbibing white spirits, I would drink this – and, for the odd utopian experience, blend of this and the new make from Glen Grant in Scotland. Get those proportions right and this little gin revolution will be a thing of the past... Which reminds me: blending the different Buffalo Trace White Dogs can be a thing of endless fun, and occasional surprises, too...(and something I concocted from those here has already outscored the individual bottlings...!) *57% (114 proof).*

Buffalo Trace White Dog Wheated Mash bott 9065011647M **(94.5) n22.5 t24 f24 b24** An earthier, oiler version with the spices taking their time to arrive but do so at exactly the same moment the sugars begin to open up. A little more chocolate than before, also. *57% (114 proof).*

Other American Whiskey

Breckenridge Colorado Whiskey PX Cask Finish Aged a Minimum of at least Three Years batch no. 2 db **(84.5) n22 t22 f20.5 b20** Some enjoyable early spice amid the fruity, prune-rich soup. But, ultimately, flat as a witch's tit. *45% (90 proof).*

Breckenridge Colorado Whiskey Sauternes Finish Aged a Minimum of at least Three Years batch no.1 db **(82.5) n22 t21.5 f20 b19** Very clean grape with no shortage of over-ripe greengages on display. But it is hard to follow the narrative, as the grape and grain appear to largely cancel the other out. A little furriness at the death? *45% (90 proof).*

◈ **Cadée Distillery Medusa American Whiskey** Finished in Madeira Wine Barrels db **(92.5) n23.5** how can you not be seduced by that marriage of intense spicy tannin, moist ginger cake and cherries? **t23** As soft a landing as falling into a bag of feathers, rather than snakes. The spices appear to be stitched into the velvety fabric **f23** long and a more refined continuation of before; **b23** an almost infinitely huge improvement on the ugly old hag I had in my glass last time I tasted this brand. A disarming softness and controlled sweetness, offset by the late buzzing spice, make for a charming whiskey. *40% (80 proof).*

Cascade Blonde American Whiskey bott code: L8081ZX222 1458 **(85.5) n22 t22 f20.5 b21** An exceptionally easy ride, soft and avoiding any big flavours without ever lacking character. The thin finish apart, abounds with tannin and roasty promise. *40% (80 proof).*

Charbay R5 Lot No. 4 Hop Flavored Aged 28 Months French oak barrels, distilled from Bear Republic Racer 5 IPA db **(72) n17 t19 f18 b18** I'm sure Charbay once did a distillation from a hopped beer which worked agreeably well: I remember it, as it is an unusual occurrence. Most hopped whiskeys (if, indeed they are whiskeys, which I dispute) really don't work. This is one such failure, though there is a pleasant round of chocolate on the delivery. *49.5% (99 proof).*

⬧ **Downslope Double Diamond Whiskey Aged 2 Years** triple casked, Cabernet Sauvignon finish, cask no. 321 db **(81.5) n22 t20.5 f19 b20** The Cab Sauv is all over nose like a 1970s hairpiece. But the fresh fruitiness fails to materialise on the palate which is at times puckeringly tart and towards the end painfully dry and bitter. *40% (80 proof). sc.*

Early Times Kentucky Whisky bott code: A027161143 3125362 **(89) n22.5 t22.5 f21.5 b22.5** The fact they are using what they term on the label as "reused cooperage" means this is Kentucky Whisky as opposed to Kentucky Bourbon, which requires virgin oak (and before you ask, YES, bourbon is a whisky...!). So, while it may not be a mighty fine Kentucky bourbon, brimming as it is with all kinds of liquorice and molasses this is still mighty fine Kentucky whisky...!! *40% (80 proof).*

⬧ **Falls Church Distillers Church Burn** batch no. 1, finished in habanero porter barrels **(79) n19 t19 f21 b20** Way too many tobacco notes on the nose and delivery. Redeems itself slightly late on as the sugars and spices mount. *46% (92 proof).*

⬧ **J Mattingly White House 13 Whiskey (88) n22.5 t23.5 f20.5 b21.5** For the most part an agreeable whiskey which runs out of steam long before the end. The nose and delivery are both charged with deeply attractive classical spiced hickory and liquorice notes impressively sweetened with light molasses. The finish is thin fare by comparison. *68.5% (137 proof).*

⬧ **Knaplund Barrel Select Port Finished Whiskey** barrel no. PFW02, aged 3 years in new American white oak barrels, finished in used 55l port barrels at Knaplund Distillery, Denmark **(89) n22.5** vanilla ice cream with a blackcurrant sauce...; **t22.5** crisp and salivating with the fruit calling every shot. Even a little kiwi fruit at the sharper end of this. Decent, well-weighted, spices make their mark; **f22** back to a butterscotch and blackcurrant tart. A few dark cherries to end the evening...; **b22** I have to say that I really enjoyed this. But there was a nagging feeling in me that the whiskey itself was nowhere to be seen, or had so heavily vanished into the fruit all traces had been lost. Maybe the vanilla and butterscotch were its last remains. But the whisky man inside me always laments at the loss of a whisky within a whisky... *50% (100 proof). sc. 196 bottles.*

⬧ **Michter's Small Batch Original Sour Mash** batch no. 20B203, bott code: A2005800203 **(93) n23** superbly supple as well as subtle spice presence, the major corn attack giving the toastier notes, sugars and spices an oily, rounded feel...; **t23** light heather honey moves towards muscovado sugars. Again the corn surges through and with it comes the toastier notes, though any bitterness is handsomely offset by the healthy honey; **f23.5** very pleasing soft spice sitting comfortably with the corn and light molasses; **b23.5** an exceptionally comfortable ride which goes big on the corn oil. *43% (86 proof).*

⬧ **Micther's Toasted Barrel Finish Kentucky Sour Mash Whiskey** batch no. 19G1244, bott code: A192171244 **(93) n23** I have yet to encounter a toasted barrel finish whiskey that is not pretty much up to its armpits in caramel. That's the extra sugars drawn from the oak, not the fake stuff. And this lives up to expectations. A real throbbing spiciness bodes well for later down the line; **t23.5** fabulously thick delivery, corn oil mingling with natural toffees to make a soft yet sumptuous delivery and follow through. A little small grain fizz really ups the complexity and balance levels; **f23** oh, those wonderful spices and ulmo honey on the corn and caramel...; **b23.5** just such great chewing whisky. Sipping? Forget it! What a great whiskey! And shows batch 1249 just how it should be done. *43% (86 proof).*

⬧ **Michter's Toasted Barrel Finish Kentucky Sour Mash Whiskey** batch no. 19H1249, bott code: A192201249 **(89) n22.5** saturated in caramel, the creamy toffee trumps the delicate and clever spices; **t22** silky soft with thick corn oils mingling with chewy caramel; **f22.5** more complex as the corn dissipates slightly. The spices re-emerge, but it is barely a whisper...; **b22** toasted oak can work with a bourbon, but it is a tough ask to get the balance right. I have yet to encounter such a finish with the natural caramels being raised significantly. And it is here that it is too easy to lose the complexity and the overall direction of the bourbon. Plenty to enjoy, nonetheless. *43% (86 proof).*

◈ **Michter's Unblended American Whiskey** batch no. 20C371, bott code: A2000760371 **(91) n23** a celebration of all things sugary – and, specifically, all things brown sugary...; a lovely layering of gentle hickory softens matters and gives it a distinctive Kentucky aroma; **t22.5** here we go! It's those brown sugars, crisp and melting in the mouth. The liquorice is little more than a nudge and a hint; **f22** elegant; **b23.5** all low key, yet spick and span. A kind of bourbon, but in miniature... 41.7% (83.4 proof).

◈ **Obtainium Light Whiskey** db **(88.5) n21.5 t22.5 f22 b22.5** Curiously, I'm tasting this Light Whiskey entirely in the dark... And I have to say that the fruit-charged delivery is like a blast to the head: massive. A whiskey you can chew until your tongue drops off with a muscovado rich delivery to fair make you wince...in pleasure. Big, brooding...and bloody delicious. Oh, and "light" it most certainly ain't... 67.3% (134.4 proof).

◈ **Sagamore Spirit Brewer's Select Destihl Brewery Imperial Stout Barrel Finish** batch no. 1A **(85) n21.5 t22 f21 b21** Well, if you are looking for something very different, I may have found it for you. At times you feel the rye is about to take off, but then it is gagged while the traditional sharper edges of the grain are filed down and rounded off. Many whiskeys are bitter-sweet. This one is very bitter-slightly sharp. Then very bitter-creamy soft. I think odd would be an accurate and not unkind description. 47.5% (95 proof). Straight rye whiskey finished in Imperial Stout beer barrels.

◈ **Sagamore Spirit Brewer's Select Sierra Nevada Rye Ale Barrel Finish** batch no. 1A **(89) n22.5** the rye takes a dual role of both being slightly shrill and gentle, offering a degree fruitiness that is usually sharp but here dulled into polite sugary sweetness; **t22.5** ah! Rye! The grains announce their charms at three-quarter volume, but always with an eye to a crunchy sub-plot. But the crunch is muted by a waves of creamy vanillas; **f22** silky vanilla with a charming rye tang; **b22** being a massive fan of the Sierra Nevada brewery, I was hoping this would be from a barrel of one of the less hopped beers I sampled there once. And, from the relatively carefree attitude of the rye, it certainly seems to be. Not too much damage to the rye at all. 47.5% (95 proof). Straight rye whiskey finished in rye ale barrels.

◈ **Sagamore Spirit Calvados Finish** batch no. 1A **(95) n23.5** the apple certainly readily attaches itself to the already fruity, crisp "rye" fascinating...and quite well matched. Love the delicate cinnamon sub strata...; **t24** now there is one serious fruitfest! The rye retains its fabulously salivating qualities and is unmistakable in its ability to allow the Demerara sugars to blossom. Meanwhile the apple adds a less brittle yet still well-matched fruitiness; **f23.5** very decent, busy and complex spice (again on the cinnamon spectrum) now as the tannins build; **b24** I am probably moved to say that this is the first specially finished bourbon or rye that I have tasted that actually works...ever! The crisp, sharp fruity element of the Calvados seems a very natural fit for the crisp, sharp fruity element of the grain. I so thoroughly enjoyed this! Bravo! This is sheer class. 50.6% (101.2 proof). A blend of straight rye whiskies.

Sagamore Spirit Cognac Finish batch no. 1A **(86.5) n22.5 t22 f21 b21** The stupendous marzipan on the nose and heather honey delivery apart, too much on the hard, bitter and unyielding side. 52.5% (105 proof).

Sagamore Spirit Sagamore Reserve Moscatel Barrel Finished Whiskey batch no. 1A **(91.5) n23 t23.5 f22 b23** Pretty well balanced with no flavour cul-de-sacs. 50.6% (101.2 proof).

Sagamore Spirit Port Finish batch no. 1C **(90.5) n23.5 t23.5 f21 b22.5** Though not the greatest fan of wine finished American whiskies, this one has got it absolutely spot on. And, thankfully, it doesn't call itself a rye, though that is the base spirit. 50.5% (101 proof).

Sagamore Spirit Sagamore Reserve Vintner's Finish batch no. 1A **(85.5) n22 t22 f20.5 b21** A cumbersome whisky where the fruit strangles the grain but leaves a little too much bitterness hanging around after the super-soft and salivating delivery. 49.2% (98.4 proof).

◈ **Taconic Distillery Mizunara Cask** db **(94) n22.5** the fruit is taking no prisoners at first. Slowly, though, it relaxes to allow a light liquorice note through...; **t24** talk about lush! As on the nose, the fruit has the first say on both the mouthfeel and flavour, with a ulmo-honey softened fruitiness holding fort. Then successive waves of liquorice and hickory knock the door down to allow through the more masculine tannins...; **f23.5** a beautiful fade of fruit-kissed spices. Toasty and comfortably warming...; **b24** no easy matter to make a subtle whiskey out of a cask such as this. But they have succeeded brilliantly. Of its style, as good as I have ever encountered. 53.5% (107 proof).

Wild Turkey Master's Keep Revival Aged 12 to 15 Years batch 001, oloroso sherry cask finish, bott code: LL\GD130911 db **(86.5) n22 t23 f20 b21.5** A boxer's nose: flat. And offers no punch whatsoever. That said, not normally a great fan of this whiskey style. However, this is better than most and the delivery itself offers ten seconds of beauty as a Demerara/rye sharpness is caressed by the fruit. But it is too brief and the weakness in the oloroso is visible late on. 50.5% (101 proof).

Canadian Whisky

The vastness of Canada is legendary. As is the remoteness of much of its land. But anyone who has not yet visited a distillery which sits serenely on the shores of Lake Manitoba more or less bang in the middle of the country and, in early Spring, ventures a few miles out into the wilderness, has really missed a trick.

Because there, just a dozen miles from the remotest distillery of them all, Gimli, you can stand and listen to the ice crack with a clean, primeval crispness unlike any other thing you will have experienced; a sound once heard by the very first hunters who ventured into these uncharted wastes. And hear a distant loon call its lonely, undulating, haunting song, its notes scudding for miles along the ice and vanishing into the snow which surrounds you. Of all the places on the planet, it is the one where you will feel a sensation as close to nature - and your insignificance - as you are likely to find.

It was also a place where I felt that, surely, great whisky should be made. But in the early days of the Gimli distillery there was a feeling of frustration by the blenders who used it. Because they were simply unable to recreate the depth and complexity of the legendary Crown Royal brand it had been built to produce in place of the old, now closed, distilleries to the east. When, in their lab, they tasted the new Crown Royal against the old there were furrowed brows, a slight shaking of heads and an unspoken but unmistakable feeling of hopeless resignation.

To understand why, we have to dispense with the nonsense which appears to have been trotted out by some supposed expert in Canadian whisky or other who has, I have been

advised by quite a few people I meet at my tastings, been writing somewhere that Canada has no history of blending from different distilleries. Certainly that is now the perceived view of many in the country. And it is just plain wrong: only a maniac would write such garbage as fact and completely undersell the provenance of Canadian whisky. Crown Royal, when in its pomp, was a meticulous blending of a number of different whiskies from the Seagram empire and by far the most complex whisky Canada had to offer.

The creases in the furrowed brows deepened as the end of the last century approached. Because the key distilleries of LaSalle, Beupre and Waterloo were yielding the very last of their stocks, especially top quality pure rye, and although the much lighter make of Gimli was of a high standard, they had not yet been able to recreate the all- round complexity as when adding the fruits of so many great distilleries together. The amount of experimentation with yeasts and distilling speeds and cutting times was a wonder to behold. But the race was on: could they, before the final stocks ran dry, produce the diversity of flavours to match the old, classic distilleries which were now not just closed but in some cases demolished?

When I had sat in the LaSalle blending lab for several days in the 1990s and worked my way through the near extinct whiskies in stock I recognised in Beupre a distillery which, had it survived, probably might have been capable of producing something as good, if not better, than anything else on this planet. And it was clear just what a vital contribution it made to Crown Royal's all round magnificence.

So I have monitored the Crown Royal brand with interest, especially since Gimli and the brand was acquired by Diageo some 15 years ago. And anyone doubting that this really was a truly great whisky should have accompanied me when I visited the home of my dear friend the late Mike Smith and worked our way through his astonishing Crown Royal collection which showed how the brand's taste profile had evolved through the ages.

And, at last, it appears all that hard work, all those early days of experimentation and fine tuning at Gimli have paid off. For while the standard Crown Royal brand doesn't yet quite live up to its starry past, they have unleashed upon us a whisky which dazzles, startles and engulfs you in its natural beauty like an early spring morning on Lake Manitoba.

The whisky is called Crown Royal Northern Harvest Rye. It was Jim Murray's World Whisky of the Year 2016: batch L5085 N3 had redefined a nation's whisky.

The fact it should have achieved this at a time when Canadian whisky is at a nadir, with far too many brands dependent on adding too many unacceptable things as flavouring agents, is providential. It shows that keeping the grains at a maximum to be the flavouring agent is the way to define a nation's whisky style: rye whisky by name, rye whisky by nature. So perhaps it is no great surprise that five years on Canada has done it again and pulled off the Whisky Bible World Whisky of the Year for a second time with the 2021 edition. The closest whisky in style to Northern Harvest is Alberta Premium. And when they let this astonishing whisky loose at cask strength there was no stopping it. By anything worldwide.

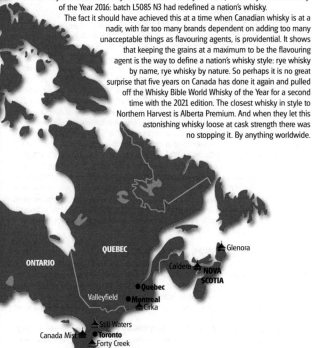

Jim Murray's Whisky Bible Canadian Whisky of the Year Winners

2004	Seagram's VO
2005	Seagram's VO
2006	Alberta Premium
2007	Alberta Premium 25 Years Old
2008	Alberta Premium 25 Years Old
2009	Alberta Premium
2010	Wiser's Red Letter
2011	Crown Royal Special Reserve
2012	Crown Royal Special Reserve
2013	Masterson's 10 Year Old Straight Rye
2014	Masterson's 10 Year Old Straight Rye
2015	Masterson's 10 Year Old Straight Rye
2016	Crown Royal Northern Harvest Rye
2017	Crown Royal Northern Harvest Rye
2018	Crown Royal Northern Harvest Rye
2019	Canadian Club Chronicles: Issue No. 1 41 Year Old
2020	Crown Royal Northern Harvest Rye
2021	Alberta Premium Cask Strength Rye

Canadian Distilleries
BLACK FOX FARM AND DISTILLERY Saskatoon, Saskatchewan. 2015.
⬧ **Black Fox Blended Canadian Whisky** (88) n22 t22.5 f21.5 b22 Both complex, especially on the salivating delivery, and tart. Just a little too bitter on the finish but an agreeable sub-plot of molasses throughout the piece does wonders. 47.1%. nc ncf.

⬧ **Black Fox Cask Finished Canadian Whisky** 100% Avena Sativa grain, port finish (89.5) n23 a lovely, jelly-like quality to the nose. Or, maybe blackcurrant jelly on cold porridge...; t23 the initial delivery is astounding: the oats clamber aboard the palate as though their life depends on it. They are followed by sublime spices. Then a fruity, bitter-ish cloak descends...; f21.5 ...and stays put...; b22 a great oat whisky is usually something to savour, as it is unusual to find as it delicious. You get the feeling that less wine influence would have upped the complexity here considerably. An enjoyable dram which is technically flawless. But you also know that this could have been another three or even four points better... 45.7%. nc ncf.

⬧ **Black Fox Single Grain Canadian Whisky** 100% Triticosecale, virgin oak (92) n23 sharp and busy, as this grain always should be. The tannins are soft with a light red liquorice tone. Soft fruits, too, but a surprising eucalyptus flourish...; t23.5 surprisingly dry delivery, the vanillas surging around the palate, then a slow dawning of that busy grain note noticeable on the nose; f22.5 remains creamy; slightly salty, too...; b23 my interest is always pricked when I see a distillery has chosen this rare grain – a cross between wheat and rye – because when dealt with correctly, it has the propensity to deliver a whisky big in flavour. This doesn't disappoint. 46.3%. nc ncf sc.

CENTRAL CITY BREWERS & DISTILLERS LTD. Surrey, British Columbia. 2013
Lohin McKinnon Chocolate Malt Single Malt Whisky Sauternes barrels db (80) n19 t23 f17 b21 Chocolate malt and Sauternes Barrels...? Sound like something straight out of the Glenmorangie blending lab. To taste, this is truly amazing: the closest thing to liquid Jaffa Cake biscuits I have ever encountered. So orangey...so chocolatey... Sadly, the nose and finish tell their own tale: if you are going to use wine casks from Europe, make sure they have not been sulphur treated first. 43%.

Lohin McKinnon Lightly Peated Single Malt Whisky oloroso sherry barrels db (69.5) n17.5 t19 f16 b17 A polite tip to any micro distillery planning on using European wine casks. Just don't. Or you might end up with a sulphur-ruined disaster like this. 43%.

Lohin McKinnon Muscat Wine Barrel Single Malt Whisky db (78.5) n19 t21.5 f19 b19 A reminder, were it needed, that disappointing wine casks are not just restricted to Spain. 43%.

Lohin McKinnon Niagara Wine Barrel Single Malt Whisky db **(87)** n21.5 t22.5 f21 b22 If memory serves, it was these poor chaps who ended up with malt shewing the dangers of maturing whisky in sherry butts. They have wisely gone closer to home for their wine cask this time: Niagara. And this wasn't a barrel that fell over the Falls (well, I don't think so, anyway) but from one of the local vineyards. And the result is a full-flavoured but eye-watering experience, certainly sulphur free, but with enough under-ripe gooseberry to keep your eyes watered for quite a while. Just needed an extra year or two in cask maybe for a more meaningful relationship between fruit and oak. Tart but very tasty. 43%.

Lohin McKinnon Peated Single Malt Whisky db **(95.5)** n23.5 t24 f23.5 b24.5 This is genuinely top rate, outstandingly distilled and matured peated whisky 43%.

Lohin McKinnon Tequila Barrel Finished Single Malt Whisky db **(92)** n23 t23 f22.5 b23.5 A fascinating and salivating addition to the whisky lexicon. 43%.

Lohin McKinnon Wine Barrel Finished Single Malt Whisky finished in B.C. VQA Okanagan Valley Back Sage Vineyard Pipe wine barrels db **(90.5)** n22 t23 f22.5 b23 Impressive balance here with the fruit doing enough but not too much. 43%.

DEVINE SPIRITS Saanichton, British Columbia. 2007.

Glensaanich Single Malt batch no. 2 db **(86)** n21.5 t22 f21 b21.5 An unexpected tobacco note on the nose mixes it with the malt. The oil wades in to soften, releasing an attractive degree of bruyere honey which covers the slightly more bitter notes with aplomb. 45%.

Glensaanich Single Malt Whisky batch no. 4 db **(88)** n22.5 t23 f20.5 b22 As the first bottling I encountered of this was superb and the second not so, I was curious to see what a pour from the bottle would bring forth this time. Well, something that sits somewhere between the two but with a character all its own. 45%.

Glensaanich Quarter Cask Ancient Grains batch no. 1 db **(91.5)** n23 t23 f22 b23.5 A beautiful little essay in complexity. The varied grains spelt, emmer, einkorn, khorosan and, of course, locally grown organic BC barley have been put together to delicious and fascinating effect. A real entertainer, especially when warmed for a while. 45%.

FORTY CREEK Grimsby, Ontario. 1992.

Forty Creek Confederation Oak Reserve lot no. 1867-L, finished in Canadian wine barrels **(94)** n23 t23.5 f23.5 b24 Forty Creek feel relaxed with this brand and seem to know how to pull the strings for near maximum effect. Very clean, too. 40%.

❖ **Forty Creek Confederation Oak Reserve** lot no. 1867-M, finished in Canadian wine barrels, bott code: BG/HL12447 **(94.5)** n23.5 diced banana and hay lofts. Such a delicate and ethereal quality to this...! t23.5 so sensual on delivery. The mouthfeel is buttery and caressing, the impact of controlled molasses, Dundee fruitcake and madeira cake, too, plus lashing of vanilla is dangerously sexy: a refined joy; f23.5 the oils plus the encroaching tannins make this not only long but fabulously layered for so late in the game. The spices build, as does the chocolate raisin, but never too high; b24 just so charming and elegant. It's the quiet ones you have to watch... 40%.

Forty Creek Copper Pot Reserve bott code: DGIHC12074 **(89.5)** n22.5 big fruity ignition; t23 the house style lushness goes into overdrive, though here the spices arrive a lot earlier and there is far more meaningful laying to the bitter-sweet fruit; f21 just a little tangy and untidy; b23 they have remained very true to style since this brand first hit the shelves. The finish could do with a clean-up, though. 43%.

❖ **Forty Creek Copper Pot Reserve** bott code: DGIHK01391 **(95.5)** n23 fruity, with a tapestry of grape skin and mango chutney; t24 one of the best mouthfeels and deliveries from a Forty Creek for a very long time. Rich with no hints of a cloying nature, then an explosion of complexity as varied cocoa tones, from bitter to milk chocolate captures and controls the fruit so by the midpoint, when the fuller tannins arrive, the layering and complexity hit a delirious height. At times there is a rum-like quality to this; f24 long and drying, the grape skin apparent on the nose now abundant at the death. But it is the slow build of the Old Jamaica chocolate candy so late on that wins your heart; b24.5 another stupendous Canadian from a distillery that has re-found its brilliance. This is the cheese to their Confederation oak chalk... And don't ye knock it all back at once... 43%.

Forty Creek Double Barrel Reserve lot no. 267, finished in once used American bourbon barrels **(87)** n21.5 t22.5 f21 b22 Incredibly lush, but perhaps a tad too incredibly lush. Those caramel notes dominate with too much of a velvet fist, though it does briefly open out for some enjoyable oaky interplay, though all a little muffled. The finish is somewhat off key, alas. 40%.

❖ **Forty Creek Double Barrel Reserve** lot no. 272, finished in once mellowed American bourbon barrels, bott code: DGIIA09007 **(91)** n23 the vaguest bourbon edge to this with a sliver of red liquorice. This sits comfortably with the heather honey and peach; t22 a non-committal delivery, stuck in neutral it appears to take its time to decide in which direction to proceed. Eventually it heads towards a muscovado sugar sweet oiliness and a subtle build up of vanilla and butterscotch; **f23** very happy in its own skin now, the oils have lessened slightly while the layering of sugars and ulmo honey is giving the lightest spice pep; **b23** badly needs the Murray Method to get this one singing in harmony. When it does, just sit back, listen...and be entertained. 40%.

Forty Creek Premium Barrel Select bott code: DGIHC14075 **(81)** n21.5 t22 f18.5 b19 Massively thick on delivery, fruity but, sadly, the sulphur has returned. Decent spice, though. 40%.

⬩ **Forty Creek Premium Barrel Select** bott code: DGIIB11069 **(88.5)** n22 t22.5 f22 b22 A silky soft arrangement which ensures the fruity element always has pride of place and the juicy, marzipan sweetness is controlled. A little dull at the death, spices apart, but this is as friendly as a relatively rich whisky can get. 40%.

GLENORA Glenville, Nova Scotia. 1989.

Glen Breton Rare Aged 10 Years bott 10 db **(89.5)** n22 t23 f22 b22.5. An impressive whisky: one of the best bottlings of this age for some while and showing the malt at full throttle. 43%

HIGHWOOD DISTILLERS High River, Alberta. 1974.

Highwood Distillers Centennial Whisky db **(84.5)** n21.5 t22 f20 b21 Toffee and raisin. Tangy, though the finish dries significantly. 40%.

Highwood Distillers Ninety 5 Year Old Whisky db **(86.5)** n21.5 t22 f21.5 b21.5 A sweet, simplistic whisky which ramps up some very attractive spices. 45%.

Highwood Distillers Ninety 20 Year Old Whisky db **(90)** n23.5 t22.5 f22 b22 This is a grand old man of Canadian whisky yet sprightly and full of very simple Canadian tales... 45%.

Canadian Rockies 10 Year Old **(84.5)** n21.5 t22 f20.5 b20.5. Resplendent in all its chewy one-dimensional caramel. 40%. Taiwan Exclusive.

Canadian Rockies Aged 17 Years bott code: 8127 **(92)** n23 typical light and gentle aroma with the accent on lightly sweetened vanilla; **t23.5** gorgeous mouthfeel: again, light and fragile but enough oils to soften the impact. A mix of light ulmo honey and vanilla, before soft natural caramels and spices fill the mid-ground; **f22**. Delicate even on the finale with the vanillas showing just a little extra tannin; **b23.5** so true to Highwood's style, this could be their signature whisky. Elegant. 50%.

Canadian Rockies 21 Year Old **(88)** n22 so light, with a mix of apple crumble and vanilla ice cream; **t22** soft and simple as you like: vanilla and docile spice; **f22** more of the same...; **b22** not sure you can find a straighter, simpler whisky... 40%. Taiwan Exclusive.

Canadian Rockies Aged 21 Years bott code 8127 **(92.5)** n23 uniquely Highwood, so sexily delicate, almost feeble, is the nose. A kind of apple and rhubarb crumble, as though steaming in the next room with Demerara sugars melting on top; **t23** and those sugars do, indeed, melt in the mouth, too! The lightest oil seems to embolden the lightest spices and vanillas as the whisky continues on its tip-toeing way; **f23** just more of the same...going on longer than might seem possible...; **b23.5** you get the feeling they have got the hang of this whisky now. Has become a classic of its sort in its own right. 46%.

Canadian Rockies 34 Year Old **(92.5)** n23 t23 f23.5 b23 The most fun I've had with a 34-year-old Canadian for quite a few years now...though that was a little hotter than this... 79.3%. Taiwan Exclusive.

THE LIBERTY DISTILLERY Vancouver, British Columbia. 2013.

⬩ **The Liberty Distillery Whiskey Canadian Rye** nbc db **(84.5)** n21 t22 f20.5 b21 Falls into the not uncommon practice in making rye – making the cut too wide. Means the oils are pretty demanding and strangle the grain itself. Not short of spices. 43%.

⬩ **The Liberty Distillery Trust Whiskey Single Grain** nbc db **(87)** n22 t22 f21.5 b21.5 Light bodied and bordering on thin. All kinds of sugars at play alongside the toffee and drying vanillas. Pleasant and untaxing. 40%.

⬩ **The Liberty Distillery Trust Whiskey Southern** nbc db **(89.5)** n22 firm but offers plenty of give on the vanilla and sugars; **t23** formidable spices erupt almost from the first moment. The grain and muscovado sugar form a juicy duet. Soon begins to toast up, deliciously; **f22** toasty spices pulses to the finish line; **b22.5** beautifully distilled with a very even balance between the big oaky spices and rich toffee and dark sugars. 43%.

MACALONEY CALEDONIAN DISTILLERY Victoria, British Columbia. 2016.

⬩ **Macaloney's Caledonian Glenloy Island Single Malt Whisky Whisky Maker's Signature Expression** Kentucky bourbon, re-charred red wine & sherry casks, bott Apr 20 db **(90.5)** n22 a very slight wobble from the cut on first sniff, but tune that out and it's plain sailing as a beautiful ripe date note mingles sumptuously with the malt; **t23** thick almost at times syrupy with a rich mix of malty vanilla and grape forming into a fruity treacle toffee. The salivating juiciness is both a surprise and delight; **f22.5** some beautiful toasty notes, liberally sprinkled with raising and a persistent maltiness makes for glorious and delicately spiced finale. **b23** when in my Canadian base, Victoria, after a day's tasting I'll settle down at my Club to dine on that prince of fish, the halibut, to allow its tender meat and exquisite flavours to massage my tired taste buds. As I was examining Victorian whisky today, but in Lockdown UK rather than British Columbia, I had a halibut here, instead, perfectly baked in enough tin foil to forge a coat of armour...and not allow a single atom of juice to escape. Tasting this malt both before and after the melt-in-the-mouth fish (but certainly not with) was an experience I can thoroughly recommend. This, is by far and away, the best thing from Macaloney's I have tasted this year. *46%. nc ncf. 1,276 bottles.*

◇ **Macaloney's Caledonian Invermallie Island Single Malt Whisky** European Moscatel barrique, cask no. 03, bott May 20 db **(84)** n19 t22.5 f21 b21.5 Can't say this is quite the best exhibition of malt-making I've ever encountered, the nougat notes on the nose not being the most attractive. But picks up on delivery to an extent, where the malt actually becomes quite butch in part but, as it progresses and despite the best attention of the gentle ulmo honey, the balance is never quite there. *46%. nc ncf sc. 287 bottles.*

◇ **Macaloney's Peated Mac Na Braiche Island Single Malt Spirit** nbc, db **(81.5)** n21 t22 f18.5 b20 A head-scratcher of a malt. Whatever happened to the character and personality? It has peat and it comes from a distillery I know, from having sampled from their maturing stock, is not short of characterful and good quality malt. But even allowing for the slightly wide cut, you expect more; instead you appear to get some kind of overwhelming flat-caramel rich fruitiness cancelling out the peat. A bemusing dram. Not unpleasant, save an obvious cask niggle on the finish. Just far, far too dull and ordinary elsewhere. *46%. nc ncf.*

Victoria Caledonian Mac Na Braiche Single Malt Spirit Moscatel white wine 225l barrique made with European oak, nbc, db **(88.5)** n21.5 t22 f22.5 b22.5 A lip-smackingly fulsome malt. The nose suggests a slight untidiness to the distillate, which is pretty normal for a new distillery. But the mix of icing sugar and sultana really makes for a lovely experience once on the palate. *50%. nc ncf sc.*

Victoria Caledonian Mac Na Braiche Single Malt Spirit port wine 225l barrique made with white American oak, nbc, db **(86.5)** n21 t22.5 f22 b21 A pretty clumsy maturing spirit where the profound grapey notes is too big for the malt and oaky body in which it is housed. Trips over itself a bit along the way, though given time this should settle into something substantial. *50%. nc ncf sc.*

Victoria Caledonian Mac Na Braiche Single Malt Spirit shaved, toasted and re-charred red wine 225l barrique made with white American oak, nbc, db **(93)** n22.5 t23 f24 b23.5 Technically, this is too young to be called whisky. The reality in the glass is that whisky is exactly what this is, whether it conforms to the manufactured rigidity of law not. Put it another way: there has been many a technical whisky I have tasted this year and last which, from its performance on the nose and palate, is stretching realms of credulity to its maximum limits. This, however, not only ticks all the boxes required in terms of desirability but adds a few extra on for good measure. There is, it must be said, just a vaguest technical flaw, in that some of the cut here was a bit wider than perfectly desired. But that minor blemish falls by the wayside once the barley begins to kick in and the maple syrup sweetness of the cask merges with the grist. Actually, that extra cut forges the oils which gives that lovely marriage extra body to chew on. The light cocoa and heather honey finale creates a long and delightful send off. A distillery that will need careful nurturing. But on this evidence, it will be worth it. *50%. nc ncf sc.*

PEMBERTON DISTILLERY Pemberton, British Columbia. 2008.

Pemberton Organic Single Malt Whisky 2013 ex-bourbon cask, cask no. 1, dist 11 Apr 13, bott May 17 db **(85.5)** n21 t21.5 f22 b21 I was thinking: "peat and nougat...I've encountered this before". And checking the Bible, I see I have...from Pemberton, with their 2011 bottling! Lots of sweet charm from the grist, but this is a malt which struggles to go to the next step of integration. *44%. nc ncf sc.*

◇ **Pemberton Valley Single Malt Whisky** cask no. 1, 200 litre Four Roses ex-bourbon barrel, dist 20 Sept 10, bott 13 Mar 20 db **(88)** n22 t23 f21 b22 A far slicker malt than their previous expressions over the years. Still a niggling degree of feint. But the barley gives full value for money with a confident and intense performance. Rather like the delicate hickory that flits around the nose and the midpoint. Enjoyable. *44%. nc ncf sc.*

◇ **Pemberton Valley Single Malt Whisky** 120 litre French oak apple brandy cask, dist 22 Nov 14, bott 9 Mar 20 db **(85)** n20.5 t22 f21 b21.5 Doesn't hold back on the flavours. Thick with malty, apple-ey nougat. The last note again underlines the weakness of the cut, but the influence of the oak – and the juicy properties of the barley – are first class. *44%. nc ncf sc.*

◆◆◆ **Pemberton Valley Single Malt Whisky** 200 litre Heaven Hill ex-bourbon barrel, dist 14 Sept 12, bott 13 Mar 20 db **(85.5) n20 t22.5 f21.5 b21.5** Very much in the house style of hairy, bare-chested malt. But not the greatest cut to start out upon and too many feints for satisfaction. *44%. nc ncf sc.*

◆◆◆ **Pemberton Valley Single Malt Whisky** 200 litre Woodford Reserve ex-bourbon barrel, dist 10 Jun 14, bott 9 Mar 20 db **(90) n21.5 t23.5 f22 b23** A much better, more beautifully balanced and rounded malt from Pemberton. Helped by starting off with a much superior spirit than usual. Not perfect, but the extra chocolate nougat notes from the cut fit in very comfortably with the beautifully intense barley. Chewy and delightfully weighted and paced. This is on a different level altogether to anything I have seen from them before. The extra tannin towards the end not only offers weight, but a charming spiciness and depth, too... *44%. nc ncf sc.*

SHELTER POINT DISTILLERY Campbell River, British Columbia. 2011.

Shelter Point Distillery Artisanal Cask Strength Whisky American oak, finished in French oak db **(91) n22.5 t23.5 f22 b23** Looks as though the law in Canada now says you even have to have the barrels from both English and French language... A beautifully complex and intense malt. *54.8%. 1,200 bottles.*

Shelter Point Artisanal Single Malt Whisky Distiller's Select db **(94.5) n23 t24 f23.5 b24** When I initially tasted this distillery's very first maturing cask quite a little while ago now, the evidence provided by the lightly yellowing spirit left me fully confident that they would, with great care, be capable of producing a very high class malt. They have not let me down. This is truly beautiful. *46%. nc ncf.*

◆◆◆ **Shelter Point Double Barreled Single Malt Whisky** finished for 335 days in Quails Gate Pinot Noir cask, bott 2019 db **(89) n22** the unrelentingly dry character of the Quails Gate squeezes this until the malt grains squeak. Tight and mildly foreboding; **t23** at first the delivery is non-committal – the grape and grain in a standoff. Then soft oils break the stranglehold and things relax, the highpoint being the rich fruit and nut chocolate middle amid a surprisingly salivating period; **f21.5** tightens very slightly again, especially at the slightly bitter finish; **b22.5** whisky from one of my favourite Canadian distilleries maturing in a barrel from one of my favourite Pinot Noir winemakers. Quails Gate is usually pretty dry and medium bodied, sometimes a tad heavier. Shelter Point malt is delicate. The balance, as might be expected is patchy. But when it works, it does so beautifully...; *50%. nc ncf.*

Shelter Point Double Barreled Single Malt Whisky French oak finish, bott Jul 18 db **(94) n23.5 t23.5 f23.5 b24** The label kindly informs us that this has spent no less than 1993 hours being finished in French oak. Now, in case you are wondering, that is 83 days: roughly 2 months and 22 days. And if you think they have not been quite specific enough, that is 119,580 minutes. Or, to put it another way, 7,174,800 seconds. Maybe had it been 7,174,801 that might just have done the trick to get those extra points for Canadian whisky of the year.... *50%. nc ncf. 1,131 bottles (That's 28,275 standard 3cl Canadian measures by the way...).*

◆◆◆ **Shelter Point Double Barreled Whisky** finished for 152 days in Quails Gate Old Vines Foch cask, batch no. 4, bott 2019 db **(86) n22 t21 f22 b21** Nowhere near the usual high standard of Shelter Point. The wine has overwhelmed the malt and seldom is there cohesion. Juicy in part with the odd cocoa note. But not an unqualified success. *50%. nc ncf. 1,644 bottles.*

Shelter Point Montfort District Lot 141 batch 2018 db **(92) n22 t23.5 f23 b23.5** Still a little young at crucial moments. But, my word, this whisky from the Oyster River is sexy stuff, indeed... *46%. nc ncf. 1,224 bottles.*

◆◆◆ **Shelter Point Single Cask Quails Gate Old Vines Foch Reserve Finish** bott 2019 db **(84.5) n22 t22.5 f20 b20** A hard, tight whisky which is unforgiving. The fruit seems detached and the whole metallic and tart. The big, juicy flavour delivery apart, fails to find happiness on the palate. *46%. nc ncf sc. 228 bottles. Single Cask Release no. 2.*

◆◆◆ **Shelter Point Single Cask Virgin Oak Finish** db **(95.5) n23.5** you don't have to be much of a whisky detective to spot all the clues on this nose: so choc-a-bloc with racy, intense tannin, there has to be virgin oak involvement somewhere – such a nose can come from nowhere else. And also, there isn't great age involved here, either. Or, rather, there hasn't been a long wedding between the barley and oak. This is flash tannin, like water pouring down rivers after a cloud-burst; **t24** perhaps it took me the fifth mouthful to fully realise just how stunning the experience on the palate is. The layering of the oak is lip-smackingly glorious and offers a gorgeous depth topped by cherry and dark chocolate, plus spices and liquorice: it is not a tune but a symphony; **f23.5** the barley finds its place to shine, intense now, making full use of its relative youth to magnify the impact of the grain; **b24.5** stunningly well distilled and matured: an absolute pearl from the distillery on the Oyster River... *56.8%. nc ncf sc. 174 bottles. Edition no. 3.*

◆◆◆ **Shelter Point Smoke Point Whisky** peat finished, bott 2019 db **(92.5) n23** a distinguished aroma – a kind of cross between barley dust from a filling silo and the lazy but significant peat reek of a recently emptied Islay cask. Youthful, but achingly attractive; **t23** clean, beautifully distilled barley at its most intense, then several layers of light smoke which builds into something heavier and sweeter; **f23** the climate of growing sweetness drops as a sudden vanilla chill sets in while the peat becomes a little sootier; superb oils and a dash of spice lengthens the finale considerably; **b23.5** even the healthy dose of peat injected into this with a high-quality finish can't entirely hide away the youthful nature of this malt. But when something is this fresh, mouth-watering and simply alive, then perhaps you don't want it to. Oh, for the vitality of youth... *55%. nc ncf. 1,044 bottles.*

SHERINGHAM DISTILLERY Sooke, **British Columbia. 2015.**

Sheringham Whisky Red Fife grain: Red Fife/barley, ex-bourbon cask, bott 2019 db **(86) n21.5 t22 f21 b21.5** Not technically a perfect whisky, but the initial produce of new distilleries very seldom are. The usual light feint at work here which adds on the extra oils and slight bitterness on the finish. But provides, also, an attractive chewability to the abundant sweet caramels extracted from an excellent ex-bourbon cask. A work in progress, for sure. But enough good points not to forsake this distillery from Sooke. *45%.*

Sheringham Whisky Woodhaven grain: corn/Red Fife/barley, new American oak cask, bott 2019 db **(91) n23 t23 f22.5 b22.5** A much better made spirit than the bourbon cask bottling, while the virgin oak does no harm whatsoever. A mouth-filling joy of a malt. *45%.*

SPIRIT OF YORK Toronto, **Ontario. 2015.**

Spirit of York 100% Rye db **(93.5) n24.5 t23.5 f22 b23.5** Whoever engineered this, their first-ever whisky bottling, must have been using the Lawrenceburg, Indiana, rye as its blueprint, including virgin oak casks. Matches its intensity and clarity in so many ways, though perhaps not at the death. For a first whisky from Toronto's famous and historic distilling district, the distillers from the Spirit of York should take a bow: this is memorable and authentic stuff distilled, romantically, in part of the old Gooderham and Worts Building...! Toronto is well and truly back on the whisky distilling map... *46% (92 proof).*

STILLWATERS DISTILLERY Concord, **Ontario. 2009.**

Stalk & Barrel 100% Rye Single Cask Whisky **(82.5) n18 t21.5 f22 b21** An ashy, dry rye not helped by the feints. But certainly not short on character, the grain full on and commanding and a layer of heather honey sorting out the required sweetness. Even some wonderful chocolate tones towards the finish. *46%. sc.*

Stalk & Barrel 100% Rye Single Cask Whisky **(86.5) n20 t23 f21.5 b22** Despite the light feintiness, this really does rack up some big rye notes. Rock hard from nose to finish – save for the oils from the wide cut – the delivery and afterglow offer a stupendous degree of grain and spice. Technically not perfect, but worth discovering just for the uncompromising ride. *60.2%. sc.*

Stalk & Barrel Single Malt Whisky **(78) n19 t22 f18 b19** Well, it's malty: you can say that about it. But the feints as well as giving a nougat feel to this, does very little that is positive to the tangy finish. *46%. sc.*

Stalk & Barrel Single Malt Whisky **(84) n19 t22.5 f21.5 b21** Full on malty, chocolate-laden spiced toffee nougat. Once past the so-so nose, becomes pretty enjoyable. *60.2%. sc.*

YUKON BREWING Whitehorse, **Yukon. 1997.**

Two Brewers Yukon Single Malt Release 09 Special Finishes db **(87.5) n22 t22 f21.5 b22** You don't really associate The Yukon with softness, silkiness and all things rather twee. A bit like Michael Palin's lumberjack, surely it should be all masculine and...butch. Well, not this girlie. As sweet and fruity as a bride on her wedding night. *46%. 1,340 bottles.*

Two Brewers Yukon Single Malt Release 10 Classic db **(92) n22.5 t23.5 f23 b23.5** An explosion of flavours on delivery gives lie to the gentle, non-committal, though, clean, nose. Just brilliantly toasty with a breathtaking blend of ulmo honey and molasses. Chewy, salivating and no quarter given as the light liquorice and tannins go in for the kill. *58%. 1,000 bottles.*

Two Brewers Yukon Single Malt Release 14 Innovative db **(89.5) n22.5 t22.5 f22 b22.5** Despite the volley of spices on both nose and delivery, this is still a real soft cutie. The texture is devoid of any gnarled edges, but all kinds of coffee notes percolate through. Like a whisky distilled at the campfire of the Klondike gold rush prospectors. Oh, and they obviously had a sweet tooth, as well. *46%.*

〰 **Two Brewers Yukon Single Malt Release 15 Special Finishes** bott Apr 19 db **(89) n22 t22.5 f22 b22.5** The sharp tanginess of a pastel fruit candy busy at work here. Decent barley layering, but it is playing second fiddle to the fruit...maybe even third to the oak-dominated spice. A real softy on the palate, though. Juicy, refreshing and at times even intriguing. A very friendly malt. *43%. 1,258 bottles.*

⬧ **Two Brewers Yukon Single Malt Release 16 Classic** bott Jun 19 db **(94) n23 t24 f23.5 b23.5** Any lover of Neapolitan ice cream will appreciate this one. The mix of vanilla, raspberry and chocolate make for a dessert-like feel to this beautiful whisky The malt is almost three dimensional in its busy sharpness. And full marks to the distiller, too. What a job he did keeping the cut clean, yet saving enough oils to spread the flavours further and longer than could reasonably be expected. Classic? They're not joking! There's a gem up in them thar Yukon hills... *43%. 1,280 bottles.*

⬧ **Two Brewers Yukon Single Malt Release 17 Innovative** bott Oct 19 db **(87) n21.5 t22 f22 b21.5** Not unattractive. But overly sweet, meaning the balance is skewed. A light icing sugar sweetness appears to have settled in with the grist to slightly over emphasise the juiciness of the barley, while the light feints on shew are left a little too unchecked. An enjoyable malt, but with a few reservations. *46%. 1,090 bottles.*

Canadian Single Rye
CIRKA DISTILLERIES Montréal, Quebec. 2014.

⬧ **Cirka Premier Whisky 93/07 Québécois Réserve Paul Cirka** 3 years in new American oak #3, 5 weeks in Oloroso sherry casks db **(82) n22 t21.5 f19.5 b19** Fantastic to see a new distillery making 100% rye whisky in Canada. It warms the heart! Not so good, though, is to see the grain vanish without trace under an uncompromising blanket of fruit, so the rye's unique qualities cannot be heard and enjoyed. A smattering of sulphur from the oloroso butt does it no favours, either. Still, I look forward to seeing this distillery flourish. It deserves to. *46%. nc ncf.*

Canadian Blended Whisky

Alberta Premium (95.5) n24 t25 f22.5 b24 It has just gone 8am and the Vancouver Island sky is one of clear blue. My windows are open to allow in some chilly, early Spring air and, though only the first week of March, an American robin sits in the arbutus tree, resplendent in its now two-toned leaves, calling for a mate, as it has done since 5.15 this morning, his song blending with the lively trill of the house finches and the doleful, maritime anthem of the gull. It seems the natural environment of Alberta Premium, back here to its rye-studded best after a couple I tasted socially in Canada last year appeared comparatively dull and restrained. I am tasting this from Bottle Lott No L93300197 and it is classic, generating all I expect and now demand. A national treasure. *40%*

⬧ **Alberta Premium Aged 20 Years** db **(72) n19.5 t20.5 f15 b17** Singularly the biggest disappointment of the year. A strange cold tea and tobacco note has infiltrated what is usually the most rock-solid rye in the business. This is my beloved Alberta Premium.... unrecognisable. They have got this so wrong... *42%.*

⬧ **Alberta Premium Cask Strength Rye** bott code: L9212ADB013408:16 db **(97.5) n24.5** a bold but on message aroma, the rye ganging up en-masse, mainly firm and unyielding but just enough spearmint and thinned eucalyptus to ensure complexity levels are satisfied; **t24.5** the delivery should be exhibited at the Museum of Canada because even the smallest mouthful simply ejaculates the most rampant toasty rye notes known to mankind. This is huge, yet the sure-footed elegance of the oaky vanillas and the tannin-stained spices ensure this isn't a one-man show...or do I mean one grain show? A succulence to the oils, balanced perfectly by ulmo and manuka honeys ensure for the most chewable Canadian mouthful possibly ever....and yet this is constantly salivating, from the very first nanosecond ...just how does it do it....? **f24** just lie back and think of the spices...; **b24.5** Truely world-class whisky from possibly the world's most underrated distillery. How can something be so immense yet equally delicate? For any whisky lover on the planet looking for huge but nearly perfectly balanced experience, then here you go. And with rye at its most rampantly beautiful, this is something to truly worship. Daily. *65.1%.* 🏆

Bearface Aged 7 Years Triple Oak Canadian Single Grain ex-bourbon barrels, finished in French oak red wine barrels & Hungarian oak, bott no. H1418W1MH **(88.5) n22 t22.5 f22 b22** About as soft as whisky gets. If they could find a way of tuning out some of the caramel, they'd definitely have a more satisfying whisky. *45.5%.*

⬧ **Bearface One Eleven Series** batch no. 1, nbc **(89) n22** the one part smoked Agave kicks the living shit out of the ten parts of Canadian....which are conspicuous by their absence...; **t23** it's the mouthfeel that really stars here: a genteel oiliness embraces and gently massages. But the balance between bitter-sweet is also pretty impressive. As on the nose, the Mexican influence dominates...; **f22** a light smokiness – almost elements of breakfast bacon...; **b22** OK, this is one very weird Canadian whisky. But is it enjoyable? Well, anyone who says it isn't is telling you a Bearfaced lie... *42.5%. Ten parts Bearface cut with one part Agave Espadin.*

⬧ **Benjamin Chapman 7-Year Whiskey** nbc **(84.5) n21 t 21.5 f21 b21** A pretty straight up and downer with a big, bland emphasis on toffee. Soft, otherwise thin, with some gentle spices kicking in as the oak at last gets a word in. Canadian with an "e". Interesting. *45% (90 proof). 3 Badge Beverage.*

Black Velvet (78) n18 t20 f20 b20. A distinctly off-key nose is compensated for by a rich corn and vanilla kick on the palate. But that famous spice flourish is a distant memory. Another big caramel number. *40%*

Caldera Distilling Hurricane 5 Whisky batch no. 0001 **(87.5) n21.5 t22 f22 b22.** Silky, soft. But lashings of toffee and sugars. Decent spices balance things up a little. *40% (80 proof)*

Canadian Club 100 Proof (89) n21 t23 f22 b23. If you are expecting this to be a high-octane version of the standard CC Premium, you'll be in for a shock. This is a much fruitier dram with an oilier body to absorb the extra strength. An entertaining blend. *50%.*

Canadian Club 100% Rye (92) n23 t23.5 f22.5 b23 Will be interesting to see how this brand develops over the years. Rye is not the easiest grain to get right when blending differing ages and casks with varied histories: it is an art which takes time to perfect. This is a very attractive early bottling, though my money is on it becoming sharper in future vattings as the ability to show the grain above all else becomes more easily understood. Just so wonderful to see another excellent addition to the Canadian whisky lexicon. *40% (80 proof)*

✧ **Canadian Club 1858 Original Blended Canadian Whisky** American oak barrels, bott code: L0042FFB325471529 **(92) n23** a languidly soft and soothingly sweet aroma, golden syrup and spices ensuring a charming complexity; **t23.5** pure silk. The spices arrive immediately to pepper the palate and ensure immediate action. The buttery oils move towards melt-in-the-mouth ulmo honey; **f22.5** long and still lush thanks to the embrace of those fabulous. Vanilla joins forces with the ulmo honey to see off the drier oaky elements; **b23** one of those quiet, understated and criminally underrated whiskies which pays back close scrutiny handsomely. *40%.*

Canadian Club Chairman's Select 100% Rye (81.5) n21 t21.5 f20 b19. A bemusing whisky. The label proudly announces that here we have a whisky made from 100% rye. Great news: a Canadian eagerly anticipated. But the colour – a deep orange – looks a bit suspicious. And those fears prove well founded when the taste buds, as well as the nose, go looking for the rye influence in vain. Instead we have a massive toffee effect, offset by some busy spice. Colouring has ruined many a great whisky...and here we have a painful example. What a waste of good rye... *40%*

Canadian Club Chronicles: Issue No. 1 Water of Windsor Aged 41 Years (97) n24.5 t24 f24 b24.5 Have I had this much fun with a sexy 41-year-old Canadian before? Well, yes I have. But it was a few years back now and it wasn't a whisky. Was the fun we had better? Probably not. It is hard to imagine what could be, as this whisky simply seduces you with the lightness and knowledgeable meaning of its touch, butterfly kissing your taste buds, finding time after time your whisky erogenous zone or g spots ... and then surrendering itself with tender and total submission. *45% (90 proof).*

✧ **Canadian Club Chronicles Aged 42 Years** bott code: L19260IW **(96.5) n24** unquestionably the most delicate nose of the year, the vanillas and icing sugar crust seeming to be only a few atoms thick. Spices trickle and crawl about as though terrified of breaking anything, the tannins stating their age not so much with a whisper but by thought transference. There is also, mysteriously, a light salty note, too: like everything else, nothing like a statement but a hint of a hint...; **t24** it is a caress. A kiss. At most an intimate nibble. Every single note is one of sensuality: a tease, a torment. Again, the vanillas lead the way - once you recognise that's what they are: something akin to ice cream with a butterscotch topping. The sugars, at first light and playful, gather into something much closer to ulmo honey, complete with a glycerine waxiness. This is buttery and about as full as it gets, especially when it thickens into the unique voluptuous beauty of Corsican heather honey...; **f24** just ridiculous. As serene as a whisky gets, and more effortlessly seductive. There are countless types of vanilla and ulmo honey to be getting on with here. Just surrender and let it all wash over you; **b24.5** I have just tasted one of the top ten whiskies of the year for absolute certain. Simply spellbinding. *45% (90 proof). Issue No. 2.* 🏆

Canadian Club Premium (92) n23 t22.5 f23 b23.5. A greatly improved whisky which now finds the fruit fitting into the mix with far more panache than of old. Once a niggardly whisky, often seemingly hell-bent on refusing to enter into any form of complexity: but not now! Great spices in particular. I'm impressed. *40%*

Canadian Five Star Rye Whisky (83) n21 t22 f20 b20. An entirely tame, well behaved Canadian which celebrates the inherent sweetness of the species. That said, the immediate impact on the palate is pretty delicious with a quick, flash explosion of something spicy. But it is the deft, satin-soft mouthfeel which may impress most. *40%*

Canadian Hunter (85.5) n20.5 t21 f22 b22. Remains truly Canadian in style. The toffee has diminished, allowing far more coffee and cocoa to ensure a delightful middle and finish. *40%*

Canadian Mist (78) n19 t20.5 f18.5 b20. Much livelier than previous incarnations despite the inherent, lightly fruited softness. *40%*

Canadian Mist At Least 36 Months Old bott code: L 171007 3133317 **(87.5) n**21.5 **t**22.5 **f**21.5 **b**22 An old-fashioned style of Canadian which is big on the grain and softens out further with the moderate intervention of fruit and caramel. Doesn't stint on the late spice, either. A lovely every day kind of Canadian. *40% (80 proof).*

Canadian Pure Gold (82) n21.5 **t**20.5 **f**20 **b**20. Full-bodied and still a notably lush whisky. The pure gold may have more to do with the caramel than the years in cask but the meat of this whisky still gives you plenty to chew over. I especially enjoy the gradual building of spices. *40%*

Centennial 10 Year Limited Edition (88.5) n21.5 **t**23 **f**22 **b**22. Retains its usual honey-flavoured breakfast cereal style, but the complexity has increased. Busy and charming. *40%*

Century Reserve 8 Years Old Premium (82) n20 **t**21 **f**20 **b**21. Clean vanilla caramel. *40%*

Century Reserve Custom Blend 15 Years Plus (88.5) n21.5 **t**22 **f**23 **b**22. After two days of being ambushed in every direction, or completely steamrollered by Canadian caramel, my tastebuds are in total shock. Caramel kept to an absolute minimum so that it hardly registers at all. Charming and refined drinking. *40%*

Century Reserve 21 Years Old (91.5) n23.5 **t**23 **f**23 **b**22. Quite beautiful, but a spirit that is as likely to appeal to rum lovers as whisky ones. *40%*

Crown Royal (86) n22 **t**23.5 **f**19.5 **b**21. The Crown has spoken and it has been decreed that this once ultra grainy old whisky is taking its massive move to a silky fruitiness as far as it can go. It was certainly looking that way last time out; on this re-taste (and a few I have unofficially tasted) there is now no room for doubt. If you like grape, especially the sweeter variety, you'll love this. The highpoint is the sublime delivery and starburst of spice. The low point? The buzzy, unhappy finale. The Grain Is Dead. Long Live The Grape! *40%*

Crown Royal bott code: 318 B4 2111 **(87.5) n**22 **t**23 **f**21 **b**21.5 Carries on in the same style as above. But at least the finish is a lot happier now with welcome ulmo honey extending further and the spices also working overtime. Still a little residual bitterness shows more work is required but, unquestionably, keep on this course and they'll soon be getting there. *40%*

Crown Royal Black (85) n22 **t**23 **f**18.5 **b**21.5. Not for the squeamish: a Canadian which goes for it with bold strokes from the off which makes it a whisky worth discovering. The finish needs a rethink, though. *45%*

Crown Royal Blender's Select Bourbon Whiskey db **(91) n**22 **t**23.5 **f**22.5 **b**23 A pretty classic Canadian very much in the Crown Royal mould. *44% (88 proof).*

Crown Royal Bourbon Mash Bill bott code: L8 N04 N7 db **(94.5) n**23.5 **t**23.5 **f**23.5 **b**24 Whiskies like this do so much to up the standing of Canadian whisky. *40% (80 proof).*

Crown Royal Cornerstone Blend (85.5) n21 **t**22 **f**21 **b**21.5. Something of a mish-mash, where a bold spiciness appears to try to come to terms with an, at times, random fruity note. One of the most curious aspects of this quite different whisky is the way in which the weight of the body continues to change. Intriguing. *40.3% (80.6 proof)*

Crown Royal DeLuxe (91.5) n23.5 **t**23 **f**22.5 **b**22.5 Some serious blending went into this. Complex. *40% (80 proof)*

Crown Royal Hand Selected Barrel (94.5) n23.5 **t**24 **f**23.5 **b**23.5 If this is a single barrel, it boasts extraordinary layering and complexity *51.5% (103 proof)*

Crown Royal Limited Edition (87) n22 **t**22.5 **f**20.5 **b**22. A much happier and productive blend than before with an attractive degree of complexity but the more bitter elements of the finish have been accentuated. *40%*

Crown Royal Noble Collection 13 Year Old Bourbon Mash bott code: L8037 2S 00108:06 db **(96) n**24.5 **t**24 **f**23.5 **b**24 It's Canadian, Jim: but not as we know it... Deliciously going places where no other Canadian has gone before... *45% (90 proof).*

⬥ **Crown Royal Noble Collection French Oak Cask Finished** bott code: L9 079 2S 001 db **(93.5) n**23.5 not often the nose gets massaged, but that's the feeling you get here as the lazy vanillas, sugars and butterscotch mixes with a curiously yeasty sharpness to greet you...; **t**23.5 typical Canadian silk toffee. But the interspersed heather honey and sticky dates does no harm to the complexity; **f**23 more sweet dates working alongside a delicious tannin buzz, but in the designated style, all is soft and drowsy...; **b**23.5 all the time Crown Royal produce additions to their portmanteau such as this, then the perception of Canadian whisky will continue to rise in the public's esteem. Also, moving away from a dependency on wine casks for a flavour profile is also no bad thing. *40% (80 proof).*

Crown Royal Northern Harvest Rye bott code L5085 N3 **(97.5) n**25 **t**24.5 **f**23.5 **b**24.5 This is the kind of whisky you dream of dropping into your tasting room. Rye, that most eloquent of grains, not just turning up to charm and enthral but to also take us through a routine which reaches new heights of beauty and complexity. To say this is a masterpiece is barely doing it justice. *45%*

⬥ **Crown Royal Northern Harvest Rye** bott code: L5093 N5 **(94.5) n**23.5 ah! From the very first sniff we can see that the rye doesn't sparkle like 24 carat jewels here, as it so often does with this brand. Instead, we have a heavyweight. A dusky aroma thickset with caramel and vanilla, with the grain having to punch its sugary fist through the fatter blanket, spices coming to its aid; **t24** the delivery is at first sharp and salivating, just teeming with all kinds of rye-induced goodies. For a wonderful moment it is brittle and salivating, as it should be. But soon those duller tones depicted on the nose make their presence felt and we are swimming in those promised caramels. The spices, though, keep their shape and intensity; **f23.5** a long finish thanks to some subtle oils, some gentle chocolate presence, but again it is the caramel dominating, though the rye still brings some Demerara sugars into play before the grand finale; **b23.5** a slightly different animal to last year's Canadian champion: this doesn't even begin to match the sharpness and clarity of that batch. This, instead, takes a more intense and enveloping persona. Beautiful in its own way. But not quite in the same league as those cut-glass, ultra-complex bottlings which set it either as the world's best, or at least in the top five. That said...this is still stunning whisky of a sublime standard. Curiously, a Northern Harvest Rye which works better at lower temperatures, rather than benefitting from the Murray Method, as is usually the case. *45% (90 proof).*

Crown Royal Northern Harvest Rye bott code: 095 B1 0247 db **(95.5)** n24 t24 f23.5 b24 Not quite the same beguiling intensity as the batch which once won the Whisky Bible's World Whisky of the Year, but what an absolute salivating treat of a whisky this remains...as sprightly and fresh as any NHR I have tasted yet. *45% (90 proof).*

Crown Royal Northern Harvest Rye bott code: L8 353 N5 **(97)** n25 t24 f23.5 b24.5 Having spent a little while in Canada over the last year, I have had the pleasure of a few stunning Northern Harvest Ryes in that time. But I admit I did a double-take when this bottling turned up in my lab for the official sample tasting. It was by far the darkest example of this brand I had ever seen – and I admit that I feared the worst, as that can often mean the sharp complexity which is the hallmark of a whisky such as this can be compromised. I need not have worried: the glass is almost shattering from the enormity of vivid delights contained therein. A stunning whisky, as usual, but they will have to ensure that the colour returns to its lighter gold, perhaps with slightly younger casks, to guarantee the fresh style remains, as this could easily have become a dullard. This, though, is anything but. *45% (90 proof).*

Crown Royal Reserve bott code: 3046A52219 db **(88)** n22 t23 f21 b22 Not sure if this is complex or just confusing. The excellent moments are as good as the lesser moments are not. 40%.

Crown Royal Special Reserve (96) n24 t24 f24 b24 Complex, well weighted and simply radiant: it is like looking at a perfectly shaped, gossamer clad Deb at a ball. The ryes work astonishingly well here (they appear to be of the malted, ultra-fruity variety) and perhaps to best effect after Alberta Premium, though now it is a hard call between the two. 40%

Crown Royal XR Extra Rare lot no. L7064 N4 **(93.5)** n24 t23 f23 b23.5. Just about identical to the previous bottle above. The only difference is on the finish where the rye, fortified with spice, decides to hang back and battle it out to the death; the toffee and vanilla make a controlled retreat. Either the same bottling with a slightly different stance after a few years in the bottle, or a different one of extraordinary high consistency. 40%

Crown Royal XO (87.5) n22 t21 f22.5 b22. With an XO, one might have hoped for something eXtraOrdinary or at least eXOtic. Instead, we have a Canadian which carried on a little further where their Cask No 16 left off. Always a polite, if rather sweet whisky, it falls into the trap of allowing the Cognac casks a little too much say. Only on the finish, as the spices begin to find channels to flow into, does the character which, for generations, set Crown Royal apart from all other Canadians begin to make itself heard: complexity. 40% WB15/398

Gibson's Finest Aged 12 Years (77) n18 t20 f19 b20. Unlike the Sterling, going backwards rather than forwards. This is way too syrupy, fruity and toffee impacted. Despite the very good spice, almost closer to a liqueur than a true whisky style. 40%

Gibson's Finest Rare Aged 18 Years (95.5) n24 t24.5 f23.5 b23.5 So far ahead of both Sterling and the 12, it is hard to believe they are from the same stable. But make no mistake; this is pure thoroughbred: truly world class. 40%

Gooderham & Worts Four Grain blend no. A.A1129 **(94)** n23 t24 f23.5 b23.5 Four there's a jolly good whisky..worts and all...! 44.4%

Gooderham & Worts Little Trinity Three Grain Blend (94) n23.5 t24 f23 b23.5 Beautifully complex but will still suit those with catholic tastes... 45%. *Ultra-Rare Craft Series.*

⬧⬧⬧ **Heavens Door The Bootleg Series Canadian Whisky 26 Years Old 2019** finished in Japanese Mizunara oak casks **(96)** n24 the Japanese casks – which play only a minor role in most Japanese whisky – thump home here with almost a primitive intensity. The tannins are sharp, but never vicious and form a butterscotch-sweet interplay with drier vanillas and even a hint of lavender on the conservative sugars; **t24** the nose may be angular and stretched, but the delivery propels the corn oils to the fore, accompanied by bold, striking spices – as warm as the deeper molasses notes are earthy and intensely sweet; **f23.5** perhaps the only weakness is a little bitterness as the more intense oaks make their mark, but that is more a contrast against the big sugar surge than any fault-line in the whisky itself.. But a light liquorice note helps carry the considerable load; **b24.5** it thrills me when I see Canadian whisky take on this advanced form of complexity, rather than rely on the false promises of fruit juice. A standing ovation to those responsible for this delightful and star quality Canadian. *55.75% (111.5 proof). 3,797 bottles.*

Hiram Walker Legends Series Guy Lafleur (87.5) **n**21.5 **t**22.5 **f**21.5 **b**22 A kind of classic present day style Canadian with plenty of fruit muscling in on the corn. Easy going and very drinkable. *40%. Legends Whisky Series.*

Hiram Walker Legends Series Lanny McDonald (85) **n**21.5 **t**21.5 **f**21 **b**21 Looks like they are taking a maple leaf out of the Welsh Whisky Company's books by launching whiskies in honour of great fellow countrymen. A friend informs me Lanny McDonald was an ice hockey player. So I suspect he had a touch more personality than this rather sweet straight up and downer. *40%. Legends Whisky Series.*

Hiram Walker Legends Series Wendel Clark (94) **n**23.5 **t**23.5 **f**23 **b**24 Being English, don't know about Wendel Clark being a legend...but this whisky certainly is... *41.6%.*

J.P. Wiser's 18 Year Old db (94) **n**22.5 **t**24 **f**23.5 **b**24 Exceptionally creamy but maintains the required sharpness. *40%.*

J.P. Wiser's 18 Years Old bott code 54SL24 L16341 (94) **n**23 **t**24 **f**23 **b**24 Some great blending here means this is a slight notch up on the bottling above, though the styles are almost identical. Main differences here concern the fruit aspect: more prolific and spicier on the nose and then added moist date on the delivery. Significantly, there is more honey on the longer finish, also. Remains a deliciously rounded and satisfying whisky. *40%.*

J. P. Wiser's 35 Year Old (96) **n**23.5 **t**24 **f**24 **b**24.5 Many, many years ago I tasted Canadian older than this in the blending lab. But I have never seen it before at this age as an official bottling. What I had before me on the lab table could not have engineered this style, so this is as fascinating as it is enjoyable. *50%. Ultra-Rare Craft Series.*

J. P. Wiser's Dissertation (89) **n**22 **t**22 **f**22 **b**22.5 A distinctive and quite different style being handsome, a little rugged but always brooding. *46.1%.*

J.P. Wiser's Double Still Rye (94) **n**23.5 the rye is gorgeously crisp, its natural fruity notes augmented by spearmint; **t**23.5 every bit as salivating and full-flavoured as the nose predicts. Not as crunchy, maybe, until the Demerara sugars ram themselves home. But the spices arrive in the first few moments and continue building until they become quite a force; **f**23.5 long, oily, with that spice still impacting positively; **b**23.5 big, superb rye: a genuine triumph from Wiser's. *43.4%*

J.P. Wiser's Hopped Whisky (77) **n**18 **t**21 **f**19 **b**19. Sorry chaps: one has to draw the line somewhere. But, despite my deep love for great beer, as a whisky this really isn't my kind of thing. Oh, and by the way: been tasting this kind of thing from Germany for the last decade... *40%*

J.P. Wiser's Last Barrels Aged 14 Years (94.5) **n**24.5 **t**23.5 **f**23.5 **b**23.5 You don't need to be pulsing with rye to ensure a complex Canadian of distinction. *45%*

J. P. Wiser's Rye 15 Year Old (89) **n**22 **t**22.5 **f**22.5 **b**22 Doesn't do too much. But what it does do, it does big... *40%.*

J. P. Wiser's Rye Triple Barrel bott code L16331 54SL24 (85.5) **n**22 **t**21.5 **f**21 **b**21 Three types of toffee barrel by the looks of it. Pleasant but lacking complexity. *45%.*

J. P. Wiser's Seasoned Oak Aged 19 Years seasoned 48 months, bott code L18114EW0814 (87.5) **n**22.5 **t**23 **f**20.5 **b**21.5 Some high-octane tannin trumps all, though some rich fruit – moist dates especially - rounds off the peppery oak. Enjoys a glossy, coppery but unravels somewhat at the death with a furry, off-key finale. Some lovely, lilting moments but the balance seems controlled. *48%. Rare Cask Series. Exclusive to the LCBO.*

J.P. Wiser's Triple Barrel (85.5) **n**22 **t**21.5 **f**21 **b**21. The barrels, whatever their number, appear to be no match for the big caramel theme. *40% (80 proof)*

J. P. Wiser's Triple Barrel Aged 10 Years bott code: L17258 (89) **n**22 **t**23 **f**21.5 **b**22.5 The finale apart, this is a celebration of the gentler side of whisky *40%.*

Lot 40 Cask Strength (88.5) **n**23.5 **t**24 **f**20 **b**22 At last! Lot 40 at full strength! You will not read this anywhere (or anything to do with my many whisky creations over the last 25 years as journalists can sometimes be a pathetically narrow-minded and jealous bunch disinclined to tell the true story if it doesn't suit their own agenda) but when I first created the style for Lot 40 a great many years back the first thing I proposed was that it should be a rye at cask strength. The idea was liked in principle but regarded way too radical for its time and dropped. So I helped come up with a weaker but still excellent rye. This is a different style to what I had in mind as the oak gives a slant I would have avoided. But it gladdens my heart to see it nonetheless. *53%. Ultra-Rare Craft Series.*

Lot No. 40 Rye Whisky bott code 54SL24 L16344 (96) **n**24 **t**24 **f**23.5 **b**24.5 Now this is very close to the rye I had in mind when first involved in putting this whisky together the best part of a couple of decades ago. Much more complex and satisfying than the previous re-introduced bottling I encountered...which in itself was magnificent. Here, though, the honey I had originally tried to lasso has been brilliantly recaptured. Happy to admit: this is better than my early efforts. There really is a Lot going on... Classic! *43%*.

Masterson's 10 Year Old Straight Rye Whiskey batch no. 016 **(94) n23 t23 f24 b24** One of the most beautiful finishes to any whisky on the planet this year. *45% (90 proof).*

Pendleton 1910 Aged 12 Years Rye (83) n21 t22 f20 b20. Pleasant enough. But if it wasn't for the small degree of spice pepping up this fruitfest, it would be all rather too predictable. *40%*

Pike Creek (92) n22 t23.5 f23 b23.5 A whisky that is more effect over substance, for this really has to be the softest, silkiest world whisky of 2015. And if you happen to like your taste buds being pampered and chocolate is your thing, this Canadian has your name written all over it. *40%*

Pike Creek French, Hungarian & American oak casks **(89) n23 t22.5 f21.5 b22** You know you have a great nose on your hands when a fly drowns in your whisky even before you get a chance to taste it... Decent stuff keeping your taste buds at full stretch. *45%*.

Pike Creek 10 Years Old finished in port barrels **(80) n21.5 t22.5 f17 b19.** The delivery is the highlight of the show by far as the fruit takes off backed by delicate spices and spongy softness. The nose needs some persuading to get going but when fully warmed, gives a preview of the delivery. The furry finish is a big disappointment, though. *40%*

Pike Creek 10 Year Old Rum Barrels Finish bott code 54SL24 L16174 EW07:30 **(86.5) n22 t22.5 f20 b22** A far happier fellow than the Port finish, for sure – even though the slight furriness on the finale is a bit of a bore. Before reaching that point, though, there is a velvet revolution involving much honey. *42%.*

Pike Creek 21 Year Old Single Malt Cask Finish (87.5) n21 t23.5 f21.5 b21.5 Pleasant and fruity. As silky as you like with a moist date and spiced theme. But, doubtless, through the cask finish, the age and accompanying complexities seems to have been lost in translation somewhere... *45%. Ultra-Rare Craft Series.*

Rich and Rare (79) n20 t20 f20 b19. Simplistic and soft. One for toffee lovers. *40%*

Rich and Rare Reserve (86.5) n19.5 t21 f23.5 b22.5. Actually does what it says on the tin, certainly as to regard the "Rich" bit. But takes off when the finish spices up and even offers some ginger cake on the finale. Lovely stuff. *40%*

Royal Reserve Gold (94.5) n24 t23.5 f23 b24. Retains its position as a classy, classy Canadian that is an essay on balance. Don't confuse this with the much duller standard bottling: this has been moulded in recent years into one of the finest – and among its country's consumers - generally most underrated Canadians on the market. *40%*

Sam Barton Aged 5 Years bott code: L814502B **(86.5) n21 t22 f21.5 b22** A much improved blend of late with a much studier structure after the clean, now classically Canadian nose. Good spice buzz and lots of easy charm. *40%. La Martiniquaise.*

Seagram's Canadian 83 (86.5) n21 t22 f21.5 b22. A vastly improved blend which has drastically cut the caramel to reveal a melt-in-the-mouth, slightly crisp grain. There are some citrusy edges but the buttery vanilla and pleasing bite all go to make for a chic little number. *40%*

Seagram's VO (91) n22 t23.5 f22.5 b23. With a heavy heart I have to announce the king of rye-enriched Canadian, VO, is dead. Long live the corn-dominant VO. Over the years I have seen the old traditional character ebb away: now I have let go and have no option other than to embrace this whisky for what it has become: infinitely better than a couple of years back; not in the same league as a decade ago. But just taking it on face value, credit where credit is due. This is an enjoyably playful affair, full of vanilla-led good intention, corn and complexity. There is even assertive spice when needed and the most delicately fruity edge...though not rye-style. Thoughtfully blended and with no little skill, I am impressed. And look forward to seeing how this develops in future years. A treat which needs time to discover. *40%*

Signal Hill Whisky bott no. 181560932 **(82) n21.5 t21.5 f19 b20** There is no little irony that a hill which dramatically juts 470 feet out of the sea to present one of Canada's most startling and historical points should be represented by a whisky that is so intransigently flat... *40%. ncf.*

Stalk & Barrel Canadian Whisky Blue Blend (91) n22.5 impressive vanilla layering; lovely lime blossom honey sweetness; **t23** silky and salivating, again the honey thread wins the day, this time acacia to the fore; **f22.5** beautiful oils hug every contour, the thin fingers of honey reaching out still to all four corners; **b23** supremely easy-going Canadian. Such a treat. *40%.*

Stalk & Barrel Canadian Whisky Red Blend (84.5) n19 t22 f21.5 b22 Hefty and spicy, the caramel and vanillas dominate Quite a lingering finish. *43%.*

Union 52 (90.5) n23 t23 f22.5 b23 A very different type of Canadian which is as busy as it gets. *40%.*

Western Gold Canadian Whisky (91) n23 t23 f22.5 b22.5. Clean and absolutely classic Canadian: you can't ask for much more, really. *40%*

Scottish Malts

For those of you deciding to take the plunge and head off into the labyrinthine world of Scotch malt whisky, a piece of advice. And that is, be careful who you take your advice from. Because, too often, I hear that you should leave the Islays until you have tackled the featherlight Speysiders and the bolder, weightier Highlanders. This is just complete, patronising nonsense. The only time that rings true is if you are tasting a number of whiskies in one day. Then leave the smoky ones till last, so the lighter chaps get a fair hearing.

I know many people who didn't like whisky until they got a Talisker from Skye inside them, or a Lagavulin to swamp their tastebuds with oily iodine. The fact is, you can take your map of malt whisky, start at any point and head in whichever direction you feel. There are no hard and fast rules. Certainly with over 1,600 tasting notes for Scottish malts here you should have some help in picking where this journey of a lifetime begins.

It is also worth remembering not always to be seduced by age. It is true that many of the highest scores are given to big-aged whiskies. The truth is that the majority of malts, once they have lived beyond 25 years or so, suffer from oak influence rather than benefit. Part of the fun of discovering whiskies is to see how malts from different distilleries perform to age and type of cask. Happy discovering.

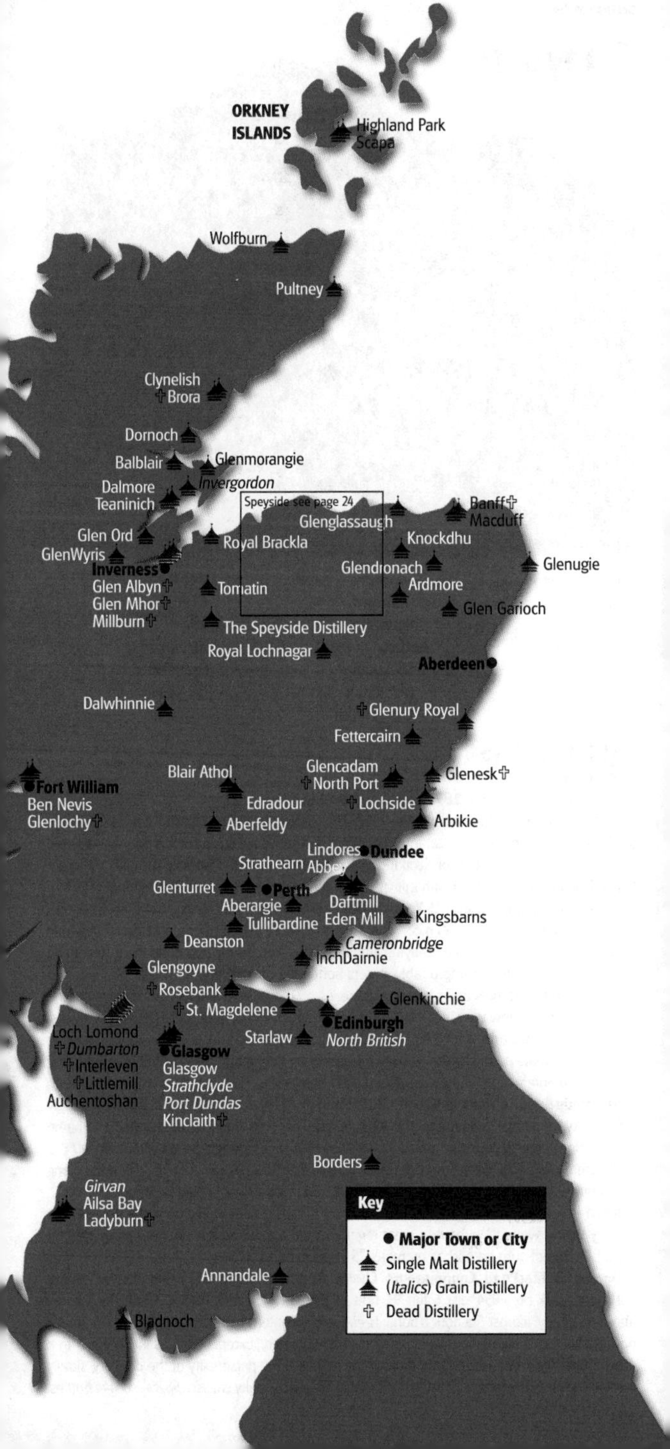

ORKNEY ISLANDS
Highland Park
Scapa

Wolfburn
Pultney

Clynelish
Brora

Dornoch
Balblair Glenmorangie
Dalmore *Invergordon*
Teaninich

Glen Ord
GlenWyris Royal Brackla
Inverness
Glen Albyn Tomatin
Glen Mhor
Millburn
The Speyside Distillery
Royal Lochnagar

Speyside see page 24

Glenglassaugh
Knockdhu
Glendronach
Ardmore
Glen Garioch

Banff
Macduff
Glenugie

Aberdeen

Dalwhinnie

Glenury Royal
Fettercairn

Blair Athol
Glencadam
North Port Glenesk
Edradour Lochside
Aberfeldy Arbikie

Fort William
Ben Nevis
Glenlochy

Lindores
Strathearn Abbey **Dundee**
Glenturret
Aberargie **Perth**
Tullibardine Daftmill
Eden Mill Kingsbarns
Deanston *Cameronbridge*
InchDairnie

Glengoyne
Rosebank
St. Magdelene Glenkinchie
Loch Lomond Starlaw **Edinburgh**
Dumbarton
Interleven *North British*
Littlemill
Auchentoshan **Glasgow**
Glasgow
Strathclyde
Port Dundas
Kinclaith

Borders

Girvan
Ailsa Bay
Ladyburn

Annandale

Bladnoch

Key	
●	**Major Town or City**
▲	Single Malt Distillery
▲	(*Italics*) Grain Distillery
✝	Dead Distillery

Speyside

Distilleries by Town

Dufftown
Glenfiddich
Convalmore
Balvenie
Kininvie
Glendullan

Mortlach
Dufftown
Pittyvaich

Rothes
Speyburn
Glen Grant
Caperdonich

Glenrothes
Glenspey

Keith
Aultmore
Strathmill
Glen Keith
Strathisla

SINGLE MALTS
ABERFELDY

Highlands (Perthshire), 1898. Bacardi. Working.

Aberfeldy Aged 12 Years bott code: L19032249021553 db **(78.5) n20 t20.5 f19 b19** Reduced to 40% and then rammed with caramel for colouring. And we are talking at this age, when tasted in good bourbon casks, one of Scotland's more delightful and effortlessly complex whiskies. Instead we are still presented with this absolute non-event of a bottling. Bewildering. 40%.

◈ **Aberfeldy Guaranteed 15 Years** finished in red wine casks, batch no. 2919, bott code: L19291ZA8021209 db **(92) n22.5** the nose is no more than a caress, and the most gentle and constant comes from an underlying lime note. This sits comfortably amid the toffee apple and spice; **t23** somehow, improbably, it gets softer still on delivery: the malts play peek-a-boo with gentle caramels and salivating grape. As on the nose, the spices are always around somewhere; **f23.5** now we enter into a far more nuanced world, drier and toastier. But always that fruit, that spice and, above all, that caressing softness are constantly to be had; **b23** no easy task to create a whisky that is both exceptionally gentle and delicate but without being bland and uninteresting. They have pulled it off here! 43%.

Aberfeldy Aged 16 Years bott code: L16118ZA805 db **(83.5) n21 t21 f20.5 b21** An astonishingly dull whisky for its age. Sweet and soft for sure, but very little character as it appears to bathe in rich toffee. If you want a safe, pleasant whisky which says very little, here's your dram. 40%.

Aberfeldy Aged 21 Years bott code: L18092ZA803 db **(88) n22 t22.5 f21.5 b22** Poodles along pleasantly but feels like a Fiat Uno engine in what, for this distillery, should be Jaguar XK... 40%.

Aberfeldy Aged 25 Years db **(85) n24 t21 f19 b21.** Just doesn't live up to the nose. When Tommy Dewar wrote, "We have a great regard for old age when it is bottled," as quoted on the label, I'm not sure he had as many as 25 years in mind. 40%.

Gordon & MacPhail Connoisseurs Choice Aberfeldy Aged 25 Years first fill sherry puncheon, cask no. 4054, dist 6 Jun 93, bott 21 Jun 18 **(94.5) n23.5 t24 f23 b24** Don't know about Aberfeldy: almost Aberlour a'bunagh-esque in the intensity of its sherry attack. And make no mistake: this is high grape, faultless oloroso at work here. Except, this presents the fruit in a much more clear, untroubled form, making the power of the personality of the distillery, slowly work its way into the picture which it does thanks to its rich, malty chassis. 58.8%. sc. 444 bottles.

ABERLOUR

Speyside, 1826. Chivas Brothers. Working.

Aberlour 10 Years Old db (87.5) n22.5 t22 f21 b22. Remains a lusty fellow though here nothing like as sherry-cask faultless as before, nor displaying its usual honeyed twinkle. *43%*

Aberlour 12 Years Old Double Cask db (89) n22 t23 f21.5 b22.5 A delicately poised malt which makes as much ado about the two different oak types as it does the fruit-malt balancing act. *40%*

Aberlour 12 Years Old Double Cask Matured db (88.5) n22 t22.5 f22 b22. Voluptuous and mouth-watering in some areas, firmer and less expansive in others. Pretty tasty in all of them. *43%*

Aberlour 12 Years Old Non Chill-Filtered db (87) n22.5 t22 f21 b21.5. There are many excellent facets to this malt, not least the balance between barley and grape and the politeness of the gristy sugars. But a sulphured butt has crept into this one, taking the edge off the excellence and bringing down the score like a cold front drags down the thermometer. *48%. ncf.*

Aberlour 12 Years Old Sherry Cask Matured db (88) n23 t22 f21 b22. Could do with some delicate extra sweetness to take it to the next level. Sophisticated nonetheless. *40%*

Aberlour 15 Years Cuvee Marie d'Ecosse db (91) n22 t24 f22 b23. This always was a deceptive lightweight, and it's got lighter still. It is sold primarily in France, and one can assume only that this is God's way of making amends for that pretentious, over-rated, caramel-ridden rubbish called Cognac they've had to endure. *43%*

Aberlour 15 Year Old Double Cask Matured db (84) n23 t22 f19 b20. Brilliant nose full of vibrant apples and spiced sultana, but then, after a complex, chewy, malt-enriched kick-off, falls surprisingly flat on its face. *40%*

Aberlour 15 Year Old Sherry Finish db (91) n24 t22 f23 b22 Quite unique: freaky, even. Really a whisky to be discovered and ridden. Once you acclimatize, you'll adore it. *43%*

Aberlour 16 Years Old Double Cask Matured traditional oak & sherry oak casks, bott code: L N2 27 2019/05/14 db (88) n22.5 t22 f21.5 b22 None of the dreaded S word here, so well done sherry butts. But this is underpowered in this day and age for the kind of malt it could be. The lack of oils are crucial. *40%.*

Aberlour 18 Years Old db (91) n22 t22 f24 b23 Another high performance distillery age-stated bottling. *43%*

Aberlour 100 Proof db (91) n23 t23 f22 b23. Stunning, sensational whisky, the most extraordinary Speysider of them all...which it was when I wrote those official notes for the bottling back in '97, I think. Other malts have superseded it now, but on re-tasting I stand by those original notes, though I disassociate myself entirely with the rubbish: "In order to savour Aberlour 100 at its best add 1/3 to 1/2 pure water." *57.1%*

Aberlour A'Bunadh Batch No. 57 Spanish Oloroso sherry butts db (81) n20.5 t22.5 f18 b20 Read my notes to batch 47, and we have a similar malt, though here there is not quite so much sparkle on delivery and there may be two rather than one butt at fault. *60.7%. ncf.*

Aberlour A'Bunadh Batch No. 61 Spanish Oloroso sherry butts db (95) n23 t24 f23.5 b24.5 Although matured in 100% sherry butts – and clean, sulphur-free ones at that – one of the most remarkable, and delicious, features of this malt is the bourbon-esque quality of the oak notes mixing in with the grape. Wow! *60.8%. ncf.*

Aberlour A'Bunadh Batch No. 63 Spanish Oloroso sherry butts db (93) n23.5 raspberry and cream Swiss Roll; t24 lush, with ulmo honey in concentrate, before juicy moist date takes control; molasses and mocha moves into midfield. Just the right degree of spices and bite; f22 a long tannin-grape mixed finale displaying just the lightest trace of bittering sulphur; b23.5 slightly lighter than some A'Bunadhs, which holds out well and seemingly clean until trace bitterness arrives. But so much to savour here. *61%. ncf.*

Aberlour Casg Annamh batch no. 0001 db (84.5) n21.5 t22.5 f19 b21.5 The nose is at first promising with nutty sherry tones dominating, then dry but with the most subtle countering muscovado and black cherry sweetness. Then comes the threat of the S word... which is confirmed on the rough, furry finish. The delivery starts with those sugars well into their stride, arriving early and mingling with the spice. Dates and figs represent the fruit with panache. *48%. ncf.*

◈ **eSpirits Shop Selection Aberlour 24 Year Old** bourbon hogshead, dist 1995, bott 2019 (94.5) n24 t24 f23 b23.5 Proof, were it needed, that the last thing Aberlour requires to underline its credentials are sherry butts. This top quality cask allows the gooseberries and greengages to present something a little special on the nose. And then the creamiest, most intense barley turns into a near foaming tirade of salivating, grassy barley and butterscotch. The finish is pretty quiet by comparison, concentrating on the salty vanillas. What a no-holds-barred experience! *61.3%. sc. 139 bottles. 10 Years of Dailydram.com.*

Liquid Treasures 10th Anniversary Aberlour 26 Year Old sherry hogshead, dist 1992, bott 2019 (86.5) n22.5 t22 f21 b21 A pithy malt in both senses which reaches into its drier, spicier fruitier side, but not much inclined to go any further. *51.9%. sc. 101 bottles.*

⟨⟨⟨ **The Perfect Fifth Aberlour 1989** cask no. 11050 **(96.5) n24** a meandering elegance and surprising degree of weight, too, with the most charming and gentle smokiness drifting around in very old-fashioned Speyside style. A classic exhibition of oak and barley interplay: perfect balance and respect for the other. There is even a surprise fruit note of sharp passion fruit: where the hell did that come from...? Could nose this all day, if I had the time...; **t24** right: so, does this complexity on the nose transfer across to the palate...? Oh, my word it certainly does! The delivery is seemingly choreographed, the malt of varied intensities – sometimes a little sharp (that passion fruit, again?), sometimes almost gristy sweet; sometimes ethereal, sometimes weightier as that minor phenol makes the most subtle of impacts - dancing across the palate without an off-note in the world; **f24** light butterscotch, lighter barley but still tan peek-a-boo smoke adding the telling late weight and gently fizzing spices for good measure. Oh, and some very late heather-honey, too, which is pretty unusual at this very late stage...; **b24.5** this malt really has pure star quality. Elegant doesn't do it justice. If you find this in a shop, snap their bloody hands off: this is Scotch malt whisky at its very best! *51.9%. nc ncf sc.* 🏆

Scotch Malt Whisky Society Cask 54.75 16 Year Old 2nd fill toasted hogshead, dist 2 Oct 02 **(94.5) n23.5 t23.5 f23.5 b24** It is so good to again find an Aberlour free of sherry, as used to be the case 30 years ago. Here, you can see clearly just how beautiful this whisky is naked. It was my choice as an outside bet for a stunner for my 750th whisky of this 2020 Bible. I have not been let down! *59.8%. sc.*

ABHAINN DEARG
Highlands (Outer Hebrides), 2008. Marko Tayburn. Working.

Abhainn Dearg New Make db **(92.5) n23 t23 f23.5 b23.** Exceptionally well made with no feints and no waste, either. Oddly salty – possibly the saltiest new make I have encountered, and can think of no reason why it should be – with excellent weight as some extra copper from the new still takes hold. Given a good cask, no reason this impressive new born son of the Outer Hebrides won't go on to become something significant. *67%*

AILSA BAY
Lowland, 2007. William Grant & Sons. Working.

Ailsa Bay db **(92.5) n23.5 t23.5 f22.5 b23** I remember years back being told they wanted to make an occasional peaty malt at this new distillery different in style to Islay's. They have been only marginally successful: only the finish gives the game away. But they have certainly matched the island when it comes to the average high quality. A resounding success of a first effort, though I'd like to see the finish offer a little more than it currently does. Early days, though. *48.9%.*

ALLT-Á-BHAINNE
Speyside, 1975. Chivas Brothers. Working.

⟨⟨⟨ **Berry Bros & Rudd Allt-á-Bhainne 23 Year Old** cask no. 125314, dist 1995, bott 2019 **(95) n24** not far off the perfect Speyside nose: intensely malty but always relaxed, citrussy without the fruit overtaking the grain and a touch of smoke, barely perceptible but adding the necessary ballast. Glorious...; **t24** after a nose like that, the delivery has to be a livewire full of juicy barley, mixed honeys and citrus. And it is. Beautifully salivating and mouth-cleansing, towards the late middle the vaguest smoke and spice begin to emerge; the texture holds surprisingly deft oils and weight; **f23** the spices continue their oscillations; **b24** I still smile when I think of conversations I held, long before this whisky was ever made, with blenders who preferred to use this distillery's malt at very young ages, especially 3- to 5-years-old because they felt it was a whisky not best suited to great age. This is coming up for nearly 25 years in cask, and there is not a wrinkle, not a single blemish. Superb! *52.7%. nc ncf sc.*

⟨⟨⟨ **Old Malt Cask Allt A'Bhainne Aged 27 Years** refill hogshead, cask no. 16942, dist May 92, bott Oct 19 **(94) n23** gorgeous moist marzipan with acacia honey and barley juice; **t23.5** the kind of delivery that makes you wonder why this distillery is not more widely appreciated: classic Speyside flightiness but with a remarkable degree of intensity to the slightly gristy barley; the spices make an announcement at the midpoint...; **f23.5**...and decide they are there to stay. Brilliant layering to the vanilla-led tannin, weaving pretty patterns with the concentrated Malteser candy; the oils cling on gamely ensuing a fabulously long finish; **b24** class in a glass. *50%. nc ncf sc. 256 bottles.*

The Whisky Chamber Allt-A-Bhainne 9 Years Old 2009 Amarone cask **(83) n21.5 t22 f19.5 b20** The trouble with the effects of an all-consuming wine cask which dramatically sweetens up the whisky, is that when there is a bitter, off-key note on the finish, as is the case here, that comes through even more loudly... *60.4%. sc.*

ANNANDALE

Lowlands, 2014. Annandale Distillery Company Ltd. Working.

꿈 **Annandale Founders' Collection Man O'Words 2016** American oak hogshead, cask no. 588 db (80) n20 t21.5 f18.5 b20 Until now they have timed, chosen and balanced their barrels with almost uncanny and certainly unerring brilliance. Not this time. Here the youth has been amplified to slightly ill-effect, giving this a vague belligerence. Add to that casks which are decidedly unhappy and we have a bottling that does this excellent distillery a grave disservice. 61.4%. sc.

꿈 **Annandale Founders' Selection Man O'Swords 2016** Spanish oak hogshead, cask no. 544 db (89) n22 the phenols have a young Marlon Brando quality. And believe me: this is very young, raw and seemingly angry...; t23 didn't quite expect that! The arrival is a sublime mix of light oils, intense malt and then a puckering smokiness; so soft and embracing...where did this come from...? f23 haphazard, borderline insane with the peat lurching around as though high on something stronger than alcohol. A little surprise hickory emerges...but then surprises are what this whisky does best...; b22.5 trying to control the goings on between peat and wine cask on a very young malt is like trying to herd cats. Both elements do as they please, whenever they want. However, sometimes they just happen to hit the right pitch at the right time, and a little magic happens. More, though, by luck than judgement... 61.1%. sc.

Annandale Man O' Sword cask no. 100, dist 2014 db (92.5) n23.5 t23 f21.5 b23.5 The strangest thing...I nosed this and thought: Jim Swan. This delightful style has the late, great whisky consultant's finger prints all over it. A young malt from a brand new distillery already punching way above its weight age-wise and in terms of complexity. Welcome to the whisky world, Annandale. And what a worthy addition you have already become. Now you just have to keep up this standard: no pressure at all... 61.6%. sc. 256 bottles.

Annandale Man O' Sword Smoulderingly Smoky once-used ex bourbon cask, cask no. 470, dist 2015 db (96.5) n24 t24.5 f23.5 b24.5 Make no mistake: new distillery or no, this is fabulously and truly faultlessly made and brilliantly matured whisky which allows every last element of the distillery's personality to be seen. What a genuine treat! What an immense start to such a new distillery! 60.2%. sc. 271 bottles.

Annandale Man O' Words cask no. 140, dist 2014 db (89.5) n22.5 t22.5 f22 b22.5 A malty delight. Had been meaning to take in Annan Athletic FC and Annandale Distillery over the last four years but my diary just wouldn't allow it. Somehow I have to make it happen. This distillery promises great things. 61.6%. sc. 273 bottles.

Annandale Man O' Words once-used ex bourbon cask, cask no. 149, dist 2015 db (94) n23 t23.5 f23.5 b24 A few months ago I was doing some quality control checks at a warehouse in Scotland and there, much to my surprise, were a whole bunch of newly filled, quietly maturing Annandale casks. You have no idea how much I wanted to take a break from my designated work to sneakily crack open a few of those Lowland barrels to see how they were getting on. I think I should arrange a return visit... Oh, and good people of Annandale, - congratulations and thank you for bottling from ex-bourbon cask. Because we can see the sheer beauty of the malt you are making, something I could not say if it was hidden under (usually faulty) wine casks or obliterated entirely by bloody PX, the scourge of world whisky today. 61%. sc. 268 bottles.

꿈 **Annandale Vintage Man O'Words 2015** once used ex-bourbon cask, cask no. 150 db (96) n24 as though concentrated grist, has squeezed a near perfect degree of lime juice, added a just-so amount of freshly cut grass. How can a whisky this young be so hypnotic on the nose...? t24 and now it is the mouthfeel which blows you away. Forget about the 61.6%. With the Murray Method the malt simply purrs onto the taste buds, the intensity of the grain growing, its youth charmingly met by sympathetic vanillas form the oak... and all this couched by a canoodling oiliness which retains every last atom of the gristy sugars for as long as possible; f23.5 spicy vanilla tingle. The malt carries its outstanding work until a late milk chocolate note signs the finale off with a flourish; b24.5 considering this is a 5-y-o whisky only, I think we are going to have to consider the possibility that we have a truly world-class distillery in our midst... So beautifully made and matured, the age seems almost irrelevant. The malt is absolutely immaculate: no malt should be quite this good as this still tender age...! 61.6%. sc. ♈

꿈 **The Whisky Chamber Annandale 4 Jahre 2015** bourbon cask (95) n24 youthful, certainly. But, so classy. At this age there is a certain balance between drier peat, youthful malt and the first budding signs of tannin that reveals a top-grade distillate in a very good bourbon cask. And this has it...; t23.5 fluting barley and then a slow but meaningful gathering of peat. As on the nose, the dosage and pace of the elements, as well as the lightly clinging oils, are exemplary; f23.5 I was expecting a new-makey sign off...and it hasn't arrived. Young, yes. But the citrus and barley sit beautifully with the now gently spiced, pulsing phenol b24 what can you say about a 4-year-old? Except that you can ask nothing more it than what you get here. Yep, 95 points for a 4-year-old. Ridiculous! Though it is worth every single mark... 59.1%. sc.

ARDBEG

Islay, 1815. Glenmorangie Plc. Working.

Ardbeg 10 Years Old db (97) n24 t24 f24 b25 Like when you usually come across something that goes down so beautifully and with such a nimble touch and disarming allure, just close your eyes and enjoy... 46%

Ardbeg 10 bottling mark L10 152 db (95) n24.5 t23.5 f23.5 b23.5 A bigger than normal version, but still wonderfully delicate. Fabulous and faultless. 46%. *Canadian market bottling in English and French dual language label.*

Ardbeg 17 Years Old earlier bottlings db (92) n23 t22 f23 b24. OK, I admit I had a big hand in this, creating it with the help of Glenmorangie Plc's John Smith. It was designed to take the weight off the better vintages of Ardbeg whilst ensuring a constant supply around the world. Certainly one of the more subtle expressions you are likely to find, though criticised by some for not being peaty enough. As the whisky's creator, all I can say is they are missing the point. 40%

Ardbeg 17 Years Old later bottlings db (90) n22 t23 f22 b23. The peat has all but vanished and cannot really be compared to the original 17-year-old: it's a bit like tasting a Macallan without the sherry: fascinating to see the naked body underneath, and certainly more of a turn on. Peat or no peat, great whisky by any standards. 40%

Ardbeg 19 Years Old db (93) n23 lower than usual phenols drift dream-like away from the glass. Look carefully and you'll find that lightly salted Digestive biscuit tannins enjoy the same foothold and the citrus has its usual seat at the table; t23 that biscuit saltiness acts as a brief spur to ramp up the early juice levels. But is fleeting and the whole dries quickly as the powdery phenols assert themselves; f23.5 the oils have thinned but have enough purchase to ensure the minty chocolate on an equal footing with the friendly phenols; b23.5 one of the sensuously understated Ardbegs that could be found in style (though with a different peat imprint) from time to time during the 1960s. 46.2%.

⟐ **Ardbeg 19 Years Old 2020 Release** db (89) n21 unusually untidy for Ardbeg. Attractive saline notes but the phenols are uneven to the point of being discordant; t23 that's much better! A quite thick set malty-smokiness drifts off towards the toasty sugars. For a moment there is an air of Ardbeg normality as the light vanillas pulse; f22.5 all understated and full of trickery. Vague minty notes blossom on the light heather-honey phenol. The oak sticks to that salty tang... and tang is the right word...; b22.5 pretty much OK and enjoyable despite the slight mess on the nose and mildly odd landing. But not sure when just OK was acceptable for Ardbeg... 46%.

Ardbeg 20 Something db (96.5) n24 t24 f24 b24.5 Such mastery over the phenols...such elegance! It is though the whisky was distilled from gossamer... 46%.

Ardbeg 21 Years Old db (96.5) n24 t24 f24 b24.5 Tap into Ardbeg with great care, like someone has done here, and there is no describing what beauty can be unleashed. For much of the time, the smoke performs in brilliant fashion somewhere between the ethereal and profound. 46%

Ardbeg 23 Year Old db (93) n22.5 t24 f23 b23.5 A malt forever treading on eggshells, trying not to disturb the tannins. As a dram, makes a nervous wreck of you, as you spend the entire time waiting for the shallow truce to be broken and the oak to declare war and come pouring in. Thankfully, it never quite happens. As all whiskies, not be taken with water. But, in this instance, a tranquilliser might not go amiss... 46.3%.

Ardbeg 1977 db (96) n25 t24 f23 b24. When working through the Ardbeg stocks, I earmarked '77 a special vintage, the sweetest of them all. So it has proved. Only the '74 absorbed that extra oak that gave greater all-round complexity. Either way, the quality of the distillate is beyond measure: simply one of the greatest experiences – whisky or otherwise – of your life. 46%

Ardbeg 1978 db (91) n23 t24 f22 b22. An Ardbeg on the edge of losing it because of encroaching oak, hence the decision made by John Smith and me to bottle this vintage early alongside the 17-year-old. Nearly ten years on, still looks a pretty decent bottling, though slightly under strength! 43%

Ardbeg An Oa db (95.5) n24 t24 f23.5 b24 I'd never say "whoa" if someone poured me an Oa... 46%.

⟐ **Ardbeg Arrrrrrrdbeg** db (84.5) n21.5 t21.5 f20.5 b21 For me, more aaarrrrgggghhh! than arrrrrrr. For a start, I hardly recognise this as an Ardbeg in style. Since when did that old Bowmore character of Victory V cough sweets hickory been part of its DNA? And what is that weak, lily-livered finish all about. The sugars come and go as they please but without being part of a set plan while the phenols wobble. Yes, of course there are some pleasant (but short-lived) phases. But Ardbeg? Just nowhere near the mark. 51.8%.

⟐ **Ardbeg Blaaack** db (92) n22.5 that unmistakable heady mix of wine cask (though not sherry, I suspect) and peat. This, as usual, gives the peat an acidic sooty disposition; t23 soft mouthfeel – perhaps a fraction too soft as the oils bind the fruit and phenols together rather than allowing their own layered marriage in the traditional house style. Still a joy, though, especially when the honey tones manage to pick a route through; **f23.5** much better now as the phenols and spices combine to give a smoky pulse while the darker sugars and chalky vanillas; **b23** still a different to feel to this than the Ardbegs of old. And though where once upon a time the move through the gears was seamless and this is just a little clunky at times, overall it works rather attractively. *46%.*

◈ **Ardbeg Blaaack Committee Release** db (86.5) **n22 t22 f21 b21.5** Just way too dull for an Ardbeg. The wine is just a little too busy filing down the edges of the malt and peat to really offer anything constructive. The result is a malt which lurches about the palate with an ungainly countenance. The spices certainly give their all, but the phenols - following an impressive start - are never allowed to make the kind of complex and stunningly balanced contribution that usually sets Ardbeg apart. *50.7%.*

Ardbeg Blasda db (90.5) **n23.5 t22.5 f22 b22.5** A beautiful, if slightly underpowered malt, which shows Ardbeg's naked self to glowing effect. Overshadowed by some degree in its class by the SMWS bottling, but still something to genuinely make the heart flutter. *40%*

Ardbeg Corryvreckan db (96.5) **n23 t24.5 f24 b25** As famous writers – including the occasional genius film director (stand up wherever you are my heroes Powell and Pressburger) – appear to be attracted to Corryvreckan, the third most violent whirlpool found in the world and just off Islay, to boot, - I selected this as my 1,500th whisky tasted for the historic Jim Murray Whisky Bible 2009. I'm so glad I did because many have told me they thought Blasda ahead of this. To me, it's not even a contest. Currently I have only a sample. Soon I shall have a bottle. I doubt if even the feared whirlpool is this deep and perplexing. *57.1%. 5000 bottles.*

Ardbeg Dark Cove db (86) **n22.5 t22.5 f19.5 b21.5.** For whatever reason, this is a much duller version than the Committee Edition. And strength alone can't explain it, or solely the loss of the essential oils from reduction. There is a slight nagging to this one so perhaps any weakness to the sherry butts has been accentuated by the reduction of oil, if it has been bottled from the same vatting – which I doubt. Otherwise, the tasting notes are along the lines of below, except with just a little less accent on the sugars. *46.5%*

Ardbeg Dark Cove Committee Edition db (90.5) **n23.5 t23 f21.5 b22.5** Big sherry and bigger peat always struggle somewhere along the line. This one does pretty well until we reach the finale when it unravels slightly. But sulphur-free. And challenging. *55%*

Ardbeg Drum db (92.5) **n23 t23.5 f22.5 b23.5** Well! I wasn't expecting that! It is as if this is from some super-fine cut, with 20% of the usual heart each way being sent back re-distillation. No idea if this is the case, but it is the only way I can think of creating a non-chillfiltered Ardbeg this clean and fragile. Quite extraordinary... *46%.*

Ardbeg Grooves db (95) **n24 t23.5 f23.5 b24** Groovy. *46%.*

Ardbeg Grooves Committee Release db (95.5) **n24** as above, except: oilier phenols adding extra depth and weight; **t23.5** as above except: a more rounded gloss to the same traits and development and much greater lustre to the sugars; **f24** as above except: longer finale and now a more apparent spice; **b24** even groovier! *51.6%.*

Ardbeg Guaranteed 30 Years Old db (91) **n24 t23 f21 b23.** An unusual beast, one of the last ever bottled by Allied. The charm and complexity early on is enormous, but the fade rate is surprising. That said, still a dram of considerable magnificence. *40%*

Ardbeg Kelpie db (95) **n24 t23.5 f23.5 b24** Beautifully crafted and cleverly – and intriguingly - structured. An understated Ardbeg for true Ardbeg lovers... *46%.*

Ardbeg Kelpie Committee Edition db (94) **n24 t24 f22.5 b23.5** As Burns might have said: I'se no speer nae to anither helpie o' Kelpie... *51.7%.*

Ardbeg Provenance 1974 bott 1999 db (96) **n24 t25 f23 b24.** This is an exercise in subtlety and charisma, the beauty and the beast drawn into one. Until I came across the 25-year-old OMC version during a thunderstorm in Denmark, this was arguably the finest whisky I had ever tasted: I opened this and drank from it to see in the year 2000. When I went through the Ardbeg warehouse stocks in 1997 I earmarked the '74 and '77 vintages as something special. This bottling has done me proud. *55.6%*

Ardbeg Uigeadail db (89) **n25 t22 f20 b22.** A curious Ardbeg with a nose to die for. Some tinkering - please guys, as the re-taste is not better - regarding the finish may lift this to being a true classic *54.1%*

Ardbeg Supernova 2019 db (92.5) **n23.5 t23 f23 b23** A kind of sub-Supernova as it has now lost much of its old explosive oomph. *53.9%.*

Ardbeg Traigh Bhan db (94.5) **n24 t23.5 f23.5 b23.5** Ah, Traigh Bhan, the remote Singing Sands beach on Islay, if memory serves. Where back in the very early 1980s, before anyone had heard of Ardbeg – or hardly Islay whisky come to that matter - you could spend a day at the silent, deserted, unknown distillery and then return to Port Ellen. And as the sun thought about setting, but before the midges (teeth freshly sharpened) came out to play, walk past a herd of goats that could win a World Championship for flatulence, and on to the Singing Sands – Traigh Bhan - where I and the lady who was unluckily destined to be, for a short time, Mrs Murray would find a remote spot to try, but only providing we were upwind from the goats, and add to the Murray clan. It as an act that began and ended with a bottle top or two full of Ardbeg 10. Magical.... Maybe I should return to those sands with a bottle of this – which, fittingly, seems, older, softer, less energetic than the elixir Ardbeg I tasted of yore - and see what happens... 46.6%.

⁓ **Ardbeg Wee Beastie Guaranteed 5 Years Old** bott code: L2395911 22/06/2020 **(91)** n24 fabulously fresh and youthful: Ardbeg as rarely seen outside the tasting lab with a resounding, pulsing phenol intensity, seemingly unconcerned by other-enthusiastic tannins... which aren't there. The distillery's citrus is in the kind of shape that starts receding at about eight-years-old from second fill bourbon **t23.5** the oily intensity of youth is there to be made the most of, as is the salivating qualities of the barley. The peat arrives as a controlled explosion of such rare and elegant beauty...but then a quieter blast of unexpected caramel. The smoke and initial joie- de- vivre seems partially extinguished and the whole quietens much more quickly than I expected; **f21.5** surprisingly tame, dull and even bitter for a young Ardbeg: well, for Ardbeg period. The peat has been gagged by toffee-vanilla; **b22** a lovely whisky, make no mistake. But for a five-year-old Ardbeg, over 35 years of experience with this distillery had conditioned me to expect just a little more. Starts off with a mesmerically youthful lustiness full of the sunny joys of a blossoming spring. Ends in the grey of a foggy autumnal evening.... 47.4%. ncf.

ARDMORE

Speyside, 1899. Beam Suntory. Working.

Ardmore 12 Year Old Port Wood Finish db **(90)** n21.5 t23.5 f22 b23 Here we have a lovely fruit-rich malt, but one which has compromised on the very essence of the complexity which sets this distillery apart. Lovely whisky I am delighted to say...but, dammit, by playing to its unique nuances it could have been so much better...I mean absolutely sensational...!46%. ncf.

Ardmore Aged 20 Years 1996 Vintage 1st fill ex-bourbon & ex-Islay casks, bott code: L723657A db **(89.5)** n22 t23 f22 b22.5 Slightly confused by this malt, for all its charm. At 20 years old this distillery projects, through its usual ex-bourbon cask portfolio of varied usages, a quite disarming complexity. To bolster it with extra oak and smoke slightly undermines the inherent subtlety of this malt which sets it apart from all others. Highly enjoyable, nonetheless. 49.3%. ncf.

Ardmore 25 Years Old db **(89.5)** n21 t23.5 f22.5 b22.5 A 25-y-o box of chocolates: coffee creams, fudge, orange cream...they are all in there. The nose may be ordinary: what follows is anything but. 51.4%. ncf.

Ardmore 30 Years Old Cask Strength db **(94)** n23.5 t23.5 f23 b24 I remember when the present owners of Ardmore launched their first ever distillery bottling. Over a lunch with the hierarchy there I told them, with a passion, to ease off with the caramel so the world can see just how complex this whisky can be. This brilliant, technically faultless, bottling is far more eloquent and persuasive than I was that or any other day... 53.7%. nc ncf. 1428 bottles.

Ardmore 1996 db **(87)** n22 t22 f21 b22. Very curious Ardmore, showing little of its usual dexterity. Perhaps slightly more heavily peated than the norm, but there is also much more intense heavy caramel extracted from the wood. Soft, very pleasant and easy drinking it is almost obsequious. 43%.

Ardmore Legacy bott code: L713757B db **(88)** n22.5 t23 f20.5 b22 That's much more like it! The initial bottling of this brand was a travesty to the distillery, seemingly making a point omitting all of the personality which makes it potentially one of the great whiskies of the world. No such problem here: a much more sympathetic rendition, though the finish is perhaps a little sharper than ideally desired. So, a massive improvement but still room for further improvement. 40%.

Berry Bros & Rudd Ardmore 9 Years Old cask no. 708628, bott 2018 **(96.5)** n24 t24 f24 b24.5 Confirmation of just what a stupendous distillery this is. For a 9-year-old, the balance defies belief. Few single malts under ten years will match this bottling this year. 52.3%. nc ncf sc.

Berry Bros & Rudd Ardmore 9 Years Old cask no. 708496, bott 2018 **(89)** n22.5 t23 f21.5 b22 An absolutely straight down the line Ardmore: still youthful but exactly what you should expect at this age from this kind of cask, though the finish does tire a little. 54.6%. nc ncf sc.

⁓ **Berry Bros & Rudd Ardmore 12 Year Old** cask no. 800961, dist 2006, bott 2019 **(90.5)** n23 that unique layering of smoke: understated hardly covers it! Some wonderful mint and lemon strands to accompany the vanilla; **t22.5** here the youthful side of its nature exhibits early. Salivating with a zesty lemon tart nose before the smoke slowly gathers weight, aided by the shy tannin; **f22** drier and almost chalky; **b22.5** one of the perennial joys of writing this book is happening across cask-strength bottlings of Ardmore being true to form. This one is slightly young for its age thinner in body than is usual. But still displays a wonderful degree of complexity even when not quite firing on all cylinders. 56.8%. nc ncf sc.

The First Editions Ardmore Aged 20 Years 1997 refill hogshead, cask no. 15307, bott 2018 **(94.5) n23.5 t23.5 f23.5 b24** A stupendous Ardmore very much on the higher end of their peating spectrum – it is even smokier than a Bowmore sitting in the glass next to it - and this smoke is used to maximum effect without for a moment overpowering and losing balance. A bit of a minor classic. *54.1%. nc ncf sc. 258 bottles.*

The John Milroy Selection Ardmore 8 Year Old refill barrel, cask no. 803059, dist 2010, bott 2019 **(86) n21.5 t22.5 f20.5 b21.5** Beautiful delivery where the peat, spices and acacia honey are in bon accord. But the ex-bourbon cask does no favours with a distinct tang on both nose and finish. *54.8%. nc ncf sc. Spirit Imports Inc.*

MacAlabur Ardmore Aged 22 Years hogshead, cask no. 149020, dist 27 Aug 96, bott 15 Oct 18 **(88) n22 t22 f22 b22** Extremely rare to find a 22-year-old barrel of Scotch malt weighing at over 60% abv. This is a bit of a freak whisky, in more ways than one! And especially enjoyable for masochists. *60.5%. nc ncf sc. 239 bottles.*

Teacher's Highland Single Malt quarter cask finish db **(89) n22.5 t23 f21.5 b22.** This is Ardmore at its very peatiest. And had not the colouring levels been heavily tweaked to meet the flawed perceptions of what some markets believe makes a good whisky, this malt would have been better still. As it is: superb. With the potential of achieving greatness if only they have the confidence and courage... *40%. India/Far East Travel Retail exclusive.*

◈ **The Whisky Agency Ardmore 1998** hogshead, bott 2018 **(89) n22** where's the smoke? Just a wisp here and there but more green apple prevalent; **t21.5** dry and malty with a slow burn of phenol just about registering; **f23.5** balances far better here, especially as the milky mocha and soft spices kicks in; again the smoke makes up the ground and mingles sexily; **b22** a very understated Ardmore, offering far less smoke than the norm. Little to write home about on the nose and delivery. But the finish is a different proposition altogether. *51.7%.*

◈ **The Whisky Chamber Ardmore 10 Jahre 2009** refill port cask **(94) n23** an apologetic wisp or two of peat appeared trapped amid the firm fruit; **t23.5** surprisingly soft delivery: the nose is pretty rigid whilst the deliver simply melts in the mouth, barley first. The smoke drifts in with menace but the hard grape ups the juiciness with a cherry drop sharpness; **f23.5** light spices and delicate fruit chocolate; **b24** enjoyable, at times refined and always complex. Certainly, the sum adds up to more than the parts. Quietly brilliant. *57.1%. sc.*

Wilson & Morgan Barrel Selection Ardmore Heavy Peat dist 2009, bott 2018 **(92) n23 t23.5 f22.5 b23** Heavy peat? I don't think so. Just a normally light peated Ardmore perhaps towards the top of its range but the smokiness amplified by the delicate touch of the oak and barley. Quite lovely. *48%.*

AUCHENTOSHAN
Lowlands, 1800. Morrison Bowmore. Working.

Auchentoshan 10 Years Old db **(81) n22 t21 f19 b19.** Much better, maltier, cleaner nose than before. But after the initial barley surge on the palate it shows a much thinner character. *40%*

Auchentoshan 12 Years Old db **(91.5) n22.5 t23.5 f22.5 b23** A delicious malt very much happier with itself than it has been for a while. *40%*

◈ **Auchentoshan Aged 12 Years** bourbon & sherry casks, bott code: L00007SB320081440 db **(86) n22.5 t22.5 f20 b21** Being triple distilled, Auchentoshan is one of Scotland's lightest, most intricate spirits to start with. Therefore, to maximise its character it needs gentle handling and the malts given free reign. This, however, is essentially sherry dominated, except perhaps for on the nose where some attractive acacia honey filters through. The delivery also has moments of complexity and clarity, but they are fleeting before the grape and tannins take command for a surfeit of dryness. The growing furry tones on the finish confirms, as detectable on the nose, that not all the butts escape the dreaded sulphur candle. *40%.*

Auchentoshan 14 Years Old Cooper's Reserve db **(83.5) n20 t21.5 f21 b21.** Malty, a little nutty and juicy in part. *46%. ncf.*

Auchentoshan 18 Years Old db **(78) n21 t21.5 f17 b19.** Although matured for 18 years in ex-bourbon casks, as according to the label, this is a surprisingly tight and closed malt in far too many respects. Some heart-warming sugars early on, but the finish is bitter and severely limited in scope. *43%*

Auchentoshan 21 Years Old db **(93) n23.5 t23 f23 b23.5** One of the finest Lowland distillery bottlings of our time. A near faultless masterpiece of astonishing complexity to be cherished and discussed with deserved reverence. So delicate, you fear that sniffing too hard will break the poor thing...! *43%.*

Auchentoshan 1979 db **(94) n23.5 t24 f23 b23.5** It's amazing what a near faultless sherry butt can do. *50.1%*

Auchentoshan 1990 27 Year Old db **(94) n23.5 t23 f24 b23.5** The fact this is triple-distilled malt has a major bearing on the structure of this excellent dram. Lighter malty and citrus notes seem able to fly above the more ingrained grape. The result is a two-toned, salivating little charmer which carries its years in a way 'Toshan was never really expected to. The mocha starts creeping in from about the halfway point, laying down a weightiness which is still in keeping with the lighter fruit. Such a delight and elegant experience with the kind of finish blenders can only dream of.... *53.1%. Selected for CWS.*

Auchentoshan American Oak db (85.5) n21.5 t22 f20.5 b21.5. Very curious: reminds me very much of Penderyn Welsh whisky before it hits the Madeira casks. Quite creamy with some toasted honeycomb making a brief cameo appearance. *40%*

Auchentoshan Blood Oak French red wine db (76.5) n20.5 t19 f18 b19. That's funny: always thought blood tasted a little sweet. This is unremittingly bitter. *48%. ncf.*

Auchentoshan Classic db (80) n19 t20 f21 b20. Classic what exactly...? Some really decent barley, but goes little further. *40%*

Auchentoshan Select db (85) n20 t21.5 f22 b21.5. Has changed shape of late, if not quality. Much more emphasis on the enjoyable juicy barley sharpness these days. *40%*

Auchentoshan Solera db (88) n23 t22 f22 b21. Enormous grape input and enjoyable for all its single mindedness. Will benefit when a better balance with the malt is struck. *48%. ncf.*

Auchentoshan The Bartender's Malt batch 01, bott code: L172249 db (94.5) n23.5 t24 f23 b24 Seeing as this was assembled by a dozen bartenders from around the world, namely Messrs Alvarado, Billing, Halsius, Heinrich, Jehli, Klus, Magro, Morgan, Schurmann, Shock, Stern and Wareing surely this is the Bartenders' Malt, not Bartender's Malt. Still, I digress. Good job, boys and (presumably) girls. Some might mark this down as a clever marketing ploy (which it may well be...). I'd rather record it as an exceptionally fine Auchentoshan. And by the way, bartenders, you have proved a point I have been making for the last 25 years: the finest cocktail is a blend of whiskies...even if from the same distillery...Now don't you go ruining this by putting ice, water, or anything else in it... *47%.*

Auchentoshan Three Wood db (76) n20 t18 f20 b18. Takes you directly into the rough. Refuses to harmonise, except maybe for some late molassed sugar. *43%*

◈ **Auchentoshan Three Wood** bourbon & Oloroso & PX sherry casks, bott code: L9274SB323011209 db (88) n22 t23 f21 b22 Three woods there may be. But it's the PX that really counts. A semi-syrupy concoction with massive chewiness. The half-expected bitter finish offers a stark contrast. *43%.*

Auchentoshan Virgin Oak db (92) n23.5 t23 f22.5 b23 Not quite how I've seen 'Toshan perform before: but would love to see it again! *46%*

Signatory Vintage Un-Chillfiltered Auchentoshan 21 Year Old 1997 refill sherry hogshead, cask no. 2911 (81) n23 t21 f18 b19 A real strange one this: the nose sets off like a champion, all roasted sultanas and herbs. But after the initial rum-like golden syrup delivery, this bitters out with a vengeance. *52.4%. sc. Exclusive to The Whisky Barrel. 168 bottles.*

Simon Brown Traders Auchentoshan bourbon cask, dist Feb 98, bott Feb 19 (90.5) n22 t23 f22.5 b23 Delightfully delicate. *43%. nc ncf sc.*

AUCHROISK
Speyside, 1974. Diageo. Working.

Auchroisk Aged 10 Years db (84) n20 t22 f21 b21. Tangy orange on the nose, the malt amplified by a curious saltiness on the palate. *43%. Flora and Fauna.*

Fadandel.dk Auchroisk Aged 7 Years 1st fill oloroso sherry cask, cask no. 82, dist 21 Dec 11, bott 20 Nov 18 (91.5) n22.5 t23 f23 b23 An audacious bottling which uses a pristine 100% sulphur-free sherry cask to breathe life into one of Speyside's lightest spirits – and, here, a very young one at that. Just admire the chutzpa because the grape makes a blistering eye-watering statement, then kindly soothes your battered taste buds by kissing them better with the most gloriously layered sultanas imaginable. A little ulmo honey adds the softest sweetness and harnesses the fruit. *59.3%. sc. 320 bottles.*

The First Editions Auchroisk Aged 24 Years 1994 refill hogshead, cask no. 15396, bott 2018 (87.5) n21 t22.5 f22 b22 I know the first-ever blender to have Auchroisk under his control never thought for a moment that this malt could last to two dozen years in the wood – he felt he had to patch it up even when he released it in its first incarnation at exactly half that age. But although the trademark thinness is evident, equally there is no denying the charm of the juicy barley melding with the delicate vanilla. Elegant, understated and always charming and engagingly delicate. *48.3%. nc ncf sc. 275 bottles.*

Hepburn's Choice Auchroisk 9 Years Old red wine hogshead, dist 2009, bott 2019 (85.5) n21.5 t22 f21 b21 Plenty of fruit but never really catches fire. *46%. nc ncf sc. 354 bottles.*

◈ **Hepburn's Choice Auchroisk 10 Years Old** rum cask, dist 2009, bott 2019 (87.5) n22 t22.5 f21 b22 Usually a disappointing malt, it appears that the rum cask has used its sugary influence to hem in the more deliciously malty aspects to wonderful effect. The finish is typically weak, nonetheless. Even so, enjoy the early salivating crispness of the barley tinged with a superb outer coating of lightly spiced heather honey. *46%. nc ncf sc. 182 bottles.*

Simon Brown Traders Auchroisk bourbon cask & port cask, dist Dec 10, bott Jan 19 **(87) n21 t22 f22 b22** A soft and even malt which goes some way in making up on the palate what it lacks on the nose. The Port was definitely on rescue mission here as the underlying body seems thin. But the grape does infuse an attractive degree of plum pudding and spice. *43%. nc ncf sc.*

AULTMORE
Speyside, 1896. Bacardi. Working.

Aultmore 12 Year Old db **(85.5) n22 t22 f20 b21.5**. Not quite firing on all cylinders due to the uncomfortably tangy oak. But relish the creamy malt for the barley is the theme of choice and for its sheer intensity alone, it doesn't disappoint; a little ulmo honey and marzipan doff their cap to the kinder vanillas. *46% WB16/028*

Aultmore of the Foggie Moss Aged 12 Years bott code: L18135ZA903 db **(92.5) n23.5** teasingly complex: the delicate oak notes combine with the barley to form a kind of dry egg nog. The adroit playfulness of the lime is almost worth getting the bottle for alone...! **t23.5** the nose suggests a salivating experience awaits...and it does! The barley almost froths in the mouth, accentuated seemingly by the quick arrival of oaky spice; the early barley sugar delights; **f22.5** true to style, dries quite quickly, a buzzing tannin having the last word; **b23** a whisky purist's delight. So delicate you can see the inner workings of this fine malt. *46%. ncf.*

Aultmore 18 Year Old db **(88.5) n22.5 t22.5 f22 b21.5** Charming, but could do with having the toffee blended out... *46%*

Aultmore of the Foggie Moss Aged 18 Years batch no. 481, bott code: L15244B100 db **(94.5) n23.5** though the distillery makes point of their using unpeated malt, a little vaguely spicy smoke drifts across the fragile nose. Gentle vanillas and the lightest dab of heather honey act as the anchor; **t24** by far the most honeyed delivery of these three impressive Aultmores, a glossy blend of ulmo and Manuka doing the trick. The sweetness lasts virtually the entire trip, a little cocoa and natural caramels filling into the mid-ground; **f23** dry and spicy; **b24** it is so satisfying when the sweetness and spices of a malt combine for near perfect harmony. Flattens towards the finish, but this is high grade malt. *46%. ncf.*

Aultmore Aged 21 Years refill hogshead, batch no. 00107, bott code: L18281ZA501 db **(95.5) n24 t24 f23.5 b24** When you get a very decent spirit filled into exceptionally good casks, the result – providing the whisky is disgorged neither too early nor late – is usually a positive one. The refill hoggies here must have been in fine fettle, for this a bit of a stunner. No, make that a classic! Potential gong material, this. *46%. nc ncf.*

Aultmore Exceptional Cask Series 21 Years Old 1996 db **(94.5) n24 t23.5 f23.5 b23.5** There is age creaking from every pore of this whisky. The nose is magnificently sensual with its orange blossom honey theme, spicy toasty tannins lurking at every corner. And those tannins carry on their impressive work, yet at the same time allowing a delicious alloy of malt and sultanas to not only thrive but fully fill the palate. Toward the end we are back to those insistent tannins which, if anything display an age greater than its given years. A malt plucked at the very right time from the warehouse: it would never have made half as good a 25-year-old. *54%. Selected for CWS.*

◈ **The Whisky Chamber Aultmore 12 Jahre 2006** bourbon cask **(91) n23** layered barley infused with varied degrees of tannin, ranging from shy vanilla to a perkier spiciness; **t23** just as you think it is heading directly into full salivation mode, the malt and vanilla thicken and put the brakes on the juiciness. What a lovely citrus kick, too...; **f22** chalky vanilla, even with a degree of surprising youthfulness; **b23** ah! Aultmore in the kind of cask it feels so at home: a reasonably well-used bourbon barrel so it can ramp up the malt content to maximum. Refreshing and delectable. *52.1%. sc.*

◈ **Whisky Illuminati Aultmore 2011** Spanish oak sherry butt, cask no. 900367 **(90.5) n22.5** an almost outrageous degree of fruit and tannin: young and virtually devoid of any malty input; **t23.5** what a fantastic delivery! Again, the fruit is in total command, though the barley presence is this time visible on the palate. But it is the spices from the tannins, gelling with the sharp sloe plum that dominates; **f22.5** oaky cocoa all the way; **b22** a sherry butt with NO sulphur whatsoever. But a malt riding this bucking bronco for dear life and making no impression on just where it will be taken. *67.5%. sc. 120 bottles.*

BALBLAIR
Highlands (Northern), 1872. Inver House Distillers. Working.

Balblair 10 Years Old db **(86) n21 t22 f22 b21.** Such an improved dram away from the clutches of caramel. *40%*

Balblair Aged 12 Years American oak ex-bourbon & double-fired American oak casks, bott code: L18/357 R18/5536 IB db **(87) n21.5 t22 f21.5 b22** There is no escaping a distinct tired cask tang to this. From the nose to the finale the oak pokes around with a little too much meanness of spirit. But it is the wonderful clarity to the barley – including a delicious citrusy freshness – which keeps the malt on course. I suspect the next bottling will be a whole lot better! *46%. nc ncf.*

Balblair Aged 15 Years American oak ex-bourbon casks, followed by first fill Spanish oak butts, bott code: L19 079 R19/5133 IB db **(93)** n23 t23.5 f23 b23 Ah, after the relative disappointment of the 12-year-old, so good to see we are right back on track here. Twenty years of very bitter experience has taught me to fear the worst and hope for the best so far as the use of sherry butts are concerned. But my hopes are rewarded here: not 100% perfect, but close enough. *46%. nc ncf.*

Balblair Aged 17 Years American oak ex-bourbon casks, followed by first fill Spanish oak butts, bott code: L19/057 R19/5097 IB db **(94)** n23.5 t24.5 f22.5 b23.5 One of the best arrivals on the palate of any Scotch whisky I have tasted this year. *46%. nc ncf. Travel Exclusive.*

Balblair Aged 18 Years American oak ex-bourbon casks, followed by first fill Spanish oak butts, bott code: L19/121 R19/5220 IB db **(83)** n22 t23 f18 b20 Balblair's luck has run out on the sherry butts. A heftier expression than the 17-year-old and the sulphur ensures there is nothing like the degree of complexity. *46%. nc ncf.*

Balblair Aged 25 Years American oak ex-bourbon casks, followed by first fill Spanish oak butts, nbc db **(91)** n23.5 t23.5 f21 b23 There has been hard work here to harmonise fruit and oak and allow the barley a say, too. But when sherry is this ripe, not the easiest stunt to pull off. Gets pretty close, though! *46%.*

Balblair 1975 db **(94.5)** n24.5 t23.5 f23 b23.5. Essential Balblair. *46%*

Balblair 1989 db **(91)** n23 t23 f22.5 b22.5. Don't expect gymnastics or the pyrotechnics of the Cadenhead 18: in many ways a simple malt, but one beautifully told. Almost Cardhu-esque in the barley department. *43%*

Balblair 1989 db **(88)** n21.5 t22 f22.5 b22. A clean, pleasing malt, though hardly one that will induce anyone to plan a night raid on any shop stocking it... *46%*

Balblair 1990 db **(92.5)** n24 t23.5 f22 b23. Tangy in the great Balblair tradition. Except here this is warts and all with the complexity and greatness of the distillery left in no doubt. *46%*

Balblair 1991 3rd Release bott 2018, bott code L18/044 R18/5054IB db **(94.5)** n23.5 t23.5 f23.5 b24 A malt embracing its passing years and has aged, silver temples and all, with great style and panache. *46%. nc ncf.*

Balblair 1997 2nd Release db **(94)** n23.5 t23.5 f23 b24 a very relaxed well-made and matured malt, comfortable in its own skin, bursting with complexity and showing an exemplary barley-oak ratio. A minor classic. *46%. nc ncf.*

Balblair 2000 2nd Release bott 2017, bott code L17/R121 db **(95.5)** n24.5 t24 f23 b24 First encountered this malt at a tasting I gave in Corsica earlier in the year. It blew away my audience while equally seducing me. Sampled back in the tasting lab, if anything it is even more stunning. The stock of this under-appreciated distillery rises by the day... *46%. nc ncf.*

Balblair 2001 db **(90.5)** n23.5 t23.5 f21.5 b22.5 A typically high quality whisky from this outrageously underestimated distillery. *46%*

◇ **The Whisky Barrel Originals Balblair 10 Years Old** 1st fill oloroso hogshead, cask no. TWB1008, dist Sept 09, bott 2019 **(91.5)** n23 there are big heavy oloroso noses: this isn't one of them. This is flighty fruit, more glacé cherry than brooding grape. As light, cheery, refreshing and sweet as you'll ever find an Oloroso cask; t23 equally limited weight on delivery. Instead of a thickset, toasty, rich delivery, we get an ethereal one, the edges tinged with sultana and ulmo honey; f22.5 some delightfully chocolate and bread and butter pudding; b23 the cleanest sherry cask you could ever wish for. And lightest: a butterfly of a sherry cask. *57.6%. sc. 298 bottles.*

BALMENACH
Speyside, 1824. Inver House Distillers. Working.

Deerstalker Balmenach 12 Years Old Highland Single Malt **(88.5)** n22.5 t22 f22 b22 Attractive, easy going malt, but struggles to get out of second gear. *43%.*

◇ **Fadandel.dk Balmenach 7 Year Old** 5 months finish in a 1st fill PX Octave, cask no. 430A, dist 17 Oct 12, bott 14 Apr 20 **(90)** n22.5 amazingly, some complexity is still to be found on this: the youthful malt packs a punch big enough to burst through the treacle-thick grape to offer a pulse of barley; t22.5 dates and figs try to strongarm the barley. It is an uneven contest; f22.5 spicy and drier at first with a little liquorice and spice on the fruit fudge fade. A little dark chocolate and cherry, too, making for a vaguely liqueur-style finale...; b22.5 this is so outrageously ridiculous, it's actually very good. The youthful malt is in mortal combat with a grapey cask of gorilla strength. Bizarre! It is probably just a grape atom away from disaster. ... but so entertaining, too... *55.4%. sc. 75 bottles.*

⬡ **Fadandel.dk Balmenach 7 Year Old** 5 months finish in a 1st fill PX Octave, cask no. 430B, dist 17 Oct 12, bott 16 Apr 20 **(84.5) n21 t22 f21.5 b20** And I thought cask 430A was dark! For its age, this is borderline opaque! Which is a bit like storm clouds over your feeble summer tent: you know you are in for it! There can be too much of a good thing and where cask 430A miraculously got away with it, this one doesn't... or come even close. Again, no off notes. But PX of this magnitude on a malt as simpering as a Balmenach is like running a fully laden, with each passenger maxing out on their luggage, freshly fuel-filled Jumbo jet over a walnut just to crack it. Hard to give marks for balance, as there simply isn't any. If you like this kind of sticky, overly-sweet, cloying thing, I suggest you buy a bottle of PX, as this is a waste of otherwise good malt. *52.8%. sc. 69 bottles.*

Hidden Spirits Balmenach 2004 cask no. BL418, bott 2018 **(94) n22.5 t24 f23.5 b24** Coconuts apart, almost the archetypal Speysider! Superb! *51.2%. sc.*

⬡ **Old Malt Cask Balmenach Aged 14 Years** refill barrel, cask no. 16791, dist Dec 04, bott Jun 19 **(94.5) n23** spiced up like a slice of bread pudding; **t24** ah....sensational! The mouthfeel, so rounded and soft, is matched by the sublime beauty of the multi-layered malt, ranging from Victoria sponge cake, through acacia honey and finishing at the midpoint with a plethora of finely tuned light, but very active spices; **f23.5** long spiced chocolate fade; **b24** glories in its complex malty freshness! A joy of a dram. *50%. nc ncf sc. 141 bottles.*

Spirit of Caledonia Balmenach cask no. 184, dist 7 Mar 07, bott 16 Jul 18 **(87.5) n21 t22.5 f22 b22** Somewhat thin, malty and with a touch of ginger. Superb ten seconds on delivery, though, when the barley goes into mouth-watering overdrive. *58.8%. Mr. Whisky.*

THE BALVENIE
Speyside, 1892. William Grant & Sons. Working.

⬡ **The Balvenie Double Wood Aged 12 Years** European oak sherry casks, bott code: L8D 7738 2309 db **(82) n22 t21 f19 b20** Pretty standard but uninspiring fare with sharp fruit pinching the palate until the furry sulphur tang arrives. Oh, how I miss Balvenie in standard bourbon casks at this age or even a little younger which gives you a chance to see how amazingly brilliant this distillery actually is. *40%.*

The Balvenie Single Barrel Sherry Cask Aged 15 Years db cask no 2075 **(58) n14 t16 f14 b14** Lovely distillery. Shame about this shockingly sulphured cask. *47.8%. sc.*

The Balvenie 16 Year Old Triple Cask db **(84.5) n22 t22.5 f19 b21** Well, after their single cask and then double wood, who saw this coming...? There is nothing about this whisky you can possibly dislike: no diminishing off notes (OK, well maybe at the very death) and a decent injection of sugar, especially early on. The trouble is, when you mix together sherry butts (even mainly good ones, like here) and first fill bourbon casks, the intense toffee produced tends to make for a monosyllabic, toffeed, dullish experience. And so it proves here. *40%*

⬡ **The Balvenie Caribbean Cask Aged 14 Years** bott code: L8D 7263 1707 db **(91.5) n23** an agreeably busy nose: you expect sugars and get it, though in a more nuanced way than you might first have though. Not so much that little sugary one associates with rum normally get from rum cask – though it is there – but a much punchier Demerara and mixed spice and even, amazingly, a playful hint of chilli...; **t23** the usual silk mouthfeel one associates with Balvenie's standard malt. With the barley still alive and well. But the tannins are up and at you early: nothing aggressive, but enough vanilla to let you know it's around. The caramelised arrival forms a central plank; **f22.5** more caramel and spice; **b23** a different kind of rum style from Balvenie to others they have done in the past, this working far better and despite a slight caramel overdose, much more complexity this time round. *43%.*

The Balvenie Double Wood Aged 17 Years db **(84) n22 t21 f20 b21.** Balvenie does like 17 years as an age to show off its malt at its most complex, & understandably so as it is an important stage in its development before its usual premature over maturity: the last years or two when it remains full of zest and vigour. Here, though, the oak from the bourbon cask has offered a little too much of its milkier, older side while the sherry is a fraction overzealous and a shade too tangy. Enjoyable, but like a top of the range Mercedes engine which refuses to run evenly. *43%.*

⬡ **The Balvenie Double Wood Aged 17 Years** European oak sherry casks, bott code: L34D 50322808 db **(95) n24** a vague saltiness lifts the over-ripe gooseberry and the plum jam to a very rich level while vanilla alongside a blend of ulmo and heather honeys to a great job of representing the oak in all its desired glory. Some older whisky lovers who remember Black Jacks, a farthing sweet, will recognise those deeper intonations; **t23.5** there's the trademark Balvenie lusciousness, slightly salty this time, backed by the cream sherry and buttery vanilla. Superb layering allowing the spices, which start slowly, to subtly make their mark; **f23** here the age has its day: a toasty speech and an anthem of liquorice sung by a lightly fruity choir. The spices how pulse with aged intent...; **b24** just fabulous to see this marriage between bourbon and sherry cask being such a happy one. Both sets of barrels are blemish-free while the weight and balance is exemplary. Luxurious in every degree and a magnificent example of the difference sulphur-free sherry butts can make to a whisky, especially as one as top drawer as The Balvenie...So deserves to be another three percent higher in strength, too... *43%*.

The Balvenie Aged 21 Years Port Wood db **(94.5)** n24 t24 f23 b23.5 What a magnificently improved malt. Last time out I struggled to detect the fruit. Here, there's no escaping. *40%*

⬦ **The Balvenie PortWood Aged 21 Years** finished in PortWood oak casks, bott code: L34D 4498 1204 db **(86)** n23.5 t22.5 f19 b21 The gnawing sulphur fade is an unfortunate ending to a malt which starts so brilliantly well. So much fresh fruit abounding here, much of it of the sugar candy variety. Those incapable of picking up sulphur are in for a treat. *40%*.

⬦ **The Balvenie The Sweet Toast of American Oak Aged 12 Years** finished in Kentucky virgin American oak barrels, bott code: L6D 6404 0603 db **(87.5)** n23 toasty, nutty tannins have their cloaks draped all over this nose. And crisp Demerara sugars form a sweet shell, with inevitable spices pinging around as though possessed; lots of bourbon-style crushed kumquat, and lemon drops too...; t22 initially a beautiful mouthfeel with the lightest of oils working well with the early sugars to give a first yielding, then stiff coating. From the first moment there is an unusually abrupt tannin trace, slightly ill-fitting...Suddenly drops off a cliff as the mid-ground threatens bitterness as the malts reduce in intensity and the early profound sugars wear thin; f21.5 simply too bitter from the harsher tannins without enough sugar to intercede; b21 not anything like carefully balanced enough. Virgin oak has to be treated carefully and with respect: that is a lot of tannin being awoken and barley is no corn or rye. Needs rebalancing as this has the potential for greatness. But not in this form. *43%. Story No. 1.*

⬦ **The Balvenie Tun 1509 Batch No. 6** bott code: L34D 5015 2608 db **(93)** n23.5 the structure to this is enough to make you groan with delight: a real coastal, seaweedy saltiness, along with a fresh sea breeze. Not your normal, Balvenie introduction. But the heather honey is not entirely unknown to the distillery, nor the firm malt layer. A mix of slightly moist and very dry date is offered up by way of a certain fruitiness; t24 a blend of heather honey and maple syrup get this malt off to a sweet start, but then it sharpens as the salt arrives. Superb barley of bewildering layering, giving the sweetness and sharpness a flickering countenance, so you are never sure if it one or the other...or simultaneously both; f22 toffee plus just an annoying little furriness late on...grrrr! b23.5 this must be from Balvenie-by-the-Sea. Amazing salt levels here, especially on the nose and early delivery. Has all the hallmarks of blender David Stewart, one of the top three at layering Scotch whisky in living memory. Just a shame about the late tang, though not too much damage done. *50.4%.*

⬦ **The Balvenie The Week of Peat Aged 14 Years** bott code: L6D 6432 1103 db **(96)** n24 a gentle drifting of peat reek over the clean vanillas, sometimes a little dense, at other times thinner and sweeter. The result, with a barely detectable degree of citrus providing an understated sharpness, as a nose you could sniff at contentedly for hours on end...; t24 a buttery gristiness is caressed by a light cloud of peat that adds both complexity and depth to the proceedings. Light liquorice and a vague molasses sweetness mingles and does its job but never interferes with a controlled oiliness which ensures intensity. The smoke now is also associated with a flickering, bitty spice which offers further texture to an already complex parade; f23.5 long. Lightly smoked. Perfectly sweetened. And still magnificently textured, especially as the vanillas confirm an outstanding oak contribution; b24.5 this could also, I suppose, be called a Weak of Peat as the phenols never really get anything like a head of steam. But, then, it never even attempts to and is quite right to concentrate on a subtlety which demonstrates the greatness of the this malt when matured in bourbon casks. One of those rare malts where the delivery and follow through on the palate is a match for a brilliant nose. Make no mistake: we have a true Speyside gem here. *48.3%. ncf. Story No. 2.* 🍷

BANFF

Speyside, 1863–1983. Diageo. Demolished.

Gleann Mór Banff Aged Over 42 Years dist 1975 **(91)** n23 t23.5 f22.5 b22 This was distilled in the same year I visited my first distillery in Scotland...and that was a bloody long time ago. Not many casks have made it from then to today, and those that have are in varying states of quality: old age does not always mean an improvement in a whisky's fortunes... often the reverse. This is a classic example of a malt which should have been bottled a little time back. But it is still massively enjoyable, throwing up the odd surprise here and there and keeping the malty script despite the militant oak. Quite an experience....*41.1%.*

BEN NEVIS

Highlands (Western), 1825. Nikka. Working.

Ben Nevis 10 Years Old 2008 batch no. 1, 1st fill bourbon, sherry and wines casks, dist 21 Apr 08, bott Sept 18 db **(86.5)** n21 t22.5 f21 b22 A robust, no holds barred malt which gets you both with the intensity of fruit and oak as well as the sheer power of the spirit itself! The varied wine casks don't perhaps gel as they might (not helped by a small sulphur note), though the intensity of the delivery may bring a pleasurable bead of sweat to the brow. 62.4%.

Ben Nevis Synergy 13 Years Old db **(88)** n22 t22 f21.5 b22.5 One of the sweetest Ben Nevises for a long time, but as chewy as ever! A bit of a lady's dram to be honest. 46%

Ben Nevis 32 Years Old 1966 dist Jun 66, bott Sept 98 db **(95.5)** n24.5 t23.5 f24 b23.5 Way back in 1998 some 1966 Ben Nevis was bottled for the US market as a "101" in 75cl bottles...but for some reason never got there. So for 20 years they slumbered peacefully in a warehouse at the distillery, entirely and blissfully forgotten, about until one day they were rediscovered by chance. That whisky, with a little softening from 20 years in glass, has now been re-consigned to 70cl bottles and at last put up for sale. What we have is a real blast from the past: a window into a Ben Nevis's distilling history, as a 32-year-old whisky bottled now from 1987 stock would certainly have a different feel. This reveals the distillery when it had the type of bite much favoured by blenders and which ensures a single malt with a singular personality. Just magnificent! 50.5%. Forgotten Bottlings Series.

꘎ **Cask & Thistle Ben Nevis 1997 Aged 22 Years** refill butt, cask no. 126 **(93.5)** n23 really impressive early tannins makes sure you know you are in the presence of an aged malt. The fruit has to stand aside until allowed to make its scented grapey presence felt; t24 one of the best texture deliveries from a Ben Nevis in years. The fruit may offer an eider-feather softness, but the scintillating spices don't allow for easy comfort; impressively, the malt makes the mid-ground with a slightly nutty vanilla surge; f23 dries as the age catches up; b23.5 a thistle can make your eye water. This cask certainly does for sure... 52.5%. sc.

The Cooper's Choice Ben Nevis 1996 21 Years Old sherry cask **(79)** n22 t21 f17 b19 As sherry butts go this, at first glance, passes muster so far as overall lack of sulphur is concerned. But there is little joy de vie to this and slowly the dreaded S word begins to gather in intensity, though never entirely dominating. A very pleasant malt I suspect for those who can't pick up sulphur; a bit of a dullard for those who can. 46%. nc ncf sc.

Glenwill Ben Nevis 1992 hogshead, cask no. 0076 **(95)** n23.5 t24 f23.5 b24 Anyone who collects distilleries in their very best form should grab a bottle of this: not a bum note to be heard. 48.7%. 217 bottles. Matisse Spirits Company.

The Golden Cask Ben Nevis 22 Years Old 1996 cask no. CM252, bott 2018 **(93.5)** n23.5 t23.5 f23 b23.5 Lovely to see a Ben Nevis at this age still capable of keeping you guessing and coming up with surprises. 46.5%. nc ncf sc. 150 bottles.

Hepburn's Choice Ben Nevis 7 Years Old wine cask, dist 2011, bott 2019 **(74.5)** n18 t19 f18.5 b19 With the furry sulphur at large, more of a whine cask... 46%. nc ncf sc. 367 bottles.

꘎ **Kingsbury Gold Ben Nevis 22 Year Old** barrel, cask no. 2118, dist 1996 **(93)** n24 blindfolded, I must admit I wouldn't have recognised this as Nevis. It's as though the barrel has sat by the sea for the last two decades, breathing in salt and ozone, and maybe a few heather and gorse bushes while it was at it...; t24 barley in insanely intense and uncorrupted form. Stunning heather honey mingles with this pristine barley...and again a saltiness drifts in to even further whet the sharpness of the flavours; f22 some bitterness is taken from a tiring barrel to undermine matters slightly. A few spicy notes kick in to counter; b23 Ben Nevis in very rare island form, with so much salt and heather hanging about it. Great to see the distillery in tip-top form. 57.2%. sc. 514 bottles.

Liquid Treasures Snakes Ben Nevis 20 Year Old dist 1998, bott 2018 **(88)** n22.5 t22 f21.5 b22 Starts off with rattling good pace, then ends as a bit of a boa. 52.1%. sc.

Saar Whisky N°9 ex bourbon barrel, sherry cask finish (01.06.17 - 23.08.18), dist 1998, bott 2018, bott code: LN9E12018 **(86)** n21.5 t22.5 f21 b21 A clean sherry cask – hurrah! The not so good news is that the malt and grape have not yet come to terms with each other, the result being a vibrant, busy but, ultimately, out of tune effort. 46.5%. ncf sc.

Single & Single Ben Nevis 1996 Aged 21 Years sherry cask **(81.5)** n22.5 t23 f16 b20 The nose shows huge fruit and nut from presumably a once dripping oloroso butt. A vague hint of something sinister under the chunky fruit...? The initial delivery is of sopping oloroso which makes for the most moist of sherry trifles. But the finish sees the tannins begin to kick in...as does the drying, off-key sulphur. Looks like someone's let loose a parcel of Ben Nevis sherry butts. This is the first of the batch I have tasted. Imperfect, as the finale reveals. By the standards of sherry butts of that day, it could have been a lot worse. 52.8%. sc.

Single Cask Collection Ben Nevis Aged 22 Years (90.5) n22.5 t23.5 f22 b22.5 sweeter than you might expect a Fino sherry to be and, thankfully, not a trace of an off note. Huge! 57.2%. sc.

Single Cask Collection Ben Nevis Aged 22 Years olorosso cask **(79.5)** n20 t21.5 f18.5 b19.5 A bit tangy and tight in the crucial areas. Good sultana thrust to the delivery, though. 51.2%. sc.

W.W. Club BNV.1 Ben Nevis Aged 20 Years American oak cask, cask no. 415, dist Sept 96, bott Feb 17 **(93)** n22.5 t23.5 f23 b24 The sheer force of the characterful spirit overcomes the oak for an enjoyable encounter. I am also noticing a distinctive salty theme to WW Club whiskies. 51.7%. sc. 235 bottles. William & Co. Spirits.

BENRIACH
Speyside, 1898. Brown-Forman. Working.

The BenRiach Aged 10 Years Curiositas Peated Malt bourbon, toasted virgin oak & rum casks, bott code: 2018/10/11 LM11452 db **(89.5) n22.5** busy and smoky, there is a hard, semi-metallic note to this where there wasn't before; **t22.5** much softer on arrival with the grist working at full throttle. A curious – or perhaps I should say curiositas - creamy texture, almost like cream soda, froths up the palate; **f22** thins now and bitter-sweet; **b22.5** unrecognisable from the original Curiositas and though the strength is back up to 46% abv, somehow the body has become lighter. Enjoyable but a head scratcher. 46%. nc ncf.

The BenRiach Aged 12 Years Matured In Sherry Wood db **(95.5) n23.5 t24 f24 b24** Since previously experiencing this the number of instances of sampling a sherry wood whisky and not finding my taste buds caked in sulphur has nosedived dramatically. Therefore, to start my tasting day at 7am with something as honest as this propels one with myriad reasons to continue the day. A celebration of a malt whisky in more ways than you could believe. 46%. nc ncf.

The BenRiach Aged 21 Years Classic bourbon barrels, virgin oak, PX sherry & red wine casks db **(90) n22.5 t23 f22 b22.5** Rich textured and complex, there is a glorious clarity to the sugars and fondant vanillas. Even the spices seem happy to dovetail into the merry mix without creating too many waves. 46%. nc

The BenRiach Aged 21 Years Tawny Port Wood Finish db **(87.5) n22 t21 f22 b21.5** I'm not sure if the cask finish was designed to impart a specific fruitiness profile or simply repair some tired old oak. In either case, it has been a partial success only. The intemperance of the tannin makes its mark in no small measure both on nose and delivery and it is only in the finish that the sugars bond strongly enough together to form a balance with the woody input. 46%.

The BenRiach Aged 21 Years Temporis Peated bourbon barrels, virgin oak, Pedro Ximenez & oloroso sherry casks db **(87.5) n22.5 t22 f21.5 b21.5** Begins nobly with a fanfare of alluring acidic peat, then strange (mainly orangey) fruit notes keeps chipping away at its integrity and ruining the song and balance. And so it also pans out on delivery, though the smoke is soon muzzled. For a flavour wave or two both smoke and fruit are in perfect harmony but it is fleeting and not worth the dull finish which follows. Enjoyable, but kind of irritating, too. 46%. nc ncf.

The BenRiach Aged 22 years Moscatel Wood Finish db **(81) n21 t23 f17 b20** Not sure any wine finish I have tasted this year has thrown up so many huge, one might even say challenging, perfumed notes which score so highly for sheer lip-smacking effect. Had this cask not given the impression of being sulphur treated what an enormous score it would have amassed...! 46%.

The BenRiach 25 Years Old db **(87.5) n21.5 t23 f21 b22.** The tranquillity and excellent balance of the middle is the highlight by far. 50%

The BenRiach Aged 25 Years Authenticus db **(91) n23 t23 f22 b23** Every moment feels as old as a Roman senator...who is eventually stabbed in the back by Oakicus. 46%.

BenRiach 35 Year Old db **(90) n23** juicy dates and plums are tipped into a weighty fruitcake; **t24** sit right back in your armchair (no..? Then go and find one...!!) having dimmed the lights and silenced the room and just let your taste buds run amok: those plums and toasted raisins really do get you salivating, with the spices also whipping up a mid-life storm; **f21.5** angular oak dries and bitters at a rate of knots; **b22** sexy fruit, but has late oaky bite. 42.5%

BenRiach Cask Strength batch 1 db **(93) n22.5 t24 f23 b23.5** If you don't fall in love with this one, you should stick to vodka... 57.2%

The BenRiach Curiositas Aged 10 Years Single Peated Malt db **(90.5) n23 t23 f22 b22.5** "Hmmmm. Why have my research team marked this down as a 'new' whisky? I wondered to myself. Then immediately on nosing and tasting I discovered the reason without having to ask: the pulse was weaker, the smoke more apologetic...it had been watered down from the original 46% to 40%. This is excellent malt. But can we have our truly great whisky back, please? As lovely as it is, this is a bit of an imposter. As Emperor Hadrian might once have said: "ifus itus aintus brokus..." 40%

The BenRiach Peated Cask Strength batch 1 db **(95) n24 t23 f24 b24** Stunning whisky magnificently distilled and, though relatively young, almost perfectly matured. 56%.

BenRiach Peated Quarter Casks db **(93) n23.5** there's a lot of peat in them barrels. The citrus is vital...; **t24** a plethora of sugars and caramel leached from the casks make for a safe landing when the smoke and malt – with a slightly new make feel - arrive in intensive form; **f22.5** the caramel continues, now with spice; **b23** though seemingly youthful in some phases, works a treat! 46%

Birnie Moss Intensely Peated db **(90) n22** youthful, full of fresh barley and lively, clean smoke; **t23.5** juicy, fabulously smoked, wet-behind the ears gristy sugars; **f22** some vanillas try to enter a degree of complexity; **b22.5** before Birnie Moss started shaving... or even possibly toddling. Young and stunning. *48%. nc ncf.*

The Great Drams Benriach 5 Years Old 2nd fill oloroso sherry barrel, cask no. 121/2013, dist 7 Nov 13, bott 26 Feb 19 **(75) n18 t20 f18 b19** A five-year-old malt matured in a lightly sulphured sherry butt does not a great dram make... *46.2%. nc ncf sc.*

Hidden Spirits Benriach 2010 Aged 8 Years Heavily Peated cask no. BH1018, bott 2018 **(91.5) n22 t23 f23 b23.5** so much personality despite its obvious youth. *50%. sc.*

⬙ **Old Malt Cask Benriach Aged 23 Years** refill hogshead, cask no. 16005, dist Mar 96, bott Oct 19 **(85) n20.5 t22.5 f21 b21** A tad too untidy and tart. The nose lets you into the secret that the malt and oak have not got on too well over the years and despite the attractive malty rally on delivery the tangy finish confirms the nose's warning. *476%. nc ncf sc. 310 bottles.*

⬙ **The Whisky Gallery Two of Wands BenRiach Aged 5 Years** refill sherry cask, cask no. 291, dist 2013, bott 2019 **(85) n21 t21.5 f21.5 b21** Any younger any they called have called this 'Embryo'. Virtually colourless, the malt has picked up little from the cask other than a rasping dryness. Some tangy malt and a new-make chocolate edge ensure some pleasure. *49%. sc. 172 bottles.*

BENRINNES

Speyside, 1826. Diageo. Working.

Benrinnes 21 Year Old ex-sherry European oak casks, dist 1992 db **(83.5) n21 t22 f19 b21.5.** Salty and tangy. Some superb cocoa moments mixing with the muscovado sugars as it peaks. But just a little too furry and bitter at the finish. *56.9%. 2,892 bottles. Diageo Special Releases 2014.*

⬙ **The First Editions Benrinnes Aged 14 Years 2005** refill barrel, cask no. 16782, bott 2019 **(88.5) n21.5 t23.5 f21.5 b22** Benrinnes at it most deliciously jaunty. The barley is on overdrive from the moment it hits the palate, making this one of the maltiest malts of the year without question. The thinness on both the nose and finish is a bridge to be crossed, but that's no good reason not to luxuriate in the very maltiest of deliveries. *56.4%. nc ncf sc. 222 bottles.*

The First Editions Benrinnes Aged 16 Years 2002 sherry butt, cask no. 15438, bott 2018 **(79) n18 t21.5 f19.5 b20** A pretty awful nose is compensated for by a boiled-sweet fruitiness and attractive accompanying very un-Benrinnes-like oils on both delivery and finish. Surprisingly assertive at times. *55.1%. nc ncf sc. 270 bottles.*

Gleann Mór Benrinnes Aged Over 24 Years **(89.5) n22.5 t23 f21.5 b22.5** One of the more impressive Benrinnes you'll find in the market place just now. On its days, it can belt out barley with the best of them. But here as well maximising the malt the subtle layering of acacia honey and vanilla sponge ensures that, with an also just-so addition of spice, you are seeing the distillery in its finest fettle. *41.1%.*

The Golden Cask Benrinnes 1995 cask no. CM248, bott 2018 **(89) n22 t22.5 f22 b22.5** A Peter Pan of a malt, refusing to grow up and making the most of its juicy vitality. *56%. nc ncf sc. 282 bottles.*

Hepburn's Choice Benrinnes 10 Years Old rum finished cask, dist 2009, bott 2019 **(84.5) n22 t22 f20 b20.5** A curious choice to put Benrinnes into rum. You start with a malty but limited distillate finding further constraints which rum casks invariably bring. The finish, predictably, does not live up to the earlier charm. *46%. nc ncf sc. 276 bottles.*

⬙ **Hepburn's Choice Benrinnes 10 Years Old** wine cask, dist 2009, bott 2019 **(83) n20 t21 f21 b21** Not a particularly bad wine cask. But the malt base is so feeble it is just incapable of making any kind of impression, or ensuring any degree of complexity. Not unpleasant, but a malt which goes precisely nowhere. *46%. nc ncf sc. 110 bottles.*

Hepburn's Choice Benrinnes 12 Years Old sherry butt, dist 2005, bott 2018 **(86.5) n21.5 t22 f21.5 b22** Benrinnes being shewn in an attractive light here thanks to some very good oak which plays alongside the lightweight malt, rather than trying to overpower it. Delicate and attractively juicy early on. *46%. nc ncf sc. 348 bottles.*

⬙ **Scyfion Choice Benrinnes 2006** pomegranate Armenian wine cask finished, bott 2019 **(91) n22.5** Benrinnes isn't Glenmorangie, or even close, so there isn't the same kind of body here for the fruit to weave itself onto, making that pomegranate and gooseberry signature a little less sturdy; **t23** decent, simplistic malt with a spicy background. The thick body makes this particularly tart and eye-watering; **f22.5** slightly gristy, vanilla...and more spice...; **b23** this is very weird. I tasted their Bashta cask vatted malt earlier in the day and got pomegranates....!!! I'm assuming this is the same cask type here: if it is, I have just impressed if not amazed myself! Well, my last girlfriend, Judy, was half Armenian: I think I know what to get her for Christmas. Lots of character and personality here. *50%. nc ncf sc. 158 bottles.*

Stronachie 18 Years Old (83.5) n21.5 t21 f20 b21. This is so much like the older brother of the Stronachie 12: shows the same hot temper on the palate and even sharper teeth. Also, the same slim-line body. Have to say, though, something strangely irresistible about the intensity of the crisp malt. 46%

Whisky Castle Benrinnes Aged 9 Years rum barrel finish, dist 2009, bott 2018 **(91)** n23 t23.5 f22 b22.5 Disarmingly orchestrated. A superior Benrinnes. 46%. nc ncf sc. 297 bottles.

World of Orchids Benrinnes 1997 20 Years Old bourbon cask, cask no. 821 **(89)** n22 t23 f22 b22 The orchids around here grow in grass. And this is the grassiest malt I have sampled in a while. Delightfully fresh, despite its age. So gristy, too. 48.9%. sc.

BENROMACH
Speyside, 1898. Gordon & MacPhail. Working.

Benromach 15 Year Old db **(78)** n20 t22 f17 b19. Some charming early moments, especially when the grape escapes its marker and reveals itself in its full juicy and sweet splendour. But it is too short lived as the sulphur, inevitably takes over. 43%

Benromach 21 Years Old db **(91.5)** n22 t23.5 f23 b23 An entirely different, indeed lost, style of malt from the old, now gone, big stills. The result is like an airier whisky which has embraced such good age with a touch of panache and grace. 43%

Benromach 30 Years Old db **(95.5)** n23.5 t24 f24 b24 You will struggle to find a 30-year-old with fewer wrinkles than this.. Magnificent: one of the outstanding malts of the year. 43%

Benromach 39 Year Old 1977 Vintage db **(94)** n23.5 t24 f23 b23.5 Just love it when a whisky creaks and complains and lets you know just how old it is...but then produces the magic that keeps alive, well and captivatingly complex after all these years. 56%

Benromach 1972 cask no. 4471 db **(94)** n23 t23.5 f23.5 b24 Has turned completely grey, but this is one sprightly malt. 55.7%. sc.

Benromach 1977 cask no. 1269 db **(87.5)** n22 t21.5 f22 b22 Plucked from the warehouse a little too late with its best days behind it. The oak is overlord here, the tannins aggressive enough to bring water to the eye, as does the grapefruit citrus kick. But by no means is all lost as the malt is proud, robust and rich and puts up a chewy rear-guard action. 49.6%. sc.

Benromach 100° Proof db **(94)** n23 t23.5 f23.5 b24 For any confused US readers, the strength is based on the old British proof strength, not American! What is not confusing is the undisputed complexity and overall excellence of this malt. 57%

Benromach 20th Anniversary Bottling db **(81)** n19 t22 f19 b21 Bit of a clumsy whisky never really feeling right on the nose or palate, though has its better moments with a big malt crescendo and a delicate minty-chocolate movement towards the late middle and early finish. 56.2%.

Benromach 2005 Sassicaia Finish db **(92.5)** n22.5 t24 f23 b23. A sassy dram! 45%

Benromach Cask No. 1 dist 1998, bott 2018 db **(89.5)** n23 like a bunch of grapes you forgot you had in the bag...; t22 fat, oily slightly off-key start but corrects itself as a tart but attractive gooseberry notes arrives; f22 dry powdery mocha; b22.5 an unusual fingerprint to this and intriguingly haphazard in its development. 60.1%.

Benromach Cask Strength 2001 db **(89)** n21.5 t23 f22 b22.5. Just fun whisky which has been very well made and matured with total sympathy to the style. Go get. 59.9%

Benromach Cask Strength 2003 db **(92)** n22.5 t23.5 f23 b23.5 Hats off to the most subtle and sophisticated Benromach I have tasted in a while. 59.4%.

Benromach Cask Strength Batch 1 dist 2008, bott 2019 db **(90.5)** n23.5 light praline sits as astride the gentle peat; just the lightest touch of parma violet; t22.5 like Cask 1, there is a slight wobble on the spirit and for a moment bares some teeth. But soon the gentle smoke returns, alongside a delicate Camp coffee note; f22 a touch of mint chocolate on the almost apologetic peat; b22.5 some smoky malts terrify people. This, I suspect, will enjoy the direct opposite effect. As friendly a peated malt as you'll ever find. 57.9%

Benromach Heritage 35 Year Old db **(87)** n22 t21.5 f22 b21.5. A busy exchange of complex tannin notes, some backed by the most faded spice and caramel. All charming and attractive, but the feeling of decay is never far away. 43%

Benromach Heritage 1974 db **(93)** n23.5 t23 f23 b23.5 Made in the year I left school to become a writer, this appears to have survived the years in better nick than I... 49.1%

Benromach Heritage 1975 db **(89)** n22 t22.5 f22 b22.5 A bottling where the malt is hanging on for grim death against the passing of time. But the discreet light honey notes do just the trick. 49.9%.

Benromach Heritage 1976 db **(86.5)** n21.5 t21 f22.5 b21.5 There are times when you can have a little too much tannin and this has crossed the Rubicon. That said, look closely on the nose for some staggering lime and redcurrant notes which escape the onslaught as well as the gorgeous butterscotch on the finish as the sugars fight back at the death in style. Some moments of genius in the oakiest of frames. 53.5%.

Benromach Organic Special Edition db **(85.5) n22 t21 f21.5 b21**. The smoky bacon crisp aroma underscores the obvious youth. Also, one of the driest malts of the year. Overall, pretty. But pretty pre-pubescent, too... *43%*

Benromach Organic 2010 db **(95.5) n24 t24 f23 b24.5** Gentle, refined and exquisitely elegant. *43%*.

Benromach Peat Smoke Batch 3 db **(90.5) n22 t23 f22.5 b23** An excellent malt that has been beautifully made. Had it been bottled at 46 we would have seen it offer an extra degree of richness. *40%*

Benromach Peat Smoke 2008 db **(85.5) n22 t22 f20.5 b21** Well, that was certainly different! The nose has the oily hallmark of a Caol Ila, though without the phenol intensity. The palate, those oils apart, is a very different tale. A unique flavour profile for sure: a kind of smoked toffee fudge which actually makes your tongue ache while tasting! And there is a bitterness, also. Normally I can spot exactly from where it originates...this one leaves me baffled...though I'd go from the distillation if pushed. *46%*.

Benromach Sherry Cask Matured Peat Smoke dist 2010, bott 2018 db **(94.5) n23.5** the kind of massive sherry and even huger peat noses that some peatophiles I know just lie in bed dreaming about....huge! Oh, and acidic and mildly aggressive, too...; **t24** wow...!! Now that's the kind of delivery I lie in bed and dream about. Perfect, not overly sweet grape, standing toe-to-toe with seriously macho phenol. Neither gives an inch...; **f23** long, with some searing spices to balance the gristy sugars; lovely milky mocha at the death; **b24** these type of whiskies so often fall flat on their face. This, by contrast, is a magnificent beast of a malt... *59.9%*.

Benromach Triple Distilled db **(88) n23** the firmness to the malt has an almost Irish pot still quality: sharp, yet with a firm, brooding disposition; **t22.5** salivating and ultra-clean. Gristy sugars melt into the mix with vanilla upping the weight; **f21.5** a slight oak-sponsored bitterness from the more antiquated casks makes its mark; **b22** the finish part, a really charming barley character pervades throughout. *50%*.

Benromach Vintage 1976 db **(89.5) n23 t23.5 f21 b22** hardly complex and shows all the old age attributes to be expected. That said...a very comfortable and satisfying ride. *46%*

Benromach Wood Finish 2007 Sassicaia db **(86.5) n22 t22 f21 b21.5**. Now back to the new distillery. Problem with this wood finish is that even when free from any taint, as this is, it is a harsh taskmaster and keeps a firm grip of any malty development – even on a dram so young. A brave cask choice. *45%*

BLADNOCH

Lowlands, 1817. David Prior. Working.

Bladnoch 10 Year Old bourbon barrels, bott code: L18/8829 db **(91) n22.5 t23 f22.5 b23** Just wonderful to see Bladnoch back in the market place again, and this time obviously receiving the kind of attention in warehouse and tasting lab it deserves. The 10-year-old was for years a Lowland staple before a succession of owners saw it all but vanish off the map. This 10-year-old suggests they have the nucleus of what can again become a much-prized dram. Though a ten-year-old, either some of the casks used in this were a lot older, or there has been heavy usage of first-fill bourbon somewhere along the line, because the tannins have an unusually significant say. The result...rather delicious and you get a hell of a lot for a ten-year-old... *46.7%. ncf.*

⟡ **Bladnoch 11 Year Old** bourbon & red wine casks, bott code: L19 WB db **(87.5) n21.5 t23 f21 b22** Certainly no escaping the full- on juiciness of the delivery which broadcasts a full on vividness of the fruit. The malt, though, offers the more alluring backbone, though the two styles have problems integrating at the death. Would love to see this without the wine. *46.7%. ncf. First Release.*

Bladnoch 15 Year Old Adela oloroso sherry casks, bott code: L18/8083 db **(91) n22 t23 f23 b23** I still feel a bit like Inspector Clouseau's boss, twitching at the mere thought of a sherry butt. But no need for alarm here: faultless oloroso influence here, indeed coming to the aid perhaps of an initial spirit which may not have been originally up to Bladnoch's excellent name. Surprisingly delightful. *46.7%. ncf.*

Bladnoch 17 Year Old Californian red wine finish db **(87.5) n22 t23 f21 b21.5** At its zenith on both nose and delivery, both imparting boiled sweet fruitiness and lustre. After that, as well as spice, a non-sulphured bitterness seeps into the proceedings. *46.7%. ncf.*

Bladnoch 27 Year Old bourbon cask finish db **(95) n24.5** the infusion of rich, clean barley with greengage, lime and vanilla is almost heady in its beauty. A soft saltiness lifts those erudite notes even further and gentle layers of orange blossom as well as Bruyere honey turns an excellent nose into truly great one; **t23.5** the finess and complexity of the spirit on the nose is further amplified by the technically perfect delivery on landing. The barley is crystalised in clarity while the very lightest of oils settle to both at weight and act as a absorbing buffer to the perkier oak tones; **f23** long with a busy, spicy tail to the weightier tannins; **b24** the best nose of a Lowlander I have encountered for a good number of years. A gem of single malt. 43%. ncf

Bladnoch Samsara Californian red wine & bourbon casks, bott code: L18/8081 db **(87)** **n21.5 t23 f21 b21.5** Wine casks at work and not a sulphur atom in sight. However, there is no escaping a certain unscheduled bitterness or the fact that perhaps some of the malt was technically not the greatest ever distilled in Bladnoch's history. The result is a patchy experience, delicious in part, but bitty and bitter in others. Lush though on delivery and the plusses are big ones. 46.7%. ncf.

⬧ **Bladnoch Talia 26 Year Old** red wine casks nbc db **(89.5) n23.5** we are almost heading towards Kentucky territory as the light red liquorice intertwangles with the juicy barley...but then a big whoosh of grape arrives; **t22.5** light and bouncy on the palate, the barley having a certain brittleness and no shortage of chutzpah. But...whoosh...in comes that wine...! **f21.5** pleasant, but technically untidy. A little gnawing dryness amid the uneven malt and fruit fade; **b22** have to say, knowing Bladnoch as well as I do (and loving it even more intensely!) I was a little frustrated by the heavy-handedness of the grape which carries all before it. There is still a residual juiciness from the barley 44%. ncf. 2020 Release.

⬧ **Bladnoch Single Cask 2020/01** California red wine hogshead, cask no. 38, dist Jan 08, bott Mar 20 db **(90) n22.5** the grape dominates, a degree of sharpness and spice almost alien to a distillery whose nose is usually a byword for yielding, sweet maltiness; **t23** a lovely voluptuousness to the fruit on delivery is at odds with the crisper nose, though a brittleness does develop as the muscovado sugars kick in; **f22** long, a little too sweet at times and surprisingly oily. Not a single off note and an impressive countering dryness as the vanilla begins to build; **b22.5** a very bold wine influence tends to wipe out the usual charming malt character offered up by Bladnoch at this age. But the wine cask is clean and clear in its design, ensuring a wonderfully flavoursome experience. Though if blind-tasted, I wouldn't have picked Bladnoch in 50 increasingly desperate guesses... 56%. nc ncf sc. 289 bottles.

Cask 88 Bladnoch 27 Year Old sherry hogshead, sherry quarter cask finish, cask no. 877589 **(84.5) n21.5 t20.5 f21.5 b21** Some whiskies are born great, some achieve greatness and some have greatness thrust upon them. This is the latter. Except more like greatness thrust upon them...but missed. Some almost grotesque grape at work here. 51.3%. nc ncf sc. 88 bottles. Eighty Eight Series.

BLAIR ATHOL
Highlands (Perthshire), 1798. Diageo. Working.

Blair Athol 23 Year Old ex-bodega European oak butts db **(90.5) n23 t23.5 f21.5 b22.5** Very often you think: "Aha! Here's an un-sulphur-treated sherry-matured malt!" And then find long into the finish that the taint turns up and sticks with you for another 20 minutes. Is there a slight trace on this late on? Yes. But it is one of the lightest and least concerning I have encountered this year. Which leaves you with plenty of luscious grape to enjoy... 58.4%. 5,514 bottles. Diageo Special Releases 2017.

⬧ **Blair Athol Distillery Exclusive Bottling** batch no. 01, refill, rejuvenated & American oak ex-bourbon casks, bott code: L9316DQ002 db **(94) n23** enticingly nutty, the sugar development seems to be arrested by the elegant oaky tones and light caramel. The vaguest spice prickle, but it makes all the difference...; **t24** every outstanding malt has a degree of layering – and this has it in droves. Particularly impressive are the varied sugars, three types in particular: caramel, Demerara and light molasses. Maybe a fourth with the very vaguest faintest hint of maple syrup. But all this mixes and blends in with the slightly toasted barley **f23.5** gorgeous spiced cocoa and residual nuttiness – quality! **b23.5** a distillery that has come so far away from its days as a producer of fodder malt for Bells, when the spirit was thin and inconsequential, it is now a malt to be sought after and savoured rather than snubbed. This expression really underlines not just the high quality that this distillery is now capable of but also its depth of character. Delightful. 48%. 6,000 bottles.

⬧ **Acla Selection Summer Edition Blair Athol 29 Year Old** hogshead, dist 1988, bott 2018 **(82.5) n20 t22 f20.5 b20** Maybe not distilled at the greatest time in the distillery's history, a malt that is down to the bare bones as little body is evident. Some interesting fruit pastel tones on delivery, but at no time does this malt ever find any kind of meaningful equilibrium. 51.9%.

The First Editions Blair Athol Aged 23 Years 1995 sherry butt, cask no. 15758, bott 2019 **(78) n19 t21.5 f18.5 b19** The fruit flourishes briefly, but the sulphur kicks in quite quickly. 55.7%. nc ncf sc. 289 bottles.

⬧ **Hepburn's Choice Blair Athol 11 Years Old** wine cask, dist 2009, bott 2019 **(78) n19 t20 f19 b20** My 13th whisky of the day...which says it all. A very tight wine cask which closes all avenues for development. A closed and closed case... 46%. nc ncf sc. 181 bottles.

Old Malt Cask Blair Athol Aged 23 Years sherry butt, cask no. 15757, dist Aug 95, bott Feb 19 **(74.5) n18 t20 f18 b18.5** Guess. The clue comes in the bit that comes after "Aged 23 Years"... *50%. nc ncf sc. 321 bottles.*

◈ **Old Malt Cask Blair Athol Aged 24 Years** sherry butt, cask no. 17193, dist Jun 95, bott Sept 19 **(88) n21.5 t22.5 f22 b22** Fat and malty, the sherry butt makes no great impression, other than perhaps upping the viscosity slightly. Some lovely spices in action with the vanilla. Busy and satisfying. *50%. nc ncf sc. 294 bottles.*

World of Orchids Blair Athol 1988 29 Years Old bourbon cask, cask no. 509 **(87) n21.5 t22.5 f21 b22** You can almost hear this malt panting after such a long journey, for which the spirit was ill-prepared for in a cask like this. The oak has a vice-like grip, which does bring a bit of a tear to the eye, but at least the barley is game enough to put up some sharp, not unattractive, citrusy resistance. *51.3%. sc.*

BOWMORE
Islay, 1779. Morrison Bowmore. Working.

Bowmore Aged 10 Years Spanish oak sherry casks & hogsheads, bott code: L172033 db **(92.5) n23.5 t23.5 f22.5 b23** A very happy marriage between some full on peat and decent sherry butts makes for the intense malt promised on the label. *40%.*

◈ **Bowmore Aged 12 Years** bott code: L182208 db **(86.5) n22 t22 f21 b21.5** This is some surprise package. With the phenol level being markedly down on the last bottle of this I encountered and the oils wearing thin long before the end – not assisted by the 40% abv – this Bowmore never quite gets going. Perhaps the midpoint has something to latch on to and thoroughly enjoy where the peat and oils do find accord. But it is far too short-lived. *40%.*

Bowmore "Enigma" Aged 12 Years db **(82) n19 t22 f20 b21.** Sweet, molassed and with that tell-tale Fisherman's Friend tang representing the light smoke. This Enigma hasn't quite cracked it, though. *40%. Duty Free.*

Bowmore Gold Reef oak casks db **(79) n19.5 t21 f19 b19.5.** Simple, standard (and rather boring and safe) fare for the masses gagged by toffee. *43% WB15/280*

Bowmore Aged 15 Years 1st fill bourbon casks, bott code: L172034 031 db **(88) n23.5 t22 f21 b21.5** This was going swimmingly until the caramel just went nuts. I know first-fill bourbon casks are at work here, but hard to believe that was all natural... *40%.*

Bowmore Aged 15 Years sherry cask finish, bott code: L172073 db **(91) n23 t22.5 f22.5 b23** A sherry influenced whisky outpointing a bourbon cask one....how often will you find that in this book...? *43%.*

◈ **Bowmore Aged 15 Years** bott code: L9289SB323250923 db **(94) n23.5** straight down the Victory V path, with the smoke still pretty active and alert even after all these passing years. A real allotment bonfire reek, this..; **t23.5** sugars gang together early and enjoy a toasty resonance which fits the smoke like a glove. Brilliant vanilla layering forms the key to the later complexity; **f23** creamy smoked mocha; **b24** a joyful experience with the peat in expansive mode and the Victory V cough sweet adding the right kind of toasted sugars. An easily quaffable kind of 15-year-old...not something you normally associate with a whisky of this good age. I just love to see Bowmore in this kind of mood. *43%.*

Bowmore Aged 18 Years Oloroso & Pedro Ximénez casks, bott code: L172067 060 db **(82) n20.5 t22.5 f19 b20** A dirty old nose – and I don't just mean the peat – pre-warns of the furry finish. But there is no denying the sheer joy of the voluptuous grape grappling with the phenols on delivery and in the wonderful moments just after. *43%.*

◈ **Bowmore Aged 18 Years** bott code: L9172SB322071130 db **(87) n21.5 t22 f21.5 b22** A grouchy, moody dram inclined to bite your head off. The nose is positively snarling with the peat offering no give whatsoever and happy to give you a bit of the old acid. While the delivery likewise gives your what for with a volley of dry, unforgiving, peaty expletives. The finish is no less harsh. Only a few curt molasses and hickory notes offer solace. *43%.*

Bowmore Aged 19 Years The Feis Ile Collection first fill sherry puncheon, cask no. 57,dist 13 Jan 98, bott 27 May 17 db **(97) n24 t24.5 f24 b24.5** If there was an award for the Best Cask Chosen by a Distillery Manager 2019, then it would go to this extraordinary bottling. A problem with sherry butts, even if entirely free from sulphur as this delightfully is, is their propensity to mask the actual distillery from which the whisky comes. Not here: this is as instantly and unmistakably recognisable as a Bowmore as the first three notes are as the signature of 'Goldfinger'. The salt from the No 1 warehouse, the light layering of smoke...well done distillery manager David Turner take a bow for your Bowmore....the finest I have ever tasted...! *54.3%. sc. Distillery Exclusive*

Bowmore 20 Years Old 1997 sherry cask, bott 2017 db **(95.5) n24 t24 f23.5 b24** The curtain of thick musky peat which descends on the nose leaves no doubt that we are in for one big sherried, oaky experience. And so it proves, although not quite in the fashion you might expect.

For the softness on delivery is at odds with the boldness on the nose though, slowly, rung by rung the oak begins to take an increasingly more powerful hold: it is like experiencing whisky in slow motion. The fruit is a mix of blood orange and concentrated plum, the oak (here taken to its max) and smoke together creating a peaty chocolate spine. A malt of breath-taking enormity and beauty...to be devoured in slow-motion. 54.5%. sc. 231 bottles. Selected for CWS.

Bowmore Aged 23 Years Port Matured db (86) n22 t22 f21 b21. Have you ever sucked Fisherman's Friends and fruit pastels at the same time, and thrown in the odd Parma Violet for good measure...? 50.8%

Bowmore Aged 25 Years Small Batch Release db (85.5) n21 t22 f21 b21.5. Distilled at the very heart of Bowmore's peculiar and uniquely distinctive Fisherman's Friend cough sweet era. You will never find a more vivid example. 43%

Bowmore 29 Years Old 1989 db (81.5) n20.5 t21 f20 b20 From that uniquely disjointed: Fisherman's "Friend" period of their production history. The Whisky Shop Exclusive.

Bowmore Aged 30 Years db (94) n23 t24 f23 b24 A Bowmore that no Islay scholar should be without. Shows the distillery at its most intense yet delicate; an essay in balance and how great oak, peat and fruit can combine for those special moments in life. Unquestionably one of the best Bowmores bottled this century. 43%

Bowmore Black 50 Year Old db (96.5) n25 t24 f23 b24.5 a little known fact: a long time ago, before the days of the internet and a world of whisky experts who outnumber the stars that puncture the sky on the very darkest of nights, I actually tasted the first Black Bowmore in their very basic blending lab and gave it the required seal of approval before they allowed it to hit the shelves. It wasn't a 50-year-old beast like this one, though. And it proves that though something may have reached half a century, it knows how to give pleasure on at least a par with anything younger ... 41%

Bowmore Black Rock oak casks db (87.5) n22.5 t22 f21 b22. A friendly, full bodied dram whose bark is worse than its bite. Smoked toasted fudge is the main theme. But that would not work too well without the aid of a vague backdrop cinnamon and marmalade. If you are looking for a gentle giant, they don't come more wimpish than this. 40% WB15/336

Bowmore Devil's Casks III db (92.5) n23 t23 f23.5 b23.5 a whisky created by Charles Williams, surely. So, at last....I'm in league with the devil...! Hawwww-hhaaaa-haaaaaa!!!! 56.7%

Bowmore Laimrig Aged 15 Years db (90.5) n22.5 t23.5 f22 b22.5 first things first: absolutely spot on sherry butts at work here with not a hint of an off note. But often it is hard to get smoke and sherry to gel. The exercise here is not without success, but you feel it is straining at every sinew to hit the high spots. 53.7%. 18,000 bottles.

Bowmore Mizunara Cask Finish db (90.5) n22.5 t22 f23.5 b22.5 A Bowmore like no other: not always happy in its own skin, but when it relaxes towards the finish, it positively pulses its Islay credentials. 53.9%. 2,000 bottles.

Bowmore No.1 first fill bourbon casks, bott code: L172026 db (91.5) n23 t23 f22.5 b23 Bowmore was never the most peaty of Islay's malts. But here the phenols are at their shyest. Delicate and all a rather sexy tease... 40%.

Bowmore Small Batch "Bourbon Cask Matured" db (86) n22 t22 f21 b21. A big improvement on the underwhelming previous Small Batch from this distillery, then called "Reserve", though there appears to be a naivety to the proceeding which both charm and frustrate. The smoke, hanging on the grist, is very low key. 40%.

Bowmore White Sands Aged 17 Years db (88) n20 t22 f23 b23 A muzzled malt which shouldn't work – but somehow does. 43%

The Golden Cask Bowmore 1995 cask no. CM249, bott 2018 (87) n22 t22.5 f21 b21.5 Probably not from a vintage time for Bowmore. A distinctive Victory V cough sweet nose and delivery. Delicious creaminess and viscosity and some lovely Demerara sugars on the phenols. But all very untidy and bitter from the midpoint onwards. 51.4%. nc ncf sc. 564 bottles.

The Golden Cask Bowmore 2002 cask no. CM247, bott 2018 (94.5) n23 t23.5 f24 b24 A chocolate Bowmore...! 58%. nc ncf sc. 234 bottles.

⬧ **Wemyss Malts Black Gold Bowmore 1989 30 Years Old** hogshead (82.5) n20 t22.5 f19 b21 This malt technically fails on so many levels. Something over the 30 years or so has happened to this cask that is very odd. All kinds of strange notes (most of them metallic, but also a bit of the swimming pool on the nose), that, as a blender, I'd mark off and keep away from any whisky I'm working with. Yet, despite all that, despite its metallic tang, there is also something irresistibly attractive about this brute. 50%. nc ncf sc. 175 bottles.

⬧ **Wemyss Malts Kilning The Malt Bowmore 1996 23 Years Old** hogshead (94) n23.5 a drizzle of lemon on pastel-shaded phenol. Not a hint of a hint of an off note or a molecule out of place; t23.5 you knew it'd be salivating on delivery...and it is. Despite its age, the grist is beautifully fresh and, as on the nose, the citrus and smoke meld together; icing sugars melt in the mouth; f23 only now do the tannins make any kind of meaningful contribution ganging together to pay some lip-service to the age. Labyrinthine vanillas at play; b24 if this were any more polite a malt, it'd do a curtsy before a-leaping onto your taste buds... 47.9%. nc ncf sc. 218 bottles.

◇ **Woolf/Sung The Lowest Tide Bowmore 26 Year Old 1991** Sauternes cask finish **(95)** n24 t23.5 f23.5 b24 From the very first sniff to the last dying peaty ember, this exudes class. I have long argued that high quality Sauternes cask is by far the most sympathetic of all the wine casks – and this does nothing to disprove my theory. The fruit is always around: clean at times adding candied feel. But the peat is always in control -and here, after more than a quarter of a century, the ppm levels must have been way above the usual 25 when this was made. A tactile dram clinging and kissing with maple syrup to add to the grist. What a sensational experience – in every sense! 50.9%. sc.

BRAEVAL

Speyside, 1974. Chivas Brothers. Working.

Gordon & MacPhail Connoisseurs Choice Braeval 1998 refill American hogshead, dist 1998, bott 22 Feb 18 **(84.5)** n21.5 t22 f20 b21 Not the first malt I have tasted this year which has the unmistakable hallmarks of a rushed distillate, where the stills have been fired a little too enthusiastically than is best for the whisky. The thinness to both nose and body coupled with the huge sugary outpouring as the grist and sweeter elements of the oak dominate. Then that flickering, faulting finale....59%. nc ncf sc. 185 bottles.

Kingsbury Gold Braes of Glenlivet 23 Year Old barrel, cask no. 165588, dist 1994 **(91.5)** n23.5 t23 f22 b23 You can't expect much more from an ancient Braes than this. 54.1%. sc.

BRORA

Highlands (Northern), 1819–1983. Diageo. Closed.

Brora 34 Year Old refill American oak hogsheads db **(88.5)** n22.5 t22 f22 b22 The nose kinds of sums things up perfectly: skeletal fingers of age are all over this: citrus offers sinew and a little smoke the flesh...but time is catching up... 51.9%. 3,000 bottles. Diageo Special Releases 2017.

BRUICHLADDICH

Islay, 1881. Rémy Cointreau. Working.

Bruichladdich 18 Years Old bourbon/cognac cask db **(84.5)** n23.5 t21 f20 b20. Big oak-spice buzz but thin. Sublime grapey nose, for sure, but pays a certain price, ultimately, for associating with such an inferior spirit... 46%

Bruichladdich 2005 12 Year Old fresh sherry hogshead, cask no. 998, dist 20 Jul 05, bott 2018 db **(92.5)** n23.5 t24 f23 b22 There is virtually no balance to this whisky, yet it somehow works. A whisky every home should have: if you receive a bit of a surprise in your life, this will violently shake you back into the world... 60.4%. nc ncf sc. 372 bottles. Bottled for MacAlabur.

◇ **Bruichladdich Black Art 7 Aged 25 Years** db **(95)** n23.5 pretty low voltage peat and celebrating an Muscovado sugar fruit lining; t24 salivating and sweet but, peat-wise, remarkably dull in Octomore currency. Smoked raisin and chocolate, but all far too polite and delicate; f23.5 a slightly more acidic and sooty smokiness but too little too late for greatness; some lovely milk chocolate notes filter through from the midpoint – and stick; b24 have to say I do love this whisky. One of the most complex Bruichladdichs since its conversion back to a peaty distillery with a delivery that gives you something slightly different each time you taste it....as a genuinely great 25-year-old should be. 48.4%.

Bruichladdich Islay Barley Aged 5 Years db **(86)** n21 t22.5 f21.5 b21. The nose suggests a trainee has been let loose at the stills. But it makes amends with an almost debauched degree of barley on delivery which lasts the entirety of the experience. Heavens! This is different. But I have to say: it's bloody fun, too! 50%. nc ncf.

Bruichladdich The Laddie Eight Years Old American & European oak, cask no. 16/070 db **(83)** n21.5 t22 f19 b20.5 Doesn't chime anything like so well as the Classic Laddie, for instance. The sugars surge and soar in impressive manner, the mid-range smokiness benefiting. But there is a tightness which does very few favours. 50%.

Bruichladdich Laddie Classic Edition 1 db **(89.5)** n23 t23 f21 b22.5. You probably have to be a certain vintage yourself to fully appreciate this one. Hard to believe, but I can remember the days when the most popular malt among those actually living on Islay was the Laddie 10. That was a staunchly unpeated dram offering a breezy complexity. Not sure of the age on this Retroladdich, but the similarities almost bring a lump to the throat... 46%

Bruichladdich Scottish Barley The Classic Laddie db **(78.5)** n20 t21.5 f18 b19. Not often a Laddie fluffs its lines. But despite some obviously complex and promising moves, the unusual infiltration of some sub-standard casks has undone the good of the local barley. If you manage to tune out of the off-notes, some sublime moments can still be had. 50%. nc ncf sc.

The Laddie Ten American oak db **(94.5)** n24 t23.5 f23 b24 This, I assume, is the 2012 full strength version of an Islay classic which was the preferred choice of the people of Islay throughout the 70s, 80s and early 90s. And I have to say that this is already a classic in its own right.... 46%. nc ncf.

The Laddie Sixteen American oak db **(88)** n22 huge natural caramels dipped in brine; t22.5 very even and gentle with a degree of citrus perking it up; f21.5 reverts to caramels before the tannins strike hard; b22 oak 'n' salt all the way... 46%

The Laddie Twenty Two db **(90.5)** n24 t23 f21.5 b22 Fabulous coastal malt, though the oak is a presence always felt. 46%

Octomore 7.1 5 Years Old ex-bourbon casks, cask no. 16/080 db **(96)** n23.5 t24.5 f24 b24 Fan-bloody-tastic...!! A kid of a whisky which sorts the men from the boys... 57%.

Octomore 7.2 5 Years Old bourbon & Syrah casks, cask no. 15/058 db **(81.5)** n21 t23 f18 b19.5 I love the fact that the sample bottles I have been sent under "education." Brilliant! An hilarious first. But here, if anything is to be learned by those who for some reason don't already know, is the fact that you *don't* piss around with perfection. Five-year-old Octomore in bourbon cask is a joy that has just about proved beyond description for me. Pointlessly add wine casks – and the sulphur which so often accompanies them – and you get a whisky very much reduced in quality and stature. Some superb moments on this, especially round the time of the warts-and-all delivery. But as it settles the faults of the Syrah casks slowly become clear. What a shame. And waste of great whisky. An education, indeed! 58.5%.

Octomore 10 db **(95)** n24 t24 f23 b24 When I am tasting an Octomore, it means I am in the home straight inside the stadium after running (or should I say nosing and tasting) a marathon. After this, there are barely another 20 more Scotch malts to go and I am closing in on completing my 1,200 new whiskies for the year. So how does this fare? It is Octomore. It is what I expect and demand. It gives me the sustenance and willpower to get to that crossing line. For to tell you guys about a whisky like this is always worth it...whatever the pain and price. Because honesty and doing the right thing is beyond value. Just ask David Archer. 50%.

⟩ **Octomore Edition 10.1 Aged 5 Years** PPM 107 db **(95)** n23.5 oh the peat etc....; t24 the peat...! Etc...; f23.5 oh the...etc..; b24 we've been here before. Except maybe this one has a bit more vanilla on hand, as well as some sweetening oils.... 59.8%.

⟩ **Octomore Edition 10.2 Aged 8 Years** PPM 96.9 db **(94)** n23 busy layering of hefty smoke and mildly citrussy butterscotch tart. Just a slight wobble in the tannin, I think...; t24.5 restored! The peat is not just huge, it offers both a searing acid note and also a salivating semi-bourbon style hickory sharpness; f23 the smoke fades dramatically as the vanillas take control...; b23.5 it's an interesting debate: is Octomore at its best when very young and peat has full control? Or when matured and the oak has had a chance to create a more nuanced whisky? I'd say from this evidence, and other Octomores I have seen over the years it is at is best when a little younger than this, as here the peat, despite the extraordinary complexity on the delivery, has just lost some of the power of its magic. 56.9%.

⟩ **Octomore Edition 10.3 Aged 6 Years** PPM 114 db **(96.5)** n24 oh the peat etc....; t24 the peat, the peat....!!!! Etc...; f24 bloody, hell...!!! The peat....it won't stop....!!! b24.5 bloody hell...!! What peat...!!! Yes, we have been down this road before but this one has taken us into a sooty-dry cul-de-sac. Have you ever had an enormous whisky? Yes...? Well, that'll be a little minnow you'll need to throw back against this smoke-billowing beast. 61.3%. 🍷

⟩ **Octomore Edition 10.4 Aged 3 Years** PPM 88 db **(95.5)** n24 huge peat, and for those looking for more...well, you'll find it. There are bluebells and Arbutus blossom, too. But always we come back to the peat: earthy, acidic; dry, slightly sweet from the grists...it takes on so many contradictory forms it is almost scary...; t24 you want to raise your arms and scream...!!! Yessss!!! Chocolate and smoke at its most enormous. Both challenging and yet devouring. The eyes water, the mouth salivates to uncontrollable levels, the molasses builds and builds with the toastiness...all is perfect with the world...; f23.5 a 101 variations on smoked spice...; b24 if you take this whisky for what it is: a very young hugely peated monster of a malt then you'll be very happy indeed. This is one crazy, mixed up kid. And one hell of a smoky one, too. More than great fun. It is a right of passage: for both the whisky and its consumer... 63.5%.

⟩ **Port Charlotte Aged 10 Years** db **(95)** n23.5 big peat...but just look at the way the citrus runs through the centre of those phenols cutting the smoke down to size; t24 there is more than a slight similarity here to this Port Charlotte and how Ardbeg tasted from a bourbon cask 20 years ago, but not quite so much now. The smoke has a mildly threatening but ultimately reserved character, allowing itself to build slowly but without disturbing the natural association between the malt and vanilla; f23.5 light spices and even lighter cocoa as the phenols now added weight as well as smoke; b24 very high quality and teasingly complex peated malt. 50%.

Port Charlotte Heavily Peated db **(94.5)** n23 t24 f23.5 b24 Rearrange the following two words: "giant" and "gentle". 50%

 ◈ **Port Charlotte Islay Barley 2011 Aged 6 Years** db (95) n23.5 a disarming flakiness to the peat allows both the malt and oak to have their own complex affair. While they are not looking the citrus creeps in; t24 sensational weight. The lightness of touch from the barley sugar and thin molasses you can only dream of. And a lurking presence of peat creates dark, almost sinister shadows; f23.5 so long. Beautifully oiled. Vanilla and barley stretch the point as far as they can before ulmo honey comes to the rescue. But the peat, weighty and drying, never for a moment leaves the scene; b24 there is a controlled intensity to this that is borderline frightening. A malt whisky of majestic beauty. 50%.

 ◈ **Port Charlotte Islay Barley 2012 Aged 6 Years** db (92) n23 a pretty abrasive, acidic kick to the phenol; t23.5 a softer body than the norm with more oils, contrasting vividly with the nose; f22.5 the peats have set leaving only an oily and vanilla-rich glow; b23 it has been a privilege, as well as great fun, to line up all three Port Charlottes together and compare their varying merits, their similarities, their divergencies. It has also been an education, because the beauty of whisky is that you learn from every mouthful – or should – no matter how long you have been in the game. 50%.

 ◈ **Artful Dodger Port Charlotte 8 Year Old Sauternes** cask, cask no. 2009001063 (91) n23.5 t24 f21.5 b22 Though one of the world's greatest advocates of the Sauternes cask, there are times when I think it ill advised to be used...and here is one such occasion. Port Charlotte is about peat, not fruit. And though this is a beautiful whisky in its own right, you still instinctively know that there is a neutralising process going on here with the phenols and fruit cancelling the other out. Even so, there is still much to dive into, not least the sugars which try to counter the sootier smokiness. But the finish, one feels, is unnecessarily unkempt and not in keeping with the Port Charlotte spirit or narrative. Having said all that: the delivery will leave you aghast...! 64.2%. sc.

 Dramfool 23 Port Charlotte 14 Years Old dist 24 Sept 04, bott 23 Apr 19 (86) n22 t21.5 f21 b21.5 Not what I was expecting...! A real Victory V cough sweet and hickory number once associated with Bowmore. Mouth-watering on delivery, but as a Port Charlotte never hits its straps... 53.4%. nc ncf sc. 2,999 bottles.

 Dramfool Port Charlotte 2002 16 Years Old 1st fill bourbon barrel (96.5) n24 t24 f24 b24.5 Full-on peat. Honey from a first class bourbon cask. Superb distillation. Where do you start...? 60.5%.

 ◈ **Fadandel.dk Bruichladdich 15 Year Old** fresh sherry hogshead, cask no. 1198, dist 14 Nov 03, bott 6 Nov 19 (94) n23 salty – a pit sweaty armpit, thanks to the peat; t23.5 resounding fruit, but matched by the phenols which offer an earthy contrast to the sugary fruitcake theme. The saltiness ups the malty juiciness tenfold; f23.5 drier with a light chocolate fade. The custard cream biscuit is a lovely foil for the smoke; b24 the first thing that I must note is the quality of this sherry cask. Another from Fadandel with once more not even the outline of a hint of sulphur. This is so rare, and I'd like to thank the good people of this company for the massive effort they have obviously put in to secure top quality wine casks, even if I have not enjoyed all of them quite as much as I might, though this was more to do with grape to malt ratio.... This however, is a resounding success: so difficult to pull off with a peated malt. A standing ovation to this company is deserved and I hope other whisky companies take their lead. 62.3%. sc. 157 bottles.

 ◈ **The Finest Malts Port Charlotte 15 Year Old** sherry hogshead, cask no. 1217, dist Oct 04, bott Feb 20 (81) n23 t22 f17 b19 A malt whisky denser than the fog that seems to hang permanently over Islay airport whenever I fly there... Huge peat. But not even a smogful of phenols can disguise or hide the sulphur which makes the finish such hard work and unattractive. Before then there had been some lucid peat and grape moments that bordered on delightful insanity. But the nose suggests this will end in tears...which it dutifully does. 52.1%. nc ncf sc.

 ◈ **The First Editions Bruichladdich Aged 28 Years 1991** refill hogshead, cask no. 16883, bott 2019 (95.5) n24 age is apparent on every molecule. But subtlety is the key here: the ulmo honey is most apologetic, as is the light salt raises the profile of both the gentle tannin and till fresh barley. Magnificent...; t24 the delicate oils smother the palate with a light layer of acacia honey but it's the concentrated barley – again seasoned with salt – which makes you purr loudest; f23.5 a little tang on the tannin but a real Malteser candy finale of concentrated malt; b24 spectacularly complex. A whisky technician's dream as this is so beautifully made and matured. 50.7%. nc ncf sc. 295 bottles.

 Glen Oak 17 Year Old ex-bourbon barrels (92) n23 t23 f22.5 b23.5 About as delicate as 17-year-old Islay malt gets.... 40%. Branded Spirits USA.

BUNNAHABHAIN

Islay, 1881. Burn Stewart Distillers. Working.

 Bunnahabhain Aged 12 Years db (85.5) n20 t23 f21 b21.5. Lovers of Cadbury's Fruit and Nut will adore this. There is, incongruously, a big bourbony kick alongside some smoke, too. A lusty fellow who is perhaps a bit too much of a bruiser for his own good. Some outstanding moments, though. But, as before, still a long way removed from the magnificent Bunna 12 of old... 46.3%. nc ncf.

Bunnahabhain 12 Years Old bott code: 1903372L512-1116327 db (84) n20.5 t23 f19 b21.5 Remains true to the new style of Bunna with its slightly skewed sherry notes on nose and finish compensated for by the fabulously sweet and rich ultra - grapey delivery. The sulphur does stick slightly at the death. Oh, how I would still Wester Home back to the great Bunnas of the early 1980s.... 46.3%. nc ncf.

Bunnahabhain Aged 18 Years db (93.5) n24 t24.5 f22 b23 Only an odd cask has dropped this from being a potential award winner to something that is merely magnificent... 46.3%. nc ncf.

Bunnahabhain XXV Aged 25 Years db (94) n23 t24 f23 b24 No major blemishes here at all. Carefully selected sherry butts of the highest quality (well, except maybe one) and a malt with enough personality to still gets its character across after 25 years. Who could ask for more...? 46.3%. nc ncf.

Bunnahabhain 46 Year Old db (91) n24 t23 f21.5 b22.5 Needs a good half hour in the glass to open up and have justice done to it. Perishes towards the end, but the nose and build up to that are remarkably beautiful for a whisky which normally doesn't do age very well... 42.1%.

⬩ **Bunnahabhain An Cladach bott** code: 2001007L512:3719206 db (90.5) n23 a salty, sherried fanfare. As big as it feels, there is obviously a carefully orchestrated calm to this, also; t23.5 huge delivery, the thick sweet oloroso crashing into the taste buds like storm waves into the distillery's pier. There is a sharpness, a pungency on the sub-plot while a slick of oil settles on the palate to ensure length and depth; f21.5 not technically tickety-boo, though for once the casks can't be blamed. There is a buzz which the strong vanillas and light cocoa try to erase; b22.5 for those who prefer their island whiskies to be bold and fulsome. Quite an adventure. 50%. ncf. World Traveller Exclusive.

Bunnahabhain Ceòbanach db (87.5) n21.5 t22.5 f21.5 b22. An immensely chewable and sweet malt showing little in years but much in character. A charming liquorice and acacia honey lead then a developing, dry smokiness. Great fun. 46.3%

⬩ **Bunnahabhain Cruach-Mhòna** bott code: 2000996L515:2019169 db (89) n23.5 delicate...a distinct touch of the Arbroath smokies about this one. A salty seasoning, too, and though there is an oily presence off the still, the layering of vaguely sweet vanilla helps maintain the right balance; t23 gosh! Didn't I mention oil on the nose? The lip-smacking delivery is wincingly tart, a mix of OTT feints and a salty phenol. Some lovely chocolate mousse flies in to the rescue, weighed down slightly by decent peat; f21 way too oily and slightly off key; b21.5 hard to concentrate until you have cleared the water from your eyes. It is not the strength: it is the extraordinary tartness! Technically not the greatest: the messy finish underlines that. But the nose and delivery are something else entirely. 50%. nc ncf. Travel Retail Exclusive.

Bunnahabhain Darach Ùr Batch no. 4 db (95) n24 t24.5 f23 b23.5 Because of my deep love for this distillery, with my association with it spanning some 30 years, I have been its harshest critic in recent times. This, though, is a stunner. 46.3%. nc ncf.

⬩ **Bunnahabhain Eirigh Na Greine** bott code: 1979539L512:4919127 db (89.5) n23 teasingly smoked and even more playfully spiced; complex, but oddly enough the salty body is a little on the thin side; t23 voluptuous delivery with the spices now at the vanguard and happy to mix it with the molasses and delicate phenol; f21.5 as the nose suggests, there is a surprisingly delicate structure to this which crumbles as the vanillas arrive in force; b22 a sweet, spicy, complex Bunna with a curiously thin shell. 46.3%. nc ncf. Travel Retail Exclusive.

Bunnahabhain Moine 7 Year Old Oloroso Finish db (85) n22 t23.5 f18 b21.5 The faults are apparent on both nose and finish especially. But the grape intensity of the delivery is, momentarily, something special. 60.1%.

Bunnahabhain Stiùireadair bott code: 1910838L514:1919015 db (83.5) n21 t22 f20 b20.5 Although the sherry influence is clear of any sulphur content, the grape never comes across articulately on this, either on the nose or delivery. There are some brief moments on arrival when the malt goes directly into delicious fruitcake mode but it is all too brief. From then on it never sits comfortably. The stiùireadair, the helmsman, has steered the wrong course... 46.3%. nc ncf.

Bunnahabhain Toiteach A Dhà bott code: 1767068L510:0218253 db (86) n22 t22 f21 b21 A heavyweight malt which first thumps you as hard as possible with unreconstructed peat. And after you get up off the floor from that, you are rabbit punched by chunky fruit notes. Eschews subtlety and charm for impact. But have to say it is a great improvement on the earlier Toiteach. Just a slight technical flaw to this, evident on the finish in particular. 46.3%. nc ncf.

Bunnahabhain Toiteach Un-Chillfiltered db (75.5) n18 t21 f17.5 b19. A big gristy, peaty confrontation on the palate doesn't hide the technical fault lines of the actual whisky. 46%. ncf.

The Cooper's Choice Bunnahabhain 1990 27 Years Old (91) n23 t23 f22 b23 Bunna in all its old-fashioned unpeated glory – and in fine fettle, too...! 46%. nc ncf sc.

Gleann Mór Bunnahabhain Aged Over 26 Years (91) n22 t23 f23 b23 Bunna again in its old-fashioned unpeated form. A wonderful mix of sea salt and molasses sees off the excesses of the huge oak, the tannins dominating the nose but just failing to take control of elsewhere. A greybeard older than its years, but so much to enjoy! 49.6%.

The Golden Cask Bunnahabhain 28 Years Old 1989 cask no. CM244, bott 2018 **(88)** n22 t22 f21.5 b22.5 An oddball Bunna but with some lovely touches. 45.8%. nc ncf sc. 180 bottles.

Gordon & MacPhail Discovery Range Bunnahabhain Aged 11 Years (81) n20.5 t20.5 f20 b20 Dull and very ordinary: had a personality bypass. 43%.

Hidden Spirits Bunnahabhain 2013 Aged 5 Years cask no. BU1318, bott 2018 **(87.5)** n22 t22 f21.5 b22 A bit raw in part, as you might expect. But sublimely juicy with peat rounded and balanced. The sugars melt in the mouth and the oils live long. Anyone with an age prejudice should set it aside for this little beauty. Technically, a much better made malt than their earlier peated style. 50%. sc.

◈ **Liquid Treasures From Miles Away Bunnahabhain 11 Year Old** Oloroso sherry butt, dist Mar 09, bott Mar 20 **(94)** n23 t23.5 f23.5 b24 Bunnas at this strength and age don't happen along every day. Nor do Oloroso sherry butts entirely free from sulphur: pip, pip, hurrah! So a memorable dram for all the right reasons with the grape offering honeyed riches beyond your dreams – well, certainly mine after all the poor sherry butts I've encountered this year. Fruitcake, yes. But the barley really does have a presence, too, while the maple syrup and heather honey form a bond of gentle ecstasy despite the strength. A pleasure of a dram in every sense. 66.8%. sc. 252 bottles.

◈ **Old Malt Cask Bunnahabhain Aged 27 Years** refill hogshead, cask no. 17325, dist Nov 91, bott Oct 19 **(96.5)** n24.5 ah, the layering... Textbook stuff from the days before they started peating...which means that every nuance is there and unmolested by smoke. The citrus in particular shines, a kind of lime-blossom honey sweetness weighted by a glorious butterscotch and vanilla mix; occasionally heads towards a slight bourbony note, too...; the pace, weight and complexity is borderline perfection; **t24** brilliant mouthfeel: so silky and soft with the gristy sugars from the malt still at the vanguard. Buttery and rich, but the gentle oak doesn't allow for too much OTT floweriness; **f23.5** the slow-motion movement towards spicy complexity is almost mesmerising...; **b24.5** old school Bunna at its oldest! Love it! A truly exceptional cask that demands half an hour just to get to know. 50%. nc ncf sc. 209 bottles.

◈ **The Perfect Fifth Bunnahabhain 1991** cask no. 5386 **(93)** n23.5 Bunna is found on the seashore of Islay....and this nose had been taken right to the very edge. It wreaks of salty seadog, the brine entangled with the ancient oak of the vessel; **t23.5** though the delivery is jaded, the oak having that peculiarly glassy feel unique to exhausted malts, there is also no getting away from the fact that this exudes a genteel old-worldliness than one might mistake for a 50-year-old rather than something just about approaching its 30th year. Indeed, it has managed to turn the weariness of the oak into an attribute and at the same times somehow manages to concentrate the richness of the barley tenfold...; **f22.5** tired and creaking...but still has the elegance and wherewithal to finish the job with a salty, malty flourish; **b23.5** old school, proper unpeated Bunna – the way it used to be when at its best under Highland Distillers' ownership. However, this has never been a malt that has aged particularly well and has a habit of starting to fall apart by the time it is about 25-y-o. So much to like here, indeed revere: the astonishingly salty nose and, after a faltering start, fabulous concentrated malt, thick and lush, on delivery. But after the midpoint, balance is compromised as the tannin notes fail to find a balancing malty answer. This is probably about four-years past where I'd really like it to be. Occasionally truly outstanding very old Bunnas make it through – but it is a rare phenomenon. This is borderline brilliant. Incidentally, I stayed at the Bunnahabhain distillery on holiday back in 1991: it was truly the last real vacation I ever had. 50.5%. nc ncf sc.

Scyfion Choice Bunnahabhain 2007 Pastoral cask finished, bott 2018 **(91.5)** n22.5 t23 f23 b23 Pastoral cask...? I am sure I can smell the odd member of the clergy in there and as for tasting a Bishop...let's not go there... 46%. nc ncf. 348 bottles.

◈ **Wemyss Malts The Antique Armchair Bunnahabhain 1987** butt, bott 2018 **(74)** n18 t21 f17 b18 Oh dear. Unforgiving sulphur at work. 46%. nc ncf sc. 451 bottles.

◈ **The Whisky Barrel Originals Bunnahabhain 10 Years Old** 1st fill oloroso hogshead, cask no. TWB1004, dist Sept 09, bott 2019 **(86.5)** n22 t22 f21 b21.5 A predominantly clean sherry butt at work here (the finish confirms a slight buzz), thankfully. However, the fusion of grape and grain does little in the way of complexity and when the natural caramels arrive from oak it all becomes a bit of bagpipey drone... 57.1%. sc. 292 bottles.

◈ **The Whisky Barrel Originals Bunnahabhain Staoisha 6 Years Old** 1st fill bourbon barrel, cask no. TWB1009, dist Oct 13, bott 2019 **(91.5)** n23 the peat rejoices in the sooty, acidic nip it gives the nose: this malt means business; **t23** gristy, sweet and salivating on delivery. The smoke billows about the palate like an Islay possessed; **f22.5** sharp and acidic, but softened by growing natural caramels; **b23** good to see Bunna technically where it should belong. A very well-made malt. *59.1%. sc. 265 bottles*

The Whisky Embassy Bunnahabhain Aged 9 Years cask no. 3813649, dist 2008, bott 2017 **(82.5) n21 t21 f20 b20.5** Malty but seriously struggles to find a happy combination despite a big vanilla intervention. *52.5%. nc ncf sc.*

The Whisky Embassy Bunnahabhain 2014 re-charred hogshead, cask no. 10598, dist 20 Oct 14, bott 24 Jan 19 **(89) n23 t22 f22 b22** Probably one of the peatiest Bunnas I have ever encountered. You wait for complexity to kick in, it does, but as simplistic as the peat...probably for phenol maniacs only. *59.9%. nc ncf sc. 212 bottles.*

 Wilson & Morgan Barrel Selection Bunnahabhain 1st fill sherry wood, dist 2009, bott 2019 **(81) n21.5 t23 f17 b19.5** Decent sherry giving an attractive toffee-candy feel on delivery to this malt. A sulphur influence is foretold on the nose and comes vividly true at the death... *48%.*

 Wilson & Morgan Barrel Selection Bunnahabhain 18 Year Old sherry butt, cask no. 1432, dist 2001, bott 2019 **n22.5** sultana sponge....with not much sponge but lots of sultanas...; **t23.5** a sweet and beautifully mouth-filling delivery, the oils off the wine giving both weight and intensity to the fruit, the muscovado sugars...and then the huge spices which blast their way through the mid-ground; some serious tannin follows in its train; **f21.5** the tannins have really bitten deep here and offer just a shade too much burnt raisin; **b22.5** Bunna's history with sherry butts has not been the best over the last 30 years. So I feared the worst, to be honest. But this is a very decent and honest cask with no discernible off notes. The spices are x-certificate and its only weakness is over-active tannin. Otherwise a superb whisky experience. *59.7%. sc.*

 Wilson & Morgan Barrel Selection Bunnahabhain Heavy Peat dist 2014, bott 2019 **(92.5) n23** ham-fisted peat burst out from the glass on a wave of very young grist. Decent intensity and only the slightest hint of a sharpening saltiness; **t23** biff....!!! A peat that thumps you straight in the kisser with a left hook. No gentle caresses or kisses. Bosh! Have some of that! A few basic molasses notes give a degree of sweetness, but the spices and soot rule; **f23** long lingering mix of spice and smoked mocha; **b23.5** young and not the slightest attempt at subtlety. But when you have an Islay at this age, it isn't subtlety you are looking for.... *48%.*

CAOL ILA
Islay, 1846. Diageo. Working.

Caol Ila Aged 12 Years db **(89) n23 t23 f21 b22.** A telling improvement on the old 12-y-o with much greater expression and width. *43%*

 Caol Ila Aged 18 Years bott code: L9185CM008 db **(82.5) n21.5 t22 f19 b20** Still improving – slightly. Certainly a little more sweetness early on to bolster the weak phenols. But the off kilter finish remains poor. Still one of the great mysteries of Scotch whisky in how they manage to make a bottling so unrepresentative of such a great distillery.... *43%.*

Caol Ila Aged 25 Years bott code: L71860M000 db **(95.5) n24** quite a beefy, meaty phenol kick, with something of the farmyard for good measure. Unusually for Caol Ila, a little salty, too; **t24** soft and buttery on delivery, the usual oils having taken on a more greasy feel. The sugars start to mount up impressively, while the spices become positively warm **f23.5** the smoke rumbles along with spicy mischief; **b24** even after all these years this malt can not only lay on its Islay credentials with its eyes closed, but does so with an almost haughty air, cocking a smoky snook at the passing quarter of a century... *43%.*

Caol Ila 30 Year Old refill American oak & European oak casks, dist 1983 db **(96.5) n24 t24.5 f24 b24** Indisputably, one of the most complex, well-rounded and complete Caol Ilas I have tasted since they rebuilt the distillery... *55.1%. 7,638 bottles.* Diageo Special Releases 2014.

Caol Ila Moch db **(87) n22 t22 f21 b22** I think they mean "Mocha"... *43%.*

 Abbey Whisky Caol Ila Aged 11 Years 2008 hogshead **(93) n23.5 t24 f22.5 b23** So what we have here is Caol Ila naked as it were: in the prime of its life and in what it appears to be a Third-fill hogshead. This means you get little colour and only limited interference from the cask, though what is does offer is a beautifully consistent soft vanilla sub plot. This wins because we can see just how sexy this naked body is, with its voluptuous, oily curves and its peaty, scented magnetism. This is beautifully made whisky allowing the grist a free rein on juicy sweetness. This, ladies and gentlemen, is Caol Ila exactly as nature intended... *54.2%. sc. 120 bottles.*

 Artful Dodger Caol Ila 9 Year Old 2008 **(94) n23.5 t23.5 f23 b24** As a 9-year-old, Caol Ila displaying towards the top of its form with an almost improbably degree of gristy sugars on song. Particularly impressive, though, is the laid-back smoke – this distillery can come through a lot peatier than this – and revels in its slightly ashy, drier sub-plot. Makes a mockery of the strength, as this is a real softy. *63.4%. sc.*

Cask 88 Caol Ila 9 Year Old refill hogshead, sherry quarter cask finish, cask no. 4016778 **(88.5) n23 t22.5 f21 b22** Just sorry I couldn't give them 88 points...a bitter finish takes the edge off a wonderfully intense experience. *58.2%. nc ncf sc. 88 bottles. Eighty Eight Series.*

⟨⟨⟨ **Chapter 7 Chronicle Caol Ila Small Batch 8 Year Old 1998** first fill bourbon casks, dist May 11, bott Mar 20 **(93)** n23.5 t23 f23 b23.5 A superb example as to why blenders love working with this malt from bourbon cask. Even at a relatively young 8-years-old you can see how the smoke dishes out power and softness in even doses. The house oils ensure a rounded quality but still lets the light mocha and spice notes off the oak have a good hearing. Not a sensational whisky, but simply one with a massive feel good factor. *49.2%. 893 bottles.*

Dramfool 19 Cola Ali Three 10 Years Old bourbon cask, dist 2008 **(89.5)** n22.5 t22.5 f21.5 **b22.5** Supercharged with natural caramels giving an unusual cream toffee feel to the peat. Different. Someone been fooling around...? *59.8%. nc ncf. 129 bottles.*

Endangered Drams Caol Ila 9 Year Old cask no. 4016823, dist 2008, bott 2018 **(90)** n22 t23 f22.5 b22.5 A bottle of this is in danger of being drunk in a matter of hours... *53%. nc ncf sc.*

Fadandel.dk Caol Ila Aged 7 Years 1st fill Entre Deux Mers Barrique cask, cask no. 900056, dist 10 May 11, bott 20 Nov 18 **(80.5)** n21.5 t23 f17 b19 It is quite possible that Napoleon had lesser battles than this... *60%. sc. 307 bottles.*

Fadandel.dk Treasure of Islay Caol Ila Aged 10 Years refill bourbon cask, cask no. 0007, dist May 08, bott Nov 18 **(95.5)** n24 t24 f23.5 b24 I can't remember the last time I encountered a Caol Ila so steeped in tidal tendencies as this – either for the Bible or wearing my consultant blender's hat. It is as though barnacles had to be chipped off the cask, or even the glass. A malt for those who rather like being astonished.... *58.4%. sc. 272 bottles.*

⟨⟨⟨ **The Finest Malts City Landmarks Caol Ila Aged 11 Years** bourbon barrel, cask no. 024, dist 2007, bott 2018 **(93)** n22.5 t23 f23.5 b24 An attractive, no-nonsense Caol Ila that lets the dog see the rabbit. Slightly drier nose than usual, allowing the peat to nip a little while the palate is massaged by a comforting sweetness that balances out the perfectly-weighted phenols. A lovely buttery flourish to the finale, too. Spot on for its age and cask type. *53.2%. nc ncf sc.*

⟨⟨⟨ **The First Editions Caol Ila Aged 8 Years 2010** refill hogshead, cask no. 16790, bott 2019 **(92)** n22.5 untidy, but the light smoke is thickened by the oils; t23.5 beautifully satisfying delivery. The youth engineers a salivating barley thrust, the smoke an earthy weightiness which compliments it perfectly; f22.5 long with the oils stretching out both the smoke and thickening vanillas; b23.5 the rough edges to this one act in its favour: complex and bitty, it keeps the taste buds guessing and fully entertained. *59.7%. nc ncf sc. 295 bottles.*

Gleann Mór Caol Ila Aged Over 30 Years (93.5) n23.5 t23.5 f23 b23.5 Held up over the years with seemingly little effort. The sooty dryness of the nose is like a Caol Ila half its age while it has made the most of the sugars gleaned from 30 years of maturing a cask. Meanwhile a lovely caramel-vanilla mix hangs on the oils. Big, bold, proud and in great shape. *53.6%.*

Glenwill Caol Ila 1990 hogshead, cask no. 1481 **(96)** n24 t24 f24 b24 Exemplary. *53.9%.*

⟨⟨⟨ **Gordon & MacPhail Connoisseurs Choice Caol Ila Aged 15 Years** first fill bourbon barrel, cask no. 302298, dist 10 Sept 03, bott 1 Feb 19 **(96)** n23.5 a beautiful controlled pungency to the peat with the tannins mingling to more than make up the numbers; salty and sooty; too; t24 the oils missing in the nose are soon apparent and offering a light gloss to the sweet phenols; a light molasses note sweetens the kippers; f24 the light spices which entered the fray early on stay the pace and add flair to the smoky chocolate; b24.5 classic in every sense. This is what you should expect from a Caol Ila at this age and from this type of cask...and wow! Does it deliver! Truly stunning. *55.7%. sc. 210 bottles.* 🏆

Gordon & MacPhail Connoisseurs Choice Caol Ila 1984 Aged 33 Years refill sherry hogshead, cask no. 6078, dist 11 Dec 84, bott 3 Jul 18 **(95)** n24 t24.5 f22.5 b24 When peated whiskies get to a certain age, the phenol levels drop gradually, so you are normally, on an Islay malt of over 30 years, met by a controlled gentleness: a giant tempered with age. And on the nose you might for moment suspect this to be true here. The delivery, however, soon makes a mockery of that notion as the phenols dig deep, aided and abetted by a near perfect combination of heather honey, salt and pepper all within a glazed mouthfeel; that salt, incidentally, giving the nose a particularly maritime feel. Were it not for some bitterness on the finish, the score would have been as huge as the whisky. *52.8%. sc. 216 bottles.*

Hepburn's Choice Caol Ila 7 Years Old refill hogshead, dist 2011, bott 2018 **(92)** n23 t23 f23 b23.5 If there's a case for bottling more young Caol Ila, here it is...what a beauty! *46%. nc ncf sc. 362 bottles.*

⟨⟨⟨ **Hepburn's Choice Caol Ila 8 Years Old** refill hogshead, dist 2010, bott 2019 **(87)** n21.5 t21.5 f22 b22 A light rendition with the smoke fleeting and fragmented. Youthful and fresh, it takes a little time to hit its straps. *46%. nc ncf sc. 379 bottles.*

⟨⟨⟨ **Kingsbury Gold Caol Ila 7 Year Old** Oloroso sherry hogshead, cask no. 5838, dist 2011 **(83.5)** n22.5 t22 f20 b19 When you take an apple from a tree you do so when it is ripe. When you select a big peated whisky maturing in a wine cask, you pick when it is balanced. This isn't. Got to love that farmyard nose of the year, though...!!! Sheer, unmucked-out cattle byre. *58.7%. sc. 317 bottles.*

Old Malt Cask Caol Ila Aged 9 Years wine cask, cask no. 15799, dist Sept 09, bott Feb 19 **(85.5) n21.5 t22 f21 b21** Pleasant and moderately peated. But the wine, even bringing with it a sweet, juicy softness, untidies rather than sharpens and defines. *50%. nc ncf sc. 385 bottles.*

⬧ **The Single Cask Caol Ila 2007** ex-bourbon barrel, cask no. 307362 **(94) n22.5** dry and earthy with a hint of mint to the moist bluebell woods; **t24** a shock of delicate oils on delivery, then an immediate throbbing of even more delicate spice and liquorice. The smoke both adds balance and acts as an anchor to the lighter honey notes; **f23.5** fabulous oils and glorious fade of heather honey and phenol; **b24** lightly spiced, delicately honeyed and very satisfying. So beautiful... *57.8%. nc ncf sc.*

⬧ **The Single Malts of Scotland Reserve Cask Caol Ila 10 Year Old (92) n23 t22.5 f23 b23.5** Anything but one dimensional as the peat performs circus acts here to entertain: from the high wire with an ethereal gristiness rich in molten sugar, to earthier, head in lion's mouth phenols that rumble a dull roar. And the delivery is a cannonball firing you some distance. The tannins hitch a ride on the malt's natural oils and an apologetic degree of vanilla. Oh, and did I mention the sublime late spices...? *48%.*

⬧ **The Single Malts of Scotland Reserve Cask Caol Ila 11 Year Old (86) n21 t22.5 f21.5 b21** Gristy, oily and fat. The smoke offers anthracite on the nose and little on the palate. Just not enough oak involvement and never quite gets going. *48%. nc ncf.*

CAPERDONICH
Speyside, 1898. Chivas Brothers. Closed.

Gleann Mór Caperdonich Aged Over 23 Years (86) n22 t22 f20.5 b21.5 Some beautiful banana skins on the nose. But before it slips up on the clumsy finish, the malt and spice do have a few moments of unbridled glory. A slight failing on the cask, though, means the development is limited and always borderline tangy. *59.4%.*

CARDHU
Speyside, 1824. Diageo. Working.

Cardhu 12 Years Old db **(83) n22 t22 f18 b21**. What appears to be a small change in the wood profile has resulted in a big shift in personality. What was once a guaranteed malt love-in is now a drier, oakier, fruitier affair. Sadly, though, with more than a touch of something furry. *40%*

Cardhu Aged 15 Years bott code: L8070IX00 db **(87) n22 t23 f20.5 b21.5** Decent and easy going. But hang on: this is Cardhu! It should be offering a lot more than that. Does fine until the finish when the caramel kicks in without mercy, and other off-key moments develop. But love the citrus and pineapple on the nose and the oak layering on the delivery. This is a malt which should be 100% bourbon cask, preferably no colouring and allowing its natural brilliance to dazzle. 40%.

Cardhu 18 Year Old db **(88) n22.5 t23 f20.5 b22** Very attractive at first. But when you consider what a great distillery Cardhu is and how rare stocks of 18 year old must be, have to say that I am disappointed. The fruit masks the more intricate moments one usually experiences on a Cardhu to ensure an acceptable blandness and accounts for a poor finish. Why, though, it is bottled at a pathetic 40% abv instead of an unchillfiltered 46% – the least this magnificent distillery deserves – is a complete mystery to me.*40%*

Cardhu Amber Rock db **(87.5) n22 t23 f21 b21.5**. Amber is the right colour for this: it appears stuck between green and red, not sure whether to go or not. The delivery, in which the tangerine cream is in full flow reflects the better elements of the nose. But the finish is all about being stuck in neutral. Not helped by the useless 40% abv, you get the feeling that a great whisky is trying to get out. The odd tweak and we'll have a winner. That said, very enjoyable indeed. Just even more frustrating! *40%. Diageo.*

Cardhu Gold Reserve bott code: L8024IX02 db **(86.5) n22 t22 f21 b21.5** Once, maybe two decades ago, Cardhu single malt was synonymous with malted barley shining at you from the glass in a lightly golden, gristy complexity, in near perfect harmony with bourbon casks in which it had been stored for a dozen years or so. It was very delicate in colour and even more fragile on the palate, flitting around like some exotic form of whisky sprite. The character of this malt is far removed from those halcyon days: this is dull and box-ticking, rather than its old inspiration self. That said, for a few brief moments, there is a fleeting glimpse into its past style, when a gently honeyed sheen flares and then fades. *40%.*

Game of Thrones Cardhu Gold Reserve House Targaryen db **(84) n20.5 t22 f20.5 b21** Not having a single television set in any of my three abodes dotted around the place, I have never seen Game of Thrones. Not once. I cannot tell you, even roughly, what the story is about. I have had Bibles to write, distilleries to visit, shows to perform, birds to watch. So I can't tell you whether Targaryen is a person, a place or some kind of fictional spice. Which means I cannot compare the whisky to the name to see if they somehow match. Sorry. However, if it means "a little flat with off-key fruit and plenty of toffee to chew on" then, bingo! They've nailed it. *40%.*

CLYNELISH

Highlands (Northern), 1968. Diageo. Working.

Clynelish Aged 14 Years bott code: L7285CM008 db **(86.5)** n22 some malt nips though with a vaguely salty theme. Where is the usual honey? t22.5 soft, but a degree of caramel running through this might answer a previous question. A salty vanilla coupled with a lively maltiness lifts the mid-ground; f20 much duller with an over reliance on caramel; b21 very strange. This is one of the world's true Super Distilleries, in the top five of the most beautifully complex in Scotland. Yet from this very subdued, relatively character-bypassed bottling it would be hard to tell. 46%.

◈ **Clynelish Distillery Exclusive Bottling** batch no. 01, bott code: L9204DQ001 db **(89)** n23 soft with a light spice tickle; vanilla and caramels dominates over the malt, which is unusual for this distillery; t23 the trademark honey is an intermittent visitor here, arriving in thin acacia honey strands, rather than its normal ulmo and heather honey. The malt is nowhere near so shy, offering a gristy depth and sweetness and even a slightly barley loaf element; f21 a light, unwelcome buzz accompanies the vanilla and caramel.; b22 The first batch of a distillery exclusive bottling: this should be fun. Not bad, but the finale in particular is a tad tame by Clynelish's incredibly high standards while the honey notes – and this distillery probably does honey better than any other in Scotland – have been blunted a little. Look forward to the next batch hitting the 95 point mark, where this extraordinary distillery deserves to be... 48%. 3,000 bottles.

Game of Thrones Clynelish 12 Year Old House Tyrell db **(89)** n23 t23 f21 b22 Undone slightly by the finish, but that delivery...wow! 51.2%.

◈ **Acla Selection Summer Edition Clynelish 21 Year Old** hogshead, dist 1996, bott 2018 **(89.5)** n23 t22.5 f21.5 b22.5 Even by Clynelish standards much of what to be found here is enigmatic, with the lightest ulmo honeys little more than trace elements over vanilla tones that are barely audible themselves. Underdone slight by a bitter note which creeps in from the late middle. But, elsewhere, salivates and caresses at just the right time in the right places. 45.7%.

◈ **Artful Dodger Clynelish 20 Year Old** ex-bourbon hogshead, cask no. 6526 **(89)** n22 t23 f22 b22 Surprisingly inactive on the nose for a Clynelish. But begins to make amends the moment it hits the palate with a startling saltiness to ramp up the barley. A vague phenol note adds some depth but honey, a given trait of this distillery, is conspicuous by its absence. 55.9%. sc.

Gordon & MacPhail Connoisseurs Choice Clynelish 2005 refill sherry butt, cask no. 308764, dist 14 Jun 05, bott 21 Feb 18 **(94)** n24 t25 f21.5 b23.5 Such is the fragile complexity of Clynelish my first choice for bottling would never be a sherry butt, even if in entirely tip-top nick. Well, I would have been wrong. Because had this butt not latterly shown signs of sulphur it would most certainly have picked up a major award in this year's Bible. So, forget the imperfections and, once a week, treat yourself to the ecstasy of a mouthful of this outrageously orgasmic organoleptic odyssey. 55.1%. nc ncf sc. 518 bottles.

Hidden Spirits Clynelish 1992 cask no. CY9219, bott 2019 **(96)** n24 t24.5 f23.5 b24 What a distillery...!!! 50.1%. sc.

◈ **The Single Malts of Scotland Reserve Cask Clynelish 8 Year Old** **(85.5)** n22 t22.5 f20. b21 Clynelish ordinaire. Unaccountably bitter in the wrong places. 48%.

The Whisky Embassy Clynelish Aged 23 Years refill sherry butt, cask no. 8674, dist 26 Sept 95, bott 5 Dec 18 **(93)** n23 t23.5 f22.5 b24 A near faultless sherry butt ensures this malt has a rare fruity polish, especially on delivery. The combination of Clynelish's natural, beautifully honeyed malt, unquestionably the best in the Highlands, gives even greater depth as the mouth is bathed in delightful marzipan as well as the juiciest fruit pudding imaginable, with extra figs thrown in for good measure. Though spices try to compensate, the finish does dry a little too enthusiastically, perhaps, but the overall performance is one of unquestionable elegance and quality. 54.5%. nc ncf sc.

COLEBURN

Speyside, 1897–1985. Diageo. Closed.

◈ **Gordon & MacPhail Private Collection Coleburn 1981** refill sherry hogshead, cask no. 476, dist 11 Mar 81, bott 14 Mar 19 **(94)** n25 from the days of sublime sherry butts comes a gloriously fruit intensity to the fruit that makes your almost purr. This is more than just spiced fruitcake; it goes way beyond rich fruit. This is from a sherry butt style lost to us today, where both toasty raisins and muscular tannin share the stage equally and also with rare empathy for the other. It is, without question, perfection...; t22.5 even now, after nearly 40 years, this is as hot at Hades and the top layer of skin on your palate is seared from its moorings. Yep, this is Coleburn as I remember it in its very last years when not only was the worm tub a problem, but also the speed that the stills rattled and hissed. Fortunately some sublime fruit tones come to the rescue; f23 calms down significantly – even to the point that malt becomes apparent. But the extraordinary pedigree of this classic old sherry hoggy wins the day as the layering of the lofty fruit is something to behold. Still the heat of the express distillation nips, but the fruit acts likes a generous bosom on which it can seek comfort...; **b23.5** it is a strange and interesting fact that the reason this distillery closed down was because blenders didn't much care for the whisky. Back in the 1970s and '80s it built up a deserved reputation for producing a dirty "sulphurous" whisky which many blamed on the worm coolers used in the distilling process. It is curious that the degree of sulphur detected by blenders that made it a distillery non grata was a mere infinitesimal fraction of the degree of sulphur which totally screwed up so many scores if not hundreds of thousands of sherry butts. Yet the Scotch Distillers Association, obedient handbag dogs covering the tracks of their employers and baring their teeth and yapping and snarling at anyone who doesn't feed them, passed it off as just another unique flavour for whisky. And the imagination of egotistical troublemakers such as myself. Such nauseating humbug. The fact is, when well matured the Coleburns of this world produced a beautiful malt whisky, such as this. While whisky, from whichever distillery, sitting in sherry casks treated with sulphur candles are ruined and a pox on the industry no matter however long they remain in the warehouse. And no matter what garbage blow-hards like the SWA PR (Pernicious Rot) department tell you. *55.9%. sc. 101 bottles.*

CONVALMORE

Speyside, 1894–1985. William Grant & Sons. Closed.

Convalmore 32 Year Old refill American oak hogsheads db (**96.5**) **n24 t24 f24 b24.5** Being 32 years old and bottled in 2017, these must be casks from among the very last production of the distillery before it was closed for the final time in 1985. The new spirit then, from what I remember, was not the greatest: thin and with an occasional tendency to be on the rough house side. Time, though, is a great healer. And forgiver. It has passed the last three decades turning from ugly duckling to the most elegant of swans. A sub-species, though, that is on the brink of extinction... *48.2%. 3,972 bottles. Diageo Special Releases 2017.*

Gordon & MacPhail Rare Old Convalmore 1975 (**94**) **n23 t24 f23 b24** The rarest of the rare. And in tasting, the flavour map took me back 30 years, to when I used to buy bottles of this from Gordon and MacPhail as a 10-year-old...probably distilled around 1975. The unique personality and DNA is identical on the palate as it was then; except now, of course, there is far more oak to contend with. Like finding an old lover 30 years further on: a little greyer, not quite in the same lithe shape as three decades earlier...but instantly recognisable and still very beautiful... *46%*

CRAGGANMORE

Speyside, 1870. Diageo. Working.

◈ **Cragganmore 15 Years Old 150th Anniversary** American oak, bott code: L9116DQ004 db (**94**) **n23.5** the vague freshly-bitten toffee apple note is the only concession to fruitiness you'll be offered here: this is all about rich barley and even richer tannin, to the extent that it even more towards a bourbon-style liquorice and caramel note....; **t23.5** sugars explode all over the palate on delivery. And to make it all the more fun, they take the form of differing types, ranging from salivating grist to thicker toffee-caramel with a light heather-honey tones making everything a little friendlier still; **f23** the vanillas now take a big hand with a toasty dry molasses note reminding you of the big oak input here, as do the ever-busying spices.; **b24** Cragganmore is, like most distilleries, at its very best in good American oak. Here the natural caramels have joined the tannins to create about as thick and singular a malty intrigue as you are likely to find. A big whisky, but one that is very easy to scale... *48.8%. 1,869 bottles.*

CRAIGELLACHIE

Speyside, 1891. Bacardi. Working.

Craigellachie 13 Year Old db (**78.5**) **n20 t22 f18 b18.5.** Oily and intense, it shovels on the malt for all it is worth. That said, the sulphur notes are its undoing. *46%*

Craigellachie 17 Year Old db (**88.5**) **n22** chocolate Liquorice Allsort! A tad oily and boiled vegetable. But enough malt to make the difference; **t22.5** just love that delivery. Not the cleanest. But a mix of those heavy duty oils and an almost biting vanilla-barley note is attractive in an unkempt kind of way; **f22** almost like an oil slick in a sea of oak-splintered barley; **b22** technically falls flat on its face. Yet the whole is way better than the sum of its parts... *46%*

Craigellachie Aged 17 Years bott code: L19011ZA500 db (**94**) **n23** invigorating barley: a real nip, with sharp sugars and some pointy oak, too...; **t23.5** a resounding Speyside-style delivery with the barley bouncing around the palate on delivery; the spices move in pretty sharpish before some top quality tannins add their delicate hickory depth; the elegance of the oils is both enriching...and a surprise; **f23.5** a glorious mix of malt and milky, spiced cocoa; **b24** this bottling is a great improvement on previous versions I have encountered. What an interesting and delicious dram, shewing the distillery at its best! *46%*

Craigellachie 23 Year Old db (**91.5**) n23.5 t23 f22 b23.5 Expected a little house smoke on this (the malt made here in the early 1990s always had delicate phenol), but didn't show. The honey is nothing like so shy. 46% WB16/035

Craigellachie Exceptional Cask Series 1994 bott May 18 db (**91.5**) n22.5 t23 f23 b23 How fascinating. Yes, a sherry butt and yes: there is sulphur. But this time it is not from the sherry, as the nose reveals a particular character from the condenser which does accentuate a mild sulphur character. Yet the clean wine casks tell a different, at once puckering yet juicy, story. Beautifully structured and a jaw-aching chewing malt with an unusual late salivation point. 54.8%. Bottled for Whisky L! & Fine Spirits Show.

⬦ **The First Editions Craigellachie Aged 11 Years 2008** wine cask, cask no. 16647, bott 2019 (**91**) n22.5 subtle layers of peat softens the expectant tanginess from the wine cask. Salty and intriguingly layered; t23 kerpow! A full-bloodied and entirely unsubtle assault on the taste buds, seemingly from every direction and on every front. The smoke and grape an unlikely but beautifully sweet duet which confronts the bubbling spices; f22.5 drier, insistent spice but still a light jammy sweetness at the death for balance; b23 a surprising degree of smokiness to this works quite well here, not least in taming any excesses of the wine cask. Complex and exceptionally pleasing. Probably the most surprising malt I have encountered so far this year. 59.3%. nc ncf sc. 193 bottles.

The First Editions Craigellachie Aged 12 Years 2006 sherry butt, cask no. 15087, bott 2019 (**94.5**) n23.5 t24 f23 b24 A magnificent bottling benefiting from a sherry but with not a single atom of sulphur. 59.6%. nc ncf sc. 248 bottles.

⬦ **Gordon & MacPhail Connoisseurs Choice Craigellachie Aged 13 Years** refill bourbon barrels, cask nos. 16600302, 16600303, 16600305 & 16600307, dist 29 Aug 05, bott 26 Jun 19 (**92.5**) n23 beautifully tangy citrus complements the salty tannins; t23 mega-salivating qualities as the barley is driven home by a controlled but intense oaky tailwind; f23 so much sparky vanilla; salty and slightly sharp. Nothing dull at any point here. The spices arrive late on an oily train...; b23.5 I know quite a few who are no great fans of Craigellachie. But I have always argued that in the right bourbon cask it offers a very characterful Speyside malt of unusual depth to its high quality. Thank you G&M for so eloquently proving my point. 46%. 1,314 bottles.

The Great Drams Craigellachie 11 Years Old bourbon cask, oloroso sherry cask finish, cask no. 900668/07A, dist 23 Oct 07, bott 30 Oct 18 (**80.5**) n19 t22.5 f19 b20 A very odd whisky. The sherry doesn't quite ring true, alas, as the dirty nose and finish testifies. A few moments of honeyed magic on delivery, but not enough to excuse the sub-standard sherry cask. 46.2%. nc ncf sc.

Hepburn's Choice Craigellachie 10 Years Old new sherry hogshead, dist 2008, bott 2019 (**86.5**) n22 t22 f21.5 b21 The malt and grape harmonise quite well on delivery but elsewhere had a fractious time bonding. Not a bad cask – despite the very dry finish - but has been bottled not quite at a happy time in its development. 46%. nc ncf sc. 259 bottles.

⬦ **Hepburn's Choice Craigellachie 11 Years Old** wine cask, dist 2008, bott 2019 (**85.5**) n21 t22 f21 b21.5 Tight and brusque, the out of sync tanginess gives you plenty to whine about. There is one fleeting moment just after delivery where the sweetness of both the barley and grape combine charmingly, but it is over far too quickly. 46%. nc ncf sc. 113 bottles.

MacAlabur Craigellachie Aged 12 Years first-fill bourbon barrel, cask no. 8101210, dist 23 Aug 06, bott 15 Oct 18 (**91**) n22.5 t23 f22.5 b23 There have been too many disappointing bottling of Craigellachie in recent years. Thankfully, this isn't one of them! 54.3%. nc ncf sc. 229 bottles.

⬦ **Scyfion Choice Craigellachie 2007** Saint Daniel wine cask finished, bott 2019 (**81.5**) n19 t22 f20 b20.5 The wine and malt are at odds for this thin gruel of an off-key dram. I'm afraid the saints can't be praised on this occasion. 46%. nc ncf sc. 212 bottles.

Scyfion Choice Craigellachie 2008 pomegranate wine cask finished, bott 2017 (**73**) n18 t19 f18 b18 Will be interesting to taste one of these casks not ruined by the dreaded "S" word... 46%. nc ncf sc. 268 bottles.

Simon Brown Traders Craigellachie bourbon cask, dist Oct 06, bott Feb 19 (**87**) n22.5 t22.5 f20.5 b21.5 The nose shews a degree of charm, but with caveats. Busy coriander and banana make intriguing and spicy bedfellows, but there is a warning about an oak weakness further down the line. Which does eventually arrive with an astringent bitterness. But there is, first, time to enjoy a big malty surge on delivery and a rousing spice and maple syrup follow through. 43%. nc ncf sc.

⬦ **Whisky Illuminati Craigellachie 2011** Spanish oak sherry hogshead, cask no. 900328 (**85**) n21.5 t22.5 f20 b21 Interesting to compare this with their Glentaucher's sherry offering. That sparkles from first moment to last, while this is a stodgier affair, first with a nose shorn of balance and then on the palate, the malt making no impact on the grape whatsoever. Unlike with the 'Tauchers. Good spices and pleasant chewiness plus sugary notes to enjoy. But never even hints at greatness. 67.9%. sc. 100 bottles.

DAILUAINE

Speyside, 1854. Diageo. Working.

Berry Bros & Rudd Dailuaine 21 Years Old cask no. 10608, dist 1996, bott 2018 **(91.5)** n23 t22.5 f22.5 b23.5 Not often you come across a Dailuaine that is a real joy, so hearty congratulations for BBR buyer Doug McIvor for spotting this collectors' item. And if you want to know how rare: a highly decent Dailuaine like this comes along about as often as a Charlton victory over Millwall: practically never... 46%. nc ncf sc.

⁘ **The First Editions Dailuaine Aged 12 Years 2007** sherry butt, cask no. 16641, bott 2019 **(84)** n21 t22 f20 b21 Juicy on delivery, but very limited from then on. Too dry and austere, especially in the gagged finish. 576%. nc ncf sc. 294 bottles.

⁘ **Old Malt Cask Dailuaine Aged 12 Years** sherry butt, cask no. 16640, dist May 07, bott Jun 19 **(88)** n21.5 t22.5 f22 b22 Makes a laudable attempt to get the into every square inch of your palate. Ignore the slightly restrained nose and celebrate a very above average Dailuaine where malt is not just in the centre ground, but works its way into every other aspect of the experience. A surprise package – for all the right reasons! 50%. nc ncf sc. 271 bottles.

⁘ **The Single Cask Dailuaine 1997** ex-bourbon barrel, sherry cask finish, cask no. 15563 **(85.5)** n22 t21 f21.5 b21 A sclerotic malt, set in a grapey straight jacket in which it seems unable to move. That said, it's a clean finish, the spices busy and entertaining. But all a little too stiff. Though, as Dailuaines go, I have tasted a lot worse... 52.9%. nc ncf sc.

DALLAS DHU

Speyside, 1899–1983. Closed. Now a museum.

⁘ **Gordon & MacPhail Private Collection Dallas Dhu 1969** refill sherry hogshead, cask no. 1656, dist 10 Jun 69, bott 12 Jun 18 **(96)** n24.5 the oak has impregnated every molecule to be sniffed here, giving it a weight that makes lead look like helium. To think that when this was made I was enjoying my very last days in primary school (as I then took the temperature every day for class I still, for some strange reason, remember early June was around the 70-73 degree Fahrenheit mark, so it would have been cooler for Scotland – good news for the stills). The fruit adds to this density, and here we are talking grape must, dry enough for every bickering spice to be counted, sweet enough for a lovely roast chestnut note to accompany the most delicate of smoky tones; t24 on tasting when first unveiled it is a oaky mess. Half an hour oxidisation and a little seduction via the Murray Method and we have opened this malt right out so the fruit now reveals its sweeter side: a spiced, supersoft fruit pastel which is enriched by ginger. Most remarkable, though, is that the barley is still intact enough to get you into full salivating mode before those fruitier, spicier notes kick in. A wonderful layering of barley and natural caramels ensure a rare passage of genteel elegance; f23.5 no matter what you do with this, the oak now has taken control. Well, unless you give it an hour in the glass and then an improbably fruit sugar candy emerges to see off the excesses of the tannin; b24 even in the early 1980s when I began in earnest my journeys around Scotland seeking out their rarest drams, Dallas Dhu was among the very hardest to secure. You might find the odd one here and there: indeed, if you did locate one you bought it, no questions, as you knew it might be a year or two before another surfaced. By the time I began writing about whisky full time, the distillery had been closed nine years and even then its rare bottlings were commanding high prices, making it harder to sample. So it is for that reason I have chosen this as the 1,250th whisky tasted for the Jim Murray Whisky Bible 2021. It brought a thrill to find a bottle 40 years ago. That feeling has not remotely diminished in the passing four decades. And the hour spent to understand this magnificently complex malt were as enjoyable as any of the last four months I have spent tasting... Please nose and taste with the reverence it deserves... If you open and taste immediately, it scores in the mid 80s. An hour or so employing the Murray Method...and you'll have one of the whisky experiences of your life.... 43.1%. sc. 176 bottles.

Gordon & MacPhail Rare Vintage Dallas Dhu 1979 **(94.5)** n23 t23.5 f23.5 b24 I can hardly recall the last time a bottling from this distillery popped along – depressing to think I am old enough to remember when they were so relatively common they were being sold on special offer! It was always a class act; its closure an act of whisky vandalism, whether it be preserved as a museum or not. This, even after all these years, shows the extraordinary quality we are missing day in, day out. 43%

DALMORE

Highands (Northern), 1839. Whyte and Mackay. Working.

⁘ **The Dalmore Aged 12 Years** American white oak and Oloroso sherry casks, bott code: L0029 09 29 P/011096 db **(87)** n21.5 t23 f20.5 b22 A malt which has changed tack since I last tasted it. Then, as it had been for years, the malt was lost under a blanket of caramel. Now the barley is muzzled by fruit. Attractively at first as the sugars and grape elegantly and decisively make their mark. Sadly, a furry veil, thin but unmistakable, descends to given it a coarse and bitter finish. Glad to see far less toffee in the mix. But if sherry casks must be deployed, then a malt as potentially good as Dalmore deserves clean and faultless ones. *40%.*

⟡ **The Dalmore Aged 15 Years** American white oak and finished in Oloroso sherry casks, bott code: L0034 08 35 P/011099 db **(90.5) n23** a character transplant.... now complex fruity tones, mainly lime, criss-cross the tannins. Even the odd malt note peeks out here and there...; **t22.5** malty soft (rather than exclusively toffee soft) and salivating early on. A few caramel notes drift about but come second to the plums; **f22** just a little murky here as the heavier notes finally combine and the spices buzz loudly. A little bitterness, but nothing to worry about; **b23** it speaks! Normally a whisky that has very little to say for itself. Like the Dalmore 12, looks like a malt in transformation here, though in this case with far more success. Where once, for all its years, it, like the 12, refused to offer little more than toffee, now the mouthfeel has altered and allowed the whisky itself to say a few lines. Just an odd mildly naughty sherry butt, but I suspect these will be frogmarched out for future bottlings... *40%.*

⟡ **The Dalmore Aged 18 Years** American white oak and Matusalem Oloroso sherry casks, bott code: L0030 04:17 P/011104 db **(88.5) n23 t23 f21 b21.5** There is a timelessness to the nose that takes some of us back to our first whisky experiences of the 1970s; and one presumes that it must have been enjoyed long before then, too. The fusion of malt, light kumquat and moist Dundee cake is truly classic. The mouthfeel, with its kissing oils and glistening sugars are also of noble antiquity. But from the mid-point onwards comes a wailing bitterness from the wine casks which would be better if not there. If only those sugars could be extended and the fruits happier, what a malt this would be! *43%.*

The Dalmore 21 Year Old db **(88.5) n22 t23 f21.5 b22** fat, unsubtle, but enjoyable. *42%*

The Dalmore 25 db **(88) n23.5 t22.5 f20 b22** The kind of neat and tidy, if imperfect, whisky which, were it in human form, would sport a carefully trimmed and possibly darkened little moustache, a pin-striped suit, matching tie and square and shiny black shoes. *42%.*

The Dalmore 30 Year Old db **(94) n24 t24 f22.5 b23.5** A malt, quite literally for the discerning whisky lover. Essays in complexity are rarely so well written in the glass as found here... *45%*

The Dalmore Aurora Aged 45 Years db **(90.5) n25 t22 f21.5 b22**. Sophisticated for sure. But so huge is the oak on the palate, it cannot hope to match the freakish brilliance of the nose. *45%*

The Dalmore Candela Aged 50 Years db **(96) n25 t24 f23.5 b23.5**. Just one of those whiskies which you come across only a handful of times in your life. All because a malt makes it to 50 does not mean it will automatically be great. This, however, is a masterpiece, the end of which seemingly has never been written. *50% (bottled at 45%).*

The Dalmore 1263 King Alexander III db **(86) n22 t22.5 f20 b21.5**. Starts brightly with all kinds of barley sugar, fruit and decent age and oak combinations, plus some excellent spice prickle. So far, so good...and obviously thoughtfully and complexly structured. But then vanishes without trace on finish. *40%*

The Dalmore Ceti db **(91.5) n24 t23.5 f21.5 b22.5** A Ceti which warbles rather well... *44.7%*

The Dalmore Cigar Malt Reserve Limited Edition db **(73.5) n19 t19.5 f17 b18.** One assumes this off key sugarfest is for the cigar that explodes in your face... *44%*

The Dalmore Dominium db **(89.5) n22.5 t23 f22 b22** Like so many Dalmores, starts brightly but as the caramels gather it just drifts into a soupy lump. Still, no taint to the fruit and though the finish is dull you can say it is never less than very attractive. *43%. Fortuna Meritas Collection*

The Dalmore Luceo db **(87) n22 t22 f21.5 b21.5.** Pleasantly malty, exceptionally easy going and perfect for those of you with a toffeed tooth. *40%. Fortuna Meritas Collection*

⟡ **The Dalmore Port Wood Reserve** American white oak and Tawny port pipes, bott code: L0036 00 25 P/0111 db **(92) n22.5** wow! The grape seems devoid of sugars and juice and we are left with skin at its most nose-puckering. The only relief is a light green apple note, but even that is ganged up upon by sawdust-dry vanillas...; **t23.5** more latitude towards brown sugars here and a relaxed mode. The mouthfeel fattens slightly, too. But soon the drawbridge is pulled up and we are back to a cocoa powderiness; **f22.5** puckering dry fruit stones...a little belated spice and the continuing cocoa strata; **b23.5** one of the most dry Port Wood bottlings I have ever encountered. If James Bond insisted on a whisky for his Martini, then it would probably be this. *46.5%.*

The Dalmore Regalis db **(86.5) n22.5 t21.5 f21 b21.5.** For a brief moment, grassy and busy. Then dulls, other than the spice. The caramel held in the bottling hall is such a great leveller. *40%. Fortuna Meritas Collection*

The Dalmore Valour db **(85.5) n21 t22 f21 b21.5.** Not often you get the words "Valour" and "fudge" in the same sentence. *40%. Fortuna Meritas Collection*

The Dalmore Visitor Centre Exclusive db **(95.5) n25 t24 f22.5 b24** Not exactly the easiest distillery to find but a bottle of this is worth the journey alone. I have tasted some sumptuous Dalmores over the last 30-odd years. But this one stands among the very finest. *46%*

The Dalmore Quintessence db (**91**) n22 t23.5 f22 b23.5 A late night dram after a hard day. Slump into your favourite chair, dim the lights, pour yourself a glass of this, warm in the hand and then study, quietly, for the next half hour. 45%.

⋙ **Deer, Bear & Moose Dalmore Aged 14 Years** sherry butt, dist Oct 04, bott May 19 (**84.5**) n19 t23 f20.5 b22 While the nose may be tight and unresponsive, the delivery is an orgy of golden syrup and spiced fruit. Pity the sulphur also reveals itself slightly on the finish, too... 57.4%. nc ncf. Flaviar & Friends.

⋙ **Fadandel.dk Dalmore 11 Year Old** 9 months finish in a 1st fill Oloroso octave, cask no. 800153A (**94**) n23.5 a very old-fashioned extra-dry oloroso effect – much more common in style 30 years ago than now. The oak enforces the sugar-resistant stance; t23.5 delicate dark sugars set their stall out early and await the nutty onslaught, which is quick in arriving. Despite the dryness, the malt has presence enough to ensure a quick salivating burst of barley. The midground offers a brilliant vanilla and raisin mix; f23 spices well up here to support the toasty raisins; b24 classically nutty and adroit. Such a lovely cask at work, the sophisticated style of which is so rarely found today: for those who like their Martinis very dry... 55.2%. sc. 68 bottles.

Gleann Mór Dalmore Over 13 Years (**83.5**) n21 t21.5 f20.5 b20.5 Malt ordinaire. 55.6%.

Glenwill Dalmore 1991 hogshead, cask no. 11151 (**92.5**) n22.5 t23.5 f23 b23.5 Mouthcleansing, beautifully made, high grade blending fodder. But a superb single malt instead. 46.2%. 266 bottles. Matisse Spirits Company.

Master of Malt Single Cask Dalmore 14 Year Old bourbon hogshead, dist 24 Apr 03, bott 20 Mar 18 (**95**) n23.5 t24 f23.5 b24 Well done Master of Malt! For years I have been telling people that Dalmore make a very good malt, though there has been scant evidence of this from the distillery's own caramel submerged bottlings and independent offerings, usually from less than impressive casks. Here, though, we have a naturally full bodied Dalmore I often encounter in the lab but rarely seen in public view. Excellent. Oh, and if only the standard Dalmore was this naturally magnificent. 57.8%. sc.

DALWHINNIE
Highlands (Central), 1898. Diageo. Working.

Dalwhinnie 15 Years Old db (**95**) n24 t24 f23 b24 A malt it is hard to decide whether to drink or bath in: I suggest you do both. One of the most complete mainland malts of them all. Know anyone who reckons they don't like whisky? Give them a glass of this – that's them cured. Oh, if only the average masterpiece could be this good. 43%

Dalwhinnie Winter's Gold db (**95**) n23.5 for such a remote and inland distillery, the coastal saltiness to this is remarkable... golden syrup and earthy heather-honey also at work here; t24 something of the Johnnie Walker Gold about this: there is a clarity to the malt, the citrus and vanilla which reminds one of the air when looking far away into the mountains on a cool winter's morn; f23.5 earthy to the end with the honey (ulmo, naturally!) Still the dominating theme; just a late hint of bitterness; b24 whichever blender came up with this deserves a pat on the back. 43%

Game of Thrones Dalwhinnie Winter's Frost House Stark db (**87.5**) n22 t22 f21.5 b22 This is my fourth Game of Thrones whisky I have now sampled. And, having never seen the TV series, I am beginning to get the picture: the programme is about toffee, isn't it! Because, again, caramel is the dominating factor here, somehow flattening out the higher peaks from this mountainside distillery, which happens to be one of the world's best. The delightful burst of juicy barley just after the tame delivery is all too brief. 43%.

DEANSTON
Highlands (Perthshire), 1966. Burn Stewart Distillers. Working.

⋙ **Deanston 10 Years Old Bordeaux Red Wine Cask Finish** bott code: 1952859L511:2619164 db (**91**) n22 dry to the point of making your eyes water! A real grape skin bite to this: a little acidic but charmingly clean and peppery; t22.5 the dryness transfers to the delivery which benefits from a thick oiliness that ups the chewiness considerably. The black peppers on the nose are slow out of the blocks, but once they get going they help increase the juiciness no end; f23 some lovely tannin, grape and black pepper fading into chocolate; b23.5 a cask type that seems to suit Deanston's singular style. Very attractive. Impressed with this one big time. 46.3%. ncf. Travel Retail Exclusive.

Deanston 10 Year Old PX Finish db (**83.5**) n21 t22.5 f20 b20 Displays the uncompromising sweetness of a whisky liqueur. A must-have malt for those who like their sherry influence to be way over the top. The finish, like the nose, reveals minor a dry, furry element. 57.5%.

Deanston 12 Years Old bourbon casks, bott code: 17242991509:5018106 db (**84**) n21 t22 f20 b21 All the fun is on the impact, where the barley is about as intense as anything else produced in Scotland. However, the weakness on both nose and finish points accusingly at the Deanston character of off-key feintiness. 46.3%. ncf.

Deanston 18 Year Old batch 2 db **(89.5)** n23 t22.5 f22 b22 A soft treat for the palate... 46.3%. nc ncf.

Deanston 18 Years Old 1st fill bourbon casks, bott code: 1911691L511L:2618334 db **(89.5)** n22 t23.5 f21.5 b22.5 An intense, highly enjoyable dram where the malted barley gangs up and gives the other characteristics only bit parts. 46.3%. ncf.

Deanston 20 Year Old db **(61)** n15 t16 f15 b15 Riddled with sulphur. 55.4%. nc ncf.

Deanston 40 Year Old PX Finish db **(87.5)** n22 t23 f21 b21.5 The PX is doubtless in use here to try and give a sugary wrap around the over-aged malt. Some success, though limited. This type of cask has the unfortunate habit of restricting complexity in a whisky by embracing it too tightly with its wealth of syrupy top notes. The aromas and flavours which do escape often seem brittle and clipped, and this is the case here: the whisky has no chance to tell of its 40 years in the cask – the period that counts most now is the time it has spent in PX. Love the spices, though, and the overall mouthfeel. Whatever its limitations, this still does offer a lovely dram. 45.6%.

Deanston Virgin Oak virgin oak casks, bott code: 1866939L512:4118241 db **(87.5)** n22.5 t22.5 f21.5 b21 The overall lightness of Deanston's malt is emphasised by the lingering impact of the tannin towards the finish which knocks the early balance off kilter. An attractively complex nose, though, and the acacia honey on the barley concentrate delivery, followed by zonking spice, is to die for. 46.3%. ncf.

◈ **Acla Selection Summer Edition Deanston 18 Year Old** sherry hogshead, dist 1999, bott 2018 **(88.5)** n22.5 t23 f21 b22 A busy malt, which though stretched towards the finish, underlining the fragile nature of the spirit, early on delights in a glorious mix of spice, barley and complex tannins. The vital citrussy sugars also impress. Enjoyable fayre. 49.3%.

◈ **Old Malt Cask Deanston Aged 23 Years** refill hogshead, cask no. 15954, dist Jan 96, bott Oct 19 **(86.5)** n21.5 t22 f21.5 b21.5 Despite the slight butyric on the nose, this offers plenty of juicy barley bite. A bit thin and warm but certainly not lacking in character. 50%. nc ncf sc. 322 bottles.

DUFFTOWN
Speyside, 1898. Diageo. Working.

The Singleton of Dufftown 12 Years Old db **(71)** n18 t18 f17 b18. A roughhouse malt that's finesse-free. For those who like their tastebuds Dufft up a bit... 40%

The Singleton of Dufftown Aged 15 Years bott code: L7149DM000 db **(84.5)** n21.5 t22 f20.5 b20.5 Nutty and rich on delivery. Toffee-weighted, thin and boring elsewhere. 40%.

The Singleton of Dufftown Aged 18 Years bott code: L7094DM000 db **(86.5)** n21 t22 f21.5 b22 To be honest, I was expecting a bit of a dud here, based on some 30-years-experience of this distillery. And though, for an 18-year-old, it can't be said really to hit the heights, it has – as so many less than brilliant distilleries over the years – mellowed enough with age to show a certain malty gentleness worthy of respect. 40%.

◈ **The Singleton Dufftown Malt Master's Selection** blend ref. 1106, refill, ex-sherry and bourbon casks, bott code: L9149DM003 db **(83)** n20.5 t21 f20.5 b21 The sherry and bourbon casks wipe each other out leaving a soft, occasionally malty sweetness. Absolutely nothing wrong with it, and better than some Dufftowns of times past. But I'm looking for more than flatline malt...and I don't find it. 40%.

The Singleton of Dufftown Spey Cascade db **(80)** n19 t20 f21 b20. A dull whisky, stodgy and a little dirty on the nose. Improves the longer it stays on the palate thanks mainly to sympathetic sugars and an ingratiating oiliness. But if you are looking for quality, prepare to be disappointed. 40%

The Singleton of Dufftown "Sunray" db **(77)** n20 t20 f18 b19. One can assume only that the sun has gone in behind a big toffeed cloud. Apparently, according to the label, this is "intense". About as intense as a ham sandwich. Only not as enjoyable. 40%. WB15/121

The Singleton of Dufftown "Tailfire" db **(79)** n20 t20 f19 b20. Tailspin, more like. 40%.

The Whisky Chamber Dufftown 10 Years Old 2008 bourbon cask **(85)** n21 t22.5 f20.5 b20.5 A punchy, salivating malt which works well when the Demerara sugars and intense barley combines, but found a little tangy and wanting elsewhere. A little spiced chocolate late on tames the worst excesses of the oak. 58.9%. sc.

EDRADOUR
Highlands (Perthshire), 1837. Signatory Vintage. Working.

Edradour 13 Year Old 1st fill oloroso sherry butt, dist 4 Dec 95, bott 4 May 18 db **(95)** n24 t23.5 f23.5 b24 When this whisky was distilled it was made at, then, Scotland's smallest distillery. Well, that may be so, but there is no denying that this is one absolutely huge whisky. And not only that, one where no degree of understated enormity is out step with any other:

it is a giant, but a beautifully proportioned one. The spicy, sherry trifle on steroids nose will entrap you. The staggering complexity of the sturdy tannin and muscular fruit will keep you there, spellbound. The chocolate on the finish is almost an arrogant flourish. This really is Edradour from the old school, where its old manager Puss Mitchell had laid down the law on the type of sherry butt the hefty malt had to be filled into. Were he with us now, he'd be purring... *54.2%. 661 bottles. Bottled for Whisky L! & Fine Spirits Show.*

Signatory Vintage Un-Chillfiltered Edradour 10 Year Old 2008 1st fill sherry butt (**92.5**) n23 t23 f23.5 b23 A huge, clean sherry butt at work there. Its only fault is that it rather obscures the malt for a beautiful distillery, making it a tad one-dimensional. But its overall effect is quite lovely. *58.7%. sc. Exclusive to The Whisky Barrel. 339 bottles.*

FETTERCAIRN
Highland (Eastern), 1824. Whyte and Mackay. Working.

Fettercairn Aged 12 Years bott code: L0044 15 45 P/011012 db (**88.5**) n22 t22.5 f21.5 b22.5 Well, I have to laugh. The battles with blender and dear friend Richard Richardson I have enjoyed over the last quarter of a century about the quality, or otherwise, of this malt have been ferocious though (usually) good natured. Here I have to doff my hat and give a nod to acknowledge credit where it is due. This exhibits all the distillery's normal languid nuttiness. But instead of then heading off on a tangent and into areas usually best left unexplored, as is normally the case, this actually embraces some very attractive heather honey notes which sits comfortably with both the juicier barley tones and light caramels. It all works rather well. Yes, I really rather enjoyed this one! *40%.*

Fettercairn Aged 16 Years 1st Release 2020 bott code: L0124 08:22 P/0121/6 db (**91**) n21.5 hefty and very odd. Had I not the bottle before me, I wouldn't have recognised this as a Fettercairn. Other than its inherent untidiness. But there is something else besides...; t23 immediately lush coating and then a superb mini-explosion of fruity muscovado sugars and spices. A little vanilla drifts about with some toffee; f23.5 oh, now didn't expect this....! Chocolate malt for sure....and a quick inspection of the label confirms it is there. The way it binds with a toasted toffee raisin note as well as a layering of ulmo honey is a true treat! b23 it's Fettercairn, Jim. But not as we know it. Those chocolate malt notes enter this into an entirely new dimension. The best bottling from this distillery I can remember. Love it! *46.4%.*

Fettercairn 40 Years Old db (**92**) n23 t24 f22 b23 Yes, everyone knows my views on this distillery. But I'll have to call this spade a wonderfully big, old shovel you can't help loving... just like the memory of me tattooed ol' granny... *40%. 463 bottles.*

Berry Bros & Rudd Fettercairn 11 Years Old cask no. 107750, dist 2006, bott 2018 (**80**) n21 t20 f19 b20 Pretty survivable for a Fettercairn. Lots of barley weirdness as you might expect. And that vaguely rubbery, nutty noise you always get in the background, especially at the death. But the oak is good, which helps, and the sugars and spices are in just about equal measure. Way above average. *46%. nc ncf sc.*

The First Editions Fettercairn Aged 13 Years 2005 refill butt, cask no. 15140, bott 2018 (**69**) n17 t19 f16 b17 Lots of niggle and bite. Grim, unbalanced and especially bitter towards the end. So, pretty normal for a Fettercairn, then. *59.7%. nc ncf sc. 336 bottles.*

Liquid Treasures 10th Anniversary Fettercairn 10 Year Old rum barrel, dist 2008, bott 2019 (**80.5**) n21 t22.5 f17 b19 Malty but hot and aggressive in time-honoured tradition. As is the exceptionally thin and course finale...though that is a disappointment because there is a promising, though brief buttery but malt-rich oiliness early on. A very grim finish, indeed. *57.4%. sc. 136 bottles.*

Old Malt Cask Fettercairn Aged 11 Years refill butt, cask no. 16646, dist Mar 08, bott May 19 (**78**) n19 t22 f18 b19 The nose is less than enticing, while the intense barley does have its salivating moments. But, as is the wont of Fettercairn, it never seems to gel and the finish is especially bitter and brutal. *50%. nc ncf sc. 606 bottles.*

Old Malt Cask Fettercairn Aged 13 Years refill hogshead, cask no. 15139, bott May 18 (**71**) n18 t20 f16 b17 No matter how many decades I spend doing this job, nosing and tasting Fettercairn doesn't get any easier. Proudly malty, but sharp, rock hard and even more proudly out of kilter. Thank God it was matured in a great cask. *50%. nc ncf sc. 341 bottles.*

Old Malt Cask Fettercairn Aged 14 Years refill hogshead, cask no. 15537, dist Jun 04, bott Nov 18 (**84**) n21 t22 f20 b21 No faulting the momentarily juicy malt. But one dimensional beyond belief. *50%. nc ncf sc. 314 bottles.*

GLEN ALBYN
Highlands (Northern) 1846–1983. Diageo. Demolished.

Gordon & MacPhail Rare Vintage Glen Albyn 1976 (**96**) n22.5 t24.5 f24.5 b24.5 Wow! My eyes nearly popped out of my head when I spotted this in my sample room. Glen Albyns come round as rarely as a Scotsman winning Wimbledon. Well, almost. When I used to buy this (from Gordon and MacPhail in their early Connoisseur's Choice range, as it happens) when the distillery was still alive (just) I always found it an interesting if occasionally aggressive dram. This masterpiece, though, is something else entirely. And the delivery really does take us to places where only the truly great whiskies go... 43%

GLENALLACHIE

Speyside, 1968. The GlenAllachie Distillers Co Limited. Working.

The GlenAllachie 10 Years Old Cask Strength batch 2 db (**87.5**) **n21.5 t22.5 f21.5 b22** Never thought I'd say this of a Glenallachie: but I quite enjoyed this. Despite its strength, the distillery's old trademark flamethrower character didn't materialise. The malt remains intact throughout but it is the natural caramels and vanilla from the oak which seriously catches the eye. This has spent ten years in some seriously good oak. I'll even go as far as to say that the malt-dripping delivery is rather gorgeous. *54.8%. The GlenAllachie Distillers Company.*

The GlenAllachie 12 Years Old db (**86.5**) **n21.5 t22.5 f20.5 b22** Whoever is putting these whiskies for Glenallachie together has certainly learned how to harness the extraordinary malt intensity of this distillery to its ultimate effect. Still a touch thin, at key moments, though, and the bitterness of the finish is purely down to the casks not the distillation. *46%. The GlenAllachie Distillers Company.*

The GlenAllachie 18 Years Old db (**89**) **n23 t22.5 f20 b22.5** As friendly as it gets from this distillery. *46%. The GlenAllachie Distillers Company.*

The GlenAllachie 25 Years Old db (**91.5**) **n23 t23.5 f22 b23** Around about the time this whisky was made, distillery manager Puss Mitchell, who then also had Aberlour and Edradour under his auspices, took me from time to time in his office and poured out samples of new make and maturing Glenallachie. The result, usually was a searing sensation to my mouth and a few yelps and cries from me (much to the amusement of Puss): it was then the most unforgiving – and thin - of all Scotland's malts. Indeed, when I wrote Jim Murray's Complete Book of Whisky in 1997, only one distillery in Scotland was missed out: it was Glenallachie. I had written the piece for it. But it just accidentally fell by the wayside during editing and the whisky was so ordinary I simply didn't notice. "It's a filler, Jim," said Puss as I choked on the samples. "This is for blending. It's too hot and basic for a single malt. This is no Aberlour." How extraordinary then, that the distillery now under new and focused ownership, has brought out the whisky from that very time. It is still a little thin, and on arrival it still rips into you. But the passing quarter of a century has mellowed it significantly; astonishingly. So now the sugars from the grist act as balm; the gentle tannins as peacemaker. This is, against all the odds, now a very attractive whisky. Even Puss Mitchell would have been amazed. *48%. The GlenAllachie Distillers Company.*

Abbey Whisky Glenallachie Aged 10 Years 2008 sherry butt (**87**) **n22 t22.5 f20.5 b22** Really quite like this. The strength takes some believing and definitely works in the whisky's favour, magnificently ramping up the malt contribution. Elsewhere tart and a little aggressive (nothing to do with strength), the threadbare body confirmed on the finish. But there is enough grape and muscular malt to ensure the good moments are occasionally great. *66.2%. sc. 150 bottles.*

Fadandel.dk Glenallachie 11 Year Old refill sherry butt, cask no. 900784, dist 28 Aug 08, bott 3 Sept 19 (**88**) **n22 t22.5 f21.5 b22** For a Glenallachie of this age, I have to say it's pretty damn good! A familiar lack of character on the body means that the sherry is not seriously tested from first to last and has by far too easy a match of it. Happily, this is a sound, rich cask with no obvious faults and is pretty creamy, too. A little late spice adds some verve but this is dangerously easy dramming! *62.3%. sc. 555 bottles.*

The Finest Malts Glenallachie 5 Year Old sherry hogshead, cask no. 33, dist Oct 14, bott Jan 20 (**81**) **n20 t22 f19 b20** I'm all for shewing off the vigour of young malts – always have been. But to make this work it is not a good idea to use a sulphur-treated cask. Decent sultana and spice delivery. But then goes its own furry way. *55.1%. nc ncf sc.*

Old Malt Cask Glenallachie Aged 27 Years refill hogshead, cask no. 16483, dist Jun 92, bott Oct 19 (**84**) **n21.5 t21.5 f20 b21** Although this is a malt which greatly benefits from old age, there is still some of its puppy glue from its youth, the tenuity of its body making this a fleeting and meagre experience. At least the barley gets a good run out. *50%. nc ncf sc. 296 bottles.*

GLENBURGIE

Speyside, 1810. Chivas Brothers. Working.

Ballantine's The Glenburgie Aged 15 Years Series No. 001 American oak casks, bott code: LKRM1245 2018/04/03 (**86**) **n21.5 t22 f21 b21.5** Clunking caramels clog up the nose and finish big time. But there are some interesting tannin-laden spice notes in full swing as well. 40%.

⬦ **Gordon & MacPhail Connoisseurs Choice Glenburgie Aged 20 Years** refill American hogshead, cask no. 4036, dist 22 Jul 98, bott 31 Jan 19 **(92.5) n23.5** almost too many rungs of tannin to count. But they are well spaced and serve up hickory and red liquorice with grace; **t23.5** an unusual stickiness on the palate for a Burgie, but this means the sugars go the distance They need to as the spices are bitty and biting; the malt surfs the waves...; **f22.5** though dryer, as you might expect, gentle molasses keeps up the toasty feeling; **b23** a single malt that will appeal to the bourbon-loving fraternity. Sweet and beautifully paced throughout. 55.3%. sc. 245 bottles.

Berry Bros & Rudd Glenburgie 29 Years Old cask no. 14087, dist 1989, bott 2018 **(89) n22.5 t23 f21 b22.5** An intrinsically dry dram, perfect as your pre-prandial tipple if the vermouth has run out. 46%. nc ncf sc.

Hepburn's Choice Glenburgie 10 Years Old refill hogshead, dist 2007, bott 2018 **(84) n21.5 t22 f20 b21.5** A pretty monosyllabic malt which, thanks to its youth, sticks to a grassy theme and refuses to budge. 46%. nc ncf sc. 340 bottles.

⬦ **Hepburn's Choice Glenburgie 11 Years Old** wine cask, dist 2008, bott 2019 **(83.5) n19 t22 f21 b21.5** Predominantly dry and mainly stifled. The busy spices do the malt a great service, though. 46%. nc ncf sc. 173 bottles.

⬦ **Old Malt Cask Glenburgie Aged 19 Years** refill butt, cask no. 16779, dist Nov 99, bott Apr 19 **(87.5) n21 t22.5 f22 b22** A malt that rewards a little extra time. At first glance it is austere and limited in scope. But a little bit of the Murray Method releases some previously hidden lychee juice to ensure satisfying depth and extra balance. 50%. nc ncf sc. 193 bottles.

GLENCADAM
Highlands (Eastern), 1825. Angus Dundee. Working.

Glencadam Aged 10 Years db **(95) n24 t24 f23 b24** Sophisticated, sensual, salivating and seemingly serene, this malt is all about juicy barley and balance. Just bristles with character and about as puckeringly elegant as single malt gets...and even thirst-quenching. My God: the guy who put this one together must be a genius, or something... 46%

Glencadam Aged 10 Years Special Edition batch no. 1, bott code: L1702608 CB2 db **(90.5) n22.5 t23.5 f22 b22.5** A weightier, oakier version of the standard Glencadam 10. Fascinating to see this level of oak involvement, though it further underlines what a delicate creature its spirit is... 48.2%. nc ncf. Special edition for The Whisky Shop.

Glencadam Aged 13 Years db **(94) n23.5 t24 f23 b23.5** Tasting this within 24 hours of Brechin City, the cheek by jowl neighbours of this distillery winning promotion after a penalty shoot out success in their play off final. This malt, every bit as engrossing and with more twists and turns than their seven-goal-thriller yesterday, is the perfect way to toast their success. 46%. nc ncf. 6,000 bottles.

Glencadam Aged 15 Years db **(90.5) n22.5 t23 f22 b23** The spices keep the taste buds on full alert but the richness and depth of the barley defies the years. Another exhibition of Glencadam's understated elegance. Some more genius malt creation... 46%

Glencadam Aged 17 Years Triple Cask Portwood Finish db **(93.5) n23 t24.5 f22 b24** A 17-year-old whisky truffle. A superb late night or after dinner dram, where even the shadowy sulphur cannot spoil its genius. 46%. nc ncf. 1128 bottles.

Glencadam Aged 18 Years db **(96.5) n24.5 t24 f23.5 b24.5** So, here we go again: head down and plough on with the Whisky Bible 2018. This is the first whisky tasted in anger for the new edition and I select Glencadam for the strangest of reasons: it is the closest distillery to a football ground (North British, apart) I can think of, being a drop kick from Brechin City's pretty Glebe Park ground. And why is that relevant? Well today is a Saturday and I should really be at a game but decided to start off a weekend when there are fewest interruptions and I can get back into the swing of things before settling into the rhythm of a six day tasting week. Also, Glencadam, though criminally little known beyond readers of the Whisky Bible, is among the world's greatest distilleries producing one of the most charming whiskies of them all. So, hopefully, it will be a little reward for me. And offering the bourbon cask induced natural, light gold - which perfectly matches the buzzard which has just drifted on the winds into my garden - this enticingly fills the gap between their 17- and 19- years old. Strikes me there is a fraction more first fill cask at play here than usual, ensuring not just a distinctively honeyed, bourbony edge but a drier element also. Distinguished and elegant this is a fabulous, almost unbelievable way to start the new Bible as it has the hallmarks of a malt likely to end up winning some kind of major award. Somehow I think the bar set here, one fashioned from gold, will be far too high for the vast majority that will follow over the next five months... 46%. nc ncf.

Glencadam Aged 19 Years Oloroso Sherry Cask Finish db **(84) n21.5 t22 f19.5 b21.** Mainly, though not quite, free of sulphur so the whisky after 19 years gets a good chance to speak relatively ungagged, though somewhat muffled. 46%. nc ncf. 6,000 bottles.

Glencadam Aged 25 Years db **(95)** n25 t24 f22 b24 Imagine the best-balanced team Mourinho ever produced for Chelsea. Well, it was never as good as this nose... *46%. nc ncf.*

◈ **Glencadam Reserva Andalucía Oloroso Sherry Cask Finish** sherry and bourbon casks, bott code: L20 06138 CB2 db **(91)** n22.5 a young, mildly gristy nose with a light sprinkling of delicately spiced fruit; **t23** a salivating, sugary delivery. Again the youth is hardly in question, the grist pinging all over the palate; **f22.5** dulls slightly as the grape strengthens, but the complexity is rekindled as the cocoa kicks in; **b23** Glencadam is such a charming and fragile malt, it is to be seen at its best in bourbon cask. So I was intrigued to see how they would tackle a sherry cask finish on this. First the all clear: no sulphur. Secondly, they have done justice to the malt as they have not allowed the grape to grip too tightly. Not the same charisma as the bourbon bottlings. But hugely enjoyable still, at least because the young barley continues to hold the upper hand. *46%. nc ncf.*

GLENCRAIG

Speyside, 1958. Chivas Brothers. Silent.

Cadenhead's Single Malt Glencraig 31 Years Old (92) n22.5 t23.5 f23 b23 Well done Cadenhead in coming up with one of the last surviving Glencraig casks on the planet. The feintiness shows why it was eventually done away with. But this is a malt with great distinction, too. *50.8%*

GLENDRONACH

Highlands, 1826. Brown-Forman. Working.

GlenDronach 8 Year Old The Hielan db **(82)** n20 t22 f20 b20. Intense malt. But doesn't quite feel as happy with the oil on show as it might. *46%*

The GlenDronach Aged 12 Years "Original" db **(86.5)** n21 t22 f22 b21.5. One of the more bizarre moments of the year: thought I'd got this one mixed up with a German malt whisky I had tasted earlier in the day. There is a light drying tobacco feel to this and the exact same corresponding delivery on the palate. That German version is distilled in a different type of still; this is made in probably the most classic stillhouse on mainland Scotland. Good, enjoyable whisky. But I see a long debate with distillery owner Billy Walker on the near horizon, though it was in Allied's hands when this was produced. *43%*

The GlenDronach Aged 18 Years "Allardice" db **(83.5)** n19 t22 f21 b21.5. Huge fruit. But a long-running bitter edge to the toffee and raisin sits awkwardly on the palate. *46%*

The GlenDronach Aged 18 Years Tawny Port Wood Finish db **(94.5)** n23.5 t24 f23 b24 A malt with not just an excellent flavour profile but sits on the palate as comfortably as you might snuggle into an old Jag. *46%.*

The GlenDronach Aged 21 Years Parliament db **(76)** n23 t21.5 f15 b16.5 Red-hued, myopically one dimensional, rambles on and on, sulphur-tongued, bitter and does its best to leave a bad taste in the mouth while misrepresenting its magnificent land. Now, who does that remind me of...? *48%.*

The GlenDronach 25 Years Old oloroso cask, cask no. GD#7434, dist 9 Jul 93 db **(94.5)** n23.5 t24 f23 b24 Had I any fireworks I would be setting them off outside now in celebration. I'm currently on my 1,058th whisky for the 2020 Bible and this is the first time I have tasted three sherry casks on the trot under 30-years-old that did not have a sulphur problem.... and all Glendronach's. At least I don't think this has, though there is a very late, tantalising niggle. But I can forgive that because this is your archetypal fruitcake single malt, complete with burnt raisins and glazed cherries. Toasty, tingly and just wonderful... *54.2%. sc. Bottled for The Whisky Shop.*

The GlenDronach 25 Years Old Pedro Ximénez cask, cask no. GD#5957, dist 21 May 93 db **(88.5)** n22 t22 f22.5 b22 I thought this may have been bottled for the Flat Earth Society. Because the PX, as PX has a very annoying tendency of doing, has made this very flat, indeed. Pleasant, for sure. But the usual peaks and troughs have been obliterated by the unforgiving thick sherry, though the busy spices shews there is still plenty of signs of life. Also some attractive sticky dates at the very finish. Oh, 100% sulphur-free, too! *55.6%. sc. Bottled for The Whisky Shop.*

The GlenDronach 26 Years Old oloroso cask, cask no. GD#77, dist 15 May 92 db **(81)** n19 t22.5 f19 b20.5 Strangely musty, dull and, late on, tangy. *50.3%. sc. The Whisky Shop.*

◈ **The GlenDronach Traditionally Peated** db **(89.5)** n21.5 full on smoke, but the nose is just too heavy, lopsided and vaguely off key; **t23** silky delivery but a short rubbery tone rears up early This, though, is then beaten into submission by a crashing waves of peat and spice; **f23** Jaffa cake orange, spice and phenolic remnants; **b22** a curiously untidy whisky that somehow works. Maybe by the force of will of the intense peat alone. One of those curious drams where the whole is better than the individual parts. *48%.*

GlenDronach Peated db **(93.5) n23.5 t23.5 f23 b23.5** I rarely mark the smoky whisky from a distillery which makes peat as an afterthought higher than its standard distillate. But here it is hard not to give massive marks. Only a failing cask at the very death docks a point or so... 46%

◇ **Abbey Whisky Glendronach Aged 24 Years 1993** sherry butt, cask no. 652 **(95.5) n24** classic old British Christmas cake drowning in rich fruit, molasses and brandy: simply sublime...; **t24** oh, the layering! From the first moment there is a surprising hint of chocolate – though this soon falls prey to the re-emerging sultanas and plums; **f23.5** long, increasingly toasty, with a burnt Dundee cake feel before that cocoa makes a gentle reappearance; **b24** it would be only too easy to mistake this as a duplicate of the 27-year-old below. But it isn't: here the fruit and oak is far more measured and sophisticated. Exemplary... 60.6%. sc.

◇ **Abbey Whisky Glendronach Aged 27 Years 1992** PX puncheon, cask no. 5850 **(92.5) n22.5** oh, my word...I'm in a time capsule...! Grape! Juicy, fat and lots of it...; **t23.5** the fruit hits you like a tsunami, the tannins and barley clinging for life as the juices flow almost uncontrollably; **f23** ah...some chocolate plants a flag for the great age of this malt, while beautifully matching the tasted raisin surround; **b23.5** I actually laughed out loud when I nosed this. It was like being back in my reporting days in Fleet Street again at El Vino's in the 1980s and tasting their Glendronach sherry matured malt: a massive, six-foot grapey overcoat drowning the apologetic frame of a five foot man. Once upon a time I used to dislike this whisky style because of its brash fruitiness without a trace a sympathy for the malt. Nearly 30 years on and I could almost dab at a damp eye of fondness. For this is a sherry cask without a blemish, to which sulphur is a stranger. So deep are the scars of the vile, unforgiving sulphur butts we have been forced to endure over the last three decades, today this is a whisky to be revered rather than, as it once was, mocked... 54.5%. sc.

The Whisky Shop Glendronach Aged 26 Years sherry cask, cask no. 64, dist 1992 **(96) n24 t24.5 f23.5 b24** From the creamed coffee school of drenched sherry butts. Not a single off note from this pre-Maastricht Treaty made barrel whatsoever. The kind of whisky that makes you proud to be British. 57.1%. sc. 493 bottles.

GLENDULLAN

Speyside, 1972. Diageo. Working.

Singleton of Glendullan 12 Years Old db **(87) n22 t22 f21 b22.** Much more age than is comfortable for a 12-y-o. 40%

The Singleton of Glendullan 15 Years of Age bott code: L7228DM001 db **(89.5) n22** a gentle framework of vanilla, malt and toffee; **t23** the sweetest delivery of any Glendullan I have tasted in some 40 years. A chink of malty light bursts through, then an explosion of intense molasses and fudge; **f22.5** the fudge, once burnt, is now creamier; **b22** mixed feelings. Designed for a very specific market, I suspect, and really impossible not to like. But would the real Glendullan with all its intrinsic Speyside characteristics please stand up. 40%.

The Singleton of Glendullan 18 Years of Age bott code: L6186DM000 db **(89)** n23 decent mix of Demerara sugars, dates and walnuts: have a problem locating the malt; **t22.5** a soft, sugary ultra-friendly delivery. A mix of red liquorice, light molasses and toffee; some welcome juiciness; **f21.5** the big caramel I'm afraid puts the dull in Glendullan...; **b22** a very pleasant if safe whisky where the real character of the malt is hard to unearth. 40%.

◇ **The Singleton Glendullan Classic** bott code: L5288DM000 db **(91.5) n23** the malt pulses from this, making use of some relative youth to maximise the sharpness, even to the point of a little bite; **t23** surprisingly fat delivery, again the malt at its most fulsome with a little peach skin and spice alongside; **f22.5** much drier but enough toasty sugars and late malt leakage to make for a satisfying conclusion; **b23** such an attractive freshness to this, the whole being a cross between barley sugar and fruit candy. 40%. Exclusive to Travel Retail.

Singleton of Glendullan Liberty db **(73) n17 t19 f18 b19.** For showing such a really unforgiving off key bitter furriness, it should be clamped in irons... 40% WB16/036

Singleton of Glendullan Trinity db **(92.5) n24 t23 f22.5 b23** Designed for airports, this complex little beauty deserves to fly off the shelves... 40% WB16/037

Game of Thrones The Singleton of Glendullan House of Tully db **(85.5) n21 t22 f21 b21.5** Annoyingly, the distillery style is in little evidence here so overbearing is the fudge. Some spices whizz around to inject a degree of interest. But it's an OK but one-dimensional incarnation. 40%.

GLEN ELGIN

Speyside, 1900. Diageo. Working.

Glen Elgin Aged 12 Years db **(89) n23 t24 f20 b22.** Absolutely murders Cragganmore as Diageo's top dog bottled Speysider. The marks would be several points further north if one didn't get the feeling that some caramel was weaving a derogatory spell. Brilliant stuff nonetheless. States Pot Still on label – not to be confused with Irish Pot Still. This is 100% malt... and it shows! *43%*

◈ **The Single Malts of Scotland Glen Elgin 13 Year Old Reserve Cask** (88.5) n22.5 t22 f22 b22 A distinctly undercooked Glen Elgin, probably from a third fill barrel. This means that any foibles from the cask are easily detectable, though if there are any they cannot fully compete with the juicy depths of the weak maple syrup and concentrated grist. *48%. nc ncf.*

GLENESK
Highlands (Eastern), 1897–1985. Diageo. Demolished.

Gordon & MacPhail Rare Old Glenesk 1980 (95) n23.5 t24 f23.5 b24 What a charmer: better dead than when alive, some might argue. But this has weathered the passing three and half decades with ease and really does have something of an ice cream feel to it from beginning to the end...well I suppose the distillery was located close to the seaside...One of the most understated but beautiful lost distillery bottlings of the year. *46%.*

GLENFARCLAS
Speyside, 1836. J&G Grant. Working.

Glenfarclas 10 Years Old db (80) n19 t20 f22 b19. Always an enjoyable malt, but for some reason this version never seems to fire on all cylinders. There is a vague honey sheen which works well with the barley, but struggles for balance and the nose is a bit sweaty. Still has distinctly impressive elements but an odd fish. *40%*

Glenfarclas 12 Years Old db (94) n23.5 t24 f23 b23.5 A superb re-working of an always trustworthy malt. This dramatic change in shape works a treat and suits the malt perfectly. What a sensational success!! *43%*

Glenfarclas 15 Years Old db (85.5) n21.5 t23 f20 b21. One thing is for certain: working with sherry butts these days is a bit like working with ACME dynamite... you are never sure when it is about to blow up in your face. There is only minimal sulphur here, but enough to take the edge off a normally magnificent whisky, at the death. Instead it is now merely, in part, quite lovely. The talent at Glenfarclas is unquestionably among the highest in the industry: I'll be surprised to see the same weaknesses with the next bottling. *46%*

Glenfarclas 17 Years Old db (94.5) n23.5 t24 f23 b24 When a malt is this delicate, it is surprising the difference that just 3% can make to the oils and keeping the structure together. A dram for those with a patient disposition. *43%.*

Glenfarclas 18 Years Old db (84) n21 t22 f20 b21. Tight, nutty and full of crisp muscovado sugar. *43%. Travel Retail Exclusive.*

Glenfarclas 21 Years Old db (83) n20 t23 f19 b21. A chorus of sweet, honied malt and mildly spiced, teasing fruit on the fabulous mouth arrival and middle compensates for the few blips. *43%*

Glenfarclas 25 Years Old db (84) n20 t22 f20 b22. A curious old bat: by no means free from imperfect sherry but compensating with some staggering age – seemingly way beyond the 25-year statement. Enjoys the deportment of a doddering old classics master from a family of good means and breeding. *43%*

Glenfarclas 30 Years Old db (85) n20 t22 f21 b22. Flawed yet juicy. *43%*

Glenfarclas 40 Years Old db (95) n24.5 t23.5 f23 b24 A few moments ago an RAF plane flew low over my usually quiet cottage, violently shaking the windows, silencing my parrot and turning a great spotted woodpecker feeding in my garden to stone: it was too shocked to know whether to stay or fly. And I thought, immediately: Glenfarclas 40! For when, a long time ago now, John Grant paid me the extraordinary compliment of opening his very first bottle of Glenfarclas 40 so we could taste it together, a pair of RAF fighters chose that exact moment to roar feet above his distillery forcing the opened bottle from John's startled hands and onto the lush carpet...into which the initial measures galloopingly poured, rather than our waiting glasses. And it so happened I had a new sample to hand. So, with this whisky I made a fond toast: to John. And to the RAF. *43%.*

Glenfarclas 40 Years Old db (94) n23 t23 f24 b24 Couldn't help but laugh: this sample was sent by the guys at Glenfarclas after they spotted that I had last year called their disappointing 40-year-old a "freak". I think we have both proved a point... *46%*

Glenfarclas 50 Years Old db (92) n24 t23 f22 b23 Most whiskies cannot survive such great age. This one really does bloom in the glass and the earthy, peaty aspect makes it all the more memorable. It has taken 50 years to reach this state. Give a glass of this at least an hour's inquisition, as I have. Your patience will be rewarded many times over. *44.4%*

Glenfarclas 50 Years Old III ex-Oloroso sherry casks db (88.5) n23.5 t21 f22 b22 You can actually hear it wheezing as it has run out of puff. But it is easy to recognise the mark of an old champion... *41.1%. ncf. 937 bottles.*

Glenfarclas 105 db **(95.5) n23.5 t24 f24 b24** I doubt if any restorative on the planet works quite as well as this one does. Or if any sherry cask whisky is so clean and full of the joys of Jerez. A classic malt which has upped a gear or two and has become exactly what it is: a whisky of pure brilliance... *60%*

Glenfarclas £511.19s.0d Family Reserve db **(88) n22.5 t22.5 f21 b22** Not the best, but this still ain't no two bob whisky, mister, and make no mistake... *43%*

Glenfarclas The Family Casks 1977 W18 Release 4th fill hogshead, cask no. 7281 db **(92.5) n23 t23 f23 b23.5** Where you get the feeling that a cask like the 1979 is at its zenith, this chap, as delightful as it may be, has set off on its downward path. That said, it still has a long way to go on its descent, for the structure here is still sound and although the tannins perhaps have a little too much vinegar about its personality, the sugars and the intensity of the barley remains unbowed and delicious. Just love that little chocolate wafer finale... *44.6%. sc.*

Glenfarclas The Family Casks 1978 W18 Release 4th fill hogshead, cask no. 661 db **(96) n24 t24.5 f23.5 b24** A malt which needs so much time to get to know and understand. Once you are captivated by the gooseberry nose, you stand no chance. And as bright and entrancing as the aroma may be, that is nothing compared to the complexity which unfolds on the palate. Not just in the flavours, but the textures, too. Insanely soft on delivery with an immediate move into sensual chocolate tones. Usually, that comes later, but not here. The malt for the woman of your life, first to enjoy her to seduce and/or be seduced by, and then to share together... *42.7%. sc.*

Glenfarclas The Family Casks 1979 W18 Release 4th fill hogshead, cask no. 2088 db **(95.5) n23.5 t24 f24 b24** A polished charmer capable of sweeping the most discerning whisky lover off their feet. You know it's game on when the nose doesn't just waft any old exotic fruit at you, but a little extra passion fruit and lychee no less. So not surprises that these melt-in-the-mouth fruits become the main theme, even upping the juiciness as it develops. For a perfect ending you really want a delightful, lightly spiced vanilla and chocolate mix.... and guess what you get....! Superb. *48.4%. sc.*

Glenfarclas The Family Casks 1980 W18 Release refill hogshead, cask no. 1916 db **(87.5) n22.5 t22 f21 b22** Walks with a stiff back and a creaking gait as the tannins strong-arms the malt into subservience. Some buttery barley does some important repair work. *43.3%. sc.*

Glenfarclas The Family Casks 1981 W18 Release refill hogshead, cask no. 1085 db **(89) n22 t23 f21.5 b22.5** The little bit of wear and tear on the nose and delivery is countered by soft fruit and vanillas elsewhere. With having long ago reached the exotic fruit stage of its development, it is borderline salivating. But the tannins are always lapping at the dam wall waiting to find the breach... *43.2%. sc.*

Glenfarclas The Family Casks 1982 W18 Release 4th fill hogshead, cask no. 632 db **(92) n22 t23 f23.5 b23.5** For a moment or two on delivery you wonder if tweezers are required to pick the splinters out of your tongue: certainly the big ancient oaky nose had put you on full alert. But splendid heather honey comes riding to the rescue and tones down the tannins enough to make them both enjoyable and highly effective with their spices. A lovely praline finish fits well with the style. A malt which teeters on the edge for a moment or two, but there is a happy ending. *47.1%. sc.*

Glenfarclas The Family Casks 1983 W18 Release refill hogshead, cask no. 28 db **(94.5) n23 t24.5 f23 b24** Someone has poured golden syrup over a hot cross bun. Except the barley here has managed to escape to make a fleeting appearance before the lush sultanas return. The odd moment on delivery borders on perfection, especially when the spices make their short by mercurial play. *48.8%. sc.*

Glenfarclas The Family Casks 1985 W18 Release 4th fill hogshead, cask no. 2784 db **(92) n23 t23 f22.5 b23.5** A malt which looks more concerned about holding itself together than providing a sweeping fruit and oak vista; *41.6%. sc.*

Glenfarclas The Family Casks 1986 W18 Release refill sherry butt, cask no. 4335 db **(92) n23.5 t24 f22 b22.5** If this is a refill, what was the sherry butt like when new...? This is huge, putting me in mind of a sticky plum pudding I enjoyed in Fortnum and Mason over 20 years ago which buzzed with dark sugar and spice. A slight buzz of another kind on the late finish is the only downside. *55%. sc.*

Glenfarclas The Family Casks 1987 W18 Release refill sherry butt, cask no. 3831 db **(87) n22 t22 f21.5 b21.5** Some might say silky and tannin-rich. Others might say flat and overcooked. *46%. sc.*

Glenfarclas The Family Casks 1988 W18 Release refill sherry butt, cask no. 1374 db **(96) n24 t24.5 f23.5 b24** One of the slightly drier Glenfarclases which pops up from time to time, this one almost going off the complexometer. The perfect, unblemished cask doing extraordinary things...and all of them beautiful. *49.2%. sc.*

Glenfarclas The Family Casks 1989 W18 Release sherry butt, cask no. 13010 db **(95.5)** n23.5 t24.5 f23.5 b24 Not quite a perfect butt, but it is very shapely and deserves to be bitten into.. *51.4%. sc.*

Glenfarclas The Family Casks 1990 W18 Release sherry butt, cask no. 5117 db **(89)** n23 t23 f21 b22 I remember quite a few of these sherry butts doing the rounds in the early 1990s, absolutely packed to gunnels with thick, almost opaque grape. Always nosed better than they tasted, and it is a case in point here with just a little too much bitterness towards the death despite the late mocha intervention. *51.9%. sc.*

Glenfarclas The Family Casks 1991 W18 Release sherry butt, cask no. 5675 db **(91.5)** n22 t24 f22.5 b23 If the colour doesn't scare you, then the grape will. Often malts displaying this kind of one-dimensional nose turn out to be grape-infested bores. Not this bottling. While the nose is too overwhelming for greatness, the unravelling of the sugars on the palate is as witty, eloquent and erudite as a speech from the despatch box by Jacob Rees-Mogg. So many strains of sweetness here, most muscovado-based, but also over-ripe greengages at molasses work. Entirely sulphur free, this malt could qualify for old-fashioned entertainment tax. *56.6%. sc.*

Glenfarclas The Family Casks 1992 W18 Release 4th fill butt, cask no. 5984 db **(86.5)** n22 t22 f21 b21.5 A degree of tiredness has crept into this, not normally evident in Glenfarclas' great armoury. A tightness to the tannins amplifies the lack of development from the fruit. *53.5%. sc.*

Glenfarclas The Family Casks 1993 W18 Release 4th fill butt, cask no. 4662 db **(94)** n23.5 t23.5 f23 b24 The first Glenfarclas this year I have found shewing a degree of bourbon character, especially on the nose where liquorice plays a confident and healthy part of reminding you of this whisky's good age. However, it is the texture and mouthfeel which really blows you away with this, the barley itself still playing an important role in this context, as well as the type of sugars which will work. Also in keeping the spices under control, though they are never less than warming. A superbly paced dram, this, for intriguing little sub plots and secret oaky passages. *56.8%. sc.*

Glenfarclas The Family Casks 1994 W18 Release refill sherry butt, cask no. 1581 db **(91.5)** n21 t24 f23 b23.5 I'd be lying if I said I was impressed with the nose. Which makes what comes next on the palate all the more amazing: the most intense marriage between sultana and ulmo honey. You know spices are on their way, and they arrive in no great rush, but build in harmonious intensity. But that honey never leaves the table, making this – to taste at least – an absolute gem of a bottling. *56.1%. sc.*

Glenfarclas The Family Casks 1995 W18 Release 4th fill butt, cask no. 9 db **(96)** n24 t24 f23.5 b24.5 A malt brimming with both confidence and grapey intent. The perfumed nose makes a mockery of a fourth use butt, as this is still radiating depth – though now of a distinct grape must kind – and becomes turbo charges in the honey department as a glossy fruitiness fills the mouth. Faultless, with not an atom of sulphur, and brilliantly integrated spicing. *52.1%. sc.*

Glenfarclas The Family Casks 1996 W18 Release 4th fill butt, cask no. 24 db **(94.5)** n22 t24.5 f23.5 b24.5 On nosing this you might be forgiven that you have been taken into a Jaguar showroom and shown an Audi: pleasant but a bit square and conventional. Only when you taste do you realise you are sitting in an F Type, all effervescence and power and unbelievable style, gripping your palate like the sports car hugs the road. Belt yourself in for this one...it is one delicious surprise ride... *58.9%. sc.*

Glenfarclas The Family Casks 1997 W18 Release refill sherry butt, cask no. 5134 db **(95)** n23.5 t24 f23.5 b24 Sublime. Glenfarclas doing what it does best: taking on an unusual fruity tour but with some fascinating diversions along the way. *57.1%. sc.*

Glenfarclas The Family Casks 1998 W18 Release 4th fill hogshead, cask no. 4455 db **(93.5)** n23.5 t23.5 f23 b23.5 A charming, black cherry accentuated bottling where the spices not only come out to play but act as the main focal point to the increasingly juicy body. Indeed, the intensity of the barley itself is quite superb. *54.8%. sc.*

Glenfarclas The Family Casks 1999 W18 Release refill butt, cask no. 7060 db **(85.5)** n21 t22 f21 b21.5 On the duller side of the 'Farclas family. But the light sulphur can't entirely see off the spice and minty cocoa. *56%. sc.*

Glenfarclas The Family Casks 2002 W18 Release sherry butt, cask no. 3773 db **(93)** n23 t23.5 f23 b23.5 One of those outrageously booming sherry butts displaying so many esters and so much coffee, it is easy to mistake this for an old Demerara rum. *57.8%. sc.*

Glenfarclas The Family Casks 2003 W18 Release 4th fill butt, cask no. 1963 db **(94.5)** n23 t24 f23.5 b24 Not sure if Glenfarclas had a new still in around this time, or major work to an old one, but there appears to be lots of coppery richness in play here giving a further lustre to the already eye-watering barley. The light spice and French praline thread running through this malt also marks it out as something rather special. Not the usual Glenfarclas style, other than in its usual exceptionally high quality. *58.3%. sc.*

GLENFIDDICH

Speyside, 1887. William Grant & Sons. Working.

Glenfiddich Our Original Twelve 12 Years Old Oloroso sherry & bourbon casks, bott code: L8D 8260 2611 db (82) n22 t22.5 f18 b19.5 Although they call this their "Original Twelve", I can clearly remember when Glenfiddich dispensed with their flagship unaged bottling, the celebrated fresh and juicy one that after a lifetime in ex-bourbon casks had conquered so many uncharted seas, and replaced it with a 12-year-old. And the original didn't have this degree of sherry involvement by any stretch of the imagination. The nose is attractively infused with fruit and the barley glides over the palate on delivery. It is the scratchy, bitter-ish, furry and off-key finish, revealing more of the olosoro influence than we'd really like to know, that brings the side down. 40%.

Glenfiddich Caoran Reserve Aged 12 Years db (89) n22.5 t22 f21.5 b23. Has fizzed up a little in the last year or so with some salivating charm from the barley and a touch of cocoa from the oak. A complex little number. 40%

Glenfiddich Rich Oak Over 14 Years Old new American & new Spanish oak finish db (90.5) n23 t22 f23.5 b22. Delicious, thoughtful whisky and one to tick off on your journey of malt whisky discovery. Though a pity we don't see it at 46% and in full voluptuous nudity: you get the feeling that this would have been something really exceptional to conjure with. 40%.

Glenfiddich 15 Years Old db (94.5) n23 t23 f24.5 b24 If an award were to be given for the most consistently beautiful dram in Scotland, this would win more often than not. This under-rated distillery has won more friends with this masterpiece than probably any other brand. 40%

Glenfiddich Aged 15 Years Cask Strength db (85.5) n20 t23 f21 b21.5. Improved upon the surprisingly bland bottlings of old, especially on the fabulously juicy delivery. Still off the pace due to an annoying toffee-ness towards the middle and at the death. 51%

Glenfiddich Aged 15 Years Distillery Edition American & European oak casks, bott code: L32C 4704 0908 db (95.5) n24 all kinds of chocolate and raisin fingerprints everywhere; some freewheeling sugary notes promise riches; t24 full bodied and chewy from the very start. Something of a Maryland Cookie feel to this, which a wonderful interplay between buoyant spices and maple syrup only adds positively to; f23.5 long, lingering layering and lush. More molasses than maple now but I love the late chorus of barley and Old Jamaica plain chocolate; a late spice serenade plays us out...; b24 a rumbustious malt which comes at you at full throttle. Big, muscular...but, deep down, a bit of a pussycat, too...Brilliant! 51%. ncf.

Glenfiddich 15 Years Old Solera bourbon, new oak and sherry casks, Solera vat finish, bott code: L8D 6980 2106 db (87) n22 t22.5 f20.5 b22 Have to say that this particular batch is pretty unrecognisable from the 15-year-old Solera I tasted (and helped in creating) in its first-ever form the best part of 30 years ago. The fault lines in the sherry can be detected, especially on the mildly furry finish. But this is thinner of body, too, which means the spices are a little too loud on the nose and struggling to find a counteracting partner on the palate. I do still love the oily drollness of the bitter-sweet delivery. But the middle empties rather than fills. The finish is out of sync and quarrelsome, leaving a disappointing finish to a whisky which once never disappointed. 40%.

Glenfiddich 18 Years Old db (95) n23.5 t24.5 f23 b24 At the moment, the ace in the Glenfiddich pack. If this was bottled at 46%, unchillfiltered etc, I dread to think what the score might be... 40%

Glenfiddich Aged 18 Years Small Batch Reserve Oloroso sherry & bourbon casks, batch no. 3231, bott code: L32D 4706 0606 db (91.5) n23 soft, welcoming blackberries and apple, all sharpened by a vaguely salty spiciness. A lovely oaky frame for the fruity picture to be admired to its best advantage...; t23 sensual malts soon handsomely enriched by plummy fruit. As the spices fail, then more do we move towards a fruitcake personality; f22 bitter burnt raisin. A little sulphur creeps in; b23.5 one of those malts which, cleverly, is as much about the experience of the mouthfeel and texture as it is the flavour itself. A vague weakness on the finish but, otherwise, a celebration of lustre... 40%.

Glenfiddich Age Of Discovery Aged 19 Years Bourbon Cask Reserve db (92) n23.5t24 f22 b22.5. For my money Glenfiddich turns from something quite workaday to a malt extraordinaire between the ages of 15 and 18. So, depending on the casks chosen, a year the other side of that golden age shouldn't make too much difference. The jury is still out on whether it was helped by being at 40%, which means the natural oils have been broken down somewhat, allowing the intensity and richness only an outside chance of fully forming. 40%

Glenfiddich Age Of Discovery Aged 19 Years Madeira Cask Finish db (88.5) n22.5 t22.5 f21 b22.5. Oddly enough, almost a breakfast malt: it is uncommonly soft and light yet carries a real jam and marmalade character. 40%

Glenfiddich 21 Years Old db (86) n21 t23 f21 b21. A much more uninhibited bottling with loads of fun as the mouth-watering barley comes rolling in. But still falls short on taking the hair-raisingly rich delivery forward and simply peters out. *40%*

◈ **Glenfiddich Aged 21 Years Reserva Rum Cask Finish** batch no. 64, bott code: L34D 4317 1503 db (91) n23 the barley seems locked into the rock solid sugars. Overall, a hard nose, but just enough give to allow the sugars to flourish; t23 the good old 'Fiddich juiciness is at full pelt on entry and for the first few flavour waves after. The barley appears in strands but is quietened by the effect of the clean casks; f22.5 pleasant vanillas help towards a biscuity finale; b22.5 clean, upstanding whisky from faultless casks. Just lacks that little bit of extra flavour development. *40%*

Glenfiddich 30 Years Old db (93.5) n23 t23.5 f23.5 b23.5 a 'Fiddich which has changed its spots. Much more voluptuous than of old and happy to mine a grapey seam while digging at the sweeter bourbon elements for all it is worth. Just one less than magnificent butt away from near perfection and a certain Bible Award... *40%*

◈ **Glenfiddich 30 Years Old** European Oloroso sherry & American bourbon casks, cask selection no. 00049, bott code: L34D 4828120710 db (96.5) n24 the layering of the grape could be used in lectures in how to create the perfect sherry cask Speysider. If you can count the layers and rungs to this aroma, then you are a better man than I. Incredibly well weighted and unbelievably balanced, the fruit has both an elegance and gaiety that makes every use of the marauding muscovado sugars. Brilliant..! t24.5 malt whisky comes no softer. Bizarrely, there is an attitude to this - of the burnt fruit cake variety. But the velvety tannins and barley juiciness keeps everything in check and complexity up to the maximum...especially when the lazy spices start inveigling their way in...; f24 ever seen a skylark land...? If not, then find one and study. The way the juicy fruits, the intense malts and the spices parachute on to the taste buds....well, there you have it...; b24 the move from 40% abv to 43% has made a huge difference, as little as it sounds. Taking that further step up to 46% could be a game changer for the distillery itself. Glenfiddich, 30 years ago the champion of the younger Speysider, has always been at its very best, and at its natural limit at the 18 to 21-year-old mark. This bottling reveals that things have fundamentally changed. For the better... *43%.* ☙

Glenfiddich 50 Years Old db (97) n25 t24 f24 b24 William Grant blender David Stewart, whom I rank above all other blenders on this planet, has known me long and well enough to realise that the surrounding hype, with this being the most expensive whisky ever bottled at £10,000 a go or a sobering £360 a pour, would bounce off me like a pebble from a boulder. "Honestly, David," he told my chief researcher with a timorous insistence, "please tell Jim I really think this isn't too oaky." He offered almost an apology for bringing into the world this 50-year-old babe. Well, as usual David Stewart, doyen of the blending lab and Ayr United season ticket holders, was absolutely spot on. And, as is his wont, he was rather understating his case. For the record, David, next time someone asks you how good this whisky is, just for once do away with the Ayeshire niceness instilled by generations of very nice members of the Stewart family and tell them: "Actually, it's bloody brilliant if I say so myself! And I don't give a rat's bollocks what Murray thinks." *46.1%*

◈ **Glenfiddich Fire & Cane** finished in sweet rum casks, bott code: L32D 4985 2608 db (96) n24 peat...! On a Glenfiddich...!!! But not just any old peat. Sometimes a Speysider pops up with a phenolic version which is attractive and quirky. This nose, however, is so relaxed, so happily intertwined with the layers of tannin, the islands of barley, that you feel like standing up and applauding...; not quite a giant nose...but so, so gentle...; t24 you expect the softest of landings on the palate, and that is exactly what you get: not something that adds to the is the norm so far rum casks are concerned. The phenols have a wonderfully translucent effect: thick, yet through it you can still detect the working of the barley and with increasing degrees the firmness of the cask. What sugars that are leached from the rum influence do not try to harden the arteries, but they certainly help provide an undulating effect between the softer and firmer lines; f23.5 brilliantly effective and very even spice; b24.5 I think those of us in the industry who can now be described in the "veteran" category can only smile at the prospect of tasting a full blown peaty Glenfiddich: the distillery that once stood for the cleanest, least peat influenced malt in the whole of Scotland. But when you nose and taste this, you wonder why they didn't take this route from day one, for rarely do you find a distillery that creates a peaty malt so naturally to the phenolic manor born. This is not a gimmicky whisky. No, this is something to be respected and cherished for thing of beauty it actually is. *43%. Experimental Series #4.* ☙

◈ **Glenfiddich Grand Cru Aged 23 Years** Cuvée cask finish, bott code: LA4D 9012 0210 db (90) n22.5 any Londoner who doesn't recognise this as spotted dog pudding should be sent to Europe immediately...; t23 intense malt hit the taste buds running. The fruitiness on the nose has been discarded on delivery to make way for the intrinsic interplay between vanilla and barley; **f23** a vanilla-barley co-production. Charmingly complex, especially when the spices run amok.... **b22.5** Cuvee, but not curvy. Even so, attractive and delightfully salivating in so many ways... 40%.

Glenfiddich IPA Experiment Experimental Series No 1 bott code: L34A4972141211 db **(86)** **n21.5 t22.5 f21 b21** IPA and XX...all very Greene King brewery of the early 1980s... An IPA is, by definition, extra hopped in order to preserve the beer on a long journey (to India, originally). I can't say I am picking out hop here, exactly, unless it is responsible for the off-key bitter finale. Something is interfering with the navigation and after an attractive early malty blast on delivery everything goes a little bland. 43%.

Glenfiddich Project XX Experimental Series No 2 bott code: L34B4041170207 db **(95.5)** **n24 t24 f23.5 b24** "20 minds, one unexpected whisky" goes the blurb on the label. And, in fairness, they have a point. It has been a long time since I have encountered a distillery-produced malt this exceptionally well rounded and balanced. All 20 involved should take a bow: this is Glenfiddich as it should be...xxellent, in fact! 47%.

⬦ **Glenfiddich Project XX** bott code: L34D 4210 2102 db **(90) n22** a nippy nose with a bit of the devil in it, and a slight hint of unfriendly fire from a wine cask. Intriguing, lush and balanced, though; **t24** a more fulsome and sound delivery than the flibbertigibbet nose and anyone with a weakness for the brown and liquorice one in a bag of Liquorice Allsorts will appreciate the general thrust of this! Indeed, the delivery is certainly a thing of rare beauty and balance and the sub plot of rich praline to give extra substance to liquorice is a joy to experience...; **f21** so, 20 minds worked on the creation of this malt apparently. But none of them picked up the sulphur weakness on the nose and finish... Oh well...; **b23** a flawed malt thanks to some unsound wine casks. But, that said, the overall composition is viscous, chewy and at times absolutely delicious. Impure gold... And, if finding kinder casks, a potential major award winner. 47%. ncf. Experimental Series #2.

⬦ **Glenfiddich Reserve Cask** sherry casks, Solera vat no. 2, bott code: L2D 6784 2904 db **(88.5) n21.5 t23 f21.5 b22.5** Glenfiddich, when on song, is one of my favourite distilleries: its malt can offer a clarity of flavour and effervescence that few distilleries in Scotland can match. Sherry influence has a tendency to negate that natural brilliance. However, the delivery reveals a delicious degree of that gorgeous house vitality, an effect which tapers as the grape and other influences slowly takes control. A rather delightful malt with stupendous malty sweetness on delivery and an attractive softness which is entirely in keeping with the pace of the flavour development. A lovely malt, indeed. 40%. Travel Retail Exclusive.

⬦ **Glenfiddich Select Cask** bourbon, European oak and red wine casks, Solera vat no. 1, bott code: L2D 6836 0505 db **(85.5) n21 t21.5 f21.5 b21.5** With its heavy leaning on a safe, linear toffee-raisin simplicity, some people will call this smooth. Others, like me, will call it a bit of a dullard. 40%. Travel Retail Exclusive.

⬦ **Glenfiddich Winter Storm Aged 21 Years Icewine Cask Finish Experiment** bott code: LA3 C9009 2510 db **(95) n24** a stunning nose where that half green barley-half malt character unique to this distillery is at its fullest and most effervescent: I could nose this all day...; **t24** gorgeous texture with the light oils underlining the moderate size of the stills. The juicy, delicately sweet barley is first up and explodes like a flare from storm-tossed ship; the layering of very simple barley and vanilla-rich tannin is an essay in simplicity and effect. The sweet-dry currents and sub currents create a whirlpool; **f23** heads, inexorably, towards ultra-dry cocoa and warming spices; **b24** with Storm Dennis on the warpath outside causing widespread flooding and mayhem to much of Britain, never is a whisky needed more than now. And how can you find one more fitting...? What better than to find Glenfiddich at its more juicy, crisp and alluring. Absolutely love it! Almost makes you look forward to the next storm to batter Britain... 43%. Experimental Series #3.

GLEN GARIOCH
Highlands (Eastern), 1798. Morrison Bowmore. Working.

Glen Garioch 8 Years Old db **(85.5) n21 t22 f21 b21.5.** A soft, gummy, malt – not something one would often write about a dram of this or any age from Geary! However, this may have something to do with the copious toffee which swamps the light fruits which try to emerge. 40%

Glen Garioch 10 Years Old db **(80) n19 t22 f19 b20.** Chunky and charming, this is a malt that once would have ripped your tonsils out. Much more sedate and even a touch of honey to the rich body. Toffeed at the finish. 40%

Glen Garioch 12 Years Old db **(88.5) n22 t23 f21.5 b22.**A significant improvement on the complexity front. The return of the smoke after a while away was a surprise and treat. 43%

Glen Garioch 12 Years Old db **(88) n22.5 t22.5 f21.5 b22.** Sticks, broadly, to the winning course of the original 43% version, though here there is a fraction more toffee at the expense of the smoke. 48%. ncf.

Glen Garioch 15 Years Old db (86.5) n20.5 t22 f22 b22. In the a bottling I sampled last year the peat definitely vanished. Now it's back again, though in tiny, if entertaining, amounts. 43%

Glen Garioch Aged 16 Years The Renaissance 2nd Chapter bott code: L162292 db (81) n21 t23 f18 b19 For a wonderful moment, actually two: once on the nose and then again on the delivery, you think you are heading towards some kind of Sauternes-type magnificence... then it all goes wrong. Yes, there are fleeting moments of borderline perfection. But those dull, bitter notes have by far the bigger and longer say. Perhaps the biggest disappointment of the year... 51.4%.

Glen Garioch 21 Years Old db (91) n21 t23 f24 b23 An entirely re-worked, now smokeless, malt that has little in common with its predecessors. Quite lovely, though. 43%

Glen Garioch 30 Years Old No. 503 dist 1987, bott 2017 db (89) n22.5 t23 f21.5 b22 This is from the exotic fruit school of ancient whiskies, the oak's tannin now out-manoeuvering the fruit. Perhaps moved on a little too far down a chalky, tannin-rich route though a little smoke does cushion the blow. Ancient, but still very attractive. 47.1%. Selected for CWS.

Glen Garioch 1797 Founders Reserve db (87.5) n21 t22 f22.5 b22. Impressively fruity and chewy: some serious flavour profiles in there. 48%

Glen Garioch 1958 db (90) n24 t21 f23 b22. The distillery in its old smoky clothes: and quite splendid it looks! 43%. 328 bottles.

Glen Garioch 1995 db (86) n21 t22 f21.5 b21.5. Typically noisy on the palate, even though the malty core is quite thin. Some big natural caramels, though. 55.3%. ncf.

Glen Garioch 1997 db (89) n22 t22.5 f22 b22.5 had you tasted this malt as a 15-year-old back in 1997, you would have tasted something far removed from this, with a peaty bite ripping into the palate. To say this malt has evolved is an understatement. 56.5%. Whisky Shop Exclusive.

Glen Garioch 1997 db (89.5) n22 t23 f22 b22.5. I have to say: I have long been a bit of a voice in the wilderness among whisky professionals as regards this distillery. This not so subtly muscled malt does my case no harm whatsoever. 56.7%. ncf.

Glen Garioch 1998 db (89.5) n21 t23.5 f22.5 b23 with dates this good, a chocolate-loving, non-Islamic Tuareg will adore this one... one of the best flawed whiskies I have tasted in a while... 48% WB16/039

Glen Garioch 2000 Bourbon Cask db (93.5) n23 t24 f23 b23.5 The distance this malt has travelled from the days when it was lightly peated firewater is almost beyond measure. A bourbony delight of a Highland malt. 57.3%. ncf.

◇◇◇ **Liquid Treasures 10th Anniversary Glen Garioch 8 Year Old** bourbon barrel, dist 2011, bott 2019 (87.5) n22 t22 f21.5 b22 Interesting how the old heat that used to be found on this malt back in the 1970s and '80s has returned, but the smoke which used to accompany it those days hasn't....which is a shame. Really makes a big speech on delivery and it is the malt writing the script, with the odd contribution by Demerara sugar, vanilla and natural caramels. But still pretty gruff stuff. 59.9%. sc. 132 bottles.

GLENGLASSAUGH
Speyside, 1875. Brown-Forman. Working.

Glenglassaugh 30 Year Old db (87) n22.5 t23 f20 b21.5. A gentle perambulation around soft fruitcake. Moist and nutty it still has a major job on its hands overcoming the enormity of the oak. The buzzing spices underline the oak involvement. Meek, charming though a touch furry on the finish. 44.8%.

Glenglassaugh 40 Years Old Pedro Ximénez cask, cask no. GG#3060, dist 8 Dec 78 db (88.5) n22.5 t22 f22 b22 Despite the best efforts of the molasses and life-giving PX cask, you can't help getting away from the feeling that here is one pretty exhausted malt. Both the nose and delivery in particular reveal oak tones more associated with a spent whisky. Yet it is still breathing and has energy enough to reveal a delicate complexity and grapey charm unbothered by sulphur. Then the late spices arrive like the 8th cavalry when all seems lost. It has hung on in there. Just! 46%. sc. Bottled for The Whisky Shop.

Glenglassaugh Evolution db (85) n21 t22 f21 b21. Cumbersome, oily and sweet, this youngster is still evolving. 50%.

◇◇◇ **Glenglassaugh Nauticus 1st Anniversary 8 Years Old** cask no. 288 db (91) n22.5 confident salty phenols on a bed youthful malt; t23 the youthfulness works in its favour on delivery, ensuring a powering freshness to the peat. Light Demerara sugars add to the mouth-filling, vanilla-clad jollity; f22.5 not only long, well-structured and increasingly complex as what little tannin there is blends into the phenols quite beautifully, but spices make a late and important contribution; b23 Nauticus. But nice. 56.1%. sc.

Glenglassaugh Revival new, refill and Oloroso sherry casks db (75) n19 t20 f17 b19. Rule number one: if you are going to spend a lot of money to rebuild a distillery and make great whisky, then ensure you put the spirit into excellent oak. Which is why it is best avoiding present day sherry butts at all costs as the chances of running into sulphur is high. There is some stonkingly good malt included in this bottling, and the fabulous chocolate raisin is there to see. But I look forward to seeing a bottling from 100% ex-bourbon. 46%. nc ncf.

Glenglassaugh Torfa db (90) n23.5 t22.5 f22 b22 Appears happy and well suited in its new smoky incarnation. 50%.

⋙ **Abbey Whisky Glenglassaugh Aged 7 Years 2012** Oloroso hogshead, cask no. 563 (86.5) n21.5 t21.5 f22 b21.5 Some enjoyable phases but this is a wild dog barking in the night. A beautiful creature, I'm sure, but with too many annoying traits and a distinctly mongrel feel with a vague smokiness and a vivid fruit. And with all that spice it bites, too.... 58.7%. sc.

⋙ **Woolf/Sung The Hunter Glenglassaugh 40 Year Old 1972** sherry cask (90) n22 t24 f21.5 b22.5 Presumably came out of cask in 2012 and only just been bottled. Probably on the way its strength was heading south. Well, the well-founded fears I had of this being a Glenglassaugh sherried have been alleviated: this has not been topped up in a recent sulphurous sub-standard sherry butt, as is too often the case, but this appears to have lived in only the one wood – filled long before sherry butts and the whisky within them were ruined. That said, this a bit of a thin knave, though patience while holding on the palate will reward handsomely as both the complexity of the grape and the myriad tannin tones interplay with a something approaching an art form. The finish is nowhere near so accomplished but, overall, this is a malt which makes impressive play of its great age. 42.9%. sc.

GLENGOYNE
Highlands (Southwest), 1833. Ian Macleod Distillers. Working.

Glengoyne 10 Years Old db (90) n22 t23 f22 b23 Proof that to create balance you do not have to have peat at work. The secret is the intensity of barley intertwangling with oak. Not a single negative note from first to last and now a touch of oil and coffee has upped the intensity further. 40%

Glengoyne 12 Years Old db (91.5) n22.5 t23 f23 b23 The nose has a curiously intimate feel but the tasting experience is a wonderful surprise. 43%

Glengoyne 12 Years Old Cask Strength db (79) n18 t22 f19 b20. Not quite the happiest Glengoyne I've ever come across with the better notes compromised. 57.2%. nc ncf.

Glengoyne 15 Years sherry casks db (81) n19 t20 f21 b21. Brain-numbingly dull and heavily toffeed in style. Just don't get what is trying to be created here. Some late spices remind me I'm awake, but still the perfect dram to have before bed – simply to send you to sleep. Or maybe I just need to see a Doctor... 43%. nc. Ian Macleod Distillers.

Glengoyne 17 Years Old db (86) n21 t23 f21 b21. Some of the guys at Glengoyne think I'm nuts. They couldn't get their head around the 79 I gave it last time. And they will be shaking my neck not my hand when they see the score here...Vastly improved but there is an off sherry tang which points to a naughty butt or two somewhere. Elsewhere mouth-watering and at times fabulously intense. 43%

Glengoyne 18 Years Old first-fill sherry casks db (82) n22 t22 f18 b20. Bunches of lush grape on nose and delivery, where there is no shortage of caramel. But things go downhill once the dreaded "s" word kicks in. 43%. nc. Ian Macleod Distillers.

Glengoyne 21 Years Old db (90) n21 t22 f24 b23 A vastly improved dram where the caramel has vanished and the tastebuds are constantly assailed and questioned. A malt which builds in pace and passion to delivery a final, wonderful coup-de-grace. Moments of being quite cerebral stuff. 43%

Glengoyne 25 Year Old db (95.5) n24 t24.5 f22.5 b23.5 A beautiful sherry-matured malt from the pre-cock up sulphur days. Not a single off note of note and a reminder of what a sherry cask malt meant to those of us who were involved in whisky a quarter of a century ago... 48%

Gleann Mór Glengoyne Aged Over 21 Years dist 1995 (88) n21.5 t22.5 f22 b22 The tannin really does have a big say and another year in cask might well have been one too many. But the malt, somehow never loses its structure or goal. Will divide opinion, but I certainly wouldn't turn down a second glass... 53%.

Provenance Glengoyne Aged 10 Years refill hogshead, cask no. 12104, dist Apr 07, bott Sept 17 (87) n20.5 t22 f22.5 b22 Very similar to cask 11754 above in its original malty outlook, except here some serious spice assembles from the mid-point onwards. 46%. nc ncf sc. 670 bottles.

Scotch Malt Whisky Society Cask 123.31 10 Year Old 1st fill ex-bourbon barrel, dist 29 Aug 08 (95) n23 t24.5 f23.5 b24 It was on the basis of outstanding ex-bourbon malt like this that I recommended to the current owners that they should buy the distillery – which they duly went and did. Not the sulphured sherry cask nonsense that the previous owners had also filled. So wonderful to see a cask of Glengoyne as it should be: clean, dripping with intense malt and golden syrup and forming a beautiful shape on the palate with near perfect oils. Also, have to say that I think 10-years is the optimum age for this malt in the right bourbon cask as not only do you still feel the distillery itself, but it has the rare ability to form beautiful patterns with the natural sugars from the oak. A faultless blueprint to how this distillery should taste at the decade mark. *61.8%. sc.*

GLEN GRANT
Speyside, 1840. Campari. Working.

Glen Grant 5 Years Old db (**89**) n22.5 t22 f21.5 b23. Elegant malt which has noticeably grown in stature and complexity of late. *40%*

Glen Grant Aged 10 Years db (**96**) n23.5 t24 f23.5 b24 Unquestionably the best official 10-y-o distillery bottling I have tasted from this distillery. Absolutely nails it! Oh, and had they bottled this at 46% abv and without the trimmings...my word! Might well have been a contender for Scotch of the Year. It won't be long before word finally gets around about just how bloody good this distillery is. *40%*

Glen Grant Aged 10 Years db (**96**) n24.5 t24 f23.5 b24 This is the new bottling purely for the UK market without, alas for a traditionalist like me, the famous, magnificent white label. The bottle design may not be a patch on the beautifully elegant one that had served the distillery with distinction for so long, but the malt effortlessly stands up to all scrutiny. The only difference between this and the original bottling available world-wide is a slight reduction in the work of the sugars, the muscovado ones in particular, and an upping in the green, grassy, sharper barley. Overall, this is a little drier yet slightly tarter, more reserved and stylish. My one and only regret is that it is not yet upped to 46% so the people of Britain could see a whisky, as I have so many times in the private and privileged enclave of my blending lab, as close to perfection as it comes... *40%.*

Glen Grant Aged 10 Years bott code: LRO/GE01 db (**95.5**) n24.5 t24 f23 b24 Perhaps slightly fatter than one or two other bottlings of GG10. But still bang on course with my previous observations, other than the finish not having quite the same sparkle. One of those whiskies which seems delicate and fragile, but at the same time big and robust. Just how does it do that....? *40%.*

⟐ **Glen Grant Aged 10 Years** bott code: LRO/GD26 db (**94**) n23.5 a curious yet always highly attractive nose. Sharp yet balanced by a more lumbering presence, though the malt is always the focal point. Love the lemon sherbet, too.; t23.5 a curiously young bite to this – one assumes that the third fill bourbons have been upped slightly in percentage to promote youth but there are countering measures afoot to keep the salivating qualities within reason. The malt has a trundling quality, moving from A to B without being distracted by any of the machinations of cask selection...; f23.5 a long, attractive malty spiciness turns increasingly towards caramels and vanilla; b23.5 a malt which wears its heart on its sleeve, So delicate, so fragile and easily fractured that it has to be treated with extraordinary care. Just how delicate and fragile this whisky is, just how under threat unique and beautiful malts like these are, is revealed on both nose and delivery... *40%.*

Glen Grant Aged 12 Years db (**95**) n23.5 t24 f23.5 b24 Beautifully distilled, thoughtfully matured and deeply satisfying malt. *43%.*

Glen Grant Aged 12 Years bott code: LRO/FE 03 db (**95**) n24 t24 f23 b24 A slightly different slant to previous 12-year-olds but still within the expected and brilliant spectrum. Fabulous. *43%.*

Glen Grant Aged 12 Years bott code: LRO/FK06 db (**94**) n24 t23.5 f23 b23.5 Very similar to previous bottling, with no shortage of intensity. The only difference is a little less sweetness through the mid-range between delivery and finish and a slightly bigger caramel note, instead. *43%.*

⟐ **Glen Grant Aged 12 Years** bott code: LRO/GE07 db (**92**) n23.5 light tangerine peel and bright barley. Fresh, lively and a little spice just as the tannins begin to make their mark; t23.5 initially breezy and bright with gristy sugars spilling all over the palate. Begins to flatten as the caramels arrive at the midpoint; f22 a duller more caramel-infested finale than of old; b23 a small step sideways from previous bottlings, not least because of the intensity of the malt and its relaxed attitude with the oaky vanillas then gives way to a surfeit of uncharacteristically dull toffee. Get the distinct feeling that this malt is performing well within its capabilities... *43%.*

Glen Grant Aged 12 Years Non Chill-Filtered db (**91.5**) n23 t23 f22.5 b23 In so many ways speaks volumes about what non-filtration can do to one of the world's truly great distilleries... *48%. Exclusive to travel retail.*

Glen Grant Aged 12 Years bott code: LRO/GC19 db (**94.5**) n23.5 light lychee and the most delicate barley grist; t24 fizzes on delivery as the barley goes into salivation orbit. The vanillas and butterscotch arrive early, but so to the spices to ensure there is so much life! f23 the spices still rumble, but, as you would expect from GG, the delicate nature of the barley, the mild honey notes and the kissing vanilla just makes you sigh...; **b24** that's much more like it: such balance, such dexterity...! The last time I sampled this, though delightful, it didn't quite yield the complexity I was expecting. This one is nearer expectation! *48%. ncf.*

⫸ **Glen Grant Aged 12 Years** bott code: LRO/HI18 db **(94.5) n23.5 t24 f23 b24** My rule is to never look at the previous year's scores and notes and judge the whisky at it comes. So, interesting it matches the last bottling I tasted even, I now see, down to the sectional scoring. Can't quibble with the tasting notes, either, which are pretty much identical. *48%. ncf.*

Glen Grant Aged 15 Years Batch Strength 1st Edition bott code: LRO/FG 19 db **(96.5) n23.5 t24.5 f24 b24.5** When I saw this was also 1st Edition, I thought it was the same whisky as I tasted last time. Except with a different bottling code. However, although the early personality is near identical, it really does change on the finish where the bitterness has now been eradicated. This not only improves the score to the finish, but the overall balance and performance. The entire journey is now faultless; and journeys don't often come better than this. *50%.*

Glen Grant Aged 15 Years Batch Strength 1st Edition bott code. LRO/FG 21 db **(94) n23.5** not sure a 15-year-old malt gets any more endearingly gentle than this: clean, but with a light milk chocolate attachment to the thoroughbred malt giving it an unmistakable Malteser candy effect; **t24** oh-my-word...If you think the nose is gentle, wait until you taste this. This is like a grist just melting on the tongue, spreading icing sugar in all directions, then ulmo honey and malted milk shake. A third the way in the spices arrive and with a plan, too...; **f23** just a fraction of bitterness from the oak, but the malt and ulmo honey soothe and kiss their way to the end; **b23.5** one of the maltiest malts of the year! Just a joy! *50%.*

⫸ **Glen Grant Aged 15 Years Batch Strength 1st Edition** bott code: LRO/HI16 db **(97) n24.5** just one of those 20 minute noses Glen Grant throws at you from time to time. Like shifting sands, the piece is constantly on the move and forming different shapes on the nose: one minute full of cherry blossom, the next acacia honey, then a mixture of both with butterscotch thrown in; next spices appear, tingle and vanish again, then rhubarb and custard. Simply one of my noses of the year and the Murray Method (starting from cool) will blow your mind when you realise the scope of complexity; **t24** a typical Glen Grant lightness of touch on delivery despite the strength, then a mesmerising display of juicy barley tones which gradually integrate with and then embrace the fragile tannins. Just a little extra buttery oil from the upped strength aids the longevity of these sensations and gives the mid-ground far more weight and substance than you might have expected...though the salivation levels are still high; **f24** long, languid, lilting and lush right to the very end when a little lime-blossom honey lightens the Lubek marzipan...; **b24.5** what a malt this has now become! The fact that for two successive bottlings they have blown me off my tasting desk means they appear to have nailed the personality of this malt, and in so doing extracting and then displaying the extraordinary and unique charm of this distillery. *50%.* ⚑

Glen Grant Aged 18 Years Rare Edition db **(97) n24.5** the hardest decision to make here: full marks or not. Actually, no: an even harder decision is trying to work out the leading forces behind this extraordinary nose. This is so in tune and well balanced it is impossible to nail exactly what leads and which follows. Instead, one is left mesmerised by the incredible brittleness of the barley, which seems to snap if you sniff slightly too hard; the sugars at once delicate and fruity yet with the crafted sharpness of a newly forged sword. And those tannins, somehow caught up in the overall firmness, the friability of it all. Has to be the essential Speyside nose...; **t24.5** oh, wow! When the barley does arrive this beautifully manicured, not a malty molecule out of place? The sugars are as clipped as a 1940's English actor's enunciation, and probably more precise. From somewhere light oils ooze to the surface to ensure some velvet caresses the sword. The oak builds up some steam, but the tannins never once outpoint the sugars and by the mid-ground, when a little cocoa can be detected, honours are even...; so complex it was on about the fifth go I realised just what a vital role those big early spices play; **f23.5** the firmness here is so complete, that I have only tasted whisky like this in commercially bottled form in pure Irish Pot still and rye, though here without the same intensity of spice you find in either. That said, the spices teasingly impact all the same....; **b24.5** the most crystalline, technically sublime Speysider I have tasted in a very long time... I didn't expect to find a better distillery bottled Glen Grant than their superlative 10-year-old. I was wrong... *43%.*

Glen Grant Aged 18 Years Rare Edition bott code. LRO/EE04 db **(97) n24.5 t24.5 f23.5 b24.5** See tasting notes to the Glen Grant 18 above. A different bottling, but not a single alteration in character, other than maybe just a fraction extra spice at the very end. Another Glen Grant knocking on the door of perfection. *43%.*

Glen Grant Aged 18 Years Rare Edition bott code: LRO/EE03 db **(97) n24.5 t24.5 f23.5 b24.5** So, I have chosen this as my 1,200th whisky of the 2020 Bible...which means I have tasted the last 1,000 whiskies on average at 15 samples a day, day in day out – analysing, re-analysing and describing - from morning to late evening virtually every single day without a break. Here I look for faults and weaknesses; changes, shifts of emphasis, a variation of pace as the flavours come through. And can find none. Well, maybe the vaguest hint of bitterness at the death. But this, as usual, is sublime. Though perhaps it does have two new challengers now: the Glen Grant 15 and the Glen Grant Chronicles. Didn't think it possible. But this distillery has just upped its game... *43%*.

⟨⟩ **Glen Grant Aged 18 Years Rare Edition** bott code: LRO/GB15 db **(92) n23 t23.5 f22.5 b23** A surprise bottling, this. Very unlike the Glen Grant 18s I tasted earlier in the year which were their usual bright, dazzling, mesmerising and heart-stopping selves. This is darker in colour, dimmer in flavour, full of malty riches but extra toffee, also, which appears to up the body but compromises the complexity, especially at the death. *43%*.

Glen Grant 40 Year Old db **(83.5) n22.5 t21 f20 b20.** Probably about ten summers too many. The nose threatens an oakfest, though there are enough peripheral sugars for balance and hope. Sadly, on the palate the cavalry never quite gets there.*40%*.

Glen Grant 170th Anniversary db **(89) n23.5 t23.5 f20 b22.** The odd mildly sulphured cask has slipped through the net here to reduce what was shaping to be something magnificent. Still enjoyable, though. *46%*

⟨⟩ **The Glen Grant Arboralis** bott code: LRO/HK 27 db **(90.5) n23** weighty. Takes some time to pick your way through this one: chunky toffee leads but lighter citrus and even the vaguest hint of mint ensures the complexity demanded by a GG; **t22.5** fat and swarthy, the toffees dominate at first before a semi-bourbon style red liquorice note briefly flourishes. The barley still pitches in with a lightly juicy tune, but it's all rather muted compared to the usual GG persona; **f22** really likes to play off the caramel notes. Just a light tanginess towards the finish; **b23** for a Glen Grant, this is dense stuff. One of the heaviest noses ever from the distillery I have encountered matched by a personality and flavour profile which is dark, tight, almost filled with angst. GG as I have never quite seen it before in the last 40 years. Enjoyable and stylistic but lacking that elegance, complexity and all-round finesse which sets the distillery apart from all others in Scotland and, indeed, the world. *40%*.

Glen Grant Five Decades bott 2013 db **(92) n24** the kind of aroma which leaves you transfixed: the trademark crisp, juicy barley is there in force, but the darker, deeper tones rumble with a spiced orange lead: sublimely complex; **t23.5** the delivery is full of the usual malty zest for life. There is a unique clarity to the barley of Glen Grant and here, on delivery and for a few a few moments after, this goes into overdrive. The mid ground is more muddled with tannin and burnt raisin making their presence felt; **f21.5** tangy marmalade; **b23** a nose and delivery of astonishing complexity. Hardly surprising the fade cannot keep up the pace. *46%*

Glen Grant Rothes Chronicles Cask Haven First Fill Casks bott code: LRO/FG 26 db **(96) n24 t24 f23.5 b24.5.** I think only Glen Grant can these days consistently come up with a nose which is unmistakably theirs, a malt which takes understatement to new levels. But when you look, really explore, then you sit there spellbound as its secrets slowly unfold. To give descriptors can barely do it justice, as the nose and delivery is poetry in itself. But, like a lover stripping, you are teased with one tantalising reveal after another. *46%*

⟨⟩ **Glen Grant Rothes Chronicles Cask Haven** first fill casks, bott code: LRO/HI23 db **(96) n24** the spices of the oak take no time in making their pitch. Elsewhere a moist Victoria sponge sweetness is matched by the sharper tones of orange pith and even a little bubble gum. A little smoke, perhaps...? **t24.5** there is something uniquely glorious about a great Glen Grant delivery, and you won't be let down here. It positively sashays over the taste buds on entry with all its grandiose juiciness at full tilt. Curiously, there is even the slightest smoke note on this, too, the phenol noticeable as the only weight to the personality and confirms the hints picked up on the nose; the sweetness is the muscovado-fruity type, containing a degree of other dark sugars; **f23.5** just the vaguest tang attaches itself to the slow fade of the barley and vanilla; **b24** remains, as last year, one of the most significant and alluring of all Scotland's malts. Beautiful. *46%*. ⟨⟩

⟨⟩ **Gordon & MacPhail Mr George Centenary Edition Glen Grant 1956** first fill sherry butt, cask no. 4455, dist 13 Dec 56, bott 27 Jun 19 **(97) n24** simply creaks from old age. Not quite arthritic, but the tannins certainly stiffen a few joints. The oakiness takes on something between creosote and eucalyptus – by no means an unpleasant combination. The spices nip and threaten. The key, though, is that everything holds together...; **t25** you can thank an absolutely top-of-the-range (and now extinct) sherry butt for this: this delivery is simply luxurious and at times still salivating: it is a kiss, a caress...and, as the spices assemble, a massage. The darkest of dark cherries merge with a blend of cocoa and ulmo and manuka honeys before the blueprint of rich bourbon kicks in with its classic dry liquorice and molasses. The more militant, provisional wing of the tannins don't quite want this harmony, stay their ground and carry out little guerrilla attacks as we close in towards the finish; **f23.5** drier and more urbane with firm oak holding sway and toasting up. The oak has the final say...; **b24.5** in the home stretch for the Whisky Bible 2021 and, as is my long-standing tradition, I now taste the whiskies which have a special place of honour; or from previous bottlings might well be expected to be up amongst the leading lights of the all the whiskies I will have sampled in the last year. This bottling has a special place in my heart for being the only whisky older than me...And from the greatest distillery in Scotland in terms of annually producing malt of the very highest calibre. So I have chosen this as sample number 1,225 (with just 27 more to do). This was a two hour whisky to taste. A malt which opens, closes and opens again. The Murray Method seems to take you on a journey which never ends and different temperatures will give you a different storyline each time, though the outcome is always the same. Oak. This malt is, as one might expect from such a distillery, one of the great whisky journeys. 51.7%. sc. 235 bottles. 🍷

Gordon & MacPhail Private Collection Glen Grant 1948 first fill sherry butt, cask no. 2154, dist 11 Jun 48, bott 19 Oct 18 **(95.5) n25 t23.5 f23 b24** There are no words really to describe the nose. It is 70 years old, but shews not the slightest sign of weakness. And because it comes from a time when sherry casks were entirely free from arrogance and stupidity, there was not even the remotest chance of picking up an off sulphur note. So this is a pristine aroma, taking us back to the earliest days after the war when an industry was just picking itself up from six years of hardship and international crisis and just getting back into its pre-war stride. Good oak would have been at a premium. So to find something this intact, and coming from sherry which had a crisp charm would have been a major achievement in itself. But because the cask was so clean, the wine so delicate we can now actually inspect the distillery itself... something that has been lost in the last 70 years, as most sherry casks (even if not riddled with sulphur) are so dense, the influence of the distillery is invisible. Not so here, for apparent is the sexiest degree of peat, which in itself is extraordinary. Because 70 years ago, and long before that, Speyside whisky came with a smoky hue. And here, like an insect preserved in prehistoric amber, we can see so visibly into the past it is as though we are there. To be honest, I don't really care what this whisky tastes like. Its nose alone is one of the most significant visions into the past I have seen in some 45 years of visiting distilleries and in over 20,000 whiskies tasted for the Whisky Bible. It is as though, just from this incredible nose, I have entered a time machine and returned to a long lost whisky world... 48.6%. sc. 210 bottles.

The Macphail 1949 China 70th Anniversary Glen Grant Special Edition 1 1st fill sherry butt **(97) n24.5 t24 f24 b24.5** An improbable exhibition of elegance of complexity. How is such a whisky at such an age remotely possible....? 41.4%.

The Macphail 1949 China 70th Anniversary Glen Grant Special Edition 2 cask no. 3184, first fill sherry butt, dist 24 Nov 49, bott 2 Aug 17 **(96) n24 t24.5 f23.5 b24** This is a full blown, gushing malt cocking a snook at its preposterous age, determined to reveal at every turn its lushness and vibrancy. The fruit plays more than a bit part, being the glue which holds this together, which the smoke both shocks and comforts. A real surprise package 41.7%.

Wilson & Morgan Barrel Selection Glen Grant 25 Year Old sherry finish, dist 1993, bott 2018 **(91.5) n23 t23 f23 b22.5** Very pleasant, and a spot on sherry cask at work. But perhaps a slight overkill in view of the quality of the malt which has vanished under the fruit... 54.3%.

GLENGYLE
Campbeltown, 2004. J&A Mitchell & Co. Working.

Kilkerran 12 Year Old db **(90.5) n22.5 t23 f22.5 b22.5** A malt far more comfortable at this age than some of the previous, younger, bottlings from a few years back. Has a fragile feel to it and the air of a malt which must be treated gently and with respect. 46%

GLEN KEITH
Speyside, 1957. Chivas Brothers. Working (re-opened 14th June 2013).

Glen Keith 10 Years Old db **(80) n22 t21 f18 b19**. A malty if thin dram that finishes with a whimper after an impressively refreshing, grassy start. 43%

⬦⬦⬦ **The First Editions Glen Keith Aged 26 Years 1993** refill barrel, cask no. 16784, bott 2019 **(93) n23** fantastically complex: rice and spotted dog suet puddings together with a little lightening sherbet. All this with an almost silo-full of unmalted barley...; **t24** breathtakingly salivating. Almost impossible to believe a malt of this age could be so gloriously fresh and clean...but rumbling away almost unnoticed are the tannins to underscore its vintage. But it is the melt-in-the-mouth grist and sherbet powder which concentrates the mind; **f22.5** the inevitable spices for the age sign things off with aplomb; **b23.5** for an unfashionable distillery, this can sometimes come up with the odd cracker. And here is one! 56.7%. nc ncf sc. 162 bottles.

Gordon & MacPhail Connoisseurs Choice Glen Keith Aged 24 Years refill bourbon barrel, cask no. 111152, dist 21 Sept 93, bott 13 Sept 18 **(85) n21.5 t22 f20.5 b21** A busy malt which stretches its thin sugar reserves far. But the ending is rather too oak dominated. 49.3%. sc.

Kingsbury Gold Glen Keith 22 Year Old hogshead, cask no. 171282, dist 1995 **(88) n22 t22 f22 b22** Lives on the edge, but just enough honey to see off the encroaching tannins. Sophisticated. 50%. sc. 254 bottles.

◈◈ **Liquid Treasures From Miles Away Glen Keith 27 Year Old** bourbon barrel, dist Jan 93, bott Feb 20 **(88.5) n22 t22.5 f22 b22** The buyer for Liquid Treasures seems to have a thing for thin and malty malts. Just be thankful this is in a bourbon barrel for the barley can sparkles to maximum effect. In any other cask this would have vanished out of sight. But here, at least, we have some charming citrus notes which lifts the malt both on the nose and on delivery. Little meat but a lovely shape nonetheless. *58.4%. sc. 146 bottles.*

GLENKINCHIE
Lowlands, 1837. Diageo. Working.

Glenkinchie 12 Years Old db **(85) n19 t22.5 f21.5 b22.** The last 'Kinchie 12 I encountered was beyond woeful. This is anything but. Still not firing on all cylinders and can definitely do better. But there is a fabulous vibrancy to this which nearly all the bottlings I have tasted in the last few years have sadly lacked. Impressive. *43%*

Glenkinchie 1992 The Manager's Choice db **(78) n19 t22 f18 b19.** Has a lot going for it on delivery with a barley explosion which rocks you back in your chair and has you salivating like a rabies victim. But the rest of it is just too off key. *58.1%. Diageo.*

Glenkinchie The Distillers Edition Amontillado cask-wood, dist 2005, bott 2017, bott code: L7222CM000 db **(91.5) n23 t23.5 f21.5 b23** Now that is one very elegant whisky. *43%.*

◈◈ **Glenkinchie The Royal Edinburgh Military Tattoo** bott code: L9186CM005 db **(93.5) n23** a sharp, nippy nose with the barley helped along by a salty, citrus edge; **t24** brilliant... absolutely brilliant! The delivery is a form of malt concentrate: sweet yet lush and salivating with yet more puckering barley hitting you from every angle; **f23** calms down into a more traditional vanilla and toffee 'Kinchie finale; **b23.5** one of the most flavoursome Glenkinchies I've ever encountered, really making the most of its malty disposition. Many a Glenkinchie lover will have the name of expression of this tattooed somewhere about their person... Gorgeous! *46%.*

THE GLENLIVET
Speyside, 1824. Chivas Brothers. Working.

The Glenlivet 12 Years of Age bott 2017/03/30 db **(92.5) n23 t23 f23 b23.5** Probably the best Glenlivet 12 I have tasted for quite a while...lucky Americans! An extra few percentage points of first fill bourbon cask has gone a long way here. Excellent and satisfying. *40% (80 proof)*

The Glenlivet Excellence 12 Year Old db **(87) n22 t21.5 f22 b21.5.** Low key but very clean. The emphasis is on delicate. *40%. Visitor Centre and Asian exclusive.*

The Glenlivet 18 Years of Age bott code: 2017/02/02 LKPL0386 db **(83.5) n22 t22 f19 b20.5** This is a rather flat version of a usually rich malt. Has the odd honey-charmed moment and the spices aren't hiding, either. But way too much caramel has turned the usual undulations on the palate to something of pancake proportions. A little furry at the death, also. *43%.*

The Glenlivet Alpha db **(92) n23.5 t24 f21.5 b23.** You get the feeling some people have worked very hard at creating a multi-toned, complex creature celebrating the distillery's position at the centre of Speyside. They have succeeded. Just a cask selection or two away from a potential major Bible award. Maybe for the next bottling.... *50%*

The Glenlivet Archive 21 Years of Age batch no. 0513M db **(95.5) n24 t24 f23.5 b24** Less archive and more achieve. For getting so many honey tones to work together without it getting overly sweet or syrupy really is a major achievement. *43%*

The Glenlivet Captain's Reserve finished in Cognac casks db **(89.5) n22 t23 f22 b22.5** A laid-back malt playing games being simultaneously spicy and super-soft. *40%.*

The Glenlivet Cipher db **(96.5) n24.5 t24 f23.5 b24.5** It has taken over half an hour to distil these tasting notes into something that will fit the book: we have more new entries than normal and I'm running out of room. Few whiskies I taste this year, however, will compare to this. *48%*

The Glenlivet Conglass 14 db **(92.5) n22 t23 f23.5 b24** A joyous barley and high quality oak interplay: probably what this distillery does best of all. *59.8% WB16/043*

The Glenlivet Distiller's Reserve bott code: 2019/04/01 db **(87) n21.5 t22 f21.5 b22** A soft, rotund malt designed to give minimum offence... and succeeds. Unless you are offended by the overstating of the caramels. *40%.*

The Glenlivet Founder's Reserve db **(78.5) n20 t21.5 f18 b19.** Really can't believe what a shy and passionless whisky this is (not to mention flawed). The strength gives the game away slightly as to where the malt is positioned. But I had hoped for a little more than malty tokenism. *40%*

The Glenlivet Founder's Reserve bott code: 2017/04/04 LCPL 0591 db **(88.5) n23 t22 f21.5 b22** Anyone who can remember the less than impressive start to this brand will be pretty amazed at just how deliciously approachable it is now. *40%.*

The Glenlivet 15 Years of Age French Oak Reserve bott code: 2016/12/19 LCPK 2465 db **(93) n23.5 t23 f23 b23.5** Many years ago when this first came out it wasn't very good, to be honest. Then it was re-shaped, upped a gear and became a very enjoyable dram, indeed. Now, having apparently been steered on a slightly different course again, it is just excellent... An expression that has evolved slowly but quite beautifully. 40%.

The Glenlivet The Master Distiller's Reserve bott code: 2016/10/04 LCPK 1866 db **(86.5) n22.5 t22 f20.5 b21** It is a shame the malty sparkle on the nose and delivery isn't matched by what follows. A pleasant, safe dram. But too toffee-rich and doesn't develop as this great distillery should. 40%.

The Glenlivet The Master Distiller's Reserve Small Batch batch no. 9378/006 db **(93) n23.5 t24 f22.5 b23.5** By far the best Master Distillers Reserve in Glenlivet's armoury. 40%

The Glenlivet The Master Distiller's Reserve Solera Vatted bott code: 2017/03/01 LCPL 0371 db **(89.5) n22.5 t23 f22 b22** Pretty much in line with the 2015 bottling above, except there is slightly more caramel here shaving the top off the higher notes. 40%.

The Glenlivet White Oak Reserve bott code: 2019/03/01 db **(89) n23 t23 f21 b22** Starts promisingly but fades dramatically on the toffee. 40%.

⬥ **Gordon & MacPhail Connoisseurs Choice Glenlivet Aged 14 Years** refill bourbon barrel, cask no. 800670, dist 10 Nov 04, bott 15 Jul 19 **(94.5) n23.5** acacia honey and mingling with the lightly toasted tannins suggests this will be a sweetie...; **t24** wow! And so it proves....! Ulmo honey now, playing peek-a-boo with elegant caramels and vanillas. The spices show just the right amount of devil...; the mouthfeel is just about perfect, making this a bit of a chewer...; **f23** pulsing spices I the way; light Demerara sugars keep the sweetness levels exactly where you want them to be...; **b24** The Glenlivet in maximum honey mode. Brilliant! 64%. sc. 162 bottles.

Gordon & MacPhail Connoisseurs Choice Glenlivet Aged 15 Years first fill bourbon barrel, cask no. 800772, dist 5 Nov 02, bott 6 Sept 18 **(94) n23.5 t23.5 f23 b24** A beautifully structured malt, abounding in oily barley and absorbing the top rate tannins with no difficulty whatsoever. The theme is intense malt all the way, until some gorgeous cocoa tones leach into the story late on. Exemplary. 58.4%. sc. 200 bottles.

Gordon & MacPhail Private Collection Glenlivet 1954 refill sherry butt, cask no. 1412, dist 15 Apr 54, bott 27 Apr 18 **(95) n24 t24 f23 b24** Another ancient malt which, despite coming from a sherry butt, has no difficulty proving that Glenlivet whisky was once a whole lot smokier than it is today. Indeed, this cask has withstood the test of time quite magnificently and still possesses crisp malt in its armoury to get the taste buds flowing. 41%. sc. 222 bottles.

GLENLOCHY
Highlands (Western), 1898–1983. Diageo. Closed.

Gordon & MacPhail Rare Old Glenlochy 1979 **(95) n23.5 t24 f23.5 b24** it has been many years since a bottle from this long lost distillery turned up and that was such a classic, I can remember every nuance of it even now. This shows far greater age, but the way with which the malt takes it in its stride will become the stuff of legend. I held back on tasting this until today, August 2nd 2013, because my lad David this afternoon moved into the first home he has bought, with new wife Rachael and little Abi. It is near Fort William, the remote west coast Highland town in which this whisky was made, and where David will be teaching next year. His first job after moving in, though, will be to continue editing this book, for he worked on the Whisky Bible for a number of editions as researcher and editor over the years. So I can think of no better way of wishing David a happy life in his new home than by toasting him with what turned out to be a stunningly beautiful malt from one of the rarest of all the lost distilleries which, by strange coincidence, was first put up for sale exactly 100 years ago. So, to David, Rachael & little Abigail... your new home! And this time I swallowed..46%. ncf.

GLENLOSSIE
Speyside, 1876. Diageo. Working.

Gleann Mór Glenlossie Aged Over 24 Years **(90.5) n23 t23.5 f22 b22** The ginger and allspice nose leaves you in no doubt that the oak has gouged its way into this malt. The delivery and follow though confirms it. Yet one of those nick of time bottlings, where another summer or two might have been too much. That said, absolutely nothing wrong with the delivery which takes peppery heather honey to the outer limits. 55.6%.

⬥ **Golden Glen Glenlossie Aged 22 Years** hogshead, cask no. 7108, dist 26 Nov 97, bott 27 Nov 19 **(96.5) n24** busy and intricate yet with the bluster of the tannin. The malt is crisp; the heather honey prickled by a little spice but all is softened by a buttery note which also introduces light oils. It groans its age, both in the agony of the impudent oak, but also in ecstasy because the balance on this could between the friendlier honey and the more imposing tannins hardly be bettered; **t24** a sublime delivery: moderately fat and but magnificently rich in body with the shards of honey and barley ensuring the taste buds get a wonderful peppering of personality and lightness to contra the heavier tannins. Slightly estery, as this distillery can often be, with a rich copper depth to add further lustre. The light gooseberry pie touch is fabulous **f24** delicate spices and no shortage of biscuit-like vanilla. The oils travel from the very first moment of delivery to the last dying of the rays of honey, butterscotch, cocoa and old dry banana. The barley still has the charisma to sparkle even well into the finish which still reverberates with the most brilliantly ornate spices: astounding! **b24.5** a fabulously complex individual, always popping up with the odd surprise each time you taste it. Even if you live by the Murray Method, as you should, you will be entirely forgiven for not spitting this one out. One of those whiskies that demands a leather chair on the spot for you to sink into, subdued lighting, peace and quiet, a clean atmosphere...and all the time in the world. If I were able, I'd mark this down as a 96.75...it is so closely pushing the magical 97 mark! *53.9%. 222 bottles. Bottled by The Last Drop for No. 23.* 🍷

Scotch Malt Whisky Society Cask 46.72 25 Year Old refill ex-bourbon hogshead, dist 16 Nov 92 **(93) n22.5 t23.5 f23 b24** Glen Glossy would be more apt... *53.8%. sc.*

〜 **The Whisk(e)y Company The Spirit of Glenlossie Aged 22 Years** hogshead, cask no. 7107, bott 2019 **(95.5) n24** a charming, high-class nose where the citrus tones and oaky spice seem to be a little distant from the other, thereby not forging the mesmeric qualities of the more woven cask 7108. Even so, as the malt emerges safe and sound after all these years you will be charmed off your chair...; **t24** the immediate freshness of the barley on delivery reflects its independence from the oak, which slowly pulls itself into contention and then dominance. The spices emerge about three or four flavour waves after delivery and remain a busy constant; **f23.5** now we are seeing the malt at maximum sophistication, as the layered vanilla seems to amplify the power of the spice while the delicate odd barley tone adds a gentle juiciness – and another torch to the peppers; **b24** keen-eyed observers will notice that this is the sister cask to the monumental Golden Glen bottling. This is also an essay in charm and sophistication, though lacking that almost unidentifiable charisma, that sheer magic, of its sister cask. Truly brilliant, nonetheless... *55.5%. sc. 234 bottles.*

GLEN MHOR
Highlands (Northern), 1892–1983. Diageo. Demolished.
Glen Mhor 1976 Rare Malt db **(92.5) n23 t24 f22 b23.5.** You just dream of truly great whisky sitting in your glass from time to time. But you don't expect it, especially from such an old cask. This was the best example from this distillery I've tasted in 30 years...until the Glenkeir version was unleashed! If you ever want to see a scotch that has stretched the use of oak as far it will go without detriment, here it is. What a pity the distillery has gone because the Mhor the merrier... *52.2%*

GLENMORANGIE
Highlands (Northern), 1843. Glenmorangie Plc. Working.
Glenmorangie 10 Years Old db **(94) n24 t22 f24 b24** You might find the occasional "orange variant", where the extra degree of oak, usually from a few too many first-fill casks, has flattened out the more extreme peaks and toughs of complexity (scores about 89). But these are pretty rare – almost a collector's item – and overall this remains one of the great single malts: a whisky of uncompromising aesthetic beauty from the first enigmatic whiff to the last teasing and tantalising gulp. Complexity at its most complex. *40%*

Glenmorangie 15 Years Old db **(90.5) n23** chunky and fruity: something distinctly sugar candy about this one; the barley's no slouch, either; and, just to raise the eyebrows, just the faintest waft of something smoky...; **t23** silky, a tad sultry, and serious interplay between oak and barley; a real, satisfying juiciness to this one; **f22** dries towards the oaky side of things, but just a faint squeeze of liquorice adds extra weight; **b22.5** exudes quality. *43%*

Glenmorangie 15 Years Old Sauternes Wood Finish db **(68) n16 t18 f17 b17.** I had hoped – and expected – an improvement on the sulphured version I came across last time. Oh, whisky! Why are you such a cruel mistress...? *46%*

Glenmorangie 18 Years Old db **(91) n22** pleasant if unconvincing spotted dick; **t23** sharp, eye-watering mix of fruit and mainly honeyed barley; nutty and, with the confident vanillas, forming a breakfast cereal completeness; **f23** Cocoa Krispies; **b23** having thrown off some previous gremlins, now a perfect start to the day whisky... *43%*

Glenmorangie 19 Year Old db **(94) n24 t23.5 f22.5 b24** Fruity or malty...? I can't decide...but then I don't think for a moment that you're supposed to be able to... *43%*.

Glenmorangie 25 Years Old db **(95) n24 t24 f23.5 b24** Every bit as statesmanlike and elegant as a whisky of this age from such a blinding distillery should be. Ticks every single box for a 25-year-old and is Morangie's most improved malt by the distance of Tain to Wellingborough. There is a hint of genius with each unfolding wave of flavours with this one: a whisky that will go in 99/100 whisky lover's top 50 malts of all time. And that includes the Peatheads. *43%*

Glenmorangie 30 Years Old db (72) n17 t18 f19 b18. From the evidence in the glass the jury is out on whether it has been spruced up a little in a poor sherry cask – and spruce is the operative word: lots of pine on this wrinkly. 44.1%

Glenmorangie Allta db (89) n22.5 t23 f21.5 b22 This is a very different 'Morangie: the Allta, could well be for Alternative. Because while the distillery is rightly famed for its cask innovation, there is no barrel style I can think of on the planet which can shape the malt in this unique way. So either grain or yeast is the deciding factor here – perhaps a mixture of both (and you can rule out water!). My money is on yeast, as the only ever time I've come across something quite like this was in a lab in Kentucky with some experimental stuff. The perfect Glenmorangie to confuse your friends by... 51.2%.

Glenmorangie Artisan Casks db (93) n23 t23.5 f23 b23.5. If whisky could be sexed, this would be a woman. Every time I encounter Morangie Artisan, it pops up with a new look, a different perfume. And mood. It appears not to be able to make up its mind. But does it know how to pout, seduce and win your heart...? Oh yes. 46%

Glenmorangie Astar db (93) n24 t23.5 f22 b23.5 Astar has moved a long way from the first bottling which left me scratching my head. This is one of the maltiest of all their range, though the lightness of touch means that any bitterness can be too easily detected. 52.5%.

Glenmorangie Bacalta db (87) n22 t22.5 f21 b21.5. Unusually for a Glenmorangie the narrative is muffled and indistinct. Has some lovely moments, but a bit sharp and lacking in places. 46%

Glenmorangie Cadboll db (86.5) n21 t23.5 f20.5 b21.5 Every year a challenging new breed of Glenmorangie appears to be thrown into the mix, as though to fully test the taste buds. This is this year's offering: different again, with neither the nose nor finish quite up to par with the outstanding delivery – indeed, the finale is pretty bitter, indeed. But the texture and intensity of the barley on arrival is borderline brilliant, as is the most wonderful caramel which frames it with a buttery sweetness. 43.1%.

Glenmorangie Companta Clos de Tart & Rasteau casks, dist 27 Jan 99, bott 14 Nov 13 db (74) n17 t20 f18 b19. "I don't think you'll be a fan of this one, Jim" said the Glenmorangie blender to me, letting me know the sample was on its way. How right he was. Have to say there is some breath-taking fruit to be had before the sulphur does its worst. 46%. ncf.

Glenmorangie Dornoch db (94) n23.5 t23 f23.5 b24 A rare Glenmorangie which this time does not put the emphasis on fruit or oak influence. But this appears to concentrate on the malt itself, taking it through a routine which reveals as many angles and facets as it can possibly conjure. Even if the casks are from a central warehouse, at times a seascape has been created by a light salty influence – so befitting the whisky's name. A real treat. 43%

Glenmorangie Ealanta 1993 Vintage db (97.5) n24 t24 f24.5 b25 When is a bourbon not a bourbon? When it is a Scotch single malt...And here we have potentially the World Whisky of the Year. Free from the embarrassing nonsense which passes for today's sherry butt, and undamaged by less than careful after use care of second-hand bourbon casks, we see what happens when the more telling aspects of oak, the business end which gives bourbon that extra edge, blends with the some of the very finest malt made in Scotland. Something approaching one of the best whiskies of my lifetime is the result... 46%

Glenmorangie Global Travel Retail 12 Year Old db (89.5) n22 a fat, spicy nose with dates and molasses obliterating the usual delicate barley; t23 and its full on brown sugars deliver, also. Alost syrupy in its countenance, it slowly quietens towards a toasty fudge and mocha middle; f22 so much caramel. Dark and weighty with lots of chewability until late into the day; b22.5 heavy duty Morangie with subtlety and dexterity giving way to full on flavour with a cream toffee mouthfeel. 43%.

Glenmorangie Global Travel Retail 14 Year Old db (84) n22 t22 f19 b21 A pretty straightforward offering by Morangie's normally complex standards but let down by the late furry bitterness on the finish. 43%.

Glenmorangie Global Travel Retail 16 Year Old db (94.5) n23.5 t23.5 f23.5 b24 I particularly love this as the distillery in question is never in doubt: had "Glenmorangie" running through it like a stick of Blackpool rock. Despite the light phenols... 43%.

Glenmorangie Grand Vintage 1995 db (89) n23 t23 f21 b22 Some 40 years ago Glenmorangie was never considered a candidate for whiskies aged 21 and over. Not now. This holds together well...until the dying moments. 43%.

Glenmorangie Grand Vintage 1996 db (95) n23.5 t24 f23.5 b24 Principally has a firm, glazed feel to this. But he intensity of the malt takes the breath away. Too beautiful... 43%.

◇ **Glenmorangie Grand Vintage 1997** db (95) n23.5 truly classic Glenmorangie layering: the barley and warm tannins seemingly taking turns for brief snatches of gentle dominance, but it is the oak which gets greedier as time goes on; t24 top class delivery. The sugars are almost crystalline and fragile; the barley is no less crisp before a light oiliness moves in and soothes and cajoles. By the midpoint we are now in the realms of near perfect oak and grain balance met with a sharpish juiciness elevating the grassier elements of the malt; **f23.5** drier, with butterscotch on slightly burnt toast. The pace of the spice on the fade could not be better judged; **b24** such glorious weight and counterweight: a lesson in cask understanding. A classy vintage, indeed. *43%*.

Glenmorangie Lasanta sherry casks db **(68.5) n16 t19 f16 b17.5**. The sherry problem has increased dramatically rather than being solved. *46%*

Glenmorangie Lasanta Aged 12 Years sherry cask finish db **(93) n23.5 t24 f22 b23.5** A delightful surprise: every bottling of Lasanta I'd ever tasted had been sulphur ruined. But this new 12-y-o incarnation has got off to a flying start. Although a little bit of a niggle on the finish, I can live with that in the present climate. Here's to a faultless second bottling... *43%*

Glenmorangie Legends The Duthac db **(91.5) n23.5 t23.5 f21.5 b23** Not spoken to their blender, Bill Lumsden, about this one. But he's been busy on this, though not so busy as to get rid of the unwelcome you-know-what from the wine casks. Educated guess: some kind of finish involving virgin oak, or at least first fill bourbon, and sherry, probably PX on account of the intensity of the crisp sugar. *43%. ncf.*

Glenmorangie Milsean db **(94) n23 t23.5 f23.5 b24** A quite beautiful malt which goes out of its way to put the orangey in 'Morangie... *46%*

Glenmorangie Nectar D'Or db **(94.5) n23.5** the soft orange blossom honey merges beautifully with the clean barley; a vague polished leather gives an extra sparkle; **t24** the delivery is all about velvety sweetness holding just enough oak to keep the balance true. Heather honey ensures a waxy extra sweetness to the barley; **f23** dries elegantly with a delightful chalky oakiness; **b24** I was told that this was different to the last Nectar D'or as it has no age statement. To be honest, I was never aware that it had! But it doesn't matter: it is always about the blending of the malt styles from the distillery and the pursuit of balance. And what I have said about this whisky before still perfectly sums it up: an exercise in outrageously good sweet-dry balancing... *46%*

Glenmorangie Private Edition 9 Spios db **(95.5) n23 t24.5 f23.5 b24.5** Glenmorangie displaying countless layers of brilliance. Breathtakingly beautiful. *46%*

Glenmorangie Quinta Ruban 14 Year Old db **(87) n22 t22 f21 b22** Something of the sweet shop about this with the sugary fruitiness. But doesn't quite develop in structure beyond its simple – though thoroughly attractive – early confines. *46%*

Glenmorangie Signet db **(80.5) n20 t21.5 f19 b20**. A great whisky holed below the waterline by oak of unsatisfactory quality. Tragic. *46%. Travel Retail Exclusive.*

⬧ **Glenmorangie Signet** db **(94) n23.5** there is a streak of roastiness on this like a single vapour trail across an azure sky. Gently intriguing...; **t24** succulence and sharpness are delivered in one fell swoop. For a moment after that startling delivery the brain is scrambled slightly. But soon you are able to focus again on the playful fizz around the palate where mocha is the order of the day, and you fancy that buttery note even turns to milk. As for that mocha: it is liberally sweetened with molasses; **f23** long with the oak now having the louder say. But the mocha won't go easily...; **b23.5** ah, that's better! Faith and excellence has been restored! *46%*.

⬧ **Glenmorangie Signet Ristretto** db **(86.5) n22 t22.5 f21 b21** Not so sure about this one. Think I prefer my Signets non-Ristrettoed. Flies way too far towards unconstrained sweetness on delivery, but big sweetness on delivery often leaves a bit of a mess in its wake. And I have to admit I am no fan of the dishevelled, tangy finish. *46%*

Glenmorangie Taghta db **(92) n23 t23 f23 b23** A curious Glenmorangie which, unusually, appears not to be trying to make a statement or force a point. This is an old Sunday afternoon film of a dram: an old-fashioned black and whitie, (home grown and not an Ealing, or Bogie or Edward G Robinson) where, whether we have seen it before or not, we know pretty much what is going to happen, in a reassuring kind of a way... *46%*

⬧ **Glenmorangie A Tale of Cake** db **(87) n22 t23 f20 b22** So rare for acacia honey to show so early on a 'Morangie, but there it is and does a great job in offering the delicate touch to the busier spices. Sadly, there is the dull throb of an off-key cask which gets a little too loud for comfort on the finish. There are those who won't spot it, but more who will and it is a distraction from an otherwise genteel dram. *46%*.

Glenmorangie Tarlogan db **(95) n24 t24 f22.5 b23.5** Interesting. I have just tasted three new Dalmore. Identical colour and some very similar toffeed characteristics. I allowed a whisky-loving visitor to taste them, without telling him what they were. He could barely tell them apart. Here, I have three new Glenmorangies. All of a different hue. I may not like them all; we will see. But at least I know there will be remarkable differences between them. This fabulous malt radiates the countryside in a way few drams have done before. As refreshing as an early morning dip in a Scottish pond... *43%*

Glenmorangie Tayne db **(87.5) n21 t22.5 f22 b22**. Tangy back story. But also a curious early combination between butterscotch and Werther's Original candy. The malt – topped with a splash of double cream - in the centre ground, though, is the star showing. *43%. Travel Retail Exclusive.*

Glenmorangie Tùsail Private Edition db (92) n24.5 t23 f21.5 b23 Doesn't quite live up to the nose. But that would have been a big ask! From the Understated School of Glenmorangie.*46%. ncf.*

Fadandel.dk Westport Glenmorangie Aged 11 Years refill hogshead, finished in a 1st fill oloroso cask, dist 25 Sept 07, bott 11 Mar 19 (86) n21.5 t22 f21 b21.5 Not one of those sherry casks that can kill a whisky from a thousand paces. But just enough on it to take the sparkle out of the nose, follow through and finish. Plenty still to enjoy, even if the fruit and intense barley are not quite in sync. The brief clarity of the malt on delivery, though, is something to celebrate. *56.2%. sc. 272 bottles.*

GLEN MORAY
Speyside, 1897. La Martiniquaise. Working.
Glen Moray Classic 8 Years Old db (86) n20 t22 f21 b23. A vast improvement on previous bottlings with the sluggish fatness replaced by a thinner, barley-rich, slightly sweeter and more precise mouthfeel. *40%*

Glen Moray 10 Years Old Chardonnay Matured db (73.5) n18.5 t19 f18 b18. Tighter than a wine cork. *40%*

Glen Moray 12 Years Old db (90) n22.5 t22 f23 b22.5 I have always regarded this as the measuring stick by which all other malty and clean Speysiders should be tried and tested. It is still a fabulous whisky, full of malty intricacies. Something has fallen off the edge, perhaps, but minutely so. Still think a trick or two is being missed by bottling this at 40%: the natural timbre of this malt demands 46% and no less.... *40%*

Glen Moray 16 Years Old db (74) n19 t19 f18 b19. A serious dip in form. Drab. *40%*

Glen Moray 20 Years Old db (80) n22 t22 f18 b18. With so much natural cream toffee, it is hard to believe that this has so many years on it. After a quick, refreshing start it pans out, if anything, a little dull. *40%*

⬩⬩⬩ **Glen Moray Aged 21 Years Portwood Finish** db (95) n23.5 just love the hint of black pepper to slightly jar the most genteel of fruity noses out of its comfort zone. The bitter-sweet balance just couldn't be better...; t23.5 slightly fat on delivery, but immediately salivating. The Port casks have made their mark, offering a firmer touch, but the softness of the ever-sweetening malt refuses to be denied: lip-smacking...! f24 and bang on cue the spices to both lift and lengthen; ulmo honey sticks around...literally! b24 as soft and yielding on the palate as any malt you'll ever find. But not short on the complexity front, either. A true entertainer. *46.3%. ncf.*

Glen Moray Aged 25 Years Port Cask Finish dist 1988 db (88) n23 t22.5 f20.5 b22 Thought I'd celebrate Andy Murray's second Wimbledon victory, which he completed just a few minutes ago, by having another go at a Glen Moray 25-year-old (Moray is pronounced Murray). I remember last time being slightly disappointed with this expression. Well this later bottling is a little better, but nowhere near the brilliance Murray displayed in gaining revenge for Canada last year getting World Whisky of the Year. Curiously, if this is a 25-year-old and was distilled in 1988, then presumably it was bottled in 2013..the first time Murray won Wimbledon! *43%*

⬩⬩⬩ **Glen Moray Aged 25 Years Port Cask Finish** bourbon casks, dist 1994, bott code: L933659A db (93) n24 oddly, the fruit takes a back seat in the early exchanges on the nose. Instead it allows the delightful van of bourbon tones – cleverly integrated red liquorice and wafer-thin hickory – to engage with a more traditional vanilla-led tannin. The fruits lurk but have no great desire to interfere; t23.5 the mouthfeel is lush, the first flavour profile is hickory, which appears to have escaped the liquorice. As gentle spices gather into something more significant, the first tannins from the grape emerge: dry skin, bereft of meat; f22 dries even further on the wine must theme. But then dries some more, though this time from a weakness in the wine cask; b23.5 an exhibition of mind-blowing layering. The nose and delivery are a malt-lover's dream come true. *43%.*

Glen Moray 25 Year Old Port Cask Finish batch 2 db (95) n23.5 t23.5 f24 b24 Some quite first rate port pipes are involved here. Absolutely clean as a whistle and without any form of off-note. A distillery I have a very soft spot for showing very unusual depth – and age. Brilliant. *43%. 3295 bottles.*

Glen Moray Aged 25 Years Portwood Finish Rare Vintage Limited Edition bott code. 3153, dist 1986 db (87.5) n22.5 t22 f21 b22. Just get the feeling that the Port pipe has not quite added what was desired. *43%*

Glen Moray Aged 25 Years Port Cask Finish dist 1988, bott code L709759A 2017/04/07 db (94) n23 t23.5 f23.5 b24 A lovely intense malt where the Port casks leave big fruity fingerprints at every turn. *43%.*

Glen Moray 30 Years Old db **(92.5)** n23.5 it's probably the deftness of the old-fashioned Speyside smoke in tandem with the structured fruits that makes this so special; **t23.5** for a light Speysider, the degree of barley to oak is remarkable: soft, oil-gilded barley is met by a wonderful, if brief, spice prickle; **f22.5** deft layering of vanilla and cocoa; a sprinkle of muscovado sugar repels any darker oak notes; **b23** for all its years, this is comfortable malt, untroubled by time. There is no mistaking quality. 43%

Glen Moray 1984 db **(83)** n20 t22 f20 b21. Mouthwatering and incredibly refreshing malt for its age. 40%

Glen Moray 1989 db **(86)** n23 t22 f20 b21. Doesn't quite live up to the fruit smoothie nose but I'm being a little picky here. 40%

Glen Moray Bourbon Cask 1994 cask no. 42/0, bott code. 25/04/17 170635 db **(93.5)** n23.5 t23.5 f23 b23.5 For most people in England Glen Moray is a highly productive goalscorer for Brighton. But it would be great if the world woke up to just what lovely whisky can come from this much under-rated distillery. 56.4%. sc.

◈ **Glen Moray Burgundy Cask 2004 Distillery Edition** cask no. 213, bott code: L012257A 2020/05/01 db **(93)** n23 spices abound, though more from the tannins than the fruit. You know that aroma when you have finished the last glass of a particular fine Burgundy and the glass has sat empty for half an hour, the minor sediment hardening...: thin acacia honey is the glue holding this together; **t23.5** silky soft, a brief ultra-intense wave of sweet malt which appears once then disappears under the tannin and dry fruits indicated on the nose; spices burst open on impact, vanish...then saunter to the middle intensifying gently, though they are muted slightly by the thickening but short-lived oils; **f23** playfully spiced Manuka honey and burnt raisin; **b23.5** curiously, the last few Burgundy casks I had tasted from distilleries around the world, if unmolested by candles, had shewn much more breast-beating spice at work than this relatively sedate chap. But don't get me wrong, this still has plenty of fizz and much to say...all of it worth listening to. 60.1%. sc.

◈ **Glen Moray Chardonnay Cask 2003 Distillery Edition** cask no. 7670, bott code: L012257A 2020/05/01 db **(95.5)** n24 one of the most striking noses of the year: in fact my nose feels as though it has just been struck by the contents of the kitchen spice rack...with the spices still attached to the rack. A dry bread pudding nose also reeks of dried wine corks...of a particularly good vintage...; **t24** the nose doesn't prepare you for the amount of honey doing the rounds on delivery: that's if you can get your mind to focus away from the fizzing spices. This acacia honey softens the impact of the highly toasted raisin and hickory which sears into you; **f23.5** very dry as the oak manages to lose the fruit for its own brand of toastiness. The lightly oiled malt which had quietly gone about its business earlier on now makes itself much more apparent; **b24** if your thing is burnt fruitcake: smouldering, blackened raisins in particular, then I think I have just unearthed a single malt whisky just for you. A wine cask matured malt with no damaging sulphur whatsoever, which has been a rare thing this year and makes me want to cheer this bottling from the rooftops. However, there is no escaping the fact that this a form of trial by fire...or toasting to be specific. From the eye-watering, spicy and acidic nose to the honeyed finish you are offered something very different and bordering on genius. 58.9%. sc.

◈ **Glen Moray Chenin Blanc Cask 2004 Distillery Edition** cask no. 341, bott code: L012257A 2020/05/01 db **(75)** n18 t23 f16 b18 If any wine industry was worse for sulphur-treating their casks than the Spanish, it was the French. Alas, in this case. Because the sweet and voluptuous beauty of the delivery is there for all to see. 60.3%. sc.

Glen Moray Classic db **(86.5)** n22 t21.5 f21.5 b21.5. The nose is the star with a wonderful, clean barley-fruit tandem, but what follows cannot quite match its sure-footed wit. 40%

◈ **Glen Moray Elgin Classic** bott code: L929657A 2019/10/23 db **(89)** n23 the lightest dab of peat on banana cake. Some delightful grapefruity citrus tones, too, **t23** the lightness of touch means the delicate smoke holds an exaggerated position Juicy malts at first before the toffee moves in; **f21** short and a little dull; **b22** an Elgin Classic ....brushed with peat! Never thought I'd see the day. A delightful aroma of the gentlest nature. The finish, though, could do with a little less toffee. I say this as I am more than aware what a true Elgin Classic is: when my son was born in 1986 I took him to this distillery while he was just a few months old. And I had also bought him a Glen Moray 12 to open on his 21st birthday. Its colour was natural pale straw, as Glen Moray always, classically was. Some 35 years ago Gen Moray was synonymous with light natural colour and a full malty flavour. Wouldn't it be wonderful if it could be again... 40%.

Glen Moray Classic Port Cask Finish db **(89.5)** n21 t21.5 f23.5 b23.5 A malt which has to somehow work its way to the exit...and finally does so with supreme confidence and a touch of class along the way... 40%

◈ **Glen Moray Elgin Classic Cabernet Cask Finish** bott code: L820057B 2018/07/19 db **(88)** n22 t23 f21 b22 Not normally a great fan of malt with this degree of dryness on the finish. But must say I enjoyed the sophisticated pathway to the finish, if not the eye-wateringly tight finale itself. But enjoy the seasoned moist fruitcake nose and the angular, juicy berry fruits – under-ripe gooseberries in particular on delivery. Then hold on tight... 40%.

Glen Moray Elgin Classic Chardonnay Cask Finish db **(73)** n19 t19 f17 b18. Juicy. But sulphur-dulled. 40%

◈ **Glen Moray Elgin Classic Chardonnay Cask Finish** bott code: L822667C 2018/08/14 db **(83)** **n21 t22 f20 b20** You know when you have a date with a rather attractive looker you have only just met. And make a reservation at a special restaurant where, with a sinking feeling of the heart, you find out over dinner that, no matter how well you prompt and cajole, how tightly you hang on to their every dull word, that person has nothing whatsoever of interest to say; and you have so little in common that you cannot wait for the evening to end as boredom sets in. Well, that, I'm afraid, was just like tasting this malt... 40%.

◈ **Glen Moray Elgin Classic Peated Single Malt** bott code: L912557E 2019/05/06 db **(88.5)** **n22 t23.5 f21 b22** Definitely a much better all-rounder than the last bottling of this I tasted. But still palpably at the wrong strength, allowing far too much chalky vanilla given free entrance to undo the great work of the peat and the outstanding distillate. Mesmerically soft on delivery and the house mega-maltiness is soon evident, to wholly delicious effect. But the way it crumbles away on the finish is a bit of a shame. This has the potential for a malt in the 93-94 range. As it is: quite lovely...but soooo frustratingly underpowered! 40%.

◈ **Glen Moray Elgin Classic Port Cask Finish** bott code: L922067B 2019/08/08 db **(92.5)** **n22.5** firm, peppery and a tad tart. No mistaking the grape; **t23.5** a creamy maltiness blends in beautifully with the sharp tannins of the grape skin. A lovely layering of muscovado and molassed sugars go a long way; **f23** impeccably clean finish; so clean the malt is able to make itself heard. As are those persistent spices; **b23.5** another slightly underpowered malt, but it has to be said that the quality of these Port casks is exceptionally high. This is gorgeous malt at any strength. 40%.

Glen Moray Elgin Classic Sherry Cask Finish db **(85)** **n21 t22 f20.5 b21.5.** Must be a cream sherry, because this is one exceptionally creamy malt. A bit of a late sulphur tang wipes off a few marks, but the delicious grapey positives outweigh the negatives. 40%

◈ **Glen Moray Elgin Classic Sherry Cask Finish** bott code: L9150570 2019/08/30 db **(88)** **n22** though sweetness is at a premium, the spices too have a charm and the tannins no little personality. The fruit is of the dried grape skin variety...; **t23** an enticing mouthfeel. This is malt and fruit combining to caress rather than envelop while the juices flow not from the barley but the plums; **f20** not quite a perfect sherry butt at work here, but the late Demerara sugars do their best against the furriness; **b22.5** when the fruit gets into full stride it becomes quite a joy. The dangers of sherry butts though are always there as a reminder. 40%.

Glen Moray Elgin Heritage Aged 15 Years db **(74)** n19 t20 f17 b18. Dulled by some poor, sulphur-laden sherry butts. Glen Moray is one of the maltiest drams on God's earth and at its most evocative in ex-bourbon. Who needs sherry? 40%

◈ **Glen Moray Elgin Heritage Aged 15 Years** Oloroso sherry casks & ex bourbon American oak, bott code: L890127B 2019/08/14 db **(90.5)** **n23.5** a much more alert and lively nose than the Signature 15, helped along with an almost bourbon liquorice and chocolate edge to this; **t23** fabulously explosive delivery. If the fruit had been hanging back slightly on the nose, there is no such shyness here. Wonderful marriage between the fruitcake sultanas and creamy malt; **f21.5** fruit and chocolate but just slightly undone by a furry wobble at the death; **b22.5** very curious how even though this is weaker than Signature, the characteristics of the casks comes through so much more brightly, mainly thanks to less toffee apparent. The off-key sherry finale, excepted, of course. 40%.

Glen Moray Elgin Heritage Aged 18 Years db **(94)** n23.5 t24 f23 b23.5 Absolutely true to the Glen Moray style. Superb. 47%

◈ **Glen Moray Elgin Signature Aged 12 Years** American oak, bott code: L831157B 2018/11/07 db **(86)** **n23.5 t22.5 f19.5 b21** Now here's a mystery. Bourbon casks...yet a dull fruity furriness on the finish. Until that point is blazed away with that stunning malty intensity that makes Glen Moray in bourbon cask a little bit special. 48%. ncf. Cask Collection Exclusive.

◈ **Glen Moray Elgin Signature Aged 15 Years** American & sherry casks, bott code: L821157C 2018/11/07 db **(89)** **n22.5** the Oloroso is beating its chest here assuming dominance over the barley; **t22.5** typical Moray quick burst of salivation as the malt strikes; slowly the grape finds its range; **f22** lightly spiced sticky toffee pudding; **b22** another Glen Moray cut off in its prime. Pleasant but goes for impact rather than complexity. 46%. ncf. Cask Collection Exclusive.

◈ **Glen Moray Elgin Signature Elgin Classic** first fill American oak, bott code: L924157A 2019/09/23 db **(90)** **n23** despite the exclusive use of first fill bourbon, the citrus notes from the barley still ring through loud and clear. A light, dusty toffee note suggests that maybe not all the rich colour is natural. But the layering of the barley also confirms that some very judicious use of some malts at varying degrees of contact with the oak; **t23** truly classic! The delivery allows the barley to let rip before a sturdier oakiness involves itself; **f22** duller, despite the late spice and cocoa. Toffee everywhere...; **b22** hmmm! Lovely malt from this brilliant distillery. Not sure about the finish, though, where toffee abruptly ends what had been such a satisfying experience. *48%. ncf. Cask Collection Exclusive.*

Glen Moray Fired Oak Aged 10 Years db **(90) n22.5** such an attractive blend of mint humbugs and chocolate limes; **t23** the delivery is an impressive layering of alternating oaky vanilla and simplistic barley tones; juicy yet with a fabulous underlying dryness; **f22** a little feeble as the vanilla takes control a tad too easily. Some faint barley sugar persists alongside gentle spices; **b22.5** very attractive. But missing a trick at 40%: it is needing the extra oils to ramp up intensity and take into another dimension. *40%.*

⬩⬩⬩ **Glen Moray Madeira Cask Project 13 Years Old** dist 26 May 06, bott code: L012557A 2020/05/04 db **(90.5) n23** one of those malts which less kisses your nose than gives it a good fruity tweak! This is sharp, bright and purposeful; vaguely salty, too...; **t23.5** and that's just how it comes across on the palate, too. The juicier, tangier notes coming out blazing, with something approaching a kiwi fruit nip, though this is tempered by the waves of custardy vanilla; **f21.5** a little furry note to finish off with...; **b22.5** even with a cask offering just a light sulphur touch, the bountiful and slightly unusual delights of the nose and delivery in particular make its sins very easy to forgive. *46.3%. nc ncf. UK Exclusive.*

Glen Moray Mastery db **(89.5) n23.5 t22.5 f21.5 b22** Has an expensive feel to this, to be honest. But, though a huge GM fan, have to say that for all its very clean, attractive, unblemished fruit; for all its juiciness I'm afraid it's just a little bit too one-dimensional. No doubting its charm and elegance, however. *52.3%.*

Glen Moray Peated Classic db **(87.5) n21.5 t22.5 f21.5 b22**. Really never thought I'd see this distillery, once the quintessential Speyside unpeated dram, gone all smoky... A little bit of a work in progress. And a minor word to the wise to their blenders: by reducing to 40% you've broken up the oils a shade – but tellingly - too much, which can be crucial in peaty whiskies. Up to 46% next bottling and I think you'll find things fall into place – and not apart... Some minor erotic moments, though, especially on the fourth or fifth beats, when the sugars and smoked vanilla do work well together. Too fleeting, though. *40%*

⬩⬩⬩ **Glen Moray Rhum Agricole Cask Finish Project** Oloroso sherry casks & ex bourbon American oak, bott code: L921058A 2019/07/29 db **(94.5) n24** just love unusual aroma profiles – and this is pretty different. Usually Rhum agricole furnishes a far more bullish nose than this. But here the sugary effect is happy to meld into the malt and soft, supporting fruit; **t23.5** again, different. Average rum casks ensure a crisp outer edge. Here an icing sugar sweetness dissolves, all the while the salivating gristy malt building and intensifying. The grape is reduced to a low-key role, but a vital one as the grape provides weight and ballast: a bit like a leading actor reduced to character part. But a vital one...; **f23** slightly messier than the rest of the piece, but still insists on creating highly unusual flavour patterns...here with the malt at the helm but now in more in caramelised biscuit form...; **b24** a beautifully weighted malt that melts on the tongue. A highly unusual flavour profile and one that benefits from some top class blending. What a treat of a dram. *46.3%. ncf. UK Exclusive.*

Glen Moray Sherry Cask Finish 1994 cask no. 904/57, bott code. 25/04/17 170636 db **(92) n23.5 t23 f22 b23.5** Old-fashioned, traditional dry oloroso influence in its most resounding form. A must find malt for those looking to broaden their positive whisky experiences.*56.7%. sc.*

⬩⬩⬩ **Acla Selection Summer Edition Glen Moray 28 Year Old** barrel, dist 1990, bott 2018 **(91.5) n23** there's chocolate on that oak! **t22** wobbles in the oaky storm. But the ulmo honey flies to the rescue...there is hope...! **f23.5** isn't there just! The marriage of layered ulmo honey and cocoa is truly sublime. As it reaches its very long conclusion, the malt has returned but all signs of great age have vanished; **b23** a very similar experience to the OMC 28-year-old below. Except here the oak has a firmer grip, making the honey play an even more crucial role. *50.9%.*

Demijohn Glen Moray 10 Years Old (95) n23 t24 f24 b24 One of those rare whiskies which just gets better as it goes along. What a great cask in action here...! *56.4%.*

⬩⬩⬩ **The First Editions Glen Moray Aged 25 Years 1994** refill hogshead, cask no. 16609, bott 2019 **(94) n23.5** some blinding complexity here: a delicate lime note is present throughout, adding a lightness of touch. A thinnish sliver of eucalyptus underlines the age, too..; **t24** so mouth-filling on delivery. Just for a moment the house maltiness takes a back seat as an oily honey tone takes control...but the barley is soon back on track, offering wave upon wave of ulmo-honey infused maltiness...; **f23** you know the spices are coming...and here they are. But still that silky honeyed maltiness stands its ground; **b23.5** another first class offering from the First Editions portfolio. *54.6%. nc ncf sc. 339 bottles.*

Glenwill Glen Moray 1990 hogshead, cask no. 7626 **(94) n23 t23.5 f23.5 b24** Always heart-warming when a distillery which long ago thought itself incapable of producing fine, big-aged whiskies does exactly that. A little touch of ermine to a noble dram. *52.4%. 234 bottles. Matisse Spirits Company.*

Liquid Treasures 10th Anniversary Glen Moray 10 Year Old sherry hogshead, dist 2008, bott 2019 **(89) n23 t23 f21 b22** Not quite an entirely flawless hoggy at work. But the delivery is stupendous! *59.2%. sc. 134 bottles.*

⬦ **Old Malt Cask Glen Moray Aged 28 Years** refill hogshead, cask no. 16610, dist Oct 91, bott Oct 19 **(90) n22.5** tiring, but just enough malty life to balance out the more exhausted oaky tones; **t22** those jaded oak notes strike first. But, as on the nose, the vanilla, ulmo honey and malt combine, fitfully at first to save the day...; **f23** and now go into overdrive as the finale stretches out to accommodate the increasing complexity; the honey travels a surprisingly long distance; **b22.5** has all the marks of an old timer just about on its last legs, but still capable of one final, elegant hurrah! *50%. nc ncf sc. 270 bottles.*

⬦ **Scyfion Choice Glen Moray 2007** Areni Noir wine cask finished, bott 2019 **(85) n22 t23.5 f18.5 b21** A malt boasting a sublime delivery as the ripe fruits and spices gang together to let rip. Likewise, the follow-through is an outstanding display of layered fruit candy leading down to a small reservoir of malt. Just a little furry tang on the finale though that turns into gnawing sulphur. *50%. nc ncf sc. 132 bottles.*

⬦ **Scyfion Choice Glen Moray 2007** Foursquare rum cask finished, bott 2019 **(91.5) n23.5** beautifully balanced: Glen Moray's famous malt intensity holds firm, though alongside a dash of citrus the rum also gives a variation of sweetness; **t23** now the rum eclipses the barley with some ease, a gentle creaminess washing over the barley. Chewy, elegant and delicate; **f22** a little bitterness squeezes in as the tannins bite alongside the spices; **b23** it is perhaps ironic that the owner of the Foursquare distillery in Barbados shares my slight weariness of cask finishes (in my case because over 25 years I have tasted a disproportionately high number of unimpressive ones) yet here is one of his casks being used to finish a single malt. And, I have to say, doing a good job of it. *46%. nc ncf sc. 97 bottles.*

The Whisky Chamber Glen Moray 11 Years Old 2007 bourbon cask **(89.5) n22.5 t23 f22 b22** A typical Glen Moray Maltfest! *58.4%. sc.*

GLEN ORD
Highlands (Northern), 1838. Diageo. Working.

Glen Ord Aged 12 Years db **(81) n20 t23 f18 b20.** Just when you thought it safe to go back...for a while Diageo ditched the sherry-style Ord. It has returned. Better than some years ago, when it was an unhappy shadow of its once-great self, but without the sparkle of the vaguely-smoked bottling of a year or two back. Nothing wrong with the rich arrival, but the finish is a mess. I'll open the next bottling with trepidation... *43%*

Singleton of Glen Ord 12 Years Old db **(89) n22.5 t22.5 f22 b22** A fabulous improvement on the last bottling I encountered. Still possesses blood oranges to die for, but greatly enhanced by some sublime spices and a magnificent juiciness. *40%*

The Singleton of Glen Ord 14 Year Old db **(95.5) n23.5 t24.5 f23.5 b24** Sheer quality. The distillery revealed in all its astonishing complexity. *57.6%. Diageo Special Releases 2018.*

The Singleton of Glen Ord Aged 15 Years European & American oak casks, bott code: L8038DM003 db **(90.5) n23 t23.5 f21.5 b22.5** The fun of the label on many a bottle of whisky is just how far removed the described tasting notes are to what is actually poured from the bottle. Here, there are no quibbles from me: the promised ginger and chocolate come true! *40%.*

Singleton of Glen Ord 32 Year Old db **(91) n23.5 t23 f22 b22.5.** Delicious. But if ever a malt has screamed out to be at 46%, this is it. *40%*

⬦ **The Singleton Glen Ord Distillery Exclusive** batch no. 01, bott 2019, bott code: L9193DQ0002 db **(95.5) n24.5** one of the noses of the years: the Liebfraumilch suggests this must be as near as damn it natural colour and the breathtakingly delicate nature of the malt itself conforms nothing is impeding even the most intricate aromas – even those represented by the odd atom or two – from playing their part. The main theme here is grapefruit, but there is a twist of lychee and fresh green grist from relatively young malt, but not so young that light tannin notes have become attached. Also, look out for the sexiest little layer of peat, visible only because the this is the cleanest nose of any distillery bottling this year...; **t23.5** salivating...??? Not half! The barley is a staggering exhibition of fresh, citrus-kissed barley grist as on the nose accompanied with the most brilliantly disguised smokiness – easily overlooked, but there to be savoured when you realise the part it plays. A thin layer of marzipan appears to represent the oak's contribution. All of this is a teasing dovetailing of immaculate finesse. And what of that salivating sweetness.? Grist aplenty for sure, but a little lime blossom honey adds to the fruity character...but delicately, of course...; **f23.5** being so light, the headier oak notes have a chance to form in slightly greater depth, but the gentle spice, light milk chocolate and settling smoke ensures there are still many facets to this malt in action to the very last moment; **b24** It is unfortunate that the Glen Ord distillery is not the easiest in Scotland to get to. But while they have this bottle in their shops, get plane, boat, go-cart, train, pushbike, helicopter, space hopper, parachute, pogo stick, glider, Harley- Davidson, horse, foot-scooter, paraglider, huskies, jet ski, cannon, roller skates, bobsleigh, canoe, Penny Farthing, Zeppelin, windsurf, camel, sedan, jet propulsion pack, elephant, raft, auto-rickshaw, lawnmower, crutches....absolutely bloody ANYTHING to get you there. Because this is the great Gen Ord unplugged, naked and as beautiful as you'll ever find it. *48%. 6,000 bottles.*

GLENROTHES
Speyside, 1878. Edrington. Working.

The Glenrothes 10 Years Old sherry seasoned oak casks db **(80.5) n19 t22.5 f19 b20** Neither a nose or finish I much care for: tight, a little tangy and out of sync. But I certainly approve the delivery which shows no such constraints and celebrates the voluptuousness of its maltiness. *40%. nc. The Soleo Collection.*

The Glenrothes 12 Years Old sherry seasoned oak casks db **(68) n17 t19 f15 b17** Sulphur addled. *40%. nc. The Soleo Collection.*

The Glenrothes 18 Years Old sherry seasoned oak casks db **(87) n22 t22.5 f21 b21.5** Nutty and hefty, there is always a slight tang to this which slightly reduces the intricate nature of the barley. The off-key finish confirms not all is well, but this being the truly brilliant distillery it is, an inner depth of barley and ulmo honey ensures there always something to treasure from this dram. *43%. nc. The Soleo Collection.*

The Glenrothes 25 Years Old sherry seasoned oak casks db **(86) n23 t22 f19.5 b21.5** The nose is the star turn here, shewing some of the complexity you might demand of a 25-year-old malt. The adroitness of the barley ripe Chinese gooseberry is particularly alluring. But after a surprisingly malt delivery and a volley of pleasant sultana, it is the finish (again) which reveals a furry weak link. *43%. nc. The Soleo Collection.*

The Glenrothes Whisky Maker's Cut first fill sherry seasoned oak casks db **(95) n23.5** a semi-simplistic nose of happy, dry oloroso dominating in fruitiness, but delighted to let in the sharply tannin-rich oak; **t23.5** ah...! No faulting that at all...! A sublime burst of rounded grape, sweetened marginally by the odd busy significant strand of molasses; spices move into position early on; **f24** even late on there is an attractive salivating element to this, but the late sherry trifle, enriched with chocolate source, is deeply attractive; **b24** unspoiled casks at work. An absolute must for sherry cask lovers. *48.8%. nc. The Soleo Collection.*

◇◇ **Cadenhead's Glenrothes 18 Year Old** port cask, dist 2001 **(87.5) n21 t23.5 f21 b22** Having spent the last couple of decades running away from any Glenrothes matured in a wine cask, have to admit I took this whisky on with more than a degree of trepidation. The dry, penurious nose makes you start looking for the hills...when suddenly you are stopped in your tracks by the sheer voluptuousness, the honey-laden generosity of the delivery that makes delicious celebration of the stunning grape. There is little else to cling on to with any warmth after that – perhaps a little salty chocolate and spice maybe. But that delivery...just wow! *53.6%. 246 bottles. Cadenhead Shop Series 2019 Baden.*

The Cooper's Choice Glenrothes 1997 19 Years Old Jurancon finish **(91) n22.5** a vaguely phenolic note fits beautifully with the lightly sweetened Cape Gooseberry; **t23** alluringly malt from the get-go. The secondary fruitiness seems to emphasise the juiciness of the malt itself; **f22.5** pleasing spice to sex up the vanilla; **b23** a faultless cask finish but the intensity of the malt is the star of the show. Excellent! *46%. nc ncf sc.*

Hepburn's Choice Glenrothes 7 Years Old refill butt, dist 2011, bott 2019 **(76.5) n19 t20.5 f18 b19** A dull cove, the dreaded "S" word lurking in all corners. Enjoys a brief bright malty moment on delivery. *46%. nc ncf sc. 921 bottles.*

The Last Drop Glenrothes 1970 cask no. 10586 **(97) n24.5** the most complex of the trilogy, this one revealing small glimpses of myriad facets, like shards of stained glass found on an archaeological dig. The barley, even after all this time, resembles strands of freshly-plucked moist grass; the vanillas are rounded and soft – reminiscent of Lyons Maid ice cream – and, for the first time and so clean and clear is this nose, small fragments of peat can be detected, providing the most unexpected base note...; **t24** the nose is delicate and complex: the delivery mirrors this exactly. So delicate, in fact, the spices soon make their way forward, meeting little resistance from elsewhere. The malts are bitter-sweet, incredibly juicy and then...ever so slightly smoky....; **f24** a soft chocolate ice cream finale...again with those teasing shards of peat...; **b24.5** it is fascinating how the three Last Drop Glenrothes come from sister casks. But each is so different in its own way, having decided to take a slightly different course in the intervening 49 years...This one has drifted off in the general direction of perfection... *44.3%. sc.*

The Last Drop Glenrothes 1970 cask no. 10588 **(95) n24** a delicious and highly unusual mix between eggnog and bourbon. The barley is also in fine song, despite the great age; just the vaguest hint of something a little smoky, too..; **t24** surprisingly salivating on delivery, the malt really being back on track. They we come to the layering process of tannins, of varying intensities; **f23** such thick, gorgeous vanilla...; the tannins return to add some sturdy oak; **b23.5** it creaks a bit here, limps a little there. But still saunters around with the unmistakable air of whisky royalty... *43%. sc.*

The Last Drop Glenrothes 1970 cask no. 10589 **(95.5) n24** truly classic exotic fruit top quality ye olde Speyside nose...; **t24** anyone of a certain vintage who remember a British sweet called a "fruit salad" you could buy for a farthing each...well, here it is in whisky format. So silky and salivating, and the good news is that despite the oaky intervention the malt can still be enjoyed to the full...; **f23.5** just bitters slightly as those tannins really get a grip, but some lovely prickly spice does a great recovery job; **b24.5** talk about a whisky to bring back the memories...So beautiful... *44%. Sc.*

Liquid Treasures 10th Anniversary Glenrothes 21 Year Old sherry hogshead, dist 1997, bott 2019 **(89) n23 t22.5 f21 b22.5** Not quite a perfect sherry butt, but for Glenrothes, about as good as it gets. *55.8%. sc. 195 bottles.*

⟐ **Liquid Treasures 10th Anniversary Glenrothes 22 Year Old** ex rum barrel, dist 1997, bott 2019 **(90.5) n22 t23 f22.5 b23** A deeply satisfying Glenrothes where the malt, so prevalent on the nose, after the hesitation of a half-a-beat on delivery builds rapidly in and in almost bewildering intensity. The rum's contribution is easily recognised by a tightening of the sugars. But the profound juiciness of the malt makes for a dram of sheer fun and the spices ensure a rigorous subtext befitting the richness of the malt itself. Lovely! *59%. sc. 109 bottles.*

GLEN SCOTIA

Campbeltown, 1832. Loch Lomond Distillers. Working

Glen Scotia Aged 10 Years Peated first fill bourbon barrels db **(94.5) n24 t23 f23.5 b24** This entire whisky style is a throwback to the very first peated whiskies I tasted 40 years ago. Indeed, anyone still alive and able to remember Glen Garioch when it was heavily peated through its own kilns will raise an eyebrow of happy recognition... One of the greatest Glen Scotias of all time. *46%. nc ncf.*

Glen Scotia 11 Years Old 2006 cask no. 532, dist Dec 06, bott Apr 18 db **(92.5) n22.5 t23.5 f23 b23.5** Absolutely typical Glen Scotia, proudly displaying its rugged charm. *55.6%. sc. 212 bottles. Bottled for The Whisky Shop.*

Glen Scotia Aged 15 Years American oak barrels db **(91.5) n22.5 t23 f23 b23** Great to see this rather special little distillery produce something quite so confident and complete. *46%. ncf.*

Glen Scotia 18 Year Old American oak casks & first fill oloroso casks, bott code: L2/221/17 db **(95) n24 t24 f23 b24** ,y Panama is doffed in grateful thanks for the excellent use of un-sulphured clean sherry butts which give this malt a genuine lustre. And as three dimensional as its sister PX bottling is just one... *51.3%. ncf.*

Glen Scotia Aged 25 Years American oak barrels, bott 2017, bott code: L8/187/17 db **(94) n23.5 t24 f23 b23.5** So beautiful! Truly adorable – and probably a Scotia as you have never quite seen it before. Incredibly rare to find a Scotch single malt so under the thumb of a bourbon character: this must have been filled into very fresh first-fill bourbon barrels to come up with this highly American effect. Trump that! *48.8%. ncf.*

Glen Scotia 45 Year Old db **(96) n24** one of those remarkable whiskies where the oak, revealing the odd grey hair (or is that revelling in...?), appears to be holding off to ensure the salty, exotic (or do I mean erotic...?) fruits are allowed the clearest run...; **t24** immediate oak impact on delivery now. But a little maple syrup mingles with butterscotch and salted butter to ensure special things happen. Towards the mid-point orange blossom honey lands, and then melts in the mouth...; **f23.5** light walnut cake complete with crème fondant; lots of intact barley and lighter red liquorice; **b24.5** outrageously beautiful for its age with not even the hint of a beginning of a crack. Stupendous. *43.8%.*

Glen Scotia 1999 refill bourbon barrel, cask no. 455 db **(89) n22.5** a slight salty, grassy note; toffee apple; **t22.5** eye-wateringly fresh barley, but the midground fills with fudge; **f22** soft, linear caramels **b22.5** really extracts every last caramel molecule out of the cask! *60.5%. sc. Bottled for Glenkeir Whiskies.*

Glen Scotia 2008 Second Shop Bottling db **(84) n22 t21 f21 b20** Too salty and bitter for its own good *56.3%. sc.*

Glen Scotia Campbeltown 1832 American oak barrels, finished in Pedro Ximenez sherry casks, bott code: L2 087 18 db **(85.5) n22.5 t22 f20 b21** Yes, pleasant enough I suppose...but so dull! As usual there is a bitterness to a PX finish as any foibles in the oak is exaggerated massively by the sweetness of the grape, which in turn fills in all the natural ridge and furrows of the malt and leaves the flattest of whiskies. The sooner distillers and bottlers get over this PX fad the better... *46%. nc ncf.*

⟐ **Glen Scotia Campbeltown 1832** American oak & Pedro Ximenez sherry casks, bott code: L2.186 19 db **(92.5)** n23 suet pudding with extra dose of maple syrup; t23.5 my word, that PX makes its mark early. But, such a rare thing to find, the malt is brought into play early on, thereby arresting the sweetness but allowing a magnificently beautiful duet to be played by the two main characters; f23 balances out beautifully as the spices kick start late; b23 one of the best malts using PX casks on the market today. Elegant and adorable. *46%. ncf.*

Glen Scotia Campbeltown Harbour first fill bourbon casks, bott code: 23 10 2018 db **(87)** n22 t22 f21.5 b21.5 The best description of Campbeltown and its harbour was provided by 19th century whisky explorer Alfred Barnard. This malt hardly matches the whiskies you would have found of that time, and it doesn't quite match up to how you picture Campbeltown whiskies today, either. For this is very flat and far too caramel dependent, though the mix of saltiness and gentle sweetness is high attractive. The smoke unfurls at the very finish...but for all its easy attractiveness, it is still all a little too docile and tame. *40%.*

⟐ **Glen Scotia Campbeltown Harbour** first fill bourbon barrels, bott code: L20.111.20 db **(89.5)** n22.5 a thin layer of peat smoke breaks up the monopoly of the citrussy tannin; t22.5 lovely mouthfeel: soft with a few firming ribs. The malt shines briefly before the lightly spiced tannins take over; f22 just a little bitterness; b22.5 it is a very brave move to limit a malt to 100% first-fill bourbon cask, as this appears to have done, and reduce to 40% abv, because building structure and layering is almost next to impossible. Instead you are left with a take it or leave it type malt – though this does have plenty to take! Actually, I am being a little unfair because a degree of depth is supplied by the most delicate smokiness. But the scope remains restricted. *40%.*

Glen Scotia Campbeltown Malts Festival 2019 rum cask finish db **(94)** n23.5 t23.5 f23 b24 Too often rum casks can tighten a malt to the point of strangulation. Not here. Lively and outstandingly well balanced. *51.3%.*

⟐ **Glen Scotia Campbeltown Malts Festival 2020 Tawny Port Finish Aged 14 Years Peated** bott code: L4078 20 db **(93)** n23.5 pretty rare to find a Port cask with such clarity allowing the peat through with such good manners...; t23 dissolves on impact – this is as soft as it gets: silk would be like a rock by comparison. The fresh, salivating fruit bounds around with the naïve enthusiasm of a silly young squirrel, while the weightier peat offers the anchor. At even deeper levels the timber solidifies upping the chocolate output; f23 takes its time... but at last settles. And we are left with a delightfully lightly smoked chocolate liqueur...; b23.5 such fun when a distillery employs cask that are 100% clean and sulphur free. Only then can you create a malt like this with so many hidden doors to discover... *52.8%. nc ncf.*

Glen Scotia Double Cask finished in American oak & Pedro Ximenez sherry casks db **(85.5)** n22 t22 f20.5 b21. When blending, I do not like to get too involved with PX casks, unless I know for certain I can shape the effect to further or enrich the storyline on the palate. The reason is that PX means the complexity of a malt can easily come to a sticky end. That has happened here with both the malt and grape cancelling each other out. Soft and easy drinking with an excellent early delivery spike of intensity. But a dull middle and finish. And dull has never been a word I have associated with this distillery. Ever. *46%. ncf.*

⟐ **Glen Scotia Double Cask** American oak barrels & Pedro Ximenez sherry casks, bott code: L2.092.19 db **(88)** n22.5 t23 f20.5 b22 "Rich and Spicy" pronounces the label...and they are not wrong. About as succulent as it gets on delivery and there is a golden magic moment as that spice crashes into the heather honey. Undone slightly, though, by a disappointing finish. *46%. ncf.*

Glen Scotia Distillery Edition No. 6 19 Years Old first fill bourbon cask, dist Jul 99, bott Aug 18 db **(95.5)** n23.5 t24 f24 b24 One of the most charmingly, disarmingly beautiful single cask malts I have tasted this year. *579%. sc. 195 bottles.*

Glen Scotia Warehouse Edition 2005 13 Years Old recharred American oak, first fill oloroso sherry finish, dist Sept 05, bott Aug 18 db **(87.5)** n21.5 t23 f21 b21.5 Another salty offering which peaks on delivery with a huge malt and muscovado sugar burst. Flattens out thereafter and bitters out, too. *56.2%. sc.*

Glen Scotia Victoriana db **(89.5)** n23 t23 f21.5 b22 An unusual malt for a cask strength. Beyond the nose there is limited layering, instead concentrating on the malt-toffee intertwangling. *51.5%*

⟐ **Glen Scotia Victoriana Cask Strength** bott code: L4.053.19 db **(94.5)** n23.5 this has come out as gung-ho crushed hazelnut and barley. The subtlest hint of smoke makes you do a nasal double-take: is it there or not? It is...; t24 a fizzing display of ultra-lively, salivating tannins – a malt revelling in some sublime American oak. And if that isn't juicy enough, the barley pitches in to up the salivation score even further; f23 an elegant climb down. Drier, a little spice but some sexy cocoa notes moving towards praline; b24 as cheerfully bright and breezy a malt as you are likely to find and one bursting with deceptive complexity. If this is trying to depict your average bottle of whisky from Victorian Campbeltown, then it has failed miserably: it was never this good...! 54.2%. nc ncf.

 Glen Scotia Vintage 1991 American oak barrels, bott code: L8 092 19 db **(94) n23.5** salt hangs like barnacles on an ancient vessel, confirming age and character; **t24.5** no escaping the saline interference here, too. Though some gentle tangerines do lessen its grip slightly. The oak barges in, pauses and then continues its charge, though in the delayed second wave has now recruited butterscotch and ulmo honey to ensure a delicate sweetness to accompany the big spice surge. Unquestionably one of the most entertaining and complex deliveries and follow-throughs from Scotland this year; **f22.5** not quite able to keep that touch of genius going and bitters slightly; **b23.5** a very honest malt, brimming with the distillery's endearing character. Whilst tasting this whisky I was deeply saddened to learn of the death of a friend and Whisky Bible devotee, Fran Budd, a warm and charming lady who left us long before she should have done. I raise a glass of this excellent malt and toast your memory, Fran: I suspect you would have approved. 46.7%. nc ncf. Traveller Exclusive.

 The Cyprus Whisky Association Glen Scotia 10 Years Old bourbon cask, cask no. 467, dist Sept 08, bott Apr 19 **(90) n21.5** has this cask been submerged under the ocean waves for the last decade? There are lobster pots with less of a marine aroma...; **t22.5** an early saltiness but, thankfully, not on the same page as the aroma. Soon a well weighted dose of ulmo honey is on hand to give the healthy malt a certain sweet lustre; there is even a degree of juiciness at the midpoint; **f23** long, with the saline content on the rise as the sugars degrees. But still well within bounds, and a little citrus preludes the introduction of the sturdier tannins; **b23** not what I was expecting at all. The saltiest nose of the year by a country mile, or perhaps I should say by many a fathom. But that early coastal feel is tempered on delivery. 53.6%. sc. 240 bottles.

The Perfect Fifth Glen Scotia 1992 cask no. 05917, dist 22 Jan 92 **(94) n23** playful, teasing smoke offers an unlikely sharpness to the already busy barley. For its big age, this malt is alive and kicking; **t23.5** brilliant! Sublime depth to the barley which is at its juiciest and glows as the cocoa notes bring out the best of the light smoke; **f23.5** a bitter-sweet finale with the phenols swirling around and spices a-buzzing. No signs of tiredness at all as the barley still plays a big part while the oak offers both cocoa and a proud skeleton on which all else hangs; **b24** just adore that chocolate and light peat mix. Superb! 45.9%. sc.

GLEN SPEY
Speyside, 1885. Diageo. Working.
Glen Spey Aged 12 Years db **(90) n23 t22 f22 b23** Very similar to the first Glen Spey I can remember in this range, the one before the over-toffeed effort of two years ago. Great to see it back to its more natural, stunningly beautiful self. 43%

Whisky Castle Glen Spey Aged 21 Years hogshead, dist 22 Jul 97, bott 1 Sept 18 **(96.5) n23.5 t24.5 f24 b24.5** Just so wonderful to see this criminally underrated distillery displayed in the most elegant lights. As single casks go, it is as near as damn it perfection. Such beauty could bring a tear to the eye.... 55%. nc ncf sc. 185 bottles.

GLENTAUCHERS
Speyside, 1898. Chivas Brothers. Working.
Ballantine's The Glentauchers Aged 15 Years Series No.003 traditional oak casks, bott code: LKRM0071 2018/02/13 **(86) n22 t22 f21 b21** Alarm bells ring when confronted by the dull nose with a neutral fruit and caramel edge. When the palate offers something fat and glossy (that's a new one for 'Tauchers) with a dull spice development to accompany the vague fruit and caramel, the heart sinks and flashing lights join the ringing alarm. The big, boring caramel finish drives you to distraction.... If anyone on this planet has championed Glentauchers longer or louder than me, or with more heart-felt gusto, then I would like to meet them. For well over 20 years I have been telling anyone who cares to listen – and many who don't – that this is one of Scotland's finest distilleries worthy of its own proprietory bottling. It finally arrives, and instead of a malt which scores in the mid-90s, as it should (and so often has done with independent bottlings in Whisky Bibles past), we have before us something pleasant, bland and not instantly recognisable as a 'Tauchers. Frankly, it could be from any Scottish distillery as the blueprint for the nose and flavour profile is shared by many: too many. As I say, pleasant whisky. But, knowing just how good this whisky really is (using 100% bourbon cask, no colour, no chill-filtration) what a huge and crushing disappointment. A bit like going to see the Sistine Chapel and finding someone had whitewashed over it.... 40%.

Cadenhead's Cask Strength Glentauchers Aged 41 Years dist 1976 **(96) n23.5 t24.5 f23.5 b24.5** One of the world's truly great distilleries fittingly honoured in its advanced age. 42%. sc.

 Deer, Bear & Moose Glentauchers 1996 Aged 20 Years bott 2017 **(89) n22.5 t22.5 f22 b22** 'Tauchers in slightly uncharacteristic fizzy mode. The delivery virtually bubbles on arrival, despite the oily carpet of malt which helps set the scene. Indeed, this is the distillery at its most thickset, too, so the taste buds are as much assessing the mouthfeel as the flavour structure which is an unusual place to be with this distillery. Very different! 53.1%. nc ncf. 389 bottles. Flaviar & Friends.

◇◇◇ **The Great Drams Glentauchers 10 Years Old** cask no. 700435, dist 24 Jun 09, bott 1 Oct 19 **(94) n23.5** a delicious cross between a banana sandwich and egg custard tart; **t23.5** it's the enigmatic sweetness on delivery that wins you over: just a light brushing of gristy sugars to help facilitate the drier, spicier tannins that hint of chocolate mint; **f23** almost sawdusty as a delicate mocha and vanilla theme lasts longer than might be expected; **b24** comes across as one of those whiskies where the distillery doesn't even seem to try, yet effortlessly conjures up something disarmingly stylish and complex. 48.2%. nc ncf sc.

Gordon & MacPhail Connoisseurs Choice Glentauchers Aged 27 Years first fill sherry butt, cask no. 6943, dist 20 Jun 91, bott 6 Sept 18 **(95) n23.5 t24 f23.5 b24** A sherry butt in the finest fettle with not a single atom of sulphur to ruin things. From the rich sherry trifle nose you suspect you are in for a treat. And the succulent spiced grape on the mouthfeel confirms it. The lushness feel is an added bonus...but those spices...! Wow! A dry finale with a touch of mocha rounds it off. Oh, and did I mention the saltiness? Beware! An excellent sherry butt at work: the shock might kill you! It is the only one I have had this week... 56.8%. sc. 473 bottles.

◇◇◇ **Signatory Vintage Glentauchers 22 Year Old** bourbon barrel, cask no. 1404, dist 1996, bott 2018 **(94.5) n23.5** a whispering nose, lime blossom honey just as delicate as the fragile barley. The tannins show exemplary deportment; **t23.5** light strands of ulmo honey break up the far firmer oak. A drier element comes into play quite early on, but the honey always ensures the balance and mouthfeel are top drawer; **f23.5** long, distinguished, doggedly malty and with a wonderful caramelised biscuit fade; **b24** a great distillery in here in magnificent shape. 50.7%. sc. Handpicked by Acla da Fans.

Whisky Castle Glentauchers Aged 10 Years bourbon cask, dist 2007, bott 2018 **(92) n22.5 t23.5 f23 b23** Suffers a little, especially at the death, from not being cask strength. But, otherwise, superb. 46%. nc ncf sc. 500 bottles.

◇◇◇ **Whisky Illuminati Glentauchers 2011** Spanish oak sherry butt, cask no. 900364 **(95.5) n23.5** plum pudding concentrate. The 'Tauchers has vanished under a sea of delectable grape. Spicy, too...; **t24** oh, wow...!!! Stupendous oloroso intervention bringing those spices in early to complement the juiciest of molasses tones. At first the malt seems lost, but like the flotsam from an overwhelmed yacht, it floats up again, hanging onto the vanilla from the oak; the mouthfeel is lush throughout and never less than perfection; **f24** a brilliant, slow waltz played to the tune of fresh fruit and compliant spices; **b24** just so good to taste the fruits of an unspoiled sherry butt once again...it has happened so rarely in the last 20 years. And housing one of the few distilleries in Speyside that has depth enough to add subtle complexity. 63.4%. sc. 150 bottles.

GLENTURRET
Highlands (Perthshire), 1775. Edrington. Working.

Glenturret Aged 8 Years db **(88) n21 t22 f23 b22.** Technically no prizewinner. But the dexterity of the honey is charming, as this distillery has a tendency sometimes to be. 40%

The Glenturret Aged 10 Years db **(76) n19 t18 f20 b19.** Lots of trademark honey but some less than impressive contributions from both cask and the stillman. 40%

The Glenturret Aged 15 Years db **(87) n21 t22 f22 b22.** A beautifully clean, small-still style dram that would have benefitted from being bottled at a fuller strength. A discontinued bottling now: if you see it, it is worth the small investment. 40%

The Glenturret Fly's 16 Masters Edition db **(96) n24.5 t24 f23.5 b24.5** When I first found Glenturret some 30 years so ago, their whisky was exceptionally rare – on account of their size and having been closed for a very long time – but the few bottlings they produced had a very distinctive, indeed unique, feel. Then it changed as they used more Highland Distillers sherry butts which were, frankly, the kiss of death. Here, though, we appear to have reverted back to exactly how it tasted half a lifetime ago. Rich, kissed with copper and stirred with honey. It is, as is fitting to old Fly, the dog's bollocks... 44%. 1,740 bottles.

Glenturret 30 Year Old db **(94) n23 t24 f23 b24** The ultimate exhibition of brinkmanship, surely: hangs on to its integrity by a cat's whisker... 43.4%.

Glenturret Peated Drummond db **(87) n21 t23.5 f21 b21.5** The wide cut from the small still means the odd feint creeps into this one; the peat is too much on the sparse side to paper over the cracks. However, the delivery is something that has to be experienced. A new make freshness can be found all over the show, but even that gives way as the golden syrup and smoke mingle for one of the briefest yet most beautiful star quality moments of the whisky year. 58.9%.

The Glenturret Peated Edition db **(86) n20.5 t22 f21.5 b22.** Pleasant enough, for sure, even if the nose is a bit rough. But in the grand scheme of things, just another peated malt and one of no special distinction. Surely they should concentrate on being Glenturret: there is only one of those.... *43%*

The Glenturret Sherry Edition db **(78)** n19 t21 f19 b19. Not sure if this sherry lark is the best direction for this great distillery to take. *43%*

The Glenturret Triple Wood Edition db **(84)** n20 t22.5 f20 b21.5. Not the happiest of whiskies, but recovers from its obvious wounds by concentrating on the juicy grain, rather than the grape. *43%*

GLENUGIE

Highlands (Eastern). 1834–1983. Whitbread. Closed.

Deoch an Doras Glenugie 30 Years Old dist 1980, bott 2011 db **(87)** n22 t23.5 f19.5 b22. It is now 2017 and it has been six long years since this arrived in my tasting room - something I didn't expect to see again: a distillery bottling of Glenugie. Well, technically, anyway, as Glenugie was part of the Chivas group when it died in the 1980s. As far as I can remember they only brought it out once, either as a seven- or five-year-old. I think that went to Italy, so when I walked around the old site just after it closed, it was a Gordon and MacPhail bottling I drank from and it tasted nothing like this! Just a shame there is a very slight flaw in the sherry butt, but just great to see it in bottle again. *52.13%. nc ncf.*

GLENURY ROYAL

Highlands (Eastern), 1868–1985. Diageo. Demolished.

Glenury Royal 36 Years Old db **(89)** n21 t23 f22 b23. An undulating dram, hitting highs and lows. The finish, in particular, is impressive: just when it looks on its last legs, it revives delightfully. The whole package, though far from perfect, is pretty astounding. *50.2%*

Gordon & MacPhail Rare Old Glenury Royal 1984 (95.5) n23 t24 f23.5 b25 In the rare instances of the early 1980s I tasted a young Glenury, it was never this good and hardly looked up for 30 years in the cask. But this incredibly rare bottling of the malt, the best I have ever encountered from Glenury and distilled in the final days of its 117 year existence, stands its ground proudly and performs, unforgettably, the Last Post with magical honeyed notes... *46%.*

HAZELBURN *(see Springbank)*

HIGHLAND PARK

Highlands (Island–Orkney), 1795. Edrington. Working.

Highland Park 8 Years Old db **(87)** n22 t22 f22 b21. A journey back in time for some of us: this is the original distillery bottling of the 70s and 80s, bottles of which are still doing the rounds in obscure Japanese bars and specialist outlets such as the Whisky Exchange. *40%*

Highland Park 10 Year Old Ambassador's Choice db **(74)** n17.5 t20 f17.5 b19. Some of the casks are so badly sulphured, I'm surprised there hasn't been a diplomatic incident...*46%*

Highland Park Aged 12 Years db **(78)** n19 t21 f19 b19. Let's just hope that the choice of casks for this bottling as a freak. To be honest, this was one of my favourite whiskies of all time, one of my desert island drams, and I could weep. *40% WB16/048*

Highland Park Aged 15 Years db **(85)** n21 t22 f21 b21. Had to re-taste this several times, surprised as I was by just how relatively flat this was. A hill of honey forms the early delivery, but then... *40%*

Highland Park Earl Magnus Aged 15 Years 1st edition db **(76.5)** n20 t21 f17.5 b18. Tight and bitter. *52.6%. 5976 bottles.*

Highland Park Loki Aged 15 Years db **(96)** n24 t24 f23.5 b24.5 the weirdness of the heather apart, a bit of a trip back in time. A higher smoke ratio than the bottlings of more recent years which new converts to the distillery will be unfamiliar with, but reverting to the levels regularly found in the 1970s and 80s, probably right through to about 1993/94. Which is a very good thing because the secret of the peat at HP was that, as puffed out as it could be in the old days, it never interfered with the overall complexity, other than adding to it. Which is exactly the case here. Beyond excellent! *48.7%. Edrington.*

Highland Park 16 Years Old db **(88)** n23 t23 f20 b22. I tasted this the day it first came out at one of the Heathrow whisky shops. I thought it a bit flat and uninspiring. This sample, maybe from another bottling, is more impressive and showing true Highland Park colours, the finish apart. *40%. Exclusively available in Duty Free/Travel Retail.*

Highland Park Thor Aged 16 Years db **(87.5)** n22.5 t23.5 f19 b22.5. Now, from what I remember of my Norse gods, Thor was the God of Thunder. Which is a bit spooky seeing as hailstones are crashing down outside as I write this and lightning is striking overhead. Certainly a whisky built on power. Even taking into account the glitch in one or two of the casks, a dram to be savoured on delivery. *52.1%. 23,000 bottles.*

Highland Park Ice Edition Aged 17 Years db **(87) n22 t23 f21 b21.** The smoke drifts around until it finds some spices. Frustrating: you expect it to kick on but it stubbornly refuses to. Caramel and vanilla up front, then bitters out. *53.9%.*

Highland Park Aged 18 Years db **(95.5) n23.5 t24 f24 b24** If familiarity breeds contempt, then it has yet to happen between myself and HP 18. This is a must-have dram. I show it to ladies the world over to win their hearts, minds and tastebuds when it comes to whisky. And the more time I spend with it, the more I become aware and appreciative of its extraordinary consistency. The very latest bottlings have been astonishing, possibly because colouring has now been dropped, and wisely so. Why in any way reduce what is one of the world's great whisky experiences? Such has been the staggering consistency of this dram I have thought of late of promoting the distillery into the world's top three: only Ardbeg and Buffalo Trace have been bottling whisk(e)y of such quality over a wide range of ages in such metronomic fashion. Anyway, enough: a glass of something honeyed and dazzling calls... *43%*

Highland Park Aged 21 Years db **(82.5) n20.5 t22 f19 b21.** Good news and bad news. The good news is that they appear to have done away with the insane notion of reducing this to 40% abv. The bad news: a sulphured sherry butt has found its way into this bottling. *47.5%*

Highland Park Aged 25 Years db **(96) n24 t24 f24 b24** I am a relieved man: the finest HP 25 for a number of years which displays the distillery's unmistakable fingerprints with a pride bordering on arrogance. One of the most improved bottlings of the year: an emperor of a dram. *48.1%*

Highland Park Aged 30 Years db **(90) n22 t22.5 f23 b22.5** A very dramatic shift from the last bottling I tasted; this has taken a fruitier route. Sheer quality, though. *48.1%*

Highland Park 40 Years Old db **(90.5) n20.5 t22.5 f24 b23.5** Picking splinters from my nose with this one. Some of the casks used here have obviously choked on oak, and I feared the worst. But such is the brilliance of the resilience by being on the money with the honey, you can say only that it has pulled off an amazing feat with the peat. Sheer poetry... *48.3%*

Highland Park 50 Years Old dist Jan 60 db **(96.5) n24.5 t24 f24 b24** Old whiskies tend to react to unchartered territory as far as time in the oak is concerned in quite different ways. This grey beard has certainly given us a new slant. Nothing unique about the nose. But when one is usually confronted with those characteristics on the nose, what follows on the palate moves towards a reasonably predictable path. Not here. Truly unique – as it should be after all this time. *44.8%. sc. 275 bottles.*

Highland Park 2002 cask no. 3374-HCF064 db **(96) n23 t24.5 f24 b24.5** I have always through HP peaked at around 18 in mixed casks rather than 25. This is breathtaking to the point of whisky life changing and revels in its refined, complex sweetness to make a mockery of my theory. The nose apart, this has all the things that makes HP one of the world's great distilleries, and piles it on to an extent it has rarely been witnessed before. Such awesome beauty... *58.4%. sc. Bottled for Loch Fyne Whiskies.*

Highland Park 2006 cask no. 2132-HCF067 db **(91) n22.5 t23 f23 b22.5** You'd be hard pushed to recognise this as an HP unless you were told. Has many of the signature traits, but they don't click into place to create that unique style. An atypical HP, but typically delicious. *67%. sc. Bottled for The W Club.*

Highland Park Dark Origins db **(80) n19 t23 f18 b20.** Part of that Dark Origin must be cocoa, as there is an abundance of delicious high grade chocolate here. But the other part is not so much dark as yellow, as sulphur is around on the nose and finish in particular - and does plenty of damage. Genuinely disappointing to see one of the world's greatest distilleries refusing to play to its strengths and putting so much of its weight on its Achilles heel. *46.8%. ncf.*

Highland Park Earl Haakon db **(92) n22.5 t24 f22.5 b23.** A fabulous malt offering some of the best individual moments of the year. But appears to run out of steam about two thirds in. *54.9%. 3,300 bottles.*

Highland Park Einar db **(90.5) n23 t23 f22 b22.5** A curious style of HP which shows most of its usual traits but possesses an extra sharpness. *40% WB15/328*

Highland Park Freya 1st fill ex-bourbon casks db **(88.5) n22 t23 f21.5 b22.** The majestic honey on delivery makes up for some of the untidier moments. *52.10%.*

Highland Park King Christian db **(83.5) n22 t22.5 f18.5 b20.5.** A hefty malt with a massive fruit influence. But struggles for balance and to keep full control of the, ultimately, off-key grapey input. Despite the sub-standard finale, there is much to enjoy with the early malt-fruit battles on delivery that offer a weighty and buttery introduction to the diffused molasses and vanilla. But with the spice arrives the Achilles heel... *46.8%*

Highland Park Leif Eriksson bourbon and American oak db **(86) n22 t22 f21 b21.** The usual distillery traits have gone AWOL while all kinds of caramel notes have usurped them. That said, this has to be one of the softest drams you'll find. *40%. Edrington.*

Highland Park Ragnavald db (87.5) n21.5 t22 f22 b22. Thickset and muscular, this malt offers a slightly different type of earthiness to the usual HP. Even the malt has its moment in the sun. But the overall portrait hangs from the wall at a slight tilt... 45.05%

Highland Park Sigurd db (96) n23.5 t24.5 f23.5 b24.5 Breathtaking, star-studded and ridiculously complex reminder that this distillery is capable of serving up some of the best whisky the world can enjoy. 43%

Highland Park Svein db (87) n22 t22 f21.5 b21.5. A soft, friendly dram with good spice pick up. But rather too dependent on a tannin-toffee theme. 40% WB15/318

Highland Park Viking Soul Cask 13.5 Years Old 18 month sherry seasoned quarter cask finish, cask no. 700066, bott 2019 db (88.5) n22 t23.5 f21 b22 The quarter cask finish is a brave move to make after over 13 years of normality. And the extra oak really does punch through, and not always in a way that feels particularly relaxed or natural. The fruitiness arrives in sugary waves and enjoys a delightful spice flourish. But for an HP, the most rounded of all Scotland's malts, it feels a tad frantic. No faulting the fabulous delivery, though, which appears to have had the cocoa rammed forward with the grape ahead of time... 55.4%. nc ncf sc. 159 bottles. Bottled for MacAlabur.

⬦ **Artful Dodger Orkney Highland Park 14 Year Old 2004** ex-sherry butt, cask no. 18 (86.5) n22 t23 f20 b21.5 Less Artful Dodger than Jammy Dodger. The fruit envelops all aspects of this malt – on nose and delivery in particular. Deep vanilla tones hit back, as do the spices, but the dull finish brings an end to an intriguing passage of development. Perhaps by no means the worst sherry butt, but not the best, either. 58.8%. sc.

Fadandel.dk Orkney Aged 12 Years bourbon hogshead, cask no. 0001, dist 1 Sept 05, bott 26 May 18 (94.5) n23.5 t23.5 f23.5 b24 Fruity is kept secret on the label. However, this has the unique DNA of HP all over it! And if you think Heather Honey is a cliché when it comes to this distillery, then try this... 62.4%. sc. 333 bottles.

Fadandel.dk Orkney Aged 14 Years bourbon hogshead, cask no. 0008, dist 18 Aug 03, bott 25 May 18 (95.5) n23.5 t24.5 f23.5 b24 Further proof, were it needed, that the quality of HP whisky (if this is HP, which I have no doubt about) is not in question: it is just their appalling sherry butts which have been causing the problems. It needs a sublime bourbon cask like this to ram home the fact. 55.4%. sc. 342 bottles.

Fadandel.dk Orkney Aged 15 Years butt, dist 17 Sept 02, bott 18 Jan 19 (91.5) n23 t24 f21.5 b23 Intense heather honey core to this malt, but the more complex notes appear to be flattened a little by the cask type, which itself deposits a slight bitterness to the finish. But the nose and delivery are charming, with extra-intense barley and a near perfect proportion of sweetness to counter the oak. In fact, the delivery itself is truly memorable for the near perfection of its intensity, coupled with the honey's contribution. Good balancing spice, too. 58.6%. sc. 170 bottles.

⬦ **Gordon & MacPhail Connoisseurs Choice Highland Park Aged 30 Years** refill sherry butt, cask no. 1089, dist 7 Mar 89, bott 20 Mar 19 (86) n22 t22.5 f20.5 b21.5 Curious by HP standards – and probably even more curious by G&M's. When this sherry butt was first put into operation it came from a time when the quality of European oak was still very high. But, after the early, attractive vanillas peak, there is an untidy rumble to this, especially on the finish, which when accompanied by the lack of development suggests not all is well with the oak. There is a glossy feel, too, which first works in its favour, seemingly enveloping the lazy honey and vanilla. But then things go slightly askew, the same gloss acts like a shackle, refusing to allow the malt to find an escape route. A very curious HP, indeed. 51.1%. sc. 489 bottles.

The Perfect Fifth Highland Park 1987 cask no. 1531 (96.5) n24 pretty near perfect HP for its age, and one of the best examples of the distillery of that era I have nosed for a very long time. Slightly above average peat for a HP, which works perfectly in its favour. The usual heather honey has been skewed slightly by the heady mix of tannins and peat. The saltiness is profound, the oak a rich, spicy backbone. The sweetness is subtle and still honeyed, but more now a blend of Manuka and orange blossom. Truly magnificent! t24 Scotland's silkiest malt at its most silky. The bold smoke on arrival is caught in the velvet gloves of the lightly oiled barley sugar, a dark liquorice sweetness spreading as the oak makes its mark. The spices are prim, proper and just so, never moving out of their set orbit while the honey starts to make its long-awaited mark, bringing with it the light smoke; a quick surge of exotic fruit underlines the antiquity with aplomb; f24 long, increasingly smoky with the spices still teasing and forging a beautiful duet with the molassed sugars; the oak beats out an aged pulse but the phenols return to soften as well and entertain; b24.5 this is a malt whisky coming to the end of its life, like a star becomes a white dwarf before the end of its existence. In density is huge...and I mean gigantic. The oaks are about to explode...but the cask has been bottled in the nick of time where the balance is still near perfect. Fine margins...for a very fine whisky... 47.1%. sc.

Sansibar Whisky Highland Park 1999 (93.5) n23 t23.5 f23 b24 A steady, if unspectacular, HP quietly ticking all the right boxes. 49.1%.

The Whisky Embassy Highland Park Aged 14 Years cask no. 5017013, dist 2003, bott 2017 **(93.5) n23.5 t23.5 f23 b23.5** Almost identical in style to their 6993 cask, but without all the oaky flaws. The greater intensity and integration results in the smoke dovetailing with a richer, now heather honey, sweetness rather than being aloof. The lack of bitterness allows the story to be told without interruption. *53.8%. nc ncf sc.*

IMPERIAL

Speyside, 1897. Chivas Brothers. Silent.

Imperial Aged 15 Years "Special Distillery Bottling" db **(69) n17 t18 f17 b17.** At least one very poor cask, hot spirit and overly sweet. Apart from that it's wonderful. *46%*

⟫ **The Single Malts of Scotland Marriage Imperial 28 Year Old (80.5) n20.5 t21 f19 b20** For me, this is one of the most fascinating malts I will taste this year, 2020. Because 28 years ago I visited the chilly confines of this distillery quite often – and rarely found a new make that augured well for the future. The fact the distillery closed disappointed but didn't exactly surprise me. Here you can see why. The gluey nose is reminiscent of Littlemill in its last days, the delivery thin and tart. The finish, after it passes through some decent milk chocolate notes, is simply a wreck. This whisky may have soul, but there is no body...and that is why the blenders decided enough was enough. Usually the passing of three decades – or thereabouts – brings redemption to a failed distillery, Littlemill again being a case in point. Not here though. To be sampled simply as a whisky life experience rather than the expectation of great, or even particularly good, whisky. *40.88%.*

INCHGOWER

Speyside, 1872. Diageo. Working.

Inchgower 27 Year Old db **(93) n22.5 t24 f23 b23.5** Delicious and entertaining. Doesn't try to play the elegant old malt card. Instead gets stuck in with a rip-roaring attack on delivery, the fizzing spices burning deep and making the most of the light liquorice and molasses which has formed a thick-set partnership with the intense malt. The only hint of subtlety arrives towards the death as a little butterscotch tart allows a late juiciness from the barley free reign. Just love it! *43%. 8,544 bottles. Diageo Special Releases 2018.*

⟫ **Deer, Bear & Moose Inchgower Aged 22 Years** dist Sept 95, bott Dec 17 **(94.5) n23 t24 f23.5 b24** Inchgower in prime Jekyll and Hyde mode, at first the juicy, swashbuckling fruit pointing towards a malt half its age. Then, fascinatingly, a wave of tannins sweeps in bringing with it a salty, mildly earthy depth, as well as major spices... and suddenly the malt looks every bit its years. The layering on delivery is worth savouring, as it really relishes the old school griminess for a minute or two before moving into a sweeter marzipan richness with a seasidey saltiness burning into the piece. You never know what you are going to get from this distillery. But this is one of the most complete and complex versions for quite a while. A wonderful surprise. *52.1%. nc ncf sc. Flaviar & Friends.*

⟫ **Old Malt Cask Inchgower Aged 11 Years** Firkin cask, cask no. 16749, dist Jan 08, bott Mar 19 **(90.5) n22.5** the usual distillery heft and trademark untidiness, but with a dab of liquorice and chicory to beguile; **t23** huge! The weight is considerable and the molasses profound. A chewing whisky of the highest grade: lush, oily, and with ever deepening degrees of vanilla and dark sugars; **f22** slightly tangy, but a dollop of chocolate goes a long way to make amends; **b23** Firkin unbelievable: Inchgower at its most intense and startling. *50%. nc ncf sc. 59 bottles.*

INVERLEVEN

Lowland, 1938–1991. Demolished.

Deoch an Doras Inverleven 36 Years Old dist 1973 **(94.5) n24 t23.5 f23 b24** As light on the palate as a morning mist. This distillery just wasn't designed to make a malt of this antiquity, yet this is to the manor born. *48.85%. nc ncf. Chivas Brothers. 500 bottles.*

Gordon & MacPhail Private Collection Inverleven 1985 refill bourbon barrel, cask no. 562, bott 2018 **(96.5) n24 t24.5 f23.5 b24.5** I am still haunted by the day Inverleven distilled for the very last time, their manager telling me: "That's it, Jim. We're done." It was another shocking event: a great Lowland distillery which made a very consistent, malty, mildly fragile make and was absolutely excellent for blenders at about 5 years in decent second fill bourbons, and even better in firsts; and quite magnificent at about 8 years in both. Of course, the demise of Inverleven was the foretelling of the eventual closure of the unbettered Dumbarton grain distillery in which the malt complex was housed. But these were acts of whisky vandalism by a company, Allied Domecq, which never could get it right with the management of their single malts. This delicate and noble malt is a rare testimony to a distillery lost for all the wrong reasons. There is not a bum note, not a blemish. It is Lowland perfection and a whisky tragedy all rolled into one. *57.4%. 130 bottles.*

ISLE OF ARRAN

Highlands (Island–Arran), 1995. Isle of Arran Distillers. Working.

Isle of Arran Machrie Moor 5ᵗʰ Edition bott 2014 db **(91.5)** n22.5 t24 f22 b23 A few tired old bourbon barrels have taken the score down slightly on last year. But the spirit itself is nothing short of brilliant. 46% WB16/049

The Arran Malt 10 Year Old db **(87)** n22.5 t22.5 f20 b22. It has been a while since I last officially tasted this. If they are wiling to accept some friendly advice, I think the blenders should tone down on raising any fruit profile and concentrate on the malt, which is amongst the best in the business. 46%. nc ncf.

The Arran Malt 12 Years Old db **(85)** n21.5 t22 f20.5 b21 Hmmmm. Surprise one, this. There must be more than one bottling already of this. The first I tasted was perhaps slightly on the oaky side but otherwise intact and salt-honeyed where need be. This one has a bit of a tang: very drinkable, but definitely a less than brilliant cask around. 46%

The Arran Malt Aged 14 Years db **(89.5)** n22 t23.5 f21.5 b22.5. A superb whisky, but the evidence that there has been a subtle shift in emphasis, with the oak now taking too keen an interest, is easily attained. 46%. ncf.

The Arran Malt Aged 17 Years db **(91.5)** n23.5 t23.5 f21.5 b23 "Matured in the finest ex-Sherry casks" trills the back label. And, by and large, they are right. Maybe a single less than finest imparts the light furriness to the finish. But by present day sherry butt standards, a pretty outstanding effort. 46%. nc ncf. 9000 bottles. WB15/152

The Arran Malt Fino Sherry Cask Finish db **(82.5)** n21 t20 f21 b20.5. Pretty tight with the bitterness not being properly compensated for. 50%

⬦ **Acla Selection Island Edition Isle of Arran 22 Year Old** hogshead, dist 1996, bott 2019 **(86.5)** n22 t22 f21 b21.5 Punches slightly heavier than its strength and while the light heather honey tones impress, a dry, vaguely bitter, flourish to the oak detracts somewhat and closes down the conversation. 48.3%

Berry Bros & Rudd Arran 21 Years Old cask no. 370, dist 1996, bott 2018 **(96.5)** n24 t24 f24 b24.5. When my dear old friend Harold Currie built this distillery in the mid-1990s he wanted the spirit to be as close in style to Macallan as he could get it. So, when I selected the very first cuts for the very first distillation, it was Harold's wish I had I mind. This bottling was almost certainly made to the cutting points I chose and my only sadness is that Harold is no longer with us to enjoy his malt whisky coming of age. Though this is probably not from oloroso (or if it was, it was so old that very restrained fruit is imparted) – and that is just as well, as most early oloroso butts from the distillery are poor quality – it certainly matches the profile of Macallan of the same age matured in top end second fill bourbon. This is, unquestionably one of the single malt bottlings of the year. 46.4%. nc ncf sc.

Cask 88 Isle of Arran 22 Year Old dist 1997 **(73)** n19 t20 f16 b18 When a whisky turns up this colour (brown with a green tinge) in the lab you usually give it a very suspicious once-over. And here you'd have done it with good reason. 42.4%.

Golden Cask Arran Aged 21 Years cask no. CM240, dist 1996, bott 2017 **(94.5)** n23.5 t24 f23 b24 Impeccable Arran. 51.6%. sc. 254 bottles.

Single Cask Collection Arran 21 Years Old Platin Edition sherry edition **(88.5)** n22.5 t22.5 f21.5 b22 A mainly clean sherry butt doles out the fruit. 51%. sc.

W.W. Club AR.1 Arran Aged 11 Years American oak cask, cask no. 19, dist Oct 05, bott Feb 17 **(86.5)** n21.5 t22.5 f21 b21.5 Plenty of rich, creamy honey on delivery. And no little succulent malt, too. But a little too much tang towards the finish, confirming a quaver on the nose. 57.7%. sc. 321 bottles. William & Co. Spirits.

ISLE OF JURA

Highlands (Island–Jura), 1810. Whyte and Mackay. Working.

Isle Of Jura Aged 10 Years db **(79.5)** n19 t22 f19 b19.5. Perhaps a little livelier than before, but still miles short of where you might hope it to be. 40%

⬦ **Jura Aged 10 Years** American white oak bourbon barrels, aged Oloroso sherry butts, bott code: L0143 07 59 P/012028 db **(89.5)** n22.5 soft malt, sweet and a little lemon sherbet; t22 follows the nose by taking the softie route...only here goes into ultra-soft mode. Perhaps a little too much sweetness and caramel early on, but as that clears a light vanilla and raisin combination filters through; f22.5 decidedly toasty and dry. A little light molasses helps balance things; b22.5 the best part of 40 years ago I used to travel annually to Jura and stop at the hotel, the owner of which also being a director of the distillery next door. And every year I would bring back one of his hotel bottlings, complete with its label portraying a stag, usually ex-bourbon and sweet as a nut. It would be great if they could revert more towards a bottling which shewed the character of the distillery as starkly as that old hotel bottling did, as this appears to be hiding a great many things. That said, a more enjoyable Jura 10 than in the recent past: definitely on the up and worth watching. 40%.

⟨⟨⟨ **Jura Aged 12 Years** American white oak ex-bourbon barrels, aged Oloroso sherry cask finish, bott code: L80205 00:43 P/005956 db **(87.5) n22.5 t23 f20.5 b21.5** For the most part, this is an artful malt proudly portraying its coastal origins, with a sharp, malty saltiness creeping onto the nose and delivery in very respectable proportions. The mouthfeel is also a delight on entry, as is the rich chocolate fruit and nut middle. Just a shame that a rogue sherry cask has leaked some of the dreaded S element into the mix, which builds into a furry bitterness at the death. Mid Europeans devoid of the sulphur gene will devour this with joy. So much else to enjoy, though, especially that juicy delivery. I look forward to seeing the next bottling... 40%.

Isle Of Jura Aged 16 Years db **(90.5) n21.5 t23.5 t23 b23** A massive improvement, this time celebrating its salty, earthy heritage to good effect. The odd strange, less than harmonious note. But by far and away the most improved Jura for a long, long while. 40%

⟨⟨⟨ **Jura Aged 18 Years** American white oak ex-bourbon barrels and red wine casks, bott code: L0006 13:36 P/011235 db **(85.5) n21.5 t23.5 f19 b21.5** Although the nose is tight, almost mean, in its persona you are let half-fearing the worst, but wondering for the best. There is an outlandish outbreak of massive flavour on delivery, both the malt and fruit almost shrill in their proclamations of their intent. This is high juiciness in excelsis, the sugars crisp and full of grist and Demerara. And on the finish a slight chocolate note hovers, but then a degree of sulphur drifts in...as threatened by the nose. It is so frustrating when wine casks have needlessly and fatally been given the sulphur candle treatment. This has so many beautiful moments. But... 44%.

⟨⟨⟨ **Jura Aged 21 Years Tide** American white oak ex-bourbon barrels & virgin American oak casks db **(94) n23** initially quite bare and basic compared to the lightly smoked Time. But the layering of the gentle red sap more associated with young bourbon is quite a turn on...; **t23.5** a mix of treacle and vanilla make for an intense but surprisingly soft experience; **f23.5** light spices rumble over the growing caramels; dry and toasty but always in control...; delicate oils elongate the finale; **b24** not for the first time, caramel plays a big part in a Jura. But here it appears to be better weighted and structured thanks to greater tannin involvement. Pleasingly and impressively complex. 46.7%.

⟨⟨⟨ **Jura Aged 21 Years Time** American white oak ex-bourbon barrels & ex-peated malt casks db **(92) n23.5** the playful spice tweaks both your nose and that of the chunky tannin; the phenols offer an attractive deep base note; **t23.5** crystalised brown sugars formulate from the off, the tannins having a big say in matters. But it is those wisps of smoke that add structure and balance, seemingly tying together the crisper sweet notes and the earthier oakiness. Spices ping around with abandon; **f22** digestive biscuit dipped in mocha; **b23** alongside Tide, great to see Jura back offering us something that intrigues: a bit like the first Jura I ever tasted – on the island's hotel - nearly 40 years ago... 47.2%.

⟨⟨⟨ **Jura 1988** bott 2019 db **(91.5) n22** grape seemingly hangs off every atom, making for an initially tight, but eventually even fruitiness, once the oak makes its presence felt; the original spirit doesn't seem too great, but the cask influence is beautiful; **t23** the buzz of spice and tannin is soothed by the lushness and surprising sweetness offered by the wine. Spices filter through with just a little chocolate for company; **f23** long, oily... and anyone who fondly remembers Cadbury's Old Jamaica chocolate bars will be in for a treat; **b23.5** so unusually clean I wondered if this was a wine cask, almost certainly not, at work or just Demerara sugars off the oak working at their ultimate fruitiness. Or, most likely, both! 52.8%. nc ncf. 1,500 bottles.

⟨⟨⟨ **Jura 1989** American white oak ex-bourbon barrels, bott 2019 db **(83.5) n21 t22.5 f19 b21** None of the glitz and little of the balance displayed by the Two-One-Two, below. Not the most enticing of noses , though the piece rallies briefly on delivery as the intense malt is steered into position by excellent spice. Then it all unravels... 53.5%. nc ncf.

Jura One and All Aged 20 Years db **(83.5) n21 t22 f19.5 b21** A metallic tang to this. Nutty with tart, fruity borders but nothing to get excited about. Doesn't quite add up. 51%. nc ncf.

Jura One For The Road Aged 22 Years Pinot Noir finish db **(89) n23 t22.5 f21 b22** Enjoyable though ultimately a bit too straight and, just like the single road on Jura, goes nowhere... 47%. nc ncf.

Jura One For You db **(87.5) n22 t22.5 f21.5 b21.5** A straight up and down maltfest with a vaguely salty edge. Very pleasant in its own limited way, but don't spend too much time looking for complexity. 52.5%. nc ncf.

Jura Prophecy profoundly peated db **(90.5) n23.5 t23 f22 b22** Youthful, well made and I prophesy this will be one of Jura's top scorers of 2011... 46%

⟨⟨⟨ **Jura Special Wood Series French Oak** American white oak bourbon barrels, French oak cask finish, bott code: L9108 02:36 P/008522 db **(89) n22.5** the French oak appears to have brought with it French heather honey – Bruyère – to smarten this up and give the spices something to bounce against; **t23** soft delivery with an immediate malty charge. The honey also slowly materialises, though the tannins appear to have a little of the devil about them; **f21.5** just a tad untidy here and bitter. But the honey has made way for molasses; **b22** so much to enjoy here, but feel this is understrength for what it is trying to achieve, the oils breaking down too quickly and making the transition at the end a little too rugged. But a full-flavoured Jura as you have never quite seen her before! *42%*.

Jura Superstition db **(73.5)** n17 t19 f18 b18.5. I thought this could only improve. I was wrong. One to superstitiously avoid. *43%*

Jura Turas-Mara db **(82.5)** n20.5 t22 f19 b21. Some irresistible Jaffa Cake moments. *42%*.

◈ **Jura Two-One-Two** American white oak ex-bourbon barrels db **(90.5)** n23 the tannins are embroidered neatly into the lush, citrus-tinged barley; t22.5 busy on delivery – and even busier as the spices make their mark; again the oak holds all the cards and dictates, but the hickory and muscovado sugars work well together; f22 just bitters vaguely on the fade; b23 lets the tannins do the talking. And if anyone is buying this from a bar, say you'll have one, too... *47.5%. 6,000 bottles.*

◈ **Chapter 7 Jura 21 Year Old 1998** bourbon hogshead, cask no. 2144, dist Sept 98, bott Mar 20 **(87)** n22 t22.5 f21 b21.5 A first-rate bourbon cask goes a long way to seriously upping the complexity levels on this and ensuring a glorious honey theme throughout. The malt possesses a distinct nutty note from a distillate that isn't technically where it should be. *55.1%. sc. 284 bottles.*

The First Editions Jura Aged 12 Years 2006 sherry butt, cask no. 15182, bott 2018 **(86.5)** n21 t23 f21 b21.5 An exceptionally juicy bottling with attractively explosive malt on contact and the full gristy sugars still intact after a dozen years. The finish is thin and lacks any form of development. But the ultra salivating malt is an early treat. *58.9%. nc ncf sc. 267 bottles.*

Gleann Mór Isle of Jura Aged Over 20 Years (83.5) n20 t22 f20.5 b21 Not sure how a whisky of this kind of age can still be sporting a slight youthful, feinty note. The heat on the spirit also points towards a spirit rushed through the stills slightly. So, technically, not the greatest. But there is no faulting the enormity of the barley, helped slightly by the extra oils from the cut. *56.2%.*

Hepburn's Choice Jura 10 Years Old refill hogshead, dist 2008, bott 2018 **(85)** n21 t22 f20.5 b21.5 Clean, malty and simplistic. There is a bit of a tang at the death, but the barley sparkles despite the lack of illumination until that point. *46%. nc ncf sc. 334 bottles.*

Old Malt Cask Jura Aged 12 Years sherry butt, cask no. 15181, dist Apr 06, bott May 18 **(87)** n21.5 t22 f21.5 b22 A sister cask to the First Editions but, despite the extra dilution, the oils here have a greater say ensuring the finish has slightly more malty flesh. Youthful in part with a gristy spring to each barley-rich step. *50%. nc ncf sc. 312 bottles.*

KILCHOMAN
Islay, 2005. Kilchoman Distillery Co. Working.

Kilchoman 10 Years Old cask no. 150/2007, dist 20 Jul 07, bott 11 Jun 18 db **(96)** n24 t24 f23.5 b24.5 Has controlled the oils beautifully. Class in a glass. *56.5%. sc. 238 bottles. Bottled for The Whisky Shop.*

Kilchoman 10 Years Old 100% Islay cask no. 84/2008, dist 6 Mar 08, bott 19 Mar 18 db **(91)** n23.5 t23 f22 b22.5 Such is the high class of Kilchoman, even an exceptionally good malt on the whisky stage is not quite up to the distillery's normal performance. Not a bad place to be... *53.2%. sc. 239 bottles. Bottled for Loch Fyne Whiskies.*

Kilchoman 12 Years Old bourbon cask, cask no. 36/2006, dist 4 May 06, bott 21 Jun 18 db **(93.5)** n23.5 t23.5 f23 b23.5 High grade malt taking a slightly different course from this distillery's normal style. *56.9%. sc. 228 bottles. Bottled for Loch Fyne Whiskies.*

Kilchoman Private Cask Release bourbon cask, cask no. 431/2007, dist 13 Dec 07, bott 26 Feb 18 db **(96.5)** n24.5 t24 f24 b24.5 Someone fell on their feet when they bought this cask: holy crap, this is seriously good whisky! *57.2%. sc. Bottled exclusively for The Whisky Club.*

KINCLAITH
Lowlands, 1957–1975. Closed. Dismantled.

Mo Ór Collection Kinclaith 1969 41 Years Old first fill bourbon hogshead, cask no. 301453A, dist 28 May 69, bott 29 Oct 10 **(85.5)** n22 t22 f20.5 b21. Hangs on gamely to the last vestiges of life, though the oak, without being overtly aggressive, is squeezing all the breath of out of it. *46%. nc ncf sc. Release No. 2. The Whisky Talker. 164 bottles.*

KINGSBARNS
Lowland, 2014. Wemyss. Working.

Kingsbarns 2 Year Old Spirit Drink 1st fill ex-bourbon barrels db **(94)** n23 t23.5 f24 b23.5 Thought I'd bring up my 1,200th tasting note for the 2019 Whisky Bible with this maturing malt from Kingsbarns. It was an inspired choice. For although the youth is more than apparent – as it should be! – there is a surprising degree of complexity to this and balances out far better than most two year olds. For a start, the distillate was beautifully created with the cut points spot on, seemingly clean enough or the malt to flourish, but with a broadness to allow complexity to develop. Even on the nose a wonderful Cadbury's hazelnut and milk chocolate promises good things ahead and you are not remotely disappointed as the barley strikes up proudly before marzipan and mocha make their mark. Delicious! *62.8%. 1,800 bottles.*

◆ **Kingsbarns Dream to Dram** db (**94**) **n23.5** a mix of youthful charm and more relaxed maturity gives the malt a nuanced appeal. But the barley is so rich, you feel that you have just picked it from a field, dank after a late summer rain, and crushed it in your hands, even before malting. Green and clean; **t24** salivating, but not in the sharp way I was expecting from the nose. Instead a mashing of icing sugars and fresh barley mix with the light oils from the distillate to provide a seemingly simple and beautifully effacing lead. But as you concentrate, you realise so much good is happening in there; **f23** just a little tanginess as the casks and grain have not quite managed to align quite to perfection. But still no faulting the vanilla and barley fade; **b23.5** just too ridiculously good for a new distillery. The malt really does make this a Dram of Dreams, too. And if this were not a single malt, blenders would be falling over themselves to use as top dressing in a blend. So simple. Yet sublime. *46%.*

◆ **Kingsbarns Founder's Reserve #1** American oak bourbon barrel, dist 2015, bott 2018 db (**93.5**) **n23.5** no age. But, my word! The intensity of the barley is startling and there is tannin enough to ensure this is no one horse race; **t23.5** only excellent American oak can galvanise malt in this way, helping it to really ratchet up the intensity, so there is a stunning purity to help settle the semi-hidden sharp, metallic notes of a new still at work, **f23** long with very beautifully judged oils from an excellent cut. The oak has grace enough to add a little vanilla and custard without taking away from the naked charm of the barley itself; **b23.5** you really can't ask for much more from a three-year-old malt. There are no new makey signs here, though there is always the feel of a little youthful exuberance. Superbly distilled and excellently matured. And enough muscle around the spice to suggest this could have matured for a great many more years. A fledgling distillery heading in the right direction and certainly one to watch. And a perfect choice for the Whisky Bible 2021's 1,200th whisky of the year... *62.1%.*

◆ **Kingsbarns Founder's Reserve #2** STR barriques, dist 2016, bott 2019 db (**93**) **n23.5** there is a buzz from the barrique: a nose-pinching, fruit-clipped spice which for a while distracts you from the beautifully distilled firmness of the malt. Even the lightest phenol drifts around...; **t23.5** eye-wateringly sharp work from the STRs which gang up and punch your taste buds into submission. The barley then flies forth with a volley of its own, but can't entirely make itself heard above the impact of the barriques; **f23** fruit chocolate with barley sugar and vanilla; **b23** as usual the STRs force their somewhat inelegant, abrasive but mouth-filling will on the whisky. Never match a great bourbon cask for sheer panache and heart-winning charm, but sometimes, like here, for eye-watering effect they have no equal. Oh, here's a little trick for you I have been carrying out for the last decade or so: to get the full flavour from STR-matured malt, leave in a tasting glass for three or four days with a watch lid over the top. This softens the whisky into a much more sensual dram and the malt – and therefore the base characteristic of the distillate - has a far bigger say in proceedings. If you add water very slightly to reduce strength and leave, you don't get anything like the same results or complexity. Try it. But as for this bottling... Wow! What fun! And such high class, too... *61.1%.*

KNOCKANDO
Speyside, 1898. Diageo. Working.

Knockando Aged 12 Years bott code: L7229CM000 db (**82**) **n20 t22.5 f19 b20.5** My dear, late friend and mentor Jim Milne was for a very long time J&B blender and for decades this malt came under his clever jurisdiction. It was Jim who persuaded me, over a quarter of a century ago now, to publish my views on whisky, something I felt I was underqualified to do. He vehemently disagreed, so I took his advice and the rest, as they say, is history. I knew Jim's work intimately, so I know he would not be happy with his beloved Knockando in this incarnation. His Knockando was dry, making the most of the interaction between bourbon cask and delicate malt. This is sweet and, worse still, sulphur tarnished by the sherry: I doubt he would ever let grape get this kind of grip, thus negating the distillery's fragile style. Some lovely moments here for sure. But just too fleeting. *43%.*

◆ **Knockando Aged 18 Years** dist 1998, bott code: L9038CM001 db (**94**) **n23.5** malt. To the power of malt...; **t24** this barley boasts a malty intensity that is rare to match in pure atomic mass. Dense, intense, sharp, full...just sheer barley...concentrated...; **f23** still juicy to the end. Malty and spicy fade..; **b23.5** nowhere near the charm and complexity of the 21-year-old. But, my word! This has a malt intensity that is hard to match elsewhere. However, at this age you expect the casks to making a difference. But, no. The malt is in total control. Beautiful for sure. But nowhere near the overall complexity and joy of the 21-y-o... *43%.*

⟐ **Knockando Aged 21 Years Master Reserve** dist 1994, bott code: L9081CM001 db (**96.5**) **n24** this is how a Speyside at this age should be: the malt is firm yet lively enough to allow the sugars a controlled, crystalline attachment; **t24** almost beautiful enough to bring a tear to my eye. My mentor, longtime Knockando blender Jim Milne, adored fresh, juicy barley at full salivation (a la...Glen Spey) ...and he particularly appreciated the solemnity and gravitas of the Knockando malt. This appears to have both. The salivation levels are something to be almost astonished at; **f24** the malt rumbles on with a high degree of class and continued salivation in the way that it attaches to the oaky vanillas without demur. But then moves into a richer, more chocolate infested world, the barley never for a moment straying from the path, the spices never for amount raising a voice above a soft grrrr...; **b24.5** some 30 years ago I was on the original J&B training team and Knockando (I think as a 12-year-old) was used in the programme, where I would compare this against the peated malts of Islay. The Knockando I had known and worked with for many years was a bone-crushingly dry dram. Though older, this is alive and fresh. And, frankly, a delightful surprise. The 25-year-old, those three decades ago, had far more tannin per annum spent in cask in its make up and even drier...though I remember marching my students from the Craigellachie Hotel to the River Spey as the mid-summer solstice sun was rising to drink the whisky beside the fast-running waters with which it was rightfully associated. I still get letters and emails from those who experience that spectacular awakening of the whisky spirit in our souls to this very day... This is a much fresher incarnation of that reverential aged malt of the late 1980s and early '90s. And, I have to say...a little bit better,... Indeed, I am soon to embark on my 1,100th whisky of the 2021 Bible. And I cannot think of a better, more complete, single malt so far... 100% sulphur free..100% barley rich... 100% a treasure... 43%. 🍷

Knockando 1990 db (**83**) **n21 t22 f20 b20.** The most fruity Knockando I've come across with some attractive salty notes. Dry, but a little extra malty sweetness these days. 40%

KNOCKDHU

Speyside, 1894. Inver House Distillers. Working.

AnCnoc 12 Year Old db (**94.5**) **n24 t23 f23.5 b24.5** A more complete or confident Speyside-style malt you are unlikely to find. Shimmers with everything that is great about Scotch whisky... always a reliable dram, but this is stupendous. 40%

⟐ **anCnoc 12 Years Old** bott code: L19/051 R19/5082 IB db (**94**) **n23.5** green banana and lucid barley. Spices flicker and glimmer...; **t23.5** teeming barley, layered in both sweetness and intensity: there is a chewy fatness containing the juicier sugars, then a more gristy side mingling with the spice; **f23** malty to a fault, just a little duller than of yore. Heavier caramels mingle with the slightly bitter tannins; **b24** remains one of the truly beautiful, largely undiscovered great malts of Scotland. At 46% and with other minor technical adjustments, this could be a major award winner... 40%

AnCnoc 16 Years Old db (**91.5**) **n22 t23.5 f23 b23** Unquestionably the spiciest AnCnoc of all time. Has this distillery been moved to the coast..? 46%

AnCnoc 18 Years Old db (**88.5**) **n22.5 t23 f21 b22** Cleaner sherry at work here. But again, the contours of the malt have been flattened out badly. 46%. nc ncf.

⟐ **anCnoc 18 Years Old** bott code: L19/052 R19/5084 IB db (**85**) **n22 t22 f20 b21** Even one sherry butt containing sulphur in a malt as delicate as anCnoc has consequences. And these can be found on the light furry nibble on the tongue towards the end. A shame, as I had selected this as sample number 1,100 on my home-straight for the 2021 Bible. Has plenty of its old zest and brilliance, for those biologically unable to detect sulphur. 46%.

AnCnoc 22 Year Old db (**87**) **n22 t21.5 f22 b21.5.** Often a malt which blossoms before being a teenager, as does the fruits of Knockdhu; struggles to cope comfortably with the inevitable oakiness of old age. Here is such a case. 46%. Inverhouse Distillers.

AnCnoc 24 Years Old db (**94**) **n23 t24.5 f22.5 b24** Big, broad-shouldered malt which carries a lot of weight but hardly veers away from the massively fruity path. For sherry loving whisky drinkers everywhere... 46%. nc ncf.

AnCnoc 30 Years Old db (**85**) **n21 t23 f19 b22.** Seat-of-the-pants whisky that is just on the turn. Still has a twinkle in the eye, though. 49%

AnCnoc 35 Years Old bourbon and sherry casks db (**88**) **n22.5t22 f21.5 b22.** The usual big barley sheen has dulled with time here. Some attractive cocoa notes do compensate. 44.3%. nc ncf.

AnCnoc 1999 db (**95.5**) **n24 t24 f23.5 b24** I noticed as I was putting the bottle away that on their back label their description reads: "Colour: soft, very aromatic with a hint of honey and lemon in the foreground" and "Nose: amber with a slight yellow hue." Which would make this malt pretty unique. But this is worth getting for far more than just the collectors' item typo: this is brilliant whisky – one of their best vintage malts for a very long time. In fact, one of their best ever bottlings...period.46%. nc ncf. WB15/160

AnCnoc 2002 bott Mar 17, bott code: L17/089 R17/5104 IB db **(86) n21.5 t23 f20.5 b21** Overall, it is enjoyable and well spiced, but a mushy, tangy, untidy finish shows up the failings of the odd cask used. This is a distillery whose spirit yearns for ex-bourbon so its stunning naked form can be worshipped, loved and salivated over. 46%.

AnCnoc Barrow 13.5 ppm phenols db **(88) n22 t21 f23 b22** A quite peculiar Knockdhu. The usual subtle richness of texture is curiously absent. As are friendly sugars. The strange angles of the phenols fascinate, however. 46%. nc ncf. Exclusive to travel retail.

AnCnoc Blas db **(67) n16 t18 f16 b17.** Blast! Great chocolate. Shame about the sulphur.... 54%. nc ncf.

AnCnoc Black Hill Reserve db **(81) n20 t22 f19 b20.** The furriness threatened on the nose and realised at the finish does this great distillery no favours at all. 46%. nc ncf.

AnCnoc Cutter 20.5 ppm phenols db **(96.5) n24 t24 f24 b24.5** Brilliant! An adjective I am far more used to associating with anCnoc than some of the others I have had to use this year. The most Ardbeg-esque mainland malt I have ever encountered. 46%. nc ncf.

AnCnoc Peatheart batch no. 1, 40ppm, bott code: L17/301 R17/5394 db **(91.5) n22 t23.5 f23 b23** Won't be long before Peatheart becomes the peataholics' sweetheart. Curiously underperforming nose, but makes amends in style on the palate. 46%.

AnCnoc Rùdhan bott code: L16/273 R16/5391 db **(94.5) n24 t23.5 f23.5 b24** Hard to imagine a mainland Scottish distillery producing a more complex, elegant and wholly ingratiating peated malt... What a gem this is! 46%.

AnCnoc Rutter 11 ppm phenols db **(96.5) n24.5 t24.5 f23.5 b24** I remember vividly, at this great distillery's Centenary party exactly 20 years ago this summer, mentioning to the then distillery manager that I thought that the style of the malt produced at Knockdhu was perfectly geared to make a lightly malted peat along the lines of its neighbour, Ardmore. Only for a few weeks of the year I ventured. I'm pretty certain this malt was not a result of that observation, but it is heartening to see that my instincts were right: it's a sensation! 46%. ncf nc. WB15/320

LADYBURN

Lowlands, 1966–2000. William Grant & Sons. Closed.

Mo Òr Collection Rare Ayrshire 1974 36 Years Old first fill bourbon barrel, cask no. 2608, dist 10 May 74, bott 1 Nov 11 db **(89) n22 t23.5 f22 b22.5.** I had a feeling it'd be this distillery when I saw the title on the label... it couldn't be much else! Fascinating to think that I was in final countdown for my 'O' levels when this was made. It appears to have dealt with the passing years better than I have. Even so, I had not been prepared for this. For years during the very early 1990s Grant's blender David Stewart sent me samples of this stuff and it was, to put it mildly, not great. Some were the oakiest malt I ever tasted in my life. And, to compound matters further, the distillery's own bottling was truly awful. But this cask has re-written history. 46%. nc ncf sc. Release No. 4. The Whisky Talker. 261 bottles.

LAGAVULIN

Islay, 1816. Diageo. Working.

Lagavulin Aged 8 Years bott code: L7285CM013 db **(95.5) n25 t23.5 f23 b24.5** Having gone from the colouring-spoiled Cardhu to this chardonnay-hued Lagavulin in all its bourbon cask nakedness, you have to wonder: why don't they do this for all their whiskies. This was the age I first tasted Lagavulin possibly the best part of 40 years ago. It was love at first flight, and my passions – with the whisky in this beautifully natural form, though not as heavily peated now as then – have not been remotely doused. 48%.

Lagavulin Aged 12 Years bott 2017, bott code: L7089CM000 db **(94) n23.5 t23.5 f23 b24** When I first tasted Lagavulin at this age, the phenol levels were around the 50ppm mark and not the present day 35. That meant the finish offered just a little extra Islay. Even so, I challenge you not to adore this. 56.5%.

Lagavulin Aged 12 Years bott 2018, bott code: L8072CM008 db **(96) n24 t24 f23.5 b24.5** Technically, from a distilling perspective, borderline perfection. From a maturation one, slightly weaker for, although the bourbon casks give you the clearest view possible of the brilliance of the spirit, a very slight late bitterness just breaks the spell. Even so, we are talking Islay at its most truly classic. 57.8%.

Lagavulin 12 Year Old refill American oak hogsheads db **(96) n24.5 t24 f23.5 b24** I think whisky like this was invented by the whisky gods to be experienced at this full strength. Even people who do not regard themselves as peat lovers are likely to be seduced by this one. Talk about controlled power.... 56.5%. Diageo Special Releases 2017.

Lagavulin 16 Years Old db **(95) n24 t24 f23 b24** Although I have enjoyed this whisky countless times socially, it is the first time for a while I have dragged it into the Tasting Room for professional analysis for the Bible. If anyone has noticed a slight change in Lagavulin, they would be right. The peat remains profound but much more delicate than before, while the oils appear to have receded. A different shape and weight dispersal for sure. But the sky-high quality remains just the same. *43%*

Game of Thrones Lagavulin 9 Year Old House Lannister db (89.5) n22 t23.5 f21.5 b22.5 Lagavulin as I have never seen it before, the phenols being kept on a tight leash. *46%.*

◇ **Cadenhead's Lagavulin 11 Year Old** dist 2007 (96) n24 t24 f23.5 b24.5 If you are going to celebrate an anniversary, then why not pick one of the greatest distilleries in the world, choose a cask from one of its optimum ages and then make sure it is about as honest and accurate a picture of that distillery that a blender could hope for? Well, that's what's happened here. Just look at that the grist on that nose, yet as the phenols swirl around there is no mistaking the barley, either. Then, on the palate, the way in which the peat radiates around the mouth as though in slow motion, a burst of barley juice here, light liquorice there. And smoke, so stunningly controlled, everywhere. Congratulations on your anniversary. And also on this glorious, to-die-for Lagavulin. *45%. 348 bottles. 10th Anniversary of Cadenhead Switzerland bottling.*

LAPHROAIG
Islay, 1815. Beam Suntory. Working.

Laphroaig 10 Years Old db (90) n24 t23 f20.5 b22.5 Has reverted back slightly towards a heavier style in more recent bottling, though I would like to see that old oomph at the very death. Even so, this is, indisputably, a classic whisky. The favourite of Prince Charles apparently: he will make a wise judge... *40%*

Laphroaig 10 Year Old bott code: L80099MB1 db (94) n23.5 t23.5 f23.5 b24 An essay in voluptuousness. The oils speak volumes here, gathering the two-toned phenols and landing them in all corners of the palate and ensuring they stick there. The iodine kick off on the nose is like a salty trademark, the balance between the sootier phenols and juicer Demera notes a joy to experience. The finish is not so much enormous as controlled and long, with a sublime degree of mocha moving in for the last blissful moments. Glorious. Still, after all these years... *40%.*

◇ **Laphroaig 10 Year Old** bott code: L8 831 SB1 db (95) n24 just like Laphroaig: dry, even confident peat but always with that threat of sugars. Gristy, but not so gristy that the tannins don't have a balancing say. Salty and seaweedy...or is that just a romantic fancy...? t23.5 gentle oils arrive immediately on delivery, coating the palate to ensure the light, sooty dryness to take its seat in comfort while delicate leather honey tone offers just the right sweetness required for balance; f23.5 so long and so beautifully nuanced as the smoke takes varying shapes and weights, the smoke drifting from soot to cocoa effortlessly; b24 so consistent is the Laphroaig 10, that this is one of the whiskies I test myself each day with to check that my nose and palate are on song. Having done this for the last 15 years or so, I think I can recognise whether a particular bottling from this distillery is up to scratch or not. Just a word of caution: their back label recommends that you add a splash of cool water to this whisky. I thoroughly recommend you do absolutely nothing of the sort. Laphroaig is served best by the Murray Method when its untold brilliance can be seen in its myriad layers. As an experiment, I have added cool water as they suggest – and it shrinks the whisky dramatically and breaks up the oils and sugars which are then lost to us. Please, never murder this fabulous whisky so cold-bloodedly. Oh, and having tasted a few score of Laphroaig 10s over the last 40 years or so, have to say this is bang up there with the very best: it is certainly among the most complex. *40%.*

Laphroaig 10 Years Old Original Cask Strength db (92) n22 t24 f23 b23 Caramel apart, this is much truer to form than one or two or more recent bottlings, aided by the fresh, gristy sweetness and explosive spices. Wonderful! *55.7%*

Laphroaig 12 Year Old 2005 bott 2017 db (91.5) n21.5 t23.5 f23 b23.5 Here we go: one of the exceptions in whisky that proves the rule. I have long wailed about the usage of PX cask and peaty malt together. And from the nose, you think your case will be won again, for here is another example of one giant nullifying another: both the smoke and fruit cancelling the other out. Yet, confound it, the delivery shows signs of proving me wrong and the finish continues in the same fashion. For once a PX cask is allowing the peat to breathe and sing. And what's more itself kick up a juicy encore. Beyond the nose a PX and smoky giant that walks tall. Who would have thought...? *55.3%. Selected for CWS.*

Laphroaig 18 Years Old db (94) n24 t23.5 f23 b23.5 This is Laphroaig's replacement to the woefully inadequate and gutless 15-year-old. And talk about taking a giant step in the right direction. Absolutely brimming with character and panache, from the first molecules escaping the bottle as you pour to the very final ember dying on the middle of your tongue. *48%*

Laphroaig Aged 27 Years dist Oct 88 to Nov 89, bott Mar 17, bott code: L7062VB1 db (96.5) n24.5 t24 f23.5 b24.5 The 27 passing years and the added interference of fresh ex-bourbon barrels and quarter casks has taken its toll on the potency of the peat. Instead of Laphroaig pulsing with its renowned style of sea-soaked phenols, we are now faced with a dram which is more than content to allow age and gentility to be the guiding hand; so now less febrile and more cerebral. Such an honour to taste whiskies of this extraordinary yet understated magnitude. I can think of no other presently available whisky which so eloquently demonstrates that you don't have to stand a spoon up in the peat for the phenols to have such a vital input. *41.7%. ncf.*

Laphroaig Aged 30 Years db **(94)** n24 t23 f23 b24. The best Laphroaig of all time? Nope, because the 40-y-o is perhaps better still... just. However, Laphroaig of this subtlety and charm gives even the very finest Ardbeg a run for its money. A sheer treat that should be bottled at greater strength. *43%*

Laphroaig Aged 40 Years db **(94)** n23 t24 f23 b24. Mind-blowing. A malt that defies all logic and theory to be in this kind of shape at such age. The Jane Fonda of Islay whisky. *43%*

Laphroaig The 1815 Legacy Edition bott code: L7059VB1 2070 db **(92.5)** n24 t24 f21 b23.5 a sherry butt away from one of the best new whiskies of the year. *48%. Travel Retail Exclusive.*

Laphroaig Au Cuan Mòr db **(95)** n24 t24 f23 b24 You don't need to squint at the back label to be told that first fill bourbon barrels are at work here: this is where Kentucky, Jerez and Islay merges with breath-taking ease and harmony. *48%. Travel retail exclusive.*

Laphroaig Brodir Port Wood Finish bott code: L6157MB1 db **(91.5)** n24 probably one of the most old-fashioned Islay warehouse aromas I have ever encountered: that incomparable mix of smoke, oak and grape hanging thickly in a moist, salty air..; **t22** the usual gristy sugars have been silenced by the intense, moody fruit; **f23** much better balance late on as a little liquorice and treacle joins the clouds of phenols to ensure complexity; **b22.5** this is a big Laphroaig at its most brooding and taciturn. Not for when you are at your most frivolous. *48%.*

Laphroaig Four Oak bott code: L6327VB1 2359 db **(88)** n22 t22.5 f21.5 b22 Attractive, but the smoke seems a little in awe of the oak as it is unusually quiet. *40%. Travel Retail Exclusive.*

Laphroaig Lore db **(94)** n23.5 t24 f23 b23.5 Seeing how much I adore this distillery – and treasure my near 40 years of tasting its exceptional malt and visiting its astonishing home – I left this to become my 750th new whisky for the 2016 Whisky Bible. "Our richest expression ever" the label promised. It isn't. Big, fat and chunky? Tick. Bounding with phenols? Yep. Enjoyable? Aye! Richest expression ever. Nah. Not quite. Still, a friendly beast worth cuddling up with. And, whatever they say on the label, this is a stunner! *48%. ncf.*

Laphroaig Lore bott code: L7229VB1 db **(96)** n23.5 t24 f24 b24.5 Laphroaig how I've never quite seen it before – and we are talking some 40 years of intimately studying this malt: truly a lore unto itself... *48%.*

Laphroaig PX Cask bourbon, quarter and Pedro Ximenez casks db **(96)** n23.5 t24.5 f24 b24. I get the feeling that this is a breathtaking success despite the inclusion of Pedro Ximenez casks. This ultra sweet wine is often paired with smoky malt, often with disastrous consequences. Here it has worked, but only because the PX has been controlled itself by absolutely outstanding oak. And the ability of the smoke to take on several roles and personas simultaneously. A quite beautiful whisky and unquestionably one of the great malts of the year...in spite of itself. *48%. Travel Retail exclusive.*

Laphroaig Quarter Cask db **(96)** n23 t24 f24 b25 A great distillery back to its awesome, if a little sweet, self. Layer upon layer of sexed-up peatiness. The previous bottling just needed a little extra complexity on the nose for this to hit mega malt status. Now it has been achieved... *48%*

⬦ **Laphroaig Quarter Cask** bott code: L8268 db **(93)** n23 the tamest nose from this expression ever. The phenols are polite, the tannins are wimps. Lovely light lime blossom honey joins the well-behaved smoke. But on a Quarter Cask...? **t23.5** so soft, as a cushion of vanillas gives the phenols the most yielding of greetings. Honey abounds everywhere and saunters about the palate largely unchallenged. Again, as on the nose, the oak is missing in action...; **f23** just a playful little lightly smoked vanilla puffball...; **b23.5** Laphroaig Quarter Cask: where is thy sting? Easily the most strangely subdued bottlings of this great malt I have ever encountered. Make no mistake: this is still a lovely dram in its own right, but just not what I expected – or now demand – from this Islay classic. *48%. ncf.*

Laphroaig Select db **(89)** n22 t22 f23 b22 Missed a trick by not being unchillfiltered at 46%. An après-taste squint at the back label revealed some virgin oak casks had been used here, which explains much! *40%. WB15/117*

Laphroaig Triple Wood ex-bourbon, quarter and European oak casks db **(86)** n21 t21.5 f21.5 b21. A pleasing and formidable dram. But one where the peat takes perhaps just too much of a back seat. Or, rather, is somewhat neutralised to the point of directional loss. The sugars, driven home by the heavy weight of oak, help give the whisky a gloss almost unrecognisable for this distillery. Even so, an attractive whisky in many ways. *48%. ncf.*

Carn Mor Laphroaig 8 Year Old 2010 hogshead **(95)** n23.5 t24 f23.5 b24 Oh, god! How I love this!! Young Laphroaig just being allowed to be itself...! And at a criminally overlooked age for this kind of south east coast Islay. What a classic! *63.4%. sc. Exclusive to The Whisky Barrel.*

Drams by Dramtime Williamson Laphroaig 8 Year Old 2011 (93) n23 t23.5 f23 b23.5 I know people who will not touch a Scotch whisky unless it displays an age of 12 as an absolute minimum. A dram like this reveals the folly of their ways, as here we get the chance to see Laphroaig unplugged and enjoying its freedom before being cloaked in oak. Yes, there is a youthfulness to this but more than compensated for by the vibrant phenols at their most unrestrained. And the sheer fun of allowing an unfettered Islay, which has been quite beautifully made, free range over your taste buds. Most surprising is the degree of salt in the mix, which goes about intensifying the grist, smoke and light tannins. Give me a stunningly made youngster over an oldie in a dodgy cask any day. Beautiful. 59%.

The First Editions Laphroaig Aged 13 Years 2005 refill hogshead, cask no. 15534, bott 2018 (90) n22 t23 f22.5 b22.5 Charmingly understated, but never loses its distillery identity. 52.5%. nc ncf sc. 332 bottles.

The First Editions Laphroaig Aged 18 Years 2000 refill hogshead, cask no. 15530, bott 2018 (87.5) n22.5 t22 f21 b22 Sports that unmistakable, unique, "Allied Domecq" bitterness at the very death. But doesn't entirely subtract from the bold anthracite and peat nose, nor the Manuka honey on the friendly delivery. 48.8%. nc ncf sc. 204 bottles.

Gleann Mór Laphroaig Aged Over 21 Years (91) n23 t23 f22 b23 A pleasing sweet and dry interplay impresses most in this charming and spicy bottling. Some impressive coal tar on the nose, though the soot ensures a serious depth to the dryness, both on nose and finish. The spices refuse to act their age as does the excellent Manuka honey strand which doesn't just counter the phenols but actually cocks a snook at them. Great late night imbibing... 56.3%.

LINKWOOD

Speyside, 1820. Diageo. Working.

Linkwood 12 Years Old db (94.5) n23.5 t24 f23 b24 Possibly the most improved distillery bottling in recent times. Having gone through a period of dreadful casks, it appears to have come through to the other side very much on top and close to how some of us remember it a quarter of a century ago. Sublime malt: one of the most glittering gems in the Diageo crown. 43%

Berry Bros & Rudd Linkwood 12 Years Old cask no. 102, dist 2006, bott 2018 (91) n22.5 t22.5 f23 b23 Crumbs! Plays the austere Speysider with panache. 46%. nc ncf sc.

Fadandel.dk Linkwood 10 Year Old hogshead, cask no. 306465, dist 18 Nov 08, bott 5 Jun 19 (91) n22.5 t23 f22.5 b23 The sharpness on the nose could cut; the bite on the palate could leave some serious marks. This is Linkwood unleashed, maturing in a cask which allows the malt free reign and ensures it is gilded in chocolate from the midpoints onwards. Younger than its years, the grist dishes out some delightful icing sugar notes as well a delicate ulmo honey ones. The oak moves in with the cocoa and the barley does nothing to prevent it. Simple. But often simplicity works.... 59.4%. sc. 34 bottles.

Fadandel.dk Linkwood 11 Year Old 8 months finish in a 1st fill Oloroso sherry octave, cask no. 306465A (88.5) n22 t22.5 f22 b22 A perfectly sound cask with no off notes and even offering cherry blossom on the nose. Perhaps, though, the oloroso is just a little too demanding of the malt which is unable to match its bravado. The result is an enjoyable but slightly one-dimensional sherry-heavy offering, full of peppers and pep. Just not quite nuanced enough for greatness. Oh! How about that! Just as I was about push the button to send this to my Editor I noticed that the cask above is this but without the sherry. Well, as I have repeatedly said in these pages over the last 17 years: in whisky less can so often mean so much more... 57.8%. sc. 69 bottles.

Scyfion Choice Linkwood 2001 Madrasa cask finished, bott 2018 (87) n21.5 t22 f21.5 b22 A bit hefty on the oak as it appears to be missing the usual malty back up. Instead a wafer thin fruit veneer holds everything in place, except the spices which escape at will. Enjoyable. 46%. nc ncf sc. 294 bottles.

The Single Malts of Scotland Reserve Cask Linkwood 12 Year Old (92.5) n23 t23 f23 b23.5 Linkwood at its fruitiest and flightiest, concentrating on a lightness of touch that sets out to charm – and does! Lime blossom honey abounds, mixing liberally with the grassy barley to accentuate the malt while giving the limited oakiness an extra boost, too. It is so light you can even pick a molecule or two of peat here and there, though to say weight is added is stretching the imagination. The salivating never lets up from first mouthful to finish, making this joyous malt perfect for summer evenings. A minor little classic, this. 48%.

LITTLEMILL

Lowland, 1772. Loch Lomond Distillers. Demolished.

Littlemill 21 Year Old 2nd Release bourbon cask db (87) n22 t21.5 f21.5 b22. So thin you expect it to fragment into a zillion pieces on the palate. But the improvement on this as a new make almost defies belief. The sugars are crisp enough to shatter on your teeth, the malt is stone hard and fractured and, on the finish, does show some definite charm before showing its less attractive teeth...and its roots... Overall, though, more than enjoyable. *47%. nc ncf.*

Littlemill 25 Year Old db **(92.5)** n22 t24 f23 b23.5 Another example of a malt which was practically undrinkable in its youth but that is now a reformed, gentle character in older age. *52%*

Littlemill 40 Year Old Celestial Edition db **(90.5)** n23.5 t23 f22 b22.5 As we all know, when this was distilled four decades back, the new make sprang from the stills as fire water. And for the first few years in the cask it roared at and incinerated the palate of any blender foolhardy enough to try it. And so, inevitably, the distillery died. In later years it is making up for its violent youth and here offers a serene maltiness about as far removed from its original character as is possible. Enjoy the dying rays of this once vituperative spirit, now so charming in its dotage. *46.8%. 250 bottles.*

Littlemill 1964 db **(82)** n21 t20 f21 b20. A soft-natured, bourbony chap that shows little of the manic tendencies that made this one of Scotland's most-feared malts. Talk about mellowing with age... *40%*

Littlemill 2017 Private Cellar 27 Year Old db **(93)** n23 t23.5 f23 b23.5 How ironic and sad that the last casks of what were unloved – and unusable - firewater when distilled have now, after nearly three decades, calmed into a malt which is the matured embodiment of grace and finesse. *51.3%.*

Master of Malt Single Cask Littlemill 27 Year Old dist 1991 **(94.5)** n23 t24 f23.5 b24 Another old Littlemill shewing genuine elegance in its twilight years. Kind of Malteser candy with benefits from the moment it hits the palate right through to the finale. A little bourbon-style tannin on the nose doesn't quite prepare you for the chocolatey maltfest which follows... Truly delicious. I promise you: no-one, and I mean no-one, could envision it would be this good in the days when it was working.... *47.2%. sc.*

LOCH LOMOND
Highlands (Southwestern), 1966. Loch Lomond Distillers. Working.

Loch Lomond Aged 10 Years Lightly Peated bott code: 10 01 2019 db **(86)** n20.5 t22 f21.5 b22 Maybe I'm wrong, but this strikes me as being a vatting of distillation types (Inchmoan, Croftengea etc.) with their usual designated Loch Lomond straight and clean style. The result is a feinty beast, much heavier than any "Loch Lomond" I have before encountered, but buttressed with some major fudge and phenols: the Loch Lomond Monster... *40%*.

⬥ **Loch Lomond 10 Year Old 2009 Alvi's Drift Muscat de Frontignan Finish** db **(96)** n23.5 there is almost syrupy thickness to the fruit, which in itself is unusual for the depth of its pear-like lead; **t24.5** oh...my...word...!!! What happened there? My palate has just been submerged in one of the stickiest yet beautifully crafted fruit deliveries it has come across in years. This is like some kind of chocolate liqueur. Even with a slight hint of passion fruit, to up the eye-watering qualities. Salivating and so chocolatey...; **f23.5** still a little passion fruit on the finale with spices and barley running amok; **b24.5** one of those rare whiskies which is every bit as remarkable for its mouthfeel than it is for its flavour personality, which in itself borders on the unique. No, what the hell! This IS unique! A malt whose beauty you can only marvel at....I am truly blown away... *53.2%. Selected by Slijterij Frans Muthert & Dramtime.nl.*

Loch Lomond Aged 12 Years db **(93.5)** n22.5 t23.5 f23.5 b24 Great to see they now have the stocks to allow this malt to really flex its muscles... *46%. ncf.*

⬥ **Loch Lomond 12 Year Old The Open Special Edition 2020** db **(92.5)** n24 so simple... seemingly. But let the Murray Method open this up and there before you and previously hidden is labyrinthine barley, heading in countless directions...each one offering a seemingly different degree of sweetness, sometimes honeyed, sometimes of a more crystalline sugar. Such a stunner...! **t23.5** the surprising oils means the complexity doesn't quite match the nose. But there is layering enough of the malt and variance of weight of both sugars and tannins to keep you amused for some time; **f22** just a slight bitter note seeps through, noticeable only because what had gone before had been flawless; **b23** if anyone needs proof that superb whisky can be got from a relatively young malt (old when I started this game of writing about whisky in the 1980s!) just by the clever use of bourbon casks in particular, then here it is. *46%.*

⬥ **Loch Lomond Aged 14 Years Inchmoan** American oak casks, bott code: L2.080.20 db **(88.5)** n21.5 t23 f21.5 b22.5 This is like watching Charlie Chaplin sloshing paint onto a wall, or glue onto wallpaper. Slap, slap! Here everything is slapped on: the feints, the barley, the sugars, the oak. Slap, slap, slap! Love it, but don't expect subtlety, *46%. ncf. Traveller Exclusive.*

Loch Lomond 15 Year Old db **(87.5)** n21.5 t22 f22 b22 Spends a lot of its time waving its malty flag. But a slight tartness on both nose and on palate means it never quite settles into a comfortable narrative *46%.*

Loch Lomond Organic Aged 17 Years bott code: L2 120 18 db **(96.5)** n24 t24.5 f23.5 b24.5 Organic...? Orgasmic, more like! A dram which will win the hearts, minds and souls of both bourbon and scotch whisky lovers. In fact, if you don't like this, whatever the cut of your jib, you might as well give up now.. 54.9%. nc ncf.

⚜️ **Loch Lomond Aged 18 Years** American oak casks, bott code: L2.234.18 db **(95) n23** the odd atom or three of smoke cocks a snook at the prevailing light honey tones and vanillas. If your thing is understatement, then this nose will certainly turn you on...; **t24** the amalgamation of juicy barley and drier heather honey is one to celebrate. And then you get a light striping of peat-ever in concentrated enough form to in any way dominate. But the ulmo honey almost does, but so subtly, it takes a while for you to realise it is actually there...; **f23.5** so long...and more layers than a bed made up by my old mum. Some real weight now...though, oddly, it takes time before you realise it. A bit of a pattern here...; **b24.5** tasting the Loch Lomond whiskies this year has been such a pleasure. It is always heart-warming to find a distillery that uses American oak casks to best advantage and other types sparingly and with the distillery style in mind. Here is another case in point: the bourbon casks have been shaped to extract every last jot of honey out this expression, as well as complexity. I doff my Panama... 46%. ncf.

Loch Lomond The Open 18 Year Old Course Collection Carnoustie 1999 db **(92) n23 t23.5 f22 b23.5** Decided to wait until the 2018 Open at Carnoustie was in full swing before checking to see if this is up to par. Well, it is beyond that: a true double birdie as rarely is Loch Lomond this clean and malt rich. Would grace any 19th hole... 47.2%.

⚜️ **Loch Lomond Aged 18 Years Inchmurrin** American oak casks, bott code: L2.083.20 db **(95) n23.5** German caramelised biscuit; maybe a hint of ginger, too. Crisp, full of promise and very quietly hint at its age...; **t24** unquestionably the best Inchmurrin delivery and follow through I have ever encountered. The balance between heather honey, light molasses, liquorice and still crunchy, concentrated malt is no less than a work of art. Heads towards being slightly too sweet, then a volley of oak brings it back from the wire...; **f23.5** a fabulous and far from common mix between marzipan and Brazilian nut biscuit...; **b24** have to say: this is Inchmurrin revealing all its pure naked beauty. And it's some sight to behold, believe me. At this age always a good dram. Now truly a great one. 46%. ncf. Traveller Exclusive.

⚜️ **Loch Lomond 21 Year Old** db **(89.5) n22.5** a fat nose which with as much encouragement as possible tends to offer a simplistic spiced vanilla aroma on a malty plinth; **t22.5** remains fat and chewy, but now the roles are reversed: it is the malt taking up the lead with vanilla now toeing the line...; **f22** an obscure fruit note to the sweet finale with malt also helping to stave off the drier, chalkier vanillas; **b22.5** not sure if the oily style of the spirit made 21 years ago is quite as accommodating so far as complexity is concerned as most of the spirit which has come since. 46%.

Loch Lomond 25 Year Old Three Wood Matured Colin Montgomerie db **(95) n24 t23.5 f23.5 b24** I have never met Colin Montgomery, though his car and my car once parked simultaneously nose to tail in Mayfair, London, our respective personalised number plates almost touching. Mr Montgomery, I noted, was quite a large individual so was not surprised that he could persuade a small rubber ball to travel a great distance with one well-timed thwack. This whisky, then, being of a delicate and fragile nature is very much, physically, his antithesis. No doubt Colin Montgomery found the rough a few times in his long career; he certainly won't with this. 46.3%.

⚜️ **Loch Lomond 30 Year Old** db **(86) n23.5 t23 f19 b20.5** When nosing, just sit there and contemplate the spices on that fruit pudding. Wow..! But on delivery, unusually for a malt this age it is the sugars which gets the first word in, a light golden syrup number moving serenely into position with the duskier plummy tones. The spices build as advertised. But then it all starts going Pete Tong as some major furriness grows on the finish. What a shame! Until the treatment of the sherry butts kick in from three decades back, we had been on a delightful journey of unusually polished balance. But, for better or worse, it is a whisky of its times... 47%.

Loch Lomond Classic American oak casks, bott code: 17 12 2018 db **(84.5) n21 t22.5 f20 b21** Though called "Classic", the flat, chewy toffee middle and finish makes this pleasant but very un-Lomond like in character. Fudged in every sense... 40%.

Loch Lomond Cristie Kerr Vintage 2002 db **(94) n23** the vaguest hint of smoky bacon adds what little weight there is to this gentle celebration of barley; **t23.5** such a beautiful presentation of barley in all its heather-honeyed finery. Salivating, lightly oaked and perfectly spiced; **f23.5** continues in the same form, but late on a little nuttiness appears, which moves towards praline; **b24** Lomond at is malty best and cleanest. Someone in Toronto this year told me he had never found a Loch Lomond he'd ever enjoyed. I hope he discovers this minor classic... 48.1%.

Loch Lomond The Open Special Edition Distiller's Cut first fill bourbon and refill American oak casks, bott code: 12 03 2019 db **(95.5) n23.5 t25 f23 b24** One of the finest Loch Lomonds I have ever encountered. No: the finest. The distillery will go up several notches above par for anyone lucky enough to encounter this one.... 46%. ncf. Chosen for Royal Portrush.

⚜️ **Loch Lomond Original** American oak casks, bott code: L2.042 20 db **(90) n22.5** easy going malt with tannin interplay. Clean barley this time and decent spice growth...; **t23** silky and succulent, the malt is deceptive here: it is much more huge than it initially appears. A double-dimensional matiness, too, thanks to the blanket grist of restrained sweetness offering a delightful alternative to the crunchier barley tones; **f22** dries pretty nimbly as the oaky vanillas take command; **b22.5** I think this was the malt a few years back I nearly fainted from because of the feints. Many... I pause at this point because after 21,000 different samples, that's well over 100,000 mouthfulls of whisky and over 100,000 times of picking up a glass and putting it down again to write over the last 17 years, I finally knocked a charged tasting glass over the computer, thereby killing it. Death by malt. Or, rather, it was at this point it died as it had happened two samples ago. A brand new Apple Mac bought just for the Whisky Bible 2021 edition dying in its line of duty. So now an old one – with the letters e r t o a h and n obliterated by a few years' pounding has been brought out of retirement to complete the last couple of hundred whiskies (this is number 969)... Anyway, back to the Loch Lomond Original. This now a feint-free maltfest which goes easy on complexity but is big on charm. *40%.*

Loch Lomond Portrush Open Course Collection db **(82)** n22 t21.5 f19 b20 Pleasant enough start, though dulled and then damaged by the wine cask influence, with sulphur leaking through at the end. Hard going. Reminded me of when I once played Royal Portrush, on a broiling hot day nearly 20 years ago. And despite being only two inches from a hole in one, it was the most punishing and miserable afternoon of my life. From that day I have never visited another golf club to place ball on tee and decided that if I were to spend a rare afternoon in the fresh air, rather than fruitlessly chasing birdies it would be spent watching birds instead. And that is exactly what I have done since that day forth... *46.3%.*

Glengarry 12 Year Old db **(92.5)** n22.5 t23.5 f23 b23.5 Probably the most intense malt on the market today. Astonishing. And stunning.*46%. ncf.*

◈ **Inchmoan Aged 12 Years Peated** recharred American oak and refill bourbon American oak casks, bott code: L4.295,19 db **(85.5)** n20 t22.5 f21.5 b21.5 Seems as though the whole world has gone slightly mad and changed beyond recognition since I last opened a bottle of this. The only thing that hasn't changed, it seems, is the feintiness on Inchmoan. A little sweeter now, maybe. And the peat now has the distinctively chocolate mint quality of the old Merlin's Brew ice lolly. Though that lost old classic would have this licked... *46%. ncf. Loch Lomond Island Collection.*

Inchmoan 1992 Peated refill bourbon barrels db **(95)** n23 t24.5 f23.5 b24 I do believe I was at Loch Lomond distillery in 1992 while they were producing the Inchmoan strand of their output. So to see it after all this time is astonishing. No less astonishing is the sheer excellence of the malt, which here is almost a cross between a light rye-recipe bourbon and a smoky island scotch. This is a true Loch Lomond classic 48.6%. *ncf. Loch Lomond Island Collection.*

◈ **Inchmurrin Aged 12 Years** bourbon, refill and recharred casks, bott code: L2.248.18 db **(88.5)** n21.5 t23 f22 b22 Best Inchmurrin I have tasted in a good number of years. The calibre of the malt is top-notch, allowing the barley a fabulously lively, intense yet even run. Well spiced, too. Inch by Inch, it is getting there. At this rate the next bottling will be hitting the 90-mark for the Bible, once an unlikely proposition. A little cleaner on the nose and it'll be there. A bit like the distillery: a real character. *46%. ncf. Loch Lomond Island Collection.*

◈ **Inchmurrin Madeira Wood Finish** bott code: L2.185.18 db **(93)** n23 sharp fruit pastel candy; **t23.5** this is very healthy Madeira cask in full spate. The result is a flooding of lime and green banana notes...with a little custard at the mid-point; **f23** I noticed the label says the finish is dry and nutty. If only. The fruit has something to say about that. Though the cocoa powders do dry things eventually...even if the spices to get the juices flowing again...; **b23.5** well, a lush and beautifully clean Madeira cask is one way of negating any weakness on the nose. Trouble is, that fruit becomes a little too bossy....though this can be forgiven when the quality of the casks are this high. A real lip-smacking crowd pleaser. *46%. ncf. Loch Lomond Island Collection.*

The Cooper's Choice Croftengea 2007 11 Years Old Madeira finish **(87.5)** n21.5 t23 f21.5 b21.5 A typical Croftengea in that the peat is nuclear strength but the quirkiness of the stills gives it an impression of being out of focus. Not even a wine cask finish can correct it. Have to say, though: really fun whisky! *53%. nc ncf sc.*

◈ **The First Editions Inchfad Aged 14 Years 2005** refill hogshead, cask no. 16785, bott 2019 **(89)** n22 a dirty, rubbery smokiness unlike any other in Scotland; **t23** it is as though the phenolic grist has been specially concentrated for the sugars to have a remarkable say; **f21.5** after such initial sweetness must come a degree of bitterness. And you will not be disappointed...or maybe you will....; **b22.5** a brilliant example of Inchfad's truly esoteric style. *56.3%. nc ncf sc. 293 bottles.*

Hepburn's Choice Inchfad 13 Years Old refill hogshead, dist 2005, bott 2018 **(82.5)** n20.5 t22 f19.5 b20.5 A little looseness on the cuts means the oils are a tad off key and overpowering, despite the peaty meatiness. Despite its obvious faults, there is a real charm to the jammy, juicy sweetness of the barley before everything wanders off on a tangent. *46%. nc ncf sc. 345 bottles.*

◈ **Liquid Treasures 10th Anniversary Inchfad 14 Year Old** heavily peated hogsheads, dist 2005, bott 2019 (**94.5**) **n23.5 t23.5 f23.5 b24** Rarely does an Inchfad turn up in the bottle as clean and well-made as this, with the phenols at their most intense. Not an easy edition of Loch Lomond's output to find anyway, usually the feints makes for a challenging dram. Not this time, though. And while it is not quite technically perfect (not sure I've ever found an Inchfad that really is), this cask comes together in a way that is leaves you cooing like a randy woodpigeon. Just love the mintiness that attaches to the smoke and then the later praline as the nuttiness grows. Perhaps best of all, though, is the mouthfeel which varies between oily and a cocoa dryness, neither gaining control. If you use this bottle, just get it. It's a bit of a one off. *50%. sc. 144 bottles.*

Old Malt Cask Croftengea Aged 13 Years refill hogshead, cask no. 15148, dist Feb 05, bott May 18 (**87.5**) **n21.5 t23 f21.5 b21.5** A magnificently imperfect malt, groaning with all kinds of technical weaknesses. But there is no denying that the unique peat profile and those breathtakingly salivating gristy notes make for one genuinely delicious malt. *50%. nc ncf sc.*

◈ **The Single Cask Croftengea 2007** ex-wine cask, cask no. 71 (**81.5**) **n18 t21.5 f21 b21** Even at the best of times, sampling a Croftengea can be like trying to break in a particularly bloody-minded horse: you get thrown everywhere and can take one hell of a kicking. The fact that your saddle has been loosed by an unimpressive wine cask makes the job even more difficult. Hard to find a single positive about the nose but I suspect the inner masochist in me has a grudging respect for the wildness on the palate. *55.7%. nc ncf sc.*

Spirit of Caledonia Inchfad cask no. 426, dist 24 Feb 05, bott 13 Feb 19 (**86.5**) **n21.5 t22 f21.5 b21.5** That uniquely Inchfadian mix of light peat and feints. Inchfad is a pretty rare mark to find from Loch Lomond and this bottling confers on it a distinctly German style, certainly the most German of all Scotland's single malt. The grist is also on maximum sweetness, so no lacking of flavour here. *55.4%. Mr. Whisky.*

The Whisky Shop Loch Lomond Aged 15 Years cask no. 15/624-1, dist 2004 (**94.5**) **n23.5 t23.5 f23.5 b24** A distillery in its very finest clothes. *54.4%. sc.*

World of Orchids Croftengea 2007 11 Years Old bourbon cask, cask no. 58 (**90.5**) **n22 t22.5 f23 b23** Living deep in the country as I do, I think I'm perfectly qualified to call this whisky agricultural... *58.5%. sc.*

LOCHSIDE

Highlands (Eastern), 1957–1992. Chivas Brothers. Demolished.

◈ **The Whisky Agency Lochside 1981** butt, bott 2018 (**96.5**) **n24** a throwback to the days of unspoiled sherry butts, here enriching the distillery's natural tendency towards citrus with a glorious marriage of figs, dates and the drying cork of a rather fine vintage Bordeaux...; **t25** a delivery you simply do not want to end. The mouthfeel is near perfection with the weight of the fruit refusing to out-perform the still intense barley which remains, even after all these years in sherry, at the heart of this whisky. The fruit is riddled with spice and burnt raisins, but always there is heather honey on hand to keep the sweeter flame burning; **f23.5** after true perfection, what next? Well, a little bitterness arises from the oak and the spices warm up by several degrees. But in the context of age...it remains spot on...; **b24** I suspect I must be one of the very last people still working in the whisky industry who visited this distillery in the days when it was at full throttle. I was horrified by its closure way back in 1992 and thinking back on it now still fills me with great sadness. Some distilleries were awful and deserved their fate. This never for a moment did. I remember once going to see Montrose play a home game and afterwards popped into the distillery to have a word with the staff on duty. The new make then, as every time I visited, was spot on (and very warming after perishing in the main stand). And here is a magnificent example of its stunning make spending the best part of 40 years in faultless sherry oak. The result, as I expected (and the reason I left this for among the final five whiskies for the 2021 Whisky Bible) is a study of single malt Scotch: a malt of astonishing and beguiling beauty. *48.6%.* 🏆

LONGMORN

Speyside, 1895. Chivas Brothers. Working.

Longmorn 15 Years Old db (**93**) **n23 t24 f22 b24** These latest bottlings are the best yet: previous ones had shown just a little too much oak but this has hit a perfect compromise. An all-time Speyside great. *45%*

Longmorn 16 Years Old db (**84.5**) **n20.5 t22 f21 b21.** This was one of the disappointments of the 2008 edition, thanks to the lacklustre nose and finish. This time we see a cautious nudge in the right direction: the colour has been dropped fractionally and the nose celebrates with a sharper barley kick with a peppery accompaniment. The non-existent (caramel apart) finale of yore now offers a distinct wave of butterscotch and thinned honey...and still some spice. Only the delivery has dropped a tad...but a price worth paying for the overall improvement. Still a way to go before the real Longmorn 16 shines in our glasses for all to see and fall deeply in love with. Come on lads in the Chivas lab: we know you can do it... 48%

Longmorn 23 Year Old db (93) n23 t24 f23 b23.5 I can just imagine how this would be such rich top dressing for the finest blend I could concoct: as a single malt it is no less a delight. 48%. ncf.

◇ **The First Editions Longmorn Aged 21 Years 1998** refill barrel, cask no. 17324, bott 2019 (96.5) n25 profound complexity: the sweet/dry percentages are just about at the perfect 50/50 and the lightness of touch from the intricate spices has to be sniffed to be believed. Yet such is the sleight of hand from the oak's seasoning, the malt appears undisturbed and rich. I could fill this page just on the nose alone and go into poetic overdrive. I won't. But I will say this: it is unlikely I will encounter a more complex or perfectly balanced nose this year...; t24 having gone through a mental a-z on the nose so far as spices are concerned, we now do something similar on the palate with honey. Ulmo honey leads the way, though, yet without overstating its case. The flickering vanillas, caramels and hickory all give a nod to the judicious influence of an exceptional cask; f23 bitters ever so slightly, but the spices buzz with fabulous weight; b24.5 Longmorn is a malt greatly prized by the better blenders. This bottling leaves you in no doubt why...one of the single casks of the year, for sure. 56.3%. nc ncf sc. 186 bottles ☃.

Gordon & MacPhail Distillery Label Longmorn 2003 bott 18 May 17 (94.5) n23.5 t23.5 f23.5 b24 Anyone for butterscotch and Werther's Originals had better get their skates on before all this has gone... 43%.

◇ **Gordon & MacPhail Private Collection Longmorn 1966** first fill sherry butt, cask no. 610, dist 1 Feb 66, bott 22 Mar 19 (96) n25 this is not so much adorned by oak as being carved from it. The fruit – here represented by torched raisins and dried dates – is imbued into the oak like creosote into an ancient fence. This is heady stuff...and it has nothing to do with the alcohol. The sugars take their time to open up, but when they do then enjoy the mix of thick molasses and maple syrup which, mixed with ye olde fruits, stretches across the nose with the same assured ancient elegance of a Jacob Rees-Mogg lying at his most horizontally relaxed on the Government front benches; t24 after that nose, you half expect a dry, piercing attack of splinters. But it never comes. Instead, we are gifted with a delightful exhibition of thick, sensuous fruits on an oily base, not unlike, perhaps, an old fruitcake left several winters to mature, the toasted fruit and molasses shewing only glimpses of sweetness, but enough for balance and good form to be satisfied; f23 such a whisky as this can only end with an intense dryness, as the considerable tannin finds its home; b24 the colour of a greatly aged tawny port and enough oak for Henry VIII to build the biggest ship ever to set sail for Jerez and plunder as many sherry butts as he wished. Like a great wine, needs a good half hour minimum to breathe in the glass to open for best results and maximum complexity. 46%. sc. 398 bottles.

Kingsbury Silver Longmorn 13 Year Old hogshead, cask no. 13696, dist 2003 (92.5) n22.5 23 f23.5 b23.5 For years and years blenders have used Longmorn as "top dressing": a malt rich in character, high in quality and abounding in enough personality to shape the blend in the direction they wish to take it. Here you can see exactly why... 46%. sc. 336 bottles.

THE MACALLAN
Speyside, 1824. Edrington. Working.

The Macallan 10 Years Old db (91) n23 t23 f21.5 b23.5 For a great many of us, it is with the Mac 10 our great Speyside odyssey began. It has to be said that in recent years it has been something of a shadow of its former great self. However, this is the best version I have come across for a while. Not perhaps in the same league as those bottlings in the 1970s which made us re-evaluate the possibilities of single malt. But fine enough to show just how great this whisky can be when the butts have not been tainted and, towards the end, the balance between barley and grape is a relatively equal one. 40%

The Macallan Fine Oak 10 Years Old db (90) n23 t22.5 f21.5 b22 Much more on the ball than the last bottling of this I came across. Malts rarely come as understated or as clever than this. 40%

Macallan 12 Year Old db (61) n15 t16 f15 b15 An uncompromising and comprehensive essay in the present day sulphured sherry butt problem. 43% US tag CP981113

The Macallan Sherry Oak 12 Years Old db (93) n24 t23.5 f22.5 b23 I have to say that some Macallan 12 I have tasted on the road has let me down in the last year or so. This is virtually faultless. Virtually a time machine back to another era... 40%

The Macallan 12 Years Old Sherry Oak Elegancia db (86) n23 t22 f20 b21. Promises, but delivers only to an extent. 40%

The Macallan Fine Oak 12 Years Old db (95.5) n24 t24 f23.5 b24 A whisky whose quality has hit the stratosphere since I last tasted it. I encountered a disappointing one early in the year. This has restored my faith to the point of being a disciple... 40%

The Macallan Fine Oak 15 Years Old db (79.5) n19 t21.5 f19 b20. As the stock of the Fine oak 12 rises, so its 15-y-o brother, once one of my favourite drams, falls. Plenty to enjoy, but a few sulphur stains remove the gloss. 43%

The Macallan Fine Oak 17 Years Old db (82) n19.5 t22 f19.5 b21. Where once it couldn't quite make up its mind on just where to sit, it has now gone across to the sherry benches. Sadly, there are a few dissenters. 43%

The Macallan Sherry Oak 18 Years Old db (87) n24 t22 f20 b21. Underpowered. The body doesn't even come close to matching the nose which builds up the expectancy to enormous levels and, by comparison to the Independents, this at 43% appears weak and unrepresentative. Why this isn't at 46% at the very least and unambiguously uncoloured, I have no idea. 43%

The Macallan Fine Oak 18 Years Old db (94.5) n23.5 t24 f23 b24 Is this the new Fine Oak 15 in terms of complexity? That original bottling thrived on the balance between casks types. This is much more accentuated on a cream sherry persona. But this sample is sulphur-free and quite fabulous. 43%

The Macallan Fine Oak 21 Years Old db (84) n21 t22 f20 b21. An improvement on the characterless dullard I last encountered. But the peaks aren't quite high enough to counter the sulphur notes and make this a great malt. 43%

The Macallan 25 Years Old db (84.5) n22 t21 f20.5 b21. Dry with an even drier oloroso residue; blood orange adds to the fruity mix. Something, though, is not entirely right about this and one fears from the bitter tang at the death that a rogue butt has gained entry to what should be the most hallowed of dumping troughs. 43%

The Macallan Fine Oak 25 Years Old db (90) n22 t23.5 f22 b22.5 The first time I tasted this brand a few years back I was knocked off my perch by the peat reek which wafted about with cheerful abandon. Here the smoke is tighter, more shy and of a distinctly more anthracitic quality. Even so, the sweet juiciness of the grape juxtaposes gamely with the obvious age to create a malt of obvious class. 43%

The Macallan Fine Oak 25 Years Old db (89) n23 t23 f21 b22. Very similar to the Fine Oak 18. However, the signature smoke has vanished, as I suppose over time it must. Not entirely clean sherry, but much remains to enjoy. 43%

The Macallan Fine Oak 30 Years Old db (81.5) n22 t22 f18 b19.5. For all its many riches on delivery, especially those moments of great bourbon-honey glory, it has been comprehensively bowled middle stump by the sherry. Gutted. 43%

The Macallan Millennium 50 Years Old (1949) db (90) n23 t22 f22 b23. Magnificent finesse and charm despite some big oak makes this another Macallan to die for. 40%

The Macallan Lalique III 57 Years Old db (95) n24.5 t23 f23.5 b24 No experience with this whisky under an hour pays sufficient tribute to what it is all about. Checking my watch, I am writing this just two minutes under two hours after first nosing this malt. The score started at 88.5. With time, warmth, oxidation and understanding that score has risen to 95. It has spent 57 years in the cask; it deserves two hours to be heard. It takes that time, at least, not just to hear what it has to say to interpret it, but to put it into context. And for certain notes, once locked away and forgotten, to be slowly released. The last Lalique was good. But simply not this good. 48.5%

The Macallan 1824 db (88) n24 t23.5 f19 b21.5. Absolutely magnificent whisky, in part. But there are times my job is depressing...and this is one of them.. 48%

The Macallan 1824 Estate Reserve db (90.5) n22 t23 f22.5 b23 Don't know about Reserve: definitely good enough for the First Team. 45.7%

The Macallan 1824 Select Oak db (82) n19 t22 f20 b21. Soft, silky, sometimes sugary... and tangy. Not convinced every oak selected was quite the right one. 40%

The Macallan Fine Oak Master's Edition db (91) n23 t23 f22 b23 Adorable. 42.8%

The Macallan Fine Oak Whisky Maker's Selection db (92) n22 t23 f23 b24. This is a dram of exquisite sophistication. Coy, mildly cocoaed dryness, set against just enough barley and fruit sweetness here and there to see off any hints of austerity. Some great work has gone on in the lab to make this happen: fabulous stuff! 42.8%. Duty Free.

The Macallan Gold sherry oak cask db (89.5) n22 t23.5 f21.5 b22.5. No Macallan I have tasted since my first in 1975 has been sculpted to show the distillery in such delicate form. 40%

The Macallan Ruby sherry oak cask db (92.5) n23 t24 f22 b23.5. Those longer in the tooth who remember the Macallan 10 of 30 years ago will nod approvingly at this chap. Perhaps one butt away from a gong! 43%.

The Macallan Sienna sherry cask db (94.5) n23 t24 f23.5 b24. The pre-bottling sample presented to me was much more vibrant than this early on, but lacked the overall easy charm and readily flowing general complexity of the finished article. A huge and pleasing improvement. 43%.

The Macallan Rare Cask Black db (83.5) n21.5 t22 f19 b21. Pretty rich and some intense, molasses, black cherry and liquorice notes to die for. But some pretty off-key ones, too. Overall, average fare. 48%

The Macallan Select Oak db (83) n23 t21 f19 b20. Exceptionally dry and tight; and a little furry despite the early fruitiness. 40%

The Macallan Whisky Makers Edition db (76) n19 t20 f18 b19. Distorted and embittered by the horrific "S" element... 42.8%

Hard To Find Whisky Macallan Aged 30 Years sherry cask, cask no. 2824, dist 1989, bott 30 Apr 19 (93) n23.5 t24 f22.5 b23 This is the style Macallan is rightly famed for. Though finding a pure sherry-matured one with not an atom of sulphur really is a hard to find whisky. This is almost three, but not quite. Even so, it is closer to Macallan of yesteryear than 95% of others you are likely to find these days and makes a point of luxuriating in the richness of the bitter-sweet fruit. Also, Macallan fans could do worse than picking up a bottle of this and comparing it to the Master of Malt's non-sherry influenced bottling. 44.1%. sc. 98 bottles.

Heiko Thieme's 1974 Macallan 65th Birthday Bottling cask no. 16807 dist 25 Nov 74 bott Jul 08 (94) n23 t23 f24 b24 This is not whisky because it is 38%abv. It is Scottish spirit. However, this is more of a whisky than a great many samples I have tasted this year. Ageism is outlawed. So is sexism. But alcoholism isn't....!! Try and become a friend of Herr Thieme and grab hold of something a little special. 38% 238 bottles.

Master of Malt Single Cask Macallan 30 Year Old dist 1988 (93.5) n22.5 t24 f23 b23.5 The oak has its fingers on all the buttons here. This is a significant age for a Macallan and the malt is at full stretch to keep the tannins at bay. But it remains intact and even conjures up some profound barley-sugar moments to ensure the oak doesn't get all its own way. But to its great credit, even when the oak returns with a vengeance, there is no hint of bitterness, though the spice levels rise significantly. High quality. 52%. sc.

⬦ **Skene Reserve Macallan 1989 30 Year Old** 1st fill Oloroso, cask no. 152034 (76) n20 t20 f18 b18 This is a distinctly odd malt. At first I thought it was only because it was from the earliest days of when sulphur sticks were used in sherry butts like so much fertiliser was used on a crop of beans. And though I am 100% certain there are very old sulphur effects here (we are probably entering new ground in seeing the effect of candle treatment on casks over such a long period) you also get the feeling there is something else at work here stopping the development of the complexity that, had this been a 30-year-old Macallan I was tasting either from bottle or in their warehouses 30-years-ago, would have given you a result so much more different – and infinitely more beautiful and complex – than this. 43.2%. sc.

Whisky Republic Macallan 1988 mizunara cask, cask no. 18/0H003 (93) n23 t23.5 f23 b23.5 Powerful, but never overpowering. The Japanese influence is unmistakable and entertaining. 48.4%. sc.

MACDUFF
Speyside, 1963. Bacardi. Working.

The Deveron Aged 10 Years bott code: L17 284ZAB03 2327 db (94) n23.5 t23.5 f23 b24 Does the heart good to see a distillery bring their malt out as a ten-year- old – when so many think that such an age is beneath them. This shews the distillery at its most vivid and fresh, when the oak has had time to work its magic but not overstay its welcome; when the barley is still king. And, my word, its crown positively glitters gold here... 40%.

The Deveron 12 Year Old db (87.5) n22 t22 f21.5 b22. Buttery and pleasant. But feels like driving a Ferrari with a Fiat Uno engine. Woefully underpowered and slightly too flat in too many places where it should be soaring. The trademark honey notes cannot be entirely defied, however. 40%

The Deveron Aged 12 Years bott code: L172018700 db (94.5) n23.5 retains its big malt personality, though there is far more citrus about now, the oak is weightier and brings into play delicate layers of acacia honey...; t23.5 ...and it is the honey which lays the foundations for the dropped malty intro.. The mouthfeel is sexy and succulent, a light butterscotch note representing the oak; again, a citrus note hangs about, mainly time; f23 at last a little spice comes into play. But the continued complexity...just, wow! b24 Hi honey! I've homed in...! 40%.

The Deveron Aged 18 Years bott code: L181168700 db (93) n23 t24 f22.5 b23.5 Someone has started not to just fully understand this always badly underrated distillery, but put it on the map. 40%.

⬦ **Fadandel.dk Macduff 13 Year Old** barrel, cask no. 8102355, dist 27 Nov 06, bott 28 Nov 19 (92) n23 buttery barley with delightfully nuanced marzipan and vanilla...so charming...; t23.5 as on the nose, the malt has a buttery sheen which slowly breaks down into a sweeter, slightly gristy heather honey note. Sensual and mouth-watering from the very start, it keeps you puckering right up towards the finale as the spiced tannins barge in; f22.5 butterscotch and spices leading into praline; **b23** oh, thank god!! After a day of one sherry butt or wine cask finish after another at last I can taste malt...as in MALT whisky. How amazing is that! Just like the old days. And you know what...? Not only does it have personality, but it's bloody delicious! *54.2%. sc. 191 bottles.*

The First Editions Macduff Aged 21 Years 1997 refill hogshead, cask no. 15366, bott 2018 **(94) n23 t23.5 f23 b23.5** An outrageous spice bomb of a malt. Sheer, delicious entertainment. *54.4%. nc ncf sc. 288 bottles.*

The Golden Cask Macduff 26 Years Old 1992 cask no. CM251, bott 2018 **(91.5) n22 t23 f23.5 b23** What is a whisky this age doing at a strength like that....? Well, you don't often get the chance to experience a near 30-year-old malt whose abv can fair knock you back into the far recesses of your chair. *64.1%. nc ncf sc. 226 bottles.*

Hepburn's Choice Macduff 11 Years Old first fill bourbon barrel, dist 2006, bott 2018 **(88) n22.5 t22.5 f21 b22** Almost a dessert whisky, so much custard to be found.... *46%. nc ncf sc.*

Old Malt Cask Macduff Aged 21 Years refill hogshead, cask no. 15147, dist May 97, bott May 18 **(78) n20 t20 f18 b20** Sticks out like a sore thumb for the other Macduffs in this family, presumably a poor cask undoing the good of the spirit. A duff Macduff... *50%. nc ncf sc.*

Scyfion Choice Macduff 2007 Pinot Noir cask finished, bott 2019 **(90.5) n22.5 t23 f22.5 b22.5** Anyone who loves eye-wateringly sharp boiled sweets should hunt this bottling down now..! *46%. nc ncf sc. 160 bottles.*

The Whisky Chamber Macduff 12 Years Old 2006 bourbon cask **(89) n22 t23 f22 b22** A slightly simplistic, though always attractive, malt. *53.1%. sc.*

⬧ **The Whisky Gallery High Priestess Macduff Aged 8 Years** second fill bourbon barrel, cask no. 800020, dist 2011, bott 2019 **(89.5) n22.5** clean, sharp malt – makes you salivate even before you taste it...!!! **t22.5** now you really do salivate: barley rarely comes so bright and juicy. Light icing sugars on vanilla; **f22** even more delicate than the delivery (though that hardly seems possible), allowing the delicate oak a greater say than it might have expected; **b22.5** spellbindingly youthful, but technically on the money. *49%. sc. 229 bottles.*

⬧ **Wilson & Morgan Barrel Selection Macduff** 1st fill sherry wood, dist 2006, bott 2019 **(95) n24** a bit of a dark horse, this. Would be too easy only to see crystalline grape. But the Murray Method opens up many secrets, not least of all the rousing saltiness which unveils a complex degree of tannin and very light farmyard phenol. Intriguing, entertaining and beautiful...; **t24** just as on the nose, warming in the hand slightly will confirm all those complex notes found on the aroma, but here they manoeuvre in an intriguingly different way, as though all is happening in slow motion; the interplay between those oily but ridiculously delicate phenols and the most understated light fruity muscovado and cocoa is spellbinding; **f23** at last the fruit has a say, creating a light grapey covering to quieten the spices slightly; **b24** well done Wilson & Morgan for again finding an untainted sherry butt. This is big whisky that is so beautifully controlled and balanced it doesn't actually seem like it! An easy to miss stunner. *57.1%.*

World of Orchids Macduff 2003 15 Years Old bourbon cask, cask no. 106 **(89) n21 t22.5 f23 b22.5** A little on the tangy side for a bourbon cask, but the highly intense fresh barley guarantees quality. *57.9%. sc.*

MANNOCHMORE

Speyside, 1971. Diageo. Working.

Mannochmore Aged 12 Years db **(84) n22 t21 f20 b21.** As usual the mouth arrival fails to live up to the great nose. Quite a greasy dram with sweet malt and bitter oak. *43%.*

Lady of the Glen Mannochmore 2007 cask no. 13208 **(94.5) n23.5 t24 f23.5 b23.5** Mannochmore has a bit of a split perception among blenders: some adore it, some won't touch it. Well, virtually all would be fighting to get their hands on it if all samples were as spellbindingly rich and sweet as this cask. Beautifully made and benefitting from a decade or so in a top rate bourbon cask. The result is a honey-rich, spicy orgy of malt. Even boasting a cheeky hint of peat. Just brilliant. *59.4%. sc.*

MILLBURN

Highlands (Northern), 1807–1985. Diageo. Demolished.

Millburn 1969 Rare Malt db **(77) n19 t21 f18 b19.** Some lovely bourbon-honey touches but sadly over the hill and declining fast. Nothing like as interesting or entertaining as the massage parlour that was firebombed a few yards from my office twenty minutes ago. Or as smoky... *51.3%*

MILTONDUFF

Speyside, 1824. Chivas Brothers. Working.

Ballantine's The Miltonduff Aged 15 Years Series No.002 American oak casks, bott code: LKRM1193 2018/03/27 **(88.5) n23 t22 f21.5 b22** Soft, spicy, attractive but far too much one-dimensional caramel for complexity or greatness. Some decent bourbon notes filter through, though. (The Murray Method brings out the caramels further – best enjoyed at cool bottle temperature). 40%.

⟐ **Cadenhead's Whisky & More Baden Miltonduff 10 Year Old** firkin cask **(95.5) n23.5 t24 f24 b24** Firkin hell...!! This really isn't much interested in taking prisoners.! Instead it just wallows in its own swamp of spicy fruitiness and adds chocolate when required. The mouthfeel is as soft, chewy and rounded as any you'll find this year, with the accent on fat dates. As you know, I make no secret that there are some awful fruity whiskies about. This is the antithesis: a huge malt simply brimming with a fruity intensity and clarity to die for. The late mix of Venezuelan cocoa and spiced papaya is almost taking the piss. Magnificent hardly does this justice... 54.5%. sc.

⟐ **Chapter 7 Miltonduff 21 Year Old 1998** bourbon hogshead, cask no. 10142, dist Oct 98, bott Mar 20 **(94) n24 t23.5 f23 b23.5** Looking at this year's scores for, what for me, is one of the most overlooked and underrated of all the Speyside distilleries, you get the feeling that the marketing department for Miltonduff's owners should give very serious consideration into launching a cask strength, uncoloured version at their earliest opportunity. Here the malts seemingly fizz into the nose, sharp and virile despite the passing years. And there is no less malty energy on delivery, also, though a little salty seasoning appears to up the part played in the oaky incursion. Full flavoured, majorly malty and, when those gentle spices start adding their two-penn'orth things are just about complete. 49.7%. sc. 238 bottles.

⟐ **The First Editions Miltonduff Aged 29 Years 1990** refill hogshead, cask no. 16248, bott 2019 **(94) n23.5** ridiculously seductive: the involvement of the tannin is precise, measured and delightful; **t24** one of the most viscous mouthfeels I have ever encountered: actually needed to check the bottle to ensure this wasn't a liqueur...! The initial heather honey sweetness on delivery adds to the effect. But soon those tannins so clearly defined on the nose are making their presence felt from about the fourth flavour wave onwards; **f23** teasing spices as the oak plays out its wonderfully orchestrated tune; **b23.5** a belting malt which will appeal especially to those with a very sweet tooth. But it isn't all one way traffic and some outstanding oak ensures balance. 57.2%. nc ncf sc. 287 bottles.

The Golden Cask Miltonduff 8 Years Old 2009 cask no. CM245, bott 2018 **(93.5) n23 t23 f24 b23.5** For an 8-year-old, this is in need of a Zimmer frame, as it creaks and shuffles along in the oaky onslaught. There are heather honey and marzipan notes further down the line which open this up beautifully, and the chocolate tones are wonderful while the finish is stunning. But behaves far closer to an 18-year-old than a malt a decade younger! Absolutely beautiful, though, even if you do have to pick out the odd splinter. 60%. nc ncf sc. 238 bottles.

The Golden Cask Miltonduff 2009 cask no. CM254, bott 2019 **(89.5) n22 t23 f22 b22.5** Decent enough, but just has nothing like the same overall panache as cask 245. 60.1%. nc ncf sc. 228 bottles.

Hepburn's Choice Miltonduff 8 Years Old first fill bourbon barrel, dist 2009, bott 2018 **(87) n21.5 t22.5 f21 b22** Very obvious here why this is so prized as a blending malt, even at this age. Despite the eye-watering sharpness to the barley, there is no escaping that there is substance to this malt, too. So chewy and fulfilling early on, though the oak – which has surprisingly little impact for a first fill bourbon barrel - does bitter out slightly at the death. 46%. nc ncf sc. 339 bottles.

Old Malt Cask Miltonduff Aged 23 Years refill barrel, cask no. 15138, dist Feb 95, bott May 18 **(94) n23.5 t23.5 f23 b24** A very pretty whisky which carries its age effortlessly and with considerable grace. Understatedly superb. 50%. nc ncf sc. 150 bottles.

⟐ **Old Malt Cask Miltonduff Aged 25 Years** refill hogshead, cask no. 16644, dist Apr 94, bott May 19 **(95) n23.5** a light chocolatey touch to this one. A little dry and salty, too...; **t24** delicate and teasing, the spices arrive earlier than expected. And though busy, they do nothing to undermine the fabulous waves of malt which wash over the palate; **f23.5** remains malty, the chocolate returns with no little elegance; **b24** truly classy, as the finest Miltonduffs invariably are. Impeccable. 50%. nc ncf sc. 228 bottles.

⟐ **Old Malt Cask Miltonduff Aged 29 Years** refill hogshead, cask no. 16260, dist Mar 90, bott Oct 19 **(85.5) n22 t22.5 f20 b21** A sister cask to the First Editions Miltonduff (above). But this one is missing most of the lush, sweet genes and after an austere, tannin-infused start buckles somewhat under a degree of late bitterness. 50%. nc ncf sc. 277 bottles.

⟐ **The Single Cask Miltonduff 2009** sherry butt, cask no. 90030 **(88.5) n22 t22.5 f22 b22** As sherry butts go, not too bad. Perhaps a little tight towards the finish, but forgivably so. Its strength is the intensity of the grape, which is uncompromising, making the integration of the spice and move towards cocoa much more interesting than usual....quite fascinating, even. Its weakness: the uncompromising intensity of the grape.... 64.5%. nc ncf sc.

⟐ **The Whisky Barrel Originals Miltonduff 10 Years Old** 1st fill oloroso hogshead, cask no. TWB1007, dist Jul 09, bott 2019 **(91.5) n22.5** dry, with a light peppery buzz to the grape;

t23 an initial thrust of robust tannin. But this soon makes way for a sweet and spicy follow-through as the juicy fruit takes control; a little spice fizz offers some alternative entertainment; very good texture throughout; **f23** the sweetness drops, though not altogether. But the spices hurtle on...; **b23** a rare sulphur-free experience from a sherry butt of this vintage. Technically, a little one dimensional with the fruit filling most of the gaps. But the grape-malt combination works pretty well, though its beating heart is the spice. *63.4%. sc. 254 bottles.*

MORTLACH
Speyside, 1824. Diageo. Working.

Mortlach Aged 12 Years The Wee Witchie sherry & bourbon casks, bott code: L8284DM001 db **(92.5) n23** a lovely toffee and raisin theme with the barley lively enough to have a nibble at it; **t23** mouth-watering, fresh and sharp on delivery. Far more life in this than expected from the colour with the plum notes offering both depth and more salivating qualities; **f23.5** a pleasing spiciness amid the drier vanillas; **b23** clean, untainted sherry casks at work: rather lovely. *43.4%.*

Mortlach Aged 16 Years db **(87) n20 t23 f22 b22.** Once it gets past the bold if very mildly sulphured nose, the rest of the journey is superb. Earlier Mortlachs in this range had a slightly unclean feel to them and the nose here doesn't inspire confidence. But from arrival on the palate onwards, it's sure-footed, fruity and even refreshing... and always delicious. *43%*

Mortlach Aged 16 Years Distiller's Dram ex-sherry casks, bott code: L833ODM004 db **(93.5) n23.5** the underpinning oak gives a firm stage on which the kumquats and barley can choreograph their elaborate dance; **t23.5** much lighter on delivery than the nose steadies you for, the fruit juices and Demerara sugars gushing against the taste buds. Soon the oak is back in place, the tannins affording grip and delicate spice; **f23** soft vanilla and barley sugars – as well as a dry, pulsing spiciness representing age; **b23.5** after quite a long period in the doldrums, this distillery really does have the wind in its sails once more. Excellent whisky. *43.4%.*

Mortlach 18 Year Old db **(75) n19 t19 f18 b19.** When I first tasted Mortlach, probably over 30 years ago now, it really wasn't even close to this. Something went very wrong in the late '80s, I can tell you...*43.4%. Diageo.*

Mortlach 20 Year Old Cowie's Blue Seal db **(87) n22 t22 f21.5 b21.5** Pleasant, but apart from a little oak on the nose never gets round to displaying its age. The odd orange blossom honey money opens it up slightly but a shade too tame and predictable. *43.4%.*

Mortlach 25 Year Old db **(91.5) n23** just love the lemon grass alongside the liquorice and hickory; **t23.5** thick and palate-encompassing. The sugars are pretty toasty with a light mocha element in play; **f22.5** crisp finale with a return of the citrus, sitting confidently with the late spice; **b22.5** much more like it. The sugars may be pretty full on, but there is enough depth and complexity for a narrative to be told. Very much a better Mortlach on so many levels. *43.4%.*

Mortlach Rare Old db **(79) n20 t21 f19 b19.** Not rare enough... *43.4%. Diageo.*

Mortlach Special Strength db **(79.5) n20 t21.5 f19 b19.** Does whisky come any more cloyingly sweet than Mortlach...? Not in my experience.... *49%. Diageo.*

Glenwill Mortlach 1991 sherry cask, cask no. 4251 **(89.5) n23 t22.5 f22 b22** Once, there was many a blender for whom the words "Mortlach" and "sherry" in the same sentence would bring a shudder. Certainly not with this cask which, in performance, is a bit like a Jumbo Jet hanger accommodating a Spitfire. The sherry has completely dominated the malt, so there is not even a hint of barley anywhere within the flavour framework. But dripping over-ripe raisins...? This is your boy! Must admit: love the late toastiness. *53.9%. 499 bottles. Matisse Spirits Company.*

Gordon & MacPhail Connoisseurs Choice Mortlach Aged 30 Years refill American hogshead, cask no. 4839, dist 7 Dec 88, bott 11 Dec 18 **(86.5) n21 t21.5 f22 b22** Pretty enjoyable if you can grip tightly onto the arms of your chair as the tannins bite without mercy. Settles only late on as the malt regroups to add a degree of both sweetness and shape. *48.8%. sc. 129 bottles.*

Gordon & MacPhail Connoisseurs Choice Mortlach Aged 31 Years refill sherry hogshead, cask no. 425, dist 5 Feb 87, bott 3 Jul 18 **(80) n20 t22 f19 b19** About as subtle as being hit around the head by a herring dipped in unctuous sherry. Not one of Mortlach's finer moments. *54%.*

⬨ **Hepburn's Choice Mortlach 10 Years Old** wine cask, dist 2009, bott 2019 **(90.5) n23** so light, but the smoke sings beautifully with the intense barley; **t22.5** ditto on delivery: the nose in liquid form...! **f22** just dries a little to gamely; **b23** youthfully fresh and malty. But it is the low rumble of smoke on the nose, delivery and finish in particular that genuinely intrigues! Refreshing and crisp, all the same. *46%. nc ncf sc. 375 bottles.*

Highland Tiger Mortlach 2006 cask no. 15, red wine finish, dist 3 Oct 06, bott 31 Jan 19 **(87.5) n21 t22.5 f22 b22** Mortlach at its most thick-set and cloying, which is saying something. But this Tiger also has teeth and there is no denying the sheer fun as soon as the super-juicy fruit gets going on the high alcohol strength. If you want something more subtle, try a pie in the face. But in the meantime just enjoy the rounded, sweet, rumbustious outlandishness of this. *55.4%. Mr. Whisky.*

Scyfion Choice Mortlach 2005 Troyanda cask finished, bott 2018 (84.5) n21 t21 f21.5 b21 A strange malt, which feels understrength despite being close to 50% abv. Also has a certain tininess, a thin outer shell which allows little to escape. Nothing technically wrong with it, but if you wait for it to take off, you'll be there a bloody long time. *48.4%. nc ncf sc. 328 bottles.*

MOSSTOWIE
Speyside, 1964–1981. Chivas Brothers. Closed.
Rare Old Mosstowie 1979 (84.5) n21.5 t21 f21 b21. Edging inextricably well beyond its sell by date. But there is a lovely walnut cream cake (topped off with brown sugar and spices) to this which warms the cockles. Bless... *43%. Gordon & MacPhail.*

NORTH PORT
Highlands (Eastern), 1820–1983. Diageo. Demolished.
Brechin 1977 db (78) n19 t21 f18 b20. Fire and brimstone was never an unknown quantity with the whisky from this doomed distillery. Some soothing oils are poured on this troubled – and sometimes attractively honeyed – water of life. *54.2%*

OBAN
Highlands (Western), 1794. Diageo. Working.
Oban 14 Years Old db (79) n19 t22 f18 b20. Absolutely all over the place. The cask selection sits very uncomfortably with the malt. I look forward to the resumption of normality to this great but ill-served distillery. *43%*

Oban The Distillers Edition special release OD 162.FX, dist 1998, bott 2013 db (87.5) n22.5 t22.5 f21 b21.5. Some attractive kumquat and blood orange makes for a fruity and rich malt, though just a little furry towards the finish. Decent Demerara early on, too. *43%*

⟫⟫ **Oban Distillery Exclusive Bottling** batch no. 02, refill, ex-bourbon and rejuvenated casks, bott code: L9337CM008 db (91.5) n23 how's that for a mix of un-smoked gristy sugars and ulmo honey? Then the butterscotch and tannin to bind it all together...; t23.5 a super-sweet delivery that packs a beautiful malty punch. The castor sugars are never far away, though. Every atom seems to melt away...so ridiculously soft! f22 just a little bitterness as the odd tired note from the oak creeps into the action. But the lightly spiced barley still has a lot to say, even when the vanillas make their presence felt; b23 who knew that one day they'd bring out an Oban this sweet? Usually a malt with an absent-minded, salty dryness that never did anything with great intention or seemingly with a game plan. Here, though, this has been set out to be as friendly as possible. And it has most certainly succeeded! *48%. 7,500 bottles.*

Oban Little Bay db (87.5) n21 t23 f21.5 b22. A pleasant, refreshing simple dram. Clean and juicy in part and some wonderful oak-laden spice to stir things up a little. Just a little too much chewy toffee near the end, though. *43%*

Game of Thrones Oban Bay Reserve The Night's Watch db (87.5) n22 t23 f21 b21.5 Starts promisingly, even offering a saltiness you tend not to see from this distillery these days. The intense grist on the malt makes for a beautiful delivery. But flattens fast and furiously as the caramels kick in. *43%.*

PITTYVAICH
Speyside, 1975–1993. Diageo. Demolished.
Pittyvaich 28 Year Old db (86.5) n22.5 t22 f20.5 b21.5 The nose is an attractive blend of malt and hazelnut. The delivery is sweet, gristy and promising. But it thins out fast and dramatically. So limited in scope, but pleasant in the early phases. *52.1%. 4,680 bottles. Diageo Special Releases 2018.*

PORT ELLEN
Islay, 1825–1983. Diageo. Closed.
⟫⟫ **Port Ellen 9 Rogue Casks 40 Year Old** db (96) n24 the chalky vanilla hewn from 40 Scottish summers could so easily have damaged the delicate structure of the nose. Yet somehow it doesn't: the phenols have defied time and the natural order of things to maintain body enough to not just absorb the oak, but merge with it – and a few strands of citrus – to ensure a 20 minute nose: in other words, anything less than that time before tasting would be a crime as this is an unexpected piece of art.... Even more surprising is that there is an acidic bite to the peat, not unlike that you might find in a cattle byre...; t24 you have to laugh: it is like a 40-year-old version of the malt when it was just eight or ten...the gristiness is not just evident, but the malt simply melts in the mouth leaving a slightly sooty residue. The sugars, made up from both barley and heather honey, offer just the right degree of support; f23.5 I didn't for a moment expect there still to be peat working on my taste buds so late

on. But along with the prissy spices, it is. Before finally settling as the lightest oils and lightly smoked butterscotch lock in for the fade out...; **b24.5** one of the great surprise whiskies of this any many years. I didn't expect this bottling to display such astounding elegance and balance, but it does from the first moment to the last. It has taken me close on three hours to analyse this malt. Had I the space, my notes could probably take up a page of this book. But here I have simplified it over many temperatures and varying oxidisation levels. Those nine rogue casks must have been as beautifully seasoned as they come. Stunning. *50.9%.* 🏆

Port Ellen Aged 37 Years dist 1978 db **(91)** n24.5 t22.5 f22 **b22** The bark is far better than the bite: one of the great noses of the year cannot be backed up on the palate as the oak is simply too demanding. An historical experience, but ensure you spend as much time nosing as you do tasting... *55.2%. 2,940 bottles. Diageo Special Releases 2016.*

Port Ellen 37 Year Old refill American oak hogsheads & refill American oak butts db **(88)** n23 t21.5 f22 **b21.5** The oak scars the overall beauty of the malt. *51%. 2,988 bottles.*

Port Ellen 39 Years Old db **(96.5)** n24 t24 f24 **b24.5** A malt which defies time and logic, and the short-sighted individuals who closed down this distillery and later, unforgivably, ripped out its innards (despite my one-kneed imploring). Tragically beautiful. *50.9%. 1,500 bottles.*

Gleann Mór Port Ellen Aged Over 33 Years dist 1983 **(96.5)** n25 t24 f23.5 **b24** If a whisky can bring a tear to your eye, then this one will. It is too elegant and beautiful for this world... *57%. sc.*

PULTENEY
Highlands (Northern), 1826. Inver House Distillers. Working.

Old Pulteney Aged 12 Years db **(90.5)** n22 t23 f22.5 **b23** A cleaner, zestier more joyous composition than the old 43%, though that has less to do with strength than overall construction. A dramatic whisky which, with further care, could get even closer to the truth of this distillery. *40%*

Old Pulteney Aged 12 Years bott code L15/030 R15/5046 IB db **(91)** n22.5 t23 f22.5 **b23** Remarkably consistent from the bottling above. The salt continues to ensure lustre, though this bottling has a little extra – and welcome – barley gristiness. *40%. ncf.*

Old Pulteney Aged 15 Years db **(95.5)** n24 t24 f23.5 **b24** More than a night cap. One you should definitely take to bed with you... *46%.*

Old Pulteney Aged 17 Years bott code: L15/329 R15/5530 IB db **(82)** n20.5 t22.5 f19 **b20** This is usually one of the greatest whiskies bottled anywhere in the world. But not even something of Pulteney 17's usually unfathomable excellence and charisma can withstand this degree of sulphur. Much greater care has to be taken in the bottling hall to preserve the integrity of what should be one of Scotland's most beautiful offerings to the world. *46%. ncf.*

Old Pulteney Aged 18 Years db **(81)** n19 t21.5 f20 **b20.5** If you are going to work with sherry butts you have to be very careful. And here we see a whisky that is not careful enough as the sulphur does its usual damage. For those in central Europe without the "sulphur gene", then no problem as the fruit is still intact. *46%.*

Old Pulteney Aged 21 Years db **(97.5)** n25 t24 f24 **b24.5** By far and away one of the great whiskies of 2012, absolutely exploding from the glass with vitality, charisma and class. One of Scotland's great undiscovered distilleries about to become discovered, I think... and rightly so! *46%*

Old Pulteney Aged 25 Years American & Spanish oak casks, bott code: L17/282 R17/5353 IB db **(96)** n25 t23.5 f23.5 **b24** A quiet but incredibly complex reminder why this distillery is capable of producing World Whisky of the Year. Age is all around you, but degradation there is none. *46%.* 🏆

Old Pulteney 35 Year Old db **(89)** n23 t21.5 f22.5 **b22** A malt on the perimeter of its comfort zone. But there are enough gold nuggets included to make this work. Just. *46%.*

Old Pulteney Aged 40 Years db **(95)** n23.5 t23.5 f24 **b24** This malt still flies as close to the sun as possible. But some extra fruit, honey and spice now grasps the tannins by the throat to ensure a whisky of enormous magnitude and complexity *51.3%*

Old Pulteney 1990 Vintage American & Spanish casks db **(85)** n21 t23 f21 **b20.** As you know, anything which mentions sherry butts gets me nervous – and for good reason. Even with a World Great distillery like Pulteney. Oddly enough, this bottling is, as near a dammit, free of sulphur. Yee-hah! The bad news, though, is that it is also untroubled by complexity as well. It reminded me of some heavily sherried peaty jobs...and then I learned that ex Islay casks were involved. That may or may not be it. But have to say, beyond the first big, salivating, lightly spiced moments on delivery you wait for the story to unfurl...and it all turns out to be dull rumours. *46%.*

Old Pulteney 2006 Vintage first fill ex-bourbon casks, bott 2017, bott code: L17/279 R17/5452 IB db **(93)** n23 t23.5 f23 **b23.5** A beautiful, lightly salted ceremony of malt with the glycerine feel of raspberry and cream Swiss rolls. Just so love it! *46%.*

Old Pulteney Duncansby Head Lighthouse bourbon and sherry casks db **(90.5) n23 t23 f22 b22.5** Beginning to wonder if Pulteney is into making whisky or cakes. And malt straight from the oven. *46% WB15/329*

Old Pulteney Dunnet Head Lighthouse bourbon & sherry casks db **(90.5) n22 t23.5 f22 b23** Loads to chew over with this heavyweight.*46%. nc ncf. Exclusive to travel retail.*

Old Pulteney Huddart db **(88.5) n22 t22.5 f22 b22** Hopefully not named after my erstwhile physics teacher of 45 years ago, Ernie Huddart, who, annoyingly, for an entire year insisted on calling me Murphy rather than Murray, despite my constant correcting his mistake. One day he told me off for my not remembering one or other Law of Physics. When he finished berating me quite unpleasantly at high volume before my fellow classmates, I simply said: "Well, sir, that's fine coming from you. You've had a year to learn that my name is Murray and not Murphy, and still you failed!" He was so lost for words at this impudence I got away with it, though if his glare could have killed... Anyway, back to the whisky: this seemingly young, lightly smoked version shows all the hallmarks of being finished in peaty casks, as opposed to being distilled from phenolic malt, hence the slightly mottled and uneven feel to this. Odd, but attractive. Oh, and Huddart...? I think that's actually the name of the nondescript old street on which the distillery sits *46%.*

Old Pulteney Navigator bourbon & sherry casks db **(80) n19 t23 f18 b20.** Sherry butts have clearly been added to this. Not sure why, as the sulphur only detracts from the early honey riches. The compass is working when the honey and cocoa notes briefly harmonise in beautiful tandem. But otherwise, badly off course. *46%. nc ncf.*

Old Pulteney Navigator bourbon & sherry casks, bott code: L15/207 R15/5318 IB db **(78) n19 t22 f18 b19** Even further lost in sulphurous territory than before... *46%. ncf.*

Old Pulteney Noss Head Lighthouse bourbon casks db **(84) n22.5 t22 f19 b20.5.** If Noss Head was as light as this dram, it'd be gone half way through its first half decent storm. An apparent slight overuse of third and less sturdy second fill casks means the finale bitters out considerably. A shame, as the nose and delivery is about as fine a display of citrus maltiness as you'll find. *46%. Travel retail exclusive. WB15/324*

Old Pulteney Pentland Skerries Lighthouse db **(85) n21 t22 f20.5 b21.5.** A chewy dram with an emphasis on the fruit. Sound, evens enjoys the odd chocolate-toffee moment. But a little sulphur, apparent on the nose, creeps in to take the gloss off. *46%. WB15/323*

Gordon & MacPhail Connoisseurs Choice Pulteney Aged 19 Years first fill bourbon barrel, cask no. 1071, dist 26 Aug 98, bott 21 Jun 18 **(95.5) n23.5 t24 f24 b24** Malt from one of the world's very finest distilleries matured in a first- class cask. The result is inevitable. The interplay between oak and malt starts on the first molecules to hit the nose and ends only when the story is told. Can't ask any more of the spices, or their interaction with the liquorice and Manuka honey mix. Everything is perfectly paced and weighted, even the natural caramels that could so easily have tipped this towards a blander bottling. Toasty, sublimely complex and breath-taking. *57.5%. sc. 192 bottles.*

The Whisky Shop Old Pulteney Aged 12 Years Spanish oak hogshead, cask no. 1471, dist 2007 **(94.5) n23.5** blinding grape; **t23.5** the usual spice buzz of a big sherry cask; the lightest malt and marzipan stratum; **f24** gorgeous chocolate raisin; **b23.5** there's nothing like a drop of whisky in your sherry... *50.2%. sc.*

The Whisky Shop Old Pulteney 2006 cask no. 1448 **(91.5) n22.5 t23 f23 b23** Very relaxed Pulteney happy to rely on the considerable charms of ulmo honey and rich barley in unison. Juicy and sharp on delivery but finishes by whistling with its hands in its pockets. *50.2%. sc.*

ROSEBANK
Lowlands, 1840–1993. Ian Macleod. Closed- soon to re-open. (The gods have answered!)

Rosebank 21 Year Old refill American oak casks, dist 1992 db **(95.5) n23.5 t24 f24 b24** Rosebank is at its very best at eight-years-old. Well, that won't happen again, so great to see it has proven successful at 21... *55.3%. 4,530 bottles. Diageo Special Releases 2014.*

ROYAL BRACKLA
Speyside, 1812. Bacardi. Working.

Royal Brackla Aged 12 Years bott code: L18192B700 db **(85) n22 t22 f20 b21** A definite improvement on previous bottlings but, coming from Bacardi's formidable stable, I had expected more. The finish is still dull as ditch water, with nothing other than toffee to find but there is an upping of fresh fruit on both nose and delivery. *40%.*

Royal Brackla Aged 16 Years bott code: L18158B700 db **(88) n22.5** light and zesty, a little spice flickers around the caramel; **t22.5** soft, bordering luxuriant, there is a big malt and caramel hook up. But it is the all too brief, refreshing, zingy delivery which stars; **f21** still a little too much on the dull-ish caramel side; **b22** a very pleasant malt, but you get the feeling it is being driven with the handbrake on... *40%.*

Royal Brackla 21 Year Old db **(91)** n23.5 t23 f22 b22.5 Now that's much more like it! 40%

Royal Brackla Aged 21 Years bott code: L18297B701 db **(91.5)** n23 maintains its unusual but delightful lychee sweetness, that sweetness now extending to maple syrup and fudge; t23 delicate and salivating, initially shewing little sign of great age. It takes a while but the toastier tannins finally arrive; f22.5 salty, with a chocolate fudge finale; b23 where both the 12- and 16-years olds appear both to be tied to a vat of toffee, this beauty has been given its wings. Also, I remember this for being a malt with a curious lychee note, hence tasting it today. For yesterday I tasted a malt matured in a lychee liqueur barrel. Pleased to report no shortage of lychees here, either. 40%.

⟡ **Scyfion Choice Royal Brackla 2007** Banyuls wine cask finished, bott 2019 **(82)** n20 t21.5 f20.5 b20 Malty, lightly spiced, tart and never, for a moment, properly at home with itself or balanced. 46%. nc ncf sc. 150 bottles.

Single Cask Collection Royal Brackla Aged 11 Years (89) n22 t22 f22.5 b22.5 An oily and nutty offering which makes the most of its cask strength. The malt intensity is simplistic, attractive and even throughout. But it is that light chocolate-nut theme which builds and stars. 54%. sc.

⟡ **Whisky Illuminati Royal Brackla 2011** Spanish oak sherry butt, cask no. 900077 **(93)** n23 a real nuttiness to this grape – all guns are blazing; t23.5 lush and chewy with the sherry pounding the taste buds in the same way waves are pounding the British coast at this moment thanks to Storm Ciara, which is presently battering all parts of the British coastline: certainly a dram for the moment...; f23 only toward the finish does the sweetness settle towards a relaxed ulmo honey and plummy interplay. Delightful...; b23.5 every bit as punchy as the strength suggests, with the sherry influence piling in at full tilt and refusing to hold back. 68%. sc. 150 bottles.

ROYAL LOCHNAGAR
Highlands (Eastern), 1826. Diageo. Working.

Royal Lochnagar Aged 12 Years db **(84)** n21 t22 f20 b21. More care has been taken with this than some other bottlings from this wonderful distillery. But I still can't understand why it never quite manages to get out of third gear...or is the caramel on the finish the giveaway...? 40%

⟡ **Royal Lochnagar Distillery Exclusive** batch no. 01, first-fill European oak and refill casks, bott code: L9302DQ0001 db **(82)** n22 t23 f17.5 b19.5 Ultimately a dull, monotonous whisky after a promising and lively start. Love the fresh, salivating delivery and with some great spices, too. But the story ends by the midpoint. The European oak has done this no favours whatsoever, ensuring a furry, off-key finale. 48%. 5,004 bottles.

Game of Thrones Royal Lochnagar 12 Year Old House Baratheon db **(89)** n22 t22.5 f22 b22.5 Not sure when I last encountered a Lochnager of such simplicity. Friendly and impossible not to like. 40%.

⟡ **The First Editions Royal Lochnagar Aged 19 Years 2000** refill hogshead, cask no. 16350, bott 2019 **(91.5)** n23 dense heather honey and oak-fused malt: sturdy and direct; t23 puckeringly intense! The sharpness of the barley and tannin combo is softened by the glow of the honey, which softens as the spices arrive; f22.5 rich vanilla and warming spice; b23 there is no getting away from the effect of the small stills here: every sensation is in concentrate form. A kind of a head-shaking, wow! of a malt... 55.5%. nc ncf sc. 384 bottles.

ST. MAGDALENE
Lowlands, 1798–1983. Diageo. Demolished.

Linlithgow 30 Years Old dist 1973 db **(70)** n18 t18 f16 b18. A brave but ultimately futile effort from a malt that is way past its sell-by date. 59.6%

⟡ **Gordon & MacPhail Private Collection St. Magdalene 1982** refill American hogshead, cask no. 2092, dist 1 Jul 82, bott 21 Mar 19 **(96)** n24 I don't believe it: the citrus note which was a marker of its '82 vintage has withstood the test of time or, to be more precise, the test of very healthy tannin. Very good age on this: the grey hairs shew no signs of thinning, but the barley and citrus hold firm...; t24 I sit here truly amazed at what I am tasting: this, after all these years, is still salivating. The barley is identifiable and, now it has natural caramels from the oak for company, lush. The lightest heather-honey note suggests that a little smoke was once in this mix here. The butterscotch mid-ground is unusual, but confirms the oaky interception; f23.5 just the slightest hint of mocha before it begins a long journey of drying vanilla. But a light barley and spice still flit around to the very end; b24.5 it has been eight long years since a new St Magdalene turned up in my tasting room and that, like this, was distilled just a year before the closure of the distillery itself. And I can tell you for nothing, when it was made never in a million years did any of those within the distillery believe for a second that it would finally be tasted nearly 40 years after the spirit was filled into a very good American oak barrel. For a start, this was a Lowland malt that, in its lifetime, was used exclusively for blending, most of it at three and five years old. It is light in structure and flavour and conversations I had with blenders in the 1980s confirmed that they didn't trust this malt to add sufficient body to the malt content for it to be used for older blends, though that didn't stop Diageo once bringing it out as a 23-year-old. Of all the St. Mag distillates I tasted from about 1970 through to 1983, I thought 1982 the finest of the bunch, so no surprise that it has held its head high and proud here, even displaying the same citrusy undercurrent that I thought made the 10-year-old so charming way back in 1992. I have in here, not just a throwback but a little whisky miracle in my glass. This malt has no right to be this good. But, my god it is...!! 53%. sc. 161 bottles. 🏆

SCAPA

Highlands (Island–Orkney), 1885. Chivas Brothers. Working.

Scapa 12 Years Old db (88) n23 t22 f21 b22. Always a joy. 40%

Scapa 16 Years Old db (81) n21 t20.5 f19.5 b20. For it to be so tamed and toothless is a crime against a truly great whisky which, handled correctly, would be easily among the finest the world has to offer. 40%

Scapa Glansa peated whisky cask finish, batch no. GL05, bott Jul 18 db (91) n22 t23.5 f22.5 b23 A delightful whisky which could be raised several notches in quality if the influence of the caramel is diminished. 40%.

Scapa Skiren db (89.5) n22.5 t22.5 f22 b22.5 Chaps who created this: lovely, you really have to power this one up a bit... 40%

Gordon & MacPhail Connoisseurs Choice Scapa Aged 30 Years refill bourbon barrel, cask no. 10585, dist 2 Sept 88, bott 13 Sept 18 (94) n22.5 t24 f23.5 b24 One of those exceptionally rare occasions when the threatening tannins on the nose fail to materialise on the palate. Instead we have glorious display of varied honey tones far more usually associated with its neighbouring Orkney distillery. Stunning displays of light saltiness mixes brilliantly with the lime blossom honey before the spices and tannins set. A thing of beauty. 53.8%. sc. 148 bottles.

SPEYBURN

Speyside, 1897. Inver House Distillers. Working.

Speyburn Aged 10 Years bott code: L16/303 R165434 IB db (84.5) n21 t21.5 f21 b21 Appears to celebrate and even emphasises its remarkable thinness of body. As usual, juicy with a dominant toffee character. 40%.

Speyburn Aged 10 Years Travel Exclusive American oak ex-bourbon & ex-sherry casks, bott code L18/055 R18/5069 IB db (89.5) n21.5 t22.5 f22.5 b23 Really imaginative use of excellent sherry butts. An understatedly complex and delicious malt. 46%. ncf.

Speyburn Aged 15 Years American oak & Spanish oak casks, bott code L1717/253 R17/5323 IB db (91) n22 t23.5 f22 b23.5 Well done: not an off sherry butt in sight, helping to make this an enjoyably rich and fulsome malt. One of the most inventive and sympathetic Speyburns of all time. 46%.

Speyburn Aged 18 Years db (86) n22 t22.5 f20 b21.5 Nutty, malty and displaying a cocoa tendency. But the finish is a bit on the bitter side. 46%.

Speyburn Aged 25 Years db (92) n22 t24 f23 b23. Either they have re-bottled very quickly or I got the diagnosis dreadfully wrong first time round. Previously I wasn't overly impressed; now I'm taken aback by its beauty. Some change. 46%

Speyburn Arranta Casks first fill ex-bourbon casks bott code: L16/097 R16/5130 IB db (90) n22 t23 f22 b23 Speyburn at its most vocal and interesting: rather beautifully constructed. 46%.

Speyburn Bradon Orach bott code: L17/039 R17/5048 IB db (75) n19 t19 f18.5 b18.5 Remains one of the most curious distillery bottlings on Speyside and one still unable to find either its balance or a coherent dialogue. 40%.

Speyburn Hopkins Reserve Travel Exclusive bott code R18/5066 IB db (92) n23 t23 f22.5 b23.5 The kind of ultra-simplistic raw, smoky Speysider that the distillery's founder John Hopkins would have recognised – and drooled over - over a century ago... 46%. ncf.

The First Editions Speyburn Aged 12 Years 2006 sherry butt, cask no. 15539, bott 2018 (89.5) n22 t23 f22 b22.5 A clean sherry butt free from faults. Very limited complexity but the overall ride is an enjoyable one. 56.3%. nc ncf sc. 288 bottles.

Hepburn's Choice Speyburn 12 Years Old sherry butt, dist 2006, bott 2018 (87) n21.5 t22.5 f21 b22 Dry and constrained to the point of being almost paranoid in its personality. There are some lovely, fleeting sultana moments, balanced excellently by spice. But the tightness of the vanilla restricts the promised development. 46%. nc ncf sc. 708 bottles.

Old Malt Cask Speyburn Aged 13 Years sherry butt, cask no. 15306, dist Nov 04, bott Aug 18 (87.5) n22 t23 f20.5 b22 A pleasant if ultimately unexciting sherried Speyburn but boasting a real spicy sultana cake fruitiness before the unyielding intensity of the chalk-dry vanilla takes hold. A very decent and attractive malt overall. 50%. nc ncf sc. 483 bottles.

Scyfion Choice Speyburn 2008 Muscat Dolce Passione cask finished, bott 2018 **(85.5)** **n**20.5 **t**22 **f**21.5 **b**21.5 Tight and tart, this isn't the kind of malt I can get too passionate about, even if it does bring water to the eyes... *46%. nc ncf sc. 140 bottles.*

THE SPEYSIDE DISTILLERY
Speyside, 1990. Speyside Distillers. Working.

Spey 10 Year Old port casks db **(87)** **n**22 **t**22.5 **f**20.5 **b**22 Soft and nutty, there is an attractive easiness to the fruit as it makes its salivating, bitter-sweet way around the palate. Just a little bit of a tang on the finish, though. *46%. nc ncf. 3,000 bottles.*

Spey 12 Years Old limited edition, finished in new oak casks db **(85.5)** **n**21.5 **t**23 **f**19.5 **b**21.5. One of the hardest whiskies I have had to define this year: it is a curious mixture of niggling faults and charming positives which come together to create a truly unique scotch. The crescendo is reached early after the delivery with an amalgamation of acacia honey, barley sugar and butter notes interlocking with something bordering classicism. However, the nose and finish, despite the chalky oak, reveals that something was lacking in the original distillate or, to be more precise, was rather more than it should have been. Still, some hard work has obviously gone into maximising the strengths of a distillery that had hitherto failed to raise the pulse and impresses for that alone. *40%. nc. 8,000 bottles.*

Spey 18 Years Old ltd edition, fresh sherry casks db **(82.5)** **n**19 **t**23.5 **f**19 **b**21. What a shame this malt has been brushed with sulphur. Apparent on nose and finish, it still can't diminish ir detract from the joy of the juicy grape on delivery and the excellent weight as the liquorice and treacle add their gentle treasures and pleasures. So close to a true classic. *46%. nc.*

Spey Chairman's Choice db **(77)** **n**19 **t**21 **f**18 **b**19. Their Chairman's Choice, maybe. But not mine... *40%*

Spey Fumare db **(90.5)** **n**22 **t**23.5 **f**22 **b**23 A very different type of peaty malt with some surprising twists and turns. As fascinating as it is quietly delicious. I am looking at Speyside distillery in a new light...*46%. nc ncf.*

Spey Fumare Cask Strength db **(93)** **n**23 there is a cool menthol touch to perfectly match the polite loftiness of the phenol. So well groomed...; **t**23.5 sweet, smoky, salivating gristiness helps hide a slight technical flaw, like make-up over an old scar. So attractive, though...; **f**23 dries as the vanillas make a definite impact. A little diced macadamia nut fits in well with the vaguely spiced phenol and mocha; **b**23.5 unquestionably The Speyside Distillery in its prettiest pose. And this strength ensures perfect lighting... *59.3%. nc ncf. 1,500 bottles.*

Spey Royal Choice db **(87)** **n**21 **t**23 **f**21 **b**22. "I'll have the slightly feinty one, Fortescue." "Of course, Your Highness. Would that be the slightly feinty one which has a surprising softness on the palate, a bit like a moist date and walnut cake? But with a touch too much oil on the finish?" "That's the blighter! No ice, Fortescue!" "Perish the thought, Sir." "Or water, Forters. One must drink according to the Murray Method, don't you know!" "Very wise, Sir." *46%*

Spey Tenné finished in Tawny Port casks db **(90)** **n**22.5 **t**23 **f**22 **b**22.5 Upon pouring, the handsome pink blush tells you one of three things: i) someone has swiped the whisky and filled the bottle with Mateus Rosé instead; ii) I have just located where I put the pink paraffin or iii) this whisky has been matured in brand spanking new port casks. Far from a technical paragon of virtue so far as distilling is concerned. But those Tawny Port casks have brought something rather magical to the table. And glass. *46%. nc. 18,000 bottles.*

Spey Tenné Cask Strength db **(88)** **n**22.5 **t**22 **f**21.5 **b**22 Plenty of weirdness to this – and spicy fun, too! What magnificent (port?) casks they must have used for this....!! *59.5%. nc ncf. 1,500 bottles.*

Spey Trutina bourbon casks db **(90)** **n**22.5 **t**23 **f**22 **b**22.5 The best Speyside Distillery bottling I have encountered for a very long time. Entirely feint free and beautifully made. *46%. nc ncf.*

Spey Trutina Cask Strength db **(93)** **n**22.5 **t**24 **f**23 **b**23.5 Feint free and fabulous! *59.1%. nc ncf. 1,500 bottles.*

Beinn Dubh db **(82)** **n**20 **t**21 **f**21 **b**20. Mountains. Dogs. Who can tell the difference...? I suppose to a degree I can, as this has for more rummy undertones and is slightly less inclined to layering than the old Danish version. *43%*

The Golden Cask Speyside 1992 cask no. CM253, bott 2019 **(95.5)** **n**24 **t**24 **f**23.5 **b**24 Whisky from Speyside distillery – in a short, Golden, Olden period when they were distilling at a higher quality than in following years – really doesn't get better than this. *57.7%. nc ncf sc. 216 bottles.*

SPRINGBANK
Campbeltown, 1828. J&A Mitchell & Co. Working.

Springbank Aged 10 Years db **(89.5)** **n**22 **t**23 **f**22 **b**22.5. Although the inherent youthfulness of the 10-y-o has not changed, the depth of body around it has. Keeps the taste buds on full alert. *46%*

Springbank Aged 15 Years db (88.5) n22.5 t22 f22 b22. Last time I had one of these, sulphur spoiled the party. Not this time. But the combination of oil and caramel does detract from the complexity a little. *46%*

Springbank Aged 18 Years db (90.5) n23 busy in the wonderful Springbank way; delicate greengage and date; nippy; t23 yummy, mouthwatering barley and green banana. Fresh with excellent light acacia honey; f21.5 fabulous oak layering, including chocolate. A little off-key furriness from a sherry butt late on; b23 just one so-so butt away from bliss... *46%*

Springbank Aged 21 Years db (90) n22 t23 f22.5 b22.5 A few years ago I was at Springbank when they were bottling a very dark, old-fashioned style 21-year-old. I asked if I could take a 10cl sample with me for inclusion in the Bible; they said they would send it on, though I tasted a glass there and then just for enjoyment's sake. They never did send it, which was a shame. For had they, they most probably would have carried off World Whisky of the Year. This, though very good, is not quite in the same class. But just to mark how special this brand has always been to me, I have made this the 500th new single malt scotch and 700th new whisky in all of the 2015 Whisky Bible. *46%. WB15/096*

◇◇◇ **Springbank 22 Year Old Single Cask** hogshead, cask no. 582, dist May 97, bott Jan 20 db (95.5) n24 t24 f23.5 b24 It is rare these days for me to be genuinely taken aback by a whisky. But this managed it. The malt is pleasingly light in colour for its age, and certainly for a Springbank of this age. So second fill ex-bourbon, even third, possibly. Which when the tannins fire their broadside on the very first sniff...yes, there is reason to be taken aback. Of course, the trademark of this distillery is labyrinthine complexity. And though labyrinthine may be taking it a bit far here, you can still descend very deeply into this malt and have plenty of passages to explore. Certainly, I love to take the saline route here, which gives a delightful piquancy to tannin and sharpens the barley tones that float around it. So it is pleasing to see that this route can be followed on the beautifully soft delivery which just abounds in vanilla. But there is just as much thickset barley, too. This is magnificent malt which repays using the Murray Method for best results. But, as you will see, the nose is at its best at one temperature (relatively cool and the experience on the palate is at its zenith when warmed a little. Oh, and before I forget...look out for the fascinating strata of peat. Fair took me aback, it did... *55.4%. Bottled for HMMJ collection.*

Hazelburn Aged 8 Years bourbon cask, bott 2011 db (94.5) n23 t24 f23.5 b24 A very curious coppery sheen adds extra lustre and does no harm to a very well made spirit filled into top grade oak. For an eight year old malt, something extra special. *46%*

Longrow Aged 10 Years db (78) n19 t20 f19 b20. This has completely bemused me: bereft not only of the usual to-die-for smoke, its warts are exposed badly, as this is way too young. Sweet and malty, perhaps, and technically better than the marks I'm giving it – but this is Longrow, dammit! I am astonished. *46%*

Longrow 14 Years Old refill bourbon and sherry casks db (89) n24 t23.5 f19 b22.5. Again, a sherry butt proves the Achilles heel. But until then, a charmer. *46%*

Longrow Aged 18 Years db (94.5) n25 t23 f23 b23.5 If you gently peat a blend of ulmo, manuka and heather honey you might end up with something as breathtakingly stunning as this. But you probably won't... *46%. WB15/103*

◇◇◇ **Longrow 21 Year Old 2019 Release** db (92.5) n23.5 t23 f23 b23 The one thing you can safely say about the Springbank distillery is that it is idiosyncratic. And one thing you can normally say about a malt whisky is that when it has thoroughly aged the oak tones normally appear at their most powerful either upfront on delivery or at the finish. But this being from Springbank, no. Instead, massive oaky notes gather on the nose like wintertime rooks on a majestic beech tree before sunset, a noisy, ageless cacophony. Which makes you think you are in for a rather rough ride. But, no again! The smoke on the nose, like the tannin is active. Once both hit the palate they are tamed, for a while at least, to the point of docility. Natural caramels abound everywhere, even more so than peat while a little orange blossom honey offers light into the gloom. Only towards the end does the tannin reappear, a little peat for company. But always checked and balanced. A surprising dram, indeed. *46%.*

◇◇◇ **Artful Dodger Springbank 18 Year Old 2000** 1st fill sherry hogshead, cask no. 646 (96) n24 t24 f24 b24 For an 18-year-old Springbank has all the creaks and grey hairs of something a lot more than twice its age... The oak seems to date back to Robin Hood, the grape could have been from a wine shared by the disciples. This malt (some of them shewing the odd partiality to peat) bends and bows like a medieaval inn. But even so you have to say this: the balance and interplay between the delicate factions is a work of art to behold, The palate is not for a single moment molested as the tannins and gentle juices go about their business. This is a malt for that special occasion. A parent's 90th birthday perhaps; your own 60th. Your child's 30th. This is all to do with time and wisdom. And on the subject of time, less than an hour at the glass with this whisky will not do it any justice at all. The next time I taste this, it will be to celebrate the lockdown that keeps me imprisoned in the UK being lifted. It is a whisky for extraordinary moments in one's life. 45.9%. sc.

The Perfect Fifth Springbank 1993 cask no. 315, dist 28 May 93 **(96) n24** anyone who remembers the old Springbank 25-year-olds of the early 1990s will recognise this aroma as a direct descendent – indeed it is near enough identical in both weight and character. The huge, nuggety oak is faultless (this must have come from a cask which had been seasoned in the old – virtually lost – style). Salt dominates but there are dried apricots and spiced pear, too. Meanwhile the vaguest of peaty notes (and I mean the odd atom here and there!) teases away as a barely audible background noise, which automatically becomes louder the moment you spot it...; **t24** a malt on the threshold of perhaps dallying too closely with the oak. But that coastal-style bite makes just the right contact with the salty tannins and cocoa-laden phenol to make a course for more complex and satisfying port. Just enough oil makes the middle rich and promises a long finale; **f24** drier, as is to be expected, as the tannins raise their game. Still salty, but a little barley sugar and lemon juice lightens the intensity, though – happily, by not too much; the residual oils ensure the finish is of extraordinary length; **b24** a real return to the past here with Springbank in its most full-bodied, uncompromising and complex style which those of us who discovered the distillery in the 1980s remember with great affection. 52.3%. sc.

Master of Malt Single Cask Springbank 20 Year Old dist 1998 **(94.5) n23 t24 f23.5 b24** More Springbanky than a Glen Scotia. 48.1%. sc.

Sansibar Whisky Springbank 2000 (95) n23.5 t24 f23.5 b24 Just runs amok with Springbank's unique everythingness...! So much going on, it almost wears you out! 49.1%.

⬦ **The Whisky Agency Springbank 1991** hogshead, bott 2018 **(95) n24 t23.5 f23.5 b24** There are many days I'm exhausted because I have tasted nothing but poor or second-rate whisky. Then there are others, like today, when both my brain and taste buds are beaten into submission by a relentless procession of excellent to outstanding drams. Today is the latter, and my day, thankfully, is coming to an end as I head towards my 800th whisky of the year (this is number 799). This malt positively crawls of Springbankian messages: the mix of sturdy oak and varied citrus – lime marmalade leading the way – but also of an antique nature as in the aroma of ancient polished furniture. Can the delivery be quite so good? Surely not! Well, actually it isn't, but only by whisker. The fruit is stubbornly there, though more down the lime pastels this time. Then a massive injection of oaky caramel. The finish maybe a pretty routine round-up of spices and vanillas, but you are thankful for the delicate normality. And, like so many Springbanks of that era you are only afterwards left thinking: actually, there's a little peat doing the rounds, as well. Frankly if all the 1,000 plus whiskies I had to taste for the Bible were like this, I'd never get finished... 46.4%.

STRATHISLA

Speyside, 1786. Chivas Brothers. Working.

Strathisla 12 Years Old db **(85.5) n21.5 t22 f21 b21.** A slight reduction in strength from the old bottling and a significant ramping up of toffee notes means this is a malt which will do little to exert your taste buds. Only a profusion of spice is able to cut through the monotonous style. Always sad to see such a lovely distillery so comprehensively gagged. 40%.

Hidden Spirits Strathisla 15 Year Old dist 2002, bott 2018 **(89) n21.5 t23 f22 b22.5** At times simplistic, at others attractively complex. 51.2%.

STRATHMILL

Speyside, 1891. Diageo. Working.

Strathmill 25 Year Old refill American oak casks, dist 1988 db **(89) n23 t22 f22 b22** A blending malt which reveals the kind of big malty deal it offers older brands. 52.4%. 2,700 bottles. Diageo Special Releases 2014.

The First Editions Strathmill Aged 21 Years 1996 refill hogshead, cask no. 15187, bott 2018 **(94.5) n23 t24 f23.5 b24** Pure Speyside...! Beautiful. Such a badly neglected distillery: we should see far more of this around...but in the meantime just worship this! 56.2%. nc ncf sc. 208 bottles.

TALISKER

Highlands (Island–Skye), 1832. Diageo. Working.

Talisker Aged 10 Years db **(93) n23 t23 f24 b23** The deadening caramel that had crept into recent bottlings of the 10-y-o has retreated, and although that extraordinary, that wholly unique finale has still to be re-found in its unblemished, explosive entirety, this is much, much closer to the mark and a quite stupendous malt to be enjoyed at any time. But at night especially. 45.8%

⬦ **Talisker Aged 10 Years** bott code: L0045CM001 db **(84.5) n22.5 t22.5 f19 b20.5** There is a more youthful stirring to the nose than the original old 8-year-old used to possess. Decent smoke and a vague spice prickle. A kind of caramelised version of a trusty old friend.

Conversely, the attractive, silky delivery sees the smoke taking its time to make its mark though the barley is much livelier, at first offering a juicy start before the caramels take hold. But it's downhill rapidly for the finish which really dishes out the caramel before an untidy light furry touch. So, sadly, still nothing like the dashing Talisker of old (when they purposefully used only ex-bourbon casks for sharper impact and clarity), the one where as a party piece amongst friends I would buy them a double hit of this and then, after carefully nosing, taking the whole lot in one go, chewing slowly, and then let the insane spices do the rest. Just tried it: next to nothing. Just a polite buzz on delivery where once there was a nuclear explosion. Humungous amounts of toffee, though...and the later, irritating, buzz is not, alas, spice at all... 45.8%.

⬩⬩⬩ **Talisker Aged 18 Years** bott code: L0023CM001 db **(86.5) n23 t22 f20 b21.5** Like the 10-year-old, not up to the same high standards of the last bottling I tasted. Starts promisingly as a deft smokiness drifts in and out a light heather honey and lightly-salted cucumber semi-freshness. But the delivery feels weighed down by far too much toffee while the finish is bitter and uneven. Some OK moments early on. But Talisker should be so much better than this. 45.8%.

Talisker Aged 25 Years bott 2017, bott code: L7023CM000 db **(96.5) n24 t24 f24 b24.5** A malt of magnificent complexity that generously rewards time and concentration. So for some, it may not be easy to get through the forests of oak early on, but switching your senses on to full alert not only pays dividends, but is no less than this great old malt deserves or demands. 45.8%. 21,498 bottles.

Talisker 30 Years Old db **(93.5) n23 t24 f23 b23.5** Much fresher and more infinitely entertaining than the 25 year old...!!! 45.8%

Talisker 30 Years Old db **(84.5) n21 t21.5 f21 b21.** Toffee-rich and pretty one dimensional. Did I ever expect to say that about a Talisker at 30...? 53.1%

Talisker 57 Degrees North db **(95) n24 t24.5 f23 b23.5** A glowing tribute, I hope, for a glowing whisky... 57%

Talisker Dark Storm charred oak db **(92) n22 t23.5 f23 b23.5** Much more like it! Unlike the Storm, which appeared to labour under some indifferent American oak, this is just brimming with vitality and purpose. 45.8%.

Talisker Neist Point bott code: L6067CM000 db **(87) n22 t21.5 f22 b21.5** Not exactly Nil Points, but for people like me who adore Talisker (indeed, it was a visit to this distillery 43 years ago that turned my appreciation of whisky into a passionate love affair), it tastes like the malt has barely got out of second gear. Where is the fizz and bite of the peppery phenols on impact? The journey through myriad styles of smoke? The breath-taking and life-giving oomph? Not to be found in this pleasantly tame and overly sweet version, though the spices do mount to something towards the very end. It is like observing a lion that has had its teeth forcibly removed. 45.8%.

Talisker Port Ruighe db **(88) n22 t22 f22 b22.** Sails into port without changing course 45.8%.

Talisker Skye (85) n21 t22 f21 b21. The sweetest, most docile Talisker I can ever remember with the spices working hard in the background but weirdly shackled. More Toffee Sky than Vanilla... 45.8% WB16/051

Talisker Storm db **(85.5) n20 t23 f21 b21.5** The nose didn't exactly go down a storm in my tasting room. There are some deft seashore touches, but the odd poor cask –evident on the finish, also - has undone the good. But it does recover on the palate early on with an even, undemanding and attractively sweet display showing malt to a higher degree than I have seen any Talisker before. 45.8%.

The First Editions Talisker Aged 9 Years 2008 sherry butt, cask no. 15639, bott 2018 **(89.5) n22 t24 f21.5 b22** Right, not a perfect sherry butt. But its good points are breathtaking – and use the Murray Method for maximum results 54.5%. nc ncf sc. 342 bottles.

Gleann Mór Talisker Aged Over 24 Years (93) n23.5 t23 f23.5 b23 A nuttier Talisker than normal with some sweeping natural caramels drowning the noise from the peat and anthracite phenols. However, the smoke cannot be denied either on the nose, or on the mocha-sweetened, teasingly-spiced finale. 48.9%.

TAMDHU
Speyside, 1897. Ian Macleod Distillers. Working (re-opened 3rd March 2013).

Tamdhu db **(84.5) n20 t22.5 f21 b21.** So-so nose, but there is no disputing the fabulous, stylistic honey on delivery. The silkiest Speyside delivery of them all. 40%

Tamdhu Aged 10 Years oak sherry cask db **(69.5) n17 t18.5 f17 b17.** A much better malt when they stick exclusively to ex-bourbon casks, as used to be the case. 40%

Tamdhu Aged 18 Years bott code L0602G L12 20/08 db **(74.5) n19 t19 f18 b18.5.** Bitterly disappointing. Literally. 43%.

Tamdhu 25 Years Old db **(88) n22 t22 f21 b23.** Radiates quality. 43%

The First Editions Tamdhu Aged 20 Years 1997 refill hogshead, cask no. 15369, bott 2018 (88.5) n22 t22.5 f22 b22 Well spiced, malty and hugely entertaining. By no means your average Tamdhu. *55.8%. nc ncf sc. 265 bottles.*

Old Malt Cask Tamdhu Aged 19 Years refill hogshead, cask no. 14936, dist Apr 99, bott Apr 18 (79) n19 t20.5 f19 b20.5 Something of the glazed cherry and jam tart about this. That said, not a malt that hangs together particularly impressively and hints of a little grimy off note here and there. *50%. nc ncf sc. 304 bottles.*

TAMNAVULIN
Speyside. 1966. Whyte and Mackay. Working.

Tamnavulin Double Cask batch no. 0308 db (87.5) n22.5 t22.5 f21 b21.5 A bottling which deserves – and perhaps needs – to be at 46% at least. Reduced down to this strength it is levelled to a much chalkier, drier plane than it requires to fully project the oils, sugars and obvious intricacies. Entirely pleasant as it is, with an attractive clean maltiness to the thinned golden syrup as well as well-mannered spicing. But, overall, refuses to open out and develop as you might hope or expect. A 92-plus whisky just waiting to happen... *40%.*

Tamnavulin Red Wine Cask Edition No. 01 American white barrels and finished in French Cabernet Sauvignon red wine casks, batch no. 001243, bott code: L0064 22 28 P/011888 db (94) n23 there is a sharpness to this which could almost make your nose bleed: the grape has almost jammy qualities; t23.5 muscovado sugars and Demerara in cahoots. Getting toastier by the moment. As on the nose, the malt makes little forays, though prevented from going to far by the polite vanilla-rich tannins; f24 at its zenith as the juicier grape still works hard in keeping the style stable. But of the most all, confirms that these is an untainted casks where the delicate bitterness, as it grows, is perfectly in tune with the acidic fruitiness....wow! b23.5 it's like a thriller you can't put down: just gets better and more absorbing as you go along! *40%.*

Tamnavulin Red Wine Cask Edition No. 02 American white barrels and finished in Spanish Grenache red wine casks, batch no. 001075, bott code: L0139 23 10 P/012168 db (88) n22 t22 f21.5 b22.5 Pleased to report that, again, the wine casks are clean and sulphur free. But, unlike, the French Cab Sauv' bottling, this is pretty limited in overall development. A Steady Eddie dram, fat and comfortable in its fruity skin. Good spices late on. But here the bitterness does stand out a little and though enjoyable, it feels like a high-quality sports car underpowered and you are crushing the pedal to the floor for extra power and performance that just isn't forthcoming. *40%.*

Tamnavulin Sherry Cask Edition No. 02 American oak and three types of sherry casks, batch no. 30502, bott code: 23:50 L9290 P/010478 db (91) n23 Sweet Chelsea bun with all the light attendant spices; t23.5 a mix of treacle tart and mince pie. Unusually yeasty by the midpoint with a curious, pastry-like oiliness, too. The spices juxtapose with the sweeter fruit; f22 a little bitter as the burnt raisin kicks in; b22.5 I'm presuming PX is one of the sherry types here because there is a dominant stickiness to this bottling. Superb delivery, I must say! *40%.*

Old Malt Cask Tamnavulin Aged 27 Years refill hogshead, cask no. 16113, dist Dec 91, bott Oct 19 (83.5) n21.5 t21.5 f20 b21 The dank hay aroma is attractive, if not entirely technically where you want it to be, but forewarns of an off-kilter sharpness for further down the line...which duly arrives. *46.8%. nc ncf sc. 308 bottles.*

TEANINICH
Highlands (Northern), 1817. Diageo. Working.

Teaninich 17 Year Old refill American oak hogsheads & refill American oak barrels db (90) n22 t23 f22 b23 A distillery rarely celebrated in bottle by its owners. Here they have selected an age and cask profile which gets the mix between simple barley and far from taxing oak just about right. Minimalistically elegant. *55.9%. Diageo Special Releases 2017.*

The Cooper's Choice Teaninich 2009 8 Years Old Sauternes finish (91.5) n23 t23 f22.5 b23 Rarely do Sauternes casks dish out the kind of militant peppers experienced on the nose (reminded me of live crabs being freshly boiled). But settles down to its more fruity role on delivery, though the usual sweetness expected from this grape never quite arrives. *54.5%. nc ncf sc.*

Hidden Spirits Teaninich 2006 cask no. TH619, bott 2019 (94.5) n23 t24.5 f23 b24 In recent years there have been far too many bottlings that have failed to do this distillery justice. Delighted that here is another which redresses the balance. *51.7%. sc.*

TOBERMORY
Highlands (Island–Mull), 1795. Burn Stewart Distillers. Working.

Tobermory 10 Years Old db (73.5) n17.5 t19 f18 b19. The last time I tasted an official Tobermory 10 for the Bible, I was aghast with what I found. So I prodded this sample I had before me of the new 46.3% version with all the confidence Wile E Coyote might have with a failed stick of Acme dynamite. No explosions in the glass or on my palate to report. And though this is still a long way short, and I'm talking light years here, of the technical excellence of the old days, the uncomplicated sweet maltiness has a very basic charm. The nose and finish, though, are still very hard going. 46.3%

Tobermory Aged 15 Years db (93) n23.5 t23.5 f23 b23 A tang to the oils on both nose and finish suggests an over widened middle. But such is the quality of the sherry butts and the intensity of the salt-stained malt, all is forgiven. 46.3%. nc ncf.

Tobermory 42 Year Old db (94.5) n23.5 t23.5 f23.5 b24 A real journey back in time. Wonderful. 47.7%

Ledaig 18 Year Old batch 2 db (71) n16 t20 f17 b18. There are many ways to describe this whisky. Well made, alas, is not one of them. The nose sets off many alarms, especially on the feinty front. And though some exceptional oak repairs some of the damage, it cannot quite do enough. Sugary, too – and occasionally cloyingly so. 46.3%. nc ncf.

Ledaig 19 Year Old Marsala Finish db (92) n23.5 t23 f22.5 b23 Hardly textbook malt but a real gung-ho adventure story on the palate. 51%.

Ledaig Dùsgadh 42 Aged 42 Years db (96) n25 t24.5 f22.5 b24 It has to be about 30 years ago I tasted my first-ever Ledaig – as a 12 year old peated malt. This must be from the same stocks, only this has been housed in exceptional casks. Who would have thought, three decades on, that it would turn into some of the best malt bottled in a very long time. A smoky experience unlikely to be forgotten. 46.3%

Ledaig 1996 db (88) n21 t23.5 f21 b22.5 A malt you feel is at times reaching for the stars. But has to settle for an, ultimately, barren planet. 46.3%

◈ **Acla Selection Island Edition Tobermory 23 Year Old** hogshead, dist 1995, bott 2019 (94) n24 irresistible lemon sherbet...so youthful for its age, though close inspection reveals some startlingly complex tannin patterns: understatedly superb; t23.5 just has to be light and salivating...and it is. The lemony theme on the nose is not lost on the caressing early notes, the malt delicate yet proud; a few cubes of lemon drop candy also does the rounds; f23 just slightly earthier and subtly spicier; b23.5 one of the most gentle and elegant malts to comes from this island in a very long time. 49%.

◈ **Acla Selection Island Edition Ledaig 11 Year Old** hogshead, dist 2007, bott 2018 (88.5) n22.5 t22.5 f21.5 b22 The smoke offers a light, acidic fug on both nose and palate, though all the sweetness is confined to the delivery where the grist goes into overdrive. Spices are sprinkled evenly and the youth ensures the sharpness is very, very sharp! 52.6%.

◈ **Cadenhead's Authentic Collection Cask Strength Ledaig 11 Year Old** ex-bourbon cask, dist 2008, bott Sept 19 (90.5) n22 t23 f22.5 b23 If this malt was handed in as homework, it would probably be docked a few marks for being technically off the pace. But it would soon make them up again, as the oak this has been housed in perfectly matches the distillery's style, allowing a nuanced depth to the smoke and an impressive degree of barley to be seen. The nose hints at a lack of copper, and there is some evidence that the stills might have been operating slightly faster than they were comfortable with. But the nutty smokiness compensates for the thinness of body; the barley applauded for its salivating qualities. What great fun! 55.2%. sc.

◈ **Chapter 7 Ledaig 10 Year Old 2009** bourbon hogshead, cask no. 700493, dist May 09, bott Mar 20 (92.5) n23.5 t23.5 f22.5 b23 Can't remember the last time I tasted a Ledaig so technically on the money as this. I've worked with many a cask of this over the years, in the blending lab as well as in the tasting room for The Bible. The nose is pure grist, the phenols reeking from the malt as though it had just come off the mill. Consequently, the malt simply melts in the mouth with a freshness that fair brings a tear to the eye. Slowly the tannins offer a vanilla alternative...Just beautiful. 51%. sc. 351 bottles.

◈ **Chapter 7 Ledaig 24 Year Old 1995** bourbon hogshead, cask no. 189, dist Sept 95, bott Mar 20 (91.5) n23.5 t23.5 f22 b22.5 One of those peated whiskies where you aren't quite sure if the lightness of smoke is due to a lower phenol level or the passing of years. Here it is probably both. The lightly smoked butterscotch nose is a treat, the delivery an exhibition of how mouthfeel plays such a vital role. Here it is fat, chewing malt...the longer you chew the slightly peatier it gets. Only a very late bitterness can be found in the deficit column... 51.6%. sc. 242 bottles.

◈ **Gordon & MacPhail Connoisseurs Choice Ledaig Aged 12 Years** first fill sherry hogshead, cask no. 16603709, dist 13 Dec 06, bott 1 Feb 19 (87.5) n22.5 t23 f20 b22 It has taken a while to taste this. You know there's a problem but, like a slow-punctured tyre, it takes time for it to be revealed. Yes, noted a slight off-sulphur note on the nose but, thanks to the peat, it comes through on the finish very late on...actually, so late it is after you have finished the tasting. Crafty, these sulphur cask chaps. Anyway, that apart, the peat is superb and about as hairy-chested and full-on as I've seen from this distillery for a while. And the accompanying milky-marzipan demi-sweetness charms the pants off you. Just such a shame about that slow puncture. Boo....hissssssssssss.... *58.2%. sc. 329 bottles.*

Gordon & MacPhail Discovery Range Ledaig Aged 12 Years (93) n23.5 t24 f22.5 b23 Following a plethora of poor 2008 bottlings, great to come across a G&M back on track with a Ledaig in its truer style: rich, chewy, sweet, rounded and well balanced...and all traces of copper intact. A beautiful leather and chocolate sub-plot to this while the waxy heather honey is on full parade. Delicious. *43%.*

Hidden Spirits Ledaig 2007 cask no. LG719, bott 2019 **(88) n21.5 t22.5 f21.5 b22.5** Not exactly the most complex whisky out there. But if you are looking for clean, smoky and sweet then here's your boy....!!! *52.2%. sc.*

Liquid Treasures From Miles Away Ledaig 13 Year Old PX sherry butt, dist Feb 07, bott Mar 20 **(94) n23.5 t24 f23 b23.5** Delighted and greatly relieved to say to say the PX cask has not interfered with this malt and dragged it down to its excruciatingly dull level. Instead, we see the Ledaig in full vitality with a higher phenol content than normal, dishing out spices and peat reek with happy abandon. Clean, full bodied and superbly layered with what little grape there is to be found in docile mood and the sugars very much under control. Quite impossible not to love. *52.9%. sc. 252 bottles.*

Liquid Treasures Snakes Ledaig 10 Year Old bourbon hogshead, dist 2008, bott 2018 **(86) n20.5 t22.5 f21.5 b21.5** Echoes many of the failings of the Whisky Chamber 2008 (see below), though this has a slightly more substantial, gristier and juicer delivery. *59.3%. sc. 267 bottles.*

Single & Single Ledaig 2005 13 Years Old (94) n23.5 one of those bewildering Ledaig noses with the softness if matched only by the understated intensity of the smoke; **t24** if you were lulled into thinking there wasn't too much peat on the wing, the delivery soon puts you right. A huge puff of smoke hits the palate, swiftly followed by eye-tingling sooty tones plus fruity muscovado sugars. Jaw-achingly chewy, especially when the vanillas arrive in force; **f23** the spices have much to say here, though the smoke is never far from lead position. Dries despite the butterscotch development; **b23.5** this is Ledaig in very impressive form. And with the peat levels spot on. A heart winner. *58.1%. sc. 624 bottles.*

The Single Cask Tobermory 1995 ex-bourbon barrel, cask no. 1201 **(88) n23 t22.5 f20.5 b22** This malt offers a superstar, nutty nose full of intriguing light tannin-induced sugars – and is about as floral as an island whisky ever gets. But as after the initial attractive gristiness on delivery, it loses its way slightly as the oak gets a little bit to much of the upper hand, leading to a nagging bitterness. However, the better moments are very good, indeed. *54.2%. nc ncf sc.*

The Whisky Barrel Originals Ledaig 11 Years Old 1st fill oloroso hogshead, cask no. TWB1006, dist Feb 08, bott 2019 **(92.5) n23** a thick aroma that you feel you have to peel off your nose after sampling it. For a Ledaig the smoke has a density and purpose I haven't experienced for a very long time....for which I mean probably 30 years...; **t23.5** a five course delivery. The intensity on the nose is confirmed here with the peat taking no prisoners and, even after layering out, issues mini tsunamis of phenols. The heather honey sweetness is also slightly overcooked...but in keeping with the arm-wrestling peat...; **f23** a buzzing sweet spice continues to fill the palate for an improbably long time; **b23** bizarrely light for a first-fill oloroso: indeed, one of the lightest I have ever seen. But make no mistake: this is a heavyweight and there is no denying its smoky scrumminess. *63.4%. sc. 298 bottles.*

The Whisky Chamber Ledaig 10 Years Old 2008 bourbon cask **(85) n21 t22 f21 b21** An incredibly raw whisky, the nose in particular shewing a lack of copper at work, an observation confirmed by the thin finish. The main crutch for this malt is provided by the juicy peat which covers many of the obvious cracks. Not entirely without its merits. *59%. sc.*

Wilson & Morgan Barrel Selection Ledaig Traditional Oak dist 2008, bott 2018 **(87.5) n21.5 t22.5 f21.5 b22** One of a curious batch of 2008 distilled Ledaigs currently sweeping the market place. Those of you around to remember the first ever-bottlings to be brought out under the name Ledaig will weep quietly. However, this is probably the best of the bunch as there appears to be greater integrity to the malt and a more widespread richness to the smoky barley sugar; even a degree of saltiness. Not great by historic Ledaig standards, being clearly undercooked, but pretty decent amid today's offerings. *48%.*

TOMATIN
Speyside, 1897. Takara, Shuzo and Okura & Co. Working.

Tomatin 8 Years Old bourbon & sherry casks db **(89) n22 t23 f21.5 b22.5** A malt very proud of its youth. *40%. Travel Retail Exclusive.*

Tomatin 12 Year Old finished in Spanish sherry casks db **(91.5) n23 t23.5 f21.5 b23.5** For a great many years, Tomatin operated under severe financial restrictions. This meant that some of the wood brought to the distillery during this period was hardly of top-notch quality. This has made life difficult for those charged with moulding the stocks into workable expressions. I take my hat off to the creator of this: some great work is evident, despite the finish. *43%*

Tomatin 14 Year Old Port Finish db **(92.5) n23 t24 f22.5 b23** Allows the top notch port a clear road. *46%. ncf.*

Tomatin 15 Years Old American oak casks db **(89.5) n22.5 t22.5 f22 b22.5** A delicious exhibition of malt. *46%. Travel Retail Exclusive.*

Tomatin Aged 15 Years ex bourbon cask, bott 2010 db **(86) n21 t22 f21.5 b21.5.** One of the most malty drams on the market today. Perhaps suffers a little from the 43% strength as some of the lesser oak notes get a slightly disruptive foothold. But the intense, juicy barley trademark remains clear and delicious. *43% Tomatin Distillery*

Tomatin 15 Years Old bourbon barrels and Spanish Tempranillo wine casks db **(88.5) n22 t23 f21 b22.5.** Not free from the odd problem with the Spanish wine casks but gets away with it as the overall complexity and enjoyment levels are high. *52%*

Tomatin 18 Year Old db **(82) n21.5 t22 f19 b20** Sadly some sulphur on the casks which makes the finish just too dry and off key. Underneath are hints of greatness, but the sherry butt doesn't give it a chance. *46%.*

⟩⟩ **Tomatin 21 Year Old** db **(94.5) n24** there you go: a 15 minute nose. So much to discover here: the layering of the malt, alongside a clever variation of intensity; the buttery creaminess; the vaguest tangerine hint alongside new-mown grass...I could go on, as indeed you should...; **t23.5** remember that buttery note on the nose? Well, here it pops up immediately on delivery followed by a beautiful blend of gristy barley and delicate ulmo honey; **f23** not a single signal of distress from the casks after all these years, so the malt can continue its unhurried fade, at times taking on a biscuity saltiness; **b24** one of those malts which looks as though It's not even trying, but just nonchalantly produces something rather delightful and of very high class. *46%. Global Travel Retail Exclusive.*

Tomatin 25 Years Old db **(89) n22 t23 f21.5 b22.5.** Not a nasty bone in its body: understated but significant. *43%*

Tomatin 30 Year Old European & American oak casks db **(85.5) n21 t21 f22.5 b21.** Unusually for an ancient malt, the whisky becomes more comfortable as it wears its aged shoes. The delivery is just a bit too enthusiastic on the oaky front, but the natural caramels soften the journey rather delightfully. *46%. ncf.*

Tomatin 30 Years Old bott 2018 db **(93) n23 t22.5 f24 b23.5** Puts me in mind of a 29-year-old Springbank I have tasted for this Bible, which showed similar initial signs of wear and tear. But as the whisky warmed and oxidised, then so it grew in the glass and began to reveal previously hidden brilliance. This is not, perhaps, up to those gargantuan standards but what is achieved here shews the rewards for both patience and the use of the Murray Method. Patience and care are most certainly rewarded *46%.*

Tomatin 36 Year Old American & European oak db **(96.5) n24 t24.5 f23.5 b24.5** The difference between old oak and the newer stuff is brilliantly displayed here. Make no mistake: this is a masterpiece of a malt. *46%*

Tomatin 40 Years Old Oloroso sherry casks db **(87.5) n21.5 t23 f21 b22** One of those malts which offers a graceful peep at the past, when sherry butts were clean and offered nothing to fear. But no matter how good the cask time takes its toll and the intense chalkiness reveals tannins that have got slightly the better of the barley. Thankfully the grape is still intact and brings us a beautiful raisin and date depth before the chalk returns a little more determined than before. *43%. Travel Retail Exclusive.*

Tomatin 1995 Olorosso Sherry db **(82) n21 t22 f19 b20** You can peel the grape off the malt. But one of the sherry butts wasn't quite as spotless as one might hope for. The inevitable tang arrives towards the finish. *46%.*

⟩⟩ **Tomatin Amontillado Sherry 2006 Aged 12 Years Old** db **(82) n21 t22 f19 b20** You'd think from the score that sulphur plays a part here. And you'd probably be right. Just bitter and dull in all the places it shouldn't be. Those incapable of detecting sulphur will love the rich sultana delivery. *46%.*

Tomatin Cabernet Sauvignon 2002 Edition db **(82) n21 t22 f18 b21** Surprising degree of weight to this one. The fruit is not quite flawless with a little bit of a buzz on the nose and finish especially. But the rich mouthfeel and a pleasant, lush Garibaldi biscuit effect does ensure some very satisfying phases. *46%.*

Tomatin Caribbean Rum 2007 Edition db **(89.5) n22 t23 f22 b22.5** Beautifully clean malt though, as is their wont, the rum casks keep everything tight. *46%.*

⟩⟩ **Tomatin Caribbean Rum 2009 Aged 10 Years Old** db **(90.5) n22.5** clean barley with a light liquorice and Demerara sugar outer casing; **t23.5** I think the old term: "pure malt" would be the perfect description for this; **f22** the rum casks do their job and lock in the sugars for a slightly fast finish; **b22.5** as is so often the case, the rum cask has encased the malt in crisp sugar, limiting development slightly. But it also ensures the malts are at their maximum intensity. 46%.

Tomatin Cask Strength db **(80)** n19 t22 f19 b20 Stunning malt climax on delivery. But always undone by a dull, persistent off note from the cask. 57.5%.

⬧ **Tomatin Decades II** db **(91.5)** n23 when the vanilla turns to a hybrid of butterscotch and custard on the nose, then you know some decent age is involved, as well as ex-bourbon casks. Beautifully balanced and pronounced, especially when the lime blossom honey evolves; **t23** a mix of delicate sugars on delivery cleaner. A little icing sugar blends well with the thin ulmo honey and barley sugar candy. But the tannins are in quickly to also ensure creamy texture to this. The malt, soft yet confident, is always at hand; **f22.5** a dull moaning of spice on ever-thickening vanilla. Even now the malt keeps in its place without giving an inch...; **b23** Tomatin does intense malt as well as any distillery in the world. And here they give an object lesson. 46%.

Tomatin Five Virtues Series Earth Peated Malt refill hogshead oak casks db **(88)** n22 t22.5 f21.5 b22 Can honestly say I have never seen Tomatin in this kind of shape before: enjoyable once you acclimatise... 46%.

Tomatin Five Virtues Series Fire Heavily Charred Oak de-charred/re-charred oak fired casks db **(94)** n23.5 t24 f23 b23.5 High class malt with a sweet bourbon drizzle. 46%.

Tomatin Five Virtues Series Metal Bourbon Barrels first fill bourbon barrels db **(95)** n24 t24 f23 b24 There's metal enough in the "Earth" bottling. Was wondering where the metal comes into things here. As these are first fill bourbon casks, wonder if it was the type of warehouse they came from in Kentucky... Anyway, talking metal: this is pure gold... 46%.

Tomatin Five Virtues Series Water Winter Distillation sherry butts & bourbon barrels db **(72)** n18 t20 f16 b18 A small degree of molassed chocolate escapes the grim sulphured tightness of the sherry. 46%.

Tomatin Five Virtues Series Wood Selected Oak Casks French, American & Hungarian oak casks db **(90)** n22.5 t23 f21.5 b23 A Franco-Hungarian truce means the malt and bourbon casks can work their magic...Some truly brilliant and unique phrases here. 46%.

Tomatin Highland Legacy db **(88)** n22 t22.5 f21.5 b22 Clean, nutty malt but beyond that unremarkable. 43%.

Tomatin Warehouse 6 Collection 1975 db **(95.5)** n24 t23.5 f24 b24 When Jim Milne, one of Scotland's greatest-ever blenders, got back under a distillery's boardroom table after a lifetime at J&B, he chose Tomatin as his next destination. He had always appreciated the stunning consistency of its malt, especially in ex-bourbon cask. But once back in the lab again, he would ring me to tell about some ex-sherry he had located among stocks, or would send me samples and asked what I thought. This bottling reminds me very much of the samples Jim would send, although years back when it was a lot fresher. Jim, sadly, is no longer with us. But some of those casks still are. This one, naturally, shows far more grey hairs than the whiskies Jim eventually created. But it remains entirely sulphur free; and once you realise the oak is doing no harm to the fruit whatsoever other than just giving it a dry, powdery dusting, then you can go on to enjoy the still juicy, boiled sugar candy fruitiness on the palate...and even applaud the gravitas of the lightly spiced oak on its return at the finish. Jim would have approved both the complexity and charm of this malt – and he certainly wouldn't have given it an extra year, either. 46.5%.

⬧ **Tomatin Warehouse 6 Collection 1977** db **(96)** n24.5 I have just spent 20 minutes nosing this before even writing the first word. I have also taken it through the temperature points. And I'm not sure where to start! I suppose it has to be with those exotic fruits, pineapple in particular, which gives this malt its hallmark. The malts are amazingly structured: such varied intensities, such playfulness with the accompanying sugars; and the sugars themselves drift and merge – one moment a fraction toasty, the next more honeyed and sharp...; **t24** immediately into the exotic fruit: that unique marriage of top class ex-bourbon and equally fine malt spirit. As it sharpens it move into lemon blossom honey mode, though the richness of the barley is never dominated; **f23.5** just begins to bitter slightly, though it does also have a Jaffa cake chocolate-orange depth. Long and luxurious; **b24** a tale of exotic fruit. Which in turns means a story of great antiquity. Truly old school. And truly magnificent. Do not open the bottle unless you have a good half hour to study this work of art. And the Murray Method will reward you handsomely... 49%. ⬧

Cù Bòcan Creation #1 Black Isle Brewery Imperial Stout & Bacalhôa Moscatel de Setúbal wine casks db **(84.5)** n21.5 t22 f20 b21 Hands up here. Not much of a fan of whiskies shewing degrees of hops, and this one certainly does. Not like some out there, though, and the roastiness of the Imperial Stout does what it can to compensate, as does a pleasant creamy texture. But it is still more than some whisky lovers can beer... 46%.

Cù Bòcan Creation #2 Japanese Shochu & European virgin oak casks db **(93.5)** n23 t24 f23 b23.5 Not the first time I have encountered whisky matured in shochu casks. But the first time I have tasted one that has also involved European virgin oak. And a light phenol note, just for good measure. Sounds as if it should be too much. Surprisingly, though, it is a delicate malt shewing both a sharpness and much softer Brazilian biscuit feel that gives a unique identity. Only a slight bitterness to the very finish offers any degree of discord. Juicy, youthful and an absolute joy! 46%.

Cù Bòcan Signature bourbon, oloroso sherry & virgin oak casks db (82) n21.5 t21 f20 b20.5 A virgin defiled amid brimstone. 46%.

◇ **Artful Dodger Tomatin 11 Year Old 2008** ex-bourbon hogshead, cask no. 453 (88) n21 t23 f22 b22 A malt not overly troubled by tannin and still a little wet behind the ears after all this time. But this means the famous Tomatin maltiness is seen to optimum effect, like stars in a clear night sky. And that is always a delicious spectacle. 56.1%. sc.

◇ **Fadandel.dk Tomatin 10 Year Old** 3 months finish in a 2nd fill Oloroso octave, cask no. 1837A (94.5) n23 adorably intense malt with just a little delicate fruitcake on the side. A molecule or two of smoke peels off from the pack, but your nose has to be on full alert to spot it; t24 such a fabulous delivery! The malt is explosive and super salivating – Tomatin at its very best! It is weighed down slightly by a toffee-raisin jacket which slips comfortably over the barley....; f23.5 perfectly judged spice, then those layers of malt. Talk about a nuanced finale...! b24 thankfully second fill oloroso at work, which means the distillery's trademark concentrated malt character still has plenty of room in which to operate and is there to be savoured! A minor masterpiece. 59.9%. sc. 75 bottles.

Fadandel.dk Tomatin Aged 10 Years hogshead, cask no. 1837, dist 2 Apr 09, bott 8 Apr 19 (91) n22 t23 f22.5 b23.5 Few distilleries do sweet, intense malt like Tomatin, and here is a superb example. 60.2%. sc. 308 bottles.

The First Editions Tomatin Aged 23 Years 1994 refill hogshead, cask no. 15287, bott 2018 (86) n21.5 t22 f21 b21.5 A surprising malt for its age which has rigidly refused to grow up. The nose has the gristy grassiness of a malt half its age, while the oak involvement is slow out of the blocks. A slight uneven tang from the tannin late on confirms the cask wasn't helping here. 46.1%. nc ncf sc. 252 bottles.

Gordon & MacPhail Discovery Range Tomatin 2007 (92) n22 t24 f23 b23 Par for the course, this is all about intense malt – but close inspection shows there is much else besides. The light vanilla and butterscotch layering from the oak has a wonderfully light touch. And as a little cocoa begins to form, a delicious alcohol-rich Malteser candy forms. Impossible not to love. 43%.

◇ **The Single Cask Tomatin 2006** ex-bourbon barrel, PX sherry octave finish, cask no. 5777B (87) n22 t22.5 f21.5 b21 An even malt where the PX has a surprising degree of influence. As the problem can often be with PX involvement, any bitterness present is amplified by the sugary wine. Some spices relieve the slightly one-dimensional feel. Pleasant enough, but never quite feels comfortable. 53.7%. nc ncf sc.

◇ **The Whisky Chamber Tomatin 11 Jahre 2008** sherry cask (85.5) n22.5 t22 f20 b21 Eye-wateringly tart, especially at the death. Some attractive chocolate notes mixes in with the burnt raisin. But this is a malt where balance is at a premium and the tightness on the finish doesn't help the cause, either. The masochist in me does kind of enjoy the delivery, though... 56.3%. sc.

TOMINTOUL
Speyside, 1965. Angus Dundee. Working.

Tomintoul Aged 10 Years bott code: L16 02149 CB2 db (84.5) n20.5 t22 f21 b21 A very consistent dram but far too much emphasis of the chocolate toffee rather than the big malt you feel is bursting to break free. 40%.

Tomintoul Aged 12 Years Oloroso Sherry Cask Finish db (73.5) n18.5 t19 f18 b18. Tomintoul, with good reason, styles itself as "The Gentle Dram" and you'll hear no argument from me about that one. However, the sherry influence here offers a rough ride. 40%

Tomintoul Aged 12 Years Oloroso Sherry Cask Finish bott code: L17 02772 CB2 db (74.5) n20 t19 f17.5 b18 A slightly cleaner sherry influence than the last of these I tasted, but the ungentle sulphur makes short work of the "gentle dram". 40%.

Tomintoul Aged 14 Years db (91) n23.5 t23 f21.5. This guy has shortened its breath somewhat: with the distinct thinness to the barley and oak arriving a little flustered and half-hearted rather than with a confident stride; b23 remains a beautiful whisky full of vitality and displaying the malt in its most naked and vulnerable state. But I get the feeling that perhaps a few too many third fills, or under-performing seconds, has resulted in the intensity and hair-raising harmony of the truly great previous bottlings just being slightly undercooked. That said, still a worthy and delicious dram! 46%. nc ncf.

Tomintoul Aged 15 Years Portwood Finish db (94) n23 t23.5 f23.5 b24 So rare to find a wine finish which maximises the fruit to the full without allowing it to dominate. Charming.

And so clean. Probably a brilliant whisky to help repair my damaged palate after tasting yet another s******ed sherry butt. I'll keep this one handy...*46%. nc ncf. 5,820 bottles.*

Tomintoul Aged 15 Years With A Peaty Tang bott code: L17 02975 CB2 db **(89.5) n23 t23 f21.5 b22** Being a bit older than their original Peaty Tang, the phenols here are less forward. But, then, it calls itself "The Gentle Dram" and on this evidence with good reason. *40%.*

Tomintoul Aged 16 Years db **(94.5) n24.5 t23.5 f23 b23.5** Confirms Tomintoul's ability to dice with greatness. *40%*

Tomintoul Aged 21 Years db **(94) n24 t24 f22.5 b23.5** Just how good this whisky would have been at cask strength or even at 46 absolutely terrifies me. *40%.*

Tomintoul Aged 25 Years db **(95) n25 t24 f23 b23.5** A quiet masterpiece from one of Scotland's criminally under appreciated great distilleries. *43%*

Tomintoul Aged 40 Years db **(86) n22 t21 f21.5 b21.5.** Groans every single one of its 40 years. Some lovely malty moments still, as well as butterscotch. But the oak has just jogged on past the sign that said 'Greatness' and carried straight on into the woods... *43.1%. nc ncf.*

◇ **Tomintoul Seiridh Oloroso Sherry Cask** first fill Oloroso sherry butts, batch one, bott code: L19 05556 CB2 db **(87) n22 t23 f20.5 b21.5** A right old softy of a malt, the sherry ironing out any creases with the gentlest of fruity caresses. A little sulphur niggle at the end, alas. *40%. 6,000 bottles.*

Tomintoul With A Peaty Tang db **(94) n23 t24 f23 b24.** A bit more than a tang, believe me! Faultlessly clean distillate that revels in its unaccustomed peaty role. The age is confusing and appears mixed, with both young and older traits being evident. *40%*

Old Ballantruan db **(89.5) n23.5 t23 f21 b22** Profound young malt which could easily be taken for an Islay. *50%. ncf.*

Old Ballantruan Aged 10 Years bott code 1706.15 db **(94.5) n23.5 t23.5 f23.5 b24** Can't say this is a spectacular peated malt. But everything is brilliantly in proportion and so sublimely balanced. *50%. ncf.*

Old Ballantruan Aged 15 Years bott code: CBSC4 02976 db **(95) n23.5 t24 f23.5 b24** A Tomintoul classic. *50%. ncf.*

TORMORE
Speyside, 1960. Chivas Brothers. Working.

Tormore 12 Years Old db **(75) n19 t19 f19 b18.** For those who like whisky in their caramel. *40%*

Cadenhead's Authentic Collection Tormore 33 Years Old dist 1984 **(87) n23.5 t22 f20 b21.5** Even after 33 years, the sins of the distillers way back in 1984 cannot be entirely forgiven and the fault lines of the original distillate are still evident and ready to rumble. However, these weaknesses are fully compensated on the nose which deserves full study: a wonderful butterscotch and subtlest imaginable coriander spice gives the unlikely feel of ice cream in a busy vegetable-packed kitchen. The delivery, likewise, is full of molten Demerara intent. Seek some delicious entertainment here and ye shall find. *51.7%. sc. 175th Anniversary bottling.*

The First Editions Tormore Aged 29 Years 1988 refill hogshead, cask no. 15351, bott 2018 **(91.5) n23 t23 f22.5 b23** Tormore in a more soft and intricate form, benefitting latterly from an unusual sharpness to the malt which ensures the grassy barley is at full throttle. A pleasant milky trail to the muscovado sugar and cocoa finale. *44.9%. nc ncf sc. 60 bottles.*

Gordon & MacPhail Connoisseurs Choice Tormore Aged 23 Years first fill sherry butt, cask no. 5383, dist 14 Jun 95, bott 5 Sept 18 **(84) n21 t22 f20 b21** One dimensional fruit: pleasant but Tormore just doesn't have the guts to cope with this kind of cask. A little furry, too. *60.1%. sc. 615 bottles.*

◇ **Old Malt Cask Tormore Aged 26 Years** refill hogshead, cask no. 16492, dist Nov 92, bott Oct 19 **(88) n22 t22.5 f21.5 b22** Perhaps one of the most malty and gristy whiskies of such antiquity you will find this and any other year. Belies its age on so many fronts, but there is plenty to enjoy from the concentrated barley sugar delivery. Fades towards a little bitterness late on. *473%. nc ncf sc. 285 bottles.*

The Whisky Chamber Tormore 23 Years Old 1995 bourbon cask **(87) n21 t22.5 f21.5 b22** Despite the austerity of the nose, this battles back impressively with a huge if perhaps over-simplistic malt statement which makes for a real juicy cove. Don't expect complexity, but if you love crisp malt concentrate... *51.1%. sc.*

TULLIBARDINE
Highlands (Perthshire), 1949. Tullibardine Ltd. Working.

Tullibardine 15 Year Old db **(87.5) n22 t23 f21 b21.5** Starts quite beautifully but stubbornly refuses to kick on. Just adore the nuttiness on both the nose and delivery, as well as the lilting malt in the early stages which is both juicy and barley intense. There is even a light orange blossom honey note soon after...then just fades under a welter of dulling vanilla and caramel tones. Not far off being a little beauty. *43%.*

Tullibardine Aged 20 Years db (92.5) n22.5 t24 f22.5 b23.5 While there are whiskies like this in the world, there is a point to this book...*43%*

Tullibardine Aged 25 Years db (86.5) n22 t22 f21 b21.5. There can be too much of a good thing. And although the intricacies of the honey makes you sigh inwardly with pleasure, the overall rigidity and fundamentalism of the oak goes a little too far. *43%*

Tullibardine 1970 db (96.5) n25 t24.5 f23 b24s I am a professional wordsmith with a very long time in whisky. Yet words, any words, can barely do justice... *40.5%.*

Tullibardine 225 sauternes cask finish db (85) n20 t22.5 f21 b21.5. Hits the heights early on in the delivery when the honey and Lubeck marzipan are at full throttle. *43%*

Tullibardine 228 Burgundy cask finish db (82) n21 t22 f18 b21. No shortage of bitter chocolate. Flawed but a wow for those looking for mega dry malt. *43%*

Tullibardine 500 sherry cask finish db (79.5) n19 t21 f19 b20.5. The usual problems from Jerez, but the grape ensures maximum chewability. *43%*

Tullibardine Custodians Collection 1962 52 Years Old db (87.5) n22 t22 f21.5 b22 This oldie has gallantly fought in the great oak wars of 1987 to 2014 and shows some serious scars. Thankfully a little exotic fruit and citrus makes some impact on the austere tannins on the nose, but they aren't around to reduce the excesses of the finale, though a little chocolate does go a long way. The silky delivery doesn't quite hide the mildly puckering, eye-watering aggression of the tannin but butterscotch does its best to add a limp sweetness, as does the unexpected wave of juicy barley. Some fascinating old timer moments but, ultimately, a tad too ancient for its own good. *40.1%.*

⬦ **Tullibardine The Murray Cask Strength** dist 2007, bott 2019, bott code: 19/0067 db (94.5) n23.5 Tulli in tip-top form, synchronising the intense barley (at possibly its optimum age for this distillery) with faultless oak. The result is something akin to vanilla ice-cream (by the way: I see after tasting this that they use this as a descriptor on their label...!!) adorned with a citrussy syrup. Not sure the sweetness versus drier oaky levels could be better balanced; t24 that success of the balance levels on the nose are repeated on delivery....even with a little bit of interest. The heather honey is subdued allowing a feeling of age to creep into play. But the barley refuses to compromise in any way. Together they forge a nutty partnership, but not so dry that the heather-honey and muscovado sugars are stopped from their mouth-watering work; f23 now it's drier: a sprinkle of cocoa powder on the re-emerging vanillas; b24 while touring China at the back end of 2019, I met a couple of people who told me they had bought previous bottles of this brand thinking that it was related to me, and therefore must have my seal of approval. Please let me reiterate: this whisky has nothing to do with Jim Murray, a name which is itself Trademarked. I make no financial gain from this whisky, nor do I allow any whisky in the world to be named after me. I make no profit from the individual sales of whisky and, though I am a consultant blender, do not make money from the sales of any brand; nor do I have any shares in any whisky company. The only recommendation I can make for this brand is confined to my independent review of it here. *56.6%. The Marquess Collection. Sixth edition.*

Tullibardine The Murray Châteauneuf-du-Pape Finish dist 2005, bott 2018 db (91.5) n21.5 t23.5 f23 b23.5 Not too sure my Trademark lawyer's too happy about this one (yes, my name is Trademarked)... Anyway, just for the record: no, I have no connection with this whisky and I don't make any money from sales or use of the Murray name. As I know I'll be slaughtered by the socially and intellectually challenged conspiracy theorist saddoes on the Internet somewhere along the line, thought I'd better make that crystal clear. Also, if I were to have my name linked to a whisky, a wine cask of any description would be the last thing it had matured in. Even one as good as this... *40.1%. ncf. The Marquess Collection.*

Tullibardine The Murray Marsala Cask Finish dist 2006, bott 2018, bott code: 18/0167 db (86) n22 t22 f20.5 b21.5 A dry and heavy dram, very much the opposite of the standard sweet, gristy, malty affair from bourbon cask. Lots of frisky bite and nibble of delivery as the plummy fruit gets into full swing. But the tightness of the cask arrests further meaningful development. *46%. The Marquess Collection.*

Tullibardine Sovereign bourbon barrel db (89.5) n22.5 t23 f21.5 b22.5 Beautifully salivating despite the intricate oak notes. *43%*

⬦ **Cadenhead's Tullibardine 26 Year Old** sherry cask, dist 1993 (90) n23 t23 f22 b22 If nothing else this could win the award for the darkest Scotch of 2020. From sideways on it looks like my morning Sumatra/Java blend coffee: black, of course. But it certainly doesn't smell or taste like it. This is from one of those overbearing sherry butts which clamps down on all other facets of a whisky's personality faster than you can say "Jerez". The nose, though, certainly has oak enough to confirm its age but all else is grape. Delicious grape, admittedly.

And 100% sulphur free to boot. The softness of the delivery is like being kissed repeatedly by sex-starved sultanas, and their caresses are everywhere. But then it just flattens out somewhat, as big sherry so often does. How can you not love it, though...? *45.1%. 276 bottles. Cadenhead Shop Cask Series 2019 Vienna.*

⬧ **The First Editions Tullibardine Aged 27 Years 1992** refill hogshead, cask no. 16917, bott 2019 **(86.5) n22 t22 f21.5 b21** There are almost as many bourbon notes to this one as there are malt ones. The kumquats on the nose suggests Kentucky, but the sweetness you hope is going to arrive on the palate never quite materialises. Busy in part and not short of some pleasant, chewy caramel tones. But never quite nails either the rhythm or the balance. *41.1%. nc ncf sc. 81 bottles.*

Glen Oak Tullibardine 10 Year Old ex-bourbon barrels **(91)** n22.5 t23.5 f22 b23 A singular single malt full of quirks, nooks and crannies. *40%. Branded Spirits USA.*

⬧ **Old Malt Cask Tullibardine Aged 28 Years** refill hogshead, cask no. 16100, dist Sept 91, bott Oct 19 **(81) n20.5 t21.5 f19 b20** Some definite weirdness to this one – perhaps a result of the fermentation process all those long years ago. The malt is in evidence, but feels uncomfortable and incomplete. The bitterness from the cask doesn't help, either. *46.5%. nc ncf sc. 284 bottles.*

Single Cask Collection Tullibardine Aged 11 Years (93) n23 t23.5 f23 b23.5 Tully at its maltiest and most even. Salivating and bursting with youthful energy, this hits the perfect balance between a clean youth and a more grandiose ageing. Super-delicious! *56%. sc.*

WOLFBURN
Highlands (Thurso), 2012. Aurora Brewing Ltd. Working.

Wolfburn Aurora sherry oak casks db **(91.5) n22.5 t24 f22 b23** Early days at a distillery and still finding their feet with the still. The cut on this was wider than on the previous bottling I sampled, but there is no faulting the use of the 100% sulphur-free sherry butt. There is the odd aspect of genius attached to this dram, for sure. For the record: just vatted this with some OTT oak-hit sherry-cask 1954 malt in need of the kiss of life, or like a vampire in need of a virgin's blood: I suspect the first time a Wolfburn has been mixed with a 60-year-old Speysider. Result? One of the most complex and complete experiences of the last couple of months – a would-be award winner, were it commercially available! Stunning! *46%. nc ncf.*

Wolfburn Langskip bott 27 May 19 db **(94) n23 t24 f23 b24** Rich, full bodied, intense, unforgiving. A whisky that doesn't just dip its toe in the outgoing surf... *58%. nc ncf.*

Wolfburn Morven db **(91.5) n23 t23 f22.5 b23** Confirmation, were it needed, that lightly peated malt is a brilliant way of getting a distillery's whiskies out at a young age without the lack of development becoming too clear. This is a delicious and refined amble on the taste buds. *46%. nc ncf.*

Wolfburn Northland db **(88.5) n22.5 t22 f22 b22** Limited complexity but maximum charm for one so young. *46%. nc ncf.*

Wolfburn Single Malt Scotch Whisky db **(91.5) n23 t23 f22.5 b23** This is a very young malt showing an intriguing wispy smokiness, its evenness more in line with having been matured in ex-Islay casks than using low phenol barley. Still, it might have been, and, if so, perhaps reveals a style that would not have been entirely unknown to the people of Thurso when they last drank this during Victorian times. It is probably 30 years ago I was shown to a spot in the town where I was told the original distillery had been. Now it is back, and eclipses Pulteney as the producers of the most northerly mainland Scottish whisky. For all its youth, its excellence of quality glimmers from the glass: a malt as beautifully flighted as a cricket ball delivered by the most crafted of spinners. And offers a delightful turn on the palate, too. The building of a new distillery, no matter how romantic its location or story, does not guarantee good whisky. So I am delighted for those involved in a project as exhausting as this that a very good whisky is exactly what they have on their hands. *46%. nc ncf.*

Wolfburn Small Batch Release No. 128 half-sized first fill ex-bourbon barrels db **(88)** n22 t23 f21.5 b21.5 Does very well until the home straight when balance is lost. *46%. nc ncf.*

⬧ **Wolfburn Small Batch Release No. 155** first fill ex-bourbon barrels, finished for six months in fresh port hogsheads db **(93) n23** young yet complex. There is a phenol note: hard to tell if from some kind of peat or a darker note wandering in from the heftier grape tannins from the Port. Either way, works well in keeping those younger tones in check and ensuring the weight and sugars are well structured and balanced; **t23.5** super-salivating, yet rather than spiral towards the maltiness which appeared to be its first course, it instead meanders back towards a deeper fruit note... and that faux phenol. Spice threatens to rage, but then settles on a low grumble; **f23** what do you know! The malt is back again...with brass knobs! **b23.5** my word! This may be a new distillery. But they don't half produce some serious whisky... *46%. nc ncf. 5,300 bottles.*

Wolfburn Small Batch Release No. 270 half-sized first fill ex-bourbon barrels db **(92)** n23.5 t22.5 f22.5 b23.5 You'd think from the lighter colour to Wolfburn 128 this would be less developed and offering fewer flavour options. Curiously, the reverse is true, the flavours more even, satisfying and elegant. *46%. nc ncf. 6,000 bottles.*

Wolfburn Small Batch Release No. 375 half-sized first fill ex-bourbon barrels & second fill oloroso sherry hogsheads db **(87.5)** n22.5 t23 f20.5 b22 Such a wonderful nose! Fry's Turkish Delight, complete with chocolate. There is a slight niggle on the fruit but the barley is pristine. Sadly, that fruity warning comes true on the slightly furry finish. But that doesn't impair the delivery, which is an essay in honey. This distillery is a long way from anywhere, but this was close to being a minor classic. *46%. nc ncf. 5,500 bottles.*

The Cyprus Whisky Association Wolfburn Aged 4 Years quarter cask, cask no. 123/14, dist Jan 14, bott Jan 18 **(92)** n22.5 t23.5 f23 b23 This distillery really doesn't muck about, does it! Huge and makes no attempts to pretend to be otherwise. *59.8%. nc ncf sc. 160 bottles.*

UNSPECIFIED SINGLE MALTS (CAMPBELTOWN)

Cadenhead's Campbeltown Malt (92) n22 t24 f23 b23. On their home turf you'd expect them to get it right... and, my word, so they do!! *59.5%*

UNSPECIFIED SINGLE MALTS (HIGHLAND)

Asda Extra Special Highland Single Malt bott code: L6B 8127 1511 **(84.5)** n21.5 t22 f20 b21 Nutty and lush. But the degree of toffee on show makes this almost closer to being a candy liqueur than a Highland malt. Perfect...if you like toffee! *40%.*

⬧ **Compass Box Myths & Legends I (96)** n24.5 a 20 minute nose. Just sit back in a quiet room and let this malt talk to you. Engage the Murray Method and unlock the varied honey tones, the freshness of the green apples, the glory of the unblemished malt, the varying intensity of the vanilla and even the floral tones of an English garden on a late summer's evening...; **t24** if you lost count of the different honeys on the nose, don't even try and start on the palate. Such an eloquent malt, where elegance taps on the shoulder of every taste bud. The oils grease the palate and allow the sugar and vanilla an extended indulgence. The apples on the nose are not lost here, either as there is a fruit salad sweetness to add yet another super-soft dimension; **f23.5** just more of the same as you will find on the palate. Except with a little extra spice and just an occasional tannin tartness; **b24** I quite literally have no idea which distillery this is from. But those who are slightly in love with Clynelish in bourbon cask – one of the greatest experiences available in Scotch single malt whisky – will appreciate this. It may not be Clynelish, but the apples and honey make for a very creditable impersonation. By the way, I think Compass Box founder John Glaser suggests you can take ice with your whisky. Anyone adding ice or water to this deserves never to taste spectacularly great whisky again. Murray Method all the way for astonishing results... *46%.*

Glen Marnoch Highland Single Malt bott code: L12 12 18 **(91)** n22 t23 f23 b23 A beautifully even and satisfying Highlander. No great age, but so much charisma. *40%. Produced for Aldi.*

Glen Oak 28 Year Old ex-bourbon barrels **(90)** n21.5 t22.5 f23 b23 The nose is a bit scary. The experience on the palate something altogether better balanced and delightful. *40%. sc.*

Glen Turner Cask Collection Rum Cask Finish bott code: L907357A **(90.5)** n23 t22 f23 b22.5 A very well-manicured malt. *40%. La Martiniquaise.*

Glen Turner Heritage Double Cask Port Cask Finish bott code: L834657A **(94)** n23.5 t24 f23 b23.5 An impressive piece of cask finishing where the speech by the port is pretty and important, but the microphone has not been turned up too loudly. *40%. La Martiniquaise.*

Glen Turner Malt Legend Aged 12 Years bott code: L832557C **(87)** n21 t23.5 f21 b21.5 A fat, velvety malt with an attractive, lush fruitiness but just a little too much sharpness out of the oak. Plenty to enjoy. *40%. La Martiniquaise.*

Glenwill Highland Single Malt sherry butt finish **(86.5)** n22 t21.5 f21.5 b21.5 Perfectly good sherry butt at work here. However, where it has come a little unstuck is that the finishing is incomplete: they decided to bottle when the sherry has rather too over-enthusiastically filled in the peaks and troughs of the malt but not left enough character of its own The result, as is often the case, is pleasant whisky but lacking fingerprints... *40%. Matisse Spirits Company.*

Glenwill Highland Single Malt rum cask finish **(88)** n22 t22 f21.5 b22.5 An easy malt where the sugary shell of the rum comes into play infrequently. *40%. Matisse Spirits Company.*

Glenwill RV rum cask finish **(80)** n21 t21 f19 b19 Mainly toffeed, characterless and just zzzzzzzzzzz.... *40%. Quality Spirits International.*

Glenwill S = 1 sherry butt finish **(73)** n19 t21.5 f16 b17.5 S = Sulphur. *40%. Quality Spirits International.*

Grangestone Master's Selection Highland Single Malt bourbon cask finish **(87)** n22.5 t22 f21 b21.5 An attractive interplay between tannin and toffee, though the complexity is limited – especially on the simplistic finish. Good, though brief, molasses lift off on delivery. *40%. Quality Spirits International.*

Hepburn's Choice Nice 'N Peaty 11 Years Old refill hogshead, dist 2006, bott 2018 **(77)** **n18.5 t21 f19 b19.5** Peaty for sure. But usually feinty, too. *46%. nc ncf sc. 189 bottles.*

Highland Queen Majesty Classic bott code L14/8634 09.08.14 **(92) n24, t23 f22 b23** The brilliant nose isn't quite matched by the pragmatism of the overall taste experience but a blend to savour nonetheless. *40%. Tullibardine Ltd.*

Highland Queen Majesty Aged 12 Years bott code L15/8538 19/08/15 **(86.5) n22 t22 f21 b21.5** A pleasant but lazy blend considering its age. Lots of explosive malt on delivery, some with a lemon sherbet fizz. But a heavy dependence on caramel quietens the party, though a late spice surge gate-crashes to welcome effect. *40%. Tullibardine Ltd.*

Highland Queen Majesty Aged 16 Years bott code L15/8265 06 07 15 **(88) n22.5 t22.5 f21.5 b22** Enjoyable, yet leaves you with a feeling that it could have offered a little bit more. *40%. Tullibardine Ltd.*

◈ **Liquid Treasures From Miles Away Highland Malt 19 Year Old** bourbon hogshead, dist Aug 20, bott Feb 20 **(80) n19 t22 f19 b20** A malt from miles away...but not quite far enough. Very flimsy fare, despite the occasional intense barley. *55.6%. sc. 325 bottles.*

Master of Malt Highland Single Malt (86.5) n21.5 t22 f21.5 b21.5 Pleasant, absolutely middle of the road malt with a juicy, nutty and toffee-rich character. *40%.*

Muirhead's Silver Seal Aged 12 Years Highland Single Malt (87.5) n22 t22 f21 b21.5 Satisfyingly salivating. The vanillas arrive with a lemon escort from the first moment, ensuring a semi-ethereal element to this. Lightly oiled and a little nutty, just a tad too much caramel at the times you want the malt to begin to fly. *40%. Tullibardine Ltd.*

Muirhead's Silver Seal Aged 16 Years Highland Single Malt (86) n21 t23 f20.5 b21.5 A hefty malt with a battling, earthy aroma. Hits its zenith about four or five flavour waves after delivery when it strikes up a stunning spicy walnut cake and date middle. Flags towards the finish, even becoming a little flat and furry, save for the wonderful spices.... *40%. Tullibardine Ltd.*

Muirhead's Silver Seal Maturity Highland Single Malt (84) n19.5 t22 f21 b21.5 Though called "Maturity" the malt displays a youthful gristiness from time to time. Not technically the greatest nose, the malt recovers brightly on the palate with a volley of varied sugars and spice, including a light smothering of heather honey. *40%. Tullibardine Ltd.*

Sansibar Whisky Orkney 2006 (86) n21 t22 f21.5 b21.5 Stuffed solid with intense malt. But a little burn on this one, and I don't just mean from the alcohol. *60.4%.*

◈ **The Single Malts of Scotland Orkney 12 Year Old Reserve Cask (88) n21.5 t23 f21.5 b22** A slightly tired cask does not make full use of what appears to be an attractively rich spirit. Both the nose and finish reveal a slight weakness to the wood. But the delivery likewise underlines an excellent malt trying to ramp up the honey tones but getting little help from the oak. A temperamental dram but when it sparkles it's pure gold... *48%. nc ncf.*

Tesco Finest Aged 12 Years Highland Single Malt bott code L63353 **(80.5) n20 t21 f19 b20.5** Quite possibly one of the most boring single malts of all time: not recommended as a night cap as you'll doze off by the time you reach the third step on your stairs, and it won't be the effect of the alcohol. Bland barely covers it. With the amount of cream toffee found on the nose and palate not sure if this should be stocked in the Spirits or Sweets aisles. Do I like it? No. Do I dislike it? No. But if I am putting 12-year-old malt into my body, I'd like it to have some semblance of character. I suppose it was designed to offend nobody: a mute hardly can. Trouble is, it is hardly likely to get new drinkers wanting to come back and discover more about single malt, either. Oh well, I suppose that buggers up any chance of getting The Bible stocked and sold by Tesco this year. But I'm afraid they need to hear the truth. *40%.*

Whisky-Fässle Orkney 13 Year Old sherry butt, dist 2004, bott 2017 **(93.5) n23 t24 f23 b23.5** Did I expect a sherry butt quite this good? I'll be honest: I really didn't: bitter experience has taught me in recent years to be wary of the words sherry and Orkney in the same sentence. So my emergency palate cleaners were primed, but not needed. *50.5%.*

UNSPECIFIED SINGLE MALTS (ISLAND)

A.D. Rattray Cask Orkney 18 Year Old dist 1999 **(94) n23.5 t24 f23 b23.5** A beautiful and satisfying malt on a great many levels. *46%.*

◈ **The First Editions Director's Highbrow Selection Aged 13 Years 2006** refill hogshead, cask no. 16651, bott 2019 **(93) n23** saltier than a sea dog...; **t23.5** a magnificent explosion of spice and honey leaves you gasping and purring at the same moment; incredibly thick mouthfeel, though less oily and more beeswax in style; **f23** all that beeswax hangs around to allow the growing vanilla a surprising degree of intensity late on; the spices have peaked early and punched themselves out; **b23.5** with so much beeswax, a polished malt as you'd expect. *61%. nc ncf sc. 339 bottles.*

UNSPECIFIED SINGLE MALTS (ISLAY)

◇ **Aerolite Lyndsay Aged 10 Years** bott code: #4877 **(91)** n22.5 an attractive, standard Caol Ila-style nose: oily, chalky, vanilla-rich and enjoying a very even smokiness; **t23** soft and avoiding any kind of aggression. As on the nose, the smoke drifts with an even weight, a light semi-bourbonesque hickory tone mingling with the phenols. Elsewhere a gristy maltiness ensures sweetness; **f22.5** a smoky, buttery layering coats the mouth as the vanillas dry; **b23** a classic Islay unchanged in style from 30 years ago. A very pleasing experience. 46%. Atom Brands.

◇ **Angel's Nectar Single Malt Scotch Whisky Islay Edition (91.5)** n22 t23.5 f23 b23 A young Islay, but no shame in that when this well made and so beautifully matured. The peat both on nose and palate has an evenness of weight which allows the light saline edge mix with the delicate citrus without too much interruption. Fresh, salivating and incorrigibly gristy. 47%.

◇ **Arcanum Spirits Peaty Little Secret 9 Years Old** aged over 8 years in ex-bourbon hogshead, finished a full year in 1st fill Oloroso hogshead, dist 12 Jun 08, bott 19 Oct 17 **(85.5)** n22 t22 f20.5 b21 Where there 18-year-old can be held up and worshipped as an extraordinary example of balance and charm at its finest, this takes another route altogether. Finishing is an art form - and a dangerous expedition for any whisky to undertake. As you are always entering uncharted lands and there is no way of knowing when you have found the land you are looking for. Even more dangerous is introducing sherry casks. And I'm afraid that, for one reason or another, this isn't the finest quality and nor has an understanding been achieved between the two parties. (It is 8pm on a Thursday here in England – so pause here for a minute's applause for the brave and wonderful British National Health Service staff who are fighting Covid-19 head on...) What I do adore, though, is the proud cattle byre nose and delivery. Pure farmyard. 58.4%. ncf sc. 439 bottles.

Asda Extra Special Islay Single Malt bott code: L6C 7619 1109 **(88.5)** n22 peaty...; **t22.5** peaty with warming spices and underlying vanilla; **f22** silky, lingering and smoky; a tad bitter at the death; **b22** does exactly what it says on the tin...except for the alleged fruity tones which never materialise... 40%.

Cadenhead's Islay 9 Years Old (94) n23 t24.5 f23.5 b23 Only a degree of over simplicity has docked marks here. If it is perfect, clean, beautifully rounded, juicy all-enveloping peat you are after, then you might be tempted to give it a straight 100... 58.9%. sc. 175th Anniversary.

Cask Islay (91.5) n22.5 t23 f22.5 b23 Does what it says on the tin. 46%. A.D. Rattray

Demijohn 8 Year Old Islay Region (92.5) n23 t23.5 f23 b23 Clean, sweet and highly impressive youngster that has never mixed with undesirable company. 59.8%.

Demijohn 10 Years Old Port Askaig (90) n23 t22.5 f21.5 b22 The nose promises a peatiness which doesn't quite arrive on the palate. Underpowered but lovely all the same. 42%.

Eiling Lim Bessie's Dram (88) n22.5 t22.5 f21 b22 A distinctly Laphroaigian type dram complete with Allied style bitter cask (oh, I have just spotted that this is Laphroaig...!!!), is plenty to enjoy. 51.3%.

Elements of Islay AR10 (93) n23.5 t23 f23 b23.5 Not a fault, an off note, a flavour profile out of place, just sheer joy, though always on the lighter, less intense side of the distillery's spectrum. Well, just can't think what this might be... Ardbeg by any chance...? 52.4%.

◇ **Elements of Islay BW8 (86)** n21.5 t22 f21 b21.5 Thin and struggling to make a fist from first to last. Never quite hits a rhythm, with a metallic sharpness interjecting here and there, and the explosive sugars uncontrolled. Some decent chocolate is on damage limitation exercise. Not up to the normal high Elements of Islay standards though, doubtless, some Islayphiles will want to have its babies. 51.2%.

Elements of Islay CL12 (90) n23 t23 f22 b22 Wonderful iodine kick on the nose, but the oiliness gives a slightly restrictive texture once we are through the phenols and sugars of the delicious initial delivery and fabulous spice follow-through. 57.5%.

◇ **Elements of Islay CL13 (94)** n23.5 t23.5 f23 b24 This malt is in gracious mood, first offering itself up in the gristiest manner on the nose, before taking on a more weighty roll on the palate, allowing the heather honey the entire stage on which to shine while acting as the ballast. A charming Islay that swings from a dry sootiness to a butterscotch and honey tart and then onto Jamaican Blue Mountain Coffee without breaking sweat. Effortlessly, an essential Islay. 54.6%.

Elements of Islay LP10 (93.5) n23.5 t23.5 f23 b23.5 A huge dose of lychee juice is a surprise package in this otherwise docile Islay. The peat is intermittently big, but easily bossed around by the exotic fruit. Unorthodoxly beautiful. 53.9%.

Elements of Islay MA3 (91) n22 t23 f23 b23 Bit of cough sweet intensity, hickory included, to go with slightly citrusy but ultimately sooty peat 55.2%.

Elements of Islay PL6 (92) n22.5 t23 f23 b23.5 Not often you get elements of bourbon on an Islay, but the nose and finish positively quiver with tannin. Betwixt times though roaring spiciness lifts the phenols onto another plane entirely. A malt to make you sweat a bit... 55.3%.

◈ **The Finest Malts Secret Islay Distillery Aged 6 Years** sherry butt, dist Oct 13, bott Jan 20 **(89) n22 t22.5 f22 b22.5** Well, there's something for the diary: the first Islay whisky which, perhaps in conjunction with the sherry butt, offers a smokiness slightly closer to Mesquite thanks to a pretty off the wall acidity biting deep. The sherry but is clean with no sulphur, thank heavens. But, even so, the youthfulness of the malt means the two very different – and egotistical – flavour codes have had little time to strike up much of an understanding. That said, hugely enjoyable if at times a little raucous....as any self-respecting 6-year-old Islay has every right to be. *51.6%. nc ncf sc. 72 bottles.*

Finlaggan Cask Strength Islay Single Malt (88) n22.5 t23 f21.5 b21 A massive peated malt which that phenolphiles will lap up. But for its all its big Islay muscle, struggles to come together and balance out as even as might be hoped. *58%. The Vintage Malt Whisky Company.*

Finlaggan Eilean Mor Islay Single Malt (88.50) n22 t22.5 f22 b22 Oily Islay with a pleasant if limited disposition. *46%. The Vintage Malt Whisky Company.*

Finlaggan Feis Ile 2018 Vintage 2009 Islay Single Malt (95) n24 t24 f23 b24 A peated Islay in all its undisputed magnificence, Beautifully made and matured. *50%. sc.*

Finlaggan Old Reserve Islay Single Malt (91) n23 t23f22.5 b23 No great age I suspect. But the intensity and charm are profound. Unmistakably Islay! *40%.*

Finlaggan Port Finish Islay Single Malt (92.5) n23 t23.5 f23 b23.5 Huge peat at work, dry and almost coal dust-like. But its wings are initially clipped by the port before it takes off once more...to profound effect. *46%. The Vintage Malt Whisky Company.*

Finlaggan Sherry Finish Islay Single Malt (86.5) n23.5 t23 f19 b21 Delighted and relieved to report that the early damage of the sherry finish to the whisky is limited to the dampening down of what the nose suggests would have been one hell of a peaty experience, and taking the edge off the finale. Some lovely chocolate from the midpoint on...but some very late sulphur furriness confirms the sherry butt was not entirely faultless. *46%. The Vintage Malt Whisky Company.*

Glen Castle Islay Single Malt 1989 Vintage Cask 29 Years Old dist 1989, bott 2018, bott code: LHB 1477-2018 **(96) n24 t24.5 f23.5 b24** Though a single malt, this could almost be a composite of the three big South East coast distilleries, at one time or other displaying a little character trait of them all. What a little classic this is, one of the very best non-distillery bottling Islays you will find this year. And so very unusual to uncork an Islay of some 30 years standing still dishing out this degree of phenol intensity... *51%. nc ncf.*

The Ileach Cask Strength Islay Single Malt (89.5) n22 t22.5 f22 b23 A rotund, oily number where significant muscovado sugars – in full fruity mode – link stupendously with the bubbling spices to create a charming balance. The smoke chugs through evenly and unerringly like an old puffer through Hebridean waters. *58%. The Vintage Malt Whisky Company.*

Islay Storm Islay Single Malt (87) n21.5 t22 f21.5 b22 Having been caught right slap in the middle of some ferocious, frankly white knuckle, Islay storms myself over the last 40 years, this is but a five-minute passing shower. The smoke needs seeking, rather than it coming to you, and the gentle maltiness glides over the palate with all the intensity and threat of a child's rusk. Attractive, but could do with some oomph! *40%. C.S. James & Sons Ltd.*

Lady of the Glen Secret Islay 2003 cask no. 1828 **(90.5) n22 t23 f22.5 b23** Well-structured Islay with a reasonable, though not enormous, phenol presence and hefty tannin and boiled fruit candy notes at play. One of the sweeter Islays you'll encounter this year. *56.1%. sc.*

Liquid Treasures 10th Anniversary Islay Malt 10 Year Old bourbon barrel, dist 2008, bott 2019 **(90.5) n22.5 t23.5 f22 b22.5** A bit of a treat of a dram. *58.7%. sc. 171 bottles.*

Peat's Beast bott code: L 07 08 17 **(92) n22.5 t23 f23.5 b23** Nosing this whizzed me back to the late 1980s and my old office in a national newspaper in Fleet Street where, by night, I was taking my first tentative steps into the then unknown and practically non-existent medium of whisky writing. And I remember opening up a Bowmore 5-years-old bottled by Oddbins. I'm not saying this is a Bowmore, but so many features on display in that landmark bottling 30 years ago are also to be found here... *46%. ncf.*

Peat's Beast Twenty Five bott code: L1 1409-2017 11 **(88.5) n23 t23 f20 b22.5** There are far more beastly Islay whiskies than this out there – a quarter of a century in the cask means the teeth have been blunted, the claws clipped. And if you must "tame it" further, for God's sake ignore the daft advice on the label about adding water. Please use the Murray Method described on page 9. That will keep the thing alive while making it purr at full decibels... And this is so lovely (well, finish apart), it is worth listening to at full volume...which isn't very loud. *52.2%. ncf.*

Port Askaig 8 Years Old (85) n20 t22 f21.5 b21.5 Thankfully the slightly disappointing and sketchy nose isn't matched by the delivery which shows far greater harmony between the phenols and oaky vanillas. The finish, though, doesn't enjoy quite the same assuredness, despite the spice. *45.8%.*

◈ **Port Askaig Islay Aged 12 Years Spring Edition** ex-bourbon hogsheads, dist 2006 & 2007 **(95.5) n24** just bounds along with classic Islayness... Gristy smoke flutters, light salt cures and seasons. The feel of decent age, but just not too much, is spot on...; **t24** brilliant delivery with a delicate oil which stokes up the sugars and sets them against the semi-muscular phenols. Naturally, they embrace. Until now there had been a slight air of occasional youth. But now the tannins change the theme...; **f23.5** the finale chunters along with the smoke thudding against the lighter vanilla lead. The late arriving oak forms a firm backdrop form the frillier phenols; **b24** only a bourbon cask can allow the phenols to play and galivant with such fun and abandon. You get the feeling that the casks were plucked from the warehouse at exactly the right time. Fabulous! *45.8%. nc ncf. 5,000 bottles.*

Port Askaig 14 Year Old Bourbon Cask dist 2004 **(95) n24 t23.5 f23.5 b24** For those who prefer their peat to caress rather than kick. Elegant and so beautifully sensual. *45.8%.*

Port Askaig 15 Years Old sherry cask **(87.5) n22.5 t22 f21.5 b21.5** I know, I know: I have a blind spot for this kind of whisky. Rather, not blind, but not an over developed appreciation of the big smoke notes slugging it out with and then being neutralised by equally big, occasionally eye-wateringly sharp, fruit ones. At least the sherry is clean and extra marks for that. But, for me, this is just too much of a tit-for-tat malt leaving a neutral toffee fruitiness to claim the big prize. Pleasant, I grant you. But I want it to be so much more.... *45.8%.*

Port Askaig 25 Years Old (91) n23 t23.5 f21 b22.5 Bottled at the right time – another year or two would have seen a dramatic slide. But as it is, so much to quietly savour. *45.8%.*

Port Askaig 28 Years Old (92.5) n23.5 t23.5 f22 b23.5 A classically understated Islay where elegance outscores muscle. *45.8%.*

Port Askaig 33 Years Old Single Cask (95) n23.5 t24.5 f23 b24 Islay at its most coastal. Shews its age with rare elegance. Sublime. *50.3%. sc.*

Port Askaig 34 Years Old Single Cask (94) n23.5 t23.5 f23 b24 This charming whisky has decided to get old gracefully. And succeeded. *49.7%. sc.*

Port Askaig 45 Years Old (90.5) n23 t23 f22 b22.5 Even in my scaringly long career, I can probably count the number of peated malts that made it to this kind of age and then into a commercial bottling on one hand. Certainly by the end it is showing every year that has passed, but for an unexpected period the malt hangs together...sometimes surprisingly deliciously. *40.8%.*

Port Askaig 10th Anniversary Aged 10 Years refill American-oak hogsheads, first-fill bourbon casks & ex-solera casks, bott code: P/000248 **(87.5) n22 t23 f20.5 b22** Lusty and loud peat gets things off to the smokiest of starts both on the nose and palate. Grumbles a bit and rather uneven on the finish, though. But those first five crashing phenol waves on the palate, with a little orange-blossom honey attached to the smoke, ensure a brilliant opening sequence. *55.85%. nc ncf.*

Port Askaig 100 Proof (96.5) n24 t24 f24 b24.5 Just exemplary, high quality Islay: a must experience malt. If you find a more beautifully paced, weighted and elegant Islay this year, I'd like to hear about it... *57.1%.*

Port Askaig 110 Proof (91.5) n23 t23 f22.5 b23 Beautifully made and elegantly matured. *55%.*

⬦ **The Whisky Chamber Buair an Diabhail Vol. XVIII** bourbon cask **(86.5) n22 t22 f21 b21.5** It may be swamped in more smoke than a 1950s London pub, but there is something unmercifully metallic about this malt. Especially on the rigid finish. Plenty of molasses to sweeten the impact, but a whisky that is hard to embrace. *57.4%. sc.*

UNSPECIFIED SINGLE MALTS (LOWLAND)

Tweeddale Single Lowland Malt Scotch Whisky 14 Years db **(89) n21.5 t23.5 f22 b22** busy, bustling, elegant and old-fashioned...like a small borders town. *62%. nc ncf sc.*

UNSPECIFIED SINGLE MALTS (SPEYSIDE)

⬦ **Abbey Whisky Anon. Batch 3 Aged 30 Years 1988** sherry cask **(96) n24** the years pulse onto the nose with almost radiometric precision, the acidity of the grape – at times almost of a gooseberry jam quality – to the drier oaky tannins...and roving maltiness...; **t24** thumping tannins. Actually, at first they don't thump: they just knock politely, but soon patience is lost and they rattle the fruity doors demanding entry; **f23.5** huge age on the finish: the tannins almost have grey hairs. But still the fruit can dance a jig of its youth, though with a little Demerara sugar to help it around; **b24.5** those who adore Glenfarclas will find a soft spot in their hearts for this as the oaky tannin and aged-dulled fruit apes that distillery's style amazingly uncannily. This is one of the finest sherry butts I have found in action this year. Not an atom of sulphur to be seen: this is 30 year-old whisky as I tasted 30 years ago... *46.6%. sc. 153 bottles.*

A.D. Rattray Cask Speyside 10 Year Old (89) n22 t22.5 f22 b22.5 An elegant and lightly smoked malt which would double as either a pre-prandial dram, or one for the wooden hill... *46%.*

⬦ **Arcanum Spirits Arcanum One 18 Years Old** dist 26 Feb 99, bott 8 Jun 17 **(95.5) n24** sublime quality malt which unmercifully teases from the glasses. The barley is so clean and delicate, the sugars, grist and vanilla from the tannin supremely elegant and almost perfectly integrated, the citrus (especially grapefruit) tones just so full of life that it is hard to imagine this is a bit of a fogey at 18-years......; **t24** as on the nose, offers that tantalising mix of sprightly youthfulness which makes a mockery of the 18 passing summers, yet also casts a spell of malt and tannin which only slow aging can produce.... The crescendo just after delivery is the stuff of the wettest of dreams...; **f23.5** an implausibly classy procession of malts at varying levels of intensity, fading as the high-class vanilla builds. The transformation from sweet and juicy to dry and delicate is masterful...; **b24** classy, classy malt deserving the patronage of any Speysider lover. The way it maintains a degree of youthfulness and then reminds you of its decent age is such fun. Marvellous and deeply desirable whisky. 54%. ncf sc. 396 bottles.

Arcanum Spirits TR21INITY Aged Over 21 Years refill ex-bourbon barrel, dist 16 Jul 97, bott 24 Aug 18 db **(96.5) n24.5 t24 f23.5 b24.5** TR21 reminds me, touchingly, of a magazine my old dad used to bring home from work for me in the mid 1960s: TV21...never could get enough Daleks or Thunderbirds... Well this is Thunderbird 5: out of this world...and complexity like this, such utter, almost moving beauty, can only ever be achieved with a bourbon cask where all is laid bare. 52.1%. ncf sc. 222 bottles. Whisky Edition No. 3.

Asda Extra Special Speyside Single Malt bott code: L6A 8226 1412 **(81) n20 t21.5 f19 b20.5** Pleasant, soft and sweet and briefly delicious on delivery...but entirely linear. As it develops, devoid of character or personality as the big dollop of caramel and tired casks has taken its toll. 40%.

◈ **Compass Box Myths & Legends II (95) n24** a blender's dream: the malt is pure in its intensity. Whether in a blend or a vatting you pray for this and as a singleton you can just breathe its sweet malty clarity....; **t23.5** I could write the same notes as I did for the nose. Except here there is a little extra sweetness, though it is all grist related. Citrus notes are dabbed gently on the grain and light vanilla form veins through the malty body; **f23.5** yet more malt and vanilla in a simple but long and satisfying finale; **b24** incredibly lively malt on the palate. The delivery is one of the most memorable this year, aided and abetted by sublime bourbon casks allowing the malt to reveal all its naked beauty.. 46%.

Dramfool 22 Elderly Elvis Tilting 25 Years Old bourbon cask **(95) n24 t24 f23 b24** A malt which has made the use of every single day of its 25 years to compose a hit. Uh-ha! 51.2%. nc ncf. 109 bottles. Spirit of Speyside 2019 Exclusive.

Fadandel.dk Secret Speyside Aged 26 Years refill bourbon barrel, dist 17 Jun 92, bott 28 Jun 18 **(86.5) n21.5 t22 f21 b22** A bit of a tangy old cask at work here which allows the sharp, rich cerealy, barley free rein. But the balance and complexity doesn't quite fit in so comfortably. Eye-wateringly salty, too. 51.3%. sc. 72 bottles.

◈ **The Finest Malts City Landmarks Secret Speyside Aged 24 Years** bourbon barrel, cask no. 408895, dist 1994, bott 2019 **(92.5) n22.5 t24 f22.5 b23.5** A lightly honeyed offering here which, even after 24 years, is not frightened of allowing the barley to let rip. The age has crept up quietly and politely, never seemingly wanting to over-interfere. But there is a particular excellence to the saltiness which livens up the heather-honey especially early on before marzipan and caramel starts to intensify....though gently, of course. The vanillas are treading water towards the end as the malt tires. But charm and elegance are always the guiding lights here. Some whiskies wear their years well. This is one with just a little grey around the temples and never less than dapper. A great malt for long study. 49.3%. nc ncf sc.

Glenbrynth Aged 21 Years bott code L8W6323 2103 **(86.5) n22.5 t22 f21 b21** What starts off as a super-sexy nose with apple tart aplenty, tails off into a more prosaic fudge fest as the caramels get a constrictor-like grip: a bit of a bore at the end... 43%. OTI Africa.

Glen Castle Speyside Single Malt Aged 12 Years bott code: L6 7461-2017 10 05-21.14 **(87) n22 t22 f21.5 b21.5** A really lovely sweet dram with a wonderful match between barley and spice. Ridiculously easy to drink and exceptionally more-ish. The only downside is the heavy toffee aspect which dulls the obvious vivacity of the barley itself. 40%.

Glen Castle Aged 20 Years Sherry Cask Finish dist 1996 **(94) n23.5 t23.5 f23 b24** Lucky Japanese! A really satisfying, high quality single malt. 54.1%. ncf. Quality Spirits International.

Glen Castle Aged 28 Years sherry cask, dist 1996 **(96.5) n24.5 t24 f24 b24** A quality spirit from Quality Spirits: sherry butts from before the sulphur plague. Just look how magnificent this is...! Surely an award winner this year of some type... 59%. ncf. Quality Spirits International.

Glen Marnoch Speyside Single Malt bott code: L12 12 18 **(84.5) n19 t21.5 f22.5 b21.5** A malt which improves with time spent on the palate, allowing the juicy barley and sugars to build to impressive and ultimately attractive effect. The nose and delivery, though, are pretty off key. The description of the whisky on the label is interesting, but bore little resemblance to what I tasted here. 40%. Produced for Aldi.

Liquid Treasures Snakes Speyside 26 Year Old bourbon barrel, dist 1992, bott 2018 **(95) n23.5 t24 f23.5 b24** An essay in malt 'n' honey. This has been stored in some cask, I can tell you...not a single off note! 51.6%. sc. 270 bottles.

Spey River Double Cask American oak casks, bourbon cask finish **(76) n19 t21 f18 b18**. I was fascinated to see how this unusual maturation technique panned out: but I was not expecting this, or anything like. Not dissimilar to some American micro distillery malts with a tobacco character attached to the sweet sugars. Seriously odd. *40%. Quality Spirits International.*

The Whisky Agency Speyside Region Single Malt 1973 (95.5) n24 t24.5 f23.5 b24 Those into the exotic fruit school of ye olde Speysiders will be pretty delighted with this: ticks every box....with a quilled flourish. *46.9%.*

Whiskey Bottle Company Cigar Malt Lover Aged 21 Years 1st fill sherry butt, cask no. 3646, dist 1997, bott 2018 **(96) n24 t24.5 f23.5 b24** A Glenfarclas-style malt boasting a sherry cask of faultless, unimpeachable character. You don't have to smoke a cigar to enjoy this kind of whisky royalty. Indeed, to mix a malt like this with food, cigars or anything other than another glass of the same whisky must be considered, rightly, an act of treason. *54.4%. nc. 510 bottles.*

Whisky-Fässle Speyside Region 26 Year Old sherry cask, dist 1991, bott 2017 **(76) n18 t21 f18 b19** The odd fruit chocolate moment but a sulphurous sherry cask, alas.... *50.6%.*

Whisky-Fässle Speyside Region 43 Year Old sherry butt, dist 1973, bott 2017 **(87.5) n21.5 t23 f21 b22** Solid, mouth-watering fruit mixes well with the richer bourbon-style notes liquorice notes. But just too heavy on the tannins late on as the passing 43 summers catch up. *51.3%.*

⬩ **Whisky Illuminati Artis Secretum 2011** Spanish oak sherry butt, cask no. 900284 **(95.5) n24** a wonderful weaving of crushed hazelnuts and black cherry! Clean, nobly rich but never, ever overstated or uncouth; **t24.5** just fabulous! A delivery to die for from a perfect, unsulphured cask. The perfect balance evident between sweet and dry is such a rarity, and though great age to this whisky there is tannin enough to give the grape extra spice and gravitas; the mix of molasses and fruit could not offer the midground more...; **f23** long and quietens with surprising ease, then the spices pop up to keep the taste buds at full employment; **b24** a Speyside sherry butt in its finest fettle. What a complete delight... *67.1%. sc. 150 bottles.*

⬩ **Whisky Works 20 Year Old Speyside 2019/WV02./CW** finished in 20 year old Cognac casks, bott code: L9262 13:21 P/010452 **(96.5) n24** straining at the leash with grassy notes, this is making a fool of the passing years. Fresh, clean and extra green with diced cucumber, unripe gooseberry and lemon drop candy. Barley at its most fragrant. Adorable...; **t24** if you listen closely, you can hear me purring...Lime blossom honey paves the way for a succession of succulent, fresh and green note in total accord with the nose. The tannins are around, but content with adding a modest vanilla note which further enhances the sweeter, juicer persona. Slowly, spices evolve...and add further to the juiciness...; **f24** thanks to the limited intervention of the oak – though it is in there keeping things neat, tidy and a little sturdier – still the barley performs all kinds of deft tricks, aided by a light, spiced strawberry and vanilla fade...; **b24.5** on the label this whisky states: "Flavour Profile: Like an afternoon in a country garden". Well, I abandoned my tasting lab in order to taste this one afternoon in my garden, which is the quintessential country garden affording an ancient space around a 300-year-old cottage backing onto wild fields. Can't say the whisky is exactly like the world in which I live and relax. I mean, there is none of the speedwell or bird-foot trefoil; the wild rose and foxglove; the lavender or wild poppy. Nor have they managed to distil the song of the dunnock, the chiffchaff, the blackbird, the wren, the blackcap or the chaffinch; nor, as the afternoon wears on, the excitable screech of the swifts overhead or the churr of the whitethroat. But, allowing for a little poetic licence, I think I know what they are getting at... Because my garden is a little corner of Eden. And this natural, untainted whisky feels right at home in it... *47.1%. nc ncf. 1,593 bottles.*

W.W. Club MCL.1 Speyside Aged 26 Years American oak cask, cask no. 1408826, dist Jun 92, bott Jun 18 **(93) n24 t23 f22.5 b23.5** This is a Speysider from a distillery which doesn't always hit these heights at such an age. The oak has just slightly tipped over the edge, but not enough to spoil a magnificent nose, or undermine the complex elegance of the palate. *51.8%. sc. 273 bottles. Distilled at a Speyside Distillery founded in 1824. William & Co. Spirits.*

W.W. Club MCL.2 Speyside Aged 25 Years American oak cask, cask no. 1408825, dist Jun 92, bott Jun 18 **(94.5) n24 t23.5 f23 b24** As the notes above, save two vital differences. Firstly, the oak hasn't travelled too far here and we are rewarded with extra heather honey as a result. And, secondly, the saltiness is subtly more telling throughout, adding an extra piquancy to the proceedings. Small differences from its sister cask...but vital! Superb! *51.5%. sc. 276 bottles. Dist in distillery founded in 1824 William & Co. Spirits.*

UNSPECIFIED SINGLE MALTS (GENERAL)

Burns Nectar Single Malt bott code: L17/8183 **(77) n20 t19 f19 b19** An ode to toffee. *40%.*

⬩ **Compass Box Myths & Legends III (95.5) n23.5** I've always been a bit partial to a custard pie in the face...; **t24** oh, wow! Just look at that malt go! The mid-point gets really interesting as the chocolate orange kicks in: not often the salivation levels rise further down the line; **f24** just polite spice! And such gorgeous cocoa, too, drifting on the Demerara-sugared oils...; **b24**

Scottish Malts

it is noticeable that Compass Box have, by and large, reigned back on the over oaking and are back to allowing the whiskies themselves to do the talking. Another exceptionally beautiful malt from them using bourbon casks that allows the personality of the malt to come through in all its gentle but complex beauty. I just wish more blenders would take note of this. 46%.

⬦ **Darkness Aged 8 Years** sherry cask finished, bott code: #4635 **(92)** n23 the wine wins here, delicately overtaking the grain to register a layer of moist fruitcake...; t23.5 a delightful, semi-succulent grape note massages the taste buds though in doing so allows the barley a surprise moment of freedom before the spices move in to restore that fruitcake touch. The Demerara and light molasses touches are superb and cleverly never OTT; f22 the slightest furriness makes itself known though it is but a minor blemish; the raisins now toastier than ever before; b23.5 ...being the unreconstructed romantic I am, I tasted this outside in my near silent and perfectly still garden (so silent and still I can hear a train scurrying through a cutting some five miles away – only the second time I have done so in six years) without a breath of wind on the warm summer air as, long after sunset, darkness fell... And the whisky was, I must admit, as gentle as the night which had stealthily crept up and enveloped me... 47.8%. Atom Brands.

⬦ **Eternity Single Malt American Oak Matured (82.5)** n21 t21 f20 b20.5 Nutty with a vague smokiness adding weight. But the early cloying malty sweetness gives way to a dogged bitterness. 40%.

⬦ **Eternity Single Malt 12 Years Old (84)** n21.5 t21.5 f20 b21 Full bodied and malty, there is plenty to chew on here including a degree of toffee. Some redeeming spice on the bitter finish, but never quite finds a comfortable rhythm either on nose or palate. 46%.

Glen Castle Rum Cask Finish (81.5) n20 t21.5 f21 b19 It must have been over 25 years ago now that I brought to the world the first ever rum cask matured whisky, which I discovered in a long-forgotten corner of a Campbeltown warehouse. It deservedly gained great notoriety and thereafter I went out of my way to taste as many rum cask matured or finished malts as were out there. This one is unique, but for all the wrong reasons. As the sugars which normally define the crispness of the whisky appear to have been underdone by other sugars in toffee form, thus neutralising the effect. Pleasant enough. But so dull. 40%. QSI.

Glen Castle Sherry Cask Finish (80) n21 t21 f19 b19 Clean sherry at work here, it appears, though so intense is the toffee the fruit (like anything else) can barely be heard. A malt neutered by caramel. 40%. Quality Spirits International.

⬦ **Kingsbury Gold Auchindoun 22 Year Old** hogshead, cask no. 187, dist 1997 **(86)** n23 t21.5 f20.5 b21 After such a charming, citrus-laced nose with its delicate strands of malt and almost imperceptible traces of mint, what follows on the taste buds has a far bigger oaky resonance than might reasonably be expected. A bit like what appears to be a tender steak which turns out to be a little tough and gristly. 48.9%. sc. 282 bottles.

⬦ **Kingsbury Gold Culloden 15 Year Old** hogshead, cask no. 600044, dist 2004 **(92)** n23 a salty infusion of heather honey and cocoa. Pretty coastal in style, with big emphasis on the malt; t23 charming mix of intense barley and orange blossom honey. As on the nose, chocolate comes into play; those saline notes refuse to recede; f22.5 lovely salted cocoa; b23.5 one of those quiet, understated drams which could be to be easily overlooked. Worth giving a lot of extra time to in order to fully explore. 62.7%. sc. 174 bottles.

⬦ **Kingsbury Gold Kilbride 13 Year Old** barrel, cask no. 800217, dist 2006 **(94)** n23.5 confidently peated yet soft and oily in a Caol Ila style; t23.5 rich, oily and chewy, but the peat never takes liberties and allows the ulmo honey a lead role. Always elegant despite its beautifully smoked persona, helped massively by the rich vanilla from a top-class ex-bourbon cask; f23 lovely late spices intertwangle with the setting phenols; b24 very high class peated malt benefitting from 13 years in excellent oak. A peat-lover's dream! 56%. sc. 220 bottles.

⬦ **Kingsbury Gold Ruine 27 Year Old** barrel, cask no. 4406046, dist 1992 **(90)** n23 another from this Kingsbury set with a distinctive salty seashore feel. Thin ulmo and heather honeys mixing together with lemon blossom honey...but all watered down by the delicate malt; t22.5 a tart delivery which waters the eyes. The oak has kicked in hard, but the latent citrus notes rebel and fight back. Salivating, but a bit of a muddle...; f22 the oak has a slightly tired feel, but the barley is still game and belts out some cheery resistance; b22.5 a malt on the cusp of exhaustion but has enough life not to give up the ghost. Overall, as fascinating as it is delicious. 46.3%. sc. 257 bottles.

Kirkwall & St. Ola 10 Years Old cask no. 001 **(89)** n21.5 t22 f23 b22.5 Though a 10-year-old, the nose and early delivery points in a much younger direction. Slowly, though, some sumptuous heather honey begins to filter through to the point of domination. Could have done with another two years in cask just for those early gremlins to be straightened and the honey aspect to be upgraded. Ultimately, though, after the bumpy start a delicious malt. 61.3%. sc. Mr. Whisky.

224

⬦ **Matisse Single Malt Aged 19 Years (91)** n23 charmingly soft malt couched in a slightly plummy glove; t22.5 unusual for ulmo honey to arrive early in any whisky. But it does here, alongside a soft butterscotch tart semi-sweetness; f22.5 a slow fade of physalis and vanilla...; b23 a malt that operates by stealth, seemingly wanting to go unnoticed. However, perseverance will pay off for the taster. 40%. Matisse Spirits Company.

⬦ **Peat's Beast** bott code: L 20 02 19 **(89)** n22 classical peaty malt but soft and performing well within itself; t23 sets of in the same manner as the nose, though the slow build of vanilla and an cocoa start upping the complexity significantly; f22 returns to a pleasant tameness, though now with a lightly metallic finish; b22 a very safe malt by heavily peated standards, determined not to offend. 46%. ncf.

⬦ **Peat's Beast Batch Strength Pedro Ximenez** sherry wood finish, bott code: L 18 10 19 **(89.5)** n22.5 a grape-laden pie in the face of the peat; t23 ridiculously flavour-intense with little attempt at subtlety. Broad juicy grape thumps into muscular peat, nether willing to compromise. Only a healthy strand of heather honey keeps everything together; f22 slightly tangy and bitter, all of it grape related; b22 if this whisky was comedy it would be pure slapstick. 54.1%. ncf.

Saar Whisky Jahrgangsabfüllung 2019 Islay barrel, dist 2009, bott 2018, bott code: L2019 **(93.5)** n23.5 t23.5 f23 b23.5 The dram that is perfect for a sore throat... 55.5%. ncf sc.

Saar Whisky Malzbeisser ex-bourbon barrel, dist 2009, bott 2018 **(90.5)** n22.5 t23 f22.5 b22.5 If anyone wants to know what a very decent Islay whisky is all about, this will do rather well. 53.7%. ncf sc.

Saar Whisky Mandelbachtal Edition No. 2 dist 2009, bott 2018 **(88)** n22 t23 f21 b22 So much chocolate, not sure if this should be sold as a bottle or a bar... 53.7%. ncf sc.

⬦ **Skene Finest Strathdearn 2015** 1st fill Oloroso **(86)** n22 t23 f20.5 b20.5 A lively youngster bursting at the seams with juicy barley and even juicer grape. Bit of a mangle at the finish, well a complete shambles, actually, where neither of the two main elements have any idea of what to do with the other. At times I fancy a light smokiness invades, but this is so chaotic there could be a couple of Martians in there cooking tomato soup and smoking dope for all I know... 48%.

Scottish Vatted Malts
(also Pure Malts/Blended Malt Scotch)

Angels' Nectar (81) n21 t21 f19 b20. This angel has a bitter tooth... 40%

Angel's Nectar Blended Malt Rich Peat Edition (90.5) n22.5 t23 f22.5 b22.5 Excellently-made malt: sticks unerringly to the script. 46%

Ben Bracken Blended Malt Aged 12 Years (85.5) n22.5 t21 f21 b21. Quite a tight malt with a predominantly toffee theme. 40%

Berry Bros & Rudd Islay Blended Malt bott code: L18/8215 **(90.5)** n22 t23 f22.5 b23 An endearing vatting which sums up the island's whiskies without any drama but still highly attractively and with no wrong turns. 44.2%. The Classic Range.

Berry Bros & Rudd Sherry Cask Matured Blended Malt bott code: L18/8213 **(74.5)** n19 t24.5 f14 b17 With Ronnie Cox's name all over this bottle, one can safely assume that the leading light in this vatting is Glenrothes. And, of course, with Glenrothes sherry butts at work, chances are so, too, will sulphur be. Well, it is – as can be picked out on the nose and the finish especially. But, for once, it is worth undergoing the pain of the massive sulphur simply to experience the delivery which scores absolutely maximum points for the lushest of mouthfeels and the extraordinary beauty of the richness of the fruit marrying some intense barley. Between the faulty sulphur start and end is sandwiched something which, for a few spellbinding, heavenly moments, touches perfection. 44.2%. The Classic Range.

⬦ **Berry Bros & Rudd Sherry Cask Matured Blended Malt Whisky** bott code: P/001036 **(84)** n22 t21.5 f20 b20.5 Despite the early muscovado sugars which ooze all over the delivery, this turns into one of the most strangely bitter malts I have tasted in a very long time. Like a fruitcake that has been incinerated in the oven and syrup poured over it so no-one might notice... Odd! Though I'm certain there are types who will fight to the death for a bottle of this. A whisky, let us say, to divide opinion. 44.2%.

Berry Bros & Rudd Peated Cask Matured Blended Malt bott code: L18/8214 **(92)** n22 t23 f23.5 b23.5 Gentle and evenly paced. 44.2%. The Classic Range.

Berry Bros & Rudd Speyside Blended Malt (85) n20 t22.5 f21 b21.5 A lot of malt to get your teeth into. The oak isn't exactly sympathetic but the big wave of vanilla at the midpoint carries some attractive maple syrup. 44.2%. The Classic Range.

⬦ **Black Tartan 88 31 Year Old** hogshead, cask no. 00016 **(94)** n23 so much oak! But an unusual double bill of green and over-ripe gooseberry injects a balancing fruity freshness; t23.5 and it's the under-ripe gooseberry which gets its shots away on delivery. The malt helps ramp the salivating qualities up to nearly 100%...; f23.5 the long fade of malt and milk chocolate is so uncannily like a Malteser candy! **b24** the nose suggests you might be in for an overly oaky ride. It lies! This is an old dram which retains a marvellous zest for life but piles on the malt in spades. *48%. sc.*

Cadenhead's Vatted Islay 25 Year Old (89) n23 t22 f22 b22 May be wrong, but there is a feeling of something a little older than 25 in this: definitely shows its antiquity. *46%. 175th Anniversary bottling.*

⬩ **Chapter 7 Anecdote Blended Malt 24 Year Old** 2 bourbon hogsheads, dist Jul 95, bott Mar 20 **(93.5) n23** a mix of fresh and older banana mingles with the citrus laden malt; the vaguest hint of smoke burbles about; **t23.5** clean, salivating barley from the off which intensifies moments after delivery. The tannins make their mark with a delicate chocolate nut note, but it is all in slow motion; **f23.5** stays on the chocolate theme, though now very mousse-like; **b23.5** tells a quietly delicious tale. *47.9%. 424 bottles.*

Chapter 7 Island Blended Malt (91.5) n22 t23.5 f23 b23 Well done, chaps (or do I mean Chapts?).Vatting unpeated Island malt and getting the balance right is not one of the easier tasks in the whisky world. But this has been carried out wonderfully – the exclusive use of ex-bourbon helped. *49%.*

Chivas Regal Ultis bott code LPNK1759 2016/09/16 **(89.5) n22.5 t23 f21.5 b22.5** This vatted malt is the legacy of Chivas' five master blenders. But to pay real respect to them, just remove the caramel from the bottling hall. The whisky will be light coloured, for sure, but I suspect the flavour profile will blow us all away... *40%. Chivas Brothers Ltd.*

Cladach db **(91) n22 t23 f23 b23** The slightly dull, regulation nose doesn't prepare you for the fireworks ahead. The delivery quivers and shimmies and the malt takes a particularly salty course of action – seashores without the usual phenols. The saline touch allows the beautifully layered malt an extra degree of sharpness. The finish of milk chocolate malted biscuit is a quiet serenade after the earlier vividness of the barley. One hell of a surprise package! *57.1%. Diageo Special Releases 2018.*

⬩ **Compass Box The Circle** bott May 19 **(94.5) n23.5 t24 f23 b24** If a malt whisky this year proves no great age is required to create something of great beauty, then here it is. A wonderful crossover between lemon blossom honey and pear drops on the nose helps focus the attention on the clarity of the malt. Such a nose demands a delivery of great malty complexity...and you won't be disappointed. The bourbon casks add their own magic spell to proceedings, intertwangling both vanilla and butterscotch with pipette-measured exactitude and ensuring the spices play an important but never over-dominant role. Simple. Yet not. A real treat of a dram. *46%. nc ncf. 6,151 bottles.*

Compass Box Juveniles bott Sept 18 **(95) n23.5 t24 f23.5 b24** Malt whisky which, were it a metal, would be 24 carat gold. From the very first sniff right through to the last, slightly spiced pulse of flavour, it is centred on a honey-rich style but always tempered with elegant vanillas. This heather honey note is the single consistent as it changes weight and gears with rare subtlety – meaning anything less than half an hour with the Murray Method on this one would be a travesty to such a beautiful incarnation of a vatted malt. The maltiness - sometimes juicy, sometimes with a slight Horlicks-creamy twist – takes on many guises. But it cannot escape that thread of honey. *46%. nc ncf. 14,894 bottles.*

Compass Box The Lost Blend (95.5) n23 t23.5 f24.5 b24.5 I may be wrong, but I have a feeling that when the nose and flavour profile was being constructed, a little extra smoke than first planned was added. Seems that way by the manner in which the phenols just pipe up a little louder than it first seems...*46%*

Compass Box No Name bott Sept 17 **(92.5) n23 t23 f23 b23.5** I'll give it a name: Compass Box Bleedin' Delicious! *48.9%. nc ncf. 15,000 bottles.*

Compass Box No Name, No. 2 bott Feb 19 **(93.5) n23 t23.5 f23.5 b23.5** Think a lightly oiled Islay whisky where the peat is powering, but totally in sync with the overall balance of the piece. And where a light heather honey note ensures there is no bitterness and the phenols never get too acrid or sooty. Spot on wood management with this fella. *48.9%. nc ncf. 8,802 bottles.*

⬩ **Compass Box The Peat Monster** bott code: L 11 12 18 **(94.5) n23.5** a beautiful alloy of dry sootiness and all round, oilier smokiness. Quite acidic and nippy... but medium dark sugars act as a counterweight; **t23.5** Caol Ila-style oils to the fore. But the smoke doesn't immediately start out as the nose promised. Instead we are treated to waves of peat interspersed with light tannin and plentiful Demerara sugars; **f23.5** this has been matured in excellent oak, as the vanillas are faultless...not a hint of bitterness, which means the sweet smoke can carry on unsullied; **b24** this is the most complete Peat Monster I've encountered for a little while. It's all about the balance and here it manages to allow sheer enormity to come through loud and clear, but not at the expense of tact and complexity. *46%. nc ncf.*

Compass Box The Peat Monster Cask Strength (89) n23.5 t23 f20.5 b22 Plenty of peat between your teeth but deserving of some better oak. *57.3%*

Compass Box The Peat Monster Reserve (92) n23 t23.5 f22.5 b23. At times a bit of a Sweet Monster...beautiful stuff! 48.9%

Compass Box Phenomenology bott Sept 17 **(92.5) n22 t24.5 f22.5 b23.5** Once upon a time, blenders took so much notice of the blend they actually forgot to really look at what it tasted like. Decades ago more than one blender told me that he didn't taste a whisky at final strength until a sample turned up in his lab from the bottling hall. This one appears to be almost the other way round. The nose is attractive and adequate without being anything special. The delivery and follow through, though: gee what a phenomenon...! 46%. nc ncf. 7,908 bottles.

◈ **Compass Box The Spice Tree** French oak head & American oak body hybrid casks, bott code: L 28 11 18 **(96) n23.5** ulmo and heather honey in unholy cahoots...; **t25** anyone who remembers Highland Park 12 from the very early 1980s and fell deeply in love had better get here quick. Its ghost has risen and is haunting this vatting with the most sensationally rounded and complete heather-honey narrative you'll ever find. Mind-blowing...; **f23.5** just tails off slightly as the tannins make their vanilla-rich mark, though the caressing ulmo honey refuse to be shaken off. The spices have been pretty quiet until now but at last begin to grow into the picture...; **b24** don't know about The Spice Tree...Honey Tree more like.. So strikingly beautiful! 46%. 🐟

Compass Box The Story of The Spaniard 48% aged in Spanish wine casks, bott Jun 18 **(90.5) n23 t23 f22 b22.5** Often Compass Box lets the oak do the talking, occasionally too loudly. Here the tannin has a dry edge, but fits into the scenario perfectly. 43%. nc ncf.

◈ **Compass Box The Story of The Spaniard** Spanish fortified wine casks, American and French oak barrels, batch no. TS 2019-A **(83.5) n22 t23 f18.5 b20** I have had Spanish lovers: so beautiful, so passionate words alone are inadequate to describe. Close Spanish friends, their humour, sincerity, choice of great food and wine as well as good nature a man of the world only can recognise as truly priceless. Reported on Spanish football played out in front of 120,000 crowds. All exciting; always entertaining, always stretching something within you and taking you to places you have never quite been before.... This, though, doesn't. A dull nagging note keeps the whisky in check despite the sublime natural juiciness of the malt. But just too many things are off key late on. Not the kind of Spaniard I usually cosset. 43%. nc ncf.

Copper Dog batch no. 16/0673, bott code: L8127IY001 **(89) n22 t23.5 f21.5 b22** A whisky which first saw the light of day at the fabulous Craigellachie Hotel in Speyside, where I gave my first whisky lectures over a quarter of a century ago and in the 1990s wrote many chapters of my various books. The number of vatted malts we created from the whiskies in the bar... far too many to mention, though none then capable of shewing this kind of finale. 40%. The Craigellachie Hotel Scotland.

Cutty Sark Blended Malt (92.5) n22 t24 f23 b23.5. Sheer quality: as if two styles have been placed in the bottle and told to fight it out between them. What a treat! 40%.

Deerstalker Blended Malt Highland Edition (94) n23.5 t23.5 f23 b24 A quite beautiful whisky by any standards. 43%

Deerstalker Blended Malt Peated Edition (84.5) n22.5 t22 f19 b21 A slightly strange mixture: on one hand creamy, sweet and friendly, on the other somewhat metallic and harsh. Struggles to find either balance or a comfortable course. The finish is way off key and vaguely furry. 43%.

Elements of Islay Peat (91.5) n23 t24 f22 b22.5 This is rather more than elementary Islay, trust me.... 46%

Elements of Islay Peat Islay Blended Malt (94) n23 t24 f23.5 b23.5 Does everything it says on the tin – and more. Some younger elements appear to be at work here, which means the peat intensity can sometimes fly, deliciously and dramatically, off the scale. 45%.

Elements of Islay Peat Full Proof (92.5) n23.5 t23.5 f22.5 b23 A distinctly two-toned malt with the phenols seeming to be pitched quite differently. 59.3%.

◈ **Fadandel.dk MacRothes 25 Year Old** 1st fill Oloroso sherry butt, cask no. 3, dist 20 Jan 94, bott 21 Oct 19 **(89.5) n23.5** I am drifting over Denmark on a little sherried carpet, soft and luxurious in its over-ripe gooseberry and finely embroidered with spices; **t24** silk. More silk. And a little more silk if you haven't already found enough silk to be getting along with. The fruit has a voluptuousness that refuses to stretch as far as smothering, but enjoyed the cut and thrust of the spice against the teasingly tart notes and pulsing tannins...; **f20** long, the spices still healthy and intact and, incredibly, allowing a malty flourish to gently outpoint the fruit influence...such balance, char and elegance....wow! **b22** if you see a bottle of this, please be gentle with other customers and staff. But don't let anyone else get their hands on it. Mild violence is permissible and entirely understandable if provoked. However, this applies only for those lucky enough not to be able to taste sulphur which turns up here very late to the party... and then in quite an insidious manner. 56.6%. sc. 676 bottles.

◈ **The Finest Malts Blended Malt Aged 18 Years** sherry butt, dist 2001, bott 2019 **(91) n23 t24 f21 b23** Always a relief when you find the advertised sherry butt is, though not quite clean as a whistle, for this day and age not far off. And even more so when the grape doesn't dominate at all costs and spices give a much more incisive than is the norm. This is a vatted malt with huge character. And at the heart, for all the fruit, for all the spice, comes the malt which is thick, lush and true. Then there is the maple syrup running off the oak. All beautifully paced, all wonderfully integrated. Just a shame about that little late blemish. *46.1%. nc ncf sc. 72 bottles.*

⋙ **The Finest Malts City Landmarks Blended Malt Aged 25 Years** sherry hogs-head, cask no. 431, dist 1993, bott 2018 **(90) n23 t23 f21.5 b22.5** A surprising low key malt. The nose suggests we are in the land of untainted sherry casks here and celebrates with delicate oloroso and glazed cherry to join the spices and vanilla on the well set nose. And though the delivery is lush on the palate and the peppers now warming to their task, waves of natural caramels tend to ensure that development is modest after those first gorgeous spasms on entry. Subtle and satisfying, a malt that sets off like a train and then thinks better of it. There is a light buzz off the sherry butt late on, but nothing to worry about. A delightful late night dram. *52.1%. nc ncf sc.*

⋙ **The First Editions Hector Macbeth Aged 22 Years 1997** refill hogshead, cask no. 16650, bott 2019 **(93) n23.5** a little honey festival of its own: a beautiful amalgamation of ulmo and manuka, topped off with spearmint and light tannins...; **t24** waxy and lush delivery where the honey on the nose now parade in concentrated form. A wonderful butterscotch second phase keeps the experience on the delicate, sweet side; **f22** bitters slightly, but chocolate and insistent acacia honey compensates; **b23.5** whoever Hector Macbeth was, one assumes he kept bees... *53.6%. nc ncf sc. 326 bottles.*

⋙ **The First Editions John McCrae Aged 23 Years 1995** refill hogshead, cask no. 16643, bott 2019 **(86.5) n22 t22.5 f20.5 b21.5** A decent enough vatting in part. But there is perhaps a little too much tang, to reveal tiring oak. *44%. nc ncf sc. 246 bottles.*

Gleann Mór Islay Blended Malt Aged Over 8 Years (87) n22 t22 f21.5 b21.5 A robust vatted malt which, though only a standard strength bottling, rips at you like a whisky half that abv again. Moderately, sweet, not too highly peated, thin bodied and lacking couth. Fun, though! *40%.*

Gleann Mór Speyside Blended Malt Aged Over 30 Years (93) n23 t23.5 f23 b23.5 After a score years and ten, you would expect the oak to have a major say in the constitution of a whisky. And for those looking for it to have a big but not overpowering influence, then here's a malt ticking all the right boxes. While the oak threatens a little too loudly on the nose, fears that this vatting will have been over-sapped are dispelled by a glittering array of honey tones on delivery, ranging from heather to rape flower honey with a little bourbon-esque liquorice thrown into the mix. Profound and impressive. *49%.*

Gleann Mór Vatted Whisky Over 40 Years Old (92.5) n23.5 t23.5 f22.5 b23 An oldie and a goodie...Mor, please...!!! *47%*

Glenalmond Highland Blended Malt (84) n21 t22 f20.5 b20.5 Chugs along in safe, non-demanding caramel-rich fashion. *40%. The Vintage Malt Whisky Co.*

Glenbrynth Ruby 40 Year Old bott code L8V 7439 04/11/11 **(95) n24 t23.5 f23.5 b24** You cannot ask much more from a 40-year-old vatted malt than this. Amazing what a lack of colouring (and sulphured sherry casks) can do – like let the whisky speak for itself and allow you to follow its myriad paths, its highways and byways, without the route being blocked by toffee or a rabid bitterness. Each and every cask included in this great whisky should be applauded, as should the blender. *43%. OTI Africa.*

Glen Castle Blended Malt 1992 Sherry Cask Matured bott code: L7 9595-2017 12 **(96) n24 t24.5 f23.5 b24** I have no official information into what makes up this vatted malt. But this is almost identical in style to the old fashioned Glendronach 12-year-old Sherry Cask that was on the market a quarter of a century ago and more. Then I was annoyed with its OTT characteristics which swamped everything in sight. Now I hug it affectionately like a long-lost friend back from the dead, because this is sulphur-free sherried whisky – such a delight and rarity. All is forgiven... For those who truly adore big, clean sherried whisky: this will take you to a grapey heaven. *51.8%.*

Glen Castle Blended Malt 1990 Sherry Cask Matured 28 Years Old bott code: LHB 1479-2018 **(96) n24 t24 f24 b24** Anyone who wants to know the difference between ye olde great, untainted sherry butts and the poor and unacceptable offerings we have been subjected to for the last 25 years should grab a bottle of this. Old school brilliance. And beauty. Just...wow! Old Time sherry at its most accessible....and mind-blowing. *55.2%. nc ncf.*

Glen Castle Blended Malt 1992 Sherry Cask Matured bott code: L7 9595-2017 12 **(95.5) n24 t24 f23.5 b24** Just brilliant whisky to be savoured and cherished, restoring my faith in sherry – very few butts from this era survived the sulphury onslaught – and the perfect after dinner or very late night dram. *46.8%.*

Glen Turner Heritage Double Wood Bourbon & Madeira casks, bott code. L311657A **(85.5) n21.5 t22 f21 b21.** A very curious amalgamation of flavours. The oak appears to be in shock with the way the fruit is coming on to it and offers a bitter backlash. No faulting the crisp delivery with busy sugar and spice for a few moments brightening the palate. *40%.*

Glen Turner Pure Malt Aged 8 Years L525956A **(84) n**20 **t**22 **f**22 **b**20. A lush and lively vatting annoyingly over dependent on thick toffee but simply brimming with fabulously mouth-watering barley and over-ripe blood oranges. To those who bottle this, I say: let me into your lab. I can help you bring out something sublime!! *40%*

Hogwash Blended Malt Scotch Whisky Blend No. 08 bott code: LBB 3C 4353 **(85.5) n**21.5 **t**22 **f**21 **b**21 Juicy in part. And if you are looking for a gentle, soft, refined, complex, gentleman of a vatted malt...this isn't it. *40%. Produced for Aldi.*

Johnnie Walker Green Label 15 Years Old (95) n24 **t**23.5**f**23.5 **b**24. God, I love this stuff... this is exactly how a vatted malt should be and one of the best samples I've come across since its launch. *43%. Diageo.*

◇◇ **Johnnie Walker Green Label Aged 15 Years** bott code: L9076DN002 **(91) n**23 despite the good age, there is a fresh, grassy greenness on this reminiscent of a much younger malt. Some toffee wanders into the frame, but it is that fresh mown grass which dominates; **t**23.5 again, a malt defying its years with an early overture of stupendous barley in its most natural and carefree form. But before the real complexity levels get going, a little spice and toffee kicks in; **f**22 a big spicy, toffee buzz, some of that buzz having a vaguely furry tang; **b**22.5 really lovely malt, but would dearly like to see the degree of toffee reduced on this as you feel there is so much going on that can't quite be named. *43%.*

Le Gus't Selection X Speyside Blended Malt 39 Years Old sherry cask, cask no. 4 **(94.5) n**23.5 **t**24 **f**23 **b**24 Truly Xcellent. *60.4%. sc. 109 bottles.*

Le Gus't Selection XI Speyside Blended Malt hogshead, cask no. 403 **(91) n**22.5 **t**23 **f**22.5 **b**23 Appears to have good age to this and a little bit of class. *49.7%. sc. 262 bottles.*

Liquid Treasures Entomology Wardhead Over 21 Years Old (88.5) n22 **t**22.5 **f**21.5 **b**22.5 All the classic signs of a malt which really struggles with great age: so even at 21 the barley is fracturing to allow the oak an ungainly foothold. Lots to savour, though. *55.5%.*

Liquid Treasures Entomology Williamson Over 6 Years Old (87.5) n21.5 **t**22 **f**22 **b**22 A beautifully young and raw whisky which tears at your taste buds like a hawk's talon on its prey. Sound peat mingles with decent Demerara sugars and though a few tannin notes gets through, the malt's youth is never in doubt. *59.6%.*

The Loch Fyne The Living Cask 1745 (94.5) n23.5 **t**23.5 **f**23.5 **b**24 One of the best whiskies ever created at quarter to six in the evening... and one quite impossible not to love. *46.3%.*

Loch Fyne Living Cask batch no. 6 **(88.5) n**23 **t**22.5 **f**21 **b**22 Well Batch 6 appears to be living and breathing peat... *43.6%.*

Macaloney's TWA Cask Series Benrinnes & Glenlossie ex-bourbon casks, finished in re-toasted red wine barriques **(89) n**22.5 **t**22.5 **f**22 **b**22 Not a malt for the faint-hearted: the fruit dominates and makes little effort to integrate, leaving the oak to make a violent, forced entry. *57.2%. ncf 1,198 bottles.*

Macaloney's TWA Cask Series Blair Athol & Macduff ex-bourbon casks, finished in re-toasted red wine barriques **(88.5) n**22.5 **t**23 **f**20.5 **b**22.5 Have to admit that those wine barrels, though not faultless, certainly have a charm and do all they can to accentuate any honey notes lurking. *58%. ncf 797 bottles.*

Macaloney's TWA Cask Series Caol Ila & Bunnahabhain ex-bourbon casks, finished in re-toasted red wine barriques **(93) n**23 **t**23.5 **f**23 **b**23.5 About as juicy a peated malt as you'll ever find! Something for everyone. *55.6%. ncf. 918 bottles.*

MacNair's Lum Reek 12 Years Old (89) n22 **t**22.5 **f**22 **b**22.5 Interesting chimneys they have in this part of Scotland, which appears to reek marzipan and apple blossom where you might expect, coal, peat or wood...! *46%. The GlenAllachie Distillers Company.*

MacNair's Lum Reek 21 Years Old (91) n22.5 **t**23 **f**22.5 **b**23 A wild malt tamed it seems to me and certainly not lacking in personality *48%. The GlenAllachie Distillers Company.*

MacNair's Lum Reek Peated (88.5) n22 **t**22 **f**22 **b**22.5 Has the consistency of a nail file wrapped in velvet. Enough edges to this to draw blood. But the modest smoke soothes and kisses better. The salivating maltiness another surprise. Not quite like any other vatted malt I have before encountered. And have to admit: I kind of begrudgingly like it, though McNair's appear to always include a malt that can pick a fight with itself in a 5cl miniature...! *46%. The GlenAllachie Distillers Company.*

Matisse 12 Year Old Blended Malt (93) n23.5 **t**23 **f**22.5 **b**23. Succulent, clean-as-a-whistle mixture of malts with zero bitterness and not even a whisper of an off note: easily the best form I have ever seen this brand in. Superb. *40%. Matisse Spirits Co Ltd.*

Matisse Aged 12 Years (79) n17 **t**21 **f**20 **b**21. Not sure if some finishing or re-casking has been going on here to liven it up. Has some genuine buzz on the palate, but intriguing weirdness, too. Don't bother nosing this one. *40%. The Matisse Spirits Co Ltd.*

Mo'land (82) n21 **t**22 **f**19 **b**20. Extra malty but lumbering and on the bitter side. *40%.*

Monkey Shoulder batch 27 **(79.5)** n21 t21.5 f18 b19. Been a while since I lasted tasted this one. Though its claims to be Batch 27, I assume all bottlings are Batch 27 seeing as they are from 27 casks. This one, whichever it is, has a distinctive fault found especially at the finale, which is disappointing. Even before hitting that point a big toffeed personality makes for a pleasant if limited experience. 40%. *William Grant & Sons.*

Old Perth Blended Malt 23 Years Old dist 1994, bott code: 18/182 **(95)** n24 t23.5 f23.5 b24 Creakier than a haunted mansion. But full of much more welcoming spirits. This shows its oaky age with the same pride a veteran might display his war wounds. Not even a hint of a single off note: amazing! 44.9%. nc ncf.

Old St. Andrews Aged 10 Years Twilight batch no. L1058 G1048 **(91.5)** n22.5 t23.5 grassy, f22.5 b23 As clean a contact as you ever hope to make and travels a long way. 40%.

Old St. Andrews Aged 10 Years Twilight batch no. L3017 G2716 **(91)** n22 t23.5 f22.5 b23 Takes a different course from the previous batch, eschewing the sharper tones for a more rumbling, deeper and earthier character. Very much above par. 40%.

Old St. Andrews Aged 12 Years Fireside batch no. L2446 G2557 **(89)** n22.5 t22 f22.5 b22 Perfect for those who can't make their mind up between a malt and a G&T in the 19th hole... 40%.

Old St. Andrews Aged 12 Years Fireside batch no. L2927 G2716 **(93)** n23 t23 f23.5 b23.5 Returns to its usual high quality brand which usually makes the cut. 40%.

Old St. Andrews Aged 15 Years Nightcap batch no. L2519 G2557 **(86.5)** n21.5 t22.5 f21 b21.5 A little more fizz on delivery than their last round but then again the finish ends up lost in the long grass. Just too much caramel effect from somewhere. 40%.

Old St. Andrews Aged 15 Years Nightcap batch no. L2976 G2716 **(86)** n22 t21.5 f21 b21.5 Well, this certainly is a nightcap: I fell asleep waiting for something to happen. Pleasant honey at times and chewy toffee but a bit short on the charisma front. 40%.

Poit Dhubh 8 Bliadhna (90) n22.5 t23.5 f21.5 b22.5. Though the smoke which marked this vatting has vanished, it has more than compensated with a complex beefing up of the core barley tones. Cracking whisky. 43%. ncf. Pràban na Linne.

Poit Dhubh 12 Bliadhna (77) n20 t20 f18 b19. Toffee-apples. Without the apples. 43%. ncf. Pràban na Linne.

Poit Dhubh 21 Bliadhna (86) n22 t22.5 f21 b20.5. Over generous toffee has robbed us of what would have been a very classy malt. 43%. ncf. Pràban na Linne.

Queens & Kings Kenneth I. MacAlpin (86) n22 t22 f20.5 b21.5 A brittle, unyielding vatting softened only by delicate smoke and a little but attractive Manuka honey, though the late vanilla is a bit aggressive. 53.7%.

Queens & Kings Mac Bethad mac Findláich (91) n23 t23 f23 b23.5 Sharp, vivacious, fresh, clean and pulsing. A smoky malt to celebrate here, seemingly making the most of no great age to maximise the salivation levels. Whoever put this together should take a bow, as the taste buds are never given a moment's peace... 54.1%. Mr. Whisky.

Queens & Kings Mary of Guise (87.5) n22 t22 f21.5 b22 Anyone who has chewed on tart, under-ripe gooseberries in the garden will recognise this whisky's profile. Malty and invigorating, though. 53.4%. Mr. Whisky.

Queens & Kings Mary, Queen of Scots (91.5) n22.5 t23 f23 b23 A very comfortable assembling of malt. Impressed. 55.6%. Mr. Whisky.

Royal Salute 21 Year Old Blended Malt (88.5) n23 t22 f21.5 b22 Malt and caramel-themed throughout. 40%.

Saar Whisky Gruwefreund sherry hogshead, dist 2009, bott 2018 **(87)** n22 t22.5 f20.5 b22 Though from a sherry hoggy, it is youthful, salivating malt which dominates, though the bitter-ish out of sync finish doesn't do much for the overall picture. 53.4%. ncf sc. Vatted Malt from the Orkney Distilleries.

◇ **Scyfion Choice Westport 1996** Argaman Jezreel cask finished, bott 2019 **(94.5)** n23.5 dry. A lovely grape must feel to this, setting off spices that are light and proportionate to both the malt and tannin...; t24 now that really does the trick so far as the delivery is concerned: very controlled fruit with limited sugars, juicy and seemingly barley to the salivation properties slightly later down the track. Gentle but confident spice; f23 the fruit has vanished here, unless that is still a grape skin dryness. Totally in sync with the lingering malt and high grade tannin...; b24 now, having a lot of close Jewish friends I certainly know where these casks come from. And as they have not been sulphur treated (probably not Kosher, thankfully) I'm not at all surprised this very high quality wine produces casks which can certainly add a degree of sophistication to a malt. 49.1%. nc ncf sc. 102 bottles.

◇ **Scyfion Choice Westport 1996** Bashta cask finished, bott 2019 **(94.5)** n23.5 pomegranates and gooseberries make for a sharp but sweet nose, the ulmo honey mixing in with the malt to soften things down; t24 one of the deliveries of the year: so astonishingly clean, the semi-fruit note seems to herd the barley up for one of the maltiest concoctions I have enjoyed this year...; **f23** now for the spice. And, my word! Does this stuff warm things up...! **b24** I'd be lying if I said I knew what the hell a Bashta cask was. But all I can say is, if this is an example of it then the Scots should drop sherry (please, God!), PX in particular, and get this in its place. One of the real surprises of the year and one of my favourites for sure for offering something very different, yet still managing to keep the signature of the distillery burnishing brightly. *50%. nc ncf sc. 77 bottles.*

Selkie batch no. 001, bott code: L13/9097 **(94) n23.5 t23.5 f23 b24** The label keeps abreast of this alluring whisky. I'd happily chew on a nip of this any day... *40%. House of MacDuff.*

Selkie batch no. 002 **(80) n20 t23 f18 b20** Must be the ugly sister. The nose, finish and overall balance aren't a patch on batch 1. But impossible not to fall in love a little with the mid-point peak, which is rich, alive with creamy mocha and maintains that salty character. Now that bit does get my seal of approval... *50%. House of MacDuff.*

⬧ **Shackleton Blended Malt** bott code: L8123 11:52 P/004904 **(85.5) n22.5 t22 f20 b21** An old-fashioned dusting of smoke plus a layering of Demerara ensures a certain gravitas is maintained through this vatted malt, starting at the come-to-me nose and continuing throughout the broad body on the palate. Falls away at the end, though, when too much bitterness sneaks in. *40%.*

Shetland Reel Batch No. 1 (72) n18 t22 f15 b17 I am just glad that the sulphur comes from dodgy casks used in this vatting of other distillery's malts and not their own. If this isn't a great lesson for the Shetland lads not to touch sherry butts with a pole that can stretch from Lerwick to Norway, I don't know what is. *47%. 1,800 bottles.*

Shetland Reel Batch No. 2 (90) n23.5 t23 f21 b22.5 A rogue sherry butt cannot entirely undo the many excellent qualities of this vatting. *47%. 1,800 bottles.*

Shetland Reel Batch No. 3 (93) n23.5 t23.5 f22.5 b23.5. It has been many a long year since I last visited the Shetlands but the salty bite to this, plus the peat reek on the breeze means someone has created a style well in keeping with the feel of those far off isles. A very satisfying dram. *47%. 1,800 bottles.*

⬧ **Shetland Reel Finished in Shetland Blended Malt Whisky** ex-sherry casks, bott code: 248/19 **(79) n20 t20 f19 b20** Tight, dry and doesn't sit very prettily... *47%.*

Smokestack Blended Malt (87) n22 t21.5 f22 b21.5 The jolting delivery seems to vividly portray an unusual sharpness on the nose, despite the profound peat. An angular, elbowing malt on nose and arrival but finally relaxes to allow the sugars and oils to combine for a far more attractive, distinguished finale. *46%. The Vintage Malt Whisky Company.*

Son of a Peat batch no. 01 **(91) n23.5 t23 f22 b23** Peaty, but not just for peat's sake... *48.3%. nc ncf. Flaviar.*

Spirit of Caledonia Flaitheanas 18 Years Old (94) n23.5 t24 f23 b23.5 Now that is a proper vatted malt...!!! *578%. Mr Whisky.*

St. Ola 8 Year Old 2010 Orcadian Blended Malt (94) n23 t23.5 f23.5 b24 A young, fresh-faced whisky which just bowls you over with its charm. The high strength ensures the oils remain intact for maximum length and volume. I just wish more whiskies were like this! *66.6%. The Whisky Barrel. 82 bottles.*

⬧ **Water Proof** batch no. 001 **(86) n21.5 t22.5 f20.5 b21.5** A toffee and raisin style malt which certainly hits a crescendo with the caramel and the sugars have a distinctively grapey quality. But, as pleasant as it is, it is just a little too one-paced and single threaded in style. Also a slight niggle on the finish which matches the bright yellow label... *45.8%. Macduff International.*

⬧ **Wemyss Malts Family Collection Blooming Gorse Blended Malt** batch no. 2018/03 **(89.5) n22.5 t23 f22 b22** The gorse is probably my favourite plant. It reminds me of Dartford Warblers, great grey shrikes and stonechats. All of which I have often found around this stunning evergreen of vibrant yellow flower. It also has a sting to its tail, being an unmercifully prickly cove, and woe betide anyone daft enough to fall into it. So I was expecting a malt of beauty and bite. Well this one's a pretty thorn-less gorse with not quite enough polish to match the vividness of the flower. Except perhaps on the delivery, when the frail honey notes grow into something of a crescendo; and though spices do happen along they have none of the spite of the real thing... But if you are looking for a charmingly malty and delicately sweet offering, then you won't be disappointed. *46%. nc ncf. 6,900 bottles.*

⬧ **Wemyss Malts Family Collection Flaming Feast Blended Malt** batch no. 2018/04 **(87) n21.5 t23 f21 b21.5** Pleasant enough. Juicy in part, malty and spicy. But from the mid-point onwards, just too flaming dull. *46%. nc ncf. 6,000 bottles.*

Wemyss Family Collection Treacle Chest 1st fill ex-sherry hogsheads, batch no. 2017/02 **(84.5) n21.5 t22.5 f20 b20.5** There appears to be mainly clean sherry butts at work here: not perfect but by comparison to most, not too bad. And a mix of date and prune briefly fill the palate on delivery. But after that the lights appear to be switched off and though one can grope around in the dark and enjoy oneself to some extent, there is surprisingly little to stimulate the taste buds after. Just too flat by half. *46%. nc ncf. 6,300 bottles.*

Wemyss Family Collection Vanilla Burst 1st fill ex-bourbon barrels, batch no. 2017/01 **(86.5)** n22.5 t22.5 f20 b21.5 A pleasant experience. But you can't help feeling that the casks are slightly neutralising each other rather than adding layers of complexity. The nose does express vanilla and the odd hickory note and the delivery, well, delivers. But by the time we reach the finale there is little in reserve. *46%. nc ncf. 4,800 bottles.*

Wemyss Malts The Hive (87) n21.5 t22 f22 b21.5 A lush, easy-drinking dram but one with a surprising lack of high spots: it is as though someone has made the common but fatal mistake of putting together styles that have cancelled each other out – certainly at this strength - rather than bringing the best out of and enhancing the other. No lack of honey and spice, for sure, but also toffee aplenty. *46%. ncf.*

Wemyss Malts The Hive Batch Strength batch 001 **(90.5)** n22 t23.5 f22 b23 A lovely malt which is heavily dependent on the honey and spice. And there is nothing wrong with that! *54.5%. ncf. 6,000 bottles.*

◈ **Wemyss Malts The Hive Blended Malt Whisky** batch no. 002 **(91.5)** n23 charming and complex. The light heather honey tones has a spicy back-lift while the vanilla helps the sweeter strains show their softer side; t23.5 a strange vacuum on the first beat, then the honey comes rushing in to fill the void. Heather honey again, and a slightly thinner acacia honey tone for a mere trilling sweetness. Intense, but beautifully controlled; f22 something of a vanilla wafer to accompany the spice; b23 a malt greatly bolstered by the upping of the strength since its last bottling, which makes the honey positively buzz... *55.5%. ncf. 9000 bottles.*

◈ **Wemyss Malts Nectar Grove Blended Malt** Madeira wine cask finished, batch no. 001 **(95)** n23 no off notes, but even so the grape has a bit of a stranglehold here and it takes some cajoling to get the fruit to open into a more expansive fruitcake vane; t24.5 brilliant! Just absolutely bloody brilliant! The best wine opening to any whisky I have tasted so far this year. Where the nose is hard work, this just ruptures onto the palate disgorging all its richest, most oily and spicy secrets in the process, not to mention a shed load of muscovado sugar. Amazingly, there is a faint malt note still detectable and this works sublimely with the toastier tannins; f23.5 just the beautiful rhythmic pulsing of the spices is all you need....; b24 just blown away by this. Nectar, indeed...! *54%. nc ncf.*

Wemyss Nectar Grove Madeira Wine Cask Finished (88.5) n22.5 t22.5 f21.5 b22 Soft and beautifully honeyed. *46%. nc ncf.*

Wemyss Malts Peat Chimney (84.5) n21.5 t21.5 f21 b20.5 A sharp, muddled malt whose unbalanced kippery nose is a peaty indication of what is to follow. Each avenue explored appears to narrow into a dead end: a tight, restricted, frustrating experience. *46%. ncf.*

Wemyss Malts Peat Chimney Batch Strength batch 001 **(87.5)** n22 t23 f21 b21.5 Much more comfortable and happy with itself than the 46% version, mainly thanks to the extra oils allowing the molasses to integrate to greater effect with the smoke. But the tinny, off kilter finale shows that some elements here simply refuse to bond. *57%. ncf. 6,000 bottles.*

◈ **Wemyss Malts Peat Chimney Blended Malt** batch no. 002 **(95)** n24 fabulous intertwangling between peat reek and anthracite; t24 oh, what a scrumptuous, faultless mouthfeel. For a moment you forget about the flavours themselves as you are so caught up in the pure sensuality of the soft oils. On fourth taste you get the fuller picture the entangled smoke and first muscovado then molassed sugars; f23.5 dark chocolate with a woofer base of peat; b23.5 another massive jump in quality from their previous bottling. Captured not just the intensity of the smoke this time, but the harmony surrounding it. No great age, but when everything fits into place, there doesn't need to be. Lovely, lovely stuff. *57%. ncf. 9000 bottles.*

Wemyss Malts Spice King (90) n23.5 t22.5 f22 b22 A lovely malt, but beyond the nose the spices of note are conspicuous by their absence and not a patch on those found on The Hive... *46%. ncf.*

Wemyss Malts Spice King Batch Strength batch 001 **(95.5)** n23.5 t24.5 f23.5 b24 Notably different in character and storyline to the 46% version...and here spices are in no shortage whatsoever...! Stunningly gorgeous. *56%. ncf. 6,000 bottles.*

◈ **Wemyss Malts Spice King Blended Malt** batch no. 002 **(89)** n21.5 a little bit of youth pepped by some half-baked tannin...; t23 there we go! Hold tightly onto the reins as this bronco is bucking. The spices are upfront and at times sear. The sugars are ribald and raw; f22 the lack of age is apparent again as the tannins trip over themselves clumsily; b22.5 I remember last time out with this vatted malt I felt a little swizzed by the lack of spice. No such complaints this time: a real rip-roaring malt! *58%. ncf. 9000 bottles.*

◈ **Wemyss Malts Velvet Fig Aged 25 Years Blended Malt** sherry casks **(87)** n22.5 t22.5 f21 b21 No off notes. Sadly, just one of those occasions when the casks married together here have not gelled quite as one might have hoped. Attractively soft delivery and for a few moments the fruit apparent has a genuinely complex moment or two. But then it falls apart slightly as various strands fail to tie or simply find dead ends. I do love the mouthfeel on delivery, though. *42.3%. nc ncf. 5,000 bottles.*

The Whisky Cask Company Peatside 7 Year Old P.X. sherry cask, bott Feb 17 **(84.5) n22 t21.5 f21 b20** This is my 1,110th new whisky for the 2019 Whisky Bible, and it seems like my 1,000th peat and PX sample. Very few of them particularly excite me. Usually, just too uncouth and showy I'm afraid...a bit like a young person staggering noisily along a Spanish resort in the early hours from one nightclub to another, deliberately wearing very little and no better for alcohol. *60.3%. 317 bottles.*

Whisky D'arche 5 Ans D'âge lot no. 250817 **(90.5) n22.5 t23 f22 b23** What a joy of a whisky! Such is the joy of youth! *43% (86 proof).*

Whisky-Fässle Blended Malt 24 Year Old sherry hogshead, dist 1993, bott 2018 **(94) n23.5 t23 f23.5 b24** Sherry influence but elegant and clean as a whistle! *54.3%.*

The Whisky Works King of Trees 10 Year Old Blended Malt part-finished in native Scottish oak **(89.5) n22 t23 f22 b22.5** A native malt matured in native oak. As neat as the whisky. The fabled tightness of Scottish oak certainly comes out with the punchy tannin on the finish. But the barley itself is crystalline and crisp. *46.5%. nc ncf. 2,157 bottles.*

◈ **Wilson & Morgan Barrel Selection Westport 15 Year Old** Marsala finish, dist 2004, bott 2019 **(86) n22 t22 f21 b21** Westport at this age when in its usual ex-bourbon garb can be a delightful fellow, abounding with all kinds of lively barley tones. The Marsala intervention has stripped that away, alas. Instead we have sulphur traces making this a very uncomfortable fit, especially at the death when everything is squeezed eye-wateringly tight. Hard as nails and sharp, with that nagging off-key finale despite a late hint of cocoa. A shame. *59.5%.*

World of Orchids Blend of Islay Malt sherry cask finish, bott 2019 **(92) n23 t23.5 f22.5 b23** So often sherry and peat cancel each other out. Here they may not exactly work in tandem, but they certainly ensure some spectacularly intense and juicy moments. One for the thrill-seekers... *53.5%.*

SCOTTISH RYE
ARBIKIE
Highlands, 2013. Working.

Arbikie Highland Rye Aged 3 Years Single Grain Scotch charred American oak, Pedro Ximenez barrels, cask nos. 9, 11 & 16, dist 2015 db **(86.5) n21 t22 f21.5 b22** And finally...now for something completely different. The final whisky I shall taste for the Jim Murray Whisky Bible 2020, the 1,252st, is Scotland's first commercially bottled rye whisky. It is being sampled here straight after tasting the world's ultimate rye, Sazerac and Handy from Buffalo Trace, but I was so impressed with this distillery trying something so different, I wanted them to bring the curtain down on this year's Whisky Bible. After tasting 20,027 whiskies for this book since 2003 you would have thought that amongst them would have been the odd Scottish rye or two. But no: no such thing existed. Until now. Is it a classic? No. Is it historic? Most certainly. Is it any good? Well, it isn't bad, but could be a lot better, especially if they got away from this hysteria sweeping the industry in which PX casks have to be used for everything. Had they asked me the very last cask they should use, I would have told them PX...simply because it smothers a distillery's character to death. And here even the rye, the most toothsome grain of them all, vanishes under a welter of moist dates; though a tobacco character (of concern) on the nose is not extinguished. Am I disappointed? No. Because getting rye right is not at all easy and for a new distillery it is even harder. But they would help themselves by ditching the PX and giving the grain a chance to speak. I look forward to visiting them before the 2021 Bible is published and see what they are up to. In the meantime, congratulations. And here's to reaching for the stars... and touching them. *46%. nc ncf. 998 bottles.*

◈ **Arbikie Highland Rye Aged 4 Years Cask Selection Single Grain Scotch** charred American oak, Armagnac barrels, cask nos. 3, 5, 13 & 14, dist 2015 db **(89) n21.5** no escaping the wide cut here. Equally, the rye is unmissable, too. A curious mix of oils and crisp fruitiness and sugars which increasingly err toward molasses; **t23.5** so sensual! The oils are so soft yet rich and this coating allows the sugars to drip from every taste bud, The rye tones grow exponentially – though that little tobacco note I think I detected last time also finds a place in the flavour line-up. Moist dates and even a surprising degree of heather honey all make for a mouth-filling experience; **f21.5** just bitters slightly as the oils kick back into play; **b22.5** a massive lurch upwards in character and quality from their initial bottling, this time the grain is given a platform to perform and entertain. And doesn't it take the opportunity with both hands! A dense rye, still slightly thick from the wide cut. But the sugars are profound and delicious. So much personality – and still room for improvement as their experience increases. Exciting times! *46%. nc ncf. 1,220 bottles.*

Scottish Grain

It's a bit weird, really. Many whisky lovers stay clear of blended Scotch, preferring instead single malts. The reason, I am often told, is that the grain included in a blend makes it rough and ready. Yet I wish I had a twenty pound note for each time I have been told in recent years how much someone enjoys a single grain. The ones that the connoisseurs die for are the older versions, usually special independent bottlings displaying great age and more often than not brandishing a lavish Canadian or bourbon style.

Like single malts, grain distilleries produce whisky bearing their own style and signature. And, also, some display characteristics and a richness that can surprise and delight. Most of the grains available in (usually specialist) whisky outlets are pretty elderly. Being made from either maize or wheat helps give them either that Canadian or, depending on the freshness of the cask, an unmistakable bourbony style. So older grains display far greater body than is anticipated.

That was certainly underlined in most beautiful and emphatic style by last year's Scotch Grain Whisky of the Year. The Last Drop Dumbarton 1977 had all that you should demand from a magnificent grain and more.

The fact that it was from Dumbarton was significant. For years, right up until its tragic and unnecessary closure in 2002, this distillery made the core grain for the Ballantine's blends and it was, following the closure of Cambus, without question the producer of the highest quality grain in Scotland. I had worked with it many times in the blending lab and it was as though I had the finest marble to sculpt from.

Dumbarton and Cambus have long been my two favourite grain distilleries, not least because both are thick with character. So no great surprise, then, that the Jim Murray Whisky Bible 2021 Single Grain of the Year is from Cambus.

Again, a single cask, this time from the American bottlers Perfect Fifth. And not only was this the most compelling grain I encountered in the market place this year, but also within the blending lab where I also tasted many a grain of varying ages. What worries me, though, is how many Cambuses are left out there of this quality still to be unearthed. Very few, I suspect.

Jim Murray's Whisky Bible Scottish Grain of the Year Winners	
2004-07	N/A
2008	Duncan Taylor Port Dundas 1973
2009	The Clan Denny Dumbarton Aged 43 Years
2010	Duncan Taylor North British 1978
2011	The Clan Denny Dumbarton Aged 40 Years
2012	The Clan Denny Cambus 47 Years Old
2013	SMWS G5.3 Aged 18 Years (Invergordon)
2014	The Clan Denny Dumbarton 48 Years Old
2015	The Sovereign Single Cask Port Dundas 1978
2016	The Clan Deny Cambus 25 Years Old
2017	Whiskyjace Invergordon 24 Year Old
2018	Cambus Aged 40 Years
2019	Berry Bros & Rudd Cambus 26 Years Old
2020	The Last Drop Dumbarton 1977
2021	The Perfect Fifth Cambus 1979

Single Grain Scotch

CALEDONIAN Lowland, 1885. Diageo. Demolished.

The Cally 40 Year Old refill American oak hogsheads, dist 1974 db **(88.5)** n23.5 t23 f20 **b22** This poor old sod is tiring before your nose and taste buds. But it hangs on grimly to give the best show it can. Quite touching, really...we are witnessing first hand the slow death of a once great distillery. *53.3%. 5,060 bottles. Diageo Special Releases 2015.*

The Sovereign Caledonian 35 Years Old refill hogshead, cask no. 14271, dist Feb 82, bott Oct 17 **(87)** n22 t22 f21 **b22** Caledonian MacBrayn? Caledonian Canal? Caledonian Sea? Amazingly salty and coastal, more so than any grain I have encountered before. Has its unique and oddly delicious charm,but runs out of legs well before the finale. *46.9%. nc ncf sc. 154 bottles.*

CAMBUS Lowland, 1836. Diageo. Closed.

Cambus Aged 40 Years dist 1975 db **(97)** n24.5 t24 f23.5 **b25** I chose this as my 600th whisky for Bible 2018: a tragically lost distillery capable of making the finest whisky you might expect to find at 40 years of age. And my hunch was correct: this is flawless. *52.7%. 1,812 bottles. Diageo Special Releases 2016.*

Berry Bros & Rudd Cambus 26 Years Old cask no. 61972, dist 1991, bott 2018 **(96.5)** n24 t24 f24 **b24.5** Few whiskies this year have displayed so many beguiling twists and turns: a true gem of a grain, though always a bit of a rum do. I can imagine my dear friend of nearly three decades, Doug McIvor, leaping from his seat when he unearthed this sample.... something as rare as any kind of satisfying Charlton Athletic experience... *55.1%. nc ncf sc.*

The Cooper's Choice Cambus 1991 refill sherry butt, cask no. 61982, bott 2018 **(90)** n23.5 t24 f20.5 **b22** A very good whisky from the Swedish Whisky Fed which will probably make it to the quarter finals of any whisky competition – and then lose to an English malt... *58.5%. sc. Bottled for the Swedish Whisky Federation.*

The Perfect Fifth Cambus 1976 cask no. 05916, dist 27 Oct 76 **(93)** n23.5 t24 f22 **b23.5** An impressive example of the what then was arguably the finest grain distillery in Scotland. The structure is sound and the Canadian style of whisky is exactly what should be expected of a fine corn Cambus of this age. There is a slightly nagging bitterness caused by the tiring oak, but the inherent sweetness controls this well. The sugar-spice balance is pretty near perfection. Has the odd fault, but the complexity of the sweet riches outweigh those slightly bitter failings. *576%. sc.*

◈◈◈ **The Perfect Fifth Cambus 1979** cask no. 900003 **(96.5)** n23.5 just classic. The corn oils and ulmo honey are in a love clinch...; **t24.5** now I'm in one...with the glass...! The ulmo honey spreads around your palate like your lover on a rug before a log fire... And now the oak is gorgeously embedded into the corn. So the mouthfeel plays an equal role to the flavours... and they are luxurious and delicate in the extreme. A fragile blend of acacia and heather honey on one higher pitch, ulmo honey on a deeper, and here even with a light coconut touch...; **f24** no bitter notes, which so often happens at this age and after so much honey on display. Just a slow sunset of corn oils, still the ulmo honey and now a wonderful but measured degree of pattering spice...; **b24.5** given the right cask and the right time, Cambus is as good as anything distilled in Scotland. Here we see it in sublime form: no major faults from the cask... and certainly not the distillate. How many varying forms and densities of sweetness can you find on one whisky? Well here's your chance to find out...get counting...! *53.2%. nc ncf sc.* 🍸

Sansibar Whisky Cambus 1991 bott 2019 **(88)** n22 almost rum-like with sweet estery qualities; **t23** incredibly sweet delivery, but spices arrive early to harmonise. No shortage of golden syrup; **f21** bitters out as the cask gives way...; **b22** a rather weak bourbon cask has done this no favours. Some superb moments. *47.7%.*

The Sovereign Cambus 29 Years Old refill hogshead, cask no. 15010, dist Sept 88, bott Apr 18 **(86)** n22 t22.5 f20.5 **b21** Lots of fat and bubble gum at play here. Some superb moments on the corn, but never feels entirely at ease with itself, thanks to some stuttering oak. *45.6%. nc ncf sc. 299 bottles.*

The Sovereign Cambus 30 Years Old refill hogshead, cask no. 14857, dist 1988 **(94)** n23.5 t24 f23 **b23.5** A good hundred years ago, this grain was bottled and marketed as an equal to a single malt. If the distillery was still alive today a similar campaign would not bring in many complaints. A beauty! *45.2%. nc ncf sc. 313 bottles. Exclusive to The Whisky Barrel.*

The Whisky Cask Company Cambus 27 Years Old bourbon barrel, cask no. 286, dist 24 Sept 91, bott 29 Nov 18 **(95.5)** n24 t24 f23.5 **b24** ridiculously beautiful. *576%. sc. 286 bottles.*

CAMERONBRIDGE Lowland, 1824. Diageo. Working.

◈◈◈ **Artful Dodger Cameronbridge 35 Year Old** bourbon barrel **(94.5)** n23.5 t24 f23 **b24** Soft and succulent all the way, this is a masterclass in how to ramp up the natural caramels without losing shape or interest. Light traces of ulmo honey also generate controlled sweetness but it is what feels like corn oil that makes a huge difference, stretching the narrative further than originally seemed possible and allowing the delicate spices and sweeter vanillas plenty of room and time interact. Burnt fudge towards the finish underscores the age. Ridiculously charming. *52.2%.*

⬩ **Liquid Treasures From Miles Away Cameronbridge 38 Year Old** bourbon barrel, dist Feb 82, bott Feb 20 (94.5) n23.5 t23.5 f23.5 b24 Textbook grain whisky seemingly made from corn as there is a Canadian-style corn oil and vanilla richness to this which really extracts the last nuance out from the syrupy sugars. Lush, lengthy and benefitting from a sublime bourbon barrel which ensures a perfect measure of sugars adds to the depth. When these older Cameronbridges are on form they are really something to behold. And this is a faultless stunner. *48.6%. sc. 140 bottles.*

Old Particular Cameronbridge 26 Years Old refill hogshead, cask no. 12233, dist Oct 91, bott Dec 17 (93) n23 t23.5 f23 b23.5 A Scotch that wanted to be a bourbon when it grew up... *51.5%. nc ncf sc. 569 bottles.*

The Sovereign Cameronbridge 26 Years Old refill butt, cask no. 14752, dist Oct 91, bott Feb 18 (79) n19 t22 f18 b20 Sweet and fruity but curiously tight on the nose and finish. *56.9%. nc ncf sc. 481 bottles.*

⬩ **The Whisky Barrel Originals Cameronbridge 37 Years Old** refill bourbon barrel, cask no. TWB1005, dist Feb 82, bott 2019 (86.5) n22 t23.5 f20 b21 As you'd expect from a C'Bridge of this vintage, there is plenty to involve your taste buds and enjoy. But, equally, there is a little frustration of the dustiness on the nose and emaciated body towards the finish – something not normally expected. That essentially leaves the delivery and follow through to enjoy – and it doesn't let you down, the ulmo honey and spices forming a delightful partnership and not without a Canadian feel. The remainder disappoints. *51%. sc. 164 bottles.*

World of Orchids Cameron Brig 1991 26 Years Old bourbon cask, cask no. 031 (94.5) n23.5 t23.5 f23.5 b24 Truly faultless. Cameron Bridge must have had a hell of a bee invasion back in 1991...! *56.4%. sc.*

CARSEBRIDGE Lowland, 1799. Diageo. Demolished.

The Sovereign Carsebridge 44 Years Old refill hogshead, cask no. 14189, dist May 87, bott Sept 17 (90) n22.5 t23 f22 b22.5 Very attractive, but about as sweet as you'd like a whisky to go. *50.9%. nc ncf sc. 150 bottles. The Whisky Barrel 10th Anniversary bottling #7.*

DUMBARTON Lowland, 1938. Pernod Ricard. Demolished.

Fadandel.dk Dumbarton 30 Years Old cask no. 25241, dist 18 Mar 87, bott 27 Mar 17 (86) n22 t22.5 f20 b21.5 A clumsy grain festooned with honey and spice, but little ability to bring them happily together. Delicious early on but bitters out as the oak finally cracks. *57.2%. sc. 168 bottles.*

The Last Drop Dumbarton 1977 cask no. 140000004 (97) n24.5 almost a cross between a high class bourbon and rye blend, the Demerara sugars magically crisp and clean. Blenders used Dumbarton grain for firmness and backbone. Here, even the nose has a spine to it... vanillas drift around like snow on the wind, the tannins proffering the most understated of spices...; t24.5 how can a delivery of a whisky over 40 years old be this salivating? This clean? This brittle? Again, it is Demerara to the fore, but now the corn oils coat it with a luxurious softness. Light caramels drift on while, like on the nose, the spice takes its time to make a furtive entry; f23.5 long, with the vanilla and spice now seeing out the show. The caramels to harden and crisp up in true Dumbarton fashion; b24.5 Last Drop have been and done it again. They've only gone and found a near faultless barrel from what was once, before it was needlessly destroyed, a near faultless grain distillery. Nothing unusual you'd say, except that this spent 42 years in oak, giving it plenty of time to go wrong. Nothing did, so you have a pristine example of a grain distilled in the year I returned to the UK having hitch-hiked through Africa. And in my flat in Melton Mowbray, which also housed my Press Agency, would always sit a bottle of Chivas Regal...a very different, lighter and more delicate blend than you see today. And this barrel, most likely, was filled to be added to another bottling of Chivas, 12 years on. Instead, it remained in a warehouse seeking perfection...and as near as damn it finding it. *48.7%. sc.*

Scotch Malt Whisky Society Cask G14.5 31 Year Old 2nd fill ex-bourbon barrel, dist 1 Oct 86 (96) n24 t24 f23.5 b24.5 The confident solidity of this grain stands out like Dumbarton Rock...one of the great whiskies of the year, anywhere in the world. *50.6%. sc.*

Single Cask Collection Dumbarton 30 Years Old bourbon barrel (96) n24 t24.5 f23.5 b24 Taste a whisky like this and you'll fully understand why I regard the destruction of this distillery as one of the greatest criminal acts ever perpetrated against the Scotch whisky industry by the Scotch whisky industry. *52.1%. sc.*

The Sovereign Dumbarton 30 Years Old refill barrel, cask no. 14247, dist Mar 87, bott Sept 17 (92) n23 t23.5 f22.5 b23 Beautiful stuff and those who appreciate Canadian will particularly benefit. But a little tiredness to the oak reminds you of its great age. 55.3%. nc ncf sc. 160 bottles. The Whisky Barrel 10th Anniversary bottling #6.

The Sovereign Dumbarton 30 Years Old refill barrel, cask no. 14327, dist Mar 87, bott Oct 17 **(94) n23.5 t24 f23 b23.5** Practically a re-run of the Single Cask Dumbarton 30, except not all the dots on the sugars are joined. That said, still a whisky work of art. 50.2%. nc ncf sc. 135 bottles.

The Sovereign Dumbarton 31 Years Old refill hogshead, cask no. 15477, dist 1987 **(92) n22.5** a light lavender note introduces a bourbon weightiness; **t23.5** ah....the trademark stiff spine delivery. Rock hard sugars are surrounded by more forgiving corn notes. A slight oiliness to fill the mouth, but the spice-sugar battle is the main attraction through to the finish...; **f23** ....and more of the same...! **b23** Dumbarton's style stood alone among Scotland's grain distilleries: its idiosyncratic style is in full spate here. 50.5%. nc ncf sc. 207 bottles. Exclusive to The Whisky Barrel.

The Sovereign Dumbarton 31 Years Old bourbon barrel, cask no. 15801, dist Mar 87, bott Feb 19 **(86.5) n22 t22.5 f20.5 b21.5** Unusually grassy and fresh for a Dumbarton. The firmness arrives later than normal, though with it an unfortunate bitterness from the cask. 43.5%. nc ncf sc. 186 bottles.

The Whisky Barrel Dumbarton 30 Year Old barrel, cask no. 13436, dist 1987 **(96.5) n24 t24.5 f24 b24** Dumbarton at anything from 21to 30 is about as good as grain whisky gets (hence why Ballantine's can be sensational), providing it has lived in the right cask. And this is the right cask...56.7%. sc. 197 bottles.

GARNHEATH Lowland, 1964. Inver House Distillers. Demolished.

The Cooper's Choice Garnheath 48 Year Old dist 1967, bott 2016 **(96) n24 t24 f24 b24** It is an honour to experience a whisky both so rare and gorgeous. Perhaps not the most complex, but what it does do is carried out close to perfection. A must find grain. 41.5%. nc ncf sc. The Vintage Malt Whisky Co.

GIRVAN Lowland, 1963. William Grant & Sons. Working.

The Girvan Patent Still Over 25 Years Old db **(84.5) n21.5 t21.5 f20.5 b21.** A pretty accurate representation of the character these stills were sometimes quietly known for at this time, complete with some trademark sulphury notes – presumably from the still, not cask, as I do pick up some balancing American white oak character. 42%. nc.

The Girvan Patent Still No. 4 Apps db **(87) n21.5 t22 f21.5 b22.** A first look at probably the lightest of all Scotland grain whiskies. A little cream soda sweetens a soft, rather sweet, but spineless affair. The vanillas get a good, unmolested outing too. 42% WB15/369

Berry Bros & Rudd Girvan 12 Years Old cask no. 532388/9, dist 2006, bott 2018 **(94) n23 t24 f23 b24** If you wondered why Grant's blends have been so good for so many years, then try out this straight down the line example of their 12-year-old grain. If I were asked in a tasting to describe what I should expect from this distillery at this age, then really this bottling has completely nutshelled it! This is when average equals excellence. 46%. nc ncf sc.

Dramfool 20 Girvan 11 Years Old bourbon cask, dist 2007 **(87) n21.5 t22.5 f21 b22** An old cask has resulted in some major inaction between the oak and the grain. Indeed, we get a very clear look at the spirit itself, which is no bad thing considering how sweet and lush it is. But lacks desired development. 65.1%. nc ncf. 162 bottles.

Dramfool 21 Girvan 11 Years Old bourbon cask, ex-Lagavulin sherry octave, dist 2007 **(92) n23 t23.5 f22 b23.5** The influence of the peat far outweighs any grape notes. Indeed, because of the light character of the spirit, the smoke travels a long way. 64.4%. nc ncf. 64 bottles.

🔹 **Fadandel.dk Girvan 13 Year Old** barrel, cask no. 532404, dist 11 Jul 06, bott 30 Aug 19 **(86.5) n22.5 t23 f20 b21** Characteristic fatness surrounded by friendly sugars and marzipan makes for a delicious nose and opening. Sexy spices, too. But not the best finish I've seen from this distillery, being a tad bitter and generally askew. 61.2%. sc. 203 bottles.

The First Editions Girvan Aged 38 Years refill hogshead, cask no. 14749, bott 2018 **(95) n23.5 t24 f23.5 b24** Wears its age and gravity lightly: this is wonderful grain whisky. 50.3%. nc ncf sc. 302 bottles.

The Great Drams Girvan 11 Years Old cask no. 300609, dist 27 Jun 07, bott 27 Feb19 **(91.5) n22.5 t23.5 f22.5 b23** Any softer or more shy and this grain would barely escape from your glass. But with some cajoling you end up with a very accurate representation of this distillery for its age. 46.2%. nc ncf sc.

Lady of the Glen Girvan 1991 cask no. 54459 **(89.5) n22.5 t23 f22 b22.5** Though seemingly soft and yielding, the sturdy subplot maximises the otherwise limited oak influence. Good spice prickle while late sugars are able to counter the encroaching bitterness. 43.2%. sc.

Liquid Treasures Entomology Girvan Over 28 Years Old ex-bourbon barrel, dist 1989, bott 2018 **(86.5) n23 t22 f20.5 b21** A typical pea-souper of a Girvan, thick on the nose with sugary promise and no shortage of oak-encouraged vanilla depth then eye-smartingly sweet delivery with golden syrup mixing in with the oils. A warming sub plot as the spices build but a little disappointing as the oak gives way to bitterness. *52.7%*.

Old Particular Girvan 27 Years Old refill hogshead, cask no. 12191, dist Dec 89, bott Nov 17 **(91) n24 t22.5 f22 b22.5** It's all about the amazing nose, yesiree...! *51.5%. nc ncf sc. 148 bottles*.

Scyfion Choice Girvan 2006 Islay whisky cask finished, bott 2018 **(92) n23 t23.5 f22.5 b23.5** An intriguing concept brilliantly executed! *46%. nc ncf sc. 90 bottles*.

INVERGORDON Highland, 1959. Emperador Distillers Inc. Working.

Cadenhead's Single Cask International Invergordon 43 Years Old dist 1973 **(94.5) n23 t24.5 f23.5 b23.5** You are more likely to find a jagged edge on a snooker ball than you are this luscious grain! *51.3%. sc. 175th Anniversary bottling*.

Cave Aquila A Knight's Dram Invergordon 44 Years Old cask no. 20, dist Dec 72, bott Mar 17 **(95) n24 t24 f23.5 b23.5** You almost want to give the spices a standing ovation... *46.7%. sc*.

The Cooper's Choice Invergordon 1974 43 Years Old **(91) n24 t23 f21.5 b22.5** If the delivery and finish can't quite live up to the nose, that is hardly surprising. This is the aroma of all talents, offering a small grain bourbon type leathery sweetness together with a more genteel vanilla-clad Canadian of high quality. The immediate delivery has a good stab at matching that, and at first succeeds, especially with the depth of the maple syrup and honeycomb. But it understandably fades, then tires late on as the bitterness evolves. *46.5%. nc ncf sc*.

◇◇◇ **The Finest Malts City Landmarks Invergordon Aged 46 Years** bourbon barrel, cask no. 32, dist 1972, bott 2018 **(93.5) n23.5** gentle vanilla and corn oil. Uncomplicated but very alluring and effective...; **t23.5** simplistic white sugars dissolve on impact forming a juicy frame in which gentle layers of vanilla form and intertwine. Plenty of natural caramels; **f23** Curiously for a grain, there is almost a profound maltiness to this; a very slight bitterness of the oak, but nothing drastic; **b23.5** time appears to be lost on this one. No great bowing and scraping to the oak. Good age is apparent, but only if you really think about it...Such elegance. *49.9%. nc ncf sc*.

The First Editions Invergordon Aged 45 Years refill barrel, cask no. 14772, bott 2018 **(94) n23.5 t24 f23 b23.5** Almost a halfway house between ancient grain and a simplistic liqueur. But not so sweet as to be beyond a thing of beauty. *49.6%. nc ncf sc. 230 bottles*.

◇◇◇ **Single & Single Invergordon 1974 45 Years Old (94.5) n23** sharp and fruity. Lots of sugar candy, including pear drops. Not a nose you normally associate with the 45-year-old grain...; **t23.5** a degree of sharpness and bite on arrival: spices curl their lips early and salivation levels rise through the roof; **f24** natural caramel link arms with the like cocoa tones. Molasses keep the sweetness going. A faultless finish which lingers on the light oils, buzzes on the delicate spices...and not a hint of bitter oak weariness in sight; **b24** just how you want an old grain to be. Still full of life after all these years... *46.6%. sc. 156 bottles*.

Single Cask Collection Invergordon 26 Years Old rum barrel finish **(87) n22 t22.5 f21 b21.5** Soft and sweet in the time-honoured Invergordon tradition. But with this amount of sugar at work, it needs to breathe and evolve. Rum casks have a tendency to clip a whisky's wings so, though a very decent and soothing grain, the fun comes to a slightly premature and bitter end. *574%. sc*.

The Sovereign Invergordon 30 Years Old refill hogshead, cask no. 15012, dist May 87, bott Apr 18 **(88) n23 t23 f20.5 b21.5** Promises so much, but the oak can't quite match the deal. *51.6%. nc ncf sc. 314 bottles*.

LOCH LOMOND Highland, 1966. Loch Lomond Group. Working.

Loch Lomond Single Grain db **(93) n23** crisp sugars are willing to absorb the vanilla; **t23.5** indeed, the sugars on the nose are indicative of a sweet grain, for the delivery centres around the maple syrup lead. The oak is something like most anchors at work: barely visible to invisible; **f23** the oaks do have a say, though you have to wait a while on the long finale. A little spice arrives, too; **b23.5** elegant grain; keeps the sweetness controlled. *46%*

◇◇◇ **Loch Lomond Single Grain Peated** db **(91) n22** more like bonfire smoke, rather than peat. But smoky it is and with a real acidic nip to it, too...; **t23.5** surprisingly, the delivery isn't as soft and oily as their usual mouthfeel for LL Grain. This has a more clipped personality and that includes the Demerara sugars. But just love that flavour explosion shock waves in when the smoke and spices suddenly seem to wake to the fact they are there – and really let you know about it....! **f22.5** settles down a smoky rumble with a light vanilla and muscovado sugar accompaniment; **b23** different, intriguing...and beautifully weighted. Love it! *46%*.

LOCHSIDE Highland, 1957. Pernod Ricard. Demolished.

The Cooper's Choice Lochside 44 Year Old dist 1964, bott 2015 **(92.5) n23.5** not unlike a bourbon-Canadian blend (yes, I have encountered such a thing) where a muscular coconut-honey candy theme dominates the subservient vanilla; **t24** salivating and soft, corn oils drift among the obliging sugars without a care in the world; you can hear the tannins knocking, but only the spices gain entry; **f22** back to a coconut toffee thread; bitters late on; **b23** it's hangs on in there, giving in to its age only in the final moments... *41.2%. nc ncf sc. The Vintage Malt Whisky Co.*

NORTH BRITISH Lowland, 1885. Diageo & Edrington. Working.

Berry Bros & Rudd North British 20 Years Old cask no. 224754, dist 1996, bott 2017 **(94.5)** **n23.5 t24 f23 b24** Let's say you are a blender working on a high grade 21-year-old blend and a sample of this came into your lab as you worked out the next year's batch. You would be thrilled. This gives everything you'd want as it is far from neutral and a few casks of those would bolster your honey profile to sort out any oak from elsewhere which have gone a bit dry and gung ho early on. Exemplary. *54.8%. nc ncf sc.*

Gordon & MacPhail Connoisseurs Choice North British Aged 28 Years first fill sherry puncheon, cask no. 73847, dist 23 Oct 90, bott 29 Nov 18 **(82.5) n21 t21.5 f21 b19** Huge grape, under which the distillery and grain vanishes entirely. Simply too one-dimensional. Delicious as in part it may be, you might as well get a bottle of sherry. *61%. sc. 181 bottles.*

The Sovereign North British 21 Years Old refill hogshead, cask no. 14409, dist Oct 96, bott Nov 17 **(87) n22.5 t22 f21 b21.5** A workmanlike grain keeping true to its age and type so far as a blender is concerned, the sharp clarity of the vanilla-tinged icing sugar more than useful. Likewise, the both lush yet underlyingly firm body would be of great use, especially with the marshmallow sweetness. The slight bitterness on the fade can be compensated for in a blend, though harder when a singleton like this. *54.8%. nc ncf sc. 219 bottles.*

⟐ **The Whisky Gallery The Magician North British Aged 5 Years** oak barrel, cask no. 291, dist 2006, bott 2019 **(94) n22.5 t24 f23.5 b24** Beautifully distilled and really well matured in a barrel which allows the grain to reveal its full character: with North British, that means a lot. Though young there is still marzipan on the nose and sublime heather honey on delivery. A little grassy, too, while the late spices are superb. Any blender would give his right arm to work with a grain of this quality in a 5-year-old blend. Indeed, good enough to mix in with some of your better non-sherried malts up to the age of about 15-year-old as you could create something very interesting with this chap, especially with that light oiliness which means a little of this goes a long way. *49%. sc. 242 bottles.*

Whisky Krüger North British 26 Years Old 1991 bott 2017 **(88) n22** a faint spice fizz. But its ultra-friendly vanilla all the way; **t23** juicy, sugar coated corn; **f21** oily vanilla; **b22** despite the sugars a curiously flat grain, but sweet in all the right places. *48.6%. sc.*

NORTH OF SCOTLAND Lowland, 1957. North of Scotland Distilling Co. Silent.

The Pearls of Scotland North of Scotland 1971 dist Dec 71, bott Apr 15 **(95.5) n25 t23.5 f23 b24** What a beautifully elegant old lady...and one with virtually no wrinkles... *43.6%*

PORT DUNDAS Lowland, 1811. Diageo. Demolished.

Port Dundas 52 Year Old refill American oak hogsheads db **(96) n24.5 t24 f23.5 b24** Note to all other grain whisky bottlers: bourbon casks every time to show the distillery in its true colours: NEVER sherry casks...! *44.6%. 725 bottles. Diageo Special Releases 2017.*

The Cooper's Choice Port Dundas 1999 18 Years Old Marsala finish **(87) n21.5 t22.5 f21 b22** Pleasant enough, especially on delivery with the big grape and delicate spice interplay. But otherwise I don't get it. Grain whisky isn't full-bodied enough to react with wine casks and offer any serous complexity. And this is a lost distillery here being overwhelmed so its unique character is lost. That said, if you are looking simply for delicious, muscular spiced fruit, here's your dram! *53%. nc ncf sc.*

⟐ **The Great Drams Port Dundas 10 Years Old** cask no. 800202, dist 13 Oct 09, bott Feb 20 **(92.5) n23** a gorgeously soft, vaguely oily custard tart, with a little powdered sugar; **t23.5** that almost lyrical light waxiness to the delivery that is so Port Dundas: god, how I miss this distillery! The sweetness appears to be perfectly measured. Mashed over-ripe banana and ulmo honey make perfect accomplices; **f23** and elegant spicy buzz hangs on the delicate oil; **b23** wonderful to see a grain whisky marketed at an age us blenders tend to thoroughly enjoy using it at. A grain like this will be found in virtually all top blending labs and this sample has the benefit of coming from cask that hadn't at some stage been sulphur treated. So this Port Dundas at 10 is pretty typical as to how I was tasting it 30 years ago at the same age. Timeless. *48.2%. nc ncf sc.*

The Sovereign Port Dundas 27 Years Old refill hogshead, cask no. 14451, dist Feb 90, bott Nov 17 **(91.5) n23** Fox's Party Rings biscuits; **t23.5** light corn oils can't distract from the German caramelised biscuit; **f22** most of the oils have burned off to leave roasty bourbon creams; **b23** simply takes the biscuit. *51.5%. nc ncf sc. 258 bottles.*

That Boutique-y Whisky Company Port Dundas 25 Year Old batch 1 **(95) n24 t24 f23 b24.5** A little bit special... *48.2%. 115 bottles.*

World of Orchids Port Dundas 24 Year Old bourbon cask, dist 1989 **(92) n22 t24 f23 b23** Don't expect great complexity...just a whole lot of technically faultless deliciousness. *56.1%.*

STRATHCLYDE Lowland, 1927. Pernod Ricard. Working.

◇ **Artful Dodger Strathclyde 27 Year Old** bourbon barrel, cask no. 110035 **(89.5) n22 t23 f22 b22.5** Old school Strathclyde before a small fortune was spent cleaning the place up. This has its traditional "dirty" feel, which over the years has given so many blends a particular character. At 27 years some of the natural blemishes have transformed into a chewy heather-honey tone, with a little manuka and Marmite thrown in. The firmness on the finish is its signature. *51.8%. sc.*

Glasgow Gardens Festival 30th Anniversary Strathclyde 30 Year Old 1988 cask no. 62125, dist 9 Jun 88, bott 10 Jun 18 **(87) n22 t23 f20.5 b21.5** I think I remember Hunter Laing bringing out a 30-year-old Strathclyde last year which surprised me with its gentle good manners. This is probably much closer to what I was expecting, with the rough edges of the distillery at that time clearly on display here, despite a flurry of superb golden syrup notes on delivery. *54.3%. sc. Exclusive to The Whisky Barrel. 138 bottles.*

Old Particular Strathclyde 11 Years Old sherry butt, cask no. 11952, dist Nov 05, bott Jul 17 **(91) n22 t23.5 f22 b23.5** Not just a sherry butt! But a clean, 100% untainted, entirely sulphur-free sherry butt! Fabulous! *55.5%. nc ncf sc. 638 bottles.*

The Sovereign Strathclyde 28 Years Old refill barrel, cask no. 15804, dist Aug 90, bott Feb 19 **(90) n22.5 t23 f22 b22.5** Looks like Strathclyde were still going through a corn mash at this time, so soft, sweet and oily is this. Very un-Strathclyde for the era in its untroubled shifting through the gears. *51.1%. nc ncf sc. 198 bottles.*

The Sovereign Strathclyde 30 Years Old refill hogshead, cask no. 14448, dist Sept 87, bott Nov 17 **(90) n22 t22 f23.5 b22.5** It is as though the grain has fallen asleep after 30 years and finally wakes up late in the day. *50.7%. nc ncf sc. 175 bottles.*

That Boutique-y Whisky Company Strathclyde 30 Year Old batch 1 **(87.5) n22 t22.5 f21 b22** A grain that gives you a right punch in the throat on delivery. The sugars are profound but without structure and of very limited complexity. *53.1%. 228 bottles.*

UNSPECIFIED SINGLE GRAIN

Borders finished in Oloroso sherry casks **(66) n15 t18 f15 b18.** Finished being the operative word. Has no-one been listening regarding the total mess sherry butts are in. I wonder why I bother sometimes. Jeez... *51.7%. nc ncf. R&B Distillers.*

Haig Club toasted oak casks **(89) n21.5 t23 f22.5 b22** When I first saw this, I wasn't quite sure whether to laugh or cry. Because 25 years ago bottles of single grain whisky were the unique domain of the flat cap brigade, the miners and other working class in the Kirkcaldy area of Scotland. Their grain, Cameron Brig, would be drunk with a splash, mixed with Coke or ginger, even occasionally with Irn Bru, or straight and unmolested as a chaser to the ubiquitous kegged heavy, McEwan's lager or a bottle of Sweetheart stout. When I suggested the hierarchy at United Distillers, the forerunners of Diageo, that in their finer grains they had a product which could conquer the world, the looks I got ranged from sympathy for my lack of understanding in matters whisky to downright concern about my mental well being. I had suggested the exquisite Cambus, now lost to us like so many other grain distilleries in those passing years, should be brought out as a high class singleton. It was pointed out to me that single grain was, always had been and always will be, the preferred choice of the less sophisticated; those not wishing to pay too much for their dram. Fast forward a quarter of a century and here sits a gorgeously expensive bottle in a deep cobalt blue normally associated with Ballantine's and a very classy, heavyweight stopper. In it is a grain which, if the advertising is to be believed, is the preferred choice not of the back street bar room idlers carefully counting their pennies but of its major ambassador David Beckham: it is the drop to be savoured by the moneyed, jet-set sophisticates. My, oh my. Let's not call this hype. Let's just say it has taken some genius exec in a suit half a lifetime – and probably most of his or hers - to come around to my way of thinking and convince those in the offices on the floor above to go for it. Wonder if I qualify for 10 percent of profit for suggesting it all those years back...or, preferably, five percent of their advertising budget. Meanwhile, I look forward to watching David pouring this into some of his Clynelish and Talisker. After all, no-one can Blend it like Beckham... *40%. WB15/408*

Haig Club Clubman (87.5) n22 t22 f21.5 b22 A yieldingly soft and easy-as-you-like and at times juicy grain with a pleasant degree of light acacia honey to make friendlier still. *40%.*

Haig Club Clubman bourbon casks, bott code: L90860U002 **(87.5) n21 t22.5 f21.5 b22** Once you get past the caramel on both nose and finish it is easy to be drawn into enjoying this sweet grain which seems to glisten with acacia honey influence. *40%.*

◇ **The Tweeddale Grain of Truth Highland Single Grain** bott code: L2.282.19 09.10.2019 **(92.5) n23** a strangely dry and strained, almost grumbling, smokiness. The smoke feels as though it's been stretched to its fullest, leaving a peculiarly ashy and acidic phenol nosescape. Attractive, if austere and offering an aroma unmatched by any whisky I have encountered anywhere in the world – especially, Scotland....At given moments quite salty and seaweedy, too...; **t23.5** a surprising degree of light oils rise on delivery and cushion the impact of the smoke. There are sugars, too, (which for a moment you would swear is gristy malt) though they are soon outnumbered as the phenols soon gang together to continue its ultra-dry smoky oppression. A chalky, sooty mid-ground....; **f23** dusty cocoa powder mixed in with good old peat soot. Again a little malty sweetness lurks, but this uprising is soon ruthlessly crushed....; **b23** you could imagine some dour Victorian minister of the kirk, lashing his congregation for being the sinners, without a single hope of salvation, he believes them to be over a miserable two hours on a relentlessly grey, rain-sodden, windswept Sunday morning somewhere up in the bleakest Highlands. And when he says there can be no drinking on the Sabbath, he means all alcoholic drink...with the exception of a dram or two of Tweeddale's Grain of Truth... Aye, that should finish them off, he'd be thinking...This is distilled from a mash bill of half wheat and half peated malt. The result is uniquely sombre and austere grain which, it has to be said, is captivating in its unique and fascinating, smoky bleakness. Love it! *50%. nc ncf.*

The Whisky Works Glaswegian 29 Year Old Single Grain (92) n23.5 t23.5 f22 b23 Not often you get ginger on the nose of a grain whisky, but this one obliges. Signs of a mis-spent youth here, as this shows all the classic signs of a roughhouse whisky when young, a bit of the Gorbals, and though still shewing the odd scar or two, now has a real touch of polished old school, debonair recalcitrance about it. *54.2%. nc ncf. 1,642 bottles.*

WoodWinters The Five Distinguished and Rare Aged 39 Years (93) n22.5 t24 f23 b23.5 A grain of marvellous pedigree and integrity, at least equal to the vast majority of single malts whiskies you will find...*51%. sc. 330 bottles.*

Vatted Grain

Angus Dundee Distillers Blended Grain 50 Year Old (91.5) n23 as old and creaking as a soon to retire Chelsea centre-half. Has given great service, but definitely a few cracks where there had been none a few years before. That said, the very light eucalyptus and heather honey work together charmingly; **t23.5** as silky as an Antonio Conte title winning side. Soaks up layers of tannins and counter attacks quickly with thrusting vanilla and ulmo honey; **f22** good spice helps deflect from the tiring oak; **b23** just champion...! *40.1%.*

⬥ **Compass Box Hedonism** first fill American oak casks, batch no. MMXIX-A, bott 28 Feb 19 **(91) n23** the vanilla is out in force, supported and sweetened by a mildly spiced fusion of acacia and ulmo honeys. Soft, but alluringly rich, too...; **t23** still a bit of a fatty on delivery, but this time the lushness doesn't consume all. Deft sugars - distinctly melt-in-the-mouth in style – which, as on the nose, mingles with light spices in just-so proportions; **f22.5** a touch of the Swiss Rolls in consistency here. Dries back towards the creamy vanilla which runs the nose, so to speak: a finish not to be sneezed at...; **b22.5** after suffering at the hands of so many sulphurous sherry casks over the last month, I have sought sanctuary in John Glaser's Hedonism, a safe wine cask-free zone. It was a sensible choice... *43%. nc ncf.*

Compass Box Hedonism Maximus (93.5) n25 t22.5 f23 b23. Bourbon Maximus... *46%*

Compass Box Hedonism The Muse bott Feb 18 **(89) n23 t23 f21 b22** A fruit fly landing in a whisky while it is waiting to be tasted is always a good sign: these things know where to find sweetness. *53.3%. nc ncf.*

Compass Box Hedonism Quindecimus (88.5) n22.5 t22 f22 b22 Sweet and refreshingly ordinary grain. Well made and unspectacularly delicious. *46%*

Count Cristo bott code: L7117HA8 **(89) n22.5 t22.5 f22 b22** "Learning does not make one learned: there are those who have knowledge and those who have understanding. The first requires memory and the second philosophy." This is a whisky worth trying to understand. *40%.*

The Sovereign Blended Grain 28 Years Old bourbon barrel, cask no. 13327, dist Dec 64, bott Mar 17 **(96) n24.5 t24 f23.5 b24** May be completely wrong, but a theory. There is a dryness here which suggests big age, maybe so big that the strength of a barrel fell below 40%abv... so had to be added to another to restore it back to whisky again. As I say: just a theory. But it'd fit the structure of this beautifully fragile old grain perfectly. *47.9%. nc ncf sc. 221 bottles.*

William Grant & Sons Rare Cask Reserves 25 Years Old Blended Grain Scotch Whisky (92.5) n23 t23.5 f23 b23. A really interesting one, this. In the old days, blenders always spent as much time vatting the grains together as they did the malts, for if they did not work well as a unit it was unlikely harmony would be found in their blend. A long time ago I was taught to, whenever possible, use a soft grain to counter a firmer one, and vice versa. Today, there are far fewer blends to choose from, though 25 years ago the choice was wider. So interesting to see that this grain is soft-dominated with very little backbone at all. Delicious. But screams for some backbone. *47%. Exclusive to The Whisky Shop.*

Scottish Blends

If any whisky is suffering an identity crisis just now, it must be the good old Scottish blend.

Once the staple, the absolute mainstay, of the Scotch whisky industry it has seen its market share increasingly buried under the inexorable, incoming tide that is single malt. But worse, the present-day blender has his hands tied in a way no previous generation of blenders has had before.

Now stocks must be monitored with a third eye, one that can judge the demand on their single malt casks and at increasingly varied ages. Worse, the blender cannot now, as once was the case, create blends with subtly shifting textures - the result of carefully using different types of grain. So many grain distilleries have closed in the last quarter of a century that now most blends seem remarkably similar to others. And there is, of course, the problem of sherry butts which has been fully documented over the years in the Whisky Bible.

For Jim Murray's Whisky Bible 2018 I tasted or re-tasted 128 blends in total, a quite significant number. And there is no doubt that the lack of choice of grain for blenders is beginning to pose a problem for the industry. What was particularly noticeable was the number of blends which now lack a crisp backbone and have softened their stance, making them chewy and pliable on the palate but often lacking the crispness which can maximise the complexity of the malts on display. By the time you add in the caramel, the results can sometimes be just a little too cloying.

Naturally, it was the bigger blenders - those possessing by far the largest stocks - who best escaped this narrowing down of style among the younger blends in particular, and this year it was that thoroughbred blend known even by our grand-parents and great-grandparents, White Horse, which really caught the eye...and palate.

But, not for the first time, it has been the Ballantine stable which this year gave me most pleasure. On my travels around the world I caught up with their entire range at one time or another, but the 30-Year-Old Ballantine's was the one which simply ticked every box, several times over. As a great blend should, it seamlessly combined complexity with elegance...and achieved this without evidently trying. A reminder of what a great blended Scotch should be. Johnnie Walker Black Label achieves this year after year, as does Ballantine's 17. This year, though, Ballantine's 30 did it a little better....

Jim Murray's Whisky Bible Scottish Blend of the Year Winners	
2004/5	William Grant's 21 Year Old
2006	William Lawson Aged 18 Years
2007	Old Parr Superior 18 Years Old
2008	Old Parr Superior 18 Years Old
2009	The Last Drop
2010	Ballantine's 17 Years Old
2011	Ballantine's 17 Years Old
2012	Ballantine's 17 Years Old
2013	Ballantine's 17 Years Old
2014	Ballantine's 17 Years Old
2015	The Last Drop 1965
2016	The Last Drop 50 Years Old
2017	The Last Drop 1971
2018	Compass Box The Double Single
2019	Ballantine's 17 Years Old
2020	Ballantine's 17 Years Old
2021	Ballantine's 30 Years Old

Scottish Blends

100 Pipers bott code LKVK2677 2016/07/01 **(74) n18 t19 f19 b18** These 100 Pipers deserve an award. How can they have played for so many years and still be so off key and out of tune? It is an art form, I swear. I feel like giving the blend a special gong for so many years of consistent awfulness. *40%. Chivas Brothers Ltd.*

❖ **Artful Dodger Blended Scotch 41 Year Old** ex-bourbon hogshead **(95.5) n24 t24 f23.5 b24** Now and again, one of those ultra-sensuous whiskies turns up in my tasting room...and you melt into the glass as you sample it. Here's one such occasion where the blender, either 41-years-ago, or now, has understood how the grains can layer and structure a blend, and how the malt can fuse with the tannins and more caramelised elements. The result is a blend that you would chew, except it dissolves before you get the chance. The grain-malt ratio looks to be pretty spot on, as is the spice which nibbles and harries warmly, but without a hint of aggression. Just ahhhhhh.... *494%. sc.*

The Antiquary bott code L 02 08 16 **(86) n20 t22 f22 b21** Appears to be going along the present day trend of spongy, super soft grain which doesn't always do the best of favours to the obviously high quality malt in here. Pleasantly sweet and chewy with an attractive base note. *40%. Tomatin Distillery.*

The Antiquary Aged 12 Years bott code L 17 12 15 **(87.5) n21.5 t22 f22 b22** The smoke I so well remember from previous bottlings appears to have dispersed. Instead we have an ultra-lush blend dependent on molasses and spice to punch through the major toffee. *40%.*

The Antiquary Aged 21 Years bott code 2016/02/29 LK30215 **(92.5) n23 t23.5 f23 b23** If you are not sure what I mean by a beautifully paced whisky, try this and find out. *43%.*

The Antiquary Aged 35 Years bott code L 24 08 15 **(96.5) n24 t24 f24 b24.5** Enjoy some of the grains involved in this beauty: their type and ability to add to the complexity is, tragically, a dying breed: the hardest whisky I have found so far to spit out...and I'm on dram number 530....! Antiquary's late, great blender, Jim Milne, would shed a tear of joy for this creation of unreconstructed beauty and brilliance, as this was just out of his school of elegance. *46%.*

Ballaglass Blended Scotch Whisky (85) n21 t22 f21 b21. Perfectly enjoyable, chewy – but clean – blend full of toffee and fudge. Very good weight and impressive, oily body. *40%.*

Ballantine's 12 Years Old (87) n21 t22 f21 b23. The kind of old-fashioned, mildly moody blend Colonel Farquharson-Smythe (retired) might have recognised when relaxing at the 19th hole back in the early '50s. Too good for a squirt of soda, mind. *40%. Chivas Bros.*

Ballantine's 17 Years Old (97.5) n24.5 t24 f24 b25 Now only slightly less weighty than of old. After a change of style it has comfortably reverted back to its sophisticated, mildly erotic old self. One of the most beautiful, complex and stunningly structured whiskies ever created. Truly the epitome of great Scotch. *43%.* 🍷

Ballantine's Aged 21 Years (94) n23.5 t24 f23.5 b24 Even though the strength has been reduced, presumably to eke out rare stocks, the beauty of this blend hasn't. *40%*

Ballantine's Aged 30 Years (95.5) n24.5 t24 f23 b24 A fascinating malt, slightly underpowered perhaps, which I have had to put to one side and keep coming back to see what it will say and do next... *40%.*

Ballantine's Aged 30 Years bott code LKRK1934 2016/05/16 **(96) n24.5 t24 f22.5 b24** Practically a replay of the bottle I tasted last year, right down to that very late, barely perceptible furriness. Simply one of the world's most sensual drams... *40%. Chivas Brothers Ltd.* 🍷

Ballantine's Barrel Smooth finished in double charred barrels, bott code: 2018/11/08 **(87.5) n22 t22 f21.5 b22** A cream toffee-rich blend concentrating on molasses and caramel. A real super-soft member of the Ballantine's family, but possessing only a fraction of the age-statement bottlings' complexity. *40%.*

Ballantine's Finest bott code LKEK4068 2016/10/04 **(96) n23.5 t24 f24 b24.5** The consistency and enormity of this blend fair staggers me. It is often my go to blend when travelling the world as I pretty much know what I'll get, within its normal parameters. This bottling has a little extra sweetness on the smoke but exceeds expectation on the finish with a slightly more clever use of the spices and Demerara sugars as they merge with the peat. Just such a big and satisfying experience. *40%. Chivas Brothers Ltd*

Ballantine's Hard Fired (86.5) n22 t22 f21 b21.5. Despite the smoky and toasty elements to this, you're left waiting for it to take off....or even go somewhere. Perhaps just a little too soft, friendly and grain indulgent. Decent, enjoyable blend, of course, but a little out of the Ballantine's usual circle of high class friends. *40%*

Ballantine's Limited release no. A27380 (96) n24 t24.5 f23.5 b24 Each Limited release has a slightly different stance and this one holds its posture with more debonair, lighter-on-foot poise. The vague furry note of recent bottlings is missing here or, rather, is of the least consequence. The fruit, also, is more of a sheen than a statement more room for the malt and vanilla to play and the spices to impart age. It may be soft on both nose and palate –

especially the delivery – as the grains have obviously been vatted to create minimum traction, but it is a blend of quiet substance. Another Ballantine's brand this year hitting the 96 or more mark. Astonishing, absolutely astonishing...more a case of Ballantine's Unlimited... 40%.

Ballantine's Master's bott code LKAK1001 2016/03/09 **(85) n21 t22 f21 b21** The label promises a "fresh take" on this blend. And I admit, it is far more agreeable than before with a little coconut oil and apple helping to give it a lift and the sugars herded into attractive use. But still far too dependent of caramel input, which may round the whisky but flattens it all rather too well. 40%. *Chivas Brothers Ltd.*

Bell's Original (91) n23 t22.5 f22.5 b23 Your whisky sleuth came across the new version for the first time in the bar of a London theatre back in December 2009 during the interval of "The 39 Steps". To say I was impressed and pleasantly surprised is putting it mildly. And with the whisky, too, which is a massive improvement on the relatively stagnant 8-year-old especially with the subtle extra smoky weight. If the blender asks me: "Did I get it right, Sir?" then the answer has to be a resounding "yes". 40%

Bells 8 Years Old (85) n21.5 t22.5 f20 b21. Some mixed messages here: on one hand it is telling me that it has been faithful to some of the old Bells distilleries – hence a slight dirty note, especially on the finish. On the other, there are some sublime specks of complexity and weight. Quite literally the rough and the smooth. 40%. *Diageo.*

⟡ **Berry Bros & Rudd The Perspective Series No.1 21 Year Old** bott 2019 **(90) n22.5** light, teasingly fruity and sweet roast chestnut coming off the brazier; **t22.5** the softest of deliveries, helped along the way by lychee and strands of barley; the grain is more noticeable by texture than flavour; **f22** drier, pithy fruit tones, pleasing spice and light tannins as the age is at last acknowledged; **b23** one of those highly unusual blends where the influence of the grain takes a back seat. 43%. *6,300 bottles.*

Black & White (91) n22 t23 f22.5 b23.5 This one hasn't gone to the dogs: quite the opposite. I always go a bit misty-eyed when I taste something this traditional: the crisp grains work to maximum effect in reflecting the malts. A classic of its type. 40%. *Diageo.*

Black Bottle (74.5) n18 t20.5 f17 b18. Barely a shadow of its former, great self. 40%.

Black Bottle bott code 2038310 L3 16165 **(94.5) n23.5 t23.5 f23.5 b24** Not the byword for macho complexity it was 15 years ago but after a lull in its fortunes it is back to something that can rightfully boast excellence. Brilliant. 40%.

Black Bottle 10 Years Old (89) n22 t23 f22 b23 A stupendous blend of weight and poise, but possessing little of the all-round steaming, rampaging sexuality of the younger version... but like the younger version showing a degree less peat: here perhaps even two. Not, I hope, the start of a new trend under the new owners. 40%

Black Dog 12 Years Old (92) n21 t23 f24 b24. Offering genuine sophistication and élan. This minor classic will probably require two or three glass-fulls before you take the bait... 42.8%

Black Grouse (94) n23 t24 f23 b24. A superb return to a peaty blend for Edrington for the first time since they sold Black Bottle. Not entirely different from that brand, either, from the Highland Distillers days with the smokiness being superbly couched by sweet malts. 40%

The Black Grouse Alpha Edition (72.5) n17 t19.5 f17 b18. Dreadfully sulphured. 40%

Black Hound (83) n21 t21.5 f21 b20.5 Here's to Max! Max grain in this but no complaints here as the relatively limited caramel doesn't spoil the enjoyment of what feels like (though obviously isn't) a single distillery output. Crisp at first, then succulent, chewy cream toffee. 40%. *Quality Spirits International.*

Black Scott 3 Years Old bott code: 3L08460154 **(85.5) n20.5 t22 f21.5 b21.5** Pretty standard, though not unattractive fare. The nose is a bit of a struggle but relaxes on delivery and even entertains with a spicy blitz. 40%. *Toorank Productions BV.*

Black Stripe (77) n19 t20 f19 b19 Untidy without character. 40%.

Blend No. 888 bott code L15/8185 **(84.5) n21 t22 f20.5 b21** Light, breezy and sweet, this is grain dominant and makes no effort to be otherwise. Soft, untaxing and pleasant. 40%. *House of MacDuff.*

Boxes Blend (90) n22.5 t23.5 f21 b23. A box which gets plenty of ticks. 40.9%. *ncf.*

Buchanan's De Luxe 12 Years Old (82) n18 t21 f22 b21. The nose shows more than just a single fault and the character simply refuses to get out of second gear. Certainly pleasant, and some of the chocolate notes towards the end are gorgeous. But just not the normal brilliant show-stopper! 40%. *Diageo.*

Buchanan's Master bott code: L7313CE001 **(94.5) n24 t23.5 f23 b24** Some 40-odd years ago I was in love with Buchanans: it was one of the truly sophisticated blends from which I learned so much and this pays homage to the legacy. On the down side the grains are nowhere near so complex and the vague furry bitterness at the end tells its own tale. But I doff my Panama to blender Keith Law in genuine respect: works like this don't just happen and this is a blended Scotch worthy of the name. 40%.

Castle Rock (81) n20 t20.5 f20 b20.5. Clean and juicy entertainment. 40%

Catto's Aged 25 Years bott code RV9499 **(94.5) n23 t24 f23 b24.5** A far better experience than the last time I officially tasted a Catto's 25 seven or eight years ago. Both malts and grains are of the charming style once associated with Catto's Rare : so jaw-droppingly elegant... 40%. International Beverage Holdings Ltd.

Catto's Deluxe 12 Years Old bott code L 18 03 16 **(86.5) n21.5 t22 f21.5 b21.5** A safe, sweet and sumptuous blend which places major emphasis on the molasses. Won't win any beauty contests but there is a weighty earthiness, also. 40%. International Beverage Holdings Ltd.

Catto's Rare Old Scottish bott code L 25 01 16 **(83) n20.5 t21 f20.5 b21** Once fresh as dew on morning grass, this has changed in recent years with a different grain profile which no longer magnifies the malt. Adopted a rougher, more toffeed approach from its once clean cut personality: not even a close approximation of the minor classic it once was. 40%. International Beverage Holdings Ltd.

◇ **Chapter 7 Blended Scotch 26 Year Old 1993** sherry butt, dist Dec 93, bott Mar 20 **(77) n22 t22 f16 b17** A blend, by definition, should be about layering and complexity and, if desired, not allowing any single trait dictate to the rest. So this blend fails because although the sherry cask is rich and sweet but, sadly, nowhere near sulphur free, the story is fruit and grain. And then sulphur. A lot of sulphur, in fact... Which after the malts have matured for 26 years minimum is a bit sad. A Chapter that needs serious re-writing. 44.9%. sc. 618 bottles.

Chequers Deluxe (78.5) n19.5 t20 f19 b20. Charm, elegance, sophistication...not a single sign of any of them. Still if you want a bit of rough and tumble, just the job. 40%. Diageo.

The Chivas 18 Ultimate Cask Collection First Fill American Oak (95.5) n24 t23.5 f24 b24 Immeasurably superior to any Chivas 18 I have tasted before. A true whisky lover's whisky... 48%. ncf.

Chivas Regal Aged 12 Years bott code 2017/01/31 LPAL 0162 **(93) n23 t23.5 f22.5 b24** Last year I was in a British Airways Business Lounge somewhere in the world and spotted at the bar two different Chivas Regal 12s: the labels had differing designs. I asked for a glass of each and tried them side by side. The first one, from the older label, was the pleasant but forgettable blend I expected and knew so well. The newer version wasn't: had it not been time to get my flight I would have ordered a second glass of it....and I can't remember the last time I did that. What I have here is something very much like that surprise Chivas I discovered. This is, unquestionably, the best Chivas 12 I've encountered for a very long time (and I'm talking at least 20 years): pretty impressive use of the understated smoke, especially on the nose, which works well with that date and walnut toffee. I really could enjoy a second glass of this, though still a very different, delicate animal to the one I grew up with in the mid-70s. Actually, I just have had a second glass of this: delicious....! 40%. Chivas Brothers Ltd.

Chivas Regal Aged 15 Years finished in Grande Champagne Cognac casks, bott code: 2018/07/19 **(89) n23** superb, scampering nose with gentle fruit and spice fizzing around the caramel facade; **t22.5** very sweet delivery, even slightly gristy, super soft with a liquorice and toffee follow through; **f22** toasty fudge; **b22.5** can't quite escape the over-zealous caramel. But there is an undoubted charm to this and extra clever use of the sweeter elements to good effect. Probably one of the softest and most moreish whiskies launched in the last year or so. 40%.

Chivas Regal Aged 18 Years bott code LKRL0346 2017/01/30 **(86) n22 t22 f21 b21** A great improvement on the last bottling I encountered with a pleasing chewiness and understated spiciness. But this remains far too dependent on a big caramel surge for both taste and structure. 40%. Chivas Brothers Ltd.

Chivas Regal Aged 25 Years bott code 2017/03/01 LPML0373 **(95.5) n24.5 t24.5 f22.5 b24** This is quite brilliant whisky. Maybe just one sherry butt away from what would almost certainly have been among the top three whiskies of the year... 40%. Chivas Brothers Ltd.

Chivas Regal Extra (86) n20 t24 f20.5 b21.5. Chivas, but seemingly from the Whyte and MacKay school of thick, impenetrable blends. The nose may have the odd undesirable element and the finish reflects those same trace failings. But if chewy date and walnuts in a sea of creamy toffee is your thing, then this malt is for you. This, though, does show genuine complexity, so I have to admit to adoring the lush delivery and early middle section: the mouthfeel is truly magnificent. Good spice, too. Flawed genius comes to mind. 40%

Chivas Regal The Chivas Brother's Blend Aged 12 Years bott code 2016/04/12 LPEK0613 **(81.5) n21 t21.5 f19 b20** Oh, brother! Fabulous texture but a furry finish... 40%.

Chivas Regal Mizunara bott code: LPBM0253 2018/02/06 **(89.5) n22.5 t23 f22 b22** For years the Japanese copied everything the Scotch whisky industry did, not quite realising – or perhaps willing to believe – that many of their indigenous whiskies were of world class standard deserving respect and discovery in their own right. Now the Scots have, for the first time I'm aware of, openly copied the Japanese– and celebrated the fact. The Japanese oak used within the marrying process does appear to have given an extra impetus and depth to this blend. Definitely offers an extra dimension to what you'd expect from a Chivas. 40%.

Clan Campbell bott code LR3 1047 13/09/05 **(89) n21.5 t23 f22 b22.5** Amazing what happens when you reduce the colouring Last time I tasted this I could barely find the whisky for all the toffee. Now it positively shines in the glass. Love it! 40%. *Chivas Brothers Ltd.*

Clan Campbell rum barrel finish, bott code: 2018/04/04 **(90.5) n22 t23.5 f22 b23** This blend is all about impact and staying power. All kinds of rum and caramel incursions, but a really lovely broadside on the palate. 40%.

Clan Campbell Dark rum barrel finish, bott code 2017/03/29 LPHL 0570 **(89.5) n22 t23 f22 b22.5** Putting my rum blender's hat on here, can't think which barrels they used to get this degree of colour and sweetness. Still, I'm not arguing; it's a really lovely, accommodating dram. 40%. *Chivas Brothers Ltd.*

Clan Gold 3 Year Old (95) n23.5 t24 f23.5 b24. A blend-drinkers blend which will also slay the hearts of Speyside single malt lovers. For me, this is love at first sip... 40%

Clan Gold Blended 15 Years Old (91) n21.5 t23 f23.5 b23 An unusual blend for the 21st century, which steadfastly refuses to blast you away with over the top flavour and/or aroma profiles and instead depends on subtlety and poise despite the obvious richness of flavour. The grains make an impact but only by creating the frame in which the more complex notes can be admired. 40%

Clan Gold Blended 18 Years Old (94.5) n23 t24 f23.5 b24. Almost the ultimate preprandial whisky with its, at once robust yet delicate, working over of the taste buds by the carefully muzzled juiciness of the malt. This is the real deal: a truly classy act which at first appears to wallow in a sea of simplicity but then bursts out into something very much more complex and alluring. About as clean and charming an 18-year-old blend as you are likely to find. 40%

Clan Gold 18 Years of Age bott code L6X 7616 0611 **(95) n24 t24 f23 b24** Nothing like as juicy and cleverly fruity as it once was, yet marriage between malt and grain seldom comes more happy than this... 40%. *Quality Spirits International.*

Clan Gold Finest bott code L10Z 6253 1902 **(83) n20 t21 f21 b21** Sweet, silky, soft and caramel heavy. Decent late spice. 40%. *Quality Spirits International.*

Clan MacGregor (92) n22 t24 f23 b23 Just gets better and better. Now a true classic and getting up there with Grant's. 43%

Clan Murray bott code L9X 7694 1411 **(86) n20 t22.5 f21.5 b22** For the avoidance of doubt: no, this not my blend. No, I am not the blender. No, I do not get a royalty from sales. If I could have had a tenner for each time I've had to answer that over the last decade or so I could have bought my own island somewhere, or Millwall FC... Anyway, back to the whisky. Far better nose than it has shown in the past and the delivery has an eye-watering bite, the finish a roguish spice. Rough-ish but very ready... 40%. *The BenRiach Distillery Co. Ltd.*

Clansman (80.5) n20.5 t21 f19 b20. Sweet, grainy and soft. 40%. *Loch Lomond.*

Clansman bott code L3/170/15 **(84) n21 t22 f20 b21** More to it than of old, though still very soft, the dark sugars and spice have a very pleasant input. 40%. *Loch Lomond Group.*

The Claymore (85) n19 t22 f22 b22. These days you are run through by spices. The blend is pure Paterson in style with guts etc, which is not something you always like to associate with a Claymore; some delightful muscovado sugar at the death. Get the nose sorted and a very decent and complex whisky is there to be had. 40%. *Whyte & Mackay Distillers Ltd.*

Cliff Allen bott 20 07 18, bott code: L1524 015503 **(87) n21.5 t22 f21.5 b22** Though grain heavy, there is a pleasing sweetness to accompany the enveloping softness. Attractive spice prickle, too, as well as decent balance. 40%. *BBC Spirits.*

Compass Box Delilah's Limited Release Small Batch American oak **(92.5) n23 t23.5 f23 b23** blends rarely come more honeyed, or even sweeter, than this with every last sugary element seemingly extracted from the oak. My only sorrow for this whisky, given its American theme, was that it wasn't bottled as a 101 (ie 50.5% abv) instead of the rather underpowered 80 proof – because you have the feeling this would have become pretty three dimensional and leapt from the glass. And then down your throat with serious effect. 40%. nc ncf. *WB15/171*

Compass Box Delilah's XXV American oak & sherry casks **(82) n20.5 t22.5 f18 b21** A blend with an astonishing degree of natural caramels in play, giving the whole piece a soft, chewy feel with both sugars and spices coming off at a tangent. Sadly, the sherry input is distracting on the nose and distinctly tangy and furry towards the end. 46%. nc ncf.

Compass Box The Double Single bott Mar 17 **(97) n24.5 t25 f23.5 b24** By no means the first time I have encountered a single malt and grain in the same bottle. But I am hard pressed to remember one that was even close to being this wonderful...This is Compass Box's finest moment... 46%. nc ncf. *5,838 bottles.*

Compass Box Great King St. Artist's Blend (93) n24 t23 f22.5 b23.5. The nose of this uncoloured and non-chill filtered whisky is not dissimilar to some better known blends before they have colouring added to do its worst. A beautiful young thing this blend: nubile, naked and dangerously come hither. Compass Box's founder John Glaser has done some memorable work in recent years, though one has always had the feeling that he has still been learning his trade, sometimes forcing the issue a little too enthusiastically. Here, there is absolutely no doubting that he has come of age as a blender. *43%. nc ncf.*

Compass Box Great King Street Experimental Batch #00-V4 bott Sept 13 (93) n22.5 t24 f23 b23.5. A blend combining astonishing vibrancy with oaky Russian roulette. Not a dram to do things by halves... *43%. 3,439 bottles.*

Compass Box Great King Street Experimental Batch #TR-06 bott Sept 13 (92) n22 t23.5; f23 b23.5 I think this one's been rumbled... *43%.*

Compass Box Great King Street Glasgow Blend (88.5) n22 t23.5 f21 b22 Just the odd note seems out of place here and there: delicious but not the usual Compass Box precision. 43%

◇◇ **Compass Box Great King St Glasgow Blend** batch no. GB 209, bott 8 Aug 19 (89) n23 I adore the earthy quality to this: the peat doesn't dominate but ensures a rich resonance on which the nuanced sugars and vanillas hang. Just a mystery off-balanced note brings the score down slightly; t23.5 it is like Demerara sugar cubes dipped into malt. For though this a is a blend, there must a high malt content as the barley pokes out from everywhere; f20.5 some light chocolate, but also that out of kilter, bitter note apparent on the nose here too; b22 perhaps a rogue cask away from an award. *43%. nc ncf.*

Compass Box The Circus bott Mar 16 (93) n23 t23.5 f23 b23.5 Scotland's very own Clown Royal... *49%. nc ncf. 2,490 bottles.*

Compass Box This Is Not A Luxury Whisky bott Aug 15 (81) n20 t21.5 f19.5 b20. Correct. *53.1%. nc ncf. 4,992 bottles.*

◇◇ **Compass Box Rogue's Banquet** (94.5) n23.5 just step back, take your time and hunt out the subtlety of this blend: the citrus notes amid the Demerara is such a clever touch, as is the weightier chestnut puree; t23.5 enveloping oils massage the taste buds and all is genteel and soft. Malt springs out from here and there to up the juiciness. But it is the grains which seem to steer the boat; f23.5 light ulmo honey and vanilla, alongside faint spices, serves as a very acceptable - and long - exit; b24 quite a different tack from Compass Box, really concentrating on the daintiness a blend might reveal despite the sometimes voluptuous body. Helped along by sublime cask selection. Gorgeous. *46%.*

Consulate (87) n21.5 t22 f22 b21.5 I assume this weighty and pleasant dram was designed to accompany Passport (whose chewiness it now resembles) in the drinks cabinet. I suggest, if buying them, use Visa. *40%. Quality Spirits International.*

Crawford's (83.5) n19 t21 f22 b21.5. A lovely spice display helps overcome the caramel. *40%.*

Cutty Black (83) n20 t23 f19 b21. Both nose and finish are dwarfed and flung into the realms of ordinariness by the magnificently substantial delivery. Whilst there is a taint to the nose, its richness augers well for what is to follow; and you won't be disappointed. At times it behaves like a Highland Park with a toffeed spine, such is the richness and depth of the honey and dates and complexity of the grain-vanilla background. But those warning notes on the nose are there for good reason and the finish tells you why. Would not be surprised to see this score into the 90s on a different bottling day. *40%. Edrington.*

Cutty Sark (78) n19 t21 f19 b19. Crisp and juicy. But a nipping furriness, too. *40%*

Cutty Sark bott code L60355 L7 (84.5) n21 t22 f20 b21.5 To some extent an improvement on a couple of years back when this blend was vanishing in character. But could still do with some urgent extra restorative work. For as long I can remember the grain on this was crisp and brought the sharpest, juiciest notes imaginable from the Speyside malts: indeed, that was its trademark character. Now, like so many standard blends, it is bubble gum soft and spreads the sugars evenly with the malts fighting to be heard. Only very mild sulphur tones to the crippling ones I had previously found. But it really does need to re-work the grain...if it can find it. *40%.*

Cutty Sark Aged 12 Years (92) n22 t24 f23 b23 At last! Cutty 12 at full sail...and blended whisky rarely looks any more beautiful! *40%. Edrington.*

Cutty Sark Aged 15 Years (82) n19 t22 f20 b21. Attempts to take the honey route. But seriously dulled by toffee and the odd sulphured cask. *40%. Edrington.*

Cutty Sark Aged 18 Years (88) n22 t22 f22 b22 Lost the subtle fruitiness which worked so well. Easy-going and attractive. *43%*

Cutty Sark Aged 25 Years (91) n21 t23.5 f22.5 b23 Magnificent, though not quite flawless, this whisky is as elegant and effortlessly powerful as the ship after which the brand was named... *45.7%. Berry Bros & Rudd.*

Cutty Sark Prohibition Edition American oak, bott code L0401W L4 11/18 (91) n21.5 t25 f20 b24.5 Probably the best label and presentation of any whisky in the world this year: sheer class. On the back label they use the word authentic. Which is a very interesting concept. Except authentic whisky sent to the USA back in the 1920s wouldn't have that annoying and debilitating rumble of sulphur, detectable on both nose and finish. And I suspect the malt content would have been higher – and the grain used showing far more of a corn-oily character. That all said, I doubt the blender of the day would have achieved better delivery or balance: indeed, this delivery has to be one of the highlights of the whisky year. You will not be surprised to discover my resolve cracked, and I swallowed a full mouthful of this special blend. And, gee: it was swell, bud... 50%. *Edrington*.

Cutty Sark Storm (81.5) n18 t23.5 f19.5 b20.5. When the wind is set fair, which is mainly on delivery and for the first six or seven flavour waves which follow, we really do have an astonishingly beautiful blend, seemingly high in malt content and really putting the accent on ulmo honey and marzipan: a breath-taking combination. This is assisted by a gorgeous weight to the silky body and a light raspberry jam moment to the late arriving Ecuadorian cocoa. All magnificent. However, as Cutty sadly tends to, sails into sulphurous seas. 40%. *Edrington*.

Demijohn Finest Blended Scotch Whisky (88) n21 t22 f23 b22 OK, now that's spooky. You really don't expect tasting notes written ten years ago to exactly fit the bill today. But that is exactly what happens here: well maybe not quite exactly. Ten years ago I wrote of the "wonderful firmness of the grain" where today, like 90% of all blends, it is much more yielding and soft than before. Thankfully, it hasn't detracted from the enjoyment. 40%.

Dew of Ben Nevis Supreme Selection (77) n18 t20 f20 b19. Some lovely raspberry jam Swiss roll moments here. But the grain could be friendlier, especially on the nose. 40%

Dewar's Aged 12 Years The Ancestor bott code: L17338ZA80109:20 **(87) n21.5 t22 f21.5 b22** A welcoming blend, relying mainly on softer grains which suck you in and caress you. A little orange peel and tart tannin helps give the blend vibrancy, but there is always a slight murkiness hanging around, too, which becomes more apparent at the death. 40%.

Dewar's Aged 15 Years The Monarch bott code: L18340ZA800 1326 **(81) n21 t21.5 f18 b20.5** Sweet and chewy in part, but the fuzzy finish abdicates. 40%.

Dewar's Aged 18 Years The Vintage bott code: L19030ZA8051642 **(96.5) n24** a gentle fruitiness centres around both unripe and over-ripe greengages, which offer both a sharpness and sweeter friendliness. Spices are close to the surface but refuse to break; tannins provide the anchor; **t24.5** sublime grain at work here. That is the key to the blend, finding one that can both absorb and reflect the malt at work...and this is does here almost to perfection; the key to the sweetness is its refined and relaxed balancing act with the much drier oak. The most charming heather honey pulls this off, and still has room for the sweeter fruity moments; **f23.5** a long, sophisticated finish lacking now the earlier glossy oils, but instead concentrating on the vanillas and spiced butterscotch; **b24.5** this is how an 18-year-old blend should be: complex, noble and both keeping you on the edge of your seat as you wonder next what will happen, and falling back into its furthest recesses so you can drift away on its beauty... A blend that upholds the very finest traditions of the great Dewar's name. 40%.

Dewar's Aged 25 Years The Signature bott code: L18081ZA8011034 **(96) n24** high grade marzipan caresses and teases the nose, while the grains exude a softness which on excavation reveals a much firmer side; a lovely candy floss sweetness completes the extraordinary aroma; **t24** that super-soft grain on the nose turns up first and simply melts away out of existence. The residue is a gently malty spiciness which gathers in tannins by the second. The harder, secondary grain now forms the spine on which all this hangs; **f24** long, lightly spiced and back to the marzipan as the circle is completed; **b24** a 25-year-old blend truly worthy of that mantle. Always an honour to experience a whisky that has been very cleverly sculpted, not haphazardly slung together: a blender's blend. I doff my Panama to the blender. 40%. 🍷

Dewar's Double Double Aged 21 Years Blended Scotch Whisky finished in oloroso sherry casks, bott code: L19106ZA500 **(88) n23.5 t23.5 f18.5 b22.5** Another blender's blend. Or would have been 30 years ago. But doesn't seem to quite take into account the Russian roulette decision to add extra oloroso into the mix – Russian roulette with only one empty chamber that is... 46%.

Dewar's Double Double Aged 27 Years Blended Scotch Whisky finished in Palo Cortado sherry casks, bott code: L19106ZA501 **(96.5) n24** if I didn't have a book to write I could nose this all day: the peat, seemingly stand alone, shifts gear to weave brilliantly amid the crisper grain tones: sublime...and very, very cleverly done; **t24** fabulous delivery with the grain upholding that brittle sharpness displayed on the nose. But then gives way slowly to let in both the now smoke and voluptuous peat; the fruit offers a secondary fruitiness to the Speyside/Highland malts which present a grassy, honey freshness; **f24** although long, although the best part of three decades old, somehow the malty juiciness lasts right to the very death. The peat, also, revels in its two-towned complexity until the very final flavour rays finally set...; **b24.5** a blend not scared to embrace its peaty side. And sherry butts free from sulphur. A double miracle at work. And one of the best new blends I have tasted for a year or two. Superb. 46%.

Dewar's Double Double Aged 32 Years Blended Scotch Whisky finished in PX sherry casks, bott code: L19107ZA501 **(86.5) n21.5 t24 f20.5 b20.5** I clocked the PX influence before I was aware it was officially finished in that cask type. After the staggeringly beautiful and vivid 27-year-old, this is very much a case of following the Lord Mayor's show. Yes, the sherry influence is pristine and untainted by sulphur, and the spices do a grand job. But to put a 30 year old blend into PX is like restoring an Old Master with a nine inch brush dipped into a gloss finish. Lovely in places (the astonishing delivery shews just how much sublime complexity was originally around)...but could have been so much more... *46%.*

⬥ **Dewar's Illegal Smooth Mezcal Cask Finish Aged 8 Years** bott code: L20027ZA8002254 **(88)** n23 t23 f20 b22 There is not the remotest doubt in my mind that of all the blending companies of Scotland, it is Dewar's that in recent years have upped their game most and returned to their once given place amongst the greats. This is probably just a cask away from adding to their rich tapestry of sublime blends. But, sadly, a little sulphur has entered the fray here – not a massive amount, but enough to dull the glitter from a potentially 24 carat blend. With the muscular grape sparring with the crisp grain and fulsome malt, at first this was going rather well, especially with the lightly spiced undertone. Look forward to seeing the next bottling... *40%.*

Dewar's White Label bott code: L18241ZA204 2203 **(82)** n20 t21 f20 b21 A great improvement on the last White Label I tasted (though nowhere near my great love of the 1970s!) but some murky grain still apparent. Definite layering and structure here, though. *40%.*

Dhoon Glen (86) n21 t22 f21.5 b21.5 Full of big flavours, broad grainy strokes and copious amounts of dark sugars including chocolate fudge and now a little extra spice, too. Goes dhoon a treat... *40%. Lombard Scotch Whisky Ltd.*

Dimple 12 Years Old (86.5) n22 t22 f21.5 b21. Lots of sultana; the spice adds aggression. *40%.*

Dimple 15 Years Old (87.5) n20 t21 f24 b22.5. Only on the late middle and finish does this particular flower unfurl and to magnificently complex effect. The texture of the grains in particular delight while the strands of barley entwine. A type of treat for the more technically minded of the serious blend drinkers among you. *40%. Diageo.*

⬥ **Dimple Golden Selection** (84.5) n21 t22 f20.5 b21 A clumsy, untidy bottling with a little too much bitterness on both nose and finish. The odd heather honey note drifts about and some saving busy spice, too. But too easily the honey turns to burnt honeycomb, especially noticeable on the dry finale. Certainly the caramels add to the ungainly narrative. *40%.*

⬥ **Eternity Diamond Reserve Old Premium Blend** Oloroso sherry cask finish **(86)** n21 t22 f21.5 b21.5 Enjoy the chocolate notes which pop up at regular intervals and the chewy mouthfeel which accommodates them perfectly. Just not sure about those gin notes which appear to pepper this blend...and have cost points. *40%.*

⬥ **Eternity Royal Reserve Noble Blend** ex-bourbon casks **(89)** n22.5 not the remotest interest in offering great depth, this makes the most of the delicate citrus tones; t22 grainy with vanillas and tannins to the fore. For a moment a little hit of juniper, which is not particularly welcome; f22.5 sweet with a modicum of grist before fragile spices arrive; b22 determined to stay on the delicate side of the tracks, has both a pleasing sweetness, weight and mouthfeel throughout. Sometimes, though, it reminds me of a Geneve... *40%.*

The Famous Grouse bott code L4812TL1 25/08 **(88.5)** n22.5 t23 f21 b22 Changed its stance a few years back from light blend to a middle-weighted one and has worked hard to keep that position with thoughtful use of the phenols. Unlike many other brands it has not gone colouring mad and the little toffee apparent does nothing to spoil the narrative and complexity: I doff my hat. *40%.*

The Famous Grouse Gold Reserve (90) n23.5 t23 f21.5 b22 Great to know the value of the Gold Reserve is going up...as should the strength of this blend. The old-fashioned 40% just ain't enough carats. *40%. Edrington Group.*

The Famous Grouse Married Strength (82.5) n19 t22 f20 b21.5. The nose is nutty and toffeed. But despite the delightful, silky sweetness and gentle Speyside-style maltiness which forms the main markers for this soft blend, the nose, like the finish, also shows a little bitter furriness has, sadly, entered into the mix. Not a patch on the standard Grouse of a decade ago. *45.9% WB16/019*

The Famous Grouse Mellow Gold sherry & bourbon casks **(85)** n20 t23.5 f20 b21.5. While the nose and finish tell us a little too much about the state of the sherry butts used, there is no harm tuning into the delivery and follow though which are, unquestionably, beautiful. The texture is silk normally found on the most expensive lingerie, and as sexy as who you might find inside it; while the honey is a fabulous mix of ulmo and orange blossom. *40%*

The Famous Grouse Smoky Black (87) n22 t22 f21 b22. Black Grouse by any other name. Flawed in the usual tangy, furry Grouse fashion. But have to say there is a certain roughness and randomness about the sugars that I find very appealing. A smoky style that Bowmore lovers might enjoy. A genuinely beautiful, smoky, ugly, black duckling. Sorry, I mean Grouse. *40%*

Firean blend no. 005, bottling line. 003, bott code. L17066 **(91.5)** n23 t23.5 f22 b23 Does the heart good encounter to encounter a blend so happy to embrace its smokier self. Deliciously impressive. *40%. Burlington Drinks.*

Fort Glen The Blender's Reserve Aged 12 Years (88.5) n21.5 t23 f21.5 b22.5 An entirely enjoyable blend which is clean and boasting decent complexity and weight. *40%*

Fort Glen The Distiller's Reserve (78) n18 t22 f19 b19. Juicy, salivating delivery as it storms the ramparts. Draws down the portcullis elsewhere. *40%. The Fort Glen Whisky Company.*

Fraser MacDonald (85) n21 t21.5 f21 b21.5. Some fudge towards the middle and end but the journey there is an enjoyable one. *40%. Loch Lomond Distillers.*

Gairloch (79) n19 t20 f20 b20. For those who like their butterscotch at 40% abv. *40%*

Gleann Mór Blended Whisky 18 Year Old (87) n21.5 t23 f20.5 b22. A few passages in this are outstanding, especially when the delicate honey appears to collide with the softest smoke. A slight bitterness does jar somewhat, though the softness of the grain is quite seriously seductive *43.9%*

Gleann Mór 40 Year Old Blend (94) n23 t23.5 f23.5 b24 Some 52-year-old Carsebridge makes up about a fifth of this blend, but I suspect the big oak comes from one of the malts. A supreme old whisky which cherishes its age. *44.6%.*

Glenalba Aged 22 Years Sherry Cask Finish batch no. JS/322, lot no. 0745C, dist 1993 (90) n22 t23.5 f23.5 b21 A pristine sherry effect. No off notes whatsoever. If there is a downside, it is the fact that the sherry evens out the complexity of the blend. I mean, surely...that has to be the purpose of a blend: complexity and balance, right....? That said, for the experience alone...all rather lovely and deserving of further exploration...! *40%*

Glenalba Aged 25 Years Sherry Cask Finish batch no. SE/425, lot no. 0274J, dist 1990 (89) n22 t23.5 f22.5 b21.5 A lovely whisky, though again the unreconstructed sherry effect does few favours to the overall layering and balance. Maybe the vaguest hint of something with the 'S' word, though very low key... *40%*

Glen Brynth (70.5) n18 t19 f16 b17.5. Bitter and awkward. *43%*

Glenbrynth Premium Three Year Old (82) n19 t21 f21 b21 An enormously improved, salivating, toasty blend making full use of the rich muscovado sugars on display. Good late spice, too. *43%. OTI Africa.*

Glenbrynth 8 Year Old (88) n21.5 t22 f22.5 b22. An impressive blend which improves second by second on the palate. *40%. OTI Africa.*

Glenbrynth Pearl 30 Year Old Limited Edition (90.5) n22.5 t23.5 f21.5 b23 Attractive, beautifully weighted, no off notes...though perhaps quietened by toffee. Still a treat of a blend. *43%. OTI Africa.*

Glenbrynth Pearl 30 Year Old bott code L8V 7410 28/11/11 (88) n22.5 t22.5 f21 b22 A genuinely strange blend. Not sure how this whisky was mapped out in the creator's mind. A hit and miss hotchpotch but when it is good, it is very good.. *43%. OTI Africa.*

The Glengarry bott code L3/301/15 (80) n19 t21 f20 b20 A brand that would once make me wince has upped its game beyond recognition. Even has the nerve to now possess an attractively salivating as well as silky disposition. *40%. Loch Lomond Group.*

Glen Lyon (85) n19 t22.5 f22 b21.5. Works a lot better than the nose suggests: seriously chewy with a rabid spice attack and lots of juices. For those who have just retired as dynamite testers. Unpretentious fun. *43%. Diageo.*

Glen Talloch Choice Rare & Old (85.5) n20.5 t22.5 f21 b21.5. A very pleasing sharpness to the delivery reveals the barley in all its Speyside-style finery, The grain itself is soothing, especially when the caramel notes kick in. *40%. ncf.*

Glen Talloch Gold Aged 12 Years (85) n21 t22 f21 b21. Impressive grain at work insuring a deft, velvety caress to the palate. Mainly caramel speaking, despite the age, though there is an attractive spice buzz towards the thin-ish finish. *40%*

Glen Talloch Peated (77) n18 t20 f20 b19 The awful tobacco nose needs some serious work on it. The taste is overly sweet, mushy and shapeless, like far too many blends these days. Requires a complete refit. *40%. Boomsma Distillery.*

Glory Leading Aged 32 Years (88.5) n22.5 t22.5 f21.5 b22 At times a little heavy handed and out of sync. But the overall experience is one of stunningly spiced enjoyment. *43%*

Glory Leading Blended Scotch Whisky 30 Years Old American oak casks (93) n22.5 t23 f23.5 b24 a big, clever, satisfying blend which just gets better and better... though not too sure about the Crystal Palace style eagle on the label. Even so, love it! *43%*

Golden Piper (86.5) n22 t21 f22 b21.5. A firm, clean blend with a steady flush through of diverse sugars. The grain does all the steering and therefore complexity is limited. But the overall freshness is a delight. *43%. Whisky Shack.*

Goldfield bott code: L17 02796 CB1 (86) n21 t21.5 f21.5 b22 These days I am minded to give an extra mark to any blend that is not carrying a sulphur trace from the grain receptacles. So an extra mark here, for sure, for this fat and full-flavoured blend which, despite its unashamed cream toffee roundness, enjoys enough spice to punch through for bite, as well as some late hickory. *40%.*

The Gordon Highlanders (86) n21 t22 f21 b22. Lush and juicy, there is a distinctive Speysidey feel to this one with the grains doing their best to accentuate the developing spice. Plenty of feel good factor here. *40%. William Grant & Sons.*

Grand Macnish bott code L16/8404 **(85.5) n21.5 t22 f21 b21** Never a blend for the lily-livered this brand has always been a byword for a whisky with big character. It can still claim that, except now we have a much more absorbing grain at play which undermines the blend's former maltiness. *40%. MacDuff International Ltd.*

Grand Macnish 12 Years Old (86) n21 t22 f21.5 b21.5. A grander Grand Macnich than of old with the wonderful feather pillow delivery maintained and a greater harmonisation of the malt, especially those which contain a honey-copper sheen. *40%. MacDuff.*

Grand Macnish Black Edition charred Bourbon casks, bott code L15 8863 **(94.5) n24 t23.5 f23 b24** A blended whisky classic. *40%. MacDuff International Ltd.*

◇ **Grand Macnish Double Matured Aged 15 Years Sherry Cask Edition** ex-bourbon barrels, Jerez Oloroso sherry butt finish, batch no. 002, bott code: P/000837 **(94) n23.5** so impressive: ripe greengages and gooseberries, all with the added piquancy of extra spice; **t23.5** melt-in-the-mouth grains soften further as light muscovado sugars and sultanas get involved. As on the nose, the spices play a delightfully even game. Always borderline salivating; **f23** extra weight and bitterness as the oak evolves. But residual fruit and sugars are happy to balance matters out; **b24** delighted to report that the sherry involvement is without blemish. This Grand Macnish is very grand, indeed. *43%. Macduff International.*

Grant's Aged 12 Years bott code: L6X 6682 1305 **(96) n24 t24 f23.5 b24.5** There is no doubting that their 12-year-old has improved dramatically in recent years. Doubtless better grain than their standard blend, but also a slightly braver use of phenols has paid handsome dividends. Sits proudly alongside Johnny Walker Black as one of the world's must have 12-year-old blends. For me, the perfect daily dram. *40%.*

Grant's Cask Editions No. 1 Ale Cask Finish bott code: L1X 7354 1809 **(91) n22.5** attractive Demerara firmness and even a malty swirl; the green, youthful freshness charms; **t23** juicy delivery and firmer than the Family Reserve with much more sharpness and clarity; big sugars build; **f22.5** a pleasing spiced mocha fade; **b23** a much cleaner, more precise blend than when this was first launched, with less noticeable beer character: impressive. *40%.*

Grant's Cask Editions No. 2 Sherry Cask Finish bott code: L3Z 7760 0211 **(84.5) n21.5 t22 f20 b21** A lovely fresh, fruity and salivating edge to this even boasting an early honeyed sheen. Complexity has been sacrificed for effect, however. *40%.*

Grant's The Family Reserve bott code: L3A 8017 1711 **(85) n21 t22 f21 b21** What was once the very finest, most complex nose in the entire Scotch whisky lexicon is now, on this evidence, a mushy shadow of its former self. Where once there was a judicious mix of softer and firmer grain to ensure the malts could make the most eloquent of speeches, now there is just a spongy sweetness which shouts loud enough to silence the poetry. If you like your blend fat, sweet, chewy, softer than quicksand and boasting a bitter, vaguely off-key finale here you go. But for those of us who once revered Grant's as the greatest of all standard blends, a whisky whose artistry once gilt-framed the very finest Scotland had to offer, this will not be a glass of cheer. I cannot blame the blender: he can work only with what he has available. And today, after a succession of nonsensical grain distillery closures (nonsensical to anyone who understands whisky, but not the soul-less bean counters who haven't the first clue) the choice in his lab is limited. It would be like blaming the manager of Bradford City for being a third tier football club because they won the FA Cup in 1910. Times change. And not, sadly, always for the better... *40%.*

Grant's Signature bott code: L1Z 7468 1609 **(79) n19 t22 f18 b20** Smudged. *40%.*

◇ **The Great Drams Blended Cask Series 7 Years Old** batch no. 2, bott Feb 20 **(89.5) n22.5** green, clean and youthful, this is a rare blend that appears to have no base notes whatsoever. Both the grains and malts are at the flighty end of the scale; **t23** every bit as fresh and salivating as the nose promises. A surprising degree of saltiness, too, as the barley hits the odd shrill note while the sugars are of melt-in-the-mouth icing sugar-gristiness; **f22** in come the spices; **b22** an exceptionally bright and clean blend to be applauded. But it was like listening to the violins without a single cello to be had. *46.2%.*

The Great Macaulay (86.5) n22 t21.5 f21.5 b21.5 The character is one mainly of trudging, attractive caramel bolstered by busy, warming spice. The nose shows some degree of complexity. By no means unpleasant. *40%. Quality Spirits International.*

◇ **Green Isle Deluxe** bott code: #4878 **(91.5) n22.5** pungent peat is both penetrating but also a soft pillow for the gentle grains; **t23** from the nose it was obvious the grain would be yielding, but it is still a surprise when it arrives this softly. The smoke puffs around the palate like a steam train. The salivating qualities are a real bonus; **f23** you half expect spices to arrive here...and slightly behind schedule they do; **b23** for those who like their blends sending out unambiguous smoke signals. A deep, simplistic but satisfying blend. *40%. Atom Brands.*

Green Plaid 12 Years Old (89) n22 t23 f22 b22 Beautifully constructed; juicy. 40%.

Guneagal Aged 12 Years (85.5) n21 t22.5 f20.5 b21.5. The salty, sweaty armpit nose gives way to an even saltier delivery, helped along by sweet glycerine and a boiled candy fruity sweetness. The finish is a little roughhouse by comparison. 40%. William Grant & Sons.

Haddington House (81) n20 t21 f20 b20 Good grief! This has changed since I last tasted it over a decade ago. Gone is its light, bright juicy character and in its place a singularly sweet, cloying blend due, I suspect, to a very different grain input. 40%. Quality Spirits International.

Haig Gold Label (88) n21 t23 f22 b22 What had before been pretty standard stuff has upped the complexity by an impressive distance. 40%. Diageo.

The Half Century Blend batch no. 4 (95) n24 t24 f23 b24 A rich malt making an absolute nonsense of its age statement. A fruitcake theme then moves into far maltier territory, but it is the sheer beauty of the lush mouthfeel which blows you away. Dark summer cherries and chocolate Maltesers melt into the other while light spices offer a third dimension. The is even a Farley's Rusk moment, though totally in keeping with the narrative... Oh, and look out for the flawless, teasingly understated seem of ulmo honey, too. Stunning. For its age: breathtaking. 45.6%. The Blended Whisky Company.

Hankey Bannister (84.5) n20.5 t22 f21 b21. Lots of early life and even a malt kick early on. Toffee later. 40%. Inverhouse Distillers.

Hankey Bannister 12 Years Old (86.5) n22 t21.5 f21 b22. A much improved blend with a nose and early delivery which makes full play of the blending company's Speyside malts. Plenty of toffee on the finish. 40%. Inverhouse Distillers.

Hankey Bannister 21 Years Old (95) n23.5 a fruity ensemble, clean, vibrant and loath to show its age t24 as juicy as the nose suggests, except for the odd rumble of distant smoke; a firm, barley-sugar hardness as the grains keep control; f23.5 the arrival of the oak adds further weight and for the first time begins to behave like a 21-y-o; long, now with decent spice and with some crusty dryness at the very death; b24 with top dressing like this and some obviously complex secondary malts, too, how can it fail? 43%.

Hankey Bannister 25 Years Old (91) n22.5 t24 f21.5 b23 Follows on in style and quality to 21-year-old. Gorgeous. 40%

Hankey Bannister 40 Years Old (89). n22 t23 f22 b22. This blend has been put together to mark the 250th anniversary of the forging of the business relations between Messrs. Hankey and Bannister. And although the oak creaks like a ship of its day, there is enough verve and viscosity to ensure a rather delicious toast to the gentlemen. Love it! 44%. Inverhouse.

Hankey Bannister 40 Year Old (94) n23.5 t23.5 f23 b24. Pure quality. The attention to detail is sublime. 44.3%. Inverhouse Distillers.

Hankey Bannister Heritage Blend (92) n23 t24 f22 b23 Just so soft and sensual...46%.

Harveys Lewes Blend Eight Year Old batch 4 (93) n23.5 t23 f23 b23.5 First tasted this in the front parlour of legendary Harvey's brewer Miles Jenner's home just after Christmas. It tasted quite different from their previous bottlings – and quite superb. Nosed and tasted now several months on in the cold analytical light of a tasting room...helped along with that deft addition of subtle peat, it still does. Superb! 40%

Hazelwood 18 Year Old (88) n23.5 t22.5 f20.5 b22 Until the final furry moments, a genuine little, understated, charmer. 40%. William Grant & Sons.

Hazelwood 21 Year Old (74) n19 t20 f17 b18. Some decent acacia honey tries to battle against the bitter imbalance. 40%. William Grant & Sons.

Hazelwood 25 Year Old (89.5) n22 t23 f22 b22.5 Distinctly chunky. 40%. WG & Sons.

High Commissioner bott code L2/305/16 (87.5) n21.5 t22.5 f21.5 b22 Boasts an unusually well balanced disposition for a young blend, not at all cowered into being a one trick caramelled pony. Instead, we are treated to a fulsome array of huskier and duskier notes, especially the molasses mixing with a hint of phenol. Delicious. 40%. Loch Lomond Group.

High Commissioner Aged 7 Years Lightly Peated bott code: 22 06 2018 (89) n22.5 t22 f22 b22.5 A seemingly simple malt with a lot of complexity if you want to find it. 40%.

Highland Baron (88.5) n22 t22.5 f22 b22 Has seriously upped the smoke and honey ratio in recent years. Deserves its Baronetcy. 40%. Lombard Scotch Whisky Ltd.

Highland Bird bott code L9Z 6253 2302 (83.5) n21 t21 f20.5 b21 I've had a few of these over the years, I can tell you. Glasses of this whisky, as well. As for the blend, this is by far and away the cleanest, enjoyable and most well-balanced yet: a dram on the up. 40%. QSI.

Highland Black Special Reserve Aged 8 Years bott code: L9A 7064 2906 (86) n21.5 t22 f21 b21.5 Soft, silky, distinctly friendly and unerringly sweet, But definitely a touch too heavy on the toffee. Produced for Aldi.

Highland Harvest Organic Scotch Whisky (76) n18 t21 f19 b18. A very interesting blend. Great try, but a little bit of a lost opportunity here as I don't think the balance is quite right. But at least I now know what organic caramel tastes like... 40%

Highland Mist (88.5) n20.5 t23 f22.5 b22.5 Fabulously fun whisky bursting from the bottle with character and mischief. Had to admit, broke all my own rules and just had to have a glass of this after doing the notes... 40%. *Loch Lomond Distillers.*

Highland Piper (79) n20 t20 f19 b20. Good quaffing blend – if sweet - of sticky toffee and dates. Some gin on the nose – and finish. 40%

Highland Pride (86) n21 t22 f21.5 b21.5. A beefy, weighty thick dram with plenty to chew on. The developing sweetness is a joy. 40%. *Whyte & Mackay Distillers Ltd.*

Highland Queen Blended Scotch Whisky (86.5) n22 t21 f21.5 b22. Lots of grains at play here. But what grains?! Clean and crisp with a superb bite which balances the softening mouthfeel attractively. Old fashioned and delicious. 40%

Highland Queen bott code L12 356 **(87)** n22.5 t22.5 f20.5 b21.5 If the caramels on this could be reduced slightly what a brilliant blend we'd have on our hands here. As it is, the nose is a hotbed of complex intrigue with earthier and lighter honeyed notes combining sublimely while the delivery allows the sugars, vanillas and spices room to make their cases. Bar the spices, just all dies off a little too soon. 40%. *Tullibardine Ltd.*

Highland Queen Aged 8 Years bott code L15 071 **(89.5)** n23 t22.5 f21.5 b22.5 A classy blend showing great character and entertainment value. 40%. *Tullibardine Ltd.*

Highland Queen Aged 12 Years Blended Scotch Whisky (87) n22 t22 f21 b22. A polite, slightly more sophisticated version of the 8-year-old...but without the passion and drama! 40%

Highland Queen Aged 12 Years bott code L15 071 **(90)** n23 t22.5 f22 b22.5 A much weightier blend than it used to be, displaying excellent pace of flavour development on the palate. Decent stuff! 40%. *Tullibardine Ltd.*

Highland Queen Sherry Cask Finish bott code L16 201 **(81.5)** n19 t22 f19 b21.5 The sherry isn't exactly free from sin, and the grape easily overpowers the nuances of the blend itself. So, attractive to a degree, but... 40%. *Tullibardine Ltd.*

Highland Queen 1561 bott code L16/80 28.01.16 **(94)** n23.5 t23.5 f23 b24. As it happens, I have a home where on a living room wall is an old oil painting of Fotheringhay, where the life of Mary Queen of Scots, the Highland Queen, ended on an executioners' block in 1561. Indeed, the house is quite close by and sits near the River Nene which passes through Fotheringhay. The village itself is quiet, particularly fragrant during Spring and Summer and with an unmistakable feel of history and elegance. Not at all unlike this excellent and most distinguished blend. 40%. *Tullibardine Ltd.*

Highland Queen 1561 30 Years Old bott code LF13017261 261 **(88.5)** n23.5 t23.5 f19.5 b22 Shame about the finish. Until then we had one of the sweetest yet gentle blends of the year. 40%.

Highland Reserve (80) n19 t21.5 f19.5 b20 See tasting notes for 43% below. 40%.

Highland Reserve bott code B154 **(80)** n19 t21.5 f19.5 b20 An easy quaffing, silky and profoundly grained, toffee-enriched blend. 43%. *Quality Spirits International.*

Highland Warriors (82) n20 t21 f20.5 b20.5 This warrior must be wanting to raid a few grain stores... 40%. *Quality Spirits International.*

The Highland Way (82.5) n20 t21 f21 b20.5 Grainy, with a big sweet toffee middle which makes for a slightly juicy dram of a class barely distinguishable from so many other standard blends. 40%. *Quality Spirits International.*

The Highland Way bott code B445 **(83.5)** n20 t21.5 f21 b21 More Milky Way than Highland Way... Very similar to the 40% version, except some extra milk chocolate at the finish. 43%. *Quality Spirits International.*

HM The King (89.5) n23 pretty grain dominant. But at least you can nose the constituent parts without colouring clouding the issue. Busy with a light oaky-vanilla involvement; **t22** sugars arrive early, almost with a dissolving icing sugar feel to create a delightfully fresh and mouth-watering feel; **f22** busy light spice plays with the cheerful vanilla; **b22.5** so majestic to find a blend these days not swamped by artificial colouring. Royalty, indeed! 40%. *Branded Spirits USA.*

✦ **Islay Mist Aged 8 Years** bott code: L20 06871 CB2 **(93.5)** n23.5 excellent intertwangling of polite peat and Lubek marzipan...; **t23.5** so rare these days to find a blend that hits the mark with the grains. Their creamy, sweet delivery offers the perfect pillow for the ever-increasing smoke to lay its phenolic head. The midground ups in vanillas; **f22.5** such an impressive array butterscotch and peat notes gently lapping on the taste buds. The light heather honey towards the death underscores the peat and spices even more; **b24** too often their 8-year-old versions have been more a case of Islay Missed than Mist. Not this time: bullseye! I could enjoy that any evening! 40%. *Macduff International.*

Islay Mist Aged 8 Years Amontillado Napoleon Cask Finish bott code L16/8826 **(76)** n19 t20 f18 b19 For those of you not carrying the sulphur recognition gene, I suspect this will be a delight. For those of us that do, well sorry: but not tonight, Napoleon. And this sulphur is a bit of a carry on, MacDuff... 43%. *MacDuff International Ltd.*

Islay Mist Aged 8 Years Manzanilla La Gitana Cask Finish bott code L15/8293 **(85)** n21.5 t22 f20 b21.5 Lots of phenolic cough sweet properties but the fruit and smoke form a tight, enclosed union with little room for scope. The finish is rather too bitter. *40%.*

🔹 **Islay Mist Aged 8 Years Palo Cortado Wellington Finish** bott code: CBSC4 06075 05.08.19 **(81)** n20 t22 f19 b20 Tight, eye-wateringly sharp and fights against friendly integration despite the big lime marmalade theme. The niggling sulphur doesn't help at all. This Wellington has met a Napoleonic-type Waterloo... *43%. Macduff International.*

🔹 **Islay Mist Aged 10 Years** bott code: L20 07001 CB2 **(94)** n23.5 more earthy than smoky: anyone who has traipsed through sodden early spring forests will recognise – and enjoy – this musky aroma...; t23.5 superb delivery: the light maple syrup connects immediately to the phenols to soften the oaky intervention. There is even a slightly gristy twist to this as the malt really takes off; f23 a charming spice buzz enlivens the vanillas. Even at the death the malt is pounding away...; b24 a rare blend where the emphasis is squarely in the malt. One glass of this is a near impossibility.... *40%. Macduff International.*

🔹 **Islay Mist Aged 12 Years** bott code: L19 06053 CB2 **(86.5)** n21.5 t22.5 f20.5 b22 The grains are far more prevalent here than the 10-year-old, giving the blend an attractive softness at the price of complexity. Love the salivating delivery which makes up for the dull, slightly nagging finale. *40%. Macduff International.*

Islay Mist Aged 17 Years bott code L15/8826 **(96)** n24 t24 f23.5 b24.5 A truly brilliant blend that should have no water added and be spared as much time as you can afford. *40%. MacDuff International Ltd.*

🔹 **Islay Mist Aged 21 Years** bott code: L20 07315 CB2 **(94.5)** n24 if there is a more playfully teasing peatiness to any blend, then please come and show me it. Such a beautiful interplay between the smoke and the ganging tannins, though neither barely raise their voice...yet the threat from both is a constant; t23.5 now the grains take the lead, a becalming softness which keeps the smoke in place but allows the muscovado sugars and butterscotch as much liberty as they desire. Even so, spices begin to murmur gently; f23 long and still lightly played with the vanillas boasting the slightest of phenolic hues...; b24 the blender should take a bow. Jolly well played: this is quite superb! *40%. Macduff International.*

Islay Mist Deluxe bott code L16/8283 **(87)** n22 t22 f21.5 b21.5 A charmingly brazen blend, offering young peat to you with far less reserve than it once did. More an Islay Fog than Mist... *40%. MacDuff International Ltd.*

Islay Mist Peated Reserve bott code L15 9:67 **(92.5)** n23.5 t23 f22.5 b23.5 The accent is on subtlety and balance: a very classy piece of whisky engineering. *40%. MacDuff International Ltd.*

Isle of Skye 8 Years Old (94) n23 t24 f23.5 b23.5. Where once peat ruled and with its grain ally formed a smoky iron fist, now honey and subtlety reigns. A change of character and pace which may disappoint gung-ho peat freaks but will intrigue and delight those looking for a more sophisticated dram. *40%. Ian Macleod.*

Isle of Skye 21 years Old (91) n21 t23.5 f23 b23.5 What an absolute charmer! The malt content appears pretty high, but the overall balance is wonderful. *40%. Ian Macleod.*

Isle of Skye 50 Years Old (82.5) n21.5 t21 f20 b20. Drier incarnation than the 50% version. But still the age has yet to be balanced out, towards the end in particular. Early on some distinguished moments involving something vaguely smoked and a sweetened spice. *41.6%*

The Jacobite (78.5) n18 t18.5 f22 b20. Neither the nose nor delivery are of the cleanest style. But comes into its own towards the finish when the thick soup of a whisky thins to allow an attractive degree of complexity. Not for those with catholic tastes. *40%. Booker.*

James Alexander (85.5) n21 t21.5 f21.5 b21.5. Some lovely spices link the grassier Speysiders to the earthier elements. *40%. Quality Spirits International.*

James Buchanan's Special Reserve Aged 18 Years bott code: L7237CE001 **(89)** n22.5 t24 f20.5 b22 A blend I have known and admired a very long time. Since indeed, my beard was black and I carried not an extra ounce of weight. And I am still, I admit, very much in love with, though she has betrayed me with a Spanish interloper... *40%.*

🔹 **James Buchanan's Special Reserve Aged 18 Years** bott code: L0003CE001 **(95.5)** n24 moist Genoa cake at its moistest and most Genoaest...if Genoa means loads of ripe sultanas and raisins. Embracing and comforting.... Oh, and just love that lovely nutty oakiness which acts as a dais for those gentle but unmistakable fruits; t24 the nose had told you the grains would be at their most accommodating, and, my word, it doesn't lie! Silk doesn't quite cover it as delightful layering of malt and caramel makes room for spices and fruit, which come and go slightly more haphazardly; f23.5 long...very long. A little dark cherry, but that vanishes as light Demerara sugars and malt hang on to the vanilla-rich coattails...; b24 so understatedly complex and as always when free from any off-key sherry casks – as this is – sheer class...!!! *40%.*

James King (81) n20 t19.5 f21 b20.5 A slightly more well balanced and equally weighted blend than it once was with better use of spice and cocoa. *43%. Quality Spirits International.*

James King Aged 5 Years (84) n19.5 t21 f21.5 b21.5 While the nose never quite gets going, things are quite different on the palate. And if you find a more agreeable chocolate fudge blend this year, please let me know. *43%. Quality Spirits International.*

James King Aged 8 Years (86) n21 t21 f22 b22 A far better constructed blend than of old, with the grains far more able to deal with the demands of the caramel. Fresh and salivating early on, despite the lushness, one can even fancy spotting the odd malt note before the spiced fudge takes command. *43%. Quality Spirits International.*

James King 12 Years Old (81) n19 t23 f19 b20. Caramel dulls the nose and finish. But for some time a quite beautiful blend soars about the taste buds offering exemplary complexity and weight. *40%. Quality Spirits International.*

James King Aged 12 Years bott code B289 **(84.5) n21 t22 f20.5 b21** The malt has a far grander say than the 40% version, chipping in with an elementary Speyside note on both nose and delivery. It doesn't take long for the fudge-rich grain to take command, though. Easy, un-taxing whisky. *43%. Quality Spirits International.*

J&B Jet (79.5) n19 t20 f20.5 b20. Never quite gets off the ground due to carrying too heavy a load. Unrecognisable to its pomp in the old J&B days: this one is far too weighty and never properly finds either balance or thrust. *40%. Diageo.*

J&B Reserve Aged 15 Years (78) n23 t19 f18 b18. What a crying shame. The sophisticated and demure nose is just so wonderfully seductive but what follows is an open-eyed, passionless embrace. Coarsely grain-dominant and unbalanced, this is frustrating beyond words and not worthy to be mentioned in the same breath as the old, original J&B 15 which, by vivid contrast, was a malty, salivating fruit-fest and minor classic. *40%. Diageo.*

J&B Rare (88.5) n21.5 t22.5 f22 b22.5 I have been drinking a lot of J&B from a previous time of late, due to the death of their former blender Jim Milne. I think he would have been pretty taken aback by the youthful zip offered here: whether it is down to a decrease in age or the use of slightly more tired casks – or both – is hard to say. *40%. Diageo.*

◈ **John Barr Reserve Blend** bott code: L9287 09:38 P/010214 **(84) n21 t22 f20 b21** Never quite gels in the way I am now coming to expect from Whyte and Mackay blends. Lurches about both nose and palate as though unsure of which direction to take. The nose is a little raw, the finish bitter and lightly furry. The nuttiness between does have some attraction, though. *40%.*

Johnnie Walker Aged 18 Years bott code: L7276DN001 **(92) n23 t23.5 f22 b23.5** "The Pursuit of the Ultimate 18 year old Blend," says the label under the striding man. Well, they haven't reached their goal yet as, for all its deliciousness, this falls short of true Johnnie Walker brilliance thanks to an overly soft grain usage, when it was crying out for a variation which included a firmer, ramrod straight grain for extra mouthfeel complexity, and give something for the malts to bounce off. That said, the extra but by no means over enthusiastic use of phenols ensures impressive depth to a genuinely lovely whisky. *40%.*

Johnnie Walker Black Label 12 Years Old (95.5) n23.5 t24.5 f23.5 b24 Here it is: one of the world's most masterful whiskies back in all its complex glory. A bottle like this is like being visited by an old lover. It just warms the heart and excites. *40%. Diageo.*

◈ **Johnnie Walker Black Label 12 Years Old** bott code: L8217CA003 **(95) n23.5 n24 f23.5 b24** Just another example of this blend being in tip-top form and showing a consistency which could almost make you weep with delight. The teasing phenols coupled with its salivating properties make for something rather special. *40%.* ☫

Johnnie Walker Black Label Triple Cask Edition bott code: L8327CB009 **(92.5) n23 t23.5 f22.5 b23.5** Strange this should be in under the Black Label banner as it lacks the associated weight and delicate smokiness. Still silky and seductive, but much more naked grain on show. *40%.*

Johnnie Walker Blenders' Batch Bourbon Cask & Rye Finish bott code L7219CA002 00034598 **(89.5) n21.5 t23 f22.5 b22.5** Great to see someone have the good sense to try to make the most of rye. If they can tame the caramels the results will be better still. *40%. Diageo.*

Johnnie Walker Blender's Batch Espresso Roast bott code: L7233IH007 **(86.5) n21 t23 f21 b21.5** Well, that was different! Can't really big up the nose or finish as it is just too tangy and furry. But the delivery – probably the softest and most well-rounded of any JW I have ever encountered - really does magic up some fabulously intense mocha notes – especially when the varying coffee and chocolate tones criss-cross or merge. The spices don't do any harm, either! *43.2%.*

Johnnie Walker Blender's Batch Wine Cask Blend bott code: L7179CD002 **(91.5) n22.5 t23.5 f22 b23.5** An absolutely unique fingerprint to this member of the Walker family: none has such a fruity yet creamy profile. *40%.*

Johnnie Walker Blue Label (88) n21 t24 f21 b22 What a frustrating blend! Just so close to brilliance but the nose and finish are slightly out of kilter. Worth the experience of the mouth arrival alone. *43%. Diageo.*

◈ **Johnnie Walker Blue Label** bott code: L0010DN007 **(86) n21.5 t23 f20 b21.5** The nose tells the story of this malt without even tasting: tune out of the sulphur-tainted fruit influence and the layering of the honey, vanillas, and lightly-peated malts is a masterpiece. And for a short while you can detect the same genius on the palate. But all that counts for little when the wine influence is so off key. Spotted a thinning of the oils, too, which does little to help the finish – and upon investigation see they have dropped the strength. Remains probably the most frustrating whisky in the world! 40%.

Johnnie Walker Blue Label The Casks Edition (97) n24.5 t24.5 f23.5 b24.5. This is a triumph of scotch whisky blending. With not as much as a hint of a single off note to be traced from the tip of the nose to tail, this shameless exhibition of complexity and brilliance is the star turn in the Diageo portfolio right now. Indeed, it is the type of blend that every person who genuinely adores whisky must experience for the good of their soul....if only once in their life. 55.8%.

Johnnie Walker Blue Label Ghost & Rare bott code: L8277DN006 (96) n24 some fabulous age on this, the oak thinks about strutting ahead of the rest, but a fragile smokiness has just enough energy to keep it in line. Tingling hints of spice match the boiled gooseberry and delicate exotic fruit; t24 salivating on delivery, which is a bit of a shock when you see how much big oak backs it up. The exotic fruit shout of ye olde Speysiders comes into full view, with light molasses and smoke to ensure there is a little rough to go with the smooth; f23.5 medium length, lightly malted and still gently to the end; b24.5 there is nothing new about using dead distilleries within a blend. However, finding them in one as good as this is a pretty rare occurrence. This just creaks of old whiskies all over the show. And what a marvellous show this is...for me, far more entertaining than the standard Blue Label thanks to less sherry influence, allowing the whiskies themselves to show their talents fully. 43.8%. ☞

Johnnie Walker Double Black (94.5) n23 t23.5 f24 b24. Double tops! Rolling along the taste buds like distant thunder, this is a welcome and impressive addition to the Johnnie Walker stable. Perhaps not as complete and rounded as the original Johnnie Walker Black... but, then, what is? 40%.

☞ **Johnnie Walker Double Black** bott code: L9320CA008 (94) n23.5 one of the most citrussy JW noses I've encountered since its creation. The smoke acts as a chunky counterweight, though this is more stinting on the phenols than other bottlings of DB I have encountered; t23 softly softly does it. The grains create the gentlest platforms: a little intermediate vanilla makes its mark, but is sandwiched between a sweeter gristy smokiness and a more rumbling phenol; f23.5 just love it as a little liquorice adds muscle to the phenols, but this is all so polite...especially when a little molasses come into play to ensure a sweetish finale...always the mark of a fine grade whisky; b24 a kiss-and-tell blend with the softness of the grains making this among the most gentle of the blend on the market today, with all its attributes, even the peat, no more than a caress... 40%.

Johnnie Walker Explorers' Club Collection The Gold Route (89) n23.5 t24 f19.5 b22. Much of this blend is truly the stuff of golden dreams. Like its Explorer's Club stable mate, some attention has to be paid to the disappointing finish. Worth sending out an expedition, though, just for the beautiful nose and delivery... 40%. Diageo.

Johnnie Walker Explorer's Club Collection 'The Royal Route' (93) n24.5 t24 f21.5 b23 A fabulous journey, travelling first Class most of the way. But to have discovered more, could have been bottled at 46% for a much more panoramic view of the great whiskies on show. 40%. Diageo

Johnnie Walker Explorers' Club Collection The Spice Road (84.5) n22 t23.5 f18 b21. Sublime delivery of exceptionally intense juiciness: in fact, probably the juiciest blend released this year. But the bitter, fuzzy finish reveals certain casks haven't helped. 40%.

Johnnie Walker Gold Label Reserve (91.5) n23 t24 f22 b23. Moments of true star quality here, but the finish could do with a polish. 40%. Diageo.

☞ **Johnnie Walker Gold Label Reserve** bott code: L9214DN005 (91) n23 disciplined and subtle, there is a very slight milky, tired note from the odd cask here. That said, the malts glisten and sparkle and the bees-waxy sweetness is as prevalent as ever; the thin phenol line could disintegrate at any moment..; t24.5 improbably silky, this has one of the greatest textures of all blended scotch; the honey notes are refined and of deceptive intensity; f21.5 not quite in the same league as the delivery, with that vague milky off-note returning and the caramels having a bigger say than the high quality malts deserves; b22 a mixed bag of a bottling, with far more highs and lows than you'd normally find. Even so, the highs are of Everest proportions; 40%.

Johnnie Walker King George V db (88) n23 t22 f21 b22 One assumes that King George V is no relation to George IV. This has genuine style and breeding, if a tad too much caramel. 43%

Johnnie Walker Platinum Label Aged 18 Years (88) n22 t23 f21 b22. This blend might sound like some kind of Airmiles card. Which wouldn't be too inappropriate, though this is more Business than First... 40%. Diageo.

Johnnie Walker Red Label (87.5) n22 t22 f21.5 b22. The ongoing move through the scales quality-wise appears to suggest we have a work still in progress here. This sample has skimped on the smoke, though not quality. Yet a few months back when I was in the

BA Business Lounge at Heathrow's new Terminal Five, I nearly keeled from almost being overcome by peat in the earthiest JW Red I had tasted in decades. I found another bottle and I'm still not sure which represents the real Striding Man. *40%. Diageo.*

⁂ **Johnnie Walker Red Label** bott code: L8329T5001 **(86) n21.5 t22 f21 b21.5** Seeing as I spend half my life travelling around the globe – or at least did until Covid-19 happened along – I probably get to taste Johnnie Walker Red more than any other blend as it is a staple of the world's Airline Lounges. And I must say it is rare to find two the same as the smoke levels can differ dramatically from one bottle to the next, sometimes peat-less, at other times seemingly not far off a thinned out Caol Ila. So I must say the Striding Man has become a bit of a friend and travelling companion to me. Which makes it all the more odd and ironic that the first time I actually sit down with a bottle of Red for the Whisky Bible for a year or two this is the first to display a furry note and tang. I have noticed that for the last year it had improved impressively, more often than not with a pleasing smoky rumble and on average from the dozen or so different bottles I've sampled from around the globe, a score something like an 89 world be nearer the mark. Only moderate peating to this and the caramels are just a little too enthusiastic: it is reminiscent of when the blend went through a wobble a couple of years back.... Bet you when I'm back travelling again, the first JW Red will be a belter....! *40%.*

Johnnie Walker Select Casks Aged 10 Years Rye Cask Finish (90) n22.5 t23 f21.5 b23 With the use of first fill bourbon casks and ex-rye barrels for finishing, hardly surprising this is the JW with the most Kentuckian feel of them all. Yet it's even more Canadian, still. *46% (92 proof).*

Johnnie Walker X.R Aged 21 Years (94) n23.5 t24 f23 b23.5. How weird: I nosed this blind before seeing what the brand was. My first thought was: "mmm, same structure of Crown Royal XR. Canadian??? No, there's smoke!" Then looked at what was before me and spotted it was its sister whisky from the Johnnie Walker stable. A coincidence? I don't think so... *40%.*

Kenmore Special Reserve Aged 5 Years bott code L07285 **(75) n18 t20 f19 b18.** Recovers to a degree from the poor nose. For those who prefer their Scotch big-flavoured and gawky. *40%*

Label 5 Aged 12 Years bott code L515467C **(90) n23 t22.5 f22 b22.5** One of the easiest drams you'll find this year with just enough complexity to lift it into the higher echelons. *40%.*

Label 5 Extra Rare Aged 18 Years bott code L5301576 **(87.5) n21.5 t22.5 f22 b21.5** You have to say this is pleasant. But from an 18-year-old blend you should be saying so much more. Salivating and at times fresh and juicy, other than the late spice little gets the pulses racing in the vanilla and sugar morass. A tad too much toffee, alas. *40%.*

Label 5 Classic Black bott code L403055D **(87) n22 t22 f21 b22** A malt famed for its indifferent nose now boasts an aroma boasting complexity, layering and spice. The mix of spice and muscovado sugars elsewhere is no less appealing, though the mouthfeel is a little too fat and yielding. But what an improvement! *40%. La Martiniquaise.*

Label 5 Gold Heritage (92) n22.5 t23.5 f22 b24 A very classy blend very skilfully constructed. A stunningly lovely texture, one of the very best I have encountered for a while, and no shortage of complexity ensures this is a rather special blend. I'll even forgive the dulling by caramel and light milkiness from the tired bourbon barrel. The overall excellence outweighs the odd blemish. *40%*

Label 5 Premium Black bott code: L720856A **(84.5) n21 t22 f20.5 b21** An, at first, luscious, then later on ultra-firm blend with the accent decidedly on the grain and caramels. *40%.*

⁂ **Langs Full & Smoky (89) n22.5** quite thin and young but the smoke has a pleasantly caressing effect; **t22.5** sweet and circular on the palate with attractive oils early on. The smoke is always polite if dominant, though vanilla and hickory can be found at the mid-point; **f21.5** dries and bitters very slightly; **b22.5** light and smoky would be a more apt description. But a pleasant peaty blend all the same. *43%.* Ian Macleod Distillers.

⁂ **Langs Rich & Refined (90) n23** beautiful structure to this: nutty and warming, vaguely spiced vanillas – offering both weight and lightness of touch simultaneously; **t22.5** the grains perhaps have the braver say even on delivery, but they are assisted by a glossy oiliness which bigs up the light thread of acacia honey. The midpoint has a distinctly Mars Bar feel of nougat, chocolate and caramel working in unison; **f22** mainly spices carried on the oils; **b22.5** a thoughtfully crafted, quietly complex blend. *46%. Ian Macleod Distillers.*

⁂ **Langs Smooth & Mellow (88.5) n22.5 t22.5 f21.5 b22** No quibbling with the name of this brand! Most of the action is on the graceful nose and honey-flecked delivery which is briefly chewy. The dry and slightly bitter finish, though, doesn't try to compensate for the obvious lack in weight. That apart, agreeably easy going. *43%.* Ian Macleod Distillers.

The Last Drop 1965 American Standard Barrel **(96.5) n24 t24.5 f23.5 b24.5** Almost impossible to imagine a blended whisky to be better balanced than this. If there is a cleverer use of honey or less intrusive oak in any blended whisky bottled in the last year, I have yet to taste it. An award winner if ever I tasted one. Magnificent doesn't quite cover it... *48.6%. Morrison Bowmore. The Last Drop Distillers Ltd.*

The Last Drop 1971 Blended Scotch Whisky 45 Years Old (97) n24.5 t24 f24 b24.5 Even though I now know many of the people involved in the Last Drop, I am still not entirely sure how they keep doing it. Just how do they continue to unearth whiskies which are truly staggering; absolute marvels of their type? This one is astonishing because the grain used is just about faultless. And the peating levels can be found around about the perfect mark on the dial. Like an old Ballantine's which has sat and waited in a cask over four decades to be discovered and tell its wonderful, spellbinding and never-ending tale. Just mesmerically beautiful. 47%.

The Last Drop 50 Year Old Sherry Wood **(97) n24 t24.5 f24 b24.5** You'd expect, after half a century in the cask, that this would be a quiet dram, just enjoying its final years with its feet up and arms behind its head. Instead we have a fairly aggressive blend determined to drive the abundant fruitiness it still possesses to the very hilt. It is backed up all the way by a surprising degree of warming, busy spice. There is a hell of a lot of life in this beautiful ol' dog... 51.2%.

The Last Drop 56 Year Old Blended Scotch Whisky (96.5) n24.5 t24.5 f23.5 b24 Just one of those whiskies there is not enough time in the day for. One to share with your partner... when the lights are low and you are on your own... 47%.

Lauder's bott code L 08 10 14 4 BB **(78.5) n19 t20 f19.5 b20** For those who like whisky with their cream toffee. Decent spice fizz, though. 40%. MacDuff International Ltd.

Lauder's Aged 15 Years bott code L16/8189 **(93) n23 t23.5 f22.5 b24** Not the big fat sherry influence of a decade ago...thank heavens...!! This is a gorgeous blend for dark, stormy nights. Well, any night really... 40%. MacDuff International Ltd.

⬥ **Lauder's Aged 25 Years** bott code: P001434 2020/03/18 **(91) n23** graceful malts and grains merge. This is soft and sultry, the light lime tartness the only note to stick its head above the even sweetness; **t23** the grains are of a wallowing disposition, so enveloping and comforting...like a blanket in a chilly bedroom. But the fruity tines and the bulging, Speyside-style malt gang together for some impressive juiciness; **f22** just a little bitterness at the death, but the butterscotch and barley compensate beautifully; **b23** after two months of incarceration in my British cottage, I moved my tasting room into the garden where the air was still and the whiskies seemed to be more at home: at one with nature. In the cloudless sky a pair of swifts danced for their prey above my garden, one, its head bleached white as it faced the setting sun; the other, as it twisted and turned, reflected the powerful, dying rays off its coal-black wings. To my left a pair of great tits flew to and from their secret chamber in "Mum's" ancient apple tree on their thankless task of feeding their brood. While, just 30 feet away, a crow sat atop a fir, bellowing his mastery over all he surveyed. Meanwhile, a blackbird chinked its evening alarm, much in the way robins do at home in Frankfort. So it was when Archibald Lauder created his first blend in the first half of the 19th century; and so it is now. The finest things in life never change... 42%. MacDuff International.

Lauder's Oloroso Cask bott code L 25 01 16 4 BB **(86.5) n21.5 t24 f19 b22** A magnificent blend for those unable to nose or taste sulphur. For those who can, a nearly whisky as this is borderline brilliant. Yes, both nose and finish especially have their weakness, but the narrative of the delivery, not to mention the brilliance of the mouthfeel and overall weight and pace of the dram is sublime. Before the sulphur hits we are treated to a truly glorious Jaffa cake mix of controlled fruity sweetness as good as any blend I have tasted this year. 40%. MacDuff International Ltd.

Lauder's Ruby Cask bott code L 21 05 15 4 BB **(94) n23 t24 f23 b24** A sophisticated little gem. 40%. MacDuff International Ltd.

Lauder's Queen Mary bott code L 04 11 14 4 BB **(86.5) n22.5 t21.5 f21 b21.5** The sweet oily aroma of Angel Cake and even some roast chestnut: the nose is certainly highly attractive. This almost translates through the body of blend when the caramel allows, the grains showing an oily strain and a slightly malty kick here and there. 40%. MacDuff International Ltd.

⬥ **Liquid Treasures From Miles Away Taraansay 12 Year Old** bourbon barrel, dist Apr 07, bott Feb 20 **(92) n22.5 t23 f23 b23.5** A very pretty, flawlessly structured blend which milks every last degree of juiciness from mix of ulmo honey and light maple syrup which have been liberally sprinkled with spice. Not big on complexity, but knows how to maximise on effect, using the full body and delicate oils with aplomb. So lovely. 59.5%. sc. 249 bottles.

The Loch Fyne (89.5) n22 t23 f21.5 b23. This is an adorable old-style blend...a bit of a throwback. But no ruinous sherry notes...just clean and delicious. Well, mainly... 40%

Loch Lomond Reserve db **(86.5) n21.5 t22 f21.5 b21.5.** A spongy, sweet, chewy, pleasant blend which is more of a take as you find statement than a layering of flavour. 40%

Loch Lomond Signature bott code L3/306/15 **(86) n22 t21.5 f21 b21.5** Not quite the malty force it can be, though the sugar almonds are a treat. Succulent and gently spiced though the caramel has just a little too much force towards the end. 40%. Loch Lomond Group.

Lombard Gold Label (88) n22 t22 f22 b22 after evaluating this I read the tasting notes on the back of the label and for about the first time this year thought: "actually, the bottlers have the description pretty spot on. So tasted it again, this time while reading the notes and found myself agreeing with every word: a first. Then I discovered why: they are my tasting notes from the 2007 Whisky Bible, though neither my name nor book have been credited... A gold label, indeed... 40%.

Long John Special Reserve bott code: 2017/08/10 **(87.5) n21.5 t22.5 f21.5 b22** An honest, non-fussy blend which makes a point of stacking the bigger flavours up front so it hits the ground running. The grains and toffee shape all aspects, other than this rich delivery where the malt offers both weight and a lighter, salivating quality also; an even a gentle thread of honey. The type of blend that an offer for a refill will be seldom refused. 40%.

Lord Elcho (83.5) n20 t22 f21 b20.5 Such a vast improvement on the last bottling I encountered: this has lush grain at the front, middle and rear that entertains throughout, if a little one dimensionally. A little bit of a tweak and could be a high class blend. 40%. Wemyss Malts.

Lord Elcho Aged 15 Years (89.5) n23.5 t22.5 f21.5 b22 Three or four years ago this was a 15-year-old version of the Lord Elcho standard blend today. So, small mercies, this has moved on somewhat and now offers up a genuinely charming and complex nose and delivery. One is therefore surprised to be disappointed by the denouement, taking into account the blend's history. Some more clever and attentive work on the middle and finish would have moved this into seriously high quality blend territory. But so much to enjoy as it is. 40%. Wemyss Malts.

Lord Scot (77.5) n18.5 t20 f19.5 b19.5. A touch cloying but the mocha fudge ensures a friendly enough ride. 40%. Loch Lomond Distillers.

Lord Scot (86.5) n20 t22 f22.5 b22. A gorgeously lush honey and liquorice middle. 43%

The Lost Distilleries Blend batch 9 **(91) n23 t23.5 f22.5 b23** The distilleries may be lost to us, but on the palate they are especially at home. 52.1%. 476 bottles.

Mac Na Mara bott code L 25 08 14 2 07 48 BB **(84) n21.5 t22 f19.5 b21** As usual, a glass of tricks as the flavours come tumbling at you from every direction. Few blends come saltier and the dry vanilla forges a fascinating balance with the rampant caramel. A fraction furry at the death. 40%. Pràban na Linne Ltd.

Mac Na Mara Rum Cask Finish bott code L 23 05 16 3 BB **(86) n22.5 t22 f21 b21.5** Lost a degree of the sugary crispness normally associated with this brand and after the initial rum embrace resorts far too quickly to a caramel-rich game-plan. 40%. ncf. Pràban na Linne Ltd.

Mac's Reserve bott code: L9C 7908 0711 **(84) n21 t21.5 f21 b20.5** Perfectly acceptable, easy going soft and sweet whisky. But if they really want to pay tribute to cooper Jimmy Mackie, the Mac in question, then they should drop the toffee and let the oak do the talking. 40%.

MacArthur's bott code L16/L31 R16/5192 IB 1735 **(87.5) n21.5 t22 f21.5 b22.5** Not quite the tricky and cleverly smoked blend of a few years back. But still a weightier chap than a decade ago, not least because of the softer grain type. The malts do come through with just enough meaning to make for a well-balanced and thoroughly enjoyable offering. 40%.

MacQueens (89) n21.5 t22.5 f22.5 b22.5. I am long enough in the tooth now to remember blends like this found in quiet country hotels in the furthest-flung reaches of the Highlands beyond a generation ago. A wonderfully old-fashioned, traditional one might say, blend of a type that is getting harder and harder to find. 40%. Quality Spirits International.

MacQueens of Scotland Aged 3 Years (86) n20.5 t22 f21.5 b22 Rare to find a blend revealing its age at 3 years, though of course many are that.... and a day. Enjoyable, with attractive weight and even an ulmo honey note to partner the spices which, combined, makes it distinctively a cut above for its type. 40%. Quality Spirits International.

MacQueens of Scotland Aged 8 Years (78.5) n18 t21.5 f19 b20 A little furry and off key. 40%. Quality Spirits International.

MacQueens of Scotland Aged 12 Years (89.5) n23 t22.5 f21.5 b22.5 Some outstanding malts have gone into this charming blend. 40%. QSI.

Master of Malt Blended 10 Years Old 1st Edition (84.5) n21.5 t22.5 f20 b20.5. A pleasant enough, though hardly complex, blend benefitting from the lovely malty, then silky pick-up from delivery and a brief juicy barley sharpness. But unsettled elsewhere due, mainly, to using the wrong fit of grain: too firm when a little give was needed. 47.5%. ncf. WB15/353

Master of Malt 30 Year Old Blended Scotch Whisky (86) n21.5 t23 f20 b21.5 Typical of Master of Malt blends it is the delivery which hits fever pitch in which myriad juicy notes make a mockery of the great age. Sadly, on this occasion both the nose and finish are undone by some ungainly oak interference and, latterly quite a tang. 47.5%.

Master of Malt 40 Year Old Blended Scotch Whisky batch 1 **(93.5) n24 t23.5 f22.5 b23.5** Some outstanding oak at play here. For a blend the grains and malts appear a little isolated from the other, but the overall effect is still wonderful. 47.5%.

Master of Malt 50 Year Old Blended Scotch Whisky (92.5) n24 t23.5 f22 b23 Hard to keep all the casks of over 50 years in line. But so much else is sublime. 47.5%.

Master Of Malt St Isidore (84) n21 t22 f20 b21. Sweet, lightly smoked but really struggles to put together a coherent story. Something, somewhere, is not quite right. 41.4%

Matisse Blended Scotch Whisky (93) n23 adore the squeeze of slightly under-ripe gooseberries to sharpen the soft, acacia honey-sweetened grain. Charming...; t23.5 the flavours are a creamy rendition of the nose, with a little extra vanilla to accompany the honey; f23 long, unusually lush for a blend but a delicate barley hanging on to the end; b23.5 grain-dominated it may be, but there is malt enough – and, importantly, very well selected – to give this blend a distinctively high-end feel. Quietly impressive. 40%. Matisse Spirits Company.

Matisse 12 Years Old (90.5) n23 t23 f22 b22.5 Moved up yet another notch as this brand continues its development. Much more clean-malt oriented with a Speyside-style to the fore. Majestic and charming. 40%. Matisse Spirits Co Ltd.

Matisse Aged 12 Years (88.5) n22 t22 f22 b22.5 Creamy and pleasant, the extra tannins appear to blot out the barley which impresses so well on their standard blend, making the grain here that little bit starker. Extra spice, naturally, with the age and depth. But not quite the same elegance. 40%. Matisse Spirits Company.

Matisse 21 Years Old (86) n23 t22 f20 b21. Begins breathtakingly on the nose, with a full array of exotic fruit showing the older bourbon casks up to max effect. Nothing wrong with the early delivery, which offers a touch of honeycomb on the grain. But the caramel effect on the finish stops everything in its tracks. Soft and alluring, all the same. 40%

Matisse Aged 21 Years (80.5) n22 t22.5 f17 b19 The sulphur rumble on the finish does a dis-service to the chocolate raisin preamble. 40%. Matisse Spirits Company.

Matisse Old (85.5) n20 t23 f21 b21.5. Appears to improve each time I come across it. The nose is a bit on the grimy side and the finish disappears under a sea of caramel. But the delivery works deliciously, with a chewy weight which highlights the sweeter malts. 40%

Matisse Old Luxury Blend (92.5) n23 a lovely weight to this but without the grain being bullied by either peat or tannin. The oak interference is as it should be so the balance between a degree of freshness and outline of age offers a degree of ambiguity; t23 a slight peachy note does the job for the sweetness while the succulent mouthfeel and drier vanillas again hints at age; f23 now really starts shewing off as it reveals it has a light ulmo- and manuka honey blend in reserve and to counter the light spice buzz; b23.5 one of those very classy blends you'd rather not spit out... At 46% would probably go up a point or two. 40%. Matisse Spirits Company.

Matisse Royal (81) n19 t22 f20 b20. Pleasant, if a little clumsy. Extra caramel appears to have scuppered the spice. 40%. Matisse Spirits Co Ltd.

McArthurs (89.5) n22 t22.5 f22 b23 One of the most improved blends on the market. The clever use of the peat is exceptional. 40%. Inverhouse Distillers.

McKendrick's 3 Years Old (71) n18 t20 f16 b17 "Supple, Strong and Silky" boasts the label. Unsubtle, standard 40% abv and silky says the whisky. Cloying to a degree and with a little sulphur off note late on, presumably from the ex-sherry grain casks. Not Asda's finest. 46%. Asda

Monarch of the Glen (81) n20 t21 f20 b20 A youthful grainfest wallowing in its fat and sweet personality. 40%. Quality Spirits International.

Monarch of the Glen Aged 8 Years (82.5) n19 t20.5 f21.5 b21.5 The initially harsh grain takes time to settle but eventually finds a decent fudge and spiced mocha theme. 40%. QSI.

Monarch of the Glen Aged 12 Years (88.5) n22 a lovely fudge note goes well with the mocha; t22.5 has kept its glorious silk texture, though the fruits have vanished. Demerara sugar and chocolate hazelnut; f22 long, soft, slow raising of spice and vanilla; b22 I always enjoyed this for its unusual fruity nature. Well, the fruit has gone and been replaced by chocolate. A fair swap: it's still delicious! 40%. Quality Spirits International.

Montrose (74.5) n18 t20 f18 b18.5. A battling performance but bitter defeat in the end. 40%.

Muirhead's Blue Seal bott code L15 138 780 21 (84.5) n21.5 t21 f21 b21 A clean, uncluttered and attractive blend with heavy emphasis on grain and no shortage of caramel and spice. A distinct wisp of malt can be located from time to time. 40%. Tullibardine Ltd.

The Naked Grouse (76.5) n19 t21 f17.5 b19. Sweet. But reveals too many ugly sulphur tattoos. 40%.

Nation of Scots (92.5) n23 t23 f23 b23.5 Apparently, this is a blend designed to unite Scots around the world. Well, I'm not Scottish but it's won me over. If only more blends could be as deliciously embracing as this. 52%. Annandale Distillery.

Northern Scot (68) n16 t18 f17 b17. Heading South bigtime. 40%. Bruce and Co. for Tesco.

Oishii Wisukii Aged 36 Years (96) n24.5 t23.5 f24 b24 Normally, I'd suggest popping into the Highlander for a pint of beer. But if they happen to have any of this stuff there...break his bloody arm off: it's magnificent! 46.2%. The Highlander Inn, Craigellachie.

Old Masters G (93) n24 t23 f23 b23 A high quality blend with enough clarity and complexity to suggest they have not stinted on the malt. The nose, in particular, is sublime. Thankfully they have gone easy on the colouring here, as it this is so delicate it could have ruined the artistry. 40%. Lombard Scotch Whisky Ltd.

Old McDonald (83.5) n20 t22 f20.5 b21. Attractively tart and bracing where it needs to be with lovely grain bite. Lots of toffee, though. *43.%. The Last Drop Distillers. For India.*

Old Parr 12 Years Old (91.5) n21.5 t23.5 f23 b23.5 Perhaps on about the fourth of fifth mouthful, the penny drops that this is not just exceptionally good whisky: it is blending Parr excellence... *40%. Diageo.*

Old Parr Aged 15 Years (84) n19 t22 f21 b22. Massively massive sherry input here. Some of it is of the highest order. The nose, reveals, however, that some isn't... *43%*

Old Smuggler (85.5) n21 t22 f21 b21.5. A much sharper act than its Allied days with a new honeyed-maple syrup thread which is rather delightful. Could still do with toning down the caramel, though, to brighten the picture further. *40%. Campari, France.*

Old St. Andrews Clubhouse batch no. L2997 G2716 (87.5) n21.5 t22 f22 b22 Just a little extra grain bite to this one means the usual juiciness is down, though the slow spice build is pretty sexy. Lots of coffee-toffee tones to chew over. *40%.*

◇ **Outlaw King** bott code: L19 199 PB (90) n23 very young, vibrant malt joyfully pulsing out a sweet peatiness lightened by a charming citrus not so much sub-plot as side-plot...; t22.5 though the body is thin and very little age is evident, the smoke still works rather beautifully in conjunction with the limited vanillas. The result is a juiciness rare to a peated whisky with excellent layering towards the middle; f22 a lightly smoked, delicately spiced chocolate fade; b22.5 more of an Outlaw Queen with a delicate but shapely body like this. And, indeed, once upon a time blends displaying this degree of naked peatiness were outlawed. Blenders veered away from smokiness after the Second World war to concentrate on lighter, softer creations. With smoke very much back in vogue it is great to see a blend shewing so little reserve in its peaty intent. *40%. Annandale Distillery.*

Passport bott code LKBL0720 2017/02/24 (81.5) n20 t21 f20 b20.5 Still can't get used to the brash golden colour of the whisky that shines back at me. This was once the Passport to whisky sophistication: pale and glistening on the palate rather than from the bottle with its cut glass, precision flavour-profile – First Class in every way. Now it is fat, flat, chewy, and fudged in every sense of the word. *40%. Chivas Brothers Ltd.*

◇ **Passport** bott 2019/08/11 (83.5) n20 t21.5 f21 b21 Just a fleeting moment after the delivery when Jimmy Laing old masterpiece flashes onto the scene only to be quickly eviscerated by the uncompromising caramels. *40%*

Parkers (78) n17 t22 f20 b19. The nose has regressed, disappearing into ever more caramel, yet the mouth-watering lushness on the palate remains and the finish now holds greater complexity and interest. *40%. Angus Dundee.*

Pure Scot bott code: L 08 02 17 (87) n21.5 t22.5 f21.5 b22 The grain is both yielding and profound while the malt notes mostly are lost in a toffee swirl. Mid to late arrives spices, but complexity is at a premium and the structure perhaps a little too soft. That said, a little acacia honey goes a long way and the overall experience is very satisfying indeed, especially with the sugars always slightly ahead of the game. *40%. Bladnoch Distillery.*

Pure Scot Virgin Oak 43 virgin oak cask finish, bott code: L18/89.7 (93) n23 23.5 f23 b23.5 A sensational little blend worth finding. Not particularly complex as to regards malt and grain layering, but the integration of the tannins for a blend is a rare joy. *43%. Bladnoch Distillery.*

Queen Margot (85.5) n21.5 t22 f21 b21. A clean, silky-textured, sweet and caramel-rich blend of disarming simplicity. *40%*

Queen Margot (86) n21 t22 f21.5 b21.5. A lovely blend which makes no effort to skimp on a spicy depth. Plenty of cocoa from the grain late on but no shortage of good whiskies put to work. *40%. Wallace and Young for Lidl.*

Queen Margot Aged 5 Years (89) n22 t22.5 f22 b22.5 A very attractive blend with a most agreeable level of chewability. The chocolate orange which bolsters the yielding grain appears to suggest some good, clean sherry influence along the way. *40%*

Queen Margot Aged 8 Years (85) n21 t22 f21 b21. Pleasant, untaxing, with a hint of oaky vanilla after the sugary crescendo. *40%*

◇ **Richardson** bott L9176028 (85) N21 t21.5 f21 b21.5 A grain heavy gentle blend which emphasis sweetness over complexity. Charmingly clean, no off notes and super-easy drinking. *40%.*

Robert Burns (85) n20 t22.5 f21 b21.5. Skeletal and juicy: very little fat and gets to the mouthwatering point pretty quickly. Genuine fun. *40%. Isle of Arran.*

The Royal & Ancient (80.5) n20 t21.5 f19 b20. Has thinned out dramatically in the last year or so. Now clean, untaxing, briefly mouth-watering and radiating young grain throughout. *40%*

Royal Park (87.5) n22 t22 f22 b21.5 A significantly improved blend which though still showing toffee appears to have cut down the amount, to the advantage of the busy vanilla, Demerara sugar and increased spices. Wholly enjoyable. Incidentally, the label helpfully informs us: "Distilled and Matured in Oak Casks." Who needs stills, eh...? *40%. Quality Spirits International.*

Royal Salute 21 Years Old bott code LKSK2858 2016/07/13 **(96)** n24 t23.5 f24 b24.5 Elegant, sensual and the epitome of great blending. What else would you expect...? 40%. *Chivas Brothers.*

Royal Salute 21 Year Old The Lost Blend (95.5) n24 t24 f23.5 b24 Lost Blend...? Panic over, chaps: discovered it in my Whisky Bible tasting lab....!! And well worth finding, too.... 40%.

Royal Salute 21 Years Old The Polo Collection bott code 2017/04/25 LPNL0722 **(95)** n23.5 t23.5 f24 b24 A significantly different RS21 to the last standard bottling I came across, this being very much meatier – which is rather apt seeing that horses are involved. Mixes suave sophistication with a certain ruggedness: not unlike polo, I suppose. Not a dram to chukka away under any circumstances... 40%. *Chivas Brothers Ltd.*

Royal Salute 21 Year Old Polo Collection 3 (92) n23 t23.5 f22.5 b23 As soft as a velvet polo jumper... 46.5%.

Royal Salute 25 Year Old The Signature Blend (93) n24 t23.5 f22.5 b23 A curious blend which both underlines its age, yet with the lightness of touch, then proceeds to hide it, too. 40%.

Royal Salute 32 Years Old Union of the Crowns bott code 2017/01/17 LPNL0102 (96.5) n24 t24.5 f24 b24 I trust Nicola Sturgeon has given The Union of Crowns, this truly outstanding and worthy Scotch blend to celebrate the joining the kingdoms of England, Scotland and Ireland, her seal of approval and she will help promote it fervently as a great Scottish export... 40%.

Royal Salute 38 Years Old Stone of Destiny bott code 2016/12/20 LPNK2479 **(93.5)** n24 t23.5 f22.5 b23.5 Knowing the blender and having a pretty educated guess at the range of stocks he would have to work from, I tried to picture in my mind's eye how this whisky would nose and taste even before I opened the bottle. In particular, I tried to pre-guess the mouthfeel, a character vital especially in older blends but often overlooked by those who eventually taste it, though it actually plays a significant role without the drinker realising it. Well, both the nose and mouthfeel were just as I had imagined, though some aspects of the finish were slightly different. An engrossing and elegant dram. 40%. *Chivas Brothers Ltd.*

Royal Salute 62 Gun Salute (95.5) n24.5 t24 f23 b24 How do you get a bunch of varying whiskies in style, but each obviously growing a grey beard and probably cantankerous to boot, to settle in and harmonise with the others? A kind of Old People's Home for whisky, if you like. Well, here's how...43%. *Chivas.*

Royal Salute The Diamond Tribute (91) n23.5 t23 f21.5 b23. Ironic that a diamond is probably the hardest natural creation, yet this whisky is one of man's softest... 40%. *Chivas.*

Royal Salute The Eternal Reserve (89.5) n23 t23.5 f21 b22 One of those strange whiskies where so much happens on the nose and delivery, but much less when we head to the finish 40%

Royal Silk Reserve Aged 5 Years (92.5) n23 t23 f23 b23.5 I was lucky enough to be the first person outside the tasting lab to sample this whisky when it was launched at the turn of this century. It was quite wonderful then, it still is so today though the grains aren't quite as brittle and translucent as they were back then. Still, I admire beyond words the fact that the current blenders have eschewed the craze for obscuration by ladelling in the colouring as though lives depended on it. What we can nose and taste here in this heart-gladdeningly light (both in colour and personality) blend is whisky. As an aside, very unusual for a blend to hide its age away on the back label. 40%.

Royal Warrior (86) n21 t22 f21.5 b21.5. An entirely pleasant grain-rich, young, old fashioned blend which masters the prevalent sugars well when they appear to be getting out of hand. Extremely clean and beautifully rounded. 40%

Sandy Mac (76) n18 t20 f19 b19. Basic, decent blend that's chunky and raw. 40%. *Diageo.*

Scots Earl (76.5) n18 t20 f19 b19.5. Its name is Earl. And it must have upset someone in a previous life. Always thrived on its engaging disharmony. But just a tad too syrupy now. 40%.

Scottish Collie (78) n18 t20 f20 b20 I thought I heard you saying it was a pity: pity I never had any good whiskies. But you're wrong. I have. Thousands of them. Thousands of them. And all drams.... 40%. *Quality Spirits International.*

Scottish Collie (80) n20 t21 f19 b20 A greatly improved blend with a far more vivacious delivery full of surprising juiciness and attractively controlled sweetness. Not as much toffee influence as had once been the case, so the spices cancels out the harsh finish. 43%. *QSI.*

Scottish Leader Aged 12 Years bott code P037533 L3 09.18 16082 **(89.5)** n22 t23 f22 b22.5 A vast improvement on the last Leader 12 I encountered, this really finding a relaxed yet intriguing style. 40%.

Scottish Leader Original bott code P03 555 L 08.35 16342 **(83)** n19 t22 f21 b21 Had this been the "original" Scottish leader I tasted 20 or so years ago we'd have a lighter coloured, less caramel heavy, more malt sparkling whisky. As it is, overcomes a cramped nose to offer some excellent complexity on delivery. 40%.

Scottish Leader Signature bott code P038914 L316256 **(90.5)** n22 t23.5 f22 b23 Thoroughly enjoyable and beautifully constructed blend in which thought has clearly gone into both weight, texture and flavour profiling: not a given for blends these days. The nose and delivery are waxy with a vague honey richness; the delivery uses that honey to full effect by offering a growing firmness and then busy interplay between light oak, spices and weightier malts. Had they gone a little easier on the dumbing-down toffee, this might have bagged an award. *40%.*

Scottish Leader Supreme bott code P039255 L3 14.21 16278 **(77)** **n18.5 t20 f19 b19.5** Sticky, sweet and overly simple. *40%.*

Scottish Piper (80) n20 t20 f20 b20. A light, mildly- raw, sweet blend with lovely late vanilla intonation. *40%*

Scottish Piper bott code L17033 **(82) n20 t20 f21.5 b20.5** Continues its traditional toffee drone, though with a spicier finale than before. *40%. Burlington Drinks.*

Scottish Prince (83.5) n21 t22 f20 b20.5. Muscular, but agreeably juicy. *40%*

Sia Blended Scotch Whisky (87) n21 t22.5 f21.5 b22. Rare to find a blend that's so up front with its smoke. Doesn't scrimp on the salivation stakes or sheer chewiness, either. *43%*

Sir Edward's Aged 12 Years bott 18-09-2018, bott code: L826170-00150 **(87.5) n22 t22 f21.5 b22** Worth having around the house for the charming 1930s's-style label alone. They make big play of the brand having been around since 1891 – the year of my maternal grandmother's birth! – and even have 1891 included in the mould of the bottle. But an unnecessary over-reliance of caramel takes the score down. There is enough evidence on the early clarity and texture of the grain that this blend could hold its own and entertain thoroughly in its natural state. Rather lovely spices counter the sweetness impressively. Simple, but genuinely enjoyable whisky. *40%. Bardinet.*

Sir Lawrence bott code: L17 03274 CB2 **(87) n21 t22.5 f21.5 b22** An impressively clean blend having been matured in better quality oak. This allows you to enjoy the full-throttle delivery without fear of any tangy, off-note sub plots. The caramels do get a little too enthusiastic towards the end but before then the grain and Demerara sugars dig in for a delicious degree of mocha. *40%.*

Something Special bott code LPFK 1116 2016/06/30 **(90) n22 t22.5 f23 b22.5** One of the few blends that has actually improved in recent years. Always been an attractive, interesting if non-spectacular blend which I have enjoyed when meeting it at various bars with friends around the world. Now there is personality enough to punch through the toffee and leave you wanting more. *40%. Chivas Brothers Ltd.*

Something Special Legacy (92) n23 t22.5 f23 b23.5 Good, solid blender is David Boyd. And here he has married substance with subtlety. Lovely stuff. *40%*

❖ **The Sovereign 45 Years Old Blended Scotch** cask no. 15894, dist Dec 73, bott Mar 19 **(94.5) n23.5** natural caramels give the softest possible backdrop to the quiet but determinedly probing spices and sharpening levels of aged fruit, gooseberries in particular...; **t23.5** one of those whiskies where I had to put the glass down, put my arms to the back of my head, lie back into them and chew. Or, rather, let it dissolve. A mix of sticky dates and thinned molasses with a touch of maple honey. But the vanillas are thick, too, to absorb the sweetness; **f24** not sure where the middle ends and the finish starts. Certainly gets spicier and spikier as it progresses, but never anything remotely vicious; **b23.5** falls under the luxuriant heading for a blended scotch. Soft, silky and unravels at the most gentle of paces. *51%. sc. 300 bottles. Bottled for The Whisky Barrel.*

Stag Hunter (79) n19 t20 f20 b20 Hard to get past the gin-type nose. Not sure if this is a bottling hall issue, or if we have a blend that celebrates a botanical-style personality. *40%. Burlington Drinks.*

Storm (94) n23 t23.5 f24 b23.5. A little gem of a blend that will take you by storm. *43%.*

Teacher's Aged 25 Years batch 1 **(96.5) n24 t24.5 f23.5 b24.5** Only 1300 bottles means they will be hard pushed to create this exact style again. Worth a go, chaps: considering this is India bound, it is the Kama Sutra of blended scotch. *46%. Beam Inc. 1300 bottles. India & Far East Travel Retail exclusive.*

Teacher's Origin (92) n23 t23 f23 b23 Almost brings a tear to the eye to taste a Scotch blend that really is a blend. With a better grain input (Dumbarton, say),this perhaps would have been one of the contenders of World Whisky of the Year. Superb! *40%*

Teacher's Origin (88.5) n22 t23.5 f21 b22 A fascinating blend among the softest on the market today. That is aided and abetted by the exceptionally high malt content, 65%, which makes this something of an inverted blend, as that, for most established brands, is the average grain content. What appears to be a high level of caramel also makes for a rounding of the edges, as well as evidence of sherry butts. The bad news is that this has resulted in a duller finish than perhaps might have been intended, which is even more pronounced given the impressive speech made on delivery. Lovely whisky, yes. But something, I feel, of a work in progress. Bringing the caramel down by the percentage points of the malt would be a very positive start... *42.8%. ncf.*

Té Bheag bott code L 06 12 16 3 **(83)** **n19 t22 f21 b21** Reverted to its mucky nose of yore but though caramel has the loudest voice it has retained its brilliant spice bite. *40%. ncf.*

Tesco Special Reserve Minimum 3 Years Old bott code L6335 16/04171 **(83.5)** **n19 t22 f21.5 b21** Improved of late. Now unashamedly in the date and walnut school of blends, where before it had only dabbled; thick, uncompromisingly sweet and cloying but with enough spice and salivation to make for pleasant and characterful bit of fun. *40%.*

Ushers Green Stripe (85) **n19 t22.5 f21.5 b22.** Upped a notch or two in all-round quality. The juicy theme and clever weight is highly impressive and enjoyable. *43%. Diageo.*

Walton Royal Blend Deluxe Reserve (91.5) **n22.5 t23 f23 b23** It's amazing what a dose of good quality peaty whisky can do to a blend. Certainly ensures it stands out as a deliciously chewy – and smoky – experience.*43%*

⬧⬧⬧ **Whisky Works Quartermaster 11 Year Old Blended Scotch 2019/WV02./MX** bott code: L9263 09:08 P/010456 **(89)** **n24** oh, what joy! The malt is out in force and, seemingly unencumbered by caramel, giving as bright and brilliantly fresh display as any blend you'll find this year. But, better, still the malt and grain appear so at ease with the other, that the layering hits almost perfect. Love the orange blossom honey and the grassy barley in total harmony here...; **t24** I am almost drowning in my own saliva! This is as juicy as any blend encountered this year. But, even better, rather than just letting you stew in their barley juices, they limit the development of that and set off in a slightly creamier, more milk chocolatey direction. Buttery with the hinted sweetness of ulmo honey...but the sharper barley notes are always lurking somewhere; **f19** at first the very weakest of a furry note comes off the grains, but there is so much else going on, mainly to do with mocha, that it is hard to concentrate that particular blemish. Eventually the sulphur note builds considerably so you have no choice...; **b22** there is malt, malt, juicy to a fault, in the blend, in the blend....there is grain, grain, that proves to be a pain, in the Quartermaster's Blend. My eyes are dim, I cannot see, I'm glad I brought my nose with me. I'm glad I brought my nose with me... *46.4%. nc ncf. 1,593 bottles.*

White Horse (90.5) **n22 t23 f22.5 b23** A malt which has subtly changed shape. Not just the smoke which gives it weight, but you get the feeling that some of Diageo's less delicate malts have been sent in to pack a punch. As long as they are kept in line, as is the case here – just – we can all enjoy a very big blend. *40%. Diageo.*

⬧⬧⬧ **White Horse (94.5)** **n24** the best nose on a White Horse since the early '80s. The grains are both firm and soft, as they should be, almost shimmering on the nose, while the peat straddles the two with rare dexterity. Just the faintest trace of golden syrup...but the peat sweetens as well as deepens...; **t23.5** sublime delivery. Both the grain and phenols have locked closely together, so you can barely tell them apart. The caramels have arrived just behind the delivery and politely remove themselves to allow the grain and modicum of malt safe passage; **f23** the spices arrive with their sleeves rolled up, but decide to bathe in the serenity of the vanilla-rich grain and delicate smoke; **b24** a masterclass in how to use peat with precision to both raise the profile and complexity of a blend giving it both weight and gravitas, but never allowing it to pompously govern or overwhelm the myriad little other battles going on in the glass. A real old school blend which, I admit, is one I am drawn to when watching old black and white British movies. A charming taste of true tradition. *40%* 🏆

White Horse Aged 12 Years (86) **n21 t23 f21 b21.** Enjoyable, complex if not always entirely harmonious. For instance, the apples and grapes on the nose appear on a limb from the grain and caramel and nothing like the thoroughbred of old. Lighter, more flaccid and caramel dominated. *40%. Diageo.*

White Walker bott code: L8282KS002 **(80)** **n19 t22.5 f19 b20.5** Pouring from the top. As you might expect, there is no nose when frozen, other than the vaguely discernible, ultra clean tip of the grain. The big surprise is that there is a decent degree of flavour on delivery – again the grains at work and carrying a presentable amount of Demerara sweetness and here's the real shock...a very thick, chewable, oily body. So, early on, much more character than I expected. But the finish is as non-specific as I had feared and trails off with a certain bitterness. OK, that was it unshaken, and pouring from the top:

〰️ Now shaken: **(85.5)** **n19.5 t22 f22 b22** By shaking before pouring. You lose some of the early richness of the body. But there is a degree of oak on the aroma and the delivery and the sugars now last the pace, spreading more evenly over the scattered oils. There are now even spices at work late on in this much better-balance dram. *41.7%. Both tasted direct from the freezer (directly after two days at sub-zero temperatures) as instructed on the bottle.*

〰️ Tasted Murray Method: bott code: L8282KS002 **(90)** **n22 t23 f22.5 b22.5** a surprisingly agile and entertaining blend. Untaxing, clean, pleasantly sweet and just so easy to enjoy. *41.7%.*

⬧⬧⬧ **Whyte & Mackay** bott code: P/011524 01:36 L0049 **(88.5)** **n22 t22.5 f21.5 b22.5** Very few things in life don't change over time. But I have to say the extraordinary lushness of character of a Whyte and MacKay is one of them. Maybe I'm imagining things, but it seems to have taken its foot off the caramel slightly, allowing the malts and grains in particular to showcase their wares with a little extra confidence. The result is a subtly sweeter dram, the date and walnut cake – the blend's signature tune – still there in all its glory, but the extra vanillas of the grain in particular, slightly extra succulence of the malt both making their mark. Toasty and tasty at the finish, this is a blend that is moving almost imperceptibly towards sunnier ground. The dullest of sulphur notes on the finish prevents this from scoring even more highly: my guess it is from old sherry butts used to store the grain. But I refuse to let that spoil the overall enjoyment of this blend, of which there is much. 40%.

Whyte & Mackay Aged 13 Years bott code L6334 14/04116 **(89.5) n22 t23.5 f22 b22** Like the standard Whyte and Mackay...but thirteen years old and a little lighter... 40%.

◇ **Whyte & Mackay Aged 50 Years (96) n24.5** anyone who doesn't shut off the world for 15 minutes and devote that miniscule period of their life to simply breathing in the story of this blend, really don't deserve to have a bottle. This is rich in date and figs, not young fruit, of course. But when it is near exploding with maturity. The sugars are kept in check by the tannins which offer a salty edge to this, as well unusually gentle spices It has that rounded feel of a long marriage between grains and malts before bottling...and a high malt content to boot. Yes, rounded....but not silky as there is nothing here to lull you into a false sense of ease. The light black peppers, the varied dark sugars are always on the move and interchanging in intensity. A true delight...; **t24** a fascinating two-toned delivery. At one and the same time that rounded frame so noticeable on the nose offers delicate caress, while at the same time far more militant tannins prod and nip slightly so your tongue doesn't know whether to investigate the busier, oakier element or be attracted to the far more gentile grain. Either way the fruit builds, as do the juicier qualities – so you find a 50-year-old blend that makes you salivate – perhaps in the same way a poke in the eye makes your eyes water...; **f23.5** very toasty as the more lively sugars have mainly burned off now leaving tangier tannins which dry – though never to be point of being uncomfortable – and there are molasses enough retained for the balance never to be compromised; **b24** age issues from every pore of this blend like sweat from a long-distance runner. And this certainly has travelled a distance, as I get the feeling some of the whiskies here are well beyond their 50th birthday. A classy blend which give you the feeling of the great age like a sports car fills you with sensations of power and speed. 44.6%. 175th Anniversary. 🏆

Whyte & Mackay Triple Matured bott code 16/04120 L6329 **(86.5) n21 t23.5 f20.5 b21.5** The kind of blend you can not only stand your spoon up in but your knife - table or carving - and fork – table or pitch - as well. The nose suggests something furry is in the offing which, sadly, the finale confirms. But the delivery really is such wonderful fun! Thick with intense toffee, which shapes both its flavour and mouthfeel, and concentrated date and walnut cake. Roasty yet sweet thanks to the molasses this is about the chewiest blend on the market today. 40%.

◇ **William Cadenhead's 20 Year Old Blend** batch no. 3 **(91.5) n23 t23.5 f22 b23** There are a depressingly withering number of us who used, each year, to head to Campbeltown not to visit the distilleries - you couldn't then gain access – but to find the Cadenhead blends which had a truly unique character and offered something no other blend could get remotely near to. Indeed, I remember driving back once not with a boot full or Springbank but blended malt that I knew would get my whisky loving friends to see this type of whisky in an entirely new light. So my heart skips a beat at the sight of Cadenhead blend in a way few others these days might – we are talking close on 40 years of memories here. The grains on this one are sublime, offering both softness and rigid backbone (a style now criminally rare) but 35 years ago there was no sulphur to worry about on the sherry butts. Here a little has crept in, visible on the finish. A shame, as biting freshness on the grape early on is a salivating joy; the determined firmness of the grain to control it, a whisky lovers delight. 46%.

◇ **William Lawson** bott code: L19182ZA80 **(87) n21.5 t22 f21.5 b22** A heady, honeyed dram which puts far more emphasis on weight than most blends out there these days. The caramels do gang up momentarily, but the overall score boasts harmony...and even more honey...!! 40%.

◇ **The Woodsman** freshly built oak casks & double-scorched bourbon barrels, bott code: L0118 22:04 P/011830 **(92.5) n23** highly attractive vanilla layering with a degree of covert smokiness cleverly weighing anchor. The toffee tones are restrained; **t23** the grain ensures the flavours stick around for maximum time and achieve top billing. This is lightly oiled silk making every last atom of the heather honey count for the positive. The mid-ground heads towards nuttiness with a cocoa and marzipan depth; **f23** a gorgeous chocolate toffee/butterscotch tart hybrid, all served up on those stunning grainy oils; **b23.5** one of the things so often overlooked in a whisky is the mouthfeel. The label of this blend talks much about the wood types. But the reason they work so well is because they have created a structure to the whisky which allows you to explore those flavours to their maximum. A kind of Whyte and MacKay, but with extra depth. Very impressed! 40%.

Irish Whiskey

Of all the whiskies in the world, it is Irish which probably causes most confusion amongst both established whisk(e)y lovers and the novices.

Ask anyone to define what is unique to Irish whiskey - apart from it being made in Ireland and the water likewise coming from that isle - and the answer, if the audiences around the world at my tastings are anything to go by, are in this order: i) it is triple distilled; ii) it is never, ever, made using peat; iii) they exclusively use sherry casks; iv) it comes from the oldest distillery in the world; v) it is made from a mixture of malted and unmalted barley.

Only one of these answers is true: the fifth. Though other countries are now paying the compliment of aping this style.

And it is this type of whiskey, known as Irish Pot Still, which has again - indeed, for the tenth consecutive year - been named as Irish Whiskey of the Year. In 2016 it was the Midleton Dair Ghaelach, in 2014 and 2013 it was the Redbreast 12-years-old and in 2012 Power's John's Lane. Last year it was, just like 2017 and previously in 2015, the Redbreast 21-years-old. Redbreast 12 Cask Strength ran away with the prize in both 2019 and 2012. This year Midleton Barry Crockett Legacy has prevented the hat-trick. Considering that 25 years ago Irish Distillers had decided to end the bottling of Pure Pot Still, not bad. Just shows what a little campaigning can do.... Remarkable as it may seem, after the best part of a century of contraction within the industry, much of it as painful as it was brutal, there were only four distilleries operating on the entire island of Ireland in the autumn of 2011. Now there are over 20. The question is: how many are planning to make a Pot Still to challenge Midleton's...?

Jim Murray's Whisky Bible Irish Whiskey of the Year Winners

	Irish Whiskey	Irish Pot Still Whiskey	Irish Single Malt	Irish Blend
2004/5	Jameson	N/A	N/A	N/A
2006	Bushmills 21	N/A	N/A	N/A
2007	Redbreast 15	N/A	N/A	N/A
2008	Tyrconnel 10	N/A	N/A	N/A
2009	Jameson 07	N/A	N/A	N/A
2010	Redbreast 12	N/A	N/A	N/A
2011	Sainsbury's Dun Leire 8	N/A	N/A	N/A
2012	Powers John's Lane	N/A	Sainsbury's Dun Leire 8	N/A
2013	Redbreast 12 Year Old	Redbreast 12 C.Strength	Bushmills Aged 21	Jameson
2014	Redbreast 12 C.Strength	Redbreast 12 C.Strength	Bushmills Aged 21	Jameson
2015	Redbreast Aged 21	Redbreast Aged 21	Bushmills Aged 21	Jameson
2016	Midleton Dair Ghaelach	Midleton Dair Ghaelach	SMWS 118.3 Cooley 1991	Powers Gold Label
2017	Redbreast Aged 21	Redbreast Aged 21	Bushmills Aged 21	Jameson
2018	Redbreast Aged 21	Redbreast Aged 21	Bushmills Aged 16	Bushmills Black Bush
2019	Redbreast 12 C.Strength	Redbreast 12 C.Strength	Bushmills Aged 12	Bushmills Black Bush
2020	Redbreast 12 C.Strength	Redbreast 12 C.Strength	Bushmills Aged 21	Jameson
2021	Midleton Barry Crockett	Midleton Barry Crockett	Bushmills Port Cask Reserve	Bushmills Black Bush

Pure Pot Still

DINGLE County Kerry. 2012. Porterhouse Group.

⬩ **Dingle Pot Still Third Release** db **(93.5) n23.5** very young. But a freshly cut grass feel to this. Very clean and salivating even before you taste it...! A hint of lemon blossom honey, too...; **t23.5** wow! That really is clean and clear. As on the nose, the barley is basically untroubled by such things as tannin and has a pretty open road to display its wares. A little tanginess at the mid-ground, but the juiciness rises, as does the light marmalade now. How anyone cannot fall in love with the salivatory properties of this whiskey, I really don't know...; **f23** the finish is mainly about the chocolate, as the oak does have a say after all. But that distinctive barley-riddled juiciness still plays an impressively keen part; **b23.5** this is a very impressive pot still whiskey, by which I assume they mean there is unmalted barley. Truly wonderful and can't wait to see this mature into something rather special... 46.5%. ncf. 3,400 bottles.

KILBEGGAN County Westmeath. 1757, recommenced distilling 2007. Beam Suntory.

⬩ **Kilbeggan Single Pot Still Irish Whiskey** bott code: L19130 05/12/19 db **(89.5) n23** though the cut is generous, the honeys arrive in force – heather honey leading the pack. There is even a sweetened eucalyptus note, as well as an underlying earthiness; **t22.5** the oils from that cut gang-up early to giving that earthiness flavour form. Again, the heather honey makes an impact, especially with the thick oils, then a blossoming maltiness takes hold; **f21.5** some caramels filter through and dampen But the oils buzz and the malt and honey duet can still be heard above the background hubbub; **b22.5** the closest Pot Still to the last days of the old Jameson Distillery in Dublin I have ever tasted: this could be Redbreast from the late 1980s. 43%.

MIDLETON County Cork. 1975. Irish Distillers.

Green Spot bott code L622831252 db **(95) n23.5 t23.5 f24 b24** A slightly different weight, pace and sugar emphasis to this bottling. But remains a true classic. 40%.

⬩ **Green Spot** bott code: L921031490 db **(94) n24** the blend of over-ripe gooseberry, intense malt and sandalwood is mesmerising; a little toffee, too, which dulls things slightly; **t24** an essay in complex and understated layering. The sugars dissolve to reveal an immediately spicy undertone. Only now does the standard hardness, the unmalted grain spine, come into play. Around it a series of vanilla and butterscotch notes jostle for a major position; **f23** a relatively short finish as toffee kicks in with a degree of abandon...; **b23** what a

267

beautiful whiskey. If they could cut down on the pointless over-emphasis on the caramel and up the strength, they'd have a contender for World Whisky of the Year... 40%.

Green Spot Château Léoville Barton finished in Bordeaux wine casks, bott code L622331248 db **(79) n20 t22 f18 b19** I'd so desperately like to see this work. But, once again, far too tight and bitter for its own good. The damaging sulphur note is worthy of neither the great Green Spot or Leoville Barton names... 46%.

Green Spot Chateau Montelena Zinfandel wine cask finished, bott code: L719331280 db **(88) n23 t23.5 f19.5 b22** There is something fitting that Green Spot, an Irish Pot Still whiskey brand created many generations back by Dublin's Premier wine merchants, should find itself creating new ground...in a wine cask. Any European whisk(e)ys matured in American wine casks are thin on the ground. That they should be Chateau Montelena from Napa Valley makes this all the more remarkable. Does it work? Well, yes and no. The unique style of Irish Pot Still is lost somewhat under a welter of fruity blows and the fuzzy, imprecise finish is definitely off key. But there is no denying that it is a whiskey which does possess the odd magic moment. 46%.

◈ **Green Spot Chateau Montelena** finished in Zinfandel wine casks, bott code: L1921931293 db **(89.5) n23** tight and tart, the fruit has a distinctive nip. Not the first Irish Pot Still I've tasted today with a gooseberry feel – though where before it was ripe and bursting out of its skin, this is very sharp and green indeed...; **t23.5** deliciously salivating and even mildly confrontational. The grape dominates every aspect of the delivery, the grain not getting a word in edgeways. At the midpoint a little barley infiltrates, carried on the back of custardy vanilla; **f21** just a little awkward, furry and uncomfortable; **b22** pleasant enough, for sure. But a slight gripe that the unique Pot Still character has been over-run by the exuberance of the grape... 46%.

◈ **Method and Madness Single Pot Still** bourbon & sherry barrels, finished in Acacia wood, bott code: L91931458 db **(95) n23.5** a teasing aroma: hints of cherry blossom, hints of Turkish Delight; hints of orange-blossom honey...and somewhere, the vaguest hint of a green barley freshness; **t23.5** classic Pot Still: the moment the soft maltiness stakes its claim, a much firmer, sharper barley grist sticks its ore in. Brilliant! The result is world-class juiciness. For a moment fruit intervenes...then a massive outpouring of tannins make their mark; the presence of the ulmo honey makes not for Madness, but great sense...; **f24** a dry, wood-dominated finale - the tannins have a real attitude and would border on the austere if the barley didn't bolt back into action with a wonderful dose of rock-hard gristiness. Elegant spices spread themselves around and are in no hurry to fade...; **b24** a Pot Still creation that just gets better and better the linger you taste it. A brilliant and quite adorable exhibition of one-upmanship and profile development. 46%. ncf. Bottled exclusively for Celtic Whiskey.

Method and Madness Single Pot Irish Whiskey bourbon barrels, finished in Virgin Hungarian oak **(94) n23 t23.5 f23.5 b24** Now there was a nose! One that took me back almost 25 years to when I was visiting the Czech whisky distilleries soon after the fall of the communist regime. That whisky was matured in local oak, offering a near identical aroma to this Irish. 46%.

◈ **Method and Madness Single Pot Still** bourbon & sherry barrels, finished in wild cherry wood, bott code: L919831459 db **(96) n24** the cherry wood oozes from every molecule. Significantly, though, so, too does the Pot Still. This is the type of clean nose, that could happily spend an hour with if I had the time. Or make love to, had I energy...Sexy, sexy stuff...; **t24** rigid Pot Still – just like the old days!!! So wonderful when the Pot Still personality isn't slaughtered in the sacrificial slab of sherry. Barley crunches its way through the gears, as does a lovely Demerara undercurrent; **f24** long, distinguished, increasingly well spiced and the cherry wood won't be outdone as here is a now telling tannin note, something quite apart from oak. Still, though the crunchy sugars and barley grains to their thing. Method. Madness. Majestic...; **b24** one of the most flavoursome whiskies of the Whisky Bible 2021. A true joy to experience: Billy Leighton, I could give you a kiss! I may well have just tasted Irish Whiskey of the Year... 46%. ncf.

Method and Madness Single Pot Still Irish Whiskey sherry & American barrels, finished in French chestnut casks db **(88) n22 t23 f21 b22.5** Ah...memories of the late 1970s or perhaps very early '80s. Walking in the lonely autumnal forests surrounding the tiny French village of Evecquemont, taking my girlfriend's family's soppy Alsatian for long walks, during which I would hoover up wild sweet chestnuts by the score. Never then figured it playing a part in whisky, especially Irish. Not sure it is the perfect marriage, but certainly adds to the whiskey lexicon. 46%.

Midleton Barry Crockett Legacy American bourbon barrels, bott code L623631258 db **(95) n23.5 t24 f23.5 b24** Thank God for my dear old friend Barry Crockett. One of the top three most knowledgeable whiskey/whisky people I have known in my lifetime, you can at least be relieved that his name is synonymous with a truly great spirit. Fittingly, his whiskey is free of sherry butts, so I can just sit back and enjoy and not be on tenterhooks waiting for the first signs of a disastrous sulphur note to take hold. Indeed, the only thing that takes hold of you here is the Pot Still's stunning beauty... 46%. ncf.

◈ **Midleton Barry Crockett Legacy** American bourbon cask, bott code: L918431409 db **(96.5) n24** a surprisingly peachy personality with few of the usual spices coming through for a Pot Still. A soft, juicy maltiness, too, blending in with the growing vanillas. So indulgent and elegant...; **t24.5** the delivery is sublime. Usually Pot Still offers a firm backbone to the oilier tones. But here we have nothing other than a succession of lush tones, starting with a light prologue of maple syrup. As though in slow motion, the Pot Still begins to take hold, a growing intensity to the barely but always with the sugars on hand. At the same time the Trademark spices start as a light nip and grow in intensity; as on the nose, the vanillas play an important role, almost like warm ice cream accompanying the gathering fruits. And, make no mistake: there's the most subtle fruit thread to this, again with the peaches at the van, but now a little orange blossom honey enters the fray and pear juice...; **f23.5** there is a curious furry feel to the finale – not entirely unlike kiwi fruit. This tangy sharpness is at odds with the earlier personality of this whiskey and seems a little out of place; **b24.5** it has been my privilege and honour to have known Barry Crockett slightly over 30 years now. He, 'I and the late, much missed blender Barry Walsh championed Irish Pot still at a time when it had very much gone out of favour and the higher powers within the industry did not care one way or another if it vanished altogether. These were in days when all the Irish Pot still being used came from casks entirely free from sulphur treatment and the unique grain could be seen in all its naked glory...and what a gorgeous, passion rising stunner it was. There is now a generation within the industry who have never tasted wholly clean, unspoiled Pot Still and (from conversations I have had with them around the world) think that a tangy, bitter finish is part of its natural profile. It isn't and here you can see a style not entirely unknown three decades back. Though of the many samples of Pot Still I looked at with Barry Walsh, I don't remember any coming from bourbon that had this degree of fruitiness. Murray Method style of tasting essential here to maximise sweetness, as the sugars are the key to this easily underrated Irish. 46%. ncf. ☙

Midleton Dair Ghaelach Bluebell Forest Castle Blunden Estate finished in virgin native Irish oak hogsheads, batch no. 1, tree number 1, bott code: L628033271 db **(90.5) n22.5 t23.5 f22 b23** The vibrant pungency is matched equally by the grand dollops of natural caramel. 55.3%.

Midleton Dair Ghaelach Grinsell's Wood Ballaghtobin Estate American bourbon barrels, finished in Irish oak hogsheads, batch no. 1, tree no. 7, bott code L504031020 db **(97.5) n24 t25 f24 b24.5** What we have here, if I'm not very much mistaken, is a potential World Whisky of the Year. Rarely these days am I given an entirely new flavour profile to chew on. Not only do I have that, but I am struggling to find any faults at all. Ireland is not known for its mountains: well, it certainly has one now. 579%. ncf.

Powers Aged 12 Years John's Lane Release bott code L623731261 **(96) n23.5 t24.5 f23.5 b24.5** A slightly different slant on the toffee and fudge – and now has a degree of rye-recipe bourbon about it - but firmly remains the go to Pot Still of quite staggering beauty. 46%. ncf.

◈ **Powers John's Lane Release** American oak casks, bott code: L920631479 db **(83) n21 t22 f19 b21** Ah, great!! Matured in American oak. So, for once, no sulphur then. I taste and there, on the finish (confirming what I hadn't wanted to believe on the nose), unmistakably the grim reaper of whiskey itself: sulphur notes. How come? Grabbed the bottle and read the blurb. Not just American oak. But Iberian, too. I must teach my staff to read the small print. With whiskey, like in life, there are many catches to be found... Hold on for a toffee and sulphur ride all the way. 46%. ncf.

Powers Signature Release bott code L433231240 **(87.5) n21 t23 f21.5 b22** A much lazier version of this excellent Pot Still than I have become used to. Far too much fudge at play here, undermining the layering and complexity. Sexy and chewy for sure and a must for those into dried dates. But the usual Pot Still character is a little masked and the usual slightly off key sherry butt turns up at the very last moment. 46%. ncf.

Powers Three Swallow Release bott code L617031171 **(83.5) n21 t21 f21.5 b20** Pleasant. No off notes. But vanishes into a sea of toffee. The fact it is pure Pot Still, apparently, is actually impossible to determine, In the last six months I have seen three swallows: a barn swallow, a Pacific and a Wire-tailed. Wherever I saw them in the world, India, The Philippines, my back garden, they all swooped and darted in joyous abandon. This Three Swallow by Powers has, by vivid contrast, had its wings clipped. 40%. ncf.

◈ **Powers Three Swallow Release** American bourbon barrels & Oloroso sherry casks, bott code: L920631483 db **(84.5) n22 t21.5 f20.5 b20.5** Death by chocolate? Nope: death by toffee. Slow strangulation. If that doesn't get you, the boredom will. A fanfare for the brief burst of pot still on delivery. But it is soon ruthlessly silenced. 40%. ncf.

Redbreast Aged 12 Years bott code L634031413 db **(88.5) n22.5 t23 f21 b22** By far the flattest Redbreast I have tasted since...well, ever. Far too much reliance on obviously first-fill sherry, which had flattened out and virtually buried the unique personality of the Pot Still itself. Enjoyable, for sure. Beautiful, even, in its own way. But it should be so much better than this... 40%.

Redbreast Aged 12 Years bott code: L927731644 db **(93) n23.5** a light smothering of orange blossom honey on deep vanilla. The oakiness possesses a little church pew dustiness...; **t23** probably the softest Redbreasts delivery of all time, a restrained fruitiness taking its time to warm up and get going. A little starchy Pot Still makes its presence felt, and spices immediately after; **f23** a Cadbury's chocolate fruit and nut finale with the grain being surprisingly reticent...; lots of toffee and vanilla late on; **b23.5** one of the most docile and pacific Redbreasts I've encountered in the last 30-odd years. Lovely, though. *40%*.

Redbreast Aged 12 Years Cask Strength batch no. B1/18 db **(96) n24.5 t24.5 f23 b24** Probably one very slightly sulphured cask from World Whisky of the Year. Both nose and delivery is blarney-free Irish perfection. Worth hunting this bottle down for something truly special... *56.2%. ncf.*

Redbreast Aged 12 Years Cask Strength batch no. B2/19, bott code: L921931501 db **(95.5) n24** so wonderful to see the grain in the ascendancy. There is a real crispness to this, a sharpness than can cut, as is the case with old-style Irish Pot Still with the muscovado and Demerara sugars having the bigger input before the peach and grape juices start to soften the feel. The slow build of the spice is fabulous; **t24** oh...heavens....!!! That is so, so beautiful. A fabulous heather honey and playful molasses blend creates just the right environment for first the pompous grapiness...and then the grains steam in as though they own the place. Which I suppose they do. Magnificently choreographed, with the weight and pace of the development beyond criticism; **f23.5** long and remains lush even though the burnt raisin and fruitcake notes are turned up a notch. A vague furriness late into the death...; **b24** just like the last time I tasted this, there is just the very faintest sulphur echo. But it is miniscule and apparent only very late into the experience...and after two or three mouthfuls. Pot still at its potiest... *55.8%*.

Redbreast Aged 15 Years bott code L624931266 db **(84) n21 t22 f20 b21** When you have this much sherry influence on a whiskey, it is likely that one day you will fall foul of the odd furry butt, as is the case here. *46%. ncf.*

Redbreast Aged 15 Years bott code: L930431724 db **(80) n19 t22 f18 b21** A few too many sulphured casks for its own good. *46%*.

Redbreast Aged 21 Years bott code L612731109 db **(97) n24.5 t24 f24 b24.5** The mercifully restrained fruit and absolute total 100% absence of sulphur allows the Pot Still to display its not inconsiderable beauty unmolested and to the fullest extent. One of the world's most beautiful and iconic whisk(e)ys without doubt. The fact that so many facets of this whiskey are allowed to say their piece, yet never over-run their time and that the tenets are equally divided makes this one of the truly great whiskeys of the year. *46%. ncf.*

Redbreast Aged 21 Years bott code: L918331405 db **(94) n24** layered fruit. A little ginger pays a surprise visit and the oak is likewise laid in distinctive strata....; **t23.5** silky and spicy for the very first moments, the grain barely recognisable by flavour but by the stiffness of spine only; the salivating qualities early on seems to run hand-in-hand with the juiciest grape; **f23** a dull toffee-vanilla-grapey fade ...where is the enlivening barley...? **b23.5** this is perennially one of the contenders for the Bible's World Whisky of the Year, and once was only a single sulphured cask away from winning it. This year sulphur isn't a problem but, ironically, the sherry is. For the grape here is a little too boisterous, meaning the balance has been compromised. Lovely whisky, for sure. But when the grape dominates – and flattens - so much greatness will elude it... *46%*.

Redbreast Aged 27 Years ruby port casks, batch no. B1/19, bott code: L933633750 db **(93.5) n23.5** such a rare beast where the nose just throbs with Pot Still – even after all these years, and even with a ruby port interference. The grainy hardness is as unmistakable as it is fabulous...; **t25** again, just like the nose, the pot still has a mark all of its own – and here is probably at its starkest since anything I tasted in the mid 1990s... Others have tried to copy pot still, but the indescribable interplay between softer malt and rock-hard barley that is there, is a way that only Midleton can achieve. A delivery to die for and a follow through that defies credibility..... Perfection! **f21.5** the wine casks kick in here, but not quite as positively as I had hoped. The brilliant unmalted barley has vanished...and here is the arrogant dullness of sulphur in its place; **b23.5** if tragic can be applied to a whiskey, then it can here One minute the perfect exhibition of a wondrous whiskey type. The next, faulty obliteration... if I'm permitted a scream...... Arrrrrrggggghhhhhhh!!!!! *54.6%*.

Redbreast Aged 32 Years Dream Cask db **(96.5) n24 t24.5 f23.5 b24** A fabulous pot still very comfortable in its ancient clothes. Marvellous! *46.5%*.

Redbreast All Sherry Single Cask db **(73.5) n17 t23.5 f15 b18.** I mean: seriously guys....??? A single cask pure pot still whiskey and you bottle one with sulphur fingerprints all over it? I don't have the number of what cask this is from, so I hope yours will have come from clean sherry. If you have, you are in for a treat, because the sheer brilliance and magnitude of this whiskey was able to blot out the sulphur for a good seven or eight seconds as it reached heights of near perfection. A bowl of raspberries now and a 20 minute break to help cleanse my palate and relieve my tongue which is still seriously furred up. So frustrating, as I could see a clean butt of this getting Single Cask Whisky of the Year ... 59.9%. sc.

Redbreast Dream Cask Aged 28 Years ruby port casks, cask no. 400295, bott code: L933633750 db (**96**) **n24.5** the depth and layering of this made a liar of the label straight away – or at least the front of it. It is obvious there is more going on here than ruby port alone and an inspection of the small print reveal that oloroso and bourbon casks are at play here, too. Perhaps the cleverest, yet most easily over-looked aspect is the spice. Not just some sizzling random spice. But one that is measured and integrated. As is the fruit which varies from a cream sherry-type pillow softness to a more lusty plum pudding. There is an intrinsic toastiness, too, which mirrors the spice in its careful weight and disposition. This a 15-minute minimum Murray Method nose. And, unquestionably one of the finest in the world this year...; **t24.5** talk about cream sherry on the nose.... The marriage of oloroso and ruby port has generated the most classic cream sherry landing on the palate. But, as on the nose, is the delicate and intricate layering which sets this apart from the rest and takes this into true world class territory. There is a clever acidic touch which comes and goes, allowing the dark, salivating sugars pride and place from time to time., This is all about weight and counterweight: old-fashioned blending at is finest...; **f23** ah!...and to the Achilles heel. Toasty and an element of chocolate truffle. But that dull, bitter echo of sulphur from, presumably, the sherry butt. Not loud, but the mild furriness is indelibly there...; **b24** until the finale, this was on course for World Whisky of the Year. But that will never be won with a whiskey blemished by sulphur, and, though the mark is small, it is, alas, there.... Tragic, as this is as much an art of work as it is a whiskey... 40%. 915 bottles. ☂

Redbreast Lustau Edition sherry finish, bott code L622131242 db (**89.5**) **n22.5 t23.5 f22 b21.5** I somehow would have thought that, considering recent younger bottlings, going to the trouble of making a special sherry finish for a Redbreast is on a par with giving a gift of a barrel of sand to the Tuaregs... This bottling is attractive enough, with the fruit at its best on delivery when the whiskey goes through a spectacularly delicious phase. But this soon wears out, leaving a bitterness and slightly lopsided feel, especially at the death, as the balance struggles to be maintained. For those of you I know who refuse to touch anything sherry, this is entirely sulphur free I'm delighted to report. 46%. ncf.

Redbreast Lustau Edition Sherry Finish bott code: L930531725 db (**95**) **n23.5** brilliant spice and fruit interplay on the nose. But while that little battle goes on, the grain has a real green sharpness to it, shewing the barley in its brightest light...; **t24** a much better structured sherry influence here allowing the fruit to come in early and do its juicy, grapey thing. But then moving out of the picture so the spices, tannins and barley have the stage. The result is a complex Pot Still of dazzlingly varied texture and intensity; **f23.5** plenty of Demerara sugars – and chocolate raisin, too. The barley, though, is always on hand....; **b24** faultless sherry casks at work. And the Pot Still is firm and decisive. Who can ask for more....? Well, I could ask for the toasted almonds promised on the label, being exceedingly partial to them. The fact they never turn up is compensated for by the overall excellence...and the chocolate... 46%.

Red Spot Aged 15 Years bourbon, sherry & marsala casks, bott code: L829131516 db (**83**) **n21 t22 f19 b21** Oh, what I'd give for the days when you could taste the actual magic of the Pot Still itself, such as in the original Green Spot, rather than some lumbering fruit casks, and slightly sulphured ones at that. 46%. ncf.

Yellow Spot Aged 12 Years bourbon barrels, sherry butts & Malaga casks, bott code L622431250 db (**87**) **n22 t22 f21 b22** My previous comments stand for this, too. Except here we have a persistent bitterness towards the finish which reveals a weakness with one of the butts. An exceptionally bitty whiskey that does have its moments of soaring high, especially when the varying citrus note correlate. 46%. ncf.

Yellow Spot Aged 12 Years bourbon barrels, sherry butts and Malaga casks, bott code: L929031680 db (**92.5**) **n24** a delightful mix of Cape Gooseberry and lime blossom honey, when mixed with the fresh barley and deft tannins, gives a sensuality to the fruit which seduces with pure whiskey eroticism...; **t24** the softest mouthfeel to any Irish Pot Still I have ever encountered. A little pink grapefruit sharpness...followed by lashing of barley and creamy vanilla...; **f21.5** damn it! A slight bitter sulphur blemish carried on the warming spices; **b23** I thought the first bottlings of this were a tad out of sorts, the balance proving elusive. I backed blender Billy Leighton to crack this one eventually...and he has. This has moments of pure whiskey paradise. But the garden of Eden has a snake...and thy name is Sulphur... 46%. ncf.

UNSPECIFIED

Glendalough Pot Still Irish Whiskey tree no. 1, batch no. 1, cask no. 3, bott code: 25519 (**87.5**) **n20.5 t23.5 f21.5 b22** A bold, rich Irish weakened by the feints from the over-generous cut but strengthened thanks to the brave inclusion of local oak. Not too much that is positive can be said about the nose, alas. But the same doesn't ring true for the startling delivery which first champions the barley and then, before you have time to blink, the oak which powers through with a creamy molasses attached to the stark oak. The unravelling of the myriad sugar styles is as unique as it is delicious. A bit like a mis-firing Rolls Royce, I look forward to future bottlings when they've sorted the engine out... *43%. sc.*

◇ **Hinch Single Pot Still** nbc **(94.5)** n23.5 youthful grains make for a busy nose. The sugars have a light marzipan nuance while thin ulmo and lime blossom honey leave gentle trails. Just a touch of tobacco on the nose, too...; **t23.5** usual dual feel to this with a silky, lightly oiled maltiness providing the flesh to a firm spine. Vanilla and butterscotch arrives earlier than expected, as do the spices; **f23.5** gorgeous spice buzz beside the malt and ulmo honey. That tobacco on the nose returns slightly; **b24** quite a light Pot Still character with no great age. This gives the whiskey a very unusual personality, indeed one I cannot remember bottled before, as it is a style ignored by distillers as a singleton and in the lab I have used this type of Pot Still only within blends. Brilliant to see it get the airing it deserves. The only thing I can say against it: I know that, in my lab, this type of Pot Still sparkles best at about 51% abv when the sugars and oils seem to complement each other almost effortlessly. Hopefully the next bottling will be a little closer to that. *43%. The Time Collection.*

Single Malt
COOLEY County Louth. 1987. Beam Suntory.
Connemara bott code L9042 db **(88)** n23 t22.5 f20.5 b22. One of the softest smoked whiskies in the world which, though quite lovely, gives the impression it can't make its mind up about what it wants to be. *40%*

Connemara Aged 12 Years bott code L9024 db **(85.5)** n23 t21.5 f20 b21. The nose, with its beautiful orange, fruity lilt, puts the shy smoke in the shade. *40%*

Connemara Cask Strength bott code L9041 db **(90)** n21.5 t23 f22 b22.5. A juicy negative of the standard bottling: does its talking on the palate rather than nose. Maybe an absence of caramel notes might have something to do with that. *57.9%*

◇ **Connemara Peated Single Malt Irish Whiskey** bott code: L19109 03/10/149 db **(89)** n23 seriously sexy peat at work here, The phenols smoulder over you like the eyes possessed by an Irish redhead...; **t22.5** super-soft – perhaps too soft with the peat at first embracing then backing off as the caramels take charge; a little ulmo honey evens the sweetness; **f21.5** light spice, but even more caramel; **b22** I'm afraid I'm old and ugly enough to have been around to taste the very first ever batch of Connemara – at Cooley distillery, as it happens – after it came off the bottling line. Then the peat was rich and unhindered. Since then it has gone through a chequered career with phenols levels rising and falling like the tides at nearby Carlingford Lough. That must have been close on 30 years ago now... Pleased to say the peat is back to it old confident self..well, early on at least. But I don't remember the toffee dampening its natural spontaneity as it does here... *40%.*

Tullamore Dew Single Malt 10 Years Old db **(91.5)** n23 t23 f22.5 b23. The best whiskey I have ever encountered with a Tullamore label. Furtively complex and daringly delicate. If only they could find a way to minimise the toffee... *40%. William Grant & Sons.*

◇ **The Tyrconnell Single Malt Irish Whiskey Aged 16 Years** Oloroso & Moscatel cask finish, bott code: L19020 07/02/19 db **(94)** n23.5 possibly the cleanest and most dazzling Irish wine-matured whisky I've encountered in a couple of years. For those old enough, it will remind you of fruit sweet jars freshly opened...; **t23.5** a beautiful cross between Jaffa Cake and chocolate limes. The fruit is fresh and even allows the malt to make some excellent incursions; **f23** at last the tannins get a word in sideways, mainly caramel and vanilla, but still the spiced fruitiness endures...; **b24** so rare to find a sherry-matured Irish whiskey that isn't benighted by sulphur. An absolute treat. *46%.*

◇ **The Tyrconnell Single Malt Double Distilled Irish Whiskey** ex-bourbon casks, bott code: L18112 07/11/18 db **(87.5)** n23 t22 f21 b21.5 A thoroughbred malt offers the most gorgeous freshness on the nose while lime blossom honey does the rest. But to taste it almost falls at the first jump, unable to negotiate a fence with the clearance the nose suggests. The lightness of malt has been replaced by a slightly salivating but out of sync toffee persona; a mix between Malteser candy and MacIntosh's Toffo. A thoroughbred as I say. But carrying too much weight: was always lighter and flightier than this. So much caramel! *43%.*

Tullamore Dew Aged 10 Years Four Cask Finish bourbon, oloroso, port, madeira **(89)** n24 t23 f19.5 b22.5 Just a sherry butt or two away from complete brilliance. *40% (80 proof)*

The Wild Geese Single Malt (85.5) n21.5 t21 f22 b21. Just ignore the Wild Goose chase the labels send you on and enjoy the malt, with all its failings, for what it is (and this is pretty enjoyable in an agreeably rough and ready manner, though not exactly the stuff of Irish whiskey purists): which in this case for all its malt, toffee and delicate smoke, also appears to have more than a slight touch of feints - so maybe they were right all along...!!! *43%. Cooley for Avalon.*

DINGLE County Kerry. 2012. Porterhouse Group.

Dingle Single Malt Whisky batch no. 3 db **(87) n21 t22 f22 b22** Young, much closer in personality to new make than seasoned whiskey. In fact, reminds me of the blending lab when I'd come across a barely three-year-old Dailuaine, a Scottish Speysider, which, at this juncture of its development, is its closest flavour-type relative. Lovely, though, if you an looking for a taste of unspoiled, gently oiled maltiness – and a piece of Irish whiskey history. Clean and beautifully made. *46.5%. ncf. 13,000 bottles.*

Dingle Single Malt Whisky batch no. 4 db **(84) n20 t22 f21 b21** I always prefer to discover that a distillery makes gin because I have been there or been briefed about it. Not through sampling their whiskey. And I'm afraid there is juniper quite strongly on the nose here and few other odd flavours hitting the palate. Despite the mega dry finish, lots of malt on show and seemingly otherwise well made. *46.5%. ncf. 2,000 bottles.*

⬧ **Dingle Single Malt Whisky** batch no. 5 db **(88.5) n22 t22.5 f22 b22** Genteel malt shewing no great age but certainly celebrates an uninhibited maltiness which charms and possesses no pretentions of grandeur. Just a slight background apple cider feel to the nose, and a vague feintiness to the body. The barley is all over this, but melts towards a soft butterscotch tart finish. *46.5%. ncf.*

⬧ **Dingle Single Malt Whisky Cask Strength** batch no. 5 db **(92) n23** as on the 46.5% bottling, a slight background apple cider feel, giving the malt a sharpness it might not otherwise possess. Charming...; **t23.5** that is a fabulous delivery by any stretch of the imagination. Malted barley blends in with apple brandy with a light chocolatey background that sees off the tannin; **f22.5** a decent rumbling of spice and a few dark sugars help hide the comparative youth of the malt; juicy even now with a reminder that this malt has no great age; just a slight bitterness very late on; **b23** the extra oils work a treat on this: there is a chasm between this expression and the 46.5 version, the cask strength bottling here allowing full amplification to some otherwise understated components. *59.3%. ncf.*

MIDLETON County Cork. 1975. Irish Distillers.

Method and Madness Single Malt Irish Whiskey bourbon barrels, finished in French Limousin oak casks db **(92) n22 t23.5 f23 b23.5** A very different Irish which is quietly uncompromising and seriously tasty... *46%.*

OLD BUSHMILLS County Antrim. 1784. Casa Cuervo.

Bushmills Aged 10 Years matured in two woods db **(92.5) n23 t23 f23 b23.5.** Absolutely superb whiskey showing great balance and the usual Antrim 19th century pace with its flavour development. The odd bottle of this I have come across over the last couple of years has been spoiled by the sherry involvement. But, this, as is usually the case, is absolutely spot on. *40%*

⬧ **Bushmills Single Malt Aged 10 Years** bourbon & Oloroso casks, bott code: L8270 IB 005 db **(92.5) n23** adore the fresh zinginess to this nose, revelling in light citrus despite the close attention of sultana and toffee; **t23** salivating on impact, as Bushmills 10 should be. I still miss the old malt explosion from the days when this was 100% ex-bourbon cask, but the chocolate-toffee-sultana replacement style has its own charms and malts rarely come softer or more evenly paced; **f23** long and even more chocolate plus, now, a little extra toffee and raisin...; **b23.5** a very consistent Irish benefitting again from faultless sherry butts. *40%.*

Bushmills Aged 12 Years Single Malt Aged in Three Woods oloroso sherry & bourbon casks, Marsala cask finished, bott code: L9102IB 001 db **(89.5) n23.5 t23 f21 b22** Slightly lumpy in style, but there are some beautiful moments in there. *40%. Exclusive to Taiwan.*

⬧ **Bushmills Distillery Reserve Single Malt Aged 12 Years** bott code: L8170 IB 002 db **(95) n23.5** beautiful stratum of cocoa, apricot, heather honey and the chalkiest malt in the British Isles...; **t24** very unusual for a Bushmills of any era to kick off with a sweet delivery. But that's what you are presented with here as that heather honey kicks in, followed by layers of greengages and exploding white grape. The malt and sawdusty oak form layers alongside the toffee; **f23.5** not technically perfect, but all is forgiven as this has legs despite the lack of oils. The chocolate toffee takes over, with just a slight sultana kick here and there; **b24** what a stunning example of Bushmills this is. *40%.*

Bushmills Aged 16 Years db **(71) n18 t21 f15 b17.** In my days as a consultant Irish whiskey blender, going through the Bushmills warehouses I found only one or two sulphur-treated butts. Alas, there are many more than that at play here. 40%

⬧ **Bushmills Single Malt Aged 16 Years Rare Matured in Three Woods** Oloroso sherry, bourbon & port casks, bott code: L9249 IB 002 db **(90.5) n23** freshly halved kumquat beautifully mingling with high grade Lubeck marzipan. Light, breezy, a little salty...but a definite toffee rumble which slightly flattens things..; **t23.5** soft and salivating delivery with the malt slightly aloof from the ripe plums and cherries. But by the midpoint all contact is lost with these tantalising flavour compounds as toffee takes control; **f21.5** caramel and a very slight furry tang...; **b22.5** until the late finish barely a single off note thanks to some superb casks in use here. If only they could bring the toffee element down slight to allow a far clearer view of the excellent fruit and malt tones in play **43%**

Bushmills Aged 21 Years db **(95.5) n24.5 t24 f23.5 b24** An Irish journey as beautiful as the dramatic landscape which borders the distillery. Magnificent. *40%*

◈ **Bushmills Single Malt Aged 21 Years Rare Matured in Three Woods** Oloroso sherry, bourbon & Madeira casks, bott 2019, bott code: L9085 IB 003 db **(82) n21 t21.5 f19.5 b20** A very disappointing malt. Obviously the light dusting of tongue-numbing sulphur affects the nose and finale but some damage is already done before on the palate with a stark toffee effect that keeps complexity to a minimum. The odd honey tone here and there, and a slight saltiness, too. But, from this distillery, we should be having a whiskey in the mid-90s points-wise... *40%.*

Bushmills Distillery Exclusive Acacia Wood dist 2008, bott no. L8211 IB 01S db **(83.5) n21 t24 f18 b20.5** Not the first time I have ever tasted whiskey rounded off in acacia by a long stretch, though maybe the first after spending time – it appears – in sherry. The result for me just doesn't gel. For a start, I find the slightly imbalanced aroma a lot of hard work in getting used to, though as your nose acclimatises you can eventually pick out some half attractive buttery notes. And the finish isn't quite where it should be, with a fair bit of fuzziness at the finish. The delivery, though, is both intriguing and delicious, the acacia – as is its wont – issuing a whole batch of sugar and honey notes not normally present in whisky and never in Irish whiskey; ironically acacia honey isn't among them! Though undone by the pretty poor finish, this still represents one of the most curious and fascinating bottlings in the world over the last year. Just needs some serious tidying up before, hopefully, the next batch as the potential is great. *47%. ncf.*

◈ **Bushmills Port Cask Reserve** ruby port pipes, bott code: L8170 IB 001 db **(95.5) n24** some serious spices infiltrate the firm dark cherries. Saltier than most Bushmills, too...; **t24** much softer delivery than you'd expect from the nose. Drier and chalkier, too, in time-honoured Bushmills tradition. A little ulmo honey mixed with liquorice and Demerara sugars to provide the restrained sweetness, while the fruit heads in a light Dundee cake direction; **f23.5** lovely chocolate tones works beautifully with the fruit and nut. And more chalk as the vanilla builds; **b24** this Steamship does First Class only... *40%. The Steamship Collection.* ☙

◈ **Bushmills Rum Cask Reserve** first fill Caribbean rum casks, bott code: L9130 IB 001 db **(94) n23.5** deft and deeply appealing, it is the way that the sugars from the rum cask have helped intensify the gristiness of the youngish malt that really pleases. Light acacia honey and vanilla delight without ever over egging it...; **t23.5** silky soft and salivating: what a delivery! The barley has both a delightful flightiness and, by the mid-point, intense depth. Spices flit rather than fight and all is good on the palate; **f23** heads towards its trademark sawdusty dryness. But just enough gristy sugars and darker sugars to keep the ship afloat; **b24** the blender has really called this one right. Brilliant usage of rum casks to enrich the notoriously slight maltiness of Old Bushmills. A malt that is in full sail... *40%. The Steamship Collection.*

◈ **Bushmills Sherry Cask Reserve** Oloroso sherry butts, bott code: L9078 IB 002 db **(90.5) n22.5** delicate sultana and toffee. Light spices plus a buttery vanilla; **t22.5** soft and middling sweet on delivery. The toastier raisins meet with a blanket of Demerara sugar and caramel; **f22.5** delightfully clean, with a late malty freshness and lightly spiced chocolate fudge; **b23** clean, unsullied casks make for an easy-drinking, super-rounded Irish with an untaxing complexity. Very pleasant, indeed. *40%. The Steamship Collection.*

Bushmills Single Malt The Steamship Collection #3 Bourbon Cask db **(95) n24.5 t23.5 f23 b24** This steamship is sailing in calm seas of complexity...Take your time over this one: it is deceptively brilliant. *40%.*

The Whisky Cask Company Bushmills Capall 26 Years Old 1st fill bourbon barrel, cask no, 8391, dist 16 Oct 91, bott 26 Mar 18 **(94.5) n22.5 t24 f24 b24** Had the nose been as sensational as the experience on the palate some kind of award for this whisky would have been a certainty. Magnificent. *50.5%. sc. 175 bottles.*

The Whisky Cask Company Bushmills Madra 26 Years Old 1st fill bourbon barrel, cask no, 8386, dist 16 Oct 91, bott 26 Mar 18 **(94) n23 t24 f23 b24** A little nudge to Bushmills to make the most of their older casks, methinks. *49.4%. sc. 156 bottles.*

WEST CORK DISTILLERS County Cork. 2003. West Cork Distillers.

West Cork Irish Whiskey Bog Oak Charred Cask Matured db **(88.5) n23 t22 f21.5 b22** A little known fact: I own a 100 to 125 year-old portable Irish pot still made entirely of copper with brass handles, once owned by a Victorian or Edwardian illicit distiller. Which would explain as to why it was found in an Irish bog over 20 years ago and has been in my possession ever since. Anyway, it is extremely unlikely it ever produced a spirit which ended up quite so heavy in natural caramels... *43%. West Cork Distillers Limited.*

West Cork Irish Whiskey Glengarriff Peat Charred Cask Matured db **(90.5) n23 t22.5 f22 b23** Well, Ireland is on the way to Kentucky from here... 43%. *West Cork Distillers Limited.*

Brean Tra Single Malt Irish Whiskey db **(86.5) n21 t22 f21.5 b22** A very safe Irish. Distinctly oily and choc-a-bloc with intense if monosyllabic malt. The tannins take time to arrive but become moderately punchy. 40%. *West Cork Distillers Limited.*

Mizen Head Cask Strength Single Malt Irish Whiskey Bodega sherry casks db **(90.5) n22.5 t23.5 f22 b22.5** Well done chaps! Until the very death, barely a sulphur atom in sight! But such is the power of this distillery's love of caramel character, it even overtakes the fruit... which takes some doing! 60%. *West Cork Distillers Limited.*

UNSPECIFIED SINGLE MALTS

⬖ **Artful Dodger Irish Single Malt 15 Year Old 2002** ex-bourbon hogshead, cask no. 346 **(95) n23.5 t24 f23.5 b24** This is Irish single malt as it should be. Not vanishing behind grape thanks one type of finish or another. But out in the open, displaying its immense richness and talents – and, here, barley by the bushel-load. Clean, with intricate layering of rare intensity, the light tannins acting as the cement to the malt brick. If you ever see this bottle, just grab it. But then it might just find you, as this malt, like Irish eyes, would have a magnetic attraction. Brilliant! 57.9%. sc.

⬖ **Cadenhead's Small Batch An Irish 10 Year Old** bott Aug 19 **(91.5) n23** really charming layering to the greenish barley: clean and inviting; **t23** delightfully creamy maltiness sharpened by a citrus edges: some lovely salivating moments; **f22.5** a little salty, then dries with a sawdusty vanilla flourish; **b23** untaxing throughout, the malt tells a simple tale....well. 474%.

⬖ **Currach Single Malt Irish Whiskey Atlantic Kombu Seaweed Cask** ex-bourbon casks, finished in seaweed charred virgin oak casks, batch no. 1, bott Mar 20, bott code: 07220 **(83) n20.5 t22 f20.5 b20** Probably a whisky for the Swansea or Japanese market, where seaweed is held in high esteem. However, as a whisky in its own right I'm afraid this hits rough waters immediately, with the malt lurching around the palate as though in a gale. The sweet spot lasts far too briefly, a vague honey note well into the delivery but the tang on finish isn't one that is easy to savour. Salt is conspicuous by its absence, oddly enough, in the Whisky Bible 2020, I noted that Ireland had produced 29 different finishes in the previous year alone. This was not included amongst them. 46%. ncf. Origin Spirits Ireland.

The Dublin Liberties Copper Alley 10 Year Old Single Malt sherry cask finish, bott no. L16 280 W3 **(94.5) n23 t24 f23.5 b24** Well done, chaps! You have picked yourself a first class sulphur-free cask! What a rare treat what is this year! 46%.

The Dubliner 10 Year Old Single Malt bourbon casks, bott no. L17390-179 **(89) n22 t23 f21.5 b22.5** 'The real taste of Dublin' warbles the label in time-honoured Blarney tradition. Of course, the true, historic taste of Dublin is Irish Pot Still, that beguiling mix of malted and unmalted barley. But, in the meantime, this juicy little number will do no harm. 42%.

Dunville's VR Aged 12 Years Single Malt finished in ex-Pedro Ximénez sherry casks **(87) n23 t22.5 f20 b21.5** The success story here is on the nose: despite its Spanish inquisition, there is a profound Kentucky note leading the way, a sharp almost rye-like note with its fruity crispness. The delivery also has its moments, the riot of date and molasses in particular. The rest of the tale, much of it bitterly told, doesn't quite go so well, alas. 46%. ncf.

Dunville's VR Aged 17 Years Single Malt Port Mourant Estate rum cask finish, cask no. 195 **(91.5) n22.5 t22.5 f23 b22.5** Putting my blending hat on (which is the same one as I wear when writing the Whisky Bible) Port Mourant – known by us rum blenders as PM – trumps PX every day of the week when it comes to maturation. PM is a bit special in the rum world: it is a Guyanan rum that you add for its depth and powering coffee flavour: indeed, if you work in a rum warehouse in Guyana you can locate where the PMs are situated just by the change in aroma. This comes about by the fact that caramel is already into the cask before the rum spirit is added to it for maturation. It is a style symbolic with British Naval Rum. So where PX can be saccharine sweet and occasionally turn a whisky into something bland and uninteresting, PM is brilliant for lengthening out the finish, especially with rich mocha notes. Here, there are some sharp features it has to contend with from the first cask and a little extra time in PM might have ensured an extra softness to the finale. 57.1%. ncf sc.

Egan's Single Malt Fortitude Pedro Ximénez casks bott code: L18 003 264 **(79) n19 t22 f19 b19** Bitter and off-key. 42% (92 proof). ncf.

Egan's Single Malt 10 Aged Years bott code: US001 244 **(90) n22.5 t23.5 f22 b22.5** Rich, rounded and puts the "more" into Tullamore-based bottler...47% (94 proof). ncf.

The Exclusive Malts Irish 14 Year Old refill sherry hogshead, cask no. 200503, dist 15 Dec 03, bott Jun 18 **(86.5) n22 t22 f21 b21.5** A bewildering coming together of two irremovable forces: the peat, presumably of Cooley distillery, and a superb, faultless sherry butt. But although this cask is faultless – a rare beast in the sherry world - this has been bottled before the phenols and fruits have been able to reach a compromise. So, fun whiskey. And there is much to be said about the peat and boiled candy fruitiness. But they are too individual and each out of sync with the other. Some great moments, though! 50.5%. sc. The Whisky Barrel. 264 bottles.

Glendalough Single Malt Irish Whiskey Aged 17 Years American oak bourbon cask, Japanese Mizunara cask finish **(89.5) n21.5 t23 f22 b23** Quite a cerebral whiskey, and one with a unique fingerprint. But could have done without the juniper. 46%. ncf.

Glendalough Single Malt Irish Whiskey Aged 25 Years Tree #2 Jack's Wood American white oak bourbon cask, Spanish oloroso cask & virgin Irish oak finish **(95) n23.5 t24 f23.5 b24** No discernible problems from the oloroso, other than the very faintest long-distance buzz. Which means this is one hell of a malt. 46%. ncf.

⬧ **Hinch Peated Single Malt** nbc **(87) n22 t22 f21.5 b21.5** So rare to find a slightly feinty note in Irish, but here it is on the peaty nose and, big delivery and quarrelsome finish. A unique character, that's for sure...and what a character! Technically not quite at the races, but the peat is taking few prisoners and the oils from that wide cut ensures that the big smoke goes nowhere in a hurry. An odd whiskey, it has to be said. Knives and forks ready for this one: tuck in to enjoy... 43%. The Time Collection.

Hyde No.1 President's Cask Aged 10 Years Single Malt sherry cask finish **(85.5) n23 t22 f20 b20.5** Pleased to report the sherry butt(s) used here offer no sulphur, so a clean malt with an outstanding fruity aroma. But it does quite literally fall flat because after the initial juicy, malty entry things go a bit quiet – especially towards the middle and finish where a dull vaguely fruity but big toffee note clings like a limpet. A wasted opportunity, one feels. 46%. ncf.

Hyde No. 7 President's Cask Bodega sherry casks, bott code: 20518 **(69) n15 t19 f18 b17** Riddled with sulphur. The Germans will love it! 46%. ncf.

The Irishman Aged 12 Years first fill bourbon barrels, bott 2017 **(92) n23.5 t23 f22.5 b23** Old Bushmills like you have never quite seen her before in bottle. Works a treat. 43%. ncf. 6,000 bottles.

The Irishman 12 Years Old Florio Marsala Cask Finish cask no. 2257 **(90) n22 t23 f22.5 b22.5** A clean, unsullied cask but the grape allows the malt little room for manoeuvre. Very pleasurable though, and definitely a whisky rather than a wine..; 46%. ncf sc. 320 bottles.

The Irishman Aged 17 Years sherry cask, cask no. 6925, dist 2000 **(95.5) n24.5 t24 f23 b24** Just a year or two after this was distilled, I was crawling around the warehouses of Old Bushmills doing some blending and sampling amazingly fine, completely un-sulphured or as near as damn it un-sulphured, sherry butts – better than any I had found in Scotland in the previous several years. This style of sherry has all the hallmarks of the Bushmills butts of that time. There is trace sulphur (so this is a as near-as damn-it butt), but unless you know exactly what you are looking for it is in such small amounts it is unlikely to be detected or trouble you. This may not be from Bushmills, but if not then someone has made a good job of hiding some gems from me. If anyone can locate half a dozen of those entirely un-sulphured butts I located, then there is an Irish Whisky of the Year (at least!) in your hands... 56%. ncf sc. 600 bottles.

The Irishman Aged 17 Years sherry cask, cask no. 28657 **(94.5) n24 t24 f22.5 b23.5** It's the hoping that kills you. After 20-odd years of tasting sherry casks ruined in Jerez, you view every whisky from sherry butt, be it a full term maturation or partial, with suspicion. You hope... but sadly, that hope is terminated by grim disappointment. Here, though, we have a happy experience. Is it 100% perfect sherry butt? No. Does it damage the whiskey? Not really. This is a full-on sherry influenced Irish celebrating the grape with style. The finale shews the slightest of weaknesses, but in light of what is out there it is forgiveable (well, not quite forgiveable enough for it not to be robbed of an award in the Whisky Bible!) and forgettable. 56%. ncf sc. 600 bottles.

J. J. Corry The Flintlock No. 1 16 Year Old Single Malt Autumn 2018, cask nos. 11191, 11221 & 11233 **(95.5) n23.5** an essay in beautiful grist....; **t24** such a dazzling, uncomplicated exhibition of barley. Biscuity, gristy, intense...just stunning... **f24** light spices hover around. As does a thin layer of bruyere honey and molasses; **b24** should Ireland ever hold a Maltfest, then this should be on the altar of worship... 46%. 650 bottles.

Jack Ryan Single Malt Irish Whisky Aged 12 Years bourbon cask **(92.5) n23.5 t23 f22.5 b23.5** Deft, very clean malt whisky where decent bourbon wood adds all kinds of beautifully paced complexity. Not even a hint of an off note. Impressive. 46%

Kinahan's Heritage 10 Year Old Single Malt (93) n23 t23.5 f23 b23.5 A beautifully constructed whiskey where, very rare for a single malt these days, you can actually taste the malt itself... A treat of a whiskey. 46%.

Kinahan's Special Release Project 11 Year Old Armagnac finish, cask no. 48 **(95.5) n23 t24.5 f23.5 b24.5** This isn't good whiskey. Or even very good whiskey. It is truly great Irish whiskey. 58.9%.

⬧ **Lambay Whiskey Single Malt** finished in Cognac casks, bott code: L4329718 **(92.5) n23.5** such a lively nose, the malts being sharp, mainly clean and bolstered further by equal amounts of citrus and salt; **t24** brilliant delivery: relatively young barley arrives in myriad waves. Excellent juiciness and gristy sugars leading into a delicate fruit note. The oak and barley balance can hardly be bettered; **f22** bitters out and dries due to some kind of cask influence. A little too much toffee, too...; **b23** I've always thought that Bushmills at about 7-years-old has a special esprit de coeur (as opposed to corps!) which allowed the distillery to be seen at its freshest, most fulfilling and most true to the distillery's style. There is more than a touch of this evident here as this malt, whoever made it, boasts extraordinary verve and dash. Magnificent up until the point of the late finish when things become a little too bitter for their own good. That apart, stunning. *40%. ncf.*

Liquid Treasures 10th Anniversary Irish Malt 29 Year Old ex-rum barrel, dist 1989, bott 2019 **(94) n23.5 t23.5 f23 b24** Irish whiskies of this antiquity are as rare as leprechaun's teeth. This one is gold filled. *56.5%. sc. 127 bottles.*

Liquid Treasures Summer Dram 2018 Irish Malt Over 26 Years Old ex-bourbon barrel, dist 1992, bott 2018 **(90.5) n23.5 t23 f21.5 b22.5** the oak has taken control, here but in an entirely benign manner, bringing the barley into play here, dishing out spices there, standing back and allowing the ulmo and heather honeys to do their things at other times. Complex and beautifully paced, just shewing a degree of weariness at the finale. But don't we all...? *48.3%. sc.*

The Quiet Man 8 Year Old Single Malt Irish Whiskey bourbon casks **(89) n22 t23 f21.5 b22.5** Had the finish not dulled quite so quickly this would have scored a lot higher. Nothing less than pleasant throughout. *40%*

The Quiet Man 8 Year Old bourbon cask, bott code L18080088 **(88.5) n23 t23 f20.5 b22** Forget the finale: salute, quietly, the nose and delivery! *46%. ncf sc. 385 bottles.*

The Quiet Man 12 Year Old Kentucky bourbon casks **(93) n23 t23.5 f23 b23.5** Odd, isn't it? The owner of this brand named this whisky The Quiet Man in memory of his father, John Mulgrew, who was known by that epithet. Yet, coincidentally, it was Maurice Walsh, the grandfather of one of the greatest Irish whiskey blenders of all time, Barry Walsh, who wrote the novel The Quiet Man from which the film was made. I feel another movie coming on: The Silence of the Drams. But sssshhhh: don't tell anyone... *46%. ncf.*

The Quiet Man 12 Year Old Sherry Finished bourbon casks, finished in oloroso sherry casks, bott code: L17304295 db **(73) n18.5 t20 f16.6 b18** Ah. Sadly, the sulphur isn't quite as quiet as one might hope. *46%. ncf.*

Sansibar Irish Single Malt 1989 Japonism bott 2018 **(94.5) n23 t23.5 f24 b24** What a joy of an Irish whiskey! Shews its age at every turn, but does so with grace and proves a lovely tune can be played on an old violin... *43.7%. Joint bottling with Shinanoya.*

Sansibar Irish Whiskey 1992 bott 2018 **(89.5) n23 t23 f21.5 b22.5** A honey-drenched Irish concentrating both on nose and delivery on the buttery heather-honey at the heart of its character. The finish is a little on the hot and thin side, but this forgiveable when the vanilla and honey work so beautifully together elsewhere. *49.7%.*

The Sexton Single Malt batch no. L71861F001 **(91) n23 t23.5 f22 b22.5** Unmistakably malt from The Old Bushmills Distillery, and seemingly from sherry cask, also, as that distillery probably enjoys an above average number unsullied by sulphur. *40% (80 proof).*

Teeling Whiskey Aged 30 Years Single Malt white burgundy finish **(94.5) n23.5 t24 f23 b24** A beautifully clean, faultless wine cask makes a huge difference to a whisky...as is evidenced here. The fruit has a curiously unripe chardonnay-type sharpness and vividness to it. What fun! *46%. ncf.*

Teeling Whiskey Single Malt Vol IV Revival Aged 14 Years finished in ex-muscat barrels **(95) n23.5 t23.5 f24 b24** ...Though this muscat appears to be bang on the money... indeed, this is a stunner! *46%. nc ncf.*

Teeling Whiskey Single Malt Vol V Revival Aged 12 Years cognac & brandy casks, bott code: L18 001 088 **(90.5) n23.5 t23.5 f21 b22.5** Sharper than a newly whetted knife. *46%. nc ncf.*

Tullamore D.E.W. Single Malt Aged 14 Years four cask finish: bourbon, oloroso sherry, port & Madeira, bott code: L3 5009TD 08/01/2018 **(76) n23.5 t20 f15.5 b17** Vividly reminds me of the early 1990s when I was regularly in the tasting lab of my dear old friend the late, great Barry Walsh, going through his most recent efforts to try and perfect the balance on his embryonic Bushmills 16. This works wonderfully on the nose but is immediately fragmented on delivery, a problem Barry had to battle with for a good many months, in fact the best part of a year, before things clicked into place. But, also, in those days with a malt of that age there was no such thing as a sulphur problem, either, which there is here and wrecks the finish entirely. *41.3%.*

Tullamore D.E.W. Single Malt Aged 18 Years finished for up to six months in bourbon, oloroso sherry, port & Madeira, bott code: L3 5089TD 11/04/2018 **(88) n23 t22.5 f20.5 b22** Drop the oloroso and this malt could really take off. *41.3%. Less than 2,500 bottles.*

The Whistler Aged 7 Years Natural Cask Strength Oloroso Finished batch no. 02-0360 **(91.5) n22.5 t23.5 f22 b23.5** If you are going to round your malt off using a sherry butt probably dripping in wine when it was filled, your best option is to make the tenancy in the second cask short and then bottle at cask strength. They may not have done the former, but certainly the latter action has helped no-end, as confirmed when tasted alongside Blue Note (below). Infinitely better structure and the spices here make a big difference. Very attractive whiskey, indeed. And helped no end by a clean, sulphur-free sherry butt of the old school. I doff my Panama in finding such (mainly) unsullied sherry butts. 59%. nc ncf.

The Whistler Aged 7 Years The Blue Note Oloroso Finished (87) n22 t22 f21.5 b21.5 The great news: no sulphur! A clean sherry butt, which is a shock in itself. The less good news: the malt was a little too young and lacking in body to really be able to be much more than a vehicle for the grape. Enjoyable, rich sultana with attractive spice. But lacking in whisky-ish structure and complexity: just too much like a straight sweet sherry! 46%. nc ncf.

The Whistler Aged 10 Years How The Years Whistle By Oloroso Finished (92.5) n23 t23.5 f22.5 b23.5 A fabulously clean sherry butt which is much more at home with a broader-spectrumed malt... 46%. nc ncf.

◇ **Writer's Tears Red Head** Oloroso sherry butts (86) n21 t22.5 f21 b21.5 There are so many good things going on here: the gentle, salty orange-blossom honey which drifts across the nose; the voluptuous embrace of the malt on delivery, offering such a happy marriage between barley and spotted dick pudding. At times mouth-watering and alive. But, as on the nose and late on the finish, a dull ache of sulphur. A shame. But, still, the positive points are worth concentrating on... 46%. ncf.

Irish Vatted Malt

◇ **The Liberator Irish Malt Whiskey** Tawny port finish, batch no. one nbc (85.5) n21.5 t22 f21 b21 A big, unwieldy malt with, I have to say, a character unmatched by any Irish whiskey I have before encountered. I can't say this is technically on the money as there appears to be a number of feinty issues bubbling around from nose to finish: not something I have often encountered with Irish malt. And at times the fruit and malt characters appear to wish to spar rather than harmonise. But.... The gristy sugars and a light molasses note does make for the odd fluting and even salivating moment and the spices give some welcome pep. Though of course, those heftier feint notes do gather, as they always tend to do, for an uncomfortable finish. A malt that certainly tells a tale... 46%. 700 bottles. Inaugural Release.

Single Grain
COOLEY County Louth. 1987. Beam Suntory.
Hyde 1916 No.3 Áras Cask Aged 6 Years Single Grain bott Feb 16 (87) n22 t23 f20.5 b21.5 Cooley grain probably ranks as the best being made right now, with the loss of Dumbarton and Port Dundas in Scotland. Sadly, as deliciously rich as this is, far too much toffee on the finish rather detracts from its normal excellence. Highly enjoyable, but the flag flies nowhere near full mast. By the way: the 1916 on the label doesn't represent year of distillation or bottling. Or is there to celebrate the year of my dad's birth. No, it is something a little more political than that. 46%. ncf. 5,000 bottles.

◇ **Kilbeggan Single Grain Irish Whiskey** American oak casks, bott code: L18099 24/09/18 db (85.5) n22 t22 f21 b20.5 This is one of the finest grain distilleries in the world: certainly the best in Ireland and a match for anything at the other end of the Irish Sea. The unmistakable mouthfeel and early volley of sugars confirms that this is Cooley: there is nothing quite so beautiful. But yet again, I'm tasting a Kilbeggan brand with a massive toffee footprint. I wondered at first if it was the oak. But, no, never on a grain like this. This is caramel, as in the colouring stuff. Please, kindly, will you desist from killing your own brilliant whiskey stone dead! Thank you. 43% (86 proof).

MIDLETON County Cork. 1975. Irish Distillers.
Method and Madness Single Grain Irish Whiskey bourbon barrels, finished in virgin Spanish oak casks db (89.5) n22 t22.5 f22 b23 If you've never tasted a sweet Spanish virgin before, here's your chance... 46%.

WEST CORK DISTILLERS County Cork. 2003. West Cork Distillers.
Skibbereen Eagle Single Grain Irish Whiskey Bodega sherry casks db (88.5) n21.5 t23 f22 b22 As frictionless as the post Brexit border between Britain and Ireland shall be... 43%. West Cork Distillers Limited.

UNSPECIFIED SINGLE GRAIN
Egan's Vintage Grain 10 Aged Years bourbon casks, casked 2009, bott 2017, bott code: US001 244 (92.5) n23 t23.5 f22.5 b23.5 Such a beautiful whiskey. Don't be put off by the fact this is grain: this is exceptionally high grade Irish. Very much of the Cooley style, who happen to make the best grain whisky in the British Isles. 46% (92 proof). ncf.

Glendalough 3 Year Old Irish Single Grain sherry & Madeira butts db (**91**) **n**22 **t**23.5 **f**22.5 **b**23 A much richer and more confident grain than their first, sherry-finished version. Excellent. *43%.*

Glendalough Double Barrel Irish Whiskey first aged in American bourbon casks, then Spanish oloroso casks (**88.5**) **n**22.5 **t**23 **f**21 **b**22 A very pleasant malt but rather vague and at times a little dull. *42%*

Glendalough Single Cask Irish Whiskey Calvados XO Cask Finish cask no. 3/12 CX18 (**90**) **n**22 **t**22.5 **f**22.5 **b**23 From its nose and mouthfeel, presumably a grain whisky. If so, why don't they celebrate the fact? *42%. ncf sc. 366 bottles.*

Glendalough Single Cask Irish Whiskey Grand Cru Burgundy Cask Finish cask no. 1/BY19 (**87.5**) **n**22.5 **t**24 **f**20 **b**22 Strikes me more of a grain than a malt whisky this, not least because of the gorgeous velvety mouthfeel. The honeys on delivery are sublime: predominantly ulmo honey but a little acacia slipping in, too. There is a light fruitiness getting on the act. But the finish is undone slightly by the furry tang of a naughty wine cask. A real shame, for otherwise this would have been one hell of a score... *42%. ncf sc. 366 bottles.*

Hyde No. 5 Áras Cask 1860 Single Grain burgundy cask finished, bott Jul 16 (**86**) **n**21 **t**22.5 **f**21 **b**21.5 When I first heard about this bottling I was intrigued: one of the softest yet most charismatic grain whiskies in the world rounded off in pinot noir grape casks. Would the grape add an intriguing flintiness to the proceedings, or be of a type to soften it further? Sadly, it was the latter. Yes, sulphur free and clean (itself a minor miracle) and with plenty of chewy fruit caramels and even a little spice. But the peaks have been levelled and what is left is a pleasant, easy drinking, sweet but mainly featureless malt. *46%. ncf. 5,000 bottles.*

Teeling Whiskey Single Grain wine casks, bott Mar 17, bott code: L17 004 075 (**94**) **n**23 **t**24 **f**23 **b**24 What a beautiful grain whisky this is. Thankfully the wine casks don't interrupt the already spellbinding narrative. *46%. ncf.*

Single Rye
KILBEGGAN County Westmeath. 1757, recommenced distilling 2007. Beam Suntory.

◇ **Kilbeggan Small Batch Rye Irish Whiskey** bott code: L18094 20/09/18 db (**85.5**) **n**22.5 **t**22 **f**20.5 **b**20.5 Quite brilliant to see rye whiskey coming out of Ireland: long may it continue. However, for the next batch I'd like to see it up its game considerably, as this is surprisingly tame. Certainly the rye momentarily brightens up the nose like the sun peering through a cloud to unveil the rich colours of a country garden. But then it hides behind a cloud again, in this case one of unbudging caramel with no silver lining whatsoever. The fact that it feels that there is no finish to this, so anaemic has it become, means this whiskey is not yet aligned as it should be: something is blocking the glory of the rye. And we know it is there, for on delivery it shimmers like a pearl before disappearing through your fingers and into the depths. *43% (86 proof).*

Blends
Bushmills 12 Years Old Distillery Reserve db (**86**) **n**22.5 **t**22.5 **f**20 **b**21. This version has gone straight for the ultra lush feel. For those who want to take home some 40% abv fruit fudge from the distillery. *40%*

Bushmills 1608 400th Anniversary (**83**) **n**21 **t**21.5 **f**20 **b**20.5. Thin-bodied, hard as nails and sports a peculiarly Canadian feel. *46%. Diageo.*

Bushmills 1608 db (**87**) **n**22 **t**23 **f**20 **b**22. A blend which, through accident, evolution or design, has moved a long way in style from when first launched. More accent on fruit though, predictably, the casks aren't quite what they once were. Ignoring the furriness on the finish, there is much to enjoy on the grape-must nose and how the fruit bounces off the rigid grain on delivery. *46%*

Bushmills Black Bush (**91**) **n**23 **t**23 **f**21.5 **b**23.5. This famous old blend may be under new management and even blender. But still the high quality, top-notch complexity rolls around the glass and your palate. As beautiful as ever. *40%*

◇ **Bushmills Black Bush** (**95**) **n**24 a teasing singing of the crisp fruit notes and far from shy and tender malt: sexy and disarming; **t**24 supremely rich, making the most of the rock hard grain to fully emphasis both the juicy barley and lusciousness of the grape influence; **f**23 dries, allowing the caramel to take a bow. But the spices up their tempo to compensate **b**24 a blend that just feels so right on the palate. Remains a true work of Irish art... *40%.* 🏆

Bushmills Black Bush bott code L6140IB001 (**95**) **n**23.5 **t**24 **f**23.5 **b**24 Of all the famous old blends in the British Isles, this has probably bucked the trend by being an improvement on its already excellent self. The warehouses of Bushmills distillery boast the highest quantity of quality, unsulphured sherry butts I have encountered in the last 20 years, and this is borne out by a blend which has significantly upped the wine influence in the recipe but has not paid a price for it, as has been the usual case in Scotland. Indeed, it has actually benefitted. This is a belter, even by its normal own high standards. Truly classic and should be far easier to find than is normally the case today. *40%.*

Bushmills Original (80) n19 t21 f20 b20. Remains one of the hardest whiskeys on the circuit with the Midleton grain at its most unflinching. There is a sweeter, faintly maltier edge to this now while the toffee and biscuits qualities remain. 40%

Bushmills Red Bush bourbon casks, bott code: L7161IB001 db (92) n22 t23.5 f23 b23.5 A beautifully balanced and erudite blended Irish fully deserving of discovery. And after the preponderance of wine-finished Irish from elsewhere, it was great to taste one that hadn't already set my nerves jangling in fear of what was to come. A worthy and beautiful addition to the Bushmills range. I always knew I'd be a little bit partial to a Red Bush. 40%.

⬦ **Bushmills White Bush** bott code: L8185 IB 02S (85) n21 t22 f21 b21 For decades this was the toughest blend in all Ireland, the one you not so much cut your teeth on, but broke them. The grain was hard enough to make ships from in the dockyards and you drank this not so much for the pleasantries, but the effect. In recent years it has yielded a little to finer tastes, and though the nose still gives away absolutely nothing – except toffeed grain – at least the delivery on the palate is both clean and salivating. No off notes from second rate sherry butts. Just a sweet toffee firmness that has now also done away with the old aggressive finale. Surprisingly pleasant. 40%. Known as "White Bush" due to the white label.

⬦ **Clonakilty Irish Whiskey** batch no. NEBC002. bourbon cask, Imperial Stout Trooper cask finish (88.5) n21.5 t22.5 f22.5 b22 Just love the brightness on the delivery, especially the initial burst of malt. Beer cask finishes have embittered me over the years, but pleased to report that there is no hop interference and residue here and those strikingly juicy tones on delivery carry through unmolested. Decent cocoa at the death, too. 50.2%. ncf. 1,400 bottles. Bottled for New England Brewing Co.

Clonakilty Port Cask Finish batch no. 0012 (90) n22 t23 f22 b23 A whiskey where you're between a rock and a soft, fruity place... 43.6%. ncf. 1,000 bottles. Cask Finish Series.

Clonakilty Single Batch batch no. 003/2018 (86) n21 t22 f21.5 b21.5 Clean and salivating, this is a hard as nails, simplistic Irish dependent on toffee as its principal flavour profile. 43.6%. ncf.

⬦ **Clonakilty Single Batch The Gentle Cut** batch no. 012 (86) n22 t23 f19.5 b21.5 Starts rather beautifully, with the rigid grain allowing the sugars scope to bring forward the sugars and spices out into the open. The finish, though, is dry and off balance. 43.6%. ncf. 1,500 bottles.

The Dead Rabbit Aged 5 Years virgin American oak finished, bott no. L18001-011 (93) n23 t23.5 f23 b23.5 The rabbit is dead: long live Dead Rabbit...! Oh, Murray Method to take this from a decent to a truly excellent Irish, by the way. 44%.

The Dublin Liberties Oak Devil bott no. L17 048 W3 (94) n23.5 t23.5 f23 b24 The Cooley grain at work here is of superstar status. So beautifully balanced and the word "lush" hardly does it justice... 46%.

The Dubliner Bourbon Cask Aged batch no. 001, bott no. L0187F252 (87.5) n21.5 t22.5 f21.5 b22 A soft, clean attractive blend which peaks on delivery with a lilting juiciness which works brilliantly with the grain which is as yielding as a feathered silk pillow. Vague spices plot a course towards the bitter lemon finish. 40%.

The Dubliner Master Distiller's Reserve bourbon casks, bott no. L17718-320 (91) n23.5 well blow me...salt! More than that, tidal rock pools...; t23 crisp, juicy and lightly bathed in lime blossom honey; f22 the saltiness returns with the vanilla; b22.5 refreshing and tender. A bit of an understated treat. 42%.

Dundalgan Charred Cask Irish Whiskey db (87) n21.5 t22 f22 b21.5 This is an interesting one: you have a spirit that produces a fair chunk of oil. You then char a cask, which produces caramel. The only result possible is a thick whiskey on both nose and palate with limited scope to develop. So although the end product is the antonym of complexity, the flavours and mouthfeel are attractive and satisfying, especially if you are into malt and toffee. There are even some very late spices to stir things up a bit. 40%. West Cork Distillers Limited.

Dundalgan Irish Whiskey db (84) n21 t21 f21 b21.5 Pleasant, inoffensive, toffee-dominant and bland. 40%. West Cork Distillers Limited.

Dunville's Three Crowns (80) n19 t22 f19 b20 Three casks and Three Crowns. So three cheers for the return of one of the great names in Irish whiskey! Somewhere in my warehouse I have a few original bottles of this stuff I picked up in Ireland over the years and at auction. None I opened tasted quite like this. Have to say that, despite the rich-lip-smacking delivery, certain aspects of the tangy nose and finish don't quite gel and are a little off key. The coronation remains on hold... 43.5%.

Dunville's Three Crowns Peated (94.5) n23 t24 f23.5 b24 Even people purporting not to like peaty whisk(e)y will have a problem finding fault with this. This is a rare treat of an Irish. 43.5%.

⬦ **Egan's Centenary** finished in French Limousin XO Cognac casks nbc (94) n23 while the grain and oaks have forged a very comfortable partnership, there is enough artistry in the sugars and cunning to the vanilla to make for a complex and beautifully poised nose; t23.5

as on the nose, you get the feeling that this is grain heavy. But that doesn't matter a jot when the vanillas and Demerara sugars are so happily combined and the mouthfeel this lush. You expect spices, and they dutifully arrive, with a little bit of warmth to them, but nothing like enough to knock the balance out; **f23.5** long, lush and not a single weakness. No bitterness, but outstanding oak confirming the blend's overall excellence; **b24** so wonderful to find an Irish where both the spirit and the oak is in such deep harmony. A subtle Irish where the blender has carefully listened to what the casks are telling him. Superb. 46%. 5,995 bottles.

Feckin Irish Whiskey (81) n20 t21 f20 b20. Tastes just about exactly the feckin same as the Feckin Strangford Gold... 40%. The Feckin Drinks Co.

Flannigans Blended Irish Whiskey (87.5) n21.5 t22.5 f21.5 b22 About as mouthwatering and easy going a blended Irish as you'll hope to find. Excellent sugars and velvety body ensure the most pleasant, if simple, of rides. Even a little spice peps up the flagging finish. 40%. Quality Spirits International.

Great Oaks Cask Strength Irish Whiskey db **(90.5) n22 t23 f22.5 b23** A joyful whisky brimming with personality. 60%. West Cork Distillers Limited.

Great Oaks Irish Whiskey db **(87) n22 t22 f21.5 b21.5** Easy going, full of its signature caramel chewy sweetness. Pleasant and non-threatening. 46%. West Cork Distillers Limited.

Great Oaks New Frontiers Irish Whiskey db **(94) n23.5 t24 f23 b23.5** Very high class and inventive Irish. West Cork have seriously raised their game here and have entered a new quality dimension. 59%. West Cork Distillers Limited.

⬦ **Hinch Aged 5 Years Double Wood** ex bourbon casks & virgin American oak barrels, bott code: 16919 **(93) n23** complex, as you would hope. Nutty, as you wouldn't expect; light liquorice as you well might. But the malt pulses through, too...as it should. Very attractive...; **t23.5** the delivery isn't immediately interested in cask selection: it is the malt which explodes of the palate – youthful, sprightly and robust. Slowly the tannins zero in and make their mark, bringing a lot of spice into play in the process. The midpoint is probably the highlight, with barley sugar candy in rich association with warm tannins and red liquorice; **f23**much softer oak, but remains rich; **b23.5** a malt which works very well indeed, and deserves to. And even more so if at a greater strength and non-filtration. Impressive and highly enjoyable Irish which gives you minimum blarney and the truest flavour profile. 43%. The Time Collection.

⬦ **Hinch Aged 10 Years Sherry Cask Finish** bott code: 23519 **(89) n21.5** not the tidiest. A little green in part; **t23** ah...that's better! The nose makes no sense whatsoever, and for a start the first wave or two of the delivery offers equally little clarification. But suddenly a tidal wave of concentrated sultana rushes across the palate leaving a mix of malt and lemon drops in its wake; **f22** slightly untidy again, though with no off notes from the sherry (congratulations and heart-felt thanks to all at Hinch for that one!); **b22.5** an, at first confused and later more relaxed, Irish that offers plenty of enjoyment. So many memorable moments, but a little more care with these casks would have brought a lot more. Still, that's my blender's perfectionist hat on. Just enjoy it! 43%. The Time Collection.

⬦ **Hinch Small Batch Bourbon Cask** bott code: 16919 **(93) n23** you know when your car is running perfectly, without a note out of place on the highly tuned engine...well, so is the nose here just purring along to perfection. Some superb bourbon casks allow the malt license to thrill, the grains a license to trill...; **t23.5** a clean and uncluttered delivery save for a little toffee. Appears to be high percentage malt, as the barley really does penetrate and pulse on this. The spices are upfront and increase the already high salivation levels further; **f23** an intertwangling of vanilla, toffee and malt...; **b23.5** the bourbon casks make such a difference here. A blend which is allowed to shew both its sweeter and richer nature. 43%. The Time Collection.

Hyde No. 6 President's Reserve 1938 Commemorative Edition sherry cask finish, bott May 17 **(77) n18 t22 f18 b19** Lush grape for sure. But the very last thing I'd commemorate anything in would be a sherry cask: unless you want sulphur to give you a good Hyding.... 46%. ncf.

The Irishman Founder's Reserve Caribbean Cask Finish rum cask, cask no. 9657 **(93) n23 t23.5 f23 b23.5** This brings to an end a run of tasting six consecutive Irish whiskies, each tainted by sulphur. This, naturally, has not an atom of sulphur as, sensibly, no sherry cask was used anywhere in the maturation (three hearty cheers!). Frankly, I don't know whether to drink it, or kiss it.... 46%. ncf sc. 318 bottles.

The Irishman Founder's Reserve Florio Marsala Cask Finish cask no. 2786 **(82.5) n21 t23.5 f17.5 b20** A nipping, acidic, biting nose: borderline aggressive. But, momentarily, all is forgiven! The fruit is as lush as any delivery in the world this year, helped along by a thin maple syrup sweetness and balancing vanillas. Shame, then, about the very late sulphur tang. Whoever put the sulphur candle in this cask wants shooting: this would otherwise have been real stunner. 46%. ncf sc. 204 bottles.

The Irishman Superior Irish Whiskey bott code L6299L059 **(93) n23 t23 f23 b24.** What a quite wonderful blend: not of the norm for those that have recently come onto the market and there is much more of the Irish Distillers about this than most. Forget about the smoke promised in the tasting notes on the label...it gives you everything else but. 40%.

J. J. Corry The Battalion finished in tequila & Mezcal casks, batch no. 1, Spring 2019, bott code: L7256L1375 **(91.5) n22 t23.5 f23 b23** My Mexican hat off to the blender here, who appears to have worked exceptionally hard to ensure there was no dominance by any single party. And succeeded. 41%. 700 bottles.

J. J. Corry The Gael batch no. 1, Summer 2017, bott code: L7256L1375 **(86.5) n22 t22.5 f20.5 b21.5** An essentially bone-crushingly dry blend with a fair bit of fizz and nip here and there. Plenty of pith on both nose and delivery and soars from the prosaic to the poetic around about four flavour waves in when the malt and tannin finally combine in brief harmony. The finish, however, takes you over pretty rough terrain. Certainly the label raised a smile with the claim that this was a "Classic Irish" because I can't remember too many blends over the last four decades which included 26-year-old malt. 46%. 7000 bottles.

Jameson (95) n24.5 24 f22.5 b24 I thought I had detected in bottlings I had found around the world a very slight reduction in the Pot Still character that defines this truly classic whiskey. So I sat down with a fresh bottle in more controlled conditions...and was blown away as usual. The sharpness of the PS is vivid and unique; the supporting grain of the required crispness. Fear not: this very special whiskey remains in stunning, truly wondrous form. 40%

Jameson bott code L701012030 **(87) n22 t22.5 f21 b21.5** Now, isn't that the way it always happens! Having tasted crisp, characterful true-to-form Jamesons around the globe for the last year or so, the one I get here for a re-taste is the "other" version. Suddenly the sexiest Irish on the market has become a dullard. Where it should be soaring with Pot Still it is laden with toffee. And a little sulphur nagging on the finish doesn't help, either. Does tick the other boxes, though. But hardly representative. 40%.

Jameson 18 Years Old bott code L629231345 **(91) n22 t23 f23 b23** Definitely a change in direction from the last Jameson 18 I analysed. More grain focussed and paying less heed to the oak. 40%.

Jameson Black Barrel bott code L700431433 **(93) n23 t23.5 f23 b23.5** An improved, more sugar-laden and spicy whiskey. 40%.

⬨ **Jameson Black Barrel** double charred bourbon barrels, bott code: L932431768 **(93) n23 t23 f23.5 b23.5** Probably the softest Irish whisky I have encountered in over 40 years. But the complex sexing up by the spice raises the standard to another level. 40%.

Jameson The Blender's Dog bott code L608231059 **(91.5) n22.5 t23 f23 b23** A very slight variance on the previous sample (above) with the grain whiskey a little more dominant here despite the softer mouthfeel. All the usual tricks and intrigues though a little less orange blossom honey a tad more maple syrup, which helps lengthen the finale. 43%.

Jameson Bold bott code L617431172 **(93) n24 t23.5 f22.5 b23** Absolutely spot on with the tasting notes above. Only changes are slightly more fudge through the centre ground and a degree less bitterness on the finish, though still there. Crucially, however, the honey has a bigger late say. 40%. The Deconstructed Series.

Jameson Bow Street 18 Years Old batch no. 1/2018, bott code: L804431050 **(88.5) n22.5 t23.5 f20 b22.5** Few whiskies have such a wide flavour register between tooth-decayingly sweet and puckeringly dry. 55.3%. ncf.

Jameson Caskmates (91.5) n23.5 t23 f22 b23 Some serious elements of Jameson Gold involved in this, especially the acacia honey thread. Delightful. 40%

Jameson Caskmates IPA Edition bott code: L735315273 **(70.5) n18 t18.5 f17 b17** And you want to ruin the taste of a fine whiskey by adding the bitter taste of hops because...? Why exactly? Am I missing something here...? 40%. ncf.

Jameson Caskmates Stout Edition bott code L629315085 **(93) n22 t23.5 f24 b23.5** A very different experience to the Teeling equivalent. Here, the beer is far less prevalent on nose and taste, but makes a significant, highly positive, contribution to the mouthfeel. A super lush experience. 40%.

Jameson The Cooper's Croze bott code L608231057 **(94.5) n23.5 t24 f22.5 b24** Huh! Near enough same final score as last time, though a gentle change in emphasis and shape means the scoring itself was slightly different. Remains the most astonishingly lush and richly-flavoured of whiskeys, except on this bottling there is a bigger toffee surge, especially towards the finish and a gentle bitter tail off which has cost a half mark. Just remember: whatever anyone ever tells you, no two bottlings are identical: it is impossible. 43%. The Whiskey Makers Series.

⬨ **Jameson The Cooper's Croze** bott code: L929031684 **(94.5) n23.5** Oh, joy! No sulphur on the nose! Instead tapering strands of butterscotch and vanilla with ulmo honey taking any bite off the tannin. So lovely....; **t24** with a nose as light as that, surely the delivery has to be about mouth-watering complexity. And it is. Some barley escapes here and there, a little grassy and fresh while the mouthfeel is butterfly light but just oily enough for the sugars and lightly toasted vanillas to weigh anchor; **f23** duller, certainly. But still those spiced sugars are in play as in the ulmo honey and vanilla. All just quietly done; **b24** after a spate of pretty soul-destroying sulphur-riddled and spoiled Irish whiskeys, I could almost weep for coming across a bottling that is just as beautiful as when I tasted it last. Magnificent whiskey. *43%. ncf.*

Jameson Crested bott code L635731441 **(91) n23 t23.5 f22 b22.5** That's curious. A slight upping of the caramels here has slightly reduced the overall complexity, and the depth of the fruit. However, the bitter, off-key finish from my last sample is missing here making, when all is said and done, a slightly more satisfying all round experience. Swings and roundabouts... *40%.*

◈ **Jameson Crested** bott code: L933631800 **(85.5) n22 t23 f19.5 b21** Unquestionably dulled since its release – or re-lease, if you count the classic old Crested 10 brand. A little barley sneaks through on the nose but the degree of toffee seems to have increased exponentially. A slightly furry grape kick towards the finale, but not too untoward. Incredibly far removed from the Crested 10 I used to regularly drink over 30 years ago. Unrecognisable, in fact. *40%.*

Jameson The Distiller's Safe bott code L60331023 **(93) n24 t24 f22 b23** This brand's safe, too...at least for another bottling! As near as damn it a re-run of the last bottle I tasted, though here the butteryness kicks in sooner and there is a vague bitterness on the now chocolate-flaked finale. Still a stunner. *43%. The Whiskey Makers Series.*

Jameson Gold Reserve (88) n22 t23 f20 b22. Enjoyable, but so very different: an absolute re-working with all the lighter, more definitively sweeter elements shaved mercilessly while the thicker oak is on a roll. Some distance from the masterpiece it once was. *40%*

Jameson Lively bott code L617431174 **(85.5) n21 t22 f21.5 b21** Well you have to applaud them for keeping to the script. A couple of thumbs up from the last bottling: the impact appears to have been softened very slightly (though, sadly, via toffee) and spices at the finish do no harm at all. *40%. The Deconstructed Series.*

Jameson Round bott code L625831239 **(93.5) n22.5 t24 f23.5 b23.5** Just such a sensual whiskey... *40%. The Deconstructed Series.*

Jameson Signature bott code L617531177 **(93) n24 t23.5 f22.5 b23** No longer Signature Reserve, though every bit as good. This, though, like some other Jamesons of late appears to have an extra dose of caramel. Bring the colouring down and whiskey – and the scores here - will really fly! *40%.*

Jameson Signature Reserve (93) n23.5 t23.5 f22.5 b23.5. Be assured that Signature, with its clever structuring of delicate and inter-weaving flavours, says far more about the blender, Billy Leighton, than it does John Jameson. *40%. Irish Distillers.*

Kilbeggan bott code L7091 db **(86) n21 t22 f21.5 b21.5.** A much more confident blend by comparison with that faltering one of the last few years. Here, the malts make a significant drive towards increasing the overall complexity and gentle citrus style. *40%. Cooley.*

◈ **Kilbeggan Traditional Irish Whiskey** bott code: L19113 16/10/19 db **(88) n22 t22.5 f21.5 b22** A really lovely Irish blend, making best use of some prime grain whisky which allows the barley present to ramp up the complexity and oak likewise with the spices. Just a shade too much toffee at the death. *40% (80 proof).*

Kilbeggan 15 Years Old bott code L7048 db **(85.5) n21.5 t22 f21 b21.** My word! 15 years, eh? How time flies! And on the subject of flying, surely I have winged my way back to Canada and am tasting a native blend. No, this is Irish albeit in sweet, deliciously rounded form. However, one cannot help feeling that the dark arts have been performed, as in an injection of caramel, which, as well as giving that Canadian feel has also probably shaved off some of the more complex notes to middle and finish. Even so, a sweet, silky experience. *40%. Cooley.*

Kilbeggan 18 Year Old db **(89) n23 t21.5 f22.5 b22.** Although the impressive bottle lavishly claims "From the World's Oldest Distillery" I think one can take this as so much Blarney. It certainly had my researcher going, who lined this up for me under the Old Kilbeggan distillery, a forgiveable mistake and one I think he will not be alone in making. This, so it appears on the palate, is a blend. From the quite excellent Cooley distillery, and it could be that whiskey used in this matured at Kilbeggan... which is another thing entirely. As for the whiskey: apart from some heavy handedness on the toffee, it really is quite a beautiful and delicate thing. *40%*

Kinahan's Heritage Small Batch Blend (87.5) n22 t23 f23 b21.5. All aboard for the plush delivery, a gorgeous mix of briefly intense malt but overwhelmingly soft, sweet and embracing grain. The weak link is the tart and rough-edged finale, undermined further by a slight bitter note. But earlier there is plenty of fun to be had with the vanilla and spices. *46%.*

Kinahan's KASC Project B. 001 hybrid cask (Portuguese, American, French, Hungarian & chestnut) **(86) n20 t22 f22 b22** Well, that is different. The wood has the biggest say here, especially on the nose where the spirit is left bullied, quivering and unnoticed in some inaccessible corner. While the flavour profile is very pleasant, it certainly didn't ring true and when I later spotted the chestnut inclusion, the sensations immediately made sense. Intriguing, though. *43%.*

◈ **Lambay Whiskey Small Batch Blend** finished in Cognac casks, bott code: L4732519 21/11/19 **(92) n23** rare clarity on the nose for a blend - and by no means usual for this degree of malt to be so easy to detect. The firm grain and lively peppers form an excellent accompaniment; **t23** the silky mouthfeel is all about the grain and makes no apologies for it. Slowly the malts come into focus and both styles mingle comfortably with a delicate acacia honey sheen; **f22.5** more chalky vanillas in play, but, as on their malt, the finish has a slightly rough edge; **b23.5** the uncomfortable landing on the finish apart, this is a blend to savour with high quality malt making the most of a very sympathetic grain. Some really beautiful moments... *40%. ncf.*

Midleton Very Rare 30th Anniversary Pearl Edition db **(91) n23.5 t24 f21 b22.5** The nose and delivery will go down in Irish whiskey folklore... *53.1%*

Midleton Very Rare 1984 (70) n19 t18 f17 b16. Disappointing with little backbone or balance. *40%. Irish Distillers.*

Midleton Very Rare 1985 (77) n20 t20 f18 b19. Medium-bodied and oily, this is a big improvement on the initial vintage. *40%. Irish Distillers.*

Midleton Very Rare 1986 (79) n21 t20 f18 b20. A very malty Midleton richer in character than previous vintages. *40%. Irish Distillers.*

Midleton Very Rare 1987 (77) n20 t19 f19 b19. Quite oaky at first until a late surge of excellent pot still. *40%. Irish Distillers.*

Midleton Very Rare 1988 (86) n23 t21 f21 b21. A landmark MVR as it is the first vintage to celebrate the Irish pot-still style. *40%. Irish Distillers.*

Midleton Very Rare 1989 (87) n22 t22 f22 b21. A real mouthful but has lost balance to achieve the effect. *40%. Irish Distillers.*

Midleton Very Rare 1990 (93) n23 t23 f24 b23. Astounding whiskey: one of the vintages every true Irish whiskey lover should hunt for. *40%. Irish Distillers.*

Midleton Very Rare 1991 (76) n19 t20 f19 b18. After the Lord Mayor's Show, relatively dull and uninspiring. *40%. Irish Distillers.*

Midleton Very Rare 1992 (84) n20 t20 f23 b21. Superb finish with outstanding use of feisty grain. *40%. Irish Distillers.*

Midleton Very Rare 1993 (88) n21 t22 f23 b22. Big, brash and beautiful – the perfect way to celebrate the 10th-ever bottling of MVR. *40%. Irish Distillers.*

Midleton Very Rare 1994 (87) n22 t22 f21 b22. Another different style of MVR, one of amazing lushness. *40%. Irish Distillers.*

Midleton Very Rare 1995 (90) n23 t24 b21 b22. They don't come much bigger than this. Prepare a knife and fork to battle through this one. Fabulous. *40%. Irish Distillers.*

Midleton Very Rare 1996 (82) n21 t22 f19 b20. The grains lead a soft course, hardened by subtle pot still. Just missing a beat on the finish, though. *40%. Irish Distillers.*

Midleton Very Rare 1997 (83) n22 t21 f19 b21. The piercing pot still fruitiness of the nose is met by a countering grain of rare softness on the palate. Just dies on the finish when you want it to make a little speech. Very drinkable. *40%. Irish Distillers.*

Midleton Very Rare 1999 (89) n21 t23 f22 b23. One of the maltiest Midletons of all time: a superb blend. *40%. Irish Distillers.*

Midleton Very Rare 2000 (85) n22 t21 f21 b21. An extraordinary departure even by Midleton's eclectic standards. The pot still is like a distant church spire in an hypnotic Fen landscape. *40%. Irish Distillers.*

Midleton Very Rare 2001 (79) n21 t20 f18 b20. Extremely light but the finish is slightly on the bitter side. *40%. Irish Distillers.*

Midleton Very Rare 2002 (79) n20 t22 f18 b19. The nose is rather subdued and the finish is likewise toffee-quiet and shy. There are some fabulous middle moments, some of flashing genius, when the pot still and grain combine for a spicy kick, but the finish really is lacklustre and disappointing. *40%. Irish Distillers.*

Midleton Very Rare 2003 (84) n22 t22 f19 b21. Beautifully fruity on both nose and palate (even some orange blossom on aroma). But the delicious spicy richness that is in mid launch on the tastebuds is cut short by caramel on the middle and finish. A crying shame, but the best Midleton for a year or two. *40%. Irish Distillers.*

Midleton Very Rare 2004 (82) n21 t21 f19 b21. Yet again caramel is the dominant feature, though some quite wonderful citrus and spice escape the toffeed blitz. *40%.*

Midleton Very Rare 2005 (92) n23 t24 f22 b23. OK, you can take this one only as a rough translation. The sample I have worked from here is from the Irish Distillers blending lab, reduced to 40% in mine but without caramel added. And, as Midleton Very Rares always are at this stage, it's an absolute treat. Never has such a great blend suffered so in the hands of colouring and here the chirpiness of the pot still and élan of the honey (very Jameson Gold Label in part) show just what could be on offer given half the chance. Has wonderful natural colour and surely it is a matter of time before we see this great whiskey in its natural state. *40%*

Midleton Very Rare 2006 (92) n22 t24 f23 b23. As raw as a Dublin rough-house and for once not overly swamped with caramel. An uncut diamond. *40%*

Midleton Very Rare 2007 (83) n20 t22 f20 b21. Annoyingly buffeted from nose to finish by powering caramel. Some sweeter wisps do escape but the aroma suggests Canadian and insufficient Pot Still gets through to make this a Midleton of distinction. *40%. Irish Distillers*

Midleton Very Rare 2008 (88.5) n22 t23 f21.5 b22. A dense bottling which offers considerably more than the 2007 Vintage. Attractive, very drinkable and without the caramel it might really have hit the heights. *40%. Irish Distillers.*

Midleton Very Rare 2009 (95) n24 t24 f23 b24. I've been waiting a few years for one like this to come along. One of the most complex, cleanest and least caramel-spoiled bottlings for a good few years and one which makes the pot still character its centre piece. A genuine celebration of all things Midleton and Barry Crockett's excellence as a distiller in particular. *40%.*

Midleton Very Rare 2010 (84) n21 t22 f20 b21. A case of after the Lord Mayor's Show. Chewy and some decent sugars. But hard to make out detail through the fog of caramel. *40%*

Midleton Very Rare 2011 (81.5) n22.5 t20 f19 b20 Another disappointing version where the colour of its personality has been compromised for the sake of the colour in the bottle. A dullard of a whiskey, especially after the promising nose. *40%. Irish Distillers.*

Midleton Very Rare Irish Whisky 2012 db (89.5) n22 t23 f22 b22.5. Much more like it! After a couple of dud vintages, here we have a bottling worthy of its great name & heritage. *40%*

Midleton Very Rare Irish Whisky 2014 db (78.5) n20.5 t22 f17 b19. Must say how odd it looks to see Brian Nation's signature scrawled across the label and not Barry Crockett's. Also, I was a bit worried by this one when I saw the depth of orange hue to this whiskey. Sadly, my fears were pretty well founded. Toffee creaks from every corner making for a mainly flat encounter with what should be an uplifting Irish. Some lift at about the midway point when something, probably pot still, throws off the shackles of its jailer and emerges briefly with spice. But all rather too little, especially in the face of a dull, disappointingly flawed, fuzzy finale. Midleton Very Rare should be, as the name implies, a lot, lot better than this safe but flabby, personality bypassed offering. The most frustrating aspect of this is that twice I have tasted MVR in lab form just prior to bottling. And both were quite stunning whiskeys. That was until the colouring was added in the bottling hall. *40% WB15/416*

Midleton Very Rare 2016 (87.5) n22 t22.5 f21.5 b21.5 The grain, not exactly the most yielding, has the clearest mandate to show its uncompromising personality A huge caramel presence softens the impact and leads to a big show of coffee towards the finish. But between these two OTT beasts the Pot Still is lost completely soon after its initial delicious impact on delivery. *40%.*

Midleton Very Rare 2017 (90.5) n22 t23.5 f22 b23 Slightly less toffee than there has been, but still a fraction too much. But superb complexity levels nonetheless and one of the most attractively sweet MVRs for a little while. *40%.*

Midleton Very Rare 2018 bott code: L826431444 (88.5) n22.5 t23 f21 b22 All about understatement. But like many an Irish at the moment, just weakens towards the finish. *40%.*

⬦ **Midleton Very Rare 2019** bott code: L925431568 db (92) n23 a bright nose with myriad citrus notes: even a degree of sherbet fizz. A deft interplay by younger tones and older ones, so the grains seem fresh and lively while a little tannin slows things down to its own pace. Charming, especially when the sultanas reveal a little spice bite; t23.5 icing sugar sprinkled over vanilla...and the former melts almost instantaneously. Rare to find vanilla and butterscotch so early up in a whisky (they normally wait until the end of play before emerging). But there they are, as bright as a button; f22 just a little bitterness from the sherry casks. But it is dealt with admirably (though not entirely) by those vanillas and the lingering butterscotch. And now even a light trace of ulmo honey...; b23.5 one of the better Midletons for a while and really going full out for maximum meltdown effect. Classy, if slightly flawed. *40%.*

Mizen Head Original Irish Whiskey Bodega sherry casks db (87.5) n21.5 t22.5 f21.5 b22 Maybe this was a bit unlucky, in that I have just come from tasting Glenfarclas sherry casks of the 1980s to this. No damaging sulphur (though a little forms late on the finale), so some Brownie points there. But the lack of body to the spirit and shortage of complexity on the grape, beyond a delicious cinnamon spice, doesn't help the cause. Enjoyable, but thinner than you might expect or desire. *40%. West Cork Distillers Limited.*

Natterjack Irish Whiskey Blend No. 1 virgin American oak finish, bott code: L19/001 044 (92) n22 t23.5 f23 b23.5 A delicious whiskey and looking forward to seeing Blend No 2. But I find the label confusing: a "mash bill or malted barley and corn". Does this mean that is the distillation from a mash recipe of malt and corn? Hence the mash bill comment. Or, as I don't think they actually distilled this themselves, a blend of malt and corn whiskey? Which means that it isn't a mash bill of corn and barley. Far too vague for the consumer. Very enjoyable, nonetheless. *40%. Gortinore Distillers & Co.*

Natterjack Irish Whiskey Cask Strength virgin American oak finish **(89)** n22.5 some vivid tannins leap out and at you from the nose...frog-like...; fair bit of citrus doing the rounds; t22.5 beautiful mouthfeel. Lightly oiled but clean, followed by a procession of vanilla-led sugars. As on the nose, the tannins interject almost rudely; f22 just a little tangy and threatens to stray off-piste. But the butterscotch holds firm, again despite the intervention of some odd tannin tones...; b22 at around 40% I thought this was pretty strange whiskey: this is 50% weirder still. Enjoyable, if head-scratching stuff – though you might end up with splinters in your fingers as it seems to be the oak which causes the extra confusion... *63%. Gortinore Distillers & Co.*

Paddy (74) n18.5 t20 f17.5 b18. Cleaned its act up a little. Even a touch of attractive citrus on the nose and delivery. But where does that cloying sweetness come from? As bland as an Irish peat bog but, sadly, nothing like so potentially tasty. *40%. Irish Distillers.*

Powers (91) n23 t24 f22 b22. Is it any coincidence that in this bottling the influence of the caramel has been significantly reduced and the whiskey is getting back to its old, brilliant self? I think not. Classic stuff. *40%. Irish Distillers.*

Powers Gold Label American oak casks, bott code: L927315375 db **(83)** n21.5 t21.5 f19 b21 Three decades ago, this was always my preferred choice when drinking in Ireland. Not least because of all the blends this was the one that had by far the healthiest Pot Still involvement, and its sturdy magic was there to be savoured despite the outrageous amount of caramel that was added, making the whiskey a lot darker than its present incarnation. Today, it is virtually unrecognisable from what was the Irishman's most popular blend. The Pot Still has virtually no input whatsoever, while the sulphur attached to the sherry butts give an unfortunate, nagging, furry finale. Elsewhere the delicate heather honey notes do well. But for those of us who have loved this whiskey for almost a lifetime, it's all a bit of a disappointment... *40%. ncf.*

Powers Gold Label (96) n23 t24.5 f24 b24.5 A slightly different breed. This is not all about minute difference in strength...this is also about weight distribution and flavour pace. It is a subtly different blend...and all the better for it...Make no mistake: this is a truly classic Irish. *43.2%*

The Quiet Man Traditional Irish Whiskey bourbon casks **(88.5)** n22 t22 f22.5 b22 A gentle and genteel whiskey without an unfriendly voice. And with it I toast the memory of John Mulgrew. *40%*

Roe & Co bourbon casks, bott code: L7173NB001 006084 **(89.5)** n22 t23 f22.5 b22 A joyful Irish blend, easy drinking and basking in some outrageously good grain. But the caramel levels could do with coming down slightly for greater complexity. *45%. ncf.*

Roe & Co bourbon casks, bott code: L9227NB001 **(90.5)** n22 once you pick your way through the toffee the interplay between grain and malt becomes apparent and highly attractive; t23.5 the succulent mouthfeel is bolstered by caramel, which means the malt is only partially apparent. But the massaging grains, molasses and bickering spices make for a chewy and attractive middle; f22.5 toffee apple; b22.5 a silky, sexy massively-flavoured blend where the complexity is not only given room to thrive but the bourbon casks ensure an extra degree of rich, honey depth, too. If they could just kill the un-needed caramel, this would be such a big scorer. *45%. ncf.*

Slane Irish Whiskey Triple Casked bott code: L34638 **(86.5)** n22 t22.5 f20.5 b21.5 Soft and supine, this whisky is all about softness and mouthfeel: that feeling of a soothing friend by your side. Could do with a bit more personality on the flavour front so the simple sugars don't over dominate as they have a tendency to do here. Excellent spices slowly grow at the finish to offset the furry bitterness of, presumably, a sherry butt or two at work here. Pleasant and promising whiskey. *40%.*

Teeling Whiskey Barleywine Small Batch Barleywine finish, bott Sept 18, bott code: L18 016 270 **(84.5)** n21 t21.5 f21 b21 Well, that's a new flavour profile after all these decades in the business! Am I big fan? Well, not really. Love the cream soda texture, I admit. And the suffused sweetness But there is a lurking semi-bitterness which seems to tighten everything about it. I'm sure there are those out there, though, that will worship it. Just not me. *46%. ncf.*

Teeling Whiskey Plantation Rum Small Batch Plantation Rum finish, bott Dec 18, bott code: L18 025 336 **(88)** n22 t23 f21 b22 Works really well until the untidy finish. *46%. ncf.*

Teeling Whiskey Small Batch rum casks, bott Apr 19, bott code: L19 014 093 **(86)** n21.5 t22.5 f21 b21 A whiskey I just can't like as much as I'd like to. Certainly the delivery ticks all the boxes and offers an innate light treacle sweetness, just as one might hope. But there is an intruding bitterness – almost like hop – which interrupts the nose and finish and spoils the party a bit. Odd. *46%. ncf.*

Teeling Whiskey Trois Rivieres Small Batch rhum agricole finish, bott Jul 18, bott code: L18 001 186 **(91)** n22.5 t22.5 f22.5 b23 The most even and relaxed of the three Teeling rum expressions. What it lacks in complexity it makes up for with simple charm. *46%. ncf.*

Tullamore D.E.W. bott code: L1 5297TD 30/11/2018 **(81.5)** n21.5 t21 f19 b20 When you are using a grain as hard as this you have to be careful of the caramel as it amplifies its effects. Lots of toffee followed by a dull buzz. Still a very dull Irish. *40%. William Grant & Sons.*

Tullamore D.E.W. Aged 12 Years bourbon & oloroso sherry casks, bott code: L3 5294TD 22/11/2018 **(91.5) n23** complex, clean and superbly weighted. A lovely citrus note further freshens proceedings; **t23** the firm grain acts as the perfect skeleton on which the sherry builds the flesh. Chewy and increasingly well spiced but always fresh; **f22** long, spiced vanilla; has a shade too much toffee at the death; **b23.5** when a whiskey is this good, you wonder what the other two Tullamore blends are all about. 40%. William Grant & Sons.

Tullamore D.E.W. Caribbean Rum Cask Finish bott code: L1 5184TD 23/07/2018 **(80) n21 t20 f20 b19** Sweet, soft and a dullard of the very first order. Far more effect from the caramel than the rum casks. There may have been exotic fruit in the tasting lab. But it vanished once it entered the bottling hall. So massively disappointing. 43%. William Grant & Sons.

Uisce Beatha Real Irish Whiskey ex-Bourbon cask **(81) n21 t20.5 f19.5 b20.** The label blurb claims this is soft and subtle. That is, about as soft and subtle as if distilled from granite. Hard as nails with dominant grains; takes no prisoners at the death. 40%

West Cork Black Cask Char #5 Level bott code: L17297 db **(89) n22 t23 f22 b22** Good grief! This must be one of the most oil-rich, heavy duty blends I have encountered in my near 30 year whisky career. Either very little grain, or it is a grain distilled to a relatively low strength. Either way...good grief! 40%. West Cork Distillers Limited.

West Cork Bourbon Cask db **(87.5) n22 t22.5 f21 b22** No-one does caramel like West Cork, and even in their blend — in which their own grain has attractively thinned their hefty malt, it comes through loud and clear. Indeed, had I not known the distillery, I would have marked this down as a Canadian or a young, unfulfilled bourbon. Wonderfully soft and proffers some seriously lovely moments. 40%. West Cork Distillers Limited.

West Cork Cask Strength bott code: L17293 db **(87) n21 t23.5 f20.5 b22** Just love the power of this malt on the delivery, relentlessly, mercilessly driving home the barley, a little ulmo honey and vanilla offering a controlled sweetness. Neither the nose or finish work so well, but worth finding just for that beautiful launch. 62%. West Cork Distillers Limited.

The Whistler Oloroso Sherry Cask Finish bott code: L19/34018 141 **(83.5) n20 t22 f20 b21.5** Too much sulphur on the sherry kicks it out of tune. A shame, as some outstanding heather honey and raisin notes deserved better. 43%. nc ncf.

The Wild Geese Classic Blend Untamed (90) n22.5 t23 f22 b22.5 Appears to shew high grain content, but when that grain happens to be excellent then there are no moans from me. 43%.

The Wild Geese Fourth Centennial Untamed (87) n21.5 t22.5 f21.5 b21.5 A very firm malt, brittle almost, which crashes onto the palate in slightly ungainly style. Only in the third to sixth flavour waves does it hit some kind of rhythmic harmony, a searingly salivating experience. But the roughouse grain makes for an uncompromising finish with bite and a little attitude, which would be brilliant but for an off-key fade. 43%.

The Wild Geese Rare Irish (89.5) n22 t23 f22 b22.5 Just love this. The Cooley grain is working sublimely and dovetails with the malt in the same effortless way wild geese fly in perfect formation. A treat. 43%. Cooley for Avalon.

Writers Tears (93) n23.5 t24 f22 b23.5 Now that really was different. The first mix of pure Pot Still and single malt I have knowingly come across in a commercial bottling, but only because I wasn't aware of the make up of last year's Irishman Blend. The malt, like the Pot Still, is, I understand from proprietor Bernard Walsh, from Midleton, but the two styles mixed shows a remarkably similar character to when I carried out an identical experiment with pure pot still and Bushmills the best part of a decade ago. A success and hopefully not a one off. 40%. Writers Tears Whiskey Co.

Writers' Tears Copper Pot Florio Marsala Cask Finish Marsala hogshead, cask no. 3150 **(84.5) n22.5 t22 f20 b20** Starts brilliantly, promising so much... but then falls away dramatically at the end...And how ironic and fitting is that? I decided to taste Irish whiskeys today as it looked very likely that Ireland would beat England at Lords in their very first Test Match against them, and here was a chance to toast their historic victory. And, after skittling England out for an embarrassing 85 on the opening, incredible morning an extraordinary victory looked on the horizon. But while tasting this, Ireland themselves were blasted off the pitch and comprehensively routed, when they were all out for just 38 — the seventh lowest score in Test history. Irish writers' tears, indeed... 45%. ncf aca. 336 bottles.

Writers' Tears Double Oak American oak barrels from Kentucky & French oak Cognac casks, bott code: L9106L2273 **(89.5) n23.5 t23 f21 b22** Does really well until the last leg. 45%.

Poitín

Mad March Hare Irish Poitín bott code: L16 001 021 **(86) n20 t22.5 f21.5 b22** Full flavoured, oily and sweet there is plenty of icing sugar here to help make for an easy experience: perhaps too easy for a poitín! The nose suggests a bit more copper might not go amiss, though. And, seeing as It's poitín, why not go for a full strength version while you are at it.. 40%.

Japanese Whisky

How fitting that in the age when the sun never sets on where whisky is produced it is from the land of the Rising Sun that the finest can now be found.

Recently Japan, for the first time ever, won Jim Murray's World Whisky of the Year with its insanely deep and satisfying Yamazaki Sherry Cask(s) 2013, a result which caused predictable consternation among more than a few. And a degree of surprise in Japan itself. The industry followed that up by commanding 5th spot with a very different but truly majestic specimen of a malt showing a style unique to Japan. How impressive.

It reminded me of when, some 25 years ago, I took my old mate Michael Jackson and a smattering of non-friends on a tour of this year's Whisky Bible's Japanese Champions Yoichi distillery on Hokkaido, pointing out to them that here was a place where a malt could be made to mount a serious challenge to the best being made anywhere in the world. While there, a local journalist asked me what Japanese distillers could learn from Scotland. I caused a bit of a sharp intake of breath – and a pathetically gutless but entirely characteristic denial of association by some whisky periodical executive or other who had a clear idea which side his bread was buttered – when I said it was the other way round: it was more what the Scots could learn from the Japanese.

The reason for that comment was simple: the extraordinary attention to detail and tradition that was paid by Japanese distillers, those at Yoichi in particular, and the touching refusal to cut costs and corners. It meant that it was the most expensive whisky in the world per unit of alcohol to produce. But the quality was astonishingly high – and that would, surely, eventually reap its rewards as the world learned to embrace malt whisky made away from the Highlands and Islands of Scotland which, then, was still to happen. Ironically, it was the Japanese distillers' habit to ape most things Scottish – the reason why there is a near century-old whisky distilling heritage there in the first place - that has meant that Yoichi, or the magnificent Hakushu, has yet to pick up the Bible's World Whisky of the Year award I expected for them. Because, sadly, there have been too many bottlings over the last decade tainted by sherry butts brought from Spain after having been sulphur treated. So I was also pleasantly surprised when I first nosed – then nosed again in near disbelief – then tasted the Yamazaki 2013 sherry offering. There was not even the vaguest hint that a single one of the casks used in the bottling had been sulphur treated. The result: something as close to single malt perfection as you will have found in a good many years. A single malt which no Scotch can at the moment get anywhere near and, oddly, takes me back to the Macallans of 30 years ago.

A Japanese custom of refusing to trade with their rivals has not helped expand their export market. Therefore a Japanese whisky, if not made completely from home-distilled spirit, will instead contain a percentage of Scotch rather than whisky from fellow Japanese distillers. This, ultimately, is doing the industry no favours at all. The practice is partly down to the traditional work ethics of company loyalty an inherent, and these days false, belief, that Scotch whisky is automatically better than Japanese. Back in the late 1990s I planted the first seeds in trying to get rival distillers to discuss with each other the possibility of exchanging whiskies to ensure that their distilleries worked economically. So it can only

		Chita
White Oak ▲	Yamazaki ▲	
Togouchi ▲		●Osaka

●Fukuoka

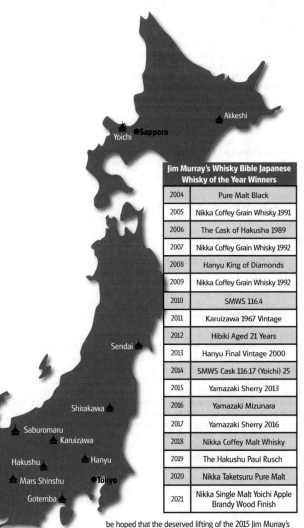

Jim Murray's Whisky Bible Japanese Whisky of the Year Winners	
2004	Pure Malt Black
2005	Nikka Coffey Grain Whisky 1991
2006	The Cask of Hakusha 1989
2007	Nikka Coffey Grain Whisky 1992
2008	Hanyu King of Diamonds
2009	Nikka Coffey Grain Whisky 1992
2010	SMWS 116.4
2011	Karuizawa 1967 Vintage
2012	Hibiki Aged 21 Years
2013	Hanyu Final Vintage 2000
2014	SMWS Cask 116.17 (Yoichi) 25
2015	Yamazaki Sherry 2013
2016	Yamazaki Mizunara
2017	Yamazaki Sherry 2016
2018	Nikka Coffey Malt Whisky
2019	The Hakushu Paul Rusch
2020	Nikka Taketsuru Pure Malt
2021	Nikka Single Malt Yoichi Apple Brandy Wood Finish

be hoped that the deserved lifting of the 2015 Jim Murray's Whisky Bible World Whisky of the Year crown, and the hitherto unprecedented international press it received has helped put the spotlight back on the great whiskies coming from the east. Because unless you live in Japan, you are likely to see only a fraction of the fabulous whisky produced there. The Scotch Malt Whisky Society should have a special medal struck as they have helped in recent years with some memorable bottlings from Japan, single cask snapshots of the greatness that is still to be fully explored and mapped.

Yet Jim Murray's Whisky Bible has provided a double-edged sword for the Japanese whisky industry. The amazing news for them was their World Whisky of the Year award precipitated sales worth billions of yen. And, consequently, a near exhaustion of stocks. The Hibiki 17 and Hakushu 12 have now vanished as brands altogether. But it means that, at long last and deservedly, whisky drinkers around the globe finally recognise that Japanese single malt can be second to no other. Their problem is how to satisfy the thirst for Japanese whisky and knowledge on what it has to offer: at the moment they cannot. But Forsyths, the Speyside-based Scottish still manufacturers, are working overtime to supply more distilling equipment for the Land of the Rising Sun. And rapidly setting whisky stocks.

Single Malts
AKKESHI 2016. Kenten Co., Ltd.

The Akkeshi New Born 2018 Foundations 1 bourbon barrel, bott Jan 2018 db **(88.5)** n22 t22 f22.5 b22 Young, clean, nutty and malty but with a very fragmented and thin body. This spirit's fragility means it will absorb the oak's influence quicker than most, a point worth bearing in mind in not too many years hence. 60%.

The Akkeshi New Born 2018 Foundations 2 Single Malt Spirit Peated bourbon barrel, bott Jun 2018 db **(94)** n23.5 t23.5 f23 b24 A fizzing, bucking bronco of a peated malt with spices zapping the taste buds with glee. The finish from this thoroughbred, is especially delightful as some chocolate joins forces with the smoke. Bodes incredibly well for the future. I can't wait to visit this distillery in the next year or two: if this is an average example of their output, exciting times lay ahead. 58%.

The Akkeshi New Born 2019 Foundations 3 Single Malt Spirit Non-Peated Hokkaido-Mizunara cask, bott Jan 2019 db **(93)** n23 t23.5 f23 b23.5 Can't wait for this beauty to become fully-fledged whisky. The freshness of the maturing new make is particularly evident on the finish. But until then the delicately tart tannin of the Mizunarna cask works its usual wonders and combines with the outstanding grist with commendable elegance. 55%.

◈ **The Akkeshi New Born 2019 Foundations 4 Malt and Grain Spirit** bott Jul 19, bott code: IGZHS **(83.5)** n21.5 t21.5 f20 b20.5 The rawness to this transgresses new make alone and enters into territory where not enough copper has been leached into the system to give this required depth and roundness. Plenty of slightly oily malt doing the rounds but balance is at a premium. 48%.

◈ **The Akkeshi Single Malt Whisky Sarorunkamuy Lightly-Peated** bott Jan 20, bott code: JAXHS **(88.5)** n22 t22.5 f21.5 b22.5 Not quite what I was expecting following some more rounded bottlings from this distillery in the past. Much thinner in body than anticipated, the smoke playing a playful game and attractively flirting with the busy, peppery spices. A little molasses and cocoa towards the end, but you feel a spine is missing for the gutsier notes to attack. A slightly strange but enjoyable malt nonetheless. 55%.

CHICHIBU 2004. Venture Whisky.

◈ **Chichibu 2012 Vintage** refill hogshead, cask no. 2089 db **(96)** n24 t24.5 f23.5 b24 Is there anything more likely to make you sigh in delight that a beautifully made peated cask-strength malt that has spent sufficient years in non-wine casks for the light tannin and sensible phenols to marry, live happily in each other's company and have begotten myriad little flavour babies? Well, that is what has happened here with the malt even having its own little room for quiet as the smoke drifts contently about elsewhere. Simplicity and excellence. Some other distillers around the world should try this sometime. They'd be surprised just what a mind-blowing treat that can be. Only a light bitterness towards the end prevents this from picking up a major Whisky Bible award. Because the delivery and first half dozen layers of follow-through has to be nigh on perfection. 60.8%. 349 bottles. Exclusive to The Whisky Exchange. ♈

◈ **Chichibu On The Way 2019** db **(94)** n23.5 t23.5 f23 b24 The one thing that Chichibu does is malt, by which I mean grist, grain and everything remotely connected. And here it is in concentrated form, even by their own dazzling standards. There is a squeeze of lemon on the nose, but for a while that is the only concession given away from barley. This is melt-in-the-mouth grist complete with dissolving icing sugar forms a natural alliance with the delicate vanilla from the oak. Such a pleasing experience. 51.5%.

EIGASHIMA 1919. Eigashima Shuzo co. ltd.

Dekanta Eigashima The Kikou Port Ellen cask, cask no. 11055, dist 2011, bott 2018 **(92)** n22.5 t23 f23.5 b23 Forget the Port Ellen cask. That is just a red herring – or, rather, a smoked herring. This is all about the barley which is thick and intense, the extra depth coming late on from the tannins and, very belatedly, from very light peat. Beyond that, the phenols barely register – which is just as well, as you don't want anything to take away from the dense purity of the malt itself. 58.4%. sc.

FUJI GOTEMBA 1973. Kirin Distillers.

The Fuji Gotemba 15 Years Old db **(92)** n21 t23 f24 b24. Quality malt of great poise. 43%.

HAKUSHU 1973. Suntory.

The Hakushu Single Malt Whisky Aged 25 Years db **(93)** n23 t24 f23 b23. A malt which is impossible not to be blown away by. 43%

The Hakushu Paul Rusch 120th Anniversary of Birth bourbon barrel, bott code LX7CJV db **(96)** n24 t24.5 f23.5 b24 There is a tipping point where a barrel has just gone over the edge, like one might at the Niagara Falls: there is no turning back and the ending is catastrophic. There is the odd moment here where you pick up a note where you realise it has moved close to that point, then myriad flavours come to the rescue to show this whisky is still very much alive and well and, like an old cowboy, basking in its great age and sun-burned charisma. Brilliant. *58%.*

HANYU 1941. Toa Shuzo Co. Ltd.
Ichiro's Malt Aged 23 Years (92.5) n23 t23.5 f23 b23. A fabulous malt you take your time over. *58%*

KARUIZAWA 1955. Mercian.
Karuizawa Pure Malt Aged 17 Years db **(90) n20 t24 f23 b23.** Brilliant whisky beautifully made and majestically matured. Neither sweetness nor dryness dominates, always the mark of a quality dram. *40%*

KURAYOSHI DISTILLERY 2015. Matsui Shuzo.
The Matsui Mizunara Cask bott code: 4 18.338 **(95) n24 t24 f23 b24** if you want to see why Japanese oak can give the indigenous whisky industry a leg up on their rivals, then it might be worth tracking this down. The flavour profile is really one, to this extent, that you see only in Japan and seems to give an extra sharpness to their malt; as though the colours on the nose and palate are pastel shaded and not just water. A quite beautiful whisky, as elegant and delicate as a demure Japanese girlfriend in a flowing silk kimono. *48%. nc ncf. BBC Spirits.*

The Matsui The Peated bott code: 4 18.338 **(87.5) n22.5 t23 f20 b22** Pleasant, though the downside is that the smoke rather detracts from the distillery's idiosyncratic charm. That said, the peat has a structure all its own, a little industrial and oily while the delivery involves some high definition grist. Its Achilles heel is the bitter-ish finale which can be predicted from the nose. *48%. nc ncf. BBC Spirits.*

The Matsui Sakura Cask bott code: 4 18.348 **(92.5) n23 t23.5 f23 b23** Matured in the wood of the cherry tree, this does impart a spicier than normal intensity, which in itself closes out the barley. Just drips with personality, however. *48%. nc ncf. BBC Spirits.*

⬩⬩⬩ **The Matsui Single Cask Mizunara Cask Single Malt** cask no. 318, bott code: 420106 **(96) n24** a nose to melt a thousand hearts... So soft...and has the magical ability to allow both the oak and the malt itself to express themselves individually and then together. It is among the rarest of gifts, and here is carried out close to perfection. Added in – as though by the molecule – is Brazilian biscuit, the finest, least sugared of marzipans, the most ticklish of spices. It is such a curious nose: seemingly dry, sometimes toasty, yet not... but with the grist and other sugars, even the odd fleeting glimpse of citrus, doing enough to ensure balance...; **t24** the texture is so ridiculously sexy – not too oily, nowhere near thin – that it takes time to start concentrating on the flavours themselves. Well, it's vaguely gristy barley which leads the way but the spices seriously ramp up the succulence levels and it becomes surprisingly mouth-watering. At the mid-point we start moving into sublime chocolate territory...and you might as well sit back and enjoy the ride...; **f24** more of this Venezuelan Porcelana cocoa with its intricate an incredibly subtle, nutty character..yet always with a little barley as a side-line...; **b24** I remember a great many years back wandering through a Japanese warehouse tasting the malt direct from mizunara casks. They were very different, not just from standard ex-bourbon, but often from each other. I remember the very finest of them had a rich texture and a middle and finish which was pretty heavy in a fine grade cocoa. Their bottling last year, though quite superb and unmistakably Japanese in style, didn't have that character found in only a small handful of the mizunaras I sampled. This has it. And how! The most Japanese of Japanese malts with its own unique signature. And one all too rarely flourished. The most complex whisky I have sampled this year so far (and this is number 1,058 - and took me over 90 minutes to nose and taste!) – and a definite contender for World Whisky of the Year. *48%. nc ncf sc. BBC Spirits.* ⬩

⬩⬩⬩ **The Matsui Single Cask Sakura Cask Single Malt** cask no. 116, bott code: 420106 **(91) n23** the tannins almost oscillate with a peppery spiciness, which in turn is quietened slightly by the oily vanillas. A slight hint of Turkish Delight here...or is it just rose petal...? **t23** the oils and tannin form an interesting and curiously different alliance to a normal malt whisky: the spices have a very different feel altogether, with a sometimes half-hearted approach. This allows the barley a little moment of glory as a brief juiciness takes hold. But a mild, jelly-like oiliness intervenes; **f22** the chalky finale I expected seems bereft of any sweetness; **b23** a slightly different aspect from this bottling from cherry wood, with slightly less weight than before and the more conservative sugars distributed evenly until the very dry finale. The spices, though prominent early on, are also a little more restrained. A very singular experience. *48%. nc ncf sc. BBC Spirits.*

KIRIN 1969. Kirin Group.

Kirin 18 Years Old db **(86.5) n22 t22 f21.5 b21.** Unquestionably over-aged. Even so, still puts up a decent show with juicy citrus trying to add a lighter touch to the uncompromising, ultra dense oak. As entertaining as it is challenging. *43%. Suntory.*

MIYAGIKYO (formerly Sendai). 1969. Nikka.

Nikka Coffey Malt Whisky db **(96) n23.5 t25 f23.5 b24** Not quite the genius of the 12-year-old. But still one of the most tactile and sensual whiskies on the world whisky stage today. *45%.*

⬙ **Nikka Whisky Single Malt Miyagikyo Apple Brandy Wood Finish** bott 2020, bott code: 6/02J161349 db **(88.5) n22 t23.5 f20.5 b22** So fascinating to compare this with the Yoichi matured in the same cask type. The Hokkaido distillery's far greater quality and versatility shines through at every level. Indeed, how can you compare against genius? It is not a fair match. This, oddly enough, struggles to make the most of the apple while the cask appears to give this malt a particular firmness which towards the end is a little wearing. That said, I really adore the delivery on this which allows the malt to let rip and pulse out some startlingly intense barley notes. But beyond the midway point it becomes a little glassy, simple and even a tad metallic. But there's no denying that big barley statement. *47%.*

SENDAI 1969. Nikka.

Scotch Malt Whisky Society Cask 124.4 Aged 17 Years 1st fill butt, dist 22 Aug 96 **(94) n24 t24 f23 b23** If there is a complaint to be made, it is that, at times, one might forget that this is a whisky at all, resembling instead a glass of highest quality oloroso. *60%. sc.*

SHINSHU MARS 1985. Hombo Shuzo Ltd

ePower Komagatake American Puncheon, dist Mar 13, bott Sept 16 **(96) n23.5 t24 f24 b24.5** Just fabulous for Japan's most malty whisky to be able to show its most intense and unique form without it being wrecked by awful sherry butts. What a malty treat this is! You could not ask for more. Well, actually you could...another glass, that is... *56.9%.*

WHITE OAK DISTILLERY 1984. Eigashima Shuzo.

White Oak Akashi Single Malt Whisky Aged 8 Years bott 2007 db **(74.5) n18.5 t19.5 f17.5 b19.** There is certainly something distinctly small still about his one, with butyric and feintiness causing damage to nose and finish. For all the early malty presence on delivery, some of the off notes are a little on the uncomfortable side. *40%*

YAMAZAKI 1923. Suntory.

The Yamazaki Single Malt Aged 18 Years db **(96) n23 t24.5 f24 b24.5** for its strength, probably one of the best whiskies in the world. And one of the most brilliantly and sexily balanced, too... All told, one glass is equal to about 45 minutes of sulphur-free satisfaction... *43%*

⬙ **The Essence of Suntory Whisky Yamazaki Distillery** Montilla wine cask, dist 2009, bott 2019, bott code: LN9BLB db **(87.5) n22 t23.5 f20.5 b21.5** Thoroughly enjoyable and a real treat for the moist fruitcake-style loving types. But for a Yamazaki this, for me, is too over the top with the distillery's subtle style lost under an avalanche of unyielding fruit. Add to that a weak sulphur note on the finish and you have a whisky that offers great beauty and intensity but only limited scope. *55%.*

⬙ **The Essence of Suntory Whisky Yamazaki Distillery** refill sherry cask, dist 2008, bott 2019, bott code: LL9BNH db **(95) n24** a 15-minute nose. In that time you might be able to establish whether this is a sweet, sultana-led aroma; or perhaps majors in toasted raisins; or whether the vanilla outweighs the butterscotch – or is it the other way round; whether the malt is gristy or slightly bready; whether the spices seem to be attached to the fruit...or is it the subtle oaks? You might work that out in 15 minutes. But I suspect you probably won't...; **t24** well, the spices may have been slightly shy on the nose. But they certainly aren't on the delivery. The onrushing fruitcake is stopped in its tracks by both the spices and a firmer tannin wall – though more of a sluice as the toasting raising appear to pass right through, the sweeter notes having been stopped in their tracks....; **f23** oh, the elegance! It just makes you smile with pleasure. All those oaky-grapey tones now down at heel to the spice...though it appears the butterscotch on the nose was the victor...because here it is the for the grand finale...; **b24** I'm not sure anyone in the world is doing sherry whisky better than Yamazaki right now. Here's another unreconstructed masterpiece from them. *53%.*

⬙ **The Essence of Suntory Whisky Yamazaki Distillery** Spanish oak, dist 2009, bott 2019, bott code: LM9BLO db **(92.5) n23.5** enchanting. Not just because of the clarity of the fruit but because of the excellent weight balance: you think it is zooming off into thick succulence...but stops short and instead gathers up some sublime tannin tones instead; **t23.5**

...oh my word: it goes and does exactly the same thing on the palate! Juicy at first, then an upgrading of the oaky intensity. The result is a wave of beautifully controlled spices perfectly arranged with the muscovado sugars; **f22** slightly dry and bitter and slightly out of sync with the remainder of the story; **b23.5** take the finish out of the equation and this is a snorter. *56%.*

YOICHI 1934. Nikka.

◇◇◇ **Nikka Whisky Single Malt Yoichi Apple Brandy Wood Finish** bott 2020, bott code: 6/02J181347 db **(96.5) n24.5** layers, layers, layers... caressing apple, kissing barley, nibbling spice; softly-brushing smoke...and all the time delicate Demerara sugars just on the fringes...; **t24** the youngish malt melts in the mouth first. But those tranquil phenols drift sublimely while the sugars have taken up a more muscovado-style stance to accommodate the flimsy and lightly acidic fruitiness..; **f24** still no great sign of age, though a little chocolate does herald the arrival of more serious tannins. The malts, though, and still with their delicate peaty accompaniment, remain fresh and juicy to the end; **b24** takes me vividly back to the day I got stuck on a warehouse roof at Yoichi distillery when filming for television many years ago. Earlier in the day I had been to a nearby farm and sampled the biggest apple off a tree I have ever seen in all my life. It was also one of the juiciness and finest-flavoured outside Somerset I had encountered. The nose, with its teasing apple edge, took me right back to that uniquely eventful moment...though thankfully I made it downstairs afterwards with no rescue necessary. By the way, great to see Yoichi still offering a malt of extraordinary finesse, even when shrouded in a cask so different to normal. Indeed, this is one of the world's great distilleries here wearing a very different costume...and still looking quite stunning. *47%.* 🍷

Vatted Malts

◇◇◇ **Kamiki Blended Malt Whisky** finished in Japanese cedar casks, batch no. 005 **(91) n22** even more cedary than their last bottling: wow! **t23** much more barley prevalent, allowing a healthy gristiness to flourish before unique tannin fingerprint start to make its mark; **f23** light oils lengthen the effect of both the sugars and those startling cedar tones. The cocoa notes I was expecting fail to materialise, though the spices up their game; **b23** such a different whisky. And it appears every batch has its own twist and take on matters. Fascinating...and delicious while it's at it... *48%. ncf.*

Kamiki Blended Malt Whisky Intense Wood finished in Japanese cedar casks, bott May 2019 **(91) n21.5 t23.5 f23 b23** While the nose is just too cedary – it is like walking into a furniture factory – the extra sugars work wonders on the whisky itself. The texture is rather dreamy, too. *48%. ncf.*

◇◇◇ **Kamiki Blended Malt Whisky Sakura Wood** finished in Japanese cedar casks, bott code: 201905 **(94) n23** cedar....!!! Concentrated....; **t23.5** sharp and even slightly taut on delivery, first getting tighter with the cedar and then relaxing with the sweeter butterscotch tart; settles down with an attractive lushness for a short while; **f23.5** slightly citrusy sugars... but then the tannins get serious..; **b24** this distillery seems hell bent on taking whisky to new cedary levels and taking us to new tannin territory. I am really beginning to get a taste for this unique stuff, though they need to work on the finish slightly to prevent the tannins from getting too frisky. *48%.*

◇◇◇ **The Kurayoshi Pure Malt** nbc **(92.5) n23** young, nutty, clean and barley barmy...! **t23.5** just as the nose promises: it's barley all the way! Gorgeously lip-smacking, it is amazingly bright and ultra-malty without throwing any weight around; **f23.5** long with spices giving a light buzz to the barley. Playful vanillas confirm the oak's involvement; **b23.5** although Japanese whisky has for a long time carved its own unique personality among the world's whiskies, this does a passable imitation of a youthful Speyside whisky celebrating its malty credentials. One of the maltiest, most cheerful whiskies of the year from any country in the world. And though no age on this, I have to say I adore it! *43%. Matsui Whisky.*

◇◇◇ **The Kurayoshi Pure Malt Aged 5 Years** nbc **(88.5) n22 t23 f21.5 b22** Now this is interesting. Appears to have a lot more about it than the non-age statement Pure Malt with the oak digging its heals in to give both gravitas and cocoa in roughly equal measures. But although the barley has presence, it has none of the joie de vivre of its presumably younger stablemate. Pleasant enough but a little stuffy and pompous. *43%. Matsui Whisky.*

◇◇◇ **The Kurayoshi Pure Malt Sherry Cask** bott code: 4 20.045 **(82) n21 t22.5 f18.5 b20** A new distillery might have to learn about the double-edged sword of sherry butts the hard way. Here the dull ache of the sulphur on the finish disappointingly rounds off the lightly honeyed and creamy delivery. Such a shame. *43%. Matsui Whisky.*

◇◇◇ **Meiyo Pure Malt Aged 15 Years Edition 2020** bott code: B9J1 **(95) n24** one of the most fragile 15-year-old whiskies you will encounter; having spent this time in Japan it is even more remarkable. The squeeze of grapefruit is as about as showy as this aroma gets.

The rest of the time it is the house style of malt and oaky vanillas mingling with uncommon elegance; **t23.5** this is melt-in-the-mouth malt: you don't have to do anything other than let the barley caress the contours of your palate and the tannins generate enough spice to offer a teasing thrill. The balance between the sweetness of the barley and drier tannins does its best to reach perfection; **f23.5** despite the lack of oils, the malt and vanillas combine with something approaching joint respect; **b24** just like its sister malt, Rei, here is a whisky that celebrates the art of blending and at every point seeks balance and symmetry. Another whisky not to be drunk in company: it deserves silence so you can benefit from the blender's skills and just allow the charm of this majestically understated whisky to gently wash over you. *40%. Bushido Series.*

◇ **Nikka Taketsuru Pure Malt Whisky** bott code: 02J14A **(95) n24 t23.5 f24 b23.5** A mildly opulent, always elegant single malt where the brightness of the barley shines like a beacon atop a Japanese mountain. Big age doesn't seem to be a factor here, with some of the malt being still fresh and flirtatious. This is one of those juicy malts that thrives on the bourbon barrel – clean and every layer of barley, sugar and oak open to scrutiny, interpretation and full enjoyment. Even the spices appear to have been calibrated to meet the malt in almost perfect synchronisation. A light buttery oiliness seems to really maximise the impact of the barley and there is a teasing is-there? isn't-there? moment as for a second you wonder if some smoke has just wandered, fleetingly, into range. Put simply: beautiful whisky in true Taketsuru tradition. *43%.*

Nikka Taketsuru Pure Malt bott no. 6/22H10 1540 **(95.5) n23.5 t24 f24 b24** Classy. *43%.*

◇ **Rei Pure Malt** bott code: B9I1 **(92) n23** the barley and gentle tannin are like lovers pressing hands and fingers together; **t23** so soft. So silky. So gentle. There appears to be the shadow of. hint of smoke, but this drifts away with the subtle vanillas; **f22.5** still a lingering gristy tone from the barley and still a caress from the post polite oak; **b23.5** very impressed with this malt. Not just for what it is, but for what it doesn't try to be. This is all about balance and elegance. And too rarely that is the case these days. No dominant features. And nothing being crushed or bullied, either. A very quiet treat; one I could enjoy any time of the day but especially before a meal. *40%. Bushido Series.*

Japanese Single Grain
CHITA 1972. Suntory.
The Chita Single Grain bott code L1610R db **(91.5) n23 t23 f22.5 b23** Spot on Corn Whiskey-type grain: could almost be a blueprint. Simple, but deliciously soft and effective. *43%.*

KUMESEN 1952.
◇ **Makoto Single Grain Whisky Aged 23 Years** bourbon cask, bott 2019 **(95.5) n24** anyone who knows and appreciates a Jaffa Cake will recognise instantly the beautifully marriage between the sweet fruit and the moodier dark cocoa. Of course, here the chocolate represents age. It does so this time with a degree of sprightliness, but also leaves no doubt to the grain's antiquity, underlined further by the depth of the spice; **t24** this style of gentleness is reserved for grain whiskies; this degree of complexity between the dates, pears, ulmo honey and butterscotch is the unique domain of greatly aged whiskies in even older casks; **f23.5** the softness of the ulmo honey continues to melt the heart; the spices remind you that this grain has been in the warehouse a good number of warm summers, but not quite warm enough to do any damage; **b24** the more I taste of this grain distillery, the greater I am impressed. What a thoroughly charming, beautifully integrated whisky. Not a single false step or off note. Unquestionably one of the friendliest and most genteel whiskies of the year. Ignore this one at your peril...it is an absolute gem. *42%. Bushido Series.* 🍷

Meiyo Single Grain Whisky Aged 17 Years bourbon cask, dist 2001, bott 2018 **(94.5) n23.5 t23.5 f23.5 b24** A Japanese Jaffa Cake... *42%. Aiko Importers, Inc.*

MIYAGIKYO 1969. Nikka.
Nikka Coffey Grain Whisky db **(94.5) n23.5 t24 f23 b24** Whisky, from any part of the globe, does not come more soft or silky than this... *45%*

Blends
◇ **The Essence of Suntory Whisky Clean Type** bott 2019, bott code: LD9JKO db **(88) n22 t22.5 f21.5 b22** Not often I come across aroma and flavour profiles entirely alien to any whisky I have before sampled – and remember last year I completed 20,000 different whiskies for the Whisky Bible alone. But different this is. The aroma – has a mix between old-fashioned Dentyne gum, new pine furniture and sweetened eucalyptus. The apparent barley sparkle on delivery is short-lived, the fade is long and drying, But all the time those unique notes on the nose cruise quietly around the palate, too. Clean...and very different! *48%.*

◇ **The Essence of Suntory Whisky Rich Type** bott 2019, bott code: LG9JPE db **(93)** n23.5 when cool the fruit note has to be chiselled off your nose, it is that solid. The Murray Method allows the grape to yield and form contours of varying intensity. It also brings the spices out from nowhere; **t23.5** again, doesn't really get cracking until warmed. And again the fruit takes on a warm plum pudding feel, salivating and sweetened with molasses. The spices have a lovely spring in their step; **f22.5** much drier: slightly burnt toast moving towards very well burnt toast...! A few late vanillas ensure balance is maintained; **b23.5** such a sensual texture. And such elegance as the fruit unfurls. Quite stunning. *48%.*

Master's Blend Aged 10 Years (87) n21 t23 f22 b21. Chewy, big and satisfying. *40%.*

Nikka Days bott no. 6222H261103 **(89)** n22.5 t22 f22 b22.5 Unquestionably the softest, least aggressive whisky I have tasted for the 2020 Whisky Bible. *40%.*

Nikka Whisky From The Barrel db **(91)** n22.5 t23 f22.5 b23 I have been drinking this for a very long time – and still can't remember a bottle that's ever let me down. *51.4%.*

◇ **The Nikka Tailored** bott code: 6/04J141353 **(88.5)** n23 I think there is a note here which may cause problems further down the line. Setting that aside, the interplay by the firm oak and muscular malt is the stuff of legend. A light bourbon tone to the tannin...but the dry fruit note troubles me...; **t24** one of the deliveries of the year. I am literally purring. The weight of the oak is substantial, but the yield with the rich barley is such that the oak is accommodated with ease and their intertwangling of textures and flavours leaves you almost rolling your eyes in delight...this is such rare and magical stuff. But hang on, I'm past the midpoint and... **f19.5** oh dear...dries and heads in the wrong direction thanks to the odd, less than top quality, sherry influence. A little chocolate tries to repair some of the damage; **b22** this was on course for super stardom...then that finish happened. The odd cask here with a sulphurous taint. Clean wine casks and this might have been on course for a very major award... *43%.*

◇ **The San-In** bott code: 619316 **(87)** n21.5 t22 f21.5 b22 A soft, clean, sweet blend with minimum complexity but still presenting an easy, not unattractive charm. *40%. Matsui Whisky.*

◇ **The San-In** ex-bourbon barrel nbc **(86)** n22 t21.5 f21 b21.5 The nose stars here: when cool deft, at times almost shy, it takes a rich vein of fresh timber and the Murray Method to up the game considerably. The odd juniper-type molecule pops up here and there. Almost perfumed at times. The delivery is at first thin and quiet. But a few flavour-waves on it's well into its stride, the grains fattening up and sweetening in one swoop. Silky vanilla is the main theme but then thins considerably and it's back to the tannins again. This really is exceptionally light, the mouthfeel of the grains trumps the tannins. *43%. Matsui Whisky.*

Sensei Whisky (86) n22 t22 f20.5 b21.5 Quite a heavy whisky with big accent on the caramel. The finish is just a shade too bitter for its own good. *40%. Aiko Importers, Inc.*

◇ **The Tottori** bott code: 4 20.070 **(87)** n21.5 t22.5 f21.5 b21.5 Mildly spicy and salivating, the grains are in control throughout, ensuring a silky countenance. Toffee plays a lead role, too. The spices ensure a good length to this. *43%. Matsui Whisky.*

◇ **The Tottori Aged in Bourbon Barrels** bott code: 4 20.069 **(89.5)** n22.5 a firm grain skeleton around which delicate malt and vanilla tones play. The tannins have the liveliest presence of them all; **t22** a vanilla and caramel fog on delivery, but this slowly clears for a far more complex oaky character emerges, the vanilla making way for light cocoa and spice; **f22** retains its warming, spicy spine and dries towards a more sawdusty character, with a little added cocoa powder; **b23** light in the house style. But much more complexity and quality about this one. Most enjoyable. *43%. Matsui Whisky.*

Yamato Japanese Whisky (87.5) n21.5 t22 f22 b22 Attractive complexity despite the thin body on this. The sweet, light mocha notes are very attractive *40%. nc. Aiko Importers, Inc.*

Other Japanese Whisky

◇ **Umiki Ocean Fused Whisky** finished in pine barrels, bott code: A **(90.5)** n22 that is odd...truly a one off. Really scratching my head working out how to describe this. Thick is probably one way: the vague saltiness and odd tannin combine to give a rare intensity you could almost cut through. The sugars are peculiar, too...a vague mix of ulmo honey and salted grist. Unique....; **t23.5** fat...yet the oils are not over the top. Not sure how that is achieved, as there is no sign of feints, either. Again, it is the sugars which hold the aces, once more of a type I find hard to describe: perhaps icing sugar with butterscotch and marzipan if I had to recreate the sensation from raw materials, or perhaps the scooping up of a bowl in which a cake is being made before it is put in the oven; **f22** dry with lightly sweetened tannins which bitter slightly at the death; **b23** it is possible something got lost in translation when they were describing the process of how this whisky comes about. Fused...? Certainly confused... What is clear from the glass – and that is where it matters, not the label – is that there is something markedly different about this whisky, offering a signature incomparable to other brands. An oddball, maybe. But one of the most fascinating whiskies I have tasted this year. *46%. ncf.*

English & Welsh Whisky

When, exactly, do you decide that a new whisky region is born? Is it like the planets forming after the Big Bang, cosmic dust gathering together to form a solid, recognisable whole?

That is the question I have had to ask myself for a long time and, since the Whisky Bible began 17 years ago, look for an answer that is beyond the hypothetical. At last I have come to a conclusion: it is, surely, when a country or region produces sufficient whisky of high enough consistency and character that its contribution to the lexicon of the world's greatest whiskies cannot be ignored. Or should that whisky be lost for any reason its effects would be greatly felt. There is no denying that this is now the case in the varied and often glorious lands to be found south of the Scottish Border.

When in 2003, on the cusp of world whisky's very own Big Bang, I sat down and tasted the whiskies for the inaugural 2004 edition of Jim Murray's Whisky Bible, Ireland boasted just three distilleries, four if you included Cooley's grain plant. Today, England and Wales provide us with three distilleries producing exceptionally high class whiskies: Penderyn, St George's and The Cotswolds. The latter is still very much in its infancy, but the quality is already beyond doubt. The English Whisky Co's remarkably consistent St George's have won numerous awards in the Whisky Bible, including this year's European Whisky of the Year.

These three distilleries are not micro distilleries. They are set up to make whisky on an industrial scale and have forged markets all over the world. On their skirt tails comes The Lakes in the beautiful Lake District while dotted around the region comes a plethora of other distilleries of varying shapes and sizes, not least the Spirit of Yorkshire Distillery in the North Yorkshire Wolds and whose maturing spirit seems as graceful as its emblem, the gannet. Bimber, in East London, have also made their mark with some fine early malts.

Over the last years I have been busy actively encouraging the larger English and Welsh distillers to create their own Whisky Association, especially as Britain has now at last left the EU. Why not? They are now their own region: they demand respect as their very own entity.

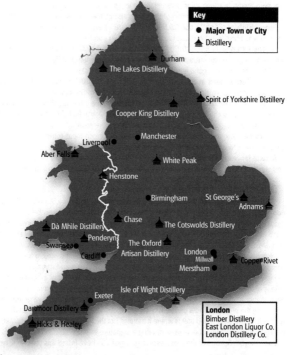

Key
- ● Major Town or City
- ⏞ Distillery

Durham
The Lakes Distillery
Spirit of Yorkshire Distillery
Cooper King Distillery
Liverpool ●
Aber Falls ⏞
● Manchester
White Peak
Henstone
● Birmingham   St George's
Adnams ⏞
Dà Mhìle Distillery
Chase   The Cotswolds Distillery
Penderyn
Swansea ●
The Oxford Artisan Distillery
Cardiff ●
London ●
Millwall
Copper Rivet
Merstham ●
Isle of Wight Distillery
Exeter ●
Dartmoor Distillery ⏞
⏞ Hicks & Healey

London
Bimber Distillery
East London Liquor Co.
London Distillery Co.

ENGLAND
ADNAMS Southwold, Suffolk. 2010. Working.

Adnams Rye Malt Whisky French oak casks, bott code: L17269 db **(90.5) n22.5 t23.5 f21.5 b23** Almost an immeasurable improvement on this distillery's early offerings. This has some serious charisma and amplifies the home-grown rye rather beautifully. 47%. ncf.

Adnams Single Malt Whisky French oak casks, bott code: L18039 db **(85.5) n22 t22 f20; b21.5** Technically not quite the ticket. But there is no faulting the big malt. 40%.

Adnams Triple Malt Whisky American oak casks, bott code: L18103 db **(91) n22.5 t23.5 f22 b23** Considering malted barley, wheat and oats have all gone into the mash, there is hardly any surprise that the nose and flavour profile is starchy and busy. Indeed, the oats have the biggest say here (a little bit of oat can go a long way in whisky!) in both aroma and on the palate; and the added sweetness from the cask gives a distinctive porridge-like feel to the delivery. But the cut is a tad wide, so the oils are a bit on the tangy side. Even so, a stylised and stylish whisky well worth experiencing, not least for that fabulous porridge delivery. A whisky to start the day with... 47%. ncf.

BIMBER DISTILLERY London. 2015. Working.

◇ **Bimber Distillery Single Malt London Whisky** re-charred American oak casks, batch no. 01/2019 db **(95.5) n23.5** the sugars radiating from the re-charred oak are hardly docile, but they never raise their voice in anger either. It is a confident aroma, sure-footed and polite, the vaguest hint of ulmo and orange blossom honey just lightening the toastiness slightly. Vanilla wafers with praline crème, too...; **t24.5** a kiss, a caress – the oils could not be better weighted. At times you half wonder if the nose is heading towards a Kentucky style and that sensation is even greater here as the tannins stake their claim. But the malt holds its ground and does so proudly and with no little charm and elegance; **f23.5** the slow unveiling of the spices is almost too good to be true... Back to the praline and vanilla found on the nose... which seems a long time ago, now...; **b24** it almost defies belief that a distillery seemingly operating for little over five minutes can come up with a whisky of such depth, magnitude, balance and all-round stunning beauty. The distillate here was of better quality than for their first bottling, and from that all else blossomed. Yet another brilliant whisky distillery is added to the already impressive English catalogue. The good people of Bimber have every right to be proud of such a malt whisky. 51.9%. nc ncf. 5,000 bottles.

◇ **Bimber Distillery Single Malt London Whisky The 1st Release** db **(90.5) n21** a slightly wide-ish cut it may have. But the crushed hazelnut and ulmo honey do a beautiful repair job....as does the concentrated malt which filters through at a leisurely pace; **t24** ohhhhh!!!! Rather than working against it, those oils do an extraordinary job of immediate intensification. As on the nose, hazelnut and ulmo abound. But now the malt is as thick as it comes, the sugars darkening the moment; **f22.5** a tapering finale, though buoyed by the gentle spice. Just a little feint on the finish, but the malt works hard to nullify its effects; **b23** a superb first bottling from a new distillery. Historic stuff. And though technically not quite on the money, this has so much charm, personality and sheer presence it is impossible not to fully enjoy. Here on St George's Day, congratulations with your astonishing entry into the whisky world, planting another English flag in the process! 54.2%. nc ncf. 1,000 bottles.

Bimber Single Malt Test Batch Sample ex-bourbon cask, cask no. 15, bott 22 May 19 db **(94.5) n23.5 t23.5 f23 b24** This cask has come on a storm with eye-watering clarity to the caramel-malt mix. The tannins have really set their stall out but superb muscovado sugars and light red liquorice softens the impact. How can this not be called a whisky....?!?!?! 57.9%. sc.

Bimber Single Malt Test Batch Sample ex-sherry cask, cask no. 38, bott 22 May 19 db **(94.5) n23 t24 f23.5 b24** Well done, Bimber! You've only gone and found yourself an absolutely flawless ex-sherry butt with not a single of atom of sulphur to be found: possibly the cleanest I have tasted this year. The mixture of ripe plummy fruit and nuttiness is a wonder to behold, as is the clarity of the grape on the palate which allows the barley to filter through at the very death. If they have set out to astound and impress, then they have succeeded. Give this another ten years for the oak to integrate and...oh, my word...! 57.8%. sc.

Bimber Single Malt Test Batch Sample re-charred cask, bott 3 Jun 19 db **(95) n23.5 t24 f23.5 b24** When I taste samples like these, it is hard not to get excited about what is to come in forthcoming years. To get something this beautiful and then stick it into a PX cask or suchlike would be something akin to industrial sabotage. Brilliantly distilled, the spirit is a perfect foil for the myriad dark sugars extracted from the oak. Malty, too. 55.6%. sc.

Bimber Single Malt Test Batch Sample virgin cask, cask no. 7, bott 22 May 19 db **(94) n24 t23.5 f23 b23.5** What a stunning natural caramel-lashed young Canadian this is. Hang on: with that heather honey and light liquorice mix with spice a bourbon, surely...no, wait a minute.... 57.7%. sc.

Artful Dodger Bimber New Make (92) n22.5 t23 f23.5 b23 An intense and creamy new make, shewing some bubblegum characteristics on the nose, but goes full throttle barley on delivery. On the sweeter end of the spectrum. *63.5%.*

COPPER RIVET DISTILLERY Chatham, Kent. 2016. Working.

Son of a Gun Cask Finished English Grain Spirit batch. 02 db (87) n22 t22 f21 b22 A much sweeter cove than their first bottling. Richer and more intense, too. Still the odd hint of copper starvation but well made and a juicier, fatter all round experience. *474%.*

COTSWOLDS DISTILLERY Shipton-on-Stour, Warwickshire. 2014. Working.

Cotswolds New Make Spirit White Pheasant db (92) n23 t23 f22.5 b23.5 Sweet, massively malty, moderately well-oiled and fabulously made. Has that late trace of cocoa which all excellent new make malts possess. Decided to taste this today as it is April 23rd: St George's Day, the day we celebrate the patron saint of England. Mind you, had you checked the BBC news website you would never know as it wasn't mentioned anywhere: but then BBC news long gave up trying to pretend to be interested in covering traditional British interests, English ones in particular. So here I sit, this time in my garden in this green and pleasant land, just a few miles from the Cotswolds itself, with barely a breath of wind and the late Spring birdsong filling the delightfully warm air. So: to St George and England, a toast. And to the disgraceful BBC: I look forward to the day when they have the licence fee ripped off them and their newsroom, preferably under new management and at long last populated with real journalists, actually starts covering relevant news and not that set to a woke agenda as, unlike this beautiful new make, they are not fit for purpose. God, I fell better for that... *63.5%. nc ncf.*

Cotswolds Single Malt Whisky Founder's Choice Batch No. 01/2019 STR American red wine casks db (89) n22 t23 f22 b22 Not quite the usual symphony of fruit and spice, but the delivery is faultless. *60.3%. nc ncf.*

Cotswolds Single Malt Whisky Founder's Choice Batch No. 02/2019 STR American red wine casks db (93) n23 t23.5 f23 b23.5 A slightly different angle from this line of bottling, with the busy spices making a huge difference to the mouthfeel. You can never get bored by a whisky like this. *60.4%. nc ncf.*

Cotswolds Single Malt Whisky 2014 Odyssey Barley Batch No. 07/2018 first fill barrels db (95) n23 t24.5 f23.5 b24 Pure English bliss... *46%. nc ncf.*

Cotswolds Single Malt Whisky 2014 Odyssey Barley Batch No. 09/2018 first fill barrels db (92) n22.5 t23 f23 b23.5 Cotswolds finest chewy toffee...! *46%. nc ncf.*

Cotswolds Single Malt Whisky 2014 Odyssey Barley Batch No. 10/2018 first fill barrels db (93) n23 t23.5 f23 b23.5 Slightly different. But works a treat. *46%. nc ncf.*

Cotswolds Single Malt Whisky 2014 Odyssey Barley Batch No. 11/2018 first fill barrels db (92) n22.5 t23 f23 b23.5 This is becoming a remarkably consistent whisky. And very high class, too. *46%. nc ncf.*

Cotswolds Single Malt Whisky 2014 Odyssey Barley Batch No. 12/2018 first fill barrels db (86) n21.5 t22 f21 b21.5 Spoke a little too soon. An enjoyable malt from the shape of the buttery barley. But the oak here has a slightly bitter twist, the problem being detectable on the nose, too. *46%. nc ncf.*

Cotswolds Single Malt Whisky 2015 Odyssey Barley Batch No. 01/2019 first fill barrels db (89) n21.5 t23 f22 b22.5 Just struggles slightly to find its way here and there. But the overall theme is delightful. *46%. nc ncf.*

Cotswolds Single Malt Whisky 2015 Odyssey Barley Batch No. 02/2019 first fill barrels db (93) n22.5 t23.5 f23 b24 The vital sugars missing from the last couple of bottlings have been re-found and celebrated. *46%. nc ncf.*

Cotswolds Single Malt Whisky 2015 Odyssey Barley Batch No. 05/2019 first fill oak barrels db (91.5) n23 a very laid-back nose where the barley reveals no great age but certainly a controlled intensity. Clean, creamy and enticing; t23 gristy sugars arrive early and hang around. The oak makes its mark gently, though the spices do prickle. It is the barley, though, from the first cascade on delivery which makes the biggest noise...; f22.5 an attractive chestnut puree sweetness amalgamates both the tannins and the barley; b23 one of those understated malts that can be too easily overlooked. Worth time and a compass... *46%. nc ncf.*

Cotswolds Single Malt Whisky Blenheim Palace Single Cask cask no. 901, STR cask db (94.5) n23.5 classical STR cask at work, with the tannin probing with a degree of urgency, bordering on irritability. The lightest slivers of jammy fruit and a sweeter thread of Fox's Butter Crinkle biscuit...; t23.5 classical STR cask at work! The thick, semi-oily barley carries a seam of rich, probing tannin that shews urgency and even a degree of irritability. Spices prickle while the buttery note on the nose formulates and gathers a little citrus along the way; f23.5 dry waves of delicate, almost manicured, vanillas: decidedly oak imbued; a little ulmo honey is rationed out to ensure balance and extra length; **b24** how could I taste this whisky at another time other than VE day: the 75th anniversary of victory in Europe for Britain and its allies against Hitler? The family home of the Churchills is Blenheim Palace – not that far from where I sample this whisky now on a stunning late Spring day. I have escaped my tasting room, my usual dungeon, to sit outside amid the orange-tipped butterflies and with a whitethroat dancing and singing its scratchy mating call; blackbirds feeding their young, while chaffinches, greenfinches, goldfinches trill and dunnocks chatter in a glorious, quintessential English setting. Even a resplendent cock pheasant (ironically the emblem of the distillery) has wandered into my garden to enjoy the moment. Doesn't he know there's a Lockdown...? *46%. nc ncf sc. 375 bottles.*

◇◇◇ **Cotswolds Single Malt Whisky Founder's Choice STR** American oak red wine casks db **(95.5) n23.5** no little lime at play here. From the natural colour you expect intensity and bulk. Instead there is a charming lightness of touch; **t24** the beauty of a whisky at this strength is that the sharpness of the wine casks is at full volume, their salivating qualities heading through the roof. The nose may be little more than a caress – but no such subtlety here are the barley gangs up into something rich and remarkable. Though this freshness and intensity points towards youth, the multi-faceted tannin suggests some serious oak interference – but not so much as to lose the plot...; **f24** long, and after that big fruit explosion, emollient and concentrating on all the softer, more honeyed aspects of the malt. Those partial to a slice of butterscotch tart will also find favour with the delicate finale...; **b24** how can one not be truly won over by the way this flits from enormity to refined elegance...? *60.5%. nc ncf.*

◇◇◇ **Cotswolds Single Malt Whisky Peated Cask Batch No. 01/2019** ex-peated Quarter casks db **(96) n24.5** at first the smoke is little more than a thin shadow, or a distant echo. Slowly, however, it builds, seemingly a molecule at a time, into something more complete, more whole. Mocha notes drift in and stick. Delicate, so delicate...; **t23.5** a degree of youth prods the salivation button, the barley thickening by the second. Soon enough tannin has intertwangled enough for age to no longer be relevant, the spices and sugars fomenting slightly through the middle; **f24** not so much a blanket of smoke, more a thin sheet. This is laid gently over the contours of the mochas-enriched tannins, gentle ulmo honey and Demerara sugars; **b24** unlikely you'll find a more perfectly balanced and complex peat cask malt than this, this year. First it is a tease. And then a complete seduction... On St. George's Day an English Whisky that is unquestionably among the world's elite this year. Amazing. *59.3%. 2,950 bottles.* 🏆

◇◇◇ **Cotswolds Single Malt Whisky Sauternes Cask Batch 01/2020** db **(86.5) n22 t22.5 f20.5 b21.5** Just a little duller than you'd like to see from a Sauternes cask. A brief Cape Gooseberry moment, but mainly we are talking a dry, biscuity vanilla and just a light furry niggle on the finish. *55.2%. nc ncf. 2020 bottles. Hearts & Crafts Range.*

◇◇◇ **Cotswolds Single Malt Whisky Sherry Release** db **(90) n22** exceptionally dry: a curious aroma of grape but with the sugars removed...; **t23** the initial hit on the palate is no sweeter than on the nose. But soon a layer of grist and muscovado sugars rush in to create a dramatic contrast: suddenly a barren palate is salivating; **f22** just slight drying bitter tone reveals a very slight flaw in the cask. But that earlier oilier, honey-lied fruit surge does enough to keep the malt on course...; **b23** a complex malt where the fruit appears to wish to play games. Very easy to join in... *50.2%. nc ncf.*

Fortnum & Mason English Single Malt cask no. 532, bott Mar 19 db **(94) n24 t23.5 f23 b23.5** So delicate...yet so big, too...! *46%. nc ncf sc.*

Fortnum & Mason English Single Malt cask no. 503, bott Jan 19 db **(90.5) n22.5 t23.5 f22.5 b22.5** Although it is obvious there is no great age to this malt, the pounding waves of tannin and the quiet elegance to the malt would have you thinking otherwise. *46%. nc ncf sc.*

Fortnum & Mason English Single Malt cask no. 527, bott Mar 19 db **(92.5) n23 t23.5 f23 b23** For a whisky of no great age, the degree of balance is both startling and wonderful. A real English treat awaits you in St. James'... *46%. nc ncf sc.*

The Boutique-y Whisky Company Cotswolds Single Malt English Whisky Aged 3 Years batch no. 1 **(92.5) n23 t23.5 f23 b23** A beautifully distilled malt which makes brilliant use of the oak's generous sugars. *50.4%. 1,783 bottles.*

EAST LONDON LIQUOR COMPANY Bow Wharf, London. 2014. Working.

East London Liquor Company Whisky London Rye new French oak, ex-bourbon & PX finish db **(88.5) n22.5 t22.5 f21.5 b22** A bewildering first bottling from this new distillery. As gingery as ginger liqueur, as dry as a gin, as confusing as a rye whisky matured in French, American and Spanish oak, one of which carried PX. It is almost impossible to say under all that what the actual spirit itself is like, though pleased to report not a single off note on both nose and finish. I really do hope they also bottle some whisky which gives us a chance to savour the grain. And remember that, in whisky, a little less can give you so much more. *46.8%. 269 bottles. Inaugural release.*

LAKES DISTILLERY Cockermouth, Cumbria. 2014. Working.

◈ **The Lakes Single Malt Whiskymaker's Reserve No. 1** bott 25 Sept 19 db (86.5) n21.5 t23 f20.5 b21.5 So, now The Lakes are off and running, too. They are now a whisky distillery for real. To be honest, I was expecting a slightly greater fanfare for a first bottling. Not the greatest distillate at work here, slightly at odds with the oak, especially at the finish. But this is a first effort and they have yet to get to understand their whisky fully. The nose struggles for identity, the barley having to overcome the grumbles of the wide-ish cut. But just love the delivery, a thickset piece full of intense barley, milk chocolate praline and even a brush with marmalade. Quite a juicy introduction. But the finish and overall balance is lacking somewhat. Early days. 60.6%.

◈ **The Lakes Single Malt Whiskymaker's Reserve No. 2 Cask Strength** PX, red wine and bourbon casks, bott code: 31 Jul 19 db (91.5) n23 the obvious youthfulness of this malt is embraced by the surprisingly lithe fruit at play here. The PX acts as a rich constant, but this is matched by the nipping spice; t23 PX lushness on arrival. But this is quickly punctured by the force of the intense barley and then a more cavalier, fresh grapiness. The spices certainly pulse with intent from the midpoint onwards; f22 just a slight bitterness and though there is natural tendency towards untidiness, especially when the vanilla arrives, the fuller PX keep things mainly in control. The spices, meanwhile, keep peppering away but now with less ferocity...; b23.5 a much more forthright and altogether happier bottling than their inaugural one. Seems as though there is marginally better distillate at play here and, if not, the PX cask has been used to act as an attractive bind for all the elements at play here, rather than dominating and boring us into submission, as can so often happen with that type of butt. Very impressed and suitably entertained... 60.9%.

SPIRIT OF YORKSHIRE DISTILLERY Hunmanby, Filey. 2016. Working.

◈ **Filey Bay Yorkshire Single Malt Whisky First Release** db (95) n23.5 green barley basking in the glow of very clean and refined cut, so there are no unwanted oils as well as limited oak to hamper the view. One moment dense in malt, the next sharp in barley, a little spice pricking; t24 both mouthfeel and taste are superb; the lightness of touch from the malt mirrors the nose, the oils restrained yet still enough to be counted and make a difference. The sugars are halfway between gristy and delicate marzipan. The tannins make an imprint but tread on nothing vital or break anything; f23.5 a slow, measured procession of vague spices plus a further extension of vanilla and barley. No off notes. No untidy loose end. No cul-de-sacs. Ends organically, just in the same way it had come together throughout; b24 I know it seems like an inappropriate thing to do when tasting the first-ever whisky bottled by a distillery, but I feel I have no option but to compare it with a distillery elsewhere. However, the Whisky Bible lives by its honesty. And I have to say that the first thing that flashed through my mind on tasting my first mouthful was: Glenfiddich! And that same thought kept recurring throughout this delightful experience. None of the whiskies you can find from that celebrated Speyside distillery today. No, I'm talking about the classic non-age statement version, for years its trademark brand, that was sadly lost a great many years ago to make way for the 12-Year-Old, one of two drams I miss most from the early days of the Malt Whisky Revolution. When you taste this, you'll see why. It is the sheer élan, the fabulous brightness of this whisky that both wins your heart and takes you back the best part of a couple of decades: youthful, fun, stunningly well made, the malt coming at you in varying intensities, never for a moment sitting still on the palate – always somewhere to go, something to do: fresh and massively satisfying. For a first-ever bottling this is right up there with the very best I have encountered. Of course it is youthful, but the tannins have presence and complexity enough to make that no issue at all. If it does, it is to make it to its own advantage. Why, this newby even has the temerity to be an identical colour to the famed old Glenfiddich. 46%. nc ncf.

◈ **Filey Bay Yorkshire Single Malt Whisky Second Release** db (93) n23 so clean, but with a marginally younger feel to the barley which dines out on its citrus freshness; t23.5 such an intense malt presence on delivery. Aided by a slightly thicker coating of oils than the First release, the fizz arrives later and hand-in-hand with earlier spices and a little more natural caramels. Still, though, the youth is more pronounced; f23 as on the nose there is a citrus buzz, this time an recognisable pink grapefruit; b23.5 another quite beautiful malt, but just lacking that priceless, enigmatic sparkle of the first bottling... 46%. nc ncf.

◈ **Filey Bay Yorkshire Single Malt Whisky Moscatel Finish** bourbon casks, finished in ex-Moscatel barrels db (94.5) n24 it is so rare to find a whisky, especially such a young one, where the fruit is weaved so finely into the malty cloth. This is rare elegance: an exhibition of control and restrain. Marriage where the two parties are on the same wavelength and give and take accordingly; t23.5 the sugar candy sweetness is met by a slightly sturdier oak presence than seen on either of the first two releases. This leads to a light chocolate mint note balancing things out; **f23** the oils gather slightly as the raisins butterscotch join with the malt for a final curtain call...; **b24** a gorgeously weighted, charismatic malt with a sublime usage of fruit which does not – and this is so rare these days - overburden. As this is called Filey Bay, for a second I'd like to make this very personal. It has since 1985 had an extraordinary special place in my heart, for professional reasons, too, and here I toast the memory of both Graham Jones the one time landlord of the Belle View at Filey, whom I never met and whose life was so tragically cut short, and his lovely mother, whom I did, who happened to be the daughter of Huddersfield Town and England legend George "Bomber" Brown. I trust you have both now found peace. *46%. nc ncf.*

Spirit of Yorkshire Maturing Malt Distillery Projects 001 db **(92)** n23 t23.5 f22.5 b23.5 A debut bottling from this outstanding new distillery and, if anything, the casks are maturing ahead of schedule. Though not legally a whisky yet, the caramel involvement from the casks is as rich as it is profound. The stunning, buttery delivery really does make maximum use of both the hugely intense barley and spice-rammed oak. The result is a spirit simultaneously soothing and warming. The most stylish treat out of Yorkshire since Geoff Boycott was in his pomp... *46%. nc ncf. 2,000 bottles.*

Spirit of Yorkshire Maturing Malt Distillery Projects 002 db **(89.5)** n22.5 t22.5 f22.5 **b22** A thinner model this time with the structure of the barley easily distinguishable. A little bit in a neither here nor there mode, but the impact of the barley sugar and butter is rather charming. *46%. nc ncf. 2,000 bottles.*

Spirit of Yorkshire Maturing Malt Distillery Projects 003 db **(95)** n23.5 t24 f23.5 **b24** Just ridiculously beautiful. The mouthfeel is as rich, oily and rounded as they could have prayed for. If anyone remembers Fox's Butter Crinkle biscuits (another brilliant Yorkshire export, this time from Batley) with affection, then they will be making a beeline for this glorious bottling. Again, the malt appears to be on steroids and has no problems coping with the teeming natural caramels from the oak. The sugars are politely muted, the bruyere honey happy to live in the shadow of the buttery barley. This distillery uses the gannet as its emblem, my favourite sea bird as it happens. And this bottling seems to match its elegance with its feather-light touch. Magnificent. *46%. nc ncf. 2,000 bottles.*

Spirit of Yorkshire Maturing Malt Distillery Projects 004 db **(88)** n23 t22.5 f21.5 **b22** Some seriously punchy tannins here. Project 04 has bite bordering on attitude, but not quite the all-round balance to allow the malt to have an even say, as has been the case with the majority of their previous bottlings. Still loads to enjoy, especially considering this is still, in these tender years, non-whisky. But by the time it grows up, some of the rougher edges should be rounded and harmony where there is currently a slight, underdeveloped discord. *46%. nc ncf. 2,000 bottles.*

ST. GEORGE'S Rowdham, Norfolk. 2006. Working.

⟡ **The English Single Malt Whisky Aged 11 Years** nbc db **(96.5)** n23.5 you almost laugh with the complexity levelled at you: the sheer impudence of the spices, arriving so early and making such bold a claim; the varied facets of the barley – varying between a crisp gristiness and a more buttery depth; the playfulness of the oak pretending at first to show severe weight, but a light touch of the Murray Method proves this to be a bluff because the other factors match it stride for stride; the fruit with its citrus tones on the back of the under-ripe banana; the honeys – plural as both ulmo and heather honeys are lightly painted onto the picture...; I could nose this all day...; **t24.5** you expect salivation. But perhaps not quite this much! The grist and icing sugars are at full throttle. Layered vanillas make their mark for the oak. But everything is underplayed, yet strangely overplayed, too, as the pulsing of these characteristics makes for a delightful depth. The spices arrive in the first nanosecond and up the juices even further; **f24** all as before, but now at a slowly beat...except for the spice. The oils gather and concentrate the weightier tannins into a drier, slightly sawdusty fade; **b24.5** the oldest whisky bottled by St George I have yet encountered, I think. But they wear the age as a princess might a tiara. Not for a moment is the freshness and clarity of the whisky lost or even compromised. Like so many of their whiskies, this malt unfurls in the glass to reveal a whisky exactly as it should be: natural, relaxed and able to display all its tricks and charms without hindrance. Excellent. *46%* 🏆.

⟡ **The English Single Malt Whisky 'Lest We Forget' 1914 - 1918** nbc db **(95.5)** n24 fresh, grassy barley with an underlying light earthiness. Just a hint of mint, too. That is near as damn it perfectly weighted...; **t23.5** the barley has a rounder and richer feel than normal for this distillery; the spices hang back to let the malt establish itself before moving in...then make up for lost time...; **f24** again, a slight mintiness on the fade...chocolate mint this time, before a pulse of passion fruit. meanwhile the malts beat in rhythm with the butterscotch tannins; **b24** probably the most touching of any whisky label I have ever encountered, it is a British Tommy silhouetted against the flag of St George. "Lest We Forget" are, of course the words used to remember those who died during the 'Great War'. Rather than taste this in my lab, I am outside in my garden to sample this, late on a warm summer's evening. At the going down of the sun I tasted....and remembered...and it gives me the chance to pay my respects to my Grandmother's three brothers who were lost in the Battle of Jutland in May 1917 (just two months after the birth of my father). A whisky worthy of their memories... *43%. 1,499 bottles.*

The English Whisky Co. Original batch no.003 18, bourbon casks db **(94.5) n24 t23.5 f23 b24** Annoyingly, I appear to have missed out on batch 2, but I remember the original version of this – batch 1 – was a little undercooked. What you have here, I am delighted to report, is the Full English....thoroughly recommend for breakfast. *43%. ncf.*

The English Whisky Co. Small Batch Release Rum Cask Matured batch no.01/2018, dist Apr 13, bott Feb 18 db **(91.5) n23 t23 f22.5 b23** A classic rum-matured style with a crisp, sugary outer shell and softer malt-rich middle. *46%. ncf.*

The English Single Malt Whisky Double Cask bourbon & oloroso sherry casks, batch no. 04/2018, dist Aug 11, bott Oct 18, nbc db **(89) n22.5 t23 f21.5 b22** A spineless, simpering malt. But in part delicious! *46%. 2,943 bottles.*

The English Single Malt Whisky Original bourbon casks, batch no. 001 19, nbc db **(90.5) n22.5 t23 f22 b23** The idea was to taste the remaining of my Australian and English whiskies during the semi-final of the cricket World Cup, as the two countries did battle. But I have had to bring the English tasting forward slightly as Surrey opener Jason Roy has made short work of the Australian bowlers. So this whisky is dedicated to another Surrey opener, John Edrich, my boyhood hero who played not just for England, but Norfolk as well...the home of this distillery. And as for this whisky: as gentle and as easy to put away as a Mitchell Starc bouncer.... *43%. ncf.*

The English Single Malt Whisky Original bourbon casks, batch no. L00120, nbc db **(89.5) n21.5 t22.5 f23 b22.5** A real youngster with the fresh, citrusy barley adorned with a surprising degree of oil. Beautifully distilled and matured in, I guess, 2nd or 3rd fill casks which allows the full magnitude of the malt to do battle with the significant oils. The late chocolate flourish rounds off the experience beautifully. One of the most refreshing malts you'll find this year without a single technical blemish. *43%. ncf.*

The English Single Malt Whisky Small Batch Release Rum Cask Matured dist Mar 14, bott Mar 20, batch no. 01/2020, nbc db **(94) n23** a firmer nose than most from this distillery, a light exoskeleton of sugar trapping the malt; **t23.5** the nose promised huge salivation and sugars...and bloody hell! It is so true to its word. The barley is at nuclear level... The sugars are first are of melt-in-the-mouth icing sugar quality. But as the light tanins evolve, a toastier move towards Demerara is made..; **f23.5** barley. Vanilla. Spice. Oil. White chocolate... **b24** so simple. Yet so complex. Just fiendishly brilliant. *46%. 1,985 bottles.*

The English Whisky Co. Smokey batch no.002 18, bourbon casks db **(94) n24 t23.5 f22.5 b24** This has to be one of the most relaxed peaty whiskies on the planet: the way it gets its smokiness across borders on the indolent. But, my word, it is so lovely... *43%. ncf.*

The English Single Malt Whisky Smokey bourbon casks, batch no. 001 19, nbc db **(92) n23.5 t23.5 f22 b23** One of those, warm sultry malts, where the peat acts as a pillow and blanket you can snuggle into. *43%. ncf.*

The English Single Malt Whisky Smokey bourbon casks, batch no. L00419, nbc db **(92.5) n23.5** dry, sooty and acidic: intense stuff..; **t23** the sugars arrive all in a breathless rush. The phenols are far less yelling here than on the nose, but integrate stunningly with the tastier tannins and molasses; **f22.5** sweet butterscotch and vanilla with a light, drier dusting of soot; **b23.5** a far more complex and confident version of the last Smokey I tasted from St George. At 46% this could be a revelation... *43%. ncf.*

The English Single Malt Whisky Smokey Oak bourbon cask, batch no. 05/2018, dist Feb 11, bott Oct 18, nbc db **(95) n24 t23.5 f23.5 b24** Where this differs from, say, an Islay is that they, almost invariably, have a softness to them which gives the smoke a billowing quality. This, by contrast, is stark and firm, so the peat has to impress by stealth and subtlety. Which it does, quite brilliantly... *46%. 1,347 bottles.*

The English Single Malt Whisky Small Batch Release Smokey Virgin peated virgin oak cask, dist Oct 12, bott Aug 19, batch no. 01/2019, nbc db **(93.5) n23.5** such a dense yet refined nose with a surprising saltiness. A real smoky bacon element to this (as opposed to kippers through lack of oil). Dry with a deft layering of muscovado sugars. The smoke is always at the forefront yet is so generous in allowing all other factors free reign..; **t23** sweet and ridiculously soft. There may not have been much oil on the nose. But it arrived here by my Jaguar's sump full. The result is two-toned malt...one smoky – and one surprisingly not; **f23.5** the oils stretch the distance, while the dark sugars and butterscotch retain their smoky credentials. Just love that understated spiciness which rumbles away in the background..; **b23.5** the nose apart, the virgin casks don't have quite the impact I expected. But there is no quarrel with the overall quality or complexity levels which are outstanding. Superb! *46%. 2,652 bottles.*

The English Single Malt Whisky Triple Distilled batch no. 01/2019, dist Jun 11, bott Jun 19 db **(96) n24 t24 f23.5 b24.5** Malt whisky of this super-delicate type are rarely found better than this. *46%. 1,462 bottles.*

The English Single Malt Whisky Virgin Oak batch no. 01/2019, dist Jul 13, bott Mar 19, nbc db (95) n23.5 t24 f23.5 b24 For those who like some whisky in their honey... This was my 500th whisky for the 2020 Bible, and it certainly lived up to the billing... Sublime. 46%. 2,689 bottles.

The Norfolk Farmers Single Grain Whisky batch no. 02/2018, bourbon cask, bott 28 Feb 18 db (96.5) n23.5 t24.5 f24 b24.5 Some people might be a little confused by the labelling of this whisky, and you have my sympathy. It is called a "single grain whisky" which kind of suggests that only one grain type has been used. Well, no, there are four: in no particular order, rye, wheat, oats and several styles of malted barley. In fact, all the grains are malted, but they didn't want to call it a "Malt Whisky" in case people automatically assumed it was a single malt like Scotch, made from 100% barley. While the "single" term reflects it is from just the one distillery, St George's in Norfolk. Complicated? Well, not half as complex as this truly beautiful and gloriously idiosyncratic malt whisky. 45%. ncf sc. 392 bottles.

The Norfolk Single Grain Parched db (96.5) n24.5 t24 f23.5 b24.5 A classic Irish "mod pot" style Irish pot still whiskey...from Norfolk! Nosed this when it was just a few months old...and it has moved on magnificently; indeed, beyond hope and expectation. Only the cat's bowler on the label and a green bottle seems to give the faintest hint towards anything Irish... For the record, by far the best Pot Still I have ever encountered made outside Ireland's shores... 45%. nc ncf sc.

The Boutique-y Whisky Company English Whisky Company Single Malt English Whisky Aged 8 Years batch no. 2 (93.5) n23.5 t23.5 f23 b23.5 Very much in the Islay style, it still has a certain St. George's quality and personality to it. Just too easy to enjoy... 52.3%. 845 bottles.

THE OXFORD ARTISAN DISTILLERY Headington, Oxford. 2017. Working.

⬩ **Exploratory Flask Series Rye** batch. 1, English oak medium char db (89.5) n21 OK, so we can pick up the odd note that shouldn't be there... But there are a lot more lies the complexed that are – and it appears to be the English oak that is coming to the rescue: the tannins have both a density yet a light porousness that lets in the attractive blood orange notes... or even may be responsible for them...; t23 thick enough to make as whisky gravy with. The rye has some beautiful, fluting moments before a mix of tannins and feints zero in. A kind of flawed genius...; f22.5 so much chocolate....! The feints are a little clumsy and usher in some tingly spices. But the vanilla and butterscotch are sound...plus that slightly indecipherable but attractive note which must be aligned to the oak; b23 now this is much more like it! Still not quite technically on the money, but the happy marriage of rye and cocoa – presumably courtesy of the English oak. For all its faults I adore this. And I suspect future bottlings could get a lot better yet, if they can iron out the wrinkles. 40.5%.

Oxford Pure Rye Spirit batch. 2 db (87.5) n21 t23 f21.5 b22 Not a bad start, though I'm sure they'll get their cuts cleaner as the making of whisky becomes second nature to them. For the best results sit the glass in some warm water for a few minutes and then allow to cool a bit (a kind of Murray Method on steroids). This removes the heavier feints and leaves a delightfully honeyed spirit rammed full of flavour and where the rye kicks off full salivation. A distillery to watch. 40%. 458 bottles.

⬩ **Oxford Pure Rye Spirit** batch. 5, new American oak casks db (83) n20 t22.5 f20 b20.5 The tobacco notes radiating from this shows that they are still a long way from really having where they want this still to be for a high-class malt of the general English style. We have something far more of the central European mould, which is briefly attractive– especially on the third and fourth waves when the rye has shaken off its oily marker to make an intense appearance. But those unwanted oils stick to the dry and untidy finish. 40%.

⬩ **Oxford Rye Distiller's Edition** new American oak cask, cask no. 101 db (76.5) n18 t20.5 f19 b19 It is very hard to get past the unhappy, butyric-type note – both on nose and palate. It is my nature to be kind to new distilleries, if always honest. But a lot is being asked of me here... I will say, though, that just after the delivery there is a very attractive ultra-malty-nutty note which is enjoyable. But it is constantly under pressure. 45%. sc. 388 bottles.

⬩ **Oxford Rye Very Special Inaugural Edition** new American oak cask, cask no. 3, dist Nov 17 db (88) n22 t22.5 f21.5 b22 Full-flavoured and chewy, this is a rye that has decidedly nougat tendencies. But it also veers at odd times towards kumquat and molasses. There is no rhyme nor rhythm to this spirit but, for all its anarchy, it certainly deals a few aces on the flavour profile. The rich chocolate as the oak gets more involved is also to be celebrated. Technically, not one for the purist. But for the flavour junkie, this has to be a big hit... 53.4%. ncf sc.

WHITE PEAK DISTILLERY Ambergate, Derbyshire. 2016. Working.

⬩ **White Peak Single Malt Spirit 24 Months Old** STR cask, bott 26 May 20 db (92) n23.5 t23 f22.5 b23 Ah, a distillery not 75 miles away from where the non-American section of the Whisky Bible is written each year and in one of my favourite areas of England. And, indeed, very close to where I would visit a girlfriend back in the late 1970s. It is a dramatic area and just a few miles from this distillery the car I was driving was once hit by lighting during a ferocious summer storm I was battling through in that part of the Peak District. Well, there's some pyrotechnics here, too, with all kinds of huge aromas and flavours meeting head on. Not least a delicate smokiness drifts across the nose, wrong-footing the chest-thumping fruit and tannins notes from the STRs. The delivery is muddled, as well it might be for a malt of this immaturity. But it is amazingly juicy, too, and the chocolate, dark cherry and grumbling smoke and spice work well from late delivery to finish. Beautifully distilled and they have invested in good wood, though I'd like to see this working in top ex-bourbon, too. When it is safe, I might just take a drive Matlock way and into the lands of my comparative youth to see what they are getting up to here. On this evidence it is looking very promising. Though, for safety's sake, I might drive with the hood of my Jag up.... *62.9%. sc.*

WALES
DA MHILE DISTILLERY Glynhynod Farm, Llandysul. 2012. Working.

Dà Mhile Single Grain Welsh Whisky db (72) n18 t20 f16 b18 I have known John Savage-Onstwedder, whom I like to think of as a friend, for the best part of 30 years and am a massive fan of his pioneering organic whisky work. And his previous whiskies have been quite superb. Things have gone wrong here, though, having been hit by a double whammy. Firstly, there is juniper all over the nose, which made me assume, correctly it transpired, that John is now involved in gin. The juniper, by the way, is annoyingly detectable on the palate, also. And secondly, he has matured this whisky in a sulphur-treated sherry cask, leading to a disastrous finish. Two pitfalls to be avoided at all costs next time round. *46%. nc ncf sc. 180 bottles. Third Edition.*

◇ **Dà Mhile Tarian Organic Single Malt Welsh Whisky** barrel no. MS1511 db **(86.5)** n21.5 t22 f21.5 b21.5 Every aspect of this malt screams "small still" at you. Or, to be precise, "new small still" as the depth of the copper on this is significant. Also, it looks as though great efforts have been made to keep the cut narrow, though still some feints have made it through – with a degree of inevitability, I must say. That smoky tobacco note on the nose, not unknown with certain German malts, is a bit of a giveaway there, and it is confirmed on the finish. But there is a rich seam of barley to be mined on the palate, for a moment or two even becoming very sweet – some intense barley sugar and maple syrup do make it into the mix. A typical new distillery first release in its occasional confusion. But if those beautifully intense moments can be harnessed and the tobacco notes eradicated, then this will become a delightfully singular malt produced by a truly singular individual. *46%. nc ncf sc.*

PENDERYN Penderyn, Aberdare. 2004. Working.

◇ **Penderyn Celt** bott code 200503 db **(95.5)** n24 quite possibly the most subtle peat nose of the year. It is there, but you can see right through it to the grist and gentle fruits beyond...; t24 one of those malts which took every piece of my will and professionalism to spit! This is less a whisky and more a lesson in seduction. The smoke has weight but no so much as to lord it above all else; the barley really does have a strong case here while the oak slowly builds but always offers structure and extra body; f23.5 how did that happen? One minute sweet on grist, then next a much drier cove concentrating on sawdust and soot...; b24 if this was a woman, I'd want to make love to it every night. And in the morning. And afternoon, if I could find the time...and energy... *43% (89 proof). nc ncf. USA Market.*

Penderyn Celt bott code 82822 db **(94)** n23 t23.5 f23.5 b24 A very different Celt: this is the quiet one, frowning upon intensity. But it is entirely impossible not to be seduced by its subtlety. *41%. ncf.*

◇ **Penderyn Celt** bott code 90165 db **(91)** n22.5 less peat, more pith...; t23 the phenols enter the fray on delivery – a lovely gristy sugar coating begins to melt in the mouth and the citrus notes found on the nose filter through; f22.5 dry, chalky and vanilla dependent. The peat now can't really be bothered...; b23 a little miserly on the phenol front. But the interplay with the fruit is a joy! *41%. nc ncf.*

◇ **Penderyn Celt** bott code 92201 db **(91.5)** n23 the smoke is wispy but layered. The malt gathers in depth and though it stokes up the vanillas, it doesn't stint on the grapefruit, either...; t22.5 very youthful with the barley grist bursting on the tongue. The smoke is puffy and powdery and makes no attempt to dominate; f23 beautiful spice and ulmo honey. Late phenols add extra weight; b23 just love this as you are never quite sure where it will take you next. A charmer, and a mystery one at that...!! *41%. nc ncf.*

◇ **Penderyn Club** rich Madeira finish, bott code 93101 db **(93.5)** n23.5 the fruit is chiselled onto the nose, so marked is it. The peppers are no less remarkable. Almost three dimensional in its vividness...; t24.5 sheer elegance and class. The spices have a rare precision to their contribution, almost perfectly weighted as an animated buffer between the intense fruit and concentrated malt. This, on the palate, is like a football team playing a deft passing game, always seeming to know where team-mates are, so nothing goes astray. A real treat to the senses and displaying an intensity that few others can match...; **f22** ah, a bit of a weakness here that could lead to relegation. So much still to enjoy with the layering of the fruit and vanilla, but there is now a nagging dull note of an imperfect cask. Still looks good, but not as good as before....; **b23.5** it noses with the elegance of Swansea City (in its Premier League days). 50%. nc ncf. Bottled for the Penderyn Club.

Penderyn Dylan Sherrywood bott code 90602 db **(87) n21.5 t23 f21 b21.5** Years and years and years ago, when I was a boy when there were wolves in Wales, and birds the colour of red-flannel petticoats whisked past the harp-shaped hills....when we rode the daft and happy hills bareback, it snowed and it snowed; and in Spain silly men did not put sulphur in innocent barrels... 41%. ncf. Icons of Wales No. 3.

Penderyn Faraday bott code 82321 db **(86) n21.5 t22 f21 b21.5** A hefty, sticky Penderyn offering little of its usual charm and complexity. Decent spices lift it from its toffee and raisin slumber. Pleasant and not unappealing, but the lamp has gone dim... 46%. ncf.

Penderyn Icons of Wales No 5/50 Bryn Terfel bourbon casks db **(96.5) n24 t24.5 f23.5 b24.5** Having seen Bryn Terfel perform live – many years ago now, I admit – I can vouch for this man's power on stage; his rare, uncanny ability to resonate with the soul. See Bryn and you get your full tenor's worth... So, this must be his alto-ego, for this is the most delicate malt ever bottled by Penderyn: ethereal, closer to the angelic voices in the closing movement of Faure's Requiem than Bryn's bass-baritone. To get that you would have needed to have added a lot of peat – and we would have ended up with Bryn Turfel....and that would never do... 41%. ncf.

◇◇ **Penderyn Legend** db **(93) n23.5** one of the most alluring noses of the Penderyn range thanks to a charming fresh vitality which never ceases. Diced apple and pear ensure there is sufficient substance to the foraging malt; **t23.5** surprisingly fat after such a waif-like nose. A gorgeous spiciness to the salivating properties here with the midground occupied by natural oak-fed caramels; **f22.5** a late bitterness creeps in but the malt still dominates; **b23.5** an exhibition in how to allow the fruit to tease, but never dominate... 43% (86 proof). nc ncf. Exclusively imported by ImpEx Beverages, Inc.

Penderyn Legend bott code 83045 db **(95.5) n23.5 t24.5 f23.5 b24** Just like having your palate kissed by a whisky nymph... This incredible, extraordinarily beautiful whisky is the undisputed master of understatement. 41%. ncf.

Penderyn Legend bott code 83048 db **(93) n23 t23.5 f23 b23.5** A beautiful malt where the oak has a fair bit to say. 41%. ncf.

◇◇ **Penderyn Legend** bott code 90252 db **(87) n22.5 t22 f21 b21.5** Just allows the dryness and slight bitterness to dominate with too much of a free hand. Plenty of malt to chew on, though, always in control. 41%. nc ncf.

◇◇ **Penderyn Legend** bott code 91172 db **(95) n23.5** another fruit-teaser on the nose: a beautiful cross between pears and grapefruit; **t24** stunning, stunning, stunning...!!! The grist melts on the tongue to form a dark-sugared accompaniment for the unprepossessing but charming fruits, sultanas quietly leading the way; **f23.5** the malt, which had formed such a porous wall on delivery makes a better fist of holding its own here. The chalky vanillas, though, give an unmistakable Penderyn feel to this...; **b24** this must have stolen the sugars from bott 90252. So elegant and well-balanced! 41%. nc ncf.

◇◇ **Penderyn Legend** bott code 913711 db **(93.5) n23** the spices, so obviously missing from the last bottling, are first out of the blocks here; **t23.5** about as big and chunky as Legend gets, the malt thick on the palate and the fruits playing lip-service; **f23.5** the oak's turn to make its mark, which it does as the fruit combines for a dry future; just adore that late chocolate sub-plot; **b23.5** as fat and chewy as some of the other legends are delicate and fragile. 41%. nc ncf.

◇◇ **Penderyn Legend** bott code 92122 db **(95.5) n23.5** drier than most, though here with a surprising smokiness: admittedly not very big on the phenol front, but this malt is always about nods and hints anyway...; **t24** that gentle smokiness arrives at the end, carrying with it more oiliness and darker sugars than is the norm. Salivating, with the fruit coming on board only when peat has quietened even further; **f23.5** long, deft malt and still that smoke lingers. A little hickory and mocha late on, too; **b24.5** adorable whisky which seems to perfect the art of quiet understatement. Such eloquent proof that in whisky less can often deliver so much more... 41%. nc ncf.

◇◇ **Penderyn Legend** bott code 92622 db **(92.5) n23** who can't be seduced by that caress of grapefruit...? **t23.5** clean barley almost to a fault: the maltiness carries a degree of salivating gristiness, the sugar slightly augmented by ulmo honey and grape; **f22.5** dry and even with the vanilla left to its own devices; **b23.5** back to its unpeated old self, and with the malt refusing to do much more than sing a duet with the delicate grape. 41%. nc ncf.

◇◇ **Penderyn Legend** bott code 93189 db **(94) n23.5** as is the style of these recent Legends, we are again talking furtive and shy, here. The malt has a light lemon-zesty freshness...but is nothing it will shout about...; **t23.5** oh, I just love this. As on the nose, the malt and citrus are melded into one. But it is all so incredibly delicate...; **f23** the malt carries on its secretive work, with now light tannins as an accomplice, rather than fruit; **b24** a malt which puts me in mind of a Town Cryer who has lost his voice. But can still whisper his message across... Brilliant! 41%. nc ncf.

⟐ **Penderyn Madeira Finish** bott code 72468 db **(93) n23** trademark chalkiness with an elegant light fruit and confident spice...just grows on the nose; **t23.5** immediately salivating a gently warming. There is a light lustre to the fruit which momentarily supercharges the sugars, though this is soon brought back into line as a saltiness emerges; **f23** long, drying and elegant. In no hurry to finish, the spices in particular; **b23.5** thought this was the perfect whisky to taste on VE Day, a British distillery working alongside an American company! Also, after a couple of sulphurous whiskies from elsewhere today, great to get onto the Penderyn Madeira finish where you know you are safe from such disappointments... 46% (92 proof). ncf. Exclusively imported by ImpEx Beverages, Inc.

Penderyn Madeira Finish bott code 83213 db **(94) n23 t24 f23 b24** Outside Scotland, hard to think of a more consistent malt whisky in the market place than this at the moment. Yet another treat. 46%. ncf.

⟐ **Penderyn Madeira Finish** bott code 83273 db **(95.5) n24** oh, wow...! Another one where a wisp of smoke has floated in, but to startling effect. There is the most subtle weight to this which just seems to add extra gravitas to the normal chalky maltiness and deft fruit: I could nose this all day...faultless...; **t24** there is no less weight on the palate, also, This has a thickness to the fruit, though it distributes its flavours lightly. A little ulmo honey and barley add extra juiciness; **f23.5** chocolate raisin...with that ridiculously subtle rumble of phenol...; **b24** if you think that Penderyn has upped its game in subtlety and complexity in recent years, then get a glass-full of this. 'Tis a thing of Welsh beauty 46%. ncf.

⟐ **Penderyn Madeira Finish** bott code 90043 db **(94) n23.5** one of the most peppery noses from Penderyn...excellent countering sweet fruitiness....so much so, fruit flies are hurling themselves into my glass for the ultimate Welsh death as I write this....!!! **t23.5** pretty rounded and boldly bodied. A softer, sweeter version where the peppers really do still have a lot to say for themselves, while the malt-laden fruit have no problems answering back; **f23** exceptionally malty; **b24** definitely a slightly different tact from this PMF, really going big on both the malt and spice. So refreshing! 46%. ncf.

⟐ **Penderyn Madeira Finish** bott code 90945 db **(91.5) n23** a reprise of bottling 72468; **t23** sumptuous and soft the barley is in tip-top form here while the vanillas are powered by the confident oak; **f22.5** drier and concentrates heavily on the barley-tannin interplay, though a little cocoa filters through...; **b23** imagine bottling 72468...but substitute chocolate for spice... 46%. ncf.

⟐ **Penderyn Madeira Finish** bott code 91992 db **(92.5) n23** earthy to the extent there is even a degree of celery at work. That normally means spice at play, too...; **t23.5** super-salivating on delivery, the malt really whipping up some serious intensity.; **f23** simplistic vanilla. But the barley and ulmo honey combination takes us in to very friendly territory; **b23** takes its foot off the complexity pedal and goes for effect. One of the most malty Penderyns for a good while. 46%. ncf.

⟐ **Penderyn Madeira Finish** bott code 92452 db **(92.5) n23** chalky sultana! **t23** the wallowing fruit gives this a slightly lazy feel, especially when the barley drifts in...though thankfully not spiceless. A little youth to this, too...; **f23** untaxing, but attractive vanilla and barley mix. A little chocolate moves in for the kill...; **b23.5** one of those malts that seems to do everything effortlessly. At times, almost too effortlessly... 46%. ncf.

⟐ **Penderyn Madeira Finish** bott code 93034 db **(89) n23** classic Penderyn Madeira Finish chalkiness, spice and laid-back fruit...; **t23.5** fabulously structured: it all comes together here – the frolicking fruit, the stupendous spice, the buccaneering barley and the chilled-out chalkiness – with the added ingredient delightful Demerara....; **f20.5** perhaps a tad tight compared to the expansive delivery; **b22** had the finish been anything like so accommodating as the rest of the experience, this would have been a very high scorer... 46%. ncf.

⟐ **Penderyn Moscatel Wine Finish** bott code 91774 db **(93.5) n23** a green, sharp nose – not entirely unlike fruit pastels. There is a little back smoke appearing from somewhere or other ensuring extra weight; **t24** an increasingly warming and salivating delivery announces this malt means business. Identically to the nose, there is a fruit pastel sharpness. But this is immediately met by that curious phenol tone and, additionally, a rich chocolate middle; **f23** untidy as the elements which had clashed so beautifully earlier no go their separate ways with less attention to harmony. So the dominance of the cocoa and fruit waivers; **b23.5** I have to say that Penderyn are making a point this year with providing us with some unique flavour profiles. A distinguished but very different experience. 59.6%. ncf. 1,456 bottles. Released August 2019.

Penderyn Myth bott code 82986 db **(88) n22.5 t23.5 f20 b22** It's a Myth, Jim. But not as we know it. 41%. ncf.

⟐ **Penderyn Myth** bott code 90641 db **(94) n23.5** talk about being alive...! The fruit. You cut yourself on it...; **t23.5** malty sherbet fizzes on the palate. All kind of lemon and lime notes abounding; **f23** light cocoa should dull the experience. But no: that there is a zesty lemon peel fade; shards of citrus still cutting deep; **b24** a real livewire of a malt. Not sure if it is that extra 2% abv (though it won't hurt!) but this one leaps from the glass to dance a merry Welsh jig around your palate. Pure entertainment. And as clean as a whisky comes. *43% (86 proof). nc ncf. Exclusively imported by ImpEx Beverages, Inc.*

⫸ **Penderyn Myth** bott code 90647 db **(91.5) n22.5** chalky pink grapefruit; **t23** salivating malt. Youthful barley conjures up some serious gristy sugars; **f23** drier now but surprisingly long. The fruitiness is playful, teasing almost; **b23** it is like a Penderyn legend being whispered, though with more emphasis on grist while the fruitiness has a definite zinginess... *41%. nc ncf.*

⫸ **Penderyn Myth** bott code 92883 db **(88.5) n22 t22.5 f22 b22** The little extra vanilla here reduces the sharpness of the fruit. Lots of flavours still working the palate, but significantly duller than most Myths. *41%. nc ncf.*

⫸ **Penderyn Oloroso Sherry Finish** bott code 91911 db **(89) n23** a pleasant, almost low key, mix of light heather honey and rich grape; **t23.5** mouth-filling and soft. Good texture and layering as the fruit views with butterscotch for a degree of dominance; **f20.5** creamy butterscotch tart wins, but just a little bitterish and untidy; **b22** if it's sherry you'll be liking... come and get it! Just the slightest hint of furriness around the edges, though. *59.6%. ncf. 1,349 bottles. Released August 2019.*

Penderyn Peated bott code 82141 db **(94.5) n23 t24 f23.5 b24** The smoke covers this malt like a satin negligee over the contours of your favourite body... *46%. ncf.*

⫸ **Penderyn Peated** bott code 90162 db **(93) n23** that teasing smokiness cannot entirely obscure the oak-fed spices and fresh Granny Smith apple; **t23.5** succulent and deft, the phenols for a moment are lost behind a small wave of healthy barley. Youthful, but with a gorgeous mocha middle; **f23** talk about apologetic oak. The tannins nibble at the barley, but it seems enough to gain a slight edge...; **b23.5** youthful, exuberant and among the most teasingly-weighed peated Penderyns... *46%. ncf.*

⫸ **Penderyn Peated** bott code 90821 db **(94) n23.5** the phenols take on a smoky bacon stance but really relish the busy spice, too. For Americans visiting Britain who are rather partial to this aroma, try smoky bacon and Cumberland sausage for breakfast...; **t23.5** fat and fulsome maltiness, then a slow spice burn...there is obviously no smoke without fire...; **f23** the oils hold sway right to the last, the spices fizzing throughout; **b24** Penderyn at its weightiest. But where it wins the heart comprehensively is that it never throws that weight around. So sexy! *46% (92 proof). ncf. Exclusively imported by ImpEx Beverages, Inc.*

⫸ **Penderyn Peated** bott code 91541 db **(92.5) n22.5** a pretty thin nose with the a light grapey note out-muscling the phenols...; **t23** salivating! The barley is on steroids while the smoke takes a back seat; **f23.5** a light, though slightly creamy mocha fade. The spices suddenly explode... **b23.5** Penderyn Peated coming at you from a very different, but still very delicious, angle... *46%. ncf.*

⫸ **Penderyn Portwood** bott code 91284 db **(86.5) n22 t22 f21 b21.5** Dull is not a word I normally link with Penderyn. But I have no problems applying it here. You know those satellite things that travel, relentlessly and without err and aberration across the night sky. But so dim you need your binoculars to make them out clearly, briefly, before they vanish into the void.... Well, this is such a whisky...Pleasant. But so bloody dull.... *46%. ncf.*

⫸ **Penderyn Portwood Grand Slam Edition 2019** bott code 91051 db **(93) n23.5** a delightful tangle of tannin and peppers but bound together by dry grape skin...; **t23.5** there's one against the head here: you are simple knocked reeling by the density of the dry, pithy grape; **f23** a lot of cocoa around to keep that ultra-dry style going. A light flicker of muscovado sugar here and there – and even, I momentarily thought, of juniper...; **b23** moments of this whisky, especially on delivery, are as tightly packed and exert as much power as your average scrum. As dry as a Ken Gorman one liner. *46%. ncf.*

⫸ **Penderyn Portwood Single Cask 12 Year Old** cask no. PT1113 db **(96) n23.5 t24 f24 b24.5** The odd thing about his fellow is that the oak plays a surprisingly low-key role for a 12-years-old. Instead it is the fruit which calls the shots – literally! – first with its airy dried date aroma then mouth-watering, eye-squinting delivery which always seems to have Venezuelan chocolate drifting around the scene. I think we have to accept that Penderyn are moving into a higher sphere than most other distilleries and the controlled enormity of some of their whiskies take a good half hour to fathom. Minimum. This is one such beast. Selecting British whisky of the year - and world whisky of the year – has just become a whole lot more interesting... *60.4%. ncf sc. Selected & imported by ImpEx Beverages, Inc.*

⫸ **Penderyn Rhiannon** sherrywood Grand Cru finish, bott code 91852 db **(96.5) n23.5** there is a mustiness of dank, mossy forests to this nose: the fruit is on a different plane, grapey and rich; **t24** a nibbling saltiness to the chocolate and raisin main theme. Pretty tart and abrasive at times, but the oak offers a steadying depth; **f24.5** still tart and mildly aggressive, the complexity is all about the cork-like dryness (by which I mean, have you ever smelt the cork of a grand-cru wine three or four hours after opening? Then you get the message...) against the tannins...though of grape, not oak...; **b24.5** a cerebral whisky playing games and tricks. Near enough perfectly balanced and different enough to set this apart from any whisky before. Few whiskies ever reach this level of complexity... 46%. Icons of Wales No. 7 🏆

Penderyn Rich Oak bott code 82504 db **(94) n23 t23.5 f23.5 b24** Jack Daniels was of Welsh descent. The layered tannins here, not entirely dissimilar to some Kentucky and Tennessee whiskey, would make him feel very much at home. Superb. 46%. ncf.

◈ **Penderyn Rich Oak** bott code 90742 db **(91) n23** Rich oak as I have never quite seen it before on the nose with walnut oil joining in with the muscovado sugars and thin molasses...; **t24** oilier, weightier and more embracing than ever before. The enormity of the delivery takes a little while to compute: never have so many faces of their malt – be it a rich nuttiness, the molasses, the mocha, the astonishingly intense maltiness – gelled together in one fell swoop. Only the spices show a degree of constraint; **f21** dried dates and even more malt. The molasses off the tannins are in no hurry to depart, either...; a little late fuzziness...; **b23** when they say "Rich" they mean rich... Penderyn at its most muscular. Probably ever.... 46%. nc ncf.

◈ **Penderyn Rich Oak** bott code 91222 db **(95.5) n24** elegant. Penderyn in typical understated and shy mode, the malt and muscovado sugars taking their time to build up a momentum...; **t24** clean, soft and sweet. A little citrus at play here before the oak begins to assume a degree of richness, a little heather-honey helping it along the way; **f23.5** powdery oak and grist make for an unusually subtle fade; **b24** as is the Penderyn way, this cleverly reveals the other side of the coin. Quietly intense and far less domineering, this is an easily overlooked gem of a whisky! 46% (92 Proof). nc ncf. Exclusively imported by ImpEx Beverages, Inc.

Penderyn Royal Welsh Whisky bott code 90532 db **(86) n22 t23 f20 b21** One of the softest deliveries of the Penderyn range, briefly enjoying a salivating grape and grain combination which for several excellent moments hit wonderful fruit and chocolate heights. But the finish is untidy and the furry buzz reveals a rogue cask in the mix. The delivery, though, is something a little special. 43%. ncf. Icons of Wales No. 6.

Penderyn Sherrywood bott code 82111 db **(94) n23 t23.5 f24 b23.5** Quite simple, but goes out of its way to do the simple things very well – and deliciously - indeed... 46%. ncf.

Penderyn Sherrywood bott code 90113 db **(86) n22.5 t22 f20.5 b21** The nose is interesting enough, but otherwise this lies flat on the palate and steadfastly refuses to sparkle. A disappointing dullard by Penderyn's high standards. 46%. ncf.

◈ **Penderyn Sherrywood** bott code 91331 db **(91.5) n23** such delicate interplay between gooseberry jam, acacia honey and tender oaky spices...; **t23** a surprising buttery note mingles with the bitter-sweet grape. The oak meanders throughout adding vanilla here and there; **f22.5** remains creamy and deft. The oak, as it should, has a keener, drier say; **b23** elegant and even: a portrait of charm itself. 46%. ncf.

◈ **Penderyn Sherrywood** bott code 92392 db **(95) n23.5** this is a ten-minute nose: it is like accustoming your eye to the night sky and seeing the ever-increasing number of stars. Here, slow analysis will allow you to discover the myriad oaky compounds which appears to let the fruit shimmer slightly in intensity; **t24** ah! Again, the delivery is far more complex than its sister bottling, the oak mixing freely with the barley to give the fruit a lesser role and generate a busy bitty-ness that includes, deliciously, cocoa and marzipan; **f23.5** fabulously long thanks to a barely detectable creaminess, but at no time stinting on the beautifully underplayed complexity. The delicate fruit notes play so well along the chocolate and hazelnut; **b24** boasting a balance and complexity which borders belief, this is one very sophisticated whisky... 46%. ncf.

◈ **Penderyn Single Cask** bourbon cask, cask no. 182/2006, bott 11 Jul 19 db **(96.5) n24.5** stunning: this exudes that unique and depressingly rare countenance of great spirit matured in outstanding oak. The result is a malty-sugary concoction to die for weight and substance, all the while enriched by sugars of magically varying intensity. All the time there is a vague echo of Kentucky... I repeat: stunning! **t24.5** hard to imagine that nose being matched, but it is. A glorious array of hazelnut oil and heather honey gives a gilded edge to the delivery and follow-through. Delicate to the point of fragility in part. But the malt really does have surprisingly strong backbone and shrugs off the grapefruit as though it isn't there; **f23.5** a delicate bourbon-style tannin which dries quite abruptly... ushering in some busy spice; **b24** this is one of those rare, magical whiskies that is not about tasting notes but the shape, depth and overall experience. Which, has to be said, is pretty close to as good as it gets... 62%. ncf sc. Selected by Harrods. 🏆

◈ **Penderyn Single Cask** bourbon cask, cask no. 2/2006 db **(95.5) n23.5 t23.5 f24.5 b24** Massively tasty, but a curious Penderyn, all the same. The precise and eye-wateringly sharp grapefruit acts as a juicy diversion away from the barley, which slowly composes itself to mount to compelling challenge. This celebrates maltiness in the same way a sex addict revels in a threesome. A malt which simply refuses to leave the taste buds alone until they finally submit. 56.8%. ncf sc.

⟨⟨⟨ **Penderyn Single Cask** ex-bourbon cask, cask no. 71/2007, dist Feb 07, bott Aug 19 db **(95) n24** chocolate Malteser candy meets Kentucky...; **t24** not sure I've before encountered a Penderyn that ladles out the barley so thickly. A secondary juicy grapefruit note tries to add a sharpness to the malt and not without success..; **f23** delightful oak and barley interplay...the malt really does blossom here; **b24** on this evidence, Penderyn is ready for a run of bourbon cask bottlings. The enormity and purity of the malt takes some believing... 58.6%. ncf sc. 196 bottles. Selected by La Maison du Whisky.

⟨⟨⟨ **Penderyn Ex-Madeira Single Cask** cask no. M524, dist Nov 13, bott Jan 20 db **(95.5) n23.5** a powerful mix of tannin, root vegetable and concentrated grape. The pepperiness is just so, while the background dark cherry-sweetness does its balancing act; **t24** all the spiced, fruity cough-sweet intensity arrives with a remarkable lushness. The oak fizzes beautifully in a gentle and busy fashion, cleverly upping the complexity and layering....; **f23.5** such a different experience. There is dark cocoa powder aplenty, though this is inextricably locked into the uniquely thick cough sweet-style cherry fruitiness **b24.5** another Penderyn it is really hard to find fault with. The most astonishing thing, perhaps, is its strength. The luxurious, creamy softness of this malt means the alcohol is barely noticeable at all...This is one very substantial whisky. 60.4%. ncf sc. Franconian Edition 2020.

⟨⟨⟨ **Penderyn Single Cask** purple moscatel finish, cask no. W23 db **(88) n22 t22.5 f21.5 b22** A tart and mildly aggressive malt. Just a little too heavy of the sharper fruit notes with the malt vanishing under a near brutal regime of murderous spices. Amazing flavour profile, I admit. But a little too vicious and blood curdling for me... 61%. ncf sc.

⟨⟨⟨ **Penderyn Single Cask** PX sherry finish, cask no. S74 db **(87) n23 t23 f20 b21** While the nose displays a highly unusual salty edge to a Penderyn, the direction of the PX involvement is predictable, though not before a superb volley of spices gather your attention early on. After a salivating entry it becomes syrupy and sticky, though the fruit does have an attractive date and walnut touch when at its best; a molassed noble rot when at its most basic. The finish, however, is furry and dull. 59.1%. ncf sc.

Penderyn Single Cask Rich Madeira Cask cask no. M334 db **(95) n23.5 t24 f23.5 b24** Rich....? You're not joking...!!! 59.1%. ncf sc. Bottled for Charles Hofer SA, Switzerland.

⟨⟨⟨ **Penderyn Single Cask** rum finished, cask no. R13 db **(93.5) n23** despite the playful nibble and bite, fruit dominates and banana in custard particularly. There is an unctuousness, too, though a little honey to cut through that; **t24** there must have been banana trees surrounding the rum warehouse where this cask first lived, for that fruit's footprint is everywhere. Creamy and increasingly sharp as the fruit, more apple and pear now, take on a more acidic character; **f23** just a little aggression starts to gee up what had been a soft and easy ride. But that creamy banana quality is still hanging around, though there is now some much drier oak to deal with; **b23.5** a very different whisky from Penderyn that at times shews just a little bit of youth, but some outstanding yumminess. Oh, and really profits under the Murray Method. 50%. ncf sc. Bottled for Schlumberger.

⟨⟨⟨ **Penderyn Single Cask** purple moscatel finish, cask no. W28 db **(88.5) n22.5 t22 f22 b22** Like Cask W23, the malt is buried under a tsunami of unforgiving grape. Certainly captures the attention but, again, the spices have little compassion and the oak is its accomplice. But providing you are tucked into your seatbelt this is an enjoyable ride, the outrageous plums offering astonishing chewiness and depth. But the corners are taken just a little too sharply. 59.8%. ncf sc.

⟨⟨⟨ **Penderyn Single Cask** ex-Tawny port cask, cask no. PT267, dist Jun 13, bott Nov 19 db **(94.5) n23.5** the fruit bounces around with a clever mix of zesty freshness and more arresting, duller peppers...; **t23.5** the nose revisited. The fruit is generous and fulsome. The malt, though present, is put into the shade. As on the nose, the spices are distinct, but attach themselves to a sombre oakiness; **f23.5** the fruit is still light enough to fly...; **b24** with its distinct pink hue, this is the most porty-looking malt of all time. But like the Tawny owl which frequents my garden, it has a certain gravitas to it too, as well as ageless elegance. 59.6%. ncf sc. Exclusive bottling for Whisky Live Manila 2020.

⟨⟨⟨ **Penderyn Single Cask** Terrantez cask finish from Blandy's Madeira Wine Lodge, cask no. 078-2, bott 6 Aug 19 db **(94.5) n24** now, that is one very proud nose! The fruit boasts a solidity, an uncompromising depth and almost regal stature. Not an atom out of place, but an almost regimented procession thick then deft grapey tones, each taking turn to hold the attention. The sugars are likewise fulsome, a mix of muscovado and molassed variety but also with a tantalising sliver of kumquat peel. Superb...; **t23.5** curiously, the delivery does not have the same initial gravitas revealed on the nose. But the fruit does soon build up into a dizzy, busy spiced concoction holding vanilla and butterscotch in major quantities; **f23** a slightly duller finish as the oak reveals its toasty nature, though the fruit does retain a creamy presence; **b24** a formidable malt where the whisky has just enough body to hold the weight of the grape without trembling. A unique assemblage of personality traits. 57.4%. ncf sc. Selected by Harrods.

Australian Whisky

It is not surprising that Australia, cast adrift it seems from the rest of the world until Captain James Cook thrust his triangulation apparatus at it some 240 years ago, has many indigenous species. The result of biodiversity having to get on with it alone, often bravely and against the odds.

From the kangaroo to the koala, the wombat to the platypus, the kookaburra to the bearded Lark. Now it is the bearded Lark (Billius Distillus) in its native Tasmanian habitat, a small creature found mainly flying around darkened buildings in the vicinity of Hobart, that has had the greatest impact on Australian whisky, and without whom there would be no chapter given only to that singular scion of the world's malt distillation family.

Bill Lark is a one-man force majeure who took a country out of a starch-knickered Victorian reactionism, so far as distilling was concerned, into one that now proudly boasts over 25 distilleries either operating or in the process of being built. And a standard achieved by many so far that is way above the norm.

We must go back to 1992, seemingly recent in the grand scheme of whisky matters but a year before many of the people I met attending a recent (though just pre-Covid) Chengdu, China, whisky festival were actually born. It was the year I gave up my work as a national newspaper journalist to become the world's first full-time whisky writer. And was the year Bill Lark began taking on the Australian government to change a law that forbade private distilling in Australia. Having got sympathetic politicians on board – always a wise move – he found his battle shorter and less bloody than expected and it was not long before he and his wife Lyn were hard at work distilling an unhopped mash made at the local – and historic – Cascade brewery. Soon their daughter, Kristy, was on board showing exceptional skill as a distiller. And next a family affair became a national one, as, inspired by the Larks, small distilleries began rising around the country. First Dave Baker, whose Bakery Hill malt scooped the Whisky Bible 2020's Southern Hemisphere Whisky of the Year, across the Tasman Straight in Melbourne and then onwards along and up the coast. A new whisky nation was born. And is growing prodigiously. Now I have given Australia its own section in Jim Murray's Whisky Bible, perhaps not before time. It is a form of award well merited, because Australian malt has constantly proved to be something worth finding: often as bold and brave as Bill Lark's vision. And, like the great man and dear friend himself, you always feel better for its company.

Key

● **Major Town or City**

🏚 **Distillery**

Adelaide
Adelaide Hills
Tin Shed Disiling Co.

Fannys Bay

Hellyers Road

Launceston
Launceston Distillery
Adams Distillery

Cradle Mountain

TASMANIA

Nant Distillery

Belgrove Distillery
Old Kempton Distillery
Shene Estate & Distillery

Spring Bay
Nonesuch

Hobart
Killara

Hobart
Devil's Distillery
Lark Distillery
Old Hobart
Sullivans Cove

2021 Australian Whisky of the Year	Adams Distillery Whisky Cask Strength

AUSTRALIA
ADAMS DISTILLERY Perth, Tasmania. 2012. Working.

Adams Distillery Tasmanian Single Malt Whisky Cask Strength 50l American oak port cask, cask no. AD 0016 db (84.5) n21 t22 f20.5 b21 Doesn't work in the same way as their peat finish bottling. The distillate itself seems less well made, resulting in some uncomfortable moments both on nose and finish. No faulting the cask, though, which throws a clean, rich, spicy, grapey beacon to bring you home. 55.5%. sc. 65 bottles.

◇ **Adams Distillery Tasmanian Single Malt Whisky Cask Strength** peated - slosh 200L Pinot Noir cask, cask no. AD 0128 db (91) n23 a complex, singular aroma where the smoke mixes with a little oil to give the fruit a slightly combative feel, as it needs to fight to make its mark; t23 the grape gains revenge on delivery, immediately elbowing the peat into the periphery. A little heather honey has to intervene before the smoke returns, though meekly; f22.5 a little spice helps the phenolic cause...; b22.5 too often wine casks and peat hit the buffers. This stays on track, even if there isn't quite enough smoke to keep this one going at full speed.. 61.2%. ncf sc. 132 bottles.

◇ **Adams Distillery Tasmanian Single Malt Whisky Cask Strength** peated - slosh 300L port cask, cask no. AD 0113 db (96) n24 sublimely structured phenol: the smoke offers myriad degrees of depth and peat intensity. Fruitcake-like sultana adds the sweeter edge; t23.5 a near perfect mouthfeel on delivery, then pow! First the smoke, then the fruit and finally the oak take turns to dominate while the spices Fester; f24.5 the glorious strands of Melton Hunt fruitcake have to give way to the chocolate-dipped phenols; b24 you've got to Hand it to them: simply brilliant! A Munster, sorry a mean monster, whisky...(I've been in Lockdown too long...) 59.5%. ncf sc. 130 bottles. ♜

Adams Distillery Tasmanian Single Malt Whisky First Release sherry cask, peat finish, cask no. 005, 012 & 013 db (90.5) n23.5 t22 f22.5 b22.5 Apart from an over indulgence of sweet fruit on delivery, this whisky ticks just about every box. 52.5%. 324 bottles.

◇ **Adams Distillery Tasmanian Single Malt Whisky Special Release** port 20L American oak cask, cask no. AD 0100 db (90) n23 love the early confidence of the tannin to bite through the layered grape. Equally, a delicate layer of smoke gives an extra rumbling degree of weight; t23.5 eye-wateringly rich. This is tart all right: jam tart, blackberry tart and plum tart;. f21 a slightly bumpy landing as the many facets of flavours can't quite find a united front; b22.5 though partially matured in bourbon cask, this is another of the Adams family of whiskies that Lurches towards fruitiness.. 55.5%. ncf sc. 26 bottles.

ADELAIDE HILLS DISTILLERY Nairne, South Australia. 2014. Working.

❧ **Native Grain Whiskey 2020** barrel no. ADP7 weeping grass, malted barley, French oak. db **(87.5)** n22.5 t23 f20.5 b21.5 Well, at least this year their offering really is a whisky. And what's more, a lifetime first for me: 20,000 different whiskies tasted for the Whisky Bible alone and this is the first I've encountered that uses the grain of weeping grass. Unless I'm mistaken, I once trod this dense-growing greenery at a farm in Tasmania while out bird watching. So thick was this stuff I remember keeping more of an eye out for snakes than avian life! However, I can report that I think it might be a very useful grain for whisky. I say think, because the use of French oak and wine barrels means you don't get a clear sight of this unique grain. With a bourbon barrel you can monitor the impact of the grass. Here, you are left wondering if it is the tannin and fruit which so blatantly obscures the finish or supplies the bitterness which undoes much of the early promise. The nose, however, is attractive and like no other: intense with a brittle sharpness. The delivery is increasingly acute yet delightfully measured before a huge rush of tannin spins it off course and leads you to a disappointingly bitter and out of alignment finale. But that is not before a beautifully on-song wave of heather-honey spreads like, well, weeping grass, all over the palate. I think the good people of Adelaide Hills might be onto a winner here. But only if they can find a formula for the finish...while keeping the late spice buzz. Perhaps the most intriguing whiskey of the 2020 Bible: thank you! Finish apart, seriously enjoyable. 46.2%. sc. 150 bottles.

ANIMUS DISTILLERY Kyneton, Victoria. 2012. Working.

Animus Distillery Alpha Whisky db **(90.5)** n23 t23.5 f22 b22.5 Impressively forceful and confident it is helped by the clean, unsullied spirit. 54.5%.

BAKERY HILL North Bayswater, Victoria. 1999. Working.

❧ **Bakery Hill The Blunderbuss** db **(90)** n22.5 t23 f22 b22.5 I can see why it has the name. The slightly thicker cut than normal manages to herd and concentrate the malt like never before. A slightly oafish dram which lets you have the barley right between the eyes. Memorable. And certainly hits the target! 52%.

Bakery Hill Classic Malt Single Malt Whisky db **(88)** n22 t22 f22 b22 A straight as a die malt which makes little attempt to veer away from its cream toffee theme. 46%. ncf.

Bakery Hill Classic Malt Cask Strength Single Malt Whisky db **(94)** n23 t23.5 f23.5 b24 Because of the lack of oils present on Baker Hill malt, it can suffer slightly when reduced. Here the whisky, oils and all, is intact we get the malt in full glory. "Classic Malt" says the label. You hear no quibbles from me... 60.5%. ncf.

❧ **Bakery Hill Death or Glory** db **(94)** n23 t23.5 f23.5 b24 Oh, my! Get the complexity on this fella! As minty as it is malty, on the nose especially, this has a colossal amount of development between the sweeter tones, mint included, and the drier oaks which act as anchor. Right in the middle of all this is sublime malt, salivating and sharp on one level, and almost biscuity and salty on another. One of those 15 minutes malts using the Murray Method to unlock a true beauty. When a malt is this on song, surely it should be called "Tunes of Glory"... 48%.

Bakery Hill Double Wood Single Malt Whisky db **(90)** n22 t23 f22.5 b23 A busy, attractive and quite full bodied Bakery Hill. 46%. ncf.

❧ **Bakery Hill Double Wood Cask Strength** db **(88)** n22.5 t22 f21.5 b22 A much flatter, steady-as-she-goes bottling with the barley subdued. Very well made, that's for sure, as there is a degree of clarity to this only obtainable from decent distillation. But the finish is slightly too bitter and twisted and sports none of the spices promised on the attractive nose. 60%.

Bakery Hill Peated Malt Single Malt Whisky db **(87.5)** n21.5 t22.5 f21.5 b22 A bit on the young and slightly wobbly side, not quite having the overall balance so monumentally displayed by the cask strength version. 46%. ncf.

Bakery Hill Peated Malt Cask Strength Single Malt Whisky db **(95.5)** n24 t24 f23 b24 Doing the Australian whiskies today (well, some of them) as England and the Aussies are battling it out in the semi-final of the cricket World Cup. Duty over pleasure means I am here tasting instead of at Edgbaston. And it is so wonderful to find David Baker's malt still very much up in smoke, a bit like Australia who have slipped to 175-7 – which doubtless means the Aussies will win.... A malt as glorious as England's bowling... 60%. ncf.

Bakery Hill Sovereign Smoke Defiantly Peated Single Malt Whisky db **(91.5)** n22.5 t23 f23 b23 A beautiful diffusion of light honey and smoke. 50%. sc.

BELGROVE DISTILLERY Kempton, Tasmania. 2010. Working.

Belgrove Distillery Rye Whisky 100% Rye barrel no. PB074, bott 11 Apr 19 db **(88.5)** n22 t22.5 f22 b22 A very different type of Belgrove rye. Actually, tasted blind I'd never have recognised it. 62.4%. ncf sc.

Belgrove Distillery Rye Whisky 100% Rye bott 11 Apr 19 db (**93**) n22.5 t24 f23 b23.5 Belgrove back to its bristling self. Full set of cutlery required for this three-course rye. 62.5%. ncf sc.

Belgrove Distillery Rye Whisky Wholly Shit Sheep Dung Smoke bott 26 Sept 18 db (**94.5**) n23.5 t23.5 f23.5 b24 A whisky coming to a baa near you... and much better than the shit I have to endure from some sulphured ex-wine casks. Yesterday I tasted whisky matured in lychee liqueur casks and plum liqueur casks; earlier today a (sulphur-treated) pomegranate wine cask. I did wonder what the hell would be next....I should have known.. 57.8%.

⬦ **Heartwood Heartgrove #2 Tasmanian Malt Whisky** spirit: rye, Muscat/sherry/sherry cask, cask no. PB052, bott 7 Feb 20 (**84**) n23 t22 f18.5 b20.5 From the distillery which last year gave me sheep dung smoked whisky, another bottling to test the mettle of my taste buds. And tested they certainly were by employing Muscat, on its day one of the boldest of the wine casks, to embolden, or perhaps overthrow, rye, the biggest flavoured of all the grains. For sheer power the muscat wins. However, you get the feeling that both the raw spirit and one of the casks wasn't up to normal high standard. The result is a bit of a mess, with the fruit dominating on both the nose and delivery, which is never less than embracing. The finish, though, is woefully off key. 54.4%. sc. 196 bottles.

BLACK GATE DISTILLERY Mendooran NSW. 2012. Working.

⬦ **Black Gate Distillery Peated Cask** cask no. BG068, dist Apr 17, bott Dec 19 db (**91.5**) n23 from the fresh kippers school of peating, though here it feels as though someone has sprinkled Demerara sugars over them...; t23 a saline and sugar mix on the lightly oiled delivery with the smoke building in intensity in a slow but determined rate; f22.5 long though the smoke diminishes as the caramels build up a head of steam; b23 the caramels dampen the peat fire a little, but no mistaking a superb whisky when you see one. 58.7%. sc.

⬦ **Black Gate Distillery Port Cask Solera Batch No. 3** db (**87**) n21.5 t22.5 f21 b22 A neat and comfortable malt, if not technically in the same league as their peated cask bottling, that seems as though it doesn't want to ruffle too many feathers. The port acts as a silky base but also ensures development and complexity is limited. 46.8%.

CHIEF'S SON DISTILLERY Somerville, Victoria. 2014. Working.

⬦ **Chief's Son Single Malt Whisky 900 Pure Malt** db (**89.5**) n22 slightly simplistic with vanilla and moscavado sugars leading; t22 a salivating delivery, though with a surprising lack of weight. A light toasted raisin note gives way to some intense barley; f23 ah, now we're talking! The vanillas break into oak-induced spicy mode, but the barley is ramping up the full-blown maltiness; b22.5 a well-made whisky which allows the malt an impressive flourish. 45%. nc ncf.

⬦ **Chief's Son Single Malt Whisky 900 Standard** db (**91**) n22.5 light caramels and a little sultana; t23 takes a little time to find its feet: the delivery is unusually quiet with delicate malt eventually filling in the void. By the midpoint it is purring along delightfully with vanilla and even a touch of praline joining the malt; f22.5 bitters out fractionally, but the lightest of creamy oils carry the cocoas onward; b23 wonderful to find an Australian that is not depending on power and/or muscular fruit. Complex and fabulously malty. 45%. nc ncf.

⬦ **Chief's Son Single Malt Whisky 900 Standard** db (**95**) n23 decidedly grapey! t23.5 no blank spots on delivery here: the fruit thunders into the taste buds with almost arrogant certainty. Surprisingly, a train of rich cocoa notes follow behind; f24.5 surprising strand of liquorice gives this a vague but delicious bourbon feel. Still the chocolate holds its place, increasingly taking a cocoa butter stance; the molassed coconut finale is a wonderful surprise, together when embraced with the chocolate....sensational...! b24 it is as though someone has put the 45% version up another gear or two...It is like taking your taste buds to the gym when they are fully worked over. And, just like a good work out, you feel so bloody good afterwards... Oh, and as this stunning malt was made at Mornington Peninsula, a warm toast to the memory of British comic legend Tim Brook-Taylor, forever associated with Mornington Crescent, who was stolen from us by Covid-19 as I wrote this Bible... 60%. nc ncf.

⬦ **Chief's Son Single Malt Whisky 900 Sweet Peat** db (**88**) n22 t22 f22 b22 The peat is little more than a gentle breeze. And even that is lost in the moderate winds of the fruit. Just a little too even and, though pleasant, you get the feeling differing forces are as much cancelling the other out as they are making for a complex malt. Even so, sweet, attractive and easy going. 45%. nc ncf.

⬦ **Chief's Son Single Malt Whisky Cask Expression** db (**93**) n23 really lovely inter-weaving between the fruit and chocolate-laden oak. So deft, despite its weight; t23 silky delivery and immediately salivating. A volley of barley reveals a pretty young malt at work here, but the assuredness of the Dundee cake allows there to be a slightly toasty edge to all that juiciness; f23.5 spiced fruit chocolate...which carries on the delicate oils for quite some time; b23.5 my very old friend, the late distillery consultant Jim Swan, would probably have cut your arm off to get a bottle of this. This was one of his preferred styles of whisky, and here it has been executed almost faultlessly. Most impressive is the way this malt just kept getting better as it went along. *47.85%. nc ncf.*

CORRA LINN DISTILLERY Relbia, Tasmania. 2015. Working.

◇ **Corra Linn Fumosus Aqua Vitae Single Malt Whisky** db (**87**) n21.5 t22.5 f21.5 b21.5 A particularly dry malt with a busy cross section of seasoning. The tannins bite a bit while a strange, meandering semi-fruitiness pitches up here and there, as does a lagging phenolic tone. An oddball malt which never quite settles on the direction it wants to take. Plenty of flavour and certainly intriguing. *56.2%.*

CRADLE MOUNTAIN WHISKY PTY LTD Ulverstone, Tasmania. Closed.

◇ **Cradle Mountain Whisky Single Malt The Long Trek** batch no. 20005 db (**95**) n23.5 slightly burnt jam sponge cake, but with none of the acidic attack. This is soft and enthralling...; t24 standing ovation for this delivery...!! Just brilliant! We have now gone from burnt jam sponge to burnt fruit cake, the raisins in particular copping it. But mixed in, as it is, with light ulmo honey and prattling peppers, we have one hell of a mouthful...; oh, and the salivation levels are right up there; f23.5 there you go...malt! Loads of it, finally battling its way through the disastrous cooking but comes out loud and proud late on with the vanilla; b24 I love a whisky with not just personality but one that's all its own. And this has it in spades. Superb! Happy anniversary! *57%. 240 bottles. 30 Year Anniversary.*

DEVIANT DISTILLERY Sandy Bay, Tasmania. 2017. Working.

Deviant Distillery Anthology 15 Single Malt Spirit heavily peated px sherry cask db (**89.5**) n21 t23 f22.5 b23 Can't say I go a bundle on the nose at this juncture of the spirit's development. But is certainly fights back on the palate as – and I do not say this either often or lightly – by the PX and smoke appear to complement each other, being superbly weighted and almost attuned to the other. A real surprise treat *47.6%.*

Deviant Distillery Anthology 16 Single Malt Spirit Pinot Noir F.O. cask, finished in a coffee cask db (**91.5**) n22.5 t23 f23 b23 For those of you looking for a spirit to wake you up first thing in the morning, here it is. You can even dip biscuits in it. Actually, the coffee isn't quite as profound as you might think...but it is there and its subtlety makes it all the more attractive. *43.7%.*

Deviant Distillery Tri Malt New Make Spirit db (**93.5**) n23 t23.5 f24 b23.5 That, in well over 40 years of visiting distilleries and tasting the juice from their stills, is the sweetest new make I have ever encountered. It is, by any yardstick, extraordinary! *55%.*

DEVIL'S DISTILLERY Hobart, Tasmania. 2015. Working.

Hobart Whisky Tasmanian Dark Mofo 2019 Winter Feast Exclusive ex-bourbon cask, rum maple finish, bott 25 Apr 19 db (**82.5**) n20 t22 f20.5 b20 Not sure what to say about this. Far more a liqueur than a whisky in character with the maple dominating the aroma to the cost of all else and the muscular sugars, though attractive, decidedly OTT. *59.1%.*

Hobart Whisky Tasmanian Single Malt Batch 19-001 ex-lightly smoked American whisk(e)y cask, bott 8 Feb 19 db (**89.5**) n22.5 t22.5 f21.5 b23 When they say lightly smoked, they ain't joking. The toffee was a much easier spot... *50.3%. 328 bottles.*

Hobart Whisky Tasmanian Single Malt Batch 19-002 ex-bourbon cask, pinot noir finish, bott 25 Apr 19 db (**94**) n23 t24 f23.5 b23.5 Like being hit by the waves of a tropical storm, one flavour smashing into you after another. Just brilliant...! *57.5%.*

Hobart Whisky Tasmanian Single Malt Batch 19-003 French oak port cask finish, bott 25 Apr 19 db (**93.5**) n23 t23.5 f23.5 b23.5 More beautifully intense than a harem... *46.4%.*

Hobart Whisky Tasmanian Single Malt Batch 19-004 bott 25 Apr 19 db (**93**) n23 t23.5 f23 b23.5 How the Devil do they make their bourbon matured malt so buttery...? *55.5%.*

Tasmanian Moonshine Company Tasmanian Malt Barrel Aged New Make port cask db (**91.5**) n23 t23 f22.5 b23 Big almost jammy fruit. But that is only half of it: a huge injection of hefty tannin has ensured backbone to the plummy muscle. And as for the spices....? Wow! A huge dose of flavours: this youngster isn't mucking about! *50%.*

FANNYS BAY DISTILLERY Lulworth, Tasmania. 2014. Working.

◇ **Fannys Bay Single Malt Tasmanian Whisky** bourbon barrel, cask no. 33 db (**89.5**) n22.5 several intriguing layers of barley of varying thickness and intensity; t23 and more of the same on delivery, though here we are now talking in concentrated form. A little bitterness from the tannins strikes back; f22 a real bitter-sweet rumble; b22 a brusque malt which certainly doesn't lack confidence. Just a little bitterness here and there weakens it slightly, though the intensity of the malt will win many friends. *63%. sc.*

Fannys Bay Tasmanian Single Malt bourbon cask, barrel no. 39, bott 2 Oct 18 db **(94.5)** n23 t24 f23.5 b24 No Port. No sherry. Just the wonderful opportunity to taste naked Fannys. This malt, like the island, shapes up perfectly. *64%. sc.*

Fannys Bay Tasmanian Single Malt port cask, barrel no. 42, bott 15 Dec 18 db **(89)** n22 t22.5 f22.5 b22 An enjoyable whisky, but with only a fraction of the complexity evident in the bourbon cask. The Port cask doesn't exactly overwhelm, but peppers and tannins apart, seems loth to allow other elements to come into play. Still very enjoyable but distinctly in your face *62%. sc.*

Fannys Bay Tasmanian Single Malt sherry cask, barrel no. 35, bott 2 Oct 18 db **(89.5)** n22.5 t23 f21.5 b22.5 The finale apart, this is a lightly fruited joy. *63.7%. sc.*

⟨⟩ **Fannys Bay Single Malt Tasmanian Whisky** sherry cask, cask no. 76 db **(91.5)** n23 magnificent intertwangling between maraschino cherries and rampant oak-edged spices; t23.5 wonderful mouthfeel on delivery. A mix of toffee and sultana mingles graciously with a healthy malt sub-plot; f22 becomes a little tame, the light spice prickle apart; b23 a more rounded and less fractious wine influenced malt than their Shiraz. Polite... and not half the fun. *64%. sc.*

⟨⟩ **Fannys Bay Single Malt Tasmanian Whisky** Shiraz cask, cask no. 61 db **(93)** n22 yes, there is a muscular tannin tone, and a spicy one, too. But the complexity you might expect is conspicuous by its absence; t24 oh my word! After that nose it was hard to see this coming. Maybe the spices. But for them to strike so early amid a sea of intense grape juice – that was a surprise. Has massive salivating properties. Dense and deeply desirous; f23 a slight salty note joins the spices in their long, nagging farewell; b24 the nose may be surprisingly non-committal. But the same can't be said once it hits the taste buds. Wow! This malt packs a fruity punch! *63%. sc.*

FLEURIEU DISTILLERY Goolwa, South Australia. 2004. Working.

Fleurieu Distillery Atlantic Crossing db **(91)** n22.5 t23 f22.5 b23 That's better: much better spirit as a starting point, ensuring a more even taste profile. Excellent complexity and weight. *52%.*

Fleurieu Distillery The Rubicon ex-Seppeltsfield Port barrels db **(89)** n22.5 t22.5 f22 b22 A muscular whisky with some big flavour egos at work. When they gel, there are some magical moments. *55%. 500 bottles.*

⟨⟩ **Tasmania Independent Bottlers Fleurieu Release 2** sherry cask, cask no. TIB FL 0011, bott Apr 19 **(86.5)** n22 t22 f21 b21.5 Not sure the wine cask has been as kind to the distillate as it might have been. Clipped to the point of being austere at times, the grape has its odd tart and lucid moment, but seems far too happy to paint a forlorn figure. The finale is just a little too dry and slightly off tune. *49.2%. sc.*

HELLYERS ROAD Havenview, Tasmania. 1999. Working.

Hellyers Road Aged 8 Years Pinot Noir Finish db **(86.5)** n22 t22 f21 b21.5 It may sound a little strange, but the Pinot Noir cask was a little too much for the whisky itself, refusing to let the malt have a meaningful presence. The result was an attractive but lop-sided feel. *61.6%.*

Hellyers Road Henry's Legacy Wey River American oak casks, Pinot Noir finish db **(88.5)** n22.5 t23 f21 b22 Wey River...? Thought for a moment we had our first whisky from my native county of Surrey...! Mouth-watering and entirely presentable single malt enlivened and enriched by an exceptionally healthy wine cask which has imparted just the right degree of sharpness and weight. Good spices, also. *60.8%.*

Hellyers Road Single Malt Whisky 12 Year Old Original db **(84.5)** n19 t22 f21.5 b22. Forget the nose and get stuck into the massive malt. *46.2%.*

Hellyers Road Original Aged 15 Years db **(92.5)** n23.5 t23.5 f22.5 b23 Almost, literally, a peach of a whisky from Hellyers...the most deft whisky ever from this distillery. *46.2%.*

Hellyers Road Original Aged 16 Years db **(90.5)** n22 t23 f22.5 b23 Put on your tin hats for this one – there is shrapnel everywhere... Carnage...and it's delicious..! *66.8%. Master Series.*

Hellyers Road Peated db **(91)** n22.5 t23.5 f22 b23 Hellyers offers a unique character in its own right. Put some pretty full-on peat into the mix and you are left with one of the most idiosyncratic whiskies in the world. And a sheer, if at times perplexing, delight...! *46.2%.*

Hellyers Road Peated Aged 14 Years db **(87.5)** n22 t23.5 f21 b21 Despite the enormity of the peat, the sheer chutzpa of the strength and sweetness for a brief few moments have you at a point of near ecstasy, the technical gremlins are still there and make themselves heard at the finish. But, my word! What a ride!!! *63%. Master Series.*

Hellyers Road Slightly Peated Aged 10 Years db **(91.5)** n23 t23 f22.5 b23 Hellyers Road has come of age in every sense: the lack of copper in their system that held them back for so long has now been mostly overcome by a mix of peat and extremely high quality oak. This is a quietly spoken little beaut. Congratulations all round: it has been a long journey... *46.2%.*

⟨⟩ **Hellyers Road Single Malt Whisky Slightly Peated Aged 15 Years** db **(92)** n23 as minty as it is malty; as low key as it is smoky...; t23.5 superb melt-in-the-mouth gristiness, with an icing sugar sweetness. The smoke rolls in like fog of the sea; f22.5 a succession of supine vanillas with the light spices, mocha and peat holding the upper hand; b23 hell, yes! *46.2%.*

KILLARA Kingston, Tasmania. 2016. Working.

Killara Distillery KD01 Cask Strength ex-port barrel db (**94**) n24 t24 f22.5 b23.5 Now, that is impressive! And that's what I call a whisky! 64.5%. 1st Release.

Killara Distillery KD02 ex-port barrel db (**94.5**) n23 t24 f23.5 b24 A very chewable and entertaining malt just dripping with flavour. 50%.

Killara Distillery KD03 ex-sherry barrel db (**90.5**) n23 t23 f22 b22.5 A genteel and understated whisky. 46%.

LARK DISTILLERY Hobart, Tasmania. 1992. Working.

Lark Single Malt Whisky Cask Strength db (**94**) n23 t24 f23.5 b23.5 Sweet, profound and with jaw-aching chewability. 58%.

Lark Single Malt Whisky Classic Cask db (**89**) n22 t23 f21.5 b22.5 Another slightly more full-bodied version. 43%.

Lark Single Malt Whisky Distillers Selection Heavily Peated Port Cask cask no. LD1016 db (**87**) n21.5 t22.5 f21 b22 A massive soup of a malt. Not quite as heavily peated as some I have experienced from Lark, and the wide cut gives a degree of oiliness which helps the lush fruit and lighter smoke meld together. Seriously big stuff but not quite so technically on the ball as usual. 46%. sc. 89 bottles.

◈ **Lark Distillery Muscat Cask Finish** db (**91.5**) n23 though giving the outward appearance of lightness, there is some serious heft on that fruit. Pretty sharp and lightly peppered, too...; t23 mouth-filling and lush, we are in major ripe greengage territory here, fortified with a dessert wine sweetness that easily copes with the chunky tannins; f22.5 dries quite prodigiously though the sharp grape never quite lets go; b23 the one thing you can say about Lark whisky: when they decide to ramp up the flavours, they don't do things by halves... 46%.

Lark Single Malt Whisky Rum Finish db (**89.5**) n22 t23.5 f22 b22.5 And again a slightly wide cut – but, again, so much personality and flavour! 55%.

◈ **Lark Distillery Sherry Matured & Sherry Finished** db (**95**) n24 a ten minute nose required here: it takes that time to get to grips with the complexity of the fruit layering. All weights, all intensities appear to be catered for. And so clean...; t23.5 a palate-kissing delivery. The delicate ulmo honey which flitted about the nose is slightly better defined here and acts as a perfect bridge to the tannin. But grape rarely comes more lush than this...; f23.5 long with the rising of intricate spices while the fruit retails a pastel lozenge quality; b24 I know Bill Lark abhors sulphur-treated sherry butts as vehemently as me. Which is why this is the only double sherry-matured whisky I picked up this year without fear that it would fail...And, of course, it didn't. It's a beaut! 50.8%.

◈ **Lark Distillery Single Malt Shiraz Cask Release 2020** ex-Shiraz casks db (**92.5**) n24 now this is just being silly! How can you have that degree of teeming grape, and yet still retain the balance? Also an undiluted blackcurrant cordial to mix in with the spices and – and get this – light barley and tannin layering; t23 playful muscovado sugars are on hand to greet the invading grape. Chewy but never overly fruity, again thanks to that sublime malt and tannin mix. Remains juicy; f22.5 just bitters slightly as the dark cherries muster; b23 have to say this is a nose and flavour profile I have never quite encountered before. Keeps just the right side of being a liqueur. Love it! 42%. 300 bottles.

◈ **Lark Distillery Symphony No. 1** db (**93**) n23.5 what's not to love about that lemon and lime marmalade on dry, malty toast...? t23 the lightness of touch from the barley is matched only by the translucence of the fruit as both coo and seduce...; f23 the oak has to have a say, and does late on as the vanillas gather. The barley still canoodles, pouts and flirts outrageously; b23.5 less a symphony and more tone poem or, to be even closer to the mark, a heart-stopping Olivia Newton-John from circa 1972... 40.2%.

Heartwood Night Thief sherry cask, cask nos. LD 654 & LD 775, bott Apr 18 (**95.5**) n24 t24 f24 b24 Though distilled at the other end of the planet, and nearly 40 years on, this bottling took me back to the very early 1980s, when I tasted a sample of Lagavulin while sitting in the distillery manager's office, the dark liquid before me having been extracted from a rare fresh sherry butt - not the normal way of maturing that great whisky in those long ago days. These days, from painful experience, not a great fan of wine and peat together. This, though is on another level: the way it should be... 64.3%. 299 bottles.

Heartwood Shot in the Dark Australian muscat cask, cask nos. LD 961, dist Nov 13, bott Mar 19 (**95**) n23.5 t24 f23.5 b24 For a shot in the dark, this hit bullseye. Anyway, after tasting that I need to lie down. I'm exhausted... 58.9%. sc. 334 bottles.

LAUNCESTON DISTILLERY Western Junction, Tasmania. 2013. Working.

◈ **Launceston Distillery Apera Cask Tasmanian Single Malt Whisky** batch no. H17:11 db (**89.5**) n23 a more vivid and brittle fruitiness than to their other bottlings; t22 this one puts the tart in fruit tart; engulfs the palate with a real livewire grapiness; f22 the grape continues its simple fruit crusade, now armed with some punchy spices and softened, at last, by cocoa; **b22.5** about as subtle as a knee in the groin and no less eye-watering. Thankfully nothing like so unpleasant and, in fact, grows on you with time. Quite a statement whisky! *46%.*

  Launceston Distillery Bourbon Cask Tasmanian Single Malt Whisky batch no. H17-14 db **(89) n22.5** you know when you slightly cut into an under-ripe gooseberry...; **t22** ...they are pretty sharp to taste, too, and my word! So is this. Takes a little while to settle – and for you to dab the water from your eyes. After the burst of barley the midground is unusually sawdusty; **f22.5** a curious late wave of citrus adds brief freshness to the powder-dry mocha; **b22** well, if you are looking for something malty, tasty and little different here's your chap. *46%.*

  Launceston Distillery Cask Strength Tawny Cask Matured Tasmanian Single Malt Whisky batch no. H17-12 db **(94) n23.5** a great cask at work here: the fruit is fit and fat with a concentrated greengage bitter-sweet sharpness. Spices have been added by the pipette; **t23.5** this is so thick and chewy your tongue starts to ache after about three or four minutes of fighting through the fruit. But the beauty is in the midground as the malt and oaky vanillas emerge for a more subtle second round; **f23** long, with a very light oil acting as a perfect foil to the custard powder and vanilla; **b24** a whisky matured in a faultless cask. No off notes and not so much fruit we are talking a one trick pony. A fruity but beautifully measured delight. *63%.*

  Launceston Distillery Peated Release Tasmanian Single Malt Whisky batch no. H17-16 db **(93) n23** one of those endearing noses, where the delicate peat is mentioned almost under its breath while the gentle vanillas and butterscotch almost match its powers; **t23.5** chocolate mint with a vanilla sub plot: very ice-creamy! **f23** long with a tantalising viscosity. Still a tad creamy with the chocolate, joined by a tannin buzz, easily lasts the course...; **b23.5** everything is understated and allows an organic development on both nose and delivery. Beautiful and elegant whisky...which should come in a cone, rather than a glass... *46%.*

  Launceston Distillery Tasmanian Single Malt Whisky Cask Strength batch no. H17-08, bourbon casks db **(94) n23 t24 f23 b24** Have to say, chaps: this is jolly good...! *62%. 225 bottles.*

  Launceston Distillery Tasmanian Single Malt Whisky Cask Strength batch no. H17-09, Tawny casks db **(91) n22.5 t23.5 f22 b22.5** Compared to their other Tawny cask offering, this has allowed the tannins to go a little too wild, thus messing with the delicate harmony. Still some whisky, mind! *63%. 200 bottles.*

  Launceston Distillery Tawny Cask Tasmanian Single Malt Whisky batch no. H17-13 db **(88.5) n22 t23.5 f21 b22** Yes, enjoyable and beautifully made. But the lack of oils, presumably by strength reduction, has left the drier aspects of the cask open to scrutiny, especially on the vaguely bitter finish. However, the late delivery and midground is a treat thanks to the light marbling of the fruit against the fabulous malt and vanilla interlay which dominates. *46%.*

LIMEBURNERS Albany, Western Australia. 2014. Working.

  Limeburners Western Australia Single Malt Whisky American Oak bott code: 219 db **(88.5) n22 t22.5 f22 b22** Just a little on the light and flighty side. Enjoyable, but if there is a problem this has been reduced to a strength the malt is not naturally happy with, the oils breaking up leaving a slightly chalky dryness. Even so, after the initial intense barley some lovely vanilla and custard notes. But up the strength by anything between three and seven per cent, and the structure and quality will be a sounder. *43%. ncf.*

  Limeburners Western Australia Single Malt Whisky Darkest Winter Cask Strength cask no. M492 db **(94) n23.5** there is more smoke on this than the "Heavy Peat". No heavy, but beautifully in context with the barley and delightful banana custard notes; **t24** fabulous... just fabulous! The malt is two-toned, offering up the juiciest grist imaginable. But there is also the sub-woofing base notes of peat, enlivened by dancing spices; **f23** we're back to the banana and vanilla again; just the most teasing lightly smoked toastiness, too; **b23.5** delighted to report that now is not the darkest winter of our discontent. In fact, I'm very contented with this, indeed... *65.2%. ncf sc. 201 bottles.*

  Limeburners Western Australia Single Malt Whisky Heavy Peat Cask Strength cask no. M221 db **(90) n22** malty, clean and virtually peatless...; **t23** superb dark sugars formulate early, with a wonderful backdrop of firm tannin. A few phenols particles float about and shuffle around with hands in pockets, barely interested; **f22** once more the dark sugars make the most of a very high quality distillate...; **b23** Sherlock Holmes. Miss Marple. Inspector Morse. Father Brown. Philip Marlow. Hercule Peroit. Maigret. Sam Spade. Paul Temple. Inspector Clouseau. Don't think any of those are Australian. But we need to call the whole lot in to find out who the fuck made off with all the peat... *61%. ncf sc. 205 bottles.*

  Limeburners Western Australia Single Malt Whisky Port Cask Cask Strength cask no. M512 db **(95.5) n23.5** the grape holds sway, but ensures a wonderful counterbalance between drier, spicier tones and more full on, sweeter fruit notes; **t24.5** a swooning delivery with near perfect mouthfeel backed up magnificently by the dark cherries and soft dates. When the molasses kicks in the salivation begins in earnest. Meanwhile the spices buzz and aren't afraid to sting; **f23.5** fabulous chocolate raisin; **b24** this one rolls its sleeves up and doesn't muck around. On the muscular side, but a bit of a softy, too... God, I love this distillery! *61%. ncf sc. 214 bottles.* ❦

McHENRY DISTILLERY Port Arthur, Tasmania. 2010. Working.

❧ **McHenry Singe Malt Whisky** 100L Makers Mark American oak cask, barrel no. 17, dist 10 Sept 14, bott 14 Jul 19 db **(88.5) n22** the thick, clean grape is slapped on with a spray gun, making short work of the light barley and tannin that tries to show its head; **t22.5** again the grape is in head-first, unable to wait for its co-stars. Sharp and sure-footed, it maximises the juiciness but never quite feels comfortable as the tannin grabs a toehold; **f22** spicy and buzzing; **b22** very pleasant but the grape makes things just a little too one-dimensional for its own good. *44%. nc sc. 250 bottles.*

MT. UNCLE DISTILLERY Walkamin, Queensland. 2001. Working.

❧ **Watkins Whisky Co. Single Malt Whisky** nbc db **(87.5) n22.5 t22.5 f20.5 b22** A distinctive malt, though one with a bit of multiple personality disorder. The nose certainly owes far more to a rum style than malt, as the esters are belted out. And there is even a hint of rye on the crisp and chipper fruitiness o the early flavour waves that follows the delivery. All this, of course, is down to an over the top cut which certainly glues up the finale. But after a number of pretty run of the mill whiskies today, this one has certainly got my nerve endings fired up. Lots of heather honey at work, too, though some of that comes from the wide-ish cut. All this care of Mark Watkins, head distiller: The Man From Uncle. And this is a very solo whisky... *43%.*

NANT DISTILLERY Bothwell, Tasmania. 2008. Working.

Nant Distillery Single Malt Whisky Port Cask cask no. 793 db **(94) n23.5 t24 f22.5 b24** Beautifully made and matured. The strength means a dreamy, super-soft malt has been created; at a fuller strength the finish would have had some extra sugars to see it through. Beautiful, nonetheless.. *43%. sc.*

Nant Distillery Single Malt Whisky White Oak Cask cask no. 951 db **(94.5) n23 t24.5 f23 b24** Some of the passages in this malt as good as any Australian malt you are likely to taste. Just brilliantly distilled. *43%. sc.*

NEW WORLD WHISKY DISTILLERY Melbourne, Victoria. 2007. Working.

Starward Nova Single Malt Australian Whisky red wine barrels, bott code: L1 19053 db **(87) n22 t22 f21.5 b21.5** Clean, thin and winey. But some superb spices do offer a narrative. *41%.*

Starward Two Fold Double Grain Australian Whisky Australian red wine barrels, bott code: 181130-A db **(84.5) n21.5 t22 f20.5 b20.5** When wine casks have this much impact on a whisky, it really has to be bottled at full strength to maintain its integrity. At this low strength the oils have been compromised and we are left with a little too much of a grape juice effect. Pleasant, for sure. But needs more structure and complexity. *40%.*

NONESUCH DISTILLERY Hobart, Tasmania. 2007. Working.

❧ **Nonesuch Single Grain** 20 litre ex-bourbon cask, cask no. 25 db **(90.5) n22** nose probing and intense. The grain holds all the cards - and quite a few are aces...; **t23.5** one of the more concentrated deliveries of the year. The tannins are just background noise, but the grains go off on one hell of a solo; **f22.5** long, lightly oiled but with a rising of the spices now; **b22.5** reminds me of some millet whisky I have tasted in the past with its intense flavour profile: a bottling for budgies. *48%. sc.*

❧ **Nonesuch Single Grain** 20 litre new French oak cask, cask no. 17 db **(93.5) n23.5** chunky! The intense grain has met its match with even more intense tannins. So peppery, too...; **t23.5** as bold as it is beautiful. All kinds of molasses and dates cling to this, though still those grains punch their way through to have a good yodel; **f23** gorgeous strains of heather-honey; **b23.5** the French oak not only stands up to the muscularity of the grain, but gives it a leg-up, too... *45%. sc.*

Nonesuch Tasmanian Single Malt ex-bourbon barrel, cask no. 3 db **(87) n22 t22 f21 b22** As a child I grew up about a mile, as the parakeet flies, from Nonsuch Park in Surrey, a place which always held an air of mystery for me. So, intrigued to discovery its near namesake whisky from down under. This is quite a perfumed article with the toasty oak holding a tight hold over the caramel. Enjoyable, but needs to relax a little. *46.9%. sc.*

❧ **Nonesuch Single Malt** 20 litre ex-bourbon cask, cask no. 22 db **(86) n22 t22.5 f20.5 b21** A splendidly malty fellow, this making good use of some light acacia honey to accompany the barley. Just loses direction a bit on the slightly bitter finish. *45.3%. sc.*

❧ **Nonesuch Single Malt** 20 litre Pinot cask, cask no. 13 db **(85.5) n22 t22.5 f20 b21** Pleasant enough, but pretty flat by Nonesuch's peculiarly complex standards. Lots of fruit and at times salivatingly enjoyable. But a little too one-dimensional after tasting their previous whiskies and not helped by the tight finale. *48%. sc.*

OLD HOBART DISTILLERY Hobart, Tasmania. 2007. Working.

Overeem Single Malt Whisky Port Cask cask no. OHD-178 db **(94.5)** n23.5 t24 f23 b24 one of those rare malts where a lot happens, but does so organically and with every shift in the gears getting the taste buds revving. *60%. sc.*

OLD KEMPTON DISTILLERY Redlands, Tasmania. 2013. Working.

Old Kempton Distillery Single Malt Pinot Noir cask, cask no. RD032 db **(85.5)** n21.5 t22 f21 b21 This is the other side of the wine cask coin, when the fruit takes over with a little too much gusto and results in a juicy but rather flat experience. The peppery spices offer most of the limited entertainment. *46%. sc.*

Old Kempton Distillery Single Malt Tokay cask, cask no. RD023 db **(91)** n22.5 t23 f22.5 b23 So many Tokay casks through the years have been wasted in the whisky world through being sulphur treated. No such worry here as the fruit gets a free hand to weave its intense, almost citrusy, magic on this malt. Just love the creaminess to this whisky and the busy, prattling spices which prevent things becoming a little too comfortable. A very satisfying experience. *46%. sc.*

⬥ **Tasmania Independent Bottlers Old Kempton Redlands Release 9** sherry cask, cask no. TIB RD 0010, bott Jul 19 **(90)** n23 t23.5 f21.5 b22 Fantastically clean throughout, the finish may be short and lacking depth. But the delivery...? Wow! *49.2%. sc. 181 bottles.*

⬥ **Tasmania Independent Bottlers Old Kempton Redlands Release 10** sherry cask, cask no. TIB RD 0027, bott Oct 19 **(87)** n22 t22.5 f21 b21.5 Rotund and fruity, there is a surprising light nougat touch to this one. The fruit is of the sweet shop variety but there is a dullness to this bottling very unlike what I was expecting. *47.9%. sc. 171 bottles.*

SHENE ESTATE DISTILLERY Pontville, Tasmania. 2014. Working.

Mackey Tasmanian Single Malt Apera sherry French oak cask db **(90.5)** n22.5 t23 f22.5 b22.5 Lush! *49%. Shene Release 3.*

Mackey Tasmanian Single Malt Tawny port French oak cask db **(81)** n21.5 t22 f18.5 b19 Still a shoot on sight policy from this distillery, which at times seems to combine astonishing oak influence with less than perfect distillate. The nose, for instance, offers a little tobacco on toast and golden syrup before the mouth-engulfing delivery, the sugars and fruit closely knitted. But the finish is a disappointment as bitterness and the tobacco return. *49%. Shene Release 2.*

SOUTHERN COAST DISTILLERS Adelaide, South Australia. 2014. Closed.

Southern Coast Single Malt Batch 007 db **(94.5)** n24 t23 f23.5 b24 This has to be the most rum oriented whisky on the planet. I thought their previous bottlings had to be slightly freakish: nothing could be that Guyana-Demerara style on purpose. But here we go again, with its massive esters. Stunning bruyere honey on both nose and delivery and light red liquorice for back up. But then those unmistakable rum notes strike, metallic almost. Superb. *46%. ncf.*

SPRING BAY DISTILLERY Spring Beach, Tasmania. 2015. Working.

Spring Bay Tasmanian Single Malt Whisky Bourbon Cask cask no. 34, dist 2016 db **(90.5)** n22.5 t23 f22 b23 A slight step up from their last bourbon cask, if I remember it correctly, the sugars more even and confident. An elegant malt *46%. sc.*

⬥ **Spring Bay Tasmanian Single Malt Whisky Rare Release Mystery Bourbon** dist 2017 db **(90.5)** n23 a rock-hard aroma, the barley chiselled onto the nose. Only on warming does a tender, sparingly used ulmo honey note come into play and transform the experience, as does the shy citrus; t23 much fatter than the nose, though it refuses to match it for sweetness...even when cajoled. Sharp, mouth-watering and grain dominant; f22.5 the oak makes its mark and time for the vanillas to dominate with a light cocoa flourish towards the finale; b22 a malt which improves tremendously using the Murray Method. Refreshing, juicy and magnificently malty. *58%. sc.*

Spring Bay The Rheban Cask Strength Tasmanian Single Malt Whisky Port Cask cask no. 37, dist 2016 db **(94)** n23.5 t23.5 f23 b24 A plum whisky...in every sense... *58%. sc.*

SULLIVANS COVE DISTILLERY Cambridge, Tasmania. 1995. Working.

⬥ **Sullivans Cove American Oak** bourbon cask, cask no. TD0267, filled 11 Apr 08, bott 26 Oct 19 db **(86.5)** n21.5 t22 f21.5 b21.5 A big malty fellow. But the bitterness at the death confirms the over exuberant cut one detects on the nose. *47.5%. sc.*

⬥ **Sullivans Cove American Oak** Tawny cask, cask no. TD0283, filled 16 May 08, bott 26 Jun 19 db **(94.5)** n24 not too dissimilar to a Guyana rum: the fruit appears to have crystallised and become a little toasted. Achingly beautiful; t24 heather- and manuka honey is blended together, with a little molasses thrown in. The fruit and barley are still intact and make for the juiciest of deliveries; **f22.5** duller and darker in tone, there is an almost inevitable buzz of spice hanging onto the tasty vanilla; **b23.5** I have crawled around warehouses in Guyana and opened 18-year-old casks with less than an aged rum feel than this little beauty. A classy malt whisky which will get the rum cognoscenti flocking... *47.3%. sc.*

⬥ **Sullivans Cove American Oak** Tawny cask, cask no. TD0324, filled 27 Oct 08, bott 1 Jun 19 db (**86.5**) **n22 t22 f21 b21.5** A much tighter whisky than cask TC0267 with none of the expansive and beguiling Demerara rum notes. Has a much younger feel all round though the mix of prunes and vanilla does impress at the midpoint. Bitters slightly and dries considerably as the spices make up ground. *47.5%. sc.*

⬥ **Sullivans Cove French Oak** Tawny cask, cask no. TD0268, filled 17 Apr 08, bott 13 Mar 19 db (**95**) **n23.5** a slight roast coffee Demerara rum style at play, with a minor sharpness attached to the tannin; **t24** now that is really impressive. The sugars which appear to be less apparent to the nose have saved themselves for the latter stages of the delivery. Then a tsunami of maple syrup and manuka honey do an impressive job; **f23.5** a dashed spicy Cove! **b24** much more along the excellent lines of the TD0283, except the more active tannins restricts the rum element in tangible degrees, but let loose the sugars. Quite beautiful, though. *47.5%. sc.*

⬥ **Sullivans Cove Old & Rare American Oak** cask no. HH0296, filled 9 May 00, bott 10 Sept 19 db (**93.5**) **n23** muscular malt lightened by a thin coating of marmalade; **t24** wow! The malt is almost eye-watering on delivery. It as the barley has been concentrated, and then concentrated some more. If it is possible to overdose on barley sugar, you'll find out now...; **f23** a much spicier narrative with the early barley somehow tamed by the oaky vanillas; **b23.5** a delightful and unusual whisky which concentrates solely on the intensity of the barley. The delivery is something to savour. *49.2%. sc.*

⬥ **Sullivans Cove Special American Oak** Apera cask, cask no. TD0214, filled 7 Nov 07, bott 15 Oct 19 db (**92**) **n22.5** the fruit wraps an avuncular and benevolent arm around the malt; **t24** rich, clean, salivating and bursting with over-ripe gooseberry and molasses. Sublime! **f22.5** just a vague bitterness on the otherwise spicy fade; **b23** can't get enough of that ultra-delicious delivery! *45.8%. sc.*

TIMBOON RAILWAY SHED DISTILLERY Timboon, Victoria. 2007. Working.

⬥ **Timboon Single Malt Whisky Bailey Street** dist 23 Apr 16, bott 13 Feb 20 db (**89**) **n22** celery!!! They've gone and given us celery...!! A touch of the Ukrainian horseradish spirit about this, too...; **t22** salivating barley. But disorganised as that vegetable note on the nose transfers to the delivery; the middle is busy during a startling metamorphosis takes place...; **f23** at last settles into a long and quite beautiful dark chocolate and ginger fade; **b22** when the nose comes across as freshly cut and salted celery, you know you are in the presence of something very different... *63.9%.*

⬥ **Timboon Single Malt Whisky Bourbon Expression** dist 14 Feb 14, bott 13 Feb 20 db (**92**) **n23** the intense barley is almost drilled into your nostrils. Like a Thommo bouncer – straight, no deviation, but upon you before you know it and right up your hooter....; **t22** myriad barley notes but trying to fight it out with the tannin-backed vanilla guerrillas....; **f24.5** at last things settle into a sensible pattern with the barley now back on track with a blindingly beautiful mosaic of malt. The chocolatey vanillas and a sensuous, creamy charm; **b22.5** takes its time to get there, but one of the best finishes of the year – anywhere on the planet! *71.1%.*

⬥ **Timboon Single Malt Whisky Christie's Cut** dist 30 Oct 14, bott 29 Jan 20 db (**88.5**) **n23 t23.5 f20 b22** Not quite the same seamless experience enjoyed with their last Christie's cut: far too much tangy bitterness on the finish here for its own good. But as for the delivery... wow! An improbable mix of jammy fruit notes and honey mixed almost into a thick paste. That is such a delicious and huge combination. *60%.*

TIN SHED DISTILLING COMPANY Adelaide, South Australia. 2013. Working.

Iniquity Gold Label Single Malt Batch 004 db (**95**) **n23 t24.5 f23.5 b24** Unquestionably Gold is the gold standard of Tin Shed's output. And I have never experienced anything so 24 carat from them than this honey monster... *60%. ncf.*

⬥ **Iniquity Gold Label Single Malt Batch 005** db (**95**) **n23.5 t24 f23.5 b24** This is knife, fork and spoon whisky, as thickset on the palate as any malt comes. Slightly different yet slightly the same as their marvellous Batch 004, this time a little extra wide cut being apparent and confirming the glutinous quality of the whisky. At lower temperatures has something of a top-rate Fijian rum about it – a definite compliment! – with a spice and busy-ness which leaves you spellbound. All kinds of manuka and heather honey tones combined here with a dash of molasses to keep that sticky feeling going. And also ensures a distinctive dry toastiness to the controlled sweetness. A five-course meal of a malt, again shewing the distillery in its most favourable light. For those who love their whiskies uncompromising and muscular, yet with a consistent honey sweetness, this might be your whisky of the year. *60%. ncf.*

⟡ **Iniquity Single Malt Batch 016** db (83.5) n21 t21 f20.5 b21 Carried on where Batch 015 left off: a bit of a Feint Fest. Has its attractive nutty moments, though. *46%. ncf.*

⟡ **Iniquity Single Malt Batch 017 The Den's Dram** db (91) n22 t22.5 f23 b23.5 The Den, of course, is where my beloved Millwall FC play, and over the years I have watched an above average number of Australians represent the side; or even Englishmen who on retirement emigrated to the land of Oz. So maybe a dram from Tim Cahill, Kevin Muscat and others, including the one and only Keith "Rhino" Stevens, whom, with my late Dad, I saw make his Lions debut at 16, and the following season I actually sponsored. A sound choice: he later helped take Millwall to the top flight for the one and only time in their history, and even went on to manage them. Now living in Australia he was, like Muscat and Cahill, a player who in each and every game gave 100% and never flinched, never compromised. Even for a 46 percenter, I think the same can be said for this malt. There is a robust, raw element at times – especially at the beginning - but as it progresses there is no little quality, too: again, a fair way of describing those Lions players during their days at The Den. That marriage of spicy steel and the deftest interplay between malt and ulmo honey makes for excellent entertainment. A dram for those looking for a full bodied but deceptive malt; and one for Antipodean Millwall legends, too... *46%. ncf.*

⟡ **Iniquity Single Malt Batch 018** db (93) n22.5 t23 f23.5 b24 Great to see that Tin Shed have got out of the little rut their malt batches lapsed into and are now back to being full of personality - and well-distilled malt all but free from feints. Or gorgeous peppery quality to the plummy nose is handsomely matched by the lush delivery where a mix of exploding greengage and toasty raisin gives the palate much to cogitate on. The late chocolate is a masterstroke. Better still, the spices never seem to run out of steam. Beautiful! *46%. ncf.*

WHIPPER SNAPPER DISTILLERY Perth, Western Australia. 2012. Working

Upshot Australian Whiskey Single Barrel barrel no. 56 db (90.5) n22.5 t23 f22 b23 A well-made, delightful whiskey but suffering from the lack of oils which is so well exploited by their game-changing, landmark 64% bottling. *43%. sc.*

Upshot Australian Whiskey Cask Strength Single Barrel batch no. 1 db (94.5) n23.5 t24 f23 b24 It has long been the tradition of the Whisky Bible to taste Australian whisky – or whiskey – on the first morning of an Ashes series. And here I am doing this again with the Aussies at 35-3. An interesting series with barely a batting side between the two teams, I won't be taking that early devastation of the Baggy Greens' top order to mean anything just yet. But I will say that if Australia need to discover how to put together something big and meaningful, with a fabulous start and carrying on from there, they could do worse than study this beaut. Western Australia now, by the way, appears to be in Kentucky... *64%. sc.*

UNSPECIFIED SINGLE MALT

⟡ **Heartwood Market Correction Tasmanian Single Malt Whisky** port, muscat, sherry, sherry cask, cask no. TD 0053, dist Oct 05, bott Jun 19 (94) n23.5 clean, over-ripe fruit on steroids; t23.5 too often a malt so swimming in grape loses its way as the malt vanishes without trace and balance is compromised. Here the fruit radiates like the rays of the rising sun. But the contours of the oak and malt are still clearly outlined to give a feel of space and perspective... beautiful...; f23 the flavour waves continue well into the finish, where spices now take the reins while butterscotch and vanilla give an oaky dryness; b24 a typical Heartwood orgy of rich, blemished fruits. I'm ripping my clothes off as I taste this now... *64.6%. sc. 280 bottles.*

⟡ **Heartwood Witch's Cauldron Tasmanian Malt Whisky** all sherry casks, cask nos. LD766, RD166 & PB121, bott 11 Dec 19 (93.5) n23 here we go: bombastic grape oozing over every grain of barley; t24 a form of conquer by numbers: the amount of grape atoms seems to see off the malt by about 20 to 1. Just as the salivation peaks and spicy kick in, then a more composed degree of vanilla softens and creates the required harmony. Maximum chewiness throughout; f23 long, with a vaguely firm metallic note having a bit of a nag at the sultana; b23.5 a typical Heartwood whisky which leaves not a single taste bud in your head unexhausted... *61.2%. 908 bottles.*

⟡ **Heartwood Wizard's Sceptre Tasmanian Malt Whisky** all sherry casks, cask nos. LD766, RD189 & PB121 (0.0015%), bott 12 Mar 20 (92.5) n23.5 fresh, dogmatic grape stamps its feet and allows little other to play. Wonderfully clean as well as intense; t23 a fat brew on the palate, the wine influence thick with stewed plums and syrupy dates is uncompromising. Out of nowhere a fabulous chocolate note is conjured up as the perfect counterpoint; f23 still those dates and plums carry out their great work. And that wonderful dark chocolate remains a match, with some dark cherry, too; b23 like the Witch's Cauldron it doesn't have to tell you this is all-sherry cask: the wine comes at you from every angle and enters every pore. But so clean and beautifully appointed, it is impossible to escape its spell. *60.7%. 332 bottles.*

European Whisky

Jim Murray's Whisky Bible 2021
European Whiskies of the Year

Austrian Whisky of the Year	J.H. Original Rye Whisky 6 Jahre Gelagert
Belgian Whisky of the Year	Braeckman Belgian Single Grain Whiskey Single Barrel Aged 12 Years
Danish Whisky of the Year	Copenhagen Single Malt Whisky First Edition
English Whisky of the Year	The English Single Malt Whisky Aged 11 Years
German Whisky of the Year	Hercynian Willowburn Exceptional Collection Aged 5 Years
Swedish Whisky of the Year	Mackmyra Svensk Single Cask Whisky Reserve The Dude of Fucking Everything
Swiss Whisky of the Year	Langatun 10 Year Old Second Edition Single Malt
Welsh Whisky of the Year	Penderyn Rhiannon

Jim Murray's Whisky Bible European Whisky of the Year Winners

	European Whisky Multiple Casks	**European Whisky Single Cask**
2004	**Waldviester Hafer Whisky 2000**	N/A
2005	**Hessicher Whisky**	N/A
2006	**Swissky Exklusiv Abfullung**	N/A
2007	**Mackmyra Preludium 03 Svensk**	N/A
2008	**Mackmyra Privus 03 Svensk**	N/A
2009	**Old Buck 2nd Release (Finland)**	N/A
2010	Santis Malt Highlander Dreifaltaigheit	**Penderyn Port Wood Single Cask**
2011	**Mackmyra Brukswhisky**	The Belgian Owl Aged 44 Months
2012	Mackmyra Moment "Urberg"	**Penderyn Bourbon Matured SC**
2013	**Penderyn Portwood Swansea**	Hicks & Healey 2004
2014	**Mackmyra "Glod" (Glow)**	Santis Malt Swiss Highlander
2015	**English Whisky Co. Chapter 14 N.P**	The Belgian Owl '64 Months'
2016	English Whisky Co. Chapter 16	**Kornog Chwee'hved 14 BC**
2017	**English Whisky Co. Chapter 14**	Langatun 6YO Pinot Noir Cask
2018	Penderyn Bryn Terfel	**The Norfolk Parched**
2019	Nestville Master Blender 8YO	**The Norfolk Farmers**
2020	Thy Whisky No. 9 Bøg Single Malt	**Penderyn Single Cask no. M75-32**
2021	**PUNI Aura Italian Single Malt**	Braeckman Single Grain Aged 12 Years

AUSTRIA
ALPEN WHISKY DISTILLERIE Frastanz. Working.

Alpenwhisky Single Malt Whisky first fill Pedro Ximenez cask, dist Jan 14, bott 21 Jan 19 db **(84.5) n20 t22 f21 b21.5** It's 7:30am and I am facing my first PX whisky of the day: be strong, Jim. Be strong. You are a pro: you can do this....Right...done it. And what can I say? Technically, a slightly better whisky than their Port cask offering. Is it more enjoyable? No. In fact, that is the problem with PX. It takes any whisky on the planet, smothers it in its one size fits all fruity, sugary overcoat and suddenly the identity and shape of the distillery is lost. No sulphur. No off notes. And just no personality. *45.5%.*

Alpenwhisky Single Malt Whisky refill port cask, dist Oct 15, bott 10 Nov 18 db **(87.5) n19.5 t24 f22 b22** This distillery should get a degree in producing monumentally huge whisky. And when it comes in at this strength, perhaps a doctorate for good measure. As usual, their whisky tends towards the feinty side. And that means something that starts out as big suddenly becomes truly massive. Yet, despite its faults, how can you not just love that mental intensity to the barley? In fact, if there is a bigger malt kick from any whisky on the planet this year, then I haven't seen it. Naturally, the finish is a delicious chocolate nougat, the Port being a bit of a bystander here, adding only a chirruping cherry sweetness. Flawed, but fabulously fulsome. *67%.*

BROGER PRIVATBRENNEREI Klaus. Working.

Broger 25 Jahre Brennerei 10 Jahre Whisky Jubiläums Edition bott code: LJU-11 db **(82.5) n21.5 t22 f19 b20** This distillery hits the heights when bottling their smokier output. This doesn't carry phenols, but has plenty of nougat to chew on, instead. Sadly, there appears to be a sherry influence here as well which is not entirely sulphur free. *46%.*

⬩ **Broger Distiller's Edition Whisky Malaga Cask** bott code: L DE-18 db **(93) n22.5** a lazy, almost criminally laid-back smokiness thinks about taking on the thrusting grape, which it could easily be a match for...but can't really be arsed; **t23.5** a very mildly wide-ish cut means there are oils enough for the sugars to mingle into. The smoke and fruit have exactly the same idea; **f23** chocolate fruit and nut; **b24** technically, it's all a bit of a nightmare with discipline at a premium. But this whisky has personality in spades and takes every opportunity to show just how much. Love it! This is pure entertainment.... *59.3%.*

⬩ **Broger Hoamat Gerste** bott code: L GE-15 db **(83.5) n20.5 t22 f20 b21** Nowhere near this distillery's usual high standards. There is a wonderful barley-packed delivery which makers you think you are back on track after the iffy nose, but it is not to be: the feints are a little too all consuming. *42%.*

DACHSTEIN DESTILLERIE Radstadt. Working

Mandlberggut Rock Whisky 5 Years bott code LWh13/4 db **(87.5) n22 t22 f21.5 b22** Another very much in the house style with a big toffee-nougat statement, though this possesses extra Manuka honey to up the sweetness. The malt has a profound say, too. Attractive whisky. *41.5%.*

⬩ **Mandlberggut Rock Whisky 5 Years** bott code LWh15 db **(87) n22 t22 f21 b22** Have to say that this is one of the most consistent whiskies in Europe. A light smattering of toffee and nougat amid the big malt. Makes for an enjoyable dram thanks to the delicate heather honey ensuring a gentle juiciness. But always with that touch of nagging feint in the background. *41%.*

DESTILLERIE FARTHOFER Öhling. Working.

Farthofer Bio-Brauweizen Hermann 2015 Single Grain Whisky feld: Kickingerfeld, reifung: mostellofass, jahr: 2015, bott code: LbWw2115 db **(84.5) n20.5 t22 f21 b21** Not exactly the most subtle whisky you'll encounter. The oils from the wide cut combine with the grain to give this a soupy effect, though the late minty chocolate notes to relieve the intensity. *40%. nc ncf sc. 202 bottles.*

⬩ **Farthofer Bio-Nackthafer 2016 Fassprobe Single Grain Whisky Fässstarke** reifung: mostellofass, jahr: 2016, abgefüllt Oct 19, bott code: LbNHW116 db **(87) n21 t22.5 f21.5 b22** A slight butyric note on the nose, which struggles alongside a sharper stonefruit tone, gets the whisky off on the wrong footing, but it then redeems itself somewhat by producing a pleasant intensity to the marzipan middle and milky chocolate finish. Good depth in just the right places. *44.6%. nc ncf sc. 224 bottles.*

⬩ **Farthofer Braugerste & Schlägler Roggen Whisky Fässstarke** reifung: mostellofass, jahr: 2014/15, abgefüllt Oct 19, bott code: LGSRW0915 db **(86) n21 t21.5 f22 b21.5** There is some hugely concentrated rye just screaming to get out, here. But a tobacco-nougat kick points towards a too generous cut. A real shame about those feints. *40%. nc ncf sc. 189 bottles.*

Farthofer Nackthafer 2015 Single Grain Whisky Fassstärke feld: Birdwiese Acker, reifung: weinbrandfass, jahr: 2015, bott code: LWNH2015 db **(88) n21.5 t22.5 f22 b22** It's 9am and I am getting my oats.... *45.7%. nc ncf sc. 866 bottles.*

Farthofer Schlägler Roggen 2014 Single Grain Whisky feld: Obere Erlgrube; reifung: weinbrandfass, jahr: 2014, bott code: LWSR2014 db **(83.5) n20 t21.5 f21 b21** For a rye, the grain is a little too non-specific and instead we have a slightly oily wide cut to contend with. *40%. nc ncf sc. 498 bottles.*

DESTILLERIE WEIDENAUER Kottes. Working

Waldviertler Dinkelwhisky bott code L10 db **(90) n22 t23 f22 b23** A cleaner (though not perfect) distillation by comparison to the last dinkelwhisky I tasted from here, though the build-up of chocolate mousse is something to behold... one for the taste buds...! *42%.*

Waldviertler Haferwhisky Classic bott code L11 db **(91) n22.5 t23 f22.5 b23** As ever, a pleasure to get my oats. *42%.*

Waldviertler Hafer Whisky Unit 2/3 Hafermalz bott code L10 db **(92.5) n22.5 t23.5 f23 b23.5** Like a sensuous massage in oaty oils... *42%.*

DISTILLERY ZWEIGER Mooskirchen. Working.

Zweiger Smoked Prisoner bott code SH/L0601/17 db **(89) n22 t22 f22.5 b22.5** Probably not the whisky of choice for officials of the European Court of Human Rights. *44%.*

EDELBRENNEREI FRANZ KOSTENZER Maurach, Working.

Whisky Alpin Single Malt Double Wood 11 Years Old bott code L1/2005 db **(88) n22 t22.5 f21 b22.5** One thing that cannot be levelled against this distillery is that it has no idea how to conjure up malt personalities previously unknown to the whisky world. It has done so again... *40%.*

Whisky Alpin Single Malt Peaty 5 Years Old bott code L1/2013 db **(89) n22 t22.5 f22 b22.5** One of the most brutally peaty whiskies I have ever encountered. The phenols hammer the palate into merciless submission, using the same force of will that tames the oily distillate. Kind of brilliant, in a truly terrifying kind of way. Outside my lab I hear the sound of distant thunder. Well, I think it's the thunder: it could well be this whisky... *46%.*

Whisky Alpin Single Malt Smoky 6 Years Old bott code L2/2011 db **(87.5) n21.5 t22.5 f21.5 b22** The distillery's distinctive nougat rich style is in full voice here. But hats off to the sturdiness of the peat which impresses in the way it is able to gather up the balm of the ulmo honey for a charming mid session. The heavier oils fur up the finish slightly. *42%.*

LAVA BRÄU Feldbach. Working.

⬦ **Bio-Whisky Smokie** dist 2015, bott code: L S 05/16 db **(92.5) n22.5** a stiflingly compact nose, keeping everything tight with minimum smoke leakage: just firmly phenolic! **t23.5** a framework of sugars give an eerie barley edge. But this is a false lead as the smoke arrives and condenses like a black hole...; **f23** beautifully arranged spices, but there is no let-up in the firmness of the peat; towards the end there is a distinct feel of the Arbroath smoky to this... though without the oils...; **b23.5** a peaty whisky which has its own unique take on things. One of the most compressed peaty whiskies I have encountered... *41.2%.*

Mehr Leben Brisky Single Malt Eiche dist 2013, bott code H 02|13 db **(87) n22 t22.5 f21.5 b22** "Brisky". Thought this was the first whisky made in Britain after the people had decided to get the hell out of Europe. But apparently not... A very well made malt with some serious loganberry on the nose – not exactly the most usual of aromas. But eventually disappears under its own weight of caramel on the palate. *40.8%.*

LEBE & GENIESSE Lagenrohr. Working

Bodding Lokn Blended Malt Nr. 3 French oak, refilled oloroso & Pedro Ximenez casks, flaschennr. 100, dist 2012 db **(90) n21.5 t23 f22.5 b23** These chaps do believe in giving their fans lots of flavour... *45%. ncf.*

Bodding Lokn Double Cask PX Master American white oak & Pedro Ximenez sherry casks, fassnr. 11/18, flaschennr. 48, dist 2012, bott Jan 19 db **(92) n22.5 t23 f23 b23.5** This unlocks at least a couple of the secrets of an enjoyable PX whisky: firstly the spirit has to have bristle and character enough to punch through the enveloping grape. And, secondly, the PX cask must be entirely free of sulphur, which this is. So, a rare treat! *55%. ncf.*

Bodding Lokn Golden Wheat Single Malt Lagerung Double Cask fass nr. 1120 & 111, gebrannt 2008 db **(91.5) n22.5 t23 f23 b23** Though perhaps a little too sweet for some, this is truly one of a kind. Almost too beautiful and demure to drink... *45%. ncf.*

Bodding Lokn Single Cask Classic American white oak cask, fassnr. 17, flaschennr. 70, dist 2013 db **(94) n23.5 t24 f23 b23.5** A delicious, beautifully made malt bursting with personality, vitality...and chocolate! *43%. ncf sc.*

Bodding Lokn Single Malt Blended Malt Nr. 2 refilled bourbon & sherry casks, dist 2011, bott 2018 db **(94) n23 t23.5 f23.5 b24** Confusingly, the label describes itself as both a single malt and a blended malt. I presume they mean it is from a single distillery but from more than one barley or perhaps cask type...though I could be wrong. Whatever it is, there is no doubting its high quality. *43%. ncf.*

Bodding Lokn Single Malt Double Cask American white oak & a 50 Litre Oloroso sherry cask, dist 2010, bott 2018 db **(88) n22 t22.5 f21.5 b22** A generous cut gives the big grape something to work on. *49.5%. ncf.*

Bodding Lokn Single Malt Double Cask Classic French Limousine oak & American white oak casks, dist 2012, bott 2018 db **(92) n22.5 t23.5 f22.5 b23.5** The limousine takes you on a very pretty journey... *43%. ncf.*

MARILLENHOF DESTILLERIE KAUSL Mühldorf. Working.

Wachauer Whisky M43 Double Oak bott code L:WD01 db **(80.5) n21 t21.5 f19 b19** This is the 1,137th whisky I have tasted for the 2020 Bible, but none of the previous 1,136 have given me quite the shock this has done. I cannot say exactly what kind of oak this has been in, other than to admit that I would not be surprised if one was a vat of cough syrup. Well, it certainly made me cough... There appears to be a huge, bitter, tannin kick, as well as sweet cherry juice. But you just can't get away from the cough mixture. A whisky to be taken three times a day after meals... *43%.*

Wachauer Whisky M48 Triple Cask bott code L:WTC1 db **(77) n19 t20 f19 b19** I have in the past greatly enjoyed whisky from this distillery. But the three offerings that have come my way this year have left me scratching my head. This begins life far closer to being a liqueur than a whisky. And though a light ginger note on the mid-point distracts you from the bizarre goings on of before, it isn't close to being enough to save it. *48%.*

Wachauer Whisky Multicorn bott code L:13WE db **(87.5) n21 t23 f21.5 b22** You get the distinct feeling that oats lay at the heart here as the mid-point give you a delightful, sticky porridge, complete with dollop of honey. But both the nose and finish are a little untidy from the barrels, the latter heading out towards a bitter tannin kick. *40%.*

PETER AFFENZELLER Alberndorf in der Riedmark. Working.

◇ **Peter Affenzeller Blend** dist 2011, bott code: L-1117105 db **(89.5) n21.5** earthy and tight; **t22** golden syrup in meltdown mode: can a whisky get any softer than this..? **f23** with the introduction of delicate spices, complexity has been achieved; **b23** A whisky with no backbone whatsoever. Softer than any bathroom essential that people have been fighting for all over the world. While there might be a slight vegetable note on the nose, the array of syrupy sugars on delivery and beyond make the aroma an irrelevance. *42%.*

◇ **Peter Affenzeller Grain** dist 2011, bott code: L-1018306 db **(89) n22** bluebell wood earthiness coupled with muscovado sugar and spice hint; **t23** if we weren't in lockdown, I'd be seeing my dentist next week because the sugary sweetness here takes some believing. Were there not some lovely strata vanilla and spice I'd not be too impressed...but instead I'm intrigued and entertained; **f22** vanilla ice cream plus wafer; **b22** any sweeter and this might qualify for a liqueur. Just stays within the boundaries of whisky, not least due to some excellent tannins planting their flag. *42%.*

◇ **Peter Affenzeller Single Malt 6 Years Old** bott code: L-1903207 db **(92) n22** just a little too hands-off on the cut. But, that said, there is an attractive sharpness to the greengages and apricot; **t23.5** you can stand down now: there is no evidence whatsoever of damaging feinty oils here, though there's confirmation enough of a wide cut. However, we have now we have moved into the realms of over-ripe figs and ulmo honey; **f23** long with muscovado sugars and manuka honey dominating until a little butterscotch tart creeps in; **b23.5** one of those unusual whiskies where the nose puts you on your guard, but the overall performance simply seduces you. *42%.*

PFANNER Vorarlberg. Working.

Pfanner Single Malt Single Barrel 2011 first fill sherry oak cask, cask no. 5, dist 16 Jun 11, bott 09 Oct 17 db **(93.5) n23 t23.5 f23 b23.5** Delightful whisky benefitting from an entirely clean sherry cask. *56.2%. sc. 412 bottles.*

Pfanner Single Malt Smokey Whisky bott code L217 db **(87.5) n21.5 t22 f22 b22** I'd love to know what they used to smoke the malt with. Rather than peat, it reminds me of some of the weird and wonderful aromas concocted over flame in distilleries in America's west coast. An engulfing, rounded mouthfeel where the sugars are maybe just a little too enthusiastic. Not a bad shout for someone with a sweet tooth, though. *43%.*

REISETBAUER Axberg, Thening. Working.

Reisetbauer 7 Year Old Distillers Choice Single Malt Whisky Chardonnay & Trockenbeerenauslese casks, bott code. 180120 db **(89) n22.5 t22.5 f22 b22** I suppose the grape style used with the chardonnay, TBA, is Austria's answer to Spain's PX or maybe Slovakian Tokay – and, having tasted quite a few over the years, you can really stand your spoon up in the darker ones. It was inevitable, then, that they would end up maturing whisky at one point. I think there is no secret of the fact that I am no great fan of PX in relation to whisky, as the intense sweetness has a tendency to kill subtlety and complexity. Because of this, this is a whisky that takes a lot longer than normal for all the nuances to filter through. A hard work whisky.. 43%.

Reisetbauer 12 Year Old Single Malt Whisky Chardonnay & Trockenbeerenauslese casks, bott code. 180120 db **(80) n19 t20.5 f20 b20** Despite the cask yet, hard to get away from the feinty nose revealing a weakness in the distillate. No amount of patience sees the TBA improve matters. 48%. 1,253 bottles.

Reisetbauer 15 Year Old Single Cask Single Malt Whisky dist 2001 db **(86.5) n20 t21.5 f23 b22** From the earliest days of this distillery, the technical flaws of the distillate are obvious. However, the malt has reacted favourably with some high class oak. The result is a whisky that grows in confidence as it goes along, like the girl who thought she was too plain to go to the ball, only to find she was as pretty as many. Late on the mix of chocolate nougat and treacle tart is rather compelling and worthy of drinking from a glass shoe.... 48%. sc. 500 bottles.

WALD4TLER GRANIT-DESTILLLERIE Hollenbach. Working.

◈ **Mayer Granit Grain-Whisky Waldstaude Waldviertler Ur-Roggen** bott code: L/14 db **(83.5) n21 t21 f21 b20.5** The oils don't know whether to twist or bust on this one, the clunking awkwardness of the over-indulgent cut making its mark on both nose and body. And though the rye bares its chest here and there, there is far too much of a gin-style flavour profile to this. Not a usual Waldviertler as I know it. 44%.

◈ **Mayer Granit Moar Whisky Gluatnest Torfrauh-Gerstenmalz** bott code: L/15 db **(88.5) n22 t22 f22.5 b22** One of those typically central European tight peated malt whiskies. Absolutely no give on this one, either on the nose or the palate: this is rock hard and rather than gently spreading the smoke around seems intent on giving you a prescribed dose of it. That said, impossible not to enjoy, especially when the molasses melt and feel it safe to come out and play. 44%.

◈ **Mayer Granit Whisky Edelprinz Mais-Roggenmalz** bott code: L/09 db **(86.5) n21 t23 f21 b21.5** Unquestionably flavoursome and full bodied with a sublime and full throttle impact from the grains on delivery. Just needs to be slightly more well controlled on the cut, though. 44%.

◈ **Mayer Granit Whisky Goldader Dinkelmalz** bott code: L/13 db **(92) n22** the slight vegetable note on here is hardly sulphurous, but infused with black peppers; **t23.5** now that is impressive! The delivery is first a wonderful announcement of the dinkel – spelt – grain at its most delicate, then a gentle wave of Demerara sugar locked in with ulmo honey; **f23** the peppers return alongside the growing vanilla and tannin; **b23.5** you are left nodding your head with approval at this one. A real touch of Austrian aristocracy at play. 44%.

◈ **Mayer Granit Whisky W4 Blended** bott code: L/15 db **(88) n21.5 t22.5 f22 b22** Light and fully entertaining, the cut is cleaner and its personality relaxed, allowing a gentle meandering of acacia honey and ginger to add sweetness and warmth in just-so quantities. Enjoyable. 42%.

WHISKY-DESTILLERIE J. HAIDER Roggenreith. Working.

J H. 12 Years Single Malt Single Cask bott code L SM 05 SL db **(94) n23 t23.5 f23.5 b24** Not quite in the same Super League as their unforgettable 13-year-old but this is a huge, uncompromising but always classy Austrian, again making the most of their generous cut. 46%.

◈ **J.H. Dark Rye Malt 6 Jahre Gelagert 100% Roggenmalz** dunkel geröstet, bott code L2 10 db **(89) n21** underlying butyric; overlaying nougat; **t23** soft and beautifully measured rye which firms up and joins forces with the molasses and honeycomb; a sublime chestnut paste creeps into the thickening mix; **f22** long, with some ginger and peppers spicing up the vanilla and ulmo honey; **b23** far less butyric (though still there) and far more nougat, this offers a much more pleasing aspect from the moment it hits the palate until the last considerable spices fade away. Some lovely roast chestnut and chocolate notes also perk this rye up considerably. Takes time to understand, but worth the effort. 41%.

J.H. Dark Rye Malt Fassfinish Ex-Laphroaig 100% roggenmalz dunkel geröstet, 9 jahre gelagert & 1 jahr fassfinish, bott code L2R08LP db **(86.5) n20 t22.5 f22 b22** I have been tasting the whisky from this excellent distillery for some 20 years or so and I know their style pretty well. Or thought I did! This is not just a departure from their consistently attractive whiskies, but here represents a flavour profile I have never before encountered in my career.... anywhere! The one weak spot is the nose, a butyric hit and out of kilter. But the flavour profile is, I can vouch on my life, entirely unique. The mix of rye and significant peat is something I have before encountered elsewhere. But take into account the distillery's own intense style off the still and you are entering previously uncharted territory. Despite the modest score by their standards, I do rather love this, not least because it even provides a minty effect which appears to chill the lips! Get past the nose and this is pure fun. 46%. ncf sc. 314 bottles.

❧ **J.H. Dark Rye Malt Peated 7 Jahre Gelagert** 100% Roggenmalz, dunkel geröstet & mit Torf geräuchert, bott code L2 P12 db **(86)** n19.5 t23 f21.5 b22 The butyric nose I spotted on this style last year is present in this bottling in even greater force. However, the double fruit delivery of intense lime and rye does its best to make amends. As fresh and citrussy as you'll ever find, with the coming through in secondary waves. But, overall, not quite at the races. *46%.*

❧ **J.H. Dark Single Malt 6 Jahre Gelagert 100% Gerstenmalz** dunkel geröstet, bott code L5 11 db **(87.5)** n21.5 t23 f21 b22 The over enthusiastically wide cut generates a spicy oiliness where it is not always wanted. Big and chewy, but a really awkward customer that seems to keep tripping over itself. *41%.*

❧ **J.H. Single Malt 6 Jahre Gelagert 100% Gerstenmalz** hell geröstet, bott code L4 11 db **(91)** n22 just a little bit on the chocolate-nougat side; t23.5 outrageous malt concentrate; f22.5 a very simplistic chocolate malt effect; b23 if anyone likes their malt malty, then they had better go no further than this: like an alcoholic version of Horlicks. *41%.*

J.H. Dark Single Malt Peated Single Cask 7 Jahre bott code L SMP 10 BRM db **(93)** n23.5 t23 f23.5 b23 Not sure if they have bothered about the malt: it just seems like peat-smoked peat turf. No, not really! But it takes a while to acclimatise to phenols this toasty, this intense. What's the Austrian for bloody hell!...? *46%. ncf sc.*

❧ **J.H. Original Rye Whisky 6 Jahre Gelagert** 60% Roggen, 40% Gerstenmalz, bott code L3 12 db **(95.5)** n23 usually nougat can be an off note. But when it now more than shadows the sharpness of the rye, it actually works pretty well; t24 oh, just so fabulous! The barley oils grip the palate first, but this is just the warm-up act for the superb explosion of rye at its most deliciously bitter-sweet. The spices are escaping immediately from the confines of the tannin...; f23.5 spiced cocoa; b24 there are few whiskies in the world that pack more flavour into a glass than Haider. Here it has gone into overdrive with the rye-barley mix offering just the right degree of thrust and juiciness. What a classic this is...! *41%.* 🏆

J.H. Original Rye 12 Jahre bott code L3S05 db **(91)** n22.5 t23 f22.5 b23 Deploy the Murray method for best results by far. *46%. ncf sc.*

J.H. Rare Selection Rye Malt 6 Jahre Fassfinish Likörwein Porteweinmethode bott code L 1R 11 db **(92)** n23 t23 f22.5 b23.5 J.H. whisky without nougat is akin to the World Cup being without one of Germany, Brazil or Spain in the semi-finals. Oh, hang on a minute... *46%. ncf sc.*

J.H. Rare Selection Rye Malt TBA Chardonnay 4 Jahre bott code L RM 13 MÜ db **(86.5)** n19 t22 f23.5 b22 Takes an age to find its niche. Unless you are willing to leave the glass open in a hot environment for an hour, the nose, sadly, doesn't work – the oils and grape make everything claustrophobic, while at least the dense delivery does allow the rye to plant its flag. The finish, though, is sublime with a rich chocolate nougat intensity aided by a two-tone fruit from the grain and grape. *46%. ncf sc.*

J.H. Rare Selection Single Malt TBA Chardonnay 4 Jahre bott code L SM 13 MÜ db **(87)** n22 t22 f21.5 b21.5 An enjoyable whisky but never seems to get the shackles off the rye. *46%. ncf sc.*

❧ **J.H. Rye Malt 6 Jahre Gelagert 100% Roggenmalz** hell geröstet, bott code L1 12 db **(88)** n22 t23 f21 b22 Overdoses very slightly on the feints. Not enough to spoil the whisky, but enough to reduce it from its normally outstanding status to just very good. Those feints are first to the nose and the delivery – and last to leave the building. But in the meantime, the rye puts up some show. *41%.*

BELGIUM
THE BELGIAN OWL Grâce-Hollogne. Working.

Belgian Owl Single Malt 36 Months bott code: LF036858 db **(90.5)** n22 t23 f22.5 b23 Young it may be, but already rather beautifully formed. *46%. nc ncf.*

❧ **Belgian Owl Single Malt 36 Months First Fill Bourbon Cask db (91)** n22.5 a youthful nutty maltiness with a squeeze of lemon; t23.5 a fabulous gristy delivery makes for one of the most mouth-watering malts on the market. Again, an ultra-salivating citrus note links with the maple syrup to ensure superb depth; f22 pleasing spices add to the simple vanillas; b23 such an improbably good whisky for something so young. This has been so beautifully distilled! *46%*

❧ **Belgian Owl Single Malt 40 Months First Fill Bourbon Single Cask No 1538333 db (92)** n23 curious. For a non-peated malt, there is a distinctive soupçon of phenols which add welcome weight to the citrussy core; t23.5 and there it is again on this superbly salivating delivery: just the lightest touch of smoke to ensure a real kaleidoscope of flavours and textures. Again, the malt is the king, the vanillas of the tannin acting as modest dais. But surprisingly oily, too. Especially early on...; f22 thinner at the death where the youth is far more apparent; some lovely Belgian chocolate late on...; b23.5 this is so young, so delicate. Beautifully distilled malt and either because or despite its age just so juicily entertaining. That vague now-you-see it, now you don't smokiness is a wonderful tease... *46%*

⬧ **Belgian Owl Single Malt 40 Months First Fill Bourbon Single Cask No 66381680** db **(90.5) n22** fragile lemon drops; very young with a distinct new make feel...; **t22.5** the delivery is a replica of the nose: light and new-makey with an distinct emphasis on delicate barley; **f23** the early barley-sugar is finding much more vanilla now to do business with as the oak influence kicks in with great charm; **b23** one of those rare malts which just gets better towards the end. Not an atom of the intricate smoke as on cask 1538333. 46%

⬧ **Belgian Owl Single Malt 40 Months First Fill Bourbon Single Cask No 6631688** db **(94.5) n23.5** young, for certain. But if this were Scotch, blenders would be fighting over this malt at this age to ensure top dressing for their higher end non-age statement blends: the clear, elegant intensity of the malt is fabulous, with a fat gooseberry sweetness to boot...; **t23.5** early oily explosion, then for one brief moment that new-make sharpness is present and intense. Then, almost immediately, swathes of oak-led vanilla and Demerara sugars and ulmo honey wade in to delicious effect...and it becomes more yummy still as the intensity of the barley itself begins to climb through the roof...; **f23.5** medium length as the early oils still hang around **b24** though a sister cask to the one above, their performances are fascinatingly different. Here the oils and weight forms early on, coating the mouth immediately for a much bigger, more chewy and better-balanced experience. It is hard to believe this malt is a mere three years old. Coming from the sister stills of the great Glen Grant distillery, Belgian Owl has planted its flag – or is that feathers? – firmly in the camp of ultra-elegant single malt. At the moment, no-one on mainland Europe can match their élan. This is really lovely stuff. 46%

Belgian Owl Single Malt 44 Months Glen Els Firkin Sherry Cask Finish bourbon cask & sherry finish, cask no. 872 db **(88) n22 t22.5 f21.5 b22** A subdued Belgian Owl which has had its wings clipped by the introduction of a sherry cask. 46%. Bottled for Kirsch Whisky.

⬧ **Belgian Owl Single Malt 12 Years Vintage No 5 Single First Fill Bourbon Cask No 4279860** db **(94.5) n23.5** nutty – a kind of marzipan of moderate sweetness. Thick barley and mild cocoa on the oak; **t23.5** so unusual for a malt of this age to see the sugars arrive ahead of all else. But the concentrated is not far behind. And then, so impressively, comes the massive chocolate tannin. For a moment it threatens to overwhelm, but then backs off allowing the various elements to integrate; **f23.5** anyone partial to an English Milky Way candy bar will rather love this...; **b24** old school Belgian Owl from their original stills. Even at the modest (by their standards) 46% abv, the intensity to the nuttiness is something to savour. 46%

⬧ **Belgian Owl 12 Years Vintage No 6 Single First Fill Bourbon Cask No 4018737** db **(96) n23.5** a light red liquorice tone underscores the age and cask type; far too many layers to count...; **t24.5** the type of delivery and follow-through that makes you purr with satisfaction. A mix of manuka honey, darker liquorice, intense barley and burnt fudge joins with outstanding light oils to make for a chewathon of near perfection; **f24** the subtle intertwangling of the most delicate spices known to man and the heather and ulmo honeys, molasses and vanillas is a dream...; **b24** heading towards Bourbonland here. Fabulous. Just fabulous. If there is a better European whisky this year, it will have to go some... 46%

⬧ **Belgian Owl 12 Years Vintage No. 07 First Fill Bourbon Single Cask No 4275925** db **(96.5) n24** the ultimate stretched tannin note on a malt: the toastiness is profound, but a glorious array of vanilla, gooseberry, heather honey and sharp barley thins and puls it so the constituent varied liquorice notes start to become identifiable. A good ten minute nose for maximum enjoyment, and no less...; **t24.5** now it is the chocolate's turn to get the full works. How many layers? How many strands of varying intensity? As delicious as it is mind-boggling; the barley somehow makes its mark among the cocoa and liquorice; **f24** so rare for clear sugars to last this kind of distance, but it does so here with ease. Butterscotch and ulmo honey lifts the vanilla to ridiculously high levels But still that chocolate and light liquorice tone pulses through, unerringly; **b24** dark Belgium chocolate at nearly 80%. Not cocoa solids, but alcohol by volume. An astonishing and absolutely delectable experience. 78.9%. nc ncf sc. 93 bottles. ⬤

⬧ **Belgian Owl Single Malt 12 Years Single Cask No 14018725** db **(96) n23.5** typically light despite the strength with pithy dryness (as in pips) balancing against the sugar-coated antique oakiness; **t24.5** maniacally intense delivery with the malt finding a superdrive to its superdrive. Salivating and icing-sugar sweet - with the same dissolvable qualities. The barley starts enormous....and gets even bigger....; **f24** so, so long... Excellent oils and add to that the depth of the heather honey and liquorice fade and we're talking something exceptional here; **b24** anyone who doesn't experience this whisky is missing out on something truly unique and beautiful. It's like going on a roller-coaster ride – in a top-of-the-range Aston Martin.... 78%.

Belgian Owl Single Malt 48 Months «By Jove» Collection No. 1 first fill bourbon cask db **(88) n21.5 t22.5 f22 b22** May this malt be a tribute to British comedy legend and proud Englishman Ken Dodd, who was lost to us during the writing of this book. By Jove, missus, what a fine day to say to that Guy Verhofstadt fellow: if you want More Europe stick a bottle of this where the sun doesn't shine and then try whistling Ode to Joy! By Jove yes, Mr Verhofstadt. What a fine day to keep pouring this excellent whisky into your diddy pal Jean-Claude Juncker's glass and see what comes first: proper Brexit or the word "when". By Jove, missus! That hair. Have you seen that Mr Verhofstadt's hair? Well, at least something's straight about him. By Jove! Tatty bye! Yes tatty bye, Mr Verhofstadt! See you at my dentist's. If we let you back in the country. Tatty bye! *46%. nc ncf.*

Belgian Owl Single Malt Distillery Intense 42 Months first fill bourbon cask, cask no. 1538181, edition 2019-02 db **(93) n22.5 t23.5 f22.5 b23.5** Never quite manages to get out of its nappy as the youth of this malt dominates from first sniff to last flavour wave. That said, the glorious, ultra-delicate lime blossom honey note lifts this way above the normal, especially in the way it combines with the cleanest barley imaginable. Such a ridiculous amount of flavour despite the new makey undertones. A bit of a paradox, this one. And a delicious one. *72.6%. nc ncf sc.*

Belgian Owl Single Malt Distillery Passion 42 Months first fill bourbon cask, cask no. 6220001, edition 2019-01 db **(91) n22.5 t23 f23 b22.5** Despite the use of first fill bourbon cask as lot of the malt's youth is on display here, on the nose especially. But very few mainland European whiskies match BO for mouthfeel, and the house toffee and barley style works wonders. *46%. nc ncf sc.*

Belgian Owl Single Malt Intense 40 Months first fill bourbon cask, cask no. 1538194, edition 2019-06 db **(92.5) n22.5 t24 f23 b23** Obvious there is no great age to this, but if you find a more salivating, concentrated barley delivery anywhere in the world this year, you will have done well! Stunning clarity to this malt which for best results, by the way, requires the Murray Method (body temperature, no water added despite the strength) and take this glorious malt full on. The rewards sparkle... *72.6%. nc ncf sc.*

Belgian Owl Single Malt Intense 40 Months first fill bourbon cask, cask no. 1538452, edition 2019-08 db **(89.5) n22 t23 f22 b22.5** The tannins have a fractionally bigger say here. Which results in slightly subdued barley but much more cream toffee. Still a beauty, though. *72.7%. nc ncf sc.*

Belgian Owl Single Malt Intense 42 Months first fill bourbon cask, cask no. 1538169, edition 2019-04 db **(93.5) n23 t23.5 f23.5 b23.5** Does exactly what it says on the tin. Everything – the toffee and barley especially are on steroids – and though youth is evident, this brings out a fabulous degree of mouth-watering qualities. Just beautifully made and matured. *72.4%. nc ncf sc.*

Belgian Owl Single Malt Passion 40 Months first fill bourbon cask, cask no. 1538449, edition 2019-07 db **(91.5) n22.5 t23.5 f22.5 b23** Another beautifully consistent cask quietly emphasising the charming, lush toffee notes and languid barley undertones. *46%. nc ncf sc.*

Belgian Owl Single Malt Passion 42 Months first fill bourbon cask, cask no. 1538178, edition 2019-05 db **(84) n21 t22 f20.5 b20.5** Tasting Belgian Owl is each year one of my highlights of writing the Whisky Bible. Very rarely do they come up with a malt which is off beam. But here is one, alas, despite its usual malty charm. Too many tangy notes as the barley and tannins refuse to unite. Bottled at the wrong time, I suspect. *46%. nc ncf sc.*

Belgian Owl Single Malt Passion 42 Months first fill bourbon cask, cask no. 6219123, edition 2019-03 db **(88) n21.5 t23 f21.5 b22** A delicious new make and natural caramel mix. The muscular and juicy barley on delivery raises the game. *46%. nc ncf sc.*

Belgian Owl Single Malt The Private Angels 60 Months first fill bourbon cask, cask no. 037/200 db **(87) n23 t22 f21 b21** Doesn't quite live up to the expectation after such a great nose which is fresh and much more on the fruity side with diced apple where there is normally toffee. On the palate, though, too much bitterness builds. *46%. nc ncf sc.*

Belgian Owl Single Malt The Private Angels 60 Months first fill bourbon cask, cask no. 038/200 db **(94) n23 t24 f23.5 b23.5** Angelic. *72.5%. nc ncf sc.*

Belgian Owl Single Malt The Private Angels 60 Months first fill bourbon cask, cask no. 039/200 db **(87.5) n23 t22.5 f20.5 b21.5** A curious pattern here emerging of the Private Angels, just shewing a little bitterness and imbalance when they are reduced from cask strength to 46%. Almost certainly this is due to the breaking up of the oils carrying the sweeter elements which counter the oaky action. At a later age more sugars from the oak may negate this. Fascinating to watch a whisky evolving. *46%. nc ncf sc.*

Belgian Owl Single Malt The Private Angels 60 Months first fill bourbon cask, cask no. 041/200 db **(91.5) n23.5 t23 f22 b23** Much better with a cask shewing no negative impact and allowing the concentrated malt an uninterrupted say; *46%. nc ncf sc.*

Belgian Owl Single Malt The Private Angels 60 Months first fill bourbon cask, cask no. 042/200 db **(96.5) n24 t24.5 f24 b24** Elegant, charming, charismatic, witty and a triumph: something everyone would want in their home and eagerly to spend time with. In other words, Belgium whisky's total antidote to Guy Verhofstadt. *72.6%. nc ncf sc.*

Belgian Owl Single Malt The Private Angels 60 Months bourbon cask, cask no. 043/200 db **(93.5) n23.5 t23.5 f22.5 b23** This malt is developing with rare panache. *46%. nc ncf sc.*

Belgian Owl Single Malt The Private Angels 60 Months bourbon cask, cask no. 044/200 db **(88.5) n23 t22 f21.5 b22** Wobbles a bit late on, but no denying the early quality. *46%. sc.*

BRAECKMAN GRAANSTOKERIJ Oudenaarde. Working

◈ **Braeckman Belgian Single Grain Whiskey Single Barrel Aged 10 Years** first fill bourbon barrel, cask no. 106, dist 2008 db **(94) n23.5** love this nose. A bright rye note pulses into the duller barley tones. Add to the mild chocolate note from the tannins and the result is something both unusual and rather delightful; **t24** excellent oils greet the delivery, and with them a battery of warming spices. Then the masterstroke: a volley of crisp, juicy, salivating grain. Love it...! **f23** the rye is spent now and the barley and vanilla exits with gentle aplomb; **b23.5** beautifully made, excellently matured and delivers impressively on the palate. Not much more you can ask. Well, less confusion on the label, perhaps. When it says single grain, I was thinking: "oh, I wonder which grain this will be" and tasted it before consulting the label. And I was immediately confused. As I was getting both rye and, slightly less prominently, unmistakable barley. And, indeed, that is the mash bill: they mean single grain as in it coming from a single distillery. Puzzle solved. Though this high grade whisky itself is more than enigmatic. Wonderful. *46%. nc ncf sc. 246 bottles.*

◈ **Braeckman Belgian Single Grain Whiskey Single Barrel Aged 10 Years Oloroso Sherry Cask Finish** first fill bourbon barrel, cask no. 218, dist 2008 db **(91) n23** clean (magnificently unsulphurous!) oloroso of a decidedly dry and nutty bent; **t23** firm and at first frisky with a pleasant interaction between the spices and fruit: a kind of cross between toffee apple, Yorkshire Parkin cake and sticky toffee pudding; **f22.5** the fruit sticks around – literally, but the grain is thin and brittle; **b22.5** first of all: standing ovation on finding such a great oloroso butt. Such a rarity to find one of this clarity. On the slightly negative side, the fruit does a good job of wiping out the usually fascinating interplay of the rye and barley grains. But I'm being hypercritical: the overall picture is a very pretty one. *60.5%. nc ncf sc. 916 bottles.*

◈ **Braeckman Belgian Single Grain Whiskey Single Barrel Aged 12 Years** first fill bourbon barrel, cask no. 83, dist 2007 db **(96.5) n23.5** not quite as well nuanced as the 10-year-old on account of some liberties taken by the muscular tannins, muzzling the clever games played by the grains. But attractive nonetheless; **t24.5** ahhhh...now that's more like it! The oils, which arrive first, act as a clarion call to the bubbling, crisp grains and rabid dark sugars which then foment the striking spices. Your taste buds are left reeling at this massive and beautifully orchestrated flavour invasion; **f24** the oils return, though now the toasty butterscotch shews the rye up in a favourable light; **b24.5** there are times when you want to stop spitting, close down the computer and just drink the whisky: this is one of them... *66.1%. nc ncf sc. 242 bottles.* ♉

BROUWERIJ PIRLOT Zandhoven. Working.

Kempich Vuur Single Malt Aged 3 Years Laphroaig quarter casks, cask no. L5, bott 24 Jan 17 db **(91) n22 t23 f23 b23** Well, those quarter casks weren't wasted! What a joy of a malt! *46%. sc.*

DISTILLERIE WILDEREN. Wilderen. Working.

◈ **Wild Weasel Finest Blend Whisky** cask no. 21, dist 2013 db **(82) n21 t21 f20 b20** Even by a weasel's standard, this is a particularly thin one. Over tame, Needs feeding and fattening. *40%. nc ncf sc.*

◈ **Wild Weasel Single Cask Single Malt Whisky** cask no. 23, dist 2013, bott 6 Dec 18 db **(88.5) n21.5 t22.5 f22.5 b22** An unusually sweet whisky: in fact an unusual single malt all round. The signature on the nose is unique, with its strangely scented softness: a kind of mix orange blossom and smothering flowers in full bloom on a very warm summer's evening. There is also a rare softness to the mouthfeel which deserves applauding, and a thick barley intensity, too. But there is something else besides, something unfathomable along the lines of those flowers on the nose, before it trails off with a burnt fudge kiss to the tannin. Rich, scented, uncommonly sweet whisky very much of its own type. *46%. nc ncf sc. 349 bottles.*

◈ **Wild Weasel Single Malt Whisky Sherry Cask Finish** cask no. 26, dist 16 Oct 13, bott 4 Dec 18 db **(88.5) n21.5 t22.5 f22 b22.5** There is something very different about the whiskies from this distillery: both fascinating and confusing. No other distillery offers a nose quite so scented, sherry finish or no. One could say, with some assurance, that this is a very feminine style of whisky, all curves, softness and scents. There is a sting in the tail, too, with the spices being quite so on the warpath towards the end, accentuated by the all-round lightness of the malt itself. No off notes, as the sherry cask is safe and sound. It is hard not to like this very singular distillery. *46%. nc ncf sc.*

IF GOULDYS FILLIERS DISTILLERY Deinze. Working.

Goldys Distillers Range 14 Years Old Belgian Single Grain Whisky Madeira cask finish, bott code: L16240900 db **(90.5) n22.5 t23 f22.5 b22.5** A big whisky, but one without muscle or threat. The Madeira cask is a little too rich to allow this whisky to move up into the next level of excellence: in whisky less is often more... *43%.*

Sunken Still 4 Years Old Belgian Single Rye Whisky bourbon barrels, bott code: L16450900 db **(85.5)** n21 t22 f21.5 b21 There is no escaping that a degree of Genève character has leaked into this rye, affecting both nose and taste. Whether it was from the filters in the bottling hall, or some other reason I can't say. Lots of positive, busy flavours at play but the incursion of the local spirit is just a little too distracting. *45%.*

STOKERIJ DE MOLENBERG Willebroek. Working.

Golden Carolus Single Malt first fill bourbon cask, Het Anker cask finish db **(88)** n22 t22.5 f21.5 b22 Cream toffee, anyone? *46%. nc ncf.*

CORSICA
DOMAINE MAVELA Aléria. Working.

P & M Red Oak Corsican Single Malt Whisky bott code L1783 db **(91.5)** n22.5 t23.5 f22.5 b23 A wonderfully understated, complex malt, despite the voluptuousness of the fruit. *42%. nc ncf. 567 bottles.*

P & M Signature Corsican Single Malt Whisky bott code L1684 db **(89.5)** n21.5 t23 f22 b23 A very charming malt which at its peak sings like a Corsican Finch. *42%. nc ncf. 6,600 bottles.*

P & M Tourbé Corsican Single Malt Whisky bott code L1682 db **(92)** n22.5 t23 f23 b23.5 A beautifully paced, gentle malt which always carries a threat on the peaty wind. *42%. nc ncf.*

P & M Aged 13 Years Corsican Single Malt Whisky bott code L2984 db **(95.5)** n23.5 t24 f24 b24 Enough oak to make a Corsican nuthatch sing with happiness. This has swallowed up the years with ease and maximised complexity. World class whisky. *42%. nc ncf. 217 bottles.*

CZECH REPUBLIC
Single Malt
RUDOLF JELÍNEK DISTILLERY Vizovice. Working.

Gold Cock Single Malt Whisky 2008 Virgin Oak Czech oak barrels, dist Feb 08, bott Mar 17 db **(96)** n24 t24 f24 b24 Not often you get gold cocks and virgins mentioned in the same sentence in a drinks guide. Or anywhere else, come to that. Equally few rampant cocks can crow so loudly; no virgin give so passionately. A consummate whisky consummated... *61.5%. nc ncf sc. 270 bottles.*

SVACH DISTILLERY Mirkovice. Working.

Svach's Old Well Whisky Peated bourbon & Porto barrels, bott 2019 db **(86)** n21.5 t22 f21 b21.5 While the smoke, on the nose especially, draws you in, the overall experience is one of a whisky with a body not quite strong enough to carry the weight of the phenols. Some decent ulmo honey early on. But this clunks around ungainly like a slim 12-year-old lad in a massive suit of armour. You know that at some stage this is going to collapse...and it does. *46.3%. sc.*

Svach's Old Well Whisky Peated Laphroaig barrel, bott 2019 db **(89)** n23 the influence of the Laphroaig cask comes out in dazzling glory: not sure I've ever encountered such massive peat transference from cask alone... Salty, too. Astonishing subtlety – love it! t22.5 charmingly soft with the vanillas and phenols floating down and landing like so many smoky snowflakes; f21 thins out rather too gamely; b22.5 well, well: if this ain't Laphroaig influenced...well, then I don't know what is. Perhaps a bit of a one trick pony, but what a trick! *42.4%. sc.*

Svach's Old Well Whisky Peated virgin oak, first fill Bohemian barrel, bott 2019 db **(90)** n22.5 once the smoke escapes the tight marking of the tannins, it has much to say; t23 the initially dull and lifeless first two flavour waves lulls you into a false sense of insecurity. What follows next is an explosion of muscovado sugar-crusted peat, the smoke getting softer after the initial shock waves; some great spices to; f22 some light oils and vanilla come into play. But the peppery peat pulses...; b22.5 very unusual...and works a treat. Superb balance and complexity: a real surprise package. *54.8%. sc.*

Svach's Old Well Whisky Unpeated bourbon & Pineau Des Charentes barrels, bott 2019 db **(91)** n22 a nose nipper: there is a tightness to the spirit and a sharpness to the fruit; t23 now, that's very much better. Fatter than anything from this distillery before, allowing the vanilla and grape to forge a charming, almost pudding-style duet; f23 superb spices and lovely butterscotch fade; b23 the higher strength suits this distillery as it ramps up the oils to ensure better weight, body and structure. A good, very clean, chewing whisky. *51.9%. sc.*

Svach's Old Well Whisky Unpeated bourbon & sherry barrels, bott 2019 db **(88.5)** n22 t23 f21.5 b22 You have to take your hats off. This is an exceptionally clean distillate – as are all this distillery's expressions – and here finding itself in no less unblemished sherry casks. That is some achievement. The grape is quite flighty, to the extent of a vague under-ripe strawberry note to the fruit on the nose. the body revels in its ultra thin style, but now helped along by a chewy candy fruitiness. Sadly, all this quickly evaporates on the unusually brief finish. *46.3%. sc.*

DENMARK
BRAENDERIET LIMFJORDEN Øster Assels. Working.

Lindorm Danish Single Malt Whisky 1st Edition db (90) n22 t22.5 f22.5 b23 This distillery appears to have created its very own understated and elegant style. Most enjoyable. *46%. ncf. 899 bottles.*

◆ **Lindorm Danish Single Malt Whisky 2nd Edition** db (94) n23.5 now this is the kind of nose that keeps me transfixed: a slight Kentucky element to this, especially as the kumquat notes thicken the earthy resonance. The spices are two-toned: both nimble and flighty as well as clumpy and businesslike; t23.5 standing ovation time! That is a one hell of a delivery: the weight is faultless. Not too heavy to overwhelm, but muscular enough to carry and oils, heftier tannins and heather honey without slowing stride. The battle between the dark sugars and the peppers at the midway point is glorious; f23 settles down for a long sunset, the rays of the peppers stretching out far and brightly; b24 an incredibly sure-footed and complex whisky for a distillery so young. Wonderful stuff! *46%. ncf. 537 bottles.*

◆ **Lindorm Danish Single Malt Whisky 3rd Edition** db (89.5) n23 notably nuttier on the nose: I was expecting citrus and found walnut cake. A thicker cut all round which means the malt goes get pretty dense. Plenty of room for heather honey, too...; t22.5 indeed, those vague feinty notes don't hang around to get to work. They immediately make for a slightly bitter star but the honey and malt combine to make the sugars count; f22 long, as the oils dictate, slightly toasty and back towards the vaguely bitter edge as the feints reassemble; b22 not so well distilled this time and though this means huge flavours, the complexity and nimble-footedness of the 2nd edition is not quite there. A real knife, fork and spoon job... *46%. ncf. 500 bottles.*

BRAUNSTEIN DISTILLERY Køge. Working.

Braunstein Danish Single Malt Cask Edition no. 2 db (94) n23.5 t23.5 f23 b24 Seriously high quality distillate that has been faithfully supported by good grade oak. Complex, satisfying, and for its obviously tender years, truly excellent malt. A welcome addition to the Scandinavian – and world! – whisky lexicon. *62.4%*

COPENHAGEN DISTILLERY Copenhagen. Working.

◆ **Copenhagen Single Malt Emmer Whisky** cask no. B001, bott 2020 db (93.5) n23 such an alluring buzz of honey and spice. This is deep, intense and challenging...and you can tell it is supposed to be. There is also, surprisingly, a slight nod towards lime peel which just lifts and lightens the load now and again. The cut could have been a little narrower – but then we wouldn't have been faced with such rare enormity...; t24 good Lord! This grain has a unique flavour profile...and here it is stomping over the taste buds for fun. Massive flavour explosion, hardly bereft of honey as both Manuka and heather form a delightful alliance with the busiest of warming spices. The grain is like a dense, freshly cut whole grain artisan loaf smeared with that delightful honey combination...; f22.5 just bitters out very slightly at the death as the previous lighter feints gather with the drier aspects of both grain and oak...; b24 if it were possible to go back in time, say 10,000 years and find that early man had somehow happened upon distillation, then the chances are it would have been Emmer, a form of wheat crop, that would have been used as the basic ingredient for fermentation. Ironic – and wholly fitting – that Scandinavia's newest distillery should also make one of their first whiskies from this rare, full-flavoured grain. And when I say full-flavoured...this was my first whisky of the day and rarely have my taste buds been awakened so stirringly and to such a rich and resounding stimulation. My 1,218th whisky for the 2021 edition (though I had encountered this at their wonderful distillery), and it is such a joy to have my nose and taste buds taken in a direction the previous 1,217 whiskies had failed to do. A superb malt which just oozes personality. *53.1%. sc. 36 bottles.*

◆ **Copenhagen Single Malt Whisky First Edition** db (96) n24 the very lightest strand of phenols woven almost imperceptibly through the sturdy, honey edged malt. Brown toast and light liquorice helps balance the drier oaks and the sweeter malt to a delightful degree. Cleanly distilled, but not so careful as to remove all the character, there is even a superb hint of yeasty marmite to accompany the Manuka honey; t24.5 outstanding delivery! The mouthfeel wins your heart at first just as much as the generous flavour profile. The malt sparkles and kicks off with that gorgeously salivating persona with, just as on the nose, a delicate phenol note adding a waspish depth. But it is the intensity of the barley which is something you can only smack your lips and admire; f23.5 good oils helping the sugars to maintain their integrity length; b24 the first-ever whisky bottled by this outstanding new distillery. I had the honour of being here when this first bottling was launched though, as is my custom, I always taste for the Bible away from the place of distillation – and I have the sample here back in my UK tasting room. But even away from the history and romance, the excellence of this whisky breezes through just as it did that day. The Danes were once known for their pork, potatoes and marzipan. Now with Copenhagen adding to the country's ever-growing fine whisky production, I think you can safely include Malt amongst their most excellent exports. *56%. 100 bottles* 🍷.

⬦ **Copenhagen Single Malt Whisky Second Edition** db **(89) n21** ah! A touch of the German stills here as a little feint leaks into the mix. Even so, malty and intense with some muscular tannin, too; **t23.5** makes amends for the nose with a delivery of brutal honesty. The barley is not just concentrated: it appears to have been concentrated from barley concentrate. The sugars are a mix of molasses and heather-honey, but really takes off as both the barley sugars and spice appear to hit their zenith at the very same moment...wow! **f22** back onto a light feint note, but the barley just carries on cruising; **b22.5** one of the most barley-intense malts to be produced not just in Scandinavia, but the whole world this year. The cut is a little too wide and undoes the nose slightly and makes an early mark on delivery. But, that said, this is the maltiest of malts with enough barley to blow your socks off... Strap yourself in for a glorious ride! Incidentally, I carefully used a little of this in a blend of all three Copenhagen bottlings. The result was the richest single malt from any distillery I have tasted in the world this year, and something around the 95 mark in points. This distillery will have to be watched closely. *57.4%*.

FARY LOCHAN DESTILLERI Give. Working.

⬦ **Fary Lochan Efterår #03** cask no. 2013-16 (sherry cask), dist 19 Nov 13, bott 19 Nov 19 db **(85.5) n20 t22.5 f21.5 b21.5** This is almost like a distillation of the distillery style itself. The less than attractive nose reminds you the cuts aren't always precise here. Then the delivery itself blasts your taste buds into orbit with one of the most joyful celebrations of the grain around, yet always kept in check by a slight tobacco note. All this backed by a light dribble of acacia honey. A Fary which alternates between beauty and the beast... *48.3%. sc. 500 bottles.*

Fary Lochan Forår db **(90) n22 t23 f22.5 b22.5** Denmark's most delicate whisky...by a distance. Youthful but quite lovely. *47%*.

⬦ **Fary Lochan Jubilæumsaftapning #01** cask no. 2012-07 (sherry cask no. 2), dist 23 Jun 12, bott 3 Dec 19 db **(92.5) n23.5** huge oloroso influence, the chunky grape meeting its match with the thick Sumatra coffee and delicate smoke...; **t23.5** lashing of burnt raisin dipped in molasses; **f22** a mild sulphur growl...but no more. The spices and raisin continue to hold their own; **b23.5** we should get down on our hands and knees and worship Sherry Cask No 2. An air punching deliciousness. *51.3%. sc. 500 bottles.*

Fary Lochan Rum Edition casks no. 2012-15 & 2012-16, dist 18 Oct 12, bott 6 Nov 17 db **(85.5) n21t22 f21 b21.5** Not entirely sure I understand the narrative of this whisky. Impressed by the odd honeyed high point. But there is an innate bitterness which runs through all sections, a wideness to the cut which offers extra oils and a general all round confusion. *64.7%. 639 bottles.*

Fary Lochan Summer batch no. 2, ex-bourbon barrels, cask nos. 2013-05, 2013-09, 2013-10 & 2013-11, bott 13 Feb 18 db **(84.5) n21 t21.5 f21 b21** Plenty of brown sugars to stir into the background coffee. But a degree of bitterness betrays a weakness in the cut. *46%. 1,715 bottles.*

MOSGAARD DISTILLERY Oure. Working.

Mosgaard New Make Spirit Organic db **(94.5) n23.5 t24 f23 b24** Outstanding new make malt. Truly exemplary, bursting with the cleanest and most intense grist you could hope for. What a fine piece of distilling this is. Put this on the market and none will mature long enough ever to reach whisky...! *68%*.

Mosgaard Peated New Make Spirit Organic 25 ppm db **(92.5) n23 t24 f22.5 b23.5** More superb new make from Mosgaard. There is a sharp interaction between the copper and phenols which offers a slight edge to this, a phenomenon which will probably pass within 18 months. But enjoy it while you can...! *66.8%*.

Mosgaard Peated Young Malt batch no. 18-02, production date. 060218, 25 ppm, bourbon barrels db **(90) n22 t22.5 f22.5 b23** The phenols come across as about half the stated dose while the oak is whipped up quite a storm. As curious as it is enjoyable. And rather beautifully made. *48%*.

Mosgaard Port Young Malt batch no. 18-03, production date. 200318 db **(84) n21 t22 f21 b20** A big whisky, but the flavour profiles are far from relaxed. The tannins are gargantuan and feel a little forced, thus knocking the fruit out of kilter. Plenty of big enjoyable flavours and spice. But balance is at a premium. *41%*.

Mosgaard Organic Single Malt Whisky oloroso cask, batch no. 1, bott 25 Mar 19 db **(88) n22 t22 f22 b22** About as steady as any whisky goes... *46.4%. 212 bottles.*

⬦ **Mosgaard Organic Single Malt Whisky** Oloroso cask, batch no. 6, bott 10 Jan 20 db **(87) n21.5 t22 f21.5 b22** Not a perfect cask, but not the worst, either. An ultra-simple tale of grape and malt that would make a good bedtime story, especially if you have had problems sleeping of late. The thickish cut ensures extra weight. I think this distillery would be better served concentrating on ex-bourbon to allow the distillery character to shine through. *46.2%*.

◇◇ **Mosgaard Organic Single Malt Whisky** peated/bourbon cask, batch no. 1, bott 14 Oct 19 db **(94)** n23 serious farmyard style: sharp and acidic. The phenols have a real edge, and are happy to use it...; **t23.5** a fantastic landing on the palate. This is clean and beautifully distilled, so both the malt and the peat profit from a rare clarity to their respective personas. Underneath it all there is an ashy dryness to the sweeter sub plot; **f23.5** long, with controlled oils and a slow crescendo on the spice; **b24** wonderfully distilled and it has blossomed in the cask. Could probably have done with a few more years for peak complexity, as this malt had a long way still to travel. Quite beautiful. *48.4%.*

Mosgaard Organic Single Malt Whisky Pedro Ximenez cask, batch no. 1, bott 22 Mar 19 db **(86.5)** n22 t22.5 f21 b21 No off notes: perfectly good butts at work here. The trouble, as can so often be the case, the PX does too much and obliterates the rest of the whisky, so only the intensely sweet grape shows. Good spice and a decent fruitcake quality. But ironic that an organic whisky is not allowed to develop organically... *46.3%. 300 bottles.*

◇◇ **Mosgaard Organic Single Malt Whisky** Pedro Ximenes cask, batch no. 3, bott 4 Jun 19 db **(87)** n21.5 t22.5 f21.5 b21.5 This distillery genuinely knows how to distil malt whisky. This is technically ship shape, but the Bristol fashion of PX cask, though clean and clear of sulphur interference, has again ill-served the malt. After a momentary attractive spasm of spice and toasty muscovado sugars, this malt flatlines into a toffee-riddled fade. Pleasant, but ultimately duller than a speech by "Just Call Me Kier" Starmer, which is seriously going some. Once more a PX cask claims an innocent victim. *46.3%.*

◇◇ **Mosgaard Organic Single Malt Whisky** Pedro Ximenez cask, batch no. 6, bott 13 Feb 20 db **(86.5)** n21.5 t22 f21.5 b21.5 I could have written this just from the nose alone: the taste is equally one-dimensional is so often the case from PX. It is like putting the malt into a sugary straight jacket. Just the slightest degree of feint to make it a little more interesting. *46.3%.*

◇◇ **Mosgaard Organic Single Malt Whisky** Port Wine cask, batch no. 1, bott 20 May 20 db **(72.5)** n18 t21.5 f16 b17 Sulphur massacred. Organic sulphur, presumably. *48.3%.*

Mosgaard Young Malt Pedro Ximenez cask finish, batch no. 18-01, production date. 170118, 25 ppm db **(86.5)** n21 t22 f22.5 b21 A very pretty whisky with plenty of fruit and nut. Technically well made. And also filled into a decent and not overly-sweet PX. However, has been bottled at a point where both the young spirit and the oak influence are at times a little at cross purposes, perhaps not helped by lazy, slightly incoherent peat. That said, the chocolate towards the finale is sublime. *41%.*

NYBORG DESTILLERI Nyborg. Working.

Nyborg Destilleri Ardor Isle of Fiona batch no. 117 db **(92.5)** n23 t23 f23 b23.5 As sweet and well controlled as Sweden's vital World Cup victory over Switzerland today. Technically, a right little beauty... *46.8%.*

Nyborg Destilleri Ardor Isle of Fiona batch no. 165 db **(89)** n22.5 t23 f21.5 b22 Keeping up their clean, malty style but this has slightly more active fruit at play here, including over-ripe greengages. Slightly more bitter than normal at the death, also. *46%. nc ncf.*

Nyborg Destilleri Danish Oak Isle of Fiona batch no. 167 db **(93)** n23 t23.5 f23 b23.5 Denmark is by far and away the least forested of all Scandinavian countries. So finding an oak tree to make a barrel from must have been a major achievement in itself. It was well worth the effort, because this is a stunner and the impact of the tannin is the least assertive of any European oak I have encountered outside of Spain. The balance of the nose is spot on with lazy harmony between grain and light toasty tannin with a little orange blossom honey as the buffer. The grist is on overdrive on the palate, the oak providing a slightly salty back up. With its Jaffa Cake sub-strata, there is much to celebrate here. *46%. nc ncf.*

SMALL BATCH DISTILLERS Holstebro. Working

◇◇ **Small Batch Distillers Edition 2017 Whisky One Peated Single Malt** db **(91)** n23 young, raw and smoky. Really sexy, as it happens...; **t22** peaty chocolate arrives early and compensates for the thin body; then it begins to spread a little haphazardly, as does the smoke; **f23.5** ah, only now towards the end do the constituent parts meet up and harmonise. First a big wave of sweet, salivating barley. The chocolate persists but now dovetails with the phenols with a degree of youthful magic; **b22.5** takes time for the brakes to be disengaged, but a malt which travels well when they do. A dram to persevere with as the first mouthful or two hardly do it justice. *52%. sc. 61 bottles.*

◇◇ **Small Batch Distillers Hjerl Hede Nr. 1 Dansk Produceret Single Malt 2019** db **(88.5)** n22 t23 f22 b21.5 Young and bristling with malty tendencies. Eye-watering in its salivating properties, a gristy sweetness is never far away. *59%. nc ncf*

Small Batch Distillers Peat by Peat 3rd Edition American white oak virgin barrels, db **(89)** n22.5 t23 f21 b22.5 It is probably this whisky's foibles that make this so attractive. *60%.*

⬦ **Small Batch Distillers Peatman Dansk Produceret Single Malt 2018** db (92) n23.5 from Denmark you might expect smoky bacon...and you won't be disappointed. There is a more acidic, sooty buzz to this, also...; t23 significant heather honey and golden syrup on the bold and youthful delivery for a moment blindsides the peat. This quickly and thickly wanders back into view with spices for company; f22.5 dense vanilla and butterscotch, lightly smoked, of course....; b23 it has been a little while since I last tasted this distillery and the first thing to strike me was the clarity of the distillate compared to previously. Beautifully run stills with now a more refined middle cut. A thoroughly enjoyable, mildly charismatic malt that sets out to stimulate both nose and palate...and succeeds handsomely. 59%. sc nc ncf.

Small Batch Distillers Peated Mystery 2nd Edition French virgin oak barrels db (88) n21.5 t23 f21 b22.5 Again, drops a few points for a few technical weaknesses, on the nose and finish especially. But the over-all picture is very pretty. 56%.

Small Batch Distillers Peated Rye db (90) n23 t22 f22.5 b22.5 Playing around my lab over the years I have experimented with amalgamating the intense aroma and flavour of rye with the depth of a smoky malt. I had come up with some interesting concoctions but none, to my memory, quite matched the unique shape of this remarkable whisky, especially on the nose. Memorable...and very beautiful. 58%.

Small Batch Distillers RugBy db (91.5) n22.5 t23.5 f22.5 b23 A profound rye which, if cleaned up a bit would represent the grain with a touch of classicism. 58%.

⬦ **Small Batch Distillers RugBy Double Cask Dansk Produceret Selected Malt Edition 2019** db (86) n21.5 t22.5 f21 b21 A bit of a bucking bronco, this, with both the nose and palate having problems coping with the youthful rye. Or perhaps it was the casks which failed to find a formula to get the best out f the grain, especially after the attractively intense delivery starts unravelling. Flavoursome and rugged, especially when the oak kicks in, harmony is always the one thing that eludes it. 46% ncf.

Small Batch Distillers RugBy Extend French virgin oak barrels db (86.5) n21.5 t23.5 f21 b20.5 No denying the impact of the rye, or its high class crisp fruitiness, which can be fully enjoyed on the astonishing delivery and for a short while beyond. But a combination of the wide cut off the still and the unforgiving tannin means the balance of the whisky is lost far too early and easily. 60%.

STAUNING WHISKEY Skjern. Working.

⬦ **Stauning Bastard Rye Whisky** Mezcal cask finish, dist 2016, bott Nov 19 db (84.5) n22.5 t22 f19 b21 With the lemon and cherry drops fizzing around with the rye on the nose, I hoped for the best. But the delivery, with the tannins taught, the rye recalcitrant and tannins testing, was something else again. The finish, though, fell prey to the wine cask. There is a word for that kind of cask... 46.3%.

⬦ **Stauning Heather** 1st fill Maker's Mark bourbon casks, dist 2013-14, bott May 19 db (86) n22.5 t22 f20 b21.5 Last time I tasted this I felt things didn't pan out as I'd have like due to a little niggling feintiness. This time the feints have gone, replaced by a nagging sulphur note on the finish. I prefer the feints! 48.7%. ncf.

Stauning Kaos dist 2014/15, bott Jun 18 db (85) n21.5 t21.5 f21 b21 A real surprise here: a mild feintiness detectable on the nose and visible on the palate from delivery to finish. That said, the acacia honey and malt thread running through this doesn't compensate entirely, but concentrate on that alone and you have a very rich and full-flavoured and lightly phenolic whisky. 46.8%.

Stauning Kaos dist 2014/15, bott Sept 18 db (90) n22 t23 f22 b23 One of those whiskies where its technical failings end up adding to the overall enormity and enjoyment of the experience. 47.1%.

⬦ **Stauning Kaos** 1st fill Maker's Mark bourbon casks & virgin Missouri white oak casks, dist 2015/16, bott Apr 19 db (96) n24 maybe this should have been called "Heather" as heather honey runs amok. The most gentle peat offers a near perfect anchor, but there is nothing flighty about the honey tones. Kaos...? This is as perfectly choreographed as they come...! t23.5 the first waves to hit the palate is pure barley...then glorious rye notes follow up with a with a succulent but much harder series of pulses. By the midpoint we have honey and spices working gorgeously in tandem; f24 a little toasty, a little smoky, a little honeyed... it seems a little bit of everything in just-so proportions; b24.5 as I taste for the Whisky Bible 2021, I needed to choose which whisky would be perfect for the 500th - set right in the middle of the Covid-19 Pandemic. Well, it just had to be this: Kaos...!!! And it was the perfect choice as it is a reminder that amid all the suffering and unhappiness, there's beauty, too. And, my word: this is a very beautiful whisky... 47.1%. ncf. ♛

⬦ **Stauning Kaos** new American oak & Maker's Mark bourbon casks, dist 2015/17, bott Feb 20 db (89) n23 the tannins have a toasty bee in their bonnet: they do not seem happy. A really huge chunk of oakiness with every sniff...; t23 haphazard and feinty, the day is saved by a stunning outbreak of chocolate praline amid the concentrated grains.; **f21** an untidy and bitter finish with an elongated drawl to the feinty furriness; **b22** well, this is certainly more chaotic than the Kaos above. Which, sadly, means it doesn't work anything like so well... 47.1%. ncf.

◈ **Stauning Peat** 1st fill Maker's Mark bourbon, 1st fill ex-oloroso sherry & virgin American white oak casks, dist 2012-14, bott Jul 19 db **(90) n23** smoke there is, but in no rip-roaring hurry to get at you. Instead, the tannins hold as much prominence as the dry, sooty phenols; **t23** a very young delivery from the malt, with the peat far more prominent now than on the nose. Ridiculously salivating, the juiciness is a joy; **f21** some sherry cask niggle on the otherwise beautifully paced, lightly smoked finale; **b23** not sure this whisky needs the sherry butt inclusion with its capricious tendencies, as the youth of the malt and the boldness of the peat were already very happy with the bourbon cask lead 48.4%. ncf.

Stauning Peat virgin cask, dist 2014, bott Jan 19 db **(95.5) n23.5 t24.5 f23.5 b24** A virgin that smokes...you have to have at least one vice in your life, I suppose. 52.1%.

Stauning Peat Festival 2018 cask no. 64, dist 2012, bott Aug 18 db **(95) n23.5 t24 f23.5 b24** The last Stauning Peated malt I encountered was a muted affair, the smoke charming rather than barnstorming. Quite the opposite here with a big, memorable statement by the phenols. And though an obviously young whisky, this is so beautifully made you cannot help but fall completely in love. A Danish Saga which turns into a classic. 47.1%. sc.

◈ **Stauning Port Smoke** Calheiros Cruz tawny port casks, nos. 357, 364, 365, 369, 381 & 394, dist 2015, bott Apr 19 db **(91) n22.5** a light heathery flourish gives this a floral but dry signature; **t23** after a juicy grape flourish, it reverts back to type on nose, getting drier by the second, the vanillas and tannins building up a spicy head of steam; **f22.5** chalky and malty; **b23** attractive, yet strangely austere – enlivened by a brief puckering fruitiness. 51.5%. ncf.

◈ **Stauning Port Smoke Cask Strength** Calheiros Cruz tawny port casks, nos. 357, 364, 365, 369, 381 & 394, dist 2015, bott Apr 19 db **(95) n23.5** where the 51.5% talks a eye-watering dry game, this has muscovado sugars meandering around the phenols; **t24** a much smokier and more pugnacious delivery than its 51.5% counterpart, the dark sugars needing no second invitation to get stuck in. Immediately salivating but despite its enormity, beautifully nuanced smoke decreasing by gentle notches to be replaced by chocolate raisin; **f23.5** very long with the full complexity still on show well into its finale; **b24** apparently, the two Port Smoke bottlings come from the same bunch of barrels, this being the full cask strength version. But there seems to be more than just strength at play here. Not sure if the percentages from each cask is different, because this has a very different narrative. A stunning Stauning for sure. 61.9%. ncf.

Stauning Rye dist 2015, bott Nov 18 db **(89) n22** a wide cut plus chiselled rye...; **t23** the muscular grain takes on a distinctly honeyed hue; salivating molten Demerara sugars; **f21.5** just a little heavy on the feints; **b22.5** the handsome bad boy of the family... 50%.

Stauning Rye dist 2016, bott Mar 19 db **(96) n24** a rye freak's rye. There is nothing like the intensity of beautifully malted rye...and it doesn't come more intense than this.... **t24.5** rye to the power of rye....multiplied by bruyere honey. Plus peppers. Also bracketed by a light salty, vanilla and butterscotch number....; **f23.5** toasted honeycomb with the most dazzling pieces **b24** don't know about Stauning... Stunning, more like...! 50%.

◈ **Stauning Rye** new American oak casks, dist 2015/16, bott Jun 19 db **(88.5) n22 t23 f21.5 b22** Raucous rye...,but a shade too much feint. Had the cut been that little tighter, this would have been something special. The rye and ulmo honey tango is gorgeous, though. 50%.

◈ **Stauning Rye** new American oak casks, dist 2016, bott Jan 20 db **(94.5) n23** the grain is on full parade here. Just a vaguely wide cut, but the sharp, intensity of the rye compensates handsomely; the tannins prod and prickle; **t24** now, I just love that! The rye arrives in double quick time and goes gung-ho from the start, spraying around delightful molasses and manuka honey notes amid liquorice and rye in concentrate. So crisp and salivating; the oak hasn't been wasting time, either and there is a huge chocolate and light liquorice presence in the near background; **f23.5** just a continuous working and re-working of the grains and tannins, always with a vague spicy bite and a softening cocoa dryness...; **b24** of all the grains in the world, only malted rye can churn out such intense flavour. Technically, not quite perfect, having this tone poem at nearly full volume more than compensates. What an experience! 50%. ncf.

Stauning Rye Cask Strength dist 2015/16, bott Feb 19 db **(92.5) n22.5 t23.5 f23 b23.5** Even with the odd imperfection from the distillation, this is still an incredible whisky to experience, just pounding with an insane degree of rye intensity. 58.7%.

Stauning Rye The Master Distiller cask no. 33, dist 2011, bott Aug 18 db **(95.5) n24 t24 f23.5 b24** This would not be out of place in the shelves of very high end Kentucky rye.... 51%. sc.

◈ **Stauning Rye Rum Cask Finish** virgin-heavy charred American white-oak casks, dist 2016, bott Jul 19 db **(87) n22 t22.5 f21 b21.5** Thickset and hefty, a little too much tannin here has negated the effect of the rye. Struggles to find quite the right kind of balance, though the initial disgorge of complex, juicy, lightly sugared tones on delivery had at first bode well. 46.5%. nc ncf.

◇◇◇ **Stauning Rye Rum Cask Finish** virgin-heavy charred American white-oak casks, dist 2016, bott Sept 19 db **(94.5) n23** sharp-as-a-knife rye, able to cut into the big tannin with ease; **t24** there are the odd moment when pulses of commanding tannin burst through, and you wonder if the game is up. But it never is, as the grain, the moment it feels its power being threatened, fights back with a juicy surge even bigger than the last one. Brilliant stuff; **f23.5** rye and chocolate at its best; **b24** struts around knowing that this is what their July bottling wanted to be. Some fabulous rye sharpness and just an all-round high-class whisky. *46.5%. nc ncf.*

Stauning Røg bott Oct 18 db **(92.5) n22 t24 f23 b23.5** I always love discovering new whisky styles, and this definitely falls into that category. Brilliantly inventive on the palate. *49.6%.*

THY WHISKY Snedsted. Working.
Thy Whisky No. 7 Bøg Single Malt ex-Olorosso fad, dist Aug 14, tappet Sept 17 db **(90.5) n22** fruit buns with a little butter; **t23** voluptuous delivery: the grape is in full flow, mixing muscovado sugars and manuka honey. Oak and barley jut through the morass to ensure some serious salivation; **f22.5** toastier tannin and a little fruit chocolate; **b23** a gorgeous late night whisky. *52.1%. nc ncf. 677 bottles.*

Thy Whisky No. 8 Fjordboen Single Malt ex-Olorosso fad, cask nos. 46 & 74, dist Mar 15, tappet May 18 db **(93.5) n23 t23.5 f23 b24** Sherry lovers will be on their knees worshipping this bottling. A truly faultless butt at work, fresh and very accessible on the palate. *51.6%. nc ncf. 569 bottles.*

Thy Whisky No. 9 Bøg Single Malt ex-Olorosso fad, cask nos. 42, 43 & 44, dist Dec 14, tappet Jan 19 db **(96.5) n24** like my old farmhouse fireplace in Melton Mowbray back in the early 1980s, when I was cleaning it out: sooty, dry...and hauntingly beautiful...; **t24** extraordinary subtlety to this: varying spiced strata amid the chocolate raisins. The delivery starts dry and builds, minor wave after another into something sweeter and alluring; **f24** lighter spices now but it is the layering of the grape which is spellbinding...what a finish! **b24.5** one of the most complete, complex and compelling whiskies I have tasted this year. A Danish masterpiece... *50.8%. nc ncf. 741 bottles.*

Thy Whisky Spelt-Rye virgin oak and ex-sherry fad, dist Mar-April 17, tappet Sept 18 db **(87.5) n21.5 t22.5 f21.5 b22** A punchy, hard-nosed whisky with lots of angular aromas and flavours. Only on delivery when the golden syrup and spelt link arm in arm does it really sit comfortably. But always salivating and sharp and the late, eye-watering tannins adds to the big personality. *46.3%. nc ncf. 644 bottles.*

TROLDEN DISTILLERY Kolding. Working.
Trolden Nimbus The Kolding Single Malt Nimbus cask no. 5 db **(93) n23 t23 f23.5 b23.5** It has been many years since I was in Kolding giving a Jim Murray whisky tasting. Indeed, so long ago, there wasn't even any Danish whisky in existence, let alone allowing the locals to savour something as delightful as this. An excellent single malt to toast many pleasant memories. *46%. nc ncf sc.*

◇◇◇ **Trolden Nimbus Danish Single Malt** cask no. 6 db **(92.5) n22.5** there's a quiet intensity to the dates and nuts which form the main thrust of this rather thick nose. Breezy peppers offer a lighter outlet; **t23.5** the density on the nose is redoubled on the palate. Golden syrup meets maple syrup meets intensely toasty tannin. Oozes in style and profound flavours... literally! **f23** more peppery towards the finale with the lightly burned butterscotch offering limited sweetness and plenty of dryness; **b23.5** a very understated whisky and it's the oils that do it. Huge weight and body, but so evenly distributed. *46%. nc ncf sc.*

◇◇◇ **Trolden Nimbus Peated Single Malt** cask no. PX db **(86.5) n22 t21.5 f22 b21** This isn't the first peat and PX fallout and it won't be the last. Only towards the very death do the two bruising elements find common ground. Until then it is an unbalanced stand-off, especially on the delivery, where they both appear to back off to create a very odd void. Peat and PX are rarely happy bedfellows and though you might find the odd charming moment – I did here briefly on the nose and certainly with the massive spices at the death – the gears grind a little too noisily. Still, I guarantee some peatophiles will find this one of the greatest experiences of their lives... *56%. nc ncf sc. 177 bottles.*

ESTONIA
MOE DISTILLERY Moe. Working.
◇◇◇ **Tamm & Rukis 100% Rye Malt Whisky** virgin American oak for 3 years, distilled from Sangaste winter rye, batch no. 1, bott 2019 db **(89) n23** how can you not be seduced by the spiced toasted honeycomb? The tannins have a proud Kentuckian feel, the esters and molasses suggesting something big and sweet about to hit the palate; **t21.5** well, certainly big, not least because of the slight feints on delivery which, as ever, are dry. But this soon burns off as the

heather honey and treacle blend sweeten up the oils and fill the mouth. It takes time, but the rye begins to make a delicious impact; f22.5 slips into happy overdrive as the rye grain now really get its act together and blends in merrily with the silky honey: we are back in Kentucky again...; b22 seeing as Estonians helped colonise America as far back as the very early 17th century, perhaps it should be no surprise Moe have decided to give this whisky a very Kentuckian slant, evident on both nose and palate. And very attractive it is, too. A fascinating and entertaining introduction by a new country to whisky. Or do I mean whiskey....? 44%.

FINLAND
THE HELSINKI DISTILLING COMPANY Helsinki. Working.

◇◇◇ **The Helsinki Distilling Co Small Batch Helsinki Whiskey Rye Malt 6th Anniversary Bottling for Viskin Ystävien Seura** new American oak, rum cask finish db (**90**) n22 agreeable peppers on the crisp rye; a little feint mugginess, but nothing like of old; t23 thumping rye hard enough to shatter your teeth. As soon as the hot spices kick in we are well into salivation mode; f22 a little bitter and toasty; b23 until I encountered this, I associated Helsinki whisky with a feinty, unbalanced whisky. Not anymore. Still a tad generous on the cut, but a massive improvement and the rye is to be found in all its most juicy glory. 59.3%. 680 bottles. Release VYS#8.

◇◇◇ **The Helsinki Distilling Co Small Batch Helsinki Whiskey Rye Malt Finnish Summer Edition 2019** American virgin oak db (**85**) n21 t23 f20 b21 Eye-watering rye intensity. But too much of a feints storm. 47.5%. 700 bottles. Release #15.

◇◇◇ **The Helsinki Distilling Co Small Batch Helsinki Whiskey Rye Malt Special Fall Release** American virgin oak, rum cask finish db (**88**) n21.5 t22.5 f22 b22 Sweet, even slightly syrupy in part a little bit of extra feint doesn't help on the complexity front. That said, the sugar-pepper ratio is impressive as is the rye crescendo about five or six flavour waves in. 47.5%. Release #14.

◇◇◇ **The Helsinki Distilling Co Small Batch Helsinki Whiskey Single Malt 4 Years Old** American virgin oak, Pedro Ximénez finish db (**93**) n23.5 not sure if they have sticky toffee pudding in Finland, but if they like this then there will be a big market for it out there. If not, they might prefer the fig and date tart, which is also evident here; t23 less Helsinki and more: Hell! Silky! Lots of stickiness to this, too. The sugars are dark, the spices pin-pricky; f23 soft with a massive juicy date and toffee presence; b23.5 right. How can we give our unpeated malt whisky the most massive flavour injection? Shove it into American virgin oak for maximum tannins. OK, that's done. What can we do next for a bit of dramatic overkill? PX, anyone? Right, we'll do that! I have seen similar attempts around the world come to grief. This one works, helped by this being the best quality distillate I've encountered from them yet. 47.5%. ncf. 80 bottles. Release #16.

◇◇◇ **The Helsinki Distilling Co Small Batch Helsinki Whiskey Single Malt 4 Years Old** small new French oak db (**92**) n22.5 the French oak appears to be churning out a very attractive, almost salty, sweet chestnut note; t23.5 massive delivery! Less oil than normal as the cut is so much cleaner but the intensity of the malt impresses first before giving way to the sugar-enriched tannins that become toastier by the moment; f23 dried manuka honey on slightly burnt toast (and, trust me, I have tasted that! And this is a ringer!); the spices rumble gamely b23 don't expect compromises: this malt fair belts it out! 56.6%. ncf. 240 bottles. Release #11.

KYRÖ DISTILLERY COMPANY Isokyrö. Working.

Rye Whisky #1 bott 10 Aug 17 db (**83.5**) n19 t21.5 f21.5 b21.5 No doubting the grain: the rye turns up big and loud, especially at the crescendo on about the fourth flavour wave. But too much oil at work here dulls the sparkle. Recovers beautifully late on with some chocolate milkshake. 47.8%.

◇◇◇ **Kyrö Single Malt Rye Whisky No. 6** bott code: L 30/01/19/A db (**88.5**) n22 t22.5 f21.5 b22.5 Feinty to a fault, there is no criticism of the extraordinary intensity of the grain itself. If Superman drank rye whisky, it would probably be this, as the enormity of the fruity personality – so much richer from being malted (a very wise choice). Heather honey bobs in and out of this, as do some black peppers but it is the crisp sharpness of the grain which makes this malt. When they have mastered their stills to reign in the feints, this is going to be one hell of a rye whisky. Watch this space. 47.2%.

◇◇◇ **Kyrö Single Malt Rye Whisky No. 8** bott code: L 25/07/19/A db (**88**) n21.5 t22 f22.5 b22 Very interesting. Much better distillate. Not quite the bee's knees. But the feints have been reduced (if not yet eradicated), though the intensity of the rye has likewise diminished, making for a more soporific experience. Here, though, the finish picks up as the rye tones congregate, the spices tumbling into the mix, too. 47.2%.

PANIMORAVINTOLA KOULU Turku. Working.

Sgoil Sherry Cask db (**90**) n23 t23.5 f21.5 b22.5 Sherry...and clean as a whistle! A sulphur-free dram from Finland. 59%. sc. 80 bottles.

TEERENPELI Lahti. Working.

Teerenpeli 7 Year Old sherry casks db **(87.5) n21.5 t22.5 f21.5 b22** Despite the sherry cask influence, it is the tannin which conquers. Hefty, dry and spicy, there is a unusual fatness to this whisky for them. *50.7%.*

Teerenpeli Islay Cask db **(95) n24 t24 f23 b24** They have pulled this one off brilliantly. The cleanness of the spirit means there is a glorious impression of a lightly, and delightfully peated malt. Really, after so many years nothing this wonderful distillery does should surprise me. *61.7%*

Teerenpeli Juhlaviski 13 Year Old bott Mar 19 db **(95) n24 t24 f23.5 b23.5** I have no idea how they do this. But nothing about this distillery is by half measures, Everything you find is at mega intensity. Amazing. *58.5%.*

◇ **Teerenpeli Kaski Single Malt Whisky** sherry cask, bott code: 1-19 db **(95) n23.5** clean grape at play, helping to give this a distinctive spotted dog pudding feel; **t23.5** brilliant! Such a rare experience: structured grape, by no means over the top, allowing the fruit to span out right across the delivery: no force, everything at ease with, in slow motion, the barley and the vanilla growing in intensity. The sugars are so well orchestrated and channelled, you don't first realise they are there...; **f24** I can't actually remember the last time I had a sherry matured malt and found that the finale – or Finnish in this case - was its greatest attribute. Here the faultless fruit has captured the spices and cocoa notes, wrapped them up in the lingering malt and sung tender fruity lullabies to them...; **b24** what a stunning piece of whisky artwork. A sherry butt revelling in a glory common 30 years ago but rarer than hen's teeth today. Pure joy. *43%. nc ncf.*

◇ **Teerenpeli Lemmon Lintu Double Wood** bourbon & rum casks db **(91) n22.5** quite a lush, soft feel to the aroma, with caramels and vanillas taking the lead; **t23** a beautiful discharge of molten sugars, mainly of the muscovado class, ensure a friendly welcome to the palate. The tannins offer an altogether different approach, threatening a tangy toastiness; **f22.5** back to butterscotch and vanilla for the gentle, and still lightly oiled, finale; **b23** certainly benefits from the Murray Method. The rum casks have cordoned off much of the more complex personality, which are fully released on being warmed. Deceptively distinguished. *43%. nc ncf. Rum Cask Whisky Trilogy.*

◇ **Teerenpeli Porti Single Malt Whisky** port wine cask finish, bott code: 1-19 db **(89) n21.5** the fruit is flexing its muscles just a little too aggressively here. Firm and with surprisingly little yield; **t22.5** salivating with a grainy firmness. Not entirely in kilter with the fruit early on, but they dovetail attractively as things progress; **f22.5** this is such a contrary malt that after the juiciness of the delivery, the dryness of the finish comes as no surprise; **b22.5** all a bit gung-ho and overly sharp. What it lacks in structure, it certainly makes up for in personality! *43%. nc ncf.*

◇ **Teerenpeli Savu Single Malt Whisky** bott code: 1-19 db **(94) n23** clean without being bland, smoky without being a heavyweight: all-round, a bit of a tease...; **t23.5** such a glorious dusting of peat makes for a sexy delivery. But, here's the rub: this time there is a fuller body and rich vanilla tones, as well as lightly fruited muscovado sugar notes, for the peat to fit around and balance against; **f23.5** the spices which had got into their stride about a third of the way into the piece are now make the most noise, using the smoke as a hailer...; **b24** the last time I tasted this, it was a classic case of the blender not having taken into account the change in structure of a whisky when reduced down to this relatively low strength. Lessons, it appears have been learned. This is better balanced and entirely whole: a whisky much more at home with itself than had previously been the case. Someone has been to Finishing School... *43%. nc ncf.*

◇ **Teerenpeli Single Malt Whisky Aged 10 Years** db **(91) n23** the malt is in concentrated but balanced mode, the vanillas being gentle but persuasive; **t23.5** ulmo honey on delivery tells you a genteel sweetness will never be too far away and a build up of malty, gristy notes confirms this. The spices are so well paced and finely tuned, they go through the gears like a Jag on automatic; **f21.5** perhaps a shade untidy as a dryer note interjects with something like abrasiveness; **b23** the last time I tasted this whisky the poor sherry casks did no favours at all. Here, if there is a sherry influence, it comes into play only at the disappointing finish: the malt and oak have by far the most important lines. A massive improvement. *43%.*

FRANCE
Single Malt
DISTILLERIE ARTISANALE LEHMANN Obernai. Working.

Elsass Whisky Single Malt Whisky Alsacien Premium db **(86) n20.5 t21.5 f22 b22.** This is about as close as you'll get to an abstract single malt. The early discordant notes of the distillate are thrown against the canvas of the malt, and then fruit is randomly hurled at it, making a juicy, then spicy, splash. The overall picture when you stand back is not at all bad. But getting there is a bit messy. *50%. ncf.*

DISTILLERIE CASTAN Villeneuve-sur-Vère. Working.

Vilanova Terrocita db **(91.5)** n23 t23.5 f22 b23 Have to admit that this is a nose and flavour profile I have never quite encountered before. What a shame it wasn't at about 55% abv, I think we might have been heading off the planet from terra firma to terro cita... 43%. ncf.

DISTILLERIE DE LAGUIOLE Laguiole. Working.

Esprit De Twelve Malt Spirit lot no. 9.5, port cask db **(90)** n22 t23 f22 b23 Clean and glimmering with sparkling malt, this spirit shews an unusual early feel for the complexities of absorbing fruit into the system. At this age has every right to be disjointed and out of sorts, but this is anything but! 52.5%. sc.

Esprit De Twelve Malt Spirit lot no. 10, pedro ximenez & port casks db **(74)** n17 t19 f18 b18 The complete opposite in quality to their Port Cask spirit. Boiled vegetable nose, off key, bitter on the palate. Grim. 48%.

⋙ **Esprit De Twelve Malt Spirit Like a Cognac** Pineau cask db **(86)** n21.5 t22 f21 b21.5 Malty, very clean very green – as it should be. Travelling through a relatively tame period of its development, here, where the cask is redacting rather than adding to the story. 65%. sc.

⋙ **Esprit De Twelve Malt Spirit Peat Project** port cask db **(92.5)** n23 t23.5 f23 b23 Beautifully distilled and massively impressive, at times having a touch of the Islays about it. Very youthful, of course, but where it is impresses most is the way the high phenol content appears controlled without losing any of its impact. And the clever way the sugars emerge from the smoke. The wine causes a slight wobble on the balance front, especially on immediate impact. But this beast has time in its favour. A great way to start the tasting day. 65%. sc.

⋙ **Esprit De Twelve Single Malt Whisky First Release** db **(89)** n22 clean and barley - rich, though with a drier, pithy note; **t22.5** impressive! The barley tries nothing fancy and does no more than open itself up for full view. And a pretty sight it is...; **f22** creamier, but still with that rich barley hue; **b22.5** it is always such a pleasure to find a new distillery which is immediately feint-free. Still pretty much on the kindergarten side of things. But there is a joy to the free-handedness of the barley and the openness of the sugars against the weightier oak. When aged slightly longer this malt has the ability to move on to greater things. 47%.

DISTILLERIE DE PARIS Paris. Working.

⋙ **Distillerie De Paris Whisky Paris Single Malt** db **(89)** n21 sacre bleu! What eezz this nose....? It is, 'ow you say? Remarkable! Technically, it is what Napoleon was for 19th century European peace.; or a 1950s Citroen was to beauty on the eye. But the failings are not so bad as to entirely spoil the overall sensation. And once you have weeded those out of your mind, you are left with the more pleasant task of enjoying the nuts and Turkish Delight...; **t23** there's an odd sensation of phenols riding across the palate. However, it is impossible to distinguish this from the oils of a heavy-handed cut, or maybe something more deliberately, if subtly, planted on the barley. Either way, you need to put your teeth in to chew this one because not only is it big in stature, but the body has a malty richness and light ulmo honey undercurrent which can make your jaw ache; **f22** a little bit of a buzz amid the vanilla as those oils from the cut make gang up slightly; **b23** usually distilleries are named after remote hamlets or villages, located as they are in the countryside where modest streams provide the cooling water and just enough people live roundabout to be employed there. Calling yourself Paris Distillery is another way of doing it....if you want to make a statement! And the whisky seems to reflect this mode of thought as this is big, earthy stuff which pumps its chest out early and is determined to make its way in the whisky world. A distillery to keep a watchful gaze upon... 43%.

DISTILLERIE DES MENHIRS Bretagne. Working.

Eddu Gold db **(93)** n22 t23 f24 b24. Rarely do whiskies turn up in the glass so rich in character to the point of idiosyncrasy. Some purists will recoil from the more assertive elements. I simply rejoice. This is so proud to be different. And exceptionally good, to boot!! 43%

Eddu Grey Rock db **(87.5)** n21.5 t22 f22 b22. A docile whisky reliant on friendly muscovado sugars which match the vanilla-oak very attractively.40%

Eddu Grey Rock Affinage Porto db **(83)** n19 t21 f22 b21 Tasting whisky from this distillery is like taking part in a lucky dip: no idea if you'll pick a winner or the booby prize. This has the uncontrollable nose of a dud, but the fruit helps it pick up on the palate to an acceptable level. Good late spices, too. 40%.

Eddu Grey Rock Brocéliande db **(86.5)** n22 t22.5 f20.5 b21.5. Dense whisky which enjoys an enjoyable molassed fruitcake theme. A bit thin and wonky towards the finish.40%

Eddu Silver Broceliande db **(92.5)** n23 t23 f23 b23.5 Pure silk. A beautiful and engaging experience. 40%.

Eddu Silver The Original db **(92.5)** n23 t23 f23.5 b23 J'adore! 40%.

DISTILLERIE DU PÉRIGOLD Sarlat. Working.

◇ **Lascaw Blended Malt Whisky Aged 12 Years** finished in Perigord truffle flavoured speciality oak barrels, bott 10/12/2019, bott code: L 65752/05/00 db **(91.5)** n23.5 delicate and beautifully structured. Beyond the vaguely sweetened tannin is an unpeated and unusual earthiness....truffle oil...? **t22** light oils skims the palate allowing a light Demerara sugar sweetness to embed. The maltiness is fragmented, perhaps because of the weakness of the spirit; **f23** now really takes off on the complexity front. There is a note for sure I have never before encountered – presumably the truffle mixing in with caramels and vanillas. Soft and truly a delight; **b23** usually I get my truffles when breakfasting at Claridge's in London, their delicate tones emanating from my stupendous Eggs Benedict. I have to confess that I cannot be certain if what I get on the nose is that rare and celebrated fungus. But what I cannot deny is that this malt does have a certain je ne sais quoi, ensuring far above average complexity and grace. Mind you, at 46% this would be so much better... *40%.*

◇ **Lascaw Blended Malt Whisky Aged 15 Years** finished in Perigord truffle flavoured speciality oak barrels, bott 04/11/2019, bott code: L 63865/05/00 db **(86) n22.5 t22.5 f20 b21** Nowhere near as finely structured as their 12-year-old and a bit of a slave to the bitterness which seems to be a threat throughout but arrives late and decisively. There is a lovely praline moment, though, as the malt peaks. *40%.*

DISTILLERIE ERGASTER Passel. Working.

◇ **ER 2015 Single Malt Whisky Tourbé No. 001** db **(94) n23.5** the phenols are rigid and disciplined. Just a little molasses accompany the firmer element, whilst elsewhere cotton wool smoke drifts away...; **t23.5** younger on delivery than on nose, but soon the barley begins to juice up the palate, the smoke playing catch up; **f23** at last some spices get in on the act: gentle, dry but telling. The smoke has now softened considerably; **b24** magnifique! A stunning first bottling from Ergaster. Very much their own style of peatiness...and what style! Encore! *45%. 1,900 bottles.*

DISTILLERIE GILBERT HOLL Ribeauvillé. Working.

Lac'Holl 8 Year Old Single Malt Whisky db **(69) n19 t20 f14 b16** If memory serves, this is the youngest Lac'Hol I have tasted. But without doubt it is the most singular and disappointing. The profile of their whisky is usually far from conventional but attractive; this one is utterly bizarre and ugly. The peculiar scenting on the Swedish aquavit-style nose, which appears to include coconut sunscreen and orange liqueur, is matched only by the finish which reminds me, late on, of Milk of Magnesia. This has not been a good tasting day: it just got a whole lot worse... *42%.*

Lac'Holl Vieil Or 10 Years Old Single Malt Whisky db **(92.5) n22.5 t23.5 f23 b23.5** A malt which gives one's taste buds a real working over. Superb balance. *42%*

Lac'Holl Junior 13 Years Old Single Malt Whisky db **(89) n22 t22.5 f22 b22.5** Wow!! Bursts from the glass with so much charisma and charm. Perhaps not technically the finest of all time, but such fun! Delicious!! *43%*

Lac'Holl 15 Years Old Single Malt Whisky db **(90.5) n23.5 t22.5 f22 b22.5** Such a rare display of barley and gristy sugars. Very impressive malt. And fabulously refreshing. *42%*

DISTILLERIE GLANN AR MOR Larmor-Pleubian. Working.

Glann Ar Mor 2019 bourbon barrels db **(89.5) n22 t23 f21.5 b22.5** This brand is usually one of the highlights of my European whisky tasting year. However, this bottling has come up a little short compared to previous years having jettisoned some of its honeyed sweetness for a much thicker, more buxom malt. Still enjoyable, the usual fudge remains in situ, even employing an extra square of chocolate. But there is also a slight bitterness which has knocked the malt out of kilter. Doubtless next year it will be back to its brilliant best. *46%.*

Kornog En E Bezh 10 Year Old bourbon barrel db **(95.5) n23 t24.5 f24 b24** Probably the first Kornog I have encountered with oak taking top billing. The tannins are profound, yet controlled on the nose. The delivery, though, takes some matching: yes, the oak is big and bustles slightly, but the malt – seemingly supercharged with deft spice and tinned maple syrup, hits heights perhaps never before reached in the history of French whisky: it is just a molecule or so away from perfect...The much drier finish soaks up the oak and the almost house cocoa style, aided by the lightest oils to further the distance. This is, by any definition or stretch of the imagination, remarkable whisky and among the best I have tasted this year... *58.9%. sc.*

Kornog Hanter-Kant 11 Year Old bourbon barrel db **(89) n22.5 t23.5 f21 b22** Not sure the quality of the spirit 11 years ago was quite up to the standards of later years. The oak certainly makes a decent contribution here, but after the malty middle things become just a little too confused. The nose is the outlet for complexity and the delivery for drama, especially with the light chocolate and maple syrup intensity. Lovely whisky, but hard to make head or tail of... *50%. sc.*

Kornog Pedro Ximenez Finish bourbon barrel db **(90.5) n22.5 t23 f22 b23** This is a top draw PX cask. And, although there is peat, thankfully it is delicate enough not to make for yet another PX-Peat bore where each twain cancels the other out. So just a playful phenol thread followed by some supersonic grape, a little maple syrup lurking about here and there. Simple complexities, so to speak. But pleasantly effective. *46%.*

Kornog Roc'h Hir 2019 bourbon barrels db **(94) n23.5 t24 f23 b23.5** Had to check the label twice. Normally one of their more feinty offerings, this has been turned on its head by not only being beautifully made with excess oils kept to a minimum but with a deft smokiness to offer layering and a better sort of weight altogether. The delivery, though, is Glann Ar Mor at the very top of its game, the richness of the gristy barley rocketing off the scales. *46%.*

Kornog Saint Erwan 2018 bourbon barrel db **(95.5) n23.5 t24 f23.5 b24.5** A malt which has gone from merely coastal in previous years to tidal. You would swear that some of the English Channel, seaweed and all, has been used to reduce this whisky while the peat used to give this such a proud richness must have been cut just yards from where waves crash against shore. Less a glass of whisky than a sojourn, with your taste buds being explored and, in turn, every aspect of the malt's integrity being re-examined back. How do you explain the tenderness of the citrus, the truffle quality of the cocoa, the myriad layering and the delicate entrance of the bruyere honey..? There are no words. Just the experience. *50%. sc.*

Kornog Saint Erwan 2019 bourbon barrel db **(92.5) n23 t24 f22 b23.5** Tries incredibly hard to capture the genius of the 2018 bottling, but falls a little short. Even so, this is still Premier League malt, though here lighter with greater salivation levels and far more intensity to the barley at the coast of its coastal feel – a kind of coastal erosion, if you like. The peat on the nose is lost slightly in the natural caramels, while there is also a slight bittering out late on. *50%. sc.*

Kornog Saint Ivy 2018 bourbon barrel db **(92.5) n23.5 t23.5 f22 b23.5** Don't remember the last St Ivy having this understated smoky thread running through it! Puts it into the same herd at the St Erwan bottlings, though the emphasis here appears to be on a lovely diced pear and citrus theme. Naturally we are talking massive juiciness here, that smoke constantly rumbling below for balance. Another lovely whisky from this excellent distillery. *59.7%. sc.*

Kornog Saint Ivy 2019 bourbon barrel db **(95) n23 t24 f24 b24** A much sharper vintage than the 2018 with passion fruit replacing the citrus. Less phenols, though still enough – and some of them are slightly anthracitish - to contribute to both weight and complexity. But the mint chocolate on the finish is what sets this apart. When the 2018 version struggles slightly with some bitterness, this enters an entirely different dimension, with the cocoa and Manuka and ulmo honey mix making this not just the best finale from this distillery, but among the top three of any malt I have tasted so far this year. Fabulous. *58.2%. sc.*

Kornog Sauternes Cask 2019 db **(81) n20 t22 f19 b20** Usually Sauternes casks offer the best returns to whisky of all the wine casks. Unless they are sulphur treated. And that would explain the overall dullness to this peaty malt and the highly unimpressive finish. *46%. sc.*

Teir Gwech bourbon barrel db **(88.5) n22 t23 f21.5 b22** A serious, simplistic blast of sweet, citrussy barley. A little too bitter on the finish, though. *46%.*

DISTILLERIE GRALLET-DUPIC Rozelieures. Working.

G.Rozelieures Whisky De Lorraine Single Malt Whisky bott code: L446 db **(87) n21.5 t22.5 f21 b22.** Exceptionally nutty. The blossoming of the sugars on delivery is always attractive, as are the complex nougat/caramel/cocoa tones. Though the feints are always a threat, the genteel pace and softness of the malt makes it well worth a look. *40%*

DISTILLERIE HEPP VUM MODERTAL Uberach. Working.

Authentic Whisky D'Alsace Whisky Single Malt Doble Fût No. 6 db **(82.5) n19 t22.5 f20 b21** Well, that was different! The nose is vaguely on the soapy side and the dry finish conjures up a late burn. The delivery, though, does have a brief spasm of enjoyably intense barley at its heart, and a little cocoa to follow through. *42%. ncf.*

Authentic Whisky D'Alsace Whisky Single Malt Doble Fût No. 7 db **(87) n21 t23 f21 b22** A much more complete malt than their No.6. The nose is a tad austere and, again, the finale requires a fire extinguisher as the degree of burn increases. But there is no doubting the beauty and integrity of the delivery, a kind of malt and chocolate bonbon, even with a Milky Way element. My word it's hot, though. *40%. ncf.*

Authentic Whisky D'Alsace Whisky Single Malt Pinot Noir & Gris db **(85) n21.5 t22.5 f20 b21** The unspoiled grape offers a magnificent salivating juiciness. But even barrels as excellent as these cannot completely cover the flame-throwing traits of the original spirit. *47%. ncf.*

Authentic Whisky D'Alsace Whisky Single Malt Russian Imperial Stout #01 db **(76) n19 t22 f16 b19** I adore malt whisky. And my cellars are never without a case of Harvey's Russian Imperial Stout. But would I drink the two together? Never! The nose, though sweet, is undone by hop and there is not enough cover on the attractive, viscous malt to see off the incendiary tendencies of the spirit. *43%. ncf.*

Authentic Whisky D'Alsace Whisky Single Malt Squaring the Circle Pinot Noir & Pinot Gris casks db **(86.5) n22 t22 t23 f20 b21.5** Hot as Hades. But at least the nose and the delivery does offer us an all to brief vision of Pinot perfection... *48.6%. ncf. 890 bottles.*

Authentic Whisky D'Alsace Whisky Single Malt Timeless Intemporel db **(81) n20 t21.5 f19 b20.5** Something a little beery about this. The late burn is as unforgiving as usual but the maltiness does have a little extra sweetness to counter the flames. *47%. ncf.*

DISTILLERIE J.ET M. LEHMANN Obernai. Working.

Elsass Single Malt Whisky Gold Aged 7 Years Bordeaux Blanc finition db **(90) n23 t22.5 f22 b22.5** Deceptive and delicious. *40%.*

Elsass Single Malt Whisky Origine Aged 7 Years Bordeaux Blanc barrel db **(90.5) n23 t23 f22b22.5** A picture of understated elegance. *40%.*

Elsass Single Malt Whisky Premium Aged 8 Years Sauternes barrel db **(94.5) n23 t24 f23.5 b24** There is no finer wine cask in which to mature whisky than a clean Sauternes one. This does nothing to undermine my argument. Truly superb. *50%.*

DISTILLERIE MEYER Hohwarth. Working.

Meyer's Le Whisky Alsacien Pur Malt No. 0395 Affinage En Fut Sauternes Finition En Fut De Bourgogne bott code: L1830656 67430 db **(90.5) n22.5 t23 f22 b23** A beautiful malt from Meyer's. Not quite technically as fine as last year's but still a treat. *40%.*

Meyer's Le Whisky Alsacien Pur Malt No. 3632 bott code: L1834296 67430A db **(86) n22 t22 f20.5 b21.5** Percy, my Meyer's Parrot, wasn't too happy with the last bottling I showed him last year, and he's still turning his beak up at this one. The feints are just a little too problematical, though a mixture of Murray Method and keeping the glass in warm water for a few minutes does help dispel the worst of them to allow some heather-honey-tinged malt to flourish. *40%.*

◇ **Meyer's Le Whisky Alsacien Pur Malt Le Fumé** bott code: L1931297 67430A db **(88) n22 t22.5 f21.5 b22** As we all know Percy, my beautiful Meyers Parrot, hasn't been too happy with this malt in the past. Now, we'll he's a little happier, especially as some of the feints have subsided giving the malt itself a far grander and more enjoyable role. Indeed, when a little ulmo honey kicks in with the vanilla it is quite a jolly affair – until the wide cut rears up late on the finish. As for Percy, we'll he's just started singing the theme tune to the BBC radio programme "The Archers", an everyday story of country folk. Must be the pure malt barley... *40%.*

Meyer's Le Whisky Artisanal Blend Superieur bott code: L1905595 67430A db **(93) n23 t23.5 f23 b23.5** A feint-free, beautifully clean Meyer's showing great understanding between the relative weights of fruit and oak. Impressive. *40%.*

Meyer's Le Whisky Artisanal Blend Superieur Affinage En Fut Sauternes Finition Pinot Noir bott code: L1833895 67430 db **(86) n21 t23 f20.5 b21.5** While the nose and finish may be less than perfect and the balance is somewhat... errr, unbalanced, there is absolutely no denying the brilliance of the delivery and the following half dozen flavour shock waves. There are a few moments of fruity genius in there. *40%.*

◇ **Meyer's Le Whisky Artisanal Pur Malt No. 08720** bott code: L1931996 67430A db **(85.5) n21 t22.5 f20.5 b21.5** Definitely an improvement on their last similar bottling. But still those feints bite deep, though now at least the barley has far more thrust than before, giving the odd delightful moment on delivery. Frustrating, as you get the feeling they could have a really top class malt here. *40%.*

UNSPECIFIED

◇ **Évadé Whisky Français Peated Single Malt** db **(87.5) n21.5 t23 f21 b22** A distinct trace of bittering tobacco running through this as the extra oils make their mark: indeed the smoke, to a non-smoker like me, has a little more to do with Gauloises than peat. But there is no denying the beauty of the delivery where the barley has been expanded for maximum flavour and the sub-plot of phenol carries delicate Demerara sugars. The bitter finish, though, is a tad tardy by comparison. *43%. Whiskies du Monde.*

◇ **Évadé Whisky Français Single Malt** bott code: 1945WDMNT db **(89) n22** the barley digs deep to overcome the leading influence of the tannin; dry and toasty nonetheless; **t22.5** the rich small still feel is underlined by the strands of heather honey; **f22** reverts to a chalky vanilla and toffee fade as the oak wrestles back control; **b22.5** even at 40%, this has a robust quality which matches the intensity of the barley. Attractive. And certainly not a malt to evade. *40%. Whiskies du Monde.*

Maison Benjamin Kuentz Aux Particules Vimes Single Malt Whisky (91) n23 t22.5 f22.5 b23 Anyone who tasted Glen Scotia during the 1980s may remember their odd slightly peated version. This has an almost identical fingerprint, except this is slightly better constructed on the palate and with none of the saltiness of the Campbeltowner. Repays the Murray Method 46%. nc ncf.

⟜ **Maison Benjamin Kuentz Aux Particules Vines Single Malt Whisky Edition 2** finished in a Grand vin de Bordeaux rouge barrel for 18 months (84.5) n20.5 t20.5 f22 b21.5 Struggles initially to find its feet. A light feint note on the nose, though a vague hickory note steadies it slightly; and it is no more precise or happy on delivery. But from the midpoint matters take an upturn as vanilla and grape melt together attractively while the oils keep the sugars on a long lead. 579%. sc.

⟜ **Maison Benjamin Kuentz Aux Particules Vines Single Malt Whisky Edition 3** Macvin barrel, finished in a Grand vin de Bordeaux rouge barrel for 8 months (87) n22 t21.5 f21.5 b22 The Bordeaux barrel has a far more significant impact after eight months than Edition 2 managed in more than twice that time. Grinds around the palate in the house style, but cannot but enjoy the Turkish Delight/Chocolate Liqueur feel to the midpoint and finish on this one. Tasty! 46%. sc.

Maison Benjamin Kuentz (D'un) Verre Printanier Single Malt Whisky (91) n22.5 t23 f22.5 b23 A delicately smoked and beautifully distilled whisky which revels in its light, malty character despite the phenols. Even lightens things further with a gentle twist of lime. A well-known style of malt, impressively achieved. 46%. nc ncf.

Maison Benjamin Kuentz Fin de Partie Single Malt Whisky (84) n21 t22 f20.5 b20.5 Very simplistic malt with not quite enough personality to go it alone without much in the way of oak back up. 46%. nc ncf.

Maison Benjamin Kuentz Le Guip Single Malt Whisky (92) n22.5 t24 f22.5 b23 This is an impressive bunch of whiskies and cask strength does their malty demeanour no harm whatsoever. Light, in the house style, with a salivating gristy barley note that makes it worth finding a bottle of this alone. The most beautifully intact maltiness of any whisky I have tasted for some while. 55%. nc ncf.

Vatted Malts

Bellevoye Bleu Whisky Triple Malt Finition Grain Fin bott code: A18184A (87.5) n21.5 t22 f22 b22 Goes pretty hefty on the tobacco note on both nose and delivery. But the wide cut delivers impressively on the chocolate nougat and even, surprisingly, a degree of chewy date alongside the malt. 40%.

Bellevoye Blanc Whisky Triple Malt Finition Sauternes bott code: A18199A (82.5) n20 t21.5 f21 b20 I am tasting in the near dark here for maximum sensory effect – and this one nearly knocked me off my chair. Certainly one of the strangest malts I have tasted this year with the most vividly citrusy nose on a Sauternes finish I have ever encountered – almost like washing up liquid. To say this whisky has a clean nose would be an understatement... Malty on the palate, but never quite feels right. 40%.

Bellevoye Rouge Whisky Triple Malt Finition Grand Cru bott code: A18200A (83) n21.5 t22 f19.5 b20 Despite the Grand Cru, there Smoke Blue as a tobacco element makes an undesired contribution. The fruit is sweet and intense, though. The finish a bit of a mess. 43%.

Bellevoye Noir Whisky Triple Malt Édition Tourbée bott code: A18232A (87) n22.5 t22 f21 b21.5 There is a certain primitive quality to the peatiness which, for all its simplistic naivety, packs no end of charm. Lots of toffee kicks in, reducing the complexity somewhat. But that peat, flighty on the nose and warming on the palate, has a distinctly more-ish quality. 43%.

GERMANY
ALTE HAUSBRENNEREI A. WECKLEIN Arnstein. Working.

Wecklain A.54 Rushburn Frankonian Single Malt barrels 8 & 19, bott code LN 1005-17 db (90) n23.5 t23 f21.5 b23 A very different, highly evocative whisky. 43%. 650 bottles.

BIRGITTA RUST PIEKFEINE BRÄNDE Bremen. Working.

Van Loon 5 Year Old Single Malt Whisky batch 2012 db (85) n21.5 t22 f20 b21.5 Usually, a little extra strength will greatly enhance a complex whisky - if given time in the glass. The exception is when the cut is already a little too wide, resulting in a lumpy, ultimately bitter effort. Where this does benefit is in the richness of the fruit and the light mocha effect. 55%.

BRENNEREI AM FEUERGRABEN Achern. Working.

⟜ **Salamansar Septem Ignis Single Malt Whisky** bott code: L99 db (86) n21.5 t22.5 f20.5 b21.5 A little kink in the distillation is revealed on both nose and finish. But no quibbles about the barley intensity which rises like mercury in the Sahara... 45%.

⟜ **Salamansar Single Cask Whisky Batch no. 1** triple wood Jamaican rum finish, bott code: L19/22 db (94.5) n23.5 what the...? Possibly the rummiest rum nose I have ever encountered in a whisky. And, unmistakably Jamaican in style. And top quality Pot Still rum to boot...! **t24** sensuous and honey-laden, a light estery sheen coats the mouth while a succession of vanilla and golden syrup tones pad around the palate; creamy butterscotch takes us towards the finish; **f23** Worther's Original candy meets a heather-honey and golden syrup hybrid, again with a rum-like estery depth keeping things chewy; **b24** most whiskies which claim "rum finish" or "Jamaican Rum finish" rarely show little more than a firm, sugary coating. This reminds me of the days in the early '90s when I was in Jamaica putting rum together. This has a kind of Longpond feel to it, with its elongated sweetness and gentle esters. Adorable whisky, which was very well distilled, incidentally. *42%. sc.*

◈ **Salamansar Single Malt Whisky Batch no. 3** triple wood, bott code: L19/24 db **(85.5)** **n22 t23 f19 b21.5** If they didn't know in Germany what a British "Jammy Dodger" smells like, then they do now. Fat, mildly unctuous and makes excellent play between the barley, grape and vanillas. Until the finale this is creamy, jammy and entertaining. Such a shame about the late sulphurous intervention. *43.7%. sc.*

BERGHOF RABEL Owen-Teck. Working.
Whisky Stube Spirit of the Cask OWEN Albdinkel Jamaika rum fass finish, destillert am 01/2012, abgefüllt am 11/2017 **(90) n21.5 t23 f22.5 b23** The spirit is not exactly faultless. But a stupendous rum cask has generated a treasure chest of untold honeyed riches. *46%.*

BRENNEREI FELLER Dietenheim-Regglisweiler. Working
◈ **Feller Valerie Amarome Cask Single Malt** db **(91) n23** fabulous! A very slight feel of German Christmas cake with a launching of sweet, busy spices The gentle tannin notes crossed with vanilla are the perfect accompaniment; **t23** immediately salivating on delivery. The mark of profound black cherry is there before a wave of spicey heather honey notes fill in the midground; **f22** a gentle mix of ginger cake and liquorice; **b23** this is one spicy Feller! *59%. nc ncf.*

Augustus Single Grain Emmer Urkorn bott code los 1001 db **(85.5) n23 t21.5 f20 b21** A fabulous nose with its fair share of kumquats, but this never registers on the palate and is unbalanced and bitter, showing an orange peel tartness. *46%. nc ncf.*

◈ **Feller Torf Single Malt** bourbon cask, bott code los 2911 db **(94) n24** the most acidic of peaty noses. And truly beautiful with it, too...; **t23.5** as every good peated whisky should, the sugars arrive with the same balancing charm as the smoky shroud which engulfs it. Though here the sugar has an unmistakable rum-like quality. Vanilla runs through the veins of this malt, momentarily softening the impact of the peat...until the acidity starts to build once more, forming layer after layer after layer...; **f23** such a charismatic make, with the smoke and sugars alternating with effortless elegance; **b23.5** what a gorgeous whisky! Adorable because it is as deft as it is enormous. *48%. nc ncf.*

◈ **Feller Valerie Rye Malt** white port cask, bott code los 901 db **(89) n22** clean and pleasingly bitter-sweet. But you get the feeling the wine has done a good job of reducing the boldness and personality of the rye. A shame...; **t23** ah...that's more like it. The grain zeroes in on the taste buds from the very first second and leave little to the imagination. This is eye-watering whisky and the fruit equally has a piercing effect; **f22** creamy and vanilla led. A little lime marmalade at the rear keeps the sharpness going; **b22** no prisoners taken here! Not the most relaxing of malts, not least because the palate is never given a chance. The wine casks seem to have the devil in them and determined to offer up the sharpest of fruits. Unusually, the rye malt acts as an accomplice rather than the boss. *60.9%. nc ncf.*

Valerie Single Malt sherry cask, bott code los 115 db **(92.5) n23.5 t23.5 f22.5 b23** First things first: no off notes – yep, a faultlessly clean sherry cask. And this surprisingly light and delicate whisky certainly takes full advantage! *46%. nc ncf.*

Valerie Single Malt French Pineau cask finish, bott code los 113 db **(94) n23.5 t24 f23 b23.5** Big difference between this and the 46% version with the oils stretching the sugars further and helping to balance out the fruit intensity. Lush, in every sense of the word... *60.3%. nc ncf.*

New Make Barley Malt dest 15 Mar 19 db **(94.5) n23.5 t24 f24 b24** Borderline incredible that a malt new make of this ultra-high strength can be with so much barley-packed flavour. But this really is the strength on the bottle – 172 proof brilliance! Have a cigar with this at your peril... *86.1%.*

New Make Barley Malt Peated bourbon cask, dest 20 Feb 18 db **(95.5) n23.5 t24 f23.5 b24.5** A truly unique take on the peaty malt whisky genre. I can see this building a cult status. Wow! *65.2%.*

BRENNEREI HENRICH Kriftel, Hessia. Working.
Gilors Single Malt Whisky Peated bourbon fass, destilliert Nov 12, abgefüllt Mar 18, bott code: L 18021 db **(88) n21.5 t22.5 f22 b22** A malt full of surprises: after a pretty scary start on the nose, it goes on a charm offensive. *42%. 336 bottles.*

Gilors Single Malt Whisky Portwein Fass destilliert Nov 15, abgefüllt Nov 18, bott code: L 18069 db **(87.5) n21 t23 f21.5 b21.5** Suffers a little from the strength of the bottling: the oils have been broken up and a few cracks appear later on. At cask strength this would have held together much better and made the most of the delightful Fry's Turkish Delight delivery. *40%. 511 bottles.*

Gilors Single Malt Whisky Portwein Finish Islay & portwein fass, destilliert Jul 13, abgefüllt Oct 18, bott code: L 18068 db **(87) n21.5 t22.5 f21.5 b21.5** It's a bumpy old road for the journey this whisky takes you on: rarely does the peat and fruit appear to be on the same wavelength once they have untangled after the excellent delivery. Juicy and not short of character, either. Enjoyable in its rough and ready way. *45%. 276 bottles.*

Gilors Single Malt Whisky PX Sherry Finish Islay & px sherry fass, destilliert Feb 14, abgefüllt Mar 19, bott code: L 19001 db **(87) n20 t23.5 f21.5 b22** Gilors seem to be cornering the market in thick set, leaden-weighted soupy whisky. Throw the distillery's generous cut into this particular mix and you really do end up with a jaw-aching single malt. Have to admit I adore the delivery once it gets into its stride and the molasses come into play. *45%. 522 bottles.*

Gilors Single Malt Whisky Sherry Fass destilliert Feb 16, abgefüllt Mar 19, bott code: L 19002 db **(86.5) n22.5 t21.5 f21.5 b21** A distinctly impressive nose to wow any and all sherry whisky lovers. But flattens out once on the palate. *40%. 654 bottles.*

BRENNEREI ZIEGLER Freudenberg, North Württemberg. Working.

◦◦◦ **Aureum Single Malt Whisky 6 Year Old Chestnut Cask** db **(91.5) n23 t23 f22.5 b23** I have long been an admirer of chestnut matured whisky, having first come across it at a remote and little-known distillery in Austria nearly 25 years ago. After all this time, this gorgeous malt reaffirms my attraction to these casks. The house creamy style is maintained as a constant. But the configuration of malt and sugars now takes on a very different shape; even the sweetness has a very tone and one, not surprisingly, unique to cask. Here the sugars boast a light lemon blossom honey tone before natural caramels intermingle... and then the malty essence of grist. No off notes from spirit of cask and despite the unique tannin character the malt is allowed to fly its flag without interference. Charming and a chestnut cask bottling that conkers many others... *48%.*

◦◦◦ **Aureum Single Malt Whisky 6 Year Old Peated** db **(90.5) n22.5 t22.5 f22.5 b23** It's the creaminess on the palate which provides the surprise package here. And probably the shyness of the peat, too. Despite its relatively tenders years, the tannins have impacted with a degree of force but have brought with the extra sugars to prop up the gristier notes. Beautifully made and fascinating cask integration of black peppers and brown sugars. The late arrival of vanilla and butterscotch tart underlines the point. A lovely cask, but the wine does take away very slightly from the malty charm of their standard bottlings. *48%.*

◦◦◦ **Aureum Single Malt Whisky 8 Year Old Portwine Cask** db **(89) n22.5 t23 f21 b22.5** To get to the vital things first: a sound cask with no off notes. That established we can thoroughly enjoy this lively malt where the Port at times threatens overkill, but a fightback of intense barley alongside the big spice and molasses means complexity always remains the leading light. A little bitterness on the finish, though thankfully it isn't sulphur. *59.2%.*

◦◦◦ **Aureum Single Malt Whisky 10 Year Old Cask Strength** db **(94) n23 t24 f23 b24** Quite often a malt which shews as much natural caramel early on as this does ends up swamped by it, lifeless and uninteresting even during the post mortem. Not this time. It is as though the malt sensed when enough was enough and instead moved on to far more interesting matters: in this case how far towards being a beautiful bourbon in character it could sail? The answer is: so close that once or twice it crosses the border and for a few moments takes on a distinctly Kentuckian hue, all liquorice and molasses in full spate. Certainly the delivery is the sweetest in Europe this year though, miraculously, never for a moment takes the cloying route and embraces pugilistic spices which come out jabbing away looking to make short work of your taste buds. Only a little gnawing bitterness – tiredness from the oak maybe – prevents a higher score, though those warming cocoa tones still offer up much to enjoy. A malt with massive character to go the distance with. *58.3%.*

◦◦◦ **Aureum Single Malt Peated New Make** db **(92) n23 t23 f22.5 b23.5** A sound and confidently made new make, free from feints of any variety and homing in deliciously on the malt. Just the right degree of gristy sweetness and oil, too. An excellent base on which to begin any malt whisky. The peat, which is far from demonstrative, is kept on a manageable and even keel. *68.5%.*

DESTILLERIE ARMIN JOBST E.K. Hammelburg. Working.

◦◦◦ **Jobst Grain Whisky 9 Jahre Madeira Cask A7 6 Jahre** Barrique fass, 3 Jahre Madeira fass db **(92.5) n22.5 t23.5 f23 b23.5** At last! An indisputably excellent bottling from Jobst after so many attempts that one way or another fell at one of the hurdles. Here it clears all the fences with something to spare (well, maybe on the nose the back hooves clip something). But off this one trots to the winners' enclosure, unquestionably a thoroughbred. How can you not applaud the measured resonance of the fruit and the way the tannins interlink with almost effortless grace. The house nutty style is there in force, but this time isn't cracked with a sledgehammer cut and even allows the grains to have some kind of say in the matter. What superb balance and character this filly has. Definitely worth a flutter on.... *50%. sc.*

❖ **Jobst Single Malt Whisky 3 Jahre Cognac-Fass No. 26** db **(81)** n17 t21 f22 b21 I think this is the distillery I once famously called a pfennig short of a Deutschmark. Never before have I made such great cents. Malty, in its very own peculiarly odd way. By the way: anyone who ever tasted the first-ever efforts of the Old Hobart distillery in Australia will be taken back 20 years or so by this nose... *58.4%. sc.*

❖ **Jobst Single Malt Whisky 4 Jahre Bourbon-Fass B4 3 Jahre** Rotwein Barrique, 1 Jahre Kentucky bourbon barrel db **(83)** n20 t23.5 f19 b20.5 There are moments when this malt is a winner. Especially when the crème chocolate is in full flow, that then moves into more praline mode. Make no mistake: that later delivery and middle is truly beautiful. The nose and finish, typical of this distillery, are best forgotten – though, sadly, the late tang ensures you can't. *43.7%. sc.*

Jobst Single Malt Whisky 4 Jahre Holzfass bott code: L SM Whisky 12 db **(82)** n19 t21 f21 b21 Incredibly sweet malt, as though the grist has been distilled into intense barley sugar candy. The spirit suffers from a generous cut, though the feinty nose proves a bark worse than its bite. *43%.*

Jobst Single Malt Whisky 5 Jahre Holzfass bott code: L SM Whisky 16 db **(80.5)** n18 t20 f21.5 b20.5 Big feints means it takes a while before the rich malt is able to settle things down. By comparison a lovely finish, but the nose and start leave something to be desired. *43%.*

❖ **Jobst Single Malt Whisky 4 Jahre Portweinfass No. 44** db **(84)** n19 t21 f22 b22 The nose is the usual technical horror show. But a subtle, untarnished grapey fruitiness offers the sexy love interest that needs saving. *43%. sc.*

❖ **Jobst Single Malt Whisky 4 Jahre Portweinfass No. 44** db **(87)** n20 t22.5 f22 b22.5 If you ever want to see why cask strength outranks a diluted version, you could do no better than sample this against their 43% version. Here the natural oils hold together the integrity of both the malt and the fruit, allowing it to fuse with the rich natural oils and overcome the weakness of the cut. Beautifully chewy and intense, the spices play out like a demented fruit cake, sweetingly warm but still in league with the intensity of the earlier sugars. Hang on and just go for the ride: it's fun! *58.8%. sc.*

Jobst Whisky 5 Jahre Holzfass Sherry Cask bott code: L 5 WhisSher 01:11 db **(85)** n20 t22 f22 b21 This distillery appears to specialise in remarkable whiskies that are loud, brash wrong in so many ways yet strangely compelling and attractive. A clean sherry cask does all in its power to inject an intense fruitiness, and succeeds. The spices are insane and the base spirit is obviously eccentric. The result is a whisky you want on technical grounds to dislike but can't help being dangerously attracted to. *46%.*

Jobst Whisky 6 Jahre Holzfass Madeira Cask bott code: L 6 WhisMad 06:10 db **(82.5)** n18.5 t22.5 f20 b21.5 Jolly well done and take a bow that Madeira cask. The grain itself offers little that is positive but the soft golden syrup and grape carries a distinct charm. *46%.*

Jobst Whisky 6 Jahre Holzfass Moscatel Cask bott code: L 6 WhisMos 06:10 db **(85)** n19.5 t22 f21.5 b22 We know what to come to expect by now: a nose a few pfennigs short of a Deutschmark, the entire currency of the whisky propped up by an outstanding cask. It really is all about the grape here, which is clean and succulent, the oils and oak giving a kind of chocolate and jam Swiss roll combo. *46%.*

❖ **Jobst Single Malt Whisky 6 Jahre Kastanien-Fass R1** db **(86.5)** n20 t22.5 f21.5 b22.5 It takes something as profound as a top-quality chestnut barrel to first control and then obliterate the edginess to the distillate. This offers a really enjoyable experience once you are past the nose and, indeed, a rich nuttiness makes the most of the silky oils and light Demerara sugars to ensure there is sublime layering to complement the mouthfeel. The spices have teeth and ensure extra depth. Pinch your nose...then enjoy...!!! *50.4%. sc.*

Jobst Whisky 9 Jahre Barrique Barrel Strength bott code: L 9 Whisky 17 db **(85.5)** n19 t23 f22 b21.5 Another poor nose. But the delivery is like receiving a cherry pie bang in the kisser. Technically a bit of a miss, but for sheer chutzpah, a resounding hit. Outrageous fruity juiciness on delivery that has to be experienced to be believed, and spices are pretty bold, too. And there really is a degree of chocolate cherry tart to this... *48.7%.*

DESTILLERIE & BRENNEREI MICHAEL HABBEL Sprockhövel. Working

Hillock 8 Year Old Single Malt Whisky 82 monate in ex bourbon fässern, 14 monate zum finish in ex Recioto fässern, bott code: L-2118 db **(87)** n22 t22 f21.5 b21.5 A soft, friendly malt determined not to upset any apple carts, but in so doing rather lays too supinely at the feet of the dominant toffee. Malt and spices apparent and, overall, quite pleasant in the German style. 45.3%.

DESTILLERIE RALF HAUER Bad Dürkheim. Working.

◈ **Saillt Mór Bad Dürkheim Whisky** Oloroso sherry peated cask, los no. 0319, fassreifung 3/16, gefüllt am 08/19 db **(93)** n23.5 an astonishing saltiness is as pronounced as the peat in the face of the thick sherry; t23 the peat positively curdles in the wine. This is big – and obviously has no intention of being anything but. There is a thick sootiness to the middle, which seems a long way removed from the early heather honey; f23 better layering now things have settled. Plenty of mocha and old fruitcake. But the spices, with their smoky accompaniment, now have teeth...; b23.5 the majority of distilleries have the alarming, and frankly depressing, habit of falling flat on their face when they combine the big two: peat and wine cask. Pleased to say, this fares far better than most. 55.6%. nc ncf.

◈ **Saillt Mór Bad Dürkheim Whisky** Pfälzer oak, los no. 0219, fass-nr. 23 & 24, jahrgang 3/14, gefüllt am 08/19 db **(91.5)** n22 a strange, slightly strangled citrus note here makes it tart in every sense; t24 where the hell did that come from....??? A blinding delivery with the gristy grains, heather honey and molasses exploding at the very same moment. Slowly the oak appears, like a forest in the distance; f22.5 spicy and now tannin-heavy; b23 if you are looking for a whisky which launches stunning flavours around your palate, then you've now found it. What a delivery... easily one of the most memorable in Europe this year! 46%. ncf.

Saillt Mór Single Cask Malt Whisky oloroso sherry cask, fass-nr. 44, jahrgang 3/14, gefüllt am 11/18 db **(81.5)** n21 t22 f19 b19.5 Fails to work on too many levels. Never manages to find a sensible balance between the grape and what appears to be a phenolic-style malt while the finish is bitter and off-key. 60.9%. sc.

Saillt Mór Single Cask Malt Whisky ruby port cask, fass-nr. 7, jahrgang 1/13, gefüllt am 11/18 db **(95)** n23.5 t23.5 f24 b24 Such a blissful yet incredibly complex malt. Just rattles the glass with its personality. 57.6%. sc.

Spirit of the Cask Saillt Mór Single Cask Malt Whisky pfälzer eiche Jamaika rum, dest Mar 14, gefüllt am Apr 19 db **(92)** n22.5 t23 f23 b23.5 A more than attractive offering, the rum cask acting like a security guard allowing little to pass outside its strict confines. A soft toffee and coffee note is the main theme, helped along with a light saltiness and even a vague hint of bourbon. But the light sugary exoskeleton ensures it keeps its shape throughout. Lovely. 45%. sc.

DESTILLERIE RIEGER & HOFMEISTER Fellbach. Working.

◈ **Rye Schwäbischer Roggenmalz-Whisky** bott code: L-RW-150819 db **(94.5)** n23.5 huge, angular rye made all the punchier by a very slight and acceptable feint kick; t24 the nose warns that this will be nothing less than a massive whisky, but doesn't prepare you for the sharp and beautifully correct rye intensity on delivery. The light feints ensure a degree of oiliness mixes the toasty vanilla in with the Demerara sweetness; f23.5 still thick and intense long into the experience, still chewy and now with chocolate and toffee, too...; b23.5 a style of whisky this distillery does wonderfully well. A real handful of a rye, bustling and muscular, allowing the earthier element of this grain full scope. 42%.

◈ **Schwäbischer Whisky Single Malt Portweinfass Finish** bott code: L-SM-230919 db **(79.5)** n19.5 t22 f19 b19 The new-mown hay reveals a slight problem along the line, probably fermentation, and the wine cask does little to rectify the matter. Certainly, it struggles to create a balance beyond the attractive delivery, as the slightly grim finish testifies. 40%.

◈ **Whisky No.4 Sherryfass Finished Schwäbischer Whisky** bott code: L-W04-010220 db **(89)** n22 a dense nose, but the grape reveals grace and quality. Attractive...; t22.5 again the wine influence hits home early and with some prominence. Lush with a prism of striking sugars that stand out against the light feints and spicy oak; f22 pastel fruits...the dark ones in particular; b22.5 an excellent sherry cask does a very good job here. At times a delicious whisky, if inconsistent. 42%.

DESTILLERIE THOMAS SIPPEL Weisenheim am Berg. Working.

Palatinatus Single Malt Whisky American Oak Peated 6 Years Old db **(92.5)** n22.5 t23.5 f23 b23.5 A sure fire winner amongst peat lovers. Simplistic, maybe. But wonderfully effective and beautifully made. 45%. 218 bottles.

◈ **Palatinatus Single Malt Whisky American Oak Peated 2014** db **(91)** n23.5 a unashamedly Islay-style smokiness to this, the phenols offering a slight acidic nose to accompany so gristy sugars: beautiful...; t23 silky arrival on the palate with icing sugar and vanilla-caramel to offer a chewiness. The peat lurks and builds deliciously; f22 just a hint of something a tad bitter and tangy; citrussy almost...; b22.5 a distillery that does peat so well. Slightly more of a tanginess on the finish this time out, though. 45%.

Palatinatus Single Malt Whisky Bordeaux Single Cask 5 Years Old db **(81.5)** n21.5 t21 f19.5 b20.5 Oddly enough, the wine cask may be sulphur-free, but not so sure about the original distillate. When the fruit shines, all is well. *57.8%. sc.*

◇ **Palatinatus Single Malt Whisky Bordeaux Single Cask Strength 6 Jahre** db **(89)** n22 curious mix of slights feints, red berries and chocolatey malt; t23 again those slight feints shew early, then a toasty raisin theme. But soon the malt has blasted off into orbit. Soft ulmo honey steadies the ship; f22 here we go, back to the air from faultless astonishing dense malt...; b22 far from technically on the money, but the flavours are huge. I should be marking this down, but find myself entranced and at its mercy! Prepare yourself for a chewathon. *54.5%. sc.*

◇ **Palatinatus Single Malt Whisky French Limousin Oak Spätburgunder Singel Cask 2014** db **(81)** n21.5 t21.5 f18.5 b19.5 Interesting tasting this after their sublime German oak bottling. That works on so many levels that this just doesn't. Bitter and unbalanced. *45%. sc.*

◇ **Palatinatus Single Malt Whisky Single Cask German Oak 2014** db **(94)** n23.5 you know when the well-suited tough stands by his boss chewing gum, daring anyone to try it... well here it is...in German tannin form. This is a quietly intense nose profile you don't muck around with...; t23.5 for one, maybe one and half beats, the barley reigns. Then in comes that unique tannin form. Tight, abrupt. But eventually with yield enough to act as backbone and most of the muscle, but still allowing the malt and accompanying sugars to offer the shape and beauty. Buttery and salivating, too...; f23 more about the caramels and spices now...; b24 profound whisky so beautifully distilled (not something I have always said about Palatinatus) and balanced. It appears that German oak bests suits this German malt. Neat! *45%. sc.*

◇ **Palatinatus Single Malt Whisky Ruby Port Single Cask First Fill 2014** db **(85.5)** n22 t21.5 f21 b21 I'm a little surprised that a first fill Port pipe didn't generate more intense fruit than is seen here. No shortage of busy flavours many of them malty. But has real problems getting them to assemble in attractive order. *45%. sc.*

EDELBRÄENDE-SENFT Salem-Rickenbach. Working.

Senft Whisky dist 2013, bott 2018, bott code: L-SW47 db **(86.5)** n20.5 t22 f22 b22 Perfect example where the wide cut on the still takes on one hand – in this case the nose in particular– but gives on another. For this is one big chewy toffee and nougat beast. *42%. nc.*

Senft Whisky Edition 79 dist 2013, bott 2018, bott code: L-WE179 db **(87.5)** n21 t22.5 f22 b22 Although, technically, the nougat style speaks volumes, there is no getting away from the fact that mix of intense toffee and chocolate to accompany it is highly attractive. A kind of distilled Milky Way candy. *47%. nc.*

◇ **Senft Whisky Edition Herbert** dist 2014, bott code: L-WE551 db **(87)** n21 t23 f21.5 b21.5 No faulting the mouthfeel which benefits from the extra oils from the wide-ish cut. Not just from the nougat school of European whisky, but at around the midpoint hits the most glorious chord of intense sweet malt, chocolate and oak-induced dry vanilla. For five or six glorious seconds as those notes align, this is stunning! *45%. nc.*

EDELBRENNEREI BISCHOF Wartmannsroth. Working.

◇ **Bischof's Rhöner Whisky Grain Whisky Aus Rhöner Weizen Single Cask** bott code: L-9 db **(85)** n21 t22.5 f20.5 b21 Not as neat and tidy as the last bottling I enjoyed from them, the feints knocking things askew here. That said, it does have its tender moments especially when the particularly nutty character softens and moves towards a light praline, even vaguely coconut hue. Spices gather, but the balance dissipates. *40%. sc.*

EDELBRENNEREI DIRKER Mömbris. Working.

Dirker Whisky Aged 4 Years Sassicaia cask, bott code L A 16 db **(80.5)** n18.5 t22.5 f19 b20.5. A deeply frustrating whisky. This is one exceptionally beautiful cask at work here and - in the mid ground - offers all kinds of toffee apple and muscovado-sweetened mocha. Sadly, the initial spirit wasn't up to the barrel's standard. This really needs some cleaning up. *53%*

EIFEL DESTILLATE Koblenz. Working.

Eifel Whisky Editions Serie 746.9 German Single Malt Whisky 10 Jahre Alt 5 jahre refill bourbon fass & wein barrique, 5 jahre Amontillado sherry barrique, bott 2019 db **(84)** n21 t21.5 f20.5 b21 A soft, toffee-rich composition. But the degree of feints visible shews how far this distillery has improved technically over the last decade. *46%. nc ncf sc. 640 Flaschen.*

Eifel Whisky Editions Serie 746.9 German Single Peated Malt Whisky 7 Jahre Alt 5 jahre refill bourbon fass & wein barrique, 2 jahre 2 x 150l first fill Moscatel sherry, bott 2019 db **(93)** n23.5 t23.5 f22.5 b23.5 When they say peated, they mean peated! This is a whisky which after this number of years and the make-up of malt and cask could easily have gone very wrong. It went very right... *46%. nc ncf sc. 858 Flaschen.*

Eifel Roggen Whisky Regional Serie Ahrtaler first fill Pinot Noir Barrique db **(94)** n23 t24 f23.5 b23.5 Eifel have found a number of ways for their rye whisky to appear in some fascinating and delicious situations. 46%.

Eifel Whisky Regional Serie Hohes Venn Quartett first fill Bordeaux barrique 3 jahre & first fill Eifel rum cask 2 jahre db **(87.5)** n21.5 t24 f20.5 b21.5 You never crack the art of blending completely until you fully understand that by adding something, you are taking away something else. This whisky is enjoyable, but is simply doing too much. The delivery, it must be said, a kind of smoky chocolate rum truffle, is to die for: one of the best deliveries anywhere this year; but it is too fleeting. Elsewhere the whisky lurches about unconvincingly, especially towards the long but uncomfortable finish. 46%. nc ncf.

Eifel Whisky Roggen Whisky Eilay 4 jahre first fill sherry barrique, 2 jahre first fill Laphroaig barrel, bott 2019 db **(87)** n22 t22 f21 b22 An interesting whisky where the fruit appearance to make a smoother ride of some turbulence elsewhere. A curious, husky, phenolic note and some oaky strangeness at the death. It is never not keeping you guessing... 46%. nc ncf sc.

Eifel Whisky Einzelfass Single Rye 2019 ex Bordeaux American oak barrique 3 jahre, first fill Malaga cask 3 jahre, dest 2013, bott 2019 db **(88)** n22 t23 f21 b22 Have to say that as a whisky per se it is enjoyable, but as a rye it is disappointing. Don't see the point of having grains with so much character drowned out by huge fruit. 50%.nc ncf sc.

Eifel Whisky Einzelfass Triple Malt 2019 refurbished French oak barrique light toast 3 jahre, first fill port cask 4 jahre, dest 2012, bott 2019 db **(89)** n23 t22 f22 b22 The oak puts a tremendous strain on the balance of this malt. But just about gets away with it. In the end proves to be quite a character. 50%. nc ncf sc.

Eifel Whisky Signatur Serie Smoky Blend 4 Jahre finish im PX sherry fass db **(88)** n22 t23 f21 b22 Another fat whisky from this distillery where the delivery is a thing of beauty but elsewhere is growls around like a malcontent. Can't help enjoying it, though. Having said that, apart from some spices, not sure what happened to the smoke... 50%. nc ncf.

ELCH WHISKY Gräfenberg. Working.

Elch Torf vom Dorf losnr.: 19/05 db **(95)** n23.5 t24 f23.5 b24 When you get a whisky that combines a fascinating narrative with clever and subtle understatement yet fortified by occasional boldness, it is hard not to be won over and seduced. Fantastic. 51%.

FESSLERMILL 1396 DESTILLERIE Sersheim. Working.

◇◇ **Mettermalt American Style Whisky** new American bourbon barrel db **(85)** n21 t21.5 f21 b21.5 American style it may be, but the closest I can think of to this is American blend. Light and lacking direction, this goes down as pleasant but far from memorable whisky. 40%. nc sc.

◇◇ **Mettermalt Classic Whisky** bott code: L200 db **(83)** n18 t22.5 f21 b21.5 When the cut is as wide as here, there will always be collateral damage. The nose is a bit of a gorgon, but there is some redemption on the resulting heather honey spice. 40%.

◇◇ **Mettermalt Single Malt Whisky** new American white oak barrel db **(86.5)** n21.5 t22 f21.5 b21.5 Dines out on the toasted honeycomb notes and spices which slalom in and out of this malt. The wide cut is equally responsible for a little extra bitterness, too. 46%. nc sc.

◇◇ **Mettermalt Single Rye Whiskey** db **(82.5)** n21 t21.5 f19.5 b20.5 The rye's fulsomeness is not in doubt. Sadly the quality of the distillate is. Far too much feint, I'm afraid. 55.5%. nc sc.

◇◇ **Mettermalt Smoky Single Rye Whiskey** ex-Laphroaig barrel db **(93)** n23 t23.5 f23 b23.5 Fabulously distilled, this is clean rye offering a crisp, fruity and salivating backdrop to the loitering phenols. The sugars are sharp and act with rare purity. Big, though it takes one a little while to realise just how...! 55.5%. nc sc.

FINCH WHISKYDESTILLERIE Nellingen, Alb-Donau. Working.

◇◇ **Finch Schwäbischer Hochland Whisky Barrel Proof 19** bott code: L19056 db **(90.5)** n22.5 a bold and complex nose of mixed grain – barley malt and wheat, I think – which bind to form a deep, resonating cord – especially when the tannins join forces; t23 a finch uncaged here, as the delivery is massive! This is huge, but always in control of the dark sugars and lighter ulmo honey which rumble magnificently; the midpoint is doused in vanilla and caramel; f22 spicier now and does a good job of diverting the attention away from the light feint; b23 As I taste this, a greenfinch calls gutterally, wheezily, to its prospective mate, while nearby a goldfinch is more than happy to use its metallic red face to dazzle, topping it off with its jaunty, equally metallic trill for good measure. Meanwhile, in the glass, this Finch entices you with its song of alluring ulmo honey and caramels. 54%.

◇◇ **Finch Schwäbischer Hochland Whisky Barrique R 19** bott code: L19130 db **(92)** n23 the spices popping up to outflank the spices remind me slightly of a wheated bourbon; creamy toffee and darker sugars drop anchor; t23 good weight, controlled oils...but always juicy in a barley-fresh kind of way. Complex and superbly paced development; **f22.5** now the vanillas dig in – and late spices, a mix of grain and oak induced; **b23.5** the model of a beautifully balanced whisky able to contain any minor lurking feints. *42%.*

    Finch Schwäbischer Hochland Whisky Private Edition Single Malt Madeira 19-1 flasche nr. 1093 von 1416, bott code: L19230 db **(93) n23** I love it when the fruit is present, but understated like here. The enigmatic sweetness keeps you sniffing, trying to unlock its meaning...; **t23** fat and chewy on delivery, the now house cream toffee not hanging around for an invite and ploughing straight in...; **f23.5** a light coating of ulmo honey adds extra juiciness to the raisins; a fabulous mix of chocolate and spices late on blend with the malt; **b23.5** it's like unwrapping a raisin toffee. An elegant Finch with much greater complexity than first seems possible.. *45%. sc.*

GUTSBRENNEREI JOH. B. GEUTING Bocholt. Working.

J.B.G Münsterländer Single Grain Whisky Aged 7 Years oloroso casks, cask nos. 9,10 & 29, dist 12 Nov 11, bott 20 Feb 18 db **(89.5) n22 t23 f22 b22.5** Probably the best distillation I have seen from this distillery with the cuts being more on the mark, while the oloroso butts are clean and drip enticingly with grape. *42%. 1,036 bottles.*

HAMMERSCHMIEDE Zorge. Working.

    The Glen Els Aged 10 Years Single Malt PX sherry casks, bott code: L1866 db **(88) n22 t23 f21.5 b21.5** Yes, yes, I know. I can hear it now: "These are perfect PX casks, without a single sulphur note. They're perfect. We went out of our way to make sure they are. And spent good money doing so... So why has Murray only given us 88 points...? He's an idiot!" Yes, they are perfect PX casks and I congratulate you: indeed, I congratulate this distillery in assembling among the best collection of wine casks I have seen from any distillery in the world. But it is not that that makes a great whisky alone. Great PX makes great PX, or perhaps a great cream sherry. But the problem for me here is the one-dimensional aspect is the malt itself, which doesn't seem to be able to make the impact it needs to. The result is the most stunning sugary delivery imaginable, and worth discovering in its own right – hence the 88 points. But not that special quality from the malt to offer balance and complexity and take it to the next level. Sorry. *52.6%. nc ncf. 750 bottles. 2018 release.*

    The Glen Els The Journey Distiller's Cut 2019 Single Malt bott code: L1879 db **(90) n22** a slightly angular off note from the stills, but the oak has been forgiving and accrued a meaningful fruitiness to give this a steaming spotted dog pudding personality; **t23** sumptuous to a fault, the malt ganging up and thickening in order to match the healthy fruit; **f22** the mild off notes are still around, but the fruit continues to radiate its juicy response; **b23** when the Coronavirus epidemic is finally over, there will be worse things to do than nip over to Glen Els to track down a bottle of this Distillery Exclusive. Rich and rewarding. *48%. nc ncf. 2,000 bottles.*

    The Glen Els Willowburn Grand Cru Claret Casks Single Malt batch no. 1, bott code: L1893 db **(68) n17 t18 f16 b17** Some Glen Els fail spectacularly. Here is one such example. Doesn't work on a single level. *46%. nc ncf. 1,000 bottles.*

    The Glen Els Willowburn Malaga Casks Single Malt batch no. 1, bott code: L1890 db **(88.5) n21.5 t22 f22.5 b22.5** An enjoyable, almost flippant, whisky which is about as relaxed as they come. The grape has no sharpness or shape but prefers to smother the malt with juicy, lightly spices Demerara-style notes. Positively grows and - glows - into its task. *46%. nc ncf. 1,000 bottles.*

    The Glen Els Willowburn Marsala Casks Single Malt batch no. 1, bott code: L1887 db **(75) n18 t19 f19 b19** Some whiskies work beautifully. This doesn't. The original distillate offered a challenge the Marsala was unable to surmount. *46%. nc ncf. 1,000 bottles.*

    The Glen Els Willowburn Moscatel Casks Single Malt batch no. 1, bott code: L1892 db **(90.5) n23** no shortage of the trademark Moscatel spice; **t22.5** eyewatering – almost shuddering to the system. The sharpness of the grape battles gamely with mildly pugnacious distillate. But it is the disarming nuttiness that wins through; **f22** a tad off piste, but the light spice added to the fruit toffee does the trick; **b23** technically a bit hit and miss. But some breathtakingly high class casks has worked wonders. *46%. nc ncf. 1,000 bottles.*

    The Glen Els Willowburn Ruby & Tawny Port Casks Single Malt batch no. 1, bott code: L1886 db **(87) n22.5 t23 f20 b21.5** The influence of the Port casks is truly fabulous: this is very high-class barrels they have put into use here. The influence of the basic distillate isn't quite of the same calibre, so as it spends longer on the palate, the less magic the wine can spread. Ruby on a Train to Nowhere, one might say... *46%. nc ncf. 1,000 bottles.*

    Hercynian Willowburn Cask Strength 2019 batch no. 1, bott code: L1889 db **(91.5) n23** there is almost a whine coming from the wine – a single grapey note that barely alters in pitch; so much toffee, too...; **t23.5** cleanly distilled malt filled into a faultless presumably sherry butt. If a German whisky comes silkier than this, I have yet to discover it; **f23** attractive mix of tannin...and toffee raisin; **b22** well-made whisky. Fruity to a fault and peppered with spice. But just a little too one dimensional for greatness. *54.8%. nc ncf. 1,000 bottles.*

⬩ **Hercynian Willowburn Exceptional Collection Aged 5 Years Single Malt** bourbon firkin cask no. V14-10, dist 2014, bott 15 Jun 19, bott code: L1902 db **(96) n24** exceptional by mainland Europe, let alone German, standards. Look for the crushed acorns. The malt is pristine and proud: concentrated yet soft enough to allow the most glorious tannins to interact with a delicate liquorice and manuka honey thread...a ten minute nose, minimum; **t24** prominent oak: sharp and rich. Praline has its fingerprints all over this, and as the malt being to leak into the mix, up come the spices; **f23.5** even more praline. No tang from a wide cut, no off notes from the cask: just stunningly well-distilled whisky allowing the oak to do its job...; **b24.5** firkin brilliant!!! A potential European Whisky of the Year. *61.9%. nc ncf sc. 36 bottles.* 🍶

HAUSBRAUEREI ALTSTADTHOF Nürnberg. Working.
Ayrer's PX Sherry Cask Finished Organic Single Malt dist 2009 db **(90) n22 t22.5 f23 b22.5** Always brave to use PX, as the intensity of the sugars can sometimes put the malt into the tightest of straight-jackets. However, this is fine, sulphur-free butt and is eventually relaxed enough for the malt to share equal billing once it finds its rhythm. *56%*

HINRICHSEN'S FARM DISTILLERY Dunsum. Working.
⬩ **Hinrichsen's Farm Distillery New Virgin Malt Spirituose Aus Gerstenmalz** lot no. 400 db **(92.5) n24 t23.5 f22 b23** The nose is of the Spirit Safe when the middle cut is running: possibly the sexiest aroma of any part of the distillery. A feint-free spirit radiating beautifully composed barley: who could ask for more? The delivery is satisfyingly intense malt aided by the lightest of oils, though the finish perhaps suggests a little more copper could do with attaching itself. But this is a very promising base for any malt whisky and true delight to sample in its own right. *42%. ncf.*

KAUZEN-BRÄU Ochsenfurt. Working.
Old Owl Feinster Fränkischer Single Malt Whisky dest 08/2013, abgef 11/2017 **(87.5) n22 t22.5 f21 b22** The barley is attractive and intense; enormous caramels coat the palate, a little spiced molasses offering an alternative, darker sweetness. A little oily late on (unlike a previous bottling of theirs I tasted), this is an attractive, untaxing single malt. *46%*.

KLEINBRENNEREI FITZKE Herbolzheim-Broggingen. Working.
⬩ **Derrina Dinkelmalz Schwarzwälder Single Malt Whisky** bott code L 5513 db **(87) n21 t21 f23 b22** Neither the nose nor delivery instil much confidence, as both are on the earthy, feinty side. However, no complaints about the finish which offers more praline than any other whisky I have tasted this year. Talk about clouds and silver linings... *43%*.

Derrina Einkorn Schwarzwälder Single Grain Whisky bott code L 11213 db **(93) n22.5 t24 f23 b23.5** Totally uncompromising in its stature, this kicks and bites like a cask strength bottling. The flavour profile explodes off the charts with a mocha and toffee delivery and follow through which is unique in its style and signature. The mouthfeel is also better than could be hoped for, the light, creamy oils filling in all cracks on the whisky and palate. What a joy to experience! *43%*.

⬩ **Derrina Einkorn-Malz Schwarzwälder Single Malt Whisky** bott code L 12012 db **(84.5) n21 t22.5 f20 b21** It looks like that the distillery has developed a code where a pretty average, feinty nose, is shorthand for a seismic outburst if chocolate somewhere down the line. Sadly the cut is far too wide for any form of greatness, as this is a bit of a rough ride. After the last brilliant bottling of Einkorn-Malz from them, this was, to say the least, disappointing... *43%*.

⬩ **Derrina Gerstenmalz Schwarzwälder Single Malt Whisky** bott code L 5413 db **(84) n19 t21.5 f22 b21.5** No doubting the enormous intensity of the barley on delivery, or its richness on follow through. But the nose leaves no doubt the cut wasn't the best and its problems stem from there. *43%*.

Derrina Gerstenmalz Torfrauch "Stark" Schwarzwälder Single Malt Whisky bott code L 13112 db **(91) n23 t23 f22.5 b22.5** If memory serves, the last peated malt I had from these fellows was a gentle, understated affair. Well, not this time: absolutely no ambiguity about this whisky at all! The peat appears to be carved from stone on the nose, so rock hard and uncompromising is it. But the delivery is every bit as gentle: the malt forms a sweet oily pouch into which the phenols are cradled. A lovely malt handsomely displaying this distillery's idiosyncratic style. *43%*.

⬩ **Derrina Granat Rotkorn Ur-Weizen Schwarzwälder Single Grain Whisky** bott code L 13912 db **(93) n22.5 t24 f23 b23.5** A sensational whisky that attacks you from the first second to the last with a plethora of unique and unorthodox flavour profiles which leave you wondering what's around the corner. The nose may be slightly caramel centric but the delivery and follow-through are a different proposition thanks to the marriage of the rich oils and the teasing, bitty grain. If you insist on identifiable landmarks, then you'll uncover butterscotch and light cream toffee, but the brilliance of this whisky is that the favours are...well...like nothing else! 43%.

Derrina Grünkern Schwarzwälder Single Grain Whisky bott code L 11013 db (88) n21.5 t22.5 f22 b22 A typical Derrina full bloodied whisky bursting at the seams with flavour. Oily, chewy the grain has a great ally in the heather honey. 43%.

Derrina Hafer Schwarzwälder Single Grain Whisky bott code L 6212 db (91) n22 t23.5 f22.5 b23 I started today's tasting with an oat whisky and now, nearly ten hours on, I taste my 25th and final whisky of the day with another one. This is far the superior of the two, more cleanly distilled and the grain far more prominent in its rich and sweet character. The blend of ulmo honey and mocha is irresistible. 43%.

◈ **Derrina Hafermalz Schwarzwälder Single Malt Whisky** bott code L 6713 db (94.5) n23.5 one of the cleanest oat whisky noses I have encountered in years: the grain is unmistakable, carrying a unique sweetness, at once dense and ethereal, which flits from praline wafers to toasted fudge; t24 a near perfect mouthfeel: like the nose, dense yet supremely light with the superb oils distributing and retaining the acacia honey on porridge theme; f23 very long and just more of the same with a slow motion fade; b24 oat whisky, when made well, is unquestionably one of the most flavoursome spirits on the planet. Here is a rare example of Hafermalz at Bundesliga standard... 43%. ♀

Derrina Karamell-Malz Gerste Schwarzwälder Single Malt Whisky bott code L 13412 db (87.5) n21.5 t22 f22 b22 One from the Central European School of Heavyweight Nougat and Toffee Whisky. You could stand a spoon up in this sweetie! 43%.

Derrina Karamell-Malz Roggen Schwarzwälder Single Malt Whisky bott code L 13512 db (77) n19 t20 f19 b19 Lots of flavour. Just not necessarily all the ones I'd expect or want to see on a rye whisky... 43%.

Derrina Karamell-Malz Weizen Schwarzwälder Single Malt Whisky bott code L 13313 db (89) n22 t22.5 f22 b22.5 Cream toffee and nuts: you are as likely to find this flavour combination in a Christmas tin of chocolates as you are on a whisky. Love it! 43%.

Derrina Khourasan Ur-Weizen Schwarzwälder Single Grain Whisky bott code L 13811 db (93.5) n23 t23.5 f23.5 b23.5 When I think Derrina, I think their wheat whisky. This is their best style and they have hit the heights again with a whisky technically superior to anything else they offer. Clean and with the oils coming less from the still and more from the grain itself. The accompaniment of heather honey and delicate spice ticks every wheat whisky box. Would love to see this at cask strength. 43%.

◈ **Derrina Müsli Schwarzwälder Single Grain Whisky** bott code L 7112 db (94.5) n23.5 where do you start? Such a complex and beautifully weighted and paced nose, certainly. But there is so much more, with the varying sweet tones, a kind of hybrid of ulmo honey, marzipan and the very lightest maple syrup, but almost too delicate to be true...; t24 the nose tells you something wonderful is happening: the delivery reinforces this. Just as the aroma, we are talking variants and hybrids of a theme, all set in a stunningly beautiful and buttery oily landscape. This is dissolve-on-delivery whisky, yet always there is a far weightier sub-text of light liquorice and molasses, though in keeping with the style it is massively understated...; f22.5 just the vaguest hint of feint as those darker, thicker tones reverberate...; b23.5 I wasn't sure if I was supposed to add milk to this and throw in a few fresh raspberries and strawberries for good measure. In the end, I tasted it using the Murray Method, which requires none of those props. And just as well, for the complexity on this is the stuff of dreams and legends. Big enough to make a film about. Indeed, it should become a cereal...(don't think the Germans will get that one!). Anyway, definitely up there as a possible award winner! 43%.

◈ **Derrina Oberkulmer Rotkorn Ur-Dinkel Schwarzwälder Single Grain Whisky** bott code L 13712 db (92.5) n23 t23.5 f23 b23 Impossible not to be delighted by the gentle elegance of this whisky, the welcoming ulmo honey on the nose matched by the light touch of Lubek marzipan and ulmo honey on delivery. To maximise this, it needs a lightness of touch from the oils...and that's exactly what it gets. 43%.

◈ **Derrina Weizenmalz Schwarzwälder Single Malt Whisky** bott code L 5713 db (93) n23.5 t23 f23 b23.5 A proudly singular style here with the distillery going great guns, as ever, with their wheated version. The odd stray feint note here and there, but this seems to ensure that the grain gains even greater weight and a more fizzy intensity to its mix of spice and light Demerara sugars. Few German whiskies can hold their salivation levels for so long and at such a high pitch. Expect your jaw to ache by the end of all the chewing. But it is a pain well worth bearing... 43%.

KORNBRENNEREI J.J. KEMPER Olpe. Working.

Spirit of the Cask Roggen Whisky Amerikanische weisseiche fass, dest Jun 15, gefüllt am Nov 18 db (89) n22 t23.5 f22 b22 Maybe not quite technically perfect, but you can't be too harsh on a whisky offering this much honey... 58.9%. sc.

KYMSEE WHISKY Grabenstätt. Working.

Kymsee Der Chiemsee-Whisky Single Malt 3 Years Old Sherry Cask Finish db **(88)** n22 t23 f21.5 b21.5 Has its faults (though not sulphur!), but the delivery is a superb mouthful. 42%.

Kymsee Der Chiemsee-Whisky Single Malt fass nr. 12, dest Dec 14 db **(87)** n22 t22 f21.5 b21.5 As usual, an attractive and competent malt from Kymsee. The barley and oak support each other deliciously early on but the increasing dryness does reveal an overall lack of sugars. 42%.

Kymsee Der Chiemsee-Whisky Single Malt Cask Strength db **(87)** n20.5 t23 f21.5 b22 Cask strength sweet nougat! 62.5%.

Kymsee Der Chiemsee-Whisky Single Malt Garrison Quarter Cask db **(92)** n23 t23.5 f22.5 b23 Charismatic distillate makes the most of a very good cask. 42%.

Kymsee Der Chiemsee-Whisky Single Malt Sherry Cask Finish fass nr. 2, dest Dec 14 db **(91)** n22.5 t23 f22.5 b23 Well balanced, elegant and satisfying. 42%.

⟐ **Kymsee Single Malt Moran Cask Strength** db **(89)** n22 lacks a little bit of copper, but the citrussy phenols are present and correct; t23 the grist wastes no time on hitting its straps ensuring the phenols are met with maximum delicate sugars. Peppery and phenolic, but the youth also reveals, like on the nose, a lightness of copper presence; f21.5 again, just a little thin on the finish; b22.5 were I in a Scottish blending lab, putting a young blend together, I wouldn't bat an eyelid if this was one of the standard Islay whiskies I had to work from. Perhaps a little thin on structure but otherwise presses all the right buttons. 58.6%.

MARDER EDELBRÄNDE Albbruck-Unteralpfen. Working.

Marder Single Malt Black Forest Reserve Cask No. 90 Single Malt 5 Years Old db **(91)** n22.5 t23 f22.5 b23 This malty monster sits prettily on the palate. 54.6%. 369 bottles.

MÄRKISCHE SPEZIALITÄTEN BRENNEREI Hagen. Working.

⟐ **DeCavo Single Malt Höhlenwhisky 3 Jahre** fass-nr. L55 db **(84.5)** n21.5 t21.5 f20.5 b21 Thin, young and the striking bitter lemon note makes the whisky wobble off its malty course. 47.3%. sc.

⟐ **DeCavo Single Malt Höhlenwhisky 5 Jahre** fass-nr. L19 db **(93.5)** n23 an impressive aroma: clean and abounding in barley. The Demerara sugars are soft and gently welcome the light vanillas onboard; t23.5 superb delivery! Starts quietly with a few early malty notes, then build in caramels and milky chocolate until they make a slightly spiced paste: this is very intense! The sugars are crystalline and agreeably crunchy; f23 a beautiful Malteser candy fade, with more spices at work now; b24 the best whisky I have encountered from this distillery, by far. Few German whiskies come maltier than this! 58.3%. sc.

NORDPFALZ BRENNEREI Höning. Working.

Taranis Pfälzer Single Malt Whisky 5 Years Old Sauternes cask, dist Winter 12 db **(87)** n21 t22 f22 b22 Just a little extra feinty nougat evident on the nose and has no second thoughts about presenting itself on the palate also. Curiously thick and lightly fruited for a Sauternes cask, offering toffee aplenty. 49.5%. sc. 166 bottles.

NUMBER NINE SPIRITUOSENMANUFAKTUR Leinefelde-Worbis, Working.

The Nine Springs Single Malt Whisky Age 3 Years batch no. 5 db **(86.5)** n19 t23 f22 b21.5 An attractive whisky, though the nose isn't entirely happy. Exceptionally sweet delivery with some serious maple syrup moments. Some red and black liquorice which underlines the bourbon-style which by the time it is in full flow late on, makes up a lot of the ground lost by the off- key nose and delivery. One careful cut away from being a classic. 45%. nc ncf.

The Nine Springs Single Malt Whisky Cask Pineau Des Charentes cask no. 119 db **(87.5)** n20 t23.5 f22 b22 The wine gives a charming polish to this malt –once on the palate. The grape is too light to make a telling difference to the off-key nose. But the spices fizz and marmalade covers the buttered toast rather beautifully. 57.9%. nc ncf sc.

The Nine Springs Single Malt Whisky Peated Breeze Edition Muscatel wine cask db **(95)** n23 t24 f24 b24 This is how fruit and peat can work together - just exploding with flavour. Beautiful! 49%. nc ncf.

SAUERLÄNDER EDELBRENNEREI Ruthen-Kallenhardt. Working.

Thousand Mountains McRaven Single Malt cask no. L 1028 05.2015 db **(85)** n20 t22 f21.5 b21.5 From the somewhat Feinty School of German whisky, it gets over a faltering start on the nose to recover with a volley of maple syrup on the palate...and a slow deliverance of barley. Ignore the nose and enjoy the flawed but tasty follow up. 46.2%. nc ncf sc.

SCHRAML - DIE STEINWALD - BRENNEREI E.K. Erbendorf. Working.

Stonewood 1818 Bavarian Single Grain Whisky 10 Jahre Alt bott code: L4118 db **(90.5)** n22 t23 f22.5 b23 A delightful, simplistic malt for its years which wrings out every last atom of barley. 45%.

◇ **Stonewood 1818 Bavarian Single Grain Whisky 10 Jahre Alt** bott code: L40120 db **(89.5)** n22 t22.5 f22.5 b22.5 Never let it be said tht this distillery doesn't perpetuate its own character. I was expecting a little feint on this...and got it. I was expecting a grassy freshness to this despite the extra weight. And got it. Really salivating and palate cleansing...and it is not often you can say that about a whisky carrying a little feint. Lovely stuff. 45%.

Stonewood Drà Bavarian Single Malt Whisky 3 Jahre Alt bott code: L1119 db **(93)** n23 t24 f22.5 b23.5 In some ways quite simple; but simply beautiful... 43%.

◇ **Stonewood Drà Bavarian Single Malt Whisky 5 Jahre Alt** bott code: L1219 db **(90.5)** n22 t23 f22.5 b23 A superbly weighted whisky abounding with malt – and further underlining that this distillery's quality is taking an upward direction as time passes. This bottling reveals the barley at that fascinating point of being just past its early youth and now happily engaging with the tannins, allowing a little heather-honey to intervene to balance out the edges. A little feint, of course, but doing no damage and even ensures extra muscle at the death. 43%.

Stonewood Smokey Monk Bavarian Single Malt Whisky 3 Jahre Alt bott code: L10118 db **(88)** n22 t22 f21.5 b22.5 One of those rare whiskies which tick the wrong boxes for technical achievement, but all the rights ones for overall enjoyment. 40%.

◇ **Stonewood Smokey Monk Bavarian Single Malt Whisky 3 Jahre Alt** db **(83)** n21 t21 f20.5 b20.5 The unrelenting feints on this means we have a Monk that got into a very bad habit... 40%.

Stonewood Woaz Bavarian Single Wheat Whisky 5 Jahre Alt bott code: L1219 db **(87)** n21.5 t22 f21.5 b22 Unmistakably wheat whisky: almost like cutting into a newly baked brown loaf and breathing in the moist fumes. But this is a slightly imperfect distillation with the prickle and oils of the wider than desired cut a distraction. Even so, the grain coupled with the light maple syrup has more than its fair share of attractions. 43%.

◇ **Stonewood Woaz Bavarian Single Wheat Whisky 7 Jahre Alt** bott code: L-120119 db **(91)** n22.5 t23 f22.5 b23 Ah, I remember this one! The wheat whisky that's like a new loaf straight out of the oven. Well it reminded me of that because that is exactly what comes across here, the steam filling the nostrils as you cut through the crusts. There is, as is this distillery's trait, a little feint turning up here and there, but the wheat is spurred on by crispy Demerara sugar so at times it has the feel of a of a British Hot Cross Bun. Not sure if you are meant to drink this or have it with your 11 O'clock coffee... 43%.

SINGOLD DESTILLERIE Wehringen. Working.

◇ **SinGold 7 Year Old** dist 19 Apr 12, bott Dec 19 db **(92)** n22.5 t23 f23.5 b23 After battling my way through a series of very average and not particularly well distilled European whiskies, I can't say what kind of relief it was to find this one. Impressively manufactured, it has also spent time in an appropriate cask, thus allowing the natural sugars to flourish and sparkle while the oak criss-crosses the piece with some excellent anchoring vanilla notes. A joy. 59.8%. sc. 249 bottles. Whisky Tasting Club Bottling.

SLYRS Schliersee-Neuhaus. Working.

◇ **Slyrs Bavarian Single Malt Whisky Aged 12 Years** American oak casks, bott code: A 3875 db **(88.5)** n22 t23 f21.5 b22 A typical Slyrsian bottling, this, with the intensity of the barley practically launching itself into orbit, despite the close attentions of vanilla-riddled oak. But also bitterness on the finish which subtracts enough to rob it of greatness. 43%.

◇ **Slyrs Bavarian Single Malt Whisky Classic** American oak casks, bott code: D09951 db **(85)** n21 t21.5 f21 21.5 Malty, rich and even minty. But by no means, alas, technically one of their better bottlings. 43%.

◇ **Slyrs Bavarian Single Malt Whisky Fifty One** bott code: A L18932 db **(91.5)** n22.5 hazelnut and chocolate mixing in with the rich, toasty barley; t23.5 molasses gets into the act early and helps give the barley some serious weight. The softness of the mouthfeel works brilliantly with the quick early spice, too: a superb delivery! f22.5 happy to fall back on to the vaguely spicy vanillas and cream toffee...remains soft and succulent; b23 Slyrs in tip-top form adding creamy dark sugars to their usual concentrated malt. Delicious! 51%.

◇ **Slyrs Bavarian Single Malt Whisky Rum Cask** Finishing bott code: C2941 db **(90.5)** n23 classic, from the point of view of the rum cask giving a real major rigid outer shell to the malt: beautiful balance and structure; t23 again, there is a crispness here oft associated with a decent rum cask, the sugars adding as much to the structure as the flavour. When the barley bursts through it so robustly; f22 just a little wide on the cut; b22.5 forget the rum: this is all about the malt! 46%.

⬥ **Sild Crannog Single Malt Whisky 2019** bott code: 3207 db **(94) n23** the smoke, rather than being a consistent plume, appears in puffs like signals atop a hill: dry, patchy...almost green with a degree of youth. A vague molasses note lingers...; **t24** the initial hit is a slightly confused one, the incomplete smoke thumping into the barley. Slowly, though, things begin to make sense and the phenols build, the sugars keep a respectful distance, vanillas caress and the natural oils give the entire picture a sheen. Indeed, these oils now ensure a softness, punctured only by the growing confidence of the spice; **f23** lightly oiled vanilla – and now the spice and smoke are one and the same; **b24** sometimes it can be the texture of a whisky that wins your heart and makes you swoon. Here is one such malt. No feints: whisky as it should be. It is not unknown for me to have sild sandwiches, sild being a type of oily fish: young herring. I'd make a sandwich of this whisky any day.... *48%.*

SPREEWOOD DISTILLERS GMBH Schlepzig. Working.

Stork Club 100% Rye New Make bott 26 Mar 19 db **(90) n22 t24 f22 b22** Surprisingly tight and quiet on both nose and finish. But the delivery is another matter entirely with explosive grain followed by exemplary new make chocolate mousse follow through. *72.01%. ncf.*

Stork Club 100% Rye Still Young Aged 2 Years heavily toasted virgin American oak casks, bott 26 Mar 19 db **(94.5) n23.5 t24 f23 b24** Still young...but grey hairs already, and all in the most distinguished places... *59.87%. ncf.*

Stork Club 100% Rye Still Young Aged 2 Years medium toasted virgin German Napoleon oak casks, bott 26 Mar 19 db **(91.5) n23 t23 f22.5 b23** On this evidence the Germans should have an annual celebration of local whisky matured in native wood: Oaktoberfest.... *59.7%. ncf.*

⬥ **Stork Club Full Proof Rye Whiskey** American & German oak, bott code: 10-19 db **(91) n23** the grain is sharp and unambiguous; a little mint to accompany the light orange and vanilla dais; **t23** immediately eye-watering as the naked rye bites, nibbles... and then sweetens: just so salivating! The wave of muscovado sugars comes as a surprise. A big vanilla presence hits the mid-point while the spices enter the fray; **f22** just a little oil from a slightly wide cut gathers, but the spices to their job; **b23** one of Germany's most consistently high-class distillers has struck again! Delightfully crafted rye. *55%.*

Stork Club Single Malt Whiskey ex-bourbon, ex-sherry & ex-Weißwein casks, lot no. 008543 L002 db **(88.5) n22.5 t22.5 f21 b22.5** Not a faultless sherry butt. But one that offers more ticks than crosses. *47%. ncf.*

Stork Club Straight Rye Whiskey ex-bourbon & ex-Weißwein casks, batch no.2, lot no. 001030 5317 db **(92) n23 t23.5 f22 b23.5** Despite the spelling of whiskey, not to be confused with the American definition of a Straight Rye: the Weisswein cask sees to that! And I doubt if it is virgin American oak in play, either. That said, no faulting the overall composition of a rather lovely rye whisky – straight or otherwise *55%. ncf.*

ST. KILIAN DISTILLERS GMBH Rüdenau. Working.

St. Kilian Turf Dog Cask Strength los no. 180409 db **(95) n24 t23.5 f23.5 b24** Technically superb. Clean as a whistle while the peat has a politeness and decorum which suggests finesse and elegance in later life. As for the 63.5% abv – rarely come across a new make as soft and less fractious. Now let's just hope they find casks good enough to match the spirit: easier said than done. *63.5%.*

The Spirit of St. Kilian Batch No. 4 16 Months Old Islay, Texas & Kentucky casks, dist 2016 db **(91) n22.5 t23 f22.5 b23** The serenity of the spirit is there for all to see: one of the softest touches to any distillery on mainland Europe, which allows the most gentle wisp of smoke to add more of a backbone than might otherwise be expected. Playful tannins help beef up the sugars and, wonderfully, the barley itself is always fully detectable. *45%. 3,000 bottles.*

The Spirit of St. Kilian Batch No. 5 27 Months Old Amarone casks from Valpolicella, dist Apr 16 db **(95) n23 t24 f23.5 b24.5** Although I adore the wine from the Valpolicella region – indeed, the region itself, I have seldom encountered whisky which has been able to harness the brilliance of the grape. The fact that sulphur gets into the mix somewhere is probably the main reason. Well, no problem with that here. And while this is not officially a whisky, the ease with which the power of the fruit is combined with outstanding oak input and then rounded off by the unmistakable and unique barley-gorged gentleness of the spirit itself makes this a special experience. Can't wait until this is officially a whisky: if they can keep this balance (much easier said than done) I can see an award or two heading this distillery's way... *50%. 4,900 bottles.*

The Spirit of St. Kilian Batch No. 6 21 Months Old France, Texas & Kentucky casks, dist 2016 db **(86.5) n21.5 t22 f22 b21.5** No mistaking the St. Kilian style of a malt spirit: softer than a baby's bum. Just not quite so sure here of the flavour profile created. Beyond the sleepy phenols the other factors seem to cancel each other out, though a few spices do begin to emerge to shake things up a little. *44.9%. 5,200 bottles.*

The Spirit of St. Kilian Batch No. 7 22 Months Old bourbon, sherry & virgin oak casks, dist 2016/17 db **(77.5) n19 t22.5 f17 b19** While the delivery is stunningly textured with a near perfect degree of sweetness, the sulphur present does little for either the nose or finish. 44%.

◈ **St. Kilian Single Malt Whisky Signature Edition One** chestnut (5%), ex bourbon (37%), ex PX sherry (18%), ex bourbon quarter casks (3%) & ex Martinique (37%) casks, dist 2016, bott 2019, los nr. 190508 db **(88) n22.5 t23 f21.5 b21** Such is the singular shape of the tannins, a kind of nondescript nuttiness, you know there is chestnut cask involvement even before you look on the label for confirmation. The only surprise is that it is a mere 5%, because it comes through a lot louder and clearer than that here, both on nose and palate. There is a mouth-filling maltiness to this, but it is constantly mithered by tannin tones that refuse to settle or agree up on their strategy and end up a little too bitter for their own good. The result is a full-flavoured but slightly incoherent whisky which sparkles best when the acacia honey gets a few clear punches in... 45%. nc ncf.

◈ **St. Kilian Single Malt Whisky Signature Edition Two** ex Amarone 50L (3%), ex Amarone 325L (61%), & ex Amarone 225L (36%) casks, dist 2016, bott 2019, los nr. 190717 db **(75.5) n18 t21.5 f17 b19** Creamy textured but tight, bitter and very limited in development. Sometimes these casks work. Sometimes, like here, they are not a success. 54.2%. nc ncf.

◈ **St. Kilian Single Malt Whisky Signature Edition Three** peated 38 ppm, ex bourbon quarter casks (6%) & ex Tennessee Whiskey (94%) casks, dist 2016, bott 2019, los nr. 191113 db **(94.5) n23.5** makes no apologies for its big smoky richness. A little saltiness, too, which does no harm to the tannins trying to make an impression, the vanillas in particular. Big, bustling, enticing and always well controlled...; **t23.5** much more creamy than the nose would have you believe; buttery, even. Also, the sugars offer far more on delivery than you'd anticipate, light molasses sitting comfortably with the phenols and taking on an increasingly toasty character as the peat becomes sootier; **f23.5** no tang, no residue other than the skeleton of the peat and vanilla-rich tannins. Confirmation of just how well this spirit was made...; **b24** a distillery which can carry off subtlety even with a thumpingly well-peated malt. When St. Kilian are on form, they really do make first-class whisky! 50%. nc ncf.

◈ **St. Kilian Single Malt Whisky Signature Edition Four** peated 54 ppm, PX sherry (51%) & Oloroso (49%) casks, dist 2016, bott 2020, los nr. 200115 db **(84) n23 t23 f17.5 b20.5** I cannot say that the teaming of PX cask and high peat is one of my favourite combinations, not least because even if there isn't sulphur being hidden away, the battle between these two super egos rarely ends in harmony – and harmony and balance is always the key to good, let alone great, whisky. There is, as it happens, some nagging bitter sulphur lurking around on this, which rather does for the finish. But I have to say that I am uncommonly impressed by both the nose and delivery where the muscular peat is allowed to battle through the grape and heroically plant its flag. A decent experience...until the sulphur kicks in... 48%. nc ncf.

STEINHAUSER GMBH Kressbronn. Working.

◈ **Brigantia Aged 8 Years Single Malt** db **(89) n22 t22 f22.5 b22.5** Not sure if this has been matured in a warehouse housing apple brandy, because there is an essence of apfel from the first sniff to the last fruity dying note. Throughout the barley is shadowed by a light fruitiness. Even when it turns spicy, there is still a fruit and nut character lurking...and that fruit, of course, is apple.... 44%.

◈ **Brigantia Single Malt ex-Brandy Single Cask** db **(87.5) n22 t21.5 f22 b22** Clean, very young, delightfully malty and salivating but has the essence of a cider brandy. 52.1%.

◈ **Brigantia Classic Single Malt** db **(90) n22 t22.5 f23 b22.5** I'm massively impressed with this. Possibly the most beautifully distilled of all the German whiskies, the malt positively shimmers on both nose and palate. I do hope, though, that they allow their malts to mature further than this, as there is no great age on display here and you get the feeling that this was just setting out on the road, rather than completing the journey. 43%.

◈ **Brigantia Islay Cask Finish Single Malt** db **(92) n22.5 t23 f23 b23.5** A distillery which has proved that it can distil beautifully needs to find an excellent cask to properly showcase its wares. This it has done to impressive effect, with the phenols singing on the nose and dancing on the palate. Understatedly elegant with some lovely toasty cocoa tones to add to the delicate smoke, spice and molasses. 46%.

◈ **Brigantia Rum Cask Finish Single Malt** db **(88) n21 t23 f22 b22** Like many rum casks before, a crisp and firm embrace allows the malt to expand in personality only so far. What it can't control is the delivery which is full-bodied and sees the malt exploding in all directions, though in a controlled manner. Light chocolate tones also please. 46%.

◈ **Brigantia Schwaben Single Malt** db **(85) n20.5 t22 f21 b21.5** Never quite seems to find its stride or narrative. The nose and finish are not particularly attractive, though the creamy vanillas and light butterscotch on delivery is more than agreeable. 45%.

◇◇ **Brigantia Sherry Cask Finish Single Malt** db (82) n21.5 t21 f19.5 b20 No sulphur on the sherry....hurrah! But that' the only really good news as this never quite finds the meaning of life with too many tangy, untidy and slightly bitter threads are left untied. Some petulant and nagging spices do ensure some entertainment. 46%.

WHISKY-DESTILLERIE DREXLER Arrach. Working.

◇◇ **Bayerwold Pure Rye Malt Whisky** los no. L19, destilliert 2/13, abgefüllt 5/19 db (82.5) n19.5 t22 f20 b21 Well, they are nothing if not consistent these Dexler chaps. Just like the last bottling of their rye I encountered, some tasty and promosing rye bound and gagged by thudding feints. 42%. 186 bottles.

◇◇ **Bayerwold Single Malt Whisky** los no. L29, destilliert 8/20/14, abgefüllt 9/20/19 db (86) n19 t23 f22 b22 As kind as you'd like to be, not too much positive can be said about the feinty, vaguely butyric nose. However, the delivery: now that's a different matter! Barley on steroids, slightly of the grassy type but the Demerara sugars inject a further succulence that boasts weight, too. The finish is patchy, but still boasts a big maltiness which overcomes many of the obvious faults. 42%. 240 bottles.

◇◇ **Drexler Arrach No. 1 Bayerwald Single Cask Malt Whisky** Bourbonfass, fass no. H36, los no. L19, destilliert Dec 15, abgefüllt Sept 19 db (87.5) n21 t22 f22 b22.5 Ah, the Drexler character all over the nose: unmistakable! Theirs is a unique style, the extra feints here drumming up a fascinating combination of chestnut and cherries – even in a bourbon cask. Dry in part and always making you wonder where it is going next. Malty late on and entertaining. 46%. nc ncf sc. 72 bottles.

◇◇ **Drexler Arrach No. 1 Bayerwald Single Cask Malt Whisky** Cognacfass, fass no. H86, los no. L19, destilliert Aug 14, abgefüllt Sept 19 db (86.5) n20 t22.5 f22 b22 While the curiously salty nose never quite works, the gathering together of the more intense flavours for the main thrust of the delivery certainly get the juices running. Again, there is a deep saline content with spices matching the candied fruit punch for punch. Light cocoa notes at the death. 46%. nc ncf sc. 192 bottles.

◇◇ **Drexler Arrach No. 1 Bayerwald Single Cask Malt Whisky** portweinfass, fass no. H110, los no. L29, destilliert Nov 14, abgefüllt Sept 19 db (89) n21 murky feints with leaking chocolate liqueur...; t23.5 here we go: the famous Drexler mouth explosion...after unpromising experience on the nose, things start to go right on the palate. It isn't pretty as it feels like a loads of ecletic notes are being thrown together, yet somehow they gel and, more, develop. Salivating and rich: if the fruit were a colour it would be metallic tinted; f21.5 typically dirty from the wide cut, but some redeeming milk chocolate and vanillas with light sugars; b23 yes, it balances, but probably more by luck than judgement. As a piece of art, this whisky comes under the Abstract movement... 46%. nc ncf sc. 85 bottles.

◇◇ **Drexler Arrach No. 1 Bayerwald Single Cask Malt Whisky** sherryfass, fass no. H48, los no. L19, destilliert Aug 11, abgefüllt Sept 19 db (92) n22.5 thick, vaguely and quietly menacing with the barley acting as a sub-plot to the plummy fruits; t23 more than an element of cherry cough medicine to this: thick, lightly oiled and spices swirling with the muscado sugars...; f23 ulmo honey mixed with plum jam on light toast. Like on the delivery there is a narrative...and, at the death, that cough sweet character again...; b23.5 so often I leave the sherry-matured whisky to the last of the pack as, more often than not, it will be the weak link of a distillery's output. I have left this to last and...struck gold! No sulphur! And, unusually for a Drexler, no weakening feints. Just lyrical malt without a bum note... 46%. nc ncf sc. 205 bottles.

WHISKY-DESTILLERIE GRUEL Owen/Teck. Working.

Tecker Single Grain Whisky Aged 10 Years Chardonnay casks db (93) n23.5 t23 f23 b23.5 Now, that is all rather beautiful... 53.2%. ncf.

WHISKY DESTILLERIE LIEBL Bad Kötzting. Working.

Coillmór Single Malt Whisky Bavaria x Toscana II Caberlot Rotwein Cask Finish cask no. 687, destilliert 08 Jun 10, abgefüllt 13 Feb 19 db (80.5) n18.5 t23 f19 b20 A fantastic cask which radiates high quality grape from the moment it hits the palate. But even that struggles against the feints from the distillate. 46%. sc. 364 bottles.

Coillmór Single Malt Whisky Bayerische Weihnacht 2018 Edition rum cask, cask no. 268, destilliert 07 Sept 11, abgefüllt 18 Oct 18 db (87.5) n21 t23 f21.5 b22 Salty and almost seaworthy. The salt forms an interesting combination with the sweeter rum notes. Fantastically chewy and fulsome delivery, though! 46%. sc. 414 bottles.

Coillmór Single Malt Whisky Bourbon Single Cask 8.5 Jahre cask no. 209, destilliert 30 May 10, abgefüllt Jan 19 db (77) n18 t21 f19 b19 Custard sweet and malty in part. But the spirit is off key. 46%. sc. 650 bottles.

Coillmór Single Malt Whisky Sherry Quarter Cask 12 Jahre destilliert März 2006, abgefüllt 19 Dec 18 db **(90.5) n22.5 t23 f22 b23** Just about unrecognisable from the three other Coillmór whiskies I tasted this year as the feints don't impact detrimentally. Loads to enjoy here. 44%. sc. 464 bottles.

WHISKY DESTILLERIE BLAUE MAUS Eggolsheim. Working.

⬩⬩ **Blaue Maus New Make** dest Sept 18, los nr. 0918 db **(95) n24 t24 f23 b24** The last time I tasted their new make it was a mind-blowing 87%abv: this is a watered down and pathetic 81%, though have to say it really does seem a lot less. Beautifully smoked and garnished in cocoa, there is so much to enjoy here. 81%. sc.

Blaue Maus Single Cask Malt Whisky German oak cask, fass/los nr. 1, destilliert May 10 db **(89.5) n22 t22.5 f22.5 b22.5** A very quiet mouse with a penchant for nougat. 40%. sc.

⬩⬩ **Blaue Maus Single Cask Malt Whisky** German oak cask, fass/los nr. 1, destilliert Jun 13 db **(88.5) n22 t23 f21.5 b22** Reminds me, this, of when I eat authentic local food in India, so busy and slowly warming are the spices. Not quite so buttery and malty as usual but the heather honey pinnacle on delivery is superb. 40%. sc.

⬩⬩ **Blaue Maus Single Cask Malt Whisky Fassstärke** German oak cask, fass/los nr. 1, destilliert Mar 02 db **(86.5) n20.5 t22 f22 b22** Feinty and chewy, the nose might be a bit of a mause trap but the extra oils on the body certainly make the most of maple syrup and delicate spices. 48.1%. sc.

Blaue Maus Single Cask Malt Whisky Fassstärke German oak cask, fass/los nr. 2, destilliert Feb 05 db **(85) n20.5 t22.5 f21 b21** One of the feinty Blaue Maus efforts, with the usual mix of drying spices and richer heather honey tones. 45.2%. sc.

⬩⬩ **Elbe 1 Single Cask Malt Whisky** German oak casks, fass/los nr. 5, destilliert Apr 08 db **(90) n21.5** gentle vanillas swell; **t23** a lovely, salivating combination of intense, well manicured malt and a succession of gentle honey notes starting with ulmo- and working through to heather-honey. Beautifully paced: so relaxed; **f22.5** surprisingly long with the honey and malt theme continuing, even when the tannins and spices make their move; **b23** gentle and elegant. 40%. sc.

⬩⬩ **Elbe 1 Single Cask Malt Whisky Fassstärke** German oak casks, fass/los nr. 1, destilliert Apr 06 db **(88) n21 t22 f22.5 b22.5** Maybe a bit wonky on the nose. But the salivating delivery is the prelude to a beautifully honeyed slow burn as the flavours build up like tributaries feeding a stream. The heather honey and light spice at the death charms. 45%. sc.

⬩⬩ **Grüner Hund Single Cask Malt Whisky** German oak casks, fass/los nr. 1, destilliert Jun 08 db **(88.5) n22.5 t22.5 f21.5 b22.** Another whisky which has suffered by the drastic weakening of strength. Some gorgeous acacia and ulmo honey notes gel well with the salt and vanilla. But dries out massively toward the end as there isn't quite muscle enough to support the structure. 40%. sc.

Grüner Hund Single Cask Malt Whisky Fassstärke German oak casks, fass/los nr. 1, destilliert Oct 05 db **(91) n22.5 t23 f22.5 b23** Usually expect a little bourbon theme, but this one is toned down. 46.7%. sc.

Grüner Hund Single Cask Malt Whisky Fassstärke German oak casks, fass/los nr. 1, destilliert Apr 04 db **(88.5) n21 t22.5 f22.5 b22.5** Peculiar. 42.1%. sc.

Jubiläums Abfüllung 2018 Single Cask Malt Whisky 16 Years Old German oak casks, fass/los nr. 1, destilliert Feb 02 db **(89.5) n22 t22 f23 b22.5** Any oilier and they would be able to sell the drilling rights. That apart, a wonderfully relaxed German whisky. 40%. sc.

Mary Read Single Cask Malt Whisky German oak cask, fass/los nr. 3, destilliert May 08 db **(89.5) n22 t22 f22.5 b22.5** Despite the jagged spices, the sugars do a superb job. 40%. sc.

⬩⬩ **Mary Read Single Cask Malt Whisky** German oak cask, fass/los nr. 4, destilliert Apr 09 db **(90) n22** a vaguely Kentuckian feel to this; **t23** red liquorice and maple syrup combine with salivating harmony. A little hickory, too, as the bourbon theme continues; **f22.5** light marzipan and barley, always that glint of Kentucky; **b22.5** always regard this as the closest thing they produce to a bourbon-style whisky. The tannins have a sweet and significant input. 40%. sc.

⬩⬩ **Old Fahr Single Cask Malt Whisky** German oak cask, fass/los nr. 2, destilliert Jun 10 db **(82) n20 t21 f20 b21** Not the old charmer I was expecting. Fahr too feinty... 40%. sc.

Old Fahr Single Cask Malt Whisky German oak cask, fass/los nr. 5, destilliert May 09 db **(89) n22.5 t22.5 f22 b22.5** Delicate and delightful. 40%. sc.

⬩⬩ **Old Fahr Single Cask Malt Whisky Fassstärke** German oak cask, fass/los nr. 1, destilliert May 05 db **(86) n20 t22.5 f21.5 b22** Once past the messy, butyric nose the flavours explode on the palate in salivating fashion, making a big play with the spiced orange blossom honey, moving them into eye-watering citruses. Technically incoherent, this certainly packs a punch. Not sure whether to love or hate it: even by Blaue Maus standards this is pretty outrageous. 52.1%. sc.

Schwarzer Pirat Single Cask Malt Whisky German oak cask, fass/los nr. 1, destilliert Mar 00 db **(90) n22 t22.5 f23 b22.5** Imagine Kentucky bourbon chocolate... 51.2%. sc.

⬦ **Schwarzer Pirat Single Cask Malt Whisky** German oak cask, fass/los nr. 1, destilliert Jul 06 db (**77**) n22 t21 f16 b18 Starts so well with nuts and citrus on the nose followed by a vague bourbon, sugary delivery...then it all goes horribly wrong as the far too bitter as spices dig in. What the hell happened there...? 40%. sc.

Schwarzer Pirat Single Cask Malt Whisky German oak cask, fass/los nr. 4, destilliert Jun 10 db (**90.5**) n22.5 t23 f22 b23 A relaxed, even, high class malt. 40%. sc.

Seute Deern Single Cask Malt Whisky German oak cask, fass/los nr. 1, destilliert Mar 10 db (**90.5**) n22 t23 f22.5 b23 For once, it is a shame that I live and work nearly five miles from the nearest shop: I could do with a Milky Way bar right now... 40%. sc.

⬦ **Spinnaker Single Cask Malt Whisky** German oak cask, fass/los nr. 1, destilliert Apr 09 db (**78**) n19 t20 f19 b20 My least favourite of the Blaue Maus cannon and it hasn't let me down again – or has, depending how you look at it. The reduction in strength has done it few favours as the butyric is still there, but the lowering in strength has upped the dry chalkiness and lowered the sugars. 40%. sc.

Sylter Ellenbrogen Single Cask Malt Whisky German oak cask, fass/los nr. 2, destilliert Feb 07 db (**86.5**) n22 t22 f21 b21.5 Changed tack from the last time I tasted this, now taking an extra dry course, at one point to near eye-watering effect. 40%. sc.

Spinnaker Single Cask Malt Whisky Fassstärke German oak cask, fass/los nr. 1, destilliert Apr 12 db (**81.5**) n19 t21.5 f20 b21 Just too aggressively spicy and dry in key places to find a good equilibrium. A touch of butyric on the nose, also. 43.5%. sc.

WHISKY-DESTILLERIE MEW Neuried. Working.

⬦ **MEW Single Malt Whisky 8 Years Old** Jamika rum finish, fass no. 1, bott 14 Apr 19, bott code: L2011 db (**91.5**) n23 heather honey and pineapple cubes. Toned down with caramel; t23.5 soft, succulent and increasingly salivating. The malt makes a stand for a few moments before the caramels move in; f22.5 remains chewy and increasingly more toasty; b22.5 far less esters than the Salamansar Jamaica rum bottling, which means less depth. A very gentle journey, and never less than delicious, but might benefit further from upping the strength slightly 42%. nc sc.

⬦ **MEW Single Malt Whisky Single Cask Collection 8 Years Old** Pedro Ximénez sherry finish, PX-fass no. 1, bott 8 Apr 19, bott code: L111 db (**86.5**) n22 t23 f20 b21.5 A well-made, clean malt tipped into an excellent but not quite unspoiled PX cask. Very attractive and much to commend it. However, the one-dimensional style of the PX rather means the flavour course is unwavering and as beautiful as this whisky may be, it lacks rather in personality. 40%. nc sc.

⬦ **MEW Single Malt Whisky Single Cask Collection 8 Years Old** Oloroso sherry finish, Oloroso-fass no. 1, bott 25 Apr 19, bott code: L222 db (**86**) n22.5 t21.5 f21 b21.5 Unerringly sherry dominated. But just a little too bitter, if you bitte... 40%. nc sc.

UNSPECIFIED

Trader Sylter Single Malt Whisky Ardmore PX cask, cask no. 36, dest Oct 14, bott Nov 18 (**89.5**) n22.5 t23.5 f21.5 b22 If was hoped that the Ardmore would infuse some magical light phenols into the character, then they were being slightly too optimistic. Any peat there may have been has been crushed out of existence by the marauding grape. But no faulting the lush fruit effect, which has a real Christmas pudding feel to it. 56.5%. sc.

Trader Sylter Single Malt Whisky PX cask, cask no. 1018, dest Dec 14, bott Nov 18 (**90.5**) n22.5 t23 f22 b23 A much better PX cask here with the malt actually getting some air- time despite thickness of the grape. Superb heather honey in the mix. 56.5%. sc.

ICELAND
EIMVERK DISTILLERY Gardabaer. Working.

⬦ **Flóki Icelandic Single Malt Whisky 3 Year Old Single Cask** ex-Flóki Young Malt casks, cask no. 21, bott 2019 db (**85.5**) n21 t22 f21 b21.5 Big and malty but a vague tobacco note hangs around, starting at the nose and holding a presence through to the very finish, which turns a tad bitter. The barley is big though at times glacial in its quality and is at its height moments after the delivery. Attractive, if a little untidy. 47%. sc.

⬦ **Flóki Icelandic Single Malt Whisky Icelandic Birch Finish** American oak, finished in Icelandic birchwood, cask no. 3, bott 2020 db (**90.5**) n22 the tannins are stark and barge their way to the front with almost indecent haste; a slightly wide cut, but acceptable; t23 controlled enormity. The wide cut promised on the nose is apparent immediately. But then so is that outrageous tannin. When they meet they form far greater harmony than on the nose, no doubt thanks to a massive dose of maple syrup and manuka heather honey. Toasted fudge for the middle and gorgeous cocoa tones, too...; f22.5 more toastiness, but the butterscotch tart and roasted hazelnut calms things charmingly; b23 birch wood...? They should have no problem flogging this... Beautifully idiosyncratic. And though the first two or three mouthfuls are a shock, once you acclimatise, so many things suddenly become visible...; *47%. sc.*

⬧ **Flóki Icelandic Single Malt Whisky Sheep Dung Smoked Reserve 3 Year Old** ex-Flóki Young Malt casks, cask no. 8, bott 2020 db **(91.5) n22 t22.5** that light feint note is hanging around, but again something else is at work to incorporate it positively into the aroma. A sweet grassy, smokiness...which, now I think about it, kind of makes sense...; **t23.5** more salivating than a saddle of lamb. Well, almost. Barley abounds, but so too, does that fresh grassy note. It can't be...surely? **f22.5** heftier, earthier now with those light feints returning, but a phenolic spiciness kicks up; **b23** and I remember the ancient days when Sheep Dip was supposed to be the avant-garde whisky... Should do well in baaaahhhs the world over... I suggest this whisky's taken neat, with neither water... nor mint sauce... *47%. sc.*

ISRAEL
THE MILK & HONEY DISTILLERY Tel Aviv-Yafo. Working.

⬧ **Milk & Honey Classic Single Malt Whisky** db **(92) n22 t23.5 f23.5 b23** A dry malt which keeps the sugars under control at all times. The result is a complex dram where the barley plays an ever-increasing part in the overall flavour structure, especially when it finds it has muscle enough to accept the growing oak without for a moment losing its poise. Reminds me of some old malt whiskies from Scotland that could be found in the early 1980s where intense malt met equally full-on oak but had personality enough to ride the storm. Loses a mark for a hint of juniper on the nose: I didn't know they made gin at this distillery. I'd bet any money now that they do. Chaps, please be more careful in your bottling hall. Otherwise, absolutely delicious. *46%.*

⬧ **The Milk & Honey Distillery Single Cask La Maison Du Whisky 2019** db **(94.5) n23 t23.5 f24 b24** On the evidence of this, we have a distillery that has to be taken very seriously, indeed. Like their Classic, the malt has a rare intensity that is nothing less than captivatingly gorgeous. At cask strength, and with no water added to break down the essential oils which carries the word even further, the malt remains honest and intact throughout, the sugars sticking rigidly to the concentrated barley. The tannins also take on an extra dimension, not entirely lacking a bourbon-esque quality with light liquorice and molasses forming complex patterns within the unrelenting purity of the malt. Made no mistake: this is truly brilliant malt whisky, the mocha towards the end offering both complexity and class to the never-ending finale. *55%. sc.*

⬧ **Milk & Honey Elements Single Malt Whisky Israeli Red Wine** db **(92.5) n22.5 t23.5 f23 b23.5** Whichever red wine they used, you get the distinct feeling that it was pretty full bodied and dry: indeed, the kind of chalky middle-eastern wines I adored with lamb. Certainly this is a fat beast on the delivery both the oils from the malt and the richer elements of the fruit combining to give the deep oaky tones a run for their money. A malt which handsomely repays time and perseverance as the Murray Method certainly unlocks far more complexity than at first seems apparent. The growth of the spices is also a feature and curiously increases its presence as the malt begins to flourish. Complex and superbly well-weighted. *46%.*

⬧ **Milk & Honey Elements Single Malt Whisky Peated** db **(84.5) n21.5 t22 f20.5 b20.5** A bit of a mess, this. Well distilled, though the half-hearted peat is never entirely convincing. But there seems to be something else at play here...gin, again, perhaps. Maybe, maybe not. Whatever, the flavour profile is confused and a little odd, the finish in particular. *46%.*

⬧ **Milk & Honey Elements Single Malt Whisky Sherry** db **(87) n21 t22.5 f21.5 b22** About a year ago I was at my home in Kentucky and had been invited to a plush event that required a tuxedo. Discovering I presently didn't have one in the USA, I went to the tailor who had faithfully served me for the last 20 years and bought from him a "brand new" penguin suit. On the evening I dressed into it for the very first time, I found that I could not get my glasses to fit into the inside jacket pocket. Which was a bit strange. Something was preventing them from going in. So I investigated and found that my brand new dinner jacket contained a silk-claret kippah. And three single one dollar bills. The kippah had been presented for the wedding of Naava and Michael Schottenstein on 12th January 2019. Mazel tov, Naava and Michael...! I wasn't quite sure what to do with this skullcap, (since when have I been Jewish? What do I want with a kippah? I have hats already!), until it was time to taste the Israeli whiskies. Then I for once removed my famous Panama and replaced it with my kippah which, as a respectful Gentile, I wear as I write this. Now everything seems right in the world. Well, almost. Seeing that this was an Israeli whisky from a sherry cask I must admit confused me. I was present – ooh, maybe 25 years ago now – when the first-ever kosher Scotch single malt was bottled. I had a good chat with the Rabbi who was present to give the whisky his thumbs up and blessing; and I distinctly remember him telling me that providing the whisky was not matured in sherry, there was no problem. Bourbon casks kosha. Sherry casks unkosher. So what's this then....? Actually, I'm scratching my non-covered bit of head to work it out. Like the peated malt, you get the feeling that there is some type of alien intervention that is playing games with the grape and sending confusing messages. The one thing that escapes the mêlée is the malt itself, which certainly manages to stand up for itself, and proudly. You know this is well made: the lusciousness of the mouthfeel confirms that. But... 46%.

ITALY
L. PSENNER GMBH Tramin an der Weinstrasse. Working.

Erético Italian Single Malt Whisky aged in grappa & sherry casks, bott code: L.19003 db **(91) n22 t23 f23 b23** The grappa cask influence is much stronger than I imagined could have been possible. Gives this whisky a unique signature...and one in italics, of course... 43%.

PUNI WHISKY DISTILLERY Glurns, Bozen. Working.

PUNI Alba Italian Single Malt batch no. 3, Marsala & Islay casks db **(95) n23.5 t24 f23.5 b24** They are getting rather good at this whisky lark, these Italians. The Marsala and Islay fit as elegantly as an Armani suit... 43%. nc ncf.

◇ **PUNI Arte I Italian Single Malt** db **(92) n23.5** the tannins bite very slightly, but the fangs are blunted by a delightful degree of lemon blossom honey; **t23** incredibly soft delivery: the teeth on the nose (so to speak) have been removed entirely. An assembly of caramels melts towards superb barley and ulmo honey; **f22.5** fades supinely, a little milk chocolate accompanying the light liquorice. The barley, though, is equal in longevity and grace; **b23** just loses something in translation by dropping to 43%. The oils aren't quite abundant enough to take this to the next level of excellence. Even so, quite beautiful, unfailingly elegant and a lovely exhibition of honey. 43%. nc ncf.

◇ **PUNI Aura Italian Single Malt** 2 years in bourbon barrels & 4 years in peated Scotch whisky casks from Islay, dist 2012, bott 2019 db **(96.5) n24** this could be a blueprint for how maturing in peated cask works – they are the only boys who can match Penderyn and Cotswolds in that skill. The binding between the bourbony, slightly honeyed tannin and the phenols is stunning...; **t24.5** a divine meeting between the reserved sooty dryness of the peat and the joyful abandon of the acacia honey and gristy barley. But this isn't about flavour alone: it is mouthfeel – with the gorgeous and cleverly weighted oils – and constant churning over the two main antagonists, the peat and the honey; **f23.5** long with a slow fade towards ulmo honey and vanilla, though the smoke always offering a mildly weighty presence; at last delicate spices arrive and play out the last moments; **b24.5** this distillery is beginning to seriously impress me: the high scores from last year were obviously no flash in the pan. Make no mistake: this is beautifully constructed malt whisky: I doubt if Michelangelo could have done better. A European Whisky of the Year contender for certain. 56.2%. nc ncf. 393 bottles 🏆.

PUNI Gold 5 Year Old Italian Single Malt ex-bourbon barrels db **(92.5) n23 t23.5 f22.5 b23.5** An understated honey fest. 43%. nc ncf.

◇ **PUNI Sole 4 Year Old Italian Single Malt** batch no. 04, bourbon barrels & Pedro Ximénez sherry casks db **(90.5) n22.5** they promise blood orange on the label, and blood orange you get! **t23.5** a luxurious mouthfeel and, for once, the PX doesn't stick its sugar-sticky beak where it isn't wanted. Instead we are treated to a beautiful wave of barley with heather honey and light muscovado sugars forming the guard of honour; **f21.5** a dull now and marginally furry for technical reasons, shall we say. But light butterscotch hangs on in there; **b23** now this is where I take my hat off and bow. Normally I face a PX cask much in the same way a revolutionary might face a firing squad. Is the PX cask 100% uncontaminated with sulphur? Actually, no it isn't. But the taint is minimal and this is a brilliant example of how to bring PX into the mix without it dominating to the deficit of all else. 46%. nc ncf.

PUNI Vina 5 Year Old Italian Single Malt Marsala casks db **(94) n23.5 t24 f23 b23.5** Amazing what happens when you put very decent malt spirit into excellent, untainted casks. Bravo!! 43%.

LIECHTENSTEIN
TELSER DISTILLERY Triesen. Closed.

Telser Liechtenstein Annual Release No. 1 Double Grain triple cask db **(92) n22.5 t24 f22 b23.5** Just incredible mouthfeel to this. And to add to the joy, the sugar profile is just about unique, the lion's share of the flavour profile dedicated to a beautifully lush malt concentrate. Liquid ulmo honey fills in the gaps. Something very different and simply brilliant. 44.6%. sc.

Telser Liechtenstein Annual Release No. 2 rum & bourbon cask db **(84.5) n20 t22 f21 b21.5** Slightly bitter and unbalanced. By this distillery's normally high standards, they have fired a blanc... 46%. sc. 150 bottles.

THE NETHERLANDS
ZUIDAM BAARLE Nassau. Working.

Millstone Dutch Single Malt Whisky Aged 10 Years American Oak bott code: 0378ZU db **(92.5) n24 t23 f22.5 b23** Bang on the money with the honey and the malt. Love it!! 43%.

Millstone Dutch Single Malt Whisky Aged 10 Years French Oak bott code: 2927 ZU db **(88.5) n22 t22 f22.5 b22** A surprise malt, this. French oak normally belts out a bit more bite and tannic pungency. Here it seems to be happy to go with the malty flow. 40%.

Millstone Dutch Single Malt Whisky Aged 12 Years Sherry Cask nbc db **(86) n22 t21.5 f21 b21.5** A clean sherry butt, but there are buts. There is a tang from the spirit itself which gives a slight feinty buzz. Characterful, but there is a dark side. 46%.

Millstone 1999 Dutch Single Malt Whisky Single Pedro Ximénez Cask nbc db **(91.5) n23 t23 f23 b22.5** I cannot say I am any kind of fan of whisky matured in PX. But here I have thought: if you can't beat 'em... The grape dominates entirely and it is, as a drinking experience, entirely enjoyable as this must have been an absolutely top quality PX cask – and one free of sulphur (a rarity back in 1999). The malt, of course, long ago waved the white flag... 46%. ncf sc. Special #2.

Millstone 2010 Dutch Single Malt Whisky Double Sherry Cask Oloroso & PX nbc db **(88) n22.5 t22 f21.5 b22** Like most PX involved whiskies, don't bother looking too hard for complexity. 46%. Special #16.

Millstone Dutch Single Malt Whisky Oloroso Sherry bott code: 0328ZU db **(81) n19 t23 f18 b21** Make no mistake: this is a fabulous, faultless sherry butt at work here. And the delivery offers grapey bliss. But, sadly, the underlying structure of the spirit itself throws up a few question marks. 46%.

◈ **Millstone Dutch Single Malt Whisky Oloroso Sherry** bott code: 0580ZU db **(84.5) n21 t21.5 f21 b21** Eye-wateringly tart. 46%.

Millstone Dutch Single Malt Whisky Peated Double Maturation American oak, Moscatel cask finish, dist 2013, nbc db **(89) n22 t22.5 f22 b22.5** An oily and deceptively full bodied whisky. Full entertainment value here. 46%. Special #14.

Millstone Dutch Single Malt Whisky Peated Pedro Ximenez bott code: 0659ZU db **(89.5) n22.5 t22 f22.5 b22.5** One of the combinations which most consistently fails around the world is peat and PX, one seemingly always cancelling out the other. Here, though, it somehow works and though complexity and elegance are at a premium, it is not short on personality. 46%.

◈ **Millstone Dutch Single Malt Whisky Peated Pedro Ximenez** bott code: 0590ZU db **(91) n22.5** the wine wisely takes a back seat while the phenols attractively dominate; **t23** whooomph!!! Take that, palate!!! The grape and peat gang together to give the taste buds a right thumping. But with feathered floves; **f22.5** back comes the smoke, but a little more brittle this time. Spices, too..; **b23** I still remain no great fan of the unholy trinity of PX, peat and barley. But. have to say that this one does have enough character, on the delivery especially, to win a few friends...me included! 46%.

Millstone Dutch Single Rye 92 Rye Whisky 100% new American oak casks, nbc db **(94) n23.5 t23.5 f23 b24** Everything I was hoping from their 100 Rye, but never got. A European mainland classic! And less of a Millstone: more of a milestone... 46%.

Millstone Dutch Single Rye 100 Rye Whisky 100% new American oak casks, bott code: 0338ZU db **(77) n19 t19 f20 b19** As the world's first, longest serving and still most full bloodied advocate of rye whisky, had to say I was looking forward to this one - the grain having been ground in a Dutch windmill, no less. However, I have problems getting past a Geneve-style nose and delivery which, as much as I like, just isn't talking "rye whisky" to me. Good cocoa on the finale, though. 50%.

◈ **Millstone Mill am oak 10 Year Old** db **(87) n21.5 t22.5 f21 b22** Bit of a curiosity this one: the crunchiness of the barley on this is as hard as the millstone which crushed the malt. Out of sync on both nose and finish – there is a distinct tang to the finish of the latter – this is all about the gorgeous sugars that meld with the barley for the bright and chewy delivery. 46%.

◈ **Single Barrel Oloroso Sherry 23 Year Old** db **(93.5) n23.5** fruitcake straight from the oven with the outer raisins crisped to a turn; **t23.5** sultry and soft, gentle weaving of plumy fruits and tannin; **f23.5** now a mx of vanilla sponge and fruitcake...always melting in the mouth; spices take their time to accrue by making their mark very warmly, indeed; **b23** a faultless sherry butt paints a very pretty picture of oloroso at its most luxuriant: delicious! The whisky, though, appears to have been lost somewhere along the line... 46%. sc. Special #18.

NORWAY
AURORA SPIRIT DISTILLERY AS Lyngseidet. Working.

◈ **Bivrost Niflheim Artic Single Malt Whisky** triple cask matured db **(88.5) n22 t23 f21 b22.5** So Norway proudly joins the roll call of world whisky nations, and with this first-ever bottling also completes the Scandinavian set. It is certainly a creature hewn from its land, as this is a malt that matches the country's rugged geology with an awe-inspiring delivery, full of peaks and valleys, inlets and fjords: it is not an easy whisky to navigate. The nose is far from perfect, revealing a feinty nature which you know will return on the finish. The Murray Method will help you burn some of those oils off and release more of the lime blossom honey that is dying to escape and reveal something a lot more enticing, sexy even. The delivery, though, is about as rugged as it comes thanks again to those big oils, but also the malt which is fighting its corner frantically. Again the honey comes up for air, but it's frantic stuff - especially when the feints make their predictable return. So, a wonderful choice for my 1,000th sample for the Whisky Bible 2021. A King amongst Scandinavian malts and an experience you can't afjord to miss... *46%. 1,622 bottles.*

MYKEN DESTILLERI AS Nordland. Working.

◇ **Myken Artic Single Malt Whisky Hungarian Touch 2019 3 Years 10 Months** db (93) **n23** salted malt. Lemon blossom honey lightens the picture; **t23.5** a truly astonishing oiliness here, especially considering this is a superb cut without a hint of feints. As on the nose, the barley is both intense and displaying a salty edge; **f23** chalkier as the vanillas kick in, but remarkably sweet and soothing as a late gristiness to the malt makes its mark; **b23.5** is a Hungarian touch salty...? Beautifully made and matured whisky that keeps things simple. *47%.*

◇ **Myken Artic Single Malt Whisky Octave Symphony 2020 4 Year Old** db (95) **n23.5** surprisingly rich and confident for a brand new distillery in a brand new distilling nation. Vanilla and an extraordinary degree of coastal saltiness... **t24** a hugely satisfying delivery. It is a malt that cruises where Demerara sugars belting out rich but crisp fruity vibe which mingles with and then marries the malt which becomes increasingly intense. Again, there is a very profound coastal saline feel to this; **f23.5** this is the point where you expect any faults in the whisky to catch up with you. But there are none: just a stunning salty-chocolate theme continued with the vanillas and malt still magnificently entangled; **b24** this is actually far better than the last eight scotch single malts I tasted: not a sulphur molecule in sight. "Robert Louis Stevenson, Robbie Burns, Robert The Bruce, Bonnie Prince Charlie, Alec Salmond, Sean Connery, The Loch Ness Monster vi har slått dem alle sammen, vi har slått dem alle sammen! Nicola Thatcher can you hear me? Margaret Sturgeon... your distilleries took a hell of a beating! Your distilleries took a hell of a beating!" *47%.*

◇ **Myken Artic Single Malt Whisky Peated Sherry 2019 3 Year Old** db (94.5) **n23.5** this is ribald peat: naked and raunchy and smeared all over with lightly salted grape; **t24** what an amazing delivery. And a mouthfeel which is one of the most remarkable I have tasted for a little while. This smoky succulence, something you encounter, when writing the Bible, only three or four times a year. Despite the peat, despite the dripping fruit juice, somehow still the malt makes its mark, a serious barley-rich core to the piece. From the midpoint the salt steams in, too...; **f23** salty vanillas as the casks get a word in. The phenols are much more abstract here...; **b24** I think they mean sherried peat... Some great complexity here. And they have been judicious in their choice of cask, which is 100% sulphur free. *47%.*

◇ **Myken Artic Single Malt Whisky Solo PX 2020 4 Year Old** db (88.5) **n22 t22.5 f22 b22** A perfectly sound, sulphur-free sherry cask. That's the good news. The not so good news is that this PX cask does what PX casks do: they wipe out any trace of the malt or the distillery identity. Except in this case for the salt, which fair rattles about the nose and palate. So, yes, very enjoyable, if at times overly sweet and sticky in a cloying, old date kind of way. But hearty congrats on them obviously going out of their way to secure a pure and clean butt. *59.7%. sc.*

PORTUGAL
VENAKKI DISTILLERY Alpiarça. Working.

◇ **Woodwork Batch No. 1 Cask Strength Blended Whisky** ex-bourbon barrels with first fill barrique of ex-Douro wine and ex-Madeira wine, bott Apr 20 db (87.5) **n21.5 t22 f22 b22** Simutaneously light and aggressive. That said, juicy, sweet and easy drinking despite the strength, but never quite achieves the depth of layering you feel it is capable of. Enjoyable. *60.5%. nc ncf.*

◇ **Woodwork Cask Strength Single Malt Whisky** matured in a 20 year old vintage port Tawny cask, first maturation in a bourbon barrel with extra maturation in a single cask first fill 500l, cask no. 1, bott Apr 20 db (93) **n23** when you get spices buzzing like so many bees then you know this is going to be one very active whisky. Especially when so much sharp fruit is keeping it company. Young, but no shortage of confidence bordering on chutzpah...; **t23.5** wow! A direct transfer of personality from nose to delivery: the spices and fruit strong arm their way around the palate, again the fruit at times taking sharp and angular turns. Dramatically so on occasion...; **f23** settles down to a light chocolate fruit fade, the sugars taking a far more molassed nuance...; **b23.5** this is the first cask from a brand new distillery? Astonishing. I chose this as whisky number 999 for the Whisky Bible 2021. And so glad I did for this is top- flight quality, clean enough not to interrupt the intricate flow of the barrel influence; hefty enough to allow a little malty breeze to ruffle fruit leaves. For a first bottling... amazing. And for an entire nation...? They have done Portugal proud... *63.8%. nc ncf sc.*

◇◇◇ **Woodwork Duoro STR Cask Strength Single Malt Whisky** first maturation in a bourbon barrel with extra maturation in a single cask first fill 225l, cask no. 8, bott Apr 20 db **(94) n23** sharp with more than a hint of saltiness to the nipping kumquat and tannin. Almost a semi-bourbon feel to this....; **t23.5** wow..! A eye-watering puckering delivery with the salivating fruit, heather honey and concentrated malt in belligerent mode and the molasses not mucking around, either; **f23.5** warming spices at full throttle as the tannins get ever toastier. A lovely dark chocolate flourish towards signs it off beautifully; **b24** you can certainly count on STR casks to kick up the piercing juiciness and it doesn't let you down here! Some statement being made here, believe me! *64.6%. nc ncf sc.*

◇◇◇ **Woodwork Duoro STR Cask Strength Single Malt Whisky** first maturation in a bourbon barrel with extra maturation in a single cask first fill 225l, cask no. 9, bott Apr 20 db **(91) n22** much more dosed up on tannins than their previous bottling. Quite heady with the exception of a lighter citrus tone; **t23.5** after the early molasses we soon hit spiced chocolate which settles more into fruit and nut! **f22.5** so much natural caramel dripping from these casks. Quite a creamy toffee by the finish; **b23** a drier, more spiced-up version of Cask 8, with a load more caramel to boot...! Another gorgeous Portuguese single malt whisky. I wonder if that is the first time that last sentence has ever been written... *64.8%. nc ncf sc.*

◇◇◇ **Woodwork Madeira Cask Strength Single Malt Whisky** first maturation in a bourbon barrel with extra maturation in a single cask first fill 225l, cask no. 10, bott Apr 20 db **(91.5) n23** the grape is practically falling off the beefed-up tannin. Some noses try to get by without causing too much of a stir. The massive oak influence on this makes no chance of that...; **t23** oh, my word! The taste apes the nose and even ups the volume. The grape arrives first, but the spices need no second invitation to join it. As the molasses formulates, the tannins steam in...; **f22.5** you can't have this degree of tannin without a little bitterness creep in. However, it is a chocolatey element develops which, alongside the fruit, makes for an attractive, if slightly oily, fade...; **b23** well, that's made a statement. Venakki are not scared of going gung-ho on the flavour front and providing edge of seat, gripping entertainment. A few little changes will be required to be made if refinement ever becomes part of their plans. But, in the meantime, sit down, fasten your seatbelt...and hold on for dear life! *63.5%. nc ncf sc.*

SLOVAKIA
NESTVILLE DISTILLERY Hniezdne. Working.
Nestville Master Blender 9 Years Old Whisky bott 20 Jun 18 db **(93) n23 t23.5 f23 b23.5** My initial thoughts on tasting this was an extraordinary marriage between malt and bourbon styles. So it came as no surprise to learn that the grains involved in this clever vatting of barrels include both wheat and corn. You need to listen carefully to this whisky, as its subtlety means much can too easily go unheard, as some of what it says is shyly and gently spoken. And such is its unique style, in foreign tongue. *46%. 1,745 bottles.*

SPAIN
DISTILERIO MOLINO DEL ARCO Segovia. Working.
DYC Aged 8 Years (90) n22 t23 f22.5 b22.5. I really am a sucker for clean, cleverly constructed blends like this. Just so enjoyable! *40%*

DYC Single Malt Whisky Aged 10 Years (91) n22 t23 f23 b23 Far more complex than it first seems. Like Segovia, where the distillery is based, worth exploring...*40%*

DESTILERÍAS LIBER Granada. Working.
Whisky Puro Malta de Granada bott code: LOTE WM 08/001 db **(86.5) n22 t22 f21 b21.5** A rock hard malt with a titanium backbone. The flavours all tend towards the slightly bitter, toasty side, other than the softer malts which briefly star on delivery. Takes time to get used to the style, but worth the effort. *40%*.

◇◇◇ **Whisky Puro Malta de Granada** bott code: LOTE 19-014 db **(88) n22 t22.5 f21.5 b22** An hospitable and friendly malt throughout. Cream toffee and raison in abundance both on nose and delivery. The finish does dry with a little quaver to the previously clear tone but the sweetness levels are well tuned and seem to act as a perfect foil to healthy tannins. Enjoyable and at higher strength could certainly make a mark. *40%*.

SWEDEN
HIGH COAST DISTILLERY Bjärtrå. Working.
High Coast Distillery Archipelago Baltic Sea 2019 bott Dec 2018 db **(95) n24 t23 f23 b24** Nautical...but nice! A deep whisky...and deeply impressive. *54.5%. nc ncf. 1,000 bottles.*

High Coast Distillery Dálvve The Signature Malt bourbon casks, batch no. 8 db **(88)** **n22.5 t22.5 f21.5 b21.5** The gentle smoke and light vanilla tones compensate for a jerky base spirit. 46%. nc ncf.

High Coast Distillery Dálvve Sherry Influence sherry & bourbon casks db **(87) n21.5** **t22.5 f21.5 b21.5** Sometimes you can a little too much going on and here is a case of the fruit and smoke never quite getting it together. Perhaps not helped by the distillate, either. Smoke, juicy fruit and chocolate to be found. But it's all a muddle. 48%. nc ncf.

High Coast Distillery Quercus III Petraea unpeated, bourbon casks, 9 month virgin oak finish, bott Oct 18 db **(89) n22.5 t23 f21 b22.5** A remarkable whisky which appears to have driven every last sugar atom out of the grist and cask. 50.8%. nc ncf.

High Coast Distillery Small Batch No. 09 oloroso sherry casks, bott Dec 18 db **(94.5)** **n23.5 t24 f23 b24** There are many great reasons to visit Taiwan. Here's another one... 56%. nc ncf. 1,200 bottles. Exclusive to Taiwan.

High Coast Distillery Visitor Center Cask batch no. 5 db **(95.5) n24 t24 f23.5 b24** That's their best use of bourbon casks yet. Superb. There are many great reasons to visit Sweden. Here's another one...Hang on a minute, I'm on my way... 50%. nc ncf.

MACKMYRA Gästrikland. Working.

Mackmyra 10 Years Single Malt art. nr. MC-008 db **(89) n22.5 t23 f21.5 b22** Taking into account the use of the number on this bottling, not sure if I should be tasting this to Ravel's Balero... 46.1%.

Mack by Mackmyra bott code:080012 db **(84.5) n21 t21.5 f21 b21** Have to admit: did a double take when I nosed this one. For the first time in a very long while I came across an independent distiller lacing their nose with added caramel, the dry dustiness coupled with the total lack of expected malt sharpness or charm giving the game away. The bland pleasantness on delivery and failure of development confirmed it. Not sure what the Swedish is for "in God's name, why ?" I'll have to find out. 40%.

Mackmyra Brukswhisky art. nr. MB-003 db **(95.5) n24 t24 f23.5 b24** Like many of Mackmyra's whiskies, your senses have to be on full alert to enjoy it to its fullest...and as the whisky deserves. This is another Swedish tease, a whisky at the end of a fingertip and searching for all your secret nerve endings... 41.4%.

⬩ **Mackmyra Brukswhisky** art. nr. MB-004 db **(95.5) n24** such a soft, tender caress of an aroma: just the most fractional degree of smoke ensures anchorage (not something I have always found with this brand) while the sweetness is dependent on a delicate marzipan touch, the malt in close attendance. The citrus is a shade heavier than previous bottlings, but it is still the lovely phenol touch which insures the weight; **t23.5** lightly salted butter gives a gloss to the clean grain. The salivation levels rise as in slow motion; the vague phenol note does likewise. The interplay is mesmeric; **f24** the slow measured delivery is matched by the fade: like the setting of the Swedish summer sun, it takes its time and the vanillas build in brightness. The one exception to all this is the spice which builds at a speed out of sync with all else around it, and with far greater intensity; **b24** having just tasted a succession of Scotch whisky brands each spoiled at the end by the unmistakable and unforgiving pollutant of sulphur; and after giving my poor, duffed-up taste buds a rest of over an hour during which time strawberries and crisps were consumed to try and neutralise the deadening effect on my palate, I have deliberately re-started my tasting day with a whisky I know to be as clean yet entertaining as can possibly be found. Was this a wise choice? You bet! Carrying a little more weight than some previous bottlings but still a real Scandinavian beauty... 41.4%.

⬩ **Mackmyra Grönt** art. nr. MC-014 db **(91) n23.5** a salt on the nose...this has the feel of malt distilled using sea water. The saline notes give everything a sharp, three-dimensional feel...; **t23.5** varoooom! Off it goes again – the barley creamy and soft but improbably intense...once more with a salty cadence; fantastic light maple syrup and milk chocolate sub-plot; **f22** once the salt dies down, it is like the sun vanishing behind a cloud...a pretty standard caramel-malt finale; **b22.5** begins life bold and with a roar and finishes with a bit of a whimper. Bloody tasty and complex, though! 46.1%.

⬩ **Mackmyra Jaktlycka** db **(87.5) n23.5 t23.5 f19 b21.5** Concentrates on the grain and associated vanillas on delivery, which is some distance away from the sexy, passion fruit nose. The finish, though, is a little off beam thanks to the casks. 46.1%.

Mackmyra Moment Efva oloroso and birch sap wine casks, warehouse: Bodås Mine, art. nr. MM-028 db **(82) n22 t21 f19.5 b20** A very dull whisky strangling Mackmyra's famous flair at birth. And certainly at the deathy, also! 46.3%. 4,111 bottles.

Mackmyra Moment Fjällmark Swedish cloudberry wine casks, fatlagrad: Bodås Gruva, art. nr. MM-026 db **(90) n22 t22.5 f22.5 b23** Having spent quite a lot of time in Sweden, I can vouch they have a lot of clouds in that country, so a cloudberry wine is truly apt. A delightful flavour profile, and one unmatched by any other whisky in the world. 42%. 4,411 bottles.

⟐ **Mackmyra Moment Lava** db **(95) n24 t24 f23 b24** Maybe this should be called Momint, for the mintiness on the delivery is amazing! Usually this note can be achieved only by long aging in cask, in the same way diamonds can only come about through volcanic activity. And this really is a gem of a whisky combining an adroit usage of smoke with the vaguest undertones of clean raisins. But it is all there to be found with the Murray Method and time, unlocking some closely guarded secrets. Even the finish has that wonderful chocolate mint fade. This is blending at its very finest and European whisky that will be among the best to be found this year. 44.4%.

Mackmyra Moment Prestige fatlagrad: Bodås Gruva, art. nr. MM-025 db **(95) n23.5 t24 f23.5 b24** This could equally have been called "Precise" because every single aroma and movement in this whisky appears to have been orchestrated and choreographed to the last detail... 46.1%. 4,111 bottles.

Mackmyra Gruvguld art. nr. MC-010 db **(93.5) n23 t24 f23 b23.5** Some whiskies possess a serious and delicious chewability. And this is one of them... 46.1%.

Mackmyra Vinterglöd art. nr. MC-011 db **(84) n21.5 t22 f20 b20.5** I couldn't quite put my finger on why this was jarring with me a little, despite the spice kick. Then, on spotting the back of the bottle "aromatic profile: mulled wine" I suddenly realised exactly why I was marking it down. The degree of spice, like mulled wine, seemed forced and aggressive rather than a natural, organic progression from the oak maturation. Curious. 46.1%.

⟐ **Mackmyra Single Cask 2nd Fill ex-Bourbon Cask Fat Nr 11638** dist 26 Feb 14 db **(95.5) n24 t24 f23.5 b24** One of those brain-busting bottlings where the dryness if so intrinsic, yet the sweetness so confident, astonishing complexity pulses from every single atom. The smokiness is of the driest, most acidic and sooty kind, and obviously makes a point of being. The sweetness is of the heather-honey variety. Surely when those two meet the result will be a mess. Not a bit of it. Instead, the sugars melt down into a more marzipan nuttiness, the smoke oils up very slightly and embraces the honey. I have no doubt that when my much-loved friend Angela opened this cask for the first time and sampled its wares a few Swedish-Italian expletives of semi-orgasmic delight issued from her lips. And with every good reason! 51.4%. sc.

⟐ **Mackmyra Single Cask 2nd Fill ex-Bourbon Cask Fat Nr 11641** dist 26 Feb 14 db **(94.5) n24 t23.5 f23 b24** A close relation to cask 11638, but with some subtle but telling differences. Here both the dryness and sweetness are both just a notch below optimum intensity: no bad thing. The result is a drizzle of aromas and flavours rather than a downpour. But then that is the beauty of second fill bourbon cask, as a blender my preferred choice of cask to make memorable things happen. Here, though, the natural caramels have a bitter say, which means there was a little less left in the tank of this cask than the last one, thereby dumbing down slightly more the more intricate nature of the sugars and tannins combined. Even so...just so lovely! 50.8%. sc.

⟐ **Mackmyra Single Cask 1st Fill Gravity Amarone Wine Cask Fat Nr 34618** db **(93.5) n23.5 t23.5 f23 b23.5** The gooseberry jam on buttered toast nose has to be one of the best aromas of the day for me – certainly the most stomach rumbling. Likewise the delivery of warming cherry fruitcake with a light cocoa powder topping is ramping my appetite up further. This must be the ultimate pre-prandial whisky. It's certainly one good enough to eat.... 50.3%. sc.

⟐ **Mackmyra Single Cask 1st Fill Gravity Amarone Wine Cask Fat Nr 36558** db **(90) n23 t23 f21.5 b22.5** A marginally drier version of the Amorone above though sharper, too. And with far more of a niggle on the finish. But then when fruit is on song, it certainly hits the high notes. 50.3%. sc.

⟐ **Mackmyra Single Cask 1st Fill Gravity Port Wine Cask Fat Nr 37574** db **(88.5) n23 t22 f21.5 b22** Peppery on the nose – almost to sneezing point. But the fruit is a little too broad, yet intense and plummy, for top vibes even though a little custard too does make it into the mix. Untidy finale. 49.6%. sc.

⟐ **Mackmyra Single Cask 1st Fill Gravity Port Wine Cask Fat Nr 38624** db **(91.5) n23 t23 f22.5 b23** A slightly more jammy personality to the grape aligned with a better integrated spiciness makes for a much more comfortable ride here. Indeed, some of the phases on this are a joy, the custard making way for a slightly drier vanilla and even a wave or two of bourbon-style liquorice. Still the finish is not quite in tune with nose and delivery. The differences between this and cask 37574 are only minor, but when they add up there is a real feel of class to this one. 49.6%. sc.

⟐ **Mackmyra Single Cask 1st Fill ex-Bourbon Calvados Cask Fat Nr 40233** dist 10 Jun 17 db **(85.5) n22 t22 f20.5 b21** Just a little too aggressive with the tannins. Austere in all the wrong places, especially the transitional ones where some deft sweetness is required but doesn't quite materialise. 49.4%. sc.

⟐ **Mackmyra Single Cask 1st Fill ex-Bourbon Calvados Cask Fat Nr 40234** dist 10 Jun 17 db **(93.5) n23 t23.5 f23 b24** Ah, that's more like it! Shews none of the aggressive intransigence of its sister cask and even a delicate degree of apple flits across both the nose and palate with something approaching elegance. Much creamier and fuller-bodied with the delicate ulmo honey and more boisterous molasses forming a beautiful counter to the drier vanillas. But the malt never stops singing, the spices accompanying and the apple teasing. Everything that cask 40233 wants to be...but isn't... 49.2%. sc.

Mackmyra Skördetid art. nr. MC-009 db **(93)** n23 t23.5 f23 b23.5 A whisky impossible not to love. 46.1%.

Mackmyra Svensk Ek art. nr. ME-002 db **(95)** n24 t23.5 f23.5 b24 Mackmyra has branched out into whisky matured from oak grown in the south of Sweden. Before I tasted this I was rooting for them. Soon I twigged that this is an avenue they must continue along. Brilliant! 46.1%.

 Mackmyra Svensk Moment 22 Swedish oak, warehouse: Bodås mine db **(95.5)** n24 very rare to find. degree of purity to peated malt, but that is exactly what the nose offers. A precision whisky of rare elegance, the slightly minty phenols working at perfect pace with the unusual, sharp oak; **t24** as with most Mackmyra, the inherent lightness of its whisky leads to an immediately juicy impact. The sugars are quickly out of the blocks, a kind of molten icing sugar impacted by a touch of molasses. Slowly, though, the vanilla and spices build a platform, the tannins even weighing in with the sweetened eucalyptus note; **f23.5** if you didn't know what Swedish oak tasted like, you will now...; **b24** a very beautiful, lightly smoked moment. In fact a great many moments: enough to put this into the taste off for European whisky of the year. Utterly adorable and puts to shame the sulphur-spattered Scotch single malt I was tasting earlier. 42.4%. 1,100 bottles.

Mackmyra Svensk Rök art. nr. MR-001 db **(95.5)** n23.5 t23.5 f24.5 b24 Forget about the peat: the secret to this whisky is its subtlety, something not normally associated with smoky whiskies. It is a whisky so constructed that its many parts take time to gather, a segment at a time, until eventually, at the very finish, the whole picture is revealed. Fascinating, and quite brilliant. Now this is real blending... 46.1%.

Mackmyra Svensk Rök/Amerikansk Ek db **(90)** n22 t23 f22.5b22.5 A huge amount of natural toffee from the barrel slightly quietens the party. 46.1%.

 Mackmyra Svensk Single Cask Whisky Reserve The Dude of Fucking Everything fatnr. 14-0304, fattyp: refill bourbon, lager: Smögen, flasknr: 30, fatfyllmning: 2014-10-06, buteljering: 2019-09-12 db **(96)** n24.5 one of the best noses of the year so far. The smoke is sweet, gentle and delicate to the point of an ethereal quality; the accompanying vanilla notes offers the same intrinsic charm. There is a citrus note...sometimes. This is love....; **t24** the delivery is as soft and teasing as the nose suggests: a yielding vanilla note allows the peat to enter...but gently and without force. The sweetness is supplied by a marriage of grist and ulmo honey. The smoke dies slightly into a sooty powder, but the intensity remained controlled; **f23.5** dry now, with most of the sugars spent and the smoke pulsing without threat...; **b24** just one of those astonishing, almost hypnotic whiskies, the nose in particular, which you find you can't tear yourself from: a bit like Agnetha Fältskog's part pure, part faltering, part fragile, part vulnerable but always haunting singing in The Day Before You Came, operating well within itself, but occasionally letting rip with a stunning, faultless, soul-piercing note to leave you in no doubt that you are in the presence of something uniquely special. And beautiful. As I taste and write this it is someone's birthday today: Happy 70th Agnetha Fältskog. 499%. sc.

 Mackmyra Vintersol art. nr. MC-013, ex-port wine casks db **(74)** n22 t20 f15 b17 Nope! After the promising (and threatening nose) becomes flat as a witch's tit and casts a less than pleasant spell on the finish. Poor casks like this are so un-Mackmyra-ish. 46.1%.

 Milroy's of Soho Mackmyra Single Cask Cloudberry wine cask finish, cask no. 19-1053 db **(78.5)** n22 t22.5 f16 b18 Well, forget about the finish which is lacking charm and mercifully short. Let's concentrate, instead, on the unique nose and delivery which has an American bubble gum quality to the fruitiness. A merry volley of salivating barley and lemon drops certainly gets the juices flowing before the aggressively hot intervention. 52.6%. sc.

 Milroy's of Soho Mackmyra Single Cask Grand Cuvée cask, cask no. 19-1057 db **(64)** n15.5 t17.5 f15 b16 This is never a convincing whisky from the moment you hit the machine shop nose. You won't be thanking the aggressive, biting vaguely petrol-headed finish, either. Quite awful. 44.1%. sc.

 Milroy's of Soho Mackmyra Single Cask Pedro Ximenez finish, cask no. 19-1054 db **(81.5)** n21.5 t22 f19 b19 Another hottie from Milroy's, though not quite so searing as their previous Mackmyras. Here, though, the average witch's tit would dwarf this whisky, as it flat-lines in texture from first moment to last. A typical PX hatchet job, offering a singular sweetness with the grain lost forever. An underlying warmth adds some comfort. 50.4%. sc.

Motörhead Whisky new American oak, batch VIII db **(91)** n23 t23 f22 b23 As someone who prefers balance and harmony in their music, be it (preferably) classical or Pink Floyd or Gryphon, I have to admit that Motörhead are anathema to me. So I feared the worst for this whisky. I shouldn't have: as raucous as the oak may be, it plays rather well. 40%.

NORRTELJE BRENNERI Norrtälje. Working.

◈ **Roslagswhisky Eko No. 1 Single Cask** batch: Bourbonfat 23-200/No3, dest Nov 13, bott 5 Feb 20 db **(86)** n21 t22.5 f21 b21.5 Exceptionally malty, making great use of the heather-honey which runs through it. A slightly unconvincing cut ensures big oils which dull and bitter just a little too much late on. *61.6%. nc ncf sc. Bottled for Cinderella Whisky Fair 2020.*

◈ **Roslagswhisky Eko Single Cask** batch: Sherry olorosfat 28-30, dest Jun 13, bott 31 Jan 20 db **(86.5)** n21.5 t21.5 f22 b21.5 A curious whisky where the distillery's thick-set style is again evident bolstered further by a chubby fruitiness. A bit untidy as the feints kick in, though now some extra cocoa and hickory tones up the complexity. *46.2%. nc ncf sc.*

◈ **Roslagswhisky Eko Single Cask** batch: Sherry olorosfat 43-250, dest Apr 16, bott 31 Jan 20 db **(91)** n22.5 t23 f22.5 b23 Oh, so much better! A cleaner, more precise distillate ensures there are no luring feints around to take the edge of the charm and complexity which abounds here. An excellent sherry cask offers a grapey gloss on the intense vanilla and muscovado sugar mix. Layered, relaxed and the slow build of the spice and its salivating consequences cannot be faulted. Now they have found the right path, I hope they can stick to it. *48.7%. nc ncf sc.*

SMÖGEN WHISKY Hunnebostrand. Working.

Smögen Aged 5 Years Single Malt Sherry Quaters db **(85)** n22.5 t22 f21 b20 You can have too much of a good thing. And here the oak is relentless and way over the top. Far too much tannin, though there is a fleeting moment early on when the oak and smoke hold hands. *61%. nc ncf sc.*

◈ **Smögen Aged 8 Years Single Malt** first fill Sauternes barriques, cask nos. 4 & 8-10/2011, dist Mar 11, bott Apr 19 db **(93)** n23 t23.5 f23 b23.5 Youthful, clean, pungent and very alive! The phenols are at the tip of a wonderful barley juiciness. Works quite brilliantly. Simple, seemingly...but so not! *57.8%. nc ncf. 1,628 bottles.*

◈ **Smögen Primör Revisited Single Malt 2019** cask no. 46-53, dist 2013 db **(95.5)** n23.5 t24.5 f23.5 b24 Yet another brutally beautiful no holds barred peat orgy from this distillery where the lush mouthfeel is matched only by the uncompromising smokiness. Young and lusty, just one mouthful battles with your taste buds for a good six or seven minutes without letting go. Superbly distilled, this is a five-course malt that is neither for the faint or feint hearted. Indeed, smogen by name and nature. *68.2%. nc ncf. 1,616 bottles.*

Smögen Svensk Single Malt Single Cask 7 Year Old Rum Finish cask no. 56/2011, dist 26 Nov 11, bott Jan 19 db **(94.5)** n23.5 t24 f23.5 b23.5 You would be hard pressed to pick this out in an identity parade alongside a gang of Islay of a similar age. Truly bursting at the seams with gristy, malty smokiness, the rum cask having a negligible effect on the overall picture. A peat-lover's multiple orgasm. *62.4%. nc ncf sc.*

SPIRIT OF HVEN DISTILLERY Sankt Ibb. Working.

◈ **Spirit of Hven Charlies Wagon Single Malt Whisky** bott code: 82T015 1333 db **(79)** n20 t22 f18 b19 I have to say that I am a big fan of this distillery, and it usually scores exceptionally well in the Bible: it has set its own bar very highly. But this malt is far from Hvenly, being off balance, at times too sweet at others too bitter and, overall, off key – especially towards the end. Very disappointing. *47.1%.*

Spirit of Hven Hvenus Rye Whisky bott code: 66R297 05736 db **(92.5)** n23.5 t23.5 f22.5 b23 Well, Having cracked the art of making great single malt whisky, they have now gone after rye. And pretty much nailed that, too... *45.6%.*

Spirit of Hven Seven Stars No. 7 Alkaid Single Malt Whisky bott code: 74S015 00655 db **(94.5)** n23.5 t24 f23 b24 Just what more can you say about this exceptional distiller?. Even when they offer a peated version of their malt, they simply refuse to settle for very good. This is excellent... *45%.*

SWITZERLAND
BAUERNHOF BRENNEREI LÜTHY Muhen. Working.

Herr Lüthy Pure Swiss Corn Böörbon cask no. 554, dest 2014, abge 2018 db **(91)** n23 t23 f22 b23 A surprising Swiss bourbon offering a chance to draw delicious flavour map of previously uncharted territory. *43%. sc.*

Herr Lüthy Pure Swiss Rye Rogge cask no. 639, dest 2014, abge 2018 db **(85)** n20.5 t22 f21.5 b21 Not the first – and won't be the last – rye whisky where the cut off the still has gone slightly askew, resulting in an over indulgence of oils. The grain dazzles briefly on delivery. Great spices, though. *56.6%. sc.*

Herr Lüthy Pure Swiss Spelt UrDinkel cask no. 501, dest 2013, abge 2018 db **(87)** n20.5 t23 f21.5 b22 The nose may not be too promising – and spelt is a bit of a challenge for any distiller – but the heather honey and butterscotch explosion on delivery more than makes up for the early problems. Hefty oils on the finale ensure the weakness is truly spelt out, but there is no shame in enjoying that beautifully sensuous arrival. *43%. sc.*

BRAUEREI FALKEN Schaffhausen. Working.

Munot Malt Single Cask Limited Edition 2015 red wine cask no. 1-111 db **(87) n22 t21.5 f22 b21.5.** Has the thin feel of a whisky distilled initially to pretty high strength. The oak has by far the biggest script to learn here and only slowly does a balancing fruitiness emerge, though it remains gentle. Clean but warming. *57.1%. sc.*

BRENNEREI STADELMANN Altbüron. Working.

Buechibärger Whisky Single Malt Fassstärke 10 Jahre herstellungsjahr 2008, fass 33 db **(92) n22.5 t23.5 f22.5 b23.5** A big whisky which carries its weight and muscle with great dignity. *55%. sc.*

DISTILLERIE ETTER Zug. Working.

Johnett Swiss Single Malt Single Cask Whisky No. 50 2 years Pinot Noir barrel, Merlot finish, dist May 10, bott Sept 18 db **(89.5) n23 t23 f21 b22.5** A real belt and braces job with the fruit! *50.3%. ncf sc. 389 bottles.*

DISTILLERIE MACARDO Strohwilen. Working.

Macardo Bourbon dist 2010, bott code 6020 db **(84.5) n20.5 t21.5 f21.5 b21** You can see where this is coming from – and where it is trying to go. But it gets stuck, literally, with bubble gum clogging up the works – on both delivery and finish. A little too sticky and indistinct. *42%.*

Macardo Single Malt dist 2010, bott code 7002 db **(92.5) n22.5 t23.5 f22.5 b23.5** An honest and attractive, beautifully distilled, single malt squeezing out every last barley note. *42%.*

LANGATUN DISTILLERY Langenthal, Kanton Bern. Working.

Langatun 10 Year Old Single Malt Chardonnay cask, cask no. 4, dist 2008, bott 2018 db **(95.5) n24 t24 f23.5 b24** One of those great moments where, 12 hours into my tasting day, I pick up a sample that is gently warmed and prepared, nose it, taste it and instantly recognise it as the best whisky of the day so far. Only afterwards I see it is Langatun which, for sheer consistency, can now be labelled as truly world class. Is it the mouthfeel? The intensity? The diaspora of sugars: Chilean ulmo honey here, Corsican bruyere honey there, a cube of muscovado tucked away there?...while the malt astonishes in its intensity and a slight fruitiness is nothing but an adornment. *49.12%. nc.*

⬧ **Langatun 10 Year Old Second Edition Single Malt** dist 18 Sept 10 db **(95) n24** how can a whisky be big yet delicately proportioned in one go...? A sublime mix of malt and spiced up lime blossom honey, with a just-so degree of healthy tannin. There is even a rum-like high ester molasses note for good measure; **t24** the delivery is the control room: fat, confident, rich and from where all the future flavours, mainly already identified on the nose, blossom and begin their slightly differing routes towards the chocolate mousse middle; **f23** fruit chocolate at first, then bitters slightly; **b24** when it comes to balance and structure of a European mainland single malt whisky, I doubt if anyone has been more consistent over the last decade than Langatun. Indeed, I always leave their whiskies to the very end of my annual European sojourn as a kind of reward to myself...and also to see if they are still worth waiting for. They are.... *61.1%.* 🍸

Langatun Cardeira Cask Finish Single Malt dist 25 Oct 10, bott 2 May 17, bott code L 0291 db **(95.5) n23.5 t25 f23 b24** Trust Langatun to come up with something very different, indeed. The effect of this less than common Portuguese wine dovetails with rare precision with the malt. The first ten seconds of the delivery is as delicious as any whisky on the planet this year. *61.4%. nc. 100 bottles.*

⬧ **Langatun Founder's Reserve 10 Year Old Single Malt** cask no. 135, dist 10 Oct 10 db **(94.5) n23.5** such charm and complexity takes time to explore and it is riveting entertainment: still a degree of green-ness despite the age an even the nuttiness has a slight youthful juiciness to it, as though not fully ripened. Meanwhile the malt is clean and unashamed of its beauty, or the fact it is prone to slight changes of mood; **t23.5** salivating with a Demerara sugar fruitiness not appearing on the nose heading straight towards a big malt and chocolate surge; **f23.5** a bitter-sweet finale with spices now a little more evident. But you are left chewing for some little time...; **b24** another Swiss to watch... *60.7%. sc.*

Langatun Nero D'Avola Cask Finish Single Malt cask no. 87, dist Feb 14, bott Feb 19 db **(89.5) n22 t23 f22 b22.5** A new flavour profile to be added to the world's whiskies. Unusually for Langatun, it's all about effect rather than complexity. *62.9%. nc sc. 100 bottles.*

Langatun Old Woodpecker chardonnay cask, cask no. 167 db **(94.5) n23.5 t23.5 f23.5 b24** A superb malt which handsomely repays patient opening up. *46%. sc.*

Langatun Old Woodpecker Organic Single Malt white wine cask, batch no. 03/19, dist 2011, bott 2019 db **(96)** n24.5 t24 f23.5 b24 Creamy and dreamy, not sure if the sweeter notes could be more beautifully in tune... Sheer woodpeckery bliss... and something to bang on about... 46%. nc.

Langatun Ruchè Cask Finish Single Malt cask no. 383, batch no. 1, dist 14 Mar 13, bott 23 Nov 18 db **(86.5)** n22 t22 f21 b21.5 Another big fruity Langatun. But this one is just a little too tart and bitter, especially on the finish. 62.8%. nc sc. 344 bottles.

Langatun White House Single Malt db **(88)** n22.5 t22.5 f21 b22 Trumps many other European whiskies, but not quite up to many of its predecessors... 45%.

SEVEN SEALS DISTILLERY AG Schweiz, working.

◇◇ **Seven Seals Age of Aquarius Single Malt Whisky Double Wood Finish** db **(81)** n21 t22 f18 b20 Big, full-bodied, smoked fish. But the sulphur on the finish means it's a malt that gets away from you... 58.7%.

◇◇ **Seven Seals Age of Aries Single Malt Whisky Triple Wood Sherry Finish** db **(86)** n23 t23 f19 b21 It is a rare thing when the peat has such a bristling countenance it is able to take on such rich fruit and come through so loud and clear. At least on the nose. And the delivery, too, where the second wave is a gorgeous heather honey thread. Sadly, the finish has a distinct and lingering sulphur kick. But even then, the sugars and smoke are still working flat out. 58.7%.

◇◇ **Seven Seals Age of the Gemini Single Malt Whisky Triple Wood Sherry Finish** db **(87.5)** n22 t23 f20.5 b22 A big, blustering, anarchic malt seemingly set on not following any particular shape or path. The nose is like kippers cooked in a plum pudding; the delivery lurches around the palate, picking up molasses here, depositing spice there, skidding and crash landing on juicy grape skins all over the place. A light vanilla touch creates some tangible sanity to the finish, though a light sulphur note is also detectable in extra time. Fun, if slightly insane... 58.7%.

◇◇ **Seven Seals Age of The Lion Single Malt Whisky Triple Wood Sherry Finish** db **(90)** n22.5 t23 f22 b22.5 Seeing I'm a lifelong supporter of The Lions – Millwall FC – it was important they got this one right! No sulphur on display here – and that makes a huge difference to the experience, even though this is one crazy, mixed up malt. A fat cut, huge tannins mined from the oak, a vague, indecipherable phenol note and untamed fruit means there is precious little structure to this...just effect. But my word! Your taste buds get the working over of their lives and if you can't enjoy something as singular as this, what's the point? 58.7%.

◇◇ **Seven Seals Age of Sagittarius Single Malt Whisky Double Wood Sherry Finish** db **(85)** n22 t23 f19 b20 A young whisky with lots of hurried tannin extraction, giving this real oaky pep. Sulphur on the finish, alas. The star turn is on delivery and just after when the sugars ripped from the cask are on full, luscious display. 58.7%.

◇◇ **Seven Seals Age of Scorpio Single Malt Whisky Triple Wood Sherry Finish** db **(88)** n22 t23 f21 b22 Though I may be a Scorpio, I certainly don't have the pugilistic tendencies that seem to be at the core of this malt's character. This distillery specialises is in big, rumbustious malts, and this is a real heavyweight forever trying to land the knockout blow. As usual there is a roughhouse, smokehouse aroma setting the phenols to go 15 rounds with the grape. They then both seem to land a haymaker that flattens the other. The cloying maple syrup and tinned prune juice middle starts to meet its match with the bitter finish. Again, the dreaded S word is present...but there is plenty to enjoy before you hit that point. 58.7%.

Seven Seals Peated Double Wood Finish db **(94.5)** n23.5 t23.5 f23.5 b24 A beautiful malt where they have got their sums right here in adding up just the required amounts of phenols, dark sugars and oak. Even the oil for body and weight is spot on. Doubtless on the sweet side, but the spice and tannin really do put the anchors on in spectacular style. Superb! 58.7%.

◇◇ **Seven Seals Lucerne Whisky Ship Single Malt Whisky Double Wood Sherry Finish** db **(94)** n23.5 t23.5 f23 b24 Beautifully made, superbly matured and delighted to say the sherry casks are not only clean, but do as little as possible to stand in the way of the beautiful phenols that drift over both nose and palate. Spices and molasses in all the right places at the right times and ticking all the right boxes. By far their best bottling of the year: in fact in a different class altogether... 58.7%.

Seven Seals Single Malt Peated Port Wood Finish db **(85.5)** n21.5 t22.5 f20.5 b21 The nose is one of good old British Black Country pork scratchings – or maybe in this case Port scratching...A malt that's about as subtle as a punch in the kisser and as rough and ready as a bare knuckle fighter. But there is a certain basic enjoyment to the fruit cake sugars on display. Technically, though, not quite at the races. 58.7%.

Seven Seals Single Malt Port Wood Finish db **(87)** n21 t22.5 f21.5 b22 A lush frenzy of fruit. A little cloying, but the spices are a treat. 58.7%.

Seven Seals Single Malt Whisky Sherry Wood Finish db **(88)** n21.5 t23 f21.5 b22 Big on the grape and even bigger on the spice and maple syrup. A bit of an untidy mishmash. But when it is good, it is very good. 58.7%.

Deciphered and Distilled. The Bible's European Guide to Whisky Labels

English	German	French
Malt	Malz	Malt
Grain	Getreide	céréales
Wheat	Weizen	blé
Barley	Gerste	orge
Rye	Roggen	seigle
Spelt	Dinkel	épeautre
Corn	Mais	maïs
Oat	Hafer	avoine
Peated	getorft	tourbé
Smoked	geraucht	fumé
Organic	biologisch	biologique
Cask	Fass	fût
Matured in/Aged in	gereift in	vieilli en
Finish	Nachreifung	déverdissage
Double Maturation	Zweitreifung	deuxième maturation
Oak	Eiche	chêne
Toasted	wärmebehandelt	grillé
Charred	ausgeflammt, verkohlt	carbonisé
Years	Jahre	ans
Months	Monate	mois
Days	Tage	journées
Chill Filtration	Kühlfiltration	filtration à froid
Non Chill Filtered	nicht kühlgefiltert	non filtré à froid
No Colouring	nicht gefärbt	non coloré
Cask Strength	Fassstärke	brut du fût
Single Cask	Einzelfass	single cask
Cask No.	Fass-Nummer	numéro du fût
Batch	Charge	Lot/charge
Distillation Date	Destillations-Datum	date de distillation
Bottling Date	Abfüll-Datum	date de mise en bouteille
Alcohol by Volume/abv	Volumenprozente/% vol.	teneur en alcool/abv
Proof (American)	amerikanische Einheit für % vol.	unité américaine

Danish	Dutch	Swedish
Malt	Gerst	Malt
Korn	graan	säd
hvede	tarwe	vete
byg	gerst	korn
rug	rogge	råg
spelt	spelt	speltvete
majs	mais	majs
havre	haver	havre
tørv	geturfd	torvrökt
røget	gerookt	rökt
organisk	biologisch/organisch	ekologisk
fad	vat	fat
modning i	gerijpt in	mognad på/lagrad på
finish	narijping/finish	slutlagrat
dobbelt modning	dubbele rijping	dubbellagrat
egetræ	eik	ek
ristet	getoast	rostad
forkullet	gebrand	kolad
år	jaren	år
måned	maanden	månader
dage	dagen	dagar
kold filtrering	koude-filtratie	kylfiltrering
ikke kold filtreret	niet koud gefilterd	ej kylfiltrerad
ikke farvet	niet bijgekleurd	inga färgämnen
fadstyrke	vatsterkte	fatstyrka
enkelt fad	enkel vat	enkelfat
fad nr.	vat nummer	fatnummer
parti/batch	serie/batch	batch
destillations dato	distillatie datum	destilleringsdatum
aftapnings dato	bottel datum	buteljeringsdatum
volumenprocent	alcoholpercentage/% vol	volymprocent/% vol.
Proof	amerikaanse aanduiding voor % vol	Amerikanska proof

World Whiskies

I have long said that whisky can be made just about anywhere in the world; that it is not writ large in stone that it is the inalienable right for just Scotland, Ireland, Kentucky and Canada to have it all to themselves. And so, it seems, it is increasingly being proved. Perhaps only sandy deserts and fields of ironstone can prevent its make physically and Islam culturally, though even that has not been a barrier to malt whisky being distilled in both Pakistan and Turkey. Whilst not even the world's highest mountains or jungle can prevent the spread of barley and copper pot.

Outside of North America and Europe, whisky's traditional nesting sites, you can head in any direction and find it being made. Australia, in particular, has gained a deserved reputation for magnificent malt though, like its finest wines, it can be hard to locate outside its own country. Indeed, Australian whiskies are of such high quality and relatively abundant that it has, like England and Wales now been rewarded with its own section in the Whisky Bible, though Australian whisky will still be found in the World Whisky awards section. World class whisky can be found in other surprisingly lush and tropical climes with Taiwan leading the way thanks to the wonderful Kavalan distillery, no stranger to the Whisky Bible awards.

Japan has long represented Asia with distinction and whisky-making there is in such an advanced state and at a high standard Jim Murray's Whisky Bible has given it its own section - and World Whisky of the Year for 2015! But while neighbouring South Korea has ended its malt distilling venture, further east, and at a very unlikely altitude, Nepal has forged a small industry to team up, geographically, with fellow malt distillers India and Pakistan. The main malt whisky from this region making inroads in world markets is India's Amrut single malt, though Paul John is also now beginning to forge a deserved following of fans. 'Inroads' is hardly doing Indian whisky justice. Full-bloodied trailblazing, more like. So good was Amrut's fantastically complex brand, Fusion, it was awarded Jim Murray's Whisky Bible 2010 Third Finest Whisky in the World. A top award repeated this year by Paul John with their astonishing Mithuna, a single malt comprising some of their oldest casks giving one of the most complete finishes of any whisky I have ever tasted. If Indian whisky wasn't on the map before, it certainly is now...

Jim Murray's Whisky Bible World Whisky of the Year Winners		
	Asian Whisky	**Southern Hemisphere Whisky**
2010	**Amrut Fusion**	N/A
2011	**Amrut Intermediate Sherry Matured**	N/A
2012	Amrut Two Continents 2nd Edition	**Kavalan Solist Fino Single Cask**
2013	N/A	**Sullivan's Cove Single Cask HH0509**
2014	Kavalan Podium Single Malt	**Timboon Single Malt Whisky**
2015	Kavalan Single Malt Whisky	**NZ Willowbank 1988 25 years Old**
2016	**Amrut Greedy Angels 46%**	Heartwood Port 71.3%
2017	**Kavalan Solist Moscatel**	Heartwood Any Port in a Storm
2018	Paul John Kanya	**Limeburner's Dark Winter**
2019	Amrut Greedy Angels 8 Years Old	**Belgrove Peated Rye**
2020	**Nantou Distillery Omar Bourbon Cask**	Bakery Hill Peated Malt
2021	**Paul John Mithuna**	Adams Distillery Tasmanian Single Malt

BRAZIL
LAMAS DESTILARIA

◇ **Nimbus Smoked Single Malte Whisky Puro Malte** lote 5, barril 10 nbc db **(93)** n23 well smoked and distinctive. Appears to be in the mesquite style but far more measured than the US offerings, and more akin to smoky bacon. Very pleasant – and becomes far more accessible the moment your nose adjusts; t23.5 a soft, lightly sweetened arrival on the palate now with even a hint of peat within the phenols, though if it is then of a type unlike any other on the planet. The mid-ground dryness is bordering on sophistication; f23 long, thanks to some unexpected oils. A lovely mocha note sits prettily beside the distinctive smokiness which, as is the case from the moment it arrives on the palate, never over-dominates, but ensures it lets you know it is there, also; b23.5 a truly unique style in all the world's whiskies: a strange but delicious mesquite/peat hybrid. So different and so delicious, it had me pouring another one – this time for fun rather than work... 40%. sc.

◇ **Plenus Whisky Single Malt Puro Malte** lote 21, barril 62/64 nbc db **(85.5)** n21.5 t21 f21.5 b21.5 Pleasant enough but, despite the barley juiciness which pops up here and there on the nose and delivery, overall a dull whisky, the buzzing spices apart. Seemingly well made, but otherwise flat and lacking much in the way of personality. Just a little too dry, as well. 40%.

◇ **Verus Whisky Single Malt Puro Malte** lote 19, barril 77/84 nbc db **(87)** n21.5 t22 f21.5 b22 An unusual whisky but one that shews some of the hallmarks of a European-style distillation. Big in malt, with feints also. Well coloured up, as much with dry tannins as toffee. This is a lively whisky, with a surprisingly delicious turn of malty phrase at the midway point, and spices, too. Though, because of the strength, the finish lacks great length and depth. 40%

TRÊS LOBOS DISTILLERY

◇ **3 Lobos Whiskey Artesanal Experience Single Malt Puro Malte 6 Anos** batch no. 2-0715, dist 17 Jul 13, bott 17 Jul 19 db **(91.5)** n23 so dry...and sweet. The malt wells up for the occasional blast. But rather than being in exotic Brazil, I have been whisked back to the UK, likley in Yorkshire to be precise... and I am sniffing at one of their local cakes, the Parkin, just before my mid-November birthday some 40 years ago with ginger and molasses at the fore...; t23 silky-soft, sensuous and salivating, the molasses on the nose has made way here for heather honey and light ginger. The malt now has a far more gristy persona, juicy and sugary...; f22.5 those spices really bite deep and dryly...and still that ginger hint continues...; b23 distilled gingerbread. A delicious malt, but one of the most ginger-infested whiskies I have encountered in a very long time. A malt with fabulous personality and joie de vivre: how Brazilian! 40%.

INDIA
AMRUT DISTILLERY

◇ **Amrut Fusion** batch no. 82, bott Jun 19 db **(90.5)** n22 green and flighty. Quite a minty aspect to the phenols which furthers the freshness; t23.5 ah...now that's much more like it! Sublime molasses mix with the relatively bold peat. The malt is so young you feel you should be patting its head and wiping its nose. The sharpness of this juvenile barley is pretty challenging, but against the odds it works well in tandem with the phenols; f22 some vanilla makes its mark which the smoke and light spice aren't quite sure where to place themselves in the scheme of things; b23 slightly more Confusion than Fusion. Again, there is a strange finish to this after a really gorgeous take off. Seems to land without any wheels or fuel everything having run out. Enjoyed this malt, but in a very different way to the Fusions of old where the layering, pace and balance were exemplary from the first moment to the last. The delivery apart, this is much more anarchic. 50%.

Amrut Greedy Angels 10 Years Old Chairman's Reserve ex bourbon cask, batch no. 01, bott 25 Jun 19 db **(94.5)** n23 t24 f23.5 b24 High quality whisky. And a must find for honey lovers... 55%. 900 bottles.

◇ **Amrut Greedy Angels Peated Rum Finish Chairman's Reserve 10 Years Old** batch no. 01, bott Oct 19 db **(95.5)** n23.5 certainly no holds barred: ultra-intense smoke holds sway; moderate fruit and spices at first, but then begin to glow...; t24 wonderful mouthfeel from the start; initially salivating barley and sharper sugars; the tannins now dig in and upping both the weight and intensity; how the previously light smoke recovers from that onslaught I really don't know but the phenols regroup and even inject a sweet maltiness at around the midway point; f23.5 mind-blowing depth to this and matched by the deft balance of the caressing smoke; emerging at the death a gorgeous fruit chocolate note that carries the distance; b24.5 keeps shewing more depth and intensity each time you taste it. Astoundingly beautiful malt of the true Amrut tradition. Sensual beyond measure and one to take your time with and cherish every erotic moment... 57.1%. 450 bottles.

Amrut Greedy Angels Peated Sherry Finish Chairman's Reserve 10 Years Old batch no. 01, bott Feb 19 db (**94**) **n**23.5 **t**24 **f**23 **b**23.5 A faultless sherry cask at work here: the rarest of the rare! So powerful the peat at times has problems making itself heard and has to content itself as being the backing group. Elegant, intense and very high quality. 60%. 324 bottles.

◇ **Amrut Indian Single Malt Whisky** batch no. 141, bott Feb 19 db (**89**) **n**22 lighter in body and more simplistic than earlier bottlings, a thin citrus sweetness hangs over this; **t**23.5 uncomplicated barley which gather and grows in intensity in almost linear fashion. At the brow of the climb it really is massively enjoyable...; **f**21.5 hmmm...that thinner quality in the finish which is just so un-Amrut! Slightly bitter...; **b**22 another puzzling bottling which at its very best is a treat, but the decline in the pleasure graph is pretty steep. 46%. nc ncf.

Amrut Kadhambham 2019 Release bott 20 Jun 19 db (**93**) **n**23 **t**23 **f**23 **b**23.5 A beautifully rich Amrut; a much heavier, maltier style than normal. 50%. 7,200 bottles.

◇ **Amrut Peated Indian Single Malt Whisky** batch no. 89, bott Feb 19 db (**86**) **n**22 **t**22.5 **f**20.5 **b**21 It is as though this whisky has had a personality transplant. The peat is thrusting and pretty confident with its sooty dryness. But the malt shews remarkable youth which probably accounts for the imbalance in the thin finish. Some good moments, but not as many as usual. 46%. nc ncf.

Amrut Peated Port Pipe Single Cask batch no. 01, bott 12 Feb 19 db (**95.5**) **n**24 **t**24.5 **f**23 **b**24 Very often a well peated malt and wine cask don't work particularly well together, one element cancelling out the other. This, it must be recorded, works a treat. It is so good, in fact, I raise this glass to the memory of Amrut's founding father, whisky visionary Neelakanta Rao Jagdale...and friend. 48%. nc ncf. The Vault Biennale Edition

◇ **Amrut Raj Igala Indian Single Malt Whisky** batch no. 20, bott Oct 19 db (**86**) **n**22.5 **t**22 **f**20.5 **b**21.5 A distinctly Speyside-style malt focussing on gentleness of touch and light caramels. As is the present Amrut style, the finish is a little feeble and bitter. But there is much to enjoy with its early grassy quality both nose and delivery. 40%.

JOHN DISTILLERIES

Paul John Brilliance db (**94.5**) **n**23.5 **t**24 **f**23.5 **b**23.5 Yet another astonishing malt from India. 46%

Paul John Chairman's Reserve db (**89**) **n**22 **t**23 **f**22 **b**22 I cannot say I am much of a fan of the mixing of PX and peat. Sometimes it works, usually it doesn't: often it is a case of two heavyweight fighters landing punches simultaneously, each knocking the other out. Well, both contestants hit the deck here but, thankfully, got up again briefly for a becalmed finish. Oh, and the really good news: 100% sulphur free...! 59.7%. ncf.

Paul John Christmas Edition batch no. 02, mfg. date 16-nov-18 db (**95.5**) **n**24 **t**24 **f**23.5 **b**24 Question: when is a big whisky not a big whisky? Answer: when it is as well balanced as this... 46%. ncf.

Paul John Classic Select Cask db (**94.5**) **n**23 **t**24 **f**23.5 **b**24 One of those whiskies which just overflows with flavour. Delicious! 55.2%. nc ncf.

◇ **Paul John Distillery Edition** db (**94.5**) **n**23.5 full of citrusy promise: light by PJ's recent standards, but no harm in that as the malt finds a mildly ethereal voice; **t**23.5 delicate but intensifying sugars bounce around the palate on arrival ensuring a mega-sweet start. The barley is all present and correct once the sweetness recedes, though the oils appear to intensify; **f**23.5 typical distillery butterscotch and vanilla with a distant wave of spice and cocoa; **b**24 compared to the enormity of the other Paul Johns I have tasted today, this is but a mere child. But what a charming one... 46%. ncf.

Paul John Exceptional db (**95**) **n**23 **t**24 **f**24 **b**24 The sheer élan of the controlled intensity is something to behold: Indian malt at its maltiest and most charmingly expressed. 47%. ncf

Paul John Kanya db (**96**) **n**23.5 **t**24 **f**24 **b**24.5 When a distillery can find honey at the very end of the its flavour range and profile, you know they have cracked it. Superb! 50%. ncf.

◇ **Paul John Mithuna** db (**97**) **n**23.5 rarely am I lost for words. But so rich and complexly entangled are these chocolates, molasses, dates, ultra-delicate spices – oh, and all slightly leavened by passion fruit – that it is only the absolute perfectionist in me that is docking the marks. Murray Method. Half an hour...whisky perception changing...; **t**24 oh, my word! Goodness gracious me! Mouthfeel...perfect. Sweetness levels...perfect. Volume of intensity... perfect. The main theme is a chocolate liqueur, with high volumes of the very finest cocoa to chew on, always oily, always able to enhance itself with a molasses sub culture and the very finest vanilla pods. But the mouthfeel...it is oily but at the same time embracing and moulded like no other whisky I have ever encountered; **f**25 so long, with the vanillas now holding sway and just the politest hint of spice. But the earlier chocolate theme still echoes around...seemingly forever... and gloriously; **b**24.5 the end of the experience is like after you have just made love...and you are unable to speak or move while your senses get back into some kind of normality. If Mithuna means "Ultimate", then it is the perfect name. Or maybe

Mithuna means "Perfect", then it is pretty close. Whichever, this is a kind of Indian version of a William Larue Weller, shewing that same extraordinary intensity, complexity and beauty. It is that very rarest of things. And, if nothing else, announces Paul John distillery on the world stage of truly great distilleries. This is a whisky to devour...while it devours you. Almost certainly destined for a top three spot in the Whisky Bible 2021. 58%. ncf. 🏆

Paul John Nirvana Unpeated Single Malt batch no. 01, mfg. date 12-nov-18 db (**94**) n24 t23.5 f23 b23.5 While writing these notes a wasp decided to fly into my tasting glass, fall into the whisky called Nirvana...and die. Ironic, or what? But wasps have a sweet tooth, so tells you all you need to know. That and the fact it climbed back in three times before it finally succumbed... 40%. ncf.

Paul John PX db (**90.5**) n22.5 t23.5 f21.5 b23 The plan was to write these tasting notes while England were playing India during the first Test match in Birmingham. England, as usual, collapsed after previously having their foot on India's throat and potentially all out for a very low score...but then blew it. So with India now favourites to win, thought I'd better get these tasted today, rather than tomorrow, while there is still a Test match. For the cricket: why do England have only one Surrey player, Sam Curran? And not surprisingly the only one to show any resistance. And as for the whisky: enjoyable with a truly brilliant delivery. But not showing the true subtlety and colours of PJ's excellent malt. 48%. ncf.

◈ **Paul John Single Cask Non Peated #4127** db (**96.5**) n24 just love that spice buzz which is a constant, never changing pitch. Because it is fascinating contrast to the lime blossom honey and lightly oiled barley which operate at a much sweeter level.; t24.5 honey....!!! I'm home! One of the single cask deliveries of the year with a blend of ulmo and heather honey thickened further by intense malt. The butterscotch and vanilla sub woofers also make a resounding mark...; f24 just more of the same over a very, very long fade. Some finest moist Danish marzipan...; b24 I think we can safely say that Paul John has now reached a stage in its development as a relatively new distillery where it can step into its warehouses and pluck out single casks of bewildering and unforgettable beauty and near perfect maturity. Here is one such cask. There are others listed in this Whisky Bible 2021, too... 58.6%. sc. 🏆

◈ **Paul John Single Cask Non Peated #6758** db (**96**) n23.5 so much vanilla and barley. Light muscovado sugars gives it a vaguely fruity feel, too...; t24.5 such a deeply satisfying mouthfeel...the acacia honey makes you purr... Barley sugar candy in its most concentrated form; f24 in the PJ tradition, a super-long fade of all the previous flavours and sensations with a shy build of spice very late on; b24 simplistic...in a complex kind of way! One of those rare malts where if you could give marks for mouthfeel alone, it would top score. A very sensuous experience...a whisky to be shared with your partner, but without a glass... 59.3%. sc.

◈ **Paul John Single Cask Peated #6086** db (**95**) n24 such a sexy nose, the peat refusing to get all gangsterish and threatening, and instead sets a course for calm persuasion. A soft spearmint nose aids the gentleness, as well as a light, salt slant to the vanillas; t23.5 healthy oils form a gloss on which the peat reflects. Light molasses ingratiate themselves, and in so doing underline the healthy maturation processes; f23.5 long, gently smoked with that salty timbre still apparent; b24 a stunning display of controlled peat seemingly revelling in the accompaniment of well-aged oak. Beautifully structured and paced. And a serious step up from their last Peated single cask. 58.9%. sc.

◈ **Paul John Single Cask Peated #6355** db (**96**) n24 immediately a bourbon-style kick hits the nose, even ahead of the phenols. Brilliant liquorice and molasses put on an elegant combined show which slowly includes the peat in its act; t24 this time it's the sugars ahead of the game: once more molasses, though seemingly in conjunction with heather-honey...which gets earthier by the moment as the peat begins to make a thick, almost sticky, contribution. As on the nose, there is a bourbon-style sub-text, red liquorice this time taking the lead....; f24 long, languid and dark chocolate giving the phenols some serious extra weight; b24 if you imagine cask 6086 as top of the range Paul John single cask, then this is the turbo-charged all-leather edition. The sheer élan for a single cask is jaw-dropping. 59.1%. sc.

Paul John Select Cask Peated (**96**) n24 t24 f24 b24 A peated malt whisky which will make a few people sit up and take even further notice of Indian whisky. World class... 46%

Paul John Tula 100% virgin American oak casks db (**96**) n23.5 t24.5 f23.5 b24.5 Think of an artist with a beautiful mind and spirit, painting, sculpting, restoring, creating...all these things have happened here as this is a work of art as much as a bottle of whisky. 58%. ncf.

◈ **Paul John Tula** (**96**) n23.5 over-ripe plums and liquorice form a soft but rich backdrop to the startling spices. The more distant background noise is a lovely manuka honey and molasses mix...all this leavened by the most insouciant of orange blossom honey notes; t24.5 after such a soft make-up on the nose, the crispness on delivery comes as a surprise. But crunchy Demerara sugars arrive in double quick time as the tannins make their mark early. The sheer power is matched only by the élan as the deep chocolate tones melt with ginger and liquorice. One crashing layer after another is a joy to behold; f24 just more of the same with a slow rising of the vanilla and spice; the notes to the original bottling hold firm; **b24** a delightful second batch of Tula with all the same stars, just the odd one or two shifting constellations. Seemingly effortless magnificence. *58%. ncf.*

RAMPUR DISTILLERY
Rampur Indian Single Malt Whisky Sherry PX Finish American oak barrels, finished in Spanish sherry PX butts db **(86) n22 t22.5 f20 b21.5** A real shame this. It is obvious that the underlying malt is very attractive. But the PX has intervened to slightly flatten and dull and then leave a sulphurous deposit on the finish. Indian distilleries have to learn, like some in Scotland and Ireland refuse to, that using Spanish oak can be a very dangerous game. *45%. ncf.*

NEW ZEALAND
WILSON DISTILLERY
⬦ **The New Zealand Whisky Collection The Oamaruvian 18 Year Old** aged 6 years in American oak, ex-bourbon casks and transferred into French oak, ex-New Zealand red wine casks for 12 years **(94) n23** for a blend, the malt is startling. A salty edge gives a charming island feel; **t23.5** oh...well done chaps! The undulating persona as the firm malt then softer grains take turns is truly luxurious. The fruit kisses while the tannins nibble; **f23.5** long and languid but also not shy of the odd tart, jammy tang...though the barley, fittingly, has the very last say...; **b24** for my 750th whisky for the Jim Murray's Whisky Bible 2021, I thought I'd travel as far as possible from my home in England which, as beautiful as it is, for the last two months has been my gaol. Way back in 1994 I travelled to the Wilson's Distillery in Dunedin to clamber through the warehouses to taste probably over 100 samples of a whisky which, then tragically unloved, has now assumed, rightfully, legendary status. Then the unique part copper part stainless steel stills were running, so I was able one minute to taste the new make, and the next sample their oldest stock and everything in between. And later in the day, travel just a couple of miles to spend time among the penguins as they dipped in and out of the sea. With my now being in my second solid month of Covid-19 lockdown, this journey back to one of the most remarkable distilleries (and now sadly lost to us) it has ever been my privilege and pleasure to visit and inspect is something I need to do once more...if in my mind's eye, only... *50%.*

UNSPECIFIED SINGLE MALT
⬦ **The New Zealand Whisky Collection Dunedin Double Cask Single Malt Whisky** small American oak, ex-bourbon casks and French oak, ex-New Zealand red wine casks **(87) n21.5 t22.5 f21.5 b21.5** A malty cove despite the intervention of wine casks and French oak. However, there is a slight discordant note that is hinted at on the nose and certainly makes its mark towards the cotton wool end. The malt, though, ploughs on regardless and finds a little milk chocolate to team up with. *40%.*

⬦ **The New Zealand Whisky Collection Oamaruvian Revolution Single Malt** small American oak, ex-bourbon casks and French oak, ex-New Zealand red wine casks **(90.5) n22.5** a fat, sweet estery note not entirely missing from some Demerara/Jamaica rum blends, especially when that light creosote and muscovado sugar fruit note kicks in. Wow! **t23** after a nose like that, the delivery cannot be anything other than forceful, and it is certainly that...! The fruit gangs up in thick plum pudding mode; **f22.5** the spices that had got lost in the maelstrom of the delivery at last find a place to be heard. Buttery and always with that shadow of slightly burnt fruit...; **b22.5** fulsome, forceful and rich, this malt doesn't pander to sophistication. Well distilled and matured. *46%.*

SOUTH AFRICA
JAMES SEDGWICK DISTILLERY
Bain's Capetown Mountain Single Grain Whisky bott code: 1869721 L5 18260 db **(87.5) n22 t22 f21.5 b22** Even though the strength of Capetown Mountain has been reduced slightly, it offers a marginally better whisky than of old with far better balance and far greater presence to ensure a more satisfying finale. Its weakness, still, is simplicity though the nip of the spice has been enhanced and fares well against the rich cream toffee. *40%.*

⬦ **Bain's Cape Mountain Whisky Single Grain** bott code: L611 28 E 19 db **(87) n21.5 t22 f21.5 b22** Well, the year of tasting this, 2020, is the year of the toilet tissue, as that is what everyone around the world has been busy collecting. But none will be as gentle and super-soft as this South African grain which appears to be distilled from MacIntosh's Cream Toffee. *43%.*

⬦ **Bain's Cape Mountain Whisky Aged 15 Years Single Grain** bott code: LA64 27K 18 db **(90.5) n23** fabulous! A genteel, low voltage but distinctive bourbon character, jam-packed with liquorice and sharper toasted tannins. Surprisingly salty, too; **t23** a lively and distinguished kick off, the heather-honey and molasses mixing with the light liquorice underscore to form a majestic whole. By the midpoint the spices are beginning to make a name for themselves; **f22** fades a little too quickly into a halfway house between egg custard and butterscotch tart; **b22.5** at times, especially on the nose, there is the unmistakable feel of antique shop here. Must make this a very collectable whisky... *52.5%.*

⬦ **Bain's Founder's Collection Aged 18 Years Single Grain Whisky Fino Cask Finish** bott code: LA64 10 D 19 db **(92) n24** one of those ten-minute noses, as it changes weight and shape as it warms and oxidises. A fascinating oaky structure as the spine to which the delicate grape attaches, which the mix of ulmo and heather-honeys amid the muscovado sugars ensure something a little special. Add that to the over-ripe gooseberry and sun-exploding greengages and you are really onto something...; **t23** not even the delivery could match that nose, but it has a damn good try! Mainly the molasses and vanillas at play, though, some toasty raisins ducking in and out, cranking up the spices along the way; **f22** the toasty bitterness begins to accelerate; **b23** works far better than the PX as this has guile and complexity. And is less sulphur challenged to boot. Charming South African whisky. *50.5%. 1,900 bottles.*

⬦ **Bain's Founder's Collection Aged 18 Years Single Grain Whisky Oloroso Cask Finish** bott code: LA64 15 D 19 db **(92) n23.5** incredibly soft grape juice backed up by moist fruit cake; **t23** the fruit dominates with a voluptuous embrace and, after starting sweetly, veers off directly towards slightly burnt Christmas pudding. For a good ten seconds after initial delivery there is enough spice prickle and honey to ensure an attractive balance and depth; **f22.5** despite the obvious lack of body, the fruit has enough toasted weight to lengthen the finale out – staying a complete softy all the way...; **b23** a plump whisky boasting a yielding softness rare among any whisky. And not a single sulphur note to be found! Delicious! *50.5%. 1,900 bottles.*

⬦ **Bain's Founder's Collection Aged 18 Years Single Grain Whisky PX Cask Finish** bott code: LA64 17 D 19 db **(88.5) n23 t23 f20.5 b22** A clean, light, delicate grain as produced at James Sedgwick versus PX Casks. Well, there can be only one winner. As you might expect, this is all about the grape. And being PX, there is a transition to the mouthfeel, ensuring that this is maximum stickiness to the already silky undercoat. The finish, I have to say, is no great shakes. But it is impossible not to be blown away by the first three or four shockwaves on delivery: concentrated dates, molasses and spice. Kind of withers on the vine after that... *50.5%. 1,900 bottles.*

TAIWAN
KAVALAN DISTILLERY

⬦ **Kavalan 40th Anniversary Limited Edition Single Malt Selected Wine Cask Matured Single Cask** cask no. LF121122043A, bott code: 2019.11.19 db **(96) n24** so rich is the grape that you will be taken aback – however experienced you are with big fruity whiskies. This is like a plum pudding mixing with a slightly uncooked Christmas cake: toasty raisin, but not burnt. Some Jamaican Blue Mountain floats around on the ether, too, so pure yet fragile is that coffee note. And, of course, there has to be spice...in this case quite nippy, though only after a very slow build up; **t24.5** brilliant...just brilliant. One of the finest deliveries of the year. The first three or four second offers an intensity and purity of flavour unlike any malt whisky I have encountered for this year's Bible. Raisins, sultanas, liquorice and plums have all been distilled down and sweetened with molasses, it seems. After the fourth flavour wave things start to lighten slightly, allowing the spices greater room to operate; **f23.5** nowhere near as dramatically memorable as those early moments, though the structure now begins to settle and as well as praline wafer and chocolate raisin is more than charming...; **b24** one huge and shapely bottle for one huge and shapely whisky. I think the cask was still diopping with wine when this was filled because the voluptuousness of the grape out-voluptuates anything I have encountered so far this year 56.3%. sc. 85 bottles. 40th Anniversary King Car Group.

Kavalan Single Malt Whisky 10th Anniversary Bordeaux Margaux Wine Cask Matured bott code: 2018.12.26 db **(95) n23.5 t24 f23.5 b24** A very quiet, understated complexity and confidence that just exudes class. Much more here than originally meets the eye...and nose. *57.8%. nc ncf sc.*

Kavalan Single Malt Whisky 10th Anniversary Bordeaux Pauillac Wine Cask Matured bott code: 2018.12.26 db **(90.5) n23 t22.5 f22 b22.5** The fruit appears to have armoured plating. This is one very, very firm and grave Monsieur. *57.8%. nc ncf sc.*

⬦ **Kavalan Single Malt Whisky Distillery Select No. 2** bott code: 2020.05.08 db **(85.5) n22 t22.5 f20 b21** Unusually for Kavalan, which usually turns on the style, they have here made the rare error of selecting casks which tend to cancel each other out rather than ensuring complexity. That leaves wilder, slightly off-key notes a blank canvas to propagate a bitter tanginess further and wider than one would have hoped. *40%.*

Kavalan Single Malt Whisky ex-Bourbon Oak bott code: 2018.06.27 db **(93.5) n23 t23 f23.5 b24** Something for everyone with a malt with early attitude but reveals some class late on, too. *46%.*

Kavalan Single Malt Whisky Kavalan Distillery Select bott code: 2018.07.17 db **(87.5) n22 t22 f22 b21.5** Must have been distilled on the silk road. As this is exceptionally soft but much simplified from the Distillery Selects of old. Very good spice fruity spice. 40%.

Kavalan Single Malt Whisky Port Cask Finish Concertmaster bott code: 2018.06.30 db **(92.5) n23 t23 f23 b23.5** Kavalan at this strength always seems a little underpowered, as if the woodwind haven't turned up for a Bruckner concert. But the elegant restraint of this whisky should certainly be admired. 40%.

Kavalan Single Malt Whisky Podium bott code: 2018.04.20 db **(88) n22 t23 f21 b22** A very fat malt but not quite shewing the usual Kavalan character. 46%.

Kavalan Distillery Reserve Single Cask Strength Rum Cask cask no. M111104056A, bott code: 2018.01.04 db **(90.5) n22.5 t23 f22 b23** On the nose it seems innocuous enough, but turns into being a huge whisky. 59.4%. sc. 401 bottles.

Kavalan Single Malt Whisky Sherry Oak bott code: 2018.06.27 db **(87.5) n22.5 t22 f21.5 b21.5** The nose leaves little doubt about the keen sherry influence but beyond the delivery the malt has surprisingly little to say. Pleasant, but hardly stirs your blood or makes you gird your loins 46%.

◈ **Kavalan Single Malt Whisky Sherry Cask Finish Concertmaster** bott code: 2019.11.15 db **(81) n21 t21 f19 b20** The driest sherry on any Kavalan I have yet encountered. Also the most uncompromisingly tight and most bitter. It could have done without that sherry finish. 40%.

Kavalan Solist Single Cask Strength Moscatel Sherry Cask cask no. MO110321014A, bott code: 2017.03.14 db **(84.5) n20 t22 f21 b21.5** Fruity for sure. But the oily, disconcerting tang is usually the result of a wide cut, not the barrel. 56.3%. nc ncf sc. 518 bottles.

Kavalan Solist Single Cask Strength Pedro Ximenez Sherry Cask cask no. PX100630027A, bott code: 2018.03.12 db **(89) n22 t23.5 f21.5 b22** Sticky and full-bodied. 56.3%. nc ncf sc.

Kavalan Solist ex-Bourbon Cask cask no. B101214030A, bott code: 2018.06.13 db **(94) n23.5 t23.5 f23 b24** A beautifully relaxed malt which shows the distillery off in a golden glow. Such class! 56.3%. nc ncf sc. 169 bottles.

Kavalan Solist Fino Sherry Cask cask no. FI00714038A, bott code: 2018.07.26 db **(94.5) n23 t24 f23.5 b24** An essay in subtlety and understatement despite the apparent bigness. 57.1%. nc ncf sc. 489 bottles.

Kavalan Solist Oloroso Sherry Cask cask no. S090102047, bott code: 2018.02.03 db **(87) n22.5 t21.5 f22 b21** Nearly three decades ago I was criticising these kind of sherry butts, then, unlike now, found exclusively in Scotland, as they were simply too heavy and cumbersome for the malt they had conjoined: rather than integrate, it had conquered. The opaque colour of the malt – almost blackcurrant juice in its darkness – offers a fair warning. The nose is attractive, especially if you happen to love oloroso sherry. But that is the problem: the whisky has vanished with barely a trace beneath it. Nonetheless, enjoyable for sure with all the spices present and correct. 57.1%. nc ncf sc. 470 bottles.

Kavalan Solist Port Cask cask no. 0090619059A, bott code: 2018.08.10 db **(95) n23.5 t24 f23.5 b24** Very much in the Kavalan house style of rich and substantially spiced - but never hot - single malt. Superb whisky from a faultless cask. 59.4%. nc ncf sc. 183 bottles.

Kavalan Vinho Barrique Cask cask no. W120614024, bott code: 2018.02.21 db **(94.5) n24 t23.5 f23 b24** Kavalan has that very rare talent for brilliance without apparent effort... 54.8%.

King Car Whisky Conductor Single Malt bott code: 2018.03.26 db **(89) n22.5 t22.5 f22 b22** Hefty malt with a rare but disarming honey thread. 46%.

◈ **Golden Gate Sunset Kavalan Single Malt Whisky Sherry Cask** cask no. S060710001 db **(94) n23.5** straight from the burnt fruitcake school of whisky. The raisins are toasted; the dates are pretty dry, too...; **t24** real blast from the past delivery: the first flavour waves here were common from early 1980s sherry butts and a collector's item today. After the initial tannin kick, every nuance is fruit related; the sugars for a moment are profound, a heady mix of muscovado and molasses; **f23** toasty and still belting out the layered fruit tones; **b23.5** absolutely delicious. But needed the malt to stand its ground just a little more firmly. What this whisky can do with is a bridge between the malt and grape... 58.6%. sc. 479 bottles. Bottled for WhiskySifu & SF Whisky, Bourbon and Scotch Society.

NANTOU DISTILLERY

Nantou Distillery Omar Cask Strength Aged 8 Years III Bourbon Cask cask no. 11090102, dist May 09, bott 1 Mar 18 db **(90.5) n23.5 t23 f21.5 b22.5** Charming and full bodied, you can see how the house style has changed slightly since this was distilled eight years ago 52.8%. sc.

Nantou Distillery Omar Cask Strength Bourbon Cask cask no. 11100221, dist Sept 10, bott 8 Jun 16 db **(93) n23 t23.5 f23 b23.5** A delightfully idiosyncratic style of intense maltiness gives this whisky a unique and dangerously drinkable disposition. Wow! 58%. sc. 206 bottles.

◈ **Nantou Distillery Omar Cask Strength Bourbon Cask** cask no. 1110613 **(93) n23** some excellent citrus tones emphasises the sharpness – and perhaps youthfulness – of the lively barley.

Fat on the nose and with exceptional balance between the sweeter elements and the drier tannins: sophisticated; the slow evolving of the fruit is delightful with apricot in particular attaching to the crisp barley; **t23.5** beautifully salivating and moderately intense. The barley coats the palate with a masterful degree of clarity: this is a clean malt but has lost nothing in personality. Spices begin to flourish around the midpoint; **f23** thinner now with the vanillas taking control. The rise of the spices has subsided, allowing a gentle malty glow to even the drier tannin; **b23.5** a beautifully made malt where subtlety is the key – even at 58% abv. There are as many quiet moments as crescendos, one emphasising the other, but this is a roller-coaster ride in subtlety. *58%*

Nantou Distillery Omar Cask Strength Bourbon cask no. 11140804, dist May 14, bott 25 May 17 db **(96.5) n24 t24.5 f23.5 b24.5** Beautifully distilled; beautifully matured. Simply stunning! One of the single casks of the year, not least for its unique and almost exhaustingly delicious style. *56%. sc. 248 bottles.*

Nantou Distillery Omar Cask Strength Lychee Liqueur Barrel Finished bott 28 Sept 17 db **(94) n23 t23.5 f23.5 b24** This whisky astounds me as much as it delights me! Curiously, lychee is a flavour sometimes picked up in well-aged Speyside-style light single malts. However, this is the first time I have ever encountered a malt matured in a lychee barrel. And it offers nothing like the cloying sweetness of say, PX. Thank god! A charming, classy malt. Oh, and the first whisky ever to include the stunning black-naped oriole (for those wondering what it is) on its label! *55%. 887 bottles.*

Nantou Distillery Omar Cask Strength Plum Liqueur Barrel Finished bott 28 Sept 17 db **(93) n23 t23.5 f23 b23.5** Another new flavour profile kindly brought to me by Nantou Distillery. And another that is absolutely impossible not to like. *53%. 795 bottles.*

Nantou Distillery Omar Cask Strength Sherry Cask cask no. 21130120, dist Jun 13, bott 1 Mar 18 db **(87.5) n22 t22.5 f22 b21** A good clean sherry cask – entirely sulphur free – but the balance between the oak and grape isn't quite there yet as the fruit is far too pugnacious. Still, the spiced-up delivery is a delight and the intensity of grape something to grapple with. *59%. sc. 246 bottles.*

⬧ **Nantou Distillery Omar Cask Strength Sherry Cask** cask no. 21130121 **(91.5) n23** had I been handed this from a sherry butt while inside a Speyside warehouse 25 years ago I wouldn't have batted an eyelid: true to style of an not overly aged malt it has that highly attractive mix of gentle grape must and slightly spiced boiled sugar candy. The spices are not just below the surface... at times they rumble and flutter to the top...; **t23** the youthfulness is barely disguised here, yet in some ways it works in its favour (and flavour!) as there is a freshness to the barley which can take on the burgeoning richness of the grape head to head. The astonishingly salivating quality makes no secret of the youth, but the intense barley leaks into every corner; **f22.5** the buzzing warmth of the spices remain untamed; the pulsing grape likewise refuses to lie low. A long and distinguished finish; **b23** not a single off note to be had. Beautifully distilled and matured, this is a malt with many years life left in it...one to lay down and forget about for two or three years...Or you can bottle now for a very fresh and clean (if underdeveloped) sherry bottling. *59.3%*

Nantou Distillery Omar Single Malt Whisky PX Solera Sherry Cask cask no. 22160006, dist Jun 08, bott Nov 18 db **(84) n22 t22 f20 b20** First things thirst. No sulphur: hurrah! The not such great news: the single malt whisky which was filled into this PX cask has vanished without trace. It will probably take archaeologists and sonar equipment to find. And this is the problem with PX, it is so all-consuming that if you are not careful you're left with massive grape. But not a single hint of an outline of the whisky itself. *52.1%. sc. 251 bottles.*

Nantou Distillery Omar Cask Strength Black Queen Wine Barrel Finished bott 29 Sept 17 db **(91) n23 t23.5 f22 b23** The sheer redness of this whisky means that you stare at it in near disbelief for a while before you even get round to tasting it. But when you do, you are well rewarded. Another very different whisky – and delicious, too! *56%. 863 bottles.*

MISCELLANEOUS

Sir John Moore Blended Whisky bott code: L-1805 **(71) n17 t19 f17 b18** It is as though their Galacian water source comes directly from the Pump Room at Bath. Or, more likely, it's the sherry butts at play. *40%. Sansutex Alimentacion. Scotch blended with Galacian water.*

Sir John Moore Blended Whisky Malta bott code: L-1812 **(73) n18 t20 f17 b18** Riddled with sulphur. Ironic when you think about it.... *40%. Sansutex Alimentacion. Scotch blended with Galacian water*

Sir John Moore Blended Whisky Malta 10 Años bott code: L-1814 **(87.5) n21.5 t22.5 f21.5 b22** Well, after the last two bottlings I was fearing the worst. But no sulphur here and instead we have an amazingly salty malt, especially on the nose, which offers up a sweet and juicy light fruitiness on the palate. The finish, like the nose, has a certain peculiarity, but when hitting the heights the sugar-tannin combination works attractively. *40%. Sansutex Alimentacion. Scotch blended with Galacian water.*

CROSS-COUNTRY VATTED WHISKIES

◈ **All Seasons Connisseur's Collection Reserve Whisky** batch no. 092, mfg. date JUL-19 **(87) n21 t22 f22 b22** Charmingly soft. Relaxed on both nose and delivery, it is happy to wallow in a toffee-rich sweetness. Sensual, not without weight and even the mildest smokiness and wraps up with a disarming degree of spice. *42.8%.*

◈ **Amrut Amalgam Malt Whisky** db **(86.5) n22 t22.5 f20 b22** Bright and juicy, the youthfulness of this malt is masked somewhat by the not inconsiderable amount of peat flowing through this. While the finish may be a bit bitter and out of sorts, the nose, delivery and early follow through have no shortage of charm. *42.8%.*

◈ **Amrut Amalgam Peated Malt Whisky** db **(81) n20 t21 f20 b20** Not remotely in the same class as their Amalgam Malt which, ironically, shews how to incorporate peat into a whisky with far greater elegance. This is an untidy malt, with harmony at a premium. Both the nose and finish are a bit on the dirty side while the delivery struggles to make sense of the apparently competing rather than unifying malts. *42.8%.*

◈ **High West Whiskey Campfire** batch no. 19K12 **(91) n23.5** the sharp hickory tones point towards a higher percentage of American whisky. Youthful with some lovely Demerara sugars mingling with the very light malt; **t22** a green, slightly unhappy delivery slowly conforms. Liquorice bites deep...but now the corn oils are almost out of control.; **f22.5** so much better now. The vanillins have landed to put out the fires but now and chocolate starts to spread...; **b23** this style of whisky, which I used to make as a party trick for my friends (and my now ex-wife in particular, and using single malt Scotch rather than blend) some 30 years ago, has a horrible habit of going wrong if you get the proportions off balance. Here it is not always quite where it wants to be, but delighted to say that eventually harmony is reached. All the elements are present and correct (if not in ideal proportions) and crank up the complexity levels....as they should. Ultimately, lovely stuff. *46% (92 proof). nc ncf. Made with straight rye whiskey, straight bourbon whiskey & blended malt Scotch whisky.*

◈ **The Lakes Distillery The One Port Cask Finished** finished in first-fill Tawny Port hogsheads, bott code: L 30 04 19 **(84.5) n22.5 t22 f19 b21** A better effort than their signature blend. But again fails ultimately because of the unwieldly, off-key finale. The nose perhaps yields a little too much to youth, but gets away with it thanks to the gristy sugars and fruits combining to make a beautifully fresh combination, though there is a weakness which may threaten later on. Likewise, the delivery is salivating, fat, malty and chewy...but tempered with a grumbling furriness at the midpoint. And this furriness goes slightly out of control at the dry finale. So much here to enjoy for sure, but... I have no idea if this is blended by an individual new to whisky or by an amateur but enthusiastic committee. Either way, for a fledgling distillery, they have to learn how important a finish is to a whisky and the amount of attention that has to be paid to it....and the quality of the casks.... Which, again, hasn't happened here. Like the Signature Blend, a naïve and ill-disciplined malt, though the early stages are just about worth the later pain, for this does at least have a delightful moment or two early on. Worth trying, though for the early moments only.... *46.6%. The Lakes (English) single malt blended with Scotch grain and malt. nc ncf.*

◈ **The Lakes Distillery The One Signature Blend** bott code: L 04 09 19 **(83.5) n22.5 t23 f18 b20** Love the marriage between the gentle phenols and natural caramels which gives the unusual aspect of the tannins outranking the peat, certainly so far as the delivery is concerned. But for all its excellent flavour development here the finish is hugely disappointing with a drying, bittering furry off-note which lets the side down. *46.6%. The Lakes (English) single malt blended with Scotch grain and malt. nc ncf.*

Lucifer's Gold bott code: L8257 **(85.5) n22 t22 f20.5 b21** A thin but pleasant blend which starts at a gallop on the palate but soon flags and bitters out slightly. Still, a delightful mouthfeel early on and the odd kick and sparkle for entertainment. *40%. A blend of bourbon and three year old grain Scotch whisky. Charter Brands.*

Mister Sam Tribute Whiskey bott code: L19011331914E db **(94.5) n24 t23.5 f23.5 b24** Big, brash...absolutely love it! What a fantastic tribute to the great whiskies of North America. I was going to say this is without parallel...but then I remembered the 49th one...*66.9% (133.8 Proof).*

The One British Blended Whisky Sherry Expression finished in Spanish sherry casks, bott code: L 01 10 18 **(94) n22.5 t23.5 f24 b24** Can't be any backstop agreement here as things are working really well between the UK, Ireland and mainland Europe with its sherry influence. Shewing all the elegance and refinement of a Jacob Rees-Mogg this, surely, should be known as the Boris Blend... *46.6%. nc ncf. 5,500 bottles.*

◈ **That Boutique-y Whisky Company World Whisky Blend (68) n18 t18 f16 b16** Maybe it was the juniper on the nose or the grapefruit at the midpoint. But as a whisky, if that is what this indeed is, I'm sorry to say is just awful. *41.6%.*

◈ **Star Walker Ultra Premium Blended Whisky Old Cask Collection** batch no. 001, mfg. date AUG.19 **(85.5) n22 t21.5 f20.5 b21.5** A satin-lined blend offering a sleek, sweet delivery. The balance is disturbed, though, by a slightly bitter intrusion. *42.8%.*

Slàinte

This is the point where I say a thank you the size of Whales to all those who have helped me write the Whiskey Bible, showing my appreciation to the many who have chipped in with their time, help and kindnesses, small and large, one way or another.

Also, of course, my usual thanks to my team of Vincent Flint-Hill, Peter Mayne, James Murray, David Rankin and, of course, the superglue that holds us all together: our very own and very special Jane Garnett, whose constant smile brightens the gloomiest of sulphur-filled days. As well as Julia Nourney and my support team of Paul and Denise Egerton, Linda Mayne, David Hartley and Julie Barrie, my personal encyclopedia. Also, Charlie Jones, Shaun Murphy and Kelly May for their magnificent assistance in Kentucky. Plus, the staff at The White Light Diner, especialy Rick and Hannah, in downtown Frankfort for getting my mornings off to the perfect start. As always, a massive hug to Heiko Thieme. Thanks, also, to those below who have provided assistance and samples for the 2013 Bible onwards. For all those who have assisted in the previous decade, we remain indebted.

Mitch Abate; Andrew Abela; Hayley Adams; Emma Alessandrini; Mary Allison; Mike Almy; Ally Alpine; Nicole Anastasi; Tommy Andersen; Wayne Anderson; Gareth andrews; Kristina Anerfält-Jansson; Clint Anesbury; Jane & Martin Armstrong; Hannah Arnold; Teemu Artukka; Scott & Sam Ashforth; Paul Aston; Kevin Atchinson; Ryan Baird; Andrew Baker; David Baker; Emma Ball; Duncan Baldwin; Clare Banner; Keith Barnes; Lauren Barrett; Hans Baumberger; Stefan Baumgart; Steve Beam; Lauren Beck; Stefan Beck; Jan Beckers; Kirsteen Beeston; Sarah Belizaire-Butler; Becky Bell; Annie Bellis; Sigurd Belsnes; Franz Benner; Alexander Berger; Akash Beri; John Bernasconi; Barry Bernstein; Stuart Bertra; Jodi Best; Marilena Bidaine; Peter Bignell; Menno Bijmolt; Lee Bilsky; Sonat Birknecker Hart; Franziska Bishof; Rich Blair; Olivier Blanc; Mike Blaum; Elisabeth Blum; René Bobrink; Andreas Boessow; Anna Boger; Arthur H. Boggs, III; Amy & Steve Bohner; Hans Bol; Mark Boley; Yvonne Bonner; Keith Bonnington; Etienne Bouillon; Borat, Birgit Bornemeier; Phil Brandon; Caroline Brel; Stephen Bremner; Rebecca Brennan; Franz Brenner; Cam Brett; Stephanie Bridge; Chris Brown; James Brown; Sara Browne; Chris Bryne; Ralf Brzeske; Michael Brzozowski; Alexander Buchholz; Ryan Burchett; Amy Burgess; Nicola Cameron; Andrew Campbell Walls; Euan Campbell; Nathan Campbell; Kimla Carsten; Lauren Casey-Haiko; Bert Cason; Stuart Cassells; Jim Caudill; Danilo Cembrero; Lisa Chandler; Thomas Chen; Yuseff Cherney; Ashok Chokalingam; Julia Christian; Morten Christensen; Michelle Clark; Claire Clark; Nick Clark; Anne-Marie Clarke; Joseph Clarkson; Fredi Clerc; Dr Martin Collis; Shelagh Considine, Peter Cooney; Mathew & Julie Cooper; Christina Conte; Gabriel Corcoran; Lynn Cross; Lauren Crothers; Rosie Cunningham; Brian Cox; Jason Craig; David Croll; Molly Cullen; Nathan Currie; Larry Currier; Benjamin Curtis; Danni Cutten; Dave Cuttino; Larry Currier; Mike DaRe; Alan Davis; Bryan Davis; Stephen Davies; Alasdair Day; Dick & Marti; Scott Dickson; Martin Diekmann; Sharton Deane; Dixon Dedman; Conor Dempsey; Paul Dempsey; Lauren Devine; Marie-Luise Dietich; Rob Dietrich; Hugo Diez; Arno Josef Dirker; Caroline Docherty; Oscar Dodd; Korrie Dodge; Angela D'Orazio; Georgia Donmall; Jean Donnay; Kellie Du; Quinzil Du Plessis; Tim Duckett; Camille Duhr-Merges; Mariette Duhr-Merges; Gemma Duncan; Shane Dunning; Christophe Dupic; Jens Drewitz; Reinhard Drexler; Jochen Druffel; Michael D'souza; Kellie Du; Jonas Ebensperger; Lenny Eckstein; Ray Edwards; Winston Edwards; Bernd Ehbrecht; Carsten Ehrlich; Ben Ellefsen; Rebecca Elliott-Smith; Lucie Ellis; Thimo Elz; Maximilian Engel; Camilla Ericsson; Beanie Espey; James Espey; Brad Estabrooke; Patrick Evans; Jennifer Eveleigh; Selim Evin; Thomas Ewers; Charlotte Falconer; Lauren Fallert; Bruce Farquhar; David Faverot; Joanna Fearnside; Angus Ferguson; Walter Fitzke; Roland Feller; Andrea Ferrari; Bobby Finan; Brigette Fine; Holly Forbes; Tricia Fox; Jean-Arnaud Frantzen; Sascha Frozza; Barry Gallagher; Hans-Gerhard Fink; Sarah Fisher; David Fitt; Walter Fitzke; Kent Fleischman; Eric Flynn; Mara Flynn; Martyn Flynn; Holly Forbes; Carole Frugier; Danny Gandert; Arno Gänsmantel; Patrick Garcia; Dan Garrison; Ralph Gemmel; Stefanie Geuting; Carole Gibson; Jonathan Gibson; Daniel Giraldo; John Glaser; John Glass; Emily Glynn; Emma Golds; Rodney Goodchild; Chloe Gordon; Jonathon Gordan; Tomer Goren; Bob Gorton; Lawrence Graham; Kelly Greenawalt; Hannah Gregory; Andrew Grey; George Grindlay; Rebecca Groom; Jason Grossmiller; Jan Groth; Viele Grube; Immanuel Gruel; Barbara Grundler; Katia Guidolin; Stefanie Geuting Josh Hafer; Jasmin Haider; Jamie Hakim; Georgina Hall; Georges Hannimann; Denis Hanns; Claire Harris; Scott E Harris; Alistair Hart; Andrew Hart; Donald Hart; Stuart Harvey; Ralf Hauer; Elizabeth Haw; Steve Hawley; Ailsa Hayes; Ross Hendry; Lianne Herbruck; Thomas Herbruck; Nils C. Herrmann; Bastian Heuser; Jennifer Higgins; Jason Himstedt; Brian Hinson; Roland Hinterreiter; Paul Hletko; Eva Hoffman; Marcus Hofmeister; Tom Holder; Julie Holl Rebsomen; Genise Hollingworth; Arlette Holmes; Bernhard Höning; Jason Horn; Mike Howlings; Emma Hurley; Alex Huskingson; Thomas B. Ide; Jill Inglis; Rachel Showalter Inman; Victoria Irvine; Hannah Irwin; Kai Ivalo; Emma Jackson; Caroline James; Richard Jansson; Amelia James; Ulrich Jakob; Andrew Jarrell; Don Jennings; Big John, Pascal Jobst; Michael John; Celine Johns; Eamonn Jones; Robert Joule; Aista Jukneviciute; Emiko Kaji; Jeff Kanof; Raphael Käser; Alfred Kausl; Christina Kavanaugh; Serena Kaye;

Colin Keegan; Joy Kelso; James Kiernan; Kai Kilpinen; Jessica Kirby; Daniel Kissling; Sara Klingberg; Martina Krainer; Franz Kostenzer; Pavlos Koumparos; Matt Kozuba; Martina Krainer; Larry Krass; Armin Krister; Karen Kushner; Sophie Lambert-Russell; Ryan Lang; Oliver Lange; Jürgen Laskowski; Sebastian Lauinger; Alan Laws; Darren Leitch; Christelle Le Lay; Danguole Lekaviciute; Cédric Leprette; Eiling Lim; Bryan Lin; Lars Lindberger; Mark T Litter; Tom Lix; Steven Ljubicic; Kelly Locker; Vincent Löhn; Richard Lombard; Alistair Longwell; Dorene Lorenz; Claire Lormier; Sarah Ludington; Valentin Lutikov; Urs Lüthy; C. Mark McDavid; James Macdonald; Jane Macduff; Jenna Macfarlane; Myriam Mackenzie; Julia Mackillop; Bethan Mackenzie; Damian & Madeleine Mackey; John Maclellan; Rosalyn MacLeod; Derek Mair; Dennis Malcolm; Jari Mämmi; Sarah Manning; Stefan Marder; Ole Mark; Amaury Markey; Gene Marra; Tim Marwood; Jennifer Masson; Gregor Mathieson; Leanne Matthews; Josh Mayr; Roxane Mazeaude; Stephen R McCarthy; Mark McDavid; Christy McFarlane; Angela Mcilrath; Catherine McKay; Mark McLaughlin; Jonny McMillan; Douglas McIvor; Heinz Meistermann; Sarah Messenger; Uwe Meuren; Raphael Meuwly; Herman C. Mihalich; Joanna Miller; Maggie Miller; Gary Mills; Tatsuya Minagawa; Clare Minnock; Ashish Misra; Euan Mitchell; Jacqueline Mitchell; Paul Mitchell; Jeroen Moernaut; Stephan Mohr; Henk Mol; Kim Møller-Elshøj; Nick Morgan; Celine Moran; Katy Moore; Maggie Morri; Elyse Morris; Michael Morris; Brendan J. Moylan; Miroslav Motyčka; Fabien Mueller; Raphael Meuwly; Dennis Mulder; Mike Müller; Tarita Mullings; Tom-Roderick Muthert; Michael Myers; Simone Nagel; Arthur Nägele; Andrew Nelstrop; Sandra Neuner; Stuart Nickerson; Alex Nicol; Jane Nicol; Jennifer Nicol; Jens Nielsen; Thorsten Niesner; Sharon Nijkerk; Zack Nobinger; Soren Norgaard; Julia Nourney; Michael Nychyk; Nathan Nye; Tom O'Connor; Sinead Ofrighil; Richard Oldfield; Linny Oliphant; Jonas Östberg; Casey Overeem; Serdar Pala; Ted Pappas; Lauri Pappinen; Allison Parc; Jason Parker; Richard Parker; Katie Partridge; Sanjay Paul; Pascal Penderak; Percy; Nadège Perrot; Jörg Pfeiffer; Alexandra Piciu; Amy Preske; Phil Prichard; Rupert Ponsonby; Andreas Poulsen; George Quiney; Rachel Quinn; George Racz; Robert Ransom; Nidal Ramini; Sarah Rawlingson; Julie Holl Rebsomen; Michael Reckhard; Guy Rehorst; Michel Reick; Bärbel & Lutz Reifferscheid; Marco Reiner; Drexler Reinhard; Carrie Revell; Frederic Revol; Kay Riddoch; Massimo Righi; Nicol von Rijbroek; Karen Ripley; Patrick Roberts; James Robertson; Dr. Torsten Römer; Mark Rosendal Steiniche; Casey Ross; Anton Rossetti; Fabio Rossi; David Roussier; Ronnie Routledge; Stephane Rouveyrol; Matthias Rosinski; Ken Rose; Miriam Rune; Michal Rusiňák; Jim Rutledge; Caroline Rylance; Simi Sagoo; Paloma Salmeron Planells; Kiran Samra; Jasmine Sangria; Carla Santoni; Colette Savage; John Savage-Onstwedder; Kirsty Saville; Manuela Savona; Ian Schmidt; Fred Heinz Schober; Karl Schoen; Lorien Schramm; Becky Schultz; Birgitta Schulze van Loon; John Scott; Chris Seale; Mick & Tammy Secor; Tad Seestedt; Tanya Seibold; Marina Sepp; Paul Shand; Steven Shand; Mike Sharples; Lorien Schramm; Rubyna Sheikh; Caley Shoemaker; Lauren Shayne Mayer; Jamie Siefken; Peter Siegenthaler; Fred Siggins; Sam Simmons; Alastair Sinclair; Thomas Sippel; Sukhinder Singh; Thomas Sippel; Thomas Smidt-Kjaerby; Aidan Smith; Barbara Smith; Beccy Smith; Gigha Smith; Phil Smith; Marianna Smyth; Gunter Sommer; Orlin Sorensen; Oliver Späth; Cat Spencer; Colin Spoelma; Alexander Springensguth; Tom Stacey; Jolanda Stadelmann; Silvia Steck; Guido Stohler Jeremy Adam Spiegel; Jolanda Stadelmann; Silvia Steck; Marlene Steiner; Vicky Stevens; Karen Stewart; Jakob Stjernholm; Katy Stollery; Greg Storm; Jarret Stuart; Jason Stubbs; Nicki Sturzaker; Peter Summer; Michael Svendsen; Henning Svoldgaard; Tom Swift; Cameron Syme; Daniel Szor; Solene Tailland; Shoko Takagi; Cheryl Targos; Chip Tate; Marko Tayburn; Elizabeth Teape; Emily Tedder; Marcel Telser; Celine Tetu; Kevyn Termet; Sarah Thacker; Johanne Theveney; Ryan Thompson; Laura Thomson; Kelly Tighe; Brian Toft; Jarrett Tomal; Cole Tomberlain; Katy Took; Hamish Torrie; Louise Towers; Hope Trawick; Matthias Trum; Anne Ulrich; Jessie Unrah; Jens Unterweger; Richard Urquhart; Stuart Urquhart; CJ Van Dijk; Rifino Valentine; Zvi A. Vapni; Lisandru Venturini; Rhea Vernon; Adam Vincent; Mariah Veis; Aurelien Villefranche; Lorraine Waddell; Josh Walker; Grace Waller; Emma Ware; Katharina Warter; Patrick Wecklein; Oswald Weidenauer; Micheal Wells; Katrin Werner; Arne Wesche; Zoe Wesseon; Anna Wilson; Georgia Wilson; Nick White; Peter White; Robert Whitehead; Lucy Whitehall; Stephanie Whitworth; Daniel Widmer; Markus Wieser; Julien Williems; George Wills; James Wills; Rinaldo Willy; Georgia Wilson; Ken Winchester; Arthur Winning; Ellie Winters; Lee Wood; Stephen Worrall; Kate Wright; Frank Wu; Tom Wyss; Junko Yaguchi; Laura Young; Kiyoyuki Yoshimura; Bettina Zannier; Jörg Zahorodnyj; Ruslan Zamoskovny; Ulrich Jakob Zeni; Rama Zuniga; Ernst Zweiger. And, as ever, in warm memory of Mike Smith.